ABBREVIATIONS

AUS.	AUSTRIA
BEL.	BELGIUM
B. H.	BOSNIA AND HERZEGOVINA
CR.	CROATIA
CZ.	CZECH REPUBLIC
DEN.	DENMARK
HUNG.	HUNGARY
LUX.	LUXEMBOURG
MAC.	FORMER YUGOSLAV REPUBLIC OF MACEDONIA
NETH.	NETHERLANDS
SLK.	SLOVAKIA
SLN.	SLOVENIA
SWITZ.	SWITZERLAND
YU.	YUGOSLAVIA

Global Marketing Strategies

Global Marketing Strategies

Third Edition

Jean-Pierre Jeannet
Professor of Marketing and International Business, and
Walter H. Carpenter Chairholder,
Babson College, Wellesley, Massachusetts

Professor of Strategy and Marketing,
International Institute for Management Development (IMD),
Lausanne, Switzerland

H. David Hennessey
Associate Professor of Marketing,
Babson College, Wellesley, Massachusetts

Associate, Ashridge Management College,
Berkhamsted, United Kingdom

HOUGHTON MIFFLIN COMPANY   Boston   Toronto
Geneva, Illinois   Palo Alto   Princeton, New Jersey

To our students and the many executives who helped light the way

Associate Editor: Susan M. Kahn
Senior Project Editors: Paula Kmetz/Chere Bemelmans
Senior Production/Design Coordinator: Jill Haber
Senior Manufacturing Coordinator: Priscilla Bailey
Marketing Manager: Robert D. Wolcott

Library of Congress Catalog Card Number: 94-76515

ISBN: 0-395-71045-6

Brief Contents

Contents

● **Part 6
Cases: Practicing Global
Marketing   629**

Preface

Since the publication of our second edition in 1992, the world of global marketing has changed substantially and in ways previously unimaginable. Whereas our second edition concentrated considerably on the events leading up to the European integration and Europe 1992, this third edition has been shaped by events elsewhere. The privatization wave going through most of Eastern Europe as a result of the tremendous political changes there have opened entire regions for global marketers. The same holds true for the changes taking place in Asia and Latin America. The exponential growth experienced by many economies in Asia increases the possibility that the Asian economies—China and India in particular—will be among the largest economic powers in the not-too-distant future. These substantial changes in the global marketing environment have shaped our new and third edition, which consequently has a much greater emphasis on the merging markets of Eastern Europe, Asia, and Latin America.

Major Features Retained

We retained a number of major features from our previous editions. *Global Marketing Strategies* continues to be aimed at the new breed of global marketing manager, regardless of nationality, industry, or company location. Our approach remains largely managerial: We look at the global marketing task through the eyes of the marketing manager. We continue to emphasize aspects of global and international marketing. As in previous editions, we maintain our strategic focus throughout. We believe that success in global marketing today is not only a function of broad cultural understanding but also modern global strategic thinking. Finally, we retain our emphasis on the practical aspects of global marketing by including numerous recent examples from well-known companies as well as full-length cases that probe international and global marketing issues in depth.

Major Changes in the Third Edition

As in our previous revision, we have made major changes in our third edition that significantly strengthen the book. We have changed the structure of the chapters and added an entirely new chapter. All the material and examples have been updated, and new cases have been added.

The text has seen major changes through combining the previous edition's Chapters 5 (International Markets) and 6 (International Buyers) into one chapter—Chapter 5, Global Markets and Buyers. The condensation of this material into one chapter allowed us to add an entire new chapter. We developed our new Chapter 7, Developing a Global Mindset, as part of our research efforts at Babson, IMD, and Ashridge into the issue of global mindset and global perspective. In this chapter, we summarize the key elements that a marketer must develop to be able to approach the global marketing challenges with a new, global mindset. The nucleus of this new chapter came from part of Chapter 8 from the previous edition, combined with material new to the field. As such, it represents another unique feature of this book and may be of interest to students and practitioners alike from not only marketing, but other business functions as well.

Several other chapters were conceptually improved to reflect new thoughts in global marketing. Chapter 8 contains several new concepts on global marketing strategies and a better structure around the notion of generic global marketing strategies. We added new art and tables, so the concepts in the chapter are now easier to grasp. Other major conceptual additions were made to Chapter 9 (Global Market Entry Strategies), where we included the most recent experience of firms in entering or reentering previously closed markets.

All chapters have received extensive updating in both examples, tables, data, and reference readings. Throughout the book, we have included the most recent examples available to us from publications all over the world. In particular, we have aimed at a full coverage of issues surrounding Eastern Europe and the tremendous changes that have taken place there since our previous edition. In several chapters we have added separate sections on Eastern Europe, and in others we have integrated discussions of Eastern Europe into the regular body of the text. The book also reflects the full political changes that took place in that region and their impact on international firms.

Another major feature of our third edition is its increased information on Asia. Although our previous editions were well documented on Japan, we have now made a special effort to include more material from the emerging economies of China, India, Korea, Taiwan, and Thailand. In some chapters, we have added specific subsections on China. We have diversified our literature search and have included periodicals from those regions to give a better balance in the examples cited in the text.

Throughout the text, we have included the expected developments coming from the adaptation of NAFTA and the most recent developments surrounding Europe, the European Union (EU), and GATT. In all of those areas, we have attempted to include the most recent examples—although we all recognize that the world is changing. To provide readers with a framework for dealing with these changes, we have included some conceptual material in Chapter 4 on new issues such as privatizations, deregulations, and liberalizations, which explains developments to date.

We have also substantially changed our selection of cases. We updated the World Paint Industry case with a more recent version (1992) and redid ICI Paints (A). Entirely new are ICI Paints (B) and a new series on the robot industry. The Worldwide Robotics Industry and ASEA Robotics AB (A) and (B) are part of a new series of cases developed at IMD that focus on global strategies for business units.

Complete Teaching Package

The teaching package for the third edition includes the *Instructor's Resource Manual with Test Bank,* a computerized test bank, and a videotape. The instructor's resource manual contains suggestions on how to design a global marketing course, student projects, answers to text questions, complete case teaching notes, and transparency masters. The test bank has been completely rewritten for this edition. In addition to true-false and multiple-choice questions, it now includes essay questions for every chapter. New to this edition is a computerized version of the test bank that allows instructors to generate and change tests easily. The videotape consists of several segments highlighting examples of global marketing that can be used to stimulate class discussion.

Acknowledgments

To write a new edition of a textbook on global marketing is a major undertaking that could not have been completed without the active support and help of a great many people. This process was especially difficult because both authors spent most of the time working on this revision during extended overseas projects. However, we hope that this has added to the global content of the material.

We are indebted to our home institution, Babson College, for generously supporting us in the manuscript stage and allowing us the flexibility to spend time overseas to develop the material for this book. To International Management Development Institute (IMD), we are indebted for their support of our case research and for allowing us to publish IMD cases in the text. To Ashridge Management College we are thankful for providing access to its extensive data base, which proved helpful in updating this new edition. And finally, we would like to express our gratitude to our colleagues at Babson, IMD, and Ashridge for their support and willingness to discuss global marketing issues, which has helped us clarify many of our concepts.

The content of the cases would not have been possible without the generous participation of a number of companies and executives: Ernst Thomke and Franz Sprecher from SMH (Swatch and Tissot cases); Ian Souter at Nestlé; Mr. Nakamoto of American Hospital Supply—Japan; John Sweeney at Puritan-Bennett; Harold Todd, Masahiro Horita, and Brian Taylor at Nippon Vicks K.K.; Herman Scopes and John Thompson at ICI Paints; and Stelio Demark and Nick Rizvi at ABB Robotics. These executives and others who prefer to remain anonymous gave generously of their time so that other practicing as well as future managers could learn from their own experiences. We would also like to thank Silvia Farmanfarma, case librarian at IMD, who has provided us crucial support in guiding our cases through the approval, release, and copyright process.

To turn the collected material and data into readable form we could always count on a number of students, graduate assistants, and research associates. Babson College students Peter Mark, John Bleh, and Sameer Kaji wrote parts of the cases used in this text. Lisa

Gibbs and Chris Murphy helped locate new resources and update tables for this edition. Susan Nye served both as graduate assistant at Babson and as research associate at IMD. Barbara Priovolos and Robert Howard wrote several of the cases at IMD. Faith Towle provided helpful editorial assistance on our new cases.

Throughout the development of this edition, as well as the previous edition, a number of reviewers have made important contributions. These reviews were extremely important in the revision and improvement of the text. We especially thank the following people:

B. G. Bizzell
Stephen F. Austin University

Jean Boddewyn
CUNY-Bernard M. Baruch College

Sharon Browning
Northwest Missouri State University

Roger J. Calantone
Michigan State University

Alex Christofides
Ohio State University

John Chyzyk
Brandon University

William Cunningham
Southwest Missouri State

Charles P. de Mortanges
University of Limburg

Dharma deSilva
Wichita State University

Susan P. Douglas
New York University

Adel I. El-Ansary
The George Washington University

Jeffrey A. Fadiman
San Jose State University

Kate Gillespie
University of Texas at Austin

John L. Hazard
Michigan State University

Joby John
Bentley College

H. Ralph Jones
Miami University

A. H. Kizilbash
Northern Illinois University

Saul Klein
Northeastern University

G.P. Lauter
The George Washington University

Sarah Maddock
University of Birmingham

Joseph L. Massie
University of Kentucky

James McCullough
The University of Arizona

Taylor W. Meloan
University of Southern California

Aubrey Mendelow
Duquesne University

Joseph Miller
Indiana University at Bloomington

Thomas Ponzurick
West Virginia University

Zahir A. Quraeshi
Western Michigan University

Samuel Rabino
Northeastern University

Pradeep Rau
University of Delaware

F. J. Sarknas
University of Pittsburgh

Chris Simango
University of Northumbria

J. Steenkamp
University of Leuven

Michael Steiner
University of Wisconsin—Eau Claire

Gordon P. Stiegler
University of Southern California

Ruth Lesher Taylor
Southwest Texas State University

L. Trankiem
California State University at Los Angeles

Phillip D. White
University of Colorado at Boulder

Van R. Wood
Texas Tech University

Attila Yaprak
Wayne State University

Poh-Lin Yeoh
University of South Carolina, Columbia

We are grateful to our publisher, Houghton Mifflin Company. Over time we have had the pleasure of working with a number of their editors who have seen this project through to its completion. We thank them for their patience, their encouragement, and their professionalism in supporting our writing efforts. Houghton Mifflin has also provided us with a first-class staff in turning the manuscript into its final form. The marketing, production, art, editorial, permissions, and manufacturing staffs have substantially added to the quality of this finished book.

Finally, we extend our greatest gratitude to our students at Babson College, at International Management Development Institute, and at Ashridge Management College for their constant help and inspiration. Their interest in global marketing issues inspired us to undertake and complete this project. Therefore, we are happy to dedicate this book to our students.

J.-P.J.
H.D.H.

Global
Marketing
Strategies

Introduction

Global Marketing: An Overview

IN THIS FIRST chapter of the text, we introduce the field of global marketing. An overview of the most important global marketing decisions is given, and the major problems likely to be encountered by international firms are highlighted. This introduction to the text also explains the conceptual framework we used to develop the book. Understanding this underlying plan will help you to quickly integrate these concepts into an overall framework for global marketing. It should also make it easier for you to appreciate the complexities of global marketing.

Global Marketing:
An Overview

● **THIS FIRST CHAPTER** *is intended to introduce you to the field of global marketing. Initially, we concentrate on the scope of global marketing, using several examples to illustrate that it is a broad-based process encompassing many types of participating firms and a wide range of activities. We next present definitions that will relate global marketing to other fields of study. We examine the differences between domestic and global marketing and explain why domestic companies often have difficulty marketing abroad. The chapter continues with a description of the major participants in global marketing. We also provide an explanation of why mastering global marketing skills can be valuable to your future career. A conceptual outline of the book concludes the chapter.*

From International Marketing to Global Marketing

The term *global marketing* has been in use only since the early 1980s. It began to assume widespread use in 1983 with the seminal article by Ted Levitt.[1] Prior to that, *international marketing,* or *multinational marketing,* was the term used most often to describe international marketing activities. However, global marketing is not just a new term for an old phenomenon; there are real differences between international marketing and global marketing. In many ways, global marketing is a subcategory of international marketing with

1. Theodore Levitt, ''The Globalization of Markets,'' *Harvard Business Review,* May–June 1983, pp. 92–102.

special importance in our present world. It has captured the attention of marketing academics and business practitioners alike, and as indicated by the title of our book, we attach considerable importance to this new type of international marketing. However, before we explain global marketing in greater detail, let us first look at the historical development of international marketing as a field and gain a better understanding of the phases through which it has passed.

Domestic Marketing

Marketing that is aimed at a single market, the firm's domestic market, is referred to as domestic marketing. In domestic marketing, the firm faces only one set of competitive, economic, and market issues and essentially must deal with only one set of customers, although the company may serve several segments in this one market. The marketing concepts that apply to domestic, or single-country, marketing are those we expect our readers are well versed in; they will not be covered further in this book.[2]

Export Marketing

The field of export marketing covers all those marketing activities involved when a firm markets its products outside its main (domestic) base of operation and when products are physically shipped from one market or country to another. Although the domestic marketing operation remains of primary importance, the major challenges of export marketing are the selection of appropriate markets or countries through marketing research, the determination of appropriate product modifications to meet the demand requirements of export markets, and the development of export channels through which the company can market its products abroad. In this phase, the firm may concentrate mostly on the product modifications and run the export operations as a welcome and profitable by-product of its domestic strategy. Because the movement of goods across national borders is a major part of an exporting strategy, the required skills include knowledge of shipping and export documentation.[3] Although export marketing probably represents the most traditional and least involved form of international marketing, it remains an important aspect for many firms. As a result, we have devoted Chapter 18 exclusively to this topic.

International Marketing

When practicing international marketing, a company goes beyond exporting and becomes much more directly involved in the local marketing environment within a given country or market. The international marketer is likely to have its own sales subsidiaries and will participate in and develop entire marketing strategies for foreign markets. At this point,

2. Philip Kotler, *Marketing Management: Analysis, Planning, Implementation and Control,* 8th ed. (Englewood Cliffs, N.J.: Prentice Hall, 1994).
3. Gerald Albaum, Jesper Strandskov, Edwin Duerr, and Laurence Dowd, *International Marketing and Export Management* (Reading, Mass.: Addison-Wesley, 1989).

the necessary adaptations to the firm's domestic marketing strategies become a main concern. Companies going international now will have to find out how they must adjust an entire marketing strategy, including how they sell, advertise, and distribute, in order to fit new market demands.

An important challenge for the international marketing phase of a firm becomes the need to understand the different environments the company needs to operate in. Understanding different cultural, economic, and political environments becomes necessary for success. This is generally described as part of a company's internationalization process, whereby a firm becomes more experienced to operate in various foreign markets. It is typical to find a considerable emphasis on the environmental component at this stage. Typically, much of the field of international marketing has been devoted to making the environment understandable and to assisting managers in navigating through the differences. The development of the cultural/environmental approach to international marketing is an expression of this particular phase.[4]

Multinational Marketing

The focus on multinational marketing came as a result of the development of the multinational corporation. These companies, characterized by extensive development of assets abroad, operate in a number of foreign countries or markets as if they were local companies. Such development led to the creation of many domestic strategies, thus the name *multidomestic strategy,* whereby a multinational firm competes with many strategies, each one tailored to a particular local market. The major challenge of the multinational marketer is to find the best possible adaptation of a complete marketing strategy to an individual country. This approach to international marketing leads to a maximum amount of localization and to a large variety of marketing strategies. Often, the attempt of multinational corporations to appear "local" wherever they compete results in the duplication of some key resources. The major benefits are the ability to completely tailor a marketing strategy to the local requirements.[5]

Multiregional Marketing

Given the diseconomies of scale of individualized marketing strategies, each tailored to a specific local environment, companies have begun to emphasize strategies for larger regions. These regional strategies encompass a number of markets, such as pan-European strategies for western Europe, and have come about as a result of regional economic and political integration. Such integration is also apparent in North America, where the United States, Canada, and Mexico have signed a far-reaching trade pact in the form of the North American Free Trade Agreement (NAFTA) in 1993. In the Pacific Rim area, regional integration took a step forward with the first Pacific Rim country summit meeting in Seattle

4. Philip R. Cateora, *International Marketing,* 8th ed. (Homewood, Ill.: Irwin, 1993).
5. Warren J. Keegan, *Global Marketing Management,* 4th ed. (Englewood Cliffs, N.J.: Prentice Hall, 1989).

in 1993, following a decade of rapid economic progress in that part of the world. Clearly, progress toward integration has been most pronounced in Europe, with the implementation of many ''Europe 1992'' initiatives and the passing of the Maastricht Treaty by most member countries of the European Community.

Companies considering regional strategies look to tie together operations in one region rather than around the globe, the aim being increased efficiency. Many firms are presently working on such solutions, moving from many multidomestic strategies in Europe toward pan-European strategies.

Global Marketing

Over the years, academics and international companies alike have become aware that opportunities for economies of scale and enhanced competitiveness are greater if they can manage to integrate and create marketing strategies on a global scale. A global marketing strategy involves the creation of a single strategy for a product, service, or company for the entire global market, encompassing many markets or countries simultaneously and aimed at leveraging the commonalties across many markets. Rather than tailor a strategy perfectly to any individual market, the company aims at settling on one general strategy that will guide itself through the world market. The management challenge is to design marketing strategies that work well across many markets. It is driven not only by the fact that markets appear increasingly similar in environmental and customer requirements but even more so by the fact that large investments in technology, logistics, or other key functions force the companies to expand their market coverage.

Thus, global marketing is the last stage in the development of the field of international marketing. While global marketers face their own unique challenges that stem from finding marketing strategies that fit many countries, the skills and concepts of the earlier stages are very important and continue to be needed. In fact, companies that take a global marketing approach will be good exporters because they will include some exporting in their strategies. Such firms will also have to be good at international marketing because designing one global strategy requires a sound understanding of the cultural, economic, and political environment of many countries. Furthermore, few global marketing strategies can exist without some local tailoring, which is the hallmark of multinational marketing. As a result, global marketing is but the last of a series of skills, all included under the broad concept of international marketing.

The Scope of International and Global Marketing

A company such as Boeing, the world's largest commercial airline manufacturer and one of the leading exporters from the United States, obviously engages in international marketing when it sells its airplanes to airlines across the globe.[6] Likewise, Ford Motor Com-

---

6. ''Overseas Sales Take Off at Last,'' *Fortune,* July 16, 1990, p. 76.

pany, which operates large manufacturing plants in several countries, engages in international marketing even though a major part of Ford's output is sold in the country where it is manufactured.

Today, however, the scope of international marketing is broader and includes many other business activities. Those of large U.S. store chains, such as Kmart and Bloomingdale's, include a substantial amount of importing. When these stores search for new products abroad to sell in the United States, they practice another form of international marketing. A whole range of service industries are involved in international marketing; many large advertising firms, banks, investment bankers, public accounting firms, consulting companies, hotel chains, and airlines now market their services worldwide.

Entertainment is another important product category with large international potential.[7] The U.S. video entertainment industry is estimated at U.S. $18 billion. Some 40 percent of this, or $8 billion, is derived from international markets, $4 billion alone from Europe. Success in Europe often makes or breaks a U.S.-made motion picture. In France, some 50 percent of airtime is accounted for by U.S.-made TV shows or films. The commercial success of the U.S. video entertainment industry was a discussion point in 1993 GATT negotiations. Disney, the large U.S.-based entertainment company, is also engaging in international and global marketing.[8] The company completed its European theme park in 1992 and has licensed another one in Japan. Despite a first-year loss of almost $930 million with Euro Disney, the company continues to expand its international business; Disney was expected to find more growth outside the United States than at home. Satellites will be used to beam programming abroad, and cable is rapidly spreading to Asia, Europe, and Latin America, requiring ever more programming.

Definitions of International and Global Marketing Management

Although much conceptual work has been accomplished in global marketing, the use of the word *global* remains unclear among many marketing academics and executives. For many, *global* is just a new or replacement term for *international*. Since it does mean something new and different to us, we plan to make use of the term in a judicious way. For us, global marketing is a subset, albeit different and distinct, of international marketing. In general, we still use the term *international* more often to describe factors that relate to the entire field and use *global* mainly when it refers to the specific new phenomena in international marketing. The term *global* was selected because it indicates clearly that a significant portion of this text will deal specifically with new concepts and strategies without neglecting the standard concepts dealing with export, international, or multinational marketing.

Having examined the scope of international and global marketing, we are now able to define it more accurately. Any definition has to be built, however, on basic definitions of marketing and marketing management, with an added explanation of the international

7. "Directors Battle over GATT's Final Cut and Print," *New York Times,* December 12, 1993, p. 24.
8. "Parks Still Spark Disney Imagination," *Advertising Age,* November 22, 1993, p. 31.

dimension. We understand *marketing* as the performance of business activities directing the flow of products and services from producer to consumer. A successful performance of the marketing function by a firm is contingent upon the adoption of the marketing concept, consisting of (a) a market focus, (b) a customer orientation, (c) an integrated marketing organization, and (d) customer satisfaction.[9] *Marketing management* is the execution of a company's marketing operation. Management responsibilities consist of planning, organizing, and controlling the marketing program of the firm.[10] To accomplish this job, marketing management is assigned decision-making authority over product strategy, communication strategy, distribution strategy, and pricing strategy. The combination of these four aspects of marketing is referred to as the *marketing mix.*

For international and global marketing management, the basic goals of marketing and the responsibilities described above remain unchanged. What is different is the execution of these activities in more than one country. Consequently, we define *international marketing management* as the performance of marketing activities across two or more countries. We are moving from single-country decisions to multicountry decisions. As we see in Figure 1.1, only two countries are involved in some situations; in other situations, dozens of countries are involved simultaneously, particularly when we speak of global marketing.

A U.S. firm exporting products to Mexico is engaged in a marketing effort across two countries: the United States and Mexico. Another U.S. firm operating a subsidiary in Mexico that manufactures and markets locally under the direction of the head office in the United States is also engaged in international marketing to the extent that the head office staff directs and supervises this effort. Consequently, international marketing does not always require the physical movement of products across national borders. International marketing occurs whenever marketing decisions are made that encompass two or more countries.

Relationships with Other Fields of Study

The field of international marketing is related to other fields of study. In its broadest terms, international marketing is a subset of *international business,* which is defined as the performance of all business functions across national boundaries. International business includes all functional areas such as international production, international financial management, and international marketing (see Figure 1.2).[11]

9. Philip Kotler, *Marketing Management,* 7th ed. (Englewood Cliffs, N.J.: Prentice Hall, 1991), p. 16–20.

10. Kotler, *Marketing Management* (8th ed.), p. 13.

11. Henry W. Lane and Joseph J. DiStefano, *International Management Behavior: From Policy to Practice,* 2nd ed. (Boston: PWS-Kent, 1992); Paul W. Beamish et al., *International Management: Text and Cases* (Homewood, Ill.: Irwin, 1991); David K. Eiteman, Arthur I. Stonehill, and Michael H. Moffet, *Multinational Business Finance,* 6th ed. (Reading, Mass.: Addison-Wesley, 1992); Alan C. Shapiro, *Multinational Financial Management,* 4th ed. (Boston: Allyn & Bacon, 1992).

FIGURE 1.1 ● International and Global Marketing

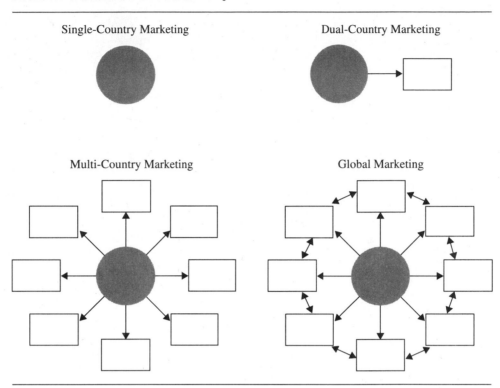

International trade theory, which explains why nations trade with each other, is a related concept. This theory is aimed at understanding product flows between countries, either in the form of exports or imports. A U.S. corporation exporting machinery to Japan would find its transactions recorded as an export in the United States, whereas the same transaction is treated as an import in Japan. In this situation, international marketing and international trade are concerned with the same phenomenon.[12]

Should the same U.S. company produce its machinery in Japan and sell locally, however, there would be no exchange of goods between the two countries. Consequently,

12. Paul R. Krugman and Maurice Obstfeld, *International Economics: Theory and Policy,* 2nd ed. (New York: Harper Collins, 1991); Francisco L. Rivera-Batiz and Luis A. Rivera-Batiz, *International Finance and Open Economy Macroeconomics,* 2nd ed. (New York: Macmillan, 1994); Jeffrey D. Sachs and B. Felipe Larrain, *Macroeconomics in the Global Economy* (Englewood Cliffs, N.J.: Prentice-Hall, 1993); Beth V. Yarbrough and Robert M. Yarbrough, *The World Economy: Trade and Finance* (New York: Harcourt Brace, 1994).

International Business

International Marketing

Global Marketing

International Trade

International Management

International Finance

FIGURE 1.2 ● International Marketing and Related Fields of Study

there would be no recognized international trading activity. However, as we have seen earlier, the U.S. company's decision to build machinery in Japan and sell it there is still considered an international marketing decision. Therefore, we can conclude that international marketing goes beyond strict definitions of international trading and includes a wider range of activities.

International marketing should not be confused with *foreign marketing,* which consists of marketing activities carried out by foreign firms within their own countries. Marketing by Brazilian firms in Brazil is, therefore, defined as foreign marketing and is not the principal focus of this book. However, Brazilian firms engaged in marketing their products in the United States are engaged in international marketing and are subject to the same concepts and principles to which U.S. firms marketing in Brazil are subject.

Using a Domestic Strategy Abroad: Risk or Opportunity?

Companies that market products or services abroad have always had to deal with a wider range of issues than those encountered by domestic firms. The following example gives some insight into the special difficulties encountered in the international market.

When a company uses an initial marketing strategy abroad, success or failure depends greatly on the market where it is used. In 1977, Apple Computer Company began distribution of its personal computer in Japan. At that time there were no other personal computer products on the market. However, by 1985, Apple still had only a very small market share, and the company had failed to achieve any significant market penetration. Japanese competitors and IBM had begun to market Japanese-language machines. The Apple could only be used by Japanese who understood English very well; thus, its market was limited to a small group. It was years later that Apple brought in a team of technicians from its head office to adapt its products to the Japanese language and built a subsidiary staff with local managers.[13]

Eventually, Apple calibrated its marketing strategy for Japan, reaching a market share of 7.5 percent in 1993. This represented a volume of about $500 million and was the fastest growing market for Apple. The cost of adapting its products to the Japanese markets has resulted in prices some 40 to 70 percent above U.S. levels. Apple's target segments were the school and home markets.[14]

Apple operated very successfully in France, where it became the leader in personal computers. In France, Apple used many of the high-visibility promotions begun in the United States, adapting them to the French environment. Apple did extremely well by focusing on in-home businesses and independent professionals, such as doctors and lawyers, achieving a market share of 35 percent in 1984, compared to 27 percent for IBM.[15]

Apple's market position internationally improved over the years and actually grew abroad while it dropped in the United States.[16] In Europe, Apple did particularly well, almost tripling sales in two years to about $1.2 billion in 1989, which amounted to almost one quarter of its worldwide sales. The success in Europe has also influenced executive positions at Apple's head office in the United States. The architects of Apple's success in France and in Europe, Jean-Louis Gassee and Michael Spindler from France and Germany, respectively, were promoted to senior positions, partly to enhance Apple's competitiveness in the U.S. market.[17]

Apple tried to duplicate a marketing strategy that had been successful in its home market. It failed initially in Japan, whereas in France it succeeded, with Apple achieving a higher market share than in its home market. The success in its European markets also caused the company to bring the lessons learned abroad back to the United States by transferring executives from abroad. Apple's example shows that success in international markets does not always require the complete adaptation of a company's strategy, but that doesn't mean one will never have to change anything. The Apple situation supports a pattern where managers will have to evaluate situations and sometimes change, sometimes adapt, and other times extend the same strategy abroad. The reasons for these patterns are explained in the next section.

13. "Apple Loser in Japan Computer Market, Tries to Recoup by Redesigning Its Models," *Wall Street Journal,* June 21, 1985, p. 30.

14. "Tokyo Product Unveiling Proves Apple's Point," *Nikkei Weekly,* February 15, 1993, p. 9.

15. "Can Apple Transplant Its Sexy French Marketing?" *Business Week,* June 10, 1985, p. 10.

16. "Apple's Woes Can't Just Be Reshuffled Away," *Business Week,* February 12, 1990, p. 32.

17. "The Toughest Job in the Computer Business," *Business Week,* March 19, 1990, p. 118.

Factors Limiting Standardization of International and Global Marketing Strategies

From an international marketing manager's point of view, the most cost-effective method to market products or services worldwide is to use the same program in every country, provided environmental conditions favor such an approach. However, invariably (as we have seen in the previous section), local market characteristics exist that may require some form of adaptation to local conditions. One of the challenges of international marketing is to be able to determine the extent to which a standardized approach may be used for any given local market. To do this, the international marketing manager must become aware of any factors that limit standardization. Such factors can be categorized into four major groups: market characteristics, industry conditions, marketing institutions, and legal restrictions.[18]

The debate over the amount or extent of standardization is one of the longest in the field of international marketing. Some see markets as becoming more similar and increasingly more global, such as those espoused by Levitt.[19] Others point out the difficulties in using a standardized approach, as has been the experience of many companies and the research of many academics.[20]

Market Characteristics

Market characteristics can have a profound effect on international marketing strategy. The *physical environment* of any country—determined by climate, product use conditions, and population size—often forces marketers to make adjustments to products to fit local conditions. Many cars in Canada come equipped with a built-in heating system that is connected to an electrical outlet to keep the engine from freezing while turned off. In warmer climates, cars are not equipped with such a heating unit but are more likely to require air conditioning. The product use conditions for lawn mowers differ considerably from one country to another. This was experienced by Flymo, a British company owned by Electrolux of Sweden. Flymo had pioneered the flying mower, hovering above the lawn without use of wheels. Very popular in the United Kingdom, the product failed in continental Europe, where lawns were much larger and mowers on wheels were therefore preferred.[21] Equally, Procter & Gamble, marketing its Cheer all-temperature brand in Japan, soon

18. This section draws heavily on Robert D. Buzzell's classic article, ''Can You Standardize Multinational Marketing?'' See *Harvard Business Review,* November–December 1968, pp. 102–113.

19. Theodore Levitt, ''The Globalization of Markets,'' *Harvard Business Review,* May–June 1983, pp. 92–102.

20. See Kamran Kashani, ''Beware of the Pitfalls of Global Marketing,'' *Harvard Business Review,* September–October 1989, pp. 91–98; ''Marketers Turn Sour on Global Sales Pitch Harvard Guru Makes,'' *Wall Street Journal,* May 12, 1988, p. 1.

21. ''Flymo Finds a Fresh Cutting Edge,'' *Financial Times,* November 2, 1988, p. 16.

learned that cold washing was required and that the product had to be reformulated to allow for the addition of fabric softener with cold water. The original Cheer formula produced insufficient suds to satisfy the Japanese consumer.[22]

A country's *population* will affect the market size in terms of volume, allowing for lower prices in larger markets. Market size, or expected sales volume, greatly affects channel strategy. Company-owned manufacturing and sales subsidiaries are often possible in larger markets, whereas independent distributors are often used in smaller countries.

Macroeconomic factors also greatly affect international marketing strategy. The income level, or gross national product (GNP) per capita, varies widely among nations— from below $100 per year for some of the world's poorest nations to above $20,000 per year for rich countries such as Kuwait, Sweden, and the United States. Countries have been categorized according to stages of economic development, ranging from a preindustrial stage to full economic maturity.[23] As can be expected, marketing environments will differ considerably according to income level. If the population's level of technical skill is low, a marketer may be forced to simplify product design to suit the local market. Pricing may be affected to the extent that countries with lower income levels show higher price elasticities for many products, compared to more developed countries. Furthermore, convenient access to credit is often restricted to buyers in developing countries. This has negative impact on the sale of capital goods and consumer durables.

Exchange rate fluctuations distort prices among countries for many products that otherwise would sell at similar prices. This leads to the problem of cross-shipping products to take advantage of price gaps. With specialization among channel members differing widely among various countries, depending on macroeconomic factors, companies often find themselves forced to adjust channel policies to compensate for the absence of the intermediary they normally rely on in their home country. Wage levels and the availability of human resources may influence a company to choose a different approach for its sales force. Since the motivation to purchase some products depends on a country's income level, advertising and promotion strategies may have to be adjusted for such changes.

Cultural and social factors are less predictable influences on the marketing environment, and they have frustrated many international marketers. Customs and traditions have the greatest effect on product categories when a country's population has had prior experience with a given product category. Although Coca-Cola has been very successful transferring its Coke brand into many countries, it has also run into difficulties with other products. Its canned coffee drink, Georgia Coffee, which met with success in Japan, did not find any acceptance elsewhere. And a soy drink that did very well in Hong Kong did not take off in the United States.[24] Viacom's MTV, a TV music channel aimed at young viewers, started broadcasting in Europe as early as 1987. Although the overall format is

22. ''After Early Stumbles, P&G Is Making Inroads Overseas,'' *Wall Street Journal,* February 6, 1989, p. B1.
23. W. W. Rostow, *The Stages of Economic Growth* (London: Cambridge University Press, 1960).
24. ''Marketers Turn Sour,'' p. 1.

very similar to the U.S. programming, the shows used in Europe are about 40 percent produced locally (other than in the United States or the United Kingdom).[25]

Language can be another hurdle for international marketing, and international marketers are focusing their attention on this problem. There are many examples of poor translations of promotional material. When McDonald's expanded into Puerto Rico in the early 1980s, the company employed U.S. TV commercials dubbed in Spanish. When prospective customers objected, the company eventually relented and developed a Spanish language campaign just for Puerto Rico. Sales showed a considerable increase.[26] This experience shows that when it comes to language, sometimes not even simple translation is enough. Slight differences in idioms can exist that are not known to the uninitiated; if neglected, they may result in poor marketing results.

Few areas have been as affected by language as the software industry has. One of the most daunting tasks for western software companies was to enter the Asian markets with products using Chinese characters. Neither IBM nor IBM-compatible PCs could make a major dent into the Japanese PC market until IBM developed DOS/V, a bilingual operating system developed in 1991 for use with Japanese language. Their success even prompted Fujitsu, a Japanese computer company, to switch from its proprietary standard to the DOS/V standard and thus offer IBM-compatible computers. DOS/V standard machines were expected to reach about 20 percent of the Japanese PC market by 1994.[27]

Industry Conditions

Industry conditions often vary by country because products frequently are in varying stages of the product life cycle. New product introduction in a country without prior experience may affect the degree of product differentiation, as only one or two versions of the product may be introduced initially. Also, a company may find itself in a situation where a country's limited awareness or prior experience requires a considerable missionary sales effort and primary demand stimulation, whereas in more mature markets the promotional strategy is likely to concentrate on brand differentiation. The level of local competition can be expected to vary substantially by country. The higher the technological level of the competition, the more an international company must improve the quality level of its products. The varying prices of local substitutes or low local production costs can be expected to influence pricing policy. In countries where competitors control channels and maintain a strong sales force, the strategy of a multinational company may differ significantly from that in a country where the company holds a competitive advantage.

Marketing Institutions

For historical and economic reasons, marketing institutions assume different forms in different countries. Practices in distribution systems often entail different margins for the

25. "Cool, Creative, and Connected," *Financial Times,* December 1, 1993, p. 12.
26. Kashani, "Marketers Turn Sour."
27. "Fujitsu Goes over to IBM Format," *Nikkei Weekly,* October 25, 1993, p. 8.

same product, requiring a change in company pricing strategy. Availability of outlets is also likely to vary by country. Mass merchandisers such as supermarkets, discount stores, and department stores are widely available in the United States and other industrialized countries but are largely absent in less developed nations in southern Europe, Latin America, and other parts of the world. Such variations may lead to considerably different distribution strategies. Likewise, advertising agencies and the media are not equally accessible in all countries, and the absence of mass media channels in some countries makes a ''pull'' strategy less effective.

Presently, eastern Europe is an area where many companies find they have to adapt to a much less developed marketing infrastructure. Xerox, in expanding its business in Czechoslovakia, found it difficult to increase its sales to independent copy shops. All copying was previously done by government-owned shops, where customers had to show identification. Sales were through only three government-owned sales outlets. Although a sufficient number of government-employed service technicians existed in the country, the company found it very difficult to find independent people willing to start copy shops, or even independent dealers for local sales.[28] The opening of eastern Europe during 1991 completely changed this situation, resulting in opportunities for numerous independent dealers.

Legal Restrictions

Legal restrictions also require consideration for the development of an international marketing strategy. Product standards issued by local governments must be observed. To the extent that they differ from one country to another, unified product design often becomes an impossibility. Tariffs and taxes may require adjustments in pricing to the extent that a product can no longer be sold on a high-volume basis. Specific restrictions may also be problematic. In Europe, restrictions on advertising make it impossible to mention a competitor's name, despite the fact that such an approach may be an integral part of the advertising strategy in the United States.

In general, legal restrictions on global marketers are in the decline. The conclusion of the GATT negotiations (Uruguay round) in December 1993 provided for a reduction in many of these barriers, in particular in tariffs where the average cut amounted to some 50 percent. However, many restrictions of a nontariff nature still have not yet been resolved, such as issues surrounding the protection of national video and film industries, subsidiaries for the production of civil aircraft, restrictions on shipping, and restrictions for many financial services sectors. With the U.S. Congress having approved this new trade agreement, the other 116 participating nations have until mid-1995 to ratify it.[29]

To carry out the international marketing task successfully, international managers have to be cognizant of all the factors that influence the local marketing environment. Frequently, they need to target special marketing programs for each country.

28. ''Dilemma of a Salesman in Prague,'' *New York Times,* December 27, 1990, p. D1.
29. ''U.S. and Europe Clear the Way for a World Accord on Trade, Setting Aside Major Disputes,'' *New York Times,* December 15, 1993, p. 1.

Major Participants in International Marketing

Several types of companies are major participants in international and global marketing. Among the leaders are multinational corporations (MNCs), exporters, importers, and service companies. These firms may be engaged in manufacturing consumer or industrial goods, in trading, or in the performance of a full range of services. What all participants have in common is a need to deal with the complexities of the international marketplace.

Multinational Corporations

Multinational corporations (MNCs) are companies that manufacture and market products or services in several countries. Typically, an MNC operates a number of plants abroad and markets products through a large network of fully owned subsidiaries. Although no clearly acceptable definition exists, MNCs are also referred to as global companies, transnational firms, or stateless corporations. For the purpose of this text, we have chosen the terms *international, multinational,* and *global* corporation. We use the term *international* to indicate a company with some international activities. The term *MNC* is reserved for a company with extensive overseas operations, including overseas manufacturing in several companies. We would call a company global if its operations span the globe and it is active in most major markets for its industry. Since *multinational (MNC)* and *global* tend to be more specific terms, we have chosen to use the term *international firm* when the issues apply to all types of firms.

According to the United Nations, there are some 37,000 firms that could be characterized as transnational corporations (TNCs). They operated some 170,000 individual affiliates all around the world, with total sales of $5.5 trillion. More than 90 percent of all TNCs are headquartered in developing countries.[30]

Fortune's list of the world's largest 500 companies shows how much international business has been developed outside the United States by large, growing firms across the world. Of the largest 500 corporations, only 161 are based in the United States; 128 are based in Japan, 40 in Britain, 32 in Germany, 30 in France, 14 in Sweden, 12 in Korea, and 9 each in Australia and Switzerland. Some 25 other countries are part of this list.[31] In *Business Week's* Global 1000 list, only 400 firms have their base in the United States.[32]

South Korea is one country with an increasing number of multinational firms. Leaders are the large conglomerates, or *chaebol,* that get involved in a number of different types of businesses. Leading is the Hyundai Group, with sales of approximately U.S. $52 billion in 1992 and some forty-four affiliate firms involved in automobile production, electrical equipment, and petrochemicals. Other leading *chaebols* are Samsung (U.S. $47.2 billion, with forty-eight affiliate firms in shipbuilding, electrical equipment, and petrochemicals),

30. "Transnational Corporations and Integrated International Production," *World Investment Report 1993* (New York: United Nations, 1993), pp. 1, 19.
31. "Guide to the Global 500," *Fortune,* July 26, 1993, pp. 188–234.
32. "The Business Week Global 1000," *Business Week,* July 12, 1993, pp. 59–107.

Lucky-Goldstar (U.S. $30.7 billion, with fifty-four affiliates in electrical equipment and chemicals), and Daewoo (U.S. $24.6 billion, with twenty-one affiliates in electrical equipment, shipbuilding, and automobiles). Some of these firms have developed and launched well-known consumer brand items in the United States and other developed markets over the past ten years.[33]

With the expansion of firms to become multinational in many countries, foreign investment in the United States increased rapidly during the 1980s. Great Britain accounted for the largest portion of foreign direct investments in the United States. For several large British firms, U.S. sales accounted for a large portion of global sales. For ICI (chemicals) and for Grand Met (acquired Pillsbury and Burger King) U.S. sales amounted to about 30 percent. For the two large German chemical firms, BASF and Hoechst, U.S. sales accounted for some 25 percent of corporate volume. For Swedish Electrolux, the U.S. volume rose to 30 percent through the acquisition of White Westinghouse. Pechiney of France has 40 percent of its corporate sales in the United States. Even some Japanese firms, such as Honda (50 percent), Mitsubishi Electric (50 percent), and Nissan (25 percent), have become dependent to a large degree on U.S. sales.[34]

Global Companies

Global companies differ from MNCs in that they pursue integrated strategies on a worldwide scale rather than separate strategies on a country-by-country basis. They tend to look at the whole world as one market and move products, manufacturing, capital, or even personnel wherever they can gain an advantage. Global firms also tend to have a strong base in all of the major economic regions of North America, Europe, and Asia's Pacific Rim countries. Products are developed for the entire world market, and the organization has undergone changes in order to be able to move from regional to product line–based profit centers. Many of the senior executives come from foreign countries.

Bartlett and Ghoshal differentiate among several types of internationally active firms. In their view, global firms operate on a world scale and tend to be heavily centralized; strategies tend to be controlled closely from the head office. In the multinational firm, each country is treated as a separate market. Multinational firms develop fairly independent clones of the parent firm in each market, with a focus on mostly local business. International firms, by contrast, have a pattern of more decentralization than global ones do, but the source of their strength is the exploitation of developments from their home market.[35]

General Electric, one of the largest U.S. corporations, is pursuing its own strategy to become a global company. Each of the company's businesses is expected to reach the number one or number two position worldwide in its respective area. However, GE from its origin has been more of an international company, based in the United States with most of its international business concentrated in Europe and Japan. In 1980, only two of its

33. ''Chaebol: Too Big to Compete?'' *Nikkei Weekly,* October 4, 1993, p. 28.

34. ''Nice View from up Here,'' *Economist,* November 24, 1990, p. 68.

35. Christopher Bartlett and Sumantra Ghoshal, *Managing Across Borders* (Boston: Harvard Business School Press, 1989).

major divisions (plastics and jet engines) were true global players. Since 1987, international revenues have risen faster than U.S. sales and accounted for 40 percent in 1993, up from just 29 percent in 1987. In the 1990s, GE began a big push into Asia, with several of its major divisions making large investments in India and China. By the year 2000, GE expects Asian markets to account for some 25 percent of total sales, almost $20 billion.[36]

Texas Instruments is pursuing globalization to compete in the very tough market for memory chips. The company designated a single design center and factory worldwide for each type of memory chip; it built two of its four new memory chip plants in Taiwan and Japan to take advantage of lower capital costs. An alliance with Hitachi of Japan helps share research costs. The global responsibility for TI's memory business is assigned to its country manager for Japan, a Japanese executive.[37]

ICI, Britain's largest chemical company and one of the world's largest, is an excellent example of a foreign-based global company. With one of the broadest product lines in the chemical industry, ICI began in 1983 to shift its traditional country-by-country organization toward a product line organization with worldwide business units. Several of these business units were headquartered outside of the United Kingdom, two of them in Wilmington, Delaware. In ICI Pharmaceuticals (today trading under the name Zeneca), worldwide responsibility for new projects allowed the company to reduce the time lag for new product introductions of drugs to different countries from as much as a dozen years to one or two. The eventual goal is to have simultaneous introductions worldwide.[38] More recently, the company announced that in the future it will put its resources behind those worldwide businesses that globally have a good chance to obtain a competitive position. The businesses will retain strategy-making responsibility, and the various country organizations will be asked to support these businesses in their individual countries in order to execute those strategies rather than have to create new strategies country by country, as was the case in previous decades.

One of the latest trends is global firms emerging from developing, or expanding, economies. These firms, different from the earlier described multinational companies, often specialize in a very particular niche and develop a global strategy during the early phase of their development. Salim Group, an Indonesian-based firm, has taken the worldwide lead in oleochemicals, oil- and fat-based chemicals used for the manufacture of detergents, cosmetics, soaps, food additives, and similar products. Salim was expected to eventually overtake both Henkel of Germany and Procter & Gamble of the United States. Salim is the only oleochemicals player in the world that has its own plantations (520,000 acres) to supply palm oil for processing. Global companies from emerging markets often start with a lucrative business in a domestic environment, far away from international competition. They exploit a unique competitive advantage by moving into the international marketplace. In the future, we can expect many more of these firms to emerge from such countries as India, Brazil, Mexico, Taiwan, Thailand, Argentina, and Venezuela.[39]

36. "GE's Brave New World," *Business Week,* November 8, 1993, pp. 64–70.
37. "How to Go Global—and Why," *Fortune,* August 28, 1989, p. 72.
38. Ibid., p. 76.
39. "Salim Targets Niche Market World-Wide," *Wall Street Journal,* September 28, 1992, p. A7.

Service Companies

Early MNCs and global companies were largely manufacturers of industrial equipment and consumer products. Many of the newer MNCs are service companies. Commercial banks, investment bankers, and brokers have turned themselves into global service networks; airlines and hotel companies have gained global status. Less noticeable are the global networks of public accounting firms, consulting companies, advertising agencies, and a host of other service-related industries. This globalization of the service sector has not been restricted to the United States alone but has been mirrored in many other countries as well.

Examples of U.S. service companies with international involvement abound. McDonald's increased its international sales from 20 percent in 1985 to 31 percent in 1989, amounting to a volume of more than $5 billion. Its international business is growing much faster than U.S. sales, where the company may have reached saturation.[40] Other major service exporters include American International Group (50 percent of revenue abroad), Citicorp (40 percent), Time Warner (communications and entertainment, 23 percent), Disney (20 percent), American Express (19 percent), Federal Express (19 percent), and Merrill Lynch (15 percent).[41] Today's service company is apt to be as global or international as any manufacturing company.

One of the newer types of service firms expanding globally is investment banks. U.S.-based investment banks are leaders in raising capital for clients worldwide, not just in the United States. Firms such as Morgan Stanley, Salomon Brothers, Goldman Sachs, and Merrill Lynch are bigger in the markets of London and Tokyo than British or Japanese firms are in the U.S. market.[42]

Exporters

Exports are an important aspect of international and global marketing. In 1992, U.S. exports totaled $448 billion. Of that, Canada ($83 billion), Japan ($48 billion), Mexico ($28 billion), and the United Kingdom ($23 billion) were the United States' biggest customers.[43]

Leading U.S. exporters were Boeing (aircraft, $17.8 billion), General Motors (cars, $11.2 billion), and General Electric (jet engines, plastic, turbines, and medical equipment, $8.6 billion). However, even for some of the largest exporters in dollar terms, the percentage of exports usually represented less than 20 percent of total sales. Companies whose exports represented a large percentage of sales were Boeing (61 percent), Sun Microsystems (49 percent), Intel (40 percent), McDonnell Douglas (33 percent), and Compaq (29

40. "McD's Faces U.S. Slowdown," *Advertising Age,* May 14, 1990, p. 1.

41. "The Stateless Corporation," *Business Week,* May 14, 1990, p. 58.

42. "Wall Street's Global Power," *Business Week,* November 1, 1993, pp. 102–115.

43. U.S. Department of Commerce, cited in *Business Almanac* (1994) (Boston: Houghton Mifflin, 1993), p. 416.

percent).[44] Leading exporters in terms of percentage of total sales are primarily firms that manufacture in the United States only, such as Boeing or McDonnell Douglas. Companies with many production sites around the world have a smaller percentage of exports. However, all multinational and global firms, even those with extensive networks of manufacturing sites around the world, tend to supply some of their markets on an export basis because few firms in today's competitive environment could produce in each market for local consumption only.

Smaller and medium-sized firms are also exporters, although the extent of their involvement differs by geographic region. In the United States, firms employing less than five hundred accounted for only 3 percent of direct foreign investments by all U.S. firms. By contrast, similar-sized Japanese firms accounted for 15 percent of their country's investment overseas, whereas the share for European firms of similar size was 7.5 percent. Only 28 percent of the smaller U.S. firms invested abroad in 1990, up from 24 percent in 1982. In general, it is felt that increasing overseas investments would accelerate the growth of exports for these smaller companies, as international sales offices lead to more overseas sales and local plants invariably import components or materials from the head office location.[45]

Some 51,000 U.S. firms export regularly, and about 87 percent of those employ fewer than five hundred. As a whole, exporting accounts for about 12 percent of U.S. GNP, up from 7.5 percent in 1987. Smaller firms have a bigger chance today due to new communications technology. Life Corp., a $5 million manufacturer of emergency oxygen kits, does almost 50 percent of all sales in the form of exports. Located in Milwaukee, the company responds to faxed inquiries usually on the same day. Videotapes of the products are then sent by air express to the potential foreign customer. Through this aggressive drive, the firm has gained customers in 43 countries.[46]

The record of European small to medium-sized exporters is quite different. In Germany, medium-sized firms are called *Mittelstand.* These firms, with sales of under DM 500 million, account for a large share of Germany's exports. As a country, Germany was the world's largest exporter several years in a row, beating out both the United States and Japan. These firms typically market industrial products, which means they are little known to most consumers. In their chosen market niche, however, they have become worldwide leaders with a clear number one position. They focus on a technical niche, a narrow product assortment, but sell worldwide. Typically, they have about a dozen sales subsidiaries abroad. Most of them maintain their own presence in the U.S. market. Although less known than such large German firms as BMW or Siemens, they have been able to do extremely well in the role of exporter.[47]

44. "*Fortune*'s Top 50 Exporters," *Fortune,* June 1992.

45. "Smaller Firms in U.S. Avoid Business Abroad," *Wall Street Journal,* August 24, 1993, p. A7.

46. "Little Companies, Big Exports," *Business Week,* April 13, 1992, pp. 70–72.

47. Hermann Simon, "Lessons from Germany's Midsize Giants," *Harvard Business Review,* March–April 1992, pp. 115–123.

Importers

Importing is as much an international marketing decision as exporting. Companies that neither export nor have multinational status may still participate in international marketing through their importing operations. Many of the largest U.S. retail chains maintain import departments that are in contact with suppliers in many overseas countries. Other major importers are MNCs that obtain products from their own plants abroad or from other clients. Among the largest U.S. importers are oil companies and subsidiaries of foreign MNCs, particularly those of European and Japanese origin.

A classic importer-only firm is Schwinn Bicycle Company. Having shifted its production over the years from the United States to the Far East, the company now sources virtually all of its bicycles from Taiwan and China. However, Schwinn markets almost none of its products outside of the United States. While this allows the company to market in a known, or domestic, market, Schwinn encounters many of the same problems faced by exporters, particularly issues related to logistics, supply, and international trade financing.[48] These aspects are primarily treated in Chapter 18.

As we have seen from this section, international and global marketing has many different types of players. Rather than specifying a particular type of participant each time, for the purpose of this text we will use *international company* or *international firm* as umbrella terms that may include MNC, global firm, exporter, importer, or global service company.

The Importance of International and Global Marketing

The globalization of markets is one of the major forces impacting on companies worldwide.[49] While it once meant forays abroad from a strong domestic market base, it has now assumed the meaning of open trade, where a company can be attacked anywhere, including its home markets. "Sanctuaries," or protected domestic markets, are rapidly disappearing. This change has increased the importance of global and international marketing to many firms and made it into the broad and pervasive activity it is today.

International and global marketing is a very broad activity and expanding rapidly. The dollar value of world trade grew by an average of 13 percent annually between 1970 and 1987.[50] As we discussed earlier, international trade is one of the important components of international and global marketing. For 1990, total world trade in merchandise reached $3,485 billion, a 13 percent rise over the previous year.[51] Table 1.1 compares world exports

48. Robert Howard and Jean-Pierre Jeannet, "Schwinn Bicycle Company," case available through the European Case Clearing House at Babson, Ltd., 1993.

49. "Welcome to the Revolution," *Fortune,* December 13, 1993, pp. 66–80.

50. "Economic and Financial Indicators: Trade," *Economist,* February 4, 1989, p. 102.

51. "Economic and Financial Judication," *Economist,* April 27, 1991, p. 110.

TABLE 1.1 ● World Exports of Manufactured Products (in Billions of Dollars)

	1985	*1986*	*1987*	*1988*	*1989*	*1990*
Food	204.50	225.05	250.65	284.45	298.95	328.95
Raw materials	64.75	72.30	90.40	104.35	108.10	104.50
Ores and minerals	36.20	36.35	39.70	47.55	54.20	52.95
Fuels	354.25	250.75	277.85	256.90	294.55	368.85
Non-ferrous metals	35.75	37.95	45.80	62.40	70.65	71.45
Total primary products	695.45	622.40	704.40	755.65	826.45	926.70
Iron and steel	69.45	73.75	79.95	99.60	108.60	109.10
Chemicals	151.55	178.60	214.65	252.75	264.60	297.65
Other semi-manufactures	124.80	152.40	185.10	214.45	230.25	264.45
Machinery and transport equipment	603.80	726.60	864.50	1010.45	1084.55	1237.20
Textiles	56.35	69.60	83.60	92.40	96.65	110.90
Clothing	49.20	63.80	82.60	88.85	97.25	113.40
Other consumer goods	136.60	170.60	210.85	246.90	269.00	312.00
Total manufactures	1191.75	1435.35	1721.25	2005.40	2150.90	2444.70
Total exports	1947.00	2136.00	2513.00	2857.00	3080.00	3485.00

Source: Data from *GATT International Trade 1990/1991,* pp. 80–87.

of manufactured products in the years 1985 through 1990. The table shows a clear upward trend in the world trade of manufactured goods. Most of this trade was concentrated in heavy machinery, transport equipment, motor vehicles, specialized machinery, and office and telecommunications equipment. The data do not include the local business of foreign-owned subsidiaries.

World trade in services—shipping, insurance, banking, and other service-related industries—increased to $690 billion in 1989[52] and now accounts for about 20 percent of total world trade. Service trade is referred to as "invisible trade" because the traded goods are abstract and difficult to quantify. Major components of service trade are transport, travel, banking, and insurance. The U.S. Department of Commerce has estimated the foreign business of U.S. service industries at about $144 billion in exports and $122 billion in imports.[53] This invisible sector of total world trade is expanding quickly and is expected to grow at a faster rate than world trade in manufactured goods and commodities. For 1989, revised U.S. export figures for services were estimated at over $100 billion, accounting for about 22 percent of U.S. exports.[54] Even education is an important service export

52. "Economic and Financial Indicators: Trade in Services," *Economist,* December 8, 1990, p. 118.
53. "Services—the Star of U.S. Trade," *New York Times,* September 14, 1986, p. 74.
54. "Nothing to Lose but Its Chains," *Economist,* September 22, 1990, p. 36.

for the U.S. economy. The tuition income U.S. educational institutions derive from foreign students has passed $5 billion annually and accounts for an important portion of the budget of many universities. China, Taiwan, Japan, India, and Korea each supply between 20,000 and 30,000 students. About half of the foreign students take graduate studies. Engineering and business administration are the favorite subjects.[55]

A substantial portion of international marketing operations does not get recorded in international trade statistics. In particular, MNC overseas sales of locally manufactured and locally sold products are not included in world trade figures. Consequently, total volume in international marketing far exceeds the volume of $2,400 billion for total world trade in 1989. Sales of overseas subsidiaries for U.S. companies are estimated at three times the value of these companies' exports.[56] Although no detailed statistics are available, this pattern suggests that the overall volume of international marketing amounts to a multiple of world trade volume.

Why Companies Become Involved in Global Marketing

Companies become involved in international markets for a variety of reasons. Some firms simply respond to orders from abroad without any organized efforts of their own, but most companies take a more active role because they have determined that it is to their advantage to pursue export business on an incremental basis. The profitability of a company can increase when fixed manufacturing costs are already committed and additional economies of scale are achieved.

For some firms, the impetus to globalize comes from a domestic competitive shock. General Electric Lighting (a division of GE) was the traditional market leader in the United States and had been in the business since 1878. In 1983, Westinghouse, its largest U.S. competitor, sold its lighting division to Philips of the Netherlands. This brought a strong foreign competitor right into GE's own backyard; yet GE was not competing in Philip's own territory in Europe. As a result, GE Lighting expanded by buying Tungsram, a Hungarian lighting company, in its first big move into eastern Europe. This was followed by the acquisition of Thorn-EMI's lighting interest, a U.K.-based unit. And in Asia, the company concluded a joint venture with Hitachi of Japan. This gave GE's international sales a boost from just 20 percent in 1988 to above 40 percent in 1993—and more than 50 percent as estimated for 1996. In Europe alone, GE Lighting's share rose to 15 percent. In the space of just a few years, the nature of the GE lighting business has thus changed from a predominantly domestic into a global business.[57]

Some companies pursue growth in other countries after their domestic market has reached maturity. Coca-Cola, a market leader worldwide in the soft drink business, finds that foreign consumers drink only 14 percent as much as Americans do. This suggests an enormous market potential outside the United States. The company already earns as much

55. ''Foreign Students: Who Are They?'' *New York Times,* November 29, 1989.
56. ''Welcome to the Revolution,'' p. 67.
57. Ibid., pp. 66–67.

as 80 percent of its operating earnings outside the United States and expects strong growth to come from Europe.[58] In eastern Germany, where Coke could only be sold after the liberalization of 1989, sales may reach $1 billion within just a few years.[59]

The Swiss-based food company Nestlé, facing maturing markets in Europe, is aiming at Asia as a major source of growth and new revenue. Developing and emerging countries accounted for just 20 percent of sales in 1992; due to above-average growth, those regions are to contribute some one-third of Nestlé's worldwide growth by the year 2000. Nestlé has targeted China as a key market, opening joint ventures in China for marketing Nescafé, Coffee-mate creamer, and milk powder. Its most recent entry was an ice cream plant in southern China through the acquisition of a Hong Kong firm's interest in the dairy business.[60]

Customers moving abroad provide reasons for many firms to follow. Major U.S. banks have shifted to serve their U.S. clients in key financial centers around the world by opening branches. Advertising agencies in the United States have created networks to serve the interests of their multinational clients. As some Japanese manufacturers opened plants in the United States, many of their component suppliers followed and built operations nearby. Not following these clients would have meant a loss of business.

Why Study Global Marketing?

You have probably asked yourself why you should study global marketing. You also may have wondered about the value of this knowledge to your future career. While it is not very likely that many university graduates find an entry-level position in international or global marketing, it is nevertheless a fact that each year U.S.-based international companies hire large numbers of marketing professionals. Since many of these firms are becoming increasingly globalized, competence in global marketing will become even more important in the future—and many marketing executives will be pursuing global marketing as a career. Other career opportunities exist with a large number of exporters, and candidates will require international marketing skills. Furthermore, many university graduates are hired each year for the marketing efforts of foreign-based companies in the United States. These companies are also looking for international and global competence within their managerial ranks.

With the U.S. service sector becoming increasingly globalized, many graduates joining service industries have found themselves confronted with international opportunities at early stages of their careers. Today, consulting engineers, bankers, brokers, and public

58. "As a Global Marketer, Coke Excels by Being Tough and Consistent," *Wall Street Journal,* December 19, 1989, p. 1.

59. "Coke Gets off Its Can in Europe," *Fortune,* August 13, 1990, p. 68.

60. "Nestlé: A Giant in a Hurry," *Business Week,* March 22, 1993, pp. 50–54.

accountants are all in need of international and global marketing skills to compete in a rapidly changing environment. Consequently, a solid understanding and appreciation of global marketing will benefit the careers of most business students, regardless of the field or industry they choose to enter.

However, as we have seen from the many examples cited in this first chapter, global and international marketing concepts do not only apply to U.S. firms expanding abroad. Companies from all countries are affected by the globalization of markets. Global firms can be headquartered just as easily in Japan, the United Kingdom, Germany, or Canada. Consequently, the concepts described in this text are meant for any aspiring global marketer, whether the person intends to start a career in the United States or elsewhere. This includes even such emerging regions as Asia, Latin America, and eastern Europe, where more and more global marketing executives will be needed to ensure the survival of firms based there.

A Need for More Global Marketers

Compared to other industrialized nations, the United States severely lacks a sufficient number of international and global marketing professionals. As active participants in international and global marketing, they play a key role in the success of international firms. In this competitive business, the United States has seen its share of world exports steadily decline. In 1953, the United States accounted for 19 percent of total world exports, more than twice the share of the second-ranked United Kingdom, with about 8 percent. At that time, Japan accounted for only 2 percent of world exports. The U.S. share of world exports was back to 12 percent in 1988, which saw the United States tied with Germany and ahead of Japan's 10 percent share. France, the United Kingdom, and Italy followed with shares of about 5 percent each.[61]

There are other indications that the United States is lagging behind other countries in global marketing. From 1870 to 1970, the United States almost always reported a positive trade balance, exporting more goods than importing. This began to change in the 1970s, and despite the large increase in earnings of the service industry, the overall balance of trade has turned substantially negative (see Figure 1.3). It has been estimated that its large trade deficit has cost the United States several million jobs. Although many reasons for this lagging performance lie beyond the control of individual companies, company management can do much to redress the imbalance. Foreign companies fight much harder than U.S. firms to retain foreign markets. Because the foreign firms' domestic markets are usually smaller than the U.S. market, foreign firms are more motivated than U.S. firms to succeed abroad.

Despite this problem, foreign trade, or international marketing, is still not given enough attention by large sectors of U.S. society. Whereas university graduates in other countries have learned one or more foreign languages as a matter of course, U.S. graduates usually have no foreign language competence. About 50,000 Japanese business

61. ''America's Place in World Competition,'' *Fortune,* November 6, 1989, p. 83.

FIGURE 1.3 ● U.S. Trade Deficit 1973–1992

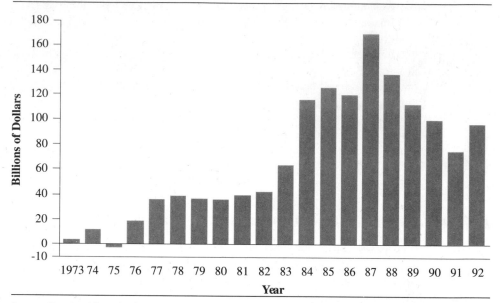

Source: Reprinted from the August 29, 1983, issue of *Business Week* by special permission, © 1983 by McGraw-Hill, Inc. 1973–1983 data from Commerce Department, Data Resources Inc.; 1984–1986 data from the United Nations, *World Economic Survey 1986*, p. 46; 1987–1988 data from *Business Week,* February 27, 1989, p. 86; 1989 *Survey of Current Business,* March 1990, p. 50; 1990 *Economist,* March 9, 1991, p. 108; 1991–1992 data from *The Statistical Abstract of the United States,* 1993, Table 1330.

professionals work in New York, all with a good understanding of English; only about 500 U.S. business professionals working in Tokyo have a good command of the Japanese language. Although it is too simplistic to associate foreign-language capabilities with effectiveness in global marketing, this comparison nevertheless serves as an indicator of interest in international business.

During the 1980s, many U.S.-based firms reduced the posting of executives overseas. Non-U.S. firms expanded at the same time. Mitsubishi, the $160 billion Japanese trading company, has half of its revenue based abroad and maintains 1,000 of its 9,900 Japanese employees overseas. Many of these executives have had more than one tour of service overseas. Some U.S.-based firms have reversed the earlier trend and are rapidly expanding opportunities for their staff overseas. Nynex, the regional telephone company, has 101 executives overseas, compared to none just a few years ago. Dell Computer expanded from 1 in 1988 to 12 in 1993; GM has 485 abroad, up 15 percent from a year earlier.[62]

Although the concepts introduced in this text are certainly important to anyone posted

62. "The Fast Track Leads Overseas," *Business Week,* November 1, 1993, pp. 64–68.

overseas in a global marketing assignment, the following section will demonstrate that these concepts have just as much validity for those of us who must "stay home."

A Need for More Global Minds

Few of us can avoid the impact of international competition today. Many of our domestic industries have fallen on hard times. Foreign competition has made enormous inroads in the manufacture of apparel, textiles, shoes, electronic equipment, and steel. As a result, these industries have become globalized (see Figure 1.4). Although foreign competition for many consumer goods has been evident for years, inroads by foreign firms in investment goods industries have been equally spectacular. By 1985, imports accounted for 20 percent of the U.S. market for industrial goods.[63] The U.S. machine tool industry found it had to appeal to the U.S. government for help because imported machine tools increased their share of domestic consumption from 25 percent in 1982 to 55 percent in 1986.[64] Management of companies competing with foreign firms requires global minds: an ability to judge the next move of foreign competitors by observing them abroad, in order to be better prepared to compete at home.

Import competition has been rising even in industries that used to be reserved largely for domestic companies. Nissin, a Japanese maker of instant noodles, started to make its dry soup called Oodles of Noodles in 1976 and, by expanding its manufacturing to a plant on each coast, now accounts for 4 percent share of the U.S. soup market, estimated at $2.3 billion. The company competes with Lipton, a traditional supplier of dry soups, by shipping smaller quantities to retailers. This results in faster product turnover at the retail level and a fresher product. Although the initial results were not successful, Nissin stayed in for the long haul and is now a successful competitor in the United States.[65] In 1983, processed food imports by the United States exceeded processed food exports for the first time.[66]

Foreign competition has also reached U.S. retailers. IKEA, a Swedish furniture retailing chain with some ninety stores worldwide in twenty-two countries and total sales of $3.2 billion, has expanded its operation into the United States. The stores have the size of six normal supermarkets and specialize in disassembled furniture. IKEA has decided on a major expansion on both coasts, and its stores have done well despite the stagnant sales in the U.S. furniture industry. In its opening in New Jersey, consumers snapped up the furniture, which was priced 20 to 40 percent below competitive prices, as the managers conceded that they had underestimated demand by 40 percent.[67]

The need to become more competitive in a global economy will force many changes on the typical company. Companies will have to become international and compete in global markets to define their own domestic markets and to keep up with global competitors

63. "America's War on Imports," *Fortune,* August 19, 1985, pp. 26–29.

64. "Cost-Cutting Will Still Be the Watchword," *Business Week,* January 12, 1987.

65. "Japan's Next Push in U.S. Markets," *Fortune,* September 26, 1988, p. 135.

66. "U.S. Food Firms Face More Imports and Rise in Foreign Plants Here," *Wall Street Journal,* November 18, 1986, p. 1.

67. "IKEA's Got 'Em Lining Up," *Fortune,* March 11, 1991, p. 72.

FIGURE 1.4 ● Globalization of Selected Industries

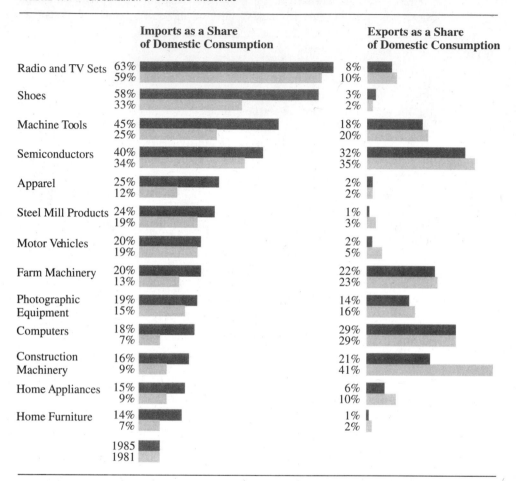

	Imports as a Share of Domestic Consumption	Exports as a Share of Domestic Consumption
Radio and TV Sets	63% / 59%	8% / 10%
Shoes	58% / 33%	3% / 2%
Machine Tools	45% / 25%	18% / 20%
Semiconductors	40% / 34%	32% / 35%
Apparel	25% / 12%	2% / 2%
Steel Mill Products	24% / 19%	1% / 3%
Motor Vehicles	20% / 19%	2% / 5%
Farm Machinery	20% / 13%	22% / 23%
Photographic Equipment	19% / 15%	14% / 16%
Computers	18% / 7%	29% / 29%
Construction Machinery	16% / 9%	21% / 41%
Home Appliances	15% / 9%	6% / 10%
Home Furniture	14% / 7%	1% / 2%

1985 / 1981

Source: Data from U.S. Commerce Department, National Association of Manufacturers, as published in *The Wall Street Journal,* October 27, 1986. Reprinted by permission of *The Wall Street Journal,* © 1986 Dow Jones & Company, Inc. All Rights Reserved Worldwide.

based in other countries. These firms will need an increasing cadre of managers who can think with a global perspective.[68] This requires not only a knowledge of other countries, economies, and cultures but a clear understanding of how the global economy works. Managers with a global perspective will also have to integrate developments in one part of the world with actions somewhere else. This means that a U.S. executive will be required

68. Jean-Pierre Jeannet, "International Management: The Age of the Global Mind," *Unternehmung,* March 1991, pp. 132–142.

to use input, facts, or ideas from all other countries for decisions in the United States so that the most efficient and best products may be marketed.

Managers with a global perspective will also be challenged to deal with new strategies that were not part of the domestic or older international business scenes. These concepts, created and developed over the past fifteen years, have been included in our text and will become apparent to the reader on a chapter-by-chapter basis. As a result, the reader will come to appreciate that the term *global* is more than just a replacement for *international*. It is a combination of a new perspective on the world and a series of new strategic concepts that add to the competitiveness of global marketing strategies. Mastering both this new outlook and the new concepts will become a requirement for firms that aspire to a position of global player in their chosen industries or market segments.

Organization of This Book

This text is structured around the basic requirements for making sound international marketing decisions. It takes into account the need to develop several types of competencies to analyze international marketing issues. The global marketer must be able to deal with decision areas on various levels of complexity. We will discuss each of these dimensions of the global marketing task before we discuss the outline for this text.

Competencies

To compete successfully in today's international marketplace, companies and their management must master certain areas. *Environmental competence,* needed to perform in the international economy, includes a knowledge of the dynamics of world economy, of major national markets, and of social and cultural environments. *Analytic competence* is needed to pull together a vast array of information and data and to assemble relevant facts. *Strategic competence* helps executives focus on the strategic or long-term requirements of their firms, as opposed to short-term, opportunistic decisions. A global marketer must also possess *functional competence,* or a thorough background in all areas of marketing. Finally, *managerial competence* is the ability to implement programs and organize effectively on a global scale.

Managers with domestic responsibility also need analytic, strategic, functional, and managerial competence. They do not need international competence. Consequently, we will isolate one component that sets international executives apart from their domestic counterparts.

Decision Areas

Successful international marketing requires the ability to make decisions not typically faced by single-country firms. These decision groupings include environmental analysis, opportunity analysis, international marketing strategies, international marketing programs, and international marketing management. Managers continuously must assess foreign environments and perform *environmental analyses* relevant to their businesses. In a second step, managers need to do an *opportunity analysis* that will tell them which products to pursue in which markets. Once opportunities have been identified, *global marketing strategies* are designed to define long-term efforts of the firm. The company then may design *global marketing programs* to determine the marketing mix. Finally, international marketing must *manage the global marketing effort,* which requires attention to planning, personnel, and organization.

Our five competence levels are closely related to the five major global marketing decision areas described above. Environmental competence is needed to perform an analysis of the international environment. Analytic competence is the basis for opportunity analysis. Sound global marketing strategies are based on strategic competence. To design global marketing programs, one needs functional competence. Finally, managerial competence is needed for managing the international marketing effort.

Chapter Organization

This text is organized around the flow of decisions, as depicted in Figure 1.5. The five decision areas are treated in several chapters that delineate the respective competence levels most appropriate for each decision area.

Chapter 1 provides an introduction and overview of global marketing and its challenges today.

Part 1, Chapters 2 through 4, is concerned with the global marketing environment. In order to build environmental competence, special emphasis is given to the economic, cultural, social, political, and legal forces companies must contend with in order to be successful.

Part 2, Chapters 5 and 6, concentrates on the global market opportunity analysis. Chapters in this section highlight international markets or countries, international buyers, and the research or analysis necessary to pinpoint marketing opportunities globally.

Chapters 7, 8, and 9, which make up Part 3, deal with strategic issues. Chapter 7 deals primarily with the mindset of the global marketer. Chapter 8 introduces the elements of global marketing strategy. Chapter 9 describes how companies can enter markets they have decided to target.

Part 4, consisting of Chapters 10 through 15, aims at developing the competence to design global marketing programs consistent with a global strategy. The chapters in this section cover product strategies, product development, pricing, channel management, communications, and advertising.

The text concludes with Part 5, Chapters 16 through 18. Here the emphasis is on building managerial competence in a global environment. Chapters 16, 17, and 18 deal with organizational and controlling issues and also with the technical aspects of the export and import trade process.

Finally, the cases at the back of the book address international and global marketing issues and will allow you to practice the concepts developed in the text. These cases feature a range of complexity levels and address different decision areas of the global marketing process. They are all based on real situations, although the names of some of the companies are disguised.

FIGURE 1.5 ● International Marketing Management

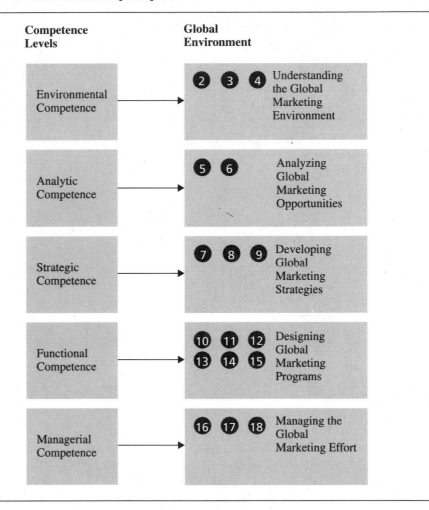

Conclusions

As a separate activity of business, global marketing is of great importance to nations, to individual companies, and to prospective managers. With markets and industries becoming increasingly globalized, most companies have to become active participants in global marketing. The competitive positions of most companies, both abroad and in their domestic markets, rests on their ability to succeed in global markets. At the same time, the economies of entire countries rest on the global marketing skills of managers. The standard of living of many people will depend on how well local industry does in the international market-place. These forces will place a premium on executive talent that is able to direct marketing operations from a global perspective. Clearly, many business professionals will need to understand the global dimension as it pertains to their functions, if they are to progress in their careers.

In assembling a trained cadre of professional global marketing executives, the United States has typically lagged behind other countries. The U.S. market is so large that domestic problems tend to overshadow global marketing opportunities. As a result, most U.S. executives develop their careers largely in a domestic setting and have little direct exposure to foreign markets. Executives in foreign countries are more apt to have traveled abroad and tend to speak one or two foreign languages. Thus, their ability to understand global complexities is more developed than is their U.S. counterparts'. All of this gives many foreign firms a considerable edge in competing for global dominance.

Although the need to develop a global competence may be clear, the circumstances that determine successful marketing practices for foreign markets are far less clear. The foreign marketing environment is characterized by a wide range of variables not typically encountered by domestic firms. This makes the job of global marketing extremely difficult. However, despite the complexities involved, there are concepts and analytic tools that can help international marketers. By learning to use these concepts and tools, you can enhance your own international and global competence. You will be able to contribute to the marketing operations of a wide range of firms, both domestic and foreign.

Questions for Discussion

1. Explain the scope of global marketing.
2. How and why does global marketing differ from domestic marketing?
3. Which do you think would be the most relevant factors limiting international marketing standardization of yogurts, automobiles, and desktop personal computers?
4. How does global marketing as a field relate to your future career in business? How would you expect to come in contact with global marketing activities?
5. Why are so many U.S. industries facing import competition?
6. Investigate one or two U.S. firms that do well abroad and analyze why they are successful.
7. Explain the major roles of multinationals (MNCs) and global corporations, as well as other types of firms in international marketing, and how they participate in this activity.
8. What do you think are the essential skills of a successful "global marketer"?
9. Which are the important skills for successful global minds?
10. List ten items most important to you that you hope to be able to understand or accomplish after studying this book.

For Further Reading

Alden, Vernon R. "Who Says You Can't Crack Japanese Markets." *Harvard Business Review,* January–February 1987, pp. 52–56.

Bartlett, Christopher, and Sumantra Ghoshal. *Managing Across Borders.* Boston: HBS Press, 1989.

Bolt, James F. "Global Competitors: Some Criteria for Success." *Business Horizons,* January–February 1988, pp. 34–41.

Buzzell, Robert D. "Can You Standardize Multinational Marketing?" *Harvard Business Review,* November–December 1968, pp. 102–113.

Kashani, Kamran. "Beware of Pitfalls in Global Marketing." *Harvard Business Review,* September–October 1989, pp. 91–98.

Kotler, Philip. "Global Standardization—Courting Danger." *Journal of Consumer Marketing,* Spring 1986, pp. 13–15.

Levitt, Theodore. "The Globalization of Markets." *Harvard Business Review,* May–June 1983, pp. 92–102.

Ohmae, Kenichi. *The Borderless World.* New York: Harper & Row, 1990.

Ohmae, Kenichi. "Managing in a Borderless World." *Harvard Business Review,* May–June 1989, pp. 152–161.

Ohmae, Kenichi. *Triad Power.* New York: Free Press, 1985.

Porter, Michael E. "The Strategic Role of International Marketing." *Journal of Consumer Marketing,* Spring 1986, pp. 17–21.

Prahalad, C. K., and Yves L. Doz. *The Multinational Mission.* New York: Free Press, 1987.

Reich, Robert B. "Who Is Them?" *Harvard Business Review,* March–April 1991, pp. 77–88.

Reich, Robert B. "Who Is Us?" *Harvard Business Review,* January–February 1990, pp. 53–64.

Reich, Robert B. *The Work of Nations.* New York: Knopf, 1991.

Simon-Miller, Françoise. "World Marketing: Going Global or Acting Local? Five Expert Viewpoints." *Journal of Consumer Marketing,* Spring 1986, pp. 5–7.

Taylor, William. "The Logic of Global Business: An Interview with ABB's Percy Barnevik." *Harvard Business Review,* March–April 1991, pp. 91–105.

World Investment Report 1993. New York: United Nations, 1993.

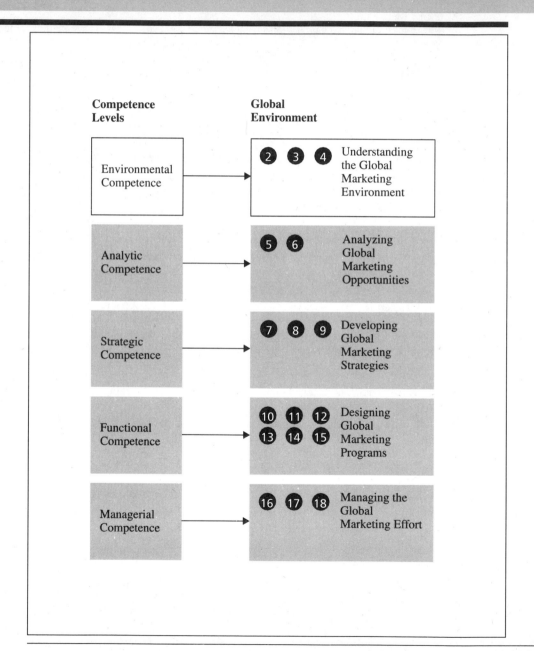

Competence
Levels

Global
Environment

Environmental
Competence

② ③ ④ Understanding
the Global
Marketing
Environment

Analytic
Competence

⑤ ⑥ Analyzing
Global
Marketing
Opportunities

Strategic
Competence

⑦ ⑧ ⑨ Developing
Global
Marketing
Strategies

Functional
Competence

⑩ ⑪ ⑫ Designing
Global
⑬ ⑭ ⑮ Marketing
Programs

Managerial
Competence

⑯ ⑰ ⑱ Managing the
Global
Marketing Effort

Part

1

Understanding the Global Marketing Environment

THIS PART OF the book introduces you to the environmental factors that influence international marketing decisions. Throughout Part 2 we maintain an analytical emphasis so that general concepts can be applied from country to country. Rather than describe a large number of environmental differences, we focus on several approaches companies adopt to cope with these differences. Our aim is to maintain a managerial point of view throughout.

In Chapter 2 we explain the nature of the various global economic forces that shape developments within individual countries as well as within the global economy. In Chapter 3 we describe the social and cultural influences that shape the local marketing environment, and in Chapter 4 we discuss the political and legal forces that affect international firms, focusing on how companies cope with these forces.

2

The Global Economy

BILLIONS OF DOLLARS *in goods and services are traded between nations each day. Businesses establish operations and borrow funds in locations throughout the world. Financial investors expeditiously purchase stocks and bonds on U.S., European, and Asian markets. Banks lend and arbitrage currencies worldwide. It is only when these transactions are interrupted or threatened that the scope and significance of the international economy are appreciated.*

The nations of the world are linked by a multidimensional network of economic, social, and political ties. As these connections become more important and complex, countries will find themselves richer but more vulnerable to foreign disturbances, and this vulnerability increasingly will move the issues surrounding international trade and finance into the political arena.

This chapter introduces the important aspects of world trade and finance. We begin by explaining comparative advantage, which is the basis for international trade. Then we explain the international system to monitor world trade, particularly the balance of payments measurement system. From this base, we describe the workings of the foreign exchange market and the cause of exchange rate movements. Finally, we discuss the international agencies that promote economic and monetary stability, as well as the strategies that countries use to protect their own economies.

International Trade: An Overview

Few individuals in the world are totally self-sufficient. Why should they be? Restricting consumption to self-made goods lowers living standards by narrowing the range and reducing the quality of goods we consume. For this reason, few nations have economies independent from the rest of the world, and it would be difficult to find a national leader willing or able to impose such an economic hardship on a country.

Foreign goods are central to the living standards of all nations. But as Table 2.1 shows, there is considerable variation among countries concerning their reliance on foreign trade. Imports are less than 13 percent of the gross domestic product (GDP) of Japan, Mexico, or the United States, whereas the Netherlands and Belgium have import-to-GDP ratios of 46 percent or more.

Even in countries that seemingly do not have a great reliance on imports (such as the

TABLE 2.1 ● Imports and Exports as a Percentage of GDP, 1991 Estimates (in Billions of Dollars)

	GDP	*Imports*	*Imports/GDP*	*Exports*	*Exports/GDP*
Industrial					
Australia	296	39	13%	39	13%
Belgium	198	120	61	118	60
Canada	602	126	21	134	22
Germany	1542	379	25	391	25
Japan	3400	218	6	200	9
Netherlands	277	127	46	134	48
Norway	111	26	23	37	34
United States	5750	486	8	417	7
Switzerland	227	65	29	59	26
Developing					
Greece	69	19	27%	7	10%
Mexico	283	36	13	28	10
Pakistan	45	8	17	6	14
Romania	26	6	23	4	16
Saudi Arabia	107	26	24	51	47
South Korea	274	83	30	72	26
Venezuela	53	10	19	16	30

Note: Estimates of GDP in local currency were converted to dollars, using the yearly average exchange rate. Figures are rounded to the nearest billion in dollars. Please note that GDP is similar to GNP, which is defined in Chapter 6, page 204. Percentages were calculated by the authors.

Source: Adapted from *World Outlook 1993.* London: Economist Intelligence Unit, January 1993.

United States), foreign goods and services do play an important role. In the United States, exports account for 75 percent of manufacturing growth.[1] For example:

> Peter Johnson, a student, is awakened in the morning by his Sony clock radio. After showering, he puts on an Italian-made jacket while listening to the latest release by Tears for Fears, a British singing group. At breakfast, he has a cup of Brazilian coffee, a bowl of cereal made from U.S.-grown wheat, and a Colombian banana. A quick glance at his Swiss watch shows him that he will have to hurry if he wants to be on time for his first class. He drives to campus in a Toyota, stopping on the way to fill the tank with gas from Saudi Arabian oil. Once in class, he rushes to take a seat with the other students, 30 percent of whom hold non-U.S. passports.

The figures given in Table 2.1 are useful for identifying the international dependence of nations, but they should be viewed as rough indicators only. In a disruption of international trade, there is little doubt that the United States would be harmed much less than the Netherlands. But how about Japan? Japan is a nation with relatively few natural resources. It survives by importing raw materials, processing them, and then exporting the finished products. Japan's import-to-GDP ratio is small (which indicates a lack of reliance on foreign trade) only because its exports are so large—therefore making its GDP large. Thus, Japan would be a major victim of trade curtailment.

So far, the focus has been on world trade for goods. Services also are an important and growing part of the world's economy. Services make up approximately 20 percent of the world's exports. Industries such as banking, telecommunications, insurance, construction, transportation, tourism, and consulting make up over half the national income of many rich economies. Services account for 70 percent of GDP in the United States and 75 percent of the employed. The leading exporters of commercial services are shown in Figure 2.1. The United States, France, and Great Britain are the largest exporters of services. Countries such as Spain, Austria, and Norway depend heavily on services, which represent over 30 percent of their exports. As the world market for services grows, developing countries fear that the powerful global service companies will steal business away from their less efficient domestic suppliers. The 1993 round of General Agreement on Tariffs and Trade (GATT) talks included freer trade in services. While the details were not finalized, the agreement was expected to create opportunities for competitive U.S. service industries.[2] Other transactions play an equally important role in world trade: International investments, foreign borrowing and lending, and grants-in-aid are essential to the health and well-being of all nations.

The Growth in World Trade

World trade has grown rapidly from about $4 trillion in 1980 to approximately 7.5 trillion in 1993.[3] This growth has been fueled by the opening of world markets. The Bretton

---

1. Susan Lee, ''Are We Building New Berlin Walls?'' *Forbes,* January 7, 1991, p. 87.
2. ''What's Next After GATT's Victory?'' *Fortune,* January 10, 1994, p. 66.
3. Ibid., p. 68.

FIGURE 2.1 ● Leading Exporters of Commercial Services, 1988

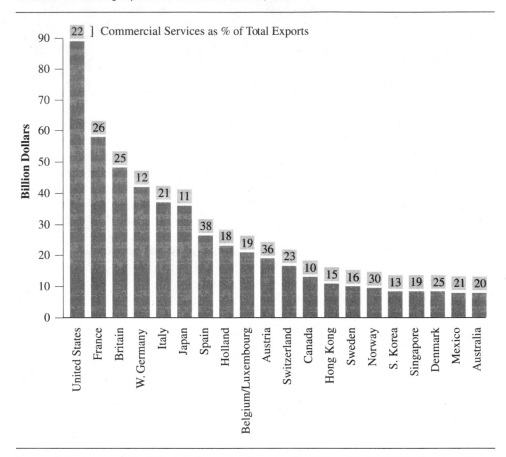

Source: ''The Survey of World Trade,'' *Economist,* September 22, 1990, p. 36. © 1990 The Economist Newspaper Limited. Reprinted with permission.

Woods conference of world leaders in 1944 led to the establishment of GATT, which will be discussed in detail later. The original group of twenty-three countries has expanded to almost one hundred. GATT has helped to reduce tariffs from 40 percent in 1947 to less than 5 percent in 1990. The reduction of tariffs and the relatively free flow of goods has increased trade by 500 percent, of which global output has gone up 200 percent.[4] The principle of free trade has led to the building of market interdependencies. As shown in Figure 2.2, major interdependencies have grown among the major trading blocks—North

4. ''The Survey of World Trade,'' *Economist,* September 22, 1990, p. 7.

FIGURE 2.2 ● World Trade Flows, 1989 (in Billions of Dollars)

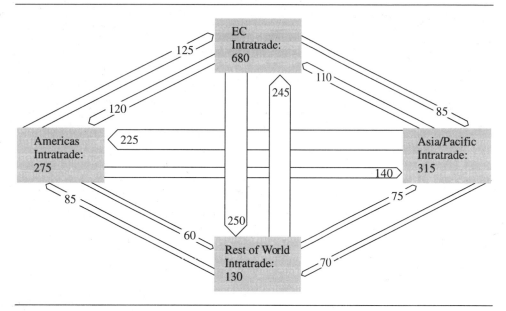

Source: "The World Economy," *Economist,* January 5, 1991, p. 22. © 1991 The Economist Newspaper Limited. Reprinted with permission.

America, Europe, Asia, and the rest of the world. If one member behaves unfairly (for example, by giving government support to a domestic industry and thereby lowering its costs, or by protecting a domestic industry by not allowing or making it difficult for foreign suppliers to enter the market, or by letting a manufacturer dump its product overseas at cut-rate prices), then other members can retaliate by excluding or limiting the culprit. Unfortunately this practice of retaliation is growing, particularly in the United States. The Omnibus Trade and Competitiveness Act of 1988 includes a section called super-301, which gives the U.S. trade representative the power to negotiate a settlement or issue a duty to offset any alleged damage. The U.S. government has used its large potential market and the power of super-301 retaliation to obtain a number of voluntary export restraints covering textiles, steel, clothing, cars, shoes, machinery, and electronics.[5] Many economists argue that when countries protect domestic industry, consumers usually pay higher prices. Understanding the economics of trade is critical to understanding the need for free trade flows from country to country.

5. Ibid., pp. 8–11.

The Basis for Trade: Absolute
Versus Comparative Advantage

Internationally traded goods and services are important to most countries, as shown in Table 2.1. Because jobs and standard of living seem to be so closely tied to these inflows and outflows, there is much debate about why particular countries find their competitive advantages in certain goods and not in others, whereas other countries have different advantages and disadvantages.

Over the past twenty years, not only has there been a dramatic rise in the volume of trade, but numerous changes have been made in its patterns as well. Countries that once exported vast amounts of steel, such as the United States, are now net importers of the metal. Other nations such as Japan, once known for inexpensive, handmade products, now compete globally in high-tech products. What caused these trade pattern changes? Why do countries that are able to produce virtually any product choose to specialize in only certain goods? Where do international cost advantages originate? In the twenty-first century, will we still think of South Korea and China as having the greatest advantage in handmade goods, or in the future will they be like Japan and Taiwan are today?

The early work of Adam Smith provides the foundation for understanding trade today. Smith saw trade as a way to promote efficiency because it fostered competition, led to specialization, and resulted in economies of scale. Specialization supports the concept of absolute advantages—that is, sell to other countries the goods that utilize your special skills and resources and buy the rest from those who have some advantage. This theory of selling what you are best at is known as *absolute advantage.* But what if you have no advantages? Will all your manufacturers be driven out of business? David Ricardo in his 1817 publication, *Principles of Political Economy,* offered his theory of comparative advantage.[6] This theory maintains that it is still possible to produce what one is best at even if someone else is better. The following sections further develop the concepts of absolute and comparative advantage, the economic basis of free trade.

Absolute Advantage

While many variables may be listed as the primary determinants of international trade, productivity differences rank high on the list. Take, for example, two countries—Spain and Germany. Suppose the average Spanish worker can produce either 400 machines or 1,600 pounds of tomatoes in one year. Over the same time period, the average German worker can produce either 500 machines or 500 pounds of tomatoes. (See example 1 in Table 2.2.) In this case, German workers can produce more machinery, *absolutely,* than Spanish workers can; whereas Spanish workers can produce more tomatoes, *absolutely,* than can their German counterparts.

Given these figures, Spain is the obvious low-cost producer of tomatoes and should

6. ''The Economies of Free Trade,'' *Economist,* September 22, 1990, p. 12.

TABLE 2.2 ● Absolute versus Comparative Advantage: Worker Productivity Examples

	Spain	Germany
Example 1		
Yearly output per worker		
Machinery	400	500
Tomatoes	1,600	500
Absolute advantage	Tomatoes	Machinery
Example 2		
Yearly output per worker		
Machinery	200	500
Tomatoes	800	1,000
Opportunity costs of production	1 machine costs 4 lb tomatoes *or* 1 lb tomatoes costs 0.25 machines	1 machine costs 2 lb tomatoes *or* 1 lb tomatoes costs 0.50 machines
Absolute advantage	None	Tomatoes Machinery
Comparative advantage	Tomatoes	Machinery

export them to Germany. Similarly, Germany is the low-cost producer of machines and should export them to Spain.[7]

Comparative Advantage

We should not conclude from the previous example that absolute differences in production capabilities are necessary for trade to occur. Consider the same two countries—Spain and Germany. Now assume that the average Spanish worker can produce either 200 machines or 800 pounds of tomatoes each year, whereas the average German worker can produce either 500 machines or 1,000 pounds of tomatoes (see example 2 in Table 2.2). Germany has an absolute advantage in both goods, and it appears as though Spain will benefit from trade because it can buy from Germany cheaper goods than Spain can make for itself. However, the basis for mutually advantageous trade is present, even here. The reason lies in the concept of comparative advantage.

Comparative advantage measures a product's cost of production, not in monetary terms but in terms of the forgone opportunity to produce something else. It focuses on

7. The concept of absolute advantage can be found in Adam Smith, *The Wealth of Nations* (New York: Modern Library, 1937). Originally published in 1776.

TABLE 2.3 ● Mutually Advantageous Trading Ratios

Tomatoes	*Machines*
1 pound tomatoes = 0.50 machines	1 machine = 4 pounds tomatoes
↕	↕
1 pound tomatoes = 0.25 machines	1 machine = 2 pounds tomatoes

tradeoffs. To illustrate, the production of machines means that resources cannot be devoted to the production of tomatoes. In Germany, the worker who produces 500 machines will not be able to grow 1,000 pounds of tomatoes. If we standardize, the cost can be stated as follows: each pound of tomatoes costs 0.5 machines, or 1 machine costs 2 pounds of tomatoes. In Spain, producing 200 machines forces the sacrifice of 800 pounds of tomatoes. Alternatively, this means that 1 pound of tomatoes costs 0.25 machines, or 1 machine costs 4 pounds of tomatoes.[8]

From the example above, we see that even though Spain has an absolute disadvantage in both commodities, it still has a comparative advantage in tomatoes. For Spain the cost of producing a pound of tomatoes is 0.25 machines, while for Germany the cost is 0.5 machines. Similarly, even though Germany has an absolute advantage in both products, it has a comparative cost advantage only in machines. It costs Germany only 2 pounds of tomatoes to produce a single machine, while in Spain the cost is 4 pounds of tomatoes.

The last step in the discussion of the comparative advantage concept is to choose a mutually advantageous trading ratio and to show how it can benefit both countries. Any trading ratio between 1 machine = 2 pounds of tomatoes (Spain's domestic trading ratio) and 1 machine = 4 pounds of tomatoes (Germany's domestic trading ratio) will benefit both nations (see Table 2.3). Suppose we choose 1 machine = 3 pounds tomatoes. Since Germany will be exporting machinery, it gains by getting 3 pounds of tomatoes rather than the 2 pounds it would have produced domestically. Likewise, because Spain will be exporting tomatoes, it gains because 1 machine can be imported for the sacrifice of only 3 pounds, rather than 4 pounds, of tomatoes if it made the machine in Spain.

Another way to think of it is in terms of the value of labor. If workers are paid relative to their output, at the end of a year a German worker could have 500 machines or 1,000 pounds of tomatoes, and a Spanish worker 200 machines or 800 pounds of tomatoes. Given the relative output of each, a German worker could trade 1 machine for 2 pounds in Germany or 4 pounds in Spain. The Spanish worker could trade a pound of tomatoes for .25 machines in Spain or .50 machines in Germany. In the end, the Spanish worker will end up with less goods because productivity is less, which means he or she will be paid less, so the goods will be cheaper than in Germany, where the output per worker is higher and therefore more expensive.

8. David Ricardo, ''Principles of Political Economy and Taxation,'' in *The Works and Correspondence of David Ricardo,* ed. Pierro Sraffa and Maurice H. Dobb (Cambridge, U.K.: University Press, 1951–1955), chap. 7.

The discussion of comparative advantage illustrates that relative rather than absolute differences in productivity can form a determining basis for international trade. Although the concept of comparative advantage provides a powerful tool for explaining the rationale for mutually advantageous trade, it gives little insight into the source of the relative productivity differences. Specifically, why does a country find its comparative advantage in one particular good or service rather than another product? Is it by chance that the United States is a net exporter of aircraft, machinery, and chemicals but a net importer of steel, textiles, and consumer electronic products? Or can we find some systematic explanations for this pattern?

The answers to these questions are of more than just academic concern; they have an impact on the standard of living and livelihood of millions of people. The importance of understanding productivity differences is especially apparent in countries where trade barriers (for example, tariffs and quotas) are about to be either erected or dismantled. For instance, during the formative years of the European Common Market, discussions centered on the economic disruptions that would occur when Germany, Italy, and France dropped their tariff barriers and permitted free trade among them. These issues have resurfaced each time a new country (such as Greece, Spain, or Portugal) has applied for membership to the European Community. They were hotly debated in 1982 when the U.S. government proposed trade liberalization measures for Latin American countries in the Caribbean Basin Initiative. Similarly, they were at the center during the Uruguay Round of GATT trade talks, which ran into difficulty over the elimination of farm subsidies by member countries.

The notion of comparative advantage requires that nations make intensive use of those factors they possess in abundance. They export *these* goods and import *those* goods for which they have a comparative disadvantage. So Hungary, with its low labor cost of one dollar per hour, will export labor-intensive goods such as unsophisticated chest freezers and table linen, while Sweden, with its high-quality iron ore deposits, will export high-grade steel.

Michael Porter argues that while the theory of comparative advantage has appeal, it is limited just to the factors of production on land, labor, natural resources, and capital. His study of ten trading nations that account for 50 percent of world exports and one hundred industries resulted in a new theory. This theory postulates that the country will have a significant impact on the competitive advantage of an industry, depending on the following factors:

1. The elements of production

2. The nature of domestic demand

3. The presence of appropriate suppliers or related industry

4. The conditions in the country that govern how companies are created, organized, and managed, as well as the nature of domestic rivalry[9]

9. Michael E. Porter, *The Competitive Advantage of Nations* (New York: Macmillan, 1990), pp. 69–175.

This view of competitive advantage does not refute the theory of comparative advantage; rather it helps explain why industries have a comparative advantage.

Balance of Payments

Newspapers, magazines, and nightly TV news programs are filled with stories relating to aspects of international business. Often, media coverage centers on the implications of a nation's trade deficit or surplus or on the economic consequences of an undervalued or overvalued currency. What are trade deficits? What factors will cause a currency's international value to change? The first step in answering these questions is to gain a clear understanding of the contents and meaning of a nation's balance of payments.

The balance of payments is an accounting record of the transactions between the residents of one country and the residents of the rest of the world over a given period of time.[10] It resembles a company's statement of sources and uses of funds. Transactions in which domestic residents either purchase assets (goods and services) from abroad or reduce foreign liabilities are considered uses (outflows) of funds because payments abroad must be made. Similarly, transactions in which domestic residents either sell assets to foreign residents or increase their liabilities to foreigners are sources (inflows) of funds because payments from abroad are received.

Listed in Table 2.4 are the principal parts of the balance of payments statement: the current account, the capital account, and the official transactions account. There are three items under the current account. The goods category states the monetary values of a nation's international transactions in physical goods. The services category shows the values of a wide variety of transactions such as transportation services, consulting, travel, passenger fares, fees, royalties, rent, and investment income. Finally, unilateral transfers include all transactions for which there is no quid pro quo (that is, gifts). Private remittances, personal gifts, philanthropic donations, relief, and aid are included within this account.

The capital account category is divided into two parts on the basis of time. Short-term transactions refer to maturities less than or equal to one year, and long-term transactions refer to maturities longer than one year. Purchases of treasury bills, certificates of deposit, foreign exchange, and commercial paper are typical short-term investments. Long-term investments are separated further into portfolio investments and direct investments.

In general, portfolio investments imply that no ownership rights are held by the purchaser over the foreign investment. Debt securities such as notes and bonds would be included under this heading. Direct investments are long-term ownership interests, such as business capital outlays in foreign subsidiaries and branches. Stock purchases are included as well, but only if such ownership entails substantial control over the foreign company. Countries differ in the percentage of total outstanding stock an individual must

10. An excellent source of historical and internationally comparable data can be found in the *Balance of Payments Yearbook,* published yearly by the International Monetary Fund.

TABLE 2.4 ● Balance of Payments

	Uses of funds	*Sources of funds*
Current Account		
1. Goods	Imports	Exports
2. Services	Imports	Exports
3. Unilateral transfers	Paid abroad	From abroad
Capital Account		
1. Short-term investment	Made abroad	From abroad
2. Long-term investments	Made abroad	From abroad
a. Portfolio investment		
b. Direct investment		
Official Transactions Account		
Official reserve changes	Gained	Lost

hold in order for an investment to be considered a direct investment in the balance of payments statements. The International Monetary Fund reports that these values range from 10 percent for widely dispersed holdings to 25 percent.[11]

Because it is recorded in double-entry bookkeeping form, the balance of payments as a whole must always have its inflows (sources of funds) equal all its outflows (uses of funds). Therefore, the concept of a deficit or surplus refers only to selected parts of the entire statement. A deficit occurs when the particular outflows (uses of funds) exceed the particular inflows (sources of funds). A surplus occurs when the inflows considered exceed the corresponding outflows. In this sense, a nation's surplus or deficit is similar to that of individuals, governments, or businesses. If we spend more than we earn, we are in a deficit position. If we earn more than we spend, we are running a surplus.

Balance of Payments Measures

Three balance of payments measures are considered to be important by many business-people, government officials, and economists. These are the balance on merchandise trade, the balance on goods and services, and the balance on current account.[12] The balance on merchandise trade is the narrowest measure because it considers only internationally traded goods. For this reason, critics feel that it is of the least practical value. They argue that the balance on merchandise trade is a vestigial remnant of the seventeenth-century

11. International Monetary Fund, *Balance of Payments Manual,* 4th ed. (Washington D.C.: International Monetary Fund, 1977), pp. 137–138.

12. The classic discussion of balance of payments is found in James Meade, *The Balance of Payments* (London: Oxford University Press, 1951).

mercantilist conviction that if one country gained from trade, the other lost.[13] In those war-torn times, domestic economic policies were geared toward ensuring that exports exceeded imports. In so doing, domestic jobs were provided, and the excess funds (usually precious metals) earned through the surpluses could be used to support armies and navies for imperialist expansions—or to defend against them. However, if jobs are the goal, there seems to be little point in separating goods from services. Both activities give jobs to willing workers.

Defenders of the measure feel that jobs connected to physical goods are more important than service-oriented jobs, and therefore the balance on merchandise trade is a useful economic indicator. They contend that if an international disruption occurred, it would be better to live in a country with textile factories, steel mills, farms, and electronics firms rather than to live in a country with a labor force of insurance clerks, computer consultants, and tourist guides.

The balance on goods and services has a direct link to most national income accounting systems. It is reported in the national income and national product statements as "net exports." If this figure is positive, a net transfer of resources is taking place from the surplus nation to the debtor nations. Many analysts feel that a negative balance is an indication that a nation is not living within its means. To have such a deficit position, the country would have to be a net borrower of foreign funds or a net recipient of foreign aid.

The most widely used measure of a nation's international payments position is the statement of balance on current account. As with the balance on goods and services statement, it shows whether a nation is living within or beyond its means. Because it includes unilateral transfers, deficits (in the absence of government intervention) must be financed by international borrowing or by selling foreign investments. Therefore, the measure is considered to be a reflection of the change in a nation's financial claims on other countries.

Exchange Rates

The purchase of a foreign good or service can be thought of as involving two sequential transactions: the purchase of the foreign currency, followed by the purchase of the foreign item itself. If the cost of buying either the foreign currency or the foreign item rises, the price to the importer increases. A ratio that measures the value of one currency in terms of another currency is called an *exchange rate.* With it, one is able to compare domestic and foreign prices.

When a currency rises in value, it is said to *appreciate.* If it falls in value, it is said to *depreciate.* Therefore, a change in the value of the U.S. dollar exchange rate from 0.50 British pounds to 0.65 British pounds is an appreciation of the dollar and a depreciation of the pound. After all, the dollar now commands more pounds while a greater number of pounds must be spent to purchase one dollar.

The strength of a domestic currency against the currency of your trading partners can

---

13. Examples of mercantilist thought can be found in Thomas Mun, "England's Treasure by Foreign Trade," in *Early English Tracts in Commerce,* ed. John McCullock (Norwich: Jarrold and Sons, 1952). See also Joseph Schumpeter, *History of Economic Analysis* (New York: Oxford University Press, 1954).

have a negative effect. For example, the Swiss franc was strong versus the dollar, pound, and yen in 1990, so when Nestlé converted its sales into dollars in the United States, yen in Japan, and pounds in the United Kingdom, it all equaled less in Swiss francs. Nestlé reported a 3.5 percent decline in sales in 1990 due to the strong Swiss franc.[14]

The strength of the yen against the dollar in 1993 had a negative effect on many Japanese businesses that export to the United States. Nissan Motor, Sony, Toshiba, Canon, and Fijitsu all expect profits to decline due to the strong yen. Canon shifted camera production to Taiwan, Malaysia, and China to offset the surging yen.[15] On the other hand, due to the decline of the dollar from 125 yen in January 1993 to 100 yen in August 1993, Ford reduced prices of its cars in Japan by 5 percent and expected to further reduce prices. The result is that Ford's sales in Japan rose 59 percent in the first seven months of 1993.[16]

The Foreign Exchange Market Unlike major stock markets, where trading is done on central exchanges (for example, the New York Stock Exchange and the London Stock Exchange), foreign exchange transactions are handled on an over-the-counter market, largely by phone, teletype, and telex. Private and commercial customers as well as banks, brokers, and central banks conduct millions of transactions on this worldwide market daily.

As Figure 2.3 shows, the foreign exchange market has a hierarchical structure. Private customers deal mainly with banks in the retail market, and banks stand ready to either buy or sell foreign exchange as long as a free and active market for the currency exists.

Not all banks participate directly in the foreign exchange market. In the United States, a bank must have a substantial volume of international business to justify setting up a foreign exchange department. Thus, most small financial intermediaries handle customers' business through correspondent banks.

Banks that have foreign exchange departments trade with private commercial customers on the retail market, but they also deal with other banks (domestic or foreign) and brokers on the wholesale market. Generally, these wholesale transactions are for amounts of one million dollars or more. Many of these trades are made on the basis of verbal agreements, and only some days later is written documentation formally exchanged.

The foreign exchange market is probably as close as one can get to the economist's proverbial ideal of pure competition. There are many buyers and sellers, no one buyer or seller can influence the price, the product is homogeneous, there is relatively free entry into and exit from the market, and there is virtually perfect worldwide information. If prices among banks differed by even a fraction of a cent, arbitragers would immediately step in for the profits they could earn risk free. Through telex machines, telephone calls, and voice boxes that lead directly into the trading rooms of other banks and brokers, participants keep abreast of the market. Positions are opened and closed minute by minute, and the pace of activity in a foreign exchange dealing room can be quite frantic.

Central banks play a key role in the foreign exchange markets because they are the ultimate controllers of domestic money supplies. When they enter the market to directly

14. "Nestlé Turnover Falls by 3.5%," *Financial Times,* January 19, 1991, p. 22.
15. "Yen Strength Threatens Corporate Profits." *Nikkei Weekly,* August 16, 1993, p. 4.
16. "In Abrupt Shift, US Intervenes to Slow Yen's Historic Rise," *Wall Street Journal,* August 20, 1993, pp. 1, 12.

FIGURE 2.3 ● Structure of the Foreign Exchange Market

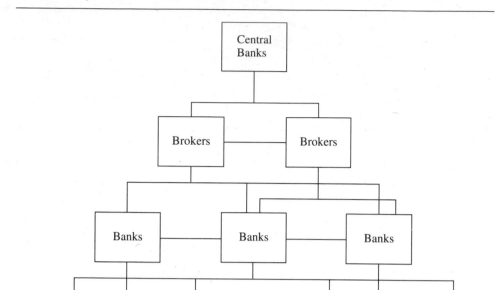

influence the exchange rate value, they deal mainly with brokers and large money market banks. Their trading is not done to make a profit but to attain some macroeconomic goal such as altering the exchange rate value, reducing inflation, or changing domestic interest rates. In general, even if central banks do not intervene in the foreign exchange markets, their actions influence exchange rate values because large increases in a nation's money supply will increase its inflation rate and lower the international value of its currency.

Causes of Exchange Rate Movements   Exchange rates are among the most closely watched and politically sensitive economic variables. Regardless of which way the rates move, some groups are hurt while other groups are helped. If a currency's value rises, domestic businesses will find it more difficult to compete internationally, and the domestic unemployment rate may rise. For example, the strong yen forced Japanese car manufacturers to raise car prices in the United States, thereby increasing the premium for Japanese cars to approximately $1,700. This caused Japan's share of the U.S. market to decline by 2.6 percent, down to 23.2 percent.[17] If the value of the currency falls, foreign goods become

17. "Trying to Rev-Up, Can Japan's Carmakers Regain Lost Ground?" *Business Week,* January 24, 1994, p. 32.

more expensive, the cost of living increases, and goods become cheaper to foreign buyers. What are the causes of these exchange rate movements, and to what extent can governments influence them?

Market exchange rates are determined by the forces of supply and demand. The greater the supply of a currency to the foreign exchange market or the lesser its demand, the lower will be its international value. Similarly, the greater the demand for a currency in the foreign exchange market or the lower its supply, the higher will be its international value. Therefore, to predict movements in a currency's international value, one must identify the participants whose transactions affect these supply and demand forces and determine which factors will cause them to change their behavior.

Identifying the international participants is a relatively easy matter because they have been implicitly mentioned already in the discussion of the balance of payments. Recall that the balance of payments is nothing more than a summary of a nation's international transactions. In the current account and the capital account, traders, speculators, and investors are the major players. To this list, we will add government participants. The following sections will show how these groups act and react to overlapping market signals.

Traders   International trade in goods and services is influenced mainly by changes in relative international prices and relative income levels. If, for example, the U.S. inflation rate exceeds that of Germany, then U.S. goods will become progressively more expensive than German goods. Consequently, U.S. consumers will begin to demand more of these foreign goods, thereby increasing the supply of dollars to the foreign exchange market (that is, increasing the demand for German marks). For the same reason, German consumers will reduce their demand for dollars (that is, reduce their supply of marks) as they purchase fewer U.S. goods. Therefore, relatively high inflation in the United States will cause the international value of the dollar to fall and the value of other currencies to rise.

Consumption is constrained by income, the ability to borrow, and the availability of credit. This is true both for individuals and nations. However, when speaking of a country's income, gross domestic product (GDP) is the most widely used measure. An increase in GDP will give the citizens of a nation the wherewithal to purchase more goods and services. Since many of the newly purchased goods are likely to be foreign, increases in GDP will raise the demand for foreign products and therefore raise the demand for foreign currencies. If, for example, the U.S. growth rate exceeds that of Germany, there will be a net increase in the demand for German marks and a lowering of the dollar's international value.[18]

Speculators   Speculators buy and sell currencies in anticipation of changing future values. If there were a widespread expectation that the Japanese yen would rise in relative

18. For an alternative point of view, see Jacob A. Frenkel and Harry Johnson, ''The Monetary Approach to the Balance of Payments: Essential Concepts and Historical Origins,'' in *The Monetary Approach to the Balance of Payments,* ed. J. A. Frenkel and H. G. Johnson (Toronto: University of Toronto Press, 1976).

value to the dollar, speculators would try to purchase yen now (that is, sell dollars) in anticipation of that change. As the demand for yen increased in the spot market and the supply of yen for dollars fell, the yen's exchange rate value would rise. (A spot market is for the immediate delivery of currency within two days of the transaction.) Similarly, as the supply of dollars increased and the demand for them decreased, the international value of the dollar relative to yen would fall. Consequently, spot market rates are very much influenced by future expectations.

Investors   One of the main factors influencing investors' decisions is the differential between international interest rates. If, for example, Italian interest rates were greater than U.S. interest rates (adjusted for such things as risk, taxability, and maturity), then investors would have an incentive to place their funds where they earned the highest return—in Italy. The supply of dollars in the foreign exchange market would rise (as U.S. investors purchased Italian securities), and the demand for dollars would fall (as Italians purchased domestic rather than U.S. securities). The effect of these investments would be to lower the value of the dollar relative to the lira.

As important as relative interest rates are to the international investment decision, expected changes in exchange rates are equally important. There can be a substantial difference between the interest rate at which funds are placed in foreign investments and the net return after repatriation. The gains made on higher foreign interest rates can be partially or fully offset by changes in a currency's value. This risk may be eliminated by contracting on the forward exchange market, but in general the forward rates are arbitraged to the point where these rates completely offset the interest rate advantage. This is why relative inflation rates reappear as an important determinant of international transactions. A relatively high domestic inflation rate is one of the major causes of a depreciation in the exchange value of a currency.[19] Therefore, a high inflation rate implies that the currency carries high nominal interest rates, an expensive spot exchange value, and a relatively cheap forward exchange rate value.

Governments   Governments enter foreign exchange markets in a variety of ways, ranging from the international purchase of goods and services to the granting of foreign aid. Perhaps the most pronounced impact governments have is as discretionary interveners in foreign exchange markets. Suppose the United States and Japan agreed to lower the dollar's value relative to the yen. To do so, dollars would have to be supplied—and yen demanded—in the foreign exchange markets.

For the United States, this would mean putting upward pressure on the domestic money supply as newly created dollars were exchanged for circulating Japanese yen. For

19. The purchasing power parity theory explains that exchange rates can be predicted by estimating relative international inflation rates. See Gustav Cassel, *The World's Monetary Problems* (London: Constable, 1921); Jacob A. Frenkel, ''Purchasing Power Parity: Doctrinal Perspective and Evidence from the 1920s,'' *Journal of International Economics,* 8 (May 1978); Jacob A. Frenkel, ''The Collapse of Purchasing Power Parity During the 1970s,'' *European Economic Review,* 16 (May 1981).

Japan, this type of intervention would mean putting downward pressure on its money supply as dollar reserves were used to take yen off the market. Because governments have such strong and direct controls over domestic money supplies, subsequent changes in other economic variables (for example, inflation rates or interest rates) will result from this activity.

International Agencies for Promoting Economic and Monetary Stability

Stability in the international economy is a prerequisite for worldwide peace and prosperity. It was for this reason that at the end of World War II a group of countries met at Bretton Woods, a small ski resort in New Hampshire, and formed both the International Monetary Fund and the World Bank (the International Bank for Reconstruction and Development). With headquarters in Washington, D.C., these two agencies continue to play major roles in the international scene. Although they have many notable achievements, perhaps their most important contribution has been to initiate forums for summit discussions of controversial financial topics.

International Monetary Fund

The major goals of the International Monetary Fund (IMF) are to promote orderly and stable foreign exchange markets, maintain free convertibility among the currencies of member nations, reduce international impediments to trade, and provide liquidity to counteract temporary balance of payments disequilibria. While the IMF has no legal powers to enforce its decisions, strong and subtle pressures can be brought to bear on noncomplying nations.

In the early years following its creation, the IMF focused its attention on restoring currency convertibility among members and ensuring that adequate liquidity existed for countries experiencing balance of payments difficulties. Free convertibility was regained by 1958, but the liquidity issue was a much more difficult problem to solve. International trade expanded rapidly over the postwar period, but international reserves in both dollars and gold grew less rapidly. To increase the amount of international liquidity and to take some of the pressure off these reserve assets, the IMF in 1970 began issuing special drawing rights (SDRs) to member nations. These SDRs (mutual book credits) gave nations the right to purchase foreign currencies, and with these currencies they could finance temporary balance of payments deficits.

In 1973, major trading nations abandoned the fixed exchange rate system set up at Bretton Woods in 1944. As a result, the need for increases in world liquidity to finance balance of payments deficits was reduced substantially. Today, the IMF has taken on some different tasks and has a somewhat new image. Prior to the 1970s, the agency funded operations with contributions from member nations, but this changed as the IMF began selling some of its gold reserves and banking part of the capital gain. In the 1980s, the IMF took another step away from the past by borrowing in the private capital markets.

Over the past decade, the IMF has begun to extend longer-term credits to the developing nations, rather than only short-term balance of payments aid. To qualify such loans, the Fund may require that countries take drastic economic steps, such as reducing tariff barriers, making businesses independent, curbing domestic inflation, and cutting government expenditures. While many nations have resented such intervention, banks worldwide have used the IMF as a screening device for their private loans to many developing countries. If countries qualify for IMF loans, they are considered for private credit.

World Bank (International Bank for Reconstruction and Development)

The World Bank, along with its sister organizations, the International Finance Corporation and the International Development Association, give long-term loans mainly to developing nations. In this sense, these three institutions are like merchant bankers (that is, suppliers of capital) for the developing nations.

The World Bank acts as an intermediary between the private capital markets and the developing nations. It makes long-term loans (usually fifteen or twenty-five years) carrying rates that reflect prevailing market conditions. By virtue of its AAA credit rating, the bank is able to borrow private funds at relatively low market rates and pass the savings to the developing nations. However, because it must borrow to obtain capital and is not funded by members' contributions, the World Bank must raise lending rates when its costs (that is, market interest rates) rise.

The International Finance Corporation (IFC) provides risk capital to fledgling companies in developing nations. For its investments, the IFC acquires stocks or bonds in the newly established businesses. After the company becomes solvent, the IFC tries to sell these securities on the domestic capital markets and to reinvest the receipts into other projects worldwide.

The International Development Association lends what may be termed *soft money* to developing nations. Funds used for these loans do not come directly from the private capital markets but are donated by member nations—meaning that they are usually taxpayer financed. Loan maturities are for fifty years, and a grace period may be granted on all payments for up to ten years. Moreover, the interest that IDA charges to debtor nations is only 0.75 percent above the agency's cost of funds.

Together these agencies have tried to encourage entrepreneurial endeavors in underdeveloped parts of the world. Their loans have focused on areas that promote domestic industry and employment. The idea is age old: ''If you give a starving man a fish, you will feed him for a day. If you teach him how to fish, you will feed him for a lifetime.''

Group of Seven

The world's leading industrial nations have established a Group of Seven, which meets regularly to discuss the world economy. Finance ministers and central bank governors from the United States, Japan, Germany, France, Britain, Italy, and Canada make up this group, referred to as G7. The group works together informally to help stabilize the world economy and reduce extreme disruptions. For example, G7 met in late January 1991 after the start of the Gulf War and issued the following statement.[20]

> Ministers and governors reviewed their economic policies and prospects and reaffirmed their support for economic policy coordination at this critical time. They noted that although growth in all their economies had slowed, expansion of the world economy continues, and the pace of activity could be expected to pick up late this year. They noted that growth remains particularly strong in Germany and Japan. Implementation of sound fiscal policies, combined with stability-oriented monetary policies, should create conditions favorable to lower global interest rates and a stronger world economy. They also stressed the importance of a timely and successful completion of the Uruguay Round [of multilateral trade talks]. The ministers and governors also discussed the situation of global financial markets in the light of uncertainties arising from the Gulf War and developments in the Soviet Union. They agreed to strengthen cooperation and to monitor developments in exchange markets. Ministers and governors are prepared to respond as appropriate to maintain stability in international financial markets.

The G7 held their nineteenth economic summit in mid-1993 in Tokyo, which resulted in a far-reaching tariff-cutting deal that finally unlocked the Uruguay Round of GATT trade talks that had languished for seven years.[21]

European Monetary System

In the early 1970s, a group of European countries established the European Joint Float agreement. The values of the currencies were fixed against one another in a narrow range of plus or minus 2.25 percent. The movement of these currencies back and forth within this range became known as the snake. The early system was later replaced by the European Monetary System (EMS), which includes the twelve members of the European Community (EC). Britain was the last to join in late 1990. The EMS includes a set of features to force member countries to regulate their economies so that their currency stays within 2.25 percent of the central rates. If a currency slips out of this band, it may be required to increase or lower interest rates to stay in line with the other currencies. The German mark is EMS's strong currency, so the exchange rate between each individual currency and the German mark is closely monitored. The EC countries have all contributed to the European Monetary Cooperation Fund, which has a pool of over $30 billion to buy or sell currency in order to keep all currencies within their acceptable band. The EMS has also developed a new currency called the European currency unit (ECU), made up of a weighted average of twelve currencies from the EC countries. The next stage after EMS is the formation of a European monetary union. This would include much closer regulation of economies and the eventual replacement of the twelve currencies with the ECU.

20. "G7 Pledges to Strengthen Cooperation," *Financial Times,* January 22, 1991, p. 7.
21. "G7 Nations Agree on Far Reaching Tariff Cuts," *Financial Times,* July 8, 1993, pp. 1–2.

The Maastricht Treaty established the European Monetary Institute (EMI) in 1993 as a precursor to a European central bank. The governors of the twelve European central banks sit on the EMI council. The single European currency could be available as soon as 1997 but may not be issued until 1999, Maastricht's deadline.[22]

While undersecretary of the U.S. Treasury, David Mulford remarked that he welcomed the idea of the European monetary union. As the Group of Seven attempts to coordinate the monetary policies of the industrialized world, it will be much easier to focus on the dollar, the yen, and the ECU.[23] With the cooperation of world leaders, a managed global economy may be possible by the year 2000. This would reduce the likelihood of recession and minimize exchange rate fluctuations.

International Trade: Does It Deserve Special Treatment?

The principles of comparative advantage can be applied to any type of trade—international, intranational, or interpersonal. But if this is true, why is there so much concern about the international sector? Few residents of Massachusetts complain about the jobs that Pennsylvania, California, or Michigan factories take away from the New England area. Is the problem that people perceive international trade as an ''us against them'' situation, while they perceive domestic trade as ''us against us''? Or are there legitimate differences when one goes beyond the national borders?[24]

One can point to some obvious factors in differentiating international from intranational trade. Varying currencies, languages, traditions, and cultures are just a few examples. But how significant are they? Switzerland, a developed but relatively small western European country, has four official languages (German, French, Italian, and Romansch) and an assortment of widely differing dialects. The country is divided into twenty-six cantons, and in most respects each canton wields more authority than does the national government. The result is a nation where rules and regulations vary canton by canton. In regards to its currency, Switzerland is bordered by Germany, France, Austria, Italy, and Lichtenstein. While the Swiss franc is the national currency, many merchants throughout the country accept payment in any of these neighboring currencies. What factors distinguish foreign from domestic trade in Switzerland? It seems that there are few, if any, distinguishing characteristics. Certainly, the ones listed above are more apparent than real. If, in general, this is true, then international trade becomes nothing more than a simple subset of broader trade issues.

22. ''Learning to Fly,'' *Economist,* January 15, 1994, p. 75.
23. ''Power to the Centre,'' *Economist,* July 7, 1990, p. 25.
24. See Lester Thurow, *The Zero Sum Society: Distribution and the Possibilities for Economic Change* (New York: Basic Books, 1980).

Protectionism and Trade Restrictions

Economists have spent considerable time identifying and quantifying the net gains from free international trade. In large part, the benefits are obvious. After all, trade by its very nature involves a voluntary exchange of assets between two parties. In the absence of coercion, the motives behind this exchange must be for mutual benefit. The controversy surfaces when domestic producers are considered. Foreign imports seem to take business away from domestic firms and to increase the domestic unemployment rate.[25]

Free trade, like all competitive or technological changes, creates and destroys; it gives and it takes away. By increasing competition, free trade lowers the price of the imported goods and raises the demand for efficiently produced domestic goods. In these newly stimulated export industries, sales will increase, profits will rise, and stock prices will climb. Clearly, consumers of the imported good and producers of the exported good benefit by these new conditions. However, it is equally clear that there are groups that are harmed as well. Domestic producers of the import-competing good are one of the most visible groups. They experience noticeable declines in market share, falling profits, and deteriorating stock prices.

It is a fact of life that there are both beneficiaries and victims from free trade, just as there are when virtually any change is made. For instance, if someone were to discover a way for people to grow three or four sets of teeth in a lifetime, most people would benefit from this discovery. Nevertheless, there exists a group of people—dentists, oral surgeons, and periodontists—who would be hurt. Should this invention be withheld from the market because this group is hurt? The true test of a discovery is not whether or not victims exist but whether the benefits outweigh the inevitable losses.[26]

Herein lies the major reason for protectionist legislation. The victims of free trade are highly visible and their losses quantifiable; governments use protectionism as a means of lessening the harm done to this easily identified group. Conversely, the individuals who are helped by free trade tend to be dispersed throughout the nation rather than concentrated in one particular region. Moreover, their monetary gain is only a fraction of the total purchase price of the commodity.

A recent study by Australia's Center for International Economies (CIE) prepared a detailed model of the international trading system in order to measure the impact of reduced protectionism on world trade. If the countries in GATT reduced their tariff and nontariff barriers by 50 percent, CIE estimates that trade would increase $750 billion: $208 billion in the United States, $245 billion in Europe, and $287 billion in Asia/Pacific.[27] The GATT agreements reached in 1993 will reduce prices U.S. consumers pay by $32.8 billion per

---

25. For details on the arguments against protectionism, see Robert Z. Lawrence and Robert E. Litan, ''Why Protectionism Doesn't Pay,'' *Harvard Business Review,* May–June 1987, pp. 60–67.

26. Leland Yeager and David G. Tuerck, *Foreign Trade and U.S. Policy* (New York: Praeger, 1976), pp. 1–11, 40–88.

27. ''Once and Future GATT,'' *Economist,* September 22, 1990, p. 39.

year. For example, $17 billion will come from liberation of the textile and apparel industry, and $1.2 billion will be from reduced agricultural production.[28]

Protectionist legislation tends to be in the form of either tariffs, quotas, or qualitative trade restrictions. This section describes these barriers and their economic effects.

Tariffs

Tariffs are taxes on goods moving across an economic or political boundary. They can be imposed on imports, exports, or goods in transit through a country on their way to some other destination. In the United States, export tariffs are constitutionally prohibited, but in other parts of the world they are quite common. Of course, the most common type of tariff is the import tariff, and it is on this tariff that we focus our attention.

Import tariffs have a dual economic effect. First, they tend to raise the price of imported goods and thereby protect domestic industries from foreign competition. Second, they generate tax revenues for the governments imposing them. It is important to recognize this duality because, often, the situations resulting from the tariffs are quite different from what was originally intended. Moreover, regardless of what the goals are (for example, increasing tax revenue or raising employment), tariffs may not be the most direct or effective means of attaining them.

Today, most nations impose import duties for the purpose of protecting domestic manufacturers. In some cases (as when they are imposed on expensive-to-store agricultural products), foreign sellers will lower their prices to offset any tariff increase. The net effect is for the consumer-paid price to differ only slightly, if at all, from the pretariff level. Consequently, the nation has greater tariff revenues but little additional protection for the domestic producers.

When tariffs do raise the price of the imported good, consumers of the imported good develop a disadvantage, whereas the import-competing industries are helped. Quite often, another unintended group is hampered as well. For example, the U.S. Department of Commerce raised duties from 27 percent to 36.5 percent on imported steel, due to foreign manufacturers' dumping of steel in the United States. While higher duties helped U.S. steel manufacturers, U.S. purchasers complained that the increased duties increased the price of steel by over 20 percent in 1993, making these purchasers less competitive in the global marketplace.[29] In another case, the Department of Commerce revoked the 63 percent import duties on advanced flat screens used on laptops, because, while the duty helped some small U.S. screen manufacturers, it hurt computer companies such as Apple, Compaq, and IBM. These companies argued that the high duty inflated the cost of their products and harmed their ability to compete abroad and would force them to shift production to other countries.[30]

28. ''GATT's Payoff,'' *Fortune,* February 7, 1994, p. 28.
29. ''Punitive Tariffs Raised Against Foreign Steel,'' *New York Times,* June 23, 1993, pp. D1, D20.
30. ''Steel Users Condemn US Trade Cases,'' *Financial Times,* June 7, 1993, p. 4; ''Duties Ended on Computer Flat Screens,'' *New York Times,* June 23, 1993, pp. D1, D18.

Quotas

Quotas are physical limits on the *amount* of goods that can be imported into a country. Unlike tariffs that restrict trade by directly increasing prices, quotas increase prices by directly restricting trade. Naturally, to have such an effect, imports must be restricted to levels below the free trade level.

For domestic producers, quotas are a much surer means of protection. Once the limit has been reached, imports cease to enter the domestic market, regardless of whether foreign exporters lower their prices. Consumers have the most to lose with the imposition of quotas. Not only are their product choices limited and the prices increased, but the goods that are imported carry the highest profit margins. Restrictions on imported automobiles, for instance, will bring in more luxury models with high-cost accessories.

Like tariffs, quotas have both revenue and protection effects. The protection effects are the most apparent because trade is unequivocally being curtailed. The revenue effects are less obvious. When a government imposes arbitrary restrictions on imported goods, companies vie for the right to conduct this limited trade. One source estimated that the net effects of the U.S. quota system on product categories such as apparel or steel cost U.S. consumers about $10 billion in 1985. Quotas protect foreign companies from competition among themselves and also tend to limit the impact on prices set by U.S. firms that can be assured a certain volume.[31] One option is for the government to auction these rights to the highest bidder. In this way, the government gains revenues similar to those earned under a tariff.[32] However, if these rights are given away (as has been done in the United States on occasion), the revenue that was earned by the government is reported as windfall profits by the domestic importers and foreign exporters.

Orderly Marketing Arrangements and Voluntary Export Restrictions

The word *quota* has come to be associated with the most selfish of protectionist legislation. There can be strong political and economic repercussions associated with such unilateral, beggar-thy-neighbor policies. To avoid these problems, the new terms *orderly marketing arrangement* and *voluntary export restriction* have been invented.[33] In general, an orderly marketing arrangement is an agreement between countries to share markets by limiting foreign export sales. Usually, these arrangements have a set duration and provide for some annual increase in foreign sales to the domestic market. South Korea and Taiwan are two countries that have negotiated orderly marketing agreements with the United States. In 1987, Korea pledged a number of steps to keep the U.S. trade deficit with that country to $7 billion. Taiwan granted more liberalized trade concessions, including a currency appre-

31. "Tariffs Aren't Great, but Quotas Are Worse," *Business Week,* March 16, 1987, p. 64.

32. Monica Langley, "The Idea of Auctioning Import Rights Appeals to Lawmakers Faced with Trade, Budget Gaps," *Wall Street Journal,* February 6, 1987, p. 44.

33. See Kent Jones, *Politics versus Economics in World Steel Trade* (London: George Allen & Unwin, 1986).

ciation, to keep its trade surplus with the United States in 1987 from passing $18 billion.[34] Voluntary restraints can take a funny twist. Mazak, a Japanese toolmaker with a factory in Kentucky, has used the voluntary restraint agreement to limit Japanese imports into the United States. In fact, Mazak prepared a video of Japanese screwdriver (assembly only) factories to show how his Tokyo competitors were circumventing the agreement.[35]

The euphemistic terms are intended to give the impression of fairness. After all, who can be against anything that is orderly or voluntary? But when one scratches beneath the surface of these so-called negotiated settlements, a different image appears. First, the negotiations are initiated by the importing country with the implicit threat that, unless concessions are made, stronger unilateral sanctions will be imposed. They are really neither orderly nor voluntary. They are quotas in the guise of negotiated agreements.

The Omnibus Trade and Competitiveness Act of 1988 gave presidents of the United States the right to negotiate orderly marketing arrangements and set countervailing duties to deal with the problems of trade deficits, protected markets, and dumping. The use of these voluntary export restraints (VERs) has spread to textiles, clothing, steel, cars, shoes, machinery, and consumer electronics. There are approximately three hundred VERs worldwide, most protecting the United States and Europe. Over fifty agreements affect exports from Japan, and another thirty-five affect South Korea.[36] Some researchers argue that the cost of these VERs to consumers far exceeds the cost of the jobs they protect. See, for example, the jobs-saved cost in the following industries:

Industry	Cost/Job saved
Carbon steel	$750,000
Shipping	270,000
Dairy	220,000
Meat	160,000
Autos	105,000
Textiles	42,000[37]

Often, the real impact of VERs is hidden in higher costs to the consumer. The voluntary restraint of Japanese cars into the United States forced Japan to send higher-priced cars to generate the maximum revenue per unit while staying within the quota. U.S. car manufacturers continued to raise their prices, and consumers paid an additional $15.7 billion from 1981 to 1984.[38]

34. "Where Sanctions Against Japan Are Really Working," *Business Week,* May 11, 1987, p. 61.
35. "Look Who's Taking Japan to Task," *Business Week,* June 4, 1990, p. 26.
36. "A Survey of World Trade," *Economist,* September 22, 1990, p. 8.
37. Michael McFadden, "Protectionism Can't Protect Jobs," *Fortune,* May 11, 1987, p. 125.
38. U.S. International Trade Commission, *The Internationalization of the Automobile Industry and*

Formal and Administrative Nontariff Trade Barriers

The final category of trade restrictions is perhaps the most problematic and certainly the least quantifiable. As sections D, E, and F of Table 2.5 show, a virtual potpourri of rules and taxes impede international trade. Not all of these barriers are discriminatory and protectionist. Restrictions dealing with public health and safety are certainly legitimate, but the line between social well-being and protection is a fine one.

At what point do consular fees, import restrictions, packaging regulations, performance requirements, licensing rules, and government procurement procedures discriminate against foreign producers? Is a French tax on automobile horsepower targeted against powerful U.S. cars, or is it simply a tax on inefficiency and pollution? Are U.S. automobile safety standards unfair to German, Japanese, and other foreign car manufacturers? Does a French ban on advertising bourbon and Scotch (but not cognac) serve the public's best interest?

Sometimes, nontariff barriers can have considerable impact on foreign competition. For decades, West German authorities forbade the sale of beer in Germany unless it was brewed from barley malt, hops, yeast, and water. If any other additives were used—a common practice elsewhere—German authorities denied foreign brewers the right to label their products as beer. Only recently has the law been struck down by the European Court of Justice.[39] In the EU, Japan has agreed to a voluntary restraint agreement limiting automobile exports to 15 percent of the EU market by 1999. What is interesting is that the nontariff trade barriers have significantly affected the share of Japanese automobiles in Europe: 2 percent in Italy and Spain, 3 percent in France, 12 percent in the United Kingdom, 16 percent in Germany, 29 percent in Switzerland, 36 percent in Denmark, and 39 percent in Finland.[40]

General Agreement on Tariffs and Trade (GATT)

Because of the harmful effects of protectionism, which were most painfully felt during the Great Depression of the 1930s, twenty-three nations banded together in 1947 to form the General Agreement on Tariffs and Trade (GATT). Over its life, GATT has been a major forum for the liberalization and promotion of nondiscriminatory international trade between participating nations. Liberalization is promoted through periodic trade rounds, or negotiations.

The principles of a world economy embodied in the articles of GATT are reciprocity, nondiscrimination, and transparency. The idea of reciprocity is simple. If one country lowers its tariffs against another's exports, then it can expect the other country to do the same. This practice of reciprocity has been important in the bargaining process to reduce tariffs. Nondiscrimination means that one country should not give one member or group

39. "EC Claims Victory as Court Overturns Germany's Age-old Ban on Beer Imports," *Wall Street Journal,* March 13, 1987, p. 29.
40. "Car Sales Charter for a Good Citizen," *Financial Times,* August 2, 1991, p. 11.

TABLE 2.5 ● Nontariff Trade Barriers

Formal trade restrictions	*Administrative trade restrictions*
A. NONTARIFF IMPORT RESTRICTIONS (PRICE-RELATED MEASURES) Surcharges at border Port and statistical taxes Nondiscriminatory excise taxes and registration charges Discriminatory excise taxes, government insurance requirements Nondiscriminatory turnover taxes Discriminatory turnover taxes Import deposit Variable levies Consular fees Stamp taxes Various special taxes and surcharges B. QUANTITATIVE RESTRICTIONS AND SIMILAR SPECIFIC TRADE LIMITATIONS (QUANTITY-RELATED MEASURES) Licensing regulations Ceilings and quotas Embargoes Export restrictions and prohibitions Foreign exchange and other monetary or financial controls Government price setting and surveillance Purchase and performance requirements Restrictive business conditions Discriminatory bilateral arrangements Discriminatory regulations regarding countries of origin International cartels Orderly marketing agreements Various related regulations C. DISCRIMINATORY FREIGHT RATES (FLAG PROTECTIONISM)	D. STATE PARTICIPATION IN TRADE Subsidies and other government support Government trade, government monopolies, and granting of concessions or licenses Laws and ordinances discouraging imports Problems relating to general government policy Government procurement Tax relief, granting of credit and guarantees Boycott E. TECHNICAL NORMS, STANDARDS, AND CONSUMER PROTECTION REGULATIONS Health and safety regulations Pharmaceutical control regulations Product design regulations Industrial standards Size and weight regulations Packing and labeling regulations Package marking regulations Regulations pertaining to use Regulations for the protection of intellectual property Trademark regulations F. CUSTOMS PROCESSING AND OTHER ADMINISTRATIVE REGULATIONS Antidumping policy Customs calculation bases Formalities required by consular officials Certification regulations Administrative obstacles Merchandise classification Regulations regarding sample shipment, return shipments, and reexports Countervailing duties and taxes Appeal law Emergency law

Source: Beatrice Bondy, *Protectionism: Challenge of the Eighties* (Zurich, Union Bank of Switzerland, 1983), p. 19. Reprinted by permission.

of members preferential treatment over other members of the group. Referred to as the "most favored nation" status, it means that you are not *most* favored but rather favored the same as the others. Transparency refers to the GATT policy that nations replace non-tariff barriers (such as quotas) with tariffs and then bind the tariff, which means to agree not to raise it. Nontariff barriers do much more harm to trade than tariffs, especially bound tariffs. Tariffs reduce uncertainty and are out in the open, so they are easier to negotiate down in the future.[41] Through these principles, trade restrictions have been effectively reduced, and price distortions have been minimized.

Although its most notable gains have been in reducing tariff and quota barriers on certain goods, GATT has also helped to simplify and homogenize trade documentation procedures, reduce qualitative trade barriers, curtail dumping (that is, selling abroad at a cost less than the cost of production),[42] and discourage government subsidies. GATT has reduced tariffs from 40 percent in 1947 to under 5 percent in 1990.

The Uruguay round of GATT talks, which lasted seven years, was finally completed in late 1993. This agreement covered the following areas.

- Agriculture: Europe will gradually reduce farm subsidies. Japan and Korea will start to import rice. The United States will reduce subsidies to growers of sugar, citrus fruit, and peanuts.

- Entertainment, pharmaceuticals, software: New rules will protect copyrights, patents, and trademarks. Developing nations will have a decade to implement patent protection for drugs. France refused to liberalize access for the U.S. film industry.

- Financial, legal, and accounting services: For the first time, these services come under the rules of international trade.

- Textiles and apparel: The strict quotas limiting imports into the United States will be phased out over ten years.

The next round of GATT talks is expected to focus on restrictions on foreign investment, government subsidies for R&D, antidumping laws, and environmental concerns.[43]

Economic Integration as a Means of Promoting Trade

There is little argument that free trade bestows net gains on trading nations—especially in the long run. The problem is that with so many entrenched, vested interest groups, it is difficult to update existing trading rules. A reduction of protectionist legislation causes

---

41. "The ITO That Never Was," *Economist,* September 22, 1990, pp. 7–8.

42. Economists prefer to define *dumping* as selling below the variable cost per unit, because only in such cases is the decision uneconomical.

43. "What's Next After GATT's Victory?" *Fortune,* January 10, 1994, pp. 66–70.

considerable short-term dislocations, putting much economic and political pressure on a nation's power structure.

As a partial step in the trade liberalization process, countries have begun to move toward limited forms of economic integration. While the degree of economic integration can vary considerably from one organization to another, four major types of integration can be identified: free trade areas, customs unions, common markets, and monetary unions. Some of these concepts will be covered in greater detail in Chapter 5.

Free Trade Areas

The simplest form of integration is a free trade area. Within a free trade area, nations agree to drop trade barriers among themselves, but each nation is permitted to maintain independent trade relations with nongroup countries. There is little attempt, at this level, to coordinate such things as domestic tax rates, environmental regulations, and commercial codes, and generally such areas do not permit resources (that is, labor and capital) to flow freely across national borders. Moreover, because each country has autonomy over its money supply, exchange rates can fluctuate relative to both member and nonmember countries.

Examples of free trade areas are the Latin American Free Trade Area and the European Free Trade Area. The North American Free Trade Agreement (NAFTA), one of the newest free trade areas, became effective in 1994. NAFTA is expected to boost trade for Mexico, Canada, and the United States and strengthen North America's position when negotiating with the European Union.

Customs Unions

Customs unions, a more advanced form of economic integration, possess the characteristics of a free trade area but with the added feature of a common external tariff/trade barrier for the member nations. Individual countries relinquish the right to set their nongroup trade agreements independently. Rather, a supranational policy-making committee makes these decisions. A historic example of a customs union was the 1834 German Zollverein, which was composed of several German states and paved the way for the eventual uniting of Germany in 1870.

Common Markets

The third level of economic integration is a common market. Here, countries have all the characteristics of a customs union, but the organization also encourages resources (labor and capital) to flow freely among the member nations. For example, if jobs are plentiful in Germany but scarce in Italy, workers can move from Italy to Germany without having to worry about severe immigration restrictions. In a common market, there is usually an attempt to coordinate tax codes, social welfare systems, and other legislation that influences resource allocation. Finally, while each nation still has the right to print and coin its own money, exchange rates among nations are often fixed or permitted to fluctuate only within a narrow band. The most notable example of a common market is the European Union (EU). Established in 1957, the EU has been an active organization for trade liberalization and continues to increase its membership size.

Monetary Unions

The highest form of economic integration is a monetary union. A monetary union is a common market in which member countries no longer regulate their own currencies. Rather, member-country currencies are replaced by a common currency regulated by a supranational central bank. With the passage of the Maastricht Treaty by EU members, the European Union could become the first major monetary union, if the treaty is implemented between 1997 and 1999, as planned.[44]

The Global Economy

The global economy is in a state of transition from a set of strong national economies to a set of interlinked trading groups. This transition has accelerated over the past few years with the fall of the Berlin Wall, the collapse of Communism, and the strengthening of the European Community into a single market. The investment by Europeans, Japanese, and Americans in each other's economies is unprecedented. U.S. companies create and sell over $80 billion per year in goods and services in Japan. Britain bought 640 companies in the United States from 1978 to 1989 and had a direct foreign investment of $250 billion in the United States, making it the biggest foreign owner of business, followed by the Dutch and Japanese.[45] There are eleven Japanese automobile assembly plants in North America, some of which will be shipping finished cars to Europe in 1991.[46] As companies globalize, manufacturing becomes more flexible, and engineers have instant access to the latest technology, we will see microchips designed in California, sent to Scotland to be fabricated, shipped to the Far East to be tested and assembled, and returned to the United States to be sold.[47]

There is no doubt the world is moving toward a single global economy. Of course there are major difficulties on the horizon, such as the development of a market-based economy in eastern Europe, a reduction of hostilities and the establishment of political stability in the Middle East and parts of eastern Europe, and stabilization and growth in the former Soviet Union. The global marketer needs to understand the interdependencies that make up the world economy in order to understand how a drop in the U.S. discount rate will affect business in Stockholm or how Britain's joining the European Monetary System will affect sales in London. As the speed of change accelerates, successful

44. ''EEA Links 17 Nations into World's Largest Free Trade Zone,'' *Financial Times,* January 1/2, 1994, pp. 1, 22.
45. John Naisbitt and Patricia Aburdene, *Mega Trends 2000* (London: Sidgwick & Jackson, 1990), pp. 9–28.
46. Kevin Done, ''Big Three Batten Down the Hatches,'' *Financial Times,* February 5, 1991, p. 18.
47. William Van Dusen Wishard, ''The 21st Century Economy,'' *Futurist,* May–June 1987, p. 23.

companies will be able to anticipate the trends and either take advantage of them or respond to them quickly. Other companies will watch the changes going on around them and wake up one day to a different marketplace with new rules.

Conclusions

We learn from the study of economics that changes in rules or in financial circumstances help some groups and hurt others. Therefore, it is important to understand that papers and speeches have particular points of view. Exchange rate movements, tariffs, quotas, and customs unions can be viewed as alternative ways to achieve economic goals. The issue is not whether a change will take place but rather *which* change will provide the most benefit with the least cost.

This chapter describes the fundamentals of international trade and finance. An understanding of the fundamentals will enable you to comprehend the technical issues raised by the media and to formulate your own views. With such an understanding, you will be able to *analyze* international economic events and *evaluate* critically the proliferation of articles being written about them.

Questions for Discussion

1. If a nation has a balance on merchandise trade deficit, can it be said that the nation has a weak currency in the international markets as well?

2. Regarding question 1, examine both the balance of payments statistics and the foreign exchange rate statistics presented in the International Monetary Fund's *International Financial Statistics.* What link, if any, do you see between Switzerland's balance on merchandise trade and the value of the Swiss franc over the past five years?

3. Calculate your individual balance of payments over the past month. What were your balance on merchandise trade, balance on goods and services, and current account balance?

4. Exchange rate changes have been called a ''double-edged sword'' because they hurt some sectors of the nation while helping other sectors. Explain why this is true.

5. If interest rates in the United Kingdom rise while those in Germany remain unchanged, explain what pressure this will put on the British pound per the German mark exchange rate.

6. Suppose the U.S. Federal Reserve reduces the rate of growth of the money supply, causing the U.S. inflation rate to fall, interest rates to rise, and economic growth to decline. What impact will these economic changes have on the actions of the participants in the foreign exchange market?

7. The concept of *comparative advantage* is one of the most powerful in all of economic theory (both at the domestic level and the international level). Explain why this is true. What does the concept show? What are its implications for international and intranational trade?

8. Suppose Brazil can produce with an equal amount of resources either 100 units of steel or ten computers. At the same time, Germany can produce either 150 units of steel or ten computers. Explain which nation has a comparative advantage in the production of computers. Choose a mutually advantageous trading ratio and explain why this ratio increases the welfare of both nations.

9. In April 1987, President Reagan imposed a tariff on goods made with Japanese semiconductors and imported into the United States. Explain which groups in the United States were helped by this action and which groups were hurt by this action. Explain why a tax on semiconductors alone would have actually lowered the level of protection given to computer manufacturers in the United States. Do you believe this action is evidence of good economic thinking? Why?

10. In terms of their economic effects on a nation's economy, explain the similarities and differences between tariffs and quotas.

11. For each of the following distinct and separate cases, explain which trade theory best describes the trading pattern cited. Briefly explain why you chose the theory you did.
    a. The opening of trade between the United States and China has resulted in U.S. importation of textiles and other handmade craftwork from China and the exportation of machinery and steel from the United States to China.
    b. Currently, the United States is a major importer of televisions from Japan. It once was a major exporter of televisions to Japan.

For Further Reading

Aggarwal, Raj. ''The Strategic Challenge of the Evolving Global Economy.'' *Business Horizons,* July–August 1987, pp. 38–44.

Foreign Exchange Information: A Worldwide Summary. New York: Price Waterhouse, 1990.

''Getting a Grip on the GATT.'' *Financial Times,* February 5, 1991, p. 18.

Hollerman, Leon. *Japan Disincorporated: The Economic Liberalization Process.* Stanford, Calif: Hoover Institution Press, 1988.

Kindleberger, Charles P., and Peter H. Lindert. *International Economics.* 7th ed. Homewood, Ill.: Irwin, 1984.

Nevin, John J. ''Doorstop for Free Trade.'' *Harvard Business Review,* March–April 1983, p. 91.

Porter, Michael E. *The Competitive Advantage of Nations.* New York: Macmillan, 1990.

Rabino, Samuel. ''An Attitudinal Evaluation of an Export Incentive Program: The Case of Disc.'' *Columbia Journal of World Trade,* Spring 1980, p. 61.

Root, Franklin R. *International Trade and Investment.* 5th ed. Cincinnati: Southwestern, 1984.

Rostow, W. W. *The Stages of Economic Growth.* 2nd ed. Cambridge, U.K.: University Press, 1971.

Schneeweis, Thomas. "A Note on International Trade and Market Structure." *Journal of International Business Studies,* 16 (Summer 1985), pp. 139–152.

The Omnibus Trade and Competitiveness Act of 1988. Washington, D.C.: International Division, U.S. Department of Commerce, 1988.

Tolchin, Martin. *Buying into America: How Foreign Money Is Changing the Face of Our Nation.* New York: Times Books, 1988.

Vernon, Raymond, "Can the U.S. Negotiate Trade Equality?" *Harvard Business Review,* May–June 1989, pp. 96–101.

Vernon, Raymond, and Debora L. Spar. *Beyond Globalism: Remaking American Foreign Policy.* New York: Free Press, 1989.

Wells, Louis T., Jr. "A Product Life Cycle for International Trade?" *Journal of Marketing,* July 1968, pp. 1–6.

"World Industrial Survey." *Financial Times,* January 15, 1991, sec. 3, pp. 1–4.

3

Cultural and Social Forces

● **IN CHAPTER 1** *we explained that the complexities of international marketing are partially caused by societal and cultural forces. In Chapter 3 we describe some of these cultural and societal influences in more detail. However, since it is not possible to list all of them—or even to fully describe the major cultures of the world—only the more salient forces are highlighted. Figure 3.1 shows the components of culture that are described in this chapter. We also provide an analytical framework that suggests to the international marketing practitioner what to look for. Thus, rather than suggesting all the possible cultural or societal factors that may affect international marketers, we concentrate on the analytical processes marketers can use to identify and monitor any of the large number of cultural influences encountered around the globe.*

A Definition of Culture

Anthropology, the study of humans, is a discipline that focuses on the understanding of human behavior. Cultural anthropology examines all human behaviors that have been learned, including social, linguistic, and family behaviors.[1] *Culture* includes the entire heritage of a society transmitted by word, literature, or any other form. It includes all

1. Charles Winick, ''Anthropology's Contributions to Marketing,'' *Journal of Marketing,* July 1961, p. 54.

FIGURE 3.1 ● Cultural Analysis

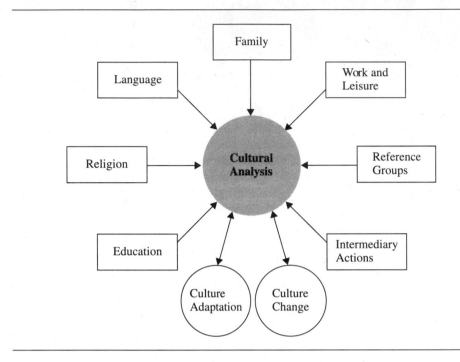

traditions, habits, religion, art, and language. Children born anywhere in the world have the same essential needs for food, shelter, and clothing. But as they grow, children will develop desires for nonessential things. The development and priority of these *wants* are based on messages from families and peers and thus are said to be a result of the culture. Culture reflects the human aspect of a person's environment; it consists of beliefs, morals, customs, and habits learned from others.

Cultural Influences on Marketing

The function of marketing is to earn profits from the satisfaction of human wants and needs. In order to understand and influence the consumer's wants and needs, marketers must understand the culture, especially in an international environment. Figure 3.2 is a diagram of how culture affects human behavior. As the figure shows, culture is embedded in elements of the society such as religion, language, history, and education. These elements send direct and indirect messages to consumers regarding the selection of goods and services. The culture we live in answers such questions as, Is tea or coffee the preferred drink? Is black or white worn at a funeral? What type of food is eaten for breakfast?

FIGURE 3.2 ● Cultural Influences on Buyer Behavior

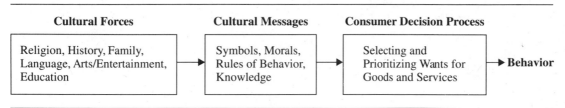

Cultural Forces	Cultural Messages	Consumer Decision Process	
Religion, History, Family, Language, Arts/Entertainment, Education	Symbols, Morals, Rules of Behavior, Knowledge	Selecting and Prioritizing Wants for Goods and Services	→ **Behavior**

Isolating Cultural Influences

One of the most difficult tasks for international marketers is assessing the cultural influences that affect their operations. In the actual marketplace there are always several factors working simultaneously, and it is extremely difficult to isolate any one factor. Frequently, *cultural differences* have been held accountable for any noticeable differences between countries. However, when environmental factors differ, what is thought to be *cultural* may in fact be attributable to other factors. Quite often, when countries with both economic and cultural differences are compared, the differences are credited solely to the varying cultural systems. The analyst should be aware that although many of the differences are culturally based, other environmental factors, such as level of economic development, political system, or legal system, may be responsible for these differences. (These other aspects of the environment will be discussed in Chapter 4.)

Language

Language is a key component of culture because most of a society's culture finds its way into the spoken language. Thus, in many ways, language embodies the culture of the society. Knowing the language of a society can become the key to understanding its culture. But language is not merely a collection of words or terms. Language expresses the thinking pattern of a culture—and to some extent even forms the thinking. Linguists have found that cultures with more primitive languages or a limited range of expression are more likely to be limited in their thought patterns. Many languages cannot accommodate modern technological or business concepts, forcing the cultural elite to work in a different language.

Forms of Address

The English language has one form of address: all persons are addressed with the pronoun *you.* Not so in many other languages. In the Germanic and Romance languages, there are always two forms, the personal and the formal address. In Japanese, there are three forms. Depending on status, a Japanese person will speak differently to a superior, a colleague, or a subordinate, and there are different forms for male and female in many expressions. These differences in language represent different ways of interacting. English, particularly as it is spoken in the United States, is much less formal than Japanese. At a recent management development course at a university in the United States with participants from many countries, the Japanese participants had first considered some Americanized nicknames. As it turned out, most of the Japanese participants preferred the Japanese way of address, which is a combination of the last name with *san* attached—for example, Endosan for Mr. Endo.[2] Consequently, knowing the Japanese language gives a foreigner a better understanding of the cultural mores regarding social status and authority. Of course, one can develop a cultural understanding or empathy by learning about a culture directly. However, just learning a foreign language can substantially help develop cultural empathy.

Overcoming the Language Barrier

International marketing communications are heavily affected by the existence of different languages. Advertising has to be adjusted to each language, and personal contacts are made difficult by a widely existing language barrier. To overcome this language barrier, businesspeople all over the world have relied on three approaches: the direct translation of written material, interpreters, and the acquisition of foreign language skills.

Translations are made for a wide range of documents, including sales literature, catalogs, advertising, and contracts. Though this increases the initial costs of entering a market, few companies can conduct their business over the long run without translating material into the language of their customers. If a company does not have a local subsidiary, competent translation agencies are available in most countries. Some companies even route their foreign correspondence through a translation firm, thus communicating with foreign clients on all matters in the client's own language. This often increases the likelihood of concluding a deal.

The use of translators is usually restricted to higher-level executives because of the higher cost. Traveling with executives and attending meetings, translators perform a very useful function when a complete language barrier exists. They are best used for a limited time only, however, and realistically cannot overcome long-term communication problems.

Both translation services and translators depend on translating one language into another. Experience shows that this also involves risks.[3] In many situations, it is almost impossible to translate fully a given meaning into a second language. When the original idea, or thought, is not part of the second culture, the translation may be meaningless. Brand names have been particularly affected by this because they are not normally translated. Consequently, a company may get into difficulty with the use of a product name in a foreign country, even though its advertising message is fully translated. General Motors'

---

2. "How 21 Men Got Global in 35 Days," *Fortune,* November 6, 1989, p. 71.
3. David A. Ricks, *Big Business Blunders: Mistakes in Multinational Marketing* (Homewood, Ill.: Dow Jones–Irwin, 1983), pp. 75–95.

experience with its Nova model is typical here. Though it could easily be pronounced in Spanish, the literal meaning is *no va,* or ''does not go.'' That was certainly not the right attribute for a car.[4]

However, the GM experience must be contrasted with a different development in Japan. There, a soft drink was launched with the brand name ''Pocari Sweat.'' To Japanese consumers, this name conveyed a positive, healthy, thirst-quenching image, resulting in a market leader. Japanese consumers reacted to the brand name strictly based upon its modern- (foreign-) sounding name, not on the content or meaning. Needless to say, this success was credited to a local firm.[5]

Today, companies tend to carefully choose product names in advance to ensure that the meaning in all major languages is neutral and positive. They also want to make sure that the name can be easily pronounced. Language differences may have caused many blunders during the period of rapid business expansion after World War II, but careful translations have now reduced the number of international marketing mistakes. However, the language barrier still remains, and companies that do more to overcome this barrier frequently achieve better results.

Another approach to the problem is to learn a foreign language. Citizens of the United States in general have been remiss in learning foreign languages, whereas citizens of other nations have invested much time and effort in language study. Although international business is increasingly being transacted in English, one should not assume that all foreign executives speak it. Furthermore, not all foreign executives speak English well enough to have serious business discussions, and still fewer can communicate fluently in written English. As a result, native English-speaking executives should not use the excuse that their counterparts speak English anyway. True, it is difficult to select a suitable language to learn. Some languages, such as Japanese or German, are spoken in only one geographic area, whereas others, such as Spanish or French, are spoken in many countries. But if marketers really believe that ''you have to speak the language of your customer,'' then there is every advantage in finding a way to communicate in the client's native language. If one considers the value of developing cultural empathy through learning a foreign language, an argument can be made that learning any language will develop such cultural skills. Looking at foreign languages from that point of view allows the student to approach learning as a developmental skill that can be applied in many ways. In a sense, by learning one foreign language, the student can learn to appreciate all different cultures. Whenever two executives get together and speak their respective languages to some extent, the chosen language is frequently the one that is better spoken. If a U.S. executive meets an Italian executive, and the Italian speaks better English than the American speaks Italian, it would be normal for the two to speak in English. Thus, as more and more executives abroad learn English, they raise the required level at which the American executive must make use of the foreign language. This is often frustrating to those who have learned a few sentences with difficulty.

4. Ibid., p. 83.
5. ''A Gaijin at the Top,'' *Financial Times,* December 27, 1991, p. 8.

Even when executives understand each other's language, there can still be plenty of room for misunderstanding. When an American executive says yes in a negotiation, this usually means "yes, I accept the terms." However, yes in Asian countries may mean four different things. First, it may mean that the other side recognizes that one is talking to them but not necessarily that they understand what is said. Secondly, it could mean that what was said was understood and was clear but not that it was agreed to. Thirdly, it may mean that the other party has understood the proposal and will consult with others about it. And finally, yes may mean total agreement. It takes skill to understand just what yes means in any type of negotiation.[6]

However, achieving some fluency in a foreign language is not the only cultural barrier to cross. At least as important is the use of nonverbal communications, or *body language.* Sometimes referred to as the "silent language," this includes such elements as touching, the distance between speakers, facial expressions, and speech inflection, as well as arm and hand gestures. Particularly the latter vary greatly according to culture.[7] The head of worldwide marketing of Parker Pen once went for a stroll with his Saudi distributor in Jidda. Suddenly, the Saudi distributor took the American's hand, and they continued to walk through the streets swinging hands. The U.S. executive found out later that this was a sign of great respect and admiration and that pulling away would have meant a great insult.[8]

One can draw two major conclusions about the impact of language on international marketing. First, a firm must adjust its communication program and design communications to include the languages used by its customers. Second, the firm must be aware that a foreign language may contain different thinking patterns or indicate varying motivations on the part of prospective clients. This is much more difficult. To the extent that such differences occur, the simple mechanical translation of messages will not suffice. Instead, the company may have to change the entire marketing message to reflect the different cultural patterns.

Religion

Many businesspeople ignore the influence religion may have on the marketing environment. Even in the United States, religion has had a profound impact, though people are not aware of it on a daily basis. Historically, the religious tradition in the United States, based on Christianity and Judaism, emphasizes hard work, thriftiness, and a simple lifestyle. These religious values have certainly altered over time; many of our modern mar-

---

6. Carl R. Ruthstrom and Ken Matejka, "The Meaning of 'Yes' in the Far East," *Industrial Marketing Management,* 19, no. 3 (August 1990), p. 191.

7. Robert Moran, "Cross-cultural Contact: Watch Your Body Language," *International Management,* May 1990, p. 84.

8. "When in Rome, or Jeddah, or Tokyo," *USA Today/International,* March 31, 1990, p. 4A.

keting activities would not exist if these older values persisted. Thrift, for instance, presumes that a person will save hard-earned wages and use these savings for purchases later on. Today, ample credit facilities exist to supplement or even supplant savings. Hard work is no longer the *raison d'être* for many U.S. consumers; more time and energy are given to leisure activities. The simple lifestyle has given way to conspicuous consumption. This latter development also affects purchasing and consumption patterns.

Christian Traditions

There still are, however, religious customs that remain a major factor in marketing today, both here and abroad. Christmas is one Christian tradition that, at least in respect to consumption, remains an important event for many consumer goods industries. Retailers traditionally have their largest sales around that time. Christmas can be used as an illustration of the substantial differences among even largely Christian societies. A large U.S.-based retailer of consumer electronics found out about these differences the hard way when it opened its first retail outlet in the Netherlands. The company planned the opening to coincide with the start of the Christmas selling season, as this would allow the firm to show a profit in the first year, and advertising space was bought accordingly in late November and December. The results were less than satisfactory, however, because major gift giving in Holland takes place not around December 25, Christmas Day, but on St. Nicholas Day, December 6, the Dutch traditional day of gift giving. Thus, the opening of the company's retail operation was late and missed the major buying season.

Many other variations surrounding Christmas gift giving can be found. In France, it is traditional to exchange gifts on January 6, often called "Little Christmas." Also different are the personifications who bring the gifts. In the United States, Santa Claus brings Christmas gifts; in the United Kingdom, Father Christmas brings them; and in German-speaking countries, gifts are brought by an angel representing the Christ Child. In German areas, Santa Claus or St. Nicholas comes on December 6 to bring small gifts and food to those children who behaved. All of these examples show that local variations of religious traditions can have a substantial impact on international marketing activities.

Islam

Religion's impact on international marketing becomes more apparent when the observer compares one religion to another. It is beyond the scope of this text to give a complete description of all world religions with specific implications for marketing. However, by using one non-Christian religion, Islam, we can document some of the potential impact. We chose Islam in view of its growing influence in many countries.

Islam is the religion of 20 percent of the world's population.[9] Islam was established by the prophet Mohammed in Mecca in A.D. 610. Thirteen years later, when Mohammed

9. Mushtaq Luqmani, Zahir Quraeshi, and Linda Delene, "Marketing in Islamic Countries: A Viewpoint," *MSU Business Topics,* Summer 1980, p. 17.

had to flee to nearby Medina, he established the first Islamic city-state.[10] By his death in 632, the holy book of Islam, the *Koran,* had been completely revealed. It is believed to contain God's own words. The *Koran* was supplemented by the *Hadith* and *Sunna,* which contain the reported words and actions of the prophet Mohammed. These works are the primary sources of guidance for all Muslims on all aspects of life.

With the expansion of the Islamic state, additional guidance was needed; as a result, the *shari'a,* or legal system, emerged. Based on the *Koran,* the *shari'a* gives details of required duties and outlines all types of human interactions. It essentially constitutes what elsewhere would be considered criminal, personal, and commercial law. These Islamic guidelines cover all aspects of human life and categorize human behavior as obligatory, merely desirable, neutral, merely undesirable, or forbidden. The principal goal is to guide human beings in their quest for salvation, because the basic purpose of human existence is to serve God. Divine guidance is to be accepted as given, and it is believed to meet both the spiritual and psychological needs of individuals, making them better social beings. The nonritual divine guidance covers, among other areas, the economic activities of society. This latter guidance offers people a wide range of choices while protecting them from evil. A set of basic values restricts economic action and should not be violated or transgressed.

The Islamic value system, as it relates to economic activities, requires a commitment to God and a constant awareness of God's presence even while the person is engaged in material work. Wealth is considered a favor of God to be appreciated; it cannot be regarded as a final goal. Wealth is to be used to satisfy basic needs in moderation. With the real ownership of wealth belonging to God, man is considered only a temporary trustee. Thus, material advancement does not entail higher status or merit. In Islam, all people are created equal and have the right of life, the right of liberty, the right of ownership, the right of dignity, and the right of education. For the true Muslim, the achievement of goals is both a result of individual efforts and a blessing from God. A Muslim should therefore not neglect the duty of working hard to earn a living.

In their work, Muslims are required to uphold the Islamic virtues of truth, honesty, respect for the rights of others, pursuit of moderation, sacrifice, and hard work. Moderation applies to virtually all situations. The resulting Islamic welfare economy is based on the bond of universal brotherhood in which the individuals, while pursuing their own good, avoid wrongdoing to others. In their economic pursuits, true Muslims not only have their own material needs in mind but accept their social obligations and thereby improve their own position with God. The Islamic culture has many specific implications for international marketers. A summary of these implications is shown in Table 3.1.

The prohibition of usury has led to quite different practices with respect to lending in Arab societies.[11] Since this law prohibits interest payments, special Islamic banks were formed. These banks maintain three types of accounts: nonprofit accounts with a very small minimum deposit and the right of immediate withdrawal without notice, profit-sharing deposit accounts, and social services funds. These banks do not charge a fixed rate of interest on loans. Instead, the "interest payment" is levied according to the profits

10. Muhammad Abdul-Rauf, "The Ten Commandments of Islamic Economics," *Across the Board,* August 1979, p. 7.
11. Ibid., pp. 15–16.

TABLE 3.1 ● Marketing in an Islamic Framework

Elements	*Implications for marketing*
Fundamental Islamic Concepts	
A. Unity. (Concept of centrality, oneness of God, harmony in life.)	Product standardization, mass media techniques, central balance, unity in advertising copy and layout, strong brand loyalties, a smaller evoked size set, loyalty to company, opportunities for brand extension strategies.
B. Legitimacy. (Fair dealings, reasonable level of profits.)	Less formal product warranties, need for institutional advertising and/or advocacy advertising, especially by foreign firms, and a switch from profit-maximizing to a profit-satisficing strategy.
C. Zakat. (2.5 percent per annum compulsory tax binding on all classified as "not poor.")	Use of "excessive" profits, if any, for charitable acts; corporate donations for charity, institutional advertising.
D. Usury. (Cannot charge interest on loans. A general interpretation of this law defines "excessive interest" charged on loans as not permissible.)	Avoid direct use of credit as a marketing tool; establish a consumer policy of paying cash for low-value products; for high-value products, offer discounts for cash payments and raise prices of products on an installment basis; sometimes possible to conduct interest transactions between local/ foreign firm in other non-Islamic countries; banks in some Islamic countries take equity in financing ventures, sharing resultant profits (and losses).
E. Supremacy of human life. (Compared to other forms of life, objects, human life is of supreme importance.)	Pet food and/or products less important; avoid use of statues, busts—interpreted as forms of idolatry; symbols in advertising and/or promotion should reflect high human values; use floral designs and artwork in advertising as representation of aesthetic values.
F. Community. (All Muslims should strive to achieve universal brotherhood—with allegiance to the "one God." One way of expressing community is the required pilgrimage to Mecca for all Muslims at least once in their lifetime, if able to do so.)	Formation of an Islamic economic community— development of an "Islamic consumer" served with Islamic-oriented products and services ("kosher" meat packages, gifts exchanged at Muslim festivals, and so forth); development of community services—need for marketing or nonprofit organizations and skills.
G. Equality of peoples.	Participative communication systems; roles and authority structures may be rigidly defined, but accessibility at any level relatively easy.
H. Abstinence. (During the month of Ramadan, Muslims are required to fast without food or drink from the first streak of dawn to sunset—a reminder to those who are more fortunate to be kind to the less fortunate and as an exercise in self-control.)	Products that are nutritious, cool, and digested easily can be formulated for Sehr and Iftar (beginning and end of the fast).

TABLE 3.1 ● Marketing in an Islamic Framework (*Continued*)

Elements	*Implications for marketing*
(Consumption of alcohol and pork is forbidden; so is gambling.)	Opportunities for developing nonalcoholic items and beverages (for example, soft drinks, ice cream, milk shakes, fruit juices) and nonchance social games, such as Scrabble; food products should use vegetable or beef shortening.
I. Environmentalism. (The universe created by God was pure. Consequently, the land, air, and water should be held as sacred elements.)	Anticipate environmental, antipollution acts; opportunities for companies involved in maintaining a clean environment; easier acceptance of pollution control devices in the community (for example, recent efforts in Turkey have been well received by the local communities).
J. Worship. (Five times a day; timing of prayers varies.)	Need to take into account the variability and shift in prayer timings in planning sales calls, work schedules, business hours, customer traffic, and so forth.
Islamic Culture	
A. Obligation to family and tribal traditions.	Importance of respected members in the family or tribe as opinion leaders; word-of-mouth communication, customer referrals may be critical; social or clan allegiances, affiliations, and associations may be possible surrogates for reference groups; advertising home-oriented products stressing family roles may be highly effective—for example, electronic games.
B. Obligations toward parents are sacred.	The image of functional products should be enhanced with advertisements that stress parental advice or approval; even with children's products, there should be less emphasis on children as decision makers.
C. Obligation to extend hospitality to both insiders and outsiders.	Product designs that are symbols of hospitality, outwardly open in expression; rate of new product acceptance may be accelerated and eased by appeals based on community.
D. Obligation to conform to codes of sexual conduct and social interaction. These may include the following:	
1. Modest dress for women in public.	More colorful clothing and accessories are worn by women at home; so promotion of products for use in private homes could be more intimate—such audiences could be reached effectively through women's magazines; avoid use of immodest exposure and sexual implications in public settings.
2. Separation of male and female audiences (in some cases).	Access to female consumers can often be gained only through women as selling agents, salespersons, catalogs, home demonstrations, and women's specialty shops.

TABLE 3.1 ● Marketing in an Islamic Framework (*Continued*)

Elements	Implications for marketing
E. Obligations to religious occasions. (For example, two major religious observances are celebrated—Eid-ul-Fitr, Eid-ul-Adha.)	Tied to purchase of new shoes, clothing, and sweets and preparation of food items for family reunions, Muslim gatherings. There has been a practice of giving money in place of gifts. Increasingly, however, a shift is taking place to more gift giving; due to lunar calendar, dates are not fixed.

Source: Mushtaq Luqmani, Zahir A. Quraeshi, and Linda Delene, "Marketing in Islamic Countries: A Viewpoint," *MSU Business Topics,* Summer 1980, pp. 20–21. Reprinted by permission.

derived from the funds employed. Thus, the depositors get earnings on their deposits, depending on the amount of profits earned by the bank. Such Islamic banks now exist in many countries, particularly Egypt, Saudi Arabia, Kuwait, Sudan, Dubai, and Jordan.

The influence of Islam is also felt in Southeast Asia. Malaysia, a country with about 52 percent of the area's population, is Muslim.[12] In that country, several business laws in banking and other areas have been made consistent with Islamic law, although in many respects a dual system exists with the British law. Greater awareness of Islamic traditions also creates new business opportunities. Kohilal is a small business catering to traditional Muslims in Malaysia. The company markets, among other items, a soap that is made of palm oil and free of animal fats. Its products are "halal" (acceptable under Islamic teaching) and typically avoid pork, pork products, and alcohol. The company also emphasizes the fact that its products are handled and distributed by devout Muslims only.[13]

Another challenge was faced by Gillette, which wanted to introduce its products in Iran. Islam discourages its followers from shaving, creating difficulties for Gillette's local distributor to secure advertising space. In the end, the distributor visited one local newspaper after another until he finally met an advertising manager without a beard. He convinced the advertising manager that shaving sometimes was unavoidable, such as when a person had a head injury as a result of an accident, and that Gillette blades would be best. The advertising manager consulted with his clergyman and, having obtained permission, accepted the ad. As a result, other newspapers followed, and Gillette Blue was launched. The company is now working on TV advertising, which is permitted only for domestically made products.[14]

Certainly, international marketers require a keen awareness of how religion can influence business. They need to search actively for any such possible influences, even when

12. "For God and Growth in Malaysia," *Economist,* November 27, 1993, p. 39.

13. "Strong Fundamentals: In Malaysia, Islam Is a Basis for Business," *Far Eastern Economic Review,* September 16, 1993, p. 74.

14. "Smooth Talk Wins Gillette Ad Space in Iran," *Advertising Age International,* April 27, 1992, pp. 1–40.

the influences are not very apparent. Developing an intitial awareness of the impact religion has on one's own culture is often very helpful in developing cultural sensitivity.

Education

Though the educational system of a country largely reflects its own culture and heritage, education can have a major impact on how receptive consumers are to foreign marketing techniques. Education shapes people's outlooks, desires, and motivation. To the extent that educational systems differ by country, we can expect differences among consumers. However, education not only affects potential consumers, it also shapes potential employees for foreign companies and for the business community overall. This will influence business practices and competitive behavior.

Executives who have been educated in one country are frequently poorly informed about educational systems elsewhere. In this section, we will indicate some of the major differences in educational systems throughout the world and explain their impact on international marketing.

Levels of Participation

In the United States, although compulsory education ends at age sixteen, virtually all students who obtain a high school diploma stay in school until age eighteen (see Table 3.2). While at high school, some 25 percent take vocational training courses. After high school, students either go on to college or find a job. About half of all high school graduates go on to some type of college.

TABLE 3.2 ● Educational Statistics of Selected Countries (in Percentages)

Country	Participation in secondary education[1]	Participation in university education[2]	Literacy rates[3]
Austria	82.00%	31.00%	98.00%
Australia	82.00	32.00	99.00
Belgium/Luxembourg	99.00	34.00	98.00
Brazil	39.00	11.00	81.10
Canada	105.00	66.00	98.00
Chile	75.00	19.00	93.40
Denmark	109.00	32.00	99.00
Germany	97.00	32.00	99.00
Greece	97.00	28.00	93.00

TABLE 3.2 ● Educational Statistics of Selected Countries (in Percentages) (*Continued*)

Country	Participation in secondary education[1]	Participation in university education[2]	Literacy rates[3]
Finland	112.00	43.00	99.00
France	97.00	37.00	99.00
Hong Kong	73.00	15.00	88.10
Hungary	76.00	15.00	98.00
India	43.00	6.00	48.20
Indonesia	47.00	7.00	77.00
Ireland	97.00	26.00	99.00
Italy	78.00	29.00	97.00
Japan	96.00	31.00	100.00
Malaysia	59.00	7.00	78.40
Mexico	53.00	15.00	87.30
Netherlands	103.00	32.00	98.00
New Zealand	88.00	41.00	98.50
Norway	98.00	36.00	100.00
Pakistan	20.00	5.00	34.80
Portugal	53.00	18.00	85.00
Singapore	69.00	35.00	86.10
South Africa	76.00	12.00	78.20
South Korea	86.00	38.00	96.30
Spain	105.00	32.00	95.00
Sweden	91.00	31.00	99.00
Switzerland	n.a.	26.00	100.00
Taiwan	85.00	n.a.	93.20
Thailand	28.00	16.00	93.00
Turkey	51.00	13.00	80.70
United Kingdom	82.00	24.00	99.00
United States	98.00	63.00	99.50
Venezuela	56.00	28.00	88.10

1. Percentage of relevant age group receiving full time education. Scores in excess of 100 percent indicate adults also participating in that education.

2. Percentage of population twenty to twenty-four years old enrolled in higher education.

3. Adult (over fifteen years) literacy rate as a percentage of population.

Source: The World Competitiveness Report 1993 (Lausanne: IMD; Geneva: World Economic Forum, 1993), pp. 662–663, 666.

This pattern is not shared by all countries. The large majority of students in Europe go to school only until age sixteen; then they join an apprenticeship program. This is particularly the case in Germany, where formal apprenticeship programs exist for about 450 job categories. These programs are under tight government supervision and typically last three years. They include on-the-job training, with one day a week of full-time school. About 70 percent of young Germans enter such a program after compulsory full-time education.[15] During the first year, they can expect to earn about 25 percent of the wages earned by a fully trained craftsman in their field. Only about 30 percent of young Germans finish university schooling. In Great Britain, the majority of young people take a job directly in industry and receive only informal on-the-job training. In the United States, about 56 percent of the work force stops at a high school education (or earlier). For those, little formal training opportunities exist. In Japan, most of the post-secondary training is provided by companies.[16]

Participation in secondary education affects literacy levels and economic development. Even with similar levels of participation in secondary education, the attitudes of some countries about the quantity and quality of education differ. For example, Japanese high school students attend class more days than students in the United States, where the school year is only 180 days long. Since students in other countries also spend a higher percentage of their school day on core academic subjects, the differences in mathematics, science, and history are 1,460 hours for high school students in the United States; 3,170 in Japan, 3,280 in France, and 3,528 in Germany.[17]

Literacy and Economic Development

The extent of education affects marketing on two levels. First, there is the problem of literacy. In societies where the average level of participation in the educational process is low, one typically finds a low level of literacy (see Table 3.2). This not only affects earning potential, and thus the level of consumption, but it determines the communication options for marketing programs, as we will see in Chapters 14 and 15. A second concern is for how much young people earn. In countries such as Germany, where many of its youth have considerable earnings by age twenty, the value, or potential, of the youth market is quite different from that in the United States, where a substantial number of youths do not enter the job market until age twenty-one or twenty-two.

Recent studies by the Organization for Economic Cooperation and Development have found a definite link between the percentage of sixteen-year-olds staying in school beyond the minimum leaving age and a country's economic well-being. Countries such as Japan, Holland, West Germany, Austria, and the United States get a high return on their educational expenses because so many young people stay in school, either in traditional or

15. "Teaching Business How to Train," *Business Week/Reinventing America,* 1992, p. 90.
16. Ibid., p. 79.
17. "U.S. Pupils Short on Basics, Study Finds," *International Herald Tribune,* May 6, 1994, p. 3.

vocational schools. Portugal, Spain, Britain, and New Zealand get a poor return on their educational expenses because so few young people continue their education.[18]

The educational system also affects the type of employees and executive talent. The typical career path of a U.S. executive involves a four-year-college program and, in many cases, a master's in business administration (M.B.A.) program. This type of executive education is rare outside the United States. Top management talent may have university degrees in other fields. For example, law is among the more popular degrees. In many areas of the world, it may be impossible to hire university graduates. In the United States, the sales organizations of many large companies are staffed strictly with university graduates. In many other countries, sales as a profession has a lower status, and it can be difficult to attract university graduates.

Different countries have substantially different ideas about education in general, and management education in particular. Overall, though differences exist between countries, traditional European education emphasizes the mastery of a subject through knowledge acquisition. In contrast, the U.S. approach emphasizes analytic ability and an understanding of concepts. Students passing through the two educational systems will probably develop different thinking patterns and attitudes. It requires a considerable amount of cultural sensitivity for an international manager to understand these differences and to make the best use of the human resources that are available.

The Family

The role of the family varies greatly between cultures, as do the roles that the various family members play. Across cultures, we find differences in family sizes, in the employment of women, and in many other factors of great interest to marketers. Particularly since the family is a primary reference group and has always been considered an important determinant of purchasing behavior, these differences are of interest.[19] Companies familiar with family interactions in western society cannot assume that they will find the same patterns elsewhere. For example, the Chinese value family above individuals or even country. People have strong ties with family members. Within a family, an individual has no rights or property—expenses are shared.[20] Therefore, product advertising appeals must focus on family benefits, not individual benefits.

One development centers around the nature of the nuclear family. The term *nuclear family* is used with reference to the immediate family group: father, mother, and children

18. "The Wealth of Nations," *Economist,* December 20, 1986, p. 101.

19. J. Barry Mason and Hazel F. Ezell, *Marketing Principles and Strategy* (Plano, Tex.: Business Publications, 1987), p. 266.

20. Ester Lee Yao, "Cultivating Guan-xi (Personal Relationships) with Chinese Partners," *Business Marketing,* January 1987, p. 64.

TABLE 3.3 ● Family Statistics of Selected Countries (in Percentages)

Country	Population growth rates[1]	Female participation in labor force[2]
Austria	0.44%	41.10%
Australia	1.50	41.60
Belgium/ Luxembourg	−0.03	41.61
Brazil	2.11	35.08
Canada	1.07	44.98
Chile	1.65	30.69
Denmark	0.10	46.06
Germany	3.43	39.20
Greece	0.26	36.90
Finland	0.43	47.01
France	0.52	43.45
Hong Kong	0.91	37.37
Hungary	−0.38	45.53
India	2.09	29.02
Indonesia	2.17	39.93
Ireland	0.07	31.60
Italy	0.05	29.02
Japan	0.48	40.75
Malaysia	2.66	35.52
Mexico	2.05	23.46
Netherlands	0.60	39.68
New Zealand	0.69	43.46
Norway	0.39	45.30
Pakistan	3.10	14.20
Portugal	0.69	43.00
Singapore	1.24	39.75
South Africa	2.25	41.00
South Korea	1.02	40.27
Spain	0.28	35.50
Sweden	0.46	47.96
Switzerland	0.70	38.32
Taiwan	1.19	37.51
Thailand	1.70	45.97

TABLE 3.3 ● Family Statistics of Selected Countries (in Percentages) (*Continued*)

Country	Population growth rates[1]	Female participation in labor force[2]
Turkey	2.32	31.06
United Kingdom	0.22	43.34
United States	0.95	44.97
Venezuela	2.65	32.21

1. Annual compound percentage change, 1983–1991.

2. Percentage of total labor force.

Source: The World Competitiveness Report 1993 (Lausanne: IMD; Geneva: World Economic Forum, 1993), pp. 636, 645.

living together.[21] In the United States, and to some degree in western Europe as well, we have found strong trends toward the dissolution of the traditional nuclear family.[22] As a result of an increasing divorce rate, the "typical" family of father, mother, and children living in one dwelling is rapidly becoming a thing of the past, or "atypical." Furthermore, families are smaller than they used to be, due to the drop in fertility rates. Also, an increasing number of women are working outside the home (see Table 3.3). These circumstances have substantially changed purchasing patterns, especially among U.S. families.

Marketers who have dealt only with U.S. consumers should not expect to find the same type of family structure elsewhere. In many societies the role of the male as head of household is more pronounced, and in some cultures (as in Asia or Latin America) the differences tend to be substantial. This male dominance coincides with a lower rate of participation by women in the labor force outside the home. On the average, this results in a lower family income, since double wage earners increase the average family income. The number of children per family also shows substantial variations by country or culture. In many eastern European countries and in Germany, one child per family is fast approaching the rule, whereas families in many developing countries are still large by western standards.

So far we have discussed only the nuclear family. However, for many cultures, the extended family—including grandparents, in-laws, aunts, uncles, and so on—is of considerable importance. In the United States, older parents usually live alone, either in individ-

21. John C. Mowen, *Consumer Behavior* (New York: Macmillan, 1987), p. 399.

22. Fabian Linder, "The Nuclear Family Is Splitting," *Across the Board,* July 1980, p. 52.

ually owned housing, in special housing for the elderly, or in nursing homes (for those who can no longer care for themselves). In countries with lower income levels and in rural areas, the extended family still plays a major role, further increasing the size of the average household.

Because the family plays such an important role as a consumption unit, marketers need to understand family roles and composition as they differ from country to country. At this point we are not so much concerned with the demographic aspects, though they will concern us as we discuss the various market opportunities in Chapters 5 and 6. Here, the primary emphasis is on the roles the individual family members play, their respective influences on each other, and the society's expectation as to what role each family member ought to play. Such an understanding is crucial for the marketing of consumer products and tends to affect both communication policy and product policy.

Work and Leisure

The attitudes a society holds toward work have been documented to have a substantial impact on a society's or culture's economic performance. David McClelland has maintained that it is not a country's external resources that determine its economic rise but its level of entrepreneurial spirit to exploit existing resources.[23] What was found to be crucial was the orientation, or attitudes, toward achievement and work. Cultures with a high level of achievement motivation were found to show a faster rise in economic development than those with low achievement motivation.

A well-known German sociologist, Max Weber, investigated the relationship between attitudes toward work and those toward religion. In his famous work published in 1904, *The Protestant Ethic and the Spirit of Capitalism,* Weber was one of the first to speculate on the influence of religion on the work ethic by demonstrating differences between Protestant and Catholic attitudes toward work. McClelland later expanded Weber's theory to cover all religions and found that economies with a more Protestant orientation exceeded economies with a Catholic orientation in per capita income. McClelland ascribed this to the Protestant (particularly Calvinist) belief that man did not necessarily receive salvation from God through work but that success in work could be viewed as an indication of God's grace. Consequently, accumulating wealth was not viewed as a shameful activity that needed to be hidden. Traditional Catholic doctrine viewed moneymaking in more negative terms. It was Weber's theory that this difference in attitude toward wealth caused Protestant societies to outperform Catholic societies in economic terms.

Thus, religion appears to be a primary influence on attitudes toward work. Observers have theorized that the Shinto religion encourages the Japanese people to have a strong patriotic attitude, which is in part responsible for Japan's excellent economic perform-

23. David C. McClelland and David G. Winter, *Motivating Economic Achievement* (New York: Free Press, 1969).

ance.[24] The low rate of economic performance in some developing countries can be attributed in part to their different attitudes toward work as dictated by their religions.

A discussion on work will usually lead to a discussion of its opposite—leisure. Different societies have different views about the amount of leisure time that is acceptable. In most economically developed countries, particularly where work has become a routine activity, leisure has become a major aspect of life. In such countries, the development of the leisure industries is an indication that leisure can be as intensely consumed as any other product. In western European countries, it is typical for employees and management alike to receive three to five weeks of vacation time and to embark on trips away from home. In Japan, official vacations may reach the same number of weeks, but employees take only a portion of it. In the United States, vacations are shorter, so people tend to use up their allotted time off. These differences in the use of leisure time reflect, to some degree, differences in attitudes toward work (see Table 3.4).

TABLE 3.4 ● Values of Selected Countries

Country	Working hours[1]	Young people's desire to work/learn vs. have fun[2]	Society's support of competitiveness[3]
Austria	1,722	5.40	6.20
Australia	1,668	5.60	4.10
Belgium/Luxembourg	1,744	5.30	5.90
Brazil	1,856	5.20	4.50
Canada	1,888	5.90	5.70
Chile	n.a.	6.30	6.20
Denmark	1,684	7.30	5.60
Germany	1,665	5.30	5.60
Greece	1,848	4.70	4.30
Finland	1,732	5.90	5.50
France	1,771	5.50	4.40
Hong Kong	2,375	6.60	8.00
Hungary	n.a.	5.30	4.40
India	2,052	6.00	5.50
Indonesia	n.a.	6.30	6.00
Ireland	1,817	6.70	5.80
Italy	1,788	5.30	4.90
Japan	2,040	5.00	8.00
Malaysia	2,167	6.70	7.20

24. Vern Terpstra, *International Marketing* (New York: Dryden Press, 1987), p. 101.

TABLE 3.4 ● Values of Selected Countries (*Continued*)

Country	Working hours[1]	Young people's desire to work/learn vs. have fun[2]	Society's support of competitiveness[3]
Mexico	1,944	5.70	5.50
Netherlands	1,727	6.00	5.10
New Zealand	n.a.	5.90	4.90
Norway	1,748	6.20	5.70
Pakistan	n.a.	3.80	4.60
Portugal	1,898	5.30	5.50
Singapore	2,042	7.50	8.60
South Africa	1,945	5.10	4.30
South Korea	1,842	6.20	5.70
Spain	1,788	4.50	4.20
Sweden	1,792	6.10	5.40
Switzerland	1,865	5.80	6.90
Taiwan	2,145	6.60	6.60
Thailand	n.a.	5.70	6.50
Turkey	n.a.	6.10	5.70
United Kingdom	1,762	4.90	4.40
United States	1,912	5.30	5.60
Venezuela	2,041	4.80	4.20

1. Average number of working hours per year.

2. Based on a survey of 2,160 executives from the countries listed, transforming the reported values (1 for having fun to 10 for working/learning) to an average.

3. Based on a survey of 2,160 executives from the countries listed, transforming the reported values (1 for least support to 10 for most support) to an average.

Source: The World Competitiveness Report 1993 (Lausanne: IMD; Geneva: World Economic Forum, 1993), pp. 676, 686, 689.

Reference Groups

The impact of reference groups on buying behavior has been documented by many writers in marketing.[25] Past experience clearly indicates that the concept of reference group influence applies to many cultures. Differences can be found in the types of relevant reference groups and in the nature of their influence on individual consumers.

25. Leon G. Schiffman and Leslie Lazar Kanuk, *Consumer Behavior,* 3rd ed. (Englewood Cliffs, N.J.: Prentice Hall, 1987), p. 374.

Peer Groups

The account of a U.S. journalist traveling in the former U.S.S.R. gives an excellent illustration of the different types of peer reference groups found abroad. The journalist became curious about the fact that many young people in Russia were wearing the same type of blue jeans and T-shirts that young people were wearing in the United States. In fact, some of the items had been acquired at very high prices on the black market. After several personal conversations, the reporter concluded that those who wore this clothing were viewed as having a sense of fashion-mindedness, and they derived a high level of status within their social groups. In contrast, U.S. consumers who wore blue jeans and T-shirts normally conveyed a sense of informality and casualness about their appearance. Indeed, the U.S. consumers wanted the opposite of their Russian counterparts. Consequently, we can observe the influence of different reference groups on the same product category as they induce consumption but satisfy different purposes. International marketers are well advised to ensure that communication programs based on specific reference groups are consistent with the cultural and social environment of that reference group in the foreign market.

Role Models

Famous sportspersons traditionally have been used in order to exploit the reference group concept. The idea is to use the prestige of accomplished athletes to promote certain products. However, not all sports are equally popular in all parts of the world. The enormous interest in baseball in the United States is shared only by certain Latin American and Asian nations and not at all in Europe. On the other hand, soccer dominates only in Europe and Latin America and not in the United States. Some sports, such as tennis or golf, have an international following, but these sports do not attract large segments of the population. Consequently, finding a sports personality that people around the world will recognize equally is difficult.

There are some reference groups of U.S. origin that appear to have substantial universal appeal. The ''American way of life'' is one phenomenon that may explain the success of many U.S. consumer products elsewhere. Though not always clearly defined, it does represent an attraction to large groups of people in most countries. What is considered American may in fact only be a cover for a modern or high-income lifestyle. Consequently, foreign consumers aspire to a high level of economic status as exemplified by the U.S. lifestyle, or the commonly held image of such a life. In any case, some companies have successfully capitalized on this lifestyle, and Americans have become a reference group for numerous products in markets abroad.

Another U.S. symbol with international appeal is the American cowboy of the ''Wild West.'' The image of a cowboy on horseback triggers substantially similar reactions in most countries, even where the cultural background is otherwise diverse. The cowboy may very well be one of the few commonly shared symbols around the world, and this may account for the success of Philip Morris's well-known Marlboro campaign featuring western scenes.

Country Image

The success of the U.S. company Levi Strauss in foreign markets can be partially credited to the penchant of foreign consumers for western-style clothing. Several U.S. manufacturers of Top-Sider shoes, such as the brands Timberland and Sperry, have enjoyed strong sales in Europe. Other U.S. firms have had more difficulty, partially because of the image foreign consumers have of shoes manufactured in the United States. Market research revealed that French manufacturers were viewed as leading in high-fashion women's shoes, whereas Italian companies dominated the market for lightweight men's shoes. Europeans viewed shoes manufactured in the United States as stiff, heavy, boxy, and lacking variety in style; manufacturers in the United States took the lead only with western boots. Once a strong image exists, it is extremely difficult to change a prevailing view.

On an international level, countries can assume the position of a reference group. Over time, various countries, or the residents of various countries, have become known for achievements in some aspects of life, culture, or industry. Other countries, thus, may attach a special quality to the behavior of these consumers or to products that originate in these countries. When the German beer Beck was touted in the United States as "the German beer that is number one in Germany," the idea was to capitalize on the image of German beer drinkers as being the most discriminating. BSN-Gervais, Danone, the French company that brewed Kronenbourg, attempted to take on Heineken, the leading exporter to the United States, by claiming "Europeans like Heineken, but they love Kronenbourg." This campaign tried to take advantage of the fact that Kronenbourg was the largest-selling bottled beer in Europe. BSN decided not to emphasize French Alsace as the origin of the beer. Since the brand name Kronenbourg sounded German to most U.S. consumers, the company was banking on the positive image of German beers in general.[26]

The U.S. brewer Anheuser-Busch faced a different problem when entering the European market. Anheuser-Busch marketed its beer as the beer brewed with "high-country barley" from Wyoming, using the German voice used in John Wayne films as the narrator. The same western theme was used in France, where Busch beer was advertised as "the beer of the men of the West." Because the United States was not recognized by Europeans as a major beer-brewing country, the company took advantage of already existing images familiar to European consumers.[27]

A survey of European consumers showed that, after their own country, they tended to prefer products made in the United States. European consumers often referred to U.S. products as innovative, fashionable, and of high quality. French consumers in the survey contradicted an often-held stereotype of being anti-American, with some 40 percent in the survey viewing U.S. products as both fashionable and innovative. Other countries surveyed were the United Kingdom, Spain, Germany, Italy, and the Netherlands.[28]

26. "Big Battle Is Brewing as French Beer Aims to Topple Heineken," *Wall Street Journal,* February 22, 1980, p. 24.
27. "Anheuser Tries Light Beer Again," *Business Week,* June 29, 1981, p. 140.
28. "Poll: Europe Favors US Products," *Advertising Age,* September 23, 1991, p. 16.

The perfume industry, for decades dominated by French firms, has been greatly affected by the "made in Paris" phenomenon. Consumers all over the world have come to admire and expect more of perfumes made by French companies. U.S. firms have tried to overcome this handicap with aggressive marketing policies and the creation of new products based on market research and new insights into perfume-making chemistry. Still, it has proved to be very difficult to enter this high-prestige market, and some U.S. cosmetic leaders have not been able to duplicate their domestic success abroad. To overcome the "made in Paris" mystique, foreign companies have acquired French cosmetic firms.

The impact of the origin of products has interested researchers for years. Numerous studies have been conducted, and the general agreement is that there is a strong correlation between country of origin and product categories. For reasons of tradition, consumers tend to attach some expertise to a certain country. For products originating in that particular country, the image tends to be higher.[29] This strongly suggests that marketing managers must carefully consider the "made in . . ." implications of their products. Where the country has a positive image, the origin of the product or company can be exploited. In other cases, the international firm may be advised to select a strategy that plays down the origin of the product. As international cosmetic firms have demonstrated in France, a positive country label can be obtained by opening operations in a particular country known for its achievements in a certain industry.

The Challenge of Cultural Change

Sometimes, what may appear to be a cultural difference may in fact be due to other influences, particularly economic ones. These other influences are subject to considerable change over short periods of time. Some examples follow.

Although Kellogg has sold Kellogg's Corn Flakes in France since 1935, it has only recently penetrated the breakfast market. The slow growth of demand for corn flakes was related to two aspects of French culinary habits. First, the French did not eat corn; 80 percent of the corn harvested in France was fed to pigs and chickens.[30] Second, of those who ate cereal for breakfast, 40 percent poured on warm milk, which didn't do much for the crunchiness or taste of corn flakes. To overcome these cultural biases, Kellogg put instructions on its cereal boxes and radically boosted television advertising with "Tony le Tigre." The average French person ate ten ounces of cereal in 1985, and Kellogg expected consumption to increase by 25 percent each year until 1990. However, the consumption

29. Martin S. Roth and Jean B. Romeo, "Matching Product Category and Country Image Perceptions: A Framework for Managing Country-of-Origin Effects," *Journal of International Business Studies,* 3rd Quarter 1992, pp. 477–497.

30. "While Americans Take to Croissants, Kellogg Pushes Corn Flakes on France," *Wall Street Journal,* November 11, 1986, p. 40.

of corn flakes in France had a long way to go to reach the average consumption of nine pounds in the United States, twelve pounds in England, and thirteen pounds in Australia.[31]

Perrier, the French producer of bottled mineral spring water, successfully launched its product in the United States despite this market's practice of consuming soft drinks, beer, or tap water instead. U.S. per capita consumption of bottled water was less than one liter, compared to fifty-five liters each in France and Italy. Despite these cultural hurdles, the French company started a major push in 1976 and increased its annual volume from 3 million to 200 million bottles in 1979, achieving a 1 percent share of the U.S. soft drink market. Though these figures may not indicate a large volume, they nevertheless indicated a considerable change in U.S. consumption habits at that time.[32]

Nowhere is the influence on culture as prevalent as with food products. However, quite a few firms have overcome cultural barriers. One such celebrated case is McDonald's, the U.S. fast-food franchise operator. The first year that McDonald's opened more restaurants abroad than in the United States was 1991. All of its top ten restaurants, measured in terms of sales and profits, are located overseas. Top stores are in Moscow, Paris, and Rome, hardly places where one would expect a typical fare of U.S.-style hamburgers to do well. In general, McDonald's restaurants overseas have sales about 25 percent higher than the average U.S. outlet.[33] In fact, one of the company's stores in Poland holds the world record for first-day sales, having served 33,000 customers on its opening day.[34] Still, there are some countries where McDonald's, with its hamburger menu, does not do well or is not represented. One of them is India, many of whose people avoid eating beef for religious reasons.[35]

More difficulties with marketing food globally have been experienced by Campbell Soup. The company's overseas sales are only about 25 percent of total volume; its brands are not easily transplanted. Italians are not interested in buying canned pasta, making Franco-American SpaghettiOs a poor performer. In Argentina, where rival CPC's Knorr brand dehydrated soup has dominated the market with 80 percent share, Campbell is the outsider with wet or canned soup. The challenge is even greater in Asia, where Campbell and other western food companies must find ways to sell food in exotic markets.[36]

Few companies have recently struggled as much with cultural differences as has Disney. The U.S.-based entertainment company owns 49 percent of Euro Disney, a large theme park built outside Paris with a $4 billion investment. The park, designed as a carbon copy of Disney World in Orlando, Florida, opened in 1992 to much fanfare and a $10 million advertising campaign aimed at some thirty European countries.[37] The theme park lost $900 million in its first full year of operation, with visitors running some 1.5 million

31. Ibid.

32. "Perrier Sales Lose Momentum as Hard Times Hit U.S. Market," *Business Standard,* July 4, 1980, p. 3.

33. "Overseas Sizzle for McDonald's," *New York Times,* April 17, 1993, p. D1.

34. "Big Mac's Counter Attack," *Economist,* November 13, 1993, p. 71.

35. "Overseas Sizzle," p. D1.

36. "Campbell: Now It's M-M-Global," *Business Week,* March 15, 1993, p. 15.

37. "Mr. Grumpy at the Door," *Financial Times,* September 1, 1993, p. 15.

below the required break-even of 11 million a year. (Critics have indicated that the park is exposed to bad weather and long winters, different from the company's U.S. properties.)[38] This experience contrasts sharply with Disney's success in Japan. Its theme park there was expected to attract 10 million visitors a year but achieved 16 million in 1991, more than 90 percent of them repeat visitors. One observer indicated that the Japanese have a deep feeling for fantasy and were not intimidated by the U.S.-manufactured icons. In fact, they wanted the undiluted American Disney. Coming to Disneyland was linked to the Japanese tea ceremony, with its rules, roles, and symbolism. Japanese attending the Disney Park knew that they were ''in'' the United States and played that role during their visit.[39]

Cultural Challenges to Marketing in Eastern Europe

The opening of eastern Europe to western businesses has created many cultural challenges. In the years following World War II, these countries had little exposure to western-style marketing. As a result, consumption habits remained at levels more typical to western Europe thirty years ago. Several U.S. companies have now made their first entry into Poland, where consumers have to learn how to deal with western-style consumer goods. Gerber, a U.S.-based baby-food maker, moved into Poland by acquiring a local company in 1991. The company needs to educate consumers in the value and use of prepared baby foods. In the United States, about 630 jars of baby food are sold for each birth; the corresponding figure is 116 in Mexico and 624 in France. In Poland, it will reach just 12 in 1993. Tradition in Poland calls for the mother to cook the baby's food. And while some mothers are now aware of the convenience of Gerber's product, only a few can yet afford it. The company is certain, however, that the market will grow substantially in the next few years.[40]

Retailers and franchise store operators have also had experience in eastern Europe. Kmart purchased thirteen stores in the Czech Republic and Slovakia. Its largest store in Bratislava, the capital of Slovakia, had sales of $40 million in the first year, surpassing all of the company's 2,400 stores in the United States. Despite this volume, the store was unprofitable due to inefficiencies, high costs, and low margins. Kmart found changing the relationship between salesclerk and consumer particularly challenging. Although the company's sales staff understand the customer concept, after forty years of communist rule its implementation is still not natural to them.[41]

The few examples reviewed in this section give a glimpse of the challenges faced by global marketers. As is evident from their experience, it is not easy to predict a product's future success or failure. Chapters 5 and 6 will provide some models to analyze different strategies for countering cultural differences. However, these examples also show that over

38. ''Is Disney Headed for the Euro-Trash Heap?'' *Business Week,* January 24, 1994, p. 52.
39. ''Japan Enters the World of Fantasy,'' *Financial Times,* May 6, 1993, p. 8.
40. ''In Poland, Gerber Learns Lessons of Tradition,'' *New York Times,* November 8, 1993, p. 1.
41. ''In East Europe, Kmart Faces an Attitude Problem,'' *New York Times,* July 7, 1993, p. D1.

time, with economic development, many traits or habits will disappear and other, more advanced ones will emerge. A marketer who faces differences between two countries must answer the question of whether these differences are cultural or simply influenced by economic development. True cultural differences are likely to survive economic development, whereas differences driven by different income levels will rapidly disappear once economic development takes off.

Adapting to Cultural Differences

Some companies have made special efforts to adapt their products or services to various cultural environments. Nowhere are these strategies more apparent than in Japan, where foreign companies have to compete in an economically developed market with greatly differing cultural patterns.

American Express had to devise a unique strategy in Japan to overcome the Japanese preference for paying in cash. Though there were about seventy million credit cards in circulation in Japan in 1980, they were rarely used. Annual charges averaged $400, compared to $1,500 in the United States. The Japanese appeared embarrassed if they could not pay in cash when out for dinner. For company entertainment, top executives frequently had their bills sent to the company, and junior executives obtained a cash advance before taking out clients. Research showed that Japanese businesspeople wanted primarily cash and security when traveling abroad. As a result, American Express offered a card that, in addition to normal charges, allowed customers to draw $2,200 in cash each month. This adaptation to Japanese requirements expanded the American Express credit card business in Japan.[42]

After years of trying, Japanese appear finally to be warming up to credit cards. Particularly younger consumers are now becoming frequent users of credit cards, and besides American Express, Visa and MasterCard are well represented.[43]

Even McDonald's, which started out in Japan decades ago with what is essentially a U.S.-style menu, came to the conclusion that for further growth it had to adapt its menu. It introduced McChao, a Chinese fried rice. Rice was an obvious first try in a country where 90 percent of the population eat rice daily. The results have been astounding. Sales have climbed 30 percent during the time McChao has been served. Even more important is the fact that 70 percent of McChao sales have been in the form of take-out food bought by single businesspeople. The company expects that eventually some 30 percent of its sales might be derived from localized menu choices.[44]

42. "Inside Japan's 'Open' Market," *Fortune,* October 5, 1981, p. 127.

43. "Japanese Consumers, Long Known Savers, Catch On to Credit," *Wall Street Journal,* April 10, 1989, p. 1.

44. "High Hopes for McChao—Japan McDonald's Expects Sales Boost from McChao Rice," *Nikkei Weekly,* February 22, 1992, p. 9.

Similar adjustments were needed for Domino's Pizza, one of the many pizza franchises active in Japan. The types of pizza favored by Japanese consumers are quite different from those favored in the United States. Although Domino's advertises its pizza as "from the U.S.A.," it offers such toppings as teriyaki gourmet pizza consisting of Japanese-style grilled chicken, spinach, onion, and corn. In addition, Domino offers squid and tuna toppings, as well as corn salad. Pizza Hut offers its Japanese customers barbecue chicken pizza as well as burdock root, potato, and macaroni salad.[45]

Cultural Analysis for International Marketing

It is not sufficient to describe cultural differences by citing only past experiences of companies. Clearly, one could never cover all of the possible mistakes or cultural differences that international firms may experience abroad. Consequently, this text is restricted to a few examples indicating the kinds of problems international firms face. However, because it is impossible to predict all the possible problems that can be encountered abroad, it becomes necessary to provide some analytical framework to deal with cultural differences.

In a classic article, James E. Lee exposed the natural tendency among executives to fall prey to a *self-reference criterion*. Lee defines the self-reference criterion as an "unconscious reference to one's own cultural values."[46] How does this work? Within each culture, we have come to accept certain truths or basic facts. These facts have become part of our experience and are, therefore, rarely challenged. As we continue our experience in one culture only, there are few occasions when such inherent beliefs can be exposed. The self-reference criterion also helps us under new circumstances. Whenever we face an unknown situation, we have an inherent tendency to fall back on prior experience to solve the new problem. There is one substantial handicap to this automatic reflex: if the new situation takes place in a different cultural environment, then the self-reference criterion may invoke past experience that is not applicable.

Lee suggests that executives, to avoid the trap of the self-reference criterion habit, approach problems using a four-step analysis. In the first step, the problem is to be defined in terms of the executive's home cultural traits, habits, or norms. Here the analyst can invoke the self-reference criterion. In a second step, the problem is to be defined in terms of the foreign cultural traits, habits, or norms. Value judgments should be avoided at this step. In the third step, the executive is to isolate the personal biases relating to the problem and determine if or how they complicate the problem. Finally, in the fourth step, the problem is to be redefined without the self-reference criterion influence in a search for the optimum solution. Consequently, the four-step approach is designed to avoid culture-bound thinking on the part of executives or companies. (We will further develop this approach in Chapter 6, where a model to analyze the entire international environment is presented.)

45. "Pizza in Japan Is Adapted to Local Tastes," *Wall Street Journal,* June 4, 1993, p. B7.
46. James E. Lee, "Cultural Analysis in Overseas Operations," *Harvard Business Review,* March–April 1966, pp. 106–114.

Businesspeople moving to another culture will experience stress and tension, often called culture shock. An individual who enters a different culture must learn to cope with a vast array of new cultural cues and expectations, as well as to identify which old ones no longer work. The authors of *Managing Cultural Differences* offer the following ten tips to deflate the stress and tension of cultural shock:

Be culturally prepared.

Learn local communication complexities.

Mix with the host and nationals.

Be creative and experimental.

Be culturally sensitive.

Recognize complexities in host cultures.

Perceive oneself as a culture bearer.

Be patient, understanding, and accepting of oneself and hosts.

Be most realistic in expectations.

Accept the challenge of intercultural experiences.[47]

Conclusions

In this chapter, we introduced you to the wide variety of possible cultural and social influences present in international marketing operations. What we have presented here represents only the tip of the iceberg, a very small sample of all the potential factors.

It is essential for international marketers to avoid a cultural bias, or the self-reference criterion, when dealing with business operations in more than one culture. As the president of a large industrial company in Osaka, Japan, once explained, our cultures are 80 percent identical and 20 percent different. The successful businessperson is the one who can identify the differences and deal with them. Of course, this is a very difficult task, and few executives ever reach the stage where they can claim to be completely sensitive to cultural differences. The analytical concepts presented at the end of the chapter will help you to deal with cultural differences. These concepts will be refined further in Chapter 6.

Questions for Discussion

1. Explain the difference between innate wants and needs and culturally derived wants and needs.

2. What process can a marketer use to ensure that an advertisement or brochure gives the desired message in an unfamiliar language?

47. Philip R. Harris and Robert T. Moran, *Managing Cultural Differences,* 2nd ed. (Houston: Gulf, 1987), pp. 212–215.

3. How would marketing automobiles to a predominantly Islamic population differ from marketing to a predominantly Christian population?

4. How do the educational systems of the United States, Japan, England, and Germany affect the marketing of banking services to young adults aged sixteen to twenty-two?

5. What aspects of the culture influence the marketing of women's designer blue jeans in different countries? How do these cultural influences affect magazine advertising?

6. The country of origin of a product is said to influence consumer demand. Why do we prefer specific products from certain countries—for example, perfume from France, electronics from Japan, and beer from Germany?

7. When entering a new market, how can one "learn" the culture?

For Further Reading

Cavusgil, S. Tamer, and Pervez N. Ghauri. *Doing Business in Developing Countries.* Lincolnwood, Ill.: Routledge, 1990.

Chao, Paul. "Partitioning Country of Origin Effects: Consumer Evaluations of a Hybrid Product." *Journal of International Business Studies,* 2nd Quarter 1993, p. 291.

Cordell, Victor V. "Effects of Consumer Preferences for Foreign Sourced Products." *Journal of International Business Studies,* 2nd Quarter 1992, pp. 251–269.

De Mente, Boye. *Chinese Etiquette and Ethics in Business.* 2nd ed. Lincolnwood, Ill.: NTC Business Books, 1994.

De Mente, Boye. *How to Do Business with the Japanese.* 2nd ed. Lincolnwood, Ill.: NTC Business Books, 1993.

Douglas, Susan, and Bernard Dubois. "Looking at the Cultural Environment for International Marketing Opportunities." *Columbia Journal of World Business,* Winter 1977, p. 102.

Geert, Hofstede. "National Cultures Revisited." *Asia-Pacific Journal of Management,* September 1984, pp. 22–29.

Graham, John L. "The Influence of Culture on Business Negotiations." *Journal of International Business Studies,* Spring 1985, pp. 81–96.

Hall, Edward T. *Beyond Culture.* Garden City, N.Y.: Anchor Press, 1976.

Harris, Philip R., and Robert T. Moran. *Managing Cultural Differences.* 2nd ed. Houston: Gulf, 1987.

Kaynak, Erdener, and S. Tamer Cavusgil. "Consumer Attitudes Towards Products of Foreign Origin: Do They Vary Across Product Class?" *International Journal of Advertising,* no. 2 (1983), pp. 147–157.

Martenson, Rita. "Is Standardization of Marketing Feasible in Culture-Bound Industries? A European Case Study." *International Marketing Review,* Autumn 1987, pp. 7–17.

Roth, Martin S., and Jean B. Romeo. "Matching Product Category and Country Image Perceptions: Framework for Managing Country-of-Origin Effects." *Journal of International Business Studies,* 3rd Quarter 1992, pp. 477–497.

Terpstra, Vern, and Kenneth David. *The Cultural Environment of International Business.* 2nd ed. Cincinnati: Southwestern, 1985.

Weiss, Stephen E. ''Negotiating with 'Romans,''' Part 1. *Sloan Management Review,* Winter 1994, pp. 51–61.

Weiss, Stephen E. ''Negotiating with 'Romans,''' Part 2. *Sloan Management Review,* Spring 1994, pp. 85–99.

4

Political and Legal Forces

IN THE FOUR *years since publication of the previous edition of this book, substantial changes have occurred on the political scene. The adoption of the North American Free Trade Agreement (NAFTA) by the U.S. government in 1993, the ratification of the Maastricht Treaty by most European countries, further upheaval in Russia, and changes in South Africa's political structure are just a few of the political events that are having a substantial impact on global marketing. The purpose of this chapter is to identify the political and legal forces that mold such important events and to demonstrate how these events influence global marketing operations.*

The first part of this chapter primarily is concerned with political factors, and the second part is devoted to the legal aspects of international marketing. The emphasis is on the regulations or laws that affect international marketing business transactions. Because many laws are actually politically inspired or motivated, it is difficult to separate political from legal forces. Nevertheless, some separation of the two areas is made to allow for a better organization of the subject matter. Figure 4.1 maps out the elements covered in the chapter and shows the relationships between them.

Dealing simultaneously with several political and legal systems makes the job of the international marketing executive a complex one. Because of these factors, many problems exist that increase the level of risk in the international marketplace. Global companies have learned to cope with such complexities by developing risk reduction strategies. These strategies are explained toward the end of the chapter.

FIGURE 4.1 ● Analyzing Political Forces

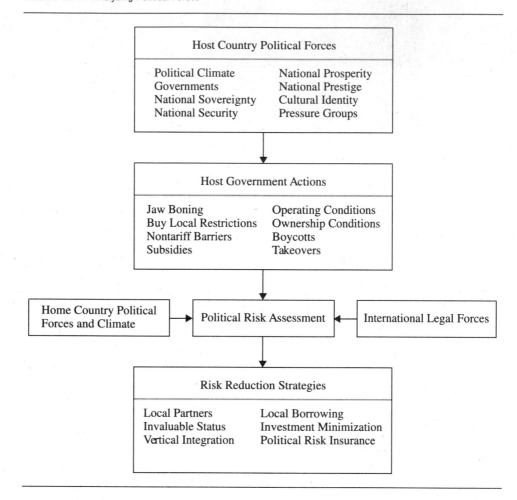

Host Country Political Forces

The rapidly changing nature of the international political scene is evident to anyone who regularly reads, listens to, or watches the various news media. Political upheavals, revolutions, and changes in government policy occur daily and can have an enormous effect on international business. As governments change, opportunities for new business may be lost or, just as often, newly gained. For the executive, this means constant adjustments to maximize new opportunities and minimize losses.

Besides the international company, the principal players in the political arena are the host country governments, the home country governments, and the transnational bodies or agencies. Although we use the term *host country* extensively in the following sections, political actions take place increasingly in an environment of *regions.* One such example is the European Community (EC, or more recently called EU for European Union). Political actions of host countries can therefore apply to an entire region, or grouping of countries. Although we do not make an explicit distinction each time, we have decided to apply the term *host country* interchangeably, to both single countries or country groupings.

The respective interactions of these groups result in a given political climate that may positively or negatively affect the operations of an international business. The difficulty for the international company stems from the fact that the firm is simultaneously subject to all these forces, which often have conflicting influence, whereas a strictly domestic corporation has to deal with only one, namely the home country political climate. The situation is further complicated by the fact that companies maintain operations in scores of countries—meaning that companies must be able to simultaneously manage many sets of political relationships. In the following sections of this chapter, we will discuss the host country political climate, the home country political climate, and transnational legal forces that regulate international trade. We also focus on political risk assessment and analyze the types of risk reduction strategies that may be employed to manage in such a complex world.

Political Climate

Any country that contains an operational unit (manufacturing, finance, sales, and so on) of an international company can be defined as a host country. By definition, international companies deal with many different host countries, each with its own political climate. In each country, the political climate is largely determined by the way the various participants interact with each other. It is influenced by the actions of the host country government and local special interest groups, as well as by the prevailing political philosophy.

Stable political climates are those in which existing relationships among the key players are not expected to change. Conversely, political climates are termed unstable when the nature of the interactions or their outcomes are unpredictable. Though the political climate of a country can be analyzed with respect to various segments of a society, for the purpose of this text we restrict ourselves to those aspects that relate to the business sectors.

Typical examples of political instability are the situations in Russia and China. Russia, which has gone through political turmoil, ended 1993 with elections that have resulted in considerable speculation as to the future direction of the country. At issue are both the pace and the direction of the economic transformation already under way.[1] In China, the political uncertainty does not stem from the present direction of the economic course. Rather, international companies are concerned with the possibility of a setback, or radical change, in China's direction at some future time.[2]

1. "Russia: From Shock Therapy to Shock Absorbers," *Business Week,* January 31, 1994, p. 49.
2. "China: Birth of a New Economy," *Business Week,* January 31, 1994, pp. 42–48.

Governments

Businesses operate in a country at the discretion of its government, which can encourage or discourage foreign businesses through a variety of measures. The government plays the principal role in host countries in initiating and implementing policies regarding the operation, conduct, and ownership of businesses. Today about 175 nations have been accepted as full members at the United Nations, giving some indication as to the large number of independent countries that exist at this time. Although each government may give the impression of acting as a single and homogeneous force, governments in most countries represent a collection of various, and at times conflicting, interests. Governments are sharply influenced by the prevailing political philosophy, existing local pressure groups or special interest groups, and the government's own self-interest. All of these factors lead to government actions that international companies must not only recognize but also actively incorporate into their marketing strategies. Of prime importance, then, is the ability to understand the rationale behind government actions.

To evaluate the political risk in a country and understand how decisions are made, examining the political structure is useful. Is it a democracy, dictatorship, monarchy, or socialist government? Knowing the political system aids understanding of the relationship between business and government. One way to classify governments is by the degree of representation of the population in government. Parliamentary governments hold regular elections so that government policies reflect the will of the people. All democracies are classified as parliamentary. Over the past decade, the world has seen a considerable shift toward democratic government. This was most apparent in eastern Europe, where Communist governments were swept away in the 1989 political upheaval. However, changes in Latin America are equally significant. In the early 1980s, true democracies existed in only a few countries, Venezuela and Costa Rica among them. Ten years later, most military dictatorships have ceased, and democratic governments govern in virtually all Latin American countries.[3]

Trying to understand governmental behavior only makes sense if there is a rational basis for leaders' actions and decisions. As many political scientists have pointed out, these actions usually flow from the government's interpretation of its own self-interest. This self-interest, often called national interest, may be expected to differ from nation to nation, but it typically includes the following goals:

1. *Self-preservation.* This is the primary goal of any entity, including states and governments.

2. *Security.* To the extent possible, each entity seeks to maximize the opportunity for continued existence and to minimize threats from the outside.

3. *Prosperity.* Improved living conditions for a country's citizens are an important and constant concern.

4. *Prestige.* Most governments or countries seek this either as an end in itself or to help reach other objectives.

3. ''Under Construction: Survey of Latin America,'' *Economist,* November 13, 1993, p. 5.

5. *Ideology.* Governments frequently protect or promote an ideology in combination with other goals.[4]

6. *Cultural identity.* Governments often intervene to protect their country's cultural identity.

The interaction of governments with foreign business interests can be understood through a basic appreciation of their national interest. The goals cited above are frequently the source of governmental actions either encouraging or limiting the business activities of international companies. Many executives erroneously believe that such limiting actions will mostly occur in developing countries. On the contrary, there are many examples of restrictive government actions in the most developed countries, which indicates the universal nature of this type of governmental behavior. Such restrictive behavior most often occurs when a government perceives the attainment of its own goals to be threatened by the activities or existence of a body beyond its total control, namely the foreign subsidiary of a company.

National Sovereignty and the Goal of Self-Preservation

A country's self-preservation is most threatened when its national sovereignty is at stake. Sovereignty gives a nation complete control within a given geographic area, including the ability to pass laws and regulations and the power to use necessary enforcement. Governments or countries frequently view the existence of sovereignty as a key to reaching the goal of self-preservation. Though sovereignty may, of course, be threatened by a number of factors, it is the relationship between a government's attempt to protect its sovereignty and a company's policies to achieve its own goals that are of primary interest to us.

Due to the fact that subsidiaries, or branch offices, of international companies are substantially controlled or influenced by decisions made in headquarters, beyond the physical or legal control of the host government, such foreign companies are frequently viewed as a danger to the host country's national sovereignty. (It is important to recognize in this context that *perceptions* on the part of host countries are typically more important than actual facts.)

Many countries limit foreign ownership of newspapers, television, and radio stations for reasons of national sovereignty. Countries fear that if a foreign company controlled these media, it could influence public opinion and limit national sovereignty. Many believe that Rupert Murdoch, the well-known Australian, became a U.S. citizen to avoid the foreign ownership limits in the United States[5] The U.K. Monopolies and Mergers Commission disallowed the sale of ICI's fertilizer business to the state-owned Finnish company Kemira Oy. Peter Lilley, the U.K. secretary of state for trade and industry, feels that selling a U.K. business to a state-owned business is a "form of Nationalization through the back door."[6]

4. Vern Terpstra and Kenneth David, *The Cultural Environment of International Business,* 3rd ed. (Cincinnati: Southwestern, 1991), p. 203.

5. "Rupert Murdoch—the Exile," *Economist,* September 29, 1990, pp. 93–94.

6. "ICI Ready to Close Leith Plant After Government Veto of Finnish Takeover," *Sunday Times,* February 3, 1991, p. 35.

Over the past few years, globalization of the world economy has caused many inter-dependencies among countries. This has led to a decrease in the expression of national sovereignty issues. In fact, the tendency at this time is for a lessening of these restrictions. A worldwide trend toward liberalization and privatization that is sweeping most countries opens up many opportunities previously closed to international firms. As a result, we will devote a special section later in this chapter to these issues.

Many attempts at restricting foreign firms have been curtailed by the worldwide General Agreement on Tariffs and Trade (GATT), the most recent version of this nego-tiated at the end of 1993. That agreement still excludes a number of issues where govern-ments, for their own interest, did not want to liberalize and will remain involved. One such area is the airline industry, where governments remain heavily involved in setting policy, restricting access to airspace or limiting landing rights. France wants to limit the access of U.S. carriers to Paris, where U.S. airlines already account for 70 percent of the inbound traffic. On most transatlantic routes, only one airline from each country can compete for traffic. Only two U.S. airlines (American and United) have landing rights at London's Heathrow Airport; this has caused disputes with governments of many countries.[7]

The Need for National Security

It is natural for a government to strive to protect its country's borders from outside forces. The military establishment typically becomes a country's principal tool to prevent outside interference. Consequently, many concerns about national security have to do with a coun-try's armed forces or related agencies. Other areas sensitive to the national security are aspects of a country's infrastructure, its essential resources, utilities, and the supply of crucial raw materials, particularly oil. To ensure their security, host governments tend to strive for control of these sensitive areas and resist any influence foreign firms may gain over such companies or agencies.

Examples of such government influence abound. The U.S. government, for one, does not typically purchase military material from foreign-controlled firms, even if they have subsidiaries in the United States. The U.S. government's involvement with the licensing of telecommunications scrambling devices is another example of sensitivity on national security. As scrambling devices for communications become more available and wide-spread, the U.S. government wants users to deposit the respective code with a national security agency. Up to now, the government, through its National Security Agency (NSA), could always listen in on international communications. The widespread use of modern scrambling devices would make such access impossible. As a result, the government pro-posed the use of a standard computer chip, ''Clipper,'' developed by the NSA, containing communications in a mathematically unbreakable code. The code would be deposited with the courts and would allow the U.S. government, with proper authorization, to listen in on

7. ''Big U.S. Airlines Fly into Foreign Barriers over Expansion Plans,'' *Wall Street Journal,* May 14, 1993, p. 1.

communications. Even more restrictive is a government attempt to use existing U.S. laws to force installation of such a chip in all computers shipped from the United States.[8]

The protection of national security interests such as defense and telecommunications through regulations requiring local sourcing is declining. This change has been influenced by two issues. First, it is not economical for each country to have its own defense and telecommunications industry. The high cost of research and development means that in many cases the small local defense supplier will have inferior technologies. Second, the European Union has agreed to open up public spending to all EU companies. This opening of European public spending has caused many U.S. and Japanese firms to form alliances with European partners and to encourage the U.S. and Japanese governments to open up their public spending markets so their industries are not shut out of European markets. For example, Japan recently agreed to open its $3 billion telecommunications market, after heavy lobbying by the U.S. government.[9]

Fostering National Prosperity

A key goal for government is to ensure the material prosperity of its citizens. Prosperity is usually expressed in national income or gross national product (GNP), and comparisons between countries are frequently made with respect to per capita income or GNP per capita figures. However prosperity is measured, most governments strive to provide full employment and an increasing standard of living. Part of this goal is to enact an economic policy that will stimulate the economic output of businesses active within its borders. International companies can assume an important role inasmuch as they add to a host country's GNP and thus enhance its income. However, any action that runs contrary to the host government's goals, though it may be in the best interest of the company, will likely cause a conflict between the foreign company and the host country government. Furthermore, a host country may take actions that unilaterally favor local industry over foreign competitors to protect its own standard of living and prosperity.

For many countries, a high level of imports represents a drain on their monetary resources and lost opportunities to expand their own industrial base. Under such circumstances, a host country may move toward a restriction of imports beyond the imposition of tariffs or customs duties. It puts up what are called nontariff barriers. Both the Italian and French governments have protected their local automobile industries from Japanese competition by using nontariff barriers. The Italian government has for many years restricted the import of Japanese automobiles to a total of 2,000 units annually. The French government, through selective use of import licenses, has limited Japanese producers to only 3 percent of the market. A new agreement between Japan and the European Union will allow more Japanese cars into Europe, although France and Italy are expected to keep

8. "Cyberspace Under Lock and Key," *New York Times,* February 13, 1994, p. E3.
9. "Japan Agrees to Open Market for Telecoms," *International Herald Tribune,* August 3, 1990, p. 11.

Japanese imports to a minimum.[10] As these examples show, government actions can frequently close an otherwise attractive market to a company.

Most host governments try to enhance a nation's prosperity by increasing its exports. To do this, some governments have sponsored export credit arrangements combined with some form of political risk insurance. (Some other methods of increasing exports are described in more detail in Chapter 18.) Particularly in Europe, heads of governments often engage in state visits to encourage major export transactions. Political observers often have pointed out that both the French president and the German chancellor spend a substantial amount of their state visits on business and trade affairs, more so than is typically the case for the president of the United States. Attracting international companies with a high export potential to open up operations in their countries is of critical interest to host governments. Frequently, such companies can expect special treatment or subsidies.

In many countries, regional or local governments can also influence decisions that affect international firms. For the U.S. location of new BMW and Daimler-Benz assembly plants, the relevant government was not a national one but state governments. Various local governments lobbied intensively for the plant. The winning state government for the Daimler-Benz plant, Alabama, had to offer a $250 million commitment in infrastructure improvements to attract the project. A year earlier, the government of South Carolina committed $150 million to attract a BMW plant.[11]

The host government's export and import policies is of interest to companies considering locating operations in a particular country. By collecting information on a government's policies or orientation, a company can make an optimal choice that may give it access to benefits not available in some other countries.

Enhancing Prestige

The pursuit of prestige has many faces; it does not always take the form of industrial achievement. While the governments of some countries choose to support team sports or individual athletes to enhance national prestige, other host governments choose to influence the business climate for the same reason. Having a national airline gives rise to national prestige. Other developed countries may prefer to see their industries achieve leadership in certain technologies such as telecommunications, electronics, robotics, or aerospace.

A host government trying to enhance its country's prestige will frequently encourage local or national companies at the expense of a foreign company. One example was the French government's intervention on behalf of the vineyard Chateau Margaux. On the grounds that it would damage national prestige to do otherwise, the Bordeaux winery was sold to a French supermarket chain despite the fact that a U.S. buyer had offered a higher price.[12] In another case, the U.S. secretary of interior raised a number of objections to the

10. ''EC Car Imports—Fiasco Turbo,'' *Economist,* September 29, 1990, pp. 90–92.

11. ''Tupelo, Miss., Concocts an Effective Recipe for Economic Health,'' *Wall Street Journal,* March 3, 1994, p. 1.

12. ''France's Erratic Policies on Investments by Foreigners Confuse Many U.S. Firms,'' *Wall Street Journal,* April 7, 1980, p. 24.

Japanese ownership of the concessions in Yosemite National Park. While the concessions are not a big business, the idea of part of Yosemite being in foreign hands challenged the nation's sense of prestige.[13]

In the future, companies will need to develop a keen sense for what constitutes national prestige as perceived by host governments. Businesspeople cannot expect host governments to have an explicit policy on such issues. Instead, they will have to derive, from a series of overt or covert government actions, some notions on national prestige. Once a company has a clear definition or idea of what constitutes prestige for a host government, it can avoid policies that are in direct conflict with government intentions or aspirations and can emphasize those actions that tend to enhance the host country's prestige.

Protecting Cultural Identity

With the global village becoming a reality, one of the major impacts felt by countries is in the area of culture. The breaking down of communications barriers has led to an increase in the activities of international, mostly U.S., media firms. These firms are most visible in entertainment, such as making and distributing movies, TV programs, videos, and music. Even more important have been the roles of TV companies through use of satellite transmission. Whereas most countries were able to determine broadcast policy on their own, the future is such that control over broadcasting, and therefore culture, is perceived to be in the hands of a few large, mostly U.S. firms.

MTV Europe is illustrative in its pan-European reach. Only about 5 percent of its regular 60 million viewers reside in the United Kingdom. Throughout the rest of Europe, MTV is available via cable television networks. Through a special limited agreement, MTV Europe is now available even to some 80 million viewers in Russia.[14] This massive invasion of foreign cultural products has created a negative reaction among European governments. During the most recent GATT negotiations, European countries, led by the French, resisted an effort to open up European markets to more foreign-made media production, particularly in movies and TV programs.[15] This led to actions in Belgium and France whereby Turner Broadcasting was barred from distributing on their national cable systems a service combining Turner's TNT movie channel and its Cartoon Network. The program was refused because it violated the EU specification of having the majority of programming produced locally. Dubbing in French was not considered "local" enough.[16]

Increasing globalization—in business, in media, and in general—is likely to produce more of such moves by host governments. International firms will therefore be well advised to understand the cultural content, or significance, of their products or services.

13. "That Tough New Line on Foreign Investment Is Only a Mirage," *Business Week,* January 21, 1991, p. 43.
14. "Lights! Camera! Europe!" *New York Times,* February 6, 1994, p. F-6.
15. "What's Next After Gatt's Victory?" *Fortune,* January 10, 1994, p. 66.
16. "Lights! Camera! Europe!" p. F-6.

Insensitivity to cultural ideals in any aspect of global marketing operations can lead to unwanted reactions.

Host Country Pressure Groups

Host country governments are not the only forces able to influence the political climate and, thus, to affect the operations of foreign companies. Other groups have a stake in the treatment of companies or in political and economic decisions that indirectly affect foreign businesses. In most instances, they cannot act unilaterally. Thus, they try to pressure either the host government or the foreign businesses to conform to their views. Such pressure groups exist in most countries and may be made up of ad hoc groups or permanently structured associations. Political parties are a common pressure group, though they frequently cannot exert much influence outside the government. Parties generally associated with a nationalist point of view frequently advocate policies restricting foreign companies. Environmental groups have had a major influence on consumers around the world, raising concerns about nuclear energy, oil transportation, waste disposal, rain forest destruction, fishing techniques, global warming, and so on. For example, scientists report that 1990 was the earth's warmest year on record since 1850, when people started recording the planet's temperature. The increased temperature is thought to be caused by human activities related to the escape of carbon dioxide, chlorofluorocarbons, and methane. There is a fear that this warming will have a drastic effect on climate, agriculture, and sea levels.[17] Du Pont, one of the world's largest producers of chlorofluorocarbons (CFCs), announced in 1988 it would stop making CFCs by 2000, hoping to offer alternatives.[18] Environmental groups also forced McDonald's to reduce its use of plastic and styrofoam packing. While McDonald's internal market research shows that environmental issues will have neither a positive nor negative impact on sales, they have agreed to work with the Environmental Defense Fund, an environmental pressure group, to reduce unnecessary and harmful waste.[19]

Some of the most potent pressure groups are found within the local business community itself. These include local industry associations and occasionally local unions. When local companies get into trouble due to foreign competition, they frequently petition the government to help by placing restrictions on the foreign competitors. In the United States, industry groups have attempted in the past to block some imports in textiles, shoes, consumer electronics, and steel. For example, the National Knitwear and Sportswear Association, which represents U.S. manufacturers of sweaters, filed a dumping complaint with the U.S. International Trade Commission against manufacturers of sweaters made in Taiwan, Hong Kong, and South Korea. The commission found in favor of the U.S. trade

17. William K. Stevens, "Separate Studies Rank '90 as World's Warmest Year," *New York Times,* January 10, 1991, p. 1.

18. "Setting the Rules," *Economist,* September 8, 1990, p. 22.

19. Martha M. Hamilton, "Will the Golden Arches Adopt a Green Tint?" *International Herald Tribune,* August 3, 1990, p. 11.

group and imposed duties of 21 percent for Taiwan, 6 percent for Hong Kong, and 1.3 percent for South Korea.[20]

Host Government Actions

In the previous section, we focused on various governmental concerns and the underlying motivations for certain political actions. In this section, we analyze some of the typical policies host governments may choose to control foreign-based businesses. The relationships between the underlying motivations and the chosen policies are also discussed. The host governments' policies are presented in order of their severity, from the least to the most severe.

Jawboning

When governments intervene in the business process in an informal way, often without a legal basis, it is called *jawboning.* Governments use this form of intervention to prevent an act that, though legal, is perceived to be contrary to their own interests or goals. The effectiveness of jawboning lies in the possibility of stronger action at a later time should the "culprit" not fall into line.

The European Union held discussions with politicians and bureaucrats in Tokyo for over a year to arrive at voluntary import quotas for cars that are expected to be imported from Japan in 1992 through 1997. The Japanese will be allowed to increase exports to Europe from 9.4 percent of the European market to 18.7 percent by 1997 (of which 10 percent will be from factories in Britain and Spain, and the other 8.7 percent will be from Japan). After 1997, the market will become fully open to the Japanese. The jawboning efforts of the EU gave the European manufacturers seven years of protection to prepare for the open market in 1998.[21]

The leverage of host governments comes from the fact that foreign companies depend on permits and approvals issued by host governments. Such favored treatment may be at risk if a company proceeds against the expressed wishes of the host government, despite the fact that no laws were violated.

Such a jawboning action was also taken by the Japanese government. In a reaction to the fall in Japanese beef prices as a result of increased imports, the Japanese government issued "administrative guidance" to restrict imports and to keep them at a certain level. Although this action was not legally binding, it reflects a step government can undertake to interfere in the free marketplace. These actions are typical for many governments, and international firms will have to be aware of their impact.[22]

20. Nancy Dunne, "U.S. Sweater Makers Elated by Anti-Dumping Victory," *Financial Times,* September 7, 1990, p. 7.
21. "EC Car Imports," *Economist,* September 19, 1990, pp. 90–92.
22. "Japan's Request to Limit Purchases of Foreign Beef Is Likely to Anger U.S.," *Wall Street Journal,* August 9, 1993, p. A9.

"Buy Local" Restrictions

Since governments are important customers of industry in virtually every country, they can use this purchasing power to favor certain suppliers. Frequently, local companies are favored over foreign imports. An industry particularly subject to such local favoritism is the telecommunications industry because telephone companies are state run in most countries. For foreign companies, the case of Japan's Nippon Telegraph & Telephone Public Corp. (NTT) was particularly problematic. For years, NTT granted contracts exclusively to a few local suppliers, virtually shutting out foreign-based companies. Pressures from foreign governments led to international agreements under the umbrella of GATT, and other international organizations have established new rules that tend to prevent direct government intervention except for cases of national security and a few other exemptions. This has also opened up opportunities for foreign firms with Japan's NTT.[23]

Few areas have recently received as much attention as the local buying preference in public sector contracts. Different from import and export transactions, these contracts frequently deal with local construction. Access to such contracts has been opened up in the EU through the Europe 1992 initiative, whereby all public sector contracts now require open bidding. The European Union has instituted a requirement to report contracts above a threshold of 5 million European currency units (ECUs) (about U.S. $5 million). Supplies contracts have a lower limit of ECU 200,000, service contracts the same. Utility supply contracts have their own limits of ECU 600,000. Contracts have to be listed with the EU official journal and are also included in a electronic database. The purpose is to give companies from all member states equal access to public contracts, and to eliminate favoring local contractors.[24]

U.S. construction companies are, with the help of the U.S. government, also trying to get access to the $250 billion Japanese public construction market. In 1989, after U.S. companies complained of unequal access, the Japanese government promised to open up the construction market to U.S. firms. Foreign firms obtained less than 1 percent of the Japanese market, compared with 6 percent for foreign firms in the United States.[25] However, even after four years of trying, only about $200 million in contracts had been rewarded.[26] A renewed effort can be expected following Japan's bribery scandals involving public construction firms and politicians. A large number of construction firms were reported to follow *dango,* a system whereby contracts are shared among competing firms and a portion of the contract is regularly used as payoff to politicians.[27] Although this scheme was not sanctioned by the Japanese government, its existence blocked international firms from gaining contracts on the basis of level competition.

---

23. "Japan Agrees to Open Market for Telecoms," *International Herald Tribune,* August 3, 1990, p. 11.

24. "Return to Tender," *Financial Times,* July 6, 1993, p. 12.

25. "U.S. Contractors Find They Rarely Get Work on Projects in Japan," *Wall Street Journal,* June 10, 1993, p. 1.

26. "Japan Heads for Clash with U.S. on Procurement," *Financial Times,* June 21, 1993, p. 4.

27. "Backs to the Wall," *Far Eastern Economic Review,* June 24, 1993, p. 59.

Nontariff Barriers

Under this heading we include any government action that is not an official custom tariff but that nevertheless inhibits the free flow of products between countries. These barriers may not necessarily add to landed costs but are more likely to result in a limitation on product flows. To a large extent, nontariff barriers are used by governments to keep imports from freely entering the home market. There are many types of measures that may be taken. A common one is import restrictions or quotas.

Nontariff barriers are hard to detect and typically are not freely listed. International Game Technology (IGT), a U.S.-based maker of slot machines, began to target Japan as a major market in 1989. The company reacted to the fact that Japanese firms were suddenly its most important competitors in the United States, and it was not selling any machines in Japan, a market with 800,000 slot machines representing about two-thirds of the total worldwide installed base. When the company wanted to enter the Japanese market with its machines, it found out that the rules for regulators were hard to find. Only the eighteen members of a small industry group could get them. On trying to join the group, IGT learned that any potential member was required to have the support of three existing members, and the candidate firm needed three years of manufacturing experience in Japan before applying. Eventually, the company found its way through the myriad of regulations with the help of a local lawyer. Even then, IGT had to navigate many different regulatory hurdles before its products would be approved for sale in Japan.[28]

There has been growth in nontariff barriers. The World Bank estimates that nontariff barriers increased from 15 percent of industrial countries' imports in 1981 to 18 percent by 1986. The Institute of International Economies estimates that if nontariff barriers were eliminated, world trade would increase by $330 billion.[29]

Subsidies

Government subsidies represent free gifts that host governments make available with the intention that the overall benefits to the economy by far exceed such grants. They are a popular instrument used both to encourage exports and to attract international companies to a certain country.

Governments may also use direct or indirect subsidies to encourage industries that will be major exporters. Exporters bring multiple benefits, since they provide employment as well as increase revenue into the country through export sales. An example of a direct subsidy is when a government agrees to pay $1.00 for each pair of shoes to help a local producer compete more effectively in foreign markets. GATT agreements outlaw direct export subsidies but usually do not prohibit indirect subsidies. An indirect subsidy is the result of a subsidy on a component of the exported product. For example, a government may provide a subsidy on the canvas used to manufacture tents, which are then exported.

28. "A Slot-Machine Maker Trying to Sell in Japan Hits Countless Barriers," *Wall Street Journal,* May 11, 1993, p. 1.
29. "A Survey of World Trade," *Economist,* September 22, 1990, p. 8.

Subsidies are one way for government to support local industries. In most countries, subsidies amount to 2–3.5 percent of the value of industrial output. The rate of subsidy in the United States is estimated to be .5 percent, whereas it is 1.0 percent in Japan. In Europe, subsidies range from 2 percent of industrial output in Germany and Britain to as much as 6–8 percent in Sweden and Ireland.[30] The logic of the subsidies is that they improve international competitiveness and create or protect jobs. The European Union has tightened its policy on state aid to industry. In cases where the state aid reduces or distorts competition, the EU can intervene and require the business to pay back the aid to the government. Peugeot, Alfa Romeo, Rover, and Renault have all been required to pay back aid they received from their governments.[31]

The treatment of local aircraft makers has also been disputed. The recent $341 increase in share capital for Aerospatiale, a French state-owned aerospace firm with a 30 percent stake in the Airbus passenger plane consortium, is considered by the U.S. government to be a hidden subsidy. The French government points toward favorable treatment of Boeing by NASA and Pentagon contracts as another form of hidden subsidies.[32] The disputes around what constitutes a subsidy and what constitutes a restraint of international trade are supposed to be dealt with through GATT. But in its most recent round, concluded in December 1993, those issues were left out due to their complexity.

Operating Conditions

Host governments have a direct influence on the operations of a foreign subsidiary by imposing specific conditions on the company's operations. The rules of conducting business may challenge the international company. For example, the requirement of *Mitbestimmung* (codetermination) in Germany necessitates the participation of labor on the management committee.[33] Limited store opening hours challenge retailers in many countries. In Germany, there is a ban on bakers working from 10:00 P.M. to 4:00 A.M. The ban dates back to World War I, when supplies were short and authorities noticed that people ate less day-old bread than fresh bread. Borden, the U.S. company that owns Wilhelm Weber, GmbH has circumvented the night use of bakers through the use of automation, including robots.[34]

Operating conditions for international firms are of particular importance when they affect the freedom to run marketing programs. Host countries may restrict international firms in the area of pricing, advertising, promoting, selling, distributing, and many other elements. Some of those restrictions, and strategies to deal with them, are included in Chapters 10–15, which deal directly with marketing mix elements. Where such operating restrictions apply to all firms, domestic and international, the competitive threat is lessened;

30. ''From the Sublime to the Subsidy,'' *Economist,* February 24, 1990, p. 85.

31. ''European State Aid—Loaded Down with Lolly,'' *Economist,* November 18, 1989, p. 127.

32. ''A French Aircraft Subsidy,'' *New York Times,* February 6, 1994, p. 2-F.

33. David Goodhart, ''Unruffled Chairman of the Club,'' *Financial Times,* January 7, 1991, p. 26.

34. Miriam Widman, ''Automating the Off-Limit Hours,'' *International Herald Tribune,* June 9, 1989, p. 13.

however, companies might still find such restrictions a problem when the way they have to operate varies from what they are accustomed to. Where operating restrictions apply to foreign or international firms only, the result will be a lessening of competitiveness, and such situations need to be seriously considered before a market is entered.

Local Content

Many host governments impose a local-content regulation that requires international firms to demonstrate that the value added derived from their products or services meets these limitations. For product-based companies, local-content laws mean that some part of the manufacturing must be done in the host country. Often, such restrictions are used to encourage local value-added activities. Occasionally, the regulations can also lead to the elimination of international competitors if the local market is not big enough to justify the manufacturing operation.

A constant point of discussion is the cars produced by Japanese transplant operations in the United States. Honda Motor Company, operating two U.S. assembly plants and assembling locally as much as two-thirds of its total U.S. sales volume, has been claiming a 50 percent local content. With less than that, Honda could not take advantage of a U.S.-Canadian free trade agreement, as it could have had with 100 percent local content. The company has had a dispute with the U.S. government on the classification of parts purchased from Japanese parts makers located in the United States. Some experts have not accepted Honda's characterization of 75 percent local content.[35] In contrast, BMW has announced that its plant to be located in South Carolina will have a local content of 80 percent so that its cars can be treated as U.S.-made cars for purposes of trade, duties, and other regulations.[36]

Enforcing local content can also result in the elimination of international competitors. The European Commission required members of the EU to ensure a majority of their television programming to be of European source.[37] In the local application of this law, France interpreted it to mean that 60 percent of its programming should be from Europe and two-thirds of that portion from France alone. A similar law was applied to radio, where the French government mandated its eight national FM stations to raise the French language content of music to 40 percent, of which half must be originating from new French talent. This 1991 ruling had earlier been the source of a trade conflict between the EU and the United States, as it was also applied to movies.[38]

Regulations imposed by host governments dealing with local content are most often found for products that are purchased by local government institutions or that are in need of local government help, as through export financing. The recent trend in international

35. "Honda: Is It an American Car?" *Business Week,* November 18, 1991.
36. "BMW Expects U.S.-Made Cars to Have 80 Percent Level of North American Content," *Wall Street Journal,* August 5, 1993, p. A2.
37. "Cultural Protectionism: Television of Babel," *Economist,* February 5, 1994.
38. "Movies Eclipse Films," *Economist,* February 5, 1994, p. 89.

trade negotiations has tended to reduce the restrictive character of some of these regulations. However, it still remains an important aspect for global marketers, and they should be aware of it.

Ownership Conditions

Host governments sometimes pursue the policy of requiring that local nationals become part owners of the foreign company. These governments believe that this guarantees fair contributions to the local economy. The restrictions can range from an outright prohibition of full foreign ownership to selective policies aimed at key industries.

One country that has used ownership conditions extensively is India. India's Foreign Exchange Regulation Act of 1973 stipulated that foreign ownership may not exceed 40 percent unless the foreign firm or Indian company belongs to a key industry, manufacturing materials such as chemicals, turbines, machinery, tractors, or fertilizers.

International Business Machines Corp. decided to leave rather than give up control. However, later changes in the government have brought a softening of India's stance, and the country is again courting firms that can contribute new technologies.[39] Coca-Cola had also decided to leave rather than share its secret formula with the Indians. In 1988, Coke began negotiations to return to India without revealing the formula.[40]

The reintroduction of Coca-Cola in the Indian market took place in 1994 with a series of ninety-second TV spots with a cast of 1,200 men, women, and children.[41] Today, the foreign direct investment law of India allows majority ownership in many industries again.[42] This demonstrates an important aspect in the control of foreign ownership. The 1960s and 1970s saw a tightening of the control over foreign ownership in many countries. During the late 1980s and particularly during the early 1990s, the trend has been toward trade liberalization. This new trend has brought the elimination of many restrictions. As a result, we will devote a special section later in this chapter to this new development, which is of crucial importance to global marketers.

Boycotts

The previously discussed policies are aimed at restricting or limiting the freedom of action of foreign firms. Boycotts, however, tend to completely shut out some companies from a given market. Typically, politically motivated boycotts tend to be directed at companies of certain origin or companies that have engaged in transactions with political enemies.

---

39. ''India: Reviving the Welcome for U.S. Business,'' *Business Week,* March 1, 1982, p. 31.

40. ''Coca-Cola Seeking to Re-Enter Huge Indian Market After 11 Years,'' *Asian Wall Street Journal,* November 21, 1988, p. 23; ''The Real Thing Returns to India,'' *Financial Times,* April 17, 1991, p. 22.

41. ''Global Gallery,'' *Advertising Age,* January 17, 1994, pp. 1–18.

42. ''India: Towards a Liberalized Economy,'' Special section, *Far Eastern Economic Review,* January 13, 1994, p. 36.

One of the most publicized boycott campaigns was the 1975 boycott waged by some Arab countries against firms that had engaged in business beyond simple export transactions with Israel. The boycott was administered by the Arab League. For example, one U.S. company on the Arab boycott list was Ford Motor Co., which supplied an Israeli car assembler with flat-packed cars for local assembly. Xerox was placed on the list after financing a documentary on Israel, and the Coca-Cola Company was added to the boycott list for having licensed an Israeli bottler. The boycott did not always include all Arab League member nations. The actual enforcement was, therefore, quite selective and differed by industry.

The Arab League boycott became considerably less relevant with the changed political situation in the Middle East. By the end of the 1980s, many countries only selectively enforced it, and after the Iraq conflict, many more countries abandoned it.[43] The U.S. government had countered the enforcement of the boycott by making it a crime for U.S. companies to refuse to deal with Israel. Baxter International, a U.S.-based hospital supply company, was found guilty in U.S. court for violating the law against cooperating with the Arab League boycott. The company was fined for its efforts to get off the boycott list. In order to enter a joint venture with Nestlé in the fast-growing nutrition market, the company had needed to get off the list. Selling its Israeli operation was viewed as a way to placate Middle Eastern customers.[44]

It is expected that with the further improvement of the ties between the Palestinians and Israel, even direct economic linkages between Arab League member states and Israel will become possible.

Takeovers

No action a host government can take is more drastic than a takeover. Broadly defined, takeovers are any host government–initiated actions that result in a loss of ownership or a direct control by the foreign company. There are, of course, several types of takeovers.[45] *Expropriation* is a formal, or legal, taking over of an operation with or without the payment of compensation. Even when compensation is paid, there are often concerns about the adequacy of the amount, timeliness of the payment, and form of payment. *Confiscation* is expropriation without any compensation. The term *domestication* is used to describe the limiting of certain economic activities to local citizens; this means a takeover by either expropriation, confiscation, or forced sales. Governments may domesticate industry by imposing one of the following requirements: transfer of partial ownership to nationals, promotion of nationals to higher levels of management, or purchase of raw materials or components produced locally. If the company cannot meet these requirements, it may be forced to sell its operations in that country.

43. "Boycott of Israel Is Said to Relax," *New York Times,* June 9, 1993, p. A5.
44. "The Case Against Baxter International," *Business Week,* October 7, 1991, p. 106.
45. Richard D. Robinson, *International Business Management* (New York: Dryden, 1973), p. 374.

TABLE 4.1 ● Host Government Goal and Policy Actions

	Goal					
Action	SELF-PRESERVATION	SECURITY	PROSPERITY	PRESTIGE	IDEOLOGY	CULTURAL IDENTITY
Jawboning	X	X	X	X	X	X
"Buy local"	X	X	X			
Nontariff barriers	X		X			
Subsidies	X		X			
Local content			X			
Operating restrictions	X	X	X			X
Ownership conditions		X				X
Boycotts					X	
Takeovers	X	X	X		X	

X = Likelihood of using given action to accomplish that goal.

At one time, studies suggested that takeovers were becoming more frequent and were a major threat to companies operating abroad. Hawkins, Mintz, and Provissiero in 1975 found a total of 170 foreign takeovers of U.S. subsidiaries registered for the period 1946 to 1973. Comparing these findings with the total of 23,282 U.S. subsidiaries operating outside the United States yielded a takeover rate of about 6 percent.[46] These statistics were supported by a broader survey of all countries by the United Nations in which 875 takeovers were identified for the 1960–1974 period.[47] Ten countries had accounted for two-thirds of all takeovers, and fifty countries registered none at all. Nationalization of international firms peaked in the mid-1970s, when up to thirty countries were involved each year, affecting as many as eighty firms. By 1985, expropriations had declined, and almost none were recorded. Instead of nationalizations, countries engaged in the massive process of privatization.[48] In general, global marketers may have to fear nationalization, and the resulting total loss of an asset, far less in the future. The loss of operating control or freedom may prove to be a far greater political risk.

This section illustrates how host governments can impact on the local operations of international companies. The section before this concentrated more on the motivations behind these governmental actions. Table 4.1 is a chart identifying and relating certain policy actions to the underlying goals discussed in this chapter. Though any combination

46. Robert G. Hawkins, Norman Mintz, and Michael Provissiero, "Government Takeovers of U.S. Foreign Affiliates," *Journal of International Business Studies,* Spring 1976, pp. 3–16.
47. Ibid.
48. "Multinationals," Survey, *Economist,* March 27, 1993, p. 19.

of goal and action is possible, past history tends to suggest that certain actions are more often associated with specific goals.

Home Country Political Forces

Managers of international companies need not only be concerned about political developments abroad. Many developments take place at home that can have a great impact on what a company can do internationally. The political development in a company's home country tends to affect either the role of the company in general, or, more often, some particular aspects of its operations. Consequently, restrictions can be placed on companies not only by host countries but by home countries as well. Therefore, an astute international manager must be able to monitor political developments both at home and abroad.

This section of the chapter will explore home country policies and actions directed at international companies. Some of these actions are unique and have only recently come into existence to any large extent.

Home Country Actions

Home countries are essentially guided by the same six interests described earlier in this chapter: self-preservation, national security, prosperity, prestige, ideology, and cultural identity. In general, a home country government wishes to have its country's international companies accept its national priorities. As a result, home country governments at times look toward international companies to help them achieve political goals. They may engage in any or all the actions outlined earlier: jawboning, nontariff barriers, subsidies, operating restrictions, and so on.

How then do home country policies differ? In the past, home country governments have tried to prevent companies from doing business on ideological, political, or national security grounds. In the extreme, this can result in an embargo on trade with a certain country. The U.S. government has taken unilateral actions in the past. Its embargo on trade with Cuba dates back to 1961, following the assumption of power of Fidel Castro. Since that time, U.S. businesses have been allowed neither to purchase nor to sell with Cuba. Any U.S. company that wants to do business with Cuba must apply for a special license, but no such applications were granted until 1993. Discussions are under way to possibly change the trade embargo.[49] Another long-running trade embargo imposed by the U.S. government related to Vietnam. Imposed in 1975, this embargo was lifted in 1994.[50]

Unilateral embargoes, those imposed by one country only, expose businesses from that country to competitive disadvantage and thus are often fought by business interests. During the embargo against Vietnam, U.S. companies were kept out while firms from

49. "U.S. Studies Expansion of Phone Links to Cuba," *New York Times,* May 29, 1993, p. 8.
50. "Clinton Lifts Ban on Trade with Vietnam," *Wall Street Journal,* February 4, 1994, p. A12.

other nations were engaging in business with a nation of 70 million consumers. By mid-1993, international firms signed off on projects worth more than $6 billion.[51] In Cuba also, only the United States applied a trade embargo. However, due to the state-controlled economy of Cuba, few investment opportunities existed for other foreign firms. This is now changing, and some European (notably Spanish and French) companies, have begun direct investments in Cuba.[52]

Because there is a risk to the competitiveness of its business if a country takes unilateral actions restricting the business community, the emphasis has shifted toward taking multilateral actions together with many other countries. Such action may come from a group of nations or, increasingly, from the United Nations. The trade embargo by the international community against South Africa was one of the first such actions. Although, as a result of consumer group pressures, many companies had left South Africa due to its apartheid regime, the embargo became applicable to a wider group of firms in the late 1980s when it was imposed by most countries. Now that the political situation in South Africa has changed and apartheid has been abolished, the United States, together with other nations, lifted the embargo in July 1991. Some forty U.S. firms have returned with investments, and more are considering returning.[53]

Other multilateral actions by the international community are the trade sanctions enforced by the United Nations against Iraq as a result of the Gulf War in 1991; this embargo substantially restricts the type of trade companies can get involved with. The most recent embargo is against Serbia and Montenegro, the survivor states of former Yugoslavia. Imposed in June 1992 and further tightened in April 1993, this embargo has virtually stopped orderly trade. Although some products reach Yugoslavia through smuggling, organized trade with international firms has almost ceased.[54]

Home Country Pressure Groups

The kinds of pressures that international companies are subject to in their home countries are frequently different from the types of pressures brought to bear on them abroad. In many ways, international companies had to deal with special interest groups abroad for a long time. But the type of special interest groups found domestically have only come into existence over the last ten to fifteen years. Such groups are usually well organized, tend to get extensive media coverage, and have succeeded in catching many companies unprepared. While part of their actions has always been geared toward mobilizing support to get the home country government to sponsor specific regulations favorable to their point of view, they have also managed to place companies directly under pressure.

International companies can come under pressure for two major reasons: (1) for the choice of their markets and (2) for their methods of business. A constant source of con-

---

51. "Look East—but Don't Touch," *Financial Times,* September 16, 1993, p. 16.
52. "Cuba's Economy Open for Business," *Economist,* December 4, 1993, p. 71.
53. "Honeywell's Route Back to South Africa Market," *New York Times,* January 31, 1994, p. D1.
54. "Serbian Companies Count the Cost of Sanctions," *Financial Times,* June 11, 1993, p. 2.

troversy involves international companies' business practices in three areas: product strategies, promotion practices, and pricing practices. Product strategies include the decision to cease marketing a certain product (such as pesticides or pharmaceuticals), usually for safety reasons. Promotional practices include the way the products are advertised or pushed through distribution channels. Pricing practices include the policy of charging higher or unfair prices.

The infant formula controversy of the early 1980s involved participants from many countries and serves as a good example of the type of pressure sometimes placed on international companies. Infant formula was being sold all over the world as a substitute or supplement for breast-feeding. Though even the producers of infant formula agreed that breast-feeding was superior to bottle-feeding, changes had started to take place in western society decades ago that brought about the decline of infant breast-feeding. Following World War II, several companies expanded their infant-formula productions in Third World countries, where birth rates were much higher than in the West. Companies that had intended their products to be helpful found themselves embroiled in controversy. Critics blasted the product, saying it was unsafe under Third World conditions. Because the formula had to be mixed with water, the critics charged that the sanitary conditions and contaminated water in developing countries led to many deaths. As a result, the critics requested an immediate stop to all promotional activities, such as nurses visiting mothers and the distribution of free samples.

Nestlé Company, as one of the leading infant-formula manufacturers, became the target of a boycott by consumer action groups in the United States and elsewhere. Under the leadership of INFACT, the Infant Formula Action Coalition, a consumer boycott of all Nestlé products was organized to force the company to change its marketing practices.[55] The constant public pressure resulted in the development of a code sponsored by the World Health Organization (WHO). This code, accepted by the Thirty-fourth WHO General Assembly in 1981 (with the sole dissenting vote from the United States), primarily covered the methods used to market infant formula. Producers and distributors could not give away any free samples, had to avoid contact with consumers, and were not allowed to do any promotion geared toward the general public. The code was subject to voluntary participation by WHO member governments.[56] The effect of this controversy was that new regulations, or codes, eventually became part of the legal system.

Boycotts can have very visible effects. The 1990 boycott against tuna caught in nets that also trap and kill dolphins caused Heinz, owner of Star-Kist, to switch to dolphin-safe tuna. The other manufacturers quickly followed suit. Avon gave in to the efforts of People for Ethical Treatment of Animals, agreeing not to use animals in testing its products. Procter & Gamble, manufacturer of Folger's coffee, did not give in to the boycott by a political advocacy group called Neighbor to Neighbor. The group accused P&G of indi-

55. "The Corporation Haters," *Fortune,* June 16, 1980, p. 126.

56. For a detailed background on the infant-formula issue, see Christopher Gale, George Taucher, and Michael Pearce, "Nestlé and the Infant Food Controversy" (A) and (B) (Lausanne: IMD; London, Ontario; University of Western Ontario, 1979).

rectly financing a brutal civil war in El Salvador because it buys its coffee beans there. Neighbor to Neighbor ran an advertisement with a cup of Folger's coffee that turns to blood when it is poured. P&G denied the claims and pulled its advertising from WHDH-TV in Boston for running the commercial.[57]

Global marketers must continue to be on the lookout for pressures from home country pressure groups or governments. International trade sanctions imposed unilaterally are likely to occur again but typically affect only marginal markets. Pressure groups with specific interests, such as animal protection groups, environmentalists, or other such focus organizations, are likely to be of greater importance as global marketing develops.

Sudden Changes in the Political Climate

The presence of political risk means that a foreign company can lose part or all of its investment in another country due to some political actions on the part of either the host country government or other pressure groups. The previous sections have detailed the various elements of political risk by describing the participants, their motivations, and their available options to participate and determine the political climate of a country. As we emphasized in the section on takeovers, the political climate of a country is hardly ever static. Instead, key decisions are often made during sudden and radical changes in the political climate of a host country. Sudden changes of power, especially when the new leadership was committed to a leftist economic and political philosophy, have frequently led to hostile political climates and takeovers. Such changes in government can happen as a result of open elections or unexpected coup d'états or revolutions.

The fall of the Iranian shah in 1980 is a typical example of a sudden change that caught many companies by surprise. The impact on U.S. business included a total of 3,848 claims—and a full 518 were for more than $250,000. The claims are being settled by the Hague Tribunal, which is dispersing funds from $1 billion of Iranian assets, which were set aside after the release of the American diplomats who had been held hostage for fourteen months. The largest single settlement was $49.8 million paid to R. J. Reynolds.[58] The damage was not only to U.S. companies. Many companies operating from Europe and Japan were forced to close either all or parts of their operations. The subsequent war between Iran and Iraq further limited the attractiveness of the area and caused additional losses to foreign investors.

For decades, sudden political change in a country meant sudden change in its economic policy, resulting in damage to international firms. As a result of the sweeping political change in eastern Europe since 1989, the splitting up of nations has actually been a dominant occurrence. The former Soviet Union has broken up into more than a dozen

57. "P&G Can Get Mad, Sure, but Does It Have to Get Even?" *Business Week,* June 4, 1990, p. 27.
58. "Slow Progress on Iran Claims," *New York Times,* November 14, 1984, pp. D1, D5.

independent nations. Yugoslavia, as well, has disintegrated into several separate countries. More recently, Czechoslovakia ceased to exist as of January 1, 1993, resulting in two independent countries, the Czech Republic and Slovakia.[59] GTECH (based in the United States), the world's largest lottery company, negotiated with Czechoslovakia in 1991 following a successful negotiation for a computerized lottery contract with Poland. Talks with Czechoslovakia concluded in 1992, but implementation was delayed due to the daunting infrastructure problems with telecommunications. The sudden border cutting the country in half meant that even transporting simple personal computers across a city suddenly became an issue. GTECH had to renegotiate the contract and establish two systems with two different currencies. The backup center in Bratislava, the city that became the new capital of Slovakia, also became the operations point for the new system for Slovakia. Both systems, now up and running, are expected to reach some 2,000 terminals in Czechia and 1,000 terminals in Slovakia.[60]

Faced with such a changing political climate, what can companies do? Internationally active companies have reacted on two fronts. First, they have started to perfect their own intelligence systems to prevent situations where they get caught unaware. Second, they have developed several risk-reducing business strategies that will help to limit the exposure, or losses, should a sudden change occur. The following sections will concentrate on these two solutions.

Political Risk Assessment

Because more than 60 percent of U.S.-based companies suffered some type of politically motivated damage between 1975 and 1980, many companies established systems to systematically analyze political risk.[61] To establish an effective political risk assessment (PRA) system, a company has to decide first on the objectives of the system. Another aspect concerns the internal organization, or the assignment of responsibility within the company. Finally, some agreement has to be reached on how the analysis is to be done.

Objectives of Political Risk Assessment

Potential risks have been described in detail in earlier sections of this chapter. Of course, companies everywhere would like to know about impending governmental instabilities so that no new investments will be placed in those countries. But even more important is the monitoring of existing operations and their political environment. Particularly with existing

59. Jean-Pierre Jeannet, ''The Marketing Challenge in Eastern Europe,'' Teaching note (European Case Clearing House), 1993.

60. ''Two for One Split,'' *Providence Sunday Journal,* May 2, 1993, sec. F, p. 1.

61. ''More Firms Are Hiring Own Political Analysts to Limit Risks Abroad,'' *Wall Street Journal,* March 30, 1981, p. 17.

operations, not much is gained by knowing in advance of potential changes in the political climate unless such advanced knowledge can also be used for future action. As a result, political risk assessment is slowly moving from predicting events to developing strategies to help companies cope with changes. But first, political risk assessment has to deal with the potential political changes. Questions must be answered, such as, Should we enter a particular country? Should we stay in a particular country? What can we do with our operations in country X, given that development Y can occur?

Organization of Political Risk Assessment

In a study conducted in 1968, more than half of the large U.S.-based international companies surveyed by the Conference Board, a U.S. research organization, indicated that company internal groups were reviewing the political climate of both newly proposed and current operations. In companies that did not have any formalized systems for political risk assessment, top executives tended to obtain firsthand information through direct contact by traveling and talking with other businesspeople.[62]

This informal and unstructured approach once spelled trouble for a U.S. company. Eaton, a diversified U.S. manufacturer, built a plant in southern Normandy, France, that was notorious for its troublesome communist union.[63] If the company had known about the labor situation, it would never have built there, of course. As a result of this and other unsatisfactory experiences, Eaton established a group of full-time political analysts at its headquarters that included former government employees with an extensive background in political risk assessment. Other companies with a full-time corporate staff included Gulf Oil, General Motors, American Can, TRW, and General Electric.[64]

The way Gulf Oil was able to make use of its political risk assessment serves as an example of the power of correct information. Gulf's small team of analysts warned of the Iranian shah's probable fall several months before it was generally anticipated. The same group supported an exploration venture in Pakistan despite the Soviet invasion of Afghanistan that had just taken place. More risky was Gulf's decision to proceed with its operations in Angola. Prior to the civil war in Angola, Gulf's analyst foresaw that a Marxist group would emerge as the most powerful force among the three factions vying for control of the country. Gulf managers felt, however, that the Marxist government would provide both a stable and a reasonable government, so they decided to invest. Angola has since become one of Gulf's most important overseas production sources.[65]

Rather than rely on a centralized corporate staff, some companies prefer to delegate

62. Franklin Root, "U.S. Business Abroad and Political Risks," *MSU Business Topics,* Winter 1968, pp. 73–80; Stephen J. Kobrin et al., "The Assessment and Evaluation of Noneconomic Environments by American Firms: A Preliminary Report," *Journal of International Business Studies,* Spring–Summer 1980, pp. 32–47.
63. "The Multinationals Get Smarter About Political Risks," *Fortune,* March 24, 1980, p. 88.
64. "The Post-Shah Surge in Political-Risk Studies," *Business Week,* December 1, 1980, p. 69.
65. "Multinationals Get Smarter," p. 87.

political risk assessment responsibility to executives or analysts located in the particular region. Exxon and Xerox both use their subsidiary and regional managers as a major source. The use of distinguished foreign policy advisers is practiced by others. Bechtel, the large California-based engineering company, made use of the services of Richard Helms, a former CIA director and U.S. ambassador to Iran. Henry Kissinger, a former U.S. secretary of state, has advised Merck, Goldman Sachs, and the Chase Manhattan Bank. General Motors and Caterpillar have also maintained outside advisory panels.[66]

Information Needs

Though expropriations and takeovers were a problem for companies in the past, companies now view other political actions as more dangerous. Some have seen delayed payments or restrictions on profit repatriation as the major problem.[67] Political stability, foreign investment, climate, profit remittance, and taxation can all be more important than the fear of expropriation. In political risk assessment, it is suggested that international companies look for answers to six broad key questions:

1. How stable is the host country's political system?
2. How strong is the host government's commitment to specific rules of the game, such as ownership or contractual rights, given its ideology and power position?
3. How long is the government likely to remain in power?
4. If the present government is succeeded, how would the specific rules of the game change?
5. What would be the effects of any expected changes in the specific rules of the game?
6. In light of those effects, what decisions and actions should be taken now?[68]

Another approach, used by an independent consultant on political risk, concentrated on viewing each country in terms of its political issues and the major political actors. The analysis was to determine which one of these actors would have the greatest influence with respect to important decisions.[69]

Several public or semipublic sources exist that regularly monitor political risk. The Economist Intelligence Unit (EIU), a sister company of the *Economist,* publishes a quarterly result in the *Economist.* The company monitors some eighty countries on the basis of twenty-seven basic factors. The factors include debt, current account position, economic policy, and political stability. The rating of 100 is used to denote highest risk. In EIU's

66. Ibid.
67. ''More Firms Are Hiring,'' p. 1.
68. Bob Donath, ''Handicapping and Hedging the Foreign Investment,'' *Industrial Marketing Management,* February 1981, p. 57.
69. ''Multinationals Get Smarter,'' p. 98.

quarterly list published at the end of 1993, Iraq was still the riskiest country, with an index of 100, followed by Russia, Ivory Coast, Kenya, Brazil, Nigeria, Poland, Venezuela, and Argentina.[70]

The *World Competitiveness Report,* an annual survey, lists political risk rankings for about thirty-five major industrial and emerging countries.[71] The ratings vary from 100 (minimum risk) to 0 points for maximum risk. The indicators used include economic expectations versus reality, economic planning failures, political leadership, external-conflict risk, corruption in government, law and order tradition, political terrorism, and the quality of bureaucracy. The results of these rankings are displayed in Figure 4.2. Different firms use different approaches and sources to assess political risk. Motorola would often use consultants to determine political risk. In 1987, for example, Motorola used consultants to evaluate the investment risk for a facility in a Southeast Asian country. A Far Eastern business information service reported on how other businesses were responding to the political climate. Another consultant analyzed financial risks. An academic analyzed factors relating to operating costs.[72]

What companies do with their assessment depends on the data they collect. Exxon, for one, integrated its political assessment with its financial plans; in cases where Exxon expects a higher political risk, the company may add 1 to 5 percent to its required return on investment.[73] Political risk assessment should also help the company stay out of a certain country when necessary. However, the collected data should be carefully differentiated so that the best decision can be made.

Risk Reduction Strategies

Determining or assessing political risk should not be a goal in itself. The value of political risk assessment is its integration of risk-reducing strategies that eventually enable companies to enter a market or remain in business. Many companies have experimented with different forms of ownership arrangements, production, and financing that were geared toward reducing political risks to an acceptable minimum. We will enlarge upon these alternatives with a discussion of the tools managers can use to deal with political risk rather than leave a market or refuse to enter one.[74]

---

70. "Risk Ratings," *Economist,* November 20, 1993, p. 128.

71. *World Competitiveness Report* (Lausanne: IMD; Geneva: World Economic Forum, 1993), p. 466.

72. "How MNCs Are Aligning Country-Risk Assessment with Bottom-Line Concerns," *Business International Weekly Report to Managers of Worldwide Organizations,* June 1, 1987, pp. 169–170.

73. "Multinationals Get Smarter," p. 88.

74. The following sections are adapted from *Insurance Decisions,* published by the CIGNA companies, Philadelphia. Reprinted by permission.

FIGURE 4.2 ● Political Risk Rating

Ranking		Index
1	Austria	90
2	Switzerland	88
3	Denmark	84
4	Australia	82
4	Netherlands	82
6	Finland	81
6	France	81
6	New Zealand	81
9	Japan	80
9	Norway	80
11	Canada	79
11	USA	79
13	Sweden	78
14	Belgium/Lux.	77
15	United Kingdom	76
16	Germany	75
17	Ircland	74
17	Portugal	74
19	Spain	72
20	Italy	66
21	Greece	64
21	Turkey	64
1	Singapore	77
1	Taiwan	77
3	Korea	75
4	Hungary	72
5	Malaysia	71
6	Chile	69
6	Mexico	69
8	Brazil	67
9	Hong Kong	66
10	South Africa	64
11	Thailand	63
12	Indonesia	60
13	Venezuela	59
14	India	50
15	Pakistan	40

Source: From *International Country Risk Guide (ICRG)*, published by Political Risk Services, IBC USA (Publications), Syracuse, New York, 1993. Graphic display reprinted from World Competitiveness Report, IMD, Lausanne, and World Economic Forum, Geneva, Switzerland. Used with permission.

Note: Indicators used: economic expectations versus reality, economic planning failures, political leadership, external conflict risk, corruption in government, military in politics, organized religion in politics, law and order tradition, racial and national tensions, political terrorism, civil war risks, political party development, quality of bureaucracy. Ratings range from 100 (minimum risk) to zero (maximum risk).

Local Partners

Relying on local partners with excellent contacts among the host country governing elite is a strategy that has been used effectively by many companies. This may range from placing local nationals on the boards of foreign subsidiaries to accepting a substantial capital participation from local investors. According to a survey done for the Conference Board, some 40 percent of U.S. companies with sales in excess of $100 million engaged in some type of joint ventures with local partners. About half of these companies claimed that their joint ventures were just as profitable as fully owned subsidiaries, and 12 percent viewed their joint ventures as even more profitable.[75] Though many host countries require some form of local participation as a condition for entering their market, many firms do it voluntarily. Diamond Shamrock, a U.S.-based company, built its chemical plant in South Korea with the help of a local partner to get more favorable operating conditions.[76]

Invaluable Status

Achieving a status of indispensability is an effective strategy for firms that have exclusive access to high technology or specific products. Such companies keep research and development out of the reach of their politically vulnerable subsidiaries and, at the same time, enhance their bargaining power with host governments by emphasizing their contributions to the economy. When Texas Instruments wanted to open an operation in Japan more than twenty years ago, the company was able, due to its advanced technology, to resist pressures to take on a local partner. This occurred at a time when many other foreign companies were forced to accept local partners.[77] The appearance of being irreplaceable obviously helps reduce political risk.

Vertical Integration

Companies that maintain specialized plants, each dependent on the others in various countries, are expected to incur fewer political risks than firms with fully integrated and independent plants in each country. A firm practicing this form of distributed sourcing can offer economies of scale to a local operation. This can become crucial for success in many industries. If a host government were to take over such a plant, its output level would be spread over too many units, products, or components, thus rendering the local company uncompetitive due to a cost disadvantage. Further risk can be reduced by having at least two units engage in the same operation to prevent the company itself from becoming

---

75. "Handicapping and Hedging," p. 61.
76. "More Firms Are Hiring," p. 17.
77. Yves L. Doz and C. K. Prahalad, "How MNCs Cope with Host Government Intervention," *Harvard Business Review,* March–April 1980, p. 152.

hostage to overspecialization. Unless multiple sourcing exists, a company could be virtually shut down if only one of its plants were affected negatively.

Local Borrowing

One of the reasons why Cabot Corp. prefers local partners is that it is then able to borrow locally instead of bringing foreign exchange to a host country.[78] Financing local operations from indigenous banks and maintaining a high level of local accounts payable maximize the negative effect on the local economy if adverse political actions were taken. Typically, host governments do not expropriate themselves, and they are reluctant to cause problems for their local financial institutions. Local borrowing, however, is not always possible, due to restrictions placed on foreign companies who may otherwise crowd local companies out of the credit markets.

Minimizing Fixed Investments

Political risk, of course, is always related to the amount of capital at risk. Given equal political risk, an alternative with comparably lower exposed capital amounts is preferable. A company can decide to lease facilities instead of buying them, or it can rely more on outside suppliers provided they exist. In any case, companies should keep exposed assets to a minimum to limit damage due to political risk.

Political Risk Insurance

As a final recourse, international companies can purchase insurance to cover their political risk. With the political developments in Iran and Nicaragua in rapid succession and the assassinations of President Park of Korea and President Sadat of Egypt all taking place between 1979 and 1981, many companies began to change their attitudes on risk insurance. Political risk insurance can offset large potential losses. For example, as a result of the United Nations Security Council's worldwide embargo on Iraq until it withdrew from Kuwait, companies will collect $100–200 million from private insurers and billions from government-owned insurers.[79]

Companies based in the United States have two sources for such insurance: government insurance or private insurance. The Overseas Private Investment Corporation (OPIC) was formed in 1969 by the U.S. government to facilitate the participation of private U.S. firms in the development of less developed countries. OPIC offers three kinds of political risk insurance in one hundred developing countries. The agency covers losses caused by currency inconvertibility, expropriation, and bellicose actions such as war and revolution.

78. "Multinationals Get Smarter," p. 98.
79. "Political Risk Insurers Fear Crisis Escalation," *Business Insurance,* 24, no. 33a (1990), p. 1.

International and Global Legal Forces

In many ways, the legal framework of a nation reflects a particular political philosophy or ideology. Just as each country has its own political climate, so does the legal system change from country to country. The legal systems of the world are based on one of four sources— common law derived from English law found in the United Kingdom, the United States, Canada, and countries previously part of the English Commonwealth; civil, or code, law based on the Roman law of written rules found in non-Islamic and non-Marxist countries; socialist law derived from the Marxist-socialist system found in China, Russia, and other socialist nations; and Islamic law derived from the Koran, found in Iran, Iraq, Pakistan, and other Islamic nations. Thus, internationally active companies find themselves in a situation where they have to conform to more than one legal system. Although this is complicated enough, the difficulty in some cases of determining whose laws apply adds further to an already complex environment.

Here we discuss some of the current major legal challenges that require adjustment and consideration at the corporate level. In later chapters, we will present the specific legal requirements covering certain aspects of the international marketing program. Such material appears in the chapters on pricing, advertising, and export mechanics, among others.

Of particular interest to us in this chapter are the laws pertaining to commercial behavior, such as laws against bribery and laws regulating competition and product liability. We also discuss the emergence of international courts.

Laws Against Bribery and Corrupt Practices

Though bribery in international business has been known to exist for years, the publicity surrounding some bribery scandals in the early 1970s caused a public furor in the United States about the practice. For example, in 1975 the U.S.-based company United Brands was accused of paying a bribe of $1.25 million in 1974 to a high government official in Honduras, later identified as that country's president,[80] to obtain a reduction of an export tax.

The Foreign Corrupt Practices Act (FCPA) of 1977 was intended to stop the payments of bribes. Though the act covers the whole range of recordkeeping and control activities of a company both in the United States and abroad, its best-known section specifically prohibits U.S. companies, their subsidiaries, and representatives from making payments to high-ranking foreign government officials or political parties. The penalties for violation can be very stiff: an executive who violates the FCPA may be imprisoned for up to five years and fined up to $10,000. The company involved may be fined up to $1 million. Though the law prohibits outright bribery, small facilitating payments are not outlawed as long as they are made to government clerks without any policymaking responsibility.[81]

---

80. "Honduran Bribery," *Time,* April 21, 1975, p. 74.

81. Hurd Baruch, "The Foreign Corrupt Practices Act," *Harvard Business Review,* January– February 1979, p. 44.

One of the principal reasons payoffs continue is due to the different attitude toward bribery by various governments. Contrary to U.S. law, the German government considers payoffs legal as long as they are made outside Germany. Furthermore, any such payments are tax deductible. As a result, many U.S.-based companies consider themselves at a disadvantage when competing for business in certain parts of the world where kickbacks are common. Some efforts have been made to help U.S. companies distinguish illegal from legal payments. The U.S. Justice Department reviews proposed transactions and lets the companies know about the legal consequences.[82] There is little likelihood that other governments will come around to accepting the U.S. positions. Europeans and Japanese view such payments as a cost of business.[83]

In a study of U.S. and Australian businesspeople, both groups reported that bribery was a major ethical problem facing international business managers.[84] There has been criticism that the FCPA has had a negative impact on U.S. companies versus their competitors who are not held to the same standard. This criticism is refuted by a macroeconomic study that found that the FCPA had not had a negative impact on U.S. export trade.[85]

Bribery exists in both developed and less developed countries. The bribery scandals involving the construction industry in Japan and Italy are well known and have even led to enormous political change in those countries. In Italy, where bribing government officials by transferring large sums of money through their political parties was common, many leading politicians and business executives have been jailed. One year later, bids for public works projects are reported to come in up to 40 percent below cost estimates based upon earlier times, and the Italian government is estimated to save up to $4.4 billion in 1994.[86] The Italian bribery scandal also involved international companies. The local executives of a U.S. advertising agency, Foote, Cone & Belding, as well as Young & Rubicam and SmithKline, were implicated in the scandal.[87]

Other parts of the world recently in the news for bribery are China and Russia. In both countries, the recent changes toward more liberalization in trade have created opportunities for local officials to approve foreign investment. One source estimated that the "connection" payments in China amounted to 3 to 5 percent of operating costs of a project.[88] Bribery is viewed differently by executives from various countries. In a recent survey in Asia, only 17 percent of Australian executives said they would offer a bribe (for

82. "U.S. Outlines Its Review of Foreign Payments," *New York Times,* March 25, 1980, p. D1.

83. "OECD Meets in Effort to Fight Bribery," *Financial Times,* February 14, 1994, p. 5.

84. Robert W. Armstrong et al., "International Marketing Ethics," *European Journal of Marketing,* 24, no. 10 (1990), p. 10.

85. John L. Graham, "The Foreign Corrupt Practices Act: A New Perspective," *Journal of International Business Studies,* Winter 1984, pp. 107–121.

86. "The Destructive Costs of Greasing Palms," *Business Week,* December 6, 1993, p. 133.

87. "Three U.S.-related Companies Dragged into Italian Investigation," *Wall Street Journal,* June 25, 1993, p. A7.

88. "Destructive Costs of Greasing Palms," p. 133.

business in Asia) if they risked losing a big sale. Japanese and U.S. executives had similar percentages at 27 and 22 percent. On the other hand, more than half of all Indonesian and Thai executives polled indicated they would bribe before losing an important client or deal. One expatriate executive noted that the Thai language did not have a word for bribe; they called it "commission."[89]

As a result of the difficulties in deciding which law applies, international companies have resorted to developing their own codes of ethics, particularly concerning bribes. When developing such a code, companies have to decide if they will apply one code worldwide or differentiate their standards by country or region. Experience over the past decade has shown that the level of ethical behavior is rising over time, and what was acceptable behavior at one time may suddenly be cause for prosecution under the local laws. As a result, companies might as well accept the highest available standard, even if it would not yet be the norm in a given country.

Rejection of a request for a payoff often puts the executive in a difficult position. One strategy is to transform the private payoff into a public gift of funds for a hospital, services for the public good, or jobs for the unemployed. These actions may satisfy the request for funds while not violating the provisions of the FCPA.[90]

Laws Regulating Competitive Behavior

Many countries have adopted laws that govern the competitive behavior of their firms. In some cases, as for the European Union, supranational bodies enforce their own laws. Unfortunately for international companies, these antitrust laws are frequently contradictory or differently enforced, adding great complexity to the job of the international executive. The United States, with its long-standing tradition of antitrust enforcement, has had considerable impact on the multinational operations of U.S. companies and increasingly on those of foreign-based companies operating in the United States.

But foreign companies entering the U.S. market may also have to deal with U.S. antitrust legislation. When Nippon Sanso attempted to buy Semi-Gas Systems, the San Jose, California, manufacturer of semiconductor equipment, the U.S. Justice Department blocked the takeover. The government said that the purchase would give Nippon Sanso 48 percent of the U.S. market, thereby reducing competition.[91]

The European Union has now its own merger task force to control mergers involving EU countries. During the first two years of existence, the task force dealt with 136 notifications. Of those, 103 dealt with short investigations of one month or less, and only a small percentage were fully investigated over four months.[92] Sometimes, international

89. "Managing in Asia," Survey, *Far Eastern Economic Review,* September 16, 1993, p. 55.

90. Jeffrey A. Fadiman, "A Traveler's Guide to Gifts and Bribes," *Harvard Business Review,* July–August 1986, pp. 122–136.

91. "That Tough Line on Foreign Investment Is Only a Mirage," *Business Week,* January 21, 1991, p. 43.

firms can get caught between competing legal systems. When ICI of the United Kingdom and Du Pont of the United States decided to swap two of their businesses, both the U.S. and European antitrust units investigated. The swap brought all of ICI's fibers business to Du Pont, which now had a dominant share both in the United States and Europe. In a parallel swap, ICI acquired the acrylics business from Du Pont, giving it stronger positions in both Europe and the United States. In the end, both transactions were approved, although it took much longer to get the U.S. approval.

Product Liability

Though there are regulations or laws that directly affect all aspects of international marketing, regulations on product liability are included here because of their enormous impact on all firms. Specific regulatory acts, or laws, pertaining to other aspects of the marketing mix—namely pricing, distribution, and promotion—have been included in other chapters.

Regulations on product liability are relatively recent and started first in the United States. Other countries, as well, have laws on product liability; a major problem for international marketers involves the differences in laws in different countries or regions. In the United States, product liability is viewed in the broadest sense, or along the lines of strict liability. For a product sold in defective condition that becomes unreasonably dangerous for the user, both producer and distributor can be held accountable.

Product liability laws have changed in Europe as well. In the mid-1970s, the European Commission proposed a set of regulations that was to supersede each member country's laws. Traditionally, the individual country laws had been rather lax by U.S. standards. In the United States, the plaintiff must prove that the product was defective at the time it left the producer's hand, whereas under the EC guidelines the manufacturers had to prove that the product was not defective when it left their control. Nevertheless, there are differences due to the different legal and social systems. In the EU, trials are decided by judges and not common jurors. And the existing extensive welfare system will automatically absorb many of the medical costs that are subject to litigation in the United States. Furthermore, it is typical for the loser in a court judgment in Europe to bear the legal costs. In the case of product liability cases, if a company is found to owe damages to a plaintiff, then it also will have to pay the plaintiff's legal costs according to typical fee standards. This differs substantially from the U.S. system, in which a winning plaintiff's lawyer typically is compensated through a predetermined percentage of the awarded damages, a practice that in the eyes of many experts has raised award damages and, as a result, liability insurance costs.

The rapid spread of product liability litigation, however, forces companies with international operations to carefully review their potential liabilities and to acquire appropriate insurance policies. Although an international marketing manager cannot be expected to know all the respective rules and regulations, executives must nevertheless anticipate

92. "Marriages Made in Brussels," *Financial Times,* January 19, 1993, p. 13.

potential exposure and, by asking themselves the appropriate questions, make sure that their firms consider all possible aspects.

Bankruptcy Laws

Bankruptcy laws vary from country to country. In the United Kingdom, Canada, and France the laws of bankruptcy favor the creditors. When a firm enters bankruptcy, an administrator is appointed. The adminstrator's job is to recover the creditors' money. In the United States, bankruptcy tends to protect the business from the creditors. Under Chapter 11, the management prepares a reorganization plan, which is voted on by the creditors. In Germany and Japan, bankruptcies are often handled by the banks behind closed doors. The national bankruptcy systems have a wide variety of standards of openness to others. Also, creditor preference varies from country to country. For example, Swiss law gives preference to Swiss creditors. There is a need for a global bankruptcy law, but until establishment of world accountancy standards, there is little chance of a global bankruptcy code.[93]

Patents, Trademarks, and Copyrights

Patents and trademarks are used to protect products, processes, and symbols. Patents and trademarks are issued by each individual country, so marketers must register every product in every country they intend to trade in. The International Convention for the Protection of Industrial Property, honored by forty-five countries, gives all nationals the same privileges when applying for patents and trademarks. Also, the agreement gives patent coverage for one year after the trademark or patent is applied for in one country, thus limiting pirating of the product in other countries. The United States has an extensive patent system open to anyone. In fact, 48 percent of the patents issued in 1988 were to foreigners. The firms receiving the most U.S. patents in 1988 were Hitachi, Toshiba, Canon, GE, Fuji Film, Philips, Siemens, IBM, Mitsubishi, and Bayer. The only U.S. firms in the top 10 were GE and IBM.[94] It does not seem that all countries have open and accessible patent systems. It took Allied Signal eleven years to get a patent on amorphous metal alloys approved in Japan. Allied Signal alleges that the Japanese patent office dragged its feet while the Ministry for Trade and Industry (MITI) launched a catch-up program with thirty-four Japanese companies.[95] The U.S. trade representative watches trading partners to ensure they are protecting intellectual property. Countries on the priority watch list—that is, subject to scrutiny—are Brazil, India, China, and Thailand.[96]

Pirating products became a significant problem in the 1980s, affecting computers, watches, designer clothes, and industrial products. The sale of counterfeit goods ranging

93. ''Bankruptcy Laws,'' *Economist,* February 24, 1990, pp. 93–94.

94. ''America's Patent System—Not Invented Here,'' *Economist,* October 24, 1989, p. 104.

95. ''American-Japanese Trade—Low Tricks in High Tech,'' *Economist,* September 29, 1990, p. 90.

96. ''Call for Stronger Action to Protect Copyrights,'' *Financial Times,* May 1, 1990, p. 4.

from Louis Vuitton bags and Rolex watches to car parts and medicines was estimated to be a hefty $150 billion a year. The United States and other industrialized countries are working together to stop this illicit trade. Washington forced a proposal for trade-related aspects of intellectual property (TRIP) on the agenda of the Uruguay round of GATT talks. The western countries wanted the TRIP proposal approved to strengthen the regulation and enforcement of intellectual property rights.[97] Patents, trademarks, and pirating will be discussed in more detail in Chapter 10.

Copyright laws and violations are becoming an increasing concern also for international executives. Disney entered China with its Chinese-speaking Mickey and Donald in 1987 but withdrew from the market in 1990 after rampant copyright violations. Following the passing of a new and stricter copyright law, Disney reentered the Chinese market in 1993.[98] Because the protection of intellectual property rights had no value in China's socialist history, many companies have had similar difficulties. Other Asian countries, Taiwan and Hong Kong in particular, have been problems for international firms due to a lack of copyright protection. Microsoft estimates it is losing as to much to piracy of its software as it sells in Asia, about $1 billion annually.[99] The European software industry estimated its total theft losses at $4.6 billion, with international trade in fakes estimated at $80 billion worldwide.[100]

The Business Software Alliance of the United States has estimated that fully 93 percent of all U.S. software sold in Taiwan is counterfeit. The respective figures for Thailand and Japan were 99 and 92 percent. However, software piracy exists all over the world. The estimate for the United States was at 35 percent. European countries ranged between 54 percent for the United Kingdom and 86 percent for Italy.[101] The importance of the copyright law for software even reached international trade discussion when the Japanese government began considering a change in the law that would allow Japanese companies to reengineer all software to make compatible products, even when the U.S. supplier would not authorize it.[102] Because of its importance to firms that depend on copyright protection, such as in the music, video, publishing, and software industries, international firms will have to pay increased attention to the enforcement of these laws.

Regulatory Trends Affecting Global Marketing

In the past, international firms had to spend a large amount of energy to protect themselves from negative political decisions. Political risk consisted largely of losing operating freedom or, in the worst case, losing the asset in a country. The tremendous political change

97. Frances Williams, "Foiling the Fakers," *Eurobusiness,* September 1990, pp. 11–14.
98. "Mickey Mouse Back in China—on Best Behavior," *Financial Times,* July 5, 1993, p. 1.
99. "Microsoft Combats Software Piracy in Greater China," Greater China Business Network, Inc.
100. "Grab That Rolex," *Far Eastern Economic Review,* August 3, 1993, p. 63.
101. "Copyright Law Proposal Worries U.S. Software Sellers," *Nikkei Weekly,* August 9, 1993, p. 1.
102. "Decompilation: A Divisive Issue," *Nikkei Weekly,* December 20, 1993, p. 8.

that has swept through the world over the past few years has actually brought a opening of trade and led to many more opportunities than in any five-year period since World War II. The key political events of total change in eastern Europe and the opening of countries such as China have significantly broadened the geographic boundaries within which international firms are allowed to participate.

Three major trends emerge, each present to different degrees in some parts of the world. The first such trend, *trade liberalization,* meaning the opening of many countries to international trade, has swept many formerly ''locked'' countries. While this has clearly been the case in the formerly socialist countries of eastern Europe, trade liberalization and the corresponding opening of borders to imports and exports have been of great importance in the merging and developing economies. The second trend of importance is *deregulation.* This trends covers the various government actions aimed at allowing market forces more influence; it has resulted in a reduction of regulatory activities primarily in the western economies but also elsewhere in the world. Finally, *privatization,* a third major trend, is today engulfing mostly the countries of eastern Europe. Governments in many countries are turning over ownership of companies, services, and agencies to private investors. We will now look at each of these trends in greater detail in an effort to understand how they have affected the global marketing strategies of international firms.

Trade Liberalization   In the early 1980s, international trade with large parts of the world was very restricted. In eastern Europe, most of Latin America, and many Asian countries such as China and India, governments tightly controlled what could be imported and thus severely restricted business opportunities for international firms. Chile, Mexico, and Argentina are countries in Latin America that began to open their borders to imports in the mid-1980s. Imports were expected to compete with high-priced local products; the resulting economic growth was then expected to lead to more export opportunities. In Mexico, this process started in 1986, when the country joined GATT. As a result, average tariffs were reduced from 22 to 9 percent, and import quotas and other trade limitations were eliminated.[103] This greatly expanded the market opportunities for international firms in Mexico from $12.5 billion to almost $40 billion in 1991.[104] The change required adjustments by international firms. Previously, any company that wanted to market its products in Mexico had to have a local production base. Now that imports are freely allowed, Cummins, a US-based diesel engine manufacturer, reduced local production and is now exporting most products from its U.S. plants.[105]

India is another country that has turned to international trade liberalization in a major way. Following its initial introduction in 1991, several steps were taken to make India a more attractive place for international firms to invest. This included a much freer regulation of foreign exchange, permission to use foreign brand names where previously not per-

103. ''Across the Rio Grande,'' *Economist,* October 9, 1993, p. 67.
104. *World Competitiveness Report, 1993,* p. 223.
105. ''No Such Thing as a Free Treaty,'' *Financial Times,* November 11, 1993, p. 13.

mitted, and the right to raise equity stakes to 51 percent in many sectors.[106] As a result of the opening of India, many international firms have entered or reentered the Indian market. Aside from Coca-Cola and Pepsi-Cola, other international companies are Morgan Stanley, a U.S. investment banking firm, Peugeot of France, Procter & Gamble, and General Electric of the United States.[107] Similar developments have led to trade liberalization between China and the rest of the world, including most of eastern Europe, as a result of the political changes that have swept through that area since 1989.[108]

Deregulation A second trend affecting global marketing is the rapid deregulation of business everywhere. The United States is generally considered to have taken the lead with its deregulation of several industries, particularly transportation, airlines, banking, and telecommunications. The general ideas of deregulation were readily absorbed by some other governments, the United Kingdom among them. As part of the European integration drive, culminating in the "Europe 1992" initiative, deregulation also became an important issue in Europe. Typically, deregulation not only acts as a barrier to government intervention but also helps in opening doors to international competition.

The European Union is slowly opening its telecommunications market. The long-held monopolies of the national telephone companies in most European countries are to give way to more open competition along the U.S. and U.K. models. While data communication has already been deregulated, the trend now is to include regular voice communications as well.[109] One Italian company believed its telephone rates in Italy were some 24 percent higher than the rates charged for the same service by British firms. Deregulation will bring more competition as the local phone companies can no longer count on their monopolies. It will also open up opportunities for other carriers, such as AT&T from the United States and the various regional operating companies. In mobile communications, these U.S. firms have already penetrated the market, usually linking up with local partners who were not previously active in telecommunications.

Similar efforts are under way in Asia, where telecommunications markets are growing rapidly.[110] Other efforts have taken place in financial markets, where substantial deregulation is under way in banking and insurance. The opening of Japanese financial markets, particularly with respect to financial derivatives, is of importance to international banks.[111] Deregulation is typically accompanied by liberalization and the opening of markets for foreign competitors. This trend, therefore, adds to the set of opportunities encountered by international firms.

106. "Back in Charge," *Far Eastern Economic Review,* July 8, 1993, p. 8.

107. "India Clears Some Foreign Investments, Sending Bullish Signal on Reform Drive," *Wall Street Journal,* June 24, 1993.

108. "Cracking the China Market," Wall Street Journal Reports, *Wall Street Journal,* December 10, 1993; "China," Financial Times survey, *Financial Times,* November 18, 1993.

109. "Telephone Upheaval in Europe," *New York Times,* May 31, 1993, p. 37.

110. "Investors Move as Asia Gets on the Phone," *Financial Times,* June 2, 1993, p. 4.

111. "Battle to Open Tokyo Markets Heats Up," *Wall Street Journal,* June 2, 1993, p. C1.

Privatization   The third trend affecting global marketing is the current rush toward privatization. Under privatization, countries sell government-owned agencies, organizations, and companies to private stockholders or other acquiring firms. Starting in the late 1970s and in the early 1980s, acts of privatization overtook nationalizations, and for the period 1990–1992, the United Nations counted more than 150 privatizations.[112] Some of the earliest examples of privatization came from the United Kingdom, where the government privatized airlines (British Airways), telecommunications companies (British Telecom), and many utilities (BAA).

The urge to privatize gained steam as the formerly socialist countries of eastern Europe began to convert to a market economy.[113] The drive toward privatization was particularly strong in Poland, the Czech Republic, and Hungary. Philip Morris, the U.S.-based food and tobacco company, was able to acquire a stake in Czechia's Tabak, a company with a tobacco monopoly. The Czech government indicated that the monopoly would eventually end; however, Philip Morris expected to get a head start through the acquisition. Many privatizations in Poland and the Czech Republic occurred through the distribution of shares, or coupons, to the local population. Nevertheless, the effort to privatize state industry in many parts of eastern Europe has resulted in significant opportunities for acquisitions for foreign firms. In Hungary, more than half of the revenue earned by the government through privatization came from foreign investors.[114]

Privatization has also become more common in other parts of the world. Argentina privatized almost its entire state holdings in a period of three years ending in 1993. This resulted in a net inflow of $19.1 billion for the sale of airlines, oil companies, gas companies, and other industrial firms.[115] Other privatization occurred in Venezuela, where the government sold a large stake to an international group headed by GTE of the United States, and in Mexico, where the government sold banks and steel companies.[116]

Privatization is also coming in a big way to western governments, where some countries have held industrial stakes for a long time. France and Italy, with long traditions for industrial holdings, will privatize some of their state-controlled industrial firms.[117] They will also sell stakes in utilities, such as telecommunications.[118] In Italy, privatization will affect large banks and many state-run oil and chemical companies.[119]

The trend toward privatization is expected to continue, with some 1,300 separate deals anticipated worldwide, not including any activity in eastern Europe. Whenever pri-

112. *World Investment Report 1993: TNCs and Integrated Production* (New York: United Nations Conference on Trade and Development, United Nations, 1993), p. 17.

113. "Altered States," *International Management Journal,* July–August 1992, pp. 58–65.

114. "Hungary's Privatization Falters after Flying Start," *Financial Times,* October 19, 1993, p. 4.

115. "Buying into Argentina Was the Easy Bit," *Financial Times,* December 7, 1993, p. 5.

116. "Argentina Races to Sell Oil Stake," *New York Times,* April 16, 1993, p. D1.

117. "State-run Groups Get Used to New Identity," *Financial Times,* January 24, 1994, p. 13.

118. "Whose Line Is It Anyway?" *Financial Times,* October 11, 1993, p. 13.

119. "After the Scandals, a Vast Sell-Off," *Business Week,* November 22, 1993, p. 56.

vatization occurs, it is typically related to a decreasing involvement of the local government in that particular industry or sector. This invariably leads to further trade liberalizations and deregulations. Both effects generate increased opportunities for international companies.

Conclusions

In this chapter, we have outlined the major political and regulatory forces facing international companies. Our approach was not so much to identify and list all possible influences or actions that may have an impact on international marketing operations. Instead, we have provided only a sample of potential acts. It is up to executives with international responsibility to devise structures and systems that deal with these environmental influences. What is important to our discussion is to recognize that companies can adopt risk reduction strategies to compensate for some of these risks but certainly not for all of them. For effective international marketing management, executives must be forward looking, anticipate potentially adversarial *or* positive changes in the environment, and not wait until changes occur. To accomplish this, a systematic monitoring system that encompasses both political and legal developments must be implemented.

The great importance such monitoring has for international firms has been demonstrated throughout this chapter. The past five years have brought enormous political changes to this world, which are affecting the global marketing operations of international firms. Although these changes have resulted in the opening of many previously closed markets, substantial uncertainties remain. In many parts of the world, the existing trend toward open market economies is still questionable; substantial political and regulatory risks remain for many countries. Past experience has demonstrated, however, that the traditional purpose of assessing political risk—to ensure that assets of firms would not be lost due to takeovers or other arbitrary host government decisions—will have to give way to finding the true opportunities that might exist. As a result, the approaches and processes used by international firms traditionally to assess political risk will have to be redirected at political opportunity assessment.[120]

Questions for Discussion

1. The telecommunications industry in Japan has traditionally been tightly controlled, with very little non-Japanese equipment allowed. What aspects of Japan's political forces may have influenced this control over the Japanese telecommunications market?

120. Ideas expressed to authors by Clifton Clarke, retired vice president for international trade at Digital and now an independent consultant.

2. What direction will the telecommunications industry take in Europe? Which way would the intentions of the European Union (Maastricht) treaty influence this direction?

3. How could a country develop its own expertise in a product that is primarily imported—for example, automobiles in Egypt?

4. Develop a political risk analysis for a country of your choice. In which direction is the country going, and what kind of effects would that have on international firms operating there?

5. What are the different methods a company can use to obtain and/or develop political risk assessment information?

6. John Deere has decided to enter the tractor market in Central America. What strategies could it use to reduce the possible effects of political risk?

7. While you are attempting to deliver a large computer system (selling price $1.4 million) to a foreign government, the minister of transportation advises that a fee of $20,000 is required to ensure proper coordination of the custom clearance delivery process. What would you do?

For Further Reading

Akhter, Humayum, and Robert F. Lusch. ''Political Risk and the Evolution of the Control of Foreign Business: Equity, Earnings, and the Marketing Mix.'' *Journal of Global Marketing,* Spring 1988, pp. 109–127.

Brewer, Thomas L., ed. *Political Risks in International Business.* New York: Praeger, 1985.

Davidow, Joel. ''Multinationals, Host Governments and Regulation of Restrictive Business Practices.'' *Columbia Journal of World Business,* Summer 1980, pp. 14–19.

Doz, Yves L., and C. K. Prahalad. ''How Multinational Corporations Cope with Host Government Intervention.'' *Harvard Business Review,* March–April 1980, pp. 149–157.

Encarnation, Dennis J., and Sushil Vachani. ''Foreign Ownership: When Hosts Change the Rules.'' *Harvard Business Review,* September–October 1985, pp. 152–160.

Graham, John L. ''The Foreign Corrupt Practices Act.'' *Journal of International Business Studies,* Winter 1984, pp. 107–121.

Harvey, Michael G., and Ilkka A. Ronkainen. ''International Counterfeiters: Marketing Success Without the Cost and the Risk.'' *Columbia Journal of World Business,* Fall 1985, pp. 37–45.

Hauptman, Gunter. ''Intellectual Property Rights.'' *International Marketing Review,* Spring 1987, pp. 61–64.

Huntington, Samuel P. ''How Countries Democratize.'' *Political Science Quarterly,* 106, no. 4 (1991–92).

Huntington, Samuel P., and Myron Weiner. *Understanding Political Development.* Boston: Little, Brown, 1987.

Huntington, Samuel P. ''The Clash of Civilizations?'' *Foreign Affairs,* 72, no. 3 (1993), pp. 22–49.

Kaikati, Jack G., and Wayne A. Label. "American Bribery Legislation: An Obstacle to International Marketing." *Journal of Marketing,* Fall 1980, pp. 38–43.

Kim, Chan W. "Competition and the Management of Host Government Intervention." *Sloan Management Review,* Spring 1987, pp. 33–39.

Lodge, George C., and Erza F. Vogel. *Ideology and National Competitiveness.* Boston: Harvard Business School Press, 1987.

Raddock, David M. *Assessing Corporate Political Risk.* Totowa, N.J.: Roowman & Littlefield, 1986.

Shapiro, Alan C. "Managing Political Risk: A Policy Approach." *Columbia Journal of World Business,* Fall 1981, pp. 63–70.

Simon, Jeffery D. "Theoretical Perspective on Political Risk." *Journal of International Business Studies,* Winter 1984, pp. 123–143.

Simon, Jeffery D. "Political Risk Assessment: Past Trends and Future Prospects." *Columbia Journal of World Business,* Fall 1982, pp. 62–71.

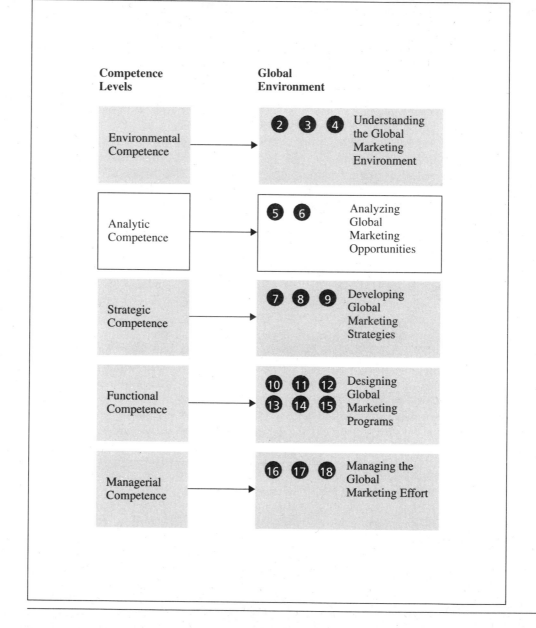

Competence
Levels

Global
Environment

Environmental
Competence

2 3 4 Understanding the Global Marketing Environment

Analytic
Competence

5 6 Analyzing Global Marketing Opportunities

Strategic
Competence

7 8 9 Developing Global Marketing Strategies

Functional
Competence

10 11 12 13 14 15 Designing Global Marketing Programs

Managerial
Competence

16 17 18 Managing the Global Marketing Effort

Part 2

Analyzing Global Marketing Opportunities

THE GLOBAL marketplace includes between 175 and 200 countries or territories. International companies are constantly searching for the most appropriate markets and the best opportunities for their firms. Analyzing, classifying, and selecting opportunities for future business is an important aspect of international marketing management. In Part 2, we concentrate on the skills necessary to do this job well.

Chapter 5 provides concepts for analyzing opportunities within countries and groups of countries. We discuss the major market segments within each country's consumer, industrial, and government sectors and analyze the differences in these segments from market to market. The next chapter of this section, Chapter 6, covers the methods by which international companies collect market data, and discusses ways to analyze this market research data for decision making.

We have given this section a largely analytic focus. Our aim in doing this has been to encourage analytic competence, which is necessary for success in international and global marketing.

5

Global Markets and Buyers

● **ASSESSMENT OF MARKET** *opportunities is an important aspect of international marketing. Every time a company decides to expand into foreign markets, it must systematically evaluate possible markets to identify the country or group of countries with the greatest opportunities. This process of evaluating worldwide opportunities is complicated for a number of reasons. First, there are between 175 and 200 countries in the world; obviously, it is difficult to examine all these opportunities. Second, due to the number of countries and resource limitations, the initial screening process is usually limited to the analysis of published data. Third, many possible markets are small, with little data available about specific consumer, business, or government needs.*

Potential buyers often vary from country to country. The buyer can be a consumer, a business, or a government. The challenge for the global marketer is to recognize the differences while looking for the similarities that cut across markets. This chapter will identify the characteristics of different buyers.

In this chapter, outlined in Figure 5.1, we first discuss the process for selecting markets, both the selection techniques and the selection criteria. Then, to illustrate the screening process, we present a detailed example of how this process can be used to select a market for dialysis equipment. In the final sections of the chapter, we discuss the rationale for grouping countries together and present the market groups

143

FIGURE 5.1 ● International Market Selection

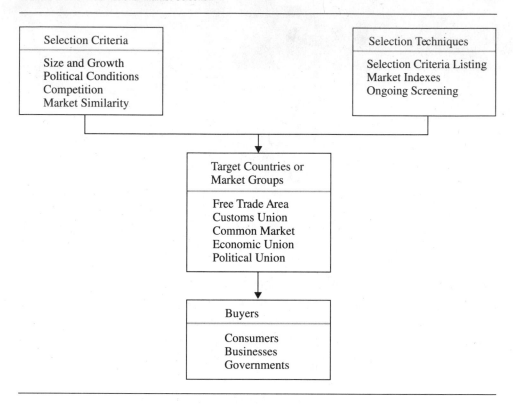

in existence around the world today. Last, we discuss the characteristics influencing the different types of buyer: consumer, business, and government.

Screening International Marketing Opportunities

Selection Stages

The assessment of international marketing opportunities usually begins with a screening process that involves gathering relevant information on each country and filtering out the less desirable countries. A model for selecting foreign markets is shown in Figure 5.2.

The model includes a series of four filters to screen out countries. It is necessary to break the process down into a series of steps due to the large number of market

FIGURE 5.2 ● A Model for Selecting Foreign Markets

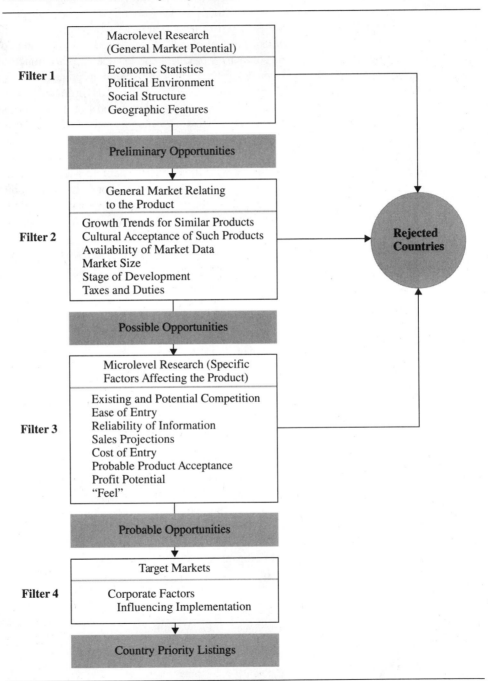

Source: R. Wayne Walvoord, ''Export Market Research,'' *Global Trade Magazine,* May 1980, p. 83. Reprinted by permission.

opportunities. Although a firm does not want to miss a potential opportunity, it cannot conduct extensive market research studies in every country of the world. (The *World Bank Atlas* includes 200 countries and territories.)[1] The screening process is used to identify good prospects. Two common errors of country screening are (1) ignoring countries that offer good potential for the company's products and (2) spending too much time investigating countries that are poor prospects.[2] Thus, the screening process allows an international company to quickly focus efforts on a few of the most promising market opportunities by using published secondary sources available in most business libraries.[3]

The first stage of the selection process uses macrovariables to discriminate between countries that represent basic opportunities and countries with little or no opportunity or with excessive risk. Macrovariables describe the total market in terms of economic, social, geographic, and political information. Often macroeconomic statistics indicate that the country is too small, as described by the gross national (or domestic) product. Possibly the gross national product seems large enough, but the personal disposable income per household may be too low. Political instability can also be used to remove a country from the set of possible opportunities.

In the second stage of the selection process, variables are used that indicate the potential market size and acceptance of the product or similar products. Often proxy variables are used in this screening process. A *proxy variable* is a similar or related product that indicates a demand for your product. For example, if you are attempting to measure the potential market size and receptivity for satellite television reception equipment, possible proxy variables may be the number of televisions per household, total sales of VCRs, or total sales of microwave ovens. The number of televisions and VCRs indicates the potential for home entertainment, and the sales of microwave ovens indicate a propensity to use advanced technologies in place of traditional appliance technology. The year-to-year growth rates and the total sales of similar or proxy products are good predictors of market size and growth. Other factors in the second stage of the selection process can also be used to screen out countries, such as the stage of economic development, taxes, and duty requirements. If you do not plan to manufacture locally, a high import duty may eliminate a country from consideration in the second stage of the screening process.

The third stage of the screening process focuses on microlevel considerations such as competitors, ease of entry, cost of entry, and profit potential. Microlevel factors influence the success or failure of a specific product in a market. At this stage of the process, marketers may be considering only a small number of countries, so it is feasible to get more detailed, up-to-date information from the U.S. Department of Commerce, the U.S. State Department, and other companies currently operating in that country. The International Trade Administration of the Department of Commerce has an office in most major

1. *World Bank Atlas 1994* (Washington, D.C.: World Bank, 1994).

2. Franklin R. Root, *Entry Strategies for International Market* (Lexington, Mass.: Lexington Books, 1994), p. 33.

3. See Susan P. Douglas and C. Samuel Craig, *International Marketing Research* (Englewood Cliffs, N.J.: Prentice Hall, 1983), pp. 306–325, for a detailed listing of secondary sources of information.

cities and can provide information and contacts for many markets. Also, customs brokers and freight forwarders can help at this stage of the process.

The focus of the screening process switches from total market size to profitability. For example, based on the current and potential competitors, how much would you need to invest to gain a particular market share? Given the prices currently charged in the market, what margin can your company expect? Given the cost of entry and the expected sales, what is the expected profit? This stage of the analysis focuses on the quantitative profit expected, but many subjective judgments are made to arrive at the expected profit. For example, an Israeli manufacturer of pipe insulation found that the market price in the United Kingdom was $10 per kilo, whereas its cost was less than $5 per kilo. This indicated a good profit potential if the company could gain access to the market.

The fourth stage of the screening process is an evaluation and rank ordering of the potential target countries, based on corporate resources, objectives, and strategies. For example, although South Africa may have the same expected potential as Venezuela, Venezuela may be given a higher priority because successful entry into Venezuela can later be followed by entry into Colombia and Bolivia.

Criteria for Selecting Target Countries

The process of selecting target countries through the screening process requires that the companies identify the criteria to be used to differentiate desirable countries from less desirable countries. Research on international investment decisions has shown that the four critical factors affecting market selection are market size and growth, political conditions, competition, and market similarity.[4] In this section, we will explain each of these factors and their uses in the market selection process.

Market Size and Growth   It is obvious that potential market size and growth are an important factor in selecting markets. The larger the potential demand for a product in a country, the more attractive it will be to a company.

Measures of market size and growth can be on both a macro and a micro basis. On a macro basis, it may be determined that the country needs a minimum set of potential resources to be worth further consideration. Table 5.1 shows a summary of potential macroindicators of market size. There are a variety of readily available statistics that are macroindicators of market size. If you are screening countries for a firm that sells microwave ovens, you may decide not to consider any country with a personal disposable income per household of less than $10,000 per year. The logic of this criterion is that if the average household has less than $10,000, the potential market for a luxury item such as a microwave oven will not be great. However, a single statistic can sometimes be deceptive. For example, a country may have an average household income of $8,000, but there may be one million households with an income of over $10,000. These one million households will be potential buyers of microwaves. One commercially available report on the

4. William H. Davidson, ''Market Similarity and Market Selection: Implications for International Market Strategy,'' *Journal of Business Research,* December 1983, pp. 439–456.

TABLE 5.1 ● Macroindicators of Market Size

Geographic Indicators

Size of the country, in terms of geographic area

Climatic conditions

Topographical characteristics

Demographic Characteristics

Total population

Population growth rate

Age distribution of the population

Degree of population density

Economic Characteristics

Total gross national product

Per capita gross national product

Per capita income (also income growth rate)

Personal or household disposable income

Income distribution

attractiveness of different countries for business is the *World Competitiveness Report.* Published annually, this report analyzes three hundred criteria to determine the overall competitiveness of the country and its strength by industry.[5]

The macroindicators of market potential and growth are usually used in the first stage of the screening process, because the data are readily available and can be used to quickly eliminate countries with little or no potential demand. The macroindicators focus on the total potential demand (population) and ability to afford a product (per capita income). However, because the macroindicators of market size are general and crude, they do not necessarily indicate a perceived need for the product. For example, a country such as Iraq may have the population and income to indicate a large potential for razors, but the consumers, many of whom are Moslems, may not feel a perceived need for the product. In the third stage of the screening process, it is recommended that microindicators of market potential be used. Microindicators usually indicate actual consumption of a company's product or a similar product, therefore indicating a perceived need. Table 5.2 shows an example of microindicators of market size.

These microindicators can be used to estimate market size. The number of households with televisions indicates the potential market size for televisions if every household purchased a new television. Depending on the life of the average television in use, one can estimate the annual demand. Although the actual consumption statistics may not be available for a certain product category, often the consumption of similar or substitute products

5. *World Competitiveness Report 1993* (Lausanne: IMD; Geneva: World Economic Forum, 1993).

TABLE 5.2 ● Microindicators of Market Size

Radios	Hotel beds
Televisions	Telephones
Cinema seats	Tourist arrivals
Scientists and engineers	Passenger cars
Hospitals	Civil airline passengers
Hospital beds	Steel production
Physicians	Rice production
Alcohol consumption	Number of farms
Coffee consumption	Land under cultivation
Gasoline consumption	Electricity consumption

are used as proxy variables. For example, in determining the market size for surgical sutures, marketers may use the number of hospital beds or doctors as a proxy variable. The number of farms may indicate the potential demand for tractors.

The macro- and microindicators of market size allow the marketer to determine or infer the potential market size. Next, the marketer needs to evaluate the risk associated with each market opportunity.

Political Conditions   The impact of a host country's political condition on market selection is described in studies by Stephan J. Kobrin and Franklin R. Root.[6] The influence of the host country's political environment was described in detail in Chapter 4. Though political risk tends to be more subjective than the quantitative indicators of market size, it is equally important. For example, the invasion of Kuwait in 1990 resulted in millions of dollars of U.S. assets being exposed to risk.

Any company can be hurt by political risk, from limitations on the number of foreign company officials and on the amount of profits paid to the parent company, to outright takeovers. There are a number of indicators that can be used to assess political risk.[7] Table 5.3 shows some indicators of political risk that may be used in country selection. Industrial disputes (strikes) can be a major disruption to business, and incidences vary greatly from country to country. For example, from 1988 to 1992, Spain lost 660 working days per 1,000 employees, whereas Japan and Switzerland each lost less than 5 days.[8]

Historically, extractive industries such as oil and mining have been susceptible to the political risk of expropriation. More recently, the financial, insurance, communication, and

6. S. J. Kobrin, "The Environmental Determinants of Foreign Direct Manufacturing Investment: An Ex-Post Empirical Analysis," *Journal of Business Studies,* Fall–Winter 1976, pp. 29–42; F. R. Root, "U.S. Business Abroad and Political Risks," *MSU Business Topics,* Winter 1968, pp. 73–80.

7. R. Rummel and David Heenan, "How Multinationals Analyze Political Risk," *Harvard Business Review,* January–February 1978, pp. 67–76.

8. "Industrial Disputes," *Economist,* January 29, 1994, p. 112.

TABLE 5.3 ● Indicators of Political Risk

Probability of nationalization	Percentage of the voters who are Communist
Bureaucratic delays	Restrictions on capital movement
Number of expropriations	Government intervention
Number of riots or assassinations	Limits on foreign ownership
Political executions	Soldier/civilian ratio
Number of Socialist seats in the legislature	

transportation industries have been targets of expropriation. As shown in Table 5.3, many aspects of political risk assessment can be analyzed based on historical data. Unfortunately, historical indicators are not always that accurate, because political conditions can change radically with a new government. Some of the syndicated services that rate political risk are the World Political Risk Forecast by Frost & Sullivan; Business International Rating of 57 Countries; Business Environment Risk Index and Political Risk Index of BERI, Ltd.; and the Economist Intelligence Unit. In addition to these major sources of information, international companies often consult banks, accounting firms, and domestic government agencies for political risk information.[9] The risk assessment services provided by Business International, Frost & Sullivan, BERI, and others are all useful long-term measures of risk. These do not preclude the need to keep attuned to the current events of the day, be they the collapse of the Berlin Wall, the invasion of Kuwait, or the crushed student uprising in Tiananmen Square. These critical events may not have been predicted by the risk assessment services; yet each had a profound effect on business.

Competition   The number, size, and quality of the competition in a particular country affect a firm's ability to enter and compete profitably.[10] In general, it is more difficult to determine the competitive structure of foreign countries than to determine the market size or political risk. Because of the difficulty of obtaining information, competitive analysis is usually done in the last stages of the screening process, when a small number of countries are being considered.

Some secondary sources are available that describe the competitive nature of a marketplace. The *Findex Directory* publishes a listing of the most readily available research reports. These reports tend to concentrate on North America and Europe, but there are some reports available on Japan, the Middle East, and South America. Such research reports usually cost between $500 and $5,000, with the average report being about $1,200. In some cases, there may not be a research report covering a specific country or product category, or it may be too expensive. Another good source of information is the U.S.

9. F. T. Haner with John S. Ewing, *Country Risk Assessment* (New York: Praeger, 1985), p. 171.
10. Igal Ayal and Zif Jehiel, ''Competitive Market Choice Strategies in International Marketing,'' *Columbia Journal of World Business,* Fall 1978, pp. 72–81.

government. The U.S. Department of Commerce and the State Department (or the equivalent in other countries) may be able to provide information on the competitive situation. Also, in almost every country, embassies employ commercial attachés whose main function is to assist home companies entering that foreign marketplace. Embassies of the foreign country being investigated may also be able to help marketers in their analysis. For example, in investigating the competition for farm implements in Spain, you can call or write the Spanish embassy in Washington, D.C. and ask for a list of manufacturers of farm implements in Spain.

Other sources of competitive information vary widely, depending on the size of the country and the product. Many of the larger countries have chambers of commerce or other in-country organizations that may be able to assist potential investors. For example, if you were investigating the Japanese market for electronic measuring devices, the following groups could assist you in determining the competitive structure of the market in Japan:

- U.S. Chamber of Commerce in Japan
- Japan External Trade Organization (JETRO)
- American Electronics Association in Japan
- Japan Electronic Industry Development Association
- Electronic Industries Association of Japan
- Japan Electronic Measuring Instrument Manufacturers Association

The final and usually most expensive way to assess the market is to go to the country and interview potential customers and competitors to determine the size and strength of the competition. As a trip to a potential market is always required before a final decision is made, it should not be overlooked as an important part of the screening process. If you are well prepared in advance, two to three days in a country talking to distributors, large buyers, and trade officials can be extremely valuable in assessing the competitiveness of the market and the potential profitability.

Market Similarity   Strong evidence exists that market similarity can be used for country selection. A study of 954 product introductions by fifty-seven U.S. firms found a significant correlation between market selection and market similarity.[11]

The concept of market similarity is simple. A firm tends to select countries based on their similarity to the home market. Therefore, when a company decides to enter foreign markets, it will first enter the markets that are most similar. For example, a U.S. firm will enter Canada, Australia, and the United Kingdom before entering less similar markets such as Spain, South Korea, or India. Measures of similarity are (1) aggregate production and transportation, (2) personal consumption, (3) trade, and (4) health and education.[12]

11. Davidson, "Market Similarity and Market Selection."
12. Ibid.

TABLE 5.4 ● Correlation of Similarity and Position in the Entry Sequence

	Similarity to the United States	*Position in investment sequence*
Canada	1	2
Australia	2	3
United Kindgom	3	1
West Germany	4	6
France	5	4
Belgium	6	10
Italy	7	9
Japan	8	5
Netherlands	9	12
Argentina	10	15
Mexico	11	8
Spain	12	13
India	13	16
Brazil	14	7
South Africa	15	14
Philippines	16	17
South Korea	17	18
Colombia	18	11

Source: Reprinted by permission of the publisher from "Market Similarity and Market Selection: Implications for International Market Strategy," by William H. Davidson, *Journal of Business Research,* vol. 11, no. 4, p. 446. Copyright 1983 by Elsevier Science Publishing Co., Inc.

As shown in Table 5.4, the selection of foreign markets tends to follow similarity very closely. Although language similarities were not measured in the study, it is worth noting that the top three markets all use the same language. Using market similarity as a selection variable is relatively simple. One can use the similarity ranking shown in Table 5.4, update it with the most recent economic data, or develop other criteria for determining similarity.

The premise behind the selection of similar markets is the desire of a company to minimize risk in the face of uncertainty. Entering a market that has the same language, a similar distribution system, and similar customers is less difficult than entering a market in which all these variables are different.

Techniques of Making Market Selection Decisions

The framework for making market selection decisions usually follows the systematic screening process shown in Figure 5.2. Different techniques can be used to accomplish the screening processes. These techniques vary from simple listings of selection criteria to complex combinations of different criteria into an index. These techniques will be discussed individually.

Listing of Selection Criteria

The simplest way to screen countries is to develop a set of criteria that are required as a minimum for a country to move through the stages of the screening process. To illustrate the screening methodology, we have outlined the screening process that can be used by a manufacturer of kidney dialysis equipment (see Table 5.5).

The minimum cutoff number for each criterion will be established by management. As we move through the screening process, the criteria become more specific. The following text will give the rationale for each of the screening criteria and cut-off point.

Macrolevel Gross National Product   Introduction of dialysis equipment in a new market requires a significant support function, including salespeople, service people, replacement parts inventory, and an ensured continuous supply of dialysate fluid, needles, tubing, and

TABLE 5.5 ● Screening Process Example: Targeting Countries for Kidney Dialysis Equipment

Filter number	Type of screening	Specific criteria
1	Macrolevel research	GDP over $15 billion GDP per capita over $1,500
2	General market factors relating to the product	Less than 200 people per hospital bed Less than 1,000 people per doctor Government expenditures over $100 million for health care Government expenditures over $20 per capita for health care
3	Microlevel factors specific to the product	Kidney-related deaths over 1,000 Patient use of dialysis equipment—over 40 percent growth in treated population
4	Final screening of target markets	Numbers of competitors Political stability

so on. Some countries lack the technical infrastructure to support such high-level technology. Therefore, management may decide only to consider countries having a minimum size of $15 billion GDP or GNP, thus excluding many of the developing economies of the world from consideration. (Note that the dialysis screening was done with 1985 data.) Also, dialysis requires substantial government support. A tradeoff then develops between acceptable expenditures for dialysis and acceptable kidney-related death rates. GDP per capita is an indicator of the level at which this tradeoff will occur. The lower the GDP per capita, the lower the expected government expenditure for dialysis equipment, given other pressing societal needs such as food and shelter. Therefore, the GDP per capita over $1,500 would have been set as a minimum. These economic factors would have limited the market to the following twenty-eight countries in the world, excluding North America:

All of Europe except Hungary

Iceland

U.S.S.R.

New Zealand

South Africa

Brazil

Venezuela

Australia

Iran

Argentina

Iraq

General Market Factors Related to the Product: Medical Concentration   Hemodialysis is a sophisticated procedure that requires medical personnel with advanced training. In order for a country to support advanced medical equipment, it requires a high level of medical specialization. Higher levels of medical concentration allow doctors the luxury of specialization in a field such as nephrology (the study of kidneys).

Management may determine that a population of less than 1,000 per doctor and a population of less than 200 per hospital bed indicate that medical personnel will be able to achieve the level of specialization needed to support a hemodialysis program. This second step of the screening process would have eliminated Iran, Iraq, Brazil, and Venezuela. As can be expected, the majority of countries with high GNP and GDP per capita have a high level of medical concentration.

Public health expenditures show the government's contribution to the medical care of its citizens—a factor of obvious importance in hemodialysis. Management may believe that countries that do not invest substantially in the health care of their population generally are not interested in making an even more substantial investment in a hemodialysis program. Thus, countries that do not have a minimum of $20 expenditure per capita or $100 million in total expenditures for health care would have been eliminated from consideration. This would have screened out Austria, Portugal, Yugoslavia, the U.S.S.R., and South

Africa. Thus, nineteen countries have the ability to purchase and satisfactorily support dialysis equipment. Dialysis programs were already under way in most of these countries.

The third stage of the screening process will identify which countries will provide the best opportunities for the sale of kidney dialysis machines.

Microlevel Factors Specific to the Product   Management may decide that there are two microlevel factors to consider: (1) the number of kidney-related deaths and (2) the growth rate of the treated patient population.

1. *Kidney-related deaths:* The number of deaths due to kidney failure is a good indicator of the number of people in each country who could have used dialysis equipment. The company will be interested only in countries with a minimum of 1,000 deaths per year due to kidney-related causes. A lower death rate indicates that the country has little need for dialysis equipment or that the market is currently being well served by competitive equipment. The Netherlands, Argentina, Norway, Switzerland, and Sweden would have been eliminated from analysis on these grounds.

2. *Growth rate of the treated patient population:* Analysis of the growth rate of the kidney treatment population demonstrates a growth in potential demand. Newly opened markets with the greatest growth potential are the best targets for a new supplier of dialysis equipment. These are the countries in which the treated patient population continues to grow at a minimum of 40 percent per year. This criterion would have excluded all but the following: Italy, with 75.1 percent; Greece, with 63.4 percent; and Spain, with 60.1 percent. Competition in all three of these markets is substantially less than in the United States, Japan, and the remainder of western Europe.

Final Screening of Target Markets   The screening process identified three target countries. To select one of these countries, an analysis of the competition and political stability is conducted. Discussions with the five major suppliers of dialysis equipment may indicate that Italy already has two local suppliers. Greece is being served by the four major European suppliers. Spain has a strong preference for U.S. equipment and is served by only one supplier. An evaluation of the political environment in each country would have indicated that Greece has a stable government; Italy's government is stable but is not increasing its medical expenditures; Spain is making a transition to a stable democracy.

After evaluating the data, management would most likely have selected Spain for the initial market entry. The final decision would have been based on the following review of each market. Greece would have been discounted as a potential market for the following reasons:

1. There is significant competition from other companies.

2. The corporate income tax is higher than that of Spain.

3. Products are subject to a "turnover" tax.

4. There is a high inflation rate.

Similarly, Italy would have been discounted for these reasons:

1. There is extensive foreign as well as local competition.
2. The projected growth for dialysis equipment is slower than in Spain.
3. Products are subject to a 14 percent value-added tax.
4. There is an extremely high inflation rate.

Spain would have been chosen for the following reasons:

1. The political outlook is stable. It appears that the transition to democracy will continue.
2. There is aggressive government support for health care.
3. There is a very high growth rate predicted for kidney equipment (23 percent).
4. Competition at this time is minimal.
5. There is no value-added tax.
6. Government subsidies for home use of dialysis equipment will stimulate demand.
7. The inflation rate is lower than in Italy or Greece.
8. U.S. products and firms have a good reputation in the country.

The screening of markets for dialysis equipment is an example of how to analyze the world market and select a few countries for entry. The screening process must be tailored to the specific product or service.

Market Indexes for Country Selection

Another technique for analyzing country selection criteria is to develop indexes that combine statistical data and allow the marketer to look at a large number of variables quickly. For example, for the past thirty years *Business International* has published market indicators that allow managers to quickly compare country opportunities. *Business International* publishes three indexes: market size, market growth, and market intensity.

Market size is the measure of total potential based on the total population (double-weighted), urban population, private consumption expenditure, steel consumption, cement and electricity production, and ownership of telephones, cars, and televisions. *Market growth* is an indicator of the rate of increase in the size of the market. The growth is determined based on an average of several indicators over five years: population, steel consumption, cement and electricity production; and ownership of passenger cars, trucks, buses, televisions, and telephones. The *market intensity* index measures the richness of a market or the concentration of purchasing power. The average world intensity is designated as 1.0, and each country is calculated in proportion to the average world intensity. Intensity is calculated for each market by averaging the per capita consumption of steel, ownership of telephones and televisions, production of cement and electricity levels, private consumption expenditure (double-weight), ownership of passenger cars (double-weight), and proportion of urban population (double-weight). Figure 5.3 shows the twenty largest coun-

FIGURE 5.3 ● *Business International* Market Indexes: Size, Growth, and Intensity of the Twenty Largest Markets

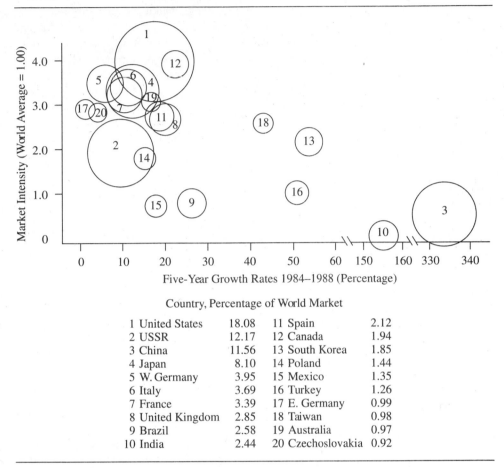

Country, Percentage of World Market

1 United States	18.08	11 Spain	2.12
2 USSR	12.17	12 Canada	1.94
3 China	11.56	13 South Korea	1.85
4 Japan	8.10	14 Poland	1.44
5 W. Germany	3.95	15 Mexico	1.35
6 Italy	3.69	16 Turkey	1.26
7 France	3.39	17 E. Germany	0.99
8 United Kingdom	2.85	18 Taiwan	0.98
9 Brazil	2.58	19 Australia	0.97
10 India	2.44	20 Czechoslovakia	0.92

Note: The position of the center of each circle shows the intensity of the market (when measured against the vertical axis) and its cumulative growth over the 1984–1988 period (when measured against the horizontal axis). The size of the circles indicates the relative size of the markets as a percentage of the total world market. See text for definitions and methodology.

Source: Business International. 1990 edition. Reprinted by permission.

tries and their percentages of the world market. The size of the circle represents the relative market size.

Ongoing Market Screening

The market screening process requires a significant amount of effort. After the target country is selected, there is a tendency to focus on the selected markets and ignore the rejected countries. However, the world market is continually changing, and countries that were rejected last year may provide significant opportunities just one year later. For example, Finland has long favored domestic banks, making it very difficult for foreign banks to operate. The move toward a single European market has caused Finland to become concerned about the limited access it provides to its banking market. So Finland's financial markets are suddenly much more accessible. The events in eastern Europe have also made countries such as Poland more attractive.

Political and economic events can also make an attractive market suddenly undesirable. Iraq and Jordan became less attractive after the invasion of Kuwait, as did Serbia and Bosnia in the former Yugoslavia, after the intense internal conflict and tight U.N. sanctions.[13] For most companies, it is necessary to have an ongoing monitoring and screening of world markets to spot new emerging opportunities, as well as to identify potential risks.

Grouping International Markets

There are many ways to group international markets. The chapters on political, economic, and cultural environments demonstrated that the interaction between these variables causes each country to be unique, therefore making it difficult to group countries together. Despite these difficulties, it is often necessary to group countries together so they can be considered as a single market or as a group of similar markets. In this segment of the chapter, we explore the rationale for grouping markets and the various ways that marketers can group countries together.

Rationale for Grouping Markets

The two principles that often drive the need for larger market groupings are critical mass and economies of scale. *Critical mass,* a term used in physics and military strategy, indicates that a minimum amount of effort is necessary before any impact will be achieved. *Economies of scale* is a term used in production situations; it means that greater levels of production result in lower costs per unit, which obviously increases profitability.

The costs of marketing products within a group of countries are lower for three reasons. First, the potential volume to be sold in a group of countries is sufficient to support a full marketing effort. Second, geographic proximity makes it easy to travel from one country to another, often in two hours or less. Third, the barriers to entry are often the same in countries within an economic grouping—for example, the European Union. Finally, in pursuing countries with similar markets, a company gains leverage with marketing programs.

---

13. ''Tighter Sanctions Unlikely to Hasten War's End,'' *Financial Times,* April 22, 1993, p. 3.

Marketing Activities Influenced by Country Groupings

The major activities used to enter a new market are market research, product development or modification, distribution, and promotion. Each of these activities can be influenced by economies of scale and critical mass. In this section, we will show how each of these four activities relates to country groupings.[14]

Market Research   In the screening process, marketers use many readily available secondary sources of market information. As stated previously, these secondary sources are acceptable for selecting target countries, but they are not sufficient to develop a marketing strategy to penetrate a specific market. Before entering a new market, the company will need to invest in the acquisition of knowledge about the specific aspects of marketing the product in each country. Normally, the following questions must be answered:

1. Who makes the purchase decisions?

2. What decision criteria do consumers use to select the product?

3. How must the product be modified?

4. What are the channels of distribution?

5. What are the competitive price levels?

These and many other questions must be answered before the first product can be shipped. The cost of this knowledge will often be higher than domestic market research, due to the distance to travel, cultural differences, and language differences. Given the sizable investment required to obtain this firsthand market knowledge, there are economies of scale if two or more countries can be included in the same market research study.

Product Development/Modification   Development of new products and modifications of current products require a large investment. Given the cost, there are obvious economies of scale when these costs are spread over a number of markets. This is particularly true if the markets are similar, so that the same modified product can be sold in a number of markets. For example, Procter & Gamble's Head & Shoulders dandruff shampoo is manufactured in a single European plant; however, the company takes advantage of European Union regulations by selling the product throughout Europe with a ''Eurobottle'' label in eight languages.[15]

Distribution   The distribution aspect of marketing is particularly important in serving international markets. In the case of exporting, the marketer is faced with all the mechanics of getting the product from the domestic market to the foreign market, which includes documentation, insurance, and financial arrangements. Also, the shipping rates will vary,

14. Vern Terpstra, ''Critical Mass and International Marketing Strategy,'' *Journal of Academy of Marketing Sciences,* Summer 1983.
15. ''Unilever Aims to Bolster Lines in U.S.'' *Wall Street Journal,* June 19, 1987, p. 6.

depending on the size of the shipment. Less than carload- or container-sized orders will be at a higher price per pound than full carloads or containers. The mechanics and shipping aspects of exporting are influenced by economies of scale and critical mass. If one only plans to ship a small amount each month to a South American country, it may not be worth the effort. Without a critical mass of business, it does not pay to learn the mechanics and process the paperwork. Also, if you do not have sufficient volumes to ship, transportation costs will escalate.

The distribution systems within foreign markets also are influenced by the number of markets served. Many distributors and dealers in foreign markets handle numerous markets. For example, Caps Gemini, a large software development and distribution firm, has operations in every European country. Given the multicountry nature of many distributors, it is usually beneficial to enter a group of similar markets through the same distribution channels.

Promotion   A major task of the international company is promotion, which includes advertising and personal selling. Advertising is used as a communication device to give customers a message about a product via television, radio, or print media. In many parts of the world, these three forms of communication cross country boundaries. For example, a message on German television will be seen in Switzerland. Also, it's much cheaper to shoot one commercial for all of Europe and to have one Euromarket manager with junior product managers for each country rather than full marketing managers at country levels.[16] So, there may be economies of scale in grouping two or more markets together when entering a new area.

Selling is a very important part of the promotional process, which usually requires a local sales force. Establishing and managing a sales force is a large fixed expense that lends itself to economies of scale. Spreading the cost of a sales office, rent, secretarial staff, sales support, sales managers, and sometimes the salesperson over two or three countries can be very cost effective.

Growth of Formal Market Groups

Countries have used the concept of market groupings for centuries. The British Commonwealth preference system linked the markets of the United Kingdom, Canada, Australia, New Zealand, India, and former colonies in Africa, Asia, and the Middle East. The growth of market groups since World War II was encouraged by the success of the European Economic Community, now called the European (EU) Union. The EU is being replaced by the European Economic Area (EEA), which includes the EU plus five (Austria, Fin-

16. ''A Universal Message, Pan-European Ads Are Increasingly Common,'' *Financial Times,* May 27, 1993, p. 18.

land, Norway, Sweden, and Ireland) of the seven members of the European Free Trade Association.[17]

As discussed in Chapter 2, a market group is created when two or more countries agree to reduce trade and tariff barriers between themselves, therefore creating a trade unit. Successful trade units or market groups are based on favorable economic, political, or geographic factors. A country will agree to join a trade unit based on one or more of these factors, *if* the expected benefits of becoming part of the trade unit exceed the disadvantages and loss of sovereignty caused by joining the group.

Economic Factors

The major benefit of every market group is usually economic. Member countries of the group experience reduced or eliminated tariffs and duties that stimulate trade between member countries. They also have common tariff barriers against firms from nonmember countries. Joining together with other countries gives members a greater economic security, reducing the impact of competition from member countries and increasing the group's strength against foreign competitors. For example, when the United States planned to impose tariffs on French cheese, Italian wine, Greek olives, and Danish ham, the twelve-nation European Union was ready to retaliate with tariffs on U.S. wheat, rice, and corn.[18]

Consumers benefit from the reduced trade barriers through lower prices. Economies that are complementary rather than directly competitive tend to make better members of a market group. Most of the problems within the European Union have revolved around agricultural products; member countries are threatened by products, such as eggs, milk, and chicken, from other member countries.

Political Factors

In most countries, the political system and its ideology are dominant forces. The political system usually reflects the aspirations of the nation. It's easy to see, then, why market groups are made up of countries with similar political aspirations. A major impetus for the original formation of the European Community was the need for a unified entity to protect against the political threat of the former U.S.S.R.

Geographic Factors

Countries that share common borders tend to function better in a market group for the simple fact that it is easier to move goods back and forth across the truck and railroad systems. Also, countries that share boundaries have experienced each other's cultures and probably have a history of trade.

17. "EEA Links 17 Nations in the World's Largest Free Trade Zone," *Financial Times,* January 1–3, 1994, p. 1.
18. "A Duty to Pay for Government Items," *Insight,* January 26, 1987, p. 46.

Types of Market Groups

There are five different types of market groups: free trade area, customs union, common market, economic union, and political union. A country may enter an agreement with another country or group of countries, using one of these five types of groups. The level of integration and cooperation between countries will depend on the type of group they form. Figure 5.4 shows which aspects of international integration are included in each type of agreement.

Major Market Groups

Market agreements that formed the major market groups are shown in Table 5.6. The next sections describe most of these market groups and the agreements that brought them together. The sections are divided according to geographic area.

Europe   Europe has four major market groups: the European Economic Area (EEA), European Union (EU), European Free Trade Area (EFTA), and Commonwealth of Independent States (CIS).

FIGURE 5.4 ● Forms of International Integration

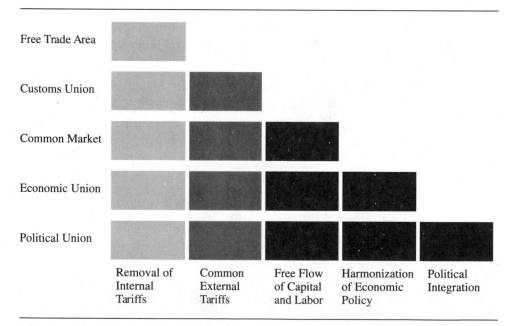

Source: Ruel K. Kahler and Roland L. Kramer, *International Marketing,* 5th ed., p. 343. Reprinted by permission of Southwestern Publishing Company.

TABLE 5.6 ● Summary of Market Agreements

Member countries	Population (in millions)	GNP (in billions of U.S. dollars)	GNP per capita (in U.S. dollars)
EUROPEAN AGREEMENTS			
European Union (EU) (customs union)			
Belgium	10	209.6	20,880
Denmark	5.2	133.9	25,930
France	57.3	1,278.7	22,300
Germany	80.6	1,846.1	23,030
Greece	10.5	75.1	7,180
Ireland	3.5	42.8	12,100
Italy	57.8	1,186.6	20,510
Luxembourg	.4	13.7	35,260
Netherlands	15.2	312.4	20,590
Portugal	9.8	73.3	7,450
Spain	39.1	547.9	14,020
United Kingdom	57.7	1,024.8	17,760
Total	347.1	6,744.9	19,432
European Free Trade Association (EFTA) (free trade area)			
Austria	7.9	174.8	17,070
Finland	5.1	116.3	22,980
Iceland	.3	6.2	23,670
Liechtenstein	.03	.5	16,964
Norway	4.3	110.5	25,800
Sweden	8.7	233.2	26,780
Switzerland	6.9	248.7	3,623
Total	33.23	890.2	26,789
Commonwealth of Independent States (CIS) (ad hoc group)			
Azerbaijan	7.1	6.3	870
Armenia	3.5	2.7	780
Belarus	10.3	30.1	2,910
Estonia	1.6	4.3	2,750
Georgia	5.5	4.7	850
Kazakhstan	16.9	28.6	1,680
Kyrgyzstan	4.5	3.6	810
Latvia	2.6	5.0	1,930
Lithuania	3.8	4.9	1,310
Moldova	4.4	5.5	1,260
Russia	148.9	397.8	2,680
Tajikistan	5.6	2.7	480
Turkmenistan	3.9	4.9	1,270

TABLE 5.6 ● Summary of Market Agreements (*Continued*)

Member countries	Population (in millions)	GNP (in billions of U.S. dollars)	GNP per capita (in U.S. dollars)
EUROPEAN AGREEMENTS (continued)			
Ukraine	52.1	87.0	1,670
Uzbekistan	21.3	18.4	860
Total	292.0	606.5	2,077
AFRICAN AGREEMENTS			
Afro-Malagasy Economic Union (economic union)			
Benin	5.0	2.0	410
Cameroon	12.2	10.0	820
Central African Republic	3.2	1.3	410
Chad	5.9	1.3	410
Gabon	1.2	5.3	4,450
Ivory Coast	12.8	8.7	670
Mali	8.9	2.7	300
Mauretania	2.1	1.1	580
Niger	8.2	2.5	300
Zaire	2.4	2.5	1,030
Total	61.9	37.4	604
East Africa Customs Union (customs union)			
Ethiopia	54.8	6.2	110
Kenya	25.8	8.5	330
Sudan	26.5	10.1	420
Tanzania	25.9	2.6	110
Uganda	17.4	2.9	170
Zambia	8.5	2.6	290
Total	158.9	32.9	207
West African Economic Community (WAEC) (common market)			
Burkina Faso	9.5	2.9	290
Ivory Coast	12.8	8.7	670
Mali	8.9	2.7	300
Mauretania	2.0	1.1	530
Niger	8.1	2.5	300
Senegal	7.8	6.1	730
Total	49.1	24.0	489
Maghreb Economic Community (common market)			
Algeria	26.3	48.3	1,830
Libya	4.8	22.9	5,410
Morocco	26.2	27.2	1,040
Tunisia	8.4	14.6	1,740
Total	65.7	113.0	1,720

TABLE 5.6 ● Summary of Market Agreements (*Continued*)

Member countries	Population *(in millions)*	GNP (in billions of U.S. dollars)	GNP per capita (in U.S. dollars)
AFRICAN AGREEMENTS (continued)			
Casablanca Group (free trade area)			
Egypt	54.8	34.5	630
Ghana	15.8	7.0	450
Guinea	6.0	3.1	510
Morocco	26.2	27.2	1,040
Total	102.8	71.8	698
Economic Community of West African States (ECOWAS) *(customs union)*			
Benin	3.2	2.1	410
Burkina Faso	9.5	2.9	290
Cape Verde	.4	.3	850
Gambia	.9	.4	390
Ghana	15.8	7.1	450
Guinea	6.0	3.1	510
Guinea-Bissau	1.0	.2	210
Ivory Coast	12.8	8.7	670
Liberia	2.7	—	—
Mali	8.9	2.7	300
Mauretania	2.0	1.1	530
Niger	8.1	2.4	300
Nigeria	101.9	32.9	320
Senegal	7.8	6.1	780
Sierra Leone	4.3	.7	170
Togo	3.9	1.6	400
Total	189.2	72.3	298
AMERICAN AGREEMENTS			
Latin American Integration Association (LAIA) *(free trade area)*			
Argentina	33	200.3	6,050
Bolivia	7.5	5.0	680
Brazil	153.9	425.4	2,770
Chile	13.6	37.1	2,730
Colombia	33.4	44.6	1,290
Ecuador	11.0	11.8	1,070
Mexico	84.9	294.8	3,470
Paraguay	4.5	6.0	1,340
Peru	22.4	21.3	950
Uruguay	3.2	10.4	3,340
Venezuela	20.3	58.9	2,900
Total	387.7	1,115.6	2,876

TABLE 5.6 ● Summary of Market Agreements (*Continued*)

	Member countries	Population (in millions)	GNP (in billions of U.S. dollars)	GNP per capita (in U.S. dollars)
AMERICAN AGREEMENTS (continued)				
North American Free Trade Agreement (free trade area)	Canada	27.8	565.8	20,320
	Mexico	84.9	294.8	3,470
	United States	255.4	5,904.8	23,120
	Total	368.1	6,765.4	18,398
Central American Common Market (common market)	Costa Rica	3.1	6.3	2,000
	El Salvador	5.4	6.3	1,170
	Guatemala	9.7	9.6	980
	Honduras	5.4	3.1	580
	Nicaragua	3.9	1.3	410
	Total	27.5	26.6	967
Andean Common Market (ANCOM) *(common market)*	Bolivia	7.5	5.1	680
	Colombia	33.4	44.6	1,290
	Ecuador	11.0	11.9	1,070
	Peru	22.3	21.3	950
	Venezuela	20.3	58.9	2,900
	Total	94.5	141.8	1,678
Southern Common Market (MerCoSur) *(common market)*	Argentina	33.0	200.3	6,050
	Brazil	153.8	425.4	2,770
	Paraguay	4.5	6.0	1,340
	Uruguay	3.1	10.4	3,340
	Total	194.4	642.1	3,303
Caribbean Community and Common Market (Caricom) *(common market)*	Antigua and Barbuda	.08	.39	4,870
	Barbados	.26	1.69	6,530
	Belize	.20	.44	2,210
	Dominica	.07	.18	2,520
	Grenada	.09	.21	2,310
	Guyana	.8	.27	330
	Jamaica	2.4	3.2	1,340
	Saint Kitts–Nevis	.04	.18	3,990
	Saint Lucia	.16	.45	2,900
	Saint Vincent	.11	.22	1,990
	Trinidad and Tobago	1.3	4.9	3,940
	Total	5.51	12.13	2,130

TABLE 5.6 ● Summary of Market Agreements (*Continued*)

Member countries	Population (in millions)	GNP (in billions of U.S. dollars)	GNP per capita (in U.S. dollars)
ASIAN AGREEMENTS			
Arab Common Market (ACM) *(common market)*			
Egypt	54.8	34.5	630
Iraq	19.1	—	—
Jordan	3.9	4.4	1,120
Syria	12.9	14.6	—
Kuwait	1.4	—	—
Total	92.1	53.5	—
Economic Cooperation Organization (ECO) *(ad hoc arrangement)*			
Afghanistan	21.5	14.5	675
Azerbaijan	7.1	6.2	870
Iran	59.8	130.9	2,190
Kazakhstan	16.9	28.6	1,680
Kyrgyzstan	4.5	3.7	810
Pakistan	119.3	49.5	410
Tajikistan	5.6	2.7	480
Turkey	58.5	114.2	1,950
Turkmenistan	3.9	4.9	1,270
Uzbekistan	21.3	18.4	860
Total	318.4	373.6	1,173
Association of South East Asian Nations (ASEAN) *(free trade area)*			
Brunei	.3	—	—
Indonesia	184.2	122.9	670
Malaysia	18.6	51.9	2,790
Singapore	2.8	44.3	15,750
Philippines	64.2	49.5	770
Thailand	67.9	106.6	1,840
Total	328.0	375.2	1,213
OTHER MAJOR COUNTRIES			
Australia	17.5	299.3	17,070
China	1,166	442.4	380
Hong Kong	5.8	89.3	15,380
India	883.5	271.6	310
Israel	5.1	67.7	13,230
Japan	124.3	3,507.8	28,220
New Zealand	3.4	41.2	12,060

TABLE 5.6 ● Summary of Market Agreements (*Continued*)

Member countries	Population (in millions)	GNP (in billions of U.S. dollars)	GNP per capita (in U.S. dollars)
OTHER MAJOR COUNTRIES (continued)			
Saudi Arabia	15.9	126.4	7,940
South Africa	39.8	106	2,670
South Korea	43.7	296.4	6,790
Yugoslavia	10.6	—	—

Source: Reprinted from *The World Bank Atlas,* © 1994, data for 1992. Used with permission.

The European Economic Area was officially begun on January 1, 1994, and includes the twelve member countries of the European Union (to be discussed later) plus five (Austria, Finland, Norway, Sweden, and Iceland) of the seven EFTA (to be discussed later) countries.[19] EEA grew out of a 1984 agreement between the EU (which was called European Community at the time) and EFTA to join together to form the European Economic Space (EES).[20] It took ten years to form the EEA because of the difficulty of getting EFTA countries to agree to the rules and policies established by the EU, especially the legal strictures against monopolies and state aid to businesses.[21] To the dismay of the other EFTA members, Switzerland voted by referendum in December 1992 not to join the EEA. Unfortunately, due to the customs union between Switzerland and Liechtenstein, the latter also could not join the EEA.

EEA is the world's largest free trade zone, with 372 million consumers and an annual gross domestic produce of $6.6 trillion.[22] EEA allows for free movement of goods, capital, services, and people across borders of these seventeen nations. EEA abides by all the EU legislation, except in the area of agricultural policy and some special provisions for fisheries, energy, and transport.[23]

Austria, Finland, Norway, and Sweden are all actively pursuing full membership into the EU by 1995 because until they are members of the EU, they cannot influence EU legislation. EEA has become a first step toward full EU membership, and a safety net if EU negotiations fail.[24]

The European Union was established in 1993 as a result of the drive toward a single market by the twelve members of the European Community (EC) in 1992. With the removal of all internal tariffs and common external tariffs and the free flow of goods,

19. "EEA Links 17 Nations," pp. 1, 22.
20. "European Economic Area," *Economist,* January 8, 1994, pp. 49–50.
21. Ibid.
22. Ibid.
23. "EEA Links 17 Nations," p. 22.
24. Ibid.

capital, and people, the EU is a true common market. The twelve members of the EU have agreed to the Maastricht Treaty, which will establish the European Monetary Union (EMU) between 1997 and 1999.[25] The EMU would unite the currencies of the EU members, with a European central bank dictating economic policy to the member country banks. The outlook for EMU is questionable, given the disagreement between the Germans, who want a strong European central bank, and the United Kingdom, Italy, and Spain, who support a more flexible approach.

The EU, referred to as the European Community until 1993, was called the European Common Market when it was established in 1958. The EU has grown from the original six countries to twelve countries, increasing its role over time through the establishment of the European Parliament, the Court of Justice, and the European currency unit (ECU).

The relaunch of the EU and the creation of the Single European Market, often referred to as ''1992,'' were initiated by Lord Cockfield. He was the British commissioner to the EU and authored the internal market white paper published on June 14, 1985.[26] The white paper explained the logic for a single market and summarized the impediments into three areas: physical barriers at frontiers, technical barriers within different countries, and barriers designed to protect fiscal regimes. It took two years for the white paper to be approved by EU members and become the Single Market Act. There was a strong logic for the single market. Europe, while bigger than the United States and Japan in population, was underperforming its two largest competitors on almost every measure. In 1987, 11.7 percent of the EU working population was unemployed, compared to 6.7 percent in the United States and 3.2 percent in Japan.[27]

The EU commissioned a number of studies to measure the potential impact of a single market. Paolo Cecchini, a senior official of the EU, coordinated thirty different studies and published the economics of 1992 in spring 1988.[28] This report, known as the Cecchini report, documented the costs of continuing in a divided market and the benefits of building an integrated one.[29] The report summarized the economic gains if the EU implemented the single market as follows:

- A rejuvenation of the EU economy, adding 4.5 percent to GDP
- A reduction in inflation, with a fall in consumer prices of 6.1 percent
- A reduction in the cost of public programs through open bidding
- The creation of 1.8 million new jobs in the EU, reducing unemployment[30]

25. ''Learning to Fly,'' *Economist,* January 15, 1994, pp. 75–76.

26. Lord Cockfield, ''Completing the Internal Market,'' white paper to the European Council (Luxembourg: Office of Publications of the European Communities, 1985).

27. Catherine Taylor and Alison Press, *1992: The Facts and Challenges* (London: Industrial Society, 1988), p. xi.

28. Nicholas Colchester and David Buchan, *Europe Relaunched* (London: Economist Books, 1990), pp. 32–33.

29. Paolo Cecchini, *The European Challenge 1992: The Benefits of a Single Market* (London: Wildwood House, 1988).

30. James W. Dudley, *1992 Strategies for the Single Market* (London: Kogan Page, 1989), pp. 34–35.

To illustrate the potential impact of 1992, consider the pharmaceutical industry. The drug industry has a separate regulatory body, applying its own criteria for approving medicines, and mutual approval of licenses is nonexistent. Each country has a different system for pricing and paying for drugs. Also, rules regarding drug advertising vary from country to country. Within the spirit of the single market, the European Union is moving on several fronts to harmonize the EU drug industry. There are plans for a central European medicines agency to open by 1996. This agency will test drugs for use throughout the EU. Also, the twelve member countries will still be able to test and license drugs, but after a company has approval in one country, the drug manufacturer will be able to request a license from the other member states, based on the principle of mutual recognition. The European Union has also stated that it plans to develop a European drug pricing system, but specific proposals have not been issued.[31] If the new approach to drug licensing is implemented, it will radically reduce the cost and time to launch drugs in Europe.

The European Free Trade Association was created in 1959 by countries that did not join the EU. EFTA, consisting of Austria, Finland, Iceland, Liechtenstein, Norway, Sweden, and Switzerland, operates as a free trade area. As the EU single market became a reality in 1992, the EFTA countries quickly negotiated to ensure they were not blocked access to the large EU market. Four of the seven EFTA members are negotiating to join the EU, and five of the seven have joined EEA, as discussed earlier. Long term, EFTA will probably play a minor role as an independent market group.

The collapse of the Berlin Wall in 1989, the breakup of the fifteen republics of the Soviet Union (e.g., Estonia, Latvia, Lithuania), and the opening of eastern Europe to free elections in 1990 resulted in the creation of the Commonwealth of Independent States. CIS is really a very loose collection of nations that replaces the Council for Mutual Economic Assistance (COMECON).

The future of CIS as a single market group is doubtful. The east European countries of Poland, Hungary, and the Czech Republic have agreed to cooperate with EFTA on trade, economic, industrial, and scientific issues; tourism; transport; communications; and environmental pollution. Given the economic and political difficulties in Russia, the former republics are more likely to cooperate with the western European groups than with Russia.

Russia, with 150 million citizens hungry for consumer goods, is the largest single market in CIS. While the risks are high, the potential is great. Hewlett-Packard had a 400 percent increase in sales in 1993, and many others (e.g., Philip Morris, RJR Nabisco, Coca-Cola, Pratt & Whitney, Bristol-Myers Squibb) have invested in Russia.[32] Otis Elevator has three joint ventures in Russia, and company president George David says, "We don't expect to make any money before the next century, but patience is the key."[33]

Prior to the collapse of the Berlin Wall in 1989, the major group of communist countries was COMECON. COMECON was formed in 1949 as a political union of eight eastern European communist countries, later joined by Cuba and Vietnam. Until 1990,

31. Clive Cookson, "In Search of Harmony to Cure Europe's Ills," *Financial Times,* March 11, 1991, p. 4.
32. "Rising in Russia," *Fortune,* January 24, 1994, pp. 93, 95.
33. Ibid., p. 95.

these ten countries were tightly controlled by the Soviet Union, and COMECON operated as an enforced political group. COMECON countries depended on the U.S.S.R. as a major customer. In exchange, the U.S.S.R. provided oil and defenses against NATO forces.

COMECON countries were dissatisfied with their forced cooperation with the U.S.S.R. At a COMECON summit in 1988, they complained about intracountry pricing, lack of currency convertibility, and slow economic growth. Matters were made worse in 1989 when the Soviets decided that trade with COMECON should be at world market pricing based on hard currency instead of rubles (the COMECON unit of account).[34] So in January 1991, the eastern European countries had to start paying for Soviet oil at world prices in hard currency. Prior to that, they were exchanging manufactured goods for Russian oil.[35] In addition to these problems, the demand for goods from East Germany and the U.S.S.R. dropped suddenly. As East and West Germany merged, East German factories struggled for survival in the new Germany and canceled contracts with their former COMECON partners.[36] Many Soviet contracts also evaporated. For example, the Ikarus bus factory in Hungary almost closed after losing most of the Soviet buyers of 15,000 buses per year.[37] COMECON was dissolved in 1992.

Africa The continent of Africa has seven major market agreements in force: Afro-Malagasy Economic Union, East Africa Customs Union, Maghreb Economic Community, Casablanca Group, Economic Community of West African States, West African Economic Community, and French African Community. The success of the EC has prompted African countries to get together to form these groups. Unfortunately, however, the groups have had little success in promoting trade and economic progress, because most African nations are small and have limited economic infrastructure to produce goods.

The French African Community (CFA) was established in 1985 as a monetary union. The member countries have fixed their currencies to the French franc. Since 1985, the combination of declining prices, tax, fiscal and monetary policies, and the appreciation of the French franc against the U.S. dollar have resulted in a 30 percent currency appreciation, which has reduced the competitiveness of exports from these countries.[38]

Latin America There are five major market agreements in Latin America: Andean Common Market, Central American Common Market, Caribbean Community and Common Market, Latin American Integration Association, and the Southern Common Market. Latin America faces a number of problems that make it difficult to achieve significant economic integration and cooperation between countries. Political turmoil, the low level of economic

34. ''COMECON—Busting Open Eastern Europe,'' *Economist,* December 16, 1989, p. 84.

35. Daniel Franklin, ''Eastern Europe's Gloomy Boom,'' in *The World in 1991* (London: Economist Publications, 1991), p. 60.

36. Anthony Robinson, ''Forward to a New Society,'' Survey—Eastern Europe in Transition, *Financial Times,* February 4, 1991, p. 11.

37. ''Welcome to This Cruel, Competitive World,'' *Economist,* August 11, 1990, p. 41.

38. ''Devaluation Is Overdue,'' Special section: Africa: A Continent at Stake, *Financial Times,* September 1, 1993, p. vii.

activity, and extreme differences in economic development from country to country are stumbling blocks to the success of these market agreements.

The Andean Common Market has sped up its reduction of tariffs with the free trade zone through the elimination of all tariffs between member countries. Economic realities have sidelined many ideological struggles in Latin America. As Ecuador's minister of industries and commerce said, "We decided to take a risk. Rather than seeing the dangers of trading with a more developed country such as Columbia, we began seeing the opportunities. If Mexico was seeking free trade with the United States, then it was because they saw opportunities of growth."[39]

The Southern Common Market, called MerCoSur, has been reducing internal barriers every six months since 1991, hoping to eliminate all tariffs by January 1, 1995. Global companies such as Monsanto, Ford, Kodak, and Volkswagen are taking advantage of this large market by investing in factories to serve the region.[40]

The Caribbean Community and Common Market (Caricom) group of thirteen Caribbean nations represents only six million people and is working closely with NAFTA to develop a trading relationship or possibly receive preferential treatment for textiles, apparel, footwear and other leather goods, and petroleum. Caricom, working with GATT, was able to eliminate the EU's import regime, which favored fruit from former European colonies such as Martinique rather than from the cheaper Caricom countries.[41]

North America   The U.S.-Canada Free Trade Agreement, which became effective in 1989, removes barriers to trade and investment for most agricultural, industrial, and service businesses. The agreement eliminates tariffs for products manufactured in either country and then exported to the other. If less than 50 percent of the manufacturing cost takes place in the United States or Canada, then the goods are subject to the normal tariff. As two-thirds of Canada's imports from the United States were already duty free, the agreement has not had a large economic impact. The main impact of the agreement is a psychological "kick in the backside," according to an economist of the Canadian Manufacturing Association.[42]

The North American Free Trade Agreement (NAFTA) was signed by the heads of state of Canada, Mexico, and the United States in October 1992 and passed by the governments in late 1993. NAFTA provides for the gradual ending of tariffs and trade barriers, over ten years for most goods and services and over fifteen years for some agricultural products.[43] NAFTA has prompted many companies to invest in Mexico. For example, PepsiCo said it plans to invest $750 million over five years in Mexico.[44]

39. "Andes Nations Regain a Taste for Free Trade," *Financial Times,* December 8, 1992, p. 6.

40. "The New World's Newest Trade Bloc," *Business Week,* May 4, 1992, pp. 50–51.

41. "Caricom Summit to Discuss NAFTA Relief," *Financial Times,* July 6, 1993, p. 4.

42. Bernard Simon, "Trade Pact Brings Canada New Hopes and Fears," *Financial Times,* February 12, 1991, p. 3.

43. "North America Free Trade," Special section, *Financial Times,* May 12, 1993, p. 27.

44. "PepsiCo to Invest About $750 Million in Mexican Market," *Wall Street Journal,* April 5, 1993, p. B2.

Middle East There are two market agreements in the Middle East: the Arab Common Market and the Economic Cooperation Organization. The Arab Common Market was formed in 1964 by Egypt, Iraq, Kuwait, Jordan, and Syria. Progress has been achieved toward the development of free trade and eliminations of tariffs between member countries. Equalization of external tariff is expected in the future. The Economic Cooperation Organization (ECO) was originally established by Pakistan, Iran, and Turkey to expand mutual trade and business ventures. In late 1992, the countries of Afghanistan, Azerbaijan, Kyrgyzstan, Turkmenistan, Uzbekistan, Kazakhstan, and Tajikistan joined ECO. Primarily Islamic countries, ECO is sizable enough, with 300 million people, to support economic initiatives.[45]

Asia The Association of South East Asian Nations (ASEAN) includes Brunei, Indonesia, Malaysia, Singapore, the Philippines, and Thailand. All ASEAN countries, except Singapore, have an abundance of labor and developing economies. Seeking closer economic integration and cooperation between the member countries, ASEAN members began cutting intra-ASEAN tariffs in 1993, working toward an ASEAN free trade area by the year 2008.[46] The aim is to reduce most tariffs with ASEAN to a maximum of 5 percent in a series of cuts over fifteen years. Cement, rubber, wooden furniture, and textiles are included in the list of fifteen items for the first seven years.[47] Whirlpool believes that by 1995 the market for large home appliances will be larger in Asia then in the United States or Europe. This is why Whirlpool formed its Asian headquarters in Singapore in 1993.[48]

The Asia Pacific Economic Cooperative (APEC) initiative includes fifteen members, the six nations of ASEAN and the United States, Australia, Canada, New Zealand, Japan, South Korea, China, Hong Kong, and Taiwan. APEC was started by the United States and Australia to promote the multilateral interests of the member countries, especially at the Uruguay round of GATT talks. The APEC trade group has been supported by U.S. president Bill Clinton as his vision of the ''new Pacific community.'' EAEC, a subgroup of APEC, excludes the ''white'' countries of the United States, Canada, Australia, and New Zealand and is considered racist by its opponents. EAEC has agreed to operate as a caucus group within the APEC and can also operate independently.[49]

Malaysia has proposed the East Asia Economic Grouping (EAEG), which will include the six members of ASEAN plus North Korea, South Korea, Japan, Taiwan, Hong Kong, Vietnam, China, Taiwan, Australia, and New Zealand.

The future of country groupings in Asia is unclear. ASEAN is a weak grouping that has not been able to harmonize its own tariff structure. APEC is a weak collection of countries to promote trade, but it is not any type of formal union; no agreements have been formatted. Some of the most successful trading countries in the world are in Asia.

---

45. ''Central Asian Republics Join Trade Grouping,'' *Financial Times,* November 30, 1992, p. 2.

46. ''Progress Toward a Free Trade Area,'' *Financial Times,* December 2, 1992, p. 12.

47. ''Fortress Asia?'' *Economist,* October 24, 1992, p. 35.

48. ''Whirlpool Plans Asian Expansion Based in Singapore,'' *Financial Times,* February 19, 1993, p. 17.

49. ''Trade Rivalries Calmed by Pacific Message,'' *Financial Times,* August 2, 1993, p. 13.

The four dragons—Japan, Taiwan, Singapore, and Hong Kong—all have developed their expertise without the protection of a market grouping.[50] Also, the largest single market in the world is China, with 1.1 billion people. As capitalism begins to take hold in China, the gross domestic product is growing at 13 percent per year, and import growth is 30 percent per year. In fact, some argue that the growth of China along with the other East Asian economies will result in a shift in world power from the West to the East.[51]

International Buyers

All buyers go through a similar process to select a product or service for purchase. While the process will be similar from country to country, the final purchase decisions will vary because of the differences in the social, economic, and cultural systems. International buyers differ by who actually makes the decision to buy, what they buy, why they buy, how they buy, when they buy, and where they buy. To assume that buyers in different countries use the same buying processes and the same selection criteria can be disastrous. When launching baby diapers worldwide, Procter & Gamble established a global marketing team in Cincinnati, believing babies' diaper needs should be the same worldwide. They later found out that while mothers in most countries are concerned about keeping their babies' bottoms dry, Japanese mothers had different needs. In Japan, babies are changed so frequently that thick absorbent diapers were not necessary and could be replaced by thin diapers that take up less space in the small Japanese home.[52]

In every marketing situation, it is important to understand potential buyers and the process they use to select one product over another. Most elements of a marketing program are designed to influence the buyer to choose one product over competitors' products. Figure 5.5 summarizes a process that can be used to analyze the buyer.

In the case of each type of buyer—consumer, business, and government—the marketer must be able to identify who the buyers are, the size of the potential market, and how they make a purchase decision. For example, in automobile purchases in Italy, who usually makes the decision, the husband or wife? When a Japanese company purchases a computer system, what type of people are involved? Is price more important than the reputation of the computer manufacturer? When a young man in Germany decides to open a savings account, what information sources does he use to select a bank?

Having set a framework for understanding international buyers, we will examine each type of buyer—consumers, businesses, and governments—in the next sections.

50. "China's Government Is in a Jam," *Economist,* January 15, 1993, p. 35.

51. "Belief in an Imminent Asian Century Is Gaining Sway," *Wall Street Journal,* May 17, 1993, p. A12.

52. Brian Dumaine, "P&G Rewrites the Rules of Marketing," *Fortune,* November 6, 1989, p. 48.

FIGURE 5.5 ● International Buyer Analysis Process

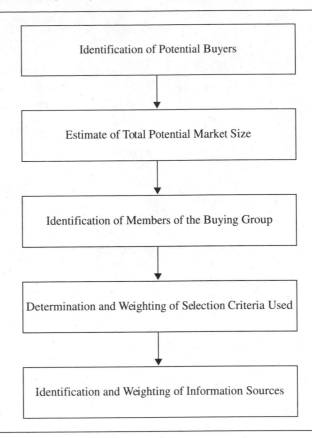

The Consumer Market

Consumers around the world have many similar needs. All people must eat, drink, and be sheltered from the elements. Once these basic needs are met, consumers will seek to improve their standard of living with a more comfortable environment, more leisure time, and an increased social status. While basic needs and the desire for an improved standard of living are universal throughout the world, people's ability to achieve these objectives is not universal. The economic, political, and social structure of countries affects the ability of consumers to fulfill their needs and the method they use. To understand a consumer market, one must examine the following four aspects of consumer behavior:

1. The ability of people to buy   *3.* Buying motives

2. Consumer needs   *4.* The buying process

Ability to Buy

To purchase a product, a consumer must have the ability to buy. The medium of exchange in most societies is currency. The ability to buy a product is affected by the amount of wealth a country possesses and the distribution of the wealth. A country accumulates wealth by the sale of goods to other countries (exports) and the sale of goods within the country. These inflows of money are offset by the outflows of money to pay for necessary imports.

A very important indicator of total consumer potential is gross national product (GNP) because it indicates the value of production in a country, which is an indicator of market size. The GNP per capita shows the value of production per consumer, which is a crude indicator of potential per consumer. The per capita national income is better than the GNP as a measure of gross consumer purchasing power, because it eliminates capital consumption and business taxes, which are not part of personal income. As shown in Table 5.6, GNP and GNP per capita can vary significantly from country to country.

The total wealth in a country is an important indicator of market potential. With a GNP per capita of $28,220 in Japan and $26,780 in Sweden, it is expected the demand for automobiles will be greater in those countries than in Niger or India, with GNPs per capita below $400.

The accumulated income (GNP) is divided among the members of a society. The government has a major influence on the distribution of wealth. A large government will take a large share of the wealth through taxes or ownership of industries. The government also sets policies and laws to regulate the distribution of wealth. For example, a graduated income tax with a 60 to 90 percent tax on high levels of income and no taxes on low levels of income will help to evenly distribute the income. The revenue that remains in the private sector will be distributed among workers, managers, and owners of the industries. Low wages and unemployment will tend to increase the size of the lower-income class. Concentration of business ownership in a few families will decrease the size of the upper class. The social structure of the country can also affect income distribution. For example, in Japan, where an emphasis is placed on group versus individual needs, 95 percent of the population reports that they are in the middle class.

Consumer Needs

Money is spent to fulfill basic human needs. One framework of consumer needs was developed by Abraham Maslow. Maslow's hierarchy of needs model explains that humans will tend to satisfy lower-level needs, such as the physiological need for food, clothing, and shelter, before attempting to satisfy higher-level needs such as safety, belongingness, or esteem. In Figure 5.6 the consumption patterns within different countries illustrate Maslow's theory. The figure shows that the structure of consumption for each country

FIGURE 5.6 ● Consumer Expenditure Patterns of Selected Countries (Percentage of Total Spending)

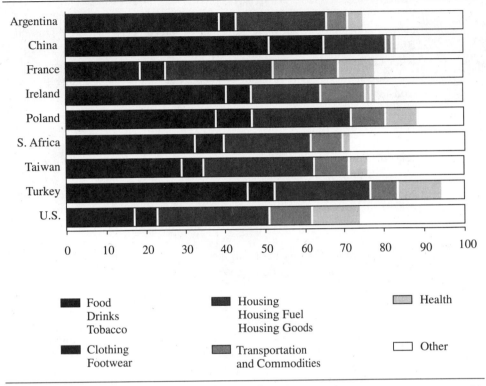

Source: *International Marketing Data and Statistics, 1992* (London: Euromonitor Publications 1992), table 1103, p. 411; *European Marketing Data and Statistics, 1991* (London: Euromonitor Publications, 1992), table 1103, pp. 248–249.

varies depending on the income per capita. A developing country, such as China, spends over 50 percent on food, whereas developed countries, such as France or the United States, spend less than 20 percent on food. While it is possible to generalize about the order of consumer purchases based on Maslow's hierarchy of needs, the patterns may vary by country.

Buyer Motivation

The ability to buy is influenced by a variety of economic elements, which are much easier to identify and qualify than elements in the motivation to buy. As mentioned earlier, all consumers have some similarities as members of the human race. Unfortunately, however, buyer behavior is not uniform among all humans. Buyer behavior is learned, primarily from the culture. As a marketer moves from culture to culture (within and between countries), buyer behavior will differ.

As we discussed in Chapter 3, culture refers to widely shared norms or patterns of behavior within a large group of people.[53] These norms can directly affect product usage. For example, mothers in Brazil feel that only they can properly prepare foods for their babies, and therefore they are reluctant to buy processed foods. This cultural norm in Brazil caused difficulty for Gerber despite the fact that its products were selling well in other Latin American countries.[54]

Social class is a grouping of consumers based on income, education, and occupation. Consumers in the same social class tend to have similar purchase patterns. The perceived class structure and the distribution of income will affect purchase behavior. Culture not only influences the consumer behavior, it also affects the conduct of businesses. Harris and Moran suggest that cross-cultural training is very important for managers to be successful in dealing with business people of different cultures.[55]

Consumers belong to a variety of different groups that also influence purchase behavior. For example, it is difficult to sell insurance in Moslem countries because religious leaders claim it is a form of usury and gambling, both of which are explicitly prohibited in the Koran.[56]

Family Structure   The structure of the family and the roles assigned to each member play an important part in determining who makes a decision and who does the influencing. Table 5.7 shows the results of a study that examined and compared decision-making roles in families from the United States and Venezuela. Nine products/services were picked, and each family surveyed was asked to identify which member made the decision to purchase the product. The overriding contrast between the two samples involved the role of the husband. More joint decisions regarding major purchases were made in the United States than in Venezuela. In all purchase decisions, except groceries and savings, the Venezuelan husband made more decisions than the U.S. husband. Families in the United States make more joint decisions than Venezuelan families.

International marketers must be aware that variations in family purchasing roles may exist in foreign markets, due to the social and cultural differences. Marketing strategy may change based on the respective role of family members. For example, a U.S. manufacturer of appliances or furniture may find it advisable to incorporate the husband into a Venezuelan marketing strategy to a larger extent than in the United States.

Family structure, particularly the number of two-parent families (versus single-parent families), will affect the level of household income. Also, families with two working parents will have a higher level of pooled income than single-parent or one-working-parent families. The pooling of incomes will positively influence the demand for consumer durables and luxury goods.

53. Henry Assael, *Consumer Behavior and Marketing Action,* 3rd ed. (Boston: Kent, 1987), p. 15.

54. Ann Helmings, ''Culture Shocks,'' *Advertising Age,* May 17, 1982, p. M-9.

55. Philip R. Harris and Robert T. Moran, *Managing Cultural Differences,* 2nd ed. (Houston: Gulf, 1987), pp. 3-24.

56. D. E. Allen, ''Anthropological Insights into Consumer Behavior,'' *European Journal of Marketing,* 5 (Summer 1971), p. 54.

TABLE 5.7 ● Mean Number of Purchase Decisions by
Product Type

Product	United States	Venezuela
Groceries		
Husband	.23	.23
Joint	.60	.69
Wife	3.20	3.08
Furniture		
Husband	.41	1.16
Joint	3.41	2.71
Wife	2.23	2.16
Major appliances		
Husband	.98	1.97
Joint	3.21	2.10
Wife	.85	.93
Life insurance		
Husband	2.65	3.38
Joint	1.23	.55
Wife	.15	.05
Automobiles		
Husband	2.59	4.16
Joint	3.06	1.42
Wife	.41	.40
Vacations		
Husband	1.00	1.51
Joint	3.68	3.18
Wife	.40	.41
Savings		
Husband	1.00	1.07
Joint	1.61	1.60
Wife	.44	.34
Housing		
Husband	.34	.87
Joint	2.47	1.82
Wife	.34	.39
Doctor		
Husband	.03	.10
Joint	.35	.42
Wife	.62	.49

Source: Robert T. Green and Isabella Cunningham, ''Family Purchasing Roles in Two Countries,'' *Journal of International Business Studies,* Spring–Summer 1980, p. 95. Reprinted by permission.

Religion   As we noted in Chapter 3, religion affects behavior patterns by establishing moral codes and taboos. What, when, and how consumers buy is a function of their religion. Traditional Catholics do not eat meat on Fridays during Lent, and Orthodox Jews are forbidden ever to eat pork. The Christian Sabbath is on Sunday, the Jewish Sabbath on Saturday, and the Moslem Sabbath on Friday. Religion influences the attitudes and beliefs of people with regard to interests, work, leisure, family size, family relationships, and so on. Many of these affect the type of products people purchase, why they buy them, and even which newspapers they read. For example, in some countries, if too much attention is given to the body in advertisements, the product may be rejected as immoral.

Educational Systems   Formal education involves public or private institutions where learning takes place in a structured environment. The literacy rate is the standard measurement used to assess the extent and success of educational systems, and it normally varies directly with economic development.

In Europe and Japan the literacy rate exceeds 90 percent (see Table 3.2), whereas in some developing countries it is below 50 percent. A low level of literacy affects marketers in two ways: first, it reduces the market for products that require reading, such as books and magazines; second, it reduces the effectiveness of advertising.

Education includes the process of transmitting skills, ideas, attitudes, and knowledge. In effect, the educational process transmits the existing culture and traditions to the next generation. Often, the goals of an educational system will include broader political goals, such as India's programs to improve agriculture and reduce the birth rate.

Consumption Patterns

It is difficult to generalize about consumer behavior in each country of the world and for every product category, because consumption patterns vary considerably. The differences are caused by consumers' ability and motivation to buy. For example, consumption patterns for wine vary tremendously from country to country. In France, as shown in Figure 5.7, the average consumption is 73 liters (19 gallons) per person, versus 1.6 liters in Japan or 8 liters in the United States. Consumption of wine in Britain has doubled during the 1980s, to 13 liters per person.

The high consumption of wine in Europe versus the United States is offset by the high U.S. consumption of soft drinks. The average American drinks five times as many soft drinks as a Frenchman, three times as many as an Italian, and two and one-half times as many as a German.[57]

Patterns of consumption also vary with services. For example, about 15 percent of the world's countries have 95 percent of all telephones. Studies by the Brookings Institution, the University of Texas, Stanford University, the University of Cairo, and Massachusetts Institute of Technology indicate that telephones have significant economic benefits to the consumer in excess of the cost and contribute to a rise in per capita income. For example, the World Bank reported that when Sri Lankan farmers received telephones,

---

57. *Beverage Industry Annual Manual* (Cleveland: Harcourt, Brace, Jovanovich, 1987), p. 16.

FIGURE 5.7 ● Wine Consumption for Selected Countries (in Liters per Person, 1989–1990)

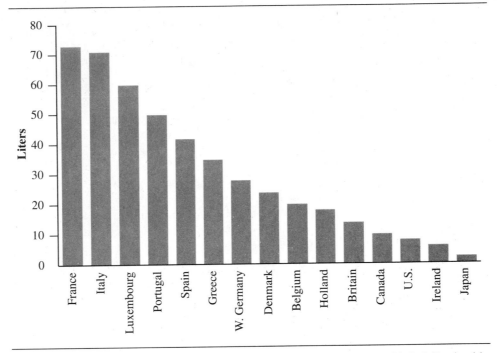

Source: Economist, December 22, 1990, p. 139. © 1990 The Economist Newspaper Limited. Reprinted by permission.

prices of produce increased from 55 percent of Colombian prices to 85 percent, due to better information.[58] The United Nations has established a fund to speed up the adoption of telephones around the world.

Business Markets

Business buyers around the world are much more predictable than consumers because they are more influenced by the economic considerations of cost and less by social or cultural factors. For example, a purchasing agent in Japan who is buying specialty steel for his company will attempt to get the best possible product at the lowest cost, which is similar to how a purchasing agent in the United States or Germany would act. The criteria that business buyers use will be much the same around the world. However, the buying process used by business buyers and the negotiation process will be influenced by local culture and will vary from country to country. The terms *business buyer* and *industrial buyer* are

58. "Third World Telephones," *Economist,* December 17, 1983, pp. 82–85.

used interchangeably in this chapter, although business buyers normally include all types of businesses, whereas industrial buyers are limited to manufacturing businesses.

Buying Motives

Industrial buying is less affected by such cultural factors as social roles, religion, and language than is consumer buying. Purchasing agents, regardless of background, will be primarily influenced by the use of the product, its cost, and delivery.

Industrial products, such as raw materials or machinery, are sold to businesses for use in a manufacturing process to produce other goods. Given that the objective of the manufacturer is to maximize profit, the critical buying criterion will focus on the perform-ance of the product purchased versus its cost. This is called the *cost-performance criterion,* and it is used along with other buying criteria such as service, dependability, and knowl-edge of the selling company.

Because the cost-performance criterion is critical, the economic situation in the pur-chasing country will affect the decision process. Cost-performance is a function of the local cost of labor and the scale of operation. As can be seen in Figure 5.8, which lists manufacturing labor cost averages in selected countries, wage levels vary from country to

FIGURE 5.8 ● Index of Manufacturing Labor Costs per Worker-Hour for Selected Countries

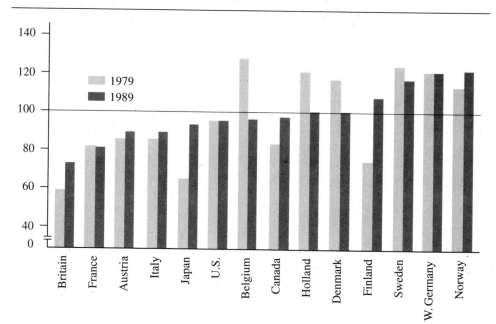

Note: United States = 100.

Source: Economist, January 20, 1990, p. 139. © 1990 The Economist Newspaper Limited. Reprinted by permission.

country. Thus, selling an industrial robot that replaces three workers in the manufacturing of a certain product will be more easily justified in Norway or Germany, where average labor costs are 20 percent more than in the United States, than it will be in Britain, where labor cost is less than 80 percent of the U.S. labor rate.

Labor costs play a key role in the level and type of manufacturing. Countries with a surplus of labor normally have lower labor costs, as supply exceeds demand. These lower pay rates result in a certain type of manufacturing that is labor intensive. Therefore, these countries will be less apt to purchase sophisticated automatic machinery, because the same job can get done with the cheaper labor. China's main objective, for example, is to import technology that optimizes its vast population. Companies wishing to export to labor-intensive countries must be aware that labor-saving measures may not be appreciated or readily applied. On the other hand, highly developed countries with a high labor rate are prime targets for automated manufacturing equipment. Countries with high labor rates have begun to see an emergence of service industries, which require human labor instead of machines. Labor in these areas is expensive, for a great deal of expertise is needed. Thus, a country normally moves from labor-intensive to capital-intensive and then to technical-intensive industry.

Factors Influencing International Purchasing

In many situations, a buyer will have the choice of purchasing a domestic product/service or a foreign product/service. The buyer's perceptions of product quality may be influenced by feelings of nationalism, the product's country of origin, and the firm's competence with international transactions. Although it is assumed that industrial buyers will be completely rational and purchase products based on concrete decision criteria such as price, quality, and performance, research has shown that professional purchases are influenced by the country of origin, even when all other variables are held constant.[59]

The international company must recognize the country-of-origin stereotypes and use this information when developing a marketing strategy. Highly nationalistic countries tend to encourage economic self-sufficiency even at the expense of economic efficiency, which will have a negative effect on the international company. A study of purchasing behavior by Swedish companies found that buyers preferred to deal with domestic suppliers but would use foreign suppliers when necessary.[60] The study also found that the purchasing firm's competence for international business is positively related to the use of international suppliers. International purchasers generally have broad market knowledge, an ability to handle foreign cultural patterns, and a knowledge of international trade techniques.[61] Given the results of this analysis, the international company should pay close attention to the

59. Phillip D. White and Edward W. Cundiff, ''Assessing the Quality of Industrial Products,'' *Journal of Marketing,* January 1978, pp. 80–86.
60. Lars Hallen, ''International Purchasing in a Small Country: An Exploratory Study of Five Swedish Firms,'' *Journal of International Business Studies,* Winter 1982, pp. 99–111.
61. Ibid.

level of nationalism in a country, the country-of-origin stereotypes, and the competence level of the purchasing function to deal with international suppliers.

Government Markets

A large number of international business transactions involve governments. For example, 80 percent of all international trade of agricultural products is handled by governments. The U.S. government buys more goods and services than any other government, business, industry, or organization in the world.[62] Selling to governments can be both time consuming and frustrating. However, governments are large purchasers, and selling to them can provide enormous returns.

The size of government purchases depends on the economic or political orientation of the country. In highly developed, free-market countries, the government has less of a role than in state-controlled markets, where most buying is under direct control of the state. Less developed countries lack the economic infrastructure to facilitate private companies; thus, governments play a major role in overseeing the purchase of foreign products. The amount of government purchases is also a function of state-owned operations. For example, in the United States the only government-owned operation is the postal system, whereas in India the government owns not only the postal system, but also the telecommunications, electric, gas, oil, coal, railway, airline, and shipbuilding industries.

The Buying Process

Governmental buying processes tend to be highly bureaucratic. In order to sell to the U.S. Department of Defense, a firm has to get on a bidding list for each branch of the armed forces. These bidding lists are issued on an annual basis; thus, a firm not able to get on the list must wait a full year to try again.

Governments make it harder for a foreign firm to sell to them; many place their own domestic firms ahead of foreign operations. Also, negotiating with foreign governments can be a very formal process. Understanding cultural differences is essential in order not to overstep boundaries.

Government procurement processes vary from country to country. The following sections describe purchasing processes in Belgium and the European Union.

Marketing to the Belgian Government[63]   In Belgium, 90 percent of all public contracts are awarded to the lowest bidder. The remaining 10 percent are granted through "invitation to tender," where factors other than price are taken into consideration. These other factors

---

62. *Selling to the Government Markets: Local, State, Federal* (Cleveland: Government Product News, 1975), p. 2.

63. The information in this section has been drawn from Business International, "How to Sell to Belgium's Public Sector," *Business Europe,* October 2, 1981, pp. 314–315.

may include the company's financial viability, technical competence, and postsale service. Central government supplies, excluding data processing and telecommunications, must be bought through the Central Supplies Office. Regional, local, and quasi-governmental bodies, such as Sabena Airlines, purchase supplies independently. Here are several recommendations to companies that wish to sell to the Belgian government:

- Manufacture in Belgium. Preference is given to a local supplier if other things are equal.

- Develop a European image. A strong EU image has favored companies such as Siemens and Philips.

- Use the appropriate language. Although both Flemish and French are officially accepted, ask which is preferred in the department that is accepting the bid.

- Emphasize the recruitment of labor following the winning of a contract. Companies are favored if they will employ Belgian people.

- When new technology is involved, get in at the beginning. It is often difficult and expensive for the government to change to a different technology at a later date.

- Whenever possible, use local contractors. The Belgian government likes a bidder to use as many local contractors as possible.

Obviously, bidding for Belgian government work is particularly difficult for suppliers with no local participation of subcontractors or manufacturing in Belgium or the EU. However, every government market has some limitations.

Public Procurement in the European Union   One of the major objectives of the 1992 Single European Market was the opening up of the public procurement markets in the European Union. Public procurement made up 15.5 percent of gross European product. Governments of Europe were only importing a small portion of their total consumption. They made almost no foreign purchases unless the goods were unavailable in local markets. For example, in 1988 the U.K. government imported only .4 percent of its requirements; in Italy it was .3 percent; in France 1.6 percent; and in Belgium 2.6 percent.[64] The European Union has actively encouraged its members to open up their government markets for the following reasons:

1. It will reduce costs of public utilities, transportation, and telecommunications through competitive bidding.

2. The cost of public administration will decline; therefore, taxes and inflation will be reduced.

3. Companies supplying governments will become more cost competitive, and their opportunity to serve customers outside the community will therefore be improved.

4. Open procurement will increase GDP by .5 percent and create 400,000 new jobs.[65]

64. Bernard Cova and Philippe Cova, "ECC Public Procurement Directives: Dropping Competitive Values," *European Management Journal,* September 1990, p. 334.
65. Dudley, *1992 Strategies,* p. 38.

To implement an open procurement policy, the EU has issued a number of directives. For example, all EU governments have agreed to remove restrictions on the purchasing of materials and to open bidding of public works projects. There is still some resistance of EU members to opening up bidding on sensitive defense-related projects.

Economic and Political Needs of Governments

Firms involved in selling to foreign governments not only must have an understanding of the political and economic structures, they must also be able to evaluate a country's industrial trends vis-à-vis the national system. Factors to be considered are the government's responsibility to industry; government priorities; national defense; high-tech, industrial efficiency; and financial self-sufficiency. The level of economic development involves not only the GNP but the state of production. China, for example, is pushing for modernization but does not want production techniques at the expense of its large labor pool. The desire to lessen unemployment is a major interest to most countries. Governments are also confronted with balance of payments problems. Trade deficits—importing more than exporting—will affect the position of a country's currency with respect to foreign currencies. The more the government imports, the more expensive the products become because the government must use more foreign exchange.

Governments tend to protect their domestic industry to reduce high unemployment and GNP deficits. Whether products are for consumer, industrial, or government use, protection in the form of tariffs, subsidiaries, and quotas is levied if domestic industries are threatened. Because the government looks out for its domestic companies, they will stay clear of those products and services for which restrictions are imposed.

Protection of domestic products and services extends beyond that imposed by foreign governments. The threat of reducing national security has governments of domestic firms employing restrictions on various products. The transfer of technology such as nuclear plants, computers, telecommunications, and military weapons is usually restricted so that these critical technologies do not get into the wrong hands.

Conclusions

The world marketplace is large and complex. The global company needs to systematically evaluate the entire world market on a regular basis to be sure that company assets are directed toward the countries with the best opportunities. The basis for an evaluation of countries should be a comparative analysis of different countries. Certain ones may be unsuitable because of their unstable political situation, and others may have little potential because their population is small or the per capita income is low. The screening process gives the firm information about market size, competition, trade regulations, and distribution systems that will form the basis for the development of a market strategy. As international firms evaluate different consumer, business, and government market opportunities, they must be aware of the nature of the differences between countries.

The nature of the world marketplace has changed as a result of the development of major regional market groups. The economic integration of a number of countries offers great opportunities to companies. Many national markets, such as those in Europe, that are small individually become significant when combined with other countries. By locating production facilities in one country of a market group, the international company has access to the other markets with little or no trade restrictions. The market groups also increase competition. Local producers who for years completely dominated their national markets due to tariff protection now face competition from many other member countries.

The development of these market groups can also have negative effects on international companies. If a company is unable or unwilling to build a manufacturing plant in a certain market group, it may be unprofitable to export to that market. There are often more regulations between market groups, making it more complicated and expensive to move goods from one group to another. Also, the market group does not necessarily reduce the complexity of the consumer and cultural differences. For example, while Germany and Spain are both in the EU, the marketing programs, products, and strategies for success in each market will probably be different.

The success of market groups formed after World War II, particularly the EU, indicates that such groups will continue to grow in the future. The potential entry of some eastern European countries into the EU, as well as the expansion of NAFTA to include other Central or South American countries, supports the growth of market groups and the growing interdependence of trading partners. International companies need to monitor the development of new groups and any changes in the structure of current groups, because changes within market groups will result in changes in market size and competition.

The largest business markets for U.S. goods are in countries that have a sophisticated industrial infrastructure, such as Canada, Japan, Germany, and England. These countries have a large industrial base, a financial basis, and a transportation network. These countries are large importers and exporters of goods and services.

Developing countries offer a different type of market opportunity. They have specific economic needs that must be met with limited financial resources. In these situations, the government is likely to get involved in the purchase process, offering concessions to get the correct product or agreement. In many cases, the government will be the decision maker.

Questions for Discussion

1. Searching for the best international opportunity often requires an analysis of all the countries of the world. How will the initial screening differ from the final screening of possible countries to enter?

2. If you were evaluating opportunities for caviar but found that no countries had data on caviar consumption, what other indicators would you use to evaluate the size of each country's market?

3. Using Figure 5.3, compare the potential for caviar consumption in Germany, India, and South Korea.

4. In the sale of hair shampoo, what are the advantages of grouping countries together rather than marketing to each country individually?

5. What are the differences between a free trade area, a customs union, and a common market? If you were marketing to a grouping of countries but only had a manufacturing plant in one of the countries, which of the three types of agreements would you prefer? Why?

6. What are the reasons for the growth in the establishment of country groupings?

7. What critical factors influence a consumer's ability to purchase a product such as a stereo system?

8. Given the data on family decision making in the United States and Venezuela in Table 5.7, how will the marketing of automobiles be different in the two countries?

9. Will the buying process be more similar from country to country for deodorant or delivery vans? Why?

10. If you are selling a product such as nuclear power plants, which are purchased mostly by governments, how would you prepare to sell to Belgium, Egypt, and Mexico? What process should be used to understand the government buying process in each of these countries?

For Further Reading

Auguier, Antoine A. *French Industry's Reaction to the European Common Market.* New York: Garland, 1984.

Behrman, Jack N. "Transnational Corporations in the New Economic Order." *Journal of International Business Studies,* Spring–Summer 1981, pp. 29–42.

Bilkey, Warren J., and Erik Nes. "Country-of-Origin: Effects on Product Evaluation." *Journal of International Business Studies,* Spring–Summer 1982, pp. 89–99.

Boisot, Max. "Territorial Strategies in a Competitive World: The Emerging Challenges to Regional Authorities." *European Management Journal,* September 1990, pp. 394–401.

Cracco, Etienne, and Guy Robert. *"The Uncommon Common Market."* In *1974 Combined Proceedings.* Ed. Ronald C. Curhan. Chicago: American Marketing Association, 1975.

Fishburn, Dudley, ed. *World in 1991.* London: The Economist Publications, 1991.

Guthery, Dennis Alan. "Income and Social Class as Indicators of Buyer Behavior in an Advanced LDC: A Case Study of Durable Good Purchases in Porto Alegre, Brazil." Paper presented at the Academy of International Business Annual Meeting, Washington, D.C., 1982.

"Here Come the Multinationals of the Third World." *Economist,* July 23, 1983, p. 55.

Hertzfeld, Jeffrey M. "Joint Ventures: Saving the Soviets from Perestroika." *Harvard Business Review,* January–February 1991, pp. 80–91.

Hilton, Andrew. "Mythology, Markets, and the Emerging Europe." *Harvard Business Review,* November–December 1992, pp. 50–54.

Kesavan, Ram, and Xin Sun. "Pacts and Impacts: A Comparative Analysis of the 1992 European Community Pact and the U.S.-Canadian Free Trade Agreement." *SAM Advanced Management Journal,* Summer 1991, pp. 4–10.

Kirkland, Richard I., Jr. "Who Gains from the New Europe?" *Fortune,* December 18, 1989, pp. 48–54.

Lal, Deepak. "Trade Blocs and Multilateral Free Trade." *Journal of Common Market Studies,* September 1993, pp. 349–358.

Lasserre, Philippe. "The New Industrializing Countries of Asia: Perspectives and Opportunities." *Long Range Planning,* June 1981, pp. 36–43.

Levy, Brian. "Korean and Taiwanese Firms as International Competitors: The Challenges Ahead." *Columbia Journal of World Business,* Spring 1988, pp. 43–52.

Lipsey, R. "The Theory of Customs Unions: A General Survey." *Economic Journal,* 70 (1960), pp. 496–513.

Longhammer, Rolf J. "The Developing Countries and Regionalism." *Journal of Common Market Studies,* June 1992, pp. 211–231.

Luqman, Mushtag, A. Quraeshi, and Linda Delene. "Marketing in Islamic Countries." *MSU Business Topics,* 3 (1980), pp. 17–26.

Masur, Sandra. "The North American Free Trade Agreement: Why It's in the Interest of U.S. Business." *Columbia Journal of World Business,* Summer 1991, pp. 98–103.

Mitchell, Vincent W., and Michael Grentorex. "Consumer Purchasing in Foreign Countries: A Perceived Risk Perspective." *International Journal of Advertising,* 9, no. 4 (1990), pp. 295–307.

Moriarty, Rowland T. *Industrial Buying Behavior.* Lexington, Mass.: D. C. Heath, 1983.

Papadopoulos, Nicolas, Louise A. Heslop, and Jozsef Beracs. "National Stereotypes and Product Evaluation in a Socialist Country." *International Marketing Review,* 7, no. 1 (1990), pp. 32–47.

Pinkerton, Richard L. "The European Community—'EC '92': Implications for Purchasing Managers." *International Journal of Purchasing and Materials Management,* Spring 1993, pp. 19–26.

Quelch, John, Erich Joachimsthalen, and Jose Luis Nueno. "After the Wall: Marketing Guidelines for Eastern Europe." *Sloan Management Review,* 32, no. 2 (1991), pp. 82–93.

Sethi, S. Prakash. "Comparative Cluster Analysis for World Markets." *Journal of Marketing Research,* August 1971, pp. 348–354.

Sethi, S. Prakash, and Richard H. Holton. "Review of Comparative Analysis for International Marketing." *Journal of Marketing Records,* November 1969, pp. 502–503.

Shipchandler, Zoher. "Change in Demand for Consumer Goods in International Markets." In *International Marketing.* 2nd ed. Ed. Subhash Jain and Lewis Tooker, Jr. Boston: Kent, 1986.

Smith-Morris, Miles, ed. *Book of Vital World Statistics.* London: Economist Books, 1990.

Staude, Gavin. "Marketing to the African Segment of the South African Market." *European Journal of Marketing,* 6 (1978), pp. 400–412.

"Survey of the Third World." *Economist,* September 23, 1989, pp. 1–58.

Weeks, John. *Population.* 5th ed. Belmont, Calif.: Wadsworth, 1994.

6

International and Global Marketing Research

● **PREVIOUSLY, WE INTRODUCED** *you to a variety of consumers, markets, and environments. Our main purpose in Chapter 6 is to provide you with a method for collecting the appropriate data and a framework in which to analyze the environment, the market, and the consumers for your product. Figure 6.1 is an overview of international market research.*

Although this chapter is written around the research issues in an international environment, our emphasis is a managerial rather than technical one. Throughout the chapter, we focus on how companies can obtain useful and accurate information that will help them to make more informed strategic and marketing decisions described in later chapters.

The Scope of International Marketing Research

International marketing research is meant to provide adequate data and cogent analysis for effective decision making on a global scale. In contrast to marketing research that has a domestic focus, international research covers a multitude of environments, and there is a scarcity of comparable, relevant data. Because of this, flexibility, resourcefulness, and ingenuity on the part of the researcher are often required in order to overcome the numerous obstacles encountered in carrying out the research task.

The analytical research techniques practiced by domestic businesses also apply to international marketing projects. The key difference is in the complexity of assignments due to the additional variables that must be dealt with. Global marketers have to judge the comparability of their data across a number of markets; they frequently are faced with making decisions based on limited data. As a result, international marketing research can

FIGURE 6.1 ● International Marketing Research and Analysis

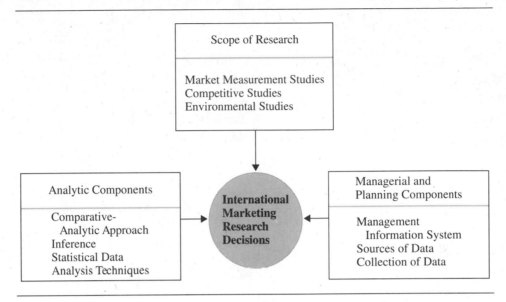

aptly be described as making the best out of limited resources. Traditionally, marketing research has been charged with the following three broad areas of responsibility:

1. *Market measurement studies.* One of the most frequent tasks of researchers is to determine the size of a market or its potential as well as a firm's sales potential. Included in this area are sales forecasts for a product. A firm's expected sales for a product in a country or set of countries are an important input into the development of an international marketing program.

2. *Competitive studies.* To provide insights about competitors, both domestic and foreign, is an important assignment for the international marketing researcher. The researcher must study the general competitive behavior of industries in the various markets within which the firm will compete.

3. *Environmental studies.* Given the added environmental complexity of global marketing, managers need factual and timely input on the international environment—particularly relating to the economic, political, and legal elements of the potential markets.

International marketing research is used to make both strategic and tactical decisions. Strategic decisions include the selection of what markets to enter, how to enter them (exporting licensing, joint venture), and where to locate production facilities. Tactical decisions are decisions about the specific marketing mix to be used in a country. Table 6.1 shows the various types of tactical marketing decisions needed and the kinds of research used to collect the necessary data.

TABLE 6.1 ● International Marketing Decisions Requiring Marketing Research

Marketing mix decision	Type of research
Product policy	Focus groups and qualitative research to generate ideas for new products
	Survey research to evaluate new product ideas
	Concept testing, test marketing
	Product benefit and attitude research
	Product formulation and feature testing
Pricing	Price sensitivity studies
Distribution	Survey of shopping patterns and behavior
	Consumer attitudes toward different store types
	Survey of distributor attitudes and policies
Advertising	Advertising pretesting
	Advertising posttesting, recall scores
	Surveys of media habits
Sales promotion	Surveys of response to alternative types of promotion
Sales force	Tests of alternative sales presentations

Source: Susan P. Douglas and C. Samuel Craig, *International Marketing Research,* © 1983, p. 32. Reprinted by permission of Prentice Hall, Inc., Englewood Cliffs, New Jersey.

New product development or product adaptation will require product benefit research and product testing to meet environmental conditions, customer tastes, and competitive constraints. For example, CPC International did consumer research on Skippy peanut butter in Hungary. They found no question as to the taste, look, and packaging, but Hungarian consumers were critical about the texture. Chunky style was favored over creamy style. This research helped focus the advertising and direct in-store displays and sampling.[1]

Advertising, sales promotion, and sales force decisions all require data from the local market in the form of testing. The type of information required is often the same as that required in domestic marketing research, but the process is more complex due to the variety of cultures and environments.

The Importance of International Marketing Research

The complexity of the international marketplace, the extreme differences that exist from country to country, and the frequent lack of familiarity with foreign markets accentuate

1. "Hungary for Skippy, CPC Spreads Peanut Butter Brand in New Market," *Advertising Age,* September 2, 1991, p. 36.

the importance of international marketing research. Before making market entry, product position, or market mix decisions, a marketer must have accurate information about the market size, market needs, competition, and so on. Marketing research provides the necessary information to avoid the costly mistakes of poor strategies or lost opportunities.

Marketing research can guide product development for a foreign market. Based on a research study conducted in the United States, one U.S. firm introduced a new cake mix in England. Believing that homemakers wanted to feel that they participated in the preparation of the cake, the U.S. marketers devised a mix that required homemakers to add an egg. Given the success in the U.S. market, the marketers confidently introduced the product in England. The product failed, however, because the British did not like the fancy American cakes. They preferred cakes that were tough and spongy and could accompany afternoon tea. The technique of having homemakers add an egg to the mix did not eliminate basic taste and stylistic differences.[2]

Whirlpool found that market research can help speed up market entry. While fewer than one-third of European households owned microwave ovens, research suggested that European consumers would buy a microwave that performed like a conventional oven. Whirlpool introduced a model that incorporated a broiler coil for top browning and a unique dish that sizzles the underside of the food. This new product, the Crisp, is now Europe's best-selling microwave.[3]

Challenges in Planning International Research

International marketing researchers face five principal challenges:

1. Complexity of research design

2. Lack of secondary data

3. Costs of collecting primary data

4. Coordination of research and data collection across countries

5. Establishing comparability and equivalence[4]

While domestic research is limited to one country, international research includes many countries. The research design is made more complex because the researcher defining the possible target market must choose which countries or segments should be researched. This initial step in the research process is further complicated by limited secondary information. Even if the appropriate secondary information exists, it may be difficult to locate and acquire. Thus, researchers are forced either to spend considerable resources finding

---

2. David A. Ricks, *Big Business Blunders: Mistakes in Multinational Marketing* (Homewood, Ill.: Dow Jones–Irwin, 1983), pp. 129–130.

3. ''How to Listen to Consumers,'' *Fortune,* January 11, 1993, p. 77.

4. Susan P. Douglas and C. Samuel Craig, *International Marketing Research* (Englewood Cliffs, N.J.: Prentice Hall, 1983), pp. 16–19.

such data or to accept the limited secondary data that are available. In many countries, the cost of collecting primary data is substantially higher than in the domestic market. This is particularly the case for developing countries. Consequently, researchers have to make tradeoffs between the need for more accurate data and the limited resources available to accomplish the tasks.

Even gathering demographics from country to country is no easy task. There are a wide variety of problems with using national census data. For example, the U.S. census is taken every ten years. Canada and Japan do one every five years. Germany did one in 1987, twenty-seven years after its previous census in 1960. While the United States, Canada, Australia, New Zealand, Mexico, Sweden, and Finland collect income data, most countries do not. Educational levels can be used to determine socioeconomic status, but educational systems vary widely from country to country, making comparisons very crude. Switzerland and Germany publish data on noncitizens. Canada collects data on religion. Both these topics are excluded from the U.S. census. Marital status and head of household information varies from country to country. Ireland only recognizes single, married, or widowed. Latin America often combines cohabiting with marital categories. These major differences from country to country make even the simplest demographic analysis very challenging.[5]

Because companies can ill afford for each subsidiary to obtain its own expensive primary data, coordination of research and data collection across countries becomes necessary. The borrowing of research results from one country to another is hindered by the general difficulty of establishing comparability and equivalence among various research data. Definitions of housewives, socioeconomic status, incomes, and customers vary widely in Europe, even where the research is measuring the same thing.[6] Full comparability can only be achieved when identical procedures are used. A recent study found that, even with the same scales measuring the same attributes of products, different cultures exhibit different degrees of reliability due to different levels of awareness, knowledge, and familiarity.[7] With research capabilities differing from country to country, global marketing research administration becomes a real challenge. Companies that can successfully manage this task will be in a situation to avoid costly duplication of research.

Along with all the problems of data collection and comparability, balancing between the needs of the national subsidiaries and the headquarters of the multinationals can pose a challenge. Market research agencies report that treading the diplomatic path between head office staff and national subsidiaries of multinational firms is probably the biggest problem they face on global research projects. This obstacle is increasingly recognized as companies make the conceptual switch to treating Europe as a single market.[8]

5. Donald B. Pittenger, ''Gathering Foreign Demographics Is No Easy Task,'' *Marketing News,* January 8, 1991, p. 23.

6. Tom Lester, ''Common Markets,'' *Marketing,* November 9, 1989, p. 41.

7. Ravi Parameswaran and Attila Yaprak, ''A Cross-National Comparison of Consumer Research Measures,'' *Journal of International Business Studies,* Spring 1987, p. 45.

8. Robin Cobb, ''Client Diplomacy,'' *Marketing,* May 17, 1990, p. 31.

Conceptual Framework: The Comparative Analytic Approach

We have discussed the scope of marketing research situations and the difficulties encountered in conducting research. Although an understanding of the difficulties of collecting information for foreign markets helps to increase the quality of information obtained, an overall conceptual framework is necessary to provide the analyst with the relevant questions to ask. Consequently, this section of the chapter focuses on building a framework that can guide international marketing managers in the formulation of market research studies.

Pioneered by T. A. Hagler in the late 1950s, comparative research actually led to the establishment of international marketing as a discipline.[9] Comparative marketing focuses on the entire marketing system, but this macro approach becomes less important as specific problems at the company level need to be analyzed. However, the comparative approach can be adapted to specific micromarketing problems.

Marketing as a Function of the Environment

Comparative marketing analysis emphasizes the study of the marketing process in its relationship to the environment. The marketing process is viewed as a direct function of environment. Under changed environmental conditions, the existing marketing processes are also expected to change. In a dual-country analysis employing the comparative approach, the marketing environment in one country is investigated with respect to its effect on the marketing process. The resulting functional relationship is transferred to a second country, whose environment may be known but whose marketing process will be assessed based on the earlier analysis of the relationship between the marketing process and the environment in another country.

This situation is illustrated in Figure 6.2.[10] The comparative marketing analysis allows the researcher to understand the relationship between the environment and the marketing process in one country and then to transfer that knowledge to another country, *adjusting* for differences in the environment.

Example: McDonald's   In the United States (the home country), McDonald's obtained its tremendous success through an aggressive, well-structured marketing mix. The elements may be described as follows:

● *Product/service design:* A standardized product of high and consistent quality emphasizing speed of service and long opening hours

9. Jean Boddeyn, ''A Framework for Comparative Marketing Research,'' *Journal of Marketing Research,* May 1966, pp. 149–153; *Comparative Management and Marketing* (Glenview, Ill.: Scott, Foresman, 1969).

10. Jean-Pierre Jeannet, ''International Marketing Analysis: A Comparative-Analytic Approach,'' working paper, 1981.

FIGURE 6.2 ● Managerial Approach to Comparative Analysis

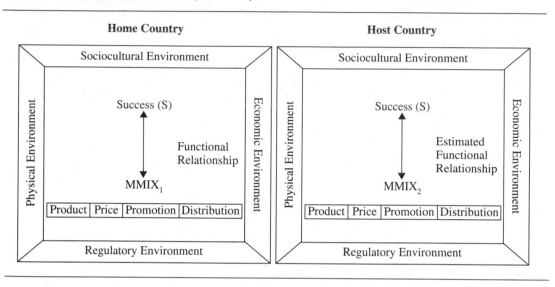

● *Price:* A low price policy

● *Distribution:* Placing restaurants in areas where customers primarily live—suburban and urban locations

● *Promotion:* A strong advertising campaign that focuses on the consumer, particularly young people, via heavy use of television promotion

In the early 1970s, several other countries were targeted for possible expansion, and an assessment had to be made as to the best approach for McDonald's to pursue. The traditional approach views success in the United States as a function of McDonald's effective marketing strategy or as a direct result of the company's own efforts. The comparative analytic approach advanced here, however, views McDonald's success as a function of a given set of marketing mix variables that are effective due to the country's environment. The main emphasis falls on the environmental variables that allowed McDonald's marketing mix to be successful.

The difference between the two approaches is important. The comparative analytic view sees McDonald's primarily as having been able to take advantage of an existing opportunity, whereas the traditional approach views McDonald's success primarily as a direct result of its own efforts.

Viewing the Marketing Mix as a Function of the Environment   Viewing the marketing mix as a function of the existing environment emphasizes an environmental view of the marketing process.[11] The focus now is on the existing environment that enables a given

11. Robert Bartels, ''Are Domestic and International Marketing Dissimilar?'' *Journal of Marketing,* July 1968, pp. 56–61.

marketing mix to be successful. This view is of great importance. Success is no longer defined as unilateral or solely a function of the marketing mix. Thus, the company is viewed as taking advantage of a given opportunity rather than creating one by its own actions.

Understanding the Marketing Environment

The first step in the comparative analytic approach is to look at the environmental factors. The critical environmental variables may be grouped into four major categories: physical, social, economic, and regulatory.

Physical Variables   Included in physical variables are physical constraints with respect to the conditions of the product's use or the physical properties of the particular market. These are population, population density, geographic area, climate, and the physical conditions of the product's use (surroundings, space and size requirements, and so on). Variables such as population have an effect on the absolute size of any target market and, similar to climate, tend to be subject to little change over time. The physical use conditions relate to a product's function in any given environment. As a result, we view the consumption of the product or service as a *physical event* directly influenced by physical environmental variables that have to be recognized to determine a marketing mix.

Turning again to the McDonald's example, several variables from the physical environment have contributed toward McDonald's success in the United States. An important influence on McDonald's distribution or location policies was the concentration of the U.S. population in suburbia. Opening 4,000 units in the United States was possible due to the absolute size of the population, which is about 248 million people. It is important to recognize that the market size is often finite and that any country with a different population would, of course, not offer the same opportunities, all things being equal. The physical use conditions of McDonald's are less restrictive because they are directly shaped by the firm's policies and the building of outlets. The situation is different in cases where consumers take products home for consumption and are restricted by their own physical environments, such as apartment or kitchen size.

Social Variables   Social variables include all relevant factors from the social and cultural background of any given marketing environment, including cultural background (race, religion, customs, habits, and languages), educational system, and social structure (individual roles, family structure, social classes, and reference groups).

As we have mentioned before, the social environment is a primary influence on the role expectations of buyers and sellers, regardless of the differences in the physical environment. Since the social environment does not change rapidly over time, many domestic marketers can lose sight of the fact that they've subconsciously chosen a marketing mix that incorporates many social values. Defining the social forces that impact on a marketing mix is the first step in shedding the cultural bias that affects so many managers unknowingly.

In the case of McDonald's, several social and cultural forces greatly affected its success. For one, the value that U.S. society placed on time favored the consumption of meals with minimum time effort. Saving time, in fact, created the desire for meals purchased outside the home on an unplanned or impulse basis. The result was a burgeoning demand for low-priced food that was available any time and that could be purchased with minimum shopping effort. Another important factor was the prevailing family structure in the United States and the trend toward a youth-oriented culture. In the 1960s and 1970s, the decision-making role had changed to such an extent that children often made the selection of a place to eat. McDonald's special emphasis on children and teenagers as advertising targets was successful largely because the strategy capitalized on these existing social trends.

The changing role of the wife in the typical U.S. household resulted in an ever increasing number of women accepting employment outside the home. Whether this resulted in a lower valuation of the home-cooked meal in a social sense is debatable; nevertheless, it greatly increased the acceptability of eating meals outside the home.

Not to be underestimated is the habit or heritage of the hamburger itself. Truly, the hamburger represents a long-standing tradition of the U.S. food and restaurant scene, and hamburger made up the daily meal of many Americans before McDonald's arrived on the scene. It is fair to state, then, that the company's success stemmed to a considerable degree from the selection of an already existing and widely popular product. Aside from the type of service, the product did not represent an innovation. Of course, there are other reasons for dining out, and U.S. customers often make other choices, but the social and cultural influences to a large extent prepared the ground for the success of an operation such as McDonald's.

What is important then is to isolate the salient social and cultural variables that have an impact on the success of a company's products or services. The combined sociocultural variables create the *sociocultural event* that becomes an essential part of the consumption and use of any product or service. Understanding the nature of the sociocultural event in one country as the starting point for analyzing the respective variables in another country is the basis of the comparative analytic model.

Economic Variables   Under the economic category, we include all aspects of the economic environment, on both a macro and micro level, such as GNP, GNP per capita, price levels, income distribution, and prices of competitive products and services.

Economic considerations affect most consumption or buying decisions. To the extent that income levels of consumers differ from country to country, the tradeoffs consumers make in order to maximize economic satisfaction are different. Different price levels for products also cause changes in buying behavior even under a constant income level. The international marketer must isolate the specific income and price variables to arrive at a given combination, termed the *economic event,* that affects the success of a given product or service. The comparative analytic model suggests that the elements and nature of the economic event with regard to another market can largely be found by first investigating the relevant factors in a company's home market.

For McDonald's, a significant variable of the economic environment was the income level of the U.S. population and the resulting disposable income available for frequent visits to fast-food restaurants. It is still more expensive to frequent a fast-food outlet than to prepare an equivalent meal at home; consequently, the success of fast-food outlets does not so much stem from their price advantage over food purchased in stores. Instead, it was the *relative price advantage* of fast-food restaurants over the more traditional, simple diner-type restaurants that ensured their tremendous success. Consuming a meal at a place such as McDonald's becomes an economic event to the extent that economic variables are introduced into the consumer's decision-making process affecting the particular product or service choice.

Regulatory Variables   The regulatory environment includes all actions of governments or agencies influencing business transactions such as commercial law or codes, consumer protection laws, product liability laws, regulatory agencies (for example, the FDA, U.S. Department of Commerce and ICC), local regulations, and zoning laws.

Regulations do not tend to stimulate needs or demands for services and products. Instead, they act in an *enabling manner* (or disabling manner, depending on the point of view) by restricting choices for the international corporation or prescribing the nature of its marketing effort. Companies have to be aware of the particular regulations that make an existing marketing program effective, because such an approach may not be duplicated in other countries even if it were desirable from a business point of view.

The possible effect of the regulatory environment can be illustrated by returning to our example. Certainly, the use of television advertising to reach children was one of the reasons for McDonald's success in the United States. But in many other countries, particularly those in Europe, such advertising is banned outright. On an operational level, it may be difficult to get teenage help in some countries or impossible to keep operating during hours customary in the United States. Since the United States has in many ways a more liberal regulatory environment, companies often face situations where operations cannot be carried out in the accustomed fashion. This is true even when the target customers in other countries would respond positively to U.S. methods or practices and the relevant physical, economic, and social events indicate that their use would be beneficial.

Analyzing Environmental Variables

The importance of environmental variables to international marketing has been emphasized by previous writers. Robert Bartels highlighted physical, social, and economic variables in his environmental marketing concept.[12] Robert Buzzell included a similar set of variables in his analysis of elements that may prevent a standardization of marketing programs across several countries.[13] Furthermore, Warren Keegan concentrated on the same variables as

12. Ibid.
13. Robert D. Buzzell, ''Can You Standardize Multinational Marketing?'' *Harvard Business Review,* November–December 1968, pp. 102–113.

influencing extension versus adaptation decisions for product design or communications strategy.[14] The comparative analytic approach is different in that it focuses on the situational and selects the salient environmental variables that may affect the product's or service's success in any country. Since the selected environmental variables are the ones most clearly related to the success of a product or service in the home country, they can be referred to as *success factors.*

Traditionally, marketers have viewed success factors as variables under marketing management's control. With the comparative analytic approach, success factors are treated as a function of the environment, which means that success is recognized as a function of a given scenario of outside factors not always subject to management's control. Typically, marketing programs succeed because managements take advantage of opportunities or positive constellations of success factors. Therefore, we are ''allowed'' to be successful provided we spot the opportunity. This view results in a greater appreciation of the role that environmental variables play in marketing and also tends to avoid traditional tendencies to overestimate the impact of management's own actions in the marketplace.

The comparative analytical approach provides a methodology for marketers to analyze their success in current markets as a function of the marketing mix and the environment. It also provides an approach for isolating the critical environmental variables. These variables become the focus of the international market research process. In the McDonald's example, the variables we analyzed were population, population density, family structure, role of the mother, income levels, and availability of advertising media to reach children. As we look at other countries, we must examine these environmental variables and adjust McDonald's marketing mix appropriately.

The Research Process

Although conducting marketing research internationally usually adds to the complexity of the research task, the basic approach remains the same for domestic and international assignments. Either type of research is a four-step process:

1. Problem definition and development of research objectives
2. Determination of the sources of information
3. Collection of the data from primary and secondary sources
4. Analysis of the data and presentation of the results

While these four steps may be the same for both international and domestic research, problems in implementation may occur because of cultural and economic differences from country to country.

---

14. Warren J. Keegan, ''Multinational Product Planning: Strategic Alternatives,'' *Journal of Marketing,* January 1969, p. 58.

Problem Definition and Development of Research Objectives

In any market research project, the most important task is to define what information you are after. This process, which can take weeks or months, determines the choice of methodologies, the types of people you wish to interview, and the appropriate time frame in which to conduct your research.[15]

Problems may not be the same in different countries or cultures. This may reflect differences in socioeconomic conditions, levels of economic development, cultural forces, or the competitive market structure.[16] For example, bicycles in a developed country may be competing with other recreational goods, such as skis, baseball gloves, or exercise equipment; whereas in a developing country, they may be a form of basic transportation competing with small cars, mopeds, and scooters.

The comparative analytic approach can be used to isolate the critical environmental variables in the home market. These variables should be included in the problem definition and research objectives.

Determination of Data Sources

For each assignment, researchers may choose to base their analyses on primary data (data collected specifically for this assignment) or to use secondary data (already collected and available data). Since costs tend to be higher for research based on primary data, researchers usually exhaust secondary data first. Often called desk research or library research, this approach depends on the availability of material and its reliability. Secondary sources may include government publications, trade journals, and data from international agencies or service establishments such as banks or advertisement agencies.

The quality of government statistics is definitely variable. For example, Germany reported that industrial production was up by 0.5 percent in July 1993 but later revised this figure, reporting that production actually declined by 0.5 percent, an error of 100 percent in the opposite direction. An *Economist* survey of twenty international statisticians rated the quality of statistics from thirteen developed countries, based on objectivity, reliability, methodology, and timeliness. The leading countries were Canada, Australia, Holland, and France, while the worst were Belgium, Spain, and Italy.[17]

Although a substantial body of data exists from the most advanced industrial nations, secondary data are less available for developing countries. Not every country publishes a census, and some published data are not considered reliable. In Nigeria, for example, the population total is of such political importance that published census data are generally believed to be highly suspect. For reasons such as this, companies sometimes have to proceed with the collection of primary data in developing countries at a much earlier stage than in the most industrialized nations.

15. Michael Brizz, ''How to Learn What Japanese Buyers Really Want,'' *Business Marketing,* January 1987, p. 72.
16. Douglas and Craig, *International Marketing Research,* pp. 16–19.
17. ''The Good Statistics Guide,'' *Economist,* September 11, 1993, p. 65.

Data Collection

Collecting Secondary Data   For any marketing research problem, the analysis of secondary data should be a first step. Although not available for all variables, often data are available from public and private sources at a fraction of the cost of obtaining primary data.

Collection of data includes the task of calling, writing, or visiting the potential secondary sources. Often, one source will lead to another source until you find the desired information or determine that it does not exist. A good approach to locating secondary sources is to ask yourself who would know about most sources of information on a specific market. For example, if you wanted to locate secondary information on fibers used for tires in Europe, you may consider asking the editor of a trade magazine on the tire industry or the executive director of the tire manufacturing association or the company librarian for Akzo, a Dutch company that manufactures fibers. Also, most business libraries will have some type of directory of secondary information, such as:

International Directory of Published Research, vol. 14 (London: Arlington Management Publications, 1994)

Directory of U.S. and Canadian Marketing Surveys and Services (Kline Publishing, 1994)

Findex: Directory of Market Research Reports, Studies and Surveys, 1995

On-line databases, microfilm, and compact disks also are excellent sources of information available in most business libraries. Searches on these systems can quickly identify articles, books, and financial information on most business topics, marketing, and companies. Some of these on-line data sources follow:

Datastream International (Dun & Bradstreet)

Textline (Reuters Limited)

DunsPrint (Dun & Bradstreet)

Harvest, Marketing Research (Harvest Information Services)

ABI/Inform (University Microfilms)

It would be impractical to list all the secondary data sources available on international markets, but some secondary data sources would be banks, consulates, embassies, foreign chambers of commerce, libraries with foreign information sections, foreign magazines, public accounting firms, security brokers, and state development offices in foreign countries. A good business library and the local U.S. Department of Commerce are always good places to start a search for secondary data. Table 6.2 lists some of the major sources of published secondary data.

There are problems associated with the use of secondary data, namely (1) lack of necessary data, (2) level of accuracy of the data, (3) lack of comparability of the data, and (4) age of the data. In some cases, no data have been collected. For example, many countries have little data on the number of retailers, wholesalers, and distributors. In Ethiopia and Chad, no population statistics are available.

TABLE 6.2 ● Major Sources of Secondary Data

U.S. DEPARTMENT OF COMMERCE

  Foreign Trade Report: U.S. exports by commodity and by country

  Global Market Surveys: Global market research on targeted industries

  Country Market Surveys: Detailed reports on promising countries covering fifteen industries

  Business America: Magazine presenting domestic and international business news

  Overseas Marketing Report: Trade forecasts, regulations, and market profiles prepared for all countries

INTERNATIONAL MONETARY FUND

  International Financial Statistics: Monthly report on exchange rates, inflation, deflation, country liquidity, etc.

NATIONAL TECHNICAL INFORMATION SERVICES

  Market Share Reports: Reports the size of 88 markets and identifies export opportunities

UNITED NATIONS

  Yearbook of Industrial Statistics: Statistics of minerals, manufactured goods, electricity, and gas

  Statistical Yearbook: Population, production, education, trade, wages

  Demographic Yearbook: Population, income, marriages, deaths, literacy

WORLD BANK

  Country Economic Reports: Macroeconomic and industry trends

  World Development Report: Population, investment, balance of reports, defense expenditures

BUSINESS INTERNATIONAL

  Business International Data Base: Economic indicators, GNP, wages, foreign trade, production, and consumption

EUROMONITOR PUBLICATIONS

  European Marketing Data and Statistics: Population, employment, production, trade, standard of living, consumption, housing, communication

PREDICASTS

  Worldcasts: Economics, production, utilities

THE ECONOMIST

  E.I.U. World Outlook: Forecasts of trends for 160 countries

  Marketing in Europe: Product markets in Europe—food, clothing, furniture, household goods, appliances

---

The accuracy of data varies from country to country, with data from highly industrialized nations likely to be more accurate than data from developing countries.[18] This is a result of the mechanism for collecting data. In industrialized nations, relatively reliable procedures are used for national accounting and for collecting population and industry statistics. In developing countries, where a major portion of the population is illiterate, the data may be based on estimates or rudimentary procedures. Also, statistics could be manipulated for political reasons. For example, a study by the International Labor Organization found actual unemployment to be over 10 percent in Russia, compared with the official figure of 2 percent.[19]

Data may not be directly comparable from country to country. The population statistics in the United States are collected every ten years, whereas population statistics in Bolivia are collected every twenty-five years. Also, countries may calculate the same statistic but in different ways. For example, there are a number of indicators of national wealth. Gross national product (GNP) is the gross value of production in a country. Gross domestic product (GDP) is the value of all goods and services produced and is often used in place of GNP. GDP per capita is one of the most common measures of market size, suggesting the economic wealth of a country per person. Recently, the International Monetary Fund (IMF) decided that the normal practice of converting local currency of GDP into dollars at market exchange rates understates the true size of developing economies relative to rich ones. Therefore, IMF has decided to use purchasing power parities, which take into account the difference in international prices. As shown in Table 6.3, GDP per head is much higher based on purchasing power. For example, the GDP per head in China jumped from $370 to $2,460, an increase of 935 percent.[20]

Another problem with GDP statistics is the hidden, or underground, economy not shown in government statistics. For example in Greece, Spain, and Italy, the hidden economy is 20–30 percent of GDP, while in Japan and Switzerland it is less than 4 percent of GDP.[21] When using official GDP statistics, it is important to remember that they do not reflect the true size of the economy.

In 1990, *Economist* examined ten reports on the economies of eastern Europe. The GDP ranged from $4,000 per person to $13,000 per person for East Germany. The use of gross statistics of national production is very challenging. These crude measures of national wealth can often be very misleading.[22]

Finally, age of the data is a constant problem. Population statistics are usually two to five years old. Industrial production statistics can be one to two years old. With different growth rates, it is difficult to use older data to make decisions.

18. Ibid., p. 79.

19. "Politics and Current Affairs," *Economist,* February 5, 1994, p. 4.

20. "Chinese Puzzles, Developing Countries Are Less Poor Than Official Figures Suggest," *Economist,* May 15, 1993, p. 83.

21. "Working in the Shadows," *Economist,* February 12, 1994, p. 81.

22. "Grossly Deceptive Product," *Economist,* March 10, 1990, p. 99.

TABLE 6.3 ● Market Exchange Rates and Purchasing Power Parity in Developing Countries, 1992

	GDP per Capita $		GDP purchasing power parity ($ billions)
Country	MARKET EXCHANGE RATES	PURCHASING POWER PARITY	
China	$ 370	$2,460	$2,870
India	275	1,255	1,105
Brazil	2,525	4,940	770
Mexico	3,700	6,590	590
Indonesia	650	2,770	510
South Korea	6,790	8,635	380
Thailand	1,780	5,580	320
Pakistan	400	2,075	240
Argentina	6,870	5,930	190
Nigeria	275	1,560	190
Egypt	655	3,350	180
Philippines	820	2,400	155
Malaysia	2,980	7,110	130

Source: Copyright © 1993 The Economist Newspaper Group, Inc. Reprinted with permission.

To test the quality of secondary data, marketers should investigate the following:

1. When were the data collected?

2. How were the data collected?

3. What is the expected level of accuracy?

4. Who collected the data, and for what purpose?

Collecting Primary Data   If secondary data are not available or usable, the marketer will need to collect primary data. Experienced global researchers indicate that while secondary data may be available, going directly to potential consumers, distributors, and retailers may sometimes be less expensive in the long run than spending considerable time in libraries, embassies, and trade associations.

Once secondary sources of information have been exhausted, the next step is to collect primary data that will meet the specific information requirements for making the management decision. Often primary sources will reveal data not available from secondary sources. For example, Siar Research International found that over 50 percent of Kazakhstan men shave every day, while most Azerbaijan men shave only once a week.[23]

Sources of primary data are those in the target country who will purchase or influence the purchase of products. They are consumers, businesses, or governments. Collecting the

23. ''Sharp as a Razor in Central Asia,'' *Economist,* June 5, 1993, p. 36.

appropriate data requires the development of a process to do so. The primary data collection process involves developing a research instrument, selecting a sample, collecting the data, and analyzing the results. These steps are the same in domestic and multinational environments. The process of collecting data in different cultures creates a number of challenges for the international marketer. These challenges include comparability of data, willingness of the potential respondent to participate, and ability of the respondent to understand and communicate.

Comparability of data is important irrespective of whether research is conducted in a single-country or multicountry context. Research conducted in a single country may be used at a later date to compare with the results of research in another country.[24] For example, if a product is tested in France and is successful, the company may decide to test the Italian market. The test used for the Italian market must be comparable with the test in the French market to assess the possible outcome in Italy. Significant differences exist from country to country. For example, a survey of Europeans found the French twice as likely as the European average (22 percent versus 11 percent) to try a product endorsed by a celebrity.[25] Obviously, that research would have a big impact on how a new product is marketed in France.

A second challenge in research is the willingness of the potential respondent. For example, in many cultures a man will consider it inappropriate to discuss his shaving habits with anyone, especially with a female interviewer. Respondents in the Netherlands or Germany are notoriously reluctant to divulge information on their personal financial habits; the Dutch are more willing to discuss sex than money. Through careful planning, researchers can design instruments and techniques to overcome or avoid cultural limitations.[26] For example, in some cultures, it may be necessary to enlist the aid of a local person to obtain cooperation.

Another challenge in survey research involves translation from one language to another. Translation equivalence is important, first to ensure that the respondents understand the question and second to ensure that the researcher understands the response. Idiomatic expressions and colloquialisms are often translated incorrectly. For example, the French translation of a *full* airplane became a *pregnant* airplane; in German, a *"Body by Fisher"* became a *corpse by Fisher.*[27] In a recent case, Braniff found its translation of *to be seated in leather* became *to be seated naked* in Spanish.[28] To avoid these translation errors, experts suggest the technique of back-translation.[29] First, the questionnaire is translated from the home language into the language of the country where it will be used, by a bilingual who is a native speaker of the foreign country. Then this version is translated

24. Douglas and Craig, *International Marketing Research,* p. 132.

25. "Hunting the Euro-Consumer," *Financial Times,* June 28, 1993, p. 4.

26. Robin Cobb, "Marketing Shares," *Marketing,* February 22, 1990, p. 44.

27. Ricks, *Big Business Blunders,* p. 83.

28. "Braniff, Inc.'s Spanish Ad Bears Cause for Laughter," *Wall Street Journal,* February 9, 1987, p. 5.

29. R. Brislin, "Back-Translation for Cross-Cultural Research," *Journal of Cross Cultural Psychology,* 1 (1970), pp. 185–216.

TABLE 6.4 ● Comparison of European Data Collection Methods

	France	*The Netherlands*	*Sweden*	*Switzerland*	*U.K.*
Mail	4%	33%	23%	8%	9%
Telephone	15	18	44	21	16
Central location/streets	52	37	—	—	—
Home/work	—	—	8	44	54
Groups	13	—	5	6	11
Depth interviews	12	12	2	8	—
Secondary	4	—	4	8	—

Source: Emanuel H. Demby, ''ESOMAR Urges Changes in Reporting Demographics, Issues Worldwide Report,'' *Marketing News,* January 8, 1990, p. 24. Reprinted by permission of the American Marketing Association.

back to the home language by a bilingual who is a native speaker of the home language. Another translation technique is parallel translation, in which two or more translators translate the questionnaire. The results are compared, and differences are discussed and resolved.

Data can be collected by mail, by telephone, or face to face. The technique will vary by country. The European Society for Opinion and Market Research (ESOMAR) recently reported on interviewing techniques used in Europe. As shown in Table 6.4, face-to-face interviews at home or work are very popular in Switzerland and the United Kingdom, while interviews in shopping areas are popular in France and the Netherlands. Telephone interviewing dominates Swedish data collection.[30]

Data collection and privacy concerns being raised in the European Union (EU) may affect market research globally. One of the EU directives on data privacy states that respondents cannot be asked sensitive questions without prior written permission.[31] This could seriously limit the use of telephone interviews that may ask questions related to health problems, political beliefs, sex habits, and so on. All twelve EU nations have some type of data privacy legislation regarding the use and sale of consumer research data. This legislation will restrict the use of market research data in Europe.[32]

In Japan, personal, face-to-face discussions are recommended instead of telephone or mail questionnaires.[33] Although personal interviews are expensive and time consuming, the Japanese preference for face-to-face contact suggests that personal interviews yield

30. Emanual H. Demby, ''ESOMAR Urges Changes in Reporting Demographics, Issues Worldwide Report,'' *Marketing News,* January 8, 1990, p. 24.

31. ''CMOR Is Part of a Response to a Worldwide Problem,'' *Marketing News,* August 16, 1993, p. A6.

32. ''Data Privacy Legislation All the Rage in Europe,'' *Marketing News,* August 16, 1993, p. A7.

33. Brizz, ''How to Learn,'' p. 72.

better information than data collected by mail or telephone. In fact, Japanese managers are skeptical about western-style marketing research. Senior and middle managers will often go into the field and speak directly with consumers and distributors. This technique of collecting information called "soft data," though less rigorous than large-scale consumer studies, gives the manager a real feel for the market and the consumers.[34]

Recently, Japanese firms have begun to do more market research. For example, Matsushita (Panasonic) visited 10 million households in 1992 to determine consumer needs for electronic products.[35]

Another technique for collecting marketing research data is focus groups. The researcher assembles a set of six to twelve carefully selected respondents to discuss a product. The focus group is often used at the early stage of a new product concept to gain valuable insights from potential consumers. The research company assembles the participants and leads the discussion, avoiding the potential bias from a company representative. Of course, the discussion leader must speak in the mother tongue of the participants. Representatives of the company can observe the focus group via video or audio taping, through a one-way mirror, or sitting in the room. In some countries such as Japan, it may be difficult to get participants to criticize a potential product. Experienced focus group companies are resourceful at using questioning techniques and interpreting body language to get the full value from this research technique.[36]

Sample Selection   After developing the instrument and converting it to the appropriate language, the researcher will determine the appropriate sample design. Due to its advantage of predicting the margin of error, researchers generally prefer to use probability sampling. The great power of a probability sample lies in the possibility of predicting the corresponding errors: (1) sampling errors, or the chance of not receiving a true sample of the group investigated; (2) response errors, or the deviation of responses from the facts due to either incorrect recall or unwillingness to tell the truth; and (3) nonresponse errors, or uncertainty of the views held by members of the sample that were never reached.[37] For these reasons, probability samples are generally preferred by researchers.

In many foreign countries, however, the existing market infrastructure and the lack of available data or information substantially interfere with attempts to use probability samples. Sampling of larger populations requires the availability of detailed census data, called *census tracks,* and maps from which probability samples can be drawn. Where such data are available, they are often out of date. Thus, stratification is prevented.[38] Further

34. Johny K. Johansson and Ikujiro Nonaka, "Market Research the Japanese Way," *Harvard Business Review,* May–June 1987, pp. 16–22.

35. "Marketing in Japan, Taking Aim," *Economist,* April 24, 1993, p. 74.

36. Catherine Bond, "Market Research—Spy in a Corner," *Marketing,* August 17, 1989, p. 35.

37. Paul E. Green and Donald S. Tull, *Research for Marketing Decisions,* 4th ed. (Englewood Cliffs, N.J.: Prentice Hall, 1978), pp. 111–112.

38. W. Boyd Harper, Jr., Ronald E. Frank, William F. Massy, and Mostafa Zoheir, "On the Use of Marketing Research in the Emerging Economies," *Journal of Marketing Research,* 1 (November 1964), pp. 20–23.

difficulties arise from inadequate transportation that may prevent fieldworkers from actually reaching selected census tracks in some areas of the country. Sampling is particularly difficult in countries having several spoken languages, because carrying out a nationwide survey is impractical.

Research Techniques

A variety of analytic techniques can be used in international marketing research. Although these techniques may be used in domestic marketing research, they are often modified to deal with the complexities of international markets.

Demand Analysis

Demand for products or services can be measured at two levels: aggregate demand, for an entire market or country, and company demand, as represented by actual sales. The former is generally termed *market potential,* whereas the latter is referred to as *sales potential.* A very useful concept developed by Richard Robinson views both market and sales potential as a filtering process (see Figure 6.3). According to Robinson, demand or potential demand

FIGURE 6.3 ● Market Potential and Sales Potential Filter

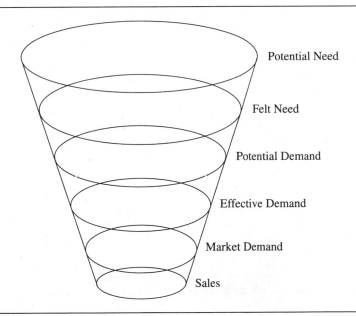

Potential Need

Felt Need

Potential Demand

Effective Demand

Market Demand

Sales

Source: Reprinted from *Internationalization of Business,* 2nd edition, by Richard D. Robison, p. 36. Copyright © 1984 with permission of the author.

can be measured at six successive levels, the last and final level representing actual sales by the firm.[39] The six levels of demand are explained as follows.

Potential Need   Of course, the country's consumers will not purchase the product if there is no need. Therefore, the researcher has to pose the question: Is there a potential need, either now or in the future? Potential need for a product or service is primarily determined by the demographic and physical characteristics of a country. The determinants are a country's population, climate, geography, natural resources, land use, life expectancy, and other factors termed part of the physical environment. The potential need could only be realized if all consumers in a country used a product to the fullest extent regardless of social, cultural, or economic barriers. This represents the ideal case that actually may never be reached.

Felt Need   Though a potential need as defined above may exist to the uninvolved observer, one should not assume that everyone in a market actually feels a need for the product or service under investigation. Due to different life styles, some consumers may not feel a need for a product. For instance, though a farmer in a developing country who drives his produce to a local market in an animal-drawn cart potentially has a use for a pickup truck, he actually may not feel the need for one. Thus, felt need is substantially influenced by the cultural and social environment, including the amount of exposure consumers or buyers have to modern communications. The key task for the researcher is to evaluate the extent to which the potential need is culturally and socially appropriate among the target customers.

Potential Demand   The felt need represents the aggregate desire of a target population to purchase a product. However, lack of sufficient income may prevent some customers from actually purchasing the product or service. The result is the potential demand, or the total amount the market would be ready to absorb. Economic variables preventing the realization of sales are generally beyond the control of any individual company. For example, the average income per household may seem to indicate a large demand for washing machines, but the distribution of income is skewed so that 10 percent of the population has 90 percent of the wealth. To identify if potential demand is blocked, a firm must look at income distribution data.

Effective Demand   Though potential demand might exist, regulatory factors might prevent prospective customers from being able to satisfy their demand. Included are regulations on imports, tariffs, and foreign exchange; specific regulations on product standards with respect to safety, health, pollution; legal aspects such as patents, copyrights, trademarks; fiscal controls such as taxes, subsidies, or rationing and allocations; economic regulations, including price controls and wage controls; and political regulations, including restrictions

39. Richard D. Robinson, *Internationalization of Business,* 2nd ed. (Chicago: Dryden Press, 1984), p. 36.

on buying foreign goods, the role of the government in the economy, and the power of the government to impose controls.

The presence of any of the above cited factors can cause the potential demand to be reduced to a lower level—in other words, to effective demand. Therefore, marketing research needs to uncover the extent to which regulatory factors are present and to determine the possible actions a firm may take to avoid some of the impact on demand.

Market Demand   The extent to which the effective demand can be realized depends substantially on the marketing infrastructure available to competing firms in a country. The degree to which a country's transportation system has been developed is important, as well as its efficiency in terms of cost to users. Additional services that marketers use regularly are storage facilities, banking facilities (particularly for consumer credit), available wholesale and retail structure, and advertising infrastructure. The absence of a fully developed marketing infrastructure will cause market demand to be substantially below effective demand. Marketing research will determine the effectiveness of the present marketing system and locate the presence of any inhibiting factors.

Sales Potential   The actual sales volume that a company will realize in any country is essentially determined by its competitive offering vis-à-vis other firms who also compete for a share of the same market. The resulting market share is determined by the relative effectiveness of the company's marketing mix. In determining sales potential, the researcher will have to assess whether the company can meet the competition in terms of product quality and features, price, distribution, and promotion. The assessment should yield an estimate of the company's market share, given the assumptions about the company's mode of entry (see Chapter 9) and marketing strategy (see Chapter 8).[40]

The difficulty, of course, lies in determining the various demand levels and collecting the facts that can be used to determine actual potential and sales forecasts. Consider a situation in which a company is investigating a market that already has had experience with the product to be introduced. In such a case, the research effort is aimed at uncovering the data on present sales, usage, or production to arrive at the market demand (see Figure 6.3). Consequently, this is primarily an effort in collecting data from secondary information sources or commissioning professional marketing research through independent agencies when necessary.

Analysis by Inference

Available data from secondary sources are frequently of an aggregate nature and do not satisfy the specific needs of a firm focusing on just one product at a time. A company must usually assess market size based on very limited data on foreign markets. In such cases, market *assessment by inference* becomes a necessity. This technique uses available facts about related products or other foreign markets as a basis for inferring the necessary

40. Franklin R. Root, *Entry Strategies for International Markets* (Lexington, Mass.: Lexington Books, 1987), p. 41.

information for the market under analysis. Market assessment by inference, a low-cost method that is analysis based, should take place before a company engages in any primary data collection at a substantial cost. Inferences can be made based on related products, related markets' sales, and related environmental factors.

Related Products   Few products are consumed or used alone without any ties to other prior purchases or products in use. Relationships exist, for example, between replacement tires and automobiles on the road and between electricity consumption and the use of appliances. In some situations, it may be possible to obtain data on related products and their uses as a basis for inferred usage of the particular product to be marketed. From experience in other, similar markets, the analyst is able to apply usage ratios that can provide for low-cost estimates. For example, the analyst can determine the number of replacement tires needed per *X* automobiles on the road. A clear understanding of usage patterns can be gained from performing a comparative analysis as described earlier.

Related Markets' Size   Quite frequently, if market size data are available for other countries, this information can be used to derive estimates for the particular country under investigation. For example, consider that market size is known for the United States and estimates are required for Canada, a country with a comparable economic system and consumption patterns. Statistics for the United States can be scaled down by the relative size of either GNP, population, or other factors to about one-tenth of U.S. figures. Similar relationships exist in Europe, where the known market size of one country can provide a basis for an inference about a related country. Of course, the results are not exact, but they provide a basis for further analysis. The cost and time lag for collecting primary market data often force the analyst to use the inference approach.

Related Environmental Factors   A more comprehensive analysis can be provided after a full comparative analysis as outlined previously. After data are collected on the relevant environmental variables for a given product, an inference may be made on the market potential. The estimate's reliability would depend on the type of data available on the success factors. Actual data on success factors are of course preferable to inferences based on the demand structure in a related market. Reed Moyer described a series of additional methods suited for forecasting purposes that often involve the use of historic data.[41] Some of these methods are described in abbreviated form.

Analysis of Demand Patterns   By analyzing industrial growth patterns for various countries, researchers can gain insights into the relationship of consumption patterns to industrial growth. Relationships can be plotted between gross domestic product per capita and the percentage of total manufacturing production accounted for by major industries. During earlier growth stages with corresponding low per capita incomes, manufacturing tends to center on necessities such as food, beverages, textiles, and light manufacturing. With grow-

41. Reed Moyer, ''International Market Analysis,'' *Journal of Marketing Research,* 5 (November 1968), pp. 353–360.

ing incomes, the role of these industries tends to decline, and heavy industry assumes a greater importance. By analysis of such manufacturing patterns, forecasts for various product groups can be made for countries at lower income levels, since they often repeat the growth patterns of more developed economies.

Similar trends can be observed for a country's import composition. With increasing industrialization, countries develop similar patterns modified only by each country's natural resources. Energy-poor countries must import increasing quantities of energy as industrialization proceeds, whereas energy-rich countries can embark on an industrialization path without significant energy imports. Industrialized countries import relatively more food products and industrial materials than manufactured goods, which are more important for the less industrialized countries. Understanding these relationships can help the analyst determine future trends for a country's economy and may help determine future market potential and sales prospects.

Multiple-Factor Indexes

This technique has already been successfully used by domestic marketers. It entails the use of proxies to estimate demand if the situation should prevent the direct computation of a product's market potential. A multiple factor measures potential indirectly, using proxy variables that intuition or statistical analysis reveals to be closely correlated to the potential for the product under review.

A good example for such an approach is Ford Motor's analysis for its overseas tractor business.[42] To evaluate the attractiveness of its various overseas markets, the company developed a scale and rated each country on attractiveness and competitive strength. These two dimensions were measured based on the following:

Country attractiveness	*Competitive strength*
Market size	Market share
Market growth rate	Product fit
Government regulations	Contribution margin
Price controls	Profit per unit
Nontariff barrier	Profit percentage, net of dealer cost
Local content	
Economic and political stability	Market support
Inflation	Quality of distribution system
Trade balance	Advertising versus competition
Political stability	

These items were evaluated by Ford's executives and rated on a ten-point scale for each item. The items are combined based on the relative weight of each item to determine

42. Gilbert D. Harrell and Richard O. Kiefer, "Multinational Strategic Market Portfolios," *MSU Business Topics,* Winter 1981, pp. 5–15.

the coordinates of the X and Y axes. Figure 6.4 illustrates Ford's use of the market evaluation system for Ford's key countries. The weights are indicative of the firm's effort to rank markets via multiple-factor indexes.

Competitive Studies

As every marketer knows, results in the marketplace do not depend only on researching buyer characteristics and meeting buyer needs. To a considerable extent, success in the marketplace is influenced by a firm's competition. Companies competing on an international level have to be particularly careful with monitoring competition, because some of the competing firms will most likely be located abroad, thus creating additional difficulties in keeping abreast of the latest developments.

When Honda first entered the U.S. motorcycle industry in 1959, the British and U.S. motorcycle firms that dominated the industry did not pay much attention. Honda's entry with a 50-cc bike posed little threat to the macho bikes by Harley Davidson and Triumph. But thirty years later, 80 percent of the bikes are Japanese competing from 50 cc to 1,400 cc. Many companies fail to spot competitors until it is too late. Swiss watchmakers were blind-sided by competitors not even in the same business. While the Swiss were making increasingly more complex mechanized watches, Casio launched basic digital watches that sold at half the price of cheap mechanical watches. Only with the launch of the fashionable electronic Swatch watch in 1985 were the Swiss able to regain some of their lost market.[43]

First, a company will have to determine who its competitors are. The domestic market will certainly provide some input here. However, it is of great importance to include any foreign company that either presently is a competitor or may become one in the future. For many firms, the constellation of competitors will most likely change over time. One U.S. company, Caterpillar, could consider other domestic competitors its major competitors both domestically and abroad. More recently, the Japanese firm Komatsu has established itself as the second-largest firm for earthmoving equipment, forcing Caterpillar to concentrate more resources on this new competitor.[44] Therefore, included in a company's monitoring system should be *all* major competitors, both domestic and foreign. The monitoring should not be restricted to activity in the competitors' domestic market only but must include competitors' moves anywhere in the world. Many foreign firms first innovate in their home markets, expanding abroad only when the initial debugging of the product has been completed. Therefore, a U.S. firm would lose valuable time if, say, a Japanese competitor's action would only be picked up on entry into the U.S. market. Any monitoring system needs to be structured in such a way as to ensure that competitors' actions will be spotted wherever they tend to occur first. Komatsu, Caterpillar's major competitor worldwide, subscribed to the *Journal Star,* the major daily newspaper in Caterpillar's hometown, Peoria, Illinois. Also important are the actions taken by subsidiaries; they may signal future moves elsewhere in a company's global network of subsidiaries.

43. "Competing with Tomorrow," *Economist,* May 12, 1990, p. 85.
44. "Komatsu on the Track of Cat," *Fortune,* September 20, 1981, pp. 164–174.

FIGURE 6.4 ● Key-Country Matrix

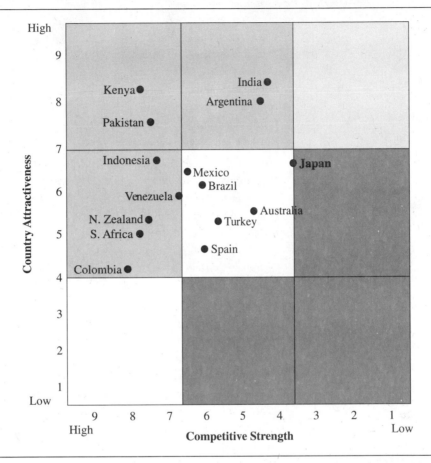

Source: Gilbert D. Harrell and Richard O. Kiefer, ''Multinational Strategic Market Portfolios,'' MSU Business Topics, Winter 1981, p. 13. Reprinted by permission.

Table 6.5 contains a list of the type of information a company may wish to collect on its competitors. Aside from the general business statistics, a competitor's profitability may shed some light on the capacity to pursue new business in the future. Learning about others' marketing operations will allow the investigating company to assess, among other things, the market share to be gained in any given market. Whenever major actions are planned, it is extremely helpful to know what the likely reaction of competitive firms will be and to include them in a company's contingency planning. And, of course, monitoring a competitor's new products or expansion programs may give early hints on future competitive threats.

TABLE 6.5 ● Monitoring Competition: Facts to Be Collected

Overall company statistics
Sales and market share profits
Balance sheet
Capital expenditures
Number of employees
Production capacity
Research and development capability

Marketing operations
Types of products (quality, performance, features)
Service and/or warranty granted
Prices and pricing strategy
Advertising strategy and budgets
Size and type of sales force
Distribution system (includes entry strategy)
Delivery schedules (also spare parts)
Sales territory (geographic)

Future intentions
New product developments
Current test markets
Scheduled plant capacity expansions
Planned capital expenditures
Planned entry into new markets/countries

Competitive behavior
Pricing behavior
Reaction to competitive moves, past and expected

Analysis that focuses on studying the products of key competitors can often miss the real strength of the competitor. To understand an industry and where it is headed over the next five years, studying the core competencies in an industry is important. For example, Chaparral Steel, a profitable U.S. steelmaker, sends its managers and engineers to visit competitors, customers, and suppliers' factories to identify the trends and skills that will lead steelmaking in the future. Chaparral also attends trade shows and visits university research departments to spot new competencies that may offer an opportunity or pose a threat.[45]

45. C. K. Prahalad and Gary Hamel, "The Core Competence of the Corporation," *Harvard Business Review,* May–June 1990, pp. 79–91.

There are numerous ways to monitor competitors' activities. Thorough study of trade or industry journals is an obvious starting point. Also, frequent visits can be made to major trade fairs where competitors exhibit their products. At one such fair in Texas, Caterpillar engineers were seen measuring Komatsu equipment.[46] Other important information can be gathered from foreign subsidiaries located in the home markets of major competitors. The Italian office equipment manufacturer, Olivetti, assigned a major intelligence function to its U.S. subsidiary because of that unit's direct access to competitive products in the U.S. marketplace. A different approach was adopted by the Japanese pharmaceutical company, Esei, which opened a liaison office in Switzerland, home base to several of the world's leading pharmaceutical companies.

There is a widespread impression that U.S. and European firms are much less vigilant than their Asian competitors. For example, Mitsubishi has between 650 and 800 employees in New York to gather intelligence information about their U.S. competitors. The South Koreans are not far behind; the intelligence systems of their three largest trading companies were developed by an ex-colonel of the South Korean military intelligence. The systems require real-time reporting to a central processing unit by every branch manager around the world.[47] The examples from Japan and Korea suggest that a business intelligence system requires a coordinated effort that draws on the knowledge of the entire organization. To keep track of a firm's competitors is an important international research function. The effort is most effectively performed on a permanent basis rather than ad hoc. To give it the status of a permanent monitoring operation, responsibilities need to be assigned to personnel well placed to carry out this important activity.

Environmental Studies

Frequently it becomes necessary to study the international environment beyond the customary monitoring function that most international executives perform. Of particular interest are the economic, physical, sociocultural, and political environments.

In any focus on the economic environment, the primary interest will be on the economic activity in target countries. Major economic indicators are GNP growth, interest levels, industrial output, employment levels, and the monetary policy of the country under investigation. Studies focusing on a country are frequently undertaken when a major decision regarding that country has to be made. This could include a move to enter the country or to significantly increase the firm's presence in that market through large new investments.

Also frequently studied are the international economy and the role of the various supranational organizations as these affect the business climate for international companies. For example, it is important for companies active in Europe to learn about the possible impact or likelihood of new regulations or decisions of the European Union. Frequently,

46. Ibid.

47. Benjamin Gilad, ''The Role of Organized Competitive Intelligence in Corporate Strategy,'' *Columbia Journal of World Business,* Winter 1989, p. 32.

reviews of such agencies or groups are ordered when a major move is imminent and information is needed on the potential impact of these decisions.

Since the physical environment tends to be the most stable aspect of the foreign marketing environment, such studies are frequently made for major market entry decisions or when the introduction of a new product requires a special analysis of that particular aspect of the environment. Included within the physical environment are population and related statistics on growth, age composition, birthrates, and life expectancy, as well as data on the climate and geography of a country.

Of particular interest is the sociocultural environment already described in some detail in Chapter 3. The salient factors include social classes, family life, life styles, role expectations of the sexes, reference groups, religion, education, language, customs, and traditions. Market researchers have classified these statistics as psychographics. The primary interest to the international company is the potential effect of these variables on the sale of its products. Since the sociocultural environment is also unlikely to change over the short run and changes that do occur tend to be of a more gradual nature, such studies are most likely ordered when a major marketing decision in the local market is contemplated. As a company gains experience in any given country, its staff and local organization accumulate considerable data on the social and cultural situation that can be tapped whenever needed. Therefore, a full study of these environmental variables is most useful when the company does not already have a base in that country and past experience is limited.

Frequently management will investigate the regulatory environment of a given country because those influences can substantially affect marketing operations anywhere. Today, regulatory influences can originate with both national and supranational organizations. National bodies tend to influence the marketing scene within the borders of one country only, whereas supranational agencies have a reach beyond any individual country. National regulations may include particular rulings affecting all businesses, such as product liability laws, or may be targeted at individual industries only. In the United States, the latter type would include regulatory agencies such as the U.S. Food and Drug Administration (FDA) and the U.S. Department of Commerce. Examples of supranational regulations are those issued by the European Union with respect to business within the member nations, and the United Nations' Center for Transnational Corporations' nonbinding code of conduct for international companies.

Regulatory trends can be of great importance to international companies and may even lead to new opportunities. It is generally accepted by most observers that U.S. safety and emission control regulations for passenger automobiles are the most stringent to be found anywhere in the world. Recognizing this fact, the French company Peugeot has maintained a small beachhead in the U.S. market, even with a small and insignificant sales volume, primarily to gain the experience of engineering cars under these stringent conditions. The company feels that this experience can be usefully applied elsewhere as other countries adopt similar regulations. Consequently, a company will not monitor the regulatory environment to adopt products and marketing operations to meet with only local success. In addition, firms may find it useful to keep informed about the latest regulations regarding their business in countries that have preceded other countries with pertinent legislation even if they may not conduct any business there.

Developing a Global Information System

Companies that already have or that plan to become global marketers must look at the world marketplace to identify global opportunities. To evaluate the full range of opportunities requires a global perspective for market research. Although many global players started in the triad of North America, Japan, and Europe, this only represents 15 percent of the planet's population. Eastern Europe offers interesting opportunities, with a combined GNP from the former East Germany, Hungary, and Czechoslovakia that is larger than the GNP of China. This region has relatively well-trained and low-paid workers. Indonesia, the fifth-most populated country in the world, has recently cut government paperwork by 67 percent in an effort to stimulate growth and attract foreign investors. India, the second-largest country with 800 million people, has been eliminating regulations to open its markets. For example, in 1988, Indians bought 6 million television sets, up from only 150,000 sets a decade earlier.[48] In approaching the marketplace from a global perspective, companies need to look at not only countries but also industries and segments.

The forces that affect industry should be analyzed to determine the competitiveness of the industry and the role of the major forces such as buyers, suppliers, new entrants, substitutes, and competitors.[49] In addition, companies need to look for global industry shifts and position themselves to take advantage of them. For example, a retailer examining the do-it-yourself market may notice that the car servicing industry is shifting due to changes in automotive technology. With the mechanical reliability of modern cars, the maintenance needs of second-hand car owners beyond the warranty are limited to a few options that do not require skilled labor on complex equipment. These repairs can be done in specialty workshops at a lower cost and more conveniently than at the authorized dealer.[50] Predicting this type of industry shift opens opportunities for the vigilant company.

Globalization also means that companies are looking for new ways to segment markets, especially where demographics fail. There is a trend toward classifying consumers based on life styles, attitudes, and preferences rather than nationalities. If you plan to build a global brand, you need segments that are similar regardless of nationality.[51]

Another challenge to the global company is the sharing of information regarding customers, markets, competitors, and marketing approaches. For example, the marketing manager for the chemical divison who is evaluating the global tape industry should have easy access to research done by other parts of the company that also may have looked at that business. While it sounds like an easy task, it is not. Imperial Chemical Industries (ICI), with 130,000 employees worldwide, launched an ''Experience Databank'' to capture

48. Thomas A. Stewart, ''How to Manage in a New Era,'' *Fortune,* January 15, 1990, p. 29.

49. Michael E. Porter, *Competitive Strategy: Techniques for Analyzing Industries and Competitors* (New York: Free Press, 1980).

50. Xavier Gilbert and Paul Stebel, ''Taking Advantage of Industry Shifts,'' *European Management Journal,* 7, no. 4 (1990), p. 399.

51. Mary Goodyear, ''Bold Approaches to Brave New Worlds,'' *Marketing Week,* March 23, 1990, pp. 52–55.

its marketing knowledge. The database stores information from all over the world, covering every part of the market process. It draws on the experience of different businesses, territories, and functions within ICI, as well as from other international companies. Anyone in the country can contact the Market Focus Bureau, which manages the service, to search the database for particular needs. This is one approach to helping share the experience throughout the company.

The demand for quality multicountry research has spurred the market research industry to expand beyond traditional national boundaries. Mintel, primarily a U.K.-based market research company, changed its name to Mintel International to reflect its concentration on the world market. Industry experts expect a rapid increase in the demand for multicountry research.[52]

Nielsen introduced its first pan-European research service called Quartz, which provides simulated market tests based upon consumer reactions in five European countries. Twenty-five multinationals, including Nestlé, Procter & Gamble, and BSN, have already signed up for the service. Europanel, a consortium of Europe's leading consumer panel companies has developed a pan-European service called the European Market Measurement Database. It tracks the movement of consumer goods throughout western Europe, based on information from 55,000 households. The global research companies have purchased a number of national market research companies. For example, Nielsen bought companies in Denmark, Holland, and Italy to expand its European operations. With the acquisitions, Nielsen reports track 25,000 European householders on an ongoing basis.[53]

Global market research companies often publish monthly industry reports that cover specific product categories. They supply the industry with a wide variety of secondary research. Also, they can be called on to conduct primary research where necessary. The largest international research companies are shown in Table 6.6.

To assist decision making about marketing on a global scale, researchers must provide more than data on strictly local factors within each country. All firms that market their products in overseas markets require information that allows analysis across several countries or markets. However, leaving each local subsidiary or market to develop its own database does not usually result in an integrated marketing information system (MIS). Instead, authority to develop a centrally managed MIS must be assigned to a central location, with reports given directly to the firm's chief international marketing officer. Jagdish Sheth made a very effective case for a centralized marketing research staff that would monitor buyer needs on a worldwide basis.[54] Sheth favors the establishment of a longitudinal panel in selected geographical areas encompassing all major markets, present and potential. By assessing client needs on a worldwide basis, the company ensures that products and services are designed with all buyers in mind. This avoids the traditional pattern

52. Donna Dawson, ''Booming Reports,'' *Marketing,* December 14, 1989, p. 37.

53. Elena Bowers, ''Powerhouses Tear Down Europe Borders,'' *Advertising Age,* June 11, 1990, pp. S-14–16.

54. Jagdish N. Sheth, ''A Conceptual Model of Long-Range Multinational Marketing Planning,'' *Management International Review,* no. 4–5 (1971), pp. 3–10.

TABLE 6.6 ● Top Ten Market Research Companies

	1992 international non-U.S. revenue (in millions of dollars)
A. C. Nielson	$790
IMS International	391
Research International	123
MRB Group	65
Global Market Research	50
Millward Brown	46
Information Resources	35
Walsh International	32
Goldfarb Corp.	15
Louis Harris & Associates	14

Source: R. Craig Endicott, ''European Dream Captivates Researchers,'' *Advertising Age,* December 18, 1993, pp. 5–6.

of initially designing products for the company's home market and looking at export or foreign opportunities only once a product has been designed.

A principal requirement for a worldwide MIS is a standardized set of data to be collected from each market or country. Though the actual data collection can be left to a firm's local units, they will do so according to central and uniform specifications.

Conclusions

In this chapter, we discussed the major challenges and difficulties in securing necessary data for international marketing. We have shown that effective marketing research is based on a conceptual framework combined with a thorough but flexible use of conventional marketing research practices. The major difficulties are the lack of basic data on many markets and the likelihood that research methods will have to be adapted to local environments. The final challenge of international marketing research is to provide managers with a uniform database covering all the firm's present and potential market. This will allow for cross-country comparisons and analysis as well as the incorporation of worldwide consumer needs into the initial product design process. Given the difficulties in data collection, to achieve this international comparability of data is indeed a challenge for even the most experienced professionals.

The value of market research cannot be understated, especially in new developing markets. The managing director of Digital Equipment Corporation's Asian region offers the following advice to executives considering the China market:

> Aggressively conduct market research—talk to companies with experience in the market. Most executives are willing to share the lessons they have learned. In addition, work closely with the American Chamber of Commerce in Hong Kong and the U.S. Consulates and embassies. The officials are aggressive in promoting U.S. companies and they are very knowledgeable about local conditions.[55]

Questions for Discussion

1. Why is it so difficult to do marketing research in multicountry settings?

2. Comparative marketing analysis is a powerful technique that provides the basis for the study of international marketing. What is the comparative approach, and how do you apply it to multicountry environments?

3. What are the advantages and disadvantages of secondary and primary data in international marketing?

4. If you were estimating the demand for bathroom cleaners, what type of inference analysis would you use? Give a specific example.

5. If you headed Kodak, how would you monitor reactions around the world to a major competitor such as Fuji Film?

For Further Reading

Davis, Harry L., Susan P. Douglas, and Alvin J. Silk. "Measure Unreliability: Hidden Threat to Cross-National Marketing Research." *Journal of Marketing,* Spring 1981, pp. 98–109.

Douglas, Susan P., and Samuel Craig. *International Marketing Research.* Englewood Cliffs, N.J.: Prentice Hall, 1983.

Green, Robert, and Philip D. White. "Methodological Considerations in Cross National Consumer Research." *Journal of International Business Studies,* Fall–Winter 1976, pp. 81–88.

Jaffee, E. D. "Multinational Marketing Intelligence: An Information Requirements Model." *Management International Review,* 19, no. 2 (1979), pp. 53–60.

Miller, Cyndee. "Anyone Ever Hear of Global Focus Groups?" *Advertising Age,* May 27, 1991, p. 14.

Murray, J. Alex. "Intelligence Systems of the MNCs." *Columbia Journal of World Business,* September–October 1972, pp. 63–71.

Netemeyer, Richard G., Srinivas Durvasula, and Donald R. Lichtenstein. "A Cross-National Assessment of the Reliability and Validity of the CETSCALE." *Journal of Market Research,* August 1991, pp. 320–327.

55. "Digital Equipment Corporation's China Strategy: Building a Foundation for the Long Term" (Greater China Business Network, 1993), pp. 19–23.

Permut, Steven F. ''The European View of Marketing Research.'' *Columbia Journal of World Business,* Fall 1977, p. 94.

Peterson, Robin T. ''Screening Is First Step in Evaluating Foreign Market.'' *Marketing News,* November 9, 1990, p. 13.

''Research Companies Push Global Expansion.'' *Advertising Age,* March 8, 1993, p. 31.

Samli, A. Coskun. ''An Approach to Estimating Market Potential in East Europe.'' *Journal of International Business Studies,* Fall–Winter 1977, pp. 49–55.

Wind, Yoram, and Susan Douglas. ''International Market Segmentation.'' *European Journal of Marketing,* 6, no. 1 (1972), p. 18.

Winters, Lewis C. ''International Psycholographics.'' *Marketing Research: A Magazine of Management and Application,* September 1992, pp. 48–49.

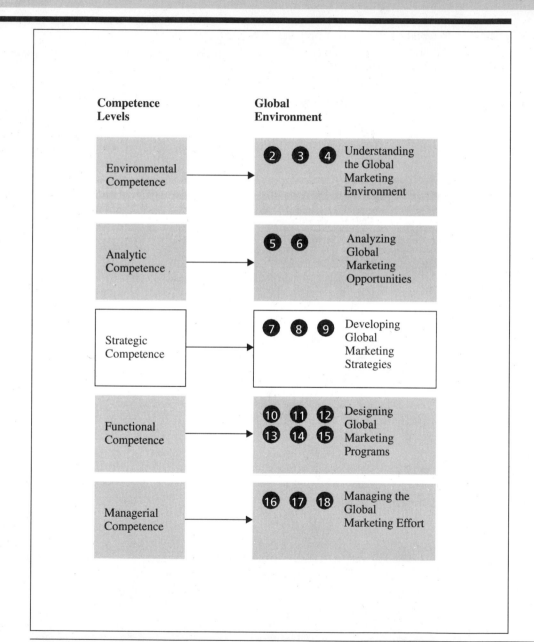

**Competence
Levels**

**Global
Environment**

Environmental
Competence

② ③ ④ Understanding
the Global
Marketing
Environment

Analytic
Competence

⑤ ⑥ Analyzing
Global
Marketing
Opportunities

Strategic
Competence

⑦ ⑧ ⑨ Developing
Global
Marketing
Strategies

Functional
Competence

⑩ ⑪ ⑫ Designing
Global
⑬ ⑭ ⑮ Marketing
Programs

Managerial
Competence

⑯ ⑰ ⑱ Managing the
Global
Marketing Effort

PART 3

Developing Global Marketing Strategies

INCREASINGLY, INTERNATIONAL COMPANIES are being asked to design their business strategies from a global point of view. Globalized business strategies require an ability to look at business and competitive developments all over the world and to digest often conflicting information into a workable plan. Global strategies require skills and conceptual understanding that are different from those required for developing domestic strategies.

In this section, we concentrate on the global strategies international firms must be able to develop to be successful. No company can be all things to all people, and international managers have to learn to focus and build on their company's strengths. Future international marketing managers need to have the strategic competence necessary to develop global marketing programs that will ensure the success of their firms.

Chapter 7 deals with the global mindset required of future international marketing managers. Chapter 8 concentrates on the major strategic decisions faced by firms active in global marketing. The chapter will introduce the most recent concepts on globalization of marketing strategies. The various alternative entry strategies will be the subject of Chapter 9.

7

Developing a Global Mindset

● **THE SLOGAN** "**THINK** *globally, act locally" is frequently used to describe the managerial challenge faced by global marketers.*[1] *It captures the need to think in global terms about a business or a market while, at the same time, doing some local tailoring to meet the particular requirements of the local customers. In this chapter, we give some background on what is meant by thinking globally. If this is a truly different type of thinking, requiring a new mindset (namely a global one), one should be able to differentiate it from a more traditional mindset. We have therefore decided to offer detailed ideas about what this new global marketer with a global perspective ought to be able to do, how he or she should be able to think, and what kind of skills could be expected from such a person. This chapter is different from others, as it does not focus to the same extent on existing business practice. Instead, we concentrate on developing new analytic tools that will make the adoption of a global perspective more likely.*

The Four Types of Marketing Mindsets[2]

The mindset is the outlook or frame of mind that the marketer carries around the world. The global perspective, or mindset, is characterized by a different view of the opportunities

1. Gurcharan Das, "Local Memoirs of a Global Manager," *Harvard Business Review,* March–April 1993, pp. 38–47.
2. Jean-Pierre Jeannet, "The Age of the Global Mind," *Unternehmung,* 45, no. 2 (1991), pp. 132–142.

and the facts of the world market. The global marketing perspective is more encompassing than the domestic, international, or even multinational perspective. It is a new, truly different dimension in managerial thinking that transcends traditional labels and shapes the outlook of global marketers. (See Figure 7.1 for a more detailed account of the concepts discussed in this chapter.)

Domestic Perspective

The *domestic perspective* is characterized by the fact that all basic anchor points of a marketer are from a single, his or her domestic, market or country. A marketing executive

FIGURE 7.1 ● The Global Mindset

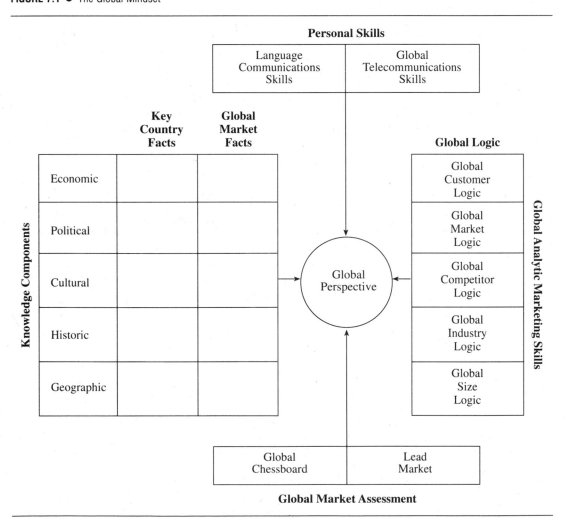

growing up in the United States and professionally active in the U.S. market only has a single-country, domestic mindset. The same is true for a German manager growing up and living in Germany only. Thus, the domestic mindset is always single-country in nature. As we all know, marketers must constantly refer to their own experience as they go about making marketing decisions. The facts are not always spelled out, and executives typically ''fill in the blanks'' from their own cultural experience. The domestic mind tends to fill in those blanks from its own domestic market or cultural perspective.

Falling back on one's own cultural or domestic experience base comes very naturally to executives. As we showed in Chapter 3, violating cultural norms in another country often occurs because executives, or companies, go to a different country and automatically transfer some of the underlying assumptions to a different place. The reverse, however, is also true. When data from a different country are available, executives with a domestic perspective will often find that set of data meaningless, or discomfiting, preferring instead business data from their own country.

The concept of the domestic perspective is not new to global and international marketing. For some time, executives have referred to such a perspective as ethnocentric, or bound in only one culture.[3] This reaction of rejecting data, facts, or readings from elsewhere is sometimes referred to as the not-invented-here (NIH) syndrome, a concept well known in engineering and scientific circles. It generally results in the rejection of new ideas that are not homegrown and stands in the way of adopting best practice in marketing, particularly when the product originated in some distant other market.

International Perspective

Marketing executives with an international perspective have broadened their reference points to other markets, typically through some longer international or overseas stay. A Japanese executive who has spent four years with the U.S. subsidiary can be expected to have broadened his perspective to an international one, allowing for incorporation of Japanese and U.S. reference points in that person's mind.

In many firms, executives are sent on international assignments for the simple reason that this broadens their perspective. The number of Americans working for U.S. firms overseas is estimated at about 250,000.[4] There are many expatriate employees from other countries as well. While working overseas provides a new perspective for the manager, substantial barriers exist that limit opportunities. For one, sending a manager overseas is more costly than hiring locals. The experience of Tetra Laval, a Swedish firm, indicates that moving a French manager to the United States cost 50 percent more than hiring a local (U.S.) manager. Conversely, moving a U.S. manager into France and providing the required overseas package drove up costs to 150 percent above hiring a local (French) manager.[5] The extra costs include cost-of-living allowances, different taxation schemes, and the higher costs of sending an entire family to a different country.

3. Howard V. Perlmutter, ''The Tortuous Evolution of the Multinational Corporation,'' *Columbia Journal of World Business,* January–February 1969, p. 12.

4. ''Thriving in a Foreign Environment,'' *New York Times,* December 5, 1993, p. F17.

5. ''The Unmaking of a Myth,'' *International Management,* December 1993, p. 48.

An international experience can take several different forms. Many students spend some time abroad in overseas university programs. To the extent that they have contact with the local environment, some international experience is gained. Likewise, the large number of international students in U.S. business schools gain international experience through their stay in the United States. At Babson College in Massachusetts, all full-time M.B.A. students are required to participate in an international component, taking them overseas to a certain country.

All such experiences provide an international perspective as the student or executive gains in-depth knowledge of a foreign country. Although it is international experience in just one country, many experts believe that such a manager would be less subject to the NIH syndrome. By broadening the domestic, single-country perspective to an international (dual-country) view, the individual would in all likelihood respond better to an initiative in a new country than would the domestic-minded executive, for whom any international contact would be a first-time affair.

Multinational Perspective

A still smaller set of executives, having gone through several overseas experiences or assignments, has reached a multinational perspective. These executives know more than one overseas country well. Often, their assignments span a region, or even more than one region. In many large international firms, such as Citibank, Nestlé, Unilever, and BP, executives have a series of assignments, each of which may be three to four years, in different locations. These executives not only become knowledgeable about one market or culture but have also learned how to master a new one, not yet experienced.

The cadre of executives with the multinational perspective are, however, still largely bound by their cultural and foreign experiences. Their skill derives from the detailed knowledge of those markets they have experienced. While characterizing the multinational perspective as incorporating a greater quantity of in-depth international experience is fair, it still is not to be confused with a global perspective, the unique mindset we wish to describe in more detail in the next section.

Global Perspective

Whether we call the global perspective gaining a global view, a global mindset, global brains, or some other term, we are stepping into a type of perspective fundamentally different from the three previously described. The global perspective encompasses all cultures or nationalities; it might be described as a mind hovering like a satellite over the earth.[6] This calls for a manager with a capability to maintain equal ''mental'' distance from all regions of the world. However, this should not be construed as a person without any cultural anchor. Rather, the executive with the global perspective maintains that point of view with respect to his or her business or profession. A personal cultural anchor point is still required for personal balance.

6. Kenichi Ohmae, *The Borderless World* (London: Collins, 1990), chap. 2, pp. 17–31.

International and multinational perspectives depend on experience gained from direct contact with one or several other countries and cultures. The marketing executive with a global perspective achieves that view throughout the world, even for areas where no direct prior experience exists. That becomes essential because managers who receive global responsibility for a product, a segment, a category, or some other project could not possibly have been exposed to all those countries before.

That a marketing executive who wants to achieve a global perspective will have to think differently about the world should be clear. The following sections of this chapter establish more clearly what those differences are. We will concentrate on the particular knowledge required for a global perspective, the new global analytic skills to be applied, the strategic concepts to be understood, the personal skills to be mastered, and the managerial capabilities to be acquired.

Although we have not said so up to this point, the global mindset is also an attitude. Executives with that global mind display an innate curiosity about the developments of this world. They recognize a need for continued, permanent, lifelong learning, because much of what they know becomes obsolete over time. Executives who aspire to a global mindset need to recognize the integration of industries into a global economy. In this new world, they must see their industry as an interconnected whole and appreciate that events generated in this dynamic drive the shape of their industry and their customer needs over time. This global mindset, then, is as much an attitude as it is a capability to exercise a certain set of analytic skills.[7]

Knowledge Components of the Global Perspective

In the previous section, we described the kind of outlook, or mindset, a marketing manager with a global perspective would bring to an assignment. Although such an outlook is important, it cannot suffice alone. The marketing manager with a global perspective will need knowledge of a set of facts about the world markets. The knowledge components described in this section are basic but not necessarily complete. However, the ones we discuss would most likely account for a vast majority of the necessary factual knowledge; they might serve as a guide to aspiring global marketing managers who are just in the process of acquainting themselves with the world. Again, with the world constantly changing, such knowledge can never be viewed as final or static. It is in constant need of updating.

Key Market Knowledge

With the world consisting of more than two hundred countries and territories, it would be impossible for anyone to have a firsthand and factual knowledge of all of these countries.

---

7. The authors are indebted to Clifton Clarke, formerly with Digital Equipment Corp. and now an independent consultant, for his observations on the attitudinal dimensions of the global mindset.

Instead, a knowledge of *key markets* would have to suffice. We describe key markets as the top twenty markets in a given industry, recognizing that the list of top twenty might change depending on product line. Since in most countries, 80 percent or more of the economic activity can be expected to come from the top twenty markets, we have structured the knowledge components around such a list. For the purpose of this book, we use the listing of the top twenty countries by gross national product (GNP) as a measure (Table 7.1). Since these markets are of global strategic value, marketing managers need to understand the parameters that shape the dynamics in those markets.

Economic Knowledge

While statistical knowledge has some value, marketing managers need even more to have an understanding of the economic situation in a key market. It would be important to know the present stage of the economic cycle. Another part of required knowledge would be the type of economic system and the structure of the economy. The marketer with a global perspective ought to know economic developments in the key markets, so that a clear tapestry of the economic activity emerges. Key areas of market economic knowledge are

TABLE 7.1 ● Top 20 Countries by US$ GNP (1991)

Country	GNP (US$ billion)
United States	$5,695
Japan	3,370
Germany	1,586
France	1,191
Italy	1,128
United Kingdom	1,016
Canada	570
Spain	522
Brazil	395
China	373
Netherlands	287
Australia	282
Korea	281
India	265
Switzerland	242
Mexico	234
Sweden	231
Belgium/Luxembourg	213
Taiwan	180
Indonesia	111

Source: *The World Competitiveness Report 1993,* IMD (Lausanne) and World Economic Forum (Geneva).

TABLE 7.2 ● Key Areas of Market Economic Knowledge

GNP	Export volume
GNP growth	Import volume
GNP per capita	Foreign trade position
Major industrial sectors	Monetary policies
Inflation rate	Foreign reserve position
Interest level	Employment level

listed in Table 7.2. However, real understanding comes from combining these facts into a composite understanding of the present and future economic situation of the key markets.

Political Knowledge

The global marketing manager needs to know the current and future political trends for each key market. This will certainly consist of knowledge of the important political institutions and a sense as to how the country is governed. Among other things, managers need to know the importance of the various political parties, their political programs, something about their leaders, and a sense of the electoral chances for success. Country analysis, as it has been practiced traditionally, will not be sufficient to understand the dynamics in key markets. Companies have to learn to understand the key drivers in the industrial policies of countries. Increasingly, governments strive for added competitiveness, often in the form of generating more exports. The resulting economic policies affect players in that country and, due to the global economy, often radiate across other countries. When new policies are adopted, as in the United States' intent to reform health care, they not only affect all players in the health-care industry in the United States. These actions ripple through the entire world, influencing that industry's companies worldwide.

Cultural Knowledge

Each key market has its own cultural heritage.[8] A manager with a global perspective is expected to understand those major cultural traits and appreciate them, as they may shape customers or business executives in the market. Such cultural knowledge would certainly include an understanding of the type of language, or languages, spoken. This would include knowing in the case of Brazil that Portuguese was the official language, whereas for Belgium it would be French and Flemish (Dutch). Additional knowledge of particular literature, arts, or music might be important. (In the case of Japan, for example, it would mean some understanding of such traditional arts as kabuki and No.) Included in cultural

8. Vern Terpstra and Kenneth David, *The Cultural Environment of International Business,* 2nd ed. (Cincinnati: Southwestern, 1985).

knowledge would be an understanding of the religious background of the key country. As we explained in detail in Chapter 3, the business environment is significantly affected if the country has a Christian, Muslim, or other religious tradition. For many countries, some understanding of the more popular local sports may be part of knowing the culture.

Historic Knowledge

Executives often underestimate the value of knowing a country's history. Many developments that appear to be of a short-term political nature are driven by longer-term historical experiences of a country. How groups of executives relate to each other is also influenced by that heritage. While global marketers typically know the historical background of their own country, few know the key historical developments that shaped the present in their relevant key markets. Marketers need not know history for history's sake but should learn the relevant historical facts that still shape, or influence, the political and economic life of a country in the present time. Looking over the list of top twenty economies (Table 7.1) would quickly indicate where gaps exist. As the tragic developments in a country such as the former Yugoslavia demonstrate, the actions we witness today are rooted in history, dating back as many as six hundred years.[9]

Geographic Knowledge

Part of a thorough understanding of a key market is knowledge of its geography. This may include knowing the locations of key cities and the logistics of getting in and out of the country. Knowing the size of a country, its key dimensions, and its topographic features is also part of geographic knowledge.[10]

Understanding Global Market Facts

Up to now, we have discussed knowledge about a company's key markets. Those facts are about individual countries only. A much larger body of knowledge about the ''global'' economy, politics, history, culture, and geography embraces all countries and plays an increasingly important role in today's business environment. A marketing manager with a global perspective would appreciate this overarching global data structure just as much as each individual key market.

Understanding *global economic forces,* rather than individual-country economic forces, requires knowledge about world trade, international economic structures, and the various international institutions that play a role in the creation of the global economy. Many of those—including the International Monetary Fund (IMF), the General Agreement on Tariffs and Trade (GATT), the Group of 7 (G7, consisting of the leaders of the largest

9. Ferdinand Schevill, *A History of the Balkans* (New York: Dorset, 1991).

10. Philip R. Cateora, *International Marketing,* 7th ed. (Homewood, Ill.: Irwin, 1990), chap. 7, p. 209.

seven economies of the world), and regional bodies such as the European Union (EU), the North American Free Trade Agreement (NAFTA), and ASEAN—have been described in earlier chapters in greater detail. In this category, we include understanding the current global economic trends that shape the structure of the world economy over the next decades.[11]

The equivalent body of knowledge in the political realm consists of understanding how *global political forces* affect the global marketing environment. This knowledge goes beyond the political structures of any individual country but includes the role played by bodies such as the United Nations and an appreciation of the geopolitical realities of the day. The disappearance of Communist regimes in eastern Europe could not be treated as a single-country event alone but would need to be understood in the context of world political forces.[12]

Country-specific history has also its equivalent in a new body of knowledge that we could describe as world history. The understanding required is not the knowledge of just one country but the historical trends and development over time, including a group of countries, a region, or even the entire world. Paul Kennedy's *Rise and Fall of the Great Powers* is but one example of such a new body of historical knowledge that aims at a global perspective in history.[13] Equivalent knowledge exists on *world culture,* where the current media trends might be included; *world geography,* where a clear understanding of world trade patterns and trade routes could be included; and the history of *world trade.*[14]

The Importance of Acquiring Global Key Market Knowledge

To some extent, the knowledge we are describing in this section may be viewed as strictly factual, the kind contained in a library. However, executives do not always consult their library when making decisions about the importance of key markets. Rather, any decisions can be made based upon erroneous, unverified knowledge and thus can result in less than optimal global marketing strategies. Significantly ''underestimating'' a country's population without checking might lead to the elimination of a market that otherwise would need to be part of a global marketing strategy. Many recent studies have shown that knowledge about key market or world affairs varies considerably between countries and that U.S. managers particularly may be approaching global marketing battles with less factual knowledge than managers from other countries have.[15] A realistic strategy of acquiring knowledge of key markets and the global marketplace thus can be an important ingredient in the success of individual executives and companies.

11. Robert B. Reich, *The Works of Nations* (New York: Knopf, 1991).

12. Henry Kissinger, *Diplomacy* (New York: Simon & Schuster, 1994).

13. Paul Kennedy, *The Rise and Fall of the Great Powers* (New York: Random House, 1987). See also Paul Kennedy, *Preparing for the Twenty-First Century* (New York: Random House, 1993).

14. Fernand Braudel, *The Wheels of Commerce* (Berkeley: University of California Press, 1992).

15. ''What's Going On?'' *Wall Street Journal,* March 30, 1994, p. A16.

Global Analytical Marketing Skills

Acquiring a global marketing perspective is not dependent only on acquiring global marketing facts. Marketing managers who want to plot strategy with a global perspective will be challenged to process the vast amount of data they acquire in a different way. In this section, we will center in on the thinking and analytic routines the minds of executives have to go through as they chart global marketing strategies from a large set of data.

For space reasons, we do not give a complete summary of the analytic competence required by global marketers. Basic marketing analysis, used for both single-country and multicountry situations, will not be covered here. We concentrate on some of the unique marketing analytic skills, concepts, and tools that are relevant primarily in global marketing. These topics are grouped around the concept of a *global logic,* with special emphasis on how it applies to global marketing.

The Global Logic Concept

Writers have used the term *global logic* in the past to connote a given relationship in global markets.[16] Here we use *global logic* as a *condition in the marketplace that requires a company to adopt a global strategy.* When the global logic is very strong, there is almost a mandate to pursue its operations on a global scale. Furthermore, if the global logic were violated, the firm presumably would suffer negative competitive consequences. Wherever present, the company facing a global logic in its business must accommodate that logic or suffer competitively.

Whereas the global logic applies to the entire business strategy of a firm, the more specific *global marketing logic* describes the forces that demand the adoption of a global marketing strategy. The global marketer must understand the source of the global marketing logic, as the strategic response might differ. The sources of a global marketing logic might rest with the customer base, thus creating a global *customer* logic. They may also come from the market and purchasing approaches, resulting in a global *market* logic. The strategies pursued by competitors are at the source of the global *competitor* logic. Another source is related to the industry and the relevant key success factors, creating a global *industry* logic. And finally, the presence of a strong critical mass can lead to the global *size* logic. We will now explore each of these sources of global marketing logic in more detail.

Global Customer Logic

A company faces a global customer logic when its customers demand the same product in most countries and, in particular, when the same customer purchases a given product or service in many different locations, or countries. However, in few cases is the nature of demand so homogeneous that there are virtually no differences among countries. More

16. Ohmae, *Borderless World,* p. 114.

likely, levels of similarities and dissimilarities exist. How does the marketer answer the question, "Do we have a global customer?" (See Figure 7.2.)

Analyzing the nature of the demand across countries is a starting point. Traditionally, companies have segmented their business or markets along product/market and country/geographic territories. This traditional matrix, depicted in Figure 7.3, captures the view that, as a company moves from one country to the next, significant changes occur in its marketing environment. The traditional view, emphasizing the country or geographic differences, is characterized through the presence of fat vertical lines, each one of these lines representing significant country differences. A company viewing its business this way would constantly emphasize the difference in its global marketing strategies. However, due to the differences, once a company is in a given country, experience can be leveraged through to other product lines. This we call leveraging on the vertical axis.

The opposite view may be taken by a company that finds that while country differences exist, still larger and more significant differences exist across segments, product lines, or industry sectors. In that situation, the horizontal lines depicted between the segments are drawn as "fat," with the vertical lines separating countries as finer lines. In such a situation, the emphasis on the analysis is on the horizontal axis, where leverage occurs across a segment, product line, or sector. Similarities across countries are significant and can be exploited. We describe this as the horizontal view.

The marketer with a global perspective will discern the differences between geographic differences and segment-specific similarities. For products more rooted in customs, such as food, differences along geographic lines may be greater than those across segment lines. As one moves more toward new technological products and into industrial products

FIGURE 7.2 ● Global Customer Logic

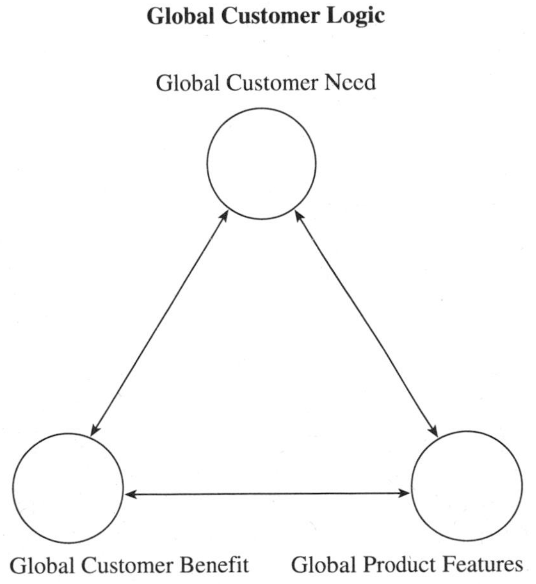

Global Customer Logic

Global Customer Need

Global Customer Benefit   Global Product Features

FIGURE 7.3 ● Global Market Segmentation Matrix

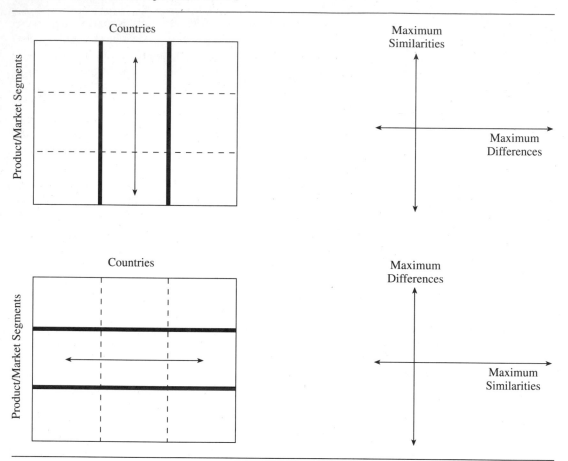

and services, the geographic differences are often smaller than the segment or industry differences.

Although such an analysis might show to what extent a market may differ across many countries, a company has other ways to test for global customer logic.

More likely, a partial global customer logic may exist. Few products, particularly consumer products, are demanded by consumers in exactly the same form, because the comparison across countries is lacking. The ultimate form of global product, which entails essential similarity in features and form, is rarely achieved. This is a function of the differences in requirements among countries.

If a given underlying need for a product or service exists across many countries, this is a *global need*. A product or service subject to global need would show its presence worldwide, with consumers in most countries indicating such a need. Many generic needs such as the need for communications, food, and so on are global needs. Marketing products that fit a global need could be undertaken with multidomestic approaches, offering each country its own version of that product bundle. Whether or not a product or service would be subject to a still more powerful global logic would depend on other things.

The second phase of customer globalization occurs at the benefit level. Companies whose customers derive the same benefit from a product or service will face a much more far-reaching form of global logic. Benefits touch on marketing communications. When a company needs to accommodate a *global benefit,* it will sooner or later move toward some form of global communications development.

When customers desire similar features in products, a company is said to face a *global product logic.* Similarity in features allows companies to standardize products and to market more homogeneous products across world markets.

Companies may not face all customer logic in the same way. A company may face a global product logic, requiring homogeneous products, but encounter significant differences in benefits sought among customers. For other firms, the opposite may be true; a customer base seeks similar benefits around the world but requires different product features. Companies have to be ready to accommodate different levels and intensity of global logic, with corresponding differences in the strategic response.

Global Market Logic

The section on global customer logic concentrated on customer requirements. Aside from what they buy, customers also show different forms of purchasing behavior and processes. A company is subject to a global market logic to the extent that its customers search the world for best products as opposed to purchasing within a given local market only. In many industries, the time has passed when a customer buys within the confines of one country only. While this is less the case in consumer goods markets, industrial buyers are becoming accustomed to look for the best bargain on an international, regional, even world-wide basis.

Automobile companies' purchasing behavior for parts used in assembling cars provides an example.[17] Total parts costs have traditionally accounted for 50 percent of total product costs for carmakers. Typically, parts purchases are sent out for bid each year, splitting supply contracts among several companies to ''bid down'' prices. In recent years, these companies have begun to pay more attention to parts cost as a way to increase efficiency. In some of the high-technology sectors of parts (e.g., automotive electronics, which includes automatic breaking systems or engine management systems), research costs have amounted to about 10 percent of parts costs for parts suppliers. With each part supplier paying for its own research to fit components into specific car models, car companies have in fact paid for the same set of research costs several times. This has led some companies —GM was first among them—to concentrate parts purchases on just a few suppliers, or even one supplier, per model and to give them a contract over the entire model life cycle.

17. ''The World Automotive Suppliers,'' *Financial Times,* June 28, 1993, Survey, sec. IV.

Parallel to this development, car companies have begun to insist on best prices and now engage in worldwide sourcing. Rather than purchasing from a number of nearby plants, a car company will source a greater distance away for lower costs. In some cases, parts are flown in by cargo aircraft from long distances away on a regularly determined schedule, ''just in time.'' This has changed the way companies purchase parts and locate plants, making the entire world the shopping plaza for firms that no longer source in the same country or nearby. Thus, the automotive parts and components industry has become subject to a strong global market logic wherein buyers, car companies in this case, search the world for the best bargain. Many car components suppliers have had to adjust to this demand, often turning local firms into global suppliers if they wanted to survive.[18] The presence of global sourcing or global purchasing practices in an industry is therefore one of the strongest indications of the presence of a significant global market logic.

The presence of a gray market is another indicator. Gray markets exist where prices for a given product or service between two countries are widely different. Customers aware of that price difference begin to purchase in the low-price area and move the products into the high-price area. These gray market activities are not illegal, and in Chapter 13 we explore this phenomenon in greater detail. However, we need to understand that industries where such activities persist are subject to the global market logic. Many international firms experience this phenomenon constantly. One U.S. pharmaceutical company reported that a significant portion of its products sold through Dutch drugstores were in fact purchased in France through unofficial channels. The price differences between France and the Netherlands were significant and were largely caused by different pricing mechanisms applied by the various governments. Behavior such as that of the buyers in the Netherlands demonstrates a transparent market, with buyers well informed as to where better prices exist. Again, when companies face such purchasing behavior, they need to accommodate the global market logic through specific global marketing strategies.

This test of global market logic is therefore often present in industry or business-to-business markets. It happens far less in consumer marketing, because individual consumers usually buy a given product or service in one location only. Citicorp, the leading U.S.-based international bank, has encountered a similar requirement among its wealthy customers looking for private banking services. The company began to offer a Citigold service to upwardly mobile Asian private customers with access to banking services wherever Citicorp has a branch—worldwide.[19] For some leisure or travel-related products, such as films, hotels, or even telephone services, a global market logic exists because travelers demand these products to be present wherever they are.

Global Competitor Logic

When the need to develop a global marketing strategy stems from the behavior of a company's major competitors, we are speaking of a *global competitor logic.* Global pressures rooted in competitive actions can be observed from specific competitive patterns. First and

18. Jean-Pierre Jeannet, ''Siemens AT: Brazil Strategy'' (Lausanne: IMD Institute, 1993).
19. ''Capturing the Global Consumer,'' *Fortune,* December 13, 1993, p. 166.

foremost, a firm might face global competitor logic when the company encounters the same competitors consistently wherever it markets. In some industries, particularly those of industrial equipment, a small set of internationally active companies pursue major orders, such as for aircraft, power plant, turbines, and similar large installations. Whenever a large public tender is opened up, the same sales teams pursue the contract, independent of the country in question. This is a clear sign of global competitor logic. The presence of other, globally active players, who can reach into most markets, requires all players to adopt a global marketing strategy to remain competitive themselves.

In an extreme situation, leading companies engage in what we call a *global chess game.* Picturing the world market as a chessboard, the global chess game implies a consistent, direct, and competitor-oriented move that is highly cognizant of the various market positions of each player. The competitive situations of Pepsi-Cola versus Coca-Cola, or Kodak versus Fuji Film, or Caterpillar versus Komatsu are typical of such competitive games, where two players face off worldwide and pursue competitive advantages in many territories.[20] As in a chess game, the competitors' moves are very open and visible, and each company needs to think about the next move of the opponent.

The presence of significant global competitor logic is derived from the number of relevant competitive theaters. Companies must understand when they are competing in a single, global competitive theater, or arena, where the eventual outcome or ranking denotes their competitive position on a worldwide basis. In one global competitive arena, it will make sense to consider market share on a global, not national, basis. Indicating the presence of a single competitive arena is the fact that the outcome in the world market race is more important than the ranking in any single national market. For a company such as Boeing, the global market share for wide-bodied passenger jets is more important than the market share in any given country.

A company might find, rather than one global theater, many individual-country theaters, thus calling for country-by-country competition. In such a case, looking at market share and competitive position on a country-by-country basis would be more relevant. Intermediate strategies are called for by regional competitive theaters, where the relevant unit of analysis then becomes the region, such as Europe, North America, or Asia. Global competitive logic is strongest where the company faces one relevant global theater and weakest when the relevant competitive theater is one country. (See Figure 7.4.)

Recent developments in some industries have shown, however, that care must be exercised in the analysis of global competitive theaters. An analysis in the white goods industry in 1980 might not have found much presence of any global competitor logic, as main players were confined to regions (e.g., U.S. firms to the United States and European firms to parts of Europe). The aggressive competitive behavior of one single player, in this case Electrolux, that led to the acquisition of Zanussi, a major Italian producer, and White Westinghouse, a major U.S. company, in the 1980s has transformed an entire industry.[21]

20. Stephen Allen, Case Series: ''Note on the Construction Machinery Industry'' (ECCH no. 393-068-5), ''Caterpillar and Komatsu in 1988'' (ECCH no. 393-069-1), ''Caterpillar and Komatsu in 1992'' (ECCH no. 393-070-1).

21. Christopher Lorenz, ''The Birth of a Transnational,'' *McKinsey Quarterly,* Autumm 1989, p. 72.

FIGURE 7.4 ● Global Competitive Theaters

Global Competitive Theaters

Country-Specific Theaters

Regional Theaters

Global Theater

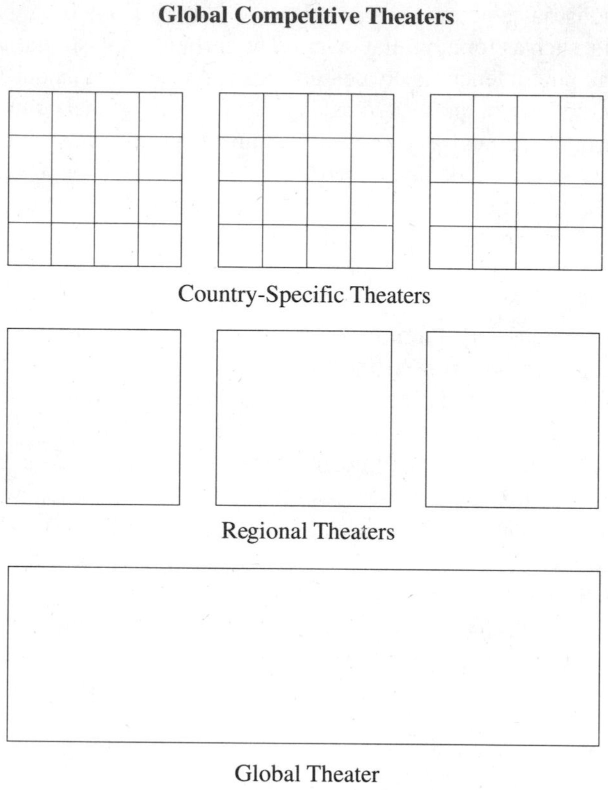

Major U.S. firms such as Maytag, Whirlpool, and GE all reacted, moving aggressively into Europe.[22] These moves were triggered by a perceived threat to their position by Electrolux. In such a way, an industry with little global competitor logic was transformed into an industry with an overwhelming global logic.[23] Firms without any accommodation of that global logic risk competitive disadvantage over the longer term. There are many other industries where a sudden shock move by one major player brought about a complete competitive reorganization and a sudden emergence of a global competitive logic.

22. "On the Verge of a World War in White Goods," *Business Week,* November 2, 1987, p. 41.
23. Stephen Allen, Case Series: "Note on the European Major Home Appliance Industry—1990" (ECCH no. 393-091-5), "Whirlpool Corporation" (ECCH no. 393-095-1), "Electrolux" (ECCH no. 393-094-1), "General Electric: Major Appliances" (ECCH no. 393-093-1).

Global Industry Logic

Conceptually, every industry requires some basic dos and don'ts of its participants. A company that violated these competitive rules would invariably suffer competitive disadvantage and, in the long run, go out of business. These basic rules of competition, required from any player that wants to be a member of this industry, have traditionally been called *key success factors* (KSFs).[24] When an industry is characterized by similar KSFs across the world, a global industry logic exists that would make transferring this experience from one country to another important.

Each company, successful in its home market, has learned how to deliver on the KSFs in its industry. An important indicator of global industry logic is the transferability of these KSFs across the world. If the lessons of competition and the basic competitive requirements for a company to sustain itself in an industry are essentially the same, the first and most important condition for a global industry logic exists. When a company competes in a global industry, leveraging any experience across many countries becomes of great importance. Firms that do this effectively gain a competitive advantage.

The presence of a significant global industry logic will often draw competitors into leveraging their experience into other countries, therefore also creating a secondary effect in the global competitor logic. The experience in the white goods industry serves as an example. As mentioned above, Electrolux was the first player to pursue a global strategy, prompting many competitors into pursuing the same for fear of competitive disadvantage. The cause of Electrolux's original intent to change its strategy from essentially a country-by-country or even regional one centering on Scandinavia to pursuing a broader global strategy rested with some new assumptions. The Electrolux managers were not tempted by a sudden emergence of customers who all wanted the same appliances. Instead, they realized that while appliances were different on the outside from country to country, the important components hidden from view were essentially the same. As costs for appliances became an important element, the costs for key components could only be driven down if the company gained economies of scale on compressors, pumps, and other elements present in millions of appliances.[25]

Electrolux believed that a competitive cost position for large component volume was dependent on gaining market share by acquiring other appliance makers in foreign countries. Electrolux was able to combine its component manufacturing with that of the acquired firms, reducing costs and investing in new models otherwise not affordable. This fundamental economic logic in the appliance business was not just restricted to Electrolux's local market but applied to the world market as a whole. It was on this global industry logic that the company acted, causing a competitive effect that changed the entire industry worldwide. Leveraging this type of component system may play a role in one industry. But in other industries, companies may be able to leverage some other parts of the

24. Kenichi Ohmae, *The Mind of the Strategist* (New York: McGraw-Hill, 1992), chap. 3.

25. ''White Goods Empire: 400 Villages Crown Electrolux Market King,'' *Business International,* August 11, 1986, p. 250.

value chain. Whether a strong global industry logic exists in a given industry will depend on the presence of such leverage points.

Global Size Logic

A very particular logic is the one driven by critical mass. For many firms, a minimal size of a key activity needs to be sustained before they can safely compete in a given industry. The presence of some form of critical mass in the economics of an industry therefore easily relates to a global logic if that necessary critical mass cannot be achieved anymore in a single market. When companies need to pursue global markets to get over the critical mass hurdle, a global size logic exists.

Such critical mass issues exist in many industries. In the telecommunications industry, the development of a new public switching system may cost as much as U.S. \$2 billion.[26] In pharmaceuticals, the development of a new drug, ranging from compound development through to toxicology and testing, tends to cost about \$230 million.[27] In both instances, the amount of money a company may pay for research and development is limited. In few industries does this limit exceed 10 percent of sales/revenue. Whatever the acceptable percentage in a given industry, the relationship determines the volume the company needs to sell to pay off the entire development of a system or new product. In many industries, the minimal sales level to be achieved over the product life cycle exceeds the volume a company can expect to obtain in even as large a market as the United States. In the case of a new pharmaceutical drug, one company reported requiring annual sales of \$200 million for a new product.[28] As a result, companies pursue markets overseas to pay off the large fixed amount inherent in the development of a new product or system.

The pursuit of new markets to pay off initial large investments for development is at the heart of the global size logic. What many of these companies have found is that the development or adjustment of an initial product to new markets is minor, once the first step has been taken. While we have cited mostly high-technology companies or industries so far, the same development can be seen in the motion-picture industry, where true profitability often can only be achieved from foreign sales. Critical mass may be encountered in many ways. It may consist of a reservations or computer system in one industry or the logistics system for another. Each industry must be analyzed separately and may show different patterns.

This section has focused on major global logics and how they might influence the companies and their global strategies. We have described five prototypes, or generic global

26. ''Job of Wiring China Sets Off Wild Scramble by Telecom Giants,'' *Wall Street Journal,* April 5, 1994, p. 1.

27. ''Successful but Cautious,'' *Financial Times,* July 23, 1991, p. 1, Sect. III, Survey on Pharmaceuticals.

28. ''Research Moves to Sharper Focus,'' *Financial Times,* March 23, 1994, p. 5, Survey, Pharmaceuticals: Research and Development.

logic forces; conceivably, different companies may be exposed to others. In analyzing global logic, however, it is very important to determine which logic is the major source of the global pressure. Depending on the source of the global logic, companies may have to pursue different strategies to accommodate that force. Managers with a global perspective will be able to quickly determine the type of global logic and thus the corresponding global marketing strategy that is best suited for a company in a given industry.

Global logic is not a geographically limited concept. Once a global logic exists in a given industry, companies from all parts of the world are subject to it, provided their markets are integrated into the world market. In principle, the global logic in a given industry applies not only to competitors in the United States or Europe but equally to those in less developed countries or emerging markets.

Global Market Assessment

To bring a global perspective to the analysis of marketing opportunities requires a different approach to the analysis of data. Traditionally, international marketers did a large amount of their analysis on a country-by-country basis. By contrast, marketing with a global perspective requires that additional analytic market assessment skills be acquired. This section introduces such new skills and concepts. They are to be viewed as additional skills to those already described in Chapter 6.

The World Market as a Global Chessboard

In the earlier passage on global competitor logic, we spoke of global chess. Rather than describing the rules of this game, we will concentrate on drawing analogies between the world market and the chessboard (see Figure 7.5). The global chessboard is not a square board consisting of sixty-four equal squares. Rather, it consists of many squares, one for

FIGURE 7.5 ● The Global Chessboard

The Global Chessboard Differs

● Has One Square For
  Each Country
  (175–200)

● The Squares Are Not All
  Equal in Size
  (Driven by GNP)

● The Board Changes During Play
  (Political and Economic
  Developments)

FIGURE 7.5 ● The Global Chessboard (*Continued*)

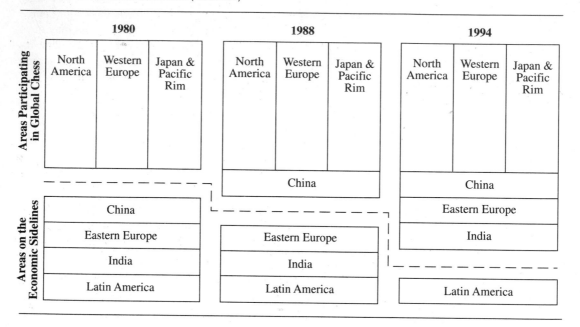

each of the approximately two hundred countries that presently exist. Also contrary to regular chess, where each space is of equal size, the spaces on the global chessboard vary in size. In this game, square sizes represent market size, or GNP: countries with large GNPs are presented by large squares, countries with small GNPs by correspondingly smaller ones. The United States, as the country with the largest GNP representing about 20 percent of world GNP, would make up 20 percent of this global chessboard. Other countries would follow, each in proportion to its GNP.

Similar to regular chess, the rules of the game in global chess require the capture of the most-important pieces on the board. However, contrary to regular chess, the global chessboard is a moving board, with the various squares subject to constant change driven by the particular dynamics of changing economic circumstances of the countries involved. Despite the large number of global chess pieces, the ones that really count are those where companies can move products, services, people, capital, and profits freely across borders. Countries that are behind insurmountable barriers or that do not allow free transfer of imports or exports are excluded from global chess, as any market position in those countries cannot be leveraged to other countries.

Traditionally, the major members of the global chessboard were markets considered part of the triad, contributing some 75 percent of world GNP.[29] Consisting of Europe

29. Kenichi Ohmae, *Triad Power: The Coming Shape of Global Competition* (New York: Free Press, 1985), pp. 122–124.

(western Europe then), the United States, and Japan, the triad market area was important for any global marketer. Having a strong position in at least two of the three areas and a credible presence in the third was viewed as critical for global success. L'Oreal, the world's largest cosmetics company, has a market share of 22 percent in Europe, compared to only 7.5 percent in the United States. Leadership in cosmetics is hotly contested with Procter & Gamble of the United States and Unilever, another European firm. With the U.S. market accounting for the largest share in the sixty billion dollar global cosmetics market, eventual global leadership will be decided on the outcome of the U.S. market battle. The U.S. market has become, therefore, a "must" market for L'Oreal, causing it to invest disproportionately more in that market than elsewhere.[30]

The triad concept, in the eyes of Kenichi Ohmae, was helpful to create a sense of priorities among the many existing countries. In some ways, it consisted of selecting a few key markets from the global chessboard. That global chessboard, however, has undergone substantial changes in the past few years. Not only has it gained many additional markets, pushing the total up toward two hundred, but the world marketplace has also seen different countries rise in importance and others decrease. If we define the relevant part of the chessboard as those countries open to free trading, we have seen a boom in the creation of new relevant markets.

The tremendous political changes leading to liberalization, privatization, and deregulation have led to many countries joining the global chessboard. In addition to the traditional industrialized countries consisting of Organization for Economic Cooperation and Development (OECD) members (western Europe, the United States, Canada, Japan, Australia, and New Zealand), other major countries have risen in importance. This includes the group of Asian countries (South Korea, Tiawan, Hong Kong, Singapore) typically described as the "Tigers" for their aggressive export drive.

Recent newcomers to the global chessboard include China (where relatively open trade is now possible), India, and a number of Latin American countries (notably Brazil, Mexico, Argentina, and Chile). As all of these countries begin to abandon their old restrictive trade practices, they become important pieces in the global chess game for market dominance. The same is the case for the former eastern European countries. Over the last five years, the major expansion in the global chessboard has forced a rethinking of the triad concept. The relevant free market is now distributed into three major trading regions: North America, consisting of the United States, Canada, and Mexico, bound together in NAFTA; Europe, consisting of the twelve EU countries and the associate countries of the European Free Trade Area (EFTA) forming the European Economic Area (EEA); and finally Asia, consisting of Japan, China, and the many Asian Pacific Rim countries that are growing rapidly.

The dynamics of the global chessboard do not only include the many new countries joining in through trade liberalization. Some of these countries, China and India notably, are experiencing substantial growth, as we explained in earlier chapters. That growth is represented with an ever larger square on the global chessboard represented by China, thus enhancing its importance in the competitive calculations of global firms. A market such

30. "Can the Queen of Cosmetics Keep Her Crown?" *Business Week,* January 17, 1994, p. 90.

as China, shut off from the rest of the world economy, not accessible for international firms via imports or exports, would be a far less important piece on the global chessboard.

Although we can imagine the world as a global chessboard with each country represented by its size of GNP, individual firms competing in their own specific industry will be required to see the chessboard as showing countries where each country, or local market, is represented with respect to the market size of that industry. The chessboard for Ford will be determined by the size of the automotive markets in the various countries. The chessboard of IBM or Apple will be represented by the size of the computer markets. Global marketers, therefore, face chessboards that differ by industry and on which each industry will have its own key markets as determined by size.

The telecommunications market provides an excellent example of the shifting importance of individual countries on the overall global chessboard. The fastest-growing market for telecommunications installations today is China, with annual spending expected to reach eight billion dollars by 1995.[31] This contrasts with only two billion dollars per year in 1990. The reason for this enormous growth is the need to bring more phone lines into China, where the density of telephones was less than two phones per one hundred inhabitants in 1994, amounting to no more than forty million lines. By the year 2000, the Chinese government intends to increase phone density to ten lines per one hundred inhabitants—still behind the United States, where the density was fifty lines per one hundred inhabitants. However, the investment necessary to reach the goal by the year 2000 amounts to building the equivalent of one regional U.S. operating company (referred to as ''Baby Bell'') every single year. Telecommunications firms that must invest large sums of money to develop the next generation of digital systems may find it critical to participate in the Chinese market for future competitiveness. Some experts have indicated that China might well become the largest market for telecommunications networking and infrastructure equipment. Should this come to pass, the Chinese market would become the cornerstone of any global marketing strategy of telecommunications firms.

Global marketers aspiring to a global perspective will need to constantly evaluate the state of the global chessboard. This evaluation, leading to the importance of key markets, not only will have to be made on present data but needs to consider growth rates and the state of the chessboard many years out. This must occur at both the macroeconomic level and the particular industry level relevant to the company.

Marketers will not only have to develop a new sense of understanding and of evaluating one country at a time but most obtain a sense of importance of one piece of the global chessboard versus the rest of the pieces.

Lead Market Logic

Once the global chessboard relevant to a particular industry and a particular company has been determined, the marketer with a global perspective will need to understand the interrelationships of those markets. A major part of this consists of finding the lead market, or

31. ''Job of Wiring China Sets Off Wild Scramble by the Telecom Giants,'' *Wall Street Journal*, April 5, 1994, p. 1.

markets, relevant to a particular part of the business. The *lead market* is the particular geographic market, or country, that is ahead in its development of the rest of the world and where initial new developments tend to set a trend for other markets to follow. The lead market thus serves the function of a bellwether.[32]

The identification of a lead market has strategic importance for companies. Those who can identify their own lead markets relevant to their industry will be able to leverage learning out of those markets for the rest of their international or global operations. The knowledge about lead markets gives the global marketer a window on future opportunities. It also helps identify those countries as strategic in importance.

One can distinguish several types of lead market categories. First, there are customer-driven lead markets based upon the location of the country with the most advanced customers. A company would have to look at its industry and try to evaluate where the most-advanced customers tend to be. If those customers are concentrated on one particular country or region, we have the presence of a lead market with respect to customer demand. Charting the demand coming from that lead market might tell where the rest of the customers in other parts of the world are headed.

One can distinguish among other types of lead markets as well. Operations-based lead markets are those that contain the most efficient participants in an industry, particularly with respect to producing the products or services in question. A third category consists of the product lead market, which contains the country where the most-advanced products in that industry emerge. Again the emphasis is on industry participant, not on customer. And finally, one may distinguish the lead market based upon management systems and the companies that consistently apply the most-advanced management systems in that industry. More recently, we have applied the term *benchmarking* for measuring a company's performance against others that are best in its category. The lead market, by definition, would contain the firms against whom others would benchmark their own operations. What is different in global terms is the requirement that these benchmark operations must in fact be leading in the world, or of a world-class nature.

As with many of the concepts described earlier in this chapter, lead market identification is not a one-time exercise. Marketers who aspire to a global perspective have to monitor the performance of the lead market continuously. Furthermore, lead markets, most of which at one time were concentrated in the United States, have become dispersed, with many countries sharing in some of them over time. (See Figure 7.6.) A company must therefore understand the migration pattern of lead markets and adjust its understanding of the global chessboard accordingly. The search for lead markets is an attempt to identify the driving wheel of a complicated machine in which each country, or market, is characterized by a single cog wheel in a complex structure. (See Figure 7.7.) Marketers who understand the process and can clearly identify the ''driving'' market have an advantage. Due to its importance, we have added special sections in Chapters 8 and 9 dealing with strategic actions by which international firms can take advantage of the presence of lead markets.

32. Jean-Pierre Jeannet, ''Lead Markets: A Concept for Designing Global Business Strategies,'' working paper, IMEDE International Management Institute, May 1986.

FIGURE 7.6 ● Technology: The United States versus the World

	Lagging	Holding its own	Leading
Biotech Create an array of new materials through biotech methods	■		
Gallium arsenide Develop semiconductor materials that increase chip performance	■		
High–power microwaves Apply this technology to weapons	■		
Integrated optics Use light instead of electric charges for chip memories and signal processing	■		
Machine intelligence and robotics Incorporate human "intelligence" and actions into mechanical devices	■		
Microchips Reduce size of high–speed computers and sensitive receivers	■		
Pulsed power Develop portable devices that fire pulses of laser microwave energy	■		
Superconductors Make substances with little or no electrical resistance at up to room temperature	■		
Advanced composites Create materials that will withstand high temperatures		■	
Air–breathing propulsion Make efficient, lightweight jet engines		■	
Fiber optics Produce highly efficient fibers for communications and navigation		■	
Hypervelocity projectiles Develop hardened, high–velocity missiles with increased penetrating power		■	
Automatic target recognition Create devices to detect, classify, and track targets			■
Computational fluid dynamics Simulate flow of fluids or gases by computer			■
Data fusion Process and present large amounts of raw computer data in usable form			■
Highly sensitive radars Detect Stealth–type targets			■
Parallel processing Run processors simultaneously for high–speed computing			■
Passive sensors Monitor surroundings without emitting signals			■
Phased arrays Develop advanced radar technology with no movement of antenna			■
Signature controls Limit the telltale signals that vehicles and weapons emit			■
Simulation and modelling Test concepts and designs without building replicas			■
Software development Create more affordable and reliable software			■

Source: "Getting High Tech Back on Track," *Fortune,* January 1, 1990, p. 76. From Department of Defense data, as reprinted in *Fortune,* January 1, 1990. Copyright © 1990 The Time Inc. Magazine Company. All rights reserved.

Gray = U.S. lagging in some important areas; black = U.S. leading in most areas.

FIGURE 7.7 ● Lead Market Relationships

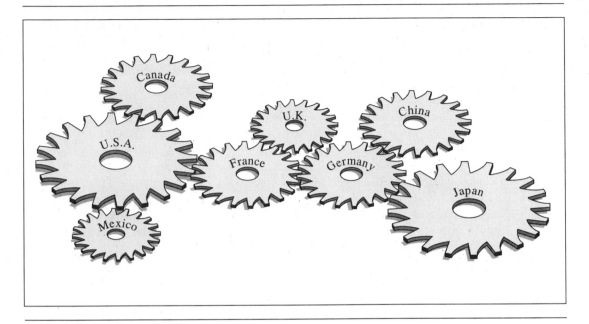

Personal Skills for a Global Perspective

Most of the previous section described analytic and conceptual requirements for a marketer with a global perspective. A few personal requirements also need to be mentioned. These skills have been identified over the years through the authors' own experience with interacting with many international executives. Some of them come from the authors' experience with sending many students on overseas assignments. In themselves, these skills do not yet add up to a global perspective. However, without them, even the conceptual understanding of a global perspective on marketing could be diminished.

Global Language Communications Skills

A first category of skills can be grouped under global language communications skills. Here we want to emphasize the language aspects, treating them separately from technological aspects of communications. Presumably, the global manager must be a multilingual manager. While this is typically the case with managers from many countries, English has reached the point of becoming the global business language. In this new global world, what is the value of learning and speaking a foreign language?

Typically, a major benefit of learning a foreign language comes from also learning about the foreign culture. However, in this global world with many major markets speaking many different languages, which one should a manager learn? This choice has baffled many students of international management. Will the language acquired also be the language that is desired some time in the future? Companies hiring young executives for future posts overseas often emphasize that having learned one language is an indication of the young executive's promise to learn another one for the next international appointment.

This pattern is illustrated by the career patterns of two former students, both of whom were hired by international firms. The first student, a U.S. national, joined a U.S. company in Latin America. The student won this assignment due to his proven Spanish language skills. After a few years, the student found himself transferred to Italy, for which he had no prior knowledge. His proven language skills in Spanish were used as an indication that he would quickly acquire another language. Our second student, also a U.S. national, had acquired some French during his undergraduate years. He was hired into the head office of a Swiss international firm where the business language was English. The company hired him because his learning of French indicated to them that the student had promise of being able to function in different environments. After an initial training period of two years, this student found himself in the newly formed subsidiary in Moscow, where again a very different language applied. These two situations illustrate the advantage of learning one foreign language, while cautioning those who do so that their particular choice of language may have little to do with the first real overseas assignment.

While learning a foreign language is still needed for longer stays in a country, most marketing executives who act in the global marketplace tend to spend little time in any one market. Moving about, making many brief trips, invariably causes them to use English as the key language in international business. Although executives in many parts of the world are increasingly familiar with English, this does not mean that their understanding is perfect. Those who work within the network of a U.S-based international company can expect to find most written documents produced everywhere to be in English. Executives working for an international firm's operation in the United States, however, may find themselves limited if they cannot speak some of the language of the head office country. This is more so for French, Italian, and German firms; the firms located in smaller countries, such as the Netherlands, Sweden, and Switzerland, tend to use English as their corporate language. When meeting local customers abroad, particularly those who are not engaged in international business per se, knowing the local language can still be important. Of course, that capability would be present in a company's local subsidiary or in a distributor or agent who can speak English.

Native English speakers use many idiomatic expressions that are not clear to those for whom English is a second language, however perfectly they may speak it. Misunderstandings thus can arise. A proven strategy is to eliminate such local, idiomatic expressions from the English spoken to arrive at something we call "global English." This capability will become ever more important, as we shall show in later chapters, such as in dealing with new forms of global organizations and global teams. Although it is important to recognize that foreign-language skills will help managers gain cultural empathy with a different culture, it is at the same time necessary to realize that a marketing executive with a global perspective will need to know the key markets for that industry. Knowledge described in the first part of our chapter will be required and can be acquired even without foreign language skills for that particular market.

Global Telecommunications Skills

A second set of important communications skills is of a more technical nature. The communications revolution has brought about new forms of international telecommunications possibilities that substantially change the nature of how international marketing gets transacted. For marketers who aspire to a global perspective, such knowledge would be critical. We cannot describe these new forms of technology here in great detail, and it is not the purpose of this text to equip all readers with that knowledge.[33] However, we can give some background and will point out the application of these techniques to the way global marketing is conducted.

Communications with customers and business partners overseas have changed substantially over the past decades. What would take weeks in regular mail has now been condensed into reaction times that approach immediate response. The real challenge is to bridge the gap between what is technologically possible and what has actually been used. To the detriment of their international marketing positions, many firms do not yet use the full technological capabilities.

Much international communication traffic travels over telephone lines. In global marketing, making international phone connections is now an everyday occurrence. With direct-access dialing to most countries, the phone has become an easy way to overcome communication gaps. Between 1981 and 1991, international calls into and out of the United States grew from 500 million to 2.5 billion per year.[34] The telephone, however, can only bridge the distance gap, giving the ability to overcome distances. It still requires that both initiator and recipient of the call be there at the same time. When calls have to be made from New York to Japan (Tokyo is fourteen hours ahead of New York), it becomes difficult to make calls at a time when both parties are in their offices. Even with Europe, where the time difference is only six hours (from the East Coast of the United States), common office time overlaps amount only to two to three hours each day.

With much of global marketing taking place in different time zones, companies have had to use other means of communicating. In the past, they used telex machines. Today, much of this communications is carried by fax machines, which are now in wide use in every type of international marketing operation. Effective communication today would be inconceivable without fax machines, and global marketing managers make heavy use of them. Faxing documents speeds up decision-making processes and has helped overcome difficulties with mail service. Similarly, use of international courier services, such as

33. *Economist,* October 23, 1993, pp. 1–20, Survey, Telecommunications.
34. ''Welcome to the Revolution,'' *Fortune,* December 13, 1993, p. 76.

Federal Express, UPS, or DHL, can speed documents across continents in just two or three days, where transmittal used to take weeks through regular mail.

The most recent advance is in data communications, placing the value of telephones into the hands of business executives in even remote areas. Combining them with mobile data transmission capabilities has extended fixed telephone networks to many parts of the world.[35] What we have come to expect in terms of on-the-desk transmission (e.g., credit card purchases), new technology makes now available on mobile networks. The effect of this new technology is to extend the reach of many firms beyond their own natural borders, bridging distance and time gaps in such a way that round-the-clock processing of orders is becoming a possibility. Electronic data interchange (EDI) exemplifies this new technology whereby companies and other organizations exchange information regularly and pass routine documents over data networks, including invoicing and payments.[36]

The rapid expansion of credit card companies and other services that depend on data transmission would not have been possible without such technological advances. Effective use of new communications technology is spawning new international businesses of substantial portions. EDS, the computer services company owned by GM, has a separate subsidiary that engages in servicing, processing, and billing for such firms. A substantial amount of that subsidiary's volume of $500 million is already taking place outside of the United States.

Electronic mail, once used only to communicate within the premises of a single firm, is now available, via regular phone lines and the Internet, for communicating with clients and companies worldwide.[37] As more and more companies avail themselves of an Internet gateway for their in-company electronic mail systems, executives have instant access to Internet's more than 25,000 computer networks.[38] The message traffic between company and outside users can be very heavy; in the case of IBM, it reached 580,000 messages in the month of January 1994 alone.[39] Although the Internet is widely accessible to most U.S. consumers, access abroad is more difficult and typically restricted to universities and businesses.[40] However, the power of Internet is not only its wide connections but also its low cost. Once a company has established a connection to the nearest host, all communications are free. Both fax and phone are much more expensive.[41]

The last step in developing an international connection is the new "groupware" software, such as Notes developed by Lotus. These software packages allow many users

35. "Mobile Data Services: Market Is Immature," *Financial Times,* June 16, 1993, p. 2, Survey, Telecommunications in Business, Sect. III.

36. "Towards a World Without Paper," *Financial Times,* October 13, 1992, p. 4, Survey, Computers and Communications.

37. "Ready to Cruise the Internet," *Business Week,* March 28, 1994, p. 180.

38. Harley Hahn and Rick Stout, *The Internet Complete Reference* (Berkeley, Calif.: Osborne McGraw-Hill, 1994).

39. "The Internet and Your Business," *Fortune,* March 7, 1994, p. 88.

40. "Technology: Wired," *Wall Street Journal,* November 15, 1993, Wall Street Journal Reports.

41. "The Race to Rewire America," *Fortune,* April 19, 1993, pp. 42–61.

of a single company to share information simultaneously, with immediate updates as if everyone were connected to the same computer or workstation. Groupware, or software for teams not all located in the same place or frequently out of the office at one time or another, has allowed firms to create virtual teams where members may in fact be located in different offices in different countries. This has affected the way these firms operate internationally.[42]

The most recent development in telecommunications concerns videoconferencing. Through connections over special telephone lines, companies have installed video systems that allow teams of managers to see each other as they talk, although they are separated by thousands of miles. With participants sitting in front of cameras and with a separate projector for documents, such conferences are becoming the norm to avoid costly and time-consuming travel. Teleconferencing also allows firms to project scarce technical specialists into the offices of their clients to support products or services and thus gain a competitive advantage. While very powerful (it does bridge the distance gap), the videoconference still requires executives at both ends to be present at the same time.

The Universal Need for Global Marketing Minds

We already pointed out in Chapter 1 that a greater need for global minds exists in today's international business. In this chapter, we explained in more detail what such a global mind, or global perspective, consists of. It is nevertheless important to indicate here that the need for marketers with a global perspective is not just limited to countries from the major industrialized nations. The need for a global perspective extends to marketers from all parts of the world, from both developed and emerging countries.

The need for a global perspective results from the pervasiveness of global logic. Any company that is part of the global economy and operating in an industry with some form of global logic will require marketing managers with a global perspective. Since the global logic works on companies large and small and is independent of the company's location, the need for the type of skills, knowledge, and concepts explained in this chapter is considered universal.

Conclusions

In this chapter, we have described the global perspective in greater detail. Acquiring a global perspective is aided by gaining knowledge about key markets and an understanding of the wider framework of the global economy and politics. Understanding the concepts

42. "Here Comes the Payoff from PCs," *Fortune,* March 23, 1992, p. 51.

of global logic and having the ability to analyze for its presence in a company's business and industry are a second prerequisite. Marketers with a global perspective will also have to adopt new ways to understand and prioritize the world market, such as through the analogy of the global chess game. And finally, the global perspective is gained through the acquisition of special communications skills that help overcome time and place differences and allow companies to project their skills beyond their own borders.

What separates the global perspective from other approaches to international and global marketing is the ability to think about the whole, the entire world, and to view each individual market in relationship to the whole world economy. This perspective, with a sense for the strategic necessity, will allow global marketers to set the right priorities and to guide their firms through a mass of potential or theoretical possibilities, not all of which can realistically be pursued. This is a sharp departure from the traditional world of analyzing individual markets one at a time. Although the single market analysis skill will still be part of the necessary tool bag of the global marketer, that alone will not suffice anymore as a guide through the multitude of possibilities.

As many more firms find themselves drawn into the global economy and forced to pursue global marketing strategies, the need for marketing managers with a capability to adopt the global perspective can be expected to rise dramatically over the next decade. A global perspective can be acquired; it is not an innate skill. Managers from all countries face the same challenge, or the same hurdles, in acquiring it. Those who do better at it are likely to gain a competitive advantage over their peers who lack it. And finally, firms with a larger cadre of marketing executives who have gained a global perspective can be expected to outperform those who lack specific human resources.

Questions for Discussion

1. How does a global perspective differ from an international or multinational perspective?
2. Explain the concept of a global logic.
3. In the automobile manufacturing industry, where do you find a global logic? Which of the sources of the global logic predominates?
4. What is the managerial meaning of the concept of the global chessboard?
5. Select a country and do a factual analysis that satisfies the section on global key markets.
6. What differentiates single market assessment from global market assessment?

For Further Reading

Bartlett, Christopher A., and Sumantra Ghoshal. "What Is a Global Manager?" *Harvard Business Review,* September–October 1992, pp. 124–132.

Hahn, Harley, and Rick Stout. *The Internet Complete Reference.* Berkeley, Calif.: Osborne, McGraw-Hill, 1994.

Ohmae, Kenichi. *Triad Power: The Coming Shape of Global Competition.* New York: Free Press, 1985.

Porter, Michael E., ed. *Competition in Global Industries.* Boston: Harvard Business School Press, 1986.

Taylor, William. ''The Logic of Global Business: An Interview of ABB's Percy Barnevik.'' *Harvard Business Review,* March–April 1991, pp. 91–105.

8

Global Marketing
Strategies

● **COMPANIES NEED TO** *make a number of strategic decisions concerning international and global marketing. First, there is the decision on global reach, which deals with the extent of internationalization and the particular geographic concentration desired for a business. Second, companies will have to decide on the appropriate market selection, dealing both with the country selection and the entry strategy to be used as each individual market is approached. Third, companies will have to make a number of managerial decisions concerning the nature of their international and global marketing programs and how they intend to manage their business. And finally, companies will have to address a number of strategic issues that shape the nature of their global marketing strategy. Strategic decisions range from selecting an appropriate geographic expansion strategy to choosing from a number of generic global marketing strategies. Other strategic elements include the decisions around product/market strategy and global competitive strategies. The purpose of this chapter is to describe the nature of these decisions, concentrating largely on the strategic elements as depicted in Figure 8.1. The other topics will be introduced as they are treated in greater detail in separate chapters.*

FIGURE 8.1 ● International and Global Marketing Decision Elements

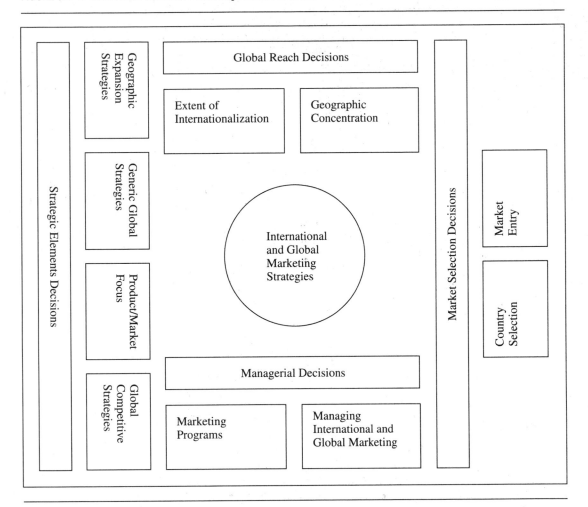

To many readers, the term *global marketing strategy* probably suggests a company represented everywhere and pursuing more or less the same marketing strategy. However,
global marketing strategies are not to be equated with global standardization, although
they may be the same in some situations. A global marketing strategy represents application
of a common set of strategic principles across most world markets. It may include, but
does not require, similarity in products or in marketing processes. A company that pursues
a global marketing strategy looks at the world market as a whole rather than at markets
on a country-by-country basis, which is more typical for the multinational firm.

    Standardization deals with the amount of similarity companies want to achieve
across many markets with respect to their marketing strategies and marketing mix.

FIGURE 8.2 ● Globalization Patterns

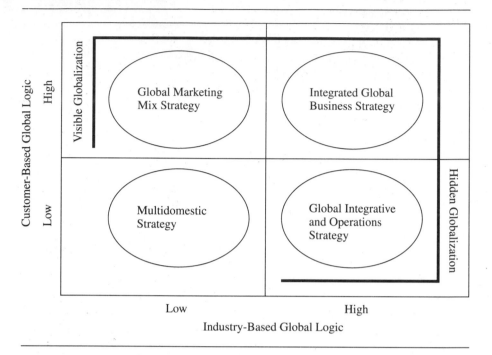

Standardization may also apply to general business policies or the modes of operation a company may want to pursue. *Globalization,* on the other hand, deals with the integration of the many country strategies and the subordination of these country strategies to one global framework. As a result, it is conceivable that one company may have a globalized approach to its marketing strategy but leave the details for many parts of the marketing plan to local subsidiaries.

Few companies will want to globalize all of their marketing operations. The difficulty then is to determine which marketing operations will gain from globalization. Such a modular approach to globalization is likely to yield greater returns than a total globalization of a company's marketing strategy.[1]

Globalization of a firm's marketing operations may take several forms. Major drivers are the differences in the environment and the different sources of global logic, as described in Chapter 7. The major sources of global logic can be grouped into two distinctive sets. Customer-based global logics, consisting of global customer or market logic, tend to affect the marketing variables such as product design, branding, and communications. Such globalization patterns frequently are taking place "in public," as globalization of products,

1. John Quelch, "Customizing Global Marketing," *Harvard Business Review,* May–June 1986, pp. 59–68.

communications, and brands is visible to all concerned. Industry-based global logics, such as competitive, industry, or size (critical mass) logic, mostly affect the integration aspects of global operations, ranging from manufacturing to research and development, logistics, and distribution. Because this type of globalization path takes place within the organization, these aspects are often hidden from view.

The two forces—customer-based and industry-based logics—combine into various paths of globalization, explaining differences in global marketing practices among international firms. When the global logic is low for both customer- and industry-based factors, companies tend to opt for multidomestic marketing strategies. Faced with strong customer-based global logic but weak industry logic as a result of differences in the competitive and industry structures across many markets, companies are able to pursue global marketing mix strategies. Confronted with different customer pressures across the world but high industry global logic, companies may adopt a global integration strategy by concentrating on synergy in operations. Finally, when both sets of global logics, industry- and customer-based ones, are strong, a firm may find an integrated global business strategy most appropriate. Figure 8.2 depicts those different globalization patterns.

Patterns of Internationalization

Whether to compete internationally is a strategic decision that will fundamentally affect the firm, including its operations and its management. For many companies, the decision to internationalize remains an important and difficult one. Typically, there are many issues behind a company's decision to begin to compete in foreign markets. For some firms, going abroad is the result of a deliberate policy decision; for others, it is a reaction to a specific business opportunity or a competitive challenge.

Opportunistic Development

Probably the most common reason for international expansion is the recognition that opportunities exist in foreign markets. Many companies, particularly those in the United States, promote their products in trade journals or through other media to their U.S. customers. These publications are also read by foreign business executives, and orders are made that are initially unsolicited. Because these transactions are usually more complicated and more involved than a routine shipment to domestic customers, the firm has to make the decision whether or not to respond at that time. The company can also adopt a more aggressive policy and actively pursue foreign customers, moving beyond filling unsolicited orders. Thus, some firms have built sizable foreign businesses by first responding to orders and then taking a more proactive approach later on. Most large, internationally active companies were built initially around an opportunistic strategy, although today these firms have moved to a more orchestrated and deliberate strategy in their approach to international marketing.

Following Customers Abroad

For a company whose business is concentrated on a few large customers, the decision to internationalize is usually made when one of its key customers moves abroad to pursue international opportunities. Many of the major U.S. automobile component suppliers are operating plants abroad to supply their customers in foreign locations. PPG Industries, a major U.S.-based supplier of car body paints to the U.S. automobile industry, did little overseas business other than licensing its technology to other foreign paint makers. In the early 1980s, the company followed its major customers abroad and began to service directly them in Europe and elsewhere. The company began to sell to non-U.S. car companies as well and achieved the leading position in supplying paints to car manufacturers worldwide.[2] Similar trends can be observed as Japanese and European automobile manufacturers set up their own operations in the United States. These moves tend to be followed by a series of component suppliers who do not want to lose out on a new business opportunity.

R. R. Donnelley & Sons Co., a U.S.-based printer of magazines, catalogs, and directories, was a largely domestic company until 1978, when it made its first foreign acquisitions. Fifteen years later, international revenue was still only 8 percent of its more than four billion dollars in sales. However, the company believed that within a decade this percentage might rise to 40 or 50 percent. The international business has developed largely on the strength of its customers' requests. Some of Donnelley's main client groups (e.g., computer firms, software houses, and telecommunications firms) are rapidly expanding overseas and want Donnelley to go with them, supplying documents and manuals overseas. The company recently acquired an Irish software translation and development company and announced a joint venture with Cincinnati Bell to study electronic yellow pages. In financial printing, another international growth segment, Donnelley opened overseas offices where lawyers can go to retrieve identical documents on computers, work on them interactively (all on real time), and then print them.[3]

The service sector has seen similar expansions triggered by client moves overseas. The establishment of international branch networks of major U.S. banks, such as Citibank and Chase Manhattan, was motivated by a desire to service key domestic clients overseas. Major U.S. advertising agencies and accounting firms have set up extensive networks of foreign offices for the same reasons. Thus, as a firm's customer base becomes international, so will the firm's own operations if it wants to maintain its business.

Pursuing Geographic Diversification

A need to diversify beyond a single country can also be behind moves to internationalize a company. Although this is less of a factor for U.S.-based companies, firms in other parts

---

2. "Remarkable Resurgence of a Highly Respected Company," *Financial Times,* March 27, 1991, p. 11, Special Survey, World Paints and Coatings.

3. "Donnelley Follows Its Customers Around the World," *Wall Street Journal,* July 1, 1993, p. B4.

of the world often do not want their operations to be dominated or to become overly dependent on the economy of a single country. Saint-Gobain, a large French company with a long-standing tradition in glass and building materials, for years followed a strategy to break out of its France-only position. Acquiring large companies in the same field in Germany and the United Kingdom, the company was able to reduce French sales to 30 percent of corporate but gain 36 percent in the rest of Europe. The acquisition of Norton Company, a U.S.-based maker of abrasives and ceramics, significantly strengthened Saint-Gobain's position in the United States, which accounted for only 20 percent of its sales before the Norton acquisition and turned a Europewide group into a worldwide group.[4]

Extending the International Market for Incremental Profit

A deliberate international expansion policy is pursued by firms that are motivated by profit potential through market extension. In industries where investment in research and development is high, companies often want to harvest past investment by introducing established products into other countries. Such a strategy is particularly profitable when additional market entries do not require substantial investments in product changes or additional research and development. This is the case for much of the computer industry, where products are substantially standardized around the world.

Ferro, a U.S.-based company in ceramics, specialty chemicals and plastics, achieved international sales of more than 55 percent of total volume. The company followed a strategy of aggressively pursuing additional payoffs for products successfully launched in the United States. This type of ''profit leverage'' was intended to use the company's foreign business to strengthen its overall competitive position, both domestically and abroad.[5]

Exploiting Countries' Different Economic Growth Rates

Growth rates are subject to wide variations among countries. A company based in a low-growth country may suffer a competitive disadvantage and may want to expand into faster-growing countries to take advantage of growth opportunities. The area of the Pacific Rim (which includes Japan, South Korea, Taiwan, China, Hong Kong, Thailand, Singapore, Malaysia, and Indonesia) experienced above-average growth rates in the second half of the 1980s, which in turn prompted many international firms to invest heavily in expanding in that region.[6]

The chemicals industry in Asia has experienced above-average growth rates, ranging between 12 percent for China and 7–9 percent for several other Asian Pacific Rim countries. This enormous growth, expected to make the Asian chemicals market the largest in the world by the year 2000, has attracted investment by many chemicals companies from the United States and Europe. ICI of the United Kingdom has spent some one billion

4. ''Saint-Gobain Pushing Worldwide Growth,'' *New York Times,* April 26, 1990, p. D5.
5. ''Ferro's Global Position Sparks Intrigue,'' *Wall Street Journal,* March 17, 1989, p. A7.
6. ''Europe's Slow Boat to Asia,'' *International Management,* November 1993, p. 28.

dollars over the last few years on plants in Taiwan, Japan, and Malaysia. Du Pont, the large U.S. chemicals company, is investing approximately one billion dollars in a chemicals and fibers complex in Singapore.[7] Another one billion dollars is expected to be spent for plants in China and other Pacific Rim countries. Plans have been announced to build a nylon materials plant in China. Additional plants have been built to produce electronic materials and synthetic fibers.[8]

The Coca-Cola Company, experiencing growth rates in Europe that were twice its U.S. market rate in the late 1980s, decided to place additional emphasis in Europe, where substantial potential exists in connection with the 1992 European integration initiative and the opening of the eastern European economies. As a result, the company felt the 1990s would be the decade of Europe.[9]

Exploiting Product Life Cycle Differences

When the market for a firm's product becomes saturated, a company can open new opportunities by entering foreign markets where the product may not be very well known. Thus, adding new markets extends the product's life cycle. Among U.S. firms following this strategy are many consumer goods marketers, such as Philip Morris, Coca-Cola, and PepsiCo. They often go into markets where the per capita consumption of their products is still relatively low. With economic expansion and the resulting improvement in personal incomes in the new market, these companies expect to experience substantial growth later on—though operations in the United States are showing little growth. One 1990 report showed that Coca-Cola sold 189 twelve-ounce servings per person annually in the United States. Its international average was only 37 servings, although this varied between 215 in Iceland, 173 in Mexico, 111 in West Germany, 61 in the United Kingdom, 35 in Japan, and 26 in France. China trailed with 0.3 servings per capita. These figures were heavily influenced by the fact that soft drinks ranked only number four for choice of drink in Europe, whereas in the United States soft drinks ranked number one. With per capita consumption in Europe only 30 percent of the U.S. levels, Coca-Cola saw a considerable future in pushing more into Europe, where colas had not yet reached maturity.[10]

Industrial products and service companies experience product life cycle differences as well. Electronic Data Systems (EDS), the largest computing services company in the United States, is exploiting its skill at outsourcing in Europe. In the United States, many companies have for many years contracted for computing services rather than having their own computer centers. EDS believes that Europe is some five years behind the U.S. trend, and Asia Pacific is still several years behind Europe. By moving in a big way into Europe, the company can ride the new trend and continue to grow more quickly than if it stayed in the United States.[11]

7. "Asia Targets Chemicals for the Next Assault on Western Industry," *Wall Street Journal,* August 4, 1993, p. 1.
8. "Western Giants Head East," *Nikkei Weekly,* April 11, 1994, p. 19.
9. "Coke Gets Off Its Can in Europe," *Fortune,* August 13, 1990, p. 69.
10. Ibid.
11. "Hungry American Eyes European Sales," *Financial Times,* March 23, 1993, p. 19.

Pursuing Potential Abroad

Despite representing the world's largest economy, the U.S. market accounts usually for little more than one-half the business in many high-technology product categories. For some of the more common product or industry categories such as food, it is a much smaller portion of the overall world market. As a result, many firms are attracted by the sheer size of the potential business abroad. The Pacific Rim countries of Korea, Taiwan, Japan, and China have very large populations and are attracting many newcomers who want to go where they see new potential.

Some firms maximize their domestic market and then reach out for more potential abroad. Anheuser-Busch has a 43 percent share of the U.S. beer market, with domestic growth slowing down. Pursuing international opportunities is an important way to rekindle growth. So Busch's international strategy is centered around Mexico, China, and Japan, where the company is engaged in a series of ventures with local brewers. The company has increased its advertising expenditures to $100 million for the marketing of Budweiser, its leading brand.[12] To help its position in China, Anheuser-Busch acquired a 5 percent interest in the Tsingtao Brewery, China's leading brewer and largest of some eight hundred companies. China's per capita beer consumption is only 7 liters, compared with 90 liters in the United States and 140 liters in Germany. The Chinese market has been growing 14 percent for the last five years, with growth of 10 percent or more expected over the next few years. While Anheuser-Busch brands sell only 200,000 cases annually, the expectation is that they will grow substantially.[13]

Duracell International, the leading U.S. maker of batteries, was also confronted with a saturated domestic market. With a 79 percent share of the U.S. battery retail market, the company saw little opportunity to grow. Duracell has aggressively pursued opportunities in eastern Europe and Asia. International volume, one-third of total sales in 1992, is expected to reach half of total sales in the near future.[14]

Internationalizing for Defensive Reasons

Sometimes companies are not interested in pursuing new growth or potential abroad but decide to enter international business for largely defensive reasons. When a domestic company sees its markets invaded by foreign firms, that company may react by entering the foreign competitor's home market in return. As a result, the company can learn valuable information about the competitor that will help in its operations at home. A company may want to slow down a competitor by denying it the cash flow from its profitable domestic operation that could otherwise be invested into expansion abroad. For these reasons, companies who had not needed to compete internationally find themselves suddenly forced to expand abroad.

12. "Anheuser-Busch Says Skoal, Salud, Prosit," *Business Week,* September 20, 1993, p. 76.
13. "Anheuser-Busch Buys Stake in Leading Chinese Brewer," *New York Times,* June 29, 1993, p. D6.
14. "Duracell Looks Abroad for More Juice," *Business Week,* December 21, 1992, p. 52.

Many U.S. companies opened operations in Japan to get closer to their most important competition. For example, major companies such as Xerox and IBM use their local subsidiaries in Japan to learn new ways to compete with the major Japanese firms in their field. Likewise, many European firms want to be represented in the U.S. market because they can learn about new opportunities more directly than if they waited in their home markets for U.S. firms to arrive with new products or technologies.

Pursuing a Global Logic

In Chapter 7, we analyzed in detail the various sources of global logic, ranging from customer logic to industry logic to size (critical mass) logic. Many firms go international and eventually globalize their business and marketing operations because they are subject to a compelling global logic. For all, the need to expand their market coverage to a global coverage will be a major determinant.

The pursuit of international opportunities in the past was driven more by reasons such as new growth, following customers, and often opportunistic strategies. Over time, many of these international firms ended up with a wide network of factories and sales offices covering many markets. Most traditional large international firms fit this mold. Although they may pursue aggressive global marketing strategies today, they did not get there on purpose. Rather, we may refer to those firms as "accidentally global," for having turned an earlier opportunistic strategy into today's calculated global marketing strategy. On the other hand, many younger firms, much more aware of the presence of global logic in their industry, realized the global imperative at an early phase of development and therefore created "purposely global" strategies. As marketers become more aware of the presence and importance of global logic for their industry and firms, more purposely global strategies will result.

Geographic Concentration

Once a company commits to extending its business internationally, management will be confronted with the task of setting some geographic or regional emphasis. A company may decide to emphasize developed nations, such as Japan or those of Europe and North America. Alternatively, some companies may prefer to pursue primarily developing countries in Latin America, Africa, or Asia. Management must make a strategic decision to direct business development in such a way that the company's overall objectives are congruent with the particular geographic mix of its activities.

Concentrating on Developed Countries

Developed countries account for a disproportionate share of world gross national product (GNP) and thus tend to attract many companies. In particular, firms with technology-intensive products have concentrated their activities in the developed world. Although competition from both other international firms and local companies is usually more intense in those markets, doing business in developed countries is generally preferred over doing business in developing nations. This is primarily because the business environment is more predictable and the investment climate is more favorable. Kraft Inc., a large U.S. food company with business worldwide, has 95 percent of its international sales in countries considered economically advanced and politically of low risk. In the developing countries, the company prefers not to own any assets and utilizes distribution or licensing agreements or works through joint ventures.[15]

Developed countries are located in North America (the United States and Canada), western Europe, and Asia (Japan, Australia, New Zealand). Although some very large international firms such as IBM operate in all of these countries, many others may be represented in only one or two areas. Very early in their development, U.S. international companies established strong business bases in Europe, more recently in Japan. Japanese firms tend to start their overseas operations in the United States and Canada and then move into Europe.

The importance of developing a competitive position in the major developed markets was first articulated by Kenichi Ohmae. Ohmae maintained that for most industries it was important to compete effectively in the three parts of the *triad* of the United States, Europe, and Japan. Companies were said to need to be strong in least two areas and have a representation in the third; real global competitors were advised to have strong positions in all three areas. The three areas of the strategic triad account for about 80 percent of most industries, thus determining the outcome of the competitive battle.[16]

Due to the importance of the triad countries in international trade, international companies expend great efforts to balance their presence such that their sales begin to mirror the relative size of the three regions. A company underrepresented in one area or another will undertake considerable investment, often in the form of acquisitions, to balance the geographic portfolio. Alcatel, Europe's largest manufacturer of telecommunications equipment, was often criticized for being underrepresented, with its 4 percent market share, in the important U.S. data transmission segment. With demand in the United States growing 10 percent annually, or more than twice the world average, the company jumped at the opportunity to purchase Rockwell International's transmission unit. This brought Alcatel's market share to 15 percent in the $5.5 billion market. Alcatel also strengthened its U.S. presence to the number two position in the telecommunications cable area with an acquisition.[17]

Europe, the third leg of the triad, has been the focus of investment from the United States and more recently from Japanese companies. Triggered by the move toward European unification that culminated in the Europe 1992 initiative (see Chapter 4 for more details), Japanese investment was substantially stepped up. Japanese foreign direct investments grew from $25 billion in 1988 to more than $55 billion in 1990. In the automobile

15. ''Kraft: Its Global Strategy,'' *World Food and Drink Report,* October 29, 1987.

16. Kenichi Ohmae, *Triad Power: The Coming Shape of Global Competition* (New York: Free Press, 1985).

17. ''Tipping the Scales of U.S. Telecoms,'' *Financial Times,* July 15, 1991, p. 17.

industry, Nissan, Toyota, and Honda have been building up their manufacturing bases in the United Kingdom. In telecommunications, NEC and Panasonic have targeted mobile phones. In consumer electronics, Sony, Toshiba, and Panasonic have built their own factories in Europe. And in construction equipment, Komatsu and other Japanese firms have reached a market share of almost one-third by 1990 for crawler-excavators.[18]

The triad is also the focus of the cable TV industry. With growth slowing in the United States and new regulation depressing profits, U.S. cable operators have moved into Europe in a big way. There they find a large customer base with considerable income; in 1992, growth in homes wired amounted to 10 percent. Already, MTV Europe, with its access to 120 million TV households in Europe, is rivaling the U.S. operations. Other U.S. networks are gearing up: QVC has plans for most of Europe; Family Channel and Sci-Fi Channel plan to target the United Kingdom first; TNT and Cartoon will target the United Kingdom and Scandinavia, Belgium, Holland, and France.[19]

Although the triad concept was first understood as referring to the United States, western Europe, and Japan, more recent use of the concept tends to emphasize three regions rather than countries. With the advent of the North American Free Trade Agreement (NAFTA), North America is a more relevant concept than just the United States. In Europe, the relevant concept is the European Union (EU), or the European Economic Area (EEA), which has been expanded to some sixteen western European countries. And finally, many firms refer to the third leg of the triad as the Asia Pacific region rather than just Japan. Including other rapidly growing Asian countries in the triad has brought about a considerably increased focus. Most European and U.S. international firms, traditionally weak in that part of the world, have recently undertaken considerable efforts to balance their market positions (see Figure 8.3).

Alcatel, the European telecommunications company whose U.S. strategy was discussed above, has placed major investments in the Asia Pacific region, with China as its cornerstone. With China expected to account for as much as 20 to 30 percent of the world telecommunications market by the year 2000, the Asia Pacific part of the triad becomes the most important one. Consequently, the world leadership in telecommunications will likely be decided by the outcome in the Asia Pacific region.[20] Whirlpool of the United States, the world's largest white goods company, will set up a regional headquarters for Asia in Singapore. The company indicated that with its past investments in Europe and Latin America, the remaining missing piece was Asia, where unit sales are expected to outpace both Europe and North America.[21]

Emphasizing Developing Countries

Developing nations differ substantially from developed nations by geographic region and by the level of economic development. Markets in Latin America, Africa, the Middle East,

18. ''The Battle for Europe,'' *Business Week,* June 3, 1991, p. 44.

19. ''Cable Has a New Frontier: The Old World,'' *Business Week,* June 28, 1993, p. 74.

20. ''Alcatel in China: The Biggest Prize,'' *Economist,* January 16, 1993, p. 68.

21. ''Whirlpool Plans Asian Expansion Based in Singapore,'' *Financial Times,* February 19, 1993, p. 17.

FIGURE 8.3 ● Intratriad Foreign Direct Investment, 1990 (in Billions of Dollars)

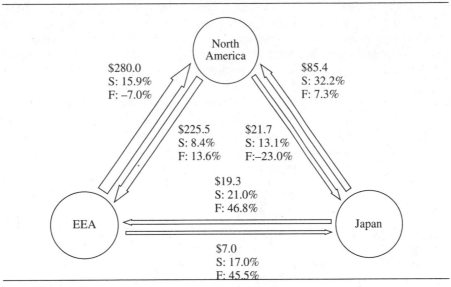

Source: United Nations Conference on Trade and Development, Division on Transnational Corporations and Investments, in *World Investment Report 1993, Transnational Corporations and Integrated International Production* (New York: United Nations, 1993), p. 44. Used with permission.

Note: Dollar figures show estimated values of stock of FDI based on data on inward and outward investment from North America and the European Economic Area (EEA), excluding Iceland and Liechtenstein. Intra–North American investment and intra-EEA in investment have been netted out. Percentages show average annual growth rates for stocks (1980–1990) and flows (1985–1991). North America includes Canada and the United States. The European Economic Area includes the European Community (EC) and the European Free Trade Association, excluding Iceland and Liechtenstein.

and Asia are also characterized by a higher degree of risk than markets in developed countries. Due to the less stable economic climates in those areas, a company's operation can be expected to be subject to greater uncertainty and fluctuation. Furthermore, the frequently changing political situations in developing countries often affect operating results negatively. As a result, some markets that may have experienced high growth for some years may suddenly experience drastic reductions in growth. In many situations, however, the higher risks are compensated for by higher returns, largely because competition is often less intense in those markets. Consequently, companies need to balance the opportunity for future growth in the developing nations with the existence of higher risk.

The past experience of international firms doing business in developing countries has not been very good. Due to trade restrictions, companies were forced to build local factories, exposing themselves to substantial risk. However, with the present trend toward global trade liberalization and privatization, many formerly closed countries have opened their borders. The result can be seen in statistics such as U.S. exports to developing countries. From 1991 to 1992, such exports grew by 13.7 percent, compared to 1.8 percent growth for exports to developed countries.[22] Traditionally, investments in Latin America countries were dominated by mining firms. Although these firms find renewed opportunities in Latin America, many other companies are joining that stayed away before.[23]

The new drive of investments in developing countries, however, no longer seeks just to use them for low-wage manufacturing. Markets such as Mexico are becoming important in themselves, and the huge populations are becoming more and more important customer groups. PepsiCo, convinced that the Mexican market is becoming important, has announced that it will invest $750 million over five years; the company is expanding its Mexican coverage by purchasing interests in local bottlers. With the ratification of the NAFTA agreement, incomes should continue to rise, creating a substantial growth in soft drinks.[24]

Expanding in Eastern Europe

The liberalization of the countries in eastern Europe has opened a large new market for many international firms. The market typically represents about 15 percent of the worldwide demand in a given industry, about two-thirds of that accounted for by Russia and other countries of the former Soviet Union. Although many companies consider this as long-term potential with little profit opportunity in the near term, a number of firms have moved to take advantage of opportunities in areas where they once were prohibited from doing business.

One example is Otis, the large U.S.-based elevator company. Already represented in all major markets of the world, the company considers the eastern European area of strategic importance, signing a series of deals since 1989. In former East Germany, Otis acquired a local company and several service companies with a total of two thousand employees. In Hungary, Otis entered a joint venture with a formerly state-owned elevator company that operates a factory and five hundred employees. In Russia, Otis signed two joint ventures with two different elevator companies. In each venture, Otis will have 55 percent ownership and will produce and market elevators for the local market. Otis was not alone in its expansion strategy. Its principal rivals, Schindler of Switzerland and Kone of Finland, ranking number two and number three respectively worldwide, both signed ventures in the same countries.[25]

Otis knows that it will take time for its eastern European ventures to return any profit. For its Russian and Ukrainian ventures, the company expects a profit in local currency by 1995. The company expected to invest about $100 million over ten years, half of this

22. ''U.S. Firms Turn to the Developing World,'' *Wall Street Journal,* August 4, 1993, p. A2.

23. ''U.S. Mining Firms, Unwelcome at Home, Flock to Latin America,'' *Wall Street Journal,* June 18, 1993, p. 1.

24. ''PepsiCo to Invest About $750 Million in Mexican Market,'' *Wall Street Journal,* March 5, 1993, p. B2.

25. ''Setting Sights on New Heights,'' *Financial Times,* March 1, 1991, p. 29.

coming from its local partners. Although the company, through its service centers, already signed up some 150,000 elevators built by companies located in the former Soviet Union, volume for new elevators took a dive. However, Otis recognized that the former Soviet Union built 40,000 elevators annually for a demand of 60,000. Although demand collapsed in the early 1980s, the company is certain that demand will come back to the original level.[26]

The first wave of investments into eastern Europe was led by companies marketing industrial equipment, such as Otis. Companies marketing consumer goods tended to enter the region later. One of the leaders was Procter & Gamble, the U.S.-based consumer products company. P&G set up regional centers for each product line, making the Czech Republic its center for detergents and Hungary the center for personal care products.[27] Procter & Gamble began its Russian operations in August 1991 in St. Petersburg. The company is slowly introducing a line of products while expanding its geographic reach. According to company surveys, only 10 to 15 percent of the Russian population could afford western consumer goods.[28]

Several luxury products companies have also entered the eastern European markets. In 1988, Mercedes-Benz was selling just 70 new cars in Russia, mostly to diplomatic customers. By 1992, volume had already grown to 3,500 units primarily to private Russians. This volume increase occurred despite hefty taxes of almost 90 percent. By 1993, the company had established some fifteen dealers. BMW's sales climbed from 500 units in 1992 to 700 units in 1993 through just three Moscow dealerships, and even Rolls-Royce has now opened a showroom in Moscow.[29] Although these volumes are still small by international standards, many companies consider this just the beginning. Toyota, the Japanese leader, sold 7,200 units in 1991. The company considers the fact that the former Soviet Union never produced more than two million vehicles annually, with customers having to wait many years for delivery, as sufficient indication that the market in Russia for cars will eventually become a multiple of that former output.[30]

Some companies are not easily deterred by dropping sales in eastern Europe as the countries move from central planning to a market economy. South Korean companies particularly have not been daunted by current problems; some of them believe the time is right to expand investments when everybody is pulling back, or hesitating to invest. Daewoo of Korea announced the investment of $100 million for a car plant in Uzbekistan, formerly part of the Soviet Union. Samsung, another Korean company, expanded its sales of consumer electronics in the former Soviet Union to $100 million. This expansion was aided by a move to sponsor the well-known Dynamo-Moscow hockey club. Bearing the Samsung name and logo, the club won the Russian hockey championship twice in a row.[31]

26. "Otis Seizes the High Ground," *International Management,* November 1992, p. 50.
27. "P&G Sets Up E. Europe Units," *Advertising Age,* June 24, 1991, p. 6.
28. "Crash Russian Course for Procter & Gamble," *New York Times,* December 19, 1993, p. 5.
29. "BMW, Mercedes, Rolls-Royce—Could This Be Russia?" *Business Week,* August 12, 1993, p. 40.
30. "Carmakers Target Former Soviet Market," *Nikkei Weekly,* April 11, 1992, p. 12.
31. "Dancing with the Bear," *Far Eastern Economic Review,* May 20, 1993, p. 56.

Country Selection

At some point, the development of an international marketing strategy will come down to selecting individual countries where a company intends to compete. There are between 175 and 200 countries and territories from which companies have to select but very few international firms end up competing in all of these markets. The decision on where to compete, the country selection decision, is one of the components of developing an international marketing strategy.

Why is country selection a strategic concern for international marketing management? Adding another country to a company's portfolio always requires some additional investment in management time and effort and in capital. Although opportunities for additional profits are usually the driving force, each additional country also represents a new business risk. It takes time to build up business in a country where the firm has not previously been represented, and profits may not show until much later on. Consequently, companies need to go through a careful analysis before they decide to move ahead.

Analyzing the Investment Climate

A complete understanding of the investment climate of a target country will help in the country selection decision. The investment climate of a country is made up of its political situation, its legal structure, its foreign trade position, and its attitude toward foreign investment or the presence of foreign companies. In general, companies will try to avoid countries with uncertain political situations. The impact that political and legal forces can have on the operations of a foreign company abroad was described in detail in Chapter 4.

A country's foreign trade position can also determine the environment for foreign firms operating there. Countries with a strong balance-of-payments surplus or strong currencies that are fully convertible are favored as good places to invest. Countries with chronic balance-of-payments difficulties and those where there are great uncertainties about the transferability of funds are viewed as risky and, as such, are less favored by foreign investors. These aspects were described in greater detail in Chapter 2. Consequently, assessing a country's investment climate will require a thorough and skillful analysis. However, investment climate is not the only determinant for a country being selected for entry.

Determining Market Attractiveness

Before a country can be selected for addition to a firm's portfolio of countries, management needs to assess the overall attractiveness of that country with respect to the firm's products or services. Initially, this requires a clear indication of the country's market size. It may consist of analyzing existing patterns of demand. Also needed are data on growth—both past and future—that will allow a firm to determine market size not only as it relates to the present situation but also with respect to potential.

Analyzing demand patterns allows a company to plot where on the product life cycle a given product or service can be located. Also, a firm may want to analyze potential competitors in that country to achieve an understanding of how it can compete. Finally, companies should get to know a new country is market enough to be able to determine if their way of competing and marketing is allowed in that country. Some markets may be very attractive, but if the firm's key strength cannot be employed, success is questionable.

The analytic approach required for an in-depth assessment of a country's market attractiveness was covered in great detail in Chapters 5, 6, and 7. Analyzing international markets and the company's prospective international buyers—the ability to perform marketing research and analysis on an international scale—is a prerequisite to sound country selection decisions.

Selecting Lead Markets

In Chapter 7, we introduced the concept of a lead market and its importance to global marketing strategists. In the context of selecting markets for special emphasis, the lead market concept can help in identifying those countries where a company should concentrate.

The United States is no longer the only lead market in many key industries. In electronics or semiconductor manufacturing, Japan has captured the lead in a number of segments. This loss of leadership to Japan and other countries has become pronounced in a number of areas of the electronics industry. The worldwide share of U.S. semiconductor manufacturers had slipped to less than 40 percent by 1990.[32] This loss was primarily a function of less investment than Japanese firms, often caused by higher financing costs in the United States. The lack of capital investment in the semiconductor industry has also caused difficulties for U.S. manufacturers of semiconductor testing equipment. In 1979, the top nine rankings were occupied by U.S. firms, led by Fairchild, Perkin-Elmer, and Applied Materials. In 1988, the list was led by two Japanese firms, Nikon and TEL Electron, and the top U.S. firm had dropped to fourth place. When Japanese firms became the world leaders in semiconductors, their position was also exploited by Japanese test equipment manufacturers.[33]

Even in the computer industry, lead markets have started to change hands. While the United States still leads in the larger computers, Japanese firms have begun to compete effectively in the smaller, newer-generation machines. While IBM and Apple lead in PCs, Toshiba of Japan is a leader in portable computers, with NEC, another Japanese company, another leading contender (behind Compaq and Zenith, both U.S. firms). The enormous potential for still smaller computers has shifted toward the Japanese. For laptop, notebook, or palm-size computers, the experience of the Japanese firms with miniaturizing has been a decided advantage.[34] Furthermore, a key component in all very small computers is a flat

32. "U.S. Semiconductor Industry Slips Further in World Markets," *Financial Times,* February 22, 1991, p. 14.

33. "Pillar of Chip Industry Eroding," *New York Times,* March 3, 1989, p. D1.

34. "Japanese Portables Threaten American Lead in Computers," *New York Times,* November 24, 1990, p. 1.

display screen. The largest maker of these is Sharp of Japan, and no credible U.S. source exists. Even those pocket-sized computers made in the United States depend on these critical components—and thus on Japanese suppliers. These developments have forced U.S. computer makers to link up with the Japanese in small models. Apple also is expected eventually to source its own laptop from Sony.[35] (See Chapter 11 for more details.)

Taiwan provides a good example of how newly industrializing countries can become lead markets by wrestling competitive positions away from developed nations. For many years behind the innovations elsewhere, Taiwanese electronics companies have now become world leaders in several important product categories. Elitegroup and First International are the world's largest independent manufacturers of printed circuit boards. GVC, another Taiwanese company, has risen to the leading position as modem producer, surpassing Hayes of the United States. For such important components as pointing devices (the computer mouse), scanners, and motherboards, Taiwan accounted for some 70 percent of the world market share in 1992. As a result of the rising importance of these firms, leading U.S. companies such as Digital, Apple, and Motorola are engaging local firms in joint design projects for microprocessors. Furthermore, Taiwan, with its efficient business culture and propensity for speed in product development, has become the site of choice for manufacturing operations. In certain industries, international firms must be present in Taiwan if they intend to keep abreast of the changes. The same applies to lead markets in other product categories, such as Singapore for disk drives.[36]

Market Entry

Having decided to select a certain country or group of countries for further market development, the company is then confronted with market entry decisions. In this phase, a company faces a series of options as to how it wants to enter the selected country. The options range from a very low level of involvement and investment, such as various forms of exporting, to more involved and investment-intensive forms of entry, such as a company-owned sales subsidiary or even a manufacturing base.

Entry strategies are of strategic importance because most companies will not be able to shift quickly from one alternative to another following initial market feedback. Depending on the type of entry strategy selected, market success may differ substantially. Furthermore, some entry strategies require a substantial amount of initial investment, and the results cannot be realized until much later. As a result, companies are very careful in finding the right amount of commitment combined with the expected results and the type of market they want to enter.

Given the importance of managing entry strategies for success in international marketing, Chapter 9 is entirely devoted to this topic. There we concentrate on documenting

35. ''Made in the U.S.A., but by Sharp,'' *New York Times,* February 22, 1991, p. D1.
36. ''Power Switch,'' *Far Eastern Economic Review,* December 16, 1993, p. 44.

the various analytic steps companies go through in making entry strategy decisions for their foreign ventures and describe influencing factors such as costs, investments, market potential, and sales volume.

Global Marketing Programs

Of the host of important decisions companies face when developing marketing programs for international markets, the most important relates to the amount of standardization versus differentiation aimed for in the various target markets. As explained in considerable detail in Chapter 1, companies face many barriers that prevent standardization or make offering standardized marketing programs very difficult. Standardization not only is to be understood in terms of product hardware but includes the ''software'' of marketing programs, such as distribution, pricing, and promotion strategies.

Whether a marketing program needs to be tailored to each individual market will not always be clear. Although local conditions may signal on the surface that such an approach may be advantageous, other concerns need to be considered. Substantial changes in a company's marketing program naturally bring additional costs. Such cost increases may occur in the production of new or additional product models, with corresponding research and engineering costs. Such incremental costs are not always justified by the incremental business volume expected. Consequently, in some cases a company may not be in a position to differentiate even though management believes the market will require it. Similar concerns apply for other marketing aspects such as advertising, distribution, or logistics.

Increasingly, companies need to consider the broader issues of globalization of their marketing programs, which will force such issues as globalized advertising, global products, or global pricing. These issues have become important as more and more international marketing decisions are made across many markets, or even worldwide, rather than the more traditional country-by-country decision-making. Developing such global programs and understanding the implications will be the focus of Chapters 10 through 15, with particular emphasis on the various elements of the marketing mix.

Global Marketing Management

How a company manages, organizes, and controls its operations greatly influences the direction it takes. Executives, both domestically and abroad, tend to adapt to a company's organizational systems, which makes the choice of organizational system important. Although the impact of the organization's design or planning and control systems is less obvious to an outside observer, these factors are nevertheless considered of strategic importance because the effect is often realized only years after such systems have been put in place.

Of major concern to a company are the organizational structure to be selected for its international operations, the location of its decision-making authority with respect to international marketing, and the nature of its planning process as it impacts on international marketing. Chapters 16 and 17 are devoted entirely to these important concerns.

Generic International Marketing Strategies

Having explored some of the key strategic decisions faced by international marketing executives, our focus will now shift to the generic global and international marketing strategies companies can adopt. Generic strategies are general classifications used to organize a large number of possible individual strategies. This is done to highlight certain general principles—no company will neatly fall into any one of these categories. Instead, most companies will fall somewhere in between categories, or they may use a combination of strategies from different categories. Furthermore, many companies actually pursue several types of strategies at once, varying them according to product line or business unit.

Dimensions

Generic international and global marketing strategies can be classified along two dimensions. Along the *geographic dimension,* the reach of a marketing operation, we can describe strategies ranging from domestic to international, regional, or global. Companies may adopt various patterns of geographic strategies. Along a second axis, the *asset dimension,* companies' generic strategies may be described in terms of asset strategies. Asset strategies may also range from domestic, single-country, to regional and eventually global. The asset strategy describes a company's investment patterns in terms of plants, logistics operations, and other physical assets.

Companies' strategies may therefore fall into several categories.[37] (See Figure 8.4 for a matrix of the patterns.) Global market strategies are pursued by those firms who serve the entire world market, and whose marketing operations stretch across the world. Global asset strategies are pursued by those firms who dot their plants, support operations, and other fixed assets across the world. Clearly, there are combinations as well. The company with a local market and asset strategy is the typical domestic company, both producing and marketing in only one market. The company with a global market strategy but local asset strategy would be the typical exporter, marketing all over the world but producing in a single market. Boeing, the passenger aircraft manufacturer, exemplifies such a strategy. When a company markets globally and its assets are also distributed globally, we may speak of a truly global company. And finally, some firms whose markets are largely domestic pursue a global asset strategy by sourcing products overseas. Such firms may be clas-

---

37. Vijay Jolly, ''Global Competitive Strategies,'' in *Strategy, Organizational Design, and Human Resource Management,* ed. Charles C. Snow (Greenwich, Conn.: JAI Press, 1989), pp. 55–110.

FIGURE 8.4 ● Markets, Asset versus Globalization Strategies

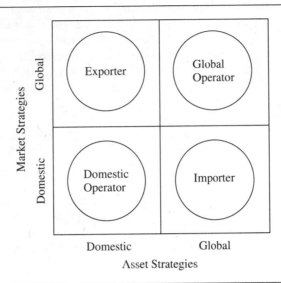

sified as classic importers. Schwinn Bicycles of the United States would typify such a strategy.[38]

A later section details the various geographic expansion strategies. The particular asset strategy followed by these companies may or may not be global and tends to play less of a role in our considerations. It becomes important only for entry strategies in a given market where sufficient market penetration is linked to entry via physical assets, such as a building or a plant.

Generic Global Marketing Strategies

In the early phases of development, global marketing strategies were assumed to be of one type only. Typically, these first types of global strategies were associated with offering the same marketing strategy across the globe. The debate centered on whether a company could gain anything from this and what the preconditions for this type of strategy would be. As marketers gained more experience, many other types of global marketing strategies became apparent. Some of those were much less involved and exposed a smaller aspect of a marketing strategy to globalization. In this section, we explore the various generic types of global marketing strategies and indicate the conditions under which they may best succeed.

38. Jean-Pierre Jeannet and Robert Howard, ''Schwinn Bicycle Company'' (European Case Clearing House, 1993).

Integrated Global Marketing Strategies   When a company pursues an integrated global marketing strategy, all aspects of the marketing strategy have been globalized. Globalization includes not only the product but also the communications strategy, pricing, and distribution, as well as such strategic elements as segmentation and positioning. Such a strategy may be advisable for companies that face completely globalized customers along the lines defined earlier. It also assumes that the way a given industry works is highly similar everywhere, thus allowing a company to unfold its strategy along similar paths in each country.

Reality tells us that such situations are rare, and complete integrated global marketing strategies will continue to be the exception. However, there are many other types of global marketing strategies; each may be tailored to specific industry and competitive circumstances.

Global Segment Strategies   A company that decides to pursue the same segment in many countries is following a global segment strategy. The company may develop an understanding of its customer base and leverage that experience around the world. In both consumer and industrial industries, significant knowledge is accumulated when a company gains in-depth understanding of a niche or segment. A pure global segment strategy will even allow for different products, brands, or advertising, although some standardization is expected. The choices may consist of competing always in the upper or middle segment of a given consumer market or for a particular technical application in an industrial segment.

Global Product Category Strategies   Possibly the least involved type of global marketing strategy is the pursuit of the global category. Leverage is gained from competing in the same category country after country and may come in the form of product technology or development costs. Selecting the form of global product category implies that the company, while staying within that category, will consider targeting different segments in each category, or varying the product, advertising, and branding according to local market requirements. Companies competing in the multidomestic way are frequently applying the global category strategy and leveraging knowledge across markets without pursuing standardization. That strategy works best if there are significant differences across markets and when few segments are present in market after market.

Global Marketing Mix Element Strategies   These strategies pursue globalization along individual marketing mix elements such as pricing, distribution, communications, or product. They are partially globalized strategies that allow a company to customize other aspects of its marketing strategy. Although various types of strategies may apply, the most important ones are global product strategies, global advertising strategies, and global branding strategies.

Global Product Strategies   Pursuing a global product strategy implies that a company has largely globalized its product offering. Although the product may not need to be completely standardized worldwide, key aspects or components may in fact be globalized. The company may elect to add a global product strategy if the product or services offered fit the description of global products discussed earlier. Global product strategies require that product use conditions, expected features, and required product functions be largely identical so that few variations or changes are needed. Companies pursuing a global product strategy are interested in leveraging the fact that all investments for producing and developing a given product have already been made. Global strategies will yield more volume, which will make the original investment easier to justify.

For a company such as Ford, achieving a global product strategy has been a long-term goal. Having failed to make its Escort model a world car in the early 1980s, Ford has launched its new Contour in the United States, based on its Mondeo model in Europe. Ford's long-term goals are to integrate Mazda, its partner in Japan, into its product planning and development process so that only one development budget of six billion dollars would be necessary for one new model. Eventually, Ford Europe might base its small-car development center in Europe, with responsibility for world markets, and its larger-sized models in the United States.[39]

Global Branding Strategies   Global branding strategies consist of using the same brand name or logo worldwide. Companies want to leverage the creation of such brand names across many markets, because the launching of new brands requires a considerable marketing investment. Global branding strategies tend to be advisable if the target customers travel across country borders and will be exposed to products elsewhere.

Spending some $140 million on its brand name, U.S.-based athletic shoe manufacturer Reebok has embarked on a global branding strategy, consolidating all of its advertising under the Leo Burnett advertising agency. The company wants to become the number one sports and fitness brand in the athletic shoe market, estimated at $12 billion, and in the process achieve a 30 percent world market share.[40]

Global branding strategies also become important if target customers are exposed to advertising worldwide. This is often the case for industrial marketing customers, who may read industry and trade journals from other countries. Increasingly, this has become important also for consumer products, where cross-border advertising through international TV channels has become common. Even in some markets such as eastern Europe, many consumers had become aware of brands offered in western Europe before the liberalization of the economies in the early 1990s. Global branding allows a company to take advantage of such existing goodwill. Companies pursuing global branding strategies may include luxury product marketers, who typically face a large fixed investment for the worldwide promotion of a product. In Chapter 15, we look at the various alternatives to global branding in more detail.

Global Advertising Strategies   Globalized advertising is generally associated with the use of the same brand name across the world. However, a company may want to use different brand names, partly for historic purposes. Many global firms have made acquisitions in

39. ''Ford Motor Chief Senses a Sea Change,'' *Financial Times,* April 11, 1994, p. 18.
40. ''Why Reebok Fired Chiat, Once and for All,'' *Advertising Age,* September 20, 1993, p. 3.

other countries resulting in a number of local brands. These local brands have their own distinguished market, and a company may find it futile to change those names. Instead, the company may want to leverage a certain theme or advertising approach that may have been developed as a result of some global customer research. Global advertising themes are most advisable where a firm may market to customers seeking similar benefits sought across the world. Once the purchasing reason has been determined as similar, a common theme may be created to address it. The difficulties encountered with selecting common themes are discussed at length in Chapter 15.

Geographic Expansion Strategies

To succeed in global marketing competition, companies need to carefully look at their geographic expansion. To some extent, a firm makes a conscious decision about its extent of internationalization by choosing a posture that may range from entirely domestic without any international involvement to a global reach where the company devotes its entire marketing strategy to global competition. Each level of internationalization will profoundly change the way a company competes and will require different strategies with respect to marketing programs, planning, organization, and control of the international marketing effort.

Domestic Strategy

A company with a strictly domestic strategy has decided not to actively involve itself in any international marketing. Clearly, such companies are not the main interest for our text, but there nevertheless are situations in which a company should not or cannot become an active participant in international marketing.

When a company has a very limited product range that appeals only to its own local market, international marketing will not be advisable unless the company is prepared to expand its product line. In many service-oriented businesses, customer relations are such that business is only done within a narrow or limited geographic trading range. To expand to new business centers, other affiliates will have to be built, again requiring considerable capital assets. Also, some industries are substantially domestic, with individual companies not directly competing beyond their own local markets. And newly started companies may not be in a position to expand abroad before their domestic market is satisfied.

Over the past twenty-five years, an ever increasing number of domestic industries have become subject to a global logic, as described in Chapter 7. These developments may have been triggered by a foreign company's arriving on the scene and changing the competitive situation. The U.S. major appliance industry serves as an excellent example of an industry that has turned from purely domestic to international in scope. Although only about 2 percent of all major appliances sold in the United States are imported and exports account for about 6 percent, foreign competitors such as Electrolux control almost 20 percent of the U.S. market. That position was achieved through the acquisition of White

Westinghouse and brands such as Frigidaire, Gibson, Kelvinator, and Tappan. With foreign competition invading its home territory and with Europe growing faster than the North American market, the major U.S. players have become active internationally: GE through a joint venture with British-owned GEC, Whirlpool through the acquisition of the Philips operation in the Netherlands, and Maytag through the acquisition of Hoover, which gave it a strong position in the United Kingdom and some Continental European markets.[41] Occurring within weeks of each other, these actions showed how quickly a purely domestic industry can turn into an international industry.[42]

With more and more industries subject to the global logic, ever fewer companies can safely select a pure global strategy. Increasingly, firms will have to accommodate the global logic by pursuing various levels of internationalization. The following sections describe different internationalization and globalization strategies companies may adopt.

Regional Expansion Strategies

Mapping out a regional strategy implies that a company will concentrate its resources and marketing efforts on one or possibly two of the world's regions. Emphasizing North America or Europe can be the result of a regional strategy. Other regions a company may want to concentrate on are Latin America, the Pacific Basin, and Asia. In such a situation, the company has expanded beyond a domestic environment but, as we will show later, has not yet reached a multinational or global state.

Companies pursue a regional expansion strategy for a number of reasons. Such firms are competing in the region of which their home market is a part; neighboring markets within the same region are invaded because of market or product similarity requiring few adaptations. Regional strategies are also encouraged when customer requirements in one region are substantially different from those in others. Under those circumstances, different sets of competitors and market structures may exist, and industry participants may not invade each other's regions or market territories. When such a fragmentation exists, a firm can compete on the basis of knowing its own region best by being closer to its customers.

The many different regional marketing strategies (see Figure 8.5) typically center around the three large trading blocs of North America (United States, Canada, Mexico), Europe, and the Asia Pacific area (Japan, Pacific Rim countries). A global strategy, by comparison, would include the major triad regions. Regional strategies may be structured around penetrating just one regional market or several markets. We speak of a North American strategy if a company has integrated its marketing strategy for the United States, Canada, and Mexico. Passage of NAFTA caused many firms to adopt an integrated North American strategy by merging the operations of the three signature countries. A pan-European strategy occurs when a firm integrates its strategy across Europe. And finally, a firm adopting a pan-Asian strategy integrates its marketing strategy across the Asia Pacific

41. "The Final Link in Whirlpool's Global Circle," *Financial Times,* June 7, 1991, p. 15; "Can Maytag's Repairman Get Out of This Fix?" *Business Week,* October 26, 1992, p. 54.
42. "A Chance to Clean Up in European White Goods," *Financial Times,* December 13, 1993, p. 23.

FIGURE 8.5 ● Regional Marketing Strategies

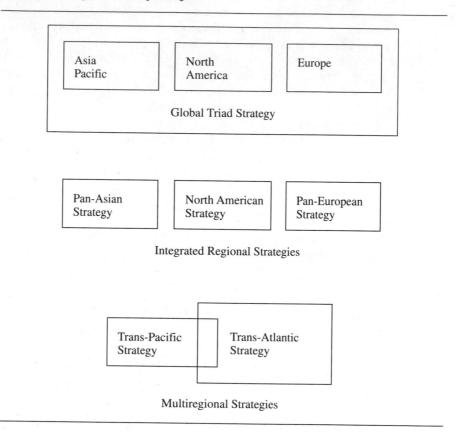

region. Companies may also integrate two regions into a trans-Pacific strategy or a trans-Atlantic strategy.

Pan-European marketing strategies have received considerable attention in the wake of the Europe 1992 initiative to create a single European market. As a result, many companies have begun to integrate their marketing strategies across Europe, striving for such things as pan-European brands, pan-European products, and pan-European advertising strategies.

In a 1992 study, some 80 percent of consumer goods companies indicated an interest in a pan-European strategy, but only a fourth admitted to having begun the process of integration, and less than 20 percent of that fourth believed their process of pan-European marketing integration had been completed. This would indicate that many firms had not yet capitalized on the opportunity for pan-European marketing integration.[43]

43. "Who Favors Branding with Euro Approach?" *Advertising Age International,* May 25, 1992, pp. 1–16.

Lever, a European company active in the detergent field, began to switch its strategy in the mid-1980s, after Procter & Gamble (its archrival from the United States) adopted pan-European strategies. Lever appointed European brand managers and started coordinating many of its policies. To avoid alienating consumers who may still require local differences, Lever has implemented this process step by step. Most brands still retain some local variations, but the company continues to strive for more uniform and standardized products across most of its European markets.[44]

Companies may pursue a single regional strategy, such as to compete only in Europe or in the Asia Pacific region. Alternatively, companies, even those covering most of the world, may decide to develop several regional strategies on the basis that integration beyond a given region does not make much sense. Such a multiregional strategy is currently pursued by Sony, the Japanese consumer electronics firm. For Asia, Europe, and the United States, the company built three largely self-sufficient industrial infrastructures that are able to handle all products from development through production. Corporate functions currently handled in Japan are decentralized to North America and Europe. Sony, with some two-thirds of its sales outside Japan, is further along in this strategy of ''global localization'' than are other Japanese firms.[45]

Wal-Mart, the leading U.S. discount retail chain, is pursuing a regional expansion strategy by advancing its business in the direction of Canada and Mexico. In Canada, Wal-Mart expanded by acquiring some 120 Woolco stores. In Mexico, Wal-Mart is acting in conjunction with a local department store company, attracted by the prospects of serving the 400 million Latin American consumers that right now cannot avail themselves of a Wal-Mart store.[46]

Regional strategies requiring the integration of a marketing strategy for one region, such as Europe, are conceptually identical to global marketing strategies. The key difference is that they are applied to a smaller set of countries. A marketer developing a pan-European strategy needs therefore to have access to the same concepts and skills as the marketer developing global strategies.

Multidomestic Marketing Strategies

Although we explore organization issues in more detail in Chapter 16, some general principles of how multidomestic firms are organized should be introduced at this point. To a large extent, international firms operating as multidomestic firms have organized their businesses around countries or geographic regions. While some key strategic decisions with respect to products and technology are made at the central or head office, the initiative of implementing marketing strategies is largely left to local-country subsidiaries. As a result, profit and loss responsibility tends to reside in each individual country. At the extreme, this leads to an organization that runs many different businesses in a number of

44. ''In Pursuit of the Elusive Euroconsumer,'' *Wall Street Journal,* April 23, 1992, p. B1.
45. ''The Emergence of a Global Company,'' *Financial Times,* October 2, 1989, p. 18.
46. ''And the Winner Is Still . . . Wal-Mart,'' *Fortune,* May 2, 1994, p. 70.

countries, therefore the term *multidomestic*. Each subsidiary represents a separate business that must be run profitably.

As we discussed in Chapter 1, multinational corporations tend to be represented in a large number of countries and the world's principal trading regions. The majority of today's large internationally active firms may be classified as pursuing multidomestic strategies.

A large number of U.S. firms listed by *Fortune* magazine in its Fortune 500 list have traditionally operated multidomestically. This includes such well-known firms as General Motors, Ford, IBM, Gillette, General Electric, and Kodak, as well as major service businesses, including Citibank and Chase Manhattan, two of the largest U.S.-based financial services organizations. Common to most of these firms is their very large percentage of sales and profits generated from overseas business. For IBM and Gillette, more than half of their volume is generated overseas. Overseas firms such as Unilever, Royal Dutch–Shell, and Nestlé are foreign-based firms with only a small portion of their sales coming from their domestic or home market. The ranks of international firms have also been joined by many Japanese firms, as well as firms from newly industrialized countries such as South Korea, Taiwan, and some developing countries.

Nestlé, the world's largest food company, though represented in most markets of the world, is a typical practitioner of the multidomestic strategy.[47] Including its operating companies such as Carnation, Rowntree, and Buitoni, among others, it has always practiced a decentralized approach to management. Local operating managers, thought to be much more in tune with local markets, are given the freedom to develop marketing strategies tailored to local needs. In the foods business, where considerable differences exist among countries' cultures and consumer habits, competitive environments, market structures, and practices, decentralization was judged by management to be imperative.[48] More recently, Nestlé has begun a move toward a more centralized management structure, which resulted in a reorganization of its U.S. operations. Following the acquisition of Carnation, a U.S. foods company, the then chief executive officer of the acquired company was in touch with the Nestlé head office only once or twice annually. Since the reorganization, the recently appointed head of Nestlé U.S. is at the company's world headquarters in Switzerland as much as one week per month.[49]

Global Product/Market Focus

As outlined earlier in this chapter, geographic extension is one of two key dimensions in the strategy of an international company. Another important dimension is concerned with the range of a firm's product and service offerings. To what extent should a company become a supplier of a wide range of products aimed at several or many market segments?

47. "Nestlé Shows How to Gobble Markets," *Fortune,* January 16, 1989, p. 74.

48. Helmut Maucher, "Global Strategies of Nestlé," *European Management Journal,* 7, no. 1 (1989), pp. 92–96.

49. "Nestlé: A Giant in a Hurry," *Business Week,* March 22, 1993, pp. 50–54.

Should a company become the global specialist in a certain area by satisfying one or a small number of target segments, doing this in most major markets around the world?

Even some of the largest companies cannot pursue all available initiatives. Resources for most companies are limited, often requiring a tradeoff between product expansion and geographic expansion strategies. Resolving this question is necessary to achieve a concentration of resources and efforts in areas where they will bring the most return. We can distinguish between two models: on the one hand, we have the broad-based firm marketing a wide range of products to many different customer groups, both domestic and overseas; on the other hand, we have the narrowly based firm marketing a limited range of products to a homogeneous customer group around the world. Both types of companies can be successful in their respective markets.

Companies such as Procter & Gamble, Unilever, and Nestlé are all examples of consumer goods firms practicing a broad-based product strategy. In most markets, these firms offer many brands and product lines. Among industrial marketers, General Electric follows a similar strategy. Some of these firms, however, are broken down into a large number of strategic business units, or divisions with a limited product range aimed at a limited market segment, and within each business unit the chosen strategy may be much more focused.

Firms with a narrow product range include Hertz and Avis, the U.S. car rental companies, and Rolex, the Swiss watch manufacturer. These firms have a common strategy of a narrow and clearly focused product line with the intent of dominating the chosen market segment across many countries. Many specialty equipment manufacturers in the fields of machine tools, electronic testing equipment, and other production process equipment tend to fit this pattern of niche, or focus, marketing.

The trend today is for companies to expect their businesses to develop a worldwide position and for some (such as GE) to become number one or two worldwide. This requires a business to develop its competitive position across all major markets, in particular across the major regions of North America, Asia Pacific, and Europe. The preference is for businesses (or strategic business units in large corporations) to focus on a particular line or segment by extending that offering around the globe. This has also led companies to pursue global marketing strategies per business line rather than corporatewide. Rather than having a single global strategy for one corporation, companies will let each operating division set the appropriate type of global strategy best suited to its markets and industry environment.

A company such as GE may pursue many different global marketing strategies, not just one. Each business is to develop its own, and there may well be different global marketing strategies for different businesses. In this sense, each business is given a global mandate which means that it is required to develop on a worldwide basis.[50] As a result, each operating division such as GE Appliances, GE Capital, GE Plastics, and GE Medical Systems has its own form of global strategy.[51] GE Capital, which concentrates on financial

50. "Jack Welch Reinvents General Electric—Again," *Economist,* March 30, 1991, p. 59.

51. "GE's Brave New World," *Business Week,* November 8, 1993, pp. 64–69.

services, is one of the largest units of its kind. GE Capital has invested heavily in Europe, where it got involved with GPA, the large Irish aircraft leasing firm, and the card finance companies of a number of European retailers. The company also invested recently in a financing company in Thailand and a vehicle fleet company in Canada.[52]

The Global Business Unit

Many firms have come to realize that a strong global presence in one given product was becoming a strategic requirement. Since traditional multinational firms, often competing through a multidomestic strategy, have realized the weakness of their unfocused patterns of global coverage, they have begun to assemble business units that have a better global focus. Many are striving to change their business to reflect more a coherent market position whereby a business consists of strong units in major markets. Avoiding globally unfocused strategies, international firms have either retrenched to become regional specialists or changed their business focus to adopt global niche strategies, selective globalization, or complete globalization (see Figure 8.6).

A strategy of *complete globalization* is selected by firms that essentially globalize all of their business units. This pattern is typical of companies such as General Electric of the United States (as discussed above) and Siemens of Germany. Such firms end up with some dozen or more globally positioned businesses, each charting its own global marketing strategy. *Selective globalization* is adopted by firms that globalize several or many businesses but also exit from others because financial resources may be limited. Examples of selective globalization include ICI of the United Kingdom, where some units, such as man-made fibers, were sold off to strengthen the market positions of others. *Global niche strategies* are selected by firms that focus on one or very few businesses worldwide and exit from others to make up for a lack of resources. Nokia, the Finnish telecommunications company, employs such niche strategies. The company exited from computers, paper, and other sectors to concentrate on cellular phones and telecommunications infrastructure.[53] Even more focused is the strategy of Newbridge, a Canadian telecommunications equipment supplier specializing in equipment for advanced networks and achieving sales of $400 million in 1994. The company competes essentially in only one product line but is a world leader for its particular applications.[54]

Competitive Strategies

This section focuses on the various competitive strategies firms can adopt in the international field. The examples given will show the impact of various geographic and product/market structures on a firm's competitive position. For our purposes, we will define competitive strategy "as the way in which a firm can compete more effectively to strengthen

52. "Global Expansion to Cap It All," *Financial Times,* March 23, 1994, p. 14.
53. "How Nokia Wins in Cellular Phones," *Fortune,* March 21, 1994, pp. 38–40.
54. "Newbridge's Joyride on the Info Highway," *Business Week,* March 28, 1994, p. 168.

FIGURE 8.6 ● Global Product/Market Strategies

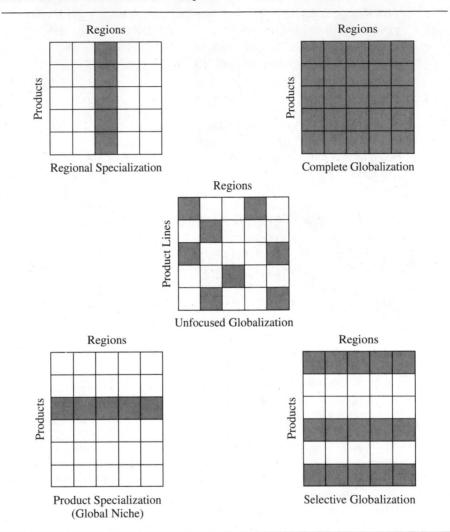

Regional Specialization

Complete Globalization

Unfocused Globalization

Product Specialization
(Global Niche)

Selective Globalization

its market position.''[55] When firms compete in the international market, their competitive strategies are likely to depend on their relevant resources and the type of competition they are meeting. At the country level, companies are apt to meet a variety of different players, ranging from local firms to multinational companies and even global firms. As we have discussed in detail in this chapter, these types of firms operate differently. Consequently, a company will have to be able to adjust to any differences in competition on a country-by-country basis.

55. Michael E. Porter, *Competitive Strategy* (New York: Free Press, 1980), p. x.

In this section, we characterize some typical matchups and make clear how competitive dynamics differ depending on the players involved. We will examine three prototype players: the local, the multidomestic, and the global firm. By describing some real competitive battles between such companies, we aim to distill some general concepts about which type of competitive strategy will work for each type of firm.

Local Company Versus Global Firm

As we have shown, global firms are able to leverage their experience and market position in one market for the benefit of another. Consequently, the global firm is often a more potent competitor for a local company. The example of how Procter & Gamble dealt with two local competitors in the Swiss disposable diaper market illustrates such a competitive dynamic.

In the mid-1970s, the Swiss market for baby diaper products consisted of cloth diapers, still the largest segment, and some disposable products such as inserts for traditional diapers.[56] Having observed the success of disposable diapers in the United States and in other larger markets, the Swiss company Moltex introduced its own version of the disposable diaper. Although a considerable habit change was needed, the company supported its product with little advertising and relied primarily on Switzerland's largest supermarket chain, Coop, for support. Moltex quickly gained a 35 percent market share.

When Procter & Gamble wanted to introduce its Pampers brand one year later, the large U.S. company found the channels blocked; Coop, its largest potential retail customer, was unwilling to stock another brand. Moltex had strengthened its hand with the trade by offering larger discounts and higher margins. In an effort to outflank the blocked channel, Pampers were introduced through drugstores, department stores, and in hospitals through heavy sampling. Once initial distribution was attained, the Pampers brand was supported with considerable advertising aimed at the consumer. Despite its distribution handicap, Pampers became the brand leader.

When Coop realized the profitability of the disposable diaper market, the chain introduced its own store brand. Moltex, up to that time the only brand carried by this chain, lost its most important distribution overnight. However, Procter & Gamble was able to continue to expand its market share and maintain dominance despite a substantial premium price, because the company had continued to build its brand image with consumers by supporting it with advertising. In the end, the supermarket chain began to carry Pampers. Moltex, having lost distribution, was relegated to a minor brand.

Why was Procter & Gamble able to overcome substantial local competition despite a late entry into the Swiss market for disposable diapers? Moltex had learned of the considerable market potential in disposable diapers by observing market trends abroad. However, the company had adopted a marketing strategy that did not consider the marketing strength of its principal and most likely competitor, Procter & Gamble, though P&G was already on the Swiss market with other products and could be expected to follow suit

---

56. For more details, see Jean-Pierre Jeannet, *Competitive Marketing Strategies in a European Context* (Lausanne: IMEDE, International Management Development Institute, 1987).

soon. Local market connections to the retail trade were not sufficient to overcome the marketing expertise of a global firm.

Our second example should make clear that local firms can in fact compete effectively against much larger international companies if they compete wisely.

Ramlösa, the leading Swedish bottler of mineral water, is a local firm that was able to compete effectively against Perrier of France, probably the most successful marketer of mineral water worldwide. Ramlösa sold its mineral water primarily in Sweden, with some minor export business to neighboring Norway and Finland. Ramlösa executives had watched Perrier invade market after market in Europe and finally dominate the premium segment for mineral water worldwide.[57]

In the early 1980s, when Perrier was repeating its attack on the premium segment of Denmark, Ramlösa executives realized that it would not be long before Perrier would invade their market also. In Sweden, Ramlösa enjoyed a market share of close to 100 percent, and it was feared an aggressive new entrant like Perrier might lower Ramlösa's share considerably. Having studied Perrier's strategy in other European markets, Ramlösa searched for a response and in 1981 finally decided to launch its own premium brand of mineral water. The company invested in expensive packaging and bottles, advertised to obtain a premium image, and increased the price by almost 50 percent although the mineral water of the premium brand was identical to that sold under its regular label. The sales volume of the premium brand did end up decreasing the sales of the regular brand, but Ramlösa was not unhappy, because the profitability of the premium brand per unit was substantially higher than its regular brand.

When Perrier finally entered the Swedish market in 1983, it followed its proven strategy of aiming at the premium spot. However, with Ramlösa already owning the premium spot with its top brand, Perrier was forced to enter on a premium versus premium strategy. This resulted in such a high price that Perrier gained very little market share over Ramlösa. By correctly spotting and predicting the Perrier strategy in advance, Ramlösa was able to design a response that prevented Perrier from unfolding the approach that had been so successful elsewhere.

Although global firms have superior resources, they often become inflexible after several successful market entries and tend to stay with standard approaches when flexibility is called for. In general, the global firms' strongest local competitors are those who watch global firms carefully and learn from their moves in other countries. With some global firms requiring several years before a product is introduced in all markets, local competitors in some markets can take advantage of such advance notice by building defenses or launching a preemptive attack on the same segment.

Multidomestic Corporation Versus Multidomestic Corporation

When two multidomestic firms clash in a single market, the battles tend to be more expensive and more drawn out than when international firms compete against local competitors. This is largely so because international firms have sufficient resources to fight it out. Such

57. Ibid.

clashes take place in many markets. However, when multinational firms compete in a certain market, there is normally no spillover into other markets, because those firms view strategy mostly on a country-by-country basis.

How two multidomestic firms, the U.S.-based CPC International and the Swiss-based Nestlé, clashed in Denmark in the 1980s serves as a typical example of a head-on collision between two large international companies.[58] Both firms are large food companies operating subsidiaries in many countries. Aside from producing in Denmark for export, both companies operated two local marketing subsidiaries distributing a full line of products to the local retail trade. Nestlé marketed instant coffee, infant food products, and bouillons under its Maggi brand name. Maggi bouillons were Nestlé's most important product line in Denmark. Competing directly against Maggi was CPC's Knorr brand of dehydrated products, which included bouillons but also soups and sauces. Nestlé controlled about 80 percent of the bouillon market, compared to CPC's 20 percent. However, CPC's Knorr brand completely dominated the sauce and soup segments.

CPC's Knorr launched an attack in the bouillon segment by substantially underpricing Maggi. When Maggi realized that it suffered a disadvantage from a smaller shelf space area due to offering only one product in that category, it countered by introducing a new dehydrated line of mixes that were not sold by Knorr in Denmark. This instantly gave Maggi more shelf space. Knorr followed suit, however. When Maggi realized that Knorr's funds for attacking in the bouillon segment came largely from its profitable sauce business, Maggi introduced a limited sauce line with low prices to reduce Knorr's cash flow. Although this paid for itself, Maggi was not able to have an impact on Knorr's profitability because the market grew due to higher competitive activity. In the end, Maggi also expanded into soups, which enabled it to improve its position and to make up for lost profits in the bouillon segment, where price competition substantially lowered profit margins after several years.

Although both CPC International and Nestlé subsidiaries fought an intense marketing battle for several years, both subsidiaries relied largely on their own financial resources and had profit and loss responsibility on a local basis. Both multinationals made available to their subsidiaries the full product development resources of their international networks. The two companies offered full lines of dehydrated products, including soups, sauces, mixes, and bouillons, in all major European markets. As a result, the Danish subsidiaries could easily and quickly launch new products that were already marketed elsewhere. However, the two subsidiaries obviously had to bear all marketing costs on their own. At no time did this intensive battle spill over into other markets, nor was it a reflection of head-office strategy to expand certain product lines in Denmark.

Global Firm Versus Global Firm

Developments in some industries have reached a point where most key competitors have attained some level of globalization. In such situations, the type of competitive behavior

58. See case series "Nestlé Nordisk A/S" (A) through (E), reprinted in Jeannet, *Competitive Marketing Strategies.*

changes, and global companies go beyond the leveraging of key developments or new product trends.

One of the longest-running global competitive battles is the competition between Coca-Cola and PepsiCo, both U.S.-based soft drink companies. Although the two companies are more evenly matched in the U.S. market, Coke's market share outside the United States leads Pepsi's by a wide margin.[59] Differences abroad come from Coke's better market position in Europe and some Asian markets, whereas Pepsi has dominated markets such as the former Soviet Union. In one important market, India, Coke withdrew in the mid-1970s due to pressures to sell part of its local subsidiary. As a result, rival Pepsi got a chance to enter, and Coke has only recently been able to get back in.[60]

In its advertising, Coca-Cola capitalizes on Coke's position as the world's most recognizable brand and product. The company spent some $240 million annually on advertising outside the United States, most of it for its Coke brand. The company is using a pool of about nine commercials from which local country managers select for their markets. By comparison, Pepsi spent $128 million outside the United States, mostly on its snack food business.[61]

The major fronts of the global cola war are now in eastern Europe and the rapidly developing countries of Asia. Besides reentering India, Coca-Cola also entered Russia, where Pepsi had an advantage in the former Soviet Union. Coca-Cola intends to have its products within reach of the world's entire population by the year 2000.[62] Not to be outdone, Pepsi launched its low-calorie soda in Japan ahead of Coca-Cola. The market developed ahead of expectations, forcing Coca-Cola to counterattack. Coca-Cola was forced to launch its caffeine-free Diet Coke ahead of schedule, forgoing a market test scheduled for later on.[63] In eastern Europe, the battle focused on Poland, where PepsiCo was forced to announce major investments in response to Coca-Cola's aggressive drive in the early 1990s. PepsiCo was slated to invest some $500 million in Poland over the next few years for both its beverage lines and its various fast-food companies. Although the market in Poland was still only $80 million in the early 1990s, its potential was viewed as large. Between 1990 and 1993, Coke invested some $200 million in the market, and PepsiCo needed to balance the threat or risk of coming in far behind Coke in this important and growing market.[64]

The battle for global dominance between Coke and Pepsi is not only fought in individual markets. It is also fought at large sports events, such as the World Cup for soccer. A company such as Coca-Cola that is dominant in some markets has the ability to cross-subsidize other markets where its competitive position is weaker.

59. "Pepsi Keeps on Going After No. 1," *Fortune,* March 11, 1991, p. 62.

60. *Fortune,* January 10, 1994, p. 16.

61. "Pepsi, Coke Focus on International Ad Efforts," *Advertising Age,* February 25, 1991, p. 32.

62. "The Ascent of Everest," *Financial Times,* January 16, 1992, p. 10.

63. "Cola Wars Bubble Over into Japan," *Nikkei Weekly,* July 10, 1992.

64. "PepsiCo to Invest $500 Million in Poland in Battle with Coke over Eastern Europe," *Wall Street Journal,* August 11, 1993, p. B6.

In some ways, global competition is like a global chess game, with a few competitors blocking each other's moves in or around key markets. What a competitor may be doing in a given market becomes more important than what potential customers desire. However, to do well in this game requires that individual-country aspirations and strategies become subordinated to the overall strategy directed from a central point.

Global Strategies for Companies Based in Emerging Economies

Much of our discussion so far has concerned itself with major international firms based in the developed economies of the United States, Europe, and Japan. One important trend, however, has been the creation of international enterprises based in countries that typically have attracted foreign investment but where businesses traditionally saw themselves as local only. In the early 1980s, international strategies by major firms in South Korea and Taiwan began to emerge. More recently, firms from Latin America and many other emerging economies have joined the select group of multinational firms.

The Thailand-based group Charoen Pokphand is a typical example of a developing global company based in an emerging country. Set up in the early 1920s by Chinese emigrants as a vegetable seed store in Bangkok, the company has expanded to become the largest animal feed supplier in Asia and the fourth-largest worldwide. It has pursued a policy of vertical integration in its feed business and has expanded into many other businesses ranging from chemicals and gasoline service stations to telecommunications. With sales of $5 billion in 1992, the company is widely expected to become one of the leading, if not *the* leading, agribusiness worldwide by the end of this century. Investments in China play a big role in its growth.[65]

Latin America has also been a place where local companies have increasingly pursued international and global strategies. Vitro, Mexico's largest glass manufacturer, and with $3.3 billion in sales its largest industrial company, has tended to pursue joint ventures with foreign investors for the Mexican market. More recently, the company acquired Anchor Glass, the second-largest U.S. glass manufacturer. This move was prompted by the expectation of trade liberalization with the United States.[66] Cemex, another Mexican company, is the largest cement producer in the Western Hemisphere and the fourth-largest worldwide. The company began its drive to internationalize with the acquisition of Mexican plants of some foreign cement companies, eventually expanding across its border into the United States.[67] In 1992, Cemex acquired two large cement plants in Spain, taking the

65. "Secrets of Cultivating $5 Billion in Sales," *Financial Times,* October 22, 1993, p. 22.
66. "Bottling Up Competitors," *Financial Times,* November 10, 1993, sect. IV, p. 4, Survey on Mexico.
67. "Cementing Global Ambitions," *Financial Times,* November 10, 1993, sect. IV, p. 4, Survey on Mexico.

company into Europe.[68] The expansion by Cemex into international markets was partly triggered by the invasion of the Mexican market by Holderbank, a Swiss-based company and the world's largest cement producer.

In the future, we can expect to see global marketing strategies adopted by firms from all parts of the world. As markets become accessible to all firms, the trend toward globalization will continue. Firms in developing and emerging economies will begin to concentrate on their own strengths and will develop global marketing strategies for a particular sector.

Conclusions

Any company engaging in international and global marketing operations is faced with a number of very important strategic decisions. At the outset, a decision in principle needs to be made committing the company to some level of internationalization. Increasingly, firms will find that international business must be pursued for competitive reasons and that it is often not an optional strategy. Once committed, the company needs to decide where the international business should be pursued, both in terms of geographic regions and specific countries. A firm's entry decision into each market and the selection of the international marketing program are additional strategic decisions.

During this decade, a changing competitive environment has considerably affected these choices. In the past, companies have moved from largely domestic or regional firms to become global. As multidomestic companies, these firms competed in many local markets and attempted to meet the local market requirements as best they could. Although many firms still approach their international marketing effort this way, an increasing number are taking a global view of their marketplace.

The global firm operates differently from the multidomestic or regional company. Pursuing a global strategy does not necessarily mean that the company is attempting to standardize all of its marketing programs on a global scale. Furthermore, a global strategy also does not imply that the company is represented in all markets of the world. Rather, global strategy is a new way of thinking about the business. Global companies are fully aware of their strengths across as many markets as possible. Consequently, the global company will build its strategy on the basis of its key skills and will enter markets where those skills are relevant.

A global company is also keenly aware of the value of global size and market share. As a result, a number of strategic decisions, such as which markets to enter, will become subject to the overall global strategy. Rather than making each market pay its way separately, a global firm may aim to break even in some markets if this will help its overall position by holding back a key competitor. As strategy begins to resemble that of a global chess game, companies have to develop new skills and learn about new concepts to survive. Understanding and exploiting the lead market principle will become more important.

68. "Cemex Embarks on a $1.85 Billion Gamble," *Financial Times,* July 22, 1992, p. 14.

Globalization of many industries today is a fact. Some companies have no choice but to become globalized; once key competitors in their industries are globalized, other firms must follow. This leads to a rethinking of the strategic choices and inevitably will lead to new priorities. Globalization is not simply a new term for something that has existed all along; it is a new competitive game requiring companies to adjust to and learn new ways of doing business. For many companies, survival depends on how well they learn this new game.

As we have seen in this chapter, *globalization* has become a multifaceted term requiring companies to carefully monitor their markets. Globalization may occur in several parts of a firm's business and may require different responses whether it occurs at the customer, market, industry, or competitor level. As a result, there are many types of global strategies a firm may choose from, moving the decision away from *whether* a global strategy toward *which* global strategy.

Questions for Discussion

1. What reasons are there for small firms to pursue an international strategy? Should they do this at all?

2. Investigate the geographic portfolio of three large Fortune 500 companies. What differences do you see, and what do you think accounts for these differences?

3. Contrast global with other types of geographic expansion strategies. In particular, how does it differ from a multinational strategy?

4. How can a local company best compete against global firms?

5. What are the major advantages of a global niche strategy?

6. Why should firms in emerging countries pursue global marketing strategies?

7. Contrast global integration strategies with global marketing strategies.

8. Contrast regional with global marketing strategies.

For Further Reading

Abegglen, James C. *Sea Change.* New York: Free Press, 1994.

Alahutta, Matti. "Growth Strategies for High Technology Challengers." Acta Polytechnica Scandinavica, Electrical Engineering Series No. 66, Helsinki University of Technology, Helsinki, 1990.

Bartlett, Christopher A., and Sumantra Ghoshal. *Managing Across Borders.* Boston: Harvard Business School Press, 1989.

Boddewyn, J. J. "Standardization in International Marketing: Is Ted Levitt in Fact Right?" *Business Horizons,* November–December 1986.

Ghoshal, Sumantra. "Global Strategy: An Organizing Framework." *Strategic Management Journal,* 8 (1987), pp. 425–440.

Ohmae, Kenichi. *Triad Power: The Coming Shape of Global Competition.* New York: Free Press, 1985.

Porter, Michael, ed. *Competition in Global Industries.* Boston: Harvard Business School Press, 1986.

Reich, Robert B. ''Who Is Them?'' *Harvard Business Review,* March–April 1991, pp. 77–88.

Simon, Hermann. ''Lessons from Germany's Midsize Giants.'' *Harvard Business Review,* March–April 1992, pp. 115–118.

Tichy, Noel, and Ram Charan. ''Citicorp Faces the World: An Interview with John Reed.'' *Harvard Business Review,* November–December 1990, pp. 135–144.

9

Global Market Entry Strategies

● **INTERNATIONAL COMPANIES MUST** *determine the type of presence they expect to maintain in every market where they compete. One major choice concerns the method of entering the selected market. A company may want to export to the new market, or it may prefer to produce locally. A second major choice involves the amount of direct ownership desired. Should the company strive for full ownership of its local operation, or is a joint venture preferable? These initial decisions on market entry tend to be of medium- to long-term importance, leaving little room for change once a commitment has been made. Therefore, it is important to treat these decisions with the utmost care. Not only is the financial return to the company at stake, but the extent to which the company's marketing strategy can be employed in the new market also depends on these decisions.*

In this chapter, we concentrate on the major entry strategy alternatives by explaining each one in detail and citing relevant company experiences. We also treat the entry strategy from an integrative point of view and offer guidance as to how a specific strategy may be selected to suit a company's needs. For an overview of all chapter topics, see Figure 9.1.

FIGURE 9.1 ● Market Entry Strategies

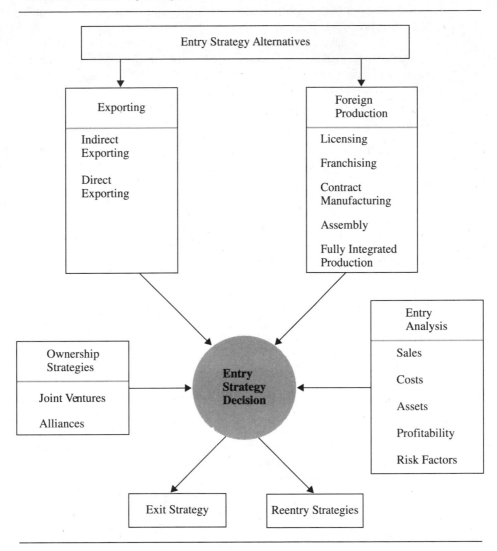

Exporting as an Entry Strategy

Exporting to a foreign market is a strategy many companies follow for at least some of their markets. Since many countries do not offer a large enough opportunity to justify local production, exporting allows a company to centrally manufacture its products for several markets and, therefore, to obtain economies of scale. Furthermore, since exports add volume to an already existing production operation located elsewhere, the marginal profitability of such exports tends to be high. A firm has two basic options for carrying out its export operations. Markets can be contacted through a domestically located (in the exporter's country of operation) intermediary—an approach called *indirect exporting*. Alternatively, markets can be reached through an intermediary located in the foreign market—an approach termed *direct exporting*. The use of various types of export intermediaries is described in detail in Chapter 12.

Indirect Exporting

Several types of intermediaries located in the domestic market are ready to assist a manufacturer in contacting foreign markets or buyers. The major advantage for using a domestic intermediary lies in that individual's knowledge of foreign market conditions. Particularly for companies with little or no experience in exporting, the use of a domestic intermediary provides the exporter with readily available expertise. The most common types of intermediaries are brokers, combination export managers, and manufacturers' export agents. Group selling activities can also help individual manufacturers in their export operations.

Even large companies may avail themselves of indirect exporting opportunities. Jaguar, the British luxury carmaker, used indirect exporting to enter the Chinese market. The company appointed Inchcape, a U.K.-based services and international marketing group, as its importer/distributor for China. The same firm is also Jaguar's importer into Hong Kong. Inchcape was to set up Jaguar China through its Inchcape Pacific distribution arm and expected to create dealerships as joint ventures. Although volume was still expected to be a low forty units in 1993, sales were anticipated to increase to one hundred units in 1994.[1]

Direct Exporting

A company engages in direct exporting when it exports through intermediaries located in the foreign markets. Under direct exporting, an exporter must deal with a large number of foreign contacts, possibly one or more for each country the company plans to enter. While a direct exporting operation requires a larger degree of expertise, this method of market entry does provide the company with a greater degree of control over its distribution channels than would indirect exporting. The exporter may select from two major types of intermediaries: agents and merchants. Also, the exporting company may establish its own sales subsidiary as an alternative to independent intermediaries. Of the about 300,000 manufacturing companies in the United States, only about 10 percent are actively exporting. Almost 85 percent of the U.S. exports, however, are accounted for by the top 250 U.S. companies, which means that a substantial amount of exporting is performed by many small to medium-sized manufacturers. Most of these companies get started by using distributors overseas. However, most foreign distributors represent other competing brands as well; they frequently push whatever brand offers the best margin.[2]

1. "Jaguar to Enter Chinese Car Market," *Financial Times,* October 4, 1993, p. 6.
2. "Made in the U.S.A.," *Business Week,* February 1988, pp. 28–34.

Successful direct exporting depends on the viability of the relationship built up between the exporting firm and the local distributor or importer. By building the relationship well, the exporter saves considerable investment costs. However, success is not always ensured. Freeman Corp., a privately held, U.S. maker of hardwood products with sales of $10 million, already had some 30 percent of its volume in exports to the Middle East and Europe. Through a Japanese trading company, Freeman contacted a Japanese firm that wanted to buy its wood products in the form of extra-thick veneer. The Japanese firm wanted to import Freeman's product, use a new slicing technology, and sell the products locally. However, when the Japanese firm ran into difficulty with the process, it stopped ordering the product. Having granted exclusive distribution rights to the Japanese trading company, Freeman was unable to change the distribution activity of the Japanese importer. To recover its investment in new machines to produce the special hardwood floor veneer, the company ended up suing the Japanese firm.[3]

The Company-Owned Sales Office (Foreign Sales Subsidiary)   Many companies export directly to their own sales subsidiaries abroad, sidestepping independent intermediaries. The sales subsidiary assumes the role of the independent distributor by stocking the manufacturer's products, selling to buyers, and assuming the credit risk. The sales subsidiary offers the manufacturer full control of selling operations in a foreign market. This may be important if the company's products require the use of special marketing skills, such as advertising or selling. The exporter finds it possible to transfer or export not only the product but also the entire marketing program that often makes the product a success.

The operation of a subsidiary adds a new dimension to a company's international marketing operation. It requires the commitment of capital in a foreign country, primarily for the financing of accounts receivables and inventory. Also, the operation of a sales subsidiary entails a number of general administrative expenses that are essentially fixed in nature. As a result, a commitment to a sales subsidiary should not be made without careful evaluation of all the costs involved.

Independent Distributor Versus Sales Subsidiary   The independent distributor earns a margin on the selling price of the products. Although the independent distributor does not represent a direct cost to the exporter, the margin the distributor earns represents an opportunity that is lost to the exporter. By switching to a sales subsidiary to carry out the distributor's tasks, the exporter can earn the same margin. For example, a manufacturer of electronic equipment exports products priced at $7,500 each (at the factory in Boston). With airfreight, tariffs, and taxes, the product's landed costs amount to $9,000 each. An independent distributor will have to price the products at $13,500 to earn a desired gross margin of 33⅓ percent. Instead, the exporter can set up a wholly owned sales subsidiary, in this case to consist of a manager, a sales manager, several sales agents, clerical staff, a warehousing operation, and the rental of both an office and a warehouse location. If the total estimated cost amounts to $450,000 annually, then the point at which the manufacturer

3. "For Japan Inc., a Kentucky Whipping," *Business Week,* November 8, 1993, p. 56.

can switch from an independent distributor to a company-owned sales subsidiary will be as follows:

$$\frac{\text{Operating costs of subsidiary}}{\text{Distributor's gross profit per machine}} = \text{unit breakeven volume}$$

$$\frac{\$450,000}{\$4,500} = 100 \text{ pieces of equipment}$$

or

$$\frac{\text{Operating costs of subsidiary}}{\text{Distributor's gross profit percentage}} = \text{dollar sales breakeven volume}$$

$$\frac{\$450,000}{33\frac{1}{3}\%} = \$1,350,000 \text{ breakeven volume}$$

With increasing volume, the incentive to start a sales subsidiary grows. On the other hand, if the anticipated sales volume is small, the independent distributor will be more efficient since sales are channeled through a distributor who is maintaining the necessary staff for several product lines. Research has shown that firms marketing products that require the development of special skills or special working relationships tend to have their own sales subsidiaries.[4]

The lack of control frequently causes exporters to shift from an independent distributor to wholly-owned sales subsidiaries. Volkswagen, the leading importer into Japan, with a volume of 53,000 VW/Audi cars, had used Yanase as its exclusive importer to Japan for almost forty years. In 1992, the company wanted to expand to a level of 100,000 units and replaced Yanase with the creation of its own sales subsidiary, Volkswagen Audi Nippon. In addition, VW entered into a cooperation with Toyota to open additional channels. Upset by this approach, Yanase signed up as the importer of Opel, GM's German subsidiary, abandoning its long-standing relationship with VW. As a result, VW expected to experience a setback in its Japanese market expansion. And Opel had to switch its previous relationship with Isuzu, a GM affiliate located in Japan, that had performed below expectations.[5]

Foreign Production as an Entry Strategy
Licensing

Under licensing, a company assigns the right to a *patent* (which protects a product, technology, or process) or a *trademark* (which protects a product name) to another company

4. Erin Anderson and Anne T. Coughlan, "International Market Entry and Expansion in Independent or Integrated Channels of Distribution," *Journal of Marketing,* January 1987, pp. 71–82.
5. "Yanase Set to Unveil Opel Distribution Deal," *Financial Times,* April 29, 1992, p. 26.

for a fee or royalty. Using licensing as a method of market entry, a company can gain market presence without an equity investment. The foreign company, or licensee, gains the right to commercially exploit the patent or trademark on either an exclusive (the exclusive right to a certain geographic region) or an unrestricted basis.[6]

Licenses are signed for a variety of time periods. Depending on the investment needed to enter the market, the foreign licensee may insist on a longer licensing period to pay off the initial investment. Typically, the licensee will make all necessary capital investments (machinery, inventory, etc.) and market the products in the assigned sales territories, which may consist of one or several countries. Licensing agreements are subject to negotiation and tend to vary considerably from company to company and from industry to industry.

Reasons for Licensing   Companies use licensing for a number of reasons. For one, a company may not have the knowledge or the time to engage more actively in international marketing. The market potential of the target country may also be too small to support a manufacturing operation. A licensee has the advantage of adding the licensed product's volume to an ongoing operation, thereby reducing the need for a large investment in new fixed assets. A company with limited resources can gain advantage by having a foreign partner market its products by signing a licensing contract. Licensing not only saves capital because no additional investment is necessary but also allows scarce managerial resources to be concentrated on more lucrative markets. Also, some smaller companies with a product in high demand may not be able to satisfy demand unless licenses are granted to other companies with sufficient manufacturing capacity.[7]

In some countries where the political or economic situation appears uncertain, a licensing agreement will avoid the potential risk associated with investments in fixed facilities. Both commercial and political risks are absorbed by the licensee.

In other countries, governments favor the granting of licenses to independent local manufacturers as a means of building up an independent local industry. In such cases, a foreign manufacturer may prefer to team up with a capable licensee despite a large market size, because other forms of entry may not be possible. International paint firms, with operations in both Europe and North America, have had difficulties penetrating the Japanese market. As a result, many have signed licensing agreements with Japanese firms. PPG of the United States and Courtaulds of the United Kingdom both licensed Nippon Paint for automotive and marine paints, respectively. Du Pont licensed Kansai, the other leading Japanese company, for its automotive paints. It was expected that these agreements, while not providing any penetration of the Japanese market, would keep the Japanese out of western markets. In other markets, however, PPG decided to stay away from licensing.[8]

---

6. For a thorough analysis of licensing among MNCs, see Piero Telesio, *Technology Licensing and Multinational Enterprises* (New York: Praeger, 1979).

7. "Licensing May Be the Quickest Route to Foreign Markets," *Wall Street Journal,* September 14, 1990, p. B2.

8. "The Pace of Change Slows," *Financial Times,* March 27, 1991, Sect. III, p. 1, Survey, World Paints and Coatings.

Disadvantages of Licensing   A major disadvantage of licensing is the company's substantial dependence on the local licensee to produce revenues and, thus, royalties, usually paid as a percentage on sales volume only. Once a license is granted, royalties will only be paid if the licensee is capable of performing an effective marketing job. Since the local company's marketing skills may be less developed, revenues from licensing may suffer accordingly. PepsiCo experienced the limitations of relying on a licensing partner in France. Pepsi was licensed through Perrier, the French mineral water company. However, the retail structure in France changed, and supermarkets emerged as important channels. Other French brands, such as Badoit and Evian, did better in those channels. The resulting decline for Perrier also had a negative impact for Pepsi, which lost almost half of its market share.[9] This led to the breakup of the relationship, PepsiCo choosing to develop the French market on its own in the future.

Another disadvantage is the resulting uncertainty of product quality. A foreign company's image may suffer if a local licensee markets a product of substandard quality. Ensuring a uniform quality requires additional resources from the licenser that may reduce the profitability of the licensing activity.

The possibility of nurturing a potential competitor is viewed by many companies as a disadvantage of licensing. With licenses usually limited to a specific time period, a company has to guard against the situation in which the licensee will use the same technology independently after the license has expired and, therefore, turn into a competitor. Although there is a great variation according to industry, licensing fees in general are substantially lower than the profits that can be made by exporting or local manufacturing. Depending on the product, licensing fees may range anywhere between 1 percent and 20 percent of sales with 3 to 5 percent being more typical for industrial products.

Conceptually, licensing should be pursued as an entry strategy if the amount of the licensing fees exceeds the incremental revenues of any other entry strategy, such as exporting or local manufacturing. A thorough investigation of the market potential is required to estimate potential revenues from any one of the entry strategies under consideration.

Franchising

Franchising is a special form of licensing in which the franchiser makes a total marketing program available, including the brand name, logo, products, and method of operation. Usually, the franchise agreement is more comprehensive than a regular licensing agreement inasmuch as the total operation of the franchisee is prescribed.

Numerous companies that successfully exploited franchising as a distribution form in their home market are exploiting opportunities abroad through foreign entrepreneurs.[10] Among these companies are McDonald's, Kentucky Fried Chicken, Burger King, and other U.S. fast-food chains with operations in Latin America, Asia, and Europe. Service com-

9. "C'est la for Coke and Pepsi," *Financial Times,* February 18, 1991, p. 15.

10. Donald W. Hackett, "The International Expansion of U.S. Franchise Systems: Status and Strategies," *Journal of International Business Studies,* Spring 1976, pp. 65–76.

panies such as Holiday Inns, Hertz, and Manpower, Inc. (a temporary employment agency) have also successfully used franchising to enter foreign markets. Some of the most extensive franchising networks are those maintained by the two leading soft drink manufacturers, Coca-Cola and PepsiCo.[11] In 1985, about 25,600 foreign outlets were maintained by U.S. franchise operators.[12]

Local Manufacturing

A common and widely practiced form of entry is the local production of a company's products. Many companies find it to their advantage to manufacture locally instead of supplying the particular market with products made elsewhere. Numerous factors such as local costs, market size, tariffs, laws, and political considerations may affect a choice to manufacture locally. The actual type of local production depends on the arrangements made; it may be contract manufacturing, assembly, or fully integrated production. Since local production represents a greater commitment to a market than other entry strategies, it deserves considerable attention before a final decision is made.

International firms with plants in Taiwan, Hong Kong, Singapore, and other foreign countries have little intention of penetrating these markets with the help of their new factories. Instead, they locate abroad to take advantage of favorable conditions that reduce manufacturing costs, and the products are slated for markets elsewhere. This cost savings strategy has been employed by many U.S. companies in the electronics industry and has more recently been adopted by Japanese and European firms as well. The motivation behind the location of plants in foreign countries may, therefore, be related at times to cost-cutting rather than to entering new markets. Such decisions, of a sourcing or production nature, are not necessarily tied to a company's international marketing entry strategy and therefore are not of concern to us here.

Contract Manufacturing   Under contract manufacturing, a company arranges to have its products manufactured by an independent local company on a contractual basis. The manufacturer's responsibility is restricted to production. Afterward, products are turned over to the international company, which usually assumes the marketing responsibilities for sales, promotion, and distribution. In a way, the international company "rents" the production capacity of the local firm to avoid establishing its own plant or to circumvent barriers set up to prevent the import of its products. Contract manufacturing differs from licensing with respect to the legal relationship of the firms involved. The local producer manufactures based on orders from the international firm, but the international firm gives virtually no commitment beyond the placement of orders.

Typically, contract manufacturing is chosen for countries with a low-volume market potential combined with high tariff protection. In such situations, local production appears advantageous to avoid the high tariffs, but the local market does not support the volume

11. Bruce Walker and Michael J. Etzel, "The Internationalization of U.S. Franchise Systems: Progress and Procedures," *Journal of Marketing,* April 1973, pp. 38–46.
12. "Franchising: Big Businesses Go Worldwide," *Financial Times,* October 7, 1985, p. 27.

necessary to justify the building of a single plant. These conditions tend to exist in the smaller countries in Central America, Africa, and Asia. Of course, whether an international company avails itself of this method of entry also depends on its products. Usually, contract manufacturing is employed where the production technology involved is widely available and where the marketing effort is of crucial importance in the success of the product.

Assembly   By moving to an assembly operation, the international firm locates a portion of the manufacturing process in the foreign country. Typically, assembly consists only of the last stages of manufacturing and depends on the ready supply of components or manufactured parts to be shipped in from another country. Assembly usually involves heavy use of labor rather than extensive investment in capital outlays or equipment.

Motor vehicle manufacturers have made extensive use of assembly operations in numerous countries. General Motors has maintained major integrated production units only in the United States, Germany, the United Kingdom, Brazil, and Australia. In many other countries, disassembled vehicles arrive at assembly operations that produce the final product on the spot. This method of shipping cars as CKDs (completely knocked downs) and assembling them in local markets is also used extensively by Ford Motor Co., American Motors' Jeep subsidiary, and most European and Japanese car manufacturers.

Often, the companies want to take advantage of lower wage costs by shifting the labor-intensive operation to the foreign market; this results in a lower final price of the products. In many cases, however, the local government forces the setting up of assembly operations either by banning the import of fully assembled products or by charging excessive tariffs on imports. As a defensive move, foreign companies begin assembly operations to protect their markets. However, successful assembly operations require dependable access to imported parts. This is often not guaranteed, and in countries with chronic foreign exchange problems, supply interruptions can occur. In some countries, as is the case for the automobile industry in Brazil, where some 70 percent of the parts are made locally, car manufacturers must engage in more than just assembly to produce for their markets.[13]

Fully Integrated Production   To establish a fully integrated local production unit represents the greatest commitment a company can make for a foreign market. Since building a plant involves a substantial outlay in capital, companies only do so where demand appears assured. International companies may have any number of reasons for establishing factories in foreign countries. Often, the primary reason is to take advantage of lower costs in a country, thus providing a better basis for competing with local firms or other foreign companies already present. Also, high transportation costs and tariffs may make imported goods uncompetitive.

Establishing Local Operations to Gain New Business   Some companies want to build a plant to gain new business and customers. Such an aggressive strategy is based on the fact that local production represents a strong commitment and is often the only way to convince clients to switch suppliers. This is of particular importance in industrial markets where service and reliability of supply are main factors in the choice of product or supplier.

13. ''Imports Take on Brazil's Car Makers,'' *Financial Times,* January 10, 1991, p. 6.

Lego, the Danish-based toy company well known for its plastic construction toys, built a factory in Brazil in the mid-1980s to penetrate a market with 140 million people but little access to its toys. As the only foreign toy company in Brazil, Lego was able to provide the local market with products that the country was prohibited from importing or allowed to only at very high duty. Brazil, with almost half its population under the age of twenty-five years, represented a great opportunity for Lego.

When Polaroid Corp. opened an assembly plant for instant cameras in the former Soviet Union in 1991, the company knew that in-country assembly was the only way to have its products sold in that country. Short of foreign exchange, Polaroid would not have been able to get access to sufficient hard currency to keep up an importing operation. Building a local assembly plant reduced the hard-currency drain, and the company could earn enough with exports of electronic components used in some of its European plants to afford importing parts needed to assemble cameras destined for the Russian market. The strategy was to earn the foreign exchange needed to purchase components needed for local assembly. Without this strategy, Polaroid would not have been able to cover the market.[14]

Establishing Foreign Production to Defend Existing Business   Many times, companies establish production abroad not to enter new markets but to protect what they have already gained. Changing economic or political factors may make such a move necessary. The Japanese car manufacturers, who had been subject to an import limitation of assembled cars imported from Japan, began to build factories in the United States in the 1980s to protect their market share.

In 1982, Honda became the first Japanese car manufacturer to set up production in the United States. In 1993, Japanese car manufacturers produced, for the first time, more cars in the United States than they exported to that country from Japan. (In 1992, Japanese exports had still outnumbered U.S. local production by some 100,000 vehicles.)[15] U.S. production is expected to increase from 2.5 million to about 2.7 million units by 1997. Major producers are Toyota, Honda, Nissan, Mitsubishi, Mazda, and Suzuki. Japanese automobile manufacturers have also built up capacities in Europe and in Asia.

As mentioned above, Japanese manufacturers' reasons for the local production were partly political, as the United States imposed import targets for several years. Also, with the value of the yen expected to increase to one hundred yen per U.S. dollar, exports from Japan would become uneconomical compared with local production. Thus, to defend market positions, Japanese car companies have approached a longer-term strategy of making cars in the region where they are sold.[16]

Moving with an Established Customer   Moving with an established customer can also be a reason for setting up plants abroad. In many industries, important suppliers want to keep

14. "Polaroid's Russian Success Story," *New York Times,* November 24, 1991, Sect. 3, p. 1.
15. "Local Auto Output in U.S. Set to Exceed Exports from Japan," *Nikkei Weekly,* December 6, 1993, p. 9.
16. "Automakers Set to Boost Global Output," *Nikkei Weekly,* June 2, 1993, p. 9.

a relationship by establishing plants near customer locations; when customers build new plants elsewhere, suppliers move too. The automobile industry, with its intricate network of hundreds of component suppliers feeding into the assembly plants, is a good example of how companies follow customers. As Japanese car manufacturers have built plants in the United States and in Canada, Japanese parts suppliers have become concerned that U.S. production will partially replace car shipments from Japan and that a reduction in parts volume will result. To counter this possibility, some four hundred component plants have been built in the United States and in Canada.[17] Bridgestone Tire Co., Japan's largest tire manufacturer, decided to set up shop in Tennessee only after Japanese automobile firms began to move manufacturing into the United States.[18] In 1988, Bridgestone acquired Firestone of the United States to become one of the largest tire companies and to help it to serve the U.S. market better.[19]

In similar fashion, Detroit's major automotive parts and component suppliers, such as tire companies and battery manufacturers, long ago opened manufacturing facilities abroad to supply General Motors' and Ford's various foreign facilities.

Shifting Production Abroad to Save Costs   When Mercedes-Benz was looking at new opportunities in the automotive market, the company targeted the luxury sports vehicle segment. In the United States, its major market, the company was suffering a 30 percent cost disadvantage against major Japanese and U.S. competitors. Mercedes-Benz decided to locate a new factory for such sports vehicles outside of Germany. (The company had up to that time never produced cars outside of Germany.) MB chose the United States because it expected total labor, components, and shipping costs to be among the lowest in the world.[20]

Ownership Strategies

Companies entering foreign markets have to decide on more than the most suitable entry strategy. They also need to arrange ownership, either as a wholly owned subsidiary (discussed above), in a joint venture, or—more recently—in a strategic alliance.

Joint Ventures

Under a joint venture (JV) arrangement, the foreign company invites an outside partner to share stock ownership in the new unit. The particular participation of the partners may vary, with some companies accepting either a minority or majority position. In most cases,

17. "Successful Transplants," *Financial Times,* March 27, 1991, p. 2, Survey, Automotive Components.
18. "A Different Kind of Tiremaker Rolls into Nashville," *Fortune,* March 22, 1982, p. 136.
19. "The World Tire Industry Survey," *Financial Times,* December 1988, Sect. III.
20. "Why Mercedes Is Alabama Bound," *Business Week,* October 11, 1993, p. 138.

international firms prefer wholly owned subsidiaries for reasons of control; once a joint venture partner secures part of the operation, the international firm can no longer function independently, which sometimes leads to inefficiencies and disputes over responsibility for the venture. If an international firm has strictly defined operating procedures, such as for budgeting, planning, and marketing, getting the JV company to accept the same methods of operation may be difficult. Problems may also arise when the JV partner wants to maximize dividend payout instead of reinvestment, or when the capital of the JV has to be increased and one side is unable to raise the required funds. Experience has shown that JVs can be successful if the partners share the same goals, with one partner accepting primary responsibility for operations matters.

Reasons for Entering into Joint Ventures   Despite the potential for problems, joint ventures are common because they offer important advantages to the foreign firm. By bringing in a partner, the company can share the risk for a new venture. Furthermore, the JV partner may have important skills or contacts of value to the international firm. Sometimes, the partner may be an important customer who is willing to contract for a portion of the new unit's output in return for an equity participation. In other cases, the partner may represent important local business interests with excellent contacts to the government. A firm with advanced product technology may also gain market access through the JV route by teaming up with companies that are prepared to distribute its products.

Many international firms have entered Japan with JVs. During the 1960s and 1970s, the Japanese market was viewed as a difficult environment, much different from other industrialized markets, and government regulations tightly controlled equity participation in ventures. When McDonald's entered Japan in 1971, it did so in a joint venture with Fujita & Company, a trading company owned by a private Japanese businessman. Den Fujita insisted on some practices that differed from the typical U.S. approach of McDonald's, such as opening the first store in the fashionable Ginza shopping district rather than going to a suburban location, and owning most of the stores rather than franchising. The success catapulted McDonald's into the position of the leading Japanese restaurant chain by 1982 and into a sales volume of $1.6 billion by 1991. This amounted to more than 10 percent of McDonald's global volume.[21]

With Fujita's skill at locating real estate and obtaining government permits for new outlets, the McDonald's Japan operation in itself was approached as a JV partner by Toys ''R'' Us. The toy manufacturer assumed McDonald's Japan's 20 percent interest in the new venture would help it land good retail sites. A more recent Fujita deal involved Blockbuster Video, where he also helped open up retail outlets.[22]

Joint Ventures to Enter Government-Controlled Economies   Joint ventures are sometimes necessary to enter countries where the economy is largely under state control. In such countries, foreign investors are only allowed to take minority positions in conjunction with local firms. In the case of government-controlled economies, this often means a joint

21. ''Den Fujita, Japan's Mr. Joint-Venture,'' *New York Times,* March 22, 1992, Sect. 3, p. 1.
22. Ibid.

venture must be signed with a government-owned firm. Given the country's large economic potential, many foreign firms have been attracted to China. Within two years of the adoption of China's law on joint ventures in 1979, more than four hundred joint venture contracts had been signed between Chinese and foreign firms. By 1991, some ten thousand joint ventures involving foreign investors had been formed in China. At least one hundred of them had been closed, not including a number of dormant ventures.[23]

Swiss-based Schindler, a leading elevator manufacturer, was the first foreign firm taking advantage of China's law on joint ventures in 1979.[24] The company took a 25 percent equity position with the goal of both becoming a major supplier of elevators in China and using the venture as a production base for its growing business in the Far East. With growth in output averaging more than 20 percent during the first six years of operation, the venture was profitable for Schindler. The company was able to beat out Hitachi and Mitsubishi, its two leading Japanese competitors, as the leader of the Chinese market. The venture developed to the satisfaction of Schindler and led to a second JV in 1988. Between the two ventures, Schindler was operating three factories on a joint venture basis with an annual output of several thousand lifts and escalators.[25]

Gillette, the U.S. razor blade manufacturer, has also gone through extensive JV experience in Japan. In the early 1980s, the company formed a first, small JV called Shenmei Daily Use Products with Chinese authorities in a province northeast of Beijing. That plant had produced older-technology blades under a local brand name for several years. However, annual production was only sixty million units in a market of one billion units, and the northern location was too far away from the booming provinces in the south. So a second JV was formed with the Shanghai Razor Blade Factory. Gillette obtained 70 percent ownership and management control. The company employs about one thousand people and has allowed Gillette to boost its market share in China from 10 percent to 70 percent. Most recently, Gillette also set up a small JV for its Oral-B toothbrush business.[26] The Gillette pattern of market entry into China follows the experience of other firms, suggesting a regional entry strategy aimed at the major regions or provinces. The entire operation might be controlled from one Chinese city, with Shanghai, Beijing, or Hong Kong the most frequently cited names.

Joint Ventures in Eastern Europe   With the liberalization of industry and trade in eastern Europe over the past few years, many international firms have pursued joint ventures in those countries. Originally, western firms were not allowed to own any stock, capital, or real estate, and joint ventures were thus the norm. Then although the political and economic situations were still in flux, restrictions on foreign investments were lifted in many countries, and foreign firms were allowed to start new companies with full ownership. Due to

23. "Foreigners Find China Ventures Difficult to Quit," *Wall Street Journal,* March 12, 1991, p. A15.
24. "Schindler Gives Chinese Business a Lift," *Financial Times,* August 29, 1986, p. 6.
25. "Swiss Lift Maker Expands in China," *Financial Times,* December 14, 1988, p. 6.
26. "Many Chinese Make Light Work of Razor Sales Targets," *Financial Times,* June 14, 1993, p. 2.

the difficulties of operating in unknown environments, many foreign firms nevertheless continue to prefer JVs with local partners.

In the former Soviet Union, about 150 JV deals were signed in 1990. Of those, about two-thirds were entered into by European firms, and about 20 percent were with U.S. companies.[27] Overall, there are about 2,800 registered JVs but only about 1,000 were estimated to be active.[28] Other sources estimate that the number of properly working JVs is less than 50.[29] The difficulties of running a JV are enormous since Russia does not yet have a market economy as we have come to know it in the West. Because of the often unreliable nature of supplies, lack of modern machinery, and technological know-how, ventures that intend to exploit cheap Russian labor or raw material often fail. Ventures aimed largely at satisfying domestic demand, with exports a secondary goal, have much greater chances for success.[30]

The structure of the McDonald's venture in Russia is a classic way of operating as an island within the country and as much as possible independent of local suppliers. With its partner, the city of Moscow, McDonald's built a $45 million processing plant to make its own beef patties, pasteurize its own milk, and bake its own buns. Raw materials for this plant, however, are obtained from Russian sources, and the company has a number of specialists working with suppliers on quality. Transportation is arranged with its own trucks. The McDonald's outlet in Moscow continues to be the company's busiest store worldwide. However, inflation, decreasing currency prices, and McDonald's insistence on selling in local currency have created uncertainty about when the company might recoup its investment. A second restaurant was opened in 1993.[31] Other companies entering JVs in former Soviet Union countries include Johnson Wax, employing some 350 workers in Kiev, Ukraine, and producing liquid detergents and shampoo. PepsiCo has employed about 270 people at its two Pizza Huts in Moscow and franchised about thirty-five Pepsi-Cola bottling plants.[32]

A more recent venture announced was between Gillette of the United States and a Russian consumer products company. Gillette built a $60 million plant and got a 65 percent stake in the operation. The goal was to produce shaving equipment and blades for the domestic Russian market. As one of the largest shaving markets in the world, the former Soviet Union was estimated to have 100 million male shavers compared to 80 million in the United States. The JV would emphasize twin-blade razors but would not produce the Sensor, Gillette's latest product generation. Eventually employing some 600 people, the Russian plant will rank among the top three production units for Gillette's worldwide operations.[33]

27. "Little Joy Flows from Soviet Joint Ventures," *Financial Times,* March 20, 1991, p. 3.

28. "Russian Roulette with Six Bullets," *Economist,* January 12, 1991, p. 65.

29. "Teaming Up to Score from Perestroika," *Financial Times,* March 28, 1990, p. 12.

30. Jeffrey M. Hertzfeld, "Joint Ventures: Saving the Soviets from Perestroika," *Harvard Business Review,* January–February 1991, pp. 80–91.

31. "Big Macs Rake in the Roubles," *Financial Times,* June 2, 1993, p. 2.

32. "Polaroid's Russian Success Story," *New York Times,* November 24, 1991, Sect. 3, p. 1.

33. "Gillette Forms Soviet Link to Make Shavers," *Financial Times,* March 5, 1991, p. 26.

Joint venture activity has also been high in eastern Europe. Hungary has attracted most of the attention so far. Few foreign ventures raised as much interest as General Electric's deal with Tungsram, a long-established Hungarian maker of electric light bulbs. Ranking fifth among light bulb manufacturers worldwide, Tungsram had its own subsidiaries in the West and had traditionally been an active exporter. GE bought 51 percent ownership for $150 million.[34] The company had annual sales of some $300 million, 70 percent of this from exports in convertible currency. The venture with Tungsram had to be seen in global terms, however. GE, number two worldwide behind Philips in lighting, had only a 2 percent market share in Europe. Tungsram's 7 percent share of the western European market was an excellent base to improve GE's overall European position.[35] The expected investment of some $50 million over the next five years to bring Tungsram up to western standards, plus the initial stake, compared well with the estimated price of $300 million for a new plant for GE in Europe, not even counting the start-up losses until volume had been reached to justify the investment.[36]

In the Czech Republic, German-based Volkswagen beat out Renault of France for a 31 percent stake in Skoda, the major Czech car manufacturer. VW is expected to raise that stake to some 70 percent by 1995. As part of the deal, VW committed to investing some six billion dollars in Skoda over the next ten years to bring it up to western standards and to expand the company's car output from 180,000 cars annually to about 400,000 by 1997. By 1993, sales volume had reached more than 200,000 units, with more than half of the units exported.[37] VW intended to increase the product range of Skoda by adding Golf- and Passat-type cars over time.[38] The Skoda brand name would be maintained, as well as Skoda's existing dealer network in Europe. Their major direction would be the growing eastern European car market that was expected to grow from two million to three million units annually, including cars for the former Soviet Union.[39]

JVs in eastern European countries have been known to be slowed down for lack of critical resources. Red tape is still a major problem for companies operating there. Access to hard currency is very limited, with special concerns for former Soviet Union countries. Negotiating business deals takes up much time, and negotiations in some countries are hampered due to a lack of laws governing property rights. As many experts have predicted, investing in eastern Europe requires patience, and companies cannot expect immediate returns.

Joint Venture Divorce: A Constant Danger   Not all joint ventures are successful and fulfill their partners' expectations. One study found that between 1972 and 1976 some ninety

---

34. "Barometer for a Changing Climate," *Financial Times,* April 10, 1990, p. 29.

35. "GE Carves Out a Road East," *Business Week,* July 30, 1990, p. 32.

36. "GE in Hungary: Let There Be Light," *Fortune,* October 22, 1990, p. 137.

37. "Costs Dispute with Prague Sours Skoda Deal," *Financial Times,* September 9, 1993, p. 4.

38. "VW and Skoda Unveil DM 9.5 Billion Strategy," *Financial Times,* December 11, 1990, p. 19.

39. "Western Car Groups Make Their Marque," *Financial Times,* April 2, 1991, p. 19.

major ventures failed in Japan alone. Many of these ventures involved large U.S.-based firms such as General Mills, TRW, and Avis. Another study showed the failure of 30 percent of investigated joint ventures formed before 1967 between U.S. companies and partners in other industrialized countries. In most cases, the ventures were either liquidated or taken over by one of the original partners.[40]

Borden Inc., a U.S.-based dairy company with worldwide sales of some $7 billion, was one of the more recent companies to experience difficulties with its JV in Japan. Originally entering Japan in the early 1970s, Borden joined up with Meiji Milk Products of Japan to form several joint ventures. Meiji had produced Borden branded ice cream since 1971 and margarine since 1983. Borden cheese was made part of a different venture in 1972. By 1990, sales for the three product categories in Japan had reached $192 million. However, Borden felt that, with the liberalization of the dairy business in Japan, a major expansion to some $400 million was possible.[41] A major disagreement developed over the ice cream business, where the Lady Borden brand had slipped from its 60 percent of imported premium to about 50 percent. Major competitors were now Häagen-Dazs and Dreyer, both U.S. entries.[42] Faced with increasing competition but also more opportunities, Borden reportedly demanded a higher performance from Meiji as a precondition for extending its arrangements. Over the talks, the companies broke up. The three agreements expired in 1990.[43]

Not all joint ventures in Japan end as failures. One of the most successful is the collaboration between Caterpillar of the United States and Mitsubishi Heavy Industries. For years, Caterpillar had a JV with Mitsubishi for the production of bulldozers and other heavy construction equipment. However, the market in Japan, where building operations must take place under very tight space situations, became increasingly attractive for excavators. These machines were never at the center for Caterpillar; so when the market took off in Japan, the company decided to form a second JV, Shin Caterpillar-Mitsubishi. But the new JV was not only for Japan. It was also made responsible for hydraulic excavator design worldwide for both Caterpillar and Mistubishi and included the Mitsubishi manufacturing in Japan. Outside Japan, Caterpillar was to remain independent for manufacturing and distribution, while all excavator products were to carry the name Caterpillar. Excavator sales of the combined company grew 75 percent, to $2.7 billion, worldwide in four years; in Japan, Mitsubishi recovered its declining market share.[44]

Corning executives, who have extensive joint venture experience, have learned a number of lessons to make joint ventures successful. Because a partner is involved in all dealings, time must be taken to explain any unilateral decisions. Richard Delude, a senior

---

40. J. Peter Killing, "How to Make a Global Joint Venture Work," *Harvard Business Review,* May–June 1982, p. 121.

41. "Borden and Meiji Part Ways, Face a Tough Road Ahead," *Tokyo Business Today,* December 1990, p. 40.

42. "Borden's Breakup with Meiji Milk Shows How a Japanese Partnership Can Curdle," *Wall Street Journal,* February 21, 1991, p. B1.

43. "Borden and Meiji Part," p. 40.

44. "Digging a Mutual Trench," *Financial Times,* March 11, 1991, p. 10.

executive at Corning, prepared the following items for a checklist for successful joint ventures:

1. Do not enter into JVs with partners that are initially overconcerned with control or how to split up if the venture should fail.

2. The venture must be able to get the resources to grow and should not be restricted technologically or geographically.

3. The venture must develop its own culture.

4. Venture managers need good access to top management at the parent companies.

5. Stay away from partners who are overly centralized and have no experience in sharing responsibility.[45]

Despite the difficulties involved, it is apparent that the future will bring many more joint ventures. Successful international and global firms will have to develop the skills and experience to manage JVs successfully, often in different and difficult environmental circumstances. And in many markets, the only realistic access to be gained will be through JVs.

Strategic Alliances

A more recent phenomenon is the development of a range of strategic alliances. Alliances are different from traditional joint ventures, in which two partners contribute a fixed amount of resources and the venture develops on its own. In an alliance, two entire firms pool their resources directly in a collaboration that goes beyond the limits of a joint venture. Although a new entity may be formed, it is not a requirement. Sometimes, the alliance is supported by some equity acquisition of one or both of the partners. In an alliance, each partner brings a particular skill or resource—usually, they are complementary—and by joining forces, each expects to profit from the other's experience. Typically, alliances involve either distribution access, technology transfers, or production technology, with each partner contributing a different element to the venture.

Technology-Based Alliances Exchanging technology for market access was the basis of the AT&T alliance with Olivetti of Italy, entered into in 1984. AT&T needed to enter the European computer market to obtain economies of scale for its U.S. operations, but it did not have any marketing contacts of its own. On the other hand, Olivetti was eager to add larger computers to its existing line. As a result, Olivetti marketed AT&T computers through its extensive distribution system in Europe. In return, Olivetti became the key supplier to AT&T for personal computers and was able to use AT&T as its distribution arm in the U.S. market.[46] However, after a quick start that involved mostly the sale of

45. "Hard Work on Joint Ventures," *Financial Times,* January 22, 1990, p. 30.

46. George Taucher, "Building Alliances (A): The American Telephone and Telegraph Company," Case GM 351, and "Building Alliances (B): Ing. C. Olivetti & Co. S.p.A.," Case GM 352 (Lausanne: IMEDE International Management Development Institute, 1986).

Olivetti-produced PCs through AT&T sales offices in the United States, the alliance lapsed when the cooperation became too one-sided. In 1989, AT&T was able to take a 20 percent stake in Italtel, the Italian state-owned telecommunications equipment company. With this alliance, AT&T hoped to gain better access to Italian telecommunications orders and elsewhere in Europe.[47]

In the more recent past, AT&T switched from concluding alliances to taking direct equity stakes in operating companies, with the aim of helping them build up the technology level of their networks and in the process being able to sell its advanced equipment. Such deals were signed in Canada with Unitel Communications, in Poland with Telfa (a company that makes switching gears and other equipment for local markets), in China through a 60 percent stake in an optical cable venture, and in India through a JV with Tata Telecom to make phone transmission equipment in India. In the former Soviet Union, AT&T took a stake in a JV near St. Petersburg to sell phone equipment and took an equity stake in a company in the Ukraine to help operate and upgrade that country's long-distance network. The most recent announcement came in China, where AT&T announced a wide-ranging agreement to assist in the modernization of China's phone system.[48]

A survey conducted by the Maastricht Economic Research Institute reviewed 4,182 alliances. Most of these technological alliances were in the biotechnology and information technology industries. The most commonly cited reasons for concluding an alliance were access to markets, exploitation of complementary technology, and a need to reduce the time taken for an innovation.[49]

One of the companies most experienced with technological alliances is Toshiba, a major Japanese electronics company. The company's first technological tie-ups go back to the beginning of this century, when it contracted to make light bulb filaments for U.S.-based General Electric. The company has since engaged in alliances with many leading international companies, among them United Technologies, Apple Computer, Sun Microsystems, Motorola, and National Semiconductor, all of the United States, as well as with European firms such as Olivetti, Siemens, Rhône-Poulenc, Ericsson, and SGS-Thomson. In 1993, Toshiba was engaged in more than a dozen major alliances. Because of its extensive experience, the company, unlike many other firms, has not had any major failures.[50]

Production-Based Alliances   Particularly in the automobile industry, a large number of alliances have been formed over the past years. These linkages fall into two groups. First, there is the search for efficiency through component linkages, which may include engines or other key components of a car. Second, companies have begun to share entire car models, either by producing jointly or by developing them together. U.S. automobile manufacturers have been very active in creating global alliances with partners, primarily in Japan. Many of these alliances are production based. With the development of a new car

47. "US Giant Plugs into Global Ambitions," *Financial Times,* August 30, 1989, p. 10.
48. "AT&T Reaches Way Out for This One," *Business Week,* March 8, 1993, p. 83.
49. "Holding Hands," *Economist,* March 27, 1993, p. 14, Survey of Multinationals.
50. "How Toshiba Makes Alliances Work," *Fortune,* October 4, 1993, p. 116.

model generation surpassing two billion dollars, companies such as Ford have created tight alliances with partners. For Ford, the major Japanese partner is Mazda, where Ford owns 25 percent of the equity. The two firms have collaborated intensively with the creation of more than ten projects over the years.[51] Other U.S. firms also have engaged in production alliances. (For more details, see Figure 9.2.)

Alliances have recently run into trouble. Volvo of Sweden and Renault of France entered a far-reaching production alliance in 1990. The two companies agreed to a series of interlocking deals. Both own 45 percent of each other's truck and bus divisions. Separately, Renault bought 25 percent of Volvo's car operation and another 10 percent of Volvo Corporation. In return, Volvo acquired 20 percent of Renault with an option for another 5 percent later on. This cooperation was expected to result in much greater synergy in trucks and buses, where the combined Renault-Volvo Group advanced to the number one spot worldwide. In cars, the level of integration was planned to be less. However, in both situations, substantial savings were expected from global purchasing, development, design, and joint production of important components.[52]

In 1993, both Volvo and Renault came to the conclusion that a full-scale merger was necessary. The major driver was the need to avoid battles over which group of shareholders, or which company, would get savings from joint cost-cutting exercises. What had begun as a venture of equals (50:50) was to turn into a 65:35 deal, with Renault of France holding the majority. Since Renault was a state-controlled company, this caused difficulties; some Volvo managers believed that France, as the major shareholder, might favor Renault in cost-cutting or employment decisions. Furthermore, Volvo had just emerged from a difficult series of years and was rapidly improving its profitability, whereas Renault was, after some successful years, moving into a period of poor financial results. In the end, the deal did not go through, because of resistance by Volvo shareholders and senior managers.[53] Following the abandonment of the full merger, the two companies decided to unravel their existing cross-shareholdings, and many of the anticipated joint projects were shelved. This shows that even two originally willing partners can have difficulties moving into a full alliance.

Honda's very successful production alliance with the U.K. carmaker Rover ran into trouble due to a change in the ownership of Rover. Originally entered into in 1983 as a joint development project for a new car model series, the relationship was broadened into production by the two companies. Rover took a 20 percent stake in Honda's new U.K. plant, and Honda in return took a 20 percent stake in Rover. They jointly developed several car models and shared production, with Honda also supplying key components to Rover. When BAe, the majority owner of Rover, wanted to sell its stake, Honda was unwilling to assume full ownership, largely because it was going through difficult financial times as a result of the worldwide industry recession. As a result, BAe sold its 80 percent stake to

51. "The Partners," *Business Week,* February 10, 1992, p. 102.

52. "Strained Alliances," *International Management,* May 1990, p. 28.

53. "Driven by the Need to Survive," *Financial Times,* September 3, 1993, p. 17; "Hard Slog to Make the Marriage Work," *Financial Times,* September 7, 1993, p. 19; "Why Volvo Kissed Renault Goodbye," *Business Week,* December 20, 1993, p. 54.

FIGURE 9.2 ● International Alliances of U.S. and Japanese Automobile Manufacturers (as of March 1993)

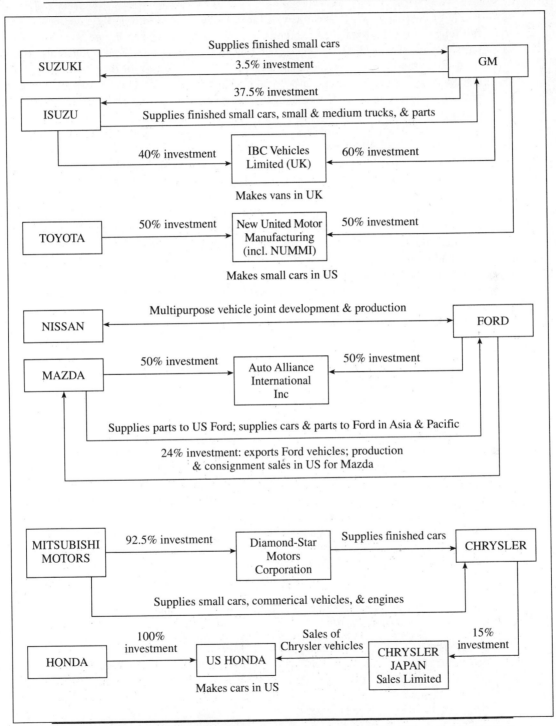

Source: Japan Automobile Manufacturers' Association. From "Japan Braces Itself for the U.S. Roadshow," *Financial Times,* August 19, 1993. Used with permission.

BMW of Germany, which was interested in Rover as a way into new car segments. The full range of off-the-road vehicle brands, such as Land Rover and Range Rover, were of particular interest to BMW. Honda, unwilling to spend more on Rover, suddenly found itself in a situation where a major competitor owned 80 percent of the shares, as well as a stake in its own production plants in the United Kingdom. The parties expected that all present projects would continue but over the years the relationship would be wound down.[54]

Distribution-Based Alliances   Alliances with a special emphasis on distribution are becoming increasingly common. General Mills, a U.S.-based company marketing breakfast cereals, had long been number two in the United States, with some 27 percent market share compared to Kellogg's 40 to 45 percent share. With no effective position outside the United States, the company entered into a global alliance with Nestlé of Switzerland. Forming Cereal Partner Worldwide, owned equally by both companies, General Mills intended to use the local distribution and marketing skills of Nestlé in Europe, the Far East, and Latin America. In return, General Mills would provide technology and the experience of how to compete against Kellogg's. Cereal Partners Worldwide (CPW) was formed as a full business unit with responsibility for the entire world except the United States. CPW passed the $250 million mark in 1992 and was well on the way to its goal of $1 billion by the year 2000, which will give it a 20 percent share outside of the United States. Already, CPW had surged beyond Quaker Oats in some markets, reaching the number two position in those countries. The venture, however, had still not yet reached breakeven.[55]

While Nestlé was getting access to a new product line, breakfast cereals, from General Mills by making its distribution network available, the company engaged in a different alliance with Coca-Cola. Forming Coca-Cola Nestlé Refreshments, the two partner companies intended to market Nestlé's new ready-to-drink coffees and teas through the Coca-Cola distribution system worldwide.[56] Nestlé had developed the products and already held a leading position in instant coffee. But ready-to-drink products are sold mainly through vending machines. This latter distribution was well known to Coca-Cola, which actually has in Georgia Brand canned coffee its leading product in Japan. It was also in Japan that Nestlé had become aware of the opportunity in ready-to-drink coffees and had already signed a JV with Otsuka Pharmaceutical.[57]

In Japan, the ready-to-drink market had sales of $4.4 billion and was growing rapidly. This fact inspired both Nestlé and Coca-Cola to work together to bring these products to

54. "Honda Strategy Derailed by BMW Takeover of Rover," *Nikkei Weekly,* February 7, 1994, p. 1; "BAe Flies Away from Rover with a Sack-Full of Cash," *Financial Times,* February 1, 1994, p. 1; "A Quick Route into New Market Segments," *Financial Times,* February 1, 1994, p. 20; "Honda Keeps Rover Projects," *Financial Times,* February 24, 1994, p. 17.

55. "Cafe au Lait, a Croissant—Trix," *Business Week,* August 24, 1992, p. 50.

56. "Coca-Cola Names Teasley as Chief of Joint Venture," *Wall Street Journal,* March 14, 1991, p. B6.

57. "War of the Sales Robots," *Forbes,* January 7, 1991, p. 294.

other markets. Both invested $100 million into the venture, which excludes the Japanese market (where both already had their own arrangements). Success elsewhere depended very much on the development and distribution of vending machines. In Japan there was some 5.4 million vending machines, some 2.2 million just for canned drinks. However, vending machines in Japan can be displayed in the streets with little fear of vandalism. Elsewhere in the world, such a strategy is not possible. This was believed to impact on the growth of such drinks outside Japan.[58]

The Future of Alliances   Although global alliances have not been around for a very long time, a few lasting ones have become models. One of the most successful is the alliance between General Electric in the United States and Snecma of France in their aircraft engine business. The partners have collaborated since 1970, combining their forces in the development of a new class of passenger aircraft engines. Commercialization did not come until 1982, but the jointly developed jet engine was a huge success. State-controlled Snecma needed a new jet engine to compete with Rolls-Royce and U.S.-based Pratt & Whitney in offering options for the European-built Airbus passenger jets. As a result, Snecma has renewed the collaboration with GE and signed on to participate again in the next generation of engines.[59]

Although many alliances have been forged in a large number of industries, the evidence is not yet in as to whether these alliances will actually become successful business ventures. Experience suggests that alliances with two equal partners are more difficult to manage than those with a dominant partner. Furthermore, many observers question the value of entering alliances with technological competitors, such as between western and Japanese firms. The challenge in making an alliance work lies in the creation of multiple layers of connections, or webs, that reach across the partner organizations. Eventually, this will result in the creation of new organizations out of the cooperating parts of the partners. In that sense, alliances may very well be just an intermediate stage until a new company can be formed or until the dominant partner takes over.[60]

Preparing an Entry Strategy Analysis

Of course, assembling correct data is the cornerstone of any entry strategy analysis. The necessary sales projections have to be supplemented with detailed cost data and financial need projections on assets. The data need to be assembled for all entry strategies under consideration (see Figure 9.3). Financial data are collected not only on the proposed venture but also on its anticipated impact on the existing operations of the international firm. The combination of the two sets of financial data results in incremental financial data

58. "Getting the Coffee Market in the Can," *Financial Times,* December 10, 1990, p. 17.
59. "A Lasting and Successful Alliance," *Financial Times,* January 8, 1991, p. 18.
60. George Taucher, "Beyond Alliances," *IMEDE Perspective for Managers,* no. 1 (Lausanne: IMEDE, 1988).

FIGURE 9.3 ● Considerations for Market Entry Decisions

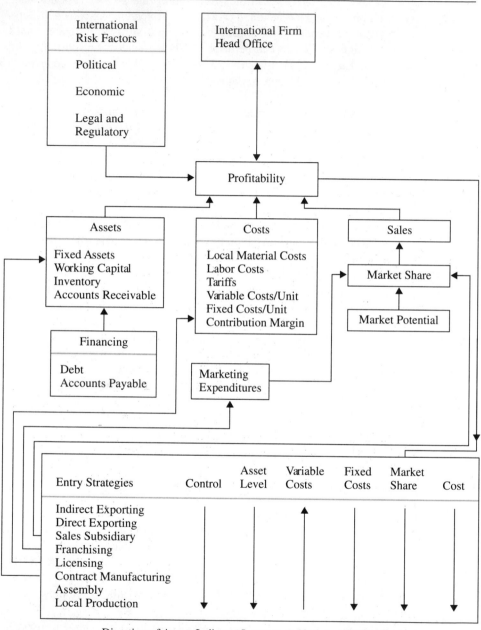

Direction of Arrow Indicates Increase or Decrease in That Factor.

incorporating the net overall benefit of the proposed move for the total company structure.

For best results, the analyst must take a long-term view of the situation. Asset requirements, costs, and sales have to be evaluated over the planning horizon of the proposed venture, typically three to five years for an average company. Furthermore, a thorough sensitivity analysis must be incorporated. This may consist of assuming several scenarios of international risk factors that may adversely affect the success of the proposed venture. The financial data can be adjusted to reflect each ''new'' set of circumstances. One scenario may include a 20 percent devaluation in the host country, combined with currency control and difficulty of receiving new supplies from foreign plants. Another situation may assume a change in political leadership, to a group less friendly to foreign investments. With the help of a sensitivity analysis approach, a company can quickly spot the key variables in the environment that will determine the outcome of the proposed market entry. The international company then has the opportunity to further add to its information on such key variables or at least to closely monitor their development.

In this section, we provide a general methodology for the analysis of entry decisions. It is assumed that any company approaching a new market is looking for profitability and growth. Consequently, the entry strategy must support these goals. Each project has to be analyzed for the expected sales level, costs, and asset levels that will eventually determine profitability (see Table 9.1).

Estimating Sales

An accurate estimate of the market share or sales volume is crucial to the entry strategy decision. Sales results will largely depend on the company's market share and the total size or potential of the market. The market share to be gained primarily is competitively determined. The foreign company can influence the market share through a strong marketing mix, which in turn is dependent on the level of financial commitment for marketing expenditures. The various types of entry strategies also allow a foreign firm to aim for varying degrees of market share. Typically, direct or indirect exporting results in a lower market share than local sales subsidiaries or local production does, due to a weaker market presence. This weaker presence causes a loss of control over local intermediaries; also, to some extent, independent firms have to be depended on to carry out the company's marketing functions.

Of course, market potential is not subject to the influence of the international firm seeking entry. The size of a local market combined with the expected market share often determines the outcome of an entry strategy analysis. Local assembly or production with correspondingly high levels of assets and fixed costs need large volumes to offset these costs, whereas exporting operations can usually be rendered profitable at much lower sales volumes than can other entry strategies.

Particularly in markets with considerable growth potential, it becomes essential to forecast sales over a longer period of time. A low expected volume right now may indicate little success for a new subsidiary, but data on volume expected later on may suggest a change in the future entry strategy. Since it is often impossible to shift quickly into another

TABLE 9.1 ● Financial Analysis for Entry Strategies

Financial variables	*Local values*
Assets 　Cash 　Accounts receivable 　Inventory 　Equipment 　Buildings 　Land 　　Total	New amount of assets needed to sustain chosen entry strategy in local market
Liabilities 　Accounts payable 　Debt 　　Total *Net Assets*	New amount of liabilities incurred due to entry strategy
Costs 　Unit variable costs (VC) 　　Material costs 　　Labor costs 　　Purchases 　　　Total	Amount of VC in newly selected operations
Fixed and semifixed costs 　Supervision 　Marketing 　General Administrative 　Expenses 　　Total *Total Unit Costs*	Local fixed costs due to selected entry mode
Sales 　*Total Sales*	Local sales of chosen entry mode

Decreases elsewhere (due to new operation)	Incremental value
Assets liquidated or no longer needed due to shift of operation	Net new assets required
Reduction or change in liabilities due to shift in operation	Net liabilities incurred
	Net asset requirement
Diseconomies of scale due to volume loss by shifting production to new subsidiary	Net variable costs across all subsidiaries resulting from new entry mode
Lost contribution if production shifted elsewhere	Net fixed burden of new entry mode Incremental total costs
Lost sales in other units of the MNC subsidiary network	Net additional sales of entry strategy

entry mode once a firm is established, special attention has to be focused on the need to ensure that the chosen entry strategy offers a long-term opportunity to maximize profits.

Estimating Costs

The international firm will have to determine the expected costs of its operation in a foreign country with respect to both manufacturing and general administrative costs. Unit variable costs may vary depending on the chosen strategy: local production, assembly, or exporting. To establish such costs, analysts must take local material costs, local wage levels, and tariffs on imports into consideration. Again, unit variable costs should be expected to vary according to the entry strategy alternatives considered.

Necessary fixed costs represent another important element in the analysis. Administrative costs tend to be much smaller for a sales subsidiary than for a local manufacturing unit. Through use of a contribution margin analysis, breakeven for several levels of entry strategies can be considered. Government regulations and laws may also affect local costs and substantially change costs over time.

Cost levels may differ substantially from country to country. Estimating and forecasting costs in the international environment required a keen sense of awareness that environmental factors of a political, economic, or legal nature can render a careful analysis invalid. Consequently, such possibilities need to be considered from the outset.

Estimating Asset Levels

The level of assets deployed greatly affects the profitability of any entry strategy. The assets may consist of any investments made in conjunction with the entrance into (or exit from, for that matter) the new market. Such investments may include working capital in the form of cash, accounts receivable, and/or inventory, or fixed assets such as land, buildings, machinery, and equipment. The amount of assets required depends to a great extent on the particular entry strategy chosen. Exporting and sales subsidiaries require an investment in working capital only, with little additional funds for fixed facilities. Local assembly and production, however, demand substantial investments. Often, local financing can reduce the net investment amount of the international firm. For an adequate comparison of the various entry strategies, an asset budget should be established for each alternative considered.

Forecasting Profitability

Conceptually, a company should maximize the future stream of earnings, discounted at its cost of capital. Other companies may prefer to concentrate on return on investment (ROI) as a more appropriate measurement of profitability. In either case, profitability is dependent on the level of assets, costs, and sales. Several exogenous international risk factors influence profitability and therefore must be included in the analysis. The outcome of such an analysis determines the selection of the entry strategy. In the following sections, each of these factors will be described and their possible impact on profitability will be indicated.

Assessing International Risk Factors   Aside from the normal business risk factors that every company also confronts in its home market, the existence of more than one economy or country involves additional risks. Each country hosting a foreign subsidiary may take actions of a political, economic, or regulatory nature that can completely obliterate any carefully drawn-up business plan. As discussed in Chapter 4, political turmoil in many parts of the world greatly affects business and investment conditions. Following the departure of the shah of Iran, for example, the country's political stability deteriorated to such an extent that business could not be conducted as usual. Many foreign operations were taken over by the government or just ceased to exist. Similar effects on businesses could be witnessed in other countries, particularly Nicaragua (in 1979) and Turkey (1978 to 1980).

As covered in Chapter 2, different economic systems add to uncertainties, which are reflected in currency changes or diverging economic trends. Manufacturing costs are particularly sensitive to various changes. Many times, a company has shifted production from one country to another on the basis of the latest cost data just to find out a few years later that costs have changed due to fluctuations of macroeconomic variables beyond company control. Local labor costs, for example, are very sensitive to local inflation and foreign currency changes; they have fluctuated considerably over the years.

Maintaining Flexibility   The ability to switch from one mode of entry into another may be an important requirement of the initial arrangement. Data General of the United States was able to shift its entry strategy following the changes in the investment laws in Japan in 1978.[61] Data General had, in 1971 signed a licensing agreement with a consortium of seven Japanese companies, called Nippon Minicomputer. A few years later, Data General realized that most of its customers in Japan were other multinationals who wanted to buy Data General minicomputers through direct purchase agreements with its head office in the United States. Since the company could not make a licensee obey such agreements, Data General negotiated first to buy a 50 percent stake in 1979, finally up to 85 percent in 1982. The local organization was changed to Nippon Data General (NDG), but Japanese management was left in place. This step approach to a integrated production and sales organization was very successful for Data General, and the company was able to obtain a leadership position in the Japanese market.

Assessing Total Company Impact   Once profitability on a local level has been established and the relevant international risk factors included, analysis must turn to the company as a whole. The expected profits of the new market entry have to be analyzed along with the overall impact on the total organization. Replacing imports with local production may cause a loss of sales or output at the existing facility, which may counterbalance the new

---

61. ''Data General Shows Friendly Takeovers Are Possible in Japan,'' *Business International,* August 6, 1982, p. 249.

profits gained from the plant opening. Such an impact may also exist with respect to assets, costs, and sales, depending on the entry strategy. As a result, the global firm aims at maximizing incremental profits achieved on incremental assets and sales. A promising opportunity abroad may suddenly appear less attractive when allowances are made for displacement in other parts of a global company.

Entry Strategy Configuration

This chapter has been dedicated to explaining the various entry strategy modes available to international and global firms. In reality, however, most entry strategies consist of a combination of different formats. We call the process of deciding on the best possible combination *entry strategy configuration.*

Rarely do companies employ a single entry mode per country. A company may open up a subsidiary that produces some products locally and imports others to round out its product line. The same foreign subsidiary may even export to other foreign subsidiaries, combining exporting, importing, and local manufacturing into one unit. Furthermore, many international firms grant licenses for patents and trademarks to foreign operations, even when they are fully owned. This is done for additional protection or to make the transfer of profits easier. In many cases, companies have bundled such entry forms into a single legal unit, in effect *layering* several entry strategy options on top of each other.

Bundling of entry strategies is the process of providing just one legal unit in a given country or market. In other words, the foreign company sets up a single company in one country and uses that company as a legal umbrella for all its entry activities. However, such strategies have become less typical—particularly in larger markets, many firms have begun to unbundle its operations.

When a company *unbundles,* it essentially divides its operations in a country into different companies. The local manufacturing plant may be incorporated separately from the sales subsidiary. When this occurs, companies may select different ownership strategies, for instance allowing a JV in one operation while keeping full ownership in another part. Such unbundling becomes possible in the larger markets, such as the United States, Germany, and Japan. It also allows the company to run several companies or product lines in parallel. ICI, the large U.K. chemicals company, operates several subsidiaries in the United States that report to different product line companies back in the United Kingdom and are independently operated. Global firms granting global mandates to their product divisions will find that each division will need to develop its own entry strategy for key markets.

Exit Strategies

Circumstances may make companies want to leave a country or market. Other than the failure to achieve marketing objectives, there may be political, economic, or legal reasons for a company to want to dissolve or sell an operation. International companies have to be aware of the high costs attached to the liquidation of foreign operations; substantial amounts of severance pay may have to be paid to employees, and any loss of credibility in other markets can hurt future prospects.

Consolidation

Sometimes, an international firm may need to withdraw from a market to consolidate its operations. This may mean a consolidation of factories from many to fewer such plants. Production consolidation, when not combined with an actual market withdrawal, is not really what we are concerned with here. Rather, our concern is a company's actual abandoning of its plan to serve a certain market or country.

In the 1970s, several U.S.-based multinational firms had to retrench their international operations and shrink back onto a U.S. base. Chrysler sold its European operations in the United Kingdom and France to European car manufacturers, mostly Peugeot, and concentrated on the U.S. market. More recently, Avon Products sold 60 percent of its successful Japanese company for some $400 million. This came after it offered 40 percent of its Japanese company to the public in 1987. The money was needed to reduce Avon's debt in the United States. Avon had started its Japanese subsidiary twenty years before and had reached sales of $285 million.[62]

Nissan, the Japanese car manufacturer, had been assembling cars in Australia since 1976. The smallest of the five assemblers, Nissan lost money after 1989. Its 10 percent market share was not sufficient to support a local assembly operation. When volume dropped to 33,000 units annually, the plant, which had a capacity for 80,000 cars, became uneconomical. Although this exit related to production only and not to the selling and dealership operations, it was nevertheless expected to impact negatively on Nissan's total volume in Australia. Other car companies are leaving countries where import levels have been lowered as part of the worldwide drive toward trade liberalization.[63]

Political Reasons

Changing political situations have at times forced companies to leave markets. Procter & Gamble, the giant U.S.-based consumer goods manufacturer, sold its Cuban subsidiary in 1958, one year before Fidel Castro won Cuba's civil war. It also disposed of its Chilean subsidiary shortly before the election victory of a leftist regime in Chile in 1970. Had the company stayed in those markets, the subsidiaries would most likely have been expropriated.

Changing government regulations can at times pose problems prompting some companies to leave a country. India is a case in point. There, the government adopted its Exchange Regulation Act in 1973 to require most foreign companies to divest themselves of 60 percent of their subsidiaries by the end of 1977. Companies that manufactured

62. "Saying Sayonara Is Such Sweet Sorrow," *Business Week,* March 12, 1990, p. 52; "Avon Agrees to Sell Rest of Japanese Unit," *New York Times,* February 22, 1991, p. D5.
63. "Auto Industry Seen Paring Operations," *Nikkei Weekly,* February 15, 1992, p. 8.

substantially for export or whose operations used advanced technology were exempted. Since IBM's Indian operation did little exporting and sold mostly older computer models, the computer manufacturer was asked to sell 60 percent of its equity to Indian citizens. Coca-Cola decided to leave the market rather than sell a controlling ownership to local investors.

Exit strategies can also be the result of negative reactions in a firm's home market. With the political situation in South Africa open to challenge on moral grounds, many multinational corporations exited that country by abandoning or selling their local subsidiaries. In 1984, some 325 U.S. companies were maintaining operations in South Africa. Two years later, this number had decreased to 265; the total amount of U.S. direct foreign investment was estimated at U.S. $1.3 billion. One of the U.S. firms that left was Coca-Cola; others included General Motors, IBM, Motorola, and General Electric. Some European firms withdrew from that country also: Alfa-Romeo of Italy, Barclays Bank of the United Kingdom, and Renault of France among them.[64]

Reentry Strategies

Several of the markets left by international firms over the past decades have changed in attractiveness, making companies reverse their exit decisions and enter those markets a second time. In India, for example, the government relaxed its restrictive ownership legislation in view of its overall policy of economic liberalization. When the restrictive Foreign Exchange Regulation Act had been introduced in India in 1973, some two hundred of five hundred companies with large investments had exited, selling their stakes to local companies. Following liberalization in August 1991, approximately one hundred firms raised their equity stakes to the allowable 51 percent. Typical of this strategy is Gillette, which had entered India with a minority stake in the mid-1980s.[65] Coca-Cola, after having left the market completely in 1977, reentered again in 1993 to counter the earlier first-time entry of rival PepsiCo. Coca-Cola accomplished its return to the Indian market by acquiring Parle, India's leading local cola company.[66] General Motors returned to India after a much longer absence. After producing cars in India from 1928 to 1953, GM left due to poor economic prospects. It later developed licensing agreements with Hindustan Motors. This developed into the announcement of a full-scale 50-50 venture to jointly produce GM models in India again.[67]

The changing situation in South Africa is largely a function of the political evolution in that country. International sanctions, as well as sanctions imposed by the U.S. govern-

64. "South Africa: Time to Stay—or Go?" *Fortune,* August 4, 1986, p. 45; "If Coke Has Its Way, Blacks Will Soon Own 'The Real Thing,'" *Business Week,* March 27, 1987, p. 56; "High Risks and Low Returns," *Financial Times,* November 25, 1986, p. 10.

65. "Back in Charge," *Far Eastern Economic Review,* July 8, 1993.

66. "Coca-Cola Invasion Starts to Worry Businessmen," *Financial Times,* November 9, 1993, p. 6.

67. "Indian Venture for 20,000 Cars a Year," *Financial Times,* May 12, 1994, p. 15.

ment and some 150 cities, states, and counties, resulted in 214 U.S. firms exiting between 1984 and 1991.[68] Since July 1991, when the ban on investing in South Africa was lifted, some of those firms have returned. Among them is Honeywell, a manufacturer of industrial controls equipment. The company returned by repurchasing the industrial distributor it had sold to local interests in 1985.[69]

The majority of the companies now entering South Africa are firms that purposely did not deal directly with that country when it remained under white minority rule. Digital Equipment waited for the formal lifting of sanctions by the African National Congress, the leading black political party, and entered on July 1, 1993. Digital was attracted by the fact that many of its key customers, such as some of the leading international oil companies, had always maintained operations there and its products had found their way to South Africa through non-Digital channels.[70]

Conclusions

The world contains between 175 and 200 individual countries or markets. Thus, entry decisions are the strategy decisions international companies must make most frequently. Since the type of entry strategy can clearly affect later market success, these decisions need to be based on careful analysis. Companies often find it difficult to break out of initial arrangements, another reason why special attention must be given to this type of decision. In some of the more difficult markets, such as Japan, making the correct entry decision can become a key competitive advantage for a firm and can unlock markets otherwise inaccessible to a foreign company.

To survive in the coming global battles for market dominance, companies have to become increasingly bolder and more creative in their entry strategy choices. Long gone are the days when entry was restricted to exporting, licensing, foreign manufacturing, and joint ventures. New concepts such as global alliances have become common, and international firms will have to include acquisitions, venture capital financing, and complex government partnerships as integral elements in entry strategy configurations. The myriad of new entry alternatives has raised the level of complexity in international marketing and will remain an important challenge for managers.

This added complexity will make detailed analysis and comparisons of entry strategy alternatives more difficult. For adequate analysis, companies have to take into consideration not only present cost structures but also the ever changing economic and political environment. Rapidly changing foreign exchange rates have changed the cost of various entry alternatives and have forced companies to shift their approach. Economic changes are likely to continue, and companies will be forced to reevaluate their entry strategy

68. "As U.S. Firms Return to Land of Apartheid, Lotus Feels Its Way," *Wall Street Journal,* Wednesday, May 26, 1993, p. 1.
69. "Honeywell's Route Back to South Africa Market," *New York Times,* January 31, 1994, p. D1.
70. "Digital Sets Up Shop in South Africa," *Boston Sunday Globe,* July 11, 1993, p. 65.

decisions on an ongoing basis. Entry strategies will rarely be permanent but will have to be adapted to the most recent situation.

Although most companies have preferences as to which entry strategy they would pursue given no objections, firms increasingly will be adopting a flexible approach. Establishing a sales subsidiary may be the best alternative for entering some countries, whereas joint ventures may be necessary to enter other countries. Managers will be forced to learn to manage with a variety of entry strategies, and they will be less able to repeat the same entry patterns all over the world. A great amount of managerial flexibility will thus be required of international companies and their executives. We can also expect that the future will bring other types of entry strategies that will challenge international managers anew.

Questions for Discussion

1. Contrast the entry strategies practiced by Boeing and IBM. What differences do you find, and what explains these differences?

2. Would entry strategies differ for companies considering Germany, Japan, and China? If so, in what way and for what reasons?

3. How will the entry strategy of a new start-up firm differ from that of a mature multinational company?

4. What difficulties and special problems can be expected from a firm practicing only franchising as an entry strategy?

5. Perform a literature search on alliances and try to determine the reasons particular alliances were made.

6. It has been speculated that alliances between Japanese and western firms work primarily to the benefit of Japanese companies. Comment.

7. Explain the concept of entry strategy configuration and the strategies of layering, bundling, or unbundling entry strategies.

For Further Reading

Alden, Vernon R. "Who Says You Can't Crack Japanese Markets?" *Harvard Business Review,* January–February 1987, p. 52.

Bleeke, Joel, and David Ernst. "The Way to Win in Cross-Border Alliances." *Harvard Business Review,* November–December 1991, pp. 127–135.

Brasch, John J. "Using Export Specialists to Develop Overseas Sales." *Harvard Business Review,* May–June 1981, pp. 6–8.

Erramilli, Krishna M., and C. P. Rao. "Service Firms' International Entry-Mode Choice: A Modified Transaction-Cost Analysis Approach." *Journal of Marketing,* 57 (July 1993), pp. 19–38.

Harrigan, Kathryn R. *Strategies for Joint Ventures.* Boston: D. C. Heath, 1985.

Hertzfeld, Jeffrey M. "Joint Ventures: Saving the Soviets from Perestroika." *Harvard Business Review,* January–February 1991, pp. 92–101.

Kanter, Rosabeth Moss. *When Giants Learn to Dance.* New York: Simon & Schuster, 1989.

Killing, J. Peter. *Strategies for Joint Venture Success.* New York: Praeger, 1983.

Kogut, Bruce, and Harbir Singh. "The Effect of National Culture on the Choice of Entry Mode." *Journal of International Business Studies,* Fall 1988, pp. 411–432.

Lawrence, Paul, and Charalambos Vlachoutsicos. "Joint Ventures in Russia: Put the Locals in Charge." *Harvard Business Review,* January–February 1993, pp. 44–54.

Parkhe, Arvind. "Interfirm Diversity, Organizational Learning, and Longevity in Global Strategic Alliances." *Journal of International Business Studies,* 4th Quarter 1991, pp. 579–601.

Pekar, Peter, Jr. "How Battle-Tested Managers Assess Strategic Alliances." *Planning Review,* July–August 1989, pp. 34–37.

Reich, Robert B., and Eric D. Mankin. "Joint Ventures with Japan Are Giving Away Our Future." *Harvard Business Review,* March–April 1986, pp. 78–86.

Root, Franklin R. *Entry Strategies for International Markets.* Revised and expanded ed. Lexington, Mass.: D. C. Heath, 1994.

Shan, Weijan. "Environmental Risks and Joint Venture Sharing Arrangements." *Journal of International Business Studies,* 4th Quarter 1991, pp. 555–578.

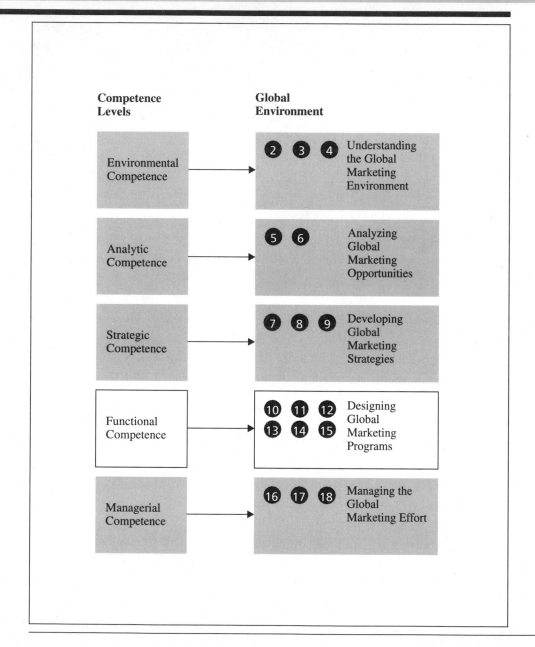

Competence Levels

Global Environment

Environmental Competence → ② ③ ④ Understanding the Global Marketing Environment

Analytic Competence → ⑤ ⑥ Analyzing Global Marketing Opportunities

Strategic Competence → ⑦ ⑧ ⑨ Developing Global Marketing Strategies

Functional Competence → ⑩ ⑪ ⑫ ⑬ ⑭ ⑮ Designing Global Marketing Programs

Managerial Competence → ⑯ ⑰ ⑱ Managing the Global Marketing Effort

Part 4

Designing Global Marketing Programs

ASSEMBLING AN INTERNATIONAL or global marketing program requires an analysis of how the international environment will affect the four major marketing mix elements: product, distribution, pricing, and communications. In Part 4, we focus on how companies adapt to different marketing environments by adjusting certain elements of their marketing programs to ensure market acceptance. In concentrating on these issues, our aim is to help you increase functional competence. Marketing managers not only must be knowledgeable about the international environment, but they also must possess the solid, functional skills necessary to compete successfully in the international marketplace.

In Chapter 10, we concentrate on product and service strategy issues for international and global markets. In Chapter 11, we discuss how to manage the new product development process in an international environment. Important distribution and channel decisions are discussed in Chapter 12. Chapter 13 outlines the differences between domestic, international, and global pricing and how companies can deal with problems arising from different prices in different markets. In Chapter 14, we give an overview of communications strategies, sales force management, and promotional policies for international companies. The final chapter in this section, Chapter 15, looks at international and global advertising and the challenges faced by companies running advertising programs simultaneously in many countries.

10

International and Global Product and Service Strategies

● **THIS CHAPTER LOOKS** *at the strategies companies can pursue to adapt their products and services to international markets. Figure 10.1 highlights the elements involved in product strategy decisions. The chapter discussion first centers on the many possible environmental factors that tend to prevent the marketing of uniform and standardized products across a multitude of markets. Attention then shifts to the various implications of selecting brand names for international markets. International firms are concerned not only with determining appropriate brand names but also with protecting those names against abuse and piracy. Subsequent sections focus on packaging and managing product lines and support services. The chapter concludes with a section on the marketing of services on a global scale. We also highlight the enormous opportunities in the service industry and explain how various companies are pursuing such challenges.*

Product Design in an International Environment

One of the principal questions in international marketing concerns the types of products that can be sold in different markets. The international firm will want to know whether existing products have to be adapted to certain international requirements or whether they can be shipped in their present form. For new products, the firm will have to select the

FIGURE 10.1 ● International and Global Product Strategies

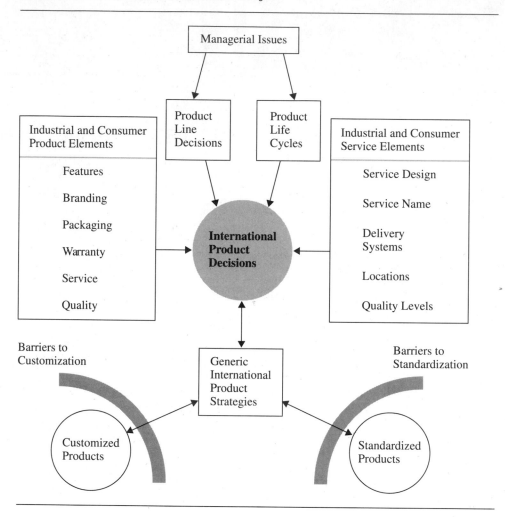

particular features their products should incorporate and to determine the desired function and performance of these features. The major elements of product design are explained in the following sections, with an emphasis on the effect of international complexities.

To select the most desirable product features is an involved decision for international marketers. The approach taken should include a thorough review of all the environmental factors that may affect product use (see Table 10.1). Furthermore, a thorough analysis should include the relative physical success factors developed in detail in Chapter 6. In all cases, however, a firm will have to picture its products in the targeted foreign market and ask the question, How would our product be used in that country? In some situations, it may be necessary to send some units to the various markets for testing purposes.

TABLE 10.1 ● Environmental Factors Requiring Product Design Changes

Environmental factors	*Design changes*
Level of technical skills	Product simplification
Level of labor costs	Automation or manualization of product
Level of literacy	Remaking and simplification of product
Level of income	Quality and price change
Level of interest rates	Quality and price change (investment in high quality may not be financially desirable)
Level of maintenance	Change in tolerances
Climatic differences	Product adaptation
Isolation (heavy repair; difficult and expensive)	Product simplification and reliability improvement
Difference in standards	Recalibration and resizing of product
Availability of other products	Greater or lesser product integration
Availability of materials	Change in product structure and fuel
Power availability	Resizing of product
Special conditions	Product redesign or invention

Source: Richard D. Robinson, *International Business Management* (Hinsdale, Ill.: Dryden Press, 1978), pp. 41–42. Reprinted by permission of the author.

Product Dimensions

Dimensions as expressed by size, capacity, or volume are subject to market and environmental influences that often require different approaches to any given market. One important factor, particularly for U.S. firms, is the selection of a metric versus a nonmetric scale. The firm must go beyond a single translation of nonmetric into metric sizes to help users or consumers understand the design of products and meet legal requirements. Simple translations do not lead to round standardized numbers, forcing companies actually to change the physical sizes of their products to conform to new standards. With Europe and Japan operating on the metric standard, the U.S. market is the only remaining major nonmetric market. Therefore, this is less of an issue for non-U.S. firms than for U.S.-based companies that normally operate on a nonmetric basis at home.

The different physical characteristics of consumers often influence product design. Swiss watch manufacturers have learned over the years to adapt their watch cases to different wrist sizes. The Japanese have smaller wrists than Americans; thus, design changes are required that do not necessarily change the function or look of the watch. A leading Italian shoe manufacturer had a similar experience exporting shoes to the United States. Research revealed that feet were not the same in every country. Americans were found to have longer toes than Italians and smaller insteps,[1] and the company learned that

1. "Three Scientists Seek U.S. Data on Genetic Engineering," *New York Times,* March 8, 1978, p. A-19.

Americans have thicker ankles and narrower, flatter feet. To produce a properly fitting shoe, the Italian company decided to make appropriate changes in its design to achieve the necessary comfort for U.S. customers. Ansell Edmont asked Japanese factory workers to test their new work gloves. They found that Japanese workers have smaller hands and shorter fingers than their counterparts in Europe and the United States and therefore require different gloves.[2]

Although product characteristics may vary from market to market, companies also look for similarities across geographic boundaries. If market segments can be identified with similar product needs that cut across geographic products, the company can reduce the number of product variations needed to serve the global marketplace. For example, in one study of four different cultural and geographic markets, researchers identified three distinct segments of fruit flavored soda drinkers. The segments were based on sensory preferences: (1) weak aroma, light color, low sweetness, and low flavor; (2) stronger aroma, medium color, medium sweetness, and stronger flavor; (3) strongest aroma, darkest color, high sweetness, and strongest flavor.[3] While products often must be tailored to the needs of different markets, more and more companies are looking for similarities across markets.

Size is often affected by the physical surroundings of product use or space. In some countries, limited living space necessitates home appliances that are substantially smaller than those found in a country such as the United States, where people live in relatively larger dwellings. Recently, U.S.-made major appliances have been imported into Japan by some discount chains. Although the volume is still small by international standards, some wealthier Japanese consumers favor these large appliances. Some of the customers have had to return them after purchase, however, because they could not get the refrigerators through their own apartment doors.[4] Winnebago Industries, the U.S. maker of recreational vehicles, encountered difficulties selling its oversized vehicles in Japan through Mitsubishi Corporation, a larger international trading company. Narrow streets in Japan and a scarcity of campgrounds with camper hookups turned out to be major impediments to sales. Similarly, Chrysler found it needed to make numerous changes to its Jeep to be successful in Japan. Underhood wiring was changed to meet Japanese standards, the owner's manual had to be revised to include big diagrams and cartoons, and each Japan-bound Jeep had to receive special quality checks to meet the standards of Japanese consumers.[5] In many countries, customers have come to expect certain products in certain sizes; thus, international firms are forced to adapt to meet these expectations.

Design Features

Invariably, international firms find they must alter some components or parts of a product because of local circumstances. One worldwide manufacturer of industrial abrasives has

2. Robert Thomas, vice president, Ansell Edmont, in a discussion with authors on July 13, 1987.

3. Howard R. Moskowitz and Samuel Rubino, ''Sensory Segmentation: An Organizing Principle for International Product Concept Generation,'' unpublished article.

4. ''Japanese Eye the Western Kitchen,'' *Financial Times,* August 10, 1989, p. 18.

5. ''The Man Who's Selling Japan on Jeeps,'' *Business Week,* July 19, 1993, pp. 56–57.

had to adjust to different raw material supply situations by varying the raw material input according to country while maintaining abrasive performance standards. Paint is another product that requires adaptation to climatic and surface circumstances. As a result, paint will differ from region to region even though the particular application may be identical.[6]

Procter & Gamble, the large U.S.-based consumer products company, found it had to adapt the formulation of its Cheer laundry detergent to fit Japanese market requirements. Cheer, initially promoted as an all-temperature product, ran into trouble because many Japanese consumers washed their clothes in cold tap water or used leftover bath water. The Japanese also liked to add fabric softeners, which tend to cut down on the suds produced by the detergent. P&G reformulated the product to work effectively in cold water with fabric softeners added and changed the positioning to superior cleaning in cold water. The brand is now one of P&G's best-selling products in Japan.[7]

Researchers have considered the U.S. customer to be particularly feature conscious.[8] Consequently, features considered necessary in the United States may not be required abroad, although others may be in greater demand. Adding the desired features can strengthen a company's marketing effort and offset the added engineering and production costs. In some local markets, customers may even expect a product to perform a function different from the one originally intended. One U.S. exporter of gardening tools found that its battery-operated trimmers were used by the Japanese as lawn mowers on their small lawns. As a result, the batteries and motors did not last as long as they would have under the intended use. Because of the different function desired by Japanese customers, a design change eventually was required.

Adapting Products to Cultural Preferences   To the extent that fashion and tastes differ by country, companies often change their styling. Color, for example, should reflect the values of each country.[9] For Japan, red and white have happy associations, whereas black and white indicate mourning. Green is an unpopular color in Malaysia, where it is associated with the jungle and illness. Green is the national color of Egypt and therefore should not be used for packaging purposes there. Textile manufacturers in the United States who have started to expand their export businesses have consciously used color to suit local needs.[10] For example, the Lowenstein Corporation has successfully used brighter colors for fabrics exported to Africa.

Scent is also subject to change from one country to another. S. C. Johnson & Son, a manufacturer of furniture polish products, encountered resistance to its Lemon Pledge

6. "Paints & Coatings: The Battle for World Markets," *Financial Times,* March 10, 1989, Section III.

7. "After Early Stumbles, P&G Is Making Inroads Overseas," *Wall Street Journal,* February 6, 1989, p. B1.

8. Montrose Sommers and Jerome Kernan, "Why Products Flourish Here, Fizzle There," *Columbia Journal of World Business,* March–April 1967, pp. 89–97.

9. Michael J. Thomas, ed., *International Marketing Management* (Boston: Houghton Mifflin, 1969), p. 35.

10. Herbert E. Meyer, "How U.S. Textiles Got to Be Winners in the Export Game," *Fortune,* May 5, 1980, p. 260.

furniture polish among older consumers in Japan. Careful market research revealed that the polish smelled similar to a latrine disinfectant used widely in Japan in the 1940s. Sales rose sharply after the scent was adjusted.[11]

Food is one of the most culturally distinct product areas. Pizza is a western product introduced in Japan in 1986 by Domino's; the original cheese and pepperoni was quickly adapted to suit Japanese tastes. Today, a variety of ingredients are available on pizza in Japan, including curry, squid, spinach, corn, tuna, teriyaki, barbecued beef, burdock root, shrimp, seaweed, apple, and rice. While Domino's and Pizza Hut battle for market share in Japan, they are faced with many Japanese imitators who offer exotic recipes and sometimes cheaper prices.[12]

Adapting Performance Standards   Manufacturers typically design products to meet domestic performance standards. As we have already seen, such standards do not always apply in other countries, and product changes are required in some circumstances. Products designed in highly developed countries often exceed the performance needed in developing Third World countries. These customers prefer products of greater simplicity, not only to save costs but to ensure better service over a product lifetime. Companies have been criticized for selling excess performance where simpler products will do. Stepping into this market gap are companies from some of the less developed countries, whose present technology levels are more in line with those the consumer needs.

The need for different product standards was behind a foreign acquisition by the Westinghouse Electric Corporation.[13] Standards for electrical equipment in the United States differed from those adopted by many foreign countries; relevant standards abroad were often set by the International Electrical Committee (IEC). Equipment based on IEC standards tended to be smaller and less costly than standard U.S. equipment. This led to a preference for IEC standard products among many developing countries. Rather than rebuilding the U.S.-made controls, Westinghouse decided to acquire a German firm specializing in IEC standard controls for use in its equipment.

Of course, manufacturers from developing countries face the opposite challenge; companies must increase the performance of their products to meet the standards of industrialized countries. In general, the necessity to increase performance tends to be more apparent as the need arises, whereas opportunities for product simplification are frequently less obvious to the observer.

Sometimes, manufacturers have to build design changes into products for overseas sales, changes that are not apparent to the buyer. These internal design changes can increase product use or performance or adapt it to a new environment. As we have seen in the case of Westinghouse, different electrical standards require product adaptation. In color television broadcasting, the U.S. system was not adopted worldwide. In Europe, countries

11. Vernon R. Alden, "Who Says You Can't Crack Japanese Markets?" *Harvard Business Review,* January–February 1987, pp. 52–56.

12. "Pizza in Japan Is Adapted to Local Tastes," *Wall Street Journal,* June 4, 1993, p. B1.

13. "Westinghouse's Gutsy Expansion Plans," *Business Week,* December 28, 1981, p. 61.

installed either a French- or a German-designed system, each requiring specially equipped TV receivers. RCA offered only its standard models in Asia, disregarding the fact that both Singapore and Malaysia, two neighboring countries, had different broadcasting systems. With the RCA model, the buyer could receive only a picture but no sound. RCA distributors in Singapore had to wait several years for the company to make the necessary adaptations.[14]

Adapting High-Technology Products   Technology-intensive and industrial products frequently find that standards for product performance differ from one country to the next. In telecommunications, the signaling standards used for U.S. switching systems differ from those used in Europe. As a result, significant barriers exist when a company wants to become an exporter. In effect, the exporter often faces the decision to become a multistandard firm. Designing and manufacturing such systems to several standards adds to the total cost, and without minimum volume a company may have to forgo export opportunities if the adaptation costs outweigh the business opportunity. For their domestic clients, Japanese manufacturers had long built machines similar to the standard U.S. machines offered by IBM, but they offered their machines with special software packages.[15] These programs were geared to the often unique needs of Japanese clients and written in a mixture of Japanese and English. The programs were not subject to easy translation. To write entirely new software packages for export markets would have been not only expensive but also extremely difficult for Japanese programmers. Under those circumstances, Hitachi, after repeated requests from its U.S. sales partner, Intel, finally accepted the idea of producing computers that were plug-compatible with IBM machines and that could also run with IBM software packages. Neither Hitachi nor other leading Japanese computer manufacturers sold machines domestically that were plug compatible with IBM at that time. In this case, the requirements of the export markets outweighed those of the domestic market.

Both Apple and IBM experienced the reverse in the Japanese market. Apple, first entering in 1979, made no significant changes in its product to meet local requirements. As a result, little software was written and the market share was always low. In 1988, however, Apple finally decided that it had to adapt and took the necessary steps to have local software houses write Japanese software. By aggressively pursuing Japanese software developers, more widely available Japanese software pushed up Apple's sales of its Macintosh line to about 50,000 units annually, double the amount of a year earlier.[16] In the personal computer (PC) market, U.S. manufacturers have been successful in converting many customers from the de facto NEC standards, which controlled 60 percent of the market, to the IBM-compatible standard. In October 1993, Fujitsu launched a line of IBM-compatible PCs, leaving NEC isolated from the rest of the world.[17]

14. ''RCA's New Vista: The Bottom Line,'' *Business Week,* July 4, 1977, p. 44.

15. Bro Uttal, ''Exports Won't Come Easy for Japan's Computer Industry,'' *Fortune,* October 9, 1978, p. 138.

16. ''Is It Finally Time for Apple to Blossom in Japan?'' *Business Week,* May 28, 1990, p. 100.

17. ''NEC Stands Alone as Fujitsu Adopts IBM PC Standard,'' *Wall Street Journal,* October 19, 1993, p. B4.

Sometimes, different standards are mandated by governments, leaving international marketers to scramble for compliance. In the United Kingdom, Caterpillar manufactures a backhoe/loader type of construction machinery for all of Europe. These machines are tractors with a bucket up-front and a digger at the back. Requirements for Germany are such that several special parts must be used. All tractors destined for Germany require a separate brake with an anti-drive-through mechanism attached to the rear axle. The operating valve for the backhoe requires a special locking capability. The steering system needs to be equipped with specially positioned valves. The bucket must be equipped with a lock for traveling. The cost of these "extras" amounts to about 5 percent of total cost. In process is the establishment of pan-European standards for construction machinery. By avoiding such country-specific standards, the European Union expects savings for industry and more competitiveness.[18]

Changing Proven Products to Meet Foreign Requirements   One of the most difficult decisions for international companies to make is whether or not to change a proven product that has sold well in the past. Sometimes, a company may be in a position to change a proven design to gain a competitive advantage because other, more tradition-bound firms declined.

Prior to 1974, French wines accounted for the largest volume of imported wines, with Italian suppliers a distant second. Since then, Italian vintners in the U.S. market have far surpassed their French competitors, who concentrated on more expensive wines. In 1979, Italian vintners even outsold the French in dollar volume. This remarkable upset of the world's most renowned wine producers was achieved by shrewd marketing and product adaptations that catered to the specific preferences of the U.S. consumer. Whereas Italians preferred their Lambrusco wine dry, light, and fruity, the U.S. population (according to data supplied by the U.S. importer) preferred a wine that was bubbly and slightly sweet, similar to popular drinks consumed with meals, such as soda. The Italians adjusted their fermentation process to produce such a wine significantly below the cost of French wines. This cost advantage was achieved with efficient bottling plants. Also, the Lambrusco wine was ready for consumption immediately upon fermentation, thus eliminating the customary two- to four-year aging process of more expensive wines. Lambrusco soon accounted for two-thirds of all Italian wines imported into the United States.[19]

Quality

The quality of a product reflects the intended function and the circumstances of product use. Consequently, as these circumstances change, it is sometimes necessary to adjust quality accordingly. Products that receive less service or care in a given country have to be reengineered to live up to the added stress. At times, there may be an opportunity to

18. "A Bumpy Ride over Europe's Traditions," *Financial Times,* October 31, 1988, p. 5.
19. "Creating a Mass Market for Wine," *Business Week,* March 15, 1982, p. 108; "The Toyota of the Wine Trade," *Fortune,* November 30, 1981, p. 155.

lower product cost by reducing the built-in quality and, in turn, reducing price to the customary purchase levels of the local market. However, this may be dangerous if company reputation can suffer in the process. Not marketing a product at all may be preferable.

Some companies go to great lengths to live up to different quality standards in foreign markets. The experience of BMW, the German automaker exporting to Japan, serves as an excellent example of the extra efforts frequently involved. BMW found that its customers in Japan expected the very finest quality. Typically, cars shipped to Japan had to be completely repainted. Even very small mistakes were not tolerated by customers. When a service call was made, the car was picked up at the customer's home and returned when completed.

International Standards[20]

Most countries have some type of organization that sets standards for business processes and practices. Groups such as the Canadian Standards Association, the British Standards Institute (BSI), and the American National Standards Institute (ANSI) all formulate standards for product design and testing. If products adhere to the standards, buyers are assured of a stated level of product quality.

Given the growth in international commerce, there are benefits to having international standards for items such as credit cards, speed codes for 35 mm film, paper sizes, screw threads, and car tires. While the national standards institutes ensure consistency within countries, an international agency is required to coordinate across countries. The country-to-country differences become immediately obvious as you try to plug in your hair dryer in various different countries.

The International Standards Organization (ISO), located in Geneva, coordinates the setting of global standards. To set an international standard, representatives from various countries meet and attempt to agree on a common standard. Sometimes they adopt the standard set by a country. For example, the British standard for quality assurance (BS5750) was adopted internationally as ISO 9000. Initially a European standard, ISO 9000 is becoming recognized in the United States.

The unification of Europe has forced the Europeans to recognize the need for multicountry standards. If Europe continues to dominate the creation of international standards through ISO, the United States and Japan will be pressured to conform. The U.S. standard-setting process is much more fragmented than Europe's. In the United States, there are over 450 different standard-setting groups, loosely coordinated by ANSI. After a standard is set by one of the 450 groups, ANSI certifies that it is an "American National Standard," of which there were 11,000 on the books in 1993.

ISO 9000 is one of the most well recognized standards. As the international quality standard, ISO 9000 ensures that an organization can consistently deliver a product or service that satisfies the customer's requirements. The number of international standards has grown from 4,917 in 1982 to 8,651 in 1992.

---

20. Charles Batchelor, "International Standards," *Financial Times,* October 14, 1993, pp. 23–25.

Branding Decisions

Selecting appropriate brand names on an international basis is substantially more complex than deciding on a brand name for just one country. Typically, a brand name is rooted in a given language and, if used elsewhere, may have either a different meaning or none at all. Ideally, marketers look for brand names that evoke similar emotions or images around the world. By past learning experience, people worldwide have come to expect the same thing from such brand names as Coca-Cola, IBM, Minolta, and Mercedes-Benz. However, it has become increasingly difficult for new entrants to become recognized unless the name has some meaning for the prospective customer. Language problems are particularly difficult to overcome. Colgate-Palmolive, the large U.S.-based toiletries manufacturer, purchased the leading toothpaste brand in Southeast Asia, ''Darkie.'' With a minstrel in blackface as its logo, the product had been marketed by a local company since 1920. After the acquisition in 1985, Colgate-Palmolive came under pressure from many groups in the United States to use a less offensive brand name. The company undertook a large amount of research to find both a brand name and logo that were racially inoffensive and yet close enough to be quickly recognized by consumers. The company changed the name to ''Darlie'' after an exhaustive search.[21]

Selection Procedures

Brand-name selection is critical. International marketers must carefully evaluate the meanings and word references in the languages of their target audiences. Can the name be easily pronounced, or will it be distorted in the local language? In China, Coca-Cola is identified by a combination of Chinese characters that are pronounced ''Coca-Cola'' but mean ''a thirst quencher that makes you happy.''[22]

Given almost unlimited possibilities for names and the restricted opportunities to find and register a desirable one, international companies spend considerable effort on the selection procedure. One consulting company specializes in finding brand names with worldwide application. The company brings citizens of many countries together in Paris where, under the guidance of a specialist, they are asked to state names in their particular language that would combine well with the product to be named.[23] Speakers of other languages can immediately react if a name comes up that does not sound well in their language. After a few such sessions, the company may accumulate as many as 1,000 names that will later be reduced to 500 by a company linguist. The client company then is asked to select 50 to 100 names for further consideration. At this point, the names are subjected to a search procedure to determine which ones have not been registered in any

21. ''Colgate Will Change Toothpaste's Name,'' *New York Times,* January 27, 1989, p. D1.

22. Murray J. Lubliner, ''Brand Name Selection Is Critical Challenge for Global Marketers,'' *Marketing News,* August 2, 1993, p. 7.

23. ''Trademarks Are a Global Business These Days, but Finding Registrable Ones Is a Big Problem,'' *Wall Street Journal,* September 4, 1975, p. 28.

of the countries under consideration. In the end, only about ten names may survive this process; from these, the company will have to make the final selection. Although this process may be expensive, it is generally considered a small cost compared with the advertising expenditures invested in the brand name over many years.

When confronted with the need to search for a brand name with international applications, a company can use the following sources:

1. An arbitrary or invented word not to be found in any standard English (or other language) dictionary, such as Toyota's Lexus.

2. A recognizable English (or foreign-language) word, but one totally unrelated to the product in question, such as the detergent Cheer.

3. An English (or other language) word that merely suggests some characteristic or purpose of the product, such as Mr. Clean.

4. A word that is evidently descriptive of the product, although the word may have no meaning to persons unacquainted with English (or the other language), such as the diapers brand Pampers.

5. Within one or more of these categories, a geographical place or a common surname, such as Kentucky Fried Chicken.

6. A device, design, number, or some other element that is not a word or a combination of words, such as 3M Company.[24]

Selection of a brand name based on these six approaches is closely related to another key issue in international branding: should the company use one brand name worldwide or should it use different names in different countries?

Single-Country Versus Global Brand Names

International marketers are constantly confronted with the decision of whether the brand name needs to be universal. Brands such as Coca-Cola and Kodak have universal use and lend themselves to an integrated international marketing strategy. With worldwide travel a common occurrence, many companies do not think they should accept a brand name unless it can be used universally. However, many product brands originated in a single market, typically the company's home market, and were given a brand name that reflected the home market's cultural background. Later extensions of such a brand name internationally can pose problems. When Bank Americard Inc. changed its logo and name to Visa in 1977, a primary consideration was bringing the card, which had been issued in over twenty countries with as many names, under the umbrella of a single, meaningful brand name.[25] The resulting name change, though expensive, led to such strong growth that Visa surpassed MasterCard to become the most widely used card in the world. This was largely because the latter did not create such a unified worldwide image.

24. George W. Cooper, ''On Your 'Mark,''' *Columbia Journal of World Business,* March–April 1970, pp. 67–76.
25. ''How a New Chief Is Turning Interbank Inside Out,'' *Business Week,* July 14, 1980, p. 109.

Of course, using the same name elsewhere is not always possible, and a change in the home market may jeopardize the positive feelings for the original name gained after years of marketing efforts. In such instances, different names have to be found. Procter & Gamble had successfully marketed its household cleaner, Mr. Clean, in the United States for some time. This name, however, had no meaning outside of countries using the English language. This prompted the company to arrive at several adaptations abroad, such as *Monsieur Propre* in France and *Meister Proper* in Germany. In all cases, however, the symbol of the genie with gleaming eyes was retained because it evoked responses abroad that were similar to those in the United States.

Private Branding Strategies

The practice of private branding, or supplying products to a third party for sale under its brand name, has become quite common in many domestic markets. Similar opportunities exist on an international scale and may be used to the manufacturer's advantage. Private branding offers particular advantages to a company with strong manufacturing skills but little access to foreign markets. Arranging for distribution of the firm's product through local distributors or companies with already existing distribution networks reduces the risk of failure and provides for rapid volume growth via instant market access. Some Japanese companies have used the private branding approach to gain market access in Europe and the United States. Ricoh serves as one of many examples.[26] Known as a manufacturer of cameras, Ricoh entered the market for small plain paper copiers (PPCs) in the early 1970s. Supply contracts were signed with Savin for the U.S. market, with Nashua of New Hampshire for Canada and Europe, and with Kalle of West Germany for Europe. With the help of these three firms, Ricoh gained 9 percent of the worldwide copier market within five years.[27]

These private branding arrangements are also called OEM (original equipment manufacturer) contracts, in which the foreign manufacturer assumes the role of the OEM. As the market grows, these arrangements become difficult to manage from the manufacturer's point of view. Nevertheless, they have opened markets more quickly and at much lower investment cost than would have been required for the Japanese firms to develop these markets on their own. Similar private branding or OEM strategies were pursued by Japanese manufacturers of videocassette recorders (VCRs) in Europe, where Japanese companies were battling Philips of the Netherlands and Grundig of Germany for market dominance.[28] Japanese companies supplied VCRs to European home electronic manufacturers with established distribution systems who did not want to invest research and funds to produce their own systems. Victor of Japan concluded long-term agreements with Saba, Nordmende, and Telefunken, all of West Germany, with Thorn Consumer Electronics of the United Kingdom, and with Thomson-Brandt of France. Matsushita Electric had similar arrangements with Blaupunkt Werke GmbH of West Germany, whereas Hitachi had an

---

26. ''PPC Marketers Take Over American Distribution,'' *Japan Economic Journal,* May 22, 1979, p. 7.

27. ''Competition Heats Up in Copiers,'' *Business Week,* November 5, 1979, p. 115.

28. ''Sony and Philips Seal Tie-up,'' *Japan Economic Journal,* October 16, 1979, p. 8.

TABLE 10.2 ● Top Ten Brands by Region

Ranking	America	Japan	Europe
1	Coca-Cola	Takashimaya	Mercedes-Benz
2	Campbell's	Coca-Cola	Philips
3	Pepsi-Cola	National	Volkswagen
4	AT&T	Matsushita	Rolls-Royce
5	McDonald's	Sony	Porsche
6	American Express	Toyota	Coca-Cola
7	Kellogg's	NTT	Ferrari
8	IBM	Japan Air Lines	BMW
9	Levi's	Nippon Airlines	Michelin
10	Sears	Seiko	Volvo

Source: The Economist. November 19, 1988, p. 80. © 1988 The Economist Newspaper Limited. Reprinted with permission.

OEM arrangement with Granada TV Rental of the United Kingdom. The latest entrant, Toshiba, signed a long-term OEM contract with Rank Radio International of the United Kingdom. In all cases, the European companies placed their own labels on the VCRs imported from Japan.

Private branding or OEM contracts are not without drawbacks for the manufacturer. With control over marketing in the hands of the distributor, the manufacturer remains dependent and can only indirectly influence marketing. For long-term profitability, companies often find that they need to sell products under their own names, even where the OEM has achieved substantial marketing success. Such partnerships often end because of conflicting interests. Ricoh, which successfully used OEM arrangements to carve out a large market share in the United States for its plain copiers, reportedly paid Savin $14.5 million in compensatory royalties to obtain the right to sell copiers under its own name, Ricoh.[29]

Global Brands

Experts disagree on what makes a global brand. However, few brands are marketed in the same way, with the same strategy, and as identical products worldwide. Furthermore, many that are actually marketed as global brands with a largely identical strategy still have not yet received major recognition beyond their own home regions. Among the top ten U.S. brands, all were of U.S. origin, and only two of the top ten in Japan were foreign brands as shown in Table 10.2.[30]

29. "PPC Marketers Take Over," p. 7.
30. "Brands: It's the Real Thing," *Economist,* November 19, 1988, p. 80.

TABLE 10.3 ● Top Ten Global Brands

	"Share of mind"	*"Esteem"*
Coca-Cola	1	6
Sony	4	1
Mercedes-Benz	12	2
Kodak	5	9
Disney	8	5
Nestlé	7	14
Toyota	8	23
McDonald's	2	85
IBM	20	4
Pepsi-Cola	3	92

Source: The Economist. September 15, 1990, p. 120. © 1990 The Economist Newspaper Limited. Reprinted with permission.

Landor, an international consulting company, surveyed some 6,000 brands among 10,000 consumers to see how many brands are truly global in recognition and esteem. According to the results, only about twenty brands have a major position in all three large markets of the United States, Japan, and Europe. The clear winner worldwide was Coca-Cola, finishing first in share of mind awareness and sixth in brand esteem, as shown in 10.3.[31]

Where appropriate, a global brand has the advantage of economies of scale in product development, manufacturing, and marketing. For example, Ford could afford to invest far more on suspension and handling because it expected sales of 700,000 units worldwide for its world car—Mordeo in Europe and Contour in the States.[32]

The validity of global brands is based on the concept of brand loyalty. When Philip Morris reduced prices worldwide on April 2, 1993, due to the impact of generic or store-brand cigarettes, it became clear that global brands may be vulnerable.[33] Many consumers in the United States and Europe seem to have correctly concluded that there is little or no difference between branded and private label products. Private label goods account for 32 percent of supermarket sales in Britain and 24 percent in France.[34]

31. "Coke's Kudos," *Economist,* September 15, 1990, p. 120.
32. "Ford Sets Its Sights on a World Car," *New York Times,* September 27, 1993, p. D1.
33. "Shootout at the Check-out," *Economist,* June 5, 1993, p. 69.
34. "The Erosion of Brand Loyalty," *Business Week,* July 19, 1993, p. 22.

Panregional Brands

Brands actively marketed in a geographic region, such as Europe, are considered panregional. (In the case of Europe, they are also called pan-European brands, or Eurobrands for short.) In the strictest sense, packaged goods marketed across Europe with the same formula, the same brand name, and the same positioning strategy, package, and advertising are said to amount to less than 5 percent of total volume in Europe.[35] Examples of such products include P&G's Pampers and Head & Shoulders, Michelin tires, and Rolex watches. Experts expect Eurobrands' share of all brands to rise, however. Another group of products, marketed with semistandardized strategies but with changes in one or more of the marketing variables, are estimated to account for as much as 40 percent of the European consumer goods business. Consequently, purely national brands may decline in share from more than 50 percent today to about one-third in the next decade.

Electrolux, the Swedish white goods (household appliances) company, made over one hundred acquisitions between 1975 and 1985, which left the company with over twenty brands sold in forty countries. Large markets such as the United Kingdom and Germany had as many as six major Electrolux brands. A study by Electrolux found a convergence of market segments across Europe, with the consumers' need for ''localness'' being primarily in terms of distribution channels, promotion in local media, and use of local names instead of product design and features. From this analysis, Electrolux developed a strategy with two pan-European brands and one or two local brands in each market. The Electrolux brand was targeted to the high-prestige, conservative consumers, and the Zanussi brand was targeted to the innovative, trend-setter consumers. The local brands were targeted to the young, aggressive urban professionals and the warm and friendly, value-oriented consumers.[36]

A survey of European consumers to determine leading brand names found that about one-fifth of the leading fifty brands are of U.S. origin, with equal amounts from Germany and France. Mercedes-Benz was the winner, followed by Philips, Volkswagen, Rolls Royce, and Coca-Cola.[37] In a later survey of more than two hundred European brand managers in thirteen countries, 81 percent indicated they were aiming for standardization and homogenization, while only 13 percent said they were leaving each country free to decide its own strategy.[38] The survey clearly indicates a strong preference for a Eurobrand strategy for most companies.

In Japan, the leading non-Japanese brands were Coca-Cola, Nestlé, Porsche, Kentucky Fried Chicken, McDonald's, BMW, Gucci, Dunhill, Louis Vuitton, and other luxury brands. Nestlé was leading among the mass-marketed brands.[39]

35. Ronald Beatson, ''The Americanization of Europe,'' *Advertising Age,* April 2, 1990, p. 16.

36. Christopher A. Bartlett and Sumantra Ghosal, ''What Is a Global Manager?'' *Harvard Business Review,* September–October 1992, p. 125.

37. ''Recognition and Respect—the Big Divide,'' *Financial Times,* November 17, 1988, p. 16.

38. ''Who Favors Branding with Euro Approach?'' *Advertising Age International*, May 25, 1992, p. I-16.

39. Ibid.

Trademarks

Because brand names or trademarks are usually backed with substantial advertising funds, it makes sense to register such brands for the exclusive use of the sponsoring firm. However, registration abroad is often hampered by a number of factors.

Different interpretations exist in different countries and may affect filing. In some countries, registration authorities may object that the name lacks the inherent distinctiveness needed for registration or that the chosen word is too common to be essential to the promotion of the product, thus allowing other firms to continue to use the name in a descriptive manner. Other countries allow registration of trademarks and renewals for actual or intended use, thus increasing the possibility that some other firm may already have registered the name. In countries where the first applicant always obtains exclusive rights, companies risk the possibility of having their brand names pirated by outsiders who apply for a new name first. The foreign company is then forced to buy back its own trademark. When a country does not allow registrations until all objections are settled, registration may be postponed for years.

Trademark and Brand Protection

Violations of trademarks have been an ever present problem in international marketing. Many companies have found themselves subject to violations by people who use either the protected name or a very similar one. Deliberate violations can usually be fought in court, though often at great expense. Violations of trademarks, or counterfeit products, are estimated to account for 3 percent of world trade, or some $60 billion in U.S. dollars, according to the International Chamber of Commerce. The Swiss watch industry has estimated its own losses at $750 million per year. French perfume makers believe that they lose 10 percent of sales to fake products each year,[40] and the U.S. Department of Commerce estimates that some 750,000 U.S. jobs have been lost due to foreign forgeries of U.S. products.

Hennessey, the French cognac producer, became alarmed when sales in some Far Eastern markets dropped by as much as 30 percent. In those areas, businessmen brought friends and clients to bars, and the choice of the cognac ordered signaled the status of both the host and guests. Cognac was ordered by the bottle, making the brand very pronounced to all. Bar operators saved the empty bottles and later refilled them with cheap cognac. In some areas, empty Hennessey bottles brought five dollars in the black market. The company retaliated by placing a tamper-proof Polaroid label on each bottle and advertising this to the target market.[41]

In India, an entire cottage industry has developed making counterfeit Scotch whiskey. Legal imports into India are virtually nonexistent and restricted to a few five-star hotels. In large cities such as Bombay or Delhi, diplomats and businesspeople sell their duty-free allocation of genuine Scotch through peddlers. The counterfeit industry, supplying iden-

40. ''Stop, Thief,'' *International Management,* September 1990, p. 48.
41. Ibid., p. 49.

tical labels, bottles, and packaging, sells its locally made liquor through these very same channels. Because customers believe they are buying genuine bottles, they are paying about $25 a bottle.[42]

Counterfeiting injures both businesses and consumers. In some cases, trademark violations can result in potential harm to the customer. Glaxo, the British pharmaceutical company, experienced counterfeiting of its best selling Zantac anti-ulcer drug. The counterfeit drug was produced in Greece, where police helped with the seizure of several thousand packages. These packages were to be shipped to the United Kingdom and sold as regular drugs in the open market.[43] A British manufacturer of surgical instruments found forged items, originating from Pakistan, appearing in several European and Third World markets. These miniature vascular clamps used to pinch arteries during heart surgery on children posed the risk of snapping during surgery.[44]

Abuses of trademarks and patents are particularly acute in ten developing countries: Taiwan, South Korea, Thailand, Singapore, Malaysia, Indonesia, the Philippines, Mexico, Brazil, and India.[45] Many industries have suffered from the effect of counterfeiters, but expensive consumer goods, automobile parts, pharmaceuticals, and software encounter particular problems. Personal computer software industry experts estimate $5.3 billion lost per year to illegal copies in Europe. In the United Kingdom, an estimated 60 percent of the PC software is pirated, 80 percent in Germany. To combat the lost sales, software companies are stepping up legal action against software pirates.[46]

International companies have gone on the offensive to defend themselves against counterfeiting. The United States passed the Trademark Counterfeiting Act of 1984, which makes counterfeiting punishable by fines of up to $250,000 and prison terms of up to five years.[47] The U.S. government has also put pressure on some foreign governments, particularly on Taiwan, to prosecute their own counterfeiters more aggressively.[48] International companies are increasingly focusing on methods to stop illegal counterfeiting. Many firms find that subcontractors, who know manufacturing processes, are becoming a problem. These companies may fulfill their regular contracts to an international company while selling extra volume on the black market. To stop such practices, new marketing systems are being developed to allow companies to monitor abuses and customers to spot counterfeit products. Polaproof by Polaroid is one tamper-proof label, holograms are another, and many invisible marketing devices or inks exist. However, given the difficulty of tracking counterfeiters and the obvious opportunities for making quick profits, counterfeiting is a problem that international companies will have to deal with for some time to come.

42. ''Bell Toll for Indian 'Scotch' Makers,'' *Financial Times,* August 29, 1990, p. 5.

43. ''Stop, Thief,'' p. 48.

44. Ibid.

45. ''Intellectual Property: Foreign Pirates Worry U.S. Firms,'' *Chemical & Engineering News,* September 1, 1986, p. 8.

46. ''Software Makers Are Pursuing Pirates Around the Globe with Fleet of Lawyers,'' *Wall Street Journal,* December 13, 1990, p. B1.

47. ''The Counterfeit Trade,'' *Business Week,* December 16, 1985, p. 64.

48. ''Taiwan Curbs Its Counterfeiters,'' *New York Times,* March 30, 1986, p. 74.

Packaging for Global Markets

Differences in the marketing environment may require special adaptation in product packaging. Changed climatic conditions often demand a change in the package to ensure sufficient protection or shelf life. The role a package assumes in promotion also depends on the market retailing structure. In countries with a substantial degree of self-service merchandising, a package with strong promotional appeal is desirable for consumer products; these requirements may be substantially scaled down in areas where over-the-counter service still dominates. In addition, distribution handling requirements are not identical the world over. In high-wage countries of the developed world, products tend to be packaged to reduce further handling by retailing employees. For consumer products, all mass merchandisers have to do is place products on shelves. In countries with lower wages and less-developed retailing structures, individual orders may be filled from larger packaged units, entailing extra labor by the retailer.

R. J. Reynolds of Winston-Salem, North Carolina, exported cigarettes to 160 countries and territories.[49] The company observed more than 1,400 different product codes covering its various brands in all markets. For its leading brand, Winston, the company needed more than 250 different packages to satisfy different brand styles and foreign government requirements. The U.S. package design was used for fewer than six markets. Differences were due to various regulations on health warnings. In Australia, the number of cigarettes contained in a package had to be printed on the package front. Some countries such as Canada require bilingual text. To avoid errors in the printing process when working with alphabets as diverse as Greek, Arabic, or Japanese, replicas of the original package were prepared in the foreign market and forwarded for production to the United States.

Specific packaging decisions affected are size, shape, materials, color, and text.[50] Size may differ by custom or by existing standards such as metric and nonmetric requirements. Higher-income countries tend to require larger unit sizes, since these populations shop less frequently and can afford to buy larger quantities each time. In countries with lower income levels, consumers buy in smaller quantities and more often. Gillette, the world's largest producer of razor blades, sells products in packages of five or ten in the United States and Europe, whereas singles are sold in some developing countries.

Packages can assume almost any shape, largely depending on customs and traditions of each market. Materials used for packaging can also differ widely. Whereas Americans prefer to buy mayonnaise and mustard in glass containers, consumers in Germany and Switzerland buy these same products in tubes. Cans are the customary material to package beer in the United States, whereas most European countries prefer glass bottles. The package color and text have to be integrated into a company's promotional strategy and therefore may be subject to specific tailoring by country. The promotional effect is of great

49. ''Tobacco Companies Face Special International Packaging Obstacles,'' *Marketing News,* February 4, 1984, p. 20.

50. Philip Kotler, *Marketing Management,* 8th ed. (Englewood Cliffs, N.J.: Prentice Hall, 1994), p. 458.

importance for consumer goods and has led some companies to attempt to standardize their packaging in color and layout. In areas such as Europe or Latin America, where the consumers frequently travel to other countries, standarized colors help identify a product quickly. This strategy depends on devising a set of colors or a layout with an appeal beyond one single culture or market. An example of a company pursuing a standardized package color is Procter & Gamble, the U.S. manufacturer of the leading detergent, Tide. The orange and white box familiar to millions of U.S. consumers can be found in many foreign markets, even though the package text may appear in the language or print of the given country.

As consumers and governments become more concerned about the environmental consequences of excess or inappropriate packaging, companies are expected to develop packaging that is environmentally friendly. Responding to consumer concern, the U.K. retailer Gainsbury examines every product it sells to ensure each uses only the minimum packaging necessary.[51]

Managing a Global Product Line

In early sections of this chapter, we covered decisions about individual products in detail. Most companies, however, manufacture or sell a multitude of products; some, such as General Electric, produce as many as 200,000 different items. To facilitate marketing operations, companies group these items into product groups consisting of several product lines. Each product line is made up of several individual items of close similarity. Quaker Oats organized its European operation into four pan-European business groups: pet food, cereals, Gatorade, and corn oil. The pan-European approach was designed to increase efficiency and take advantage of the single European market.[52]

A company with several product lines is faced with the decision to select those most appropriate for international marketing. As with each individual product or decision, the firm can either offer an identical line in its home market and abroad or, if circumstances demand, make appropriate changes. In most cases, a firm would look at the individual items within a product line and assess marketability on a product-by-product basis. As a result, the product lines abroad are frequently characterized by a narrower width than those found in a company's domestic market.

The circumstances for deletions from product lines vary, but some reasons dominate. Lack of sufficient market size is a frequently mentioned reason. Companies with their home base in large markets such as the United States, Japan, or Germany will find sufficient demand in their home markets for even the smallest market segments, justifying additional product variations and greater depth in their lines. Abroad, opportunities for

51. ''Keeping It to a Minimum,'' *Financial Times,* May 28, 1992, Special section: Packaging and the Environment, p. 5.
52. ''Quaker as a Europhile,'' *Advertising Age,* August 26, 1991, p. 26.

such segmentation strategies may not exist because the individual segments may be too small to warrant commercial exploitation. Lack of market sophistication is another factor in product line variation. Aside from the top twenty developed markets, many markets are less sophisticated and their stage of development may not demand some of the most advanced items in a product line. And finally, new product introduction strategies can impact product lines abroad. For most companies, new products are first introduced in their home markets and introduced abroad only after the product has been successful at home. As a result, the lag in extending new products to foreign markets also contributes toward a product line configuration that differs from that of the firm's domestic market.

Firms confronted with deletions in their product lines sometimes add specialized offerings to fill the gap in the line, either by producing a more suitable product or by developing an entirely new product that may not have any application outside a specific market. Such a strategy can only be pursued by a firm with adequate research and development strength in its foreign subsidiaries.

Exploiting Product Life Cycles

The existence of product life cycles immediately opens opportunities to the international firm but, on the other hand, poses additional hurdles that may complicate product strategy. Experience has shown that products do not always occupy the same position on the product life cycle curve in different countries.

New products receiving initial introduction in the world's developed markets tend to move into later life cycle stages before those in countries that receive the product at a later date. As shown in Figure 10.2, it is possible for a product to be in different stages of the product life cycle in different countries. Other countries follow, usually each according to its own stage of economic development. Consequently, although a product may be offered and produced worldwide, it is common for a product to range over several stages in the product life cycle at any point in time. The principal opportunity offered to the firm is the chance to extend product growth by expanding into new markets to compensate for declining growth rates in mature markets. A risk arises when a company enters new markets or countries too fast, before the local market is ready to absorb the new product. To avoid such pitfalls and to take advantage of long-term opportunities, international companies may follow several strategies.

During the introductory phase, a product may have to be debugged and refined. This job can best be handled in the originating market or in a country close to company research and development centers. Also, the marketing approach will have to be refined. At this stage, the market in even the more advanced countries is relatively small, and demand in countries with lower levels of economic development will hardly be commercially exploitable. Therefore, the introductory stage will be limited to the advanced markets, often the company's domestic market.

Once the product has been fully developed and a larger group of buyers has become interested, volume will increase substantially. Domestic marketing policies foresee price decreases due to volume gains and to the entry of new competitors, with an expansion of the entire market. At this stage, many firms start to investigate opportunities elsewhere by

FIGURE 10.2 ● Possible Product Life Cycle for a Product in Different Countries

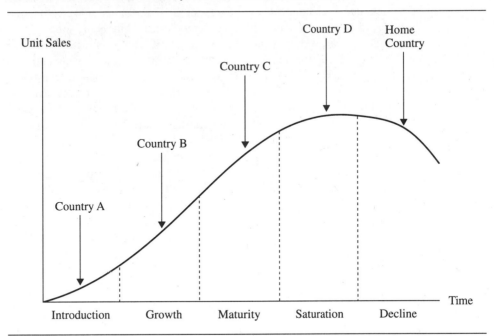

introducing the product in selective markets, where it would be in the introductory phase. This requires some adaptation of communication strategy to parallel earlier efforts in the home market, as the approach designed for the second phase, the growth stage, cannot be used. In the late 1980s and early 1990s, U.S. white goods manufacturers faced a mature market in the States, with a decline in total volume. This has led Whirlpool, GE, Hoover, and Maytag to enter the European market, which is expected to grow with the unification of western Europe and the development of eastern Europe.[53]

Bicycles are a product category that has remained in different stages of its life cycle in various countries. Of the world's 800 million bicycles, some 300 million are owned by the Chinese, up from 200 million only ten years ago. Another 45 million are owned by Indians. In China, a two-bicycle family may have as much status as a two-car family in wealthier western nations. As a result, bicycles are still in the growth phase in China but hardly are in the same category in industrialized nations.[54]

A product facing life cycle decline may be withdrawn in stages, similar to its

53. "The Deal Steps Up the U.S. Group's Drive into Europe, the Final Link in Whirlpool's Global Circle," *Financial Times,* June 7, 1991, p. 12.
54. "Pedal Power," *Economist,* January 20, 1990, p. 71.

introduction. The most advanced countries will see such a withdrawal earlier than some of the less developed markets. Volkswagen, the German automaker, offers an example of how an old design may still sell in some countries while being long gone in others. Its famous Beetle car, originally introduced in the 1930s, has been withdrawn from production everywhere but Mexico. There the Beetle remains the best-selling car and helps make VW a leading car producer. The model has been adapted for modern environmental requirements but comes only in a simple version without extras or options. The car is priced at $5,300, and the company has pledged to keep the price pegged to rises in the minimum wage. As a result, VW obtained some important tax relief.[55] Beetles still account for two-thirds of the VW's Mexican output.[56]

Stahel & Koeng, a Swiss-based maker of weaving loom shuttles, is one of the few remaining companies still supplying wooden shuttles. Modern weaving machines all are shuttleless, with annual production of some 50,000 machines compared to the 13,000 older types still produced. The company still produces some 100,000 shuttles, most of those exported to Third World countries. The old-style looms are only produced in Asia, as production in industrialized countries has shifted to the newer looms. The company has been diversifying into other products to plan for what is expected to be a limited demand for another fifteen years.[57]

As we have seen, a product cannot automatically be assumed to reach the various stages in its life cycle simultaneously in all countries; thus, flexibility in marketing strategy is required. To introduce a product abroad in stages represents a strategic decision in itself, as described later in this chapter. Though typical, the phased introduction to foreign markets may not always be in the best interest of the firm, as it may offer competitors a chance to expand locally.

Warranty and Service Policies

Buyers around the world, as do domestic consumers, expect more than just the physical benefits of a product. Clients purchase products with certain performance expectations and in their purchase choice will consider company policies for backing promises. As a result, warranties and service policies have to be considered as an integral aspect of a company's international product strategy. Companies interested in doing business abroad frequently find themselves at a disadvantage with local competitors in the area of warranties and service. With the supplier's plant often thousands of miles away, foreign buyers sometimes

55. "Miss the VW Bug? It Lives Beyond the Rio Grande," *New York Times,* October 20, 1990, p. 2.

56. "VW's Humble Hunch-back Makes a Comeback in Mexico," *Financial Times,* October 23, 1990, p. 8.

57. "Hinwiler Webschuetzen mit grosser Tradition," *Neue Zuercher Zeitung,* August 15, 1990, p. 49.

want extra assurance that the supplier will back the product. Thus, a comprehensive warranty and service policy can become a very important marketing tool for international companies.

Product Warranties

A company must address its warranty policy for international markets either by declaring its domestic warranty valid worldwide or by tailoring warranties to specific countries or markets. Although declaring worldwide warranty with uniform performance standards would be administratively simple, local market conditions often dictate a differentiated approach. In the United States, most computer manufacturers sell their equipment with a thirty- or sixty-day warranty, whereas twelve months is more typical in Europe or Japan.

Aside from the two technical decisions as to what standards should be covered under a warranty and for how long, a company would be well advised to consider the type of actual product use. If buyers in a foreign market subject the product to more stress or abuse, some shortening of the warranty period may become necessary. A company may be able to change product design to allow for different standard performance requirements. In developing countries, where technical sophistication is below North American or European standards, maintenance may not be adequate, causing more frequent equipment breakdowns. Another important factor is local competition. Since an attractive warranty policy can be helpful in obtaining sales, a firm's warranty policy should be in line with that of other firms competing in the local market.

Just how important international product warranty expectations have become is demonstrated by the experience of Perrier, the French bottled water company. In February 1990, the company had to withdraw its Perrier water from U.S. retail stores after the product was found to contain benzine above the legal limit. This U.S. test result triggered similar tests by health authorities in other countries. Soon Perrier had to withdraw its products in other countries, eventually resulting in a worldwide brand recall. This illustrates the interdependence of many products in today's open and accessible markets. Failure to maintain quality, service, or performance in one country can rapidly have a negative impact in other areas.[58]

Product Service

No warranty will be believable unless backed with an effective service organization. Although important to the consumer, service is even more crucial to the industrial buyer, since any breakdown of equipment or product is apt to cause substantial economic loss. This risk has led industrial buyers to be conservative in their choice of products, always carefully analyzing the supplier's ability to provide service in case of need.

To provide the required level of service outside the company's home base poses

58. "Brit Helps Perrier Move Beyond the Recall Crisis," *Advertising Age,* November 12, 1990, p. 54.

special problems for international companies. The selection of an organization to perform the service is an important decision. Ideally, company personnel are preferable since they tend to be better trained. However, this can only be organized economically if the installed base of the market is large enough to justify such an investment. In cases where a company does not maintain its own sales subsidiary, it is generally more efficient to turn to an independent service company or to a local distributor. To have adequate services via independent distributors requires extra training for the service technician, usually at the manufacturer's expense. In any case, the selection of an appropriate service organization should be made so that fully trained service personnel are readily available within the customary time frame for the particular market.

Closely related to any satisfactory service policy is an adequate inventory for spare parts. Because service often means replacing some parts, the company must place sufficient inventory of spare parts within reach of its markets. Whether this inventory is maintained in regional warehouses or through sales susbidiaries and distributors depends on the volume and the required reaction time for service calls. Buyers will generally want to know how the manufacturer plans to organize service before making substantial commitments.

Firms that demonstrate serious interest in a market by committing to their own sales subsidiaries are often at an advantage over firms using distributors. One German truck manufacturer that recently entered the U.S. market advertised the fact that "97 percent of all spare parts are kept in local inventory," thus assuring prospective buyers that they can get spares readily. In some instances, the difficulty with service outlets may even influence a company's market entry strategy. This was the case with Fujitsu, a Japanese manufacturer of electronic office equipment. By combining forces with TRW Inc., a U.S.-based company, Fujitsu was able to sell its office equipment in the U.S. market with the extensive service organization of TRW.

Since the guarantee of reliable and efficient service is such an important aspect of a firm's entire product strategy, investment in service centers at times must be made before any sales can take place. In this case, service costs must be viewed as an investment in future volume rather than as a recurring expense.

Marketing Services Globally

In 1992, international trade in services increased to about $1 trillion worldwide. The United States was by far the world's leading service exporter, with an annual volume of $162 billion; this represented some 38 percent of total U.S. exports. Japan had the largest service trade deficit of $48 billion.[59] International trade in services today ranges from banking to insurance, credit cards, consulting, advertising agencies, accounting, law, shipping, and even entertainment services.

59. "Trade in Services," *Economist,* January 29, 1994, p. 113.

Decisions about marketing services are related to the structure of the service itself. A firm has to decide which service to sell or offer and how the service should be designed. Again the issue of standardization needs to be addressed, although there are fewer opportunities for economies of scale by standardizing services worldwide. A company needs to decide on the content of the service it wants to offer and the manner in which the service is to be performed or consumed. Business services tend to be more standardized, and more in demand worldwide, because the needs of companies are more uniform than those of individual consumers. To a much greater degree, personal services are subject to cultural and social influences and exhibit a greater need for tailoring to local circumstances.

Business Services

The services aimed at business buyers that are most likely to be exported are those that have already met with success. The experience of U.S.-based service companies can be used as an example. Some of the services most successfully marketed abroad include financial services. Commercial banks such as Citibank, Chase Manhattan, and Bank of America have built extensive branch networks around the world, to the extent that foreign deposits and profits make up nearly half of business volume. Advertising agencies have also expanded overseas either by building branch networks or by merging with local agencies.[60] Similar strategies were followed by accounting and management consulting firms. More recently, many U.S.-based marketing research firms have expanded into foreign countries.

Opportunities for New Service Firms

Just as the U.S. economy is slowly moving to become a service economy, similar trends can be found in the economies of other developed countries in western Europe and Japan. Many types of services are in great demand abroad. For example, the international courier service is an area where several companies are vying for global positions. U.S.-based Federal Express built up its overseas business by buying Flying Tiger, the largest international cargo airline, and merging it with FedEx's international small documents and parcel service.[61] Federal Express had international revenues of $1 billion, or about 20 percent of the total. However, building up its courier service worldwide resulted in tremendous losses.[62] To recover, Federal Express scaled back operations from 125 to 16 cities in Europe and reduced the European work force from 9,200 to 2,600.[63]

Another major company in the small parcels business with global ambitions is United Parcel Service (UPS), which is using its considerable cash flow from U.S. operations to

60. Arnold K. Weinstein, ''The International Expansion of U.S. Multinational Advertising Agencies,'' *MSU Business Topics,* Summer 1974, pp. 29–35.

61. ''A Fragile Air Freight Strategy,'' *New York Times,* September 6, 1989, p. D1.

62. ''Is Federal Express an Innocent Abroad?'' *Business Week,* April 2, 1990, p. 34.

63. ''Federal Express to Trim European Operations,'' *New York Times,* March 18, 1992, p. D20.

build its international network. It took UPS some twelve years to build its German operation to 6,000 employees. To help its overseas strategy, UPS acquired several local courier companies in various countries, resulting in acquisitions costing almost $100 million.[64] UPS, however, grew its business in Europe slower than did Federal Express and was able to learn during the process. In 1992, UPS bought Star Air Parcel Service in Vienna, which will provide a gateway to eastern Europe. The company is supporting its service in thirteen countries with a pan-European media program, which includes TV spots on CNN and ITV in the United Kingdom.[65]

International accounting and consulting services are an area that saw tremendous growth in the 1980s. Major firms started to think in global terms and to expand their operations into many markets. Among the leading accounting firms, international revenue typically was larger than domestic (or U.S.) revenue. Several firms merged, so the former ''Big 8'' are now down to six.[66] Ernst & Whinney merged with Arthur Young because of the latter firm's strong international network. Peat Marwick merged with KMG, a company that was traditionally strong in Europe. Overseas expansion is important to these U.S.-based firms because revenue is growing faster abroad and margins are also better for international business. Furthermore, many of the firm's accounting clients have recently gone through globalization themselves and demand different services. Finally, the liberalization of trade in Europe under the 1992 initiative has also boosted cross-national business and mergers.

Such international mergers also create their own challenges. KPMG Peat Marwick McLintock was formed in 1987 through a merger of Peat Marwick Mitchell and KMG Thompson McLintock. The KPMG initials stand for Klynveld Peat Marwick Goerdeler. The KPMG abbreviation was to become the firm's distinctive logo or brand name. This abbreviation typically appeared before the local name of the firm's local company, such as KPMG Deutsche Treuhand in Germany. The company had difficulty in making the KPMG part a consistent brand to the financial community wherever the firm operated. International clients had a tendency to look upon the firm as KPMG, but local clients tended to associate more with the older local name of the various local operating firms, such as Treuhand in Germany.[67]

Big British and U.S. law firms are also finding numerous opportunities overseas. The unification of Europe has accelerated cross-border mergers and acquisitions. The growth of the European Union in Brussels has created a demand for lawyers to lobby the EU, and privatization of many businesses in eastern Europe has created a legal gold mine. While France and Japan have established local requirements to slow down the growth of British and U.S. firms in their countries, the legal profession will become another global service industry in the late 1990s.[68]

64. ''Mr. Smith Goes Global,'' *Business Week,* April 2, 1990, p. 69.
65. ''European Courier Dogfight Looms,'' *Advertising Age International,* April 27, 1992, p. I-6.
66. ''The Partners Revolt at Peat Marwick,'' *New York Times,* November 18, 1990, section 3, p. 1.
67. ''KPMG or Not to Be,'' *Financial Times,* November 8, 1990, p. 10.
68. ''Courts Go Global,'' *Economist,* July 18, 1992, Survey—Legal profession, p. 6.

Selling Technology Overseas

Some companies have switched from selling products to selling technology. One company that has achieved considerable success in this area is Kawasaki Steel, one of the largest steel producers in Japan.[69] Faced with a stagnant market at home and with growing reluctance by foreign governments to increase Japanese steel imports, Kawasaki turned to its eight hundred scientists and engineers to produce better steel more efficiently. This effort led to substantial cost savings at Japanese plants while tempting foreign steel operators to purchase the technology. A specially organized division composed of engineering and marketing experts began exporting this know-how. The company had engineers who could engage in a one-shot technical consulting assignment or furnish an entire turnkey plant. Other engineers were available to help important steel users, such as builders of pipelines, off-shore platforms, and shipping berths around the world. Kawasaki was not concerned about exporting technology as long as its own engineers and scientists continued to develop the new techniques. Since bringing a new steel mill on stream took years, its own scientists were expected to have advanced beyond currently installed technology. Similar opportunities were pursued by other Japanese steel manufacturers and by other companies all over the world.

United Breweries of Denmark, brewers of Carlsberg and Tuborg beer, started to exploit opportunities for selling brewing technology to those markets to which the company would have had great difficulty exporting beer.[70] The company formed Danbrew Consult Ltd. in 1970 to sell its brewing process know-how around the world. Even large U.S. breweries, such as Philip Morris's Miller brewery, have availed themselves of Danbrew's services. The company believed that in some markets it could make more money selling services and technology than marketing beer.

Services for Consumers and Individual Households

Marketing services to consumers turns out to be more difficult than selling to industrial users. Since consumer purchasing and usage patterns between countries differ to a greater degree than industry usage patterns do, many services have to be adapted to local conditions to make them successful. The U.S.-based fast-food chains were some of the first consumer service companies to pursue foreign opportunities. McDonald's, Kentucky Fried Chicken, Dairy Queen, and many others opened restaurants in Europe and Asia in large numbers.[71]

Though success came eventually, initial results were disappointing for McDonald's

69. "Kawasaki Steel: Using Technology as a Tool to Bolster Exports," *Business Week,* January 29, 1979, p. 119.

70. "Denmark's United Breweries Prospers by Selling Its Expertise as Well as Beer," *Wall Street Journal,* February 16, 1984, p. 40.

71. Donald Hackett, "The International Expansion of the U.S. Franchise Systems: Status and Strategies," *Journal of International Business Studies,* Spring 1976, pp. 65–76.

in Europe. The company had anticipated differences in taste by serving wine in France, beer in Munich and Stockholm, and tea in England, where the company also lowered the sugar content of its buns by 4 percent. But McDonald's based its first store locations on U.S. criteria and moved into the suburbs and along highways. When volume did not develop according to expectations, McDonald's quickly moved into the inner cities. Once this initial problem had been overcome, McDonald's grew very quickly abroad. In 1985, international revenue accounted for 24 percent of revenue, but by 1992 it had grown to almost 50 percent.[72] Although some local food variations have been allowed, the company operates using the same standardized manual worldwide, indoctrinating all of its franchise operations abroad with the same type of operating culture.[73]

Insurance companies have found significant opportunities in emerging markets. For example, in Shanghai, China, the American International Group (AIG) sold more than 12,000 policies in eight months. While it took AIG over ten years to get licensed in China, the company feels the opportunities are tremendous.[74]

Even producers of films for U.S. television have come to court foreign buyers.[75] In 1970, exports of U.S.-made television movies, serials, and full-length motion pictures shown on television amounted to $97 million. By 1980, sales had reached $365 million, an increase of more than 300 percent. Britain, Canada, Japan, Australia, and Brazil were believed to be the major customers. The only hurdle so far has been government quotas. In England, only 14 percent of daily airtime can go to imports; other countries enforce similar limitations. However, as governments abroad have begun to tolerate more competition, independently owned stations are being opened in many countries. This greatly increases the demand for imported programming. In Italy for instance, independent commercial television was not allowed until recently. Suddenly, fifty stations opened in Rome alone, all looking for attractive programming.

Conclusions

To be successful in foreign markets, companies need to be flexible in product and service offerings. Although a given product may have been very successful in a firm's home market, environmental differences can often force the company to make unexpected or costly changes. While a small group of products may be marketed worldwide without significant changes, most companies will find that success abroad depends on a willingness to adapt to local market requirements. Additional efforts are frequently required in product support services to assure foreign clients that the company will stand behind its products.

72. "Overseas Sizzle for McDonald's," *New York Times,* April 17, 1992, p. D1.
73. "McWorld?" *Business Week,* December 13, 1986, p. 78.
74. "AIG Sells Insurance in Shanghai, Testing Service Firms' Role," *Wall Street Journal,* July 21, 1993, pp. 1, A-9.
75. "American T.V. Abroad," *New York Times,* January 18, 1981, p. F-18.

For companies that successfully master the additional international difficulties while showing a commitment to foreign clients, success abroad can lead to increased profits and more secure market positions domestically.

Questions for Discussion

1. Generalize about the overall need for product adaptations for consumer products versus for high-technology industrial products. What differences exist? Why?

2. Which one of the factors in Table 10.1 would be of particular importance for a company such as GMC (trucks) as opposed to Atari (electronics)?

3. What are the major reasons for a company to have a worldwide brand name?

4. Under what circumstances would using different brand names in different countries be advisable?

5. Are there any differences between the international marketing of services and the international marketing of products?

For Further Reading

Ayal, Igal. "International Product Life Cycle: A Reassessment and Product Implications." *Journal of Marketing,* Fall 1981, pp. 91–96.

Bartels, Robert. "Are Domestic and International Marketing Dissimilar?" *Journal of Marketing,* July 1968, pp. 56–61.

Britt, Stewart H. "Standardizing Marketing for the International Market." *Columbia Journal of World Business,* Winter 1974, pp. 39–45.

Davidson, William H., and Richard Harrigan. "Key Decisions in International Marketing: Introducing New Products Abroad." *Columbia Journal of World Business,* Winter 1977, pp. 15–23.

Hill, John S., and Richard R. Still. "Adapting Products to LDC Tastes." *Harvard Business Review,* March–April 1984, pp. 92–101.

Jones, Barry, and Roger Ramsden. "The Global Brand Age." *Management Today,* September 1991, pp. 78–80.

Kelz, Andreas, and Brian Block. "Global Branding: Why and How?" *Industrial Management & Data Systems,* 93, no. 4 (1993), pp. 11–17.

Levitt, Theodore. "Globalization of Markets." *Harvard Business Review,* May–June 1983, pp. 92–102.

McCarthy, Michael. "Task Forces: P&G Heads Toward Global Branding." *Adweek,* April 19, 1993, pp. 1, 8.

Samiee, Saeed, and Kendall Roth. "The Influence of Global Marketing Standardization on Performance." *Journal of Marketing,* April 1992, pp. 1–17.

Samli, A. Coskun, and Rustan Kosanko. "Support Service Is the Key for Technology Transfer to China." *Industrial Marketing Management,* April 1982, pp. 95–103.

Sorenson, Ralph Z., and Ulrich E. Wiechmann. "How Multinationals View Marketing Standardization." *Harvard Business Review,* May–June 1975.

11

Developing New Products for Global Markets

● **IN CHAPTER 10,** *we focused on individual product decisions. Here we concentrate on the strategic issues of product design and development for international and global markets (see Figure 11.1). Following an analysis of the standardization versus adaptation issue, the first segment of this chapter covers a series of alternatives involving product extension, adaptation, and innovation strategies. Included is a segment on global products that deals with the complexities of designing products for many markets simultaneously. The second part of the chapter is devoted to product development strategies for international companies. Emphasis is on organizational issues, sources, and approaches that will enhance a firm's ability to innovate in a changing marketplace. We conclude the chapter with a section on the process of new product introductions.*

International Product Strategies[1]

The purpose of this section is to outline the basic product strategies a firm may select and to demonstrate their close relationship with a company's communication policy, particularly with respect to advertising.

1. This section is based on Warren J. Keegan, ''Multinational Product Planning: Strategic Alternatives,'' *Journal of Marketing,* January 1969, pp. 58–62.

FIGURE 11.1 ● International and Global Product Development Strategies

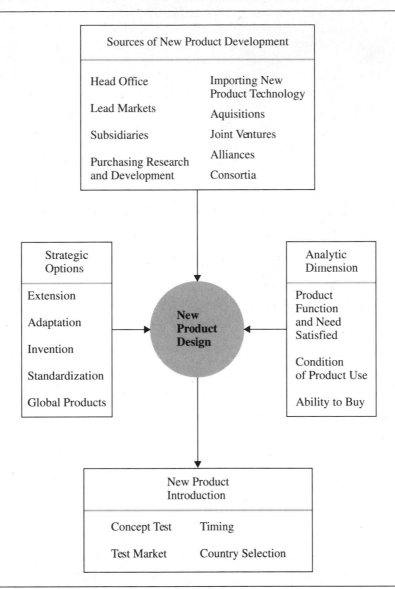

Analytic Issues: Standardization Versus Adaptation

A company's decision to pursue a specific product strategy primarily depends on three factors: (1) whether the product function or the need satisfied is the same or different in a new market, (2) whether particular conditions surrounding product use can affect company strategy; and (3) whether target market customers are financially able to buy the product. These three factors greatly influence the product strategy chosen. We will examine them in some detail before we turn to a company's strategic options.

Product Function, or the Need Satisfied   The key to the product function factor is the role the product plays in a given market. Although certain types of products may be consumed by individuals in many countries, a company cannot automatically assume that the underlying motivation to purchase is identical. Take, for example, the difference between Americans and Russians with respect to purchasing and wearing T-shirts and blue jeans. In the United States, T-shirts and jeans convey an informal attitude toward clothing and a lack of interest in any status that clothing may convey. In fact, by dressing this way, Americans give the appearance of wanting to be ordinary rather than stand out. In Russia the opposite is true. Because real blue jeans and T-shirts are in short supply, those who wear such clothing signal to society that they are aware of current fashions and are highly status conscious. In Russia, jeans and T-shirts clearly separate the individual from the rest of society. Thus, the rationale for buying them is different in these two countries and appears quite contradictory.

On the other hand, products for industrial use, such as plant machinery, are purchased the world over for the same intention or reason. Therefore, very little difference in product function or satisfied need is expected. Also, many examples of consumer goods can be pointed to for which the need to be satisfied is identical. For one, the motivation behind the purchase of razor blades is homogeneous across countries and cultures.

Differences in product function or satisfied need, even when present, do not necessarily call for a change in product design or features. The primary focus here is on the buyer and the motivation that triggers a purchase. As a psychological concept, motivation requires a corresponding response. Therefore, dissimilar purchasing motives require unique communications responses, or a change in a firm's advertising, to relate the product to these different motives.

Conditions of Product Use   Physical environmental variables combine into a physical event that determines the salient factors surrounding a product's actual use. To the extent that these events are identical within any two countries, a product may be marketed without any changes or alterations. The conditions of product use reflect the actual use or consumption of a product regardless of the motivation that triggered its purchase. In seeking opportunities for product standardization, marketers must consider the physical events surrounding product use that substantially determine the viability of the strategy.

Ability to Buy   Although purchasing power is generally not an issue in the developed countries of Europe, North America, and Asia, there are, nevertheless, hundreds of millions of potential customers in countries that simply do not have the economic resources found in more affluent markets. In such countries, the motivation to purchase a product and actual use conditions may be identical to those in affluent societies, but the products used to satisfy these demands are beyond the price that buyers can afford. Such situations may require an entirely different strategy. For example, the product can be changed so that it can be made available at a substantially lower price. Thus, substantial differences in the nature of the economic event can have a significant influence on international product strategy. General Motors' attempt to market its basic transportation vehicle (BTV) in developing countries serves as an excellent example. By sacrificing comfort, style, and performance, GM designed the BTV at costs substantially below those of traditional cars.[2]

Advantages of Product Standardization   Complete standardization of product design results in a substantial saving of production and research and development costs and will allow a company to take full advantage of economies of scale. Often, several markets can be supplied from a regional or central manufacturing plant with efficient and long production runs. Aside from these obvious advantages, production sharing and simultaneously supplying markets from several plants are important factors that support standardized output. Managers in the U.S. subsidiary of Liebherr, a large German company producing construction machinery, decided to make some changes in the basic design of an excavator that was made to identical specifications elsewhere in Europe and Latin America. To make the excavator more acceptable to U.S. customers, the Virginia-based subsidiary enlarged the fuel tank and strengthened the undercarriage. When U.S. sales dropped in the recession of 1974–1975, the company accumulated a substantial inventory of excavators. However, it could not help its European plants, filled with back orders, because of the difference in design. Obviously, the advantages gained from adaptation have to be compared to the overall loss in manufacturing flexibility.[3]

Despite the advantages of economies of scale, few companies can fully standardize their products for the many markets they serve. To bridge the gap between various local adaptations and the need to standardize some components, some international firms have moved to a new breed of products, the global product, which we will discuss later in the chapter.

Three Strategic Choices: Extension, Adaptation, Invention

A company can follow one of three basic strategies when moving into a foreign market. With respect to both its product and its communications policy, the firm can opt for an *extension* strategy, basically adopting the same approach as in its home market. The strategy of *adaptation* requires some changes to fit the new market requirements. When an entirely new approach is required, the company can adopt the strategy of *invention*. These three basic strategies can be further refined into the five strategies shown in Table 11.1 and explained in the following sections.

Strategy One: Product Extension—Communications Extension   One extension strategy calls for marketing a standardized product with the same communications strategy across the globe. Although this strategy has considerable attraction because of its cost effectiveness, it is rarely realizable for consumer products. The few exceptions include companies

2. Harvard Business School, *"General Motors Malaysia Adm. Bhd.,"* Case no. 9-574-065, HBS Case Services, Boston, Mass., 1974/1981.
3. "It's Tough Digging in the U.S.," *Fortune,* August 11, 1980, p. 146.

TABLE 11.1 ● International Product Strategies

Strategy	Product function or need satisfied	Conditions of product use	Ability to buy product	Recommended product strategy	Recommended communications strategy	Rank order from least to most expensive	Product examples
1	Same	Same	Yes	Extension	Extension	1	Soft drinks
2	Different	Same	Yes	Extension	Adaptation	2	Bicycles, motorscooters
3	Same	Different	Yes	Adaptation	Extension	3	Gasoline, detergents
4	Different	Different	Yes	Adaptation	Adaptation	4	Clothing, greeting cards
5	Same	—	No	Invention	Develop new communications	5	Hand-powered washing machines

Source: From Warren J. Keegan, ''Multinational Product Planning: Strategic Alternatives.'' Reprinted from *Journal of Marketing,* vol. 33, January 1969, pp. 58–62, published by the American Marketing Association.

in the soft drink industry and some luxury goods firms. Industrial products, with a greater homogeneity of buyers internationally, offer a somewhat greater opportunity for this strategy, but again the extension strategy is far from the norm.

   The cost effectiveness of this strategy should not be underestimated. Product adaptations entail additional research and development expenses and tooling costs, and they do not allow economies of scale to the extent possible under an extension strategy. Though less substantial, savings from the creation of only one communications strategy should also be considered. In any case, decision-makers should consider the anticipated impact on demand in the foreign market if the product is not fully suited to local tastes or preferences, as well as the potential savings. Past experience shows that rigidly enforcing a product and communication extension policy can lead to disaster and therefore should only be adopted if all requirements with respect to product function, need, use condition, and ability to buy are met.

Strategy Two: Product Extension—Communications Adaptations   When the sociocultural event surrounding product consumption differs from country to country but the use conditions as part of the physical event are identical, the same product can be marketed with a change in the communication strategy. Examples can be found among bicycle and motorcycle manufacturers. In the developing countries of Asia, Africa, and Latin America, a bicycle or motorcycle is primarily a means of transportation, whereas the same products are used in sports or for recreation purposes in the United States. This strategy is still quite cost effective, since communications adaptation represents a low-cost approach to tailoring a product to a local market.

Strategy Three: Product Adaptation—Communications Extension Strategy three is appropriate when the physical event surrounding product use varies but the sociocultural event is the same as in the company's home market. Although changes in a product are substantially more costly than changes in the communications approach, a company will follow this course when the product otherwise may not sell in a foreign market. In some cases, product formulations may be changed without the consumer knowing it, as with detergents and gasoline, so that the product can function under different environmental circumstances.

Strategy Four: Product Adaptation—Communications Adaptation When both the physical and sociocultural events vary, a strategy of dual adaptation is generally favored. To make this strategy profitable, however, the foreign market or markets need to be of sufficient volume to justify the costs of dual adaptation. Nike, a leading U.S. manufacturer of running shoes, soon found that its continued growth in Europe could not be built on jogging shoes alone. In Europe, jogging never developed to the extent it did in the United States. By far the largest sports shoe category in Europe was soccer, prompting Nike to design a shoe specifically for that market. To market the new product, Nike developed a unique promotional campaign that took into consideration the dominating positions of Adidas and Puma in the soccer shoe segment.[4] As Campbell Soup entered overseas markets, it found that tastes differed from market to market. While U.S. products such as cream of mushroom and cream of chicken were successful in some markets, watercress and duck gizzard soup was successful in China.[5]

Strategy Five: Product Invention When the ability to purchase a product is generally missing, some companies have elected to invent an entirely new product, usually by redesigning the original product to a lower level of complexity. As a result, a substantially cheaper product leads to more purchases. An example was the strategy followed by Philips, the Dutch multinational corporation. In response to the desire of many developing countries to own their own television manufacturing plants, the Dutch company redesigned its equipment and tools to suit the volume requirements of some of the world's poorest countries. The molding machines used in its European plants to produce TV cabinets cost about $150,000, an amount justified by a factory output of about 100,000 units per year. But many African countries could only support plants with an average annual output of 3,000 to 5,000 sets. By borrowing from existing technology found in automobile dashboard manufacturing, Philips eventually invented a press that cost only $2,150.[6]

Global Products

In response to the pressure for cost reduction and considering the relatively few opportunities for producing completely standardized products, many firms have moved to the

4. "Fitting the World in Sports Shoes," *Business Week,* January 25, 1982, p. 73.
5. "Campbell: Now It's M-M-Global," *Business Week,* March 15, 1993, p. 53.
6. *Wall Street Journal,* February 27, 1981.

creation of a *global product.* The global product, based on the acknowledged fact that only a portion of the final design can be standarized, builds on flexibility to tailor the end product to the needs of individual markets. This represents a move to standardize as much as possible those areas involving common components or parts. This modularized approach has become of particular importance in the automobile industry, where both U.S. and European manufacturers are moving toward the creation of world components to combat growing Japanese competitiveness.

One of the first world cars was introduced by Ford during the 1981 model year. Ford's Escort model was simultaneously assembled in the United States, Great Britain, and Germany from parts produced in ten countries. The U.S.-assembled Escort contained parts made in Japan, Spain, Brazil, Britain, Italy, France, Mexico, Taiwan, and West Germany.[7] The European assembly plants, in return, bought automatic transmissions from a U.S. plant. Ford was estimated to have saved engineering and development costs amounting to hundreds of millions of dollars because the design standardized engines, transmissions, and ancillary systems for heating, air conditioning, wheels, and seats.[8] Still, the U.S. and European Escorts were two very different cars.

The second generation of global products was started in 1981, the year the first original Escort rolled off the line, to be ready for production in 1991. With a budget of some two billion dollars, Ford designed its second-generation Escort with Mazda, the Japanese car manufacturer partly owned by Ford. The design was done by Ford engineers in the United States, with the engineering and manufacturing planning performed by the Japanese engineers at Mazda. This new model was planned for assembly in twelve different locations where Ford sells the car under its Escort name, while Mazda uses its various brand names (the 323, Protege, or Familia).

Ford's strategy was driven by the fact that product development duplication was a very costly process amounting to billions of dollars per new model. By pooling development resources, Ford was estimated to have saved as much as one billion dollars in development costs.[9]

Ford's latest global car is the Mondeo (called Contour in the United States), launched in 1993 in Europe and 1994 in the United States. Ford invested six billion dollars in the development of the new model, which includes research and development as well as two new assembly plants and four new engine plants. Ford expects to gain significant economies of scale by selling 700,000 cars a year.[10] Also, given the potential market, Ford could afford to invest significant R&D on the new suspension system.[11] While initial sales in Europe were strong, Ford will not be able to measure the success of the new car until 1995 or 1996.

As Ford was moving toward common designs for markets on three continents, some

7. *New York Times,* November 9, 1980.
8. ''Ford's Financial Hurdle,'' *Business Week,* February 2, 1981, p. 66.
9. ''How Ford and Mazda Shared the Driver's Seat,'' *Business Week,* March 26, 1990, p. 94.
10. ''Ford Mondaine or Mundane,'' *Economist,* January 8, 1993, pp. 92–94.
11. Alex Taylor III, ''Ford's $6 Billion Baby,'' *Fortune,* June 28, 1993, pp. 76–81.

Japanese car companies were moving in the opposite direction. Honda has steadily added to its development and design function in North America. Its new Honda Accord station wagon introduced in 1990 was developed from the standard Accord power train in the United States and built only in its U.S. factory. The model was exported to Japan and elsewhere.[12]

Toyota launched a new version of its popular Camry in 1991. Three inches wider than its Japanese version, the new Toyota Camry was intended to be better able to challenge the standard North American sedans of Ford and General Motors. Toyota is also developing a new large pickup truck that will be unsuitable for Japan's much narrower roads.[13]

The strategy pursued by the Japanese companies has been called a "tripolar strategy" by a Nissan executive. It allows them to spread the expensive research and development costs across a worldwide production system; the regions can help each other when demand shifts or shortages occur. Furthermore, it allows the companies to put design teams closest to the markets, thus ensuring maximum acceptance of the models.[14]

The challenge faced by Ford and other automobile manufacturers is similar to that faced by manufacturers and marketers of both industrial and consumer products all over the world. Cost pressures force them to standardize while market pressures require more customization. Conceptually, these companies will gain from increasing the standardized components in their products while maintaining the ability to customize the product at the end for each market segment. International firms will have to respond by achieving economies of scale on the core of their products—the key portion offered as a standard across all markets—by building on a series of standardized components. Different firms will have different levels of standardization, but rarely will one be able to standardize the product 100 percent. For one company, even moving from a global core representing 15 percent of the total product to 20 percent of the total product may result in a considerable cost improvement, and this may be the maximum level of standardization desirable. For another firm, the core may have to represent some 80 percent of the total product to achieve the same effect. These levels will depend on the market characteristics faced by the company or industry. The limits to possible standardization were explained in the previous chapter.

New Product Development for International and Global Markets

Developing new products or services for international and global markets offers unique challenges to a firm. In contrast to the strictly domestic company, international firms must assign development responsibilities to any one of their often numerous international subsidiaries. Aside from the question of who should perform development work, there are

12. "Honda's New Wagon: A U.S. Auto, Almost," *New York Times,* December 14, 1990, p. D1.
13. "Japan's New U.S. Car Strategy," *Fortune,* September 10, 1990, p. 65.
14. Ibid.

organizational problems to overcome that pertain to participation by experts in many subsidiaries. No doubt, the future success of international firms will depend to a substantial degree on how well firms marshal their resources on a global scale to develop new products for foreign markets.

The Organization of Head Office–Sponsored Research and Development

Most companies currently engaging in research and development on a global scale originally conducted their development efforts strictly in centralized facilities in the firm's domestic market. Even today, the largest portion of research and development monies spent by international firms is for efforts in domestically located facilities. As a result, new product ideas are first developed in the context of the domestic market, with initial introduction at home followed by a phase-in introduction to the company's foreign markets.

There are several reasons for this traditional centralized approach. First, research and development must be integrated into a firm's overall marketing strategy. This requires frequent contacts and interfacing between research and development facilities and the company's main offices. Such contacts are maintained more easily with close proximity. The argument for centralization of research and development is based on the concern that duplication of efforts will result if this responsibility is spread over several subsidiaries; centralized research and development is thought to maximize results from scarce research funds. A final important reason for centralization is the company's experience in its home, or domestic, market. Typically, the domestic market is very important to the company and, in the case of international companies based in the United States, Germany, and Japan, is often the largest market as well. As a result, new products are developed with special emphasis on the domestic market, and research and development facilities, therefore, should be close by.

While most research and development continues to be done in firms' home markets, there is a trend toward more nondomestic R&D. In the United States, for example, the amount of corporate research and development done overseas increased from $66.6 billion in 1987 to $85.6 billion in 1991.[15] This 28.5 percent increase was used to tailor products to local markets and to take advantage of R&D expertise in other countries.

Although there are many good reasons for centralizing product development at the company's head office, it will remain a challenge for the engineering and development staff of the firm to keep in mind all relevant product modifications before the design is frozen. Experience shows that later changes or modifications can be expensive. To keep a product acceptable in many or all relevant markets from the outset requires the product development staff to become globalized in the early creation. Only a globally thinking product development staff will ensure the global acceptability of a product by incorporating the maximum possible number of variations in the original product.

15. "The Big Picture, Over There," *Business Week,* April 18, 1994, p. 8.

International Lead Markets and Research and Development[16]

Prior to 1960, new developments in industry, marketing, and management tended to emerge primarily in the United States. Such developments, once accepted in the United States, were apt to be adopted later in other countries. As a result, the U.S. market served as the lead market for much of the rest of the world. In general, a *lead market* is a market whose level of development exceeds that of the market in other countries worldwide and whose developments tend to set a pattern for other countries.

Lead markets are not restricted to technological developments as embodied in product hardware. The concept covers developments in design, production processes, patterns in consumer demand, and methods of marketing. Therefore, virtually every phase of a company's operation is subject to lead market influences, although those focusing on technological developments are of special importance.

During the first half of the twentieth century, the United States achieved a position of virtual dominance as a lead market. Not only were U.S. products the most advanced with respect to features, function, and quality but they also tended to be marketed to the most sophisticated and advanced consumers and industrial buyers. This U.S. advantage was partially based on superior production methods, with the pioneering of mass production in the form of the assembly line. The U.S. advantage extended to management methods in general, and particularly to access to new consumers. The rapid development of U.S.-based international firms was to a considerable degree based on the exploitation of these advantages in applying new U.S. developments abroad and in creating extensive networks of subsidiaries across a large number of countries.

But the total U.S. lead over other countries did not last. Foreign competitors from Europe and Japan eroded the U.S. firms' advantages; as a result, no single country or market now unilaterally dominates the world economy. Though the United States may have lost its lead in steel, television, radios, shoes, textiles, and automobiles, it still leads the world in electronics, the biosciences, computers, and aerospace. (See Figure 11.2.)

Although the general-purpose computer industry is still dominated by mostly U.S. companies, with the United States still serving as the lead market, there are many signs that this position may be challenged in the future. In 1983, U.S. companies had an 81 percent share of computer sales, down to 61 percent in 1989. Over the same period, the share of Japanese companies rose from 8 percent to 22 percent. While the United States once dominated the Japanese personal computer (PC) market, U.S. manufacturers in 1992 only had 15 percent of the six billion dollar market, while NEC had 53 percent. U.S. manufacturers have rebounded with high-quality graphics, software modified for Japan, and low prices. Apple, IBM, Compaq, and Dell are the main U.S. PC suppliers in Japan.[17]

The fragmentation of lead markets led to a proliferation of centers, substantially complicating the task of keeping abreast of the latest developments in market demands,

16. This section is based on Jean-Pierre Jeannet, ''Lead Markets: A Concept for Designing Global Business Strategies,'' working paper, International Institute for Management Development (IMD), May 1986.
17. Brenton R. Schlender, ''U.S. PC's Invade Japan,'' *Fortune,* July 12, 1993, pp. 68–73.

FIGURE 11.2 ● How the United States Stacks Up in a Dozen Emerging Technologies

Technology	Compared to Japan				Compared to Europe			
	R & D		New Products		R & D		New Products	
	Status	Trend	Status	Trend	Status	Trend	Status	Trend
Advanced Materials	↔	↓	↓	↓	↑	↔	↔	↔
Advanced Semiconductor Devices	↔	↔	↓	↓	↑	↔	↔	↔
Artificial Intelligence	↑	↔	↑	↔	↑	↑	↑	↔
Biotechnology	↑	↓	↑	↓	↑	↑	↑	↔
Digital Imaging Technology	↔	↓	↓	↓	↔	↓	↓	↓
Flexible Computer-Integrated Manufacturing	↑	↔	↔	↔	↑	↓	↓	↓
High-Density Data Storage	↔	↔	↓	↓	↑	↔	↔	↔
High-Performance Computing	↑	↔	↑	↓	↑	↑	↑	↑
Medical Devices and Diagnostics	↑	↔	↑	↓	↑	↔	↔	↓
Optoelectronics	↔	↔	↓	↓	↔	↔	↑	↔
Sensor Technology	↑	↓	↔	↔	↑	↔	↔	↔
Superconductors	↔	↓	↔	↓	↔	↔	↔	↔

U.S. Status   ↑ Ahead   ↔ Even   ↓ Behind

U.S. Trend   ↑ Gaining   ↔ Holding   ↓ Losing

Source: U.S. Commerce Dept. Reprinted from the June 15, 1990 issue of *Business Week* by special permission, copyright © 1990 by McGraw-Hill, Inc.

product design, and production techniques. Even formerly developing countries, such as South Korea, have reached lead market status in some categories. In some areas of chip development, Korea is now less than twelve months behind Japan, and efforts are being made to close that gap.[18] However, to prosper in today's increasingly internationalized business climate, corporations must keep track of evolving lead markets as major sources for new product ideas. New product ideas can stem from influences in demand, processes of manufacture, and scientific discoveries; no single country should expect to play a lead role in all facets of a firm's business. This means any corporate research and development effort must look for new developments abroad rather than solely in the domestic market. For example, most U.S. and European chemical manufacturers have significant research and development efforts in Japan for advanced materials, chemicals, and pharmaceuticals. In addition to being a large market, Japan is technologically advanced in these areas, offering the chemical companies specialized expertise.[19]

The rapid international expansion of U.S.-based firms depended to a large extent on their capacity to take advantage of lessons learned in the U.S. market. This strategy was characterized by centralized research and development functions and initial product introductions in the United States. Naturally, to a large degree, the success of this strategy depends on the inputs the central research and development staff derives from its own market environment. Should any part of a company's market become subject to foreign lead market influences, the organization of a firm's research and development function will have to be adjusted. Steel companies in the United States and manufacturers of automobiles, shoes, and textiles cannot disregard developments elsewhere in the world, since the lead market for these industries is no longer the United States. To expose itself to lead market developments, Kodak invested $65 million in a research and development center in Japan that employs a staff of about two hundred people.[20] The company hired about one hundred professional researchers and directed the lab to concentrate on electronic imaging technology.[21] Other U.S. companies have built up their own R&D facilities in Japan, including Corning, Texas Instruments, IBM, Digital Equipment, Procter & Gamble, and several chemical and pharmaceutical companies such as Upjohn, Pfizer, Du Pont, and Monsanto. In 1990, U.S. companies spent $491 million to license technology from Japan compared to just $89 million eight years earlier. This speaks for the fact that Japan is increasingly becoming a lead market for many technology areas.[22]

The Japanese have also seen the need to locate research and development facilities in lead markets. For example, Nissan set up an R&D center in Detroit. Feeling that Detroit is the intellectual capital of the automotive industry, Nissan needs to be there to maintain a leading position in the global automotive industry.[23]

18. "In Korea, All Circuits Are Go," *Business Week,* July 9, 1990, p. 69.
19. "Western Firms See Japanese R&D as Key to Success," *Chemical Week,* May 20, 1992, p. 8.
20. "Kodak Invades Japan to Fight Fuji—and Learn," *Providence Sunday Journal,* December 21, 1986, p. 71.
21. "When the Corporate Lab Goes to Japan," *New York Times,* April 28, 1991, sec. 3, p. 1.
22. "Picking Japan's Research Brains," *Fortune,* March 25, 1991, p. 84.
23. "Companies Set Up Overseas R&D Bases," *Nikkei Weekly,* November 9, 1992, p. 13.

The Role of Foreign Subsidiaries in Research and Development

Foreign subsidiaries of international firms rarely play an active role in research and development unless they have manufacturing responsibilities. Sales subsidiaries may provide the central organization with feedback on product adjustments or adaptation, but generally this participation does not go beyond the generation of ideas. Past research has shown that subsidiaries may assume some research and development functions if the products require some adaptation to the local market.[24] The ensuing research and development capability is often extended to other applications unique to the local market. In many instances, however, the new product may prove to have potential in other markets, and as a result these developments get transferred to other subsidiaries and to the central research and development staff.

International subsidiaries assume special positions when lead markets change from one country to another. Countries that can assume lead market status tend to be among the most advanced industrial nations of North America, Europe, and Asia. Larger international firms quite often have subsidiaries in all these markets. A subsidiary located in a lead market is usually in a better position to observe developments and to accommodate new demands. Consequently, international firms with subsidiaries in lead markets are in a unique position to turn such units into effective "listening posts."[25] Unilever found that some countries of the world were very good at innovation in research and marketing, so it set up a global network of innovation centers. These centers were directed to expand their in-depth experience in research and marketing for Unilever's four categories of personal care products: dental, hair, deodorant, and skin. This expertise was then shared around the world.[26]

In the future, international companies will have to make better use of the talents of local subsidiaries in the development of new products. Increasingly, the role of the subsidiary as a selling or production arm of the company will have to be abandoned, and companies will have to find innovative ways to involve their foreign affiliates into the product development process. This involvement can be patterned around several role models.[27] The *strategic leader* role for developing a new range of products to be used by the entire company may be assigned to a highly competent subsidiary in a market of strategic importance. Another subsidiary with competence in a distinct area may be assigned the role of *contributor,* adapting some products in smaller but nevertheless important markets. Most subsidiaries, being of smaller size and located in less strategic markets, will be

24. Jean-Pierre Jeannet, *Transfer of Technology Within Multinational Corporations* (New York: Arno Press, 1980).

25. Raymond Vernon, "Gone Are the Cash Cows of Yesteryear," *Harvard Business Review,* November–December 1980, p. 150.

26. "Fanning Unilever's Flame of Innovation," *Advertising Age International,* November 23, 1992, p. I-3.

27. Christopher A. Bartlett and Sumantra Ghoshal, "Tap Your Subsidiaries for Global Reach," *Harvard Business Review,* November–December 1986, p. 67.

expected to be *implementers* of the overall strategy and contribute less either technologically or strategically.

Purchasing Research and Development from Foreign Countries

Instead of developing new products through its own research and development personnel, a company may acquire such material or information from independent outside sources. These sources are usually located in foreign countries that have acquired lead market status. Managers commonly read literature published by lead markets. Also, through regular visits to foreign countries and trade fairs, managers maintain close contact with lead markets. Increasingly, however, these ad hoc measures are becoming insufficient for maintaining the necessary flow of information in rapidly changing markets.

For companies without immediate access to new technology embodied in new products, the licensing avenue has been the traditional approach to gain new developments from lead markets. U.S. technology has been tapped through many independent licensing arrangements. Japanese companies have made extensive use of the licensing alternative to acquire technologies developed in countries that were lead markets from Japan's point of view. In the early 1960s, several Japanese manufacturers of earthmoving equipment signed licensing agreements with the U.S. manufacturers to obtain expertise in hydraulic power shovels.[28] Though some Japanese companies attempted to develop a new product line from their own internal resources, it was Komatsu that, based on a licensing agreement with a U.S. company, achieved leadership in Japan. By 1989, Japanese companies manufacturing earthmoving equipment owned twenty-one facilities abroad, some partly owned and others fully owned. Many firms that were originally licensers to those Japanese firms are no longer independent or have even become Japanese partners, joint ventures, or subsidiaries.[29] Though the advantage of licensing lies in its potential to teach new product technologies, there are typically some restrictions attached, such as limiting the sale of such products to specific geographic regions or countries.

A variation of the licensing agreement is the technology assistance contract with a foreign company, allowing a constant flow of information to the firm seeking assistance. Such agreements have been signed by several U.S. steel companies. Because Japanese steelmakers have achieved world leadership, steel companies all over the world, Americans among them, have tapped the former's knowledge and experience. Sumitomo Metal signed contracts with clients in nineteen countries, including U.S. Steel, for steelmaking, plate rolling, and pipe manufacturing. Other U.S. companies purchasing from Japanese companies included Armco from Nippon Steel, Inland Steel from Nippon Kokan, and Bethlehem Steel from Kawasaki Steel.[30]

The Korean firm Lucky–Gold Star is an example of a company that aggressively buys

28. *Japan Economic Journal,* October 2, 1979 and August 5, 1980.
29. "Japan's Earth Movers Look Abroad," *Financial Times,* April 11, 1989, p. 25.
30. *New York Times,* October 28, 1980.

technology abroad to assist in the development of its technologically advanced products. Over the years, the company has formed some twenty joint ventures and maintained technology cooperation agreements with more than fifty foreign firms. Lucky–Gold Star linked up with U.S.-based AT&T to manufacture electronic telephone switching gear, fiber-optic cables, and semiconductors. Entering such agreements gave the Korean firm quick access to modern technologies while allowing AT&T to build contacts within a new market.[31]

Importing as a Source of New Product Technology

Some corporations decide to forgo internally sponsored research and development, importing finished products directly from a foreign firm. Sometimes the importer assumes the role of an original equipment manufacturer (OEM) by marketing products under its own name. Two agreements made between Japanese suppliers and U.S. manufacturers serve to illustrate this strategy.

When IBM was looking for a small desktop copier to fill a gap in its product line, the company turned to a Japanese supplier, Minolta Camera Co., Ltd., instead of developing its own machine.[32] IBM's product line included photocopying machines ranging from $6,000 to $40,000 after it dropped an older model that had sold for $4,000. But in 1980, the company opened its first retail outlets, which were targeted at small businesses. The need for a small desktop model became apparent and had to be filled quickly. The Minolta-supplied model, sold as the IBM Model 102, resembled the Model EP-310, which was marketed by Minolta in the United States through a network of independent dealers.

Though the importing method gives a firm quick access to new products without incurring any research and development expenditures, a company could become dependent and lose the capacity to innovate on its own in the future. As was the case with General Electric's color TV production, economic changes can lead to reversals later on. GE had stopped production of color TV sets in the United States in the mid-1970s and sourced all such products from Matsushita in Japan. When the value of the yen rose to record levels in 1986, GE switched back to U.S. sourcing. This move was made possible because the company had earlier acquired RCA, which still operated a color TV plant in the United States.[33] Consequently, such a strategy of importing new products should be pursued with great care and possibly only in areas that do not represent the core of the firm's business and technology.

Acquisitions as a Route to New Products

Acquiring a company for its new technology or products is a strategy many firms have followed in domestic markets. To make international acquisitions for the purpose of gain-

31. "Lucky–Gold Star: Using Joint Ventures to Sprint Ahead in the High-Tech Race," *Business Week,* July 9, 1984, p. 94.

32. *Wall Street Journal,* February 18, 1981; *New York Times,* February 18, 1981.

33. "GE Will Resume Some U.S. Production of Color TVs Instead of Buying Abroad," *Wall Street Journal,* February 13, 1987, p. 6.

ing a window on emerging technologies or products is developing into an acceptable strategy for many firms. Several European firms have acquired U.S.-based electronics companies for that purpose. Siemens of then West Germany bought into Advanced Micro Devices.[34] Robert Bosch, another German firm, acquired an interest in American Micro-systems; and Philips of Holland purchased Signetics. In all these cases, the foreign firms had to pay substantial premiums over the market value of the stock as a price for access to new product development.

Japanese companies lend a good example of how the acquisition strategy can be used to get access to new products and technologies. Japanese firms are reported to have invested about $350 million in some sixty deals for a wide range of minority positions in U.S.-based high-technology firms through either joint ventures, licensing, or direct investments as minority shareholders. In 1989, Chugai Pharmaceutical acquired Gen-Probe of San Diego for $110 million to get access to the firm's products, including test kits for the detection of cancer and viral infections. The same year, Fujisawa, another Japanese pharmaceutical company, acquired Lyphomed, an Illinois-based maker of generic drugs.[35]

At the same time, Apple was rumored to be negotiating with Sony of Japan to become its supplier for laptop models. Based on their skill of miniaturization, Japanese companies had begun to take the lead in the smallest computer models, and Apple's first line of laptops was both too heavy and too small. Sourcing from Sony would be cost efficient and would give Apple the needed notebook computer model.[36]

The Joint Venture Route to New Product Development

Forming a joint venture with a technologically advanced foreign company can also lead to new product development, often at lower costs. In the 1960s and 1970s, it was largely Japanese companies that sought to attract foreign technology for the manufacture of advanced products in Japan. Many of these Japanese companies can be found in the front ranks of their industries today. Typically, these joint ventures were set up as separate entities, with their own manufacturing and marketing functions.

Other examples of this strategy can be found in France, where two French firms, Saint-Gobain-Pont-a-Mousson and Matra, entered into joint ventures with two U.S. semiconductor manufacturers, National Semiconductor and Harris Corp., with the goal of manufacturing chips in France.[37] In a similar move, the French manufacturer of machine tools, Ernault-Somur, agreed to enter a joint venture with Toyoda Machine Works of Japan, a major machine tool supplier for Toyota.[38] The French company is a major supplier of machine tools to the French automobile industry and hopes to gain access to Toyoda's experience with industrial robots, an area where Japan has assumed the lead position.

34. *Business Week,* October 17, 1977.
35. "A Shopping Spree in the U.S.," *Business Week,* June 15, 1990, p. 86.
36. "Sony, Apple Negotiating Laptop Deal," *New York Times,* October 1, 1990, p. D1.
37. "Europe's Wild Swing at the Silicon Giants," *Fortune,* July 28, 1980, p. 76.
38. *Japan Economic Journal,* September 2, 1980.

U.S. car manufacturers have also acquired parts of Japanese and other Asian firms to participate in the development of new small cars. General Motors owns a significant investment in Isuzu Motors, Ford in Mazda, and Chrysler in Mitsubishi.[39] General Motors also entered into joint ventures with Daewoo, a large Korean conglomerate, to build cars to GM's specifications. In the United States, GM jointly operated a plant with Toyota for the production of subcompact cars.[40]

When Motorola of the United States and Toshiba of Japan decided to pool their resources by swapping technology and creating a joint venture in Japan, both firms had important strategic objectives in mind. Motorola was to get access to Toshiba's production technology for mass-produced memory chips, with a chance to get back eventually into producing both one- and four-megaram chips in large numbers—a production segment that Motorola had had to abandon under intense price pressure from Japanese competitors. In return, Motorola was to give Toshiba access to its logic chips, particularly the large 32-bit microprocessors that are key components for the production of computers.[41]

Alliances for New Product Development

Many companies are finding alliances a way to share technology and research and development for competitive advantage. Alliances are not as structured as a joint venture but include some type of mutually beneficial management. For example, Electrolux, the Swedish appliance manufacturer, has an alliance with Sanyo Electric. Sanyo supplies Electrolux with sophisticated microwave ovens with sensors and "fuzzy logic" technologies that sense when the food is cooked. Electrolux also has an alliance with Sharp, which sells Electrolux washers and refrigerators in Japan. Sharp and Electrolux are jointly developing a compact dishwasher for sale in Japan.[42]

Sun Microsystem's alliance with Fujitsu Ltd. was critical to Sun's success in the workstations market. Fujitsu developed the 32-bit processor based on Sun's proprietary SPARC (scalable processor architecture). The Sun-Fujitsu alliance demonstrates how companies can leverage their individual capabilities for competitive advantage through an alliance.[43]

When IBM realized that plasma display technology was not practical in portable computers, it decided it needed access to liquid crystal displays (LCDs) and formed an alliance with Toshiba. IBM brought expertise in materials, and Toshiba had access to superior manufacturing abilities.[44] What's surprising about many alliances is that they are

39. "Detroit's New Asian Strategy," *Fortune,* December 10, 1984, p. 172.

40. *Business Week,* July 16, 1984.

41. "Toshiba's Motorola Tie-up Is Latest Bid to Bolster Its Semiconductors Business," *Wall Street Journal,* December 5, 1986, p. 35.

42. Yuko Inoue, "Have Appliance Makers Learn Cultural Lessons," *Nikkei Weekly,* September 5, 1992, p. 9.

43. Fumio Kodama, "Innovation Forged by Technology Fusion," *Nikkei Weekly,* March 1, 1993, p. 6.

44. "Moving the Lab Closer to the Marketplace," *Business Week,* Reinventing America, 1992, pp. 168–169.

between competitors, but the benefits of reduced development time and cost more than offset the negative impact of working with the competition.

Alliances can sometimes be formed by firms for some part of their business although they remain competitors in other segments. Olivetti of Italy and Canon of Japan decided to join forces to develop and market office equipment in Europe. The companies created a new joint company in Italy consisting of Olivetti production and research facilities for copiers and an infusion of capital and technology from Canon. With access to Canon's latest technology, particularly in the laser printing and electronic publishing area, Olivetti managers hoped that the new company would triple present volume—supplying both Olivetti and Canon distribution channels in Europe. Despite this cooperation, the two firms were to remain competitors in the typewriter market.[45]

The Consortium Approach

To share the huge cost of developing new products, some companies have established or joined consortia to share in new product development. Under the consortium approach, member firms join in a working relationship without forming a new entity. On completion of the assigned task, member firms are free to seek other relationships with different firms. Consortia have been used for some time in marketing entire factories or plants or in the banking industry, but they are a relatively new approach to new product research and development.

Since the development of new aircraft is particularly cost intensive, the aircraft industry offers several examples of the consortium approach to product development. The high development costs require that large passenger aircraft must be built in series of two hundred or three hundred units just to break even. Under these circumstances, several companies form a consortium to share the risk. One of the first highly successful efforts was the European Airbus, developed and produced by French, British, and German manufacturers.

For its latest generation of long-range aircraft, the 777, Boeing was facing development and launch costs of some $4 billion. Such programs could not be justified unless several airlines, including foreign ones, could be involved from the outset with large commitments. To reduce the risk, Boeing offered a 25 percent share in the project to three Japanese companies: Mitsubishi Heavy Industries, Fuji Heavy Industries, and Kawasaki Heavy Industries. These companies had been major suppliers of subassemblies for the 767 model range. It is believed that such Japanese participation was invited not only to share development costs but to help in the marketing of the planes. Japanese airlines are the largest buyers of long-range planes. The fact that All Nippon Airlines is the largest operator of Boeing 767 planes outside the United States was linked to the strong participation of Japanese firms in the production of the plane. Both Japan Airlines and All Nippon Airlines are among the key accounts sought for the launch of the Boeing 777 model range.[46] Japan

45. ''Olivetti and Canon Form Venture for Office Equipment Production,'' *Financial Times,* January 20, 1987, p. 1.
46. ''How Boeing Does It,'' *Business Week,* July 9, 1990, p. 46.

Airlines is already the world's largest operator of Boeing 747s, with a present fleet of sixty-seven airplanes and another sixty-four on order for the latest version. This underscores the need to bring in Japanese partners in the early stages of any long-range passenger plane project.[47]

Responding to the same pressures as those faced by the airplane manufacturers, the major jet engine companies have also engaged in a number of consortia. U.S.-based General Electric has had a long-term agreement with Snecma of France. The French partner took a 20 percent interest in the GE90 Model CF6 jet engine design, which was projected to cost about $1.5 billion to develop.[48] Pratt & Whitney, the other leading U.S. firm, joined a partnership with MTU, a subsidiary of the German firm Daimler-Benz.[49] MTU had previously planned to become a partner with GE, which prompted GE to look for Fiat as a new partner after the German firm decided to proceed with Pratt & Whitney.[50]

British Rolls-Royce, the smallest of the major jet engine firms, made a series of collaborative ventures with different firms. Rolls-Royce strategy has been to make project-specific ventures (see Figure 11.3). The most recent deal was made with BMW of Germany for the production of jet engines for the civil aviation market.[51]

The advantage of a consortium approach also lies in sales. The widespread participation of companies from the United States, Europe, and Japan gives partial reassurance for future sales, thus further reducing the risk to each participating company.

The consortium approach is becoming increasingly popular in several technology-intensive industries.[52] Companies in the automobile, computer, and biotechnology industries have formed cooperative agreements to share in the development and exploitation of technology. What is new to this trend is that sometimes competitors will become partners, whereas previously no cooperation would have been possible.

Internationalization of the Product Development Process

The previous section dealt primarily with the sources of product development. To bring about a total integration of the product development process for a multinational enterprise

---

47. "JAL to Buy into Lockheed Jet Maintenance Offshoot," *Financial Times,* January 7, 1991, p. 12.

48. "Snecma to Take Share in New GE Engine," *Financial Times,* January 8, 1991, p. 18.

49. "Revving Up for a Clash of Blades," *Financial Times,* September 6, 1990, p. 11.

50. "Fiat May Take 10% Stake in GE Jet Engine Development," *Financial Times,* July 4, 1990, p. 1.

51. "Modest Alliance Between Two Pioneers," *Financial Times,* May 4, 1990, p. 21.

52. Kenichi Ohmae, *Triad Power: The Coming Shape of Global Competition* (New York: Free Press, 1985), pp. 125–148.

FIGURE 11.3 ● Rolls-Royce's Main Collaborative Relationships, 1990

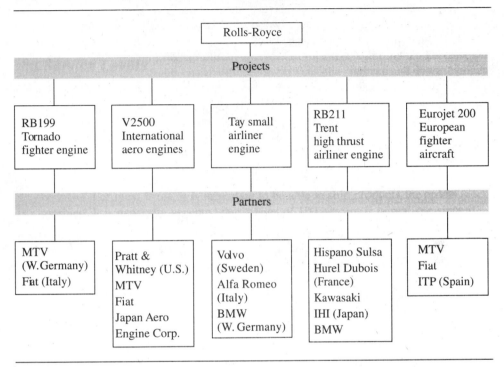

Source: *Financial Times,* May 4, 1990, p. 2. Reprinted by permission.

often requires the adoption of new organizational forms and the restructuring of the development process as a whole. The challenge in multinational product development is finding a way to combine domestic and foreign expertise so that truly international or global products can result.

The international approach to new product development is best described by an executive of Fiat, the Italian car manufacturer. "Fifteen years ago we designed cars for the Italian market. Ten years ago we began designing 'European' cars. Now we develop them for the country with the biggest market—the United States—and scale them down for the others."[53] This shift from localized to worldwide development requires that the unique or special concerns for major markets be considered from the outset of the process, rather than a company attempting to make various adaptations on the initial model or prototype. This early introduction of global considerations not only ensures that the product will

53. "To a Global Car," *Business Week,* November 20, 1978, p. 102.

achieve wide acceptance but also aims at maximizing the commonality of models to achieve economies in component manufacturing. A global product, then, is not identical in all countries. Instead, a world product is engineered from the outset with the goal of maximizing the percentage of identical components, design, and parts to the point where local needs can be met with a minimum of additional costs in tooling, engineering, and development.

To internationalize their own research, Japanese companies have made heavy investments in U.S.-based research facilities. Hundreds of Japanese scientists already work side by side with Americans in research laboratories on exchange programs. This investment aims at getting access to U.S. scientific talent. One company, Kobe Steel, announced the opening of its research center near Stanford University; another, NEC, opened a laboratory for artificial intelligence in Princeton, New Jersey.[54]

The research and development process is stimulated by ideas for new products. Global companies must identify sources of new ideas from potential markets. Microsoft sponsored a nationwide contest in Russia to develop a Russian version of Microsoft Windows. Microsoft hopes to get a good product for the Russian market as well as stimulate product development.[55] Whirlpool found it could use its customer service system not only to locate product problems but also to identify potential design improvements.[56] In some markets, local competitors may be the best source of product ideas. For example, as McDonald's eyes the market in India (where it plans to begin operations in 1995), it needs to adapt to the Hindu custom of not eating beef. Nirula's, a fast-growing fast-food outlet in India, offers burgers with lamb and mixed vegetables as an alternative to beef.[57] It is expected that McDonald's will learn from Nirula's experience.

To develop a global product also requires a different organizational setup. Changes instituted by General Motors indicate moves made by other international firms. With the advent of world cars, GM realized that the company needed closer coordination between its domestic units and its overseas subsidiaries. GM moved its overseas staff from New York to Detroit in 1978 in order to speed up communication between domestic and international staffs.[58] GM adopted the "project center" concept to manage its engineering effort. Each division or subsidiary involved in a new car design would lend engineers to a centrally organized project center, which would design, develop, and introduce the new model. Upon introduction of the model, the project center is disbanded. Of course, not every firm will find a project center approach feasible. Other alternatives include assigning primary responsibility to a subsidiary with special capability in the new product field.

54. "Japan: A Shopping Spree in the U.S.," *Business Week,* June 15, 1990, p. 87.

55. "Microsoft Urges Russian Software Bootleggers: Join Us," *Wall Street Journal,* May 18, 1993, p. B4.

56. "The Gold Mine of Data in Customer Service," *Business Week,* March 21, 1994, p. 113.

57. "Where's the Beef?" *Fortune,* January 24, 1994, p. 16.

58. "GM Plans an Offensive for Growth Overseas," *Business Week,* March 27, 1978, p. 46.

Introducing New Products to the Market

Once a product has been developed for commercial introduction, a number of complex decisions still need to be made. Aside from the question of whether to introduce the product abroad, the firm has to decide on a desirable test-marketing procedure, select target countries for introduction, and determine the timing or sequence of the introduction. With the large number of alternatives inherent in numerous possible markets, decisions surrounding new product introduction often attain strategic significance.

The determination of which product to introduce abroad depends of course on sales potential. Following a careful analysis, a list of target countries can be developed. A company then has to determine the next steps leading to actual introduction in the target countries.

Concept Tests

Once a prototype or sample product has been developed, a company may decide to subject its new creation to a series of tests to determine commercial feasibility. It is particularly important to subject a new product to actual use conditions. When the development process takes place outside the country of actual use, a practical field test can be crucial. The test must include all necessary usage steps to provide complete information. When CPC International tested the U.S. market for dehydrated soups made by its newly acquired Knorr subsidiary, the company concentrated primarily on taste tests to ensure that the final product suited U.S. consumers. Extensive testing led to soups different in formulation from those sold in Europe. CPC, however, had neglected to have consumers actually try out the product at home as part of their regular cooking activities. Such a test would have revealed consumers' discontent with the relatively long cooking time—up to twenty minutes, compared to three minutes for comparable canned soups. The company realized these difficulties only after a national introduction had been completed and sales fell short of original expectations.

The concept testing stage would be incomplete if the products were only tested in the company's domestic market. A full test in several major markets is essential so that any shortcomings can be alleviated at an early stage before costly adaptations for individual countries are made. Such an approach is particularly important in cases where product development occurred on a multinational basis, with simultaneous inputs from several foreign subsidiaries. When Volkswagen tested its original Rabbit models, test vehicles were made available to all principal subsidiaries in order to ensure that each market's requirements were met by the otherwise standardized car.

There may be some differences between concept testing for consumer products and for industrial products. Industrial products tend to be used worldwide for the same purposes under very similar circumstances. Factories for textile machinery are relatively standardized across the world so that a test in one country may be quite adequate for most others. As a result, single-country market testing may be more appropriate for industrial products.

Test-Marketing

Just as there are good reasons to test-market a product in a domestic market, an international test can give the firm valuable insights into potential future success. A key question is where the market test should be held. Companies in the United States have largely pioneered test-marketing procedures because it has been possible to isolate a given market in terms of media and distribution. This may not always be possible in smaller countries and even less so in countries where most of the media are national rather than local. If a market test were considered in a country with national TV only and print media were substituted for TV for the purpose of the test, the test would not be a true replication of the actual full-scale introduction. As a result, the opportunities for small local test markets are substantially reduced outside the United States.

To overcome the shortage of test-market possibilities, international firms often substitute the experience in one country for a market test in another. Although market tests were typical for many U.S.-based firms before full-scale introduction in the U.S. market, subsidiaries tended to use these early U.S. results as a basis for analysis. Such a strategy requires that at least one subsidiary of an international firm have actual commercial experience with a product or any given aspect of the marketing strategy before introducing the product elsewhere.

Use of the U.S. market as a test market depends on the market situation and the degree to which results can be extrapolated to other countries. Since circumstances are rarely exactly the same, early U.S. results must be regarded with caution. Also, extrapolation may only be appropriate for other advanced countries in Europe and Asia. See also our explanation of the comparative analytic approach in Chapter 6.

For firms with extensive foreign networks of subsidiaries, market tests can be used beyond the traditional mode. Another approach to test-marketing is to use a foreign country as a first introduction and proving ground before other markets are entered. In Europe, smaller markets such as the Netherlands, Belgium, Austria, and Switzerland may be used to launch a new product. Because of their size, a test would include national introduction with results applicable in other countries. When Toyota started its European sales drive, Switzerland was used as a test market, and the strategy developed by its independent Swiss distributor was later adopted elsewhere.

Special attention should be given to the lead market as a potential test market. Any new product that succeeds in its lead market can be judged to have good potential elsewhere as other markets mature. Philips, the Dutch electronics company, intended to use the United States market as its proving ground for consumer electronics products.[59] Though new products may be developed in the Netherlands, U.S. subsidiaries will market them first. Having to compete with major Japanese and U.S. manufacturers in the largest market for consumer electronics should provide input for European markets. European markets are believed ultimately to follow the consumption patterns set by U.S. consumers.

59. "In Consumer Electronics the U.S. Is a Top Target," *Business Week,* March 30, 1981, pp. 97–100.

Timing of New Product Introductions

Very early in the introduction process, a company will be faced with a decision to establish the timing and sequence of its introduction. Timing determines when a product should be introduced in a foreign market. Sequencing becomes an issue when a firm deals with several countries and must decide on a phased or simultaneous entry approach. Traditionally, firms have introduced new products first in their domestic markets to gain experience in production, marketing, and service. Foreign market introductions are attempted only after a product has proven itself in the domestic market. Research has shown, however, that the time lag between domestic and initial foreign market introduction has substantially declined.[60] From 1945 to 1950, only 5.6 percent of investigated firms introduced new products abroad within one year. By 1975, the percentage had increased to 38.7 percent, and about two-thirds were introduced abroad within five years. This time lag reduction reflects the increased capability by U.S. firms to introduce products abroad rapidly. It also reflects the rapid economic development of many advanced countries, to the point where the United States no longer leads in a number of fields. The average time lag can safely be assumed to continue to decline.

Some companies are now in a position to introduce products simultaneously in several countries. When Apple revamped its product line in 1990, the launch of the Macintosh Classic line was communicated via television broadcasts to 121 countries in a total campaign costing $45 million worldwide. Previously, Apple introduced products in the United States first, announcing shipping dates weeks or months later for its other markets. For its new line, most European countries were shipped localized versions of the original product the same week as the selling started in the United States. Japan and other Asian countries were expected to follow within just a few weeks with localized versions.[61] Simultaneous introduction depends on the company's foreign market development stage and the ability to satisfy demand. When the primary function of foreign subsidiaries is the sale of products shipped from one or a small number of central manufacturing centers, simultaneous introduction is possible as long as marketing efforts can be coordinated. This structure is typical for electronics firms. Other companies produce in many markets; thus, the manufacturing function would be strained if simultaneous introduction were attempted.

Increasingly, companies have to invest ever larger amounts for developing new technologies or products. As these investments rise, the time requirement to bring new generations of products on the market has increased, leaving less time for the commercialization of products until patent protections run out or until new competitors come out with similar products. As a result, companies have been forced to move into a rapid introduction of new products, so that we can now often talk of a global product rollout. Global rollout was practiced by Gillette with the introduction of its new Sensor razor, with simultaneous introduction in both Europe and North America.

60. William H. Davidson and Richard Harrigan, ''Key Decisions in International Marketing: Introducing New Products Abroad,'' *Columbia Journal of World Business,* Winter 1977, p. 15.
61. ''The Fruits of Flexibility,'' *Financial Times,* October 17, 1990, p. 17.

Country Selection

Although international firms have subsidiaries in numerous countries, initial product introductions have always been limited to the industrialized nations. In one study of forty-four U.S.-based firms, 83.5 percent of first introductions took place in developed countries for the 1945–1976 time period.[62] Leading target countries for the 1965–1975 period were the United Kingdom, Japan, Australia, France, and West Germany.[63]

Other research has shown that some companies use a two-step approach to new product introduction. At first, products are introduced in the most-advanced markets, with developing countries following in a second stage.[64] Many U.S.-based international firms have used their European subsidiaries as steppingstones to Latin America or eastern Europe. One electronics manufacturer transferred an innovation first to its Italian subsidiary; the Italian subsidiary then introduced it in Spain through another subsidiary there. The same company has also used its Dutch subsidiary to transfer innovations to Poland.

A firm's competitive situation abroad influences its country selection. Major subsidiaries tend to get new products first, and manufacturing subsidiaries are usually favored over sales subsidiaries. Also, each local market expects to face different competitors. This often means that the international firm will first choose a country where the firm is well entrenched over a market where competitive pressures make operating results less favorable.

Conclusions

When companies search for new markets for their products, they face the difficult choice of adapting those products to new environments. Such adaptations are frequently expensive when done after the fact. In the future, companies will increasingly consider international opportunities early in the development cycle of a new product. Incorporating international requirements early will allow new products to be immediately usable in many markets. Such a move toward internationalization of the product development cycle will result in the development of more world products. These products will be produced in modularized forms to include as many world components as possible, and they will incorporate a set of unique components to fit the product needs of individual markets. The challenge for international marketers is to find the best tradeoffs between the standardized world components of a product and the tailor-made components designed for specific markets.

Another, increasingly influential factor in new product development processes is speed. For competitive reasons, companies want to be among the first to enter with a new product or service because early entrants tend to obtain the biggest market share. To

62. Davidson and Harrigan, ''Key Decisions in International Marketing,'' p. 15.
63. Ibid.
64. Jeannet, *Transfer of Technology*.

increase speed, companies work on collaborative development processes. Furthermore, they will shrink the time it will take from first, domestic introduction until worldwide launch. In the end, many firms will undertake multicountry launches or simultaneous global product rollouts. The risk increases with such global launches because less time is available to test the product, make sure it meets the market performance, and ensure that it is sufficiently tailored to a given country.

Questions for Discussion

1. Analyze three different products (freezers, compact disks, and contact eye lenses) according to Table 11.1. What general marketing strategy recommendations do you arrive at?

2. What, in your opinion, is the future for global products?

3. How should international firms organize their new product development efforts today and in the future?

4. What is the impact of a loss of lead market position in several industries for U.S.-based corporations?

5. If you were to test-market a new consumer product today for worldwide introduction, how would you select test countries for Europe, Asia, and Latin America?

For Further Reading

Afriyie, Koti. "International Technology Transfers." In *Cooperative Strategies in International Business,* ed. Farok Contractor and Peter Lorange. Lexington, Mass.: D. C. Heath, 1987.

Behrman, J. N., and W. A. Fischer. "Transnational Corporation: Market Orientations and R&D Abroad." *Columbia Journal of World Business,* Fall 1980, pp. 55–60.

Cheng, Joseph L. C., and Douglas J. Bolon. "The Management of Multinational R&D: A Neglected Topic in International Business Research." *Journal of International Business Studies,* 1st Quarter 1993, pp. 1–18.

Crawford, Merle C. *New Products Management.* Homewood, Ill.: Irwin, 1983.

Hill, John S., and Richard R. Still. "Cultural Effects of Technology Transfer by Multinational Corporations in Lesser Developed Countries." *Columbia Journal of World Business,* Summer 1980, pp. 40–50.

Kaikati, Jack G. "Domestically Banned Products: For Export Only." *Journal of Public Policy and Marketing* 3 (1984), pp. 125–133.

Leroy, Georges. *Multinational Product Strategy.* New York: Praeger, 1976.

Mabert, Vincent A., John F. Muth, and Robert W. Schmennor. "Collapsing New Product Development Time." *Journal of Product Innovation Management,* September 1992, pp. 200–212.

Manu, Franklyn A. "Innovation, Orientation, Environment and Performance: A Comparison of U.S. and European Markets." *Journal of International Business Studies,* 2nd Quarter 1992, p. 333.

Ogbuehi, Alphonso O., and Ralph A. Bellis, Jr. "Decent Sized R&D for Global Development: Strategic Implications for the Multinational Corporation." *International Marketing Review,* 19, Issue 5 (1992), pp. 60–70.

Ronstadt, Robert. "The Establishment and Evolution of R&D Abroad." *Journal of International Business Studies,* Spring–Summer 1978, pp. 7–24.

Wind, Yoram, and Vigay Mahajan. "New Product Development Process: A Perspective for Reexamination." *Journal of Product Innovation Management,* 5, no. 4 (1988), pp. 304–310.

12

Managing International Channels

● **INTERNATIONAL MARKETING DISTRIBUTION** *decisions are similar to those in a domestic setting. What differs, of course, are the environmental influences that, in the end, may lead to substantially different policies and channel options. International marketers need to understand how environmental influences may affect these distribution policies and options. Using this knowledge, they must structure efficient channels for products on a country-by-country basis.*

This chapter discusses the structure of international distribution systems; developing a distribution strategy; and selecting, locating, and managing channel members (see Figure 12.1). We also explain the issues of international logistics, gaining access to channels, and global trends in international distribution.

The Structure of International Distribution Systems

The structure of the distribution systems available in a country is affected by the level of economic development, the personal disposable income of consumers, and the quality of the infrastructure, as well as environmental factors such as culture, physical environment, and legal/political system. Marketers who develop a distribution strategy must decide how to transport the goods from the manufacturing locations to the consumer. Although the distribution of goods can be handled completely by the manufacturer, often the goods are moved through intermediaries, such as agents, wholesalers, distributors, and retailers. An

FIGURE 12.1 ● International Distribution

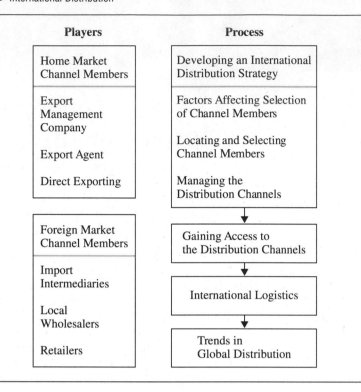

Players	Process
Home Market Channel Members	Developing an International Distribution Strategy
Export Management Company	Factors Affecting Selection of Channel Members
Export Agent	Locating and Selecting Channel Members
Direct Exporting	Managing the Distribution Channels
Foreign Market Channel Members	Gaining Access to the Distribution Channels
Import Intermediaries	International Logistics
Local Wholesalers	Trends in Global Distribution
Retailers	

understanding of the structure of available distribution systems is extremely important in the development of a strategy. The various channels available to a manufacturer are shown in Figure 12.2.

There are two major categories of channel members: (1) home country and (2) foreign. In the home country, a manufacturer can utilize the services of an export management company or an export agent, or it can use company personnel to export the products. In Chapter 9, we discussed whether or not any of these channel members should be used. In this chapter, our focus is on how to locate, select, use, and manage channel members.

Home Market Channel Members

Within your home market, a number of different types of export-related channel members can help with the export process. The most common types are export management companies and export agents. Also, a firm can bypass the help of these specialists and use internal expertise to export.

FIGURE 12.2 ● International Marketing Channel Alternatives

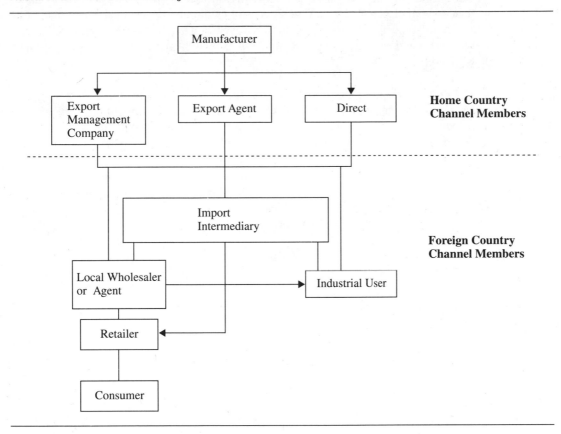

1. Bruce Seifert and John Ford, ''Export Distribution Channels,'' *Columbia Journal of World Business,* Summer 1989, p. 22.
2. Franklin R. Root, *Entry Strategies for International Markets* (Lexington, Mass.: D. C. Heath, 1994), p. 81.

Export Management Company The export management company (EMC) is a firm that handles all aspects of export operations under a contractual agreement.[1] The EMC will normally take responsibility for the promotion of goods, marketing research, credit, physical handling of the product, patents, and licensing. The population of EMCs is estimated to be 1,200 firms, representing some 10,000 manufacturers and accounting for 10 percent of U.S.-manufactured exports.[2] Arrangements between an EMC and a manufacturer will vary, depending on the services offered and the volume expected. The advantages of an EMC are that (1) little or no investment is required to enter the international marketplace, (2) no company personnel are required, and (3) the EMC will have an established network of sales offices and international marketing and distribution knowledge. One disadvantage is that the manufacturer gives up direct control of the international sales and marketing effort. Also, if the product has a long purchase cycle and requires a large amount of market development and education, the EMC may not expend the necessary effort to penetrate a new market.

Export Agents   Export agents are individuals or firms that assist manufacturers in exporting goods. They are similar to EMCs, except that they tend to provide limited services and focus on one country or one part of the world. Export agents understand all the requirements for moving goods through the customs process, but they do not provide the marketing skills that an EMC provides; these agents focus more on the sale and handling of goods. The advantage of using an export agent is that the manufacturer does not need to have an export manager to handle all the documentation and shipping tasks. One disadvantage is the export agent's limited market coverage, which requires the use of numerous export agents to cover different parts of the world.

Direct Exporting   Instead of using an EMC or export agent, a firm can export its goods directly, through in-house company personnel. Due to the complexity of trade regulations, customs documentation, insurance requirements, and worldwide transportation alternatives, people with special training and experience are necessary to handle these tasks. Also, the current or expected volume must be sufficient to support the in-house staff. As a company expands its international operations and sets up local production, the need for exporting will decrease.

Foreign Market Channel Members

As shown in Figure 12.2, once the goods have left the home market, there are a variety of channel alternatives in the international marketplace: import intermediaries, local wholesalers or agents, and retailers. Even with local manufacturing, the company will still need to get the goods from the factory to the consumers.

Import Intermediaries   Import intermediaries identify needs in their local market and find products from the world market to satisfy these needs. They will normally purchase goods in their own name and act independently of the manufacturers. As independents, these channel members use their own marketing strategies and keep in close contact with the markets they serve. A manufacturer desiring distribution in an independent intermediary's market area should investigate this channel partner as one of the ways to get its product to wholesalers and retailers in that area.

Local Wholesalers or Agents   In each country, there will be a series of possible channel members who move manufacturers' products to retailers, industrial firms, or in some cases other wholesalers. Local wholesalers will take title to the products, while local agents will not take title. Local wholesalers are also called distributors or dealers. In many cases, the local wholesaler has exclusive distribution rights for a specific geographic area or country.

The structure of wholesale distribution varies greatly from country to country. The number of wholesalers and the number of retailers per wholesaler vary according to the distribution structure and wholesale pattern of the country. For example, although Kenya and Kuwait have approximately the same number of wholesalers, the Kenya wholesaler will indirectly serve 1.8 retailers, whereas in Kuwait a wholesaler will serve 4.9 retailers.[3] Wholesale channels in Japan are very complex, with most goods going through as many as six intermediaries. This lengthy distribution channel causes Japan to have exorbitant prices—$20 for a bottle of aspirin, $72 for a package of golf balls costing $26.80 in U.S. stores.[4]

The functions of wholesalers can vary by country. In some countries, wholesalers provide a warehouse function, taking orders from retailers and shipping them appropriate quantities. Wholesalers in Japan provide the basic wholesale functions but also share risk with retailers by providing financing, product development, and even occasional managerial and marketing skills.[5]

Retailers   Retailers, the last members of the consumer distribution channel, purchase products for resale to consumers. The size and accessibility of retail channels varies greatly by country. The population per retailer varies from a low of only 40 people per retailer in Argentina to 20,000 people in Egypt.[6] Japan has a large number of retailers, with thirteen per 1,000 inhabitants, versus six in Europe or the United States. For example, Shiseido, a maker of cosmetics, has 25,000 outlets selling only their products, and Matsushita has 19,000 electrical appliance stores.[7] Until recently, all retailing in China was through state-owned stores.[8] The number of retail outlets in China has grown from 1.4 million in 1980 to 8.8 million in 1987. The ratio of state-owned to private or collective-owned stores has gone from 92/8 percent to 40/60 percent.[9] The international marketer must evaluate the available retailers in a country and develop a strategy around that structure.

Developing an International Distribution Strategy

The environmental variables of culture, physical environment, and the legal/political system, combined with the unique structure of wholesale and retail distribution systems,

3. *Statistical Yearbook 1985/86,* pp. 656–679, table 138 (United Nations, 1988).

4. Emily Thornton, ''Revolution in Japanese Retailing,'' *Fortune,* February 7, 1994, pp. 143, 146.

5. ''Why Japanese Shoppers Are Lost in a Maze,'' *Economist,* January 31, 1987, p. 62.

6. *Euromonitor International Marketing Data and Statistics,* 15th ed. (Euromonitor Publications, 1991); *European Marketing Data and Statistics,* 26th ed. (Euromonitor Publications, 1991).

7. ''Marketing in Japan—Taking Aim,'' *Economist,* April 24, 1993, p. 74.

8. Heidi Vernon-Wortzel and Lawrence H. Wortzel, ''The Emergence of Free Market Retailing in China,'' *California Management Review,* Spring 1987, pp. 59–76.

9. Guo Qiang and Phil Harris, ''Retailing Reforms and Trends in China,'' *International Journal of Retail and Distribution Management,* 18, no. 5 (1990), pp. 31–39.

complicate the development of an international distribution strategy. A distribution strategy is one part of the marketing mix, and it needs to be consistent with other aspects of the marketing strategy: product policies, pricing strategy, and communications strategy (see Figure 12.3).

Within the structure of the marketing mix, the international marketer makes the following distribution decisions:

1. *Distribution density.* Density refers to the amount of exposure or coverage desired for a product, particularly the number of sales outlets required to provide for adequate coverage of the entire market.
2. *Channel length.* The concept of channel length involves the number of intermediaries involved in bringing a given product to the market.
3. *Channel alignment and leadership.* The area of alignment deals with the structure of the chosen channel members to achieve a unified strategy.
4. *Distribution logistics.* Logistics involves the physical flow of products as they move through the channel.

FIGURE 12.3 ● Distribution Policies

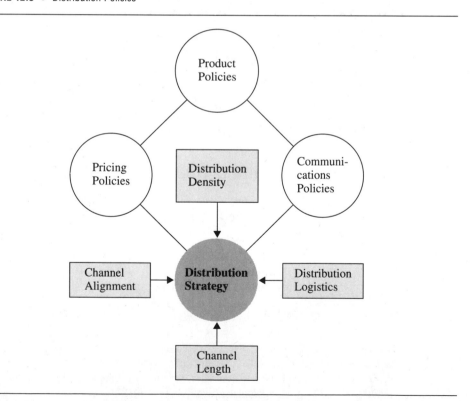

These four decision areas cannot be approached independently. The decisions are interrelated, and they need to be consistent with other aspects of the marketing strategy. While it is important to evaluate the distribution strategy logically, marketing managers are often left with an international distribution structure held over from previous managers. While the present system may limit the flexibility of a company to change, there are often numerous opportunities around the current arrangement. For example, Nordica of Italy had been selling in Japan since 1960. In 1985, the company decided it needed to change its distribution system from its exclusive distributor Daiwa Sports. Nordica reached a financial agreement with Daiwa Sports and hired the eighty-five employees who had been handling its line. These employees made up most of Nordica Japan, the company-owned sales organization in Japan, which has been very successful.[10] The following sections deal primarily with a company's distribution policies, dependence on distribution-specific variables, and its relationship to the other elements of the marketing strategy.

Distribution Density

The number of sales outlets or distribution points required for the efficient marketing of a firm's products is referred to as the *density of distribution.* The density is dependent on the shopping or buying habits of the average customer. An optimum distribution network requires the marketer to examine how customers select dealers and retail outlets by segment.[11] For consumer goods, an extensive, or wide, distribution is required if the consumer is not likely to exert much shopping effort. Such products, also called convenience goods, are bought frequently and in nearby outlets. Other products, such as appliances or clothing, are shopped for by visiting two or more stores; these require a more limited, or selective, distribution, with fewer outlets per market area. For products that inspire consumer loyalty to specific brands, called specialty goods, a very limited, or *exclusive,* distribution is required. It is assumed that the customer will search for the product desired and is willing to stop at several places until the item is located.

The key to distribution density then is the consumer's shopping behavior, the expended effort to locate a desired item. This behavior, however, may vary substantially from country to country. In the United States, for example, where per capita income is high, consumers shop for many regular-use items in supermarkets and other widely accessible outlets, such as drugstores. In other countries, particularly some with a much lower per capita income, the purchase of such items may be a less routine affair, causing consumers to exert more effort to locate such items. This allows a less extensive distribution of products. It is therefore necessary for the international marketer to assess the shopping behavior of various countries' consumers. Where consumers will buy certain goods also varies a great deal from country to country. In Germany, contact lens solution is only

10. Ian Rodger, "Nordica and Salomon Put the Boot In," *Financial Times,* August 30, 1990, p. 12.
11. Allan J. Magrath and Kenneth G. Hardy, "How Much Distribution Coverage Is Enough?" *Business Horizons,* June 1989, p. 20.

found in stores that sell eyeglasses, but in France it is also found in most drugstores. While magazines are sold in many grocery stores in the United States, in the United Kingdom they are sold almost exclusively through news agents. It is important to find out where consumers buy certain types of products early in your distribution analysis.

Retailing is exploding in many parts of Asia, where a large portion of the population is crossing the income threshold at which they start to buy entirely new categories of goods, such as packaged foods, televisions, or mopeds. This phenomenon, called "magic moments," has hit Taiwan, Indonesia, Thailand, Malaysia, and China. When a country crosses the magic moments threshold, distribution systems start to improve with modern stores. Hero Supermarkets, the local leader in Indonesia, increased sales by 18 percent in the first half of 1993; 7-Eleven stores increased sales 800 percent in three years. Led by the Japanese, retailers around the world are moving into Asia to acquire premium locations and take advantage of a fast-growing market.[12]

In the industrial sector, differences in buyer behavior or in the use of a particular product may require changes in distribution density. Since industrial products applications are more uniform around the world due to the similarity in application and use conditions, what constitutes capital equipment in one country typically is also classified as capital equipment in another nation. Differences may exist, however, among the decision-makers. In the United States, for instance, radiology supply products are sold directly to hospitals and radiology departments though hospital supply distributors. However, in France, patients must pick up radiology supplies by prescription from a pharmacy before visiting the radiology department at the hospital. In this latter case, radiology supplies have to be presold to physicians and stocked with pharmacies to be successful. This is the same strategy pursued by pharmaceutical firms. Of course, when selling to both physicians and pharmacies, the necessary distribution in France is much more extensive than it is in the United States, where only hospitals need to be contacted.[13]

Channel Length

The number of intermediaries directly involved in the physical or ownership path of a product from the manufacturer to the customer is indicative of the channel length. Long channels have several intermediaries, whereas short or direct channels have few or no intermediaries. Channel length is usually influenced by three factors: (1) a product's distribution density, (2) the average order quantities, and (3) the availability of channel members. Products with extensive distribution, or large numbers of final sales points, tend to have longer channels of distribution. Similarly, as the average order quantity decreases, products move through longer channels to add to the distribution efficiency.

Since distribution density does affect channel length, it is clear that the same factors that influence distribution density influence channel length; namely, the shopping behav-

12. "Asian Retailing: Teach Me Shopping," *Economist,* December 18, 1994, p. 64.

13. Warren J. Keegan, *Multinational Marketing Management* (Englewood Cliffs, N.J.: Prentice Hall, 1989), p. 175.

iors of customers. The average order quantity often depends on the purchasing power or income level of a given customer group. In countries with lower income levels, people often buy food on a daily basis at nearby small stores. This contrasts sharply with more-affluent consumers, who can afford to buy food or staples for one week or even a month and who don't mind traveling some distance to do this more infrequent type of shopping. In the first case, a longer channel is required, whereas a shorter channel is adequate in the latter case. The type of distributors available in a country affects the channel length. Also, the culture may demand a specific type of channel member.

Channel length does have important cost considerations. Salomon of France originally entered the Japanese ski equipment market with the giant Mitsui trading company. Mitsui insisted on taking delivery of goods through its Paris subsidiary, then transferring them to wholesalers and then to retailers. This long channel resulted in Salomon bindings being very expensive in Japan. By the time all the intermediaries took their cut, little was left for the manufacturer. As the company entered the ski boot business in 1980, it set up its own sales company that sold directly to a new breed of sport shops. In 1982, Mitsui did not renew the distribution contract on Salomon bindings.[14]

Japan is known for its lengthy, complex channels, which increase the cost of goods to consumers. Seiko Epson has bypassed Japanese channel members and begun a direct sales effort to sell its NEC and IBM-compatible PCs. Following the lead of Dell Computer, Seiko Epson hopes to attract consumers by offering significant savings through its direct marketing effort.[15]

Channel Alignment

One of the most difficult tasks of marketing is to get various channel members to coordinate their actions so that a unified approach can be achieved. The longer the channel, the more difficult it becomes to maintain a coordinated and integrated approach. On an international level, the coordinating task is made all the more difficult because the company organizing the channel may be removed by large distances from the distribution system, with little influence over the local scene. In each country, the strongest channel member will be able to dictate policies to the other channel members, though situations will vary by country. The international company will find it much easier to control the distribution channel if a local subsidiary with a strong sales force exists. In countries where the company has no local presence and depends on independent distributors, control is likely to slip to the independent distributor. This loss of control may be further aggravated if the international company's sales volume represents only a small fraction of the local distributor's business. Of course, the opposite will be true when a high percentage of the volume consists of the international corporation's products.

To achieve maximum efficiency in a channel of distribution, one participant emerges as the channel captain, or dominating member. Differences exist among countries as to

14. Ian Rodger, "Nordica and Salomon," p. 12.
15. "Seiko Epson Clones Strategy of U.S. Rival," *Nikkei Weekly,* January 17, 1994, p. 8.

who typically emerges as the dominating member. In the United States, for example, the originally strong wholesalers have become less influential, with manufacturers playing the dominant role in many channels. In Japan, on the other hand, wholesalers continue to dominate the channel structure. In many developing countries, independent distributors are very strong because they are the only authorized importers.

Different countries may require different channel strategies. Linear, a U.K. manufacturer of weather stripping for aluminum windows, uses six different distribution methods to sell in thirteen European countries. The size of the market, the distribution customers, and the way manufacturers buy dictated that different systems be used in different markets.[16] The international marketer will analyze each country with respect to the best operating mode, recognizing that it may be impossible to pursue the same strategy in all countries.

Some companies find it necessary to acquire the channel captain to further grow a market. For example, in 1994, Nike acquired Nissho Iwai Corp., the Japanese trading house that had been distributing Nike products in Japan. Nike chief executive officer Philip Knight said, "Whoever works in Japan in the coming years wins in Asia, and whoever wins in Asia will win in the world."[17] Nike felt that acquiring its Japanese distributor and converting Nissho Iwai to a wholly owned subsidiary would give it the increased control and expertise to further penetrate the Japanese market.

A different approach was chosen by Caterpillar, the large U.S. manufacturer of earthmoving equipment, for its entry into Japan. At first, the company's joint venture partner, Mitsubishi, suggested marketing equipment through existing channels. (In Japan, the manufacturers sell through large trading houses that resell and provide financing to dealers. The dealers are relatively small and leave parts inventory and service to independent repair shops.) Caterpillar preferred to market its equipment through large, independent dealers that not only sold but also serviced the equipment and maintained a sufficient parts inventory. Caterpillar recognized that its distribution strategy was a critical global strength difficult for competitors to match, so it invested heavily in building and training its dealers.[18] Thus, Caterpillar successfully implemented its traditional strategy in Japan and emerged as one of the leading earthmoving equipment manufacturers in Japan.

Distribution Logistics

Distribution logistics focuses on the physical movement of goods through the channels. An extremely important part of the distribution system, logistics will be discussed in detail later in the chapter (see "International Logistics").

16. Christopher Lorenz, "Where Variety Is the Stuff of Success," *Financial Times,* October 26, 1988, p. 31.

17. "Nike 'Just Does It' Alone with Buyout of Japan Partner," *Nikkei Weekly,* January 17, 1994, p. 10.

18. S. Tamer Cavusgil, "The Importance of Distributor Training at Caterpillar," *Industrial Marketing Management,* 19 (1990), pp. 1–9.

Factors Influencing the Selection of Channel Members

After developing a distribution strategy, a marketer then needs to identify and select appropriate distribution partners to support the overall distribution strategy. This selection of distribution partners is an extremely important decision because often the partner will assume a portion of or the entire marketing responsibility for a set of markets. The distribution decision is one of the most important elements of the entry strategy. A poor decision will often lead to lackluster performance. It is often expensive or sometimes impossible to change your distribution partner due to local laws. PepsiCo went through a yearlong court battle to terminate its twenty-two year contract with Perrier to bottle and distribute Pepsi in France. PepsiCo contended that Perrier had underperformed and had let Pepsi-Cola's share decline from 17 percent to 7 percent over the previous ten years.[19] Also, the distribution partner usually is involved in the physical movement (logistics) of products to the customers. Therefore, the success of a firm's international efforts depends on the partners it selects. A number of factors influence the selection of distribution partners. Those that have significant effect include:

1. Cost   *4.* Control
2. Capital requirement   *5.* Coverage
3. Product and product line   *6.* Synergy

Cost

Channel costs fall into three categories: initial costs, maintenance costs, and logistics costs. The *initial costs* include all the costs of locating and setting up the channel, such as executive time and travel to locate and select channel members, cost of negotiating an agreement with channel members, and the capital cost of setting up the channel. The capital cost is discussed separately in the next segment of this chapter. The *maintenance cost* of the channel includes the cost of the company's salespeople, sales managers, travel expenses, and the cost of auditing and controlling channel operations, local advertising expenses, and the profit margin of the intermediaries. The *logistical costs* include the transportation cost, storage costs, the cost of breaking bulk shipments into smaller lot sizes, and the cost for customs paperwork.

Although predicting all of these various costs when selecting different channel members is often difficult, it is necessary to estimate the cost of various alternatives. High distribution costs usually result in higher prices at the consumer level, which may hamper entry into a new market. Companies often will establish direct channels, hoping to reduce distribution cost. Unfortunately, most of the functions of the channel cannot be eliminated, so these costs show up later. A study of five different international channels of distribution

19. Alice Rawsthorn, ''Pepsi Wins Its Battle with Perrier over Marketing,'' *Financial Times,* December 18, 1992, p. 18.

found that the least profitable is exporting directly to the retailers in the host country. The most profitable channel is selling to a distributor in a country that has its own marketing channels.[20]

Capital Requirement

The capital cost of different channel alternatives can be very high. The capital cost includes the cost for inventories, the cost of goods in transit, accounts receivable, and inventories on consignment. The capital cost is offset by the cashflow patterns from a channel alternative. For example, an import distributor will often pay for the goods when they are received, before they are sold to the retailer or industrial firm. On the other hand, an agent may not receive payment until the goods reach the industrial customer or retailer. This is also true of direct sales efforts. The establishment of a direct sales channel often requires the maximum investment, whereas use of distributors often reduces the investment required. The capital cost of various distribution channels affects the company's return on investment. In the early stages of the life cycle of organizations (see Chapter 16), companies often export through a distributor or agent because they cannot afford the capital cost of setting up a direct sales effort.

Product and Product Line

The nature of a product can affect channel selection. If the product is perishable or has a short shelf life, then the manufacturer is forced to use shorter channels to get the product to the consumer faster. Delta Dairy, a Greek producer of dairy products and chilled fruit juices, was faced with increased transportation costs of shipping from Greece to France, when the United Nations banned transit across the former Yugoslavia. In addition to a 25 percent increase in production costs, Delta lost five days of product shelf life, so it set up production in Switzerland to shorten the distance to the French market.[21]

A technical product often requires direct sales or highly technical channel partners. For example, Index Technology of Cambridge, Massachusetts, sells a sophisticated software product to automate the development of software systems called computer-aided systems engineering. The company entered the United Kingdom and Australia with a direct sales effort, but to avoid start-up costs it used distributors in France, Germany, and Scandinavia. Insufficient revenues from distributors led the company to set up its own sales efforts in France and Germany, and purchase the distributor in Scandinavia. The highly sophisticated nature of the product required a direct sales effort. Nonperishable or generic, unsophisticated products, such as batteries, that are available in many types of retail stores may be distributed through a long channel that reaches many different types of retailers.

The size of the product line also affects selection of channel members. A broader

20. Warren J. Bilkey, ''Variables Associated with Export Profitability,'' presented at the 1980 Academy of International Business Conference, New Orleans, October 23, 1980.
21. ''Delta Dairy Streamlined Food Producer,'' *Financial Times,* July 8, 1993, p. 11.

product line is more desirable for channel members. A distributor or dealer is more likely to stock a broad product line than a single item. Limited product lines often must be sold through agents. If a manufacturer has a very broad, complete line, it is easier to justify the cost of a more direct channel. With more products to sell, it is easier to generate a high average order on each sales call. With a limited product line, an agent or distributor will group your product together with products from other companies to increase the average order size.

Control

Each type of channel arrangement offers a different level of control by the manufacturer. With a direct sales force, a manufacturer can control price, promotion, amount of effort, and type of retail outlet used. If these are important, the increased level of control may offset the increased cost of a direct sales force. Longer channels, particularly with distributors who take title to goods, often result in little or no control. In many cases, a company may not know who is ultimately buying the product.

Limited control is not necessarily bad, however. If the volume of sales is adequate, the manufacturer may not necessarily care where the product is being used. Also, a manufacturer can increase its level of market knowledge, its influence on channel members, and its channel control by increasing its presence in the market. For example, the manager of international sales and marketing may be located in Europe and spend all of his or her time traveling with distributor salespeople.

Coverage

Coverage refers to the geographic coverage that a manufacturer desires. Though coverage is usually easy to get in major metropolitan areas, gaining adequate coverage of smaller cities or sparsely populated areas can be difficult. Selection of one channel member over another may be influenced by the respective market coverage. To determine an agent's, broker's, or distributor's coverage, the following must be determined: (1) location of sales offices, (2) salespersons' home base, and (3) last year's sales by geographic location. The location of sales offices indicates where efforts are focused. Salespeople generally have the best penetration near their homes. Past sales clearly indicate the channel member's success in each geographic area.

Synergy

The choice of channel members or partners can sometimes be influenced by the existence of complementary skills that can increase the total output of the distribution system. This normally occurs where the potential distributor partner has some skill or expertise that will allow quicker access to the market. For example, when Compaq entered the international personal computer market, it decided to sell only through a network of strong authorized dealers. While Compaq focused on developing market applications such as sales force automation, computer-aided design, and office productivity, it used the dealers to penetrate

TABLE 12.1 ● Process of Establishing an International Distribution System

1. Develop distribution strategy
2. Establish criteria for selecting distribution partners
3. Locate potential distribution partners
4. Solicit the interest of distributors
5. Screen and select distribution partners
6. Negotiate agreements

the marketplace. Compaq's international sales grew from $20 million in 1984 to $1.33 billion in 1989 through the combination of marketing and technical expertise from Compaq and sales and implementation expertise from the authorized dealers.[22]

Locating and Selecting Channel Partners

Building an international distribution system normally takes one to three years. The process involves a series of steps that are shown in Table 12.1. The critical aspect of developing a successful system is locating and selecting channel partners.

The development of an international distribution strategy in terms of distribution density, channel length, channel alignment, and distribution logistics will establish a framework for the "ideal" distribution partners. The company's preference regarding key factors that influence selection of channel partners (cost, capital requirements, product, control, and coverage) will be used with the distribution strategy to establish criteria for the selection of partners. The strategy normally focuses the selection on one or two types of channel partners—for example, export manager's company and import distributors.

Selection criteria include geographic coverage, managerial ability, financial stability, annual volume, reputation, and so on. The following sources can be used to locate possible distribution partners:

1. *U.S. Department of Commerce.* The Agent Distributor Service is a customized service of the Department of Commerce that locates distributors and agents interested in a certain product line. Also, the department's Export Marketing Service can be used to locate distribution partners.

2. *Banks.* If the firm's bank has foreign branches, they may be happy to help locate distributors.

3. *Directories.* Country directories of distributors or specialized directories, such as those listing computer distributors, can be helpful.

22. "Compaq—in the Spirit of Europe 1992," *Economist,* May 5, 1990, pp. 32–33.

4. *Trade shows.* Exhibiting at an international trade show or just attending will expose managers to a large number of distributors and their salespeople.

5. *Competitor's distribution partners.* Sometimes a competitor's distributor may be interested in switching product lines.

6. *Consultants.* Some international marketing consultants specialize in locating distributors.

7. *Associations.* There are associations of international intermediaries or country associations of intermediaries. For example, Japan has numerous industry associations.

8. *Foreign consulates.* Most countries have a commercial attaché at their embassies or a separate consulate, both of which are helpful in locating agents/distributors in their country.

After compiling a list of possible distribution partners, the firm may send each a letter with product literature and distribution requirements. The prospective distributors can be asked to respond, if they have an interest in the firm's product line, with relevant information such as lines currently carried, annual volume, number of salespeople, geographic territory covered, credit and bank references, physical facilities, relationship with local government, and knowledge of English or other relevant languages. Firms that respond should be checked against the selection criteria. Before making a final decision, a manufacturer's representative should go to the country and talk to the industrial end users or retailers to determine the best two or three distributors.[23] While in the country, the manufacturer's representative should meet and evaluate the possible distribution partners before making a final decision.

Managing the Distribution System

Selecting the most suitable channel participants and gaining access to the market are extremely important steps in achieving an integrated and responsive distribution channel. However, without proper motivation of and control over that channel, sales may remain unsatisfactory to the foreign marketer. This section discusses the steps that must be taken to ensure the flow of the firm's products through the channel by gaining the full cooperation of all channel members.

Motivating Channel Participants

Keeping channel participants motivated is an important aspect of international distribution policies. Financial incentives in the form of higher than average gross margins can be a

23. G. Beeth, "Distributors—Finding and Keeping Good Ones," in *International Marketing Strategy,* ed. Hans Thorelli and Helmut Becker (New York: Pergamon Press, 1980), p. 261.

very powerful inducement, particularly for the management of independent distributors, wholesalers, and retailers. The expected gross margins are influenced by the cultural history of that channel. For example, if a certain type of retailer usually gets a 50 percent margin and the firm offers 40 percent, the effort may be less than expected. Inviting channel members to annual conferences and introductions of new products is also effective. By extending help to the management of distributorships in areas such as inventory control, collections, advertising, and so on, goodwill can be gained that later will be of advantage to the international firm. Special programs may also be instituted to train or motivate the channel members' sales forces.

Programs to motivate foreign independent intermediaries are likely to succeed if monetary incentives are considered along with efforts that help make the channel members more efficient and competitive. To have prosperous intermediaries is, of course, also in the interest of the international firm. These programs or policies are particularly important in the case of independents who distribute products on a nonexclusive basis. Often they are beleaguered by the principals of other products they carry; each is attempting to get the greatest possible attention from the distributor for its own purposes. Therefore, the international firm must have policies that make sure the channel members devote sufficient effort to its products.

The motivation of channel partners and the amount of effort devoted to the firm's product line are enhanced by a continuous flow of two-way information between manufacturer and distributor. The amount of effort an international firm needs to expend depends on the marketing strategy for that market. For example, if the firm is using extensive advertising to pull products through a channel, the intermediary may be expected only to take orders and deliver the product with no real sales effort. If the marketing strategy depends on the channel member's developing the market or pushing the product through the channel, then a significant sales effort will be required. As much as possible, the manufacturer should send letters, public relations releases, product news, and so on to encourage attention to its product line and reduce conflict. A study of manufacturer-distributor relationships found that more-intense contact between the export manufacturer and the distributor resulted in better performance by the distributor.[24]

In addition to telephone and mail communication, periodic visits to distribution partners can have a positive effect on their motivation and control. Visits can provide other benefits as well. By visiting the distribution partner, the firm can resolve any difficulties. Also, sales volumes can be reviewed and emphasis placed on the most important products or types of customers. Often it is helpful to travel with a channel member salesperson to gain knowledge of the marketplace and to evaluate the skills of the salesperson. The most important benefit of a visit to the channel member is that it gives a clear message that the member's performance is important to the firm. Visits strengthen the personal relationship between the manufacturer and the channel member.

24. Philip J. Rosson and I. David Ford, ''Manufacturer–Overseas Distributor Relations and Export Performance,'' presented at the 1980 Academy of International Business Conference, New Orleans, October 1980.

During these personal visits, the manufacturer can identify other ways to help and support the channel member. Strong advertising support through either national advertising or cooperative advertising can help strengthen the manufacturer's consumer franchise. Effective advertising makes it easier for the channel member to sell the manufacturer's products, which leads to increased sales and often more attention devoted to the product line.

Beware of strategies that cause conflict between manufacturers and channel members. The most common causes of channel conflict are (1) bypassing channels to sell directly to large customers, (2) oversaturating a market with too many dealers/distributors, (3) establishing too many levels in the distribution system (that is, requiring smaller distributors to buy from large ones), and (4) opening new discount channels that offer the same goods at lower prices.[25]

Recent research has shown that efforts by manufacturers to train and educate dealers in developing countries lead to increased revenue.[26] Caterpillar has faced the strong Japanese competitor Komatsu in the earthmoving equipment world market. Caterpillar found that dealer training could develop a strong competitive advantage difficult for Komatsu to copy. In fact, during the pilot of the dealer sales training program, participating dealers increased revenue by 102 percent.[27]

Controlling Channel Participants

Although motivated intermediaries will expend the necessary effort on an international company's products, there is generally no assurance that these efforts will be channeled in the right direction. Therefore, the company will want to exert enough control over channel members to help guarantee that they interpret and execute the company's marketing strategies. The firm wants to be sure that the local intermediaries price the products according to the company's policies. The same could be said for sales, advertising, and service policies. Since the company's reputation in a local market can be tarnished due to the ineffective handling of local distribution by independent intermediaries, international companies closely monitor the performance of local channel members. After the takeover of United Distillers by Guinness, the company reorganized to become a worldwide marketer of high-quality branded alcoholic drinks. In 1986, 75 percent of United Distillers volume was sold through 1,304 distributors; the company had very little control over the distribution. By 1990, the number of distributors was reduced to 470, and through acquisition or joint ventures, United Distillers had direct control over 80 percent of its distribution.[28]

25. Allan J. Magrath and Kenneth G. Hardy, ''Avoiding the Pitfalls in Managing Distribution Channels,'' *Business Horizons,* September–October 1987, p. 31.

26. Gary L. Frazier, James D. Gill, and Sudhir H. Kale, ''Dealer Dependence Levels and Reciprocal Actions in a Channel of Distribution in a Developing Country,'' *Journal of Marketing,* January 1989, pp. 50–69.

27. Cavusgil, ''Importance of Distributor Training,'' p. 5.

28. Philip Rawstorne, ''Re-shaping United Distillers,'' *Financial Times,* June 13, 1990, p. 12.

One way to exert influence over the international channel members is to spell out the specific responsibilities of each, including minimum annual sales, in the distribution agreement. Attainment of the sales goal can be required for renewal of the contract. Also, the awarding of exclusive distribution rights can be used to increase control. Typically, business is channeled through one intermediary in a given geographic area only, raising the firm's importance to the intermediary.

Frequently, exclusive rights are coupled with a prohibition against carrying directly competing products. When the small, British company Filofax (maker of binders containing customized inserts such as calendars and diaries) entered the Japanese market in 1984, it decided to use Apex Inc. as its exclusive distributor. The exclusive distributorship gave Apex the incentive to push Filofax and was successful in getting the product into 300 outlets, sixty in Tokyo, supported by heavy advertising showing Diane Keaton and Steven Spielberg using their Filofaxes. While there are 30 makers of imitation products, Filofax sells at a 50 percent price premium with high-quality packaging and a leather binder. The relationship has been very profitable for both Filofax and Apex.[29] The exclusive distributor's leverage is knowledge and expertise in the market. The leverage of the manufacturer is the patent on the product, the brand name, and possible economies of scale. Of course, the exclusive distributor can become too powerful and even evolve from a collaborator into a competitor. Many international companies limit the distribution rights to short time periods with periodic renewal. Caution is advised, however, since cancellation of distribution rights is frequently subject to local laws that do not allow a sudden termination.

Although termination of a distributor or agent for nonperformance is a relatively simple action in the United States, termination of international channel members can be very costly in many parts of the world. For example, in Honduras, the termination of an agent can cost up to five times the annual gross profits plus the value of the agent's investment, plus all kinds of additional payments. In Belgium, termination compensation for agents and distributors includes the value of any goodwill plus expenses in developing the business plus the amount of compensation claimed by discharged employees who worked on the product line. The minimum termination notice is three months.[30] As you can see, termination of a channel member can be a costly, painful process governed in almost all cases by local laws that tend to protect and compensate the channel member. Nissan, Japan's second-largest car manufacturer, expected a legal battle with its exclusive U.K. distributorship of twenty-one years. Nissan-U.K., owned by Mr. Botnar, a British entrepreneur, oversaw a network of four hundred Nissan dealers who sold 138,000 cars in the United Kingdom in 1989. Nissan sent a fax to terminate the agreement at the end of 1990[31] and started its own dealers. Botnar sued Nissan, and the case is still in court.

29. "Organized, but Not Personally," *Economist,* November 12, 1988, pp. 82–83.
30. "Guidelines for Terminating Agents and Distributors," *Export Advisor,* November 1981, p. 14.
31. John Griffiths, "Nissan to Split with U.K. Dealer After Row," *Financial Times,* December 28, 1990, p. 1.

Gaining Access to Distribution Channels

To actually gain access to distribution channels may well be the most formidable challenge in international marketing. Decisions on product designs, communications strategies, and pricing can be very complex and pose difficult choices, but once a company has made the choices, the implementation requires significant management expertise and resources. The distribution system is critical to implementing the marketing strategy.

Entry into a market can be accomplished through a variety of channel members described earlier in the chapter (see Figure 12.1). Often, the most logical channel member already has a relationship with one of your competitors, therefore limiting your access; this poses some special challenges to international marketers. Therefore, this section is aimed at illustrating alternatives companies have when, while offering an excellent product or service, they encounter difficulties in convincing channel members to carry their products.

The "Locked-Up" Channel

A channel is considered locked up when a newcomer cannot easily convince any channel member to participate despite the fact that both market and economic reasons suggest otherwise. Channel members customarily decide on a case-by-case basis what products they should add to or drop from their line. Retailers typically select products that they expect to sell easily and in volume, and they can be expected to switch sources when better opportunities arise. Similarly, wholesalers and distributors compete for retail accounts or industrial users on economic terms. They can expect to entice a prospective client to switch by buying from a new source that can offer a better deal. Likewise, manufacturers compete for wholesale accounts with the expectation that channel members can be convinced to purchase from any given manufacturer if the offer exceeds those made by competitors.

Often there are barriers that limit a wholesaler's flexibility to add or drop a particular line. The distributor may have an agreement not to sell competitive products, or its business may include a significant volume from one manufacturer, which it does not want to risk upsetting. In Japan, relationships between manufacturers, wholesalers, and retailers are long-standing in nature and do not allow channel participants to change allegiance quickly to another source because of a superior product or price. Japanese channel members develop strong personal ties, and a sense of economic dependence develops. These close ties make it very difficult for any participant to break a long-standing relationship. In some cases, most existing wholesale or retail outlets may be committed in such a way that a newcomer to the market may not find qualified channel participants.

Cultural forces may not be the only influence in blocking a channel of distribution. Competitors, domestic or foreign, may try to obstruct the entry of a new company; or the members of a channel may not be willing to take any risks by pioneering unknown products. In all of these instances, the result is a locked-up channel that severely limits access to markets. When American Standard, the world's largest supplier of plumbing fixtures, tried to enter the Korean market, it found itself locked out of the normal distributors, who were controlled by local manufacturers. American Standard looked for an alternative distribution channel that served the building trade. It found Home Center, one of the largest suppliers of homebuilding materials and appliances. With a local factory, American Standard successfully circumvented the locked channels.[32]

Manufacturers in the United States are not entirely new to the situation of the locked-up channel. Marketers of consumer goods developed the pull-type communication strategy to circumvent nonresponsive channel members by concentrating advertising directly on consumers. Manufacturers of industrial products usually can make use of independent manufacturers' representatives or agents to gain quick access to users. To use the same strategies abroad requires equally free access to communications channels in other countries. However, this access is restricted in some countries (see Chapter 15) by government regulations that forbid TV or radio advertising or allow only limited availability of these media. In the case of industrial markets, the frequent entry of new entrepreneurs as independent agents is also considerably less prevalent.

Alternative Entry Approaches

With fewer chances to outflank nonresponsive channels abroad, international marketers have developed new approaches to the difficult situation of gaining access to distribution channels.

Piggybacking   When a company does not find any channel partners with sufficient interest to pioneer new products, the practice of piggybacking may offer a way out of the situation. *Piggybacking* is an arrangement with another company that sells to the same customer segment to take on the new products as if it were the manufacturer. The products retain the name of the manufacturer and both partners normally sign a multiyear contract to provide for continuity. The new company is, in essence, "piggybacking" its products on the shoulders of the established company's sales force.

A Japanese manufacturer of soy sauce, Kikkoman, decided to piggyback on Del Monte's sales force for its entry into Mexico. The two companies had signed an earlier technical agreement allowing Kikkoman to sell Del Monte's tomato juice in Japan. Following Kikkoman's successful entry into the U.S. market, the company planned to enter several South American countries. The company also wanted to use Del Monte's existing strong retail sales network.[33] As a result of this move, Kikkoman was in a position to gain immediate distribution, a process that would have taken years to develop on its own.

Under a piggyback arrangement, the manufacturer retains control over marketing

32. Steve Glain, "American Standard Succeeds in Korea by Outflanking Local Firms' Lockout," *Financial Times,* August 26, 1993, p. A6.
33. "Kikkoman Is Due Actively to Sell Soy Sauce in Mexico in January," *Japan Economic Journal,* November 6, 1979, p. 14.

strategy, particularly pricing, positioning, and advertising. The partner acts as a ''rented'' sales force only. Of course, this is quite different from the private label strategy whereby the manufacturer supplies a marketer who places its own brand name on the product.

Joint Ventures   As discussed in Chapter 9, when two companies agree jointly to form a new legal entity, it is called a *joint venture*. Such operations have been quite common in the area of joint production. Our interest here is restricted to joint ventures in which distribution is the primary objective. Normally, such companies are formed between a local firm with existing market access and a foreign firm that would like to market its products in a country where it has no existing market access. One of the best ways to enter the Japanese market is a joint venture with a Japanese partner that is in a similar but not competitive field.[34] Many such joint ventures have been signed between Japanese firms and foreign companies eager to enter the Japanese market. Through access to the distribution channel, the Japanese partner either acts as a sales agent or opens the doors for the joint venture's sales force.

Many such joint ventures expand into production, though the original intention of the foreign partner clearly was to gain access to the distribution system. Kodak began selling in Japan in 1989 but found itself in a weak position in the mid-1980s with only fifteen people in its Tokyo office selling through four distributors. Kodak had 1 percent of the market, while Fuji had 70 percent and was attacking Kodak in the United States and Europe. Kodak formed a joint venture with Nagase Sangyo, an Osaka-based trading company specializing in chemicals, to attack Fuji in its home market. With heavy investment in plant, promotion, and distribution, Kodak had 4,500 employees in Japan and 15 percent of the market by 1990.[35]

The Mexican beer market is controlled by two companies—Femsa with a 49 percent share and Modelo with 51 percent. These two domestic producers had tied up the retail outlets with exclusivity constraints, which explains why Anheuser-Busch decided to enter Mexico through a joint venture with Modelo rather than trying to build a distribution system from scratch.[36] In another beer example, foreign beers have made little headway into the Japanese beer market, which is controlled by four domestic producers: Kirin, Asahi, Sapporo, and Suntory. These four producers have a 98 percent share of the Japanese market. To enter these locked channels, Budweiser has brewed and bottled its beer under license with Suntory since 1984. Suntory is the smallest of the four Japanese brewers, and Budweiser established a joint venture in 1993 with Kirin, the largest domestic brewer with a 49.2 percent market share. Budweiser hopes to grow its share of the Japanese market from 1.2 percent to 5 percent or even 10 percent.[37] As Komatsu, the Japanese earthmoving

34. ''Beating the System,'' *Economist,* January 31, 1987, p. 63.

35. ''The Revenge of Big Yellow,'' *Economist,* November 10, 1990, p. 103.

36. Damian Fraser, ''Mexico Provides an Attractive Brew,'' *Financial Times,* March 26, 1993, p. 19.

37. Gordon Cramp, ''Anheuser-Busch's Defection Looks Set to Shake Up Japan's Beer Market,'' *Financial Times,* July 30, 1993, p. 21.

equipment company, realized it could not overcome the strength of Caterpillar's dealer network in the United States, it formed a joint venture with Dresser Industries to strengthen its distribution.[38]

Original Equipment Manufacturers (OEMs)   In a situation in which the international manufacturer signs a supply agreement with a domestic or local firm to sell the international manufacturer's products but under the established brand name of the local firm, the arrangement is termed an *OEM agreement,* or *private labeling* (for consumer products). The foreign company uses the already existing distribution network of the local company, whereas the local company gains a chance to broaden its product lines.

The French automobile manufacturer Renault signed an OEM agreement with the U.S. truck builder Mack. The agreement provided that medium-duty diesel trucks built by Renault would be sold under the Mack name through Mack's more than three hundred dealers. Due to fuel prices, U.S. truck operators had shown a preference for the diesel trucks that always were very popular in Europe. Recognizing the opportunity, Renault signed the agreement and got immediate access to a well-entrenched distribution system. This was much easier than building one from scratch. Furthermore, selecting a well-known U.S. partner was viewed as less costly than joining a foreign company attempting to enter the same segment. The agreement was solidified by Renault's purchase of 20 percent of Mack's equity. Mack, of course, received an already proven line of medium-duty diesel trucks, thus saving the costs that it would have taken to develop its own line.[39]

Japanese companies have been particularly adept at using the OEM strategy to build whole alliances of captive markets. Matsushita, for example, marketed a substantial portion of its videotape recorders (VTRs) through OEM arrangements with RCA, Magnavox, Sylvania, Curtis Mathes, and General Electric—all U.S. companies. Likewise, another Japanese VTR producer and joint venture company distributed its products in Europe through Thorn (U.K.), Thompson-Brandt (France), Saba, Normende, and Telefunken (Germany). All of these OEMs sold joint venture company products under their own brand names.[40]

In the computer field, Japanese companies have adopted strategies that differ from those customarily chosen by U.S. computer manufacturers. For example, Hitachi sold its mainframe computers, which compete directly with IBM, through National Advanced Systems, the marketing arm of National Semiconductor in the United States. In Europe, it sells through Comparex, a joint venture of BASF and Siemens. In 1990, Hitachi formed a joint venture with Electronic Data Systems (part of General Motors) to buy National Advanced System, thereby switching from an OEM arrangement to a joint venture.[41]

Distributing in foreign markets under OEM agreements has its dangers as well. Since

38. "For Caterpillar the Metamorphosis Isn't Over," *Business Week,* April 1987, p. 72.
39. "Signal Unit Plans to Sell Trucks of Renault Unit," *Wall Street Journal,* July 27, 1978, p. 7.
40. Ibid.
41. "Hitachi Acquires Route to U.S. Market with GM Link," *Financial Times,* February 28, 1989, p. 1.

the local OEM will put its own label on the imported product, the international company does not get any access to local customers and therefore will find it difficult to achieve a strong identity in the market. This reliance on the local OEM can also pose problems when the local company's performance declines. An excellent example is the situation faced by Mitsubishi International Corporation, a large Japanese automobile manufacturer that supplied Chrysler Corporation with small cars under an OEM agreement. With Chrysler's weak financial situation from 1983 to 1985, Mitsubishi would have preferred to sell its cars directly to the U.S. market under Mitsubishi's brand name. As long as the agreement was in effect, Mitsubishi was prohibited from doing that, and its fortune in the U.S. market continued to depend on Chrysler's efforts. The OEM tie-up allows a company to reach a high volume more quickly by sacrificing independence and control over its own distribution system. Of course, a company selecting this route is partially motivated by the corresponding savings of expenses by not building its own distribution system.

Acquisitions   Acquiring an existing company can give a foreign entrant immediate access to a distribution system. Although it requires a substantial amount of capital, operating results tend to be better than those after starting a new venture, which often brings initial losses. It is often less important to find an acquisition candidate with a healthy financial outlook or top products than one with a good relationship to wholesale and retail outlets. A good example of the acquisition strategy to gain access to distribution channels was Merck's purchase of 51 percent of Japan's Banyu pharmaceutical company. Sales and profits have more than doubled since the acquisition, and Banyu is one of the fastest-growing drug companies in Japan.[42]

The Japanese car market had been difficult to enter due to the stiff tax on big cars and the limited distribution. The tax was dropped in April 1989, and Ford acquired a 35 percent stake in Autorama, a nationwide distributorship, to expand its sales. As a result, Autorama sold 44,000 cars in 1993.[43] Japanese car dealers are no longer limited to selling just Japanese cars; the exclusive arrangements have been eliminated, opening up the dealer sales networks to foreign manufacturers. In addition to a joint venture with Mazda, Ford broke new ground in 1994 by forming alliances with Nissan and Toyota dealers to sell Ford cars in Japan. According to Tokyo Nissan spokesperson Atsushi Horigose, it is likely that the Nissan dealers will sell profitable higher-priced Fords that will not compete with Nissan models.[44]

Starting New Ventures   To build one's own distribution system not only is costly but also requires patience and time. Aware of these risks, IVECO, a European truck manufacturer jointly owned by Italy's Fiat and Germany's Klockner-Humboldt-Deutz, first attempted to enter the U.S. market with an arrangement with a U.S. truck manufacturer, but an

42. Carla Rapoport, "You Can Make Money in Japan," *Fortune,* February 12, 1990, p. 45.
43. "Nissan Affiliate to Sell Ford Cars; Toyota Dealership Follows with Negotiations," *Nikkei Weekly,* January 17, 1994, pp. 1, 23.
44. Ibid., p. 23.

agreement could not be reached because IVECO refused to have its vehicles sold under an OEM contract allowing the U.S. company to put its own name on the trucks. When it started out on its own, IVECO began to realize the difficulty ahead. Each individual dealer had to be separately recruited, and sales had to be limited to the eastern and southern parts of the United States. To overcome its low profile, IVECO budgeted $2 million for an advertising campaign. The company accepted the fact that break-even volume would be at least two years away, with the actual outcome uncertain.[45] Though this strategy is higher in initial risk, it offers a company the chance to eventually control its own distribution system.

The Japanese retail market has been protected since 1973, when new stores over 500 square meters needed to get the permission of local store owners to open. Obviously, permission usually was denied! In mid-1990, the restriction was rescinded. Toys ''R'' Us opened its first store of 5,000 square meters in Niigata, a town of 500,000 people that already has sixty-three stores selling toys. Toys ''R'' Us hoped to do $13.3 million in its first year, which is eighty times the average of the current toy stores and a 50 percent share of the Niigata market. Toys ''R'' Us recently allied itself with Den Fujita, the president of McDonald's in Japan. Fujita wants to help tie Toys ''R'' Us locations with a McDonald's and a video store.[46]

International Logistics

The logistics system, also called physical distribution, involves planning, implementing, and controlling the physical flow of materials and final goods from points of origin to points of use to meet customer needs at a profit.[47] On an international scale, the task becomes more complex because so many external variables have an impact on that flow of materials or products. As geographical distances to foreign markets grow, competitive advantages are often derived from a more effective structuring of the logistics system, by either saving time or costs or increasing a firm's reliability. The emergence of logistics as a means of competitive advantage is leading companies to focus increased attention on this vital area. Many manufacturers and retailers are restructuring their logistics efforts and divesting their in-house distribution divisions in favor of outside logistics specialists.

A logistics system is expensive. It is a capital- and labor-intensive function outside of the core business of most companies and has become increasingly complex. For many concerns, it represents 16 to 35 percent of total revenues. Marks and Spencer, a U.K. retailer that operates in eight countries, found it could increase the sales per square foot and eliminate the need for most stockrooms by increasing the frequency of delivery. To

45. ''A New Challenge in Trucks,'' *Business Week,* July 3, 1978, p. 88.

46. ''Retailing in Japan—Toy Joy,'' *Economist,* January 4, 1992, p. 62.

47. Philip Kotler, *Marketing Management,* 5th ed. (Englewood Cliffs, N.J.: Prentice Hall, 1984), p. 591.

guarantee reliability the company used outside contractors.[48] In this section, we describe the objectives of an international logistics system and the individual organizational operations that have to be managed into an efficient system.

Determining Service Levels

The principal objective of the logistics system is to provide the service of dependable and efficient movement of materials or products to the user. Since any combination of logistics arrangements involves expenditures, the firm is urged to first determine the level of service desired before any implementation is made. Determining service levels is marketing management's responsibility and requires attention to the following four areas:

1. *Maximization of the number of orders shipped compared to the number of orders received.* For most firms, it is important to be able to ship products for orders received. It is generally accepted that a level of 100 percent is unrealistic since it requires the company to be prepared for all eventualities and most likely will result in high inventories. Marketing managers have to decide on an appropriate percentage, given the existing competition both here and abroad and taking into consideration the delivery systems in the particular foreign market. Since it is not possible to fill all orders received, managers have to balance the costs of maintaining a sufficient inventory with the cost of lost business because clients may place orders elsewhere if delivery is not forthcoming immediately.

2. *Minimization of the time between order submission and actual order shipment.* Aside from having the products physically on hand, the firm must reduce its reaction, or order-filling, time; there should be speedy delivery to customers. Any reduction of this order-processing time results in a reduction of the client's inventory needs and can therefore be turned into a competitive advantage. On an international level, it is unlikely that customers in all countries have the same expectation of this reaction time. Consequently, management has to pay special attention to local requirements or, where necessary, to ensure that orders submitted to one regional distribution center from different markets receive the necessary attention. It may not be feasible to have a unified, or single, policy for all markets.

3. *Minimization of the variance between promised delivery and actual delivery.* Once a customer has been promised delivery by a set date, the customer will draw down on inventory in anticipation of the new delivery. Consequently, a delay can substantially affect the client's operation, maybe even cause a loss of orders. Minimizing the variance between promised and actual delivery does not always require the fastest mode of transportation. Reliability is the key. International logistics often involves various modes of transportation subject to unexpected occurrences that upset delivery schedules. The firm that manages to insulate

48. "Distribution Services—the World's the Limit," *Financial Times,* November 6, 1990, sect. III, p. 1.

its clients from such unexpected events can gain a substantial advantage over competitors.

4. *Minimization of damage in transit.* Any shipment that reaches its destination in damaged form represents an opportunity loss to the buyer who planned for the arrival of the product. Even if an insurance settlement replaces the actual value of products damaged, the loss of business due to the absence of additional inventory cannot be replaced. International shipments are often subject to numerous adverse physical stresses due to long transit times, changes in climate, or numerous handlings at ports for transshipments. Adequate protective packaging is therefore required and may far exceed standards for domestic shipments.[49]

Logistics Decision Areas

The total task of logistics management consists of five separate though interrelated jobs:

1. Traffic or transportation management
2. Inventory control
3. Order processing
4. Materials handling and warehousing
5. Fixed facilities location management

Each of these five jobs, or decision areas, offers unique challenges to the international marketer and is described below in more detail.

Traffic or Transportation Management Traffic management deals primarily with the mode of transportation. Principal choices are air, sea, rail, and truck, or some combination thereof. Since transportation expenses contribute substantially to the costs of marketing products internationally, special attention has to be given to the selection of the transportation mode. Such choices are made by considering three principal factors: lead-times, transit times, and costs. Companies operating with long lead-times tend to use slower and therefore low-cost transportation modes such as sea and freight. For short lead-time situations, faster modes of transportation such as air and truck are used. Also important are transit times. Long transit times require higher financial costs since payments arrive later, and there are normally higher average inventories at either the point of origin or the destination. Modes of transportation with long transit times are sea or rail, whereas air or truck transportation results in much shorter transit times. Costs are the third factor considered for the decision of a mode of transport. Typically, air or truck transportation is more expensive than either sea or rail for any given distance.

Overloaded ports or transportation facilities can be hazardous and costly. With coal

49. Adapted from John F. Magee, ''The Logistics of Distribution,'' *Harvard Business Review,* July–August 1960, pp. 89–101.

again in great demand worldwide in the 1980s, U.S. coal exporters were restricted in their export shipments by bottlenecks in major ports.[50] With volumes of 90 million tons in 1980 and 110 million tons in 1985, U.S. coal exporters decided it was in their own best interest to expand port facilities. In one year alone, foreign customers paid about $1 million for waiting charges to foreign vessels waiting to load coal. At one point, 150 coal transport vessels waited at one Virginia port for an average delay of sixty to seventy days. If U.S. producers cannot guarantee speedy unloading, foreign customers may turn to other suppliers in Canada, South Africa, or Australia.

Rank Xerox found by centralizing inbound deliveries from fifteen different trucking companies to one, it reduced transport costs by 40 percent in its Holland plant. Through this and further moves to centralize logistics, it expected to save $200,000 a year. Rank Xerox expected to reduce transport cost, inventories, and warehouse costs while at the same time improving the management and control of the logistics system.[51] Some companies have found they can reduce logistics costs by cooperating with competitors. For example, Toyota and Nissan deliver each other's cars to avoid empty return trips.[52]

Inventory Control   The level of inventory on hand substantially affects the service level of a firm's logistics system. Due to the substantial costs of tied-up capital, inventory is reduced to the minimum level needed. In international operations, adequate inventories are needed as insurance against unexpected breakdowns in the logistics system. To reduce inventory levels, a number of companies have adopted the Japanese system of just-in-time deliveries of parts and components. Also, companies are developing regional manufacturing strategies to minimize cost. For example, Rank Xerox produces its models for the entire world market (except the U.S. market) in four European plants. Prior to adopting a just-in-time system, they kept buffer stocks of ten to forty days and an inventory of finished goods of ninety days. Now there is no stock for just-in-time parts and components, and an inventory of finished goods of only fifteen days. The improvements are the result of a just-in-time strategy: a reduced number of suppliers, improved quality control, and a more efficient logistics system.[53]

Order Processing   Since rapid processing of orders shortens the order cycle and allows for lower safety stocks on the part of the client, this area becomes a central concern for logistics management. The available communications technology greatly influences the time it takes to process an order. Managers cannot expect to find perfectly working mail, telephones, or telex systems everywhere. Aside from those in the United States, Europe,

50. "Inadequacy of U.S. Coal-Export Terminals Sparks Oil Money Push to Expand Capacity," *Wall Street Journal,* February 27, 1981, p. 25.

51. Michael Terry, "Logistics Firms Don New Clothes for 1992," *Financial Times,* November 6, 1990, sect. III, p. 2.

52. "Rivals Draw Distribution Truce to Cut Costs," *Nikkei Weekly,* January 31, 1994, p. 10.

53. Ibid.

and Japan, communications systems are inferior and tend to delay order processing. To offer an efficient order-processing system worldwide represents a considerable challenge to any company today. However, doing this can be turned to a competitive advantage since customers reap added benefits from such a system.

Materials Handling and Warehousing   Throughout the logistics cycle, materials and products will have to be stored and prepared for moving or transportation. How products are stored or moved is the principal concern of materials handling management. For international shipments, the shipping technology or quantities may be different, causing firms to adjust domestic policies to the circumstances. Warehousing in foreign countries involves dealing with different climatic situations, and longer average storage periods may require changing warehousing practices. In general, international shipments often move through different transportation modes than do domestic shipments. Substantial logistics costs can be saved if the firm adjusts shipping arrangements according to the prevalent handling procedures abroad.

Automated warehousing is a relatively new concept for the handling, storage, and shipping of goods. Warehouses are often adjacent to the factory, and all goods are stored automatically in bins up to twelve stories high. The delivery and retrieval of all goods are controlled by a computer system. While automated warehouses require significant up-front capital and technology, they reduce warehousing costs significantly.

Fixed Facilities Location Management   The facilities crucial to the logistics flow are, of course, production facilities and warehouses. To serve customers worldwide and to maximize the efficiency of the total logistics system, production facilities may have to be placed in several countries. In doing this, there is a tradeoff between economies of scale and savings in logistics costs.

At times, an advantage can be gained from shipping raw materials or semiprocessed products to a market for further processing and manufacture instead of supplying the finished product. These advantages arise from varying transportation costs for given freight modes or from different rates for each product category. Some companies compare the costs for several operational alternatives before making a final decision. The location of warehousing facilities greatly affects the company's ability to respond to orders once they are received or processed. A company with warehouses in every country where it does business would have a natural advantage in delivery, but such a system greatly increases the costs of warehousing and, most likely, the required level of inventory systemwide. Thus, a balance is sought that satisfies the customer's requirements on delivery and at the same time reduces overall logistics costs. Microsoft has opened a single warehouse and distribution center in Dublin, Ireland, to serve all of Europe. The new distribution center will remove the need for Microsoft to keep a warehouse and inventory in each country.[54]

54. Alan Cane, ''Microsoft Alters Distribution Chain for Europe,'' *Financial Times,* November 12, 1993, p. 20.

Managing the International Logistics System

The objective of a firm's international logistics system is to meet the company's service levels at the lowest cost. Costs are understood as total costs covering all five decision areas. Consequently, a company has to combine cost information into one overall budget typically involving many departments from several countries. The key to effective management is coordination. A situation in which managers all try to reduce costs in their individual areas either will reduce the service levels provided or force other areas to make up for the initial reduction by possibly spending more than the original savings. Consequently, companies have to look carefully at opportunities to save in one area by comparing additional costs accruing in another. This process of comparison has caused some managers to refer to the logistics system as tradeoff management.

High-quality logistics does pay off. With 50 percent of all customer complaints to manufacturers being the result of poor logistics, there are substantial rewards for good logistics that result in better service. Research by the Strategic Planning Institute revealed that companies with superior service received 7 percent higher prices and grew 8 percent faster than low-service companies. Also, on average they were twelve times more profitable.[55]

With markets becoming more scattered and dispersed over numerous countries, the opportunities for competitive advantages in international logistics grow. The firms that manage to combine the various logistics areas under the responsibility of one manager have a chance at achieving either substantial cost savings or an enhancement of their marketing position by increasing service levels at minimum costs.

Global Trends in Distribution Systems

Distribution systems throughout the world are continually evolving due to economic and social changes. A manager developing a worldwide distribution strategy must consider not only the current state of distribution but also the expected state of distribution systems in the future. Five major trends seem dominant throughout the world: (1) the growth of larger-scale retailers, (2) an increased number of international retailers, (3) the growth of direct marketing, (4) the spread of discounting, and (5) the increased role of information technology to support a distribution strategy.

Larger-Scale Retailers

There is a trend toward fewer but larger-scale retailers. As countries become more economically developed, they seem to follow a pattern of fewer, larger stores. Three factors

---

55. Neil S. Novich, ''Leading-Edge Distribution Strategies,'' *Journal of Business Strategy,* November–December 1990, p. 49.

contribute toward this trend: an increase in car ownership, an increase in the number of households with refrigerators and freezers, and an increase in the number of working wives. Although the European housewife twenty years ago may have shopped two or three times a day in local stores, the increase in transportation capacity, refrigerator capacity, and cash flow and the reduction of available shopping time have increased the practice of one-stop shopping in supermarkets. In 1987, 64 percent of households had one or more cars in the United Kingdom, making the large out-of-town store accessible. Tesco, one of the largest supermarket chains in the United Kingdom, had by 1989 shut down two-thirds of its small in-town stores (less than 10,000 square feet) in favor of large stores.[56]

The biggest change in the U.K. retail marketplace is the opening of warehouse clubs. With six clubs opening in 1993 and 1994, U.K. consumers will be able to buy goods at 25–30 percent less than at the typical retailer.[57] This trend, along with the growth of superstores, has significantly reduced the number of medium-sized and small stores. For example, the number of food stores in the Netherlands fell by 22.1 percent from 1982 to 1992, but the number of superstores increased 33.3 percent.[58]

Retail concentration has increased in most countries. Between 1980 and 1984, chains and cooperatives increased their total share of grocery trade from 75 percent to 81 percent in Britain, from 58 percent to 67 percent in West Germany, and from 44 percent to 60 percent in Holland. During the same period, the chains and cooperatives stayed at 69 percent in the United States and 43 percent in Japan.[59]

IKEA, the Scandinavian retailer, has been very successful in Europe and in the United States in luring customers into its 200,000-square-foot stores. The company had eighty-three stores in twenty countries at the end of 1989.[60] Once in the store, customers are given tape measures, catalogs, paper, and pencils. Child-care strollers are available, as well as free diapers. Each store has a restaurant with Scandinavian delicacies such as smoked salmon and Swedish meatballs. Customers can also borrow roof racks to help bring furniture home. IKEA has created a fun shopping experience that encourages people to enjoy themselves and make purchases. Sales per square foot are three times higher than in traditional furniture stores. IKEA's success has attracted the attention of Wal-Mart, Circuit City, and Stor (a U.S. retailer), which are all adopting some of IKEA's techniques.[61]

International Retailers

The number of international retailers has grown. Most originate in advanced industrial countries and spread to the developed countries of the world. For example, Sears is now

56. Suzanne Bidlake, "High Street Revival in Store," *Marketing,* October 26, 1989, p. 19.

57. Neil Buckley, "Silent Enemy Stalks the Aisles," *Financial Times,* November 30, 1993, p. 15.

58. Cacilie Rohwedder, "Europe's Smaller Shops Face Finis," *Wall Street Journal,* May 12, 1993, p. B1.

59. "Retailing: Grocer Power," *Economist,* January 10, 1987, p. 56.

60. John Thornhill, "Retailers Broaden Their Outlook," *Financial Times,* December 17, 1990, p. 3.

61. "Why Competitors Shop for Ideas at IKEA," *Business Week,* October 9, 1989, p. 88.

in Mexico, South America, Spain, and Japan; Walgreen's is in Mexico; Tandy is in Belgium, the Netherlands, Germany, the United Kingdom, and France. The internationalization of retailing includes firms originating in the United States, Canada, France, Germany, and Japan. The internationalization of retailing was started by a number of large retailers in mature domestic markets that saw limited growth opportunities at home compared to the potential opportunities overseas. This principal reason for the trend toward international retailers has led Habitat, IKEA, McDonald's, Pizza Hut, Kentucky Fried Chicken, Carrefour, Marks and Spencer, Laura Ashley, and many others to seek opportunities in Europe, the United States, and Japan. The path toward an international presence has been made smoother by a number of facilitating factors, such as enhanced data communications, new forms of international financing, and lower barriers to entry. The single European market has also motivated retailers to expand overseas as they see a number of new international retailers entering their domestic markets.[62] The trend toward international retailers allows manufacturers to build relationships with retailers who are active in a number of markets. Retailers are also expanding their global umbrellas through acquisition. For example, Kingfisher, one of the largest U.K. retailers, acquired Darty, France's largest electronics retailer, to create one of the largest nonfood retail groups in Europe.[63]

European retailers have found that it is essential to establish a unique selling position. C&A, the privately owned Dutch chain of clothing stores; the Body Shop, the U.K. natural cosmetics group; Benetton, the Italian fashion chain; IKEA, the Swedish furniture store; and Aldi, the low-priced German food retailer are all successful international retailers that have developed a distinctive style. Each has a clearly defined trading format and product range that enable it to distinguish itself in every European market. Retailing formats can be translated into other countries as long as the message is clear enough in the first place.[64]

Direct Marketing

Selling directly to the consumer by telephone, by mail, or door to door grew to a $150 billion industry in 1985, almost triple the $60 billion made in 1975 in the United States. There has also been a growth of direct marketing around the world. The complex multi-layered Japanese distribution system encouraged some foreign companies to skip the stores and go directly to consumers. The German publisher of Spiegel catalogs started selling dresses in 1986. Sharper Image and Sears have also marketed directly to Japanese consumers. High fees on bulk mailing and the difficulty of purchasing good lists have made direct marketing difficult in Japan. Shop America Ltd. took a new approach. It combined forces with 7-Eleven–Japan, which has 4,000 stores and four million customers, to distribute catalogs and place orders. Executives of 7-Eleven expected sales to reach $70 million in the first twelve months as Shop America offered high-quality, brand-name

62. Alan D. Treadgold, ''The Developing Internationalization of Retailing,'' *International Journal of Retail and Distribution Management* (1990): 18, no. 2, p. 5.

63. ''Takeover Creates Europe-wide Retailer,'' *Financial Times,* February 19, 1993, p. 15.

64. Thornhill, ''Retailers Broaden,'' p. 3.

electronic goods at 30 to 50 percent less than retail store prices.[65] The catalog sales market in Japan has grown from 640 billion yen in 1982 to 1840 billion in 1992. Major players such as L. L. Bean, Eddie Bauer, and Lands' End have entered into joint ventures with Japanese firms to exploit this growing market.[66]

The growth in direct marketing in Japan is supported by a number of demographic and technical factors. The dramatic increase in employed women from 50 percent in 1980 to 75 percent in 1987 resulted in less available shopping hours. The introduction of toll-free telephone, cable TV, videotex, and smart cards has also made it easier to shop at home.[67] Avon had an Asian sales force of 10,000 salespeople in 1981, selling more than $200 million in cosmetics directly to the consumer.[68] In Japan, Amway, the U.S. direct sales company, has been extremely successful selling through its 1.2 million distributors. The Japanese subsidiary of Amway has become the second most profitable foreign company in Japan after Coca-Cola.[69]

Direct marketing is also growing in Europe, with sales up 9 percent in 1991. There are approximately 2,000 mail-order operators in Europe covering a wide range of products. The largest mail-order market by far is Germany, followed by France and the United Kingdom. The average German spends 230 European currency units per year versus an average of ECU 100 for all Europeans or ECU 211 for the United States.[70]

In summary, the increased affluence of consumers in developed countries, a reduction in the amount of time devoted to shopping, changing lifestyles, increased acceptance of credit cards, and improved postal and telephone services have all contributed to the growth in direct marketing.

Discounting

The growth of international brands having strong consumer support due to advertising has helped discounting become a major international force, as did the elimination of required list prices. Innovative retailers have used price reductions with limited high-volume assortments to develop successful discount stores. While the Japanese are known to pay among the highest prices in the world on the Ginza, Tokyo's premier shopping district, twelve miles away in Chiba you will find discount stores and giant hypermarkets with reasonable prices. Sales at discount stores in Japan are growing at twice the rate of sales in ordinary department stores.[71]

65. "Can This Catalogue Company Crack the Japanese Marketing Maze?" *Business Week,* March 19, 1990, p. 60.

66. "Party's Over in Mail-Order Market," *Nikkei Weekly,* February 14, 1994, p. 10.

67. Nitin Sanghaui, "Non-Store Retailing in Japan," *International Journal of Retail and Distribution Management,* 18, no. 1 (1990), p. 20.

68. "Business Briefs," *World Press Review,* February 1981, p. 55.

69. Thornton, "Revolution in Japanese Retailing," p. 146.

70. Alan Shipman, "Catalogue of Woes," *International Management,* March 1993, pp. 50–51.

71. Carla Rapoport, "Ready, Set, Sell—Japan Is Buying," *Fortune,* September 11, 1989, p. 159.

Discounting is happening in many markets. Price/Costco, Inc., the biggest U.S. warehouse club operator, has opened two stores in London. Staples, the U.S. office supplies discounter, has eight stores in Germany and one in the United Kingdom.[72] Discounting has become a major segment of the U.K. retail market. Kwik Save, a discount grocery store with 780 outlets, is expanding into Scotland and will open 70 new stores per year. Carrefour, the French retail giant, has opened Europe Discount in southern England. The volume of discounters in the United Kingdom is expected to double from £4.0 billion in 1992 to £8 billion by 1996.[73]

Discounting is also becoming popular in Japan. Matsumotokiyoshi, a discount pharmaceutical chain, has opened a five-store home center in Tokyo, selling everything from cosmetics to golf clubs at 30–40 percent below competitors. Kawachiya, a discount liquor chain in Tokyo, is so busy on weekends that it must limit the number of people in the store. While discounters represent only 3.1 percent of all retail sales in Japan (1992) versus 13.5 percent in the United States, it is the fastest-growing segment of the Japanese market.[74]

Information Technology

The worldwide retail industry is moving fast toward the use of electronic checkouts that scan the bar codes on products, speeding up the checkout, reducing errors, and eliminating the need to put a price label on each item. Electronic checkout also improves the stores' ability to keep track of inventory and purchase behavior. The head of the British jewelry chain that owns Ratners, Zales, H. Samuel, and Kay Jewelers reports that twice a day each of one-thousand stores is polled and every item sold is replaced by 8:30 A.M. the following day. This computerized system gives the company a good appreciation of how fast items are selling, so it can adjust its inventory. Lines are reviewed every three months and replaced if they are not moving fast enough.[75]

Computerized retail systems have led to better monitoring of consumer purchases, low inventory, quicker stock turns, better assessment of product profitability, and the possiblity of just-in-time retailing.[76] 7-Eleven–Japan coordinates sales through its 4,000 franchised convenience stores via a computerized point-of-sale network. The typical store has only 1,000 square meters of shelf space to sell 3,500 products. The network tracks sales of products by time of day and replenishes supplies automatically with three deliveries per day.[77] Technology is one of the keys to the success of 7-Eleven in Japan, owned by

72. Carla Rapoport, "The New U.S. Push into Europe," *Fortune,* January 10, 1994, p. 73.

73. Neil Buckley, "Decade of the Deep Discount," *Financial Times,* April 21, 1993, p. 22.

74. Louise do Rosario, "Retailing Nihon-Mart," *Far Eastern Economic Review,* September 16, 1993, pp. 62–64.

75. John Thornhill, "A Sense of Urgency Makes Good Business Says Ratner," *Financial Times,* November 6, 1990, sect. III, p. VII.

76. Richard Ford, "Managing Retail Service Businesses for the 1990s: Marketing Aspects," *European Management Journal,* March 1990, p. 60.

77. "Networks' Net Profits," *Economist,* March 10, 1990, p. 30, Survey of Telecommunications.

Ito-Yokado Company, Japan's most profitable retailer. Store clerks keep track of customer preferences and inventory through a sophisticated tracking system. The clerk enters the consumer's sex and approximate age, as well as the items purchased. 7-Eleven–Japan posted a pretax profit of $680 million on $1.44 billion in 1992.[78]

Conclusions

To be successful in the marketplace, a company needs market acceptance among buyers and market access via distribution channels. Companies entering foreign markets often do so initially without substantial acceptance. Consequently, the company must guarantee some degree of market access through either effective marketing programs or sheer financial strength. To achieve access, the firm must select the most suitable members, or actors, of a channel, keeping in mind that substantial differences exist among countries on both the wholesale and the retail levels. There are major differences in distribution country to country. Local habits and cultures, planning restrictions, and infrastructure can all affect success in a new country. For example, Greece has idiosyncratic shopping hours; Germany does not allow stores over 10,000 square feet; and Italy has stringent planning restrictions. Any entrant to the Danish market needs to contend with the cooperative stores that account for 35 to 40 percent of the market.

It can also be a mistake to assume you know the market's needs, as Marks and Spencer found when they entered France. They thought fashion-conscious French shoppers would want chic clothes. But the French wanted practical clothes from M&S and went to fashion stores for their chic items.[79] Proper distribution policies have to allow for the local market's buying or shopping habits. A company should not expect to be able to use the same distribution density, channel alignment, or channel length in all its markets. The logistics system must reflect both local market situations and additional difficulties due to longer distances. To actually find willing and suitable channel members may be extremely difficult; access may only be achieved by forging special alliances with present channel members or local companies with access to them. Once the distribution system has been designed, participants still have to be motivated and controlled to ensure that the firm's marketing strategy is properly executed.

Questions for Discussion

1. Your firm is just beginning to export printing equipment. How would you assess the decision to use an export management company or an export agent versus direct exporting?

2. What are the key elements of a distribution strategy?

78. ''Listening to Shoppers' Voices,'' *Business Week/Reinventing America 1992,* p. 69.
79. Thornhill, ''Retailers Broaden,'' p. 3.

3. If you enter a new marketplace and decide to distribute the product directly to the consumer, what types of costs will you incur?

4. You have been assigned the task of selecting distributors to handle your firm's line of car batteries. What criteria will you use to select among the twenty possible distributors?

5. The performance of your agents and distributors in South America has been poor over the past three years. How will you improve the management of these agents and distributors?

6. What are the elements of an international logistics system, and how will they differ from a domestic logistics system?

7. Your firm has just entered the South Korean market for automobile parts; the major distributor is owned by a competitive manufacturer of automobile parts. What strategies can you use to gain access to this market?

8. Given the trends in distribution, what distribution strategies should a worldwide manufacturer of women's clothing consider?

For Further Reading

Bello, Daniel C., and Lee D. Dahringer. "The Influence of Country and Product on Retailer Practices." *International Marketing Review,* Summer 1985, pp. 45–52.

Bello, Daniel C., and Nicholas C. Williamson. "Contractual Arrangements and Marketing Practices in the Indirect Export Channel." *Journal of International Business Studies,* Summer 1985, pp. 65–82.

Brasch, John J. "Export Management Companies." *Journal of International Business Studies,* Spring–Summer 1978, pp. 59–72.

Cooper, James C. "Logistics Strategies for Global Business." *International Journal of Physical Distribution and Logistics Management,* 23, no. 4 (1993), pp. 12–23.

Czinkota, Michael R. "Distribution of Consumer Products in Japan." *International Marketing Review,* Autumn 1985, pp. 39–51.

Foster, Thomas. "Global Logistics Benetton Style." *Distribution,* 92, no. 10 (1993), pp. 62–66.

Klein, Saul. "Selection of International Marketing Channels." *Journal of Global Marketing,* 4, no. 4 (1991), pp. 21–37.

Price, Retha. "Channel Leadership Behavior: A Framework for Improving Channel Leadership Effectiveness." *Journal of Marketing Channels,* no. 1 (1991), pp. 87–93.

Williams, David E. "Differential Firm Advantages and Retailer Internationalization." *International Journal of Retail and Distribution Management,* 19, no. 4 (1991), pp. 3–12.

13

Pricing for International and Global Markets

● **THIS CHAPTER PROVIDES** *an overview of the key factors that affect pricing policies in an international environment. We assume that you are already aware of the basic pricing decisions that companies must make in a single-country or domestic environment. In this chapter, we focus on the unique aspects of international pricing. (See Figure 13.1 for a chapter overview.)*

The material is organized around six major issues. First we look at internal factors and company policies as they affect international pricing policies. Costs and how they affect price determination are major concerns. The second section is devoted to the market factors companies must consider in setting prices, such as competition and the income levels of various countries. The third segment focuses on the environmental variables, such as foreign exchange rates, inflation, and legal constraints, that are not controlled by individual firms but that play an important role in shaping pricing policies. The fourth section covers managerial pricing issues, such as transfer pricing—price arbitrage and countertrade— issues of great concern to companies active internationally. The chapter ends with sections on financing issues: risks and sources, two areas that have received increased attention from international firms.

FIGURE 13.1 ● International and Global Pricing Strategies

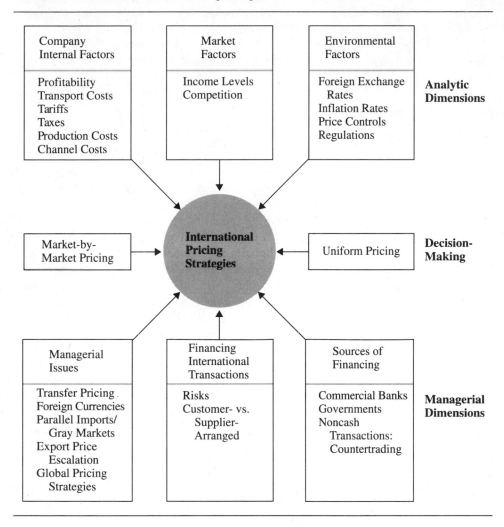

Company Internal Factors

Most companies begin pricing deliberations based on their own internal cost structure. Therefore, it makes sense to look at internal costs before considering other issues. Included under internal factors are profits and the requirement for profits as they impact internal pricing procedures.

Also of concern are international transfer costs, such as tariffs, transportation, insur-

426   PART FOUR   *Designing Global Marketing Programs*

ance, taxes, and local channel costs. Such costs frequently make exported products more expensive than domestic ones, and this fact must be taken into consideration if a company wants to compete effectively. However, such costs do not have to be taken as given. Companies can, through various actions, affect the level of these costs. It is the purpose of this section to point out the options available to companies in managing their international costs.

Profit and Cost Factors

The basis for any effective pricing policy is a clear understanding of the cost and profit variables involved. Experience shows that a clear definition of relevant costs or of profits is often difficult to achieve. On the other hand, the field of international marketing offers many examples of firms that have achieved substantial profits through flexible or nonconventional costing approaches. Therefore, understanding the various cost elements can be considered a prerequisite for a successful international pricing strategy.

According to standard accounting practice, costs are divided into two categories: fixed costs and variable costs. Fixed costs do not vary over a given range of output, whereas variable costs change directly with output. The relationship of these variables is shown in Table 13.1 using a fictitious example, Western Machine Tool, Inc., a manufacturer of machine tools selling at $60,000 per unit in the U.S. market.

The total cost of a machine tool is $54,000. Selling it at $60,000, the company will achieve a profit of $6,000 before taxes from the sale of each unit. However, if one additional unit is sold (or not sold), the marginal impact amounts to more than an additional profit of $6,000 (or loss of the same amount), because the extra cost of an additional unit

TABLE 13.1 ● Profit and Cost Calculation for Western Machine Tool, Inc.

Selling price (per unit)			$60,000
Direct manufacturing costs			
Labor	$10,000		
Material	15,000		
Energy	1,000	$26,000	
Indirect manufacturing costs			
Supervision	5,000		
Research and development contribution	3,000		
Factory overhead	5,000	13,000	
General administrative cost			
Sales and administrative overhead	10,000		
Marketing	5,000	15,000	
Full costs			54,000
Net profit before tax			$ 6,000

TABLE 13.2 ● Marginal Profit Calculation for Western Machine Tool, Inc.

Selling price (per unit)			$60,000
Variable costs			
Direct manufacturing costs			
Labor	$10,000		
Material	15,000		
Energy	1,000	$26,000	
General administrative costs			
Marketing	5,000	5,000	
Total variable costs			31,000
Contribution margin (selling price minus variable costs			$29,000

will be limited to its variable costs only, or $31,000, as shown in Table 13.2. For any additional unit sold, the marginal profit is $29,000, or the amount in excess of the variable costs. This amount may also be referred to as the *contribution margin.*

Another example is used to illustrate the relationships between variable costs, fixed costs, and contribution margin. Western Machine Tool has a chance to export a unit to a foreign country, but the maximum price the foreign buyer is willing to pay is $50,000. Machine Tool, using the full cost pricing method, argues that the company will incur a loss of $4,000 if the deal is accepted. However, since only $31,000 of additional variable cost will be incurred for a new machine because all fixed costs are incurred anyway and are covered by all prior units sold, the company can go ahead with the sale and claim a marginal profit of $19,000, using a contribution margin approach. In such a situation, a profitable sale may easily be turned down unless a company is fully informed about its cost composition.

Cost components are subject to change. By adding new output to a plant, such as new export volume, a company may achieve economies of scale that allow operation at lower costs, both domestically and abroad. Furthermore, as the experience curve indicates, companies with rapidly rising cumulative production may reap overall unit cost reductions at an increasing rate due to the higher output caused by exporting.[1]

Transportation Costs

International marketing often requires the shipment of products over long distances. Since all modes of transportation, including rail, truck, air, and ocean, depend on a considerable amount of energy, the total cost of transportation has become an issue of growing concern

1. For a detailed discussion of the experience curve concept, see Derek F. Abell and John S. Harmon, *Strategic Market Planning* (Englewood Cliffs, N.J.: Prentice Hall, 1979), chap. 3.

to international companies. High-technology products are less sensitive to transportation costs than standardized consumer products or commodities. In the latter case, the seller with the lowest transportation costs often has the advantage.

For commodities, low transportation costs can decide who gets an order. For expensive products, such as computers or sophisticated electronic instruments, transportation costs usually represent only a small fraction of total costs and rarely influence pricing decisions. For products between the two extremes, companies can substantially affect unit transportation costs by selecting new transportation methods. The introduction of container ocean vessels has made large-scale shipment of many products possible. Roll-on, roll-off ships (ro-ro carriers) have reduced ocean freight for cars and trucks to very low levels, making exporters more competitive vis-à-vis local manufacturers. The international firm must continuously search for new transportation technologies to reduce unit transportation costs and, thus, enhance competitiveness.

Tariffs

When products are transported across national borders, tariffs have to be paid unless a special arrangement exists between the countries involved. Tariffs are usually levied on the landed costs of a product, which include shipping to the importing country. Tariffs are normally assessed as a percentage of the value.

Tariff costs can have a rippling effect and increase prices considerably for the end user. Intermediaries, whether they are sales subsidiaries or independent distributors, tend to include any tariff costs in their costs of goods sold and add any operating margin on this amount. As a result, the impact on the final end-user price can be substantial whenever tariff rates are high.

The intricacies of managing through duty and regulations are illustrated by Land Rover, the British producer of the Range Rover four-wheel drive (4WD) utility vehicle, marketed in the United States since 1987. When the U.S. tariffs for trucks were increased from 2.5 percent to 25 percent to stem the imports, 4WD vehicles were classified as multipurpose vehicles subject to a higher tariff. But Land Rover complained that its $40,000 vehicle was classified as a truck, pointing out that it has four doors and not just two as the typical light truck. Thus, the higher duty was avoided. In 1991, however, the United States began to charge a 10 percent surtax on luxury vehicles above $30,000, thus potentially affecting the sales of the Range Rover. The U.S. tax authorities classified four-wheel drive vehicles as trucks, and the Range Rover again avoided the tax. To ensure compliance, however, the Range Rovers are shipped to the United States as cars to avoid the truck surcharge but have an increased weight of 6,019 pounds, from 5,997 pounds, because the tax authorities' truck definition starts at vehicles of 6,000 pounds.[2] In another case, the Court of International Trade ruled that the Nissan two-door Pathfinder was primarily designed for passengers and not cargo, so it was ordered to be classified as a passenger vehicle with a 2.5 percent duty rather than a cargo vehicle with a 25 percent

---

2. "What's in a Name?" *Economist,* February 2, 1991, p. 60.

TABLE 13.3 ● VAT Standard Rates, May 1990

	0%	5	10	15	20	25
	•	•	•	•	•	•

Spain	————●
Luxembourg	————●
West Germany	—————●
Britain	—————●
Portugal	——————●
Italy	——————●
Greece	——————●
France	———————●
Belgium	————————●
Holland	—————————●
Denmark	—————————●
Ireland	—————————●

Source: Copyright © 1990 The Economist Newspaper Group, Inc. Reprinted with permission. Further reproduction prohibited.

duty. This ruling prevented U.S. automakers from extending the cargo duty to four-door multipurpose vehicles such as minivans.[3]

Although tariffs have declined over recent years, they still influence pricing decisions in some countries. To avoid paying high duties, as we have seen in Chapter 9, companies have shipped components only and established local assembly operations because tariffs on components are frequently lower than on finished products. The automobile industry is a good example of how companies can reduce overall tariff costs by shifting the place of production and shipping of knocked-down cars to be assembled on the spot. Such a move may be called for when tariffs are especially high.

Taxes

Local taxes imposed on imported products also affect the land cost of the products. A variety of taxes may be imposed. One of the most common is the tax on value added (VAT) used by member countries of the European Union.

Each EU country sets its own value-added tax structure (see Table 13.3). However, common to all is a zero tax rate (or exemption) on exported goods. A company exporting from the Netherlands to Belgium does not have to pay any tax on the value added in the Netherlands. However, Belgian authorities do collect a tax on products shipped from the Netherlands at the Belgium rate. Merchandise shipped to any EU member country from a nonmember country, such as from the United States or Japan, is assessed the VAT rate

3. ''Nissan Ruling May Hurt Effort by Big Three,'' *Wall Street Journal,* May 17, 1993, p. A4.

on landed costs, in addition to any customs duties that may apply to those products. Eventually the EU is planning to align VAT rates among the various countries and to have the tax paid in the country of consumption, thus eliminating the payment of VAT at each border. This plan is to take effect by 1996.[4]

Local Production Costs

Up to this point, we have assumed that a company has only one producing location, from which it exports to all other markets. However, most international firms manufacture products in several countries. In such cases, operating costs for raw materials, wages, energy, or financing may differ widely from country to country, allowing a firm to ship from a particularly advantageous location to reduce prices or costs. Increasingly, companies produce in locations that give them advantages in freight, tariffs, or other transfer costs. Consequently, judicious management of sourcing points may reduce product costs and, thus, result in added pricing flexibility.

Channel Costs

Channel costs are a function of channel length, gross margin, and logistics. Many countries operate with longer distribution channels than the United States has, causing higher total costs and end-user prices because of additional layers of intermediaries. Also, gross margins at the retail level tend to be higher outside the United States. Since the logistics system in a large number of countries is also less developed than that in the United States, logistics costs, too, are higher on a per unit basis. All of these factors add additional costs to a product that is marketed internationally.

Campbell Soup Company, a U.S.-based firm, found that its retailers in the United Kingdom purchased soup in small quantities of twenty-four cans per case of assorted soups, requiring each can to be hand-packed for shipment. In the United States, the company sold one variety to retailers in cases of forty-eight cans per case, which were purchased in large quantities. To handle small purchases in England, the company had to add an additional level of distribution and new facilities. As a result, distribution costs are 30 percent higher in England than in the United States.[5]

Market Factors Affecting Pricing

Companies cannot establish pricing policies in a vacuum. Although cost information is essential, prices also have to reflect the realities of the marketplace. The challenge in pricing for international markets is the large number of local economic situations to be

4. ''Business This Week—Value-added Tax,'' *Economist,* May 12, 1990, p. 83.
5. Philip R. Cateora, *International Marketing,* 7th ed. (Homewood, Ill.: Irwin, 1990), p. 540.

considered. Two factors stand out and must be analyzed in greater detail: income levels and competition.

Income Levels

The income level of a country's population determines the amount and type of goods and services bought. When detailed income data are not available, incomes are expressed by gross national product (GNP) or gross domestic product (GDP), divided by the total population. This measure, *GNP* or *GDP per capita,* is a surrogate measure for personal income and is used to compare income levels among countries. To do so, all GNPs/GDPs have to be converted to the same currency. If you look back at Table 5.6, you'll see that GNP per capita figures for key countries were expressed in U.S. dollars.

As mentioned in Chapter 6, GNP/GDP per capita converted to dollars based on market exchange rates tends to understate the true purchasing power of a country's consumers. It is more accurate to look at developing countries' GNP or GDP per capita converted to dollars based on purchasing power parity.[6] To respond to the purchasing power of different countries, Coca-Cola prices its product as a proportion of disposable income.[7]

As a result of widely differing income and price levels, elasticity of demand for any given product can be expected to vary greatly. Countries with high income levels often display lower price elasticities for necessities such as food, shelter, and medical care. These lower elasticities in part reflect a lack of alternatives such as "doing it yourself," which forces buyers in these countries to purchase such goods even at higher prices. For example, in many countries with low income levels, a considerable part of the population has the additional alternatives of providing their own food or building their own shelters should they not have sufficient money to purchase products or services on a cash basis. Availability of such options increases price elasticity, as these consumers can more easily opt out of the cash economy than can consumers in developed economies. International companies theoretically set product price by considering the price elasticity in each country. However, there are forces at work that do not always allow this practice because prices may vary widely across several countries. The danger of disparate price levels is examined later, in the pricing segment of this chapter.

Competition

The nature and size of competition can significantly affect price levels in any given market. A firm acting as the sole supplier of a product in a given market enjoys greater pricing flexibility. The opposite is true if that same company has to compete against several other local or international firms. Therefore, the number and type of competitors greatly influence

---

6. "Chinese Puzzles, Developing Countries Less Poor Than Official Figures Suggest," *Economist,* May 15, 1993, p. 83.

7. "The Ascent of Everest, Coca-Cola's Plans for a New Global Sales Assault," *Financial Times,* January 16, 1992, p. 10.

pricing strategy in any market. The public postal, telephone, and telegraph (PTT) services of most countries are a public monopoly, allowing them to charge high rates with no threat of competition. In Europe, monthly telephone costs in Spain and Italy are over $2,000 per month for multinational concerns, while less than $1,000 in the United Kingdom. British Telecommunications in the United Kingdom no longer has a monopoly, with Mercury the second carrier. The opening of telecom markets is destroying the fortresses previously held by the PTTs.[8]

Also important is the nature of the competition. Local competitors may have different cost structures from those of foreign companies, resulting in different prices. Market prices for the same product may vary from country to country, based on the competitive situation. Heinz, the U.S.-based food company and the world leader in ketchup, with 50 percent world market share, began to expand on its 1 percent market share in Japan after a liberalization of the policy regarding some food imports. The company faced major price competition by the leading Japanese ketchup producer. However, Heinz decided not to follow suit but to keep prices at the higher level to indicate quality and to protect its profitability.[9]

But foreign companies do not always have to be at a disadvantage when competing with local companies. In the wake of the substantial appreciation of the Japanese yen in 1993, many importers found they could considerably underprice local Japanese firms. From March to September 1993, the price of Brooks Brothers ties declined 18 percent, and Apple personal computers declined 29 percent, thereby improving the competitiveness of imports versus Japanese goods.[10]

Occasionally, price levels are manipulated by cartels or other agreements among local competitors. Cartels are forbidden by law in the United States, but many foreign governments allow cartels provided they do not injure the consumer. Following a five-year long investigation, the European Union fined twenty-three western European chemical companies $80 million for the price fixing of two plastic products. The companies were found guilty of forming secret pricing cartels to keep up the price of PVC and low-density polyethylene.[11] Cartels may be officially recognized by a local government or may consist of competitors following similar pricing practices. In general, new market entrants must decide whether to accept current price levels or to set price levels different from those of the established competition.

The U.S. government has a very strict approach to cartels, and any cartel such as described above clearly would be against existing U.S. laws. Furthermore, U.S. companies may find themselves in violation of U.S. laws if they actively participate in any foreign cartel.

8. ''Europe's Telecom Monopolies Transform,'' *Wall Street Journal,* June 10, 1993, p. A6.

9. ''Ketchup War Will Be Fought to the Last Drop,'' *Financial Times,* February 21, 1990, p. 18.

10. ''Can't Get Enough of That Super-Yen,'' *Business Week,* October 4, 1993, p. 50.

11. ''Fines Unlikely to Dampen Spirits of EC Chemical Producers,'' *Financial Times,* December 22, 1988, p. 2.

Environmental Factors Affecting Price

We have thus far treated pricing as a matter of cost and market factors. A number of environmental factors also influence pricing on the international level. These external variables, uncontrolled by any individual company, include the general economic environment, foreign exchange, inflation, and government price controls. These factors restrict company decision-making authority and can become dominant concerns for country managers.

Exchange Rate Fluctuations

One of the most unpredictable factors affecting prices is foreign exchange rate movement. As the 1980s showed, world currencies can fluctuate over a short period of time. Major currencies such as the deutsche mark (Germany), yen (Japan), and franc (Switzerland) appreciated against the dollar between 1973 and 1980, followed by the opposite development in the early 1980s. In 1986 and 1987, the U.S. dollar declined again to reach record lows by 1991 compared to other major trading currencies. First, products made in the United States became cheaper than those manufactured in other countries. In the early 1980s, however, U.S. products increased again in price because of the changed value of the dollar. Then, the steep decline of the U.S. dollar in 1990 made U.S. products more competitive again. In Chapter 2, we explained the reasons behind these foreign currency fluctuations.

Though foreign exchange fluctuations can present new opportunities, they may also make operations more difficult, particularly for companies operating in countries with appreciating currencies. As the yen appreciated 16.5 percent against the U.S. dollar from January to June 1993, U.S. manufacturers were able to hold prices, while Japanese car manufacturers' prices rose. Japanese cars cost $2,300 more than U.S. equivalents, resulting in the Big Three U.S. automobiles' market share rising 4 percent while Japanese-branded vehicles went down 8.1 percent.[12]

Inflation Rates

The rate of inflation can affect product cost and may force a company to take specific action. Inflation rates have traditionally fluctuated over time and, more important, have differed from country to country. In some cases, inflation rates have risen to several hundred percent. When this happens, payment for products may be delayed for months, harming the economy because of the local currency's rapid loss of purchasing power. A company would have to use a LIFO (last-in, first-out) method of costing or, in the extreme, a FIFO (first-in, first-out) approach to protect itself from eroding purchasing power. A

12. "Hard Pedalling on the Comeback Trail," *Financial Times,* June 2, 1993, p. 17.

company can usually protect itself from rapid inflation if it maintains constant operating margins (gross margin, gross profit, net margin) and makes constant price adjustments, sometimes on a monthly basis.

Companies competing in Brazil have had to deal with inflation of more than 400 percent per year since 1987. Cash management systems become critical in dealing with high inflation. To cope with this, companies have had to develop sophisticated information systems in their prices, costs, and cash balances. Leading manufacturers in Brazil estimate their financial departments are 40 percent larger than would be necessary in a normal low-inflation climate.[13]

Because money received from a customer in thirty days is substantially less than payments made today, companies have resorted to indexing of most contracts. Substantial discounts are granted for customers paying right away, and considerable penalties are levied on customers who fail to pay within agreed time periods.[14]

In countries with extremely high inflation, companies may price in a stable currency, such as the U.S. dollar, and translate prices into local currencies on a daily basis. Vision Express, which has been very successful in Russia, charges customers in dollars to avoid the inflation that lifts prices rapidly. Most of the customers, entrepreneurs and business-people, seem to be able to get dollars.[15] The U.S. dollar was reasonably strong in 1993, appreciating against most currencies except the yen, as shown in Figure 13.2.

Price Controls

In many countries, government and regulatory agencies influence the prices of products and services. Controls may be applied to an entire economy to combat inflation; regulations may be applied only to specific industries, such as the Civil Aeronautics Board (phased out in the early 1980s) regulations for airfares in the United States. Cases in which price controls apply equally to all industries are often temporary or, as was the case in the United States, of a voluntary nature. In other cases, price increases might be permitted only when a real improvement in a product or its quality has taken place.

Other measures may be taken to prevent excessive pricing by individual companies. One such case involved Hoffmann-LaRoche & Co., A.G., a large producer of drugs and vitamins, located in Switzerland. The company had a monopoly in tranquilizers known under the brand names Valium and Librium. As a result, in 1973 the British Monopolies Commission ordered the company to reduce prices by 35 to 40 percent. Similar action was brought against Hoffmann-LaRoche by the German cartel office and by the Danish and Dutch governments. After years of litigation, Hoffmann-LaRoche was forced to reduce prices, even though the reductions were smaller than originally demanded. Higher courts, however, later rolled back all price concessions in these countries after Hoffmann-LaRoche

13. "A Roller Coaster out of Control," *Financial Times,* February 22, 1993, p. 8.

14. "Juggling with 850 Percent Inflation in Brazil," *Financial Times,* June 5, 1989, p. 18.

15. "To Succeed in Russia, U.S. Retailer Employs Patience and Local Ally," *Wall Street Journal,* May 27, 1993, p. 1.

FIGURE 13.2 ● Currencies Against the Dollar: Percentage Change, Year to September 28, 1993

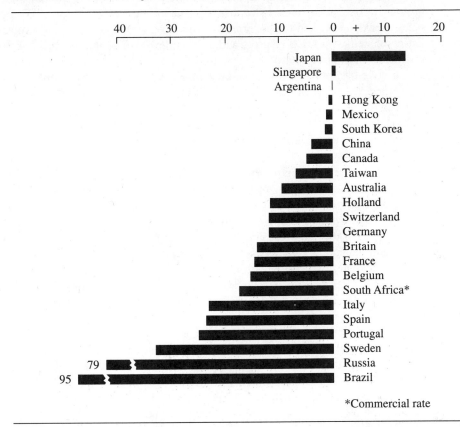

Source: Copyright © 1993 The Economist Newspaper Group, Inc. Reprinted with permission. Further reproduction prohibited.

filed suit. The Hoffmann-LaRoche experience indicates that international firms cannot always make independent pricing decisions in each country.[16]

Even in the European Union, where many aspects of the countries' economies are coordinated, methods of controlling prices for drugs may vary considerably. In the United Kingdom, drug prices are established through the Pharmaceutical Price Regulation Scheme (PPRS). Though companies are allowed to set prices for individual drugs, the government limits their overall profitability. (However, company profit targets are established through confidential negotiations and are set differently for each company.) Furthermore, the British National Health Service recently introduced price limits for drugs that qualify for

16. "The EEC Cracks Down on Price Discrimination," *Business Week,* December 7, 1981, p. 63.

customer reimbursement. RhônePoulenc Rorer, the Franco-American pharmaceutical group, cut its U.K. price on a sleeping pill called Zimovane from 98 to 16 pence to avoid being blacklisted (taken off government reimbursement).[17] Italy uses a similar restrictive list combined with price controls and varying levels of reimbursements. France uses a method of strict price controls to contain overall health costs, and Germany also maintains a restrictive list for some drugs but otherwise lets the companies set their own prices. In the United States, by contrast, prices for some drugs are established through negotiations between the drug company, the federal Medicare program, and several private insurance companies that reimburse their customers for drug costs. Otherwise, prices are set by the pharmaceutical companies, with many U.S. consumers paying out of pocket for their own drugs.[18]

In Japan, the system is different again. The Japanese government determines the prices for reimbursement of drugs made to physicians, who in turn obtain the drugs through wholesale channels of their own. Frequently, physicians end up obtaining a discount on list prices for drugs, resulting in a reimbursement that is above the physicians' own cost and thus allows them to make an extra profit. The Japanese government has combated this along with mandating reductions in the reimbursement price amounting to 9.2 percent in 1989 alone. These reductions are forced back on the pharmaceutical companies, which have to lower their own prices to keep the distribution channel at the same discount levels.[19]

The European Union is attempting to harmonize EU car prices without resorting to price controls. Twice a year, car manufacturers must publish comparative EU price lists for selected new cars. In each EU country, car prices are expected to be within 12 percent over the long term and within 18 percent over peiods of a year.[20] If car manufacturers do not stay within these differentials, they may lose the right to use selective dealer distribution in 1995. The first comparative list, released in July 1993, showed most cars were within the guidelines. The largest difference was 24 percent, found in Fiat's Cincequento between the most expensive market (France) and the cheapest (Spain).[21]

Price controls are of special concern in countries with high inflation rates. To compensate for inflation, companies must raise prices periodically. In Brazil, the government publishes a consumer price index quarterly, and companies try to increase prices quarterly with the rate of inflation. With rates of inflation over 100 percent, pricing flexibility is of great importance. This flexibility can at times come under pressure, as when a newly elected government in Brazil announced a temporary freeze on all prices and wages. With inflation running at 3 percent per day, such a loss of pricing flexibility can become a handicap for even the most astute companies.[22]

17. "Britain to Cut Price It Pays for Drugs by 2.5%," *Financial Times,* August 10, 1993, p. 14.

18. "Schools Brief: A Regulatory Overdose," *Economist,* October 18, 1986, p. 78.

19. "Long Term Benefits from Japan's Bitter Pill," *Financial Times,* June 15, 1990, p. 21.

20. "Differentials Will Be Published," *Financial Times,* February 22, 1993, p. vii—Vehicle Fleet Management.

21. "Euro Car Price List Seen as Brussels Victory," *Financial Times,* July 2, 1993, p. 2.

22. "How Business Is Hog-Tied in Brazil," *Business Week,* May 14, 1990, p. 52.

Regulatory Factors: Dumping Regulations

The practice of selling a product at a price below actual costs is referred to as *dumping*. Because of potential injuries to domestic manufacturers, most governments have adopted regulations against dumping. Antidumping actions are allowed under Article 6 of the General Agreement on Tariffs and Trade (GATT) as long as two criteria are met: "sales at less than fair value" and "material injury" to a domestic industry.[23] The first criterion is usually interpreted to mean selling abroad at prices below those in the country of origin. However, the GATT rules adopted in 1968 prohibit assessment of retroactive punitive duties and require all procedures to be open. The United States differs from GATT in its dumping regulations, determining "fair market value" and "material injury" sequentially rather than simultaneously. Also, the U.S. government will assess any duty retroactively and has on numerous occasions acted to prevent antidumping practices from injuring domestic manufacturers.

The U.S. government has taken antidumping actions on numerous occasions over the past decade. In one recent case, the U.S. government charged Asian sweater makers with dumping on a volume of $1.25 billion. In another case, dumping charges were leveled against ball-bearing imports on the basis of a suit filed by a U.S. producer.[24]

As the yen appreciated against the dollar in 1993, Japanese manufacturers had to quickly raise U.S. prices to protect themselves from allegations of selling their products in the United States at prices lower than in Japan. In August 1993, U.S. companies filed suit against Fuji, Photo Film, Nippon Steel, and Kawasaki Steel. The U.S. Department of Commerce ruled against Japanese companies 95 percent of the time, which certified that the goods were sold in the United States below the prices in Japan. The International Trade Commission (an independent agency) then hears such cases and analyzes six-month pricing data to determine if the dumping injured the U.S. manufacturers.[25]

The United States is not alone in taking antidumping action. Numerous European governments have also initiated antidumping duties for steel and other low-priced imports. In one typical action, the European Union found Japanese exporters of dot-matrix printers in violation of dumping regulations. Covering a volume of some $1.3 billion, fifteen Japanese firms were to be charged up to 47 percent of excess duties on their products. According to EC rules, these dumping charges cannot be absorbed as extra costs by the manufacturer but must be passed on as price increases to the customers.[26] International marketers have to be aware of antidumping legislation that sets a floor under export prices, limiting pricing flexibility even in the event of overcapacity or industry slowdown. On the other

23. Franklin R. Root, *International Trade and Investment,* 3rd ed. (Cincinnati: Southwestern, 1973), p. 296.

24. "When One Man's Dumping Is Another Man's Good Price," *Financial Times,* May 9, 1990, p. 10.

25. "Currency Risk—Japan's Firms Raise U.S. Prices to Avoid Dumping Charges," *Far Eastern Economic Review,* September 16, 1993, pp. 75–76.

26. "Printers Reflect Pattern of Trade Rows," *Financial Times,* December 20, 1988, p. 3.

hand, antidumping legislation can work to a company's advantage, protecting it from unfair competition.

Managerial Issues in Global Pricing

Now that we have given you a general overview of the context of international pricing, we direct your attention toward managerial issues. These recurring issues require constant management attention; they are never really considered solved. The issues are transfer pricing, quoting in foreign currencies, export price escalation, price arbitrage, and gray-market pricing.

Determining Transfer Prices

A substantial amount of international business takes place between subsidiaries of the same company. In 1983, it was estimated that in-house trading between subsidiaries accounted for 34 percent of volume among the world's 800 largest multinational companies, which accounted for about 90 percent of world trade. In 1985, Digital Equipment Corporation alone had worldwide sales of $6.7 billion, of which intercompany transfers accounted for $2 billion.

The cost to the importing or buying subsidiary depends on the negotiated transfer price agreed on by the two involved units of the international firm.[27] How these prices are set continues to be a major issue for international companies and governments alike. Because negotiations on transfer prices do not represent arm's-length negotiations between independent participants, the resulting prices frequently differ from free market prices.[28]

Companies may deviate from arm's-length prices for two reasons. They may want to (1) maximize profits or (2) minimize risk and uncertainty.[29] To pursue a strategy of profit maximization, a company may lower transfer prices for products shipped from some subsidiaries, while increasing prices for products shipped to others. The company will then try to accumulate profits in subsidiaries where it is advantageous and keep profits low in other subsidiaries.

Impact of Tax Structure   Different tax, tariff, or subsidy structures by country frequently invite such practices. By accumulating more profits in a low-tax country, a company lowers its overall tax bill and thus increases profit. Likewise, tariff duties can be reduced by quoting low transfer prices to countries with high tariffs. In cases where countries use different exchange rates for the transfer of goods as opposed to the transfer of capital or

27. "The World's In-House Traders," *Economist,* March 1, 1986, p. 61.

28. For a thorough conceptual treatment, see Jeffrey S. Arpan, *International Intracorporate Pricing* (New York: Praeger, 1972).

29. Sanjaya Lall, "Transfer-Pricing by Multinational Manufacturing Firms," *Oxford Bulletin of Economics and Statistics,* August 1973, pp. 173–175.

profits, advantages can be gained by increasing transfer prices rather than transferring profits at less advantageous rates. The same is true for countries with restrictions on profit repatriation. Furthermore, a company may want to accumulate profits in a wholly owned subsidiary rather than in one that is minority owned; by using the transfer price mechanism, it can avoid sharing profits with local partners.

Companies may also use the transfer price mechanism to minimize risk or uncertainty by moving profits or assets out of a country with chronic balance-of-payment problems and frequent devaluations. Since regular profit remittances are strictly controlled in such countries, many firms see high transfer prices as the only way to repatriate funds and thereby to reduce the amount of assets at risk. The same practice may be employed if a company anticipates political or social disturbances or a direct threat to profits through government intervention.

In actual practice, companies choose a number of approaches to transfer pricing. Market-based prices are equal to those negotiated by independent companies or at arm's length. Of thirty U.S.-based firms, 46 percent were reported to use market-based systems.[30] Another 35 percent used cost-based systems to determine the transfer price. Costs were based on a predetermined formula, which may include a standard markup for profits.

Internal Considerations Rigorous use of the transfer pricing mechanism to reduce a company's income taxes and duties and to maximize profits in strong currency areas can create difficulties for subsidiary managers whose profits are artificially reduced. In such cases, managers may be subject to motivational problems when the direct profit incentive is removed. Furthermore, company resource allocation may become inefficient since funds are appropriated to units whose profits are artificially increased; conversely, resources may be denied to subsidiaries whose income statements were subject to transfer price–induced reductions. It is generally agreed that a transfer price mechanism should not seriously impair either morale or resource allocations, since gains incurred through tax savings may easily be lost through other inefficiencies.

External Problems Governments do not look favorably on transfer pricing mechanisms aimed at reducing their tax revenues. U.S. government policy on transfer pricing is governed by tax law, particularly Section 482 of the Revenue Act of 1962.[31] The act is designed to provide an accurate allocation of costs, income, and capital among related enterprises to protect U.S. tax revenue. The U.S. Internal Revenue Service accepts the following transfer price methods:

> Market prices are generally preferred by the IRS, either based on a comparable uncontrolled price method or a resale price method. As far as cost-plus pricing is concerned, the IRS will

---

30. Scott S. Cowen, Lawrence C. Phillips, and Linda Stillabower, "Multinational Transfer Pricing," *Management Accounting,* January 1979, pp. 7–22.

31. Cowen et al., "Multinational Transfer Pricing," p. 18; Larry J. Merville and T. William Petty, "Transfer Pricing for the Multinational Firm," *Accounting Review,* 53 (October 1978), pp. 935–951.

accept cost-plus markup if market prices are not available, and economic circumstances warrant such use. Not acceptable, however, are actual cost methods. Other methods, such as negotiated prices, are acceptable as long as the transfer price is comparable to a price charged to an unrelated party.[32]

As a result of a perceived abuse of transfer pricing methods, the U.S. Internal Revenue Service undertook a major investigation of foreign subsidiaries operating in the United States. As a group, the more than 36,000 foreign-owned subsidiaries had a negative taxable income and thus paid no taxes in the mid-1980s. In particular, the IRS investigated pricing practices of foreign companies for excessively high transfer prices that tended to reduce the income produced by the foreign subsidiary in the United States. Underpayments were reported to amount to some $12 billion for the group of companies investigated. The IRS has the authority to recompute income and tax owed, by using "fair" transfer prices, and thus assess income taxes retroactively.[33]

President Clinton's election economic plan included a proposal to collect an additional $45 billion from foreign companies doing business in the United States. These foreign companies were suspected of overcharging U.S. subsidiaries to avoid U.S. taxes. While experts feel $45 billion is grossly overstated, there is the potential of $3 billion–$5 billion if the IRS is successful. The IRS settled a suit with Matsushita for $4.8 million plus interest in 1991.[34] In 1992, the IRS proposed a new set of transfer pricing rules that would calculate the internal transfer price, based on the industry profit measures.[35]

Quoting Price in a Foreign Currency

For many international marketing transactions, it is not always feasible to quote in a company's domestic currency when selling or purchasing merchandise. Although the majority of U.S. exporters quote prices in dollars, there are situations in which customers may prefer quotes in their own national currency. For most import transactions, sellers usually quote the currency of their own country. When two currencies are involved, there is the risk that a change in exchange rates may occur between the invoicing date and the settlement date for the transaction. This risk, the foreign exchange risk, is an inherent factor in international marketing and clearly separates domestic from international business. Astro-Med Inc., a small manufacturer of high-quality printers, based in Warwick, Rhode Island, experienced firsthand the reaction of a customer when the export price list was quoted in U.S. dollars. During the negotiations for a printer quoted at $200,000, its German customer balked at being presented with a price list, sales manual, and brochures,

32. Cowen et al., p. 19.

33. "IRS Seeks to Determine if Foreign Firms Owe Billions in U.S. Taxes," *Wall Street Journal,* February 20, 1990, p. A6.

34. "Clinton's Economic Proposal Faces Problem: Taxes of Foreign Companies Won't Meet Gov't," *Wall Street Journal,* November 11, 1992, p. A12.

35. "U.S. Tax Threat Plagues Japanese Firms," *Nikkei Weekly,* November 16, 1992, p. 3.

all for the U.S. market.[36] Situations occur in which an exporter is able to sign an order only if the buyer's currency is used. In such circumstances, special techniques are available to protect the seller from the foreign exchange risk.

The tools used to cover a company's foreign exchange risk are either (a) hedging in the forward market or (b) covering through money markets. Foreign exchange futures or options are also available but still represent only a small fraction of total volume. These alternatives are given because of the nature of foreign exchange. As we discussed in Chapter 2, for most major currencies, international foreign exchange dealers located at major banks quote a spot price and a forward price. The *spot price* determines the number of dollars to be paid for a particular foreign currency purchased or sold today. The *forward price* quotes the number of dollars to be paid for a foreign currency bought or sold 30, 90, or 180 days from today. The forward price, however, is not necessarily the market's speculation as to what the spot price will be in the future. Instead, the forward price reflects interest rate differentials between two currencies for maturities of 30, 90, or 180 days. Consequently, there are no firm indications as to what the spot price will be for any given currency in the future. For a review of foreign exchange markets, see Chapter 2.

A company quoting in foreign currency for purchase or sale can simply leave settlement until the due date and pay whatever spot price prevails at the time. Such an uncovered position may be chosen when exchange rates are not expected to shift or when any shift in the near future will result in a gain for the company. With exchange rates fluctuating widely on a daily basis, even among major trading nations such as the United States, Japan, Germany, and the United Kingdom, a company will expose itself to substantial foreign exchange risks. Since many international firms are in business to make a profit from the sale of goods rather than from speculation in the foreign exchange markets, managements generally protect themselves from unexpected fluctuations.

One such protection lies in the forward market. Instead of accepting whatever spot market rate exists on the settlement in thirty or ninety days, the corporation can opt to contract for future delivery of foreign currency at a firm price, regardless of the spot price actually paid at that time. This allows the seller to incorporate a firm exchange rate into the price determination. Of course, if a company wishes to predict the spot price in ninety days and is reasonably certain about the accuracy of its prediction, a choice may be made between the more advantageous of the two: the expected spot or the present forward rate. However, such predictions should only be made under the guidance of experts familiar with foreign exchange rates.

An alternative strategy, covering through the money market, involves borrowing funds to be converted into the currency at risk for the time until settlement. In this case, a company owes and holds the same amount of foreign currency, resulting in a corresponding loss or gain when settling at the time of payment. As an example, an exporter holding accounts receivable in deutsche marks (DM) and unwilling to absorb the related currency risk until payment is received may borrow deutsche marks for working capital

---

36. "Learning the Language of EC Trade," *Providence Journal-Bulletin,* March 1, 1989, p. C1.

purposes. When the customer pays in the foreign currency, the loan, also denominated in that same currency, is paid off. Any fluctuations will be canceled, resulting in neither loss nor gain.

How to Incorporate a Foreign Exchange Rate into a Selling Price Quote   To illustrate the incorporation of a foreign exchange rate into a price quote for export, assume that a U.S. company needs to determine a price quote for its plastic extrusion machinery being sold to a Canadian customer. The customer requested billing in Canadian dollars. The exporter, with a list price of U.S. $12,000, does not want to absorb any exchange risk. The daily foreign exchange rates on March 29, 1994, are U.S. $.7270 spot price for one Canadian dollar and $.7242 in the ninety days forward market.[37] The exporter can directly figure the Canadian dollar price by using the forward rate, resulting in an export price of $16,570.01 in Canadian currency. Upon shipping, the exporter would sell at $16,570.01 (in Canadian money) forward with ninety-days delivery and, with the rate of $.7242 per Canadian dollar, receive U.S. $12,000. Consequently, wherever possible, quotes in foreign currencies should be made based on forward rates, with respective foreign currency amounts sold in the forward market.

Selection of a Hedging Procedure   To illustrate the selection of a hedging procedure, assume that a U.S. exporter of computer workstations sells two machines valued at $24,000 to a client in the United Kingdom. The client will pay in British pounds quoted at the current (spot) rate (March 29, 1994) of $1.4825, or £16,188.87. This amount will be paid in three months (ninety days). As a result, the U.S. exporter will have to determine how to protect such an incoming amount against foreign exchange risk. Although uncertain about the outcome, the exporter's bank indicates that there is an equal chance for the British pound spot rate to remain at $1.4825 (Scenario A), to devalue to $1.3500 (Scenario B), or to appreciate to $1.6500 (Scenario C). As a result, the exporter has the option of selling the amount forward in the ninety days forward market, at $1.4772.

	A	B	C
Spot rate as of March 29, 1994	$1.4825	$1.4825	$1.4825
Spot rate as of June 29, 1994 (estimate)	1.4825	1.3500	1.6500
U.S. dollar equivalent of £16,188.87 at spot rates on June 29, 1994	24,000.00	21,854.97	26,711.64
Exchange gain (loss) with hedging	0	(2,145.03)	2,711.64

The alternative available to the exporter is to sell forward the invoice amount of £16,188.87 at $1.4772 to obtain a sure $23,914.20, a loss of $85.80 on the transaction. In

37. "Foreign Exchange," *Wall Street Journal,* March 30, 1994, p. C18.

anticipation of a devaluation of the pound, such a hedging strategy would be advisable. Consequently, the $85.80 represents a premium to ensure against any larger loss. However, a company would also forgo any gain as indicated under Scenario C. Acceptance for hedging through the forward market depends on the expected spot rate at the time the foreign payment is due. Again, keep in mind that the forward rate is not an estimate of the spot rate in the future.

Dealing with Parallel Imports or Gray Markets

One of the most perplexing problems international companies face is the phenomenon of different prices between countries. When such price differentials become large, individual buyers or independent entrepreneurs step in and buy products in low-price countries to reexport to high-price countries, profiting from the price differential. This arbitrage behavior creates what experts call the ''gray market'' or ''parallel imports,'' because these imports take place outside of the regular trade channels controlled by distributors or company-owned sales subsidiaries. Such price differences can occur as a result of company price strategy, margin differences, or currency fluctuations.

Pricing differently for the domestic market and export markets, U.K. car manufacturers created a price gap that caused an active parallel import market. During the late 1970s, prices for cars in the United Kingdom were increased in line with the relatively high inflation. However, the British were not in a position to pass on these increases in European export markets, thus resulting in very high car prices in the United Kingdom.[38] For example, U.K. car prices were 61 percent higher than those of Denmark when adjusted for local taxes.[39]

In response to this difference, British buyers started to go to Belgium to purchase their cars. When British Leyland and other U.K. car manufacturers tried to contain the flow of parallel imports, or gray-market cars, the British government stepped in to protect the private consumer.[40] As a result, car companies could not take direct measures against these practices other than by lowering prices in their domestic market or increasing prices abroad. European regulations permit British buyers to buy cars in Belgium and prohibit policies of car manufacturers aimed at stopping such practices.[41]

In the United Kingdom, Tesco, the supermarket group, is buying Stella Artois, the Belgian beer in France and selling it for significantly less than they could buy it from Whitbread, the U.K. brewer licensee. This gray market is putting pressure on the U.K. brewers to lower prices.[42] In the United States, Americans are going to Mexico to buy prescription drugs at a reduced price. For example, Zantac, the popular ulcer medication,

38. ''Car Prices: What Common Market?'' *Economist,* May 3, 1980, p. 75.
39. ''European Car Prices: Single Market, Double Cross?'' *Economist,* January 13, 1990, p. 48.
40. ''The Coming Car Price Crash,'' *Economist,* December 12, 1981, p. 62.
41. ''U.K. Car Pricing to Be Investigated,'' *Financial Times,* May 10, 1990, p. 22.
42. ''Brewers Fear Retail Beer Wars,'' *Financial Times,* August 13, 1993, p. 6.

costs $102 in the United States and only $22.35 for the same amount in Mexico; Xanax, for anxiety disorders, costs $55.42 in the United States versus $12.34 in Mexico.[43]

Fluctuating currency values can also create opportunities for parallel imports, as observed earlier in this chapter. This can affect even U.S. companies. Duracell, the U.S. battery producer, maintained a manufacturing facility in Belgium as well as in the United States. When the dollar began to appreciate against European currencies, some U.S. retailers and wholesalers realized they could profit by importing Belgian-made batteries. Such purchases turned out to be at least 20 percent below those of Duracell's list price in the United States. Duracell saw its profitability threatened because it earned more on U.S.-produced batteries. Although the company tried to have this practice ruled illegal, in most countries parallel imports are not against the law.[44]

For the United States alone, parallel, or gray-market, volume was estimated to be $6 billion at retail level in 1984.[45] However, parallel imports are not restricted to consumer products. With the legal situation in the United States favoring the official importer or distributor, companies have used other methods in the United States. Vivitar began to code all of its products according to the intended market. The company notified its distributors that agreements would be terminated if parallel export products were traced to them. Other camera producers changed their names on products or did not extend warranty coverage to parallel exports.

In some industries, independent businesses have sprung up to take advantage of such price differentials. These businesses, often referred to as diverters, work worldwide and are very quick to spot opportunities. A Belgian businessman acquired low-priced Colgate toothpaste in Brazil, where it was made under license for local and regional markets. This Brazilian version was sold in the United Kingdom at some 15 percent below regular retail prices. However, the Brazilian version was made with locally sourced chalk, a lower-quality version than that used by Colgate elsewhere. Furthermore, the unexpected export volume created a local shortage in a country where imports were not allowed. The practice was eventually stopped as the diverter was found guilty of selling inferior merchandise by a British court.[46]

International companies can deal with parallel, or gray, markets at two levels. Once such practices occur, a firm may use a number of strategies in a reactive way. This may range from confronting the culprit to price-cutting, supply interference, emphasis of product limitations, all the way to acquisition of the diverter involved. A number of proactive strategies may be implemented to prevent the practice from occurring at all. A company may provide product differentiation solely to prevent gray markets from developing. Strategic pricing may be used to keep prices within limits. Cooperation may be achieved with

43. "To Avoid Cost of U.S. Prescription Drugs, More Americans Shop South of the Border," *Wall Street Journal,* June 29, 1993, p. B1.

44. "Duracell Attacks U.S. Gray Market," *Financial Times,* February 23, 1984, p. 6.

45. "The Assault on the Right to Buy Cheap Imports," *Fortune,* January 7, 1985, p. 89.

46. S. Tamer Cavusgil and Ed Sikora, "How Multinationals Can Counter Gray Market Imports," *Columbia Journal of World Business,* Winter 1988, pp. 75–85.

dealers willing to cooperate. And finally, companies may use strict legal enforcement of contracts and even resort to lobbying governments with the aim of adding regulations that may prevent the practice.[47]

The pricing situation in the EU is especially interesting with the formation of the single market in 1992. Pricing differentials across Europe average only 20 percent, but certain products have a much larger difference between the highest and lowest prices: chocolate 115 percent, tomato ketchup 65 percent, beer 155 percent, yogurt 30 percent. A proactive strategy to develop a European pricing corridor is recommended by some experts. The price corridor would take into account the price elasticities of different markets and maximize the potential European profit margin rather than gravitating to the lowest price availability in Europe, if the parallel trading is successful.[48]

Product arbitrage will always occur when price differentials get too large and when transport costs are low in relation to product value. International companies will have to monitor price differentials more closely for standardized products in particular. Products that are highly differentiated from country to country are also less likely to become parallel traded.

Managing Export Price Escalation

The additional costs described earlier may raise the end-user price of an exported product substantially above its domestic price. This phenomenon, called export price escalation, may force a company to adopt any one of two strategic patterns. First, a company may realize its price disadvantage and adjust the marketing mix to account for its ''luxury'' status. By adopting such a strategy, a company sacrifices volume to keep a high unit price. Alternatively, a company may grant a ''discount'' on the standard domestic price to bring the end-user price more in line with prices paid by domestic customers. Such discounts may be justified under marginal-contribution pricing methods. Because of reduced marketing costs at the manufacturer's level, particularly when a foreign distributor is used, an export price equal to a domestic price is often not justified. Legal limits such as antidumping regulations prevent price reductions below a certain point. Customary margins, both wholesale and retail, may differ considerably among countries, with independent importers frequently requiring higher margins than domestic intermediaries do.

Global Pricing Strategies

As international companies deal with market and environmental factors, they face two major strategic pricing alternatives. Essentially, the choice is between the global, single-price strategy and the individualized country strategy.

To maximize a company's revenues, it would appear to be logical to set prices on a

47. ''Colgate Takes a Diverter to Task,'' *Financial Times,* April 14, 1989, p. 6.

48. Hermann Simon and Eckhard Kucher, ''The European Pricing Time Bomb: And How to Cope With It,'' *European Management Journal,* June 1992, pp. 136–144.

market-by-market basis, looking in each market for the best combination of revenue versus volume yielding maximum profit. This strategy was common for many firms in the early part of their international development. For many products, however, noticeable price differences between markets are taken advantage of by independent companies or channel members who see a profit from buying in lower-price markets and exporting products to high-price markets. For products that are relatively similar in many markets and for which transportation costs are not significant, substantial price differences will quickly result in the emergence of the gray market. As a result, fewer companies have the possibility of pricing on a market-by-market basis. As the markets become more transparent, the information flows more efficiently; and as products become more similar, the trend away from market-by-market pricing is likely to continue.

McDonald's, the leading U.S. fast-food chain, has taken the route of pricing its products according to local market conditions. Its key product, the Big Mac, ranges in price from $1.14 (U.S.) in Russia to $4.25 in Denmark, with most countries in the range from $2 to $4.[49] (See Table 13.4 for more comparisons.) Certainly, McDonald's can maximize its pricing according to the competitive forces of each individual country without much fear of parallel imports.

For many consumer products, there are still substantial price differences across many countries. For a selective list of consumer products across major European cities, see Table 13.5. Differences in pretax retail prices tend to hide a number of inefficiencies in retail distribution systems, such as the preponderance of large-volume and low-price chains in the United Kingdom versus the dominance of small retail shops in Italy. Other factors are competitive, such that Heinz tends to price its products lower in countries where it is not leading, and Levi's jeans prices are high in Spain, where they are viewed as fashion items rather than casual wear.[50]

Employing a uniform pricing strategy on a global scale requires that a company, which can determine its prices in local currency, will always charge the same price everywhere when the price is translated into a base currency. In reality, this becomes very difficult to achieve whenever different taxes, trade margins, and customs duties are involved. As a result, there are likely to be price differences due to those factors not under control of the company. Keeping prices identical aside from those noncontrollable factors is a challenge. Firms may start out with identical prices in various countries but soon find that prices have to change to stay in line with often substantial currency fluctuations.

Although it is becoming increasingly clear for many companies that market-by-market pricing strategies will cause difficulties, many firms have found that changing to a uniform pricing policy is rather like pursuing a moving target. Even when a global pricing policy is adopted, a company must carefully monitor price levels in each country and avoid large gaps that can then cause problems when independent or gray market forces move in and take advantage of large price differentials.

49. "Big Mac Currencies," *Economist,* April 17, 1993, p. 79.
50. "Counting Costs of Dual Pricing in the Run-up to 1992," *Financial Times,* July 9, 1990, p. 4.

TABLE 13.4 ● The Hamburger Standard

	Big Mac prices		*ACTUAL EXCHANGE RATE 13/4/93*	*IMPLIED PPP† OF THE DOLLAR*	*% LOCAL CURRENCY UNDER (−)/ OVER (+) VALUATION***
	*IN LOCAL CURRENCY**	*IN DOLLARS*			
United States‡	$2.28	2.28	—	—	—
Argentina	Peso3.60	3.60	1.00	1.58	+58
Australia	A$2.45	1.76	1.39	1.07	−23
Belgium	BFr109	3.36	32.45	47.81	+47
Brazil	Cr77,000	2.80	27,521	33,772	+23
Britain	£1.79	2.79	1.56§	1.27§	+23
Canada	C$2.76	2.19	1.26	1.21	−4
China	Yuan8.50	1.50	5.68	3.73	−34
Denmark	DKr25.75	4.25	6.06	11.29	+86
France	FFr18.50	3.46	5.34	8.11	+52
Germany	DM4.60	2.91	1.58	2.02	+28
Holland	Fl5.45	3.07	1.77	2.39	+35
Hong Kong	HK$9.00	1.16	7.73	3.95	−49
Hungary	Forint157	1.78	88.18	68.86	−22
Ireland	I£1.48	2.29	1.54§	1.54§	0
Italy	Lire4,500	2.95	1,523	1,974	+30
Japan	¥391	3.45	113	171	+51
Malaysia	Ringgit3.35	1.30	2.58	1.47	−43
Mexico	Peso7.09	2.29	3.10	3.11	0
Russia	Rouble780	1.14	686§§	342	−50
South Korea	Won2,300	2.89	796	1,009	+27
Spain	Ptas325	2.85	114	143	+25
Sweden	SKr25.50	3.43	7.43	11.18	+50
Switzerland	SwFr5.70	3.94	1.45	2.50	+72
Thailand	Baht48	1.91	25.16	21.05	−16

*Prices may vary locally.

†Purchasing-power parity: local price divided by price in United States.

**Against dollar.

‡Average of New York, Chicago, San Francisco, and Atlanta.

§Dollars per pound.

§§Market rate.

Source: Copyright © 1993 The Economist Newspaper Group, Inc. Reprinted with permission. Further reproduction prohibited.

TABLE 13.5 ● Price Comparisons of Consumer Products Across European Cities*

Product	Lowest price			Highest price			Price coefficient**
	City	RETAIL	PRETAX	City	RETAIL	PRETAX	
Bosch 500-2 power drill	Brussels	70.94	56.75	Milan	99.34	83.48	1.47
Bosch 4542 washing machine	London	462.69	402.34	Milan	672.74	565.33	1.40
Braun Silencio hair dryer	London	18.44	16.03	Athens	50.60	43.62	2.72
Coca-Cola, 1.5 L bottle	Amsterdam	.82	.69	Copenhagen	2.04	1.45	2.10
Colgate toothpaste, 100 ml	Athens	1.33	1.15	Milan	1.88	1.72	1.50
EMI compact disc: Tina Turner, "Foreign Affair"	Athens	14.39	12.41	Madrid	21.72	19.39	1.36
EMI cassette of same	London	8.7	7.57	Copenhagen	21.84	17.9	2.36
Financial Times	London	.67	.67	Copenhagen	1.54	1.54	2.30
Gillette Contour razor blades, 5-pack	Athens	1.99	1.72	Copenhagen	3.53	2.76	1.60
Heinz ketchup, 570 gm	London	.86	.86	Madrid	2.04	1.92	1.98
Hitachi 630 video recorder	London	452.17	393.19	Athens	749.64	551.21	1.40
Hoover 3726 vacuum cleaner	Luxembourg	118.31	105.63	Amsterdam	260.31	219.67	2.08
IBM 30-021 personal computer, 20MB, color display	Athens	1629.21	1404.49	Copenhagen	4065.75	3332.58	2.37
Kellogg's corn flakes, 375 gm	Amsterdam	1.26	1.06	Cologne	1.95	1.82	1.72
Kodak 35 mm Gold 100 film	Cologne	3.4	2.98	Copenhagen	5.98	4.90	1.64
Levi's 501 jeans	London	50.01	43.49	Madrid	74.65	66.85	1.53
Mars bar	London	.27	.27	Copenhagen	.67	.55	2.04
Nescafé, 200 gm	Athens	3.67	3.16	Milan	7.78	7.14	2.26
Olivetti ET65 electronic typewriter	Brussels	331.37	278.48	Lisbon	638.37	545.62	1.96
Pampers, Midi 52, boy's	Dublin	10.47	8.51	Milan	11.70	10.73	1.26
Sony 2121 television	London	536.45	466.48	Copenhagen	1091.74	894.87	1.92
Timotel shampoo, 200 ml	London	1.23	1.07	Amsterdam	2.09	1.76	1.64
Toblerone, 100 gm	Amsterdam	.85	.72	Lisbon	1.49	1.38	1.92

*Prices in ECU, converted at rate of April 27, 1990.

**Ratio of highest to lowest pretax prices.

Source: *Financial Times,* July 9, 1990, p. 4. Reprinted by permission.

Financing International Marketing Transactions

As many international marketers have observed, the ability to make financing available at a low cost can become the deciding factor that beats competitors. In the context of international marketing, financing should be understood in its broadest sense (see Figure 13.3). Not only does it consist of direct credits to the buyer, it also includes a range of activities

FIGURE 13.3 ● Financing International Marketing Transactions

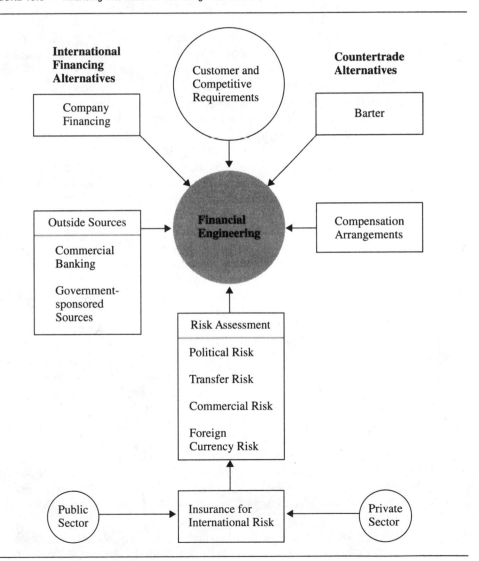

that enable the customer to afford the purchase. In this section we examine financing provided by the selling company, as well as financing through the financial community and government-sponsored agencies.

Risks

Financing international marketing transactions involves a host of risks over and above those encountered by strictly domestic operations. International companies have to be aware of these risks and understand the methods available for reducing risk to an acceptable level. The four major risks include commercial risk, foreign currency risk, transfer risk, and political risk.

Commercial risk refers to buyer ability to pay for the products or services ordered. This risk is also typical for a domestic operation. As a result, companies are accustomed to checking the financial stability of their customers and may even have internally approved credit limits. Although checking credit references in a domestic environment poses no great difficulty, such information is not always readily available in many overseas markets. Companies can rely on their banks or on foreign credit reporting agencies where such organizations exist. Past experience with a commercial customer abroad may frequently be the only indicator of a firm's financial stability.

Foreign currency risk exists whenever a company bills in a currency other than its own.[51] For U.S. companies billing in Japanese yen, a currency risk exists because the value of the yen versus the dollar is subject to market fluctuations and, therefore, cannot be determined at the outset. Foreign currency risk grows with the length of credit terms and with the instability of a foreign currency. Suppliers can insure themselves against foreign currency fluctuations, as was described in more detail earlier in this chapter.

Invoicing in their own currency, suppliers shift the currency risk to the customer. The customer may not be in a position to cover that risk, as is the case in many countries with unsophisticated financial markets. In such a case, the exporting company frequently must choose between selling in a foreign currency or having no deal at all.

Although the customer may be able to pay, payments often get delayed by bureaucracies, creating a *transfer risk*. Transfer delays prevail in countries where the foreign exchange market is controlled and where the customer has to apply for the purchase of foreign currency before payment takes place. Delays of up to 180 days beyond the credit terms agreed on are not unusual and add to the costs of exporter or supplier. In countries where a foreign exchange shortage prevents immediate payment of all foreign currency–denominated debts, complex debt restructuring negotiations may take place, causing additional delays. Many countries have had to negotiate such extensions at one time or another, including Brazil, Mexico, Argentina, Turkey, Poland, and Zaire.

Financing for international marketing operations is also subject to *political risk,* which includes the occurrence of war, revolutions, insurgencies, or civil unrest, any of which may result in nonpayment of accounts receivable. In some instances, civil unrest may

51. Chuck C. Y. Kwok, ''Hedging Foreign Exchange Exposures: Independent Versus Integrative Approaches,'' *Journal of International Business Studies,* Summer 1987, p. 33.

demand rescheduling of foreign trade debt, as in Poland in the early 1980s. In other situations, political unrest may bring about a new government that cancels foreign debt, as happened in Iran following the downfall of the shah.

The international marketer needs to understand the risks of providing financing to customers. In cases where the supplier shoulders all international risks, companies may want to build extra costs into their prices. Smaller price adjustments may be required when only a portion of the international credit risk is carried.

Customer- Versus Supplier-Arranged Financing

As discussed in this section, financing arranged by suppliers goes beyond the open account practices that will be described in Chapter 18. In this context, supplier financing is viewed as any term beyond the usual thirty to ninety days customary for open account shipment.

Because credit risks are higher for clients abroad, companies have a preference for shorter payment terms with foreign clients. However, many customers may not be able to purchase under shortened credit terms. Consequently, companies may charge an interest rate on the outstanding amount. When companies cannot get at least market interest rates, they may try to capture the additional cash through higher prices. However, most clients today are adept at comparing total costs to themselves, and opportunities for hiding interest cost behind higher list prices are limited.

Since most companies do not consider themselves to be in the business of financing their customers, they prefer to assist clients in finding suitable financing opportunities. One such exception is financing without recourse, a relatively new method (explained below) for financing shipments abroad.

Sources of Financing

Companies can choose from a wide selection of alternatives to finance international marketing transactions: traditional financing through commercial banks, government-sponsored loans, or countertrade. The international marketer is increasingly expected to be knowledgeable about complicated financial arrangements. As buyers compare acquisition costs, including any necessary financing, providing such financing becomes a matter for international marketing management to handle. The following sections are intended to offer you a general background on the most common financing alternatives practiced by many international companies today.

Commercial Banks

Commercial banks, whether domestic or foreign, are usually willing to finance transactions only to first-rate credit risks. This fact makes financing unavailable to any but the largest companies. Furthermore, commercial banks avoid long-term financing and prefer short maturities. When selecting a commercial bank, inquire about the following: size of the international department, number and locations of foreign branches or correspondent banks, charges for letters of credit, and experience with government financing programs.[52]

Commercial banks that have loaned heavily to developing countries have recently experienced difficulties with repayment and interest payments on outstanding loan portfolios. Therefore, banks located in developed countries have hesitated to lend further to developing countries, forcing exporters to look elsewhere to finance their clients.

Clients outside the developed countries of Europe and Asia have also found local financing difficult. Especially for purchases in currencies other than their own, foreign buyers in developing countries are increasingly dependent on financing from abroad. For larger industrial projects, this is now almost the rule. With commercial banks only partially able to close the gap, both buyers and suppliers are availing themselves of other financing sources.

Forfaiting: Financing Without Recourse[53]   *Forfaiting,* or financing without recourse, means that the seller of merchandise can transfer a claim, resulting from a transaction in the form of a bill of exchange, to a forfaiting house by including the term *without recourse* as part of the endorsement. The collection risk is thus transferred to the forfaiting house, and the seller receives on presentation of documents the full amount minus a discount for the entire credit period. Generally, the forfaiting houses prefer working with invoices guaranteed by the foreign banks or governments.[54] The discount varies with the country risk and the currency chosen for financing. Typical maturities range from six months to several years.

Nonrecourse financing offers the advantage of selling products over medium terms at market rates. Such transactions are not possible through commercial banks. An exporter may obtain a firm quote on a given business deal ahead of time, allowing inclusion of the discount rate into the price calculation. This ensures that the net payout meets normal profitability standards. For capital equipment–exporting countries such as Germany and Switzerland, approximately 5 to 10 percent of exports are arranged through this financing technique. However, it has limitations. For countries that are poor credit risks, forfait transactions are not possible.[55] Also, transaction size is usually under ten million dollars, although larger amounts may be financed through several institutions that together form an ad hoc consortium or syndicate.

52. This section is based upon *Forfaiting* (Zurich: Finanz A.G., 1986), p. 6.

53. U.S. Department of Commerce, *A Basic Guide to Exporting* (Lincolnwood, Ill.: NTC Business Books, 1993), p. 45.

54. "Congratulations, Exporter, Now About Getting Paid," *Business Week,* January 17, 1994, p. 98.

55. Gino Giuliato, "Forfaitierung," *Der Monat* (Swiss Bank Corporation), March 1989, p. 24.

Government-Sponsored Financing: The Export-Import Bank[56]

With the ability to assemble the best financing package often determining the sale of capital equipment or other large-volume transactions, governments all over the world have realized that government-sponsored banks can foster exports and, therefore, employment. Government-subsidized financing now exceeds that which commercial banks and exporters formerly provided. For this purpose, the United States created its Export-Import Bank (Eximbank for short) in 1934. Other countries, particularly members of the Organization for Economic Cooperation and Development (OECD), have established their own export banks, also aimed at assisting their respective exporters with the financing of large transactions. Japan committed $7.9 billion in 1987 to provide export insurance for developing countries and political risk insurance for Japanese companies investing overseas. The export insurance plan was to cover up to 97.5 percent of the value for prepaid contracts.[57]

The Export-Import Bank and its affiliated institutions, the Foreign Credit Insurance Association (FCIA) and the Private Export Funding Corporation (PEFCO), make a number of services available to U.S. exporters. Eximbank has special services for short-, medium-, and long-term financing requirements.

Short-Term Financing   Financing requirements of 180 days or less are considered short-term. For such commitments, Eximbank does not make direct financing available. Instead, through the Foreign Credit Insurance Association, Eximbank offers export credit insurance to the U.S. exporter. This insurance covers the exporter for commercial risk, such as nonpayment by the foreign buyer; political risk, such as war, revolution, insurrection, expropriation; and currency inconvertibility. The cost of such insurance averages less than half of 1 percent per $100 of gross invoice value. With such insurance in force, the exporter has the choice of carrying accounts receivable on the company records or refinancing with a commercial bank at domestic interest rates, provided the transaction is insured. In general, commercial risks are insured up to 90 percent of the invoiced value. Political risks are covered for up to 100 percent of the merchandise value, depending on the type of policy selected.

In 1983, about $7.5 billion, or 3.8 percent, of U.S. exports were insured by FCIA.[58] Total premium costs were about 0.2 percent of the insured volume. In the same year, FCIA paid out $193 million to exporters or banks financing such trade. For the past few years, U.S. firms have enjoyed lower export insurance rates than those available in other countries. Companies in Sweden and West Germany paid 3.4 and 2.3 percent respectively.

56. This segment draws heavily from official publications of the Export-Import Bank of the United States, Washington, D.C., 1979.

57. "Japan to Commit Almost $8 Billion to Trade Insurance," *Wall Street Journal,* March 31, 1987, p. 48.

58. *Der Monat* (Swiss Bank Corporation), April 1985.

Medium-Term Financing Eximbank classifies terms ranging from 181 days to five years as medium-term. To serve exporters, four special programs exist: the medium-term export credit insurance (FCIA) programs, the U.S. Commercial Bank Guarantee Program, the Discount Loan Program, and the Cooperative Financing Facility.

Several insurance alternatives are available through FCIA. Provided the foreign buyer makes a cash payment of 15 percent on or before delivery, and subject to a deductible of 10 percent, Eximbank will insure each specific transaction. Through the cooperation of nearly 300 U.S. commercial banks, Eximbank organized the U.S. Commercial Bank Guarantee Program. Under this program, Eximbank offers protection against commercial and political risks on debts acquired by U.S. banks from U.S. exporters. This coverage is now extended to more than 140 countries. Conditions for the guarantee program include a cash payment of 15 percent by the foreign buyer, a deductible of 10 percent, and passing credit checks imposed by Eximbank and the participating commercial bank. The interest rate is set by the commercial bank according to prevailing domestic market conditions.

Long-Term Financing Long-term financing by Eximbank extends from five to ten years. Under special circumstances, as in the case of conventional or nuclear power plants, financing may be arranged for longer periods. Financing may occur either by direct credit to the foreign buyer or by a guarantee of repayment of private financing arranged by the buyer. Eximbank requires a 15 percent down payment by the foreign buyer and assurance that private financing is not possible on similar terms. In the past, foreign airlines and utilities have made frequent use of such facilities to finance purchases of aircraft and power-generating equipment.

In general, Eximbank programs do not extend direct financing to the U.S. exporter. Rather, the bank closes the gap between commercial bank financing and foreign buyer needs by guarantees or financing for the foreign buyer.

The Value of Eximbank Loans to U.S. Exporters Although less than 10 percent of U.S. exports are financed through Eximbank, loans at lower than market rates are crucial to exporters of many products. In 1980, about $3 billion of Boeing Company's $5 billion in exports were financed by Eximbank.[59] In 1981, more than 2,600 firms used the services of Eximbank.[60] Researchers estimated that Eximbank operations in 1980 supported about 570,000 U.S. jobs.

Another U.S. company that relied heavily on Eximbank financing was J. I. Case, once one of the nation's leading farm equipment manufacturers. With foreign sales accounting for nearly half of Case's business, Eximbank credit helped it compete with European and Japanese manufacturers that could profit from low-cost government export financing. In 1980, a $10.4 million contract with the Dominican Republic was facilitated by an 8 percent

59. "U.S. Firms Already Cut Back Work as Result of Ex-Im Bank Restraints," *Wall Street Journal*, March 31, 1981, p. 35.
60. "U.S. Companies and Unions Fight to Save Exim Bank from Budget Knife," *Business International*, May 14, 1982, p. 153.

loan for $3.5 million to the buyers. Also in 1980, a five-year loan at 7.75 percent helped clinch a deal with Israel.[61]

Eximbank support of U.S. exporters depends on funding from the U.S. government. U.S. exporters have in the past lobbied heavily to expand Eximbank funding, hoping to receive more loans at more favorable rates. However, many critics argue that Eximbank serves large firms that are already profitable. The political debate surrounding Eximbank is expected to continue, and its lending authority will vary as Congress appropriates differing fund levels from year to year.

For smaller companies, access to the full range of government-sponsored export financing is still difficult. Large commercial banks with the sophistication to help do not like to make small loans. On the other hand, the small local banks that handle the banking business for small companies do not have the resources and experience to assist in international export financing. As a result, several U.S. states, California among them, have set up their own state-sponsored export financing schemes for transactions of about $500,000 or less. California guarantees 85 percent repayment on loans used to finance working capital or accounts receivable tied to export orders. Illinois will even lend the bank of the small firm up to 90 percent of the funds needed to make export-related loans. More than ten U.S. states have started similar programs.[62]

Competing Against Export Credit Banks of Foreign Nations   Most developed nations of North America, Europe, and Asia maintain programs to finance exports from their own countries. To the extent that internal loan conditions differ from those offered by other countries, an exporter from a given country may have an advantage. U.S. Eximbank rates are usually higher than those offered by export banks in other countries. To prevent an interest rate ''war'' from developing, leading industrial nations have agreed to minimum rates and loans for various groups of countries. Such agreements are renegotiated periodically, and the U.S. government has taken a lead in such negotiations.[63]

Eximbank has an active intermediary program to loan money to banks at 150 basis points below OECD consensus rates for loans valued at less than one million dollars. These funds are designated to finance medium and small exporters for small transactions.[64]

Governments can also help secure financing. The Taiwan government stepped in and offered loan guarantees to support the ¥ 250 million joint venture between British Aerospace and Taiwan Aerospace. This type of government support is often available for critical projects and joint ventures.[65]

61. ''Banking on Ex-Im,'' *Time,* March 2, 1981, p. 28.

62. ''States Launch Efforts to Make Small Firms Better Exporters,'' *Wall Street Journal,* February 2, 1987, p. 25.

63. ''U.S. Overcomes EEC Resistance,'' *Financial Times,* July 5, 1982, p. 4.

64. ''What's New at Eximbank and Why U.S. Exporters Should Take Another Look,'' *Business International, Weekly Report to Managers of Worldwide Operations,* March 30, 1987, pp. 98–99.

65. ''Taiwan May Underwrite BAe Venture,'' *Financial Times,* August 24, 1993, p. 14.

Financial Engineering: A New Marketing Tool   With financing costs becoming ever more important for capital goods, many companies have moved toward exploiting the best financial deal from bases around the world. A company with manufacturing bases in several countries may bid on a contract from several subsidiaries to let the client select the most advantageous package, or it may preselect the subsidiary that will bid based on available financing. Devising such financial packages is known as *financial engineering*. It is practiced by independent specialists located in leading financial centers and by international banks that have developed expertise in this field.

Massey-Ferguson, Ltd., a Canadian farm machinery manufacturer, provides an example of financial engineering.[66] Massey-Ferguson had traditionally supplied tractors to Turkey from its U.K. plants. Turkey experienced balance-of-payments difficulty, and the company had problems obtaining credit for the country. Massey-Ferguson looked to its other manufacturing bases for new sources of financing. The best deal was offered by Brazil, a country eager to expand its exports. Brazilians helped convince the Turkish customer Mafer to buy Brazilian-made equipment in U.S. dollars.

Massey sold 7,200 tractors worth $53 million to a Brazilian agency, which in turn sold to the Turkish buyer. Massey was to be paid cash, and a Brazilian state agency guaranteed payment. Thus, Brazil was able to take business of about 20,000 tractors annually from the United Kingdom because it assumed all risk for Massey-Ferguson.

Other companies are now institutionalizing financial engineering in their global operations. Some maintain full-time specialists at their international divisions who are prepared to advise operating divisions on financial engineering opportunities in bidding. One division of a company with manufacturing operations in several countries frequently submits bids from several of its plants and lets the customer select the most desirable package. This strategy works best if products are highly standardized and quality differences between the various plants are minimal.

Noncash Pricing: Countertrade

International marketers are likely to find many situations in which an interested customer will not be able to find any hard-currency financing at all. In such circumstances, the customer might offer a product or commodity in return. The supplier must then turn the product offered into hard currency. Such transactions, known as *countertrades,* are estimated to have accounted for 8 to 10 percent of world trade, or more than $200 billion in 1985. Other private sources have estimated countertrade as high as 30 percent of world trade and expect it to climb steadily in the future.[67]

The U.S. International Trade Commission surveyed 500 of the largest U.S. companies accounting for some 60 percent of U.S. exports on their use of countertrade. For 1984, the

66. "How Massey-Ferguson Uses Brazil for Export Financing," *Business Week,* March 17, 1978, p. 86.
67. "Beleaguered Third World Leads the Barter Boom," *Financial Times,* February 28, 1984, p. 6.

survey found that 5.6 percent of those firms' exports, totaling U.S. $7.1 billion, were covered by some part of a countertrade arrangement. About 80 percent of this volume was accounted for by military equipment sales. Nonmilitary countertrade grew from $285 million in 1980 to $1.4 billion in 1984.[68]

Forms of countertrade have always been popular between eastern European and CIS countries and western countries. For that region, countertrade was estimated to represent about 15 percent of international trade, twice the average for the rest of the world.[69] A study by a private research firm reported that in the early 1970s some fifteen countries insisted on countertrade in some circumstances. By the end of the 1970s this number had doubled, and by 1985 it had risen to more than fifty countries.[70] Recent political changes in the world have not eliminated the need for countertrade. The eastern European countries, including Russia, remain plagued by a scarcity of foreign exchange. Instead of involving just government-sponsored foreign trade organizations, many more private or privatized companies are now looking to help themselves through such methods. Kotva, Czechoslovakia's leading department store, could not get access to sufficient western goods even after the liberalization there in late 1989. The store traded Czech paper for Lego toys and Czech cheese for Italian vermouth.[71] To respond to this challenge, international marketers have developed several forms of countertrade (see Figure 13.4). The following sections explain each one and then examine the problems associated with each.[72]

Barter   Barter, one of the most basic types of countertrade, consists of a direct exchange of goods between two parties. In most cases, these transactions take place between two or more nations (three in cases of triangular barter). Barter involves no currency and is concluded without the help of intermediaries. Barter has become less common, while other forms of countertrade have become more popular.[73]

One of the largest barter deals in recent years, valued at about $3 billion, was signed by PepsiCo and Russia. Since 1974, PepsiCo had engaged in business with Russia, shipping soft drink syrup, bottling it into Pepsi-Cola, and marketing it within Russia. By 1989, the business had reached some 40 million cases (each containing twenty-four 8-ounce bottles). Within Russia, PepsiCo was running some twenty-six bottling plants, all producing at full capacity. The volume amounted to about $300 million for 1989. Since hard currency was not available for takeout profits, PepsiCo had entered an agreement to export

68. "Countertrade Comes out of the Closet," *Economist,* December 20, 1986, p. 89.

69. David B. Yoffie, "Barter: Looking Beyond the Short-Term Payoffs and Long-Term Threat," *International Management,* August 1984, p. 36.

70. "Countertrade Comes Out," p. 89.

71. "Czech Retailer Leads in Effort for Western Goods," *New York Times,* November 26, 1990, p. D7.

72. The terminology used in this section is based on *Barter, Compensation and Cooperation,* Publication vol. 47 IV (Zurich: Credit Suisse, 1978).

73. See Henry Ferguson, "Tomorrow's Global Manager Will Use Countertrade," *Corporate Barter and Countertrade,* July 1987.

FIGURE 13.4 ● Forms of Countertrade

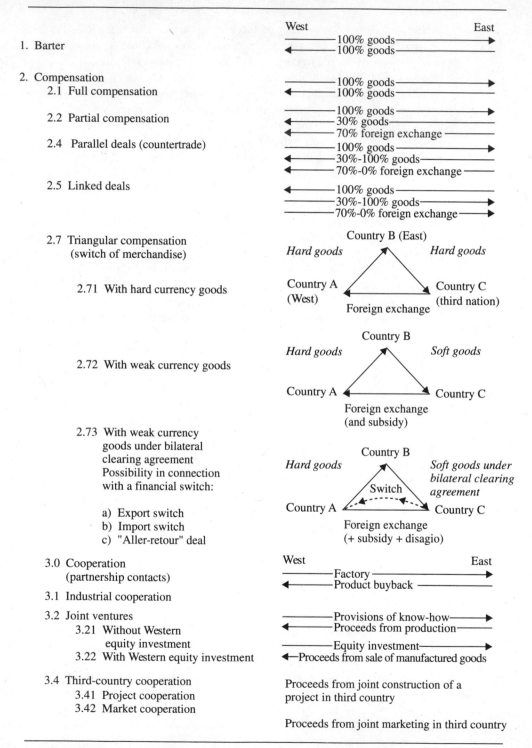

1. Barter

2. Compensation
   2.1 Full compensation

   2.2 Partial compensation

   2.4 Parallel deals (countertrade)

   2.5 Linked deals

   2.7 Triangular compensation
       (switch of merchandise)

       2.71 With hard currency goods

       2.72 With weak currency goods

       2.73 With weak currency
            goods under bilateral
            clearing agreement
            Possibility in connection
            with a financial switch:

            a) Export switch
            b) Import switch
            c) "Aller-retour" deal

3.0 Cooperation
    (partnership contacts)

3.1 Industrial cooperation

3.2 Joint ventures
    3.21 Without Western
         equity investment
    3.22 With Western equity investment

3.4 Third-country cooperation
    3.41 Project cooperation
    3.42 Market cooperation

Source: Barter, Compensation and Cooperation, Credit Suisse, Zurich, Switzerland, Vol. 47, IV, 1978, pp. 8–9. Reprinted by permission.

Stolichnaya vodka to the United States, where it was sold through an independent liquor company. That volume had reached some one million cases (each containing twelve 25-ounce bottles), or about $156 million in sales. In 1990, a new deal was signed that included the sale or the lease of at least ten Russian tanker ships ranging from 28,000 to 65,000 tons. The proceeds of these transactions are to be used to expand the ongoing PepsiCo business in Russia by expanding Pepsi-Cola into national distribution and to fund the expansion of the Pizza Hut restaurant chain.[74]

Compensation Arrangements   Compensation arrangements are transactions that include payment in merchandise or foreign exchange. Depending on the type of arrangement, the method or structure of the compensation transaction may change. One usually speaks of a compensation transaction when the value of an export delivery is offset by an import transaction or vice versa. Compensation transactions are typical for large governmental purchases, such as for defense, when a country wants to obtain some extra exports for the import of defense systems. Outstanding offset trade obligations have been estimated at about $50 billion worldwide, a large amount of that incurred by U.S.-based aerospace and defense contractors.[75] Compensation transactions may be classified into several categories, as described below.

Full versus Partial Compensation   *Full* compensation is similar to barter in that a 100 percent mutual transfer of goods takes place. However, deliveries are made and paid for separately. By signing the sales agreement, the exporter commits to purchase products or services at an amount equal to that specified in the export contract. An option exists to sell such a commitment to a third party who may take over the commitment from the exporter for a fee.

Under *partial* compensation, the exporter receives a portion of the purchase price in hard currency and the remainder in merchandise. The exporter will not be able to convert such merchandise into cash until a buyer can be found, and even then only at a discount.

A partial compensation transaction was concluded in 1981 by Honda, a Japanese car manufacturer, and the Algerian government to cover 15,000 passenger cars valued at $50 million. When Algeria could not pay in hard currency as a result of depressed crude oil volumes, that country offered to pay the entire value in oil. However, Algeria's official export price of $37.50 per barrel was above the valid spot price of $33. This would have resulted in a price discount of about 10 percent by Honda. The parties eventually agreed to compensate 40 percent of the contract value of Algeria's official export price with crude oil, and the rest was paid in hard currency. This was the first such deal for Honda.[76]

Parallel Deals   In a parallel deal, the exporter agrees to accept the merchandise equivalent of a given percentage of the export amount. Payment is received on delivery. This

---

74. ''Pepsi Will Be Bartered for Ships and Vodka in Deal with Soviets,'' *New York Times,* April 9, 1990, p. 1.
75. ''Excitement of Bartering Is Fading Away,'' *Financial Times,* June 1, 1989, Section 3, p. 111.
76. Ibid.

arrangement is intended to offset the outflow of wealth from the country when a very large purchase has been made. Within a given amount of time, the exporter searches for a specific amount of merchandise that can be bought from the country or company that purchased the products originally. Eastern European countries often include a penalty fee in case the western exporter defaults on the countertrade portion of the arrangement. Offset arrangements are a type of parallel deal gaining popularity today.

Linked Deals   Linked deals, sometimes called junctions, are a form of countertrade not frequently used. A western importer finds a western exporter willing to deliver merchandise to a country in eastern Europe or the Third World. At the same time, the inporter is released from a counterpurchase agreement by paying a premium to the exporter, who in turn organizes the counterpurchase. This transaction requires agreement of the state-controlled trading nation.

Triangular Compensation   Triangular compensation arrangements, also called *switch trades,* involve three countries. The western exporter delivers hard goods (salable merchandise) to an importing country, typically in eastern Europe. As payment, the importing country may transfer hard goods (easily salable merchandise) or soft goods (heavily discounted merchandise) to a third country in the West or in eastern Europe, which then reimburses the western exporter for the goods received. Such negotiations may become complex and time consuming. Often the assistance of skilled switch traders is required to ensure profitable participation by the western exporter.

Marc Rich & Co., a Swiss commodities firm, has been very successful in the republics of the former Soviet Union with complicated triangular arrangements. For example, in one deal, the company bought 70,000 tons of raw sugar in Brazil and shipped it to Ukraine to be processed. It paid for the processing with some of the sugar, then shipped 30,000 tons of the refined sugar 6,000 miles to several huge Siberian oil refineries, which needed the sugar for their work force. Strapped for hard currency, the oil refineries paid with 130,000 tons of low-grade A-76 gasoline, which was shipped to Mongolia. The Mongolians paid for the gasoline with 35,000 tons of copper concentrate, which was shipped across the border to Kazakhstan, where it was refined to copper metal and shipped to a Baltic port. Marc & Rich then sold the copper on the world market for hard currency and a profit.[77]

Offset Deals   One of the fastest-growing types of countertrade is offset. In an offset transaction, the selling company guarantees to use some products or services from the buying country in the final product. These transactions are particularly common when large purchases from government-type agencies are involved, such as public utilities or defense-related equipment. To land the large order for its airborne early radar system, AWACS, from the United Kingdom, Seattle-based Boeing offered to offset the purchase by 130 percent. This would commit Boeing to spend 130 percent of the purchase value on U.K. products to offset the purchase, which was competed for by a British company

---

77. "Commodity Grant: Marc Rich & Co. Does Big Deals at Big Risk in the Former USSR," *Wall Street Journal,* May 13, 1993, pp. 1 and A6.

as well. These types of transactions were first popularized by Canada and Belgium some twenty years ago and are now common for very large defense contracts in western Europe, Australia, and New Zealand. This technique has also spread to orders involving state railways or state airlines.[78]

Cooperation Agreements   Cooperation agreements are special types of compensation deals extending over longer periods of time. They may be called product purchase transactions, buyback deals, or pay-as-you-earn deals. Compensation usually refers to an exchange of unrelated merchandise, such as coal for machine tools. Cooperation usually involves related goods, such as payment for new textile machinery by the output produced by these machines.

Although sale of large equipment or of a whole factory can sometimes only be clinched by a cooperation agreement involving buyback of plant output, long-term negative effects must be considered before any deal is concluded. In industries such as steel or chemicals, the effect of high-volume buyback arrangements between western exporters of manufacturing technology and eastern European importers has been devastating. Western countries, especially Europe, have been flooded with surplus products. Negotiations among European Union members are aimed at drafting a general policy on such arrangements to avoid further disruption of their domestic industries.

International Harvester was one U.S. company with experience in buyback arrangements.[79] In 1973, the company sold the basic design and technology for a tractor crawler to Poland. At the same time, International Harvester agreed to buy back tractor components manufactured by the Polish plant. These components were shipped to a subassembly plant in the United Kingdom that served the European market. In 1976, the company sold Hungary the design for an axle. To offset this sale, the company agreed to purchase complete axles for highway trucks.

Dangers in Compensation Deals   The greatest danger in compensation arrangements stems from the difficulty of finding a buyer of the merchandise accepted as part of the transaction. Often such transactions are concluded with organizations of countries where industry is under government control. Since prices for goods in these countries are not determined by the supply and demand forces of a free market economy, merchandise transferred under compensation arrangements is often overvalued compared to open-market products. In addition, such merchandise, obviously not salable on its own, may be of low quality. As a result, the exporter may be able to sell the merchandise only at a discount. The size of these discounts may vary considerably, ranging from 10 percent to 33 percent of product value.[80] The astute exporter will raise the price of the export contract to cover such potential discounts on the compensating transaction.

The experience of a multinational chemical company serves as a good example of

78. "Countertrade Comes Out," p. 89.
79. "Countertrade," *Commerce America,* June 19, 1978, p. 1.
80. "Algeria: When Barter Is Battery," *Economist,* October 3, 1981, p. 80.

FIGURE 13.5 ● Countertrade with International Chemical Company

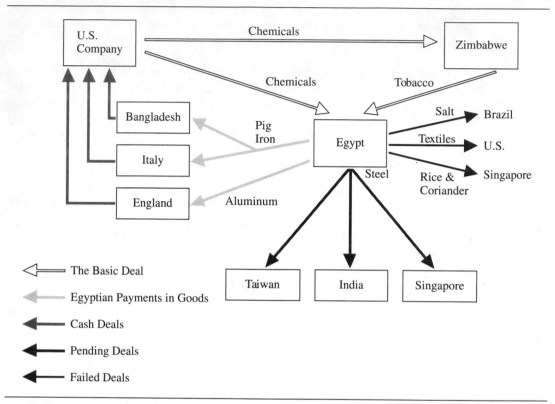

Source: The New York Times, Special Business Supplement, September 25, 1988, p. 34. Copyright ©1988 by The New York Times Company. Reprinted by permission.

the difficulties encountered in barter deals. The company had sold $8 million worth of chemicals to Zimbabwe and agreed to take payment in tobacco, which was sold to Egypt along with another $12 million worth of chemicals to that country in the process. To pay for this transaction, Egypt was offering a whole range of basic commodities and materials as payment in lieu of the $20 million cash price. A specialty company was engaged that selected appropriate products and found buyers elsewhere in the world, collecting the cash. All told, the $20 million deal with Egypt involved nine different countries and six different product categories (see Figure 13.5).[81]

81. "Barter Is His Stock in Trade," *New York Times,* September 25, 1988, pp. 32–36, *Special Business Supplement.*

Precautions for Countertrade A study of fifty-seven British companies involved in countertrade reported that the most difficult problems with countertrade were that there was no in-house use for the goods offered and the negotiations were complex and time consuming.[82]

At the conclusion of the sales agreement, the exporter should obtain a clear notion of the merchandise offered for countertrade. The description, origin, quality, quantity, delivery schedules, price, and purchasing currency in local or hard currency should be determined. With a detailed description given to a specialized trader, an estimate on the applicable discount may be rendered. The sale price of merchandise offered may be structured to include the difference between purchase amount and actual cash value. It is paramount that the western exporter not agree on any price before these other items are determined. Maintaining flexibility in negotiation requires skill and patience.

Organizing for Countertrade[83] International companies are moving toward organizing countertrade for higher leverage. Many larger firms have established specialized units whose single purpose is to engage in countertrade. Many independent trading companies offer countertrading services. Several large U.S. banks formed their own countertrade units.

Daihatsu, a Japanese automobile manufacturer, offers a good example of how a willingness to engage in countertrade can lead to a competitive advantage. Although the company is the smallest Japanese automobile manufacturer, Daihatsu has managed to become the market leader for imported cars in eastern European countries such as Poland or Hungary. In Hungary, the company went as far as to schedule its parties for retiring Japanese workers through Hungary, allowing that country to earn additional foreign exchange, which resulted in the sale of another forty cars.[84]

Conclusions

Managing pricing policies for an international firm is an especially challenging task. The international marketer is confronted with a number of uncontrollable factors out of the economic, legal, and regulatory environment that all have an impact on how prices are established in various countries. Though these influences are usually quite manageable in any given country, the difficulty of pricing across many markets arises from the price differentials that evolve out of environmental factors working in various combinations in

82. David Shipley and Bill Neale, "Industrial Barter and Countertrade," *Industrial Marketing Management,* February 1987, p. 6.

83. See also Christopher M. Korth, *International Countertrade* (Westport, Conn.: Quorum Books, 1987).

84. "Daihatsu Sets Sights on Europe," *Financial Times,* March 5, 1986, p. 4.

different countries. Managing these price differentials and keeping them within some tolerable limits are major tasks in international pricing.

One of the most critical values affecting price levels is foreign exchange rates. Today, managers find currencies moving both up and down, and the swings have assumed magnitudes that may substantially affect the competitiveness of a company. Understanding the factors that shape the directions of the foreign exchange market and mastering the technical tools that protect firms against large swings have become required skills for the international marketer. To the extent that a company can make itself less vulnerable from exchange rate movements, compared to its competitors, it may gain additional competitive advantage.

Because the relevant factors that affect price levels on an international scale are always fluctuating, the international pricing task is a never-ending process in which each day may bring new problems to be resolved. Whenever a company is slow to adapt or makes a wrong judgment, the market is very quick at adapting and at taking advantage of any weaknesses. As long as uncontrollable factors such as currency rates and inflation are subject to considerable fluctuations, the pricing strategies of international companies will have to remain under constant review. The ultimate goal is to minimize the gap between the price levels of various markets.

In this chapter, we have also examined the rather technical aspects of trade financing and countertrade. Many executives have realized that they cannot leave these trade forms to the occasional specialist but must use them as a competitive weapon against aggressive competition. If knowledge of financial engineering and countertrade is to become a competitive advantage, marketing executives negotiating such transactions must master these techniques. International companies will be forced to expose and train their executives in these aspects of trade. We can expect an increasing world trade to be attached to one or the other of these techniques.

As competition in many industries increases, companies that have maintained a policy of "cash or no deal" often face a situation of "countertrade or no deal." Companies established in industrialized countries have seen that expansion into state-controlled economies or Third World countries and the hard-currency poor countries of eastern Europe requires a willingness to engage in countertrade. Understanding countertrade has become a required background for an international marketing executive.

Questions for Discussion

1. Discuss the difficulty or desirability of having a standardized price for a company's products across all countries.

2. Why should a company not go ahead and price its products in each market according to local factors?

3. You are an exporter of industrial installations and have received a $100,000 order from a Japanese customer. The job will take six months to complete and will be paid in full at that time. Now your Japanese customer has called you and also wants a price quote in yen. What will you quote him?

4. What strategies, other than through pricing, do companies have for combating parallel imports?

5. What should be the government's position on the issue of parallel imports? Should the government take any particular actions?

6. What is meant by the term *financial engineering*?

7. How should a firm approach the decision on whether or not its exports should be insured?

8. Explain the major forms of countertrade. Under what circumstances should a company enter into such transactions?

9. What are the major risks to a firm engaging in countertrade?

For Further Reading

Baker, James C., and John K. Ryans, Jr. "International Pricing Policies of Industrial Product Manufacturers." *Journal of International Marketing,* 1, no. 3 (1982), pp. 127–133.

Burns, Jane O. "Transfer Pricing Decisions in U.S. Multinationals." *Journal of International Business Studies,* Fall 1980, pp. 21–39.

Cavusgil, S. Tamer, and Ed Sikora. "How Multinationals Can Counter Gray Market Imports." *Columbia Journal of World Business,* Winter 1988, pp. 75–85.

Dunhan, Dale F., and Mary Jane Sheffet. "Gray Markets and the Legal Status of Parallel Importation." *Journal of Marketing* 52 (July 1988), pp. 75–83.

Elderkin, Kenton W., and W. E. Norquist. *Creative Countertrade: A Guide to Doing Business Worldwide.* Cambridge, Mass.: Ballinger, 1987.

Farley, John U., James M. Hulbert, and David Weinstein. "Price Setting and Volume Planning by Two European Industrial Companies: A Study and Comparison of Decision Processes." *Journal of Marketing,* 44, no. 1 (1980), pp. 46–54.

Ferguson, Henry. "Tomorrow's Global Manager Will Use Countertrade." *Corporate Barter and Countertrade,* 1, no. 6 (1987).

Frank, Victor H., Jr. "Living with Price Control Abroad." *Harvard Business Review,* March–April 1984, pp. 137–142.

Frazer, Jill Andresky. "Controlling Global Taxes." *Inc.,* August 1993, p. 35.

Ghoshal, Animesh. "Flexible Exchange Rates and International Trade." *International Trade Journal,* 1 , no. 1 (1986), pp. 27–66.

"Global Networks, Global Pricing." *Data Communicatioins,* July 1993, p. 18.

Glowacki, Roman, and Leon Zurawicki. "Marketing for Hard Currency in Polish Domestic Markets." *Journal of Global Marketing,* 4, no. 4 (1991), p. 85.

Gut, Rainer E. "Ten Principles of International Financing." In *The International Essays for Business Decision Makers.* vol. 5. Ed. Mark B. Winchester. New York: Center for International Business and AMACOM, a division of American Management Association, 1980, pp. 217–225.

Korth, Christopher M. *International Countertrade.* Westport, Conn.: Quorum Books, 1987.

Lecraw, Donald J. "Pricing Strategies of Transnational Corporations." *Asia-Pacific Journal of Management,* January 1984, pp. 112–119.

Sinclair, Stuart. "A Guide to Global Pricing." *Journal of Business Strategy,* May–June 1993, pp. 16–19.

Sweeny, Paul. "The Transfer Price Bomb." *Global Finance,* December 1992, pp. 32–33.

Weekly, James K. "Pricing in Foreign Markets." *Industrial Marketing Management,* May 1992, pp. 173–179.

Yoffie, David B. "Barter: Looking Beyond the Short-Term Payoffs and Long-Term Threat." *International Management,* August 1984, p. 36.

14

International and Global Promotion Strategies

● **MANAGING THE COMMUNICATIONS** *process for a single market is no easy task. However, the task is even more difficult for international and global marketers who must communicate to prospective customers in many markets. In the process, they struggle with different cultures, habits, and languages.*

In this chapter, we describe the communications process when more than one country is involved and explore how a company structures its international promotion mix. (Advertising, a key element of the promotional mix, will be covered in detail in Chapter 15.) After a closer look at the differences between single-country and multicountry communications processes, we will turn to the challenge of developing a personal selling effort on an international level. Various methods of sales promotion are analyzed, and special problems involving the selling of industrial goods are highlighted.

The Single-Country Promotion Process

Before we embark on a detailed discussion of the various tools available to firms in the international promotion area, we first need to discuss the international dimension of the communications process. From studying basic marketing, you are familiar with the generalized single-country communications process. Communications flow from a source, in this case the company, through several types of channels to the receiver, in this case the customer. Channels are the mass media, both print and electronic, and the company's sales force. Communications takes place when intended content is received as the perceived content by the receiver or customer. Through a feedback mechanism, the communications sender verifies that the intended and perceived content were in fact identical.

This communications process typically is hindered by three potentially critical variables. A *source effect* exists when the receiver evaluates the received messages based on the status or image of the sender. Second, the *level of noise* caused by other messages being transmitted simultaneously tends to reduce the chances of effective communication. Finally, the messages have to pass through the receiver's, or target's, *perceptional filter,* which keeps out any messages that are not relevant to the receiver's experience. Consequently, effective communications require that the source, or sender, overcome the source effect, noise level, and perceptional filter. This is the communications process that most marketers in a domestic, or single-country, situation are familiar with.

The Multicountry Communications Process

Research evidence and experience have demonstrated that the single-country/domestic communications model is applied to consumers in other countries as well. What we also find, however, are some additional barriers to overcome: the cultural barrier, different source effects, and different noise levels. Figure 14.1 contains a multicountry communications model with the cultural barrier arising at different times in the process.

What is a cultural barrier? In any multicountry communications flow, the source and the receiver are often located in different countries and thus have different cultural environments. The kind of influence that culture can have on the marketing environment has already been discussed at length in Chapter 3. The difficulty of communicating across cultural barriers, however, lies in the danger of substituting, or falling back on, one's own

FIGURE 14.1 ● Barriers in the Multicountry Communications Process

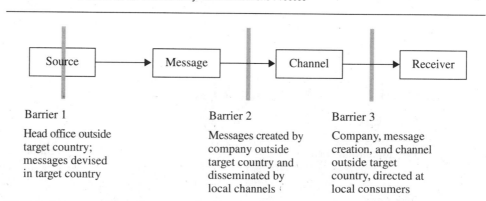

self-reference criteria in situations in which no particular information exists. This danger is particularly acute for executives who are physically removed from the target country. By moving additional decision-making responsibility into the local market, the cultural barrier will be overcome at a point closer to the source.

Even in situations where a local subsidiary has substantial decision-making authority, there will be some input from a regional or corporate head office operation. For most firms, then, some effort to overcome this cultural barrier will have to be made. In virtually all cases then, some executives will be involved in bridging two cultures. The result of not successfully bridging this gap can be failure and substantial losses.

For example, when Sara Lee's Hosiery Division was working with the retailer Marks & Spencer in the United Kingdom to introduce Hanes and L'eggs, it found significant differences between U.S. and British management. Pantyhose, which the English call tights, are a major product for Marks & Spencer, which has 20 percent of the U.K. hosiery market. Every product sold in Marks & Spencer is sold under the St. Michael brand name. After a long period of negotiations and market research, Sara Lee convinced Lord Rayner, the chairman, to use the L'eggs name with an addendum, "for St. Michael." The key reason Sara Lee was successful is it respected Marks & Spencer's expertise and tradition and focused on collaboration rather than the typical approach of "Everything you people are doing is wrong; adopt our recommendations and your sales will double."[1]

Multicountry communications may also have an impact on the source effect. A foreign company's communications may trigger different reactions than do the communications of a local firm. In cases where a positive reference group effect exists, an international company may want to exploit the situation. Frequently, however, the reaction to international firms is negative, forcing companies to deemphasize their foreign origins.

The noise level may differ due to different economic and competitive circumstances. In highly developed countries, noise from companies competing for the attention of target customers is extremely high. In some developing countries, fewer companies may vie for the attention of prospective clients. With media availability differing widely from country to country, the nature of channels used to reach target customers tends to vary. And finally, the feedback mechanisms may be subject to additional delays due to the distances involved. A recent concern in Moscow about all the foreign advertising and signs sapping the capital city of its "Russianness" led to a new requirement that all business and store displays be in Russian. This local requirement has created some additional noise and confusion for companies such as Puma, McDonald's, Benetton, Baskin & Robbins, and Reebok.[2]

Consequently, we can characterize the multicountry communications process as similar to the single-country process, though subject to considerable additional difficulties that make it a highly challenging task. The purpose of this chapter is to develop strategies that international companies can employ to overcome these additional difficulties and barriers. Therefore, we will begin our analysis by concentrating first on the different elements of the communications mix.

1. "Pushing Yankee Products in Lord Rayner's Court," *Brandweek,* July 12, 1993, pp. 26–29.
2. "The Latest Signs of Change: Russify That Name!" *New York Times,* May 25, 1993, p. A4.

International Promotion Strategies

How to manage the promotion mix internationally is a critical question for many companies. Most firms do business in a certain way and do not rethink their promotion mix regularly. However, international marketers cannot take the full availability of all promotion elements for granted. As a result, many companies find themselves in countries or situations that require an adjustment or a substantial change in their promotion mix. This section and the ones that follow are devoted to understanding how different international environments affect promotion mix decisions.

In a domestic, or single-country, environment, companies achieve a balance in their promotion mix on the basis of experience, costs, and effectiveness. For most companies, communications mix decisions require the selection of an appropriate balance between advertising and personal selling. This translates into a push versus pull strategy decision (see Figure 14.2). How different is the company's approach to marketing its products internationally?

Push-oriented Strategy

In a domestic setting, *push*-oriented marketing *strategies* emphasize personal selling rather than advertising in their promotion mix. Although very effective as a promotion tool, personal selling, which requires intensive use of a sales force, is relatively costly. Companies marketing industrial or other complex products to other firms or governmental agencies have relied on personal selling. Personal selling is usually more effective when a company is faced with a short channel. International marketers basically look at the

FIGURE 14.2 ● International and Global Promotion Strategies

personal selling requirements in the same way that marketers do in a domestic situation. However, some of the key inputs into the decision-making process need to be reviewed.

The complexity of a product usually influences how extensively personal selling is used. The level of complexity has to be compared with the readiness level of the clients. Consequently, a company selling the same products abroad as those sold domestically may find that more personal selling may be necessary abroad because some foreign clients are less sophisticated than domestic clients. A U.S. company may use the same amount of personal selling in Europe as it does in the United States but may need to put forth a greater personal selling effort in developing countries, where the product may not be well understood.

Though they may prefer personal selling as a promotion mix, many companies increasingly are using more advertising due to the high cost of maintaining a personal sales force. These costs, which are estimated to have passed $300 for a typical sales call, have motivated some companies to shift a part of the selling job to advertising.

Channel length can also be an important factor in determining the amount of personal selling or push strategy to be used. To the extent that a company faces the same channel length abroad as it does in the domestic market, no change is needed in the push strategy. However, when a company does face a longer channel because other intermediaries such as local distributors are added, the firm may be better off shifting to a pull campaign.

Pull-oriented Strategy

Pull strategy is characterized by a relatively greater dependence on advertising directed at the end user for a product or service. Pull campaigns are typical for consumer goods firms that need to approach a large segment of the market. For such companies, the economies of using mass communications such as advertising dictate a reliance on pulling the product through the distribution channel. Pull campaigns are usually advisable when the product is widely used by consumers, when the channel is long, when the product is not very complex, and when self-service is the predominant shopping behavior.

Increased or decreased reliance on pull campaigns for international marketers depends on a number of factors. Most important are access to advertising media, channel length, and the leverage the company has with the distribution channel.

Marketers accustomed to having a large number of media available may find the choice substantially limited in overseas markets. For many products, pull campaigns work only if access to electronic media, particularly TV, is guaranteed. This is the case in Japan and in some developing countries, where radio and TV stations tend to be commercially operated. However, in many European countries, advertising is restricted to print media only. In Scandinavia, no commercial television or radio stations were in existence in 1987.[3]

In many other countries, access to those media is restricted through time limits imposed by governments. Consequently, companies will find it difficult to duplicate their strategies when moving from a free environment such as the United States to the more

---

3. "Media Fact Europe," *Focus,* January 1987, p. 21.

restricted environment in Europe. Although in many countries a company may be able to shift advertising from one medium into another, it is nevertheless true that the unfolding of a full-blown push campaign as it is practiced in the United States is usually much more difficult if not impossible to do in other countries.

Channel length is a major determinant of the use of a pull campaign. Companies in complex consumer markets such as the United States often face long channels and, thus, try to overcome channel inertia by directing their advertising directly to end users. When a company markets overseas, it may face an even longer channel because local distribution arrangements are different. In the case of a country such as Japan, channels tend to be very long compared to those in the United States. As a result, a greater reliance on a pull strategy may be advisable or necessary in such countries.

Distribution leverage is also different for each company from market to market. Getting cooperation from local selling points, particularly in the retail sector, is often more difficult than in the domestic market. The fight for shelf space may be very intensive; shelf space in most markets is more limited than it is in the United States, where carrying several competing brands of a product category is customary. Under these more difficult situations, the reliance on a push campaign becomes more important. If consumers are demanding the company's product, retailers will make sure they carry it.

Push Versus Pull Strategies

In selecting the best balance between advertising and personal selling for the push versus pull decision, companies have to analyze the markets to determine the need for these two major communications mix elements. However, as we have seen, the availability of or access to any one of them may be limited. This is particularly the case for firms depending a great deal on pull policies. Many such companies find themselves limited in the use of the most powerful communications tool. How must a company adjust its communications policy under such circumstances?

When lack of access to advertising media makes the pull strategy less effective, a company may have to resort to more of a push strategy, making a greater use of personal selling. In some instances, this may already be the case when access to television advertising forces a company to use less effective media forms such as print advertising. In such circumstances, a company will employ a larger sales force to compensate for the reduced efficiency of consumer-directed promotions.

Limited ability to unfold a pull strategy from a company's home market has other effects on the company's marketing strategy. Limited advertising tends to slow the product adoption process in new markets, thus forcing the firm to accept slower growth. In markets crowded with existing competitors, newcomers will find it difficult to establish themselves when access to pull campaigns is limited.

Consequently, a company entering a new market may want to consider such situations for its planning and adjust expected results accordingly. A company accustomed to a given type of communications mix usually develops an expertise or a distinctive competence in that use. When suddenly faced with a situation in which that competence cannot be fully applied, the risk of failure or underachievement is increased. This can even affect entry strategies or the market selection process.

Personal Selling

Personal selling takes place whenever a customer is met in person by a representative of the marketing company. When doing business internationally, companies will have to meet customers from different countries. These customers may be accustomed to different business customs and may speak in a different language. That is why personal selling in an individual context is extremely complex and requires some very special skills on the part of the salesperson.

In this section, we differentiate between international selling and local selling. When a company's sales force travels across countries and meets directly with clients abroad, it is practicing *international selling.* This type of selling requires the special skill of being able to manage within several cultures. Much more often, however, companies engage in *local selling:* they organize and staff a local sales force made up of local nationals to do the selling in only one country. Managing and operating a local sales force involves different problems from those encountered by international salespersons.

International Selling (Multicountry Sales Force)

The job of the international salesperson seems glamorous. One imagines a professional who frequently travels abroad, visiting a large number of countries and meeting a large number of different businesspeople with various backgrounds. However, this type of work is quite demanding, and becoming an international salesperson requires a special set of skills.

International salespersons are needed only when companies deal directly with their clients abroad. This is usually the case for industrial equipment or business services, rarely for consumer products or services. Consequently, for our purposes, international sales will be described in the context of industrial selling.

Purchasing Behavior   In industrial selling, one of the most important parts of the job consists of finding the right decision-maker in the client company. The seller must locate the key decision-makers, who may hold different positions from company to company or from country to country.[4] In some countries, the purchasing manager may have different responsibilities or the engineers may play a greater role. The international salesperson must be able to deal effectively with buying units that differ by country.

4. Thomas V. Bonoma, ''Major Sales: Who Really Does the Buying?'' *Harvard Business Review,* May–June 1982, p. 112.

FIGURE 14.3 ● Organizational Buying Behavior in Japan: Packaging Machine Purchase Process

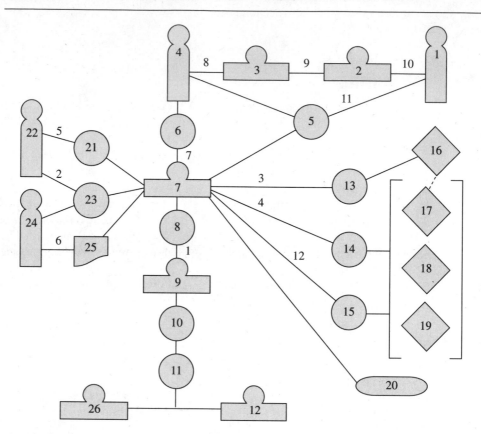

1 President	10 Request for consultation	20 Overseas machine exhibitions
2 Financial Dept.	11 Production of new product marketing plan	21 Request for testing of prototype machines
3 Sales headquarters		
4 Production chief		22 Research staff
5 Decision	12 Product Development Dept.	23 Production of basic design
6 Discussion of production and sales plans	13 Discussion on design of prototype machines	
	14 Prototype machine	24 Foreman
7 Production Dept.	15 Placement of orders	25 Production of draft plans
8 Production of packing process plan	16 Maker's design and technical staff	
	17 Supplier A	26 Marketing Dept.
9 New Products Development Committee	18 Supplier B	
	19 Supplier C	

Source: "Japanese Firms Use Unique Buying Behavior," *Japan Economic Journal,* December 23, 1980, p. 29. Reprinted by permission.

A Japanese study investigated a large corporation's process for purchasing packaging machinery.[5] The entire decision-making process took 121 days and involved twenty people from the purchasing company. In Japan, middle management is given considerable authority for purchasing. However, the staff departments responsible for the purchasing process involve all interested and affected departments in the decision-making process. In the case of the company purchasing packaging machinery, the process involved the production manager and the entire production department staff, the new product committee, the laboratory of the company, the marketing department, and the department for market development. For a detailed chart see Figure 14.3.

Buying Criteria   Aside from the different purchasing patterns found, the international salesperson may have to deal with different decision criteria or objectives on the part of the purchaser. Buyers or users of industrial products in different countries may expect to maximize different goals. However, it should be pointed out that for standardized uses for specific industries, relatively little difference between countries applies. Particularly for high-technology products, such as production equipment for semiconductor components used in the electronics industry, the applications are virtually identical regardless of whether the factory is located in Korea or in the United States.

Language   Overcoming the language barrier is an especially difficult task for the international salesperson. The personal selling effort is substantially enhanced if the salesperson speaks the language of the customer. A summary of languages spoken in European countries is shown in Table 14.1.

For some of the products marketed by an international sales force today, two trends have emerged. First, the dependency on the local language for many industries is not as strong today as it was just one or two decades ago. For many new and highly sophisticated products (e.g., electronics, aerospace), English is the language spoken by most customers. Consequently, with more and more executives speaking English in many countries, more firms have been in a position to actually market their products directly, without local intermediaries. English is widely spoken in Scandinavia and in Europe, just as it is the leading second language in Asia and Latin America. Consequently, we now see that the ability to speak a number of foreign languages is less of a necessity. However, the learning of a foreign language can be an excellent way to understand a foreign culture. Also, it continues to have a very favorable impact on the sales process.

In industries where knowledge of the local language is important, companies tend to assign sales territories to salespersons on the basis of language skills. A European multinational manufacturer of textile equipment assigns countries to its sales staff according to the languages they speak. This is more important in the traditional industries such as textile manufacturing, where businesses are more local in orientation and where English is not spoken that well by management.

5. ''Japanese Firms Use Unique Buying Behavior,'' *Japan Economic Journal,* December 23, 1980, p. 29.

TABLE 14.1 ● Languages Spoken in European Households

	HOUSEHOLDS (m)	% of adults who speak:					
		ENGLISH	FRENCH	GERMAN	ITALIAN	SPANISH	FLEMISH-DUTCH
Belgium	3.6	26%	71%	22%	4%	3%	68%
Denmark	2.1	51	5	48	1	1	1
France	20.3	26	100	11	8	13	1
West Germany	25.3	30	12	100	2	2	3
Ireland	0.85	99	12	2	1	1	—
Italy	18.5	13	27	6	100	5	—
Netherlands	5.3	50	16	61	2	2	100
Norway	1.55	80	10	20	4	2	—
Spain	10.3	n.a.	n.a.	n.a.	n.a.	100	—
Switzerland	2.5	26	55	81	17	3	—
United Kingdom	21.03	100	16	9	2	3	1

Source: Date from a Gallup survey, as published in ''European Satellite Battle Looms,'' *Financial Times,* September 16, 1985. Reprinted by permission.

Even executives who speak fairly good English may not understand all the details of product descriptions or specifications. As a result, a company can make an excellent impression by having its sales brochures translated into some of the key languages. European companies routinely produce company publications in several languages. Such translations may not be needed for Scandinavia but may go a long way in other parts of the world, where the level of English language skills is not that high.

Business Etiquette   International marketers selling to overseas markets are likely to encounter a diverse set of business practices as they move from one country to another. Since interpersonal behavior is intensely culture bound, this part of the salesperson's job will vary by country. Many differences exist for how an appointment is made, how (and whether) an introduction is made, and how much lead-time is needed for making appointments. The salesperson must also know whether or not gifts are expected or desired. When a salesperson travels to the same area repeatedly, familiarity with local customs can be expected. But for newcomers or experienced executives traveling to a new area, finding out the correct information is necessary.

For example, visiting businesspeople must attend long banquets when engaging in negotiations with the Chinese. These banquets may start in the late morning or early in the evening. Sitting mostly at a round table, the visitors will normally be seated next to the host who is expected to fill the visitor's plate at regular intervals. Foreigners are cautioned that frequent toasts are the norm and that many Chinese business hosts expect that the guest should become drunk; otherwise, the guest is believed not to have had a good time.[6] Also, business etiquette can differ from one country to another. While it is acceptable for visitors to arrive late in China, India, or Indonesia, arriving late in Hong Kong is not acceptable. Lateness causes the visitor to "lose face," which is an extremely serious matter among Hong Kong businesspeople.[7]

Since no manager can be expected to know the business customs of every country, important information can be obtained from special sources. For one, the company's own foreign market representatives or sales subsidiary can provide important information or suggestions. Also, when such access is not available, governments tend to collect data on business practices through their commercial officers posted abroad. For example, the U.S. Department of Commerce (DOC) publishes a regular series entitled "Doing Business in . . . ," which offers a wealth of helpful suggestions. Some business service companies, such as accounting firms or international banks, also provide customers with profiles of business practices in foreign countries.

Foreign businesspersons receiving visitors from the United States or any other foreign country rarely expect the foreign visitor to be familiar with all local customs. However, it is always appreciated when the visitor can indicate familiarity with the most common practices and some willingness to try to conform. Learning some foreign customs helps to generate goodwill toward the company and therefore can enhance the chance of doing business.

Negotiations Strategies Negotiations in the international arena are complicated because the negotiating partners frequently come from different cultural backgrounds. As a result, misunderstandings or misjudgments can occur that will lead to failure. To maximize the outcome in the often difficult and protracted negotiations, international sales personnel must be in tune with the cultural differences.

A common approach to cross-cultural negotiations relies on the old proverb "When in Rome, do as the Romans do." This approach, which assumes that the visitor would follow local customs and use the local language, has two problems. First, many non-Romans may be unable to act Roman beyond the normal greeting protocol. Second, most Romans will probably not act Roman themselves with a non-Roman in Rome.[8]

Although a myriad of negotiations strategies exist, concentrating on mutual needs rather than the issues is a much practiced approach. In international marketing, the salesperson, or negotiator, must first determine the true objectives and needs of the other party. When negotiating within an unknown cultural setting, this is often a challenging task. However, careful assessment of the negotiating party's needs can enhance the chance for success.

For successful negotiation, understanding the *mindscape* of the counterpart can be

6. "Chemicals in China: Capacity for Enjoyment," *Financial Times,* September 30, 1986, p. VI.
7. "Hong Kong: Executive Guide to the Territory," *Financial Times,* June 27, 1986, p. XV.
8. Stephen E. Weiss, "Negotiating with Romans," *Sloan Management Review,* Winter 1994, pp. 51–61.

very important.[9] Wenlee Ting, a noted anthropologist, defined the mindscape as "a structure of reasoning, cognition, perception, design, planning, and decision making that may vary from individual to individual and from culture to culture." Ting developed mindscape models based on the earlier work of another anthropologist, Magorah Maruyama. Building on Maruyama's work, Ting identified three common mindscapes for Hong Kong executives. Executives with an H-type mindscape tended to be interested in structured competition and the scientific organization of business. The tendency of executives with the I-type mindscape was to see separation of individual efforts as a key to higher efficiency. The G-type mindscape considered heterogeneity as a basis for mutually beneficial competition and tended to encourage differences among units. I-type mindscapes were said to be predominant among players in international finance or real estate; H-type mindscapes were predominant in family businesses; and G-type mindscapes were typical in international trading and business.[10]

The evidence further indicated that Hong Kong businesspeople negotiate well in eastern and western cultures. Skilled Hong Kong negotiators are able to engage in reasoning with western counterparts while simultaneously employing other reasoning and negotiation techniques when dealing with local groups, family members, and other business associates.[11] This suggests that successful negotiation may depend on the foreign businessperson's ability to scout out the foreign counterpart's mindscape. Careful preparation of the cultural norms prevalent in the foreign country is the starting point to successful negotiations and selling.

Timing is also an important aspect for negotiating abroad. In some countries, such as China, negotiations tend to take much more time than in the United States or some other western countries. One European company that operated a joint venture in China observed that during one annual meeting, two weeks were spent in a discussion that elsewhere might have only taken a few hours. In this situation, however, much of the time was used for interdepartmental negotiations among various Chinese agencies rather than for face-to-face negotiations with the European company.

In another instance, a European firm negotiated with a Middle Eastern country over several months for the delivery of several hundred machines. When the company representatives went into that country for the final round of negotiations, they found that the competing firm had already been there several weeks before their arrival. The European firm's representatives decided to prepare themselves for long negotiations and refused to make concessions, figuring that the competitor had most likely been worn out in the prior weeks. As it turned out, that assessment was correct, and the European company won the order by outstaying its competitor in a rather difficult negotiating environment. Obviously,

9. Alf H. Walle, "Conceptualizing Personal Selling for International Business: A Continuum of Exchange Perspective," *Journal of Personal Selling and Sales Management,* November 1986, pp. 9–17.

10. Wenlee Ting, *Business and Technological Dynamics in Newly Industrialized Asia* (Westport, Conn.: Greenwood, 1985); Magorah Maruyama, "Mindscapes and Social Theories," *Current Anthropology,* 1980, pp. 589–608.

11. Walle, "Conceptualizing Personal Selling," pp. 9–17.

unprepared sales executives may lose out to competitors if they do not understand the negotiation customs of a foreign country as they relate to the amount of time necessary to conclude a deal.

International Selling at Soudronic[12]   The sales function at Soudronic AG, a medium-sized manufacturer of welding equipment used primarily in the can-making industry, offers a good example of how an international sales force is organized and operated. Located in Switzerland, where all of its machines were produced, the company sold to can makers in some eighty countries. The selling of these machines, which welded the bodies of metal cans at very high speeds, rested with a small sales force of seven sales managers. These managers reported to two regional sales managers, who in turn reported to the manager for sales and marketing. The entire world territory had been divided into seven parts in such a way that made travel schedules more efficient, maximized the language competency of the sales force, and balanced overall workloads.

Each sales manager was responsible for all client contact in his territory. In their assigned countries, sales managers usually worked with local agents who indicated when a prospective client needed to be visited. They scheduled a visit on the next trip to that country and visited the client along with the local agent. The sales managers were technically trained to the extent that most questions could be answered on the spot. They also negotiated with clients for delivery and price terms within limits. Once a contract had been negotiated, the sales managers turned the client contact over to a service technician, although in many cases the sales manager remained in contact with the client who preferred to deal primarily with one person.

Sales managers were expected to spend 50 percent of their time with clients in the form of either local contact, telephone contact, or correspondence. As a result, the Soudronic sales staff traveled a good percentage of the time. The availability of candidates for such positions was limited. The company preferred to hire people who had a technical or engineering background together with several years of sales experience in the capital goods sector, not necessarily in the can-making industry. Prospective sales managers were also expected to have good firsthand knowledge of their assigned region, preferably through one or more years of work experience, and to have acquired the language locally. Compensation was partially on a commission and incentive basis.

Local Selling (Single-Country Sales Force)

When a company is able to maintain a local sales force in the countries where it does business, many of the difficulties of bridging the cultural gap with clients will be minimized. The local sales force can be expected to understand the local customs, and the international company typically gains additional acceptance in the market. This is primarily because local sales forces are usually staffed with local nationals. However, many chal-

12. Jean-Pierre Jeannet, *Soudronic AG,* Case (Lausanne: IMD, International Management Development Institute, 1983).

lenges remain, and the management of a local sales force often requires different strategies from those used in running a sales force in the company's domestic market.

Role of Local Sales Force and Control   When a company has decided to build a local sales force, the decision has already been made for forward integration in its distribution effort. As we learned in Chapter 9, establishing a sales force means that the company has moved to assume the full role of a local sales subsidiary, sidestepping the independent distributor. Depending on the distribution strategy adopted, the company may sell directly, as often is the case for many industrial products or business services, or indirectly through local wholesalers, as is the case for many consumer products and services. Although international companies will not make such a move unless present business volume justifies it, there are substantial benefits associated with having one's own sales force.

Control over a firm's sales activities is a frequently cited advantage for operating a company-owned local sales force. With its own sales force, the company can emphasize the products it wants to market at any time, and the company has better control over the way it is represented. In many cases, price negotiations, in the form of discounts or rebates, are handled uniformly rather than leaving these decisions to an independent distributor with different interests. Having a company sales force also ensures that the personnel are of the necessary level and qualification. Control over all of these parameters usually means higher sales compared to using a distributor sales force.

Also, the local sales force can represent an important bridge with the local business community. For industries where the buying process is local rather than international, the sales force speaks the language of the local customer, can be expected to understand the local business customs, and thus can bring the international firm closer to its end users. In many instances, local customers, though not objecting to buying from a foreign firm, may prefer to deal with local representatives of that firm. As a result, the ability of the international company to make its case heard with prospective customers is substantially enhanced.

However, local sales forces are single country, or single culture, by nature. Although they speak the language of the local customers, they often do not speak any other language. As many U.S. firms have experienced, the local sales force abroad may have a very limited understanding of English, and its understanding of the head office language is, in general, not sufficient to conduct business in that language. Furthermore, a local sales force cannot be expected to speak the languages of neighboring countries sufficiently to deal directly with such customers. In Europe, where this problem is particularly acute, language competency usually precludes a German firm from sending its sales force into France or a French firm from sending its sales force into Italy or Spain. In some countries, several different languages are spoken, and this tends to further reduce the mobility of a sales force.

Local Sales Job   The type and extent of local sales effort a company will need are dependent on its own distribution effort and the relationship to the other communications mix elements. For firms that still use distributor sales forces to a large extent, a missionary sales force with limited responsibilities may suffice. This missionary sales force would concentrate on visiting clients together with the local distributor's sales force. If the international company's sales force needs to do the entire job, a much larger sales force will be necessary. As for the international firm's domestic market, the size of the local sales force depends to a large extent on the number of clients and the desired frequency of visits. This frequency may differ from country to country, which means that the size of the sales force will differ from country to country.

The role of the local sales force needs to be coordinated with the promotion mix selected for each market. As many companies have learned, advertising and other forms of promotion can be used to make the role of the sales force more efficient. In many consumer goods industries, companies prefer a pull strategy concentrating their promotion budget on the final consumer. In such cases, the role of the sales force is restricted to gaining distribution access. However, as we have mentioned previously, there are countries in which access to communications media is severely restricted. As a result, companies may place greater emphasis on the local sales force, which affects both role definition and size.

Foreign Sales Practices   Although sales forces are employed virtually everywhere, the nature of their interaction with the local customer is unique and may affect local sales operations. For most Westerners, Japanese practices seem substantially different. Here is an example reported by Masaaki Imai, president of Cambridge Corporation, a Tokyo management consulting and recruiting firm.

When Bausch & Lomb Japan introduced its then new soft lens line into Japan, the company had targeted influential eye doctors in each sales territory for its introductory launch. The assumption was that once these leading practitioners signed up for the new product, marketing to the majority of eye doctors would be easier. One salesperson was quickly dismissed by a key customer. The doctor said that he thought very highly of Bausch & Lomb equipment but preferred regular lenses for his patients. The salesperson did not even have a chance to respond; but he decided, since it was his first visit to this clinic, to stay around for awhile. He talked to several assistants at the clinic and to the doctor's wife who was, as was typical for Japan, handling the administration of the practice.

The next morning, the salesperson returned to the clinic and observed that the doctor was very busy. He talked again with the assistants and joined the doctor's wife when she was cooking and talked with her about food. When the couple's young son returned from kindergarten, the salesperson played with him and even went out to buy him a toy. The wife was very pleased with the well-intentioned babysitter. She later explained to the salesperson that her husband had very little time to listen to any sales presentations during the day, so she invited him to come to their home in the evening. The doctor, obviously primed by his wife, received the man very warmly, and they enjoyed *sake* together. The doctor listened patiently to the sales presentation and responded that he did not want to use the soft lenses on his patients right away. However, he suggested that the salesperson try them on his assistants the next day. So on the third day, the salesperson returned to the clinic and fitted soft lenses on several of the clinic's assistants. The reaction was very favorable, and the doctor placed an order on the third day of his sales call.[13]

It is probably fair to say that salespeople in many countries would have taken the initial negative response as the final answer from the doctor and would have tried elsewhere for success. In Japan, however, the customer expects a different reaction. Japanese customers often judge from the frequency of the sales calls they receive whether the company really wants to do business. Salespeople who make more frequent calls to a potential customer than the competition does may be regarded as more sincere.

This also means that companies doing business in Japan have to make frequent sales calls to their top customers, often only for courtesy reasons. Customers get visited twice a year, usually in June and December, without necessarily discussing any business. Although this may occasionally be only a telephone call, the high frequency of visits significantly affects the staffing levels of the company-owned sales force.

Recruiting   Foreign companies have often found recruiting sales professionals quite challenging in many overseas markets. Although the availability of qualified sales personnel is a problem even in developed countries, the scarcity of skilled personnel is even more acute in developing countries. Multinational companies, accustomed to having sales staff with certain standard qualifications, may not find it easy to locate the necessary salespeople in a short period of time. One factor limiting their availability in many countries is the local economic situation. Depending on the economic cycle, the level of unemployment may be an excellent indicator as to the difficulty of finding prospects. This will limit the number of people a company can expect to hire away from existing firms unless a substantial increase over present compensation is offered.

More important, the image sales positions hold in various societies may differ substantially. Typically, sales as an occupation or career has a relatively high image in the United States. This allows companies to recruit excellent talent, usually fresh from universities, for sales careers. These university recruits can usually consider sales as a career path toward middle-management positions. Such an image of selling is rare elsewhere in the world. In Europe, many companies continue to find it difficult to recruit university graduates into their sales forces, except in such highly technical fields as computers, where the recruits are typically engineers. When sales is a less desirable occupation, the quality of the sales force may suffer. If the company wants to insist on top quality, the time it will take to fill sales positions can be expected to increase dramatically.

How then can a company approach its formation of a company-owned sales force in a local market? When the firm already operates a limited-function sales subsidiary with responsibility to deal with local distributors, existing local executives can be entrusted with the recruiting function. Where such a beachhead does not exist, the company may want to find an international sales executive presently active in one of its other markets who knows the situation and cultural context of the new market. Such executives, sometimes

13. "Salesmen Need to Make More Calls Than Competitors to Be Accepted," *Japan Economic Journal,* June 26, 1979, p. 30.

called *expatriates* because they are living outside of their own country, can be expected to build up the sales force step by step. Alternatively, executive recruiting firms have now sprung up in many countries, and these can be contacted to find the necessary personnel.

Compensation In their home markets, where they usually employ large sales forces, multinational companies become accustomed to handling and motivating their sales forces in a given way. In the United States, typical motivation programs include some form of commission or bonus for meeting volume or budget projections, as well as vacation prizes for top performers. When an international company manages local sales forces in various countries, the company is challenged to determine the best way to motivate them. Not all cultures may respond the same way, and motivating practices may differ from country to country. For example, Fiat produces trucks in Yugoslavia under an agreement with Zavodi Crvena Zastava. At one of its training sessions, the idea of paying salespeople an incentive based on profit margins was met with laughter.[14]

One of the frequently discussed topics in motivating salespeople is the value of the commission or bonus structure. U.S. companies in particular have tended to use some form of commission structure for their sales force. Although this may fluctuate from industry to industry, U.S. firms tend to use more of a flexible and volume-dependent compensation structure than European firms do. Japanese firms more often use a straight salary type of compensation. To motivate the sales force to achieve superior performance, the international company may be faced with using different compensation practices depending on the local customs.

Local Sales Force Examples Managing a local sales force tends to be different according to the requirements of any given country. Local selling is one of the marketing elements that displays relatively great variety and is frequently adjusted for local customs, even for companies where other marketing elements are standardized, such as advertising. The following examples are intended to give the reader some background on local sales force issues and practices.

Selling in Brazil[15] Ericsson do Brasil was the Brazilian affiliate of L. M. Ericsson, a Swedish multinational firm with a strong position in the telecommunications industry. The company marketed both central switching equipment for telephone companies and private exchanges (PBXs) to individual firms. The sales force for the PBX business numbered about one hundred persons and was organized geographically.

In the southern sector of Brazil, where industry was concentrated, the sales force was divided into specialists either for large PBXs, with up to two hundred external lines and several thousand internal lines, or for smaller systems called key systems, which could

---

14. "American Abroad: IVECO's Man in Yugoslavia," *Sales and Marketing Management,* June 1987, p. 77.
15. Jean-Pierre Jeannet, *Ericsson Do Brasil: Ericall System,* Case M-296 (Lausanne: IMD, International Management Development Institute, 1983).

accommodate up to twenty-five incoming lines or up to fifty internal lines. In the northern, more rural part of Brazil, this specialization could not be achieved due to fewer accounts. As a result, the northern sales offices had sales representatives that sold both large and small systems.

Ericsson's sales force was compensated partially with a fixed salary and partially with commissions. Fixed monthly salaries amounted to about $400. A good salesperson could earn about $2,000 per month when the 4 percent sales commission was added to the base salary. Special government regulations required that each salesperson be assigned an exclusive territory. If a salesperson were reassigned, the company was then liable to maintain his or her income for another twelve months. As a result, changes in sales territory had to be considered carefully. When Ericsson do Brasil was faced with the introduction of a new paging system that was to be sold to corporate clients, most of whom also bought telephone equipment, the company found it difficult to assign territories to each of its present salespersons. If it wanted to reassign territories later on, once it became clear who was good at selling paging systems over and above the telephone systems, the company would not be able to easily reassign territories without incurring compensation costs. In the end, Ericsson decided to assign the new paging system to its salespersons on a temporary basis only, thus preserving the chance to make other assignments later on without extra costs.

Wiltech India[16]   Selling in India is very different from selling in other countries. India, with the second largest population in the world, is an example of a typical developing country. Wiltech, a joint venture between the British company Wilkinson and a large Indian conglomerate, was founded to market Wilkinson technology–based razor blades in India. Founded in the early 1980s, the company needed to build up its sales force to compete against local competition. In India, there are more than 400,000 retailers or distributors of razor blades, and about 20 percent of them carry Wiltech blades.

The sales force of sixty persons primarily concentrates on urban markets. The sales representative working in a big metropolitan city directly handles one distributor and about 600 to 700 retail outlets. He or she is expected to visit the distributor every day and to make another forty to sixty sales calls per day. The sales representative accomplishes this largely on foot because the sales outlets are relatively small and are clustered close to each other. The goal is to see important retailers at least twice per month and smaller retailers once a month. The sales representative working in smaller cities may cover about a dozen distributors and some 800 to 1,000 outlets. He or she sees distributors once or twice per month and sees from thirty-five to forty outlets per day. Travel is by railway or by bus, whichever is more convenient.

Wiltech sales representatives are paid a fixed salary of 800–1,200 rupees per month (about U.S. $70 to $100). Sales representatives that achieve their quotas and productivity targets can earn another 400 to 500 rupees per month in a bonus. Expenses are paid on the basis of daily allowances for transportation, lunch, and hotel stays when necessary.

16. Jean-Pierre Jeannet, *Wiltech India,* Case M-336 (Lausanne: IMD, International Management Development Institute, 1988).

For sales representatives selling from a fixed location, this daily allowance amounts to 30 rupees per day. When traveling away from home, the daily allowance amounts to 50 rupees plus the actual transportation costs for first-class train or bus fare. Although these costs appear minimal compared to typical salaries and travel expenses paid in a developed country, they nevertheless represent a very good income in India, where per capita GNP cost of living is very low by western standards.

Alternatives to a Local Sales Force   Because building up a local sales force is both costly and time consuming, some companies have looked for alternatives without necessarily falling back on independent distributors. When competitive pressures require a rapid access to a sales force, piggybacking (as described in Chapter 12) has been practiced by some companies.

Recently, companies have entered into a wide variety of international distribution alliances. The sales alliance format differs from other ventures because the two firms that join forces do so as independent firms and not necessarily in the form of a limited joint venture. In an alliance, two companies may swap products, with one company carrying the other firm's products in one market and vice versa. Such swaps have been used extensively in the pharmaceutical industry. The short period of time left for marketing once the products have been approved and before the patents expire calls for a very rapid product roll out in as many countries as possible.

Industrial Selling

Many of the promotion strategies discussed so far are geared toward the marketing of typical consumer goods and industrial goods. However, some specific promotion methods oriented largely toward the industrial market play an important role in the international marketing of such products. The use of international trade fairs, bidding procedures for international projects, and consortium selling all have to be understood if an investment or industrial products company wants to succeed in international markets.

International Trade Fairs

Participation in international trade fairs has become an important aspect of marketing industrial products abroad. Trade fairs are ideal for exposing new customers and potential distributors to a company's product range and have been used extensively by both new-comers and established firms. In the United States, industrial customers can be reached through a wide range of media, such as specialized magazines with a particular industry focus. In many overseas countries, the markets are too small to allow for the publication of such trade magazines in only one country. As a result, prospective customers usually attend these trade fairs on a regular basis. Trade fairs also offer companies a chance to meet with prospective customers in a less formal atmosphere. For a company that is new to a certain market and does not yet have any established contacts, participation in a trade fair may be the only way to reach potential customers. There are an estimated six hundred trade shows in 70 countries every year. For example, the Cologne Trade Fair brings together 28,000 exhibitors from 100 countries with 1.8 million buyers from 150 countries. The Hanover Fair is considered the largest industrial fair in the world.[17] Other large general fairs include the Canton Fair in China and the Milan Fair in Italy.[18]

Specialized trade fairs concentrate on a certain segment of the industry or user group. Such fairs usually attract limited participation in terms of both exhibitors and visitors. Typically, they are more technical in nature. Some of the specialized trade fairs may not take place every year. One of the leading specialized fairs is the Achema for the chemical industry in Germany, held every three years. Annual fairs having an international reputation include the air shows of Farnborough, England, or Paris, where aerospace products are displayed.

Participation in trade fairs can save both time and effort for a company that wants to break into a new market and does not yet have any contacts. For new product announcements or demonstrations, the trade fair offers an ideal forum for display. Trade fairs are also used by competitors to check on each other's most recent developments. They can give a newcomer an idea of the potential competition in some foreign markets before actual market entry. Consequently, trade fairs are a means of both selling products and gathering important and useful market intelligence. Therefore, marketers with international aspirations will do well to search out the relevant trade fairs directed at their industry or customer segment and to schedule regular attendance.

Selling Through a Bidding Process

The bidding process for industrial products tends to be more complicated, particularly when major industrial equipment is involved. Companies competing for such major projects have to pass a number of stages before negotiations for a specific purchase can ever take place. Typically, companies go through a search process for new projects, then move on to prequalify for the particular project before a formal project bid or tender is submitted. Each phase requires careful management and the appropriate allocation of resources.

During the search phase, companies want to make sure that they are informed of any project worth their interest that is related to their product lines. For particularly large projects that are government sponsored, full-page advertisements may appear in leading international newspapers. More likely, companies have to have a network of agents, contacts, or former customers who will inform them of any project being considered.

In the prequalifying phase, the purchaser will frequently ask for documentation from interested companies that would like to make a formal tender. At this phase, no formal bidding or tender documents are submitted. Instead, more-general company background will be required that may describe other or similar projects the company has finished in

---

17. Brad O'Hara, Fred Palumbo, and Paul Herbig, ''Industrial Trade Shows Abroad,'' *Industrial Marketing Management,* 22 (1993), pp. 223–237.

18. ''World's Biggest Industrial Trade Fair Lures 500 U.S. Firms,'' *Industrial Marketing,* February 1981, p. 24.

the past. At this stage, the company will have to sell itself and its capabilities. A large number of companies can be expected to pursue prequalification.

In the next phase, the customer will select the companies to be invited to submit a formal bid. Usually, there will be only three to four companies. Formal bids consist of a proposal of how to solve the specific client problem at hand. For industrial equipment, this usually requires personal visits on location, special design of some components, and the preparation of full documentation, including engineering drawings for the client. The costs can be substantial and can range from a few hundred thousand dollars to several million for some very large projects. The customer will select the winner from among those submitting formal proposals. Normally, it is not just the lowest bidder who will obtain the order. Technology, the type of solution proposed, and the financing arrangements all play a role (see Chapter 13).

Once an order is obtained, the supplying company may be expected to ensure its own performance. For that purpose, the company may be asked to post a performance bond, which is a guarantee that the company will pay certain specified damages to the customer if the job is not completed within the preagreed specifications. Performance bonds are usually issued by banks on behalf of the supplier. The entire process, from finding out about a new prospect until the order is actually received in hand, may take from several months to several years, depending on the project size or industry.

Consortium Selling

Because of the high stakes involved in marketing equipment or *turnkey* projects (a plant, system, or project in which the buyer acquires a complete solution so that the entire operation can commence at the turn of a key), companies frequently band together to form a consortium. A *consortium* is a group of firms that share in a certain contract or project on a preagreed basis but act almost as one company toward the customers. Joining together in a consortium can help companies share the risk in some very large projects. A consortium can enhance the competitiveness of the members by offering a turnkey solution to the customer.

Most consortiums are formed on an ad hoc basis. For the supply of a major steel mill, for example, companies supplying individual components may combine into a group and offer a single tender to the customer. The consortium members have agreed to share all marketing costs and can help each other with design and engineering questions. The customer gets a chance to deal with one supplier only, which substantially simplifies the process. Ad hoc consortiums can be found for some very large projects that require unique skills from their members. The consortium members frequently come from the same country and, thus, expect to have a greater chance to get the contract than if they operated on their own. In situations where the same set of skills or products are in frequent demand, companies may form a permanent consortium. Whenever a chance for a deal arises, the consortium members will immediately prepare to qualify for the bidding.

Companies that market equipment that represents only a small part of a much larger project may find the consortium approach helpful because marketing costs can be shared. Preparation of bid documents is expensive and a time-consuming process. Participating in a consortium may be the only chance for a company that is faced with a client demanding a turnkey project. The selection of appropriate partners is important in this context, and chances for overseas orders may be improved if the foreign firms participating in the consortium understand the foreign buying environment.

Other Forms of Promotion

So far, our discussion has been concentrated on personal and industrial selling as key elements of the communications mix. However, next to advertising, various forms of promotion play a key role in international marketing. Usually combined under the generic title of promotions, they may include such elements as in-store retail promotions and coupons. Many of these tools are consumer goods oriented and are used less often in industrial goods marketing. In this section, we will look at sales promotion activities, as well as sports promotions and sponsorships.

Sales Promotion

In many ways, the area of sales promotion has a largely local focus. Although some form of promotions, such as coupons, gifts, and various types of reduced-price labels, are in use in most countries, strict government regulations and different retailing practices tend to limit the options for international firms (as shown in Table 14.2).

In the United States, coupons are the leading form of sales promotion. Consumers bring product coupons to the retail store and obtain a reduced price for the product. Second in importance are refund offers. Consumers who send a proof of purchase to the manufacturer will receive a refund in the form of a check. Also used, but less frequently, are cents-off labels or factory-bonus packs, which induce customers to buy large quantities due to the price incentive. Marketers of consumer goods in the United States, the primary users of these types of sales promotion, find a full array of services available to run their promotions. Companies such as A. C. Nielsen specialize in managing coupon redemption centers centrally so that all handling of promotions can be turned over to an outside contractor.

Couponing varies significantly from country to country. Coupon distribution is popular and growing in Italy. In the United Kingdom and Spain, couponing is declining. Couponing is in its infancy in Japan, with restrictions on newspaper coupons lifted in 1991. Couponing is limited in Germany, Holland, Switzerland, and Greece.[19]

In most overseas markets, price reductions in the store are usually the most important promotional tool, followed by reductions to the trade, such as wholesalers and retailers. Also of importance in some countries are free goods, double-pack promotions, and in-store displays.

19. "International Coupon Trends," *Direct Marketing,* August 1993, pp. 47–49.

TABLE 14.2 ● Concise Guide to Sales Promotion Techniques and Restrictions

Country	*Top 3 sales promotion techniques*	*Restrictions on sales promotion techniques*
Argentina	Reduced price in store Trade discounts In-store displays, promotions	Rules on lotteries, special prizes Products such as pharmaceuticals cannot be promoted through prices
Australia	Reduced price in store Trade discounts Promotional pack sizes with extra free product	Individual state coupon restrictions Promotions and trade support must be available for all stores Lotteries and games of chance subject to government authorization Some restrictions on proof of purchase
Austria	Reduced price in store Open competitions Trade discounts	No coupons Restrictions for on-pack deals
Belgium	Reduced price in store Trade discounts Extra product free	No free draws No sweepstakes
Brazil	Gift banded pack Extra product free Reduced price in store	Distribution of prizes via vouchers, contests, etc., is subject to government authorization
Canada	Reduced price in store Trade discounts Coupons	Ethical products, alcoholic beverages, cigarettes, cigars not permitted any type of sale promotion
France	Reduced price in store Trade discounts Free samples	Games of chance are usually forbidden Premiums and gifts are limited to 5% of product value and no more than 1% off
Germany	Reduced price in store Displays Trade discounts	No coupons Free goods restricted to value of about DM 0.10 No in-pack premiums or cross-product offers No free draws or money-off vouchers
Great Britain	Reduced price in store Trade discounts Coupons	Legislation on bargain offers, lotteries, sweepstakes Competitions must include a degree of skill No price promotion on categories such as pharmaceuticals
Greece	Trade discounts Special offers Reduced price in store	No coupons Gifts limited to 5% of product value
Ireland	Reduced price in store Trade discounts Extra product free	Below-cost selling License required for competitions, which must require a degree of skill
Italy	Reduced price in store Banded packs Coupons	No coupons on butter, oil, coffee No self-liquidating offer or contest or gifts Gifts limited to 8% of product value

TABLE 14.2 ● Concise Guide to Sales Promotion Techniques and Restrictions (*Continued*)

Country	Top 3 sales promotion techniques	Restrictions on sales promotion techniques
Japan	Reduced price in store Trade discounts Premiums	Some regulations regarding lotteries Some regulations on excessive gifts or premiums
Mexico	Reduced price in store Bonus packs On-pack premiums	Government authorization required No promotions based on collecting a series of labels, etc. No promotions of alcohol, tobacco products
Netherlands	Trade discounts Reduced price in store Display promotions, premiums	Legislation on gift schemes, pharmaceuticals, tobacco, games of chance
New Zealand	Reduced price in store Banded packs Coupons	No pyramid selling or trading stamps Coupons redeemable for cash only Competitions require a degree of skill Legislation on Christmas Club funds
Portugal	Trade discounts Reduced price in store Competitions	Some rules regarding lotteries and sweepstakes
South Africa	Reduced price in store Trade discounts In-store coupons, promotions	No lotteries or games of chance Restrictions on coupons, especially no conditional purchase No comparative advertising
Spain	Coupons Free goods Reduced price in store	None
Sweden	Co-op advertising and money off Local activities Coupons	No premium redemption plans Competitions must include a degree of skill Mixed offers are restricted In-pack or on-pack cross-coupons not allowed
Switzerland	Reduced price in store Trade discounts Merchandising contribution by manufacturers to trade	Laws against unfair competition No competitions, free draws, sweepstakes, money-off vouchers, or money off next purchase
United States	Coupons Refund offers Cents-off label, factory packs, and bonus packs	All promotion and trade support must include a degree of skill Mixed offers are restricted In-pack or on-pack cross-coupon not allowed

Source: From William J. Hawkes' presentation of A. C. Nielsen Company material to the International Marketing Workshop, AMA/MSI, March 1983. Reprinted by permission of A. C. Nielsen Company. Updated December 1990.

Most countries have restrictions on some forms of promotions. Frequently regulated are any games of chance, but games in which some type of skill is required are usually allowed. When reductions are made available, they often are not allowed to exceed a certain percentage of the product's purchase price. Because international firms will encounter a series of regulations and restrictions on promotions that differ among countries, there is little opportunity to standardize sales promotion techniques across many markets. This has caused most companies to make sales promotions the responsibility of local managers who are expected to understand the local customs and restrictions. Certain product categories such as tobacco face even stricter limits. Canada's 1989 Tobacco Products Control Act states: "No person shall advertise any tobacco product offered for sale in Canada." This limits Canadian tobacco manufacturers to product displays and word-of-mouth advertising.[20]

Sports Promotions and Sponsorships

With major sports events increasingly being covered by the mass media, television in particular, the commercial value of these events has increased tremendously over the last decade. Today, large sports events, such as the Olympics or world championships in specific sports, cannot exist in their present form without funding by companies, which do this either through advertising or through different types of sponsorships.

In the United States, companies have for some time purchased TV advertising space for such events as regularly broadcasted baseball, basketball, and football events. Gillette is one company that regularly uses sponsorship of the World Series to introduce new products. This is just another extension of the company's media strategy to air television and radio commercials at times when its prime target group can be found in large numbers watching TV or listening to the radio. More recently, companies have purchased similar time slots for the Olympics when they are broadcast in the United States.

In many foreign countries where commercial television advertising is restricted or not even allowed, companies do not have the opportunity to purchase air time. Given their inability to advertise tobacco in Canada, the three major companies all use sponsorships to maintain brand awareness. Imperial provides financial support for thirty sports and cultural events and ninety-seven arts groups, including the Toronto Symphony Orchestra and the Canadian Open Golf Championship.[21]

For the 1992 Winter Olympics in Albertville, France, the U.S. CBS TV network paid $243 million and had already signed up about $100 million in advertising revenue by mid-1990. NBC had purchased the U.S. rights to the 1992 Summer Olympics to be held in Barcelona, Spain, for $401 million. By mid-1990, some $38 million of advertising had been sold. The majority of revenue was expected to come from pay-per-view package events.[22]

20. "Smokers Fight to the Very Last Gasp," *Financial Times,* July 11, 1991, p. 23.

21. Ibid.

22. "Grabbing the Rings: Marketers Tie in Early with Olympics," *Advertising Age,* August 6, 1990, p. 4.

To circumvent restrictions on commercial television during sports programs, companies have purchased space for signs along the stadiums or the arenas where sports events take place. When the event is covered on television, the cameras will automatically take in the signs as part of the regular coverage. No mention of the company's product is made in any way either by the announcer or in the form of commercials. It is the visual identification that the firms are looking for.

In the case of the 1990 Football World Cup in Italy (referred to as soccer in the United States), the event extended over almost eight weeks and involved some twenty-four national teams. An estimated fifteen billion viewers watched either all the games or parts of them on television, which meant nine billion exposures for any company that had managed to obtain sign space along the playing field. Most of this was delivered in countries where from the very beginning it was difficult to get TV space; thus, it was of great importance to the firm. Ten official sponsors for the entire series of fifty-two games played by the twenty-four teams obtained exclusive advertising rights in the stadiums and in official publications. Among the sponsors were Coca-Cola, Mars, Gillette, Canon, JVC, Fuji Film, Philips, and Anheuser-Busch together with Carlsberg.[23]

With the opening of the economies of eastern Europe, sponsoring sports events is also used as a way to reach potential consumer markets. Promoters purchased the rights to the United Jersey Bank Classic and moved it to Leipzig, Germany, where several corporate sponsors paid almost $4 million to have the tennis tournament. The attraction for the sponsoring companies, which included Volkswagen, Kraft-General Foods, and American Airlines, was the TV coverage by German TV with some 30 million viewers. Also present were TV networks of several eastern European countries.[24]

To take advantage of such global sports events, a company should have a logo or brand name that is worth exposing to a global audience. It is not surprising to find that the most common sponsors are companies producing consumer goods with a global appeal such as soft drink manufacturers, consumer electronics producers, and film companies. To purchase sign space, a firm must take into consideration the popularity of certain sports. Few sports have global appeal. Football (soccer), the number one spectator sport in much of the world, still has little commercial value in the United States or in Canada. The World Cup football tournament was in the United States in 1994 for the first time. In contrast, baseball and American football have little appeal in Europe or parts of Asia and Africa. Many other sports also have only local or regional character, which requires a company to know its market and the interests of its target audience very well.

A Japanese financial services company, Orient Leasing, purchased one of Japan's twelve professional baseball teams, the Braves. As a result, the company was allowed to call the team by the company's name and promptly changed its name to the shorter Orix. Within a short time, the national awareness of the company rose from 25 to 85 percent. The total cost of running the team was estimated at about $30 million. However, the company was reducing regular advertising due to the constant exposure of the Japanese

23. "World Cup Scores Big with Sponsors," *Advertising Age,* April 30, 1990, p. 42.
24. "Look Out Wimbledon, Here Comes Leipzig," *Business Week,* September 24, 1990, p. 54.

public to Orix. This was ensured not only through the name but also by placing the Orix name on the players' uniforms.[25]

Aside from sponsoring sporting events, companies have also moved more aggressively into sponsoring direct competitors or teams. Manufacturers of sports equipment have for some time concentrated on getting leading athletes to use their equipment. For sports that have achieved international or even global reach, such as tennis, skiing, or football, an endorsement of sports products by leading athletes can be a key to success. This is why manufacturers of sports equipment have always attempted to get their equipment used by world-class athletes. In 1984, Puma sold only 15,000 tennis rackets a year. In 1985, following Boris Becker's first victory in Wimbledon and his endorsement of Puma rackets, sales jumped to 150,000 rackets.[26]

To exploit the media coverage of spectator sports, many nonsporting goods manufacturers have joined the sponsoring of specific athletes or teams. These are firms that intend to exploit the visual identification created by the media coverage. Many will remember the pictures of winning racecar drivers with all the various corporation names or logos on their uniforms. Although these promotions once tended to be mostly related to sports products, sponsors increasingly have no relationship to the sports. Sponsoring a team for competition in the sixteen Grand Prix races all over the world is estimated to cost about $45 to $60 million for one year. The main sponsor is expected to carry about one-half to two-thirds of the cost and gets to paint the cars in its colors with its logo. The expenses are substantial because the winners do not get very high purses; yet leading racecar drivers are reported to get salaries as high as $9 million for one year. In 1988, the races were broadcast in eighty-one countries over 100,000 minutes and attracted 3.3 billion viewers, resulting in some 17 billion ''viewings.'' Major sponsors were tobacco companies (Marlboro, Camel, John Player, Gitanes/Loto) and other consumer goods firms (Benetton).[27]

Companies have also become involved in bicycle racing. The U.S. convenience store chain 7-Eleven began to sponsor a team of U.S. professional riders during the 1986 Tour de France. Although the race was taking place in France, the company intended to exploit its sponsorship in the United States through extensive coverage of the race in the U.S. news media.[28] Other companies that sponsored teams included Hitachi, Toshiba, and Panasonic, all of Japan. Yet other companies sponsored the official drink or the official computer for keeping the results. All of them were attracted by the 60 million viewers all across Europe who watched the daily reports on television.[29]

Through the intensive coverage of sports in the news media all over the world, many companies continue to use the sponsorship of sporting events as an important element in their international communications programs. Successful companies have to track the inter-

25. ''Sponsorship in Japan: Benefits of Keeping an Eye on the Ball,'' *Financial Times,* May 25, 1989, p. 16.

26. ''Puma Hopes Superstar Will Help End U.S. Slump, Narrow Gap with Adidas,'' *Wall Street Journal,* February 6, 1987, p. 24.

27. ''Motor Sport Industry,'' *Financial Times,* January 26, 1990, Section 3, p. 1.

28. ''Big Money Catches Up with the Tour de France,'' *Business Week,* July 28, 1986, p. 45.

29. Ibid.

est of various countries in the many types of sports and to exhibit both flexibility and ingenuity in the selection of available events or participants. In many parts of the world, sports sponsorship may continue to be the only available way to reach large numbers of prospective customers.

Direct Marketing

Direct marketing includes a number of marketing approaches that involve direct access to the customer. Direct mail, door-to-door selling, and telemarketing are the primary direct marketing tools used in the United States. Some companies have achieved considerable success in their fields through aggressive direct marketing. Many of these firms realize that not all markets respond equally well to direct marketing. For the most part, the United States has the most developed direct marketing field.

Direct marketing, covering products purchased from an individual's home or office, brought some $70 billion in the United States in 1990. According to industry statistics, some 92 million Americans bought something from the home. Direct marketing has also grown substantially in other countries. In the United Kingdom, the Benelux countries, France, and Scandinavia, direct-mail business doubled in the 1980s.[30] The market is also growing rapidly in Asia, where it is well established in Hong Kong and Singapore. Prospects in eastern Europe are not yet clear, but experts expect it to grow there rapidly.

In Europe, despite the growth, direct marketing expenditures still only account for about one-third of all marketing expenditures compared to two-thirds in the United States. Total sales in the twelve EU member states is about one-third of the U.S. volume. Future growth appears to be largely dependent on expected regulation. In line with the EU 1992 initiative, new regulation for the direct marketing sector is under debate. Presently, direct marketing regulation is most restricted in Germany, where everything is forbidden unless specifically allowed. On the other hand, the United Kingdom and the Netherlands have more liberal regulations. As part of the EU 1992 regulations, a directive from the EU Commission is expected that will regulate the activity at the same level throughout Europe.[31]

Direct Mail

Direct mail, largely pioneered in the United States by catalog houses such as Sears, Roebuck and Montgomery Ward, is being used extensively in other countries. Successful mail-order sales require an efficient postal system and an effective collection system for the

30. "International Direct Marketing: On the Brink of Maturity," *Financial Times,* April 18, 1990, p. 15.

31. "International Direct Marketing: Largely Uncharted Territory Ahead," *Financial Times,* April 18, 1990, p. 15.

shipped products. In countries where these preconditions exist, direct mail is being used extensively by retail organizations and other service organizations such as *Reader's Digest* and credit card suppliers.

Austad, a leading U.S. catalog company marketing golf supplies, with sales of $60 million, achieved international sales of 20 percent in 1990. From a small start, international sales really took off when the company developed special catalogs for some key foreign markets. It mailed some 140,000 catalogs to Japanese customers, some 60,000 to the United Kingdom, and another 40,000 to Sweden. The company customized its catalogs to the local requirements, mailing local-language catalogs to Japan and Sweden and "English" English to the United Kingdom. All orders were shipped from the United States, incurring considerable shipping expenses per order. Austad planned to stock its products locally and, thus, cut expenses to its customers.[32]

The Japanese consumer has been reluctant to buy through the mail. To encourage more direct mail in Japan, R. R. Donnelley & Sons (a large U.S. catalog printer) launched the American Showcase Catalog in 1991 with goods from Lands' End, L. L. Bean, Orvis, Tweed's, and others. The catalog was mailed to 550,000 homes in Japan.[33]

Companies that may want to engage in direct mail will have to ensure that their mail pieces or catalogs are translated into the respective foreign language. Obtaining accurate mailing lists may also be difficult, although list brokers exist in many countries, as they do in the United States. Direct mail offers an opportunity for companies that want to extend their business beyond a limited location and even into foreign countries. In general, however, mailing of packages abroad always involves the receiver country's customs system, which tends to delay parcels considerably.

Door-to-Door Sales

Companies such as Amway and Mary Kay Cosmetics have met with considerable success in the United States. These and other firms have grown entirely by the use of door-to-door selling techniques and by employing large numbers of part-time salespersons. Some firms employ women who sell through organized home "party" demonstrations or by contacting friends in their own neighborhoods or at work. Expansion of these and other companies into foreign markets has met with mixed success.

The concept of door-to-door selling is not equally accepted in all countries. Moreover, it also may not be equally accepted to make a profit from selling to a friend, colleague at work, or neighbors. The willingness to find suitable salespeople on a part-time basis may also be limited because in some countries women or even students are not necessarily expected to work. One company that successfully transferred its direct door-to-door selling strategy from the United States to Japan is Amway. After just eleven years, Amway sales

32. "Translating a Technique into Overseas Success," *Advertising Age,* September 24, 1990, p. s-8.
33. "U.S. Mail-Order Merchants Try Japanese Markets," *New York Times,* November 5, 1991, p. D5.

reached $555 million in 1990, representing about one-fourth of total worldwide sales.[34] As a result, the Japanese operation has become Amway's largest foreign unit, with some 700,000 distributor/salespeople. Many of its distributors are working full time and are paid on a commission-only basis as in the United States. Amway's strategy of selling directly to households is a big plus in a country where the regular distribution of goods is complicated and typically goes through many steps of wholesalers and retailers. As a result, Amway, which can circumvent the difficult Japanese distribution channel structure, is now one of the most profitable foreign companies operating in Japan.[35] Amway's success has also brought it attention from Japanese companies. Japanese firms marketing competing household products through regular channels are starting to bring new products to the market to slow Amway's expansion. Other companies, such as Sharp, a leading consumer electronics firm, have hired Amway to distribute some new products in Japan.[36] As a result, the type of door-to-door selling that is the hallmark of a number of successful U.S. firms may not be limited only to the cultural background of the United States.

Telemarketing

Telemarketing, the most recent technique in direct marketing, has enjoyed explosive growth in the United States, where telephone sales amounted to $50 billion in 1990.[37] Selling by telephone allows companies to quickly access large numbers of target customers in a short period of time, something that could not be done personally. Furthermore, the high cost of personal selling has motivated many firms to augment their sales effort through telephone sales to save costs.

To make telephone sales effective abroad, an efficient telephone system is a requirement. Telephone sales for individual households may become practical when a large number of subscribers exist and when their telephone numbers can be easily obtained. However, not all countries accept the practice of soliciting business directly at home. Yet in western Europe, where the economic pressures on selling are the same as they are in the United States, companies can expect gains from effective use of telemarketing. Because of the language problems involved, companies must make sure their telemarketing sales forces not only speak the language of the local customer but do so fluently and with the correct local or regional accent. British Telecommunications, the British company operating most telephone systems in that country, maintains a telephone sales force of some 300 operators, which is believed to be the largest telephone sales operation in Europe. Other areas with substantial telephone selling activities include the Netherlands, France, Scandinavia, and Germany (where this practice is heavily restricted).[38]

On an international level, telephone sales may be helpful for business-to-business

34. *Wall Street Journal,* September 21, 1990, p. B1.
35. *Business Week,* September 4, 1989, p. 47.
36. *Financial Times,* March 22, 1990.
37. *Financial Times,* April 18, 1990, p. 15.
38. ''Cold Calls Seek a Warmer Welcome,'' *Financial Times,* June 26, 1986, p. 6.

marketing when decision-makers can be contacted quickly and when they can be identified from available directories. Since travel costs for overseas travel are considerable and direct dialing is now possible for international calls in many countries, telemarketing on a cross-country or international basis may be possible.

Conclusions

Communications in an international context are particularly challenging because managers are constantly faced with communicating to customers with different cultural backgrounds. This tends to add to the complexity of the communications task, which demands a particular sensitivity to culture, habits, and at times even different types of rational reasoning.

Aside from the cultural differences that largely affect the content and form of the communications, international firms will encounter a different set of cost constraints for the principal communications mix elements such as selling or advertising. Given such large differences from country to country with respect to sales force costs or media costs, international firms have to carefully design their communications mix to fit each individual market. Furthermore, the availability of any one individual communications mix element cannot be taken for granted. The absence of one or the other, due to either legal or economic development considerations, will force the international firm to compensate with a greater use of other mix elements.

When designing effective sales forces for local markets, international marketers need to take into consideration the challenge of international sales and the requirements for doing well. Such international sales efforts can usually be maintained for companies selling highly differentiated and complex products to a clearly defined target market. In most other situations, ones in which the products are targeted at a broader type of industrial or consumer customer group, international firms will typically have to engage a local sales force for each market. Local sales forces are usually very effective in reaching their own market or country, but they are not always able to transfer to another country because of language limitations. Building up and managing a local sales force are challenging tasks in most foreign markets and require managers with a special sensitivity to local laws, regulations, and trade practices.

Questions for Discussion

1. What factors appear to affect the extension of push or pull policies in international markets?

2. Under what circumstances should a company pursue an international versus a local selling effort?

3. What factors most often appear to make local selling different from country to country?

4. What patterns can you detect in the use of sales promotion tools across many countries?

5. To what types of companies would you suggest sponsorship in the next Olympic Games, and which sports would you recommend to them? How would such firms profit from any association with the Olympic Games?

For Further Reading

"Advertising Jingle-Jangles Through the Slump." *Economist,* September 20, 1980, pp. 85–86.

Batista, Michael J. "Recruit an International Sales Force." *Global Trade and Transportation,* August 1993, p. 32.

Blake, David H., and Vita Toros. "The Global Image Makers." *Public Relations Journal,* June 1976, pp. 10–16.

Cook, Roy A., and Joel Herche. "Assessment Centers: An Untapped Resource for Global Sales Management." *Journal of Personal Selling and Sales Management,* Summer 1992, pp. 31–38.

Dunn, S. Watson. "Effect of National Identity on Multinational Promotional Strategy in Europe." *Journal of Marketing,* October 1976, pp. 50–57.

Ferguson, Henry. "International Exhibit Marketing: A Management Approach." *Dimensions,* 1986.

Hoke, Peter. "Wunderman's View of Global Direct Marketing." *Direct Marketing,* 48 (March 1986), pp. 76–88, 153.

Japan External Trade Organization. *Sales Promotion in the Japanese Market.* Tokyo: JETRO, 1980.

Kashani, Kamran, and John A. Quelch. "Can Sales Promotion Go Global?" *Business Horizons* 33, no. 3 (May/June 1990), pp. 37–43.

McMahon, Timothy J. "Sales Automation: For Many Companies a Final Link in Global Management." *Business Marketing,* May 1993, p. 56.

Still, Richard R. "Sales Management: Some Cross-Cultural Aspects." *Journal of Personal Selling and Sales Management,* Spring–Summer 1981, pp. 6–9.

Thomas, L. R. "Trade Fairs: Gateways to European Markets." *Business America,* April 20, 1981, pp. 7–10.

Tung, Rosalie L. "Selection and Training of Personnel for Overseas Assignments." *Columbia Journal of World Business,* Spring 1981, pp. 68–78.

Weser, Robert E. *The Marketer's Guide to Selling Products Abroad.* Westport, Conn.: Quorum Books, 1989.

15

Managing International and Global Advertising

● **AT THE BEGINNING** *of this book, we defined international marketing as those marketing activities that applied simultaneously to more than one country. In the case of advertising, the volume of activity directed simultaneously toward targets in several countries is actually very small. The majority of advertising activity tends to be directed toward one country only. Despite the ''local'' nature of international advertising, it is important to recognize that the initial input, in terms of either the product idea or the basic communications strategy, largely originates in another country. Consequently, although there is a largely local aspect to most international advertising, there is also an international aspect to consider.*

Two important questions must to be answered in international advertising: (1) How much of a local versus an international emphasis should there be? (2) What should be the nature and content of the advertising itself? The first part of the chapter (see Figure 15.1) is organized around the explanation of key external factors and their influence on international advertising. The rest of the chapter focuses on the major advertising decisions and helps to explain how external factors affect specific advertising areas. Special emphasis is given to Japan, where the advertising environment differs considerably from that in the United States or Europe.

FIGURE 15.1 ● International and Global Advertising

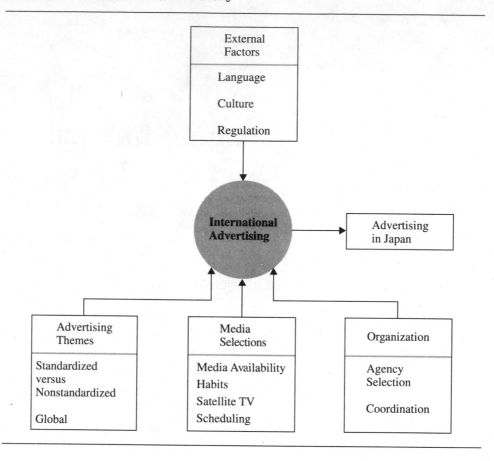

Challenges in International Advertising

Probably no other aspect of international marketing has received as much attention as international advertising. Consider the following examples:

> In Italy, "Schweppes Tonic Water" had to be reduced to "Schweppes Tonica" because "il water" turned out to be the idiom for a bathroom.

> General Motors, translating its slogan "Body by Fisher" into Flemish for its Belgium campaign, found out belatedly that the meaning was the equivalent of "Corpse by Fisher."[1]

1. David A. Ricks, Jeffrey S. Arpan, and Marilyn Y. Fu, "Pitfalls in Advertising Overseas," *Journal of Advertising Research,* December 1974, p. 48.

These are two of many mistakes that have been made in translating advertising copy from one language into another. Most, however, occurred in the 1960s, when international advertising was in its infancy. Today, most companies and advertising agencies have reached a level of sophistication that reduces the chance of translation error. This does not mean that language is not a factor to consider in today's international communications strategy. However, the industry has moved from a primary concern about translation to concerns about ways to be more efficient.

A second major cause of international advertising mistakes has traditionally been the neglect of cultural attitudes of consumers in foreign countries. Benetton, the Italian clothing manufacturer selling through stores all over the world, was one of the more recent examples of a company that ran into cultural problems with its advertising. The company launched a new campaign in fall 1989 under the theme "United Colors of Benetton," which had won awards in France. One of its ads featured a black woman breast-feeding a white baby; another had a black and a white man locked together in handcuffs. The ads came under protest from U.S. civil rights groups and had to be withdrawn. Benetton also fired its advertising agency, Eldorado of France, the creator of the ads.[2]

Such examples show that, even when the language or translation hurdle is correctly overcome, there still remains the need to consider the cultural and social background of the target market. Mistakes based on a misinterpretation of cultural habits are more difficult to avoid, though substantial progress has been made by international marketers to ward staying away from the most obvious violations. However, the avoidance of either translation or cultural errors will not be enough to produce an effective advertising campaign. Although we will initially concentrate on approaches to overcome such cultural difficulties, we will eventually emphasize critical issues around organizing campaigns internationally.

Overcoming the Language Barrier

Most of the translation blunders referred to in the previous section were due to literal translations performed outside of the target country. The translators, not always in contact with the culture of the target country, were unable to judge the actual meaning of the translated copy for the target audience. Furthermore, the faulty translation could not be checked by the executives involved, because they too were from a different culture and did not possess the necessary foreign language skills.

With the opening of the economies in eastern Europe to advertising, many companies had looked for translators. Some found out that those translators who had fled those countries many years ago wrote correct but outmoded copy.[3]

Today, the traps of faulty translations can be avoided through the involvement of local nationals or language experts. Typically, international marketers have any translations checked by either a local advertising agency, their own local subsidiary, or an independent distributor located in the target country. Because international firms are active in a large

2. International Advertising Supplement, *Financial Times,* December 7, 1989, p. 3.
3. "How to Advertise in Eastern Europe," *Financial Times,* October 31, 1989, p. 14.

number of countries and thus require the use of many languages, today's international marketers can find an organizational solution to the translation errors of the past. Many errors can still occur, however, if the foreign language copy is typeset incorrectly or by inexperienced typesetters. This is particularly true for non-Roman letters.[4]

In the European Union, there are nine official languages. As a result, this puts a special emphasis on the ability to communicate visually rather than through the various languages. It is expected that graphics will be used more effectively in print media, too. Even the satellite TV service Sky Channel has discovered that not everyone in Europe speaks English and that, if given a chance, most people like to watch programs in their own language. Super Channel, the other satellite channel, moved to trilingual program service, and rather than offer pan-European programs, the operators of satellite channels in Europe are moving into the direction of multiregional programming.[5]

Adjusting to a local language often requires changes in the product name or positioning. For example, Procter & Gamble found that Head & Shoulders shampoo had no meaning in Chinese, so the revised Chinese name means "see flying silk," to fit the concept of looking and feeling good.[6]

Overcoming the Cultural Barrier

When international marketers fail due to misinterpretation of the local culture, they usually do so because they advocated an action that was inconsistent with the local culture or because the appeal chosen was inconsistent with the motivational pattern of the target culture. Advocating the purchase of a product whose use is inconsistent with the local culture will result in failure, even if the appeal chosen did not violate that culture per se. However, companies can also fail if only the appeal, or message employed, is inconsistent with the local culture, even if the action promoted is not. Consequently, a foreign company entering a new market has to be aware of both cultural aspects: the product's use and the message employed.

When Procter & Gamble, the U.S. consumer goods manufacturer, promoted its Camay soap in Japan in 1983, it ran into unexpected trouble. In the TV commercial, a Japanese woman was bathing when her husband walked into the bathroom. She began telling him about her new beauty soap, but the husband, stroking her shoulder, hinted that suds were not on his mind. This very popular ad from Europe flopped because it was bad manners for a Japanese man to intrude on his wife.[7]

To ensure that a message is in line with the existing cultural beliefs of the target market, companies can use resources similar to those used to overcome the translation

4. "A Not-So-Funny Thing Happened on the Way to the Printer," *Business Marketing,* February 1987, p. 113.

5. "Reaching United Europe Won't Be a Simple Task," *Advertising Age,* April 9, 1990, p. 31.

6. "Why There's Still Promise in China," *Fortune,* February 27, 1989, p. 99.

7. "After Early Stumbles, P&G Is Making Inroads Overseas," *Wall Street Journal,* February 6, 1989, p. B1.

barriers. Local subsidiary personnel or local distributors can judge the cultural content of the message. Also helpful are advertising agencies with local offices. International marketers cannot possibly know enough about all the cultures they will come into contact with. However, it is the responsibility of the international executive to make sure that knowledgeable local nationals have given enough input so that the mistake of using an inappropriate appeal with respect to the local culture will be avoided.

For successful advertising in Nigeria, Africa's largest and most populous nation, the standard advertising patterns used in other countries will not necessarily work.[8] Gulda beer ads showed a large, rough-hewn man in a blue-jean jacket based on the American movie character Shaft. The person was shown holding a mug, and the brown glass bottle of Gulda beer rested on the table. The slogan "Gulda man, Gulda man, sure of his taste, proud to be different" was used. However, this ad did not appear to promote the brand. Research showed that Nigerian consumers of beer felt that good beer came only in green bottles. They also noted that the person in the Gulda ad was always drinking alone; for many Nigerians, drinking beer was a social activity. The ad was finally changed. Gulda was presented in a green bottle, the theme was changed to "Gulda makes you feel real fine," and the setting was changed to show elegant people drinking together. Sales volume increased dramatically.

Helene Curtis, a major company in the hair care market, tailored its advertising to suit the cultural differences of the various national markets while keeping intact the underlying theme of catering to the changing needs of the customer's hair. Hair care is different by national character, and hair type also differs by region. Middle-class women in Spain rarely wash their own hair, whereas the opposite is true among British women. In Japan, Japanese women are fearful of overwashing their hair and removing its protective oils. As a result, the company needed to tailor its messages carefully to each national culture.[9]

Procter & Gamble was pleased by the initial success of its Vidal Sassoon Wash & Go shampoo in Poland. P&G launched it in August 1991 with a major advertising campaign and whistle-stop tour by Vidal Sassoon, the British-born hairdresser. It captured 30 percent of the market. Unfortunately, sales plummeted as rumors began that Wash & Go caused dandruff and hair loss. P&G had tried to use its U.S. commercials in Poland. They seemed to be too brash, causing 75 percent of the Poles to dislike the ads. Also, some believe the rumors were started by the numerous entrepreneurial hairdressers who felt Vidal Sassoon would open shops in Poland and threaten their business. P&G hoped to revive Wash & Go with new advertising that would educate the consumers.[10]

Judging the appropriateness of a product or service for a culture is substantially more difficult than making a judgment only on the type of advertising to be employed. In Chapter 3 we discussed the nature of cultural and social forces, and in Chapter 6 we covered the evaluation of market potential for products. Here, we restrict ourselves to a discussion of the advertising aspects of cultural analysis.

8. "Of Ads and Elders: Selling to Nigerians," *New York Times,* April 20, 1987, p. D10.
9. "Haircare Creates a Parting of the Ways," *Financial Times,* September 7, 1989, p. 12.
10. "Wash & Get into a Lather in Poland," *Financial Times,* May 28, 1992, p. 10.

The Impact of Regulations on International Advertising

Although there are numerous situations where differing customer needs require tailor-made advertising campaigns, in many instances the particular regulations of a country prevent firms from using standardized approaches, even when they would appear desirable. When Coca-Cola internationally launched its theme, "Coke adds life," in the late 1970s, Scandinavian countries and Thailand refused the slogan because it was considered an overclaim. Eventually, the company was able to overturn the countries' prohibition after some considerable lobbying effort.[11] In countries such as Malaysia, regulations are a direct outgrowth of changing political circumstances. Following the growing influence of Moslem fundamentalists in many parts of the world, Malaysia, a country with a large Moslem population, outlawed ads showing women in sleeveless dresses and pictures showing underarms. These were considered offensive by strict Moslem standards. Obviously, this caused considerable problems to marketers of deodorant products.[12]

Advertising for cigarettes and tobacco products is under strict regulation in many countries.[13] In France, R. J. Reynolds, the manufacturer of Camel cigarettes, was prohibited from showing humans smoking cigarettes. The company finally overcame the restrictions by showing a smiling camel smoking a Camel cigarette.[14] On the other hand, cigarette advertising was permitted in Greece, when it was the only member of the European Union to do so. Although a ban existed on cigarette ads for television and radio, no limits were placed on print advertising and posters.[15] On March 14, 1990, the European Parliament voted a complete ban of tobacco advertising throughout the European Union.[16] By the end of 1990, few of the largest fifty tobacco markets were expected to be without significant regulations on tobacco advertising; in as many as twenty of them, outright bans may be in effect.[17]

Advertising to children is also an area facing considerable regulation. General Mills, when marketing its Action Man soldiers in Germany, could not simply translate its copy into German. The company was forced to produce a very different television commercial by reducing the tone of the speaker's voice and the violence. Instead of showing the toy soldiers holding machine guns and driving tanks, they were shown unarmed and driving a jeep.[18] Kellogg could not use a commercial produced in the United Kingdom for its

11. "Curbs on Ads Increase Abroad as Nations Apply Standards of Fairness and Decency," *Wall Street Journal,* November 25, 1980, p. 56.

12. Ibid.

13. "Defending the Rights of Marlboro Man," *Economist,* April 21, 1990, p. 84.

14. Ibid.

15. "Greece: No Limits on Ads for Cigarettes," *International Herald Tribune,* October 1, 1984, p. 15.

16. "Advertising: Single Marketing," *Economist,* March 24, 1990, p. 64.

17. "Defending the Rights," p. 84.

18. "Countries' Different Ad Rules Are Problem for Global Firms," *Wall Street Journal,* September 27, 1984, p. 33.

continental European business. The reference to Kellogg's cereals' iron and vitamin contents were not permissible in the Netherlands. The child wearing the Kellogg T-shirt in the original commercial had to be edited out for use in France, where children are forbidden to endorse a product. And the key line ''Kellogg's makes their cornflakes the best they have ever been'' would have been disallowed in Germany because of a prohibition against making competitive claims.[19]

As part of the Europe 1992 initiative, the European Union is debating a series of rulings that could have great impact on advertising in Europe. The discussions involve both efforts toward greater harmonization and the extent of regulation. Greater harmonization is generally viewed as desirable throughout Europe and potentially would result in equal regulations for advertising. This would greatly enhance the potential for pan-European marketing campaigns and bring greater advertising efficiency. Also at issue is also the extent of regulation. Draft directives covering such areas as tobacco advertising, pharmaceuticals, and food claims tend to incorporate the most restrictive national regulations in many areas. Consequently, marketers are afraid that the end effect is ''harmonizing the restrictions instead of harmonizing the freedoms.''[20]

Other regulations companies may encounter cover the production of advertising material. Some countries require all advertising, particularly television and radio, to be produced locally. As a result, it has become a real challenge for international advertisers to find campaigns that can be used in as many countries as possible to save on the production costs. Such campaigns are, however, only possible if a company has sufficient input from the very beginning on the applicable legislation so this can be taken into account.

Selecting an Advertising Theme
Standardization Versus Nonstandardization

For international marketers with products sold in many countries, the basic decision tends to center around the appropriate level of standardization for the advertising theme and its creative execution. As a result of early failures in the 1950s by inexperienced international companies that employed a totally standardized approach, companies shifted to the other extreme by allowing each market to design its own campaign. In the mid-1960s, European-based advertising executives started to discuss the possibility of greater standardization. Erik Elinder was among the first to advocate the benefits of a more standardized approach.[21]

19. Ibid.

20. ''Next Challenge: Re-regulation: 1992 Adding Up to Tough Ad Restrictions,'' *Advertising Age,* September 10, 1990, p. 57.

21. Erik Elinder, ''How International Can Advertising Be?'' *International Advertiser,* December 1961, pp. 12–16; ''How International Can European Advertising Be?'' *Journal of Marketing,* April 1965, pp. 7–11.

Elinder argued that European consumers are increasingly "living under similar conditions although they read and speak different languages."[22]

A study by BBDO of the "Eurowoman," which included 1,000 interviews with women from twenty-six countries, found there is a consistent profile of the Eurowoman. The study found that communications to European women often depend on the stereotype of either the sexy bimbo or the veteran housewife, ignoring the working female. The research identified an opportunity to improve European advertising with women through the use of the workingwoman image and the recognition that today's woman has humor, confidence, and individuality.[23]

Elinder also pointed out that much of the European consumption has become international and that mass media coverage in several areas overlaps national boundaries. With people thinking and living more and more alike, why should advertising be different for each market?

Some of the barriers to standardized advertising, which include structural and organizational problems, could prevent companies from selecting a more standardized approach.[24] Among the factors preventing standardization are the absence of international advertising agencies with offices in many countries, the lack of interest among some companies in imposing stricter controls over their local operations, the proliferation of languages, and the diversity of media characteristics by country.

What are the advantages of, or even the needs for, standardizing more of the firm's international advertising? First, there is the concern that *creative* talent is scarce and that one effort to develop a campaign will produce better results than forty or fifty efforts. This particularly applies to countries for which the marketing or advertising experience is limited. A second advantage centers around the economics of a global campaign. To develop an individual campaign in many countries creates costs for photographs, layouts, and the production of television commercials. In a standardized approach, these production costs can be reduced, and more funds can be spent on purchasing space in the media. One company, Levi Strauss, paid as much as $550,000 for one series of TV commercials. By reusing its commercials in many countries, the company saved in production costs. Furthermore, the company was able to spend more on the original version and thus produce a better advertisement.[25] A third reason for a standardized approach is found in global brand names. Many companies market products under a single brand name in several countries within the same region. With the substantial amount of international travel occurring today and the considerable overlap in media across national borders, companies are interested in creating a single image to avoid any confusion caused through local campaigns that may be in conflict with each other. L'Oréal, the French cosmetics company, was one company that aimed for a uniform identity for its international customer group.[26]

22. "How International Can European Advertising Be?" p. 9.

23. "Advertisers Glimpse Their Dream Woman," *International Management,* March 1993, p. 21.

24. Illmar Roostal, "Standardization of Advertising for Western Europe," *Journal of Marketing,* October 1963, pp. 15–20.

25. "Ads Astride the World," *Financial Times,* April 13, 1989, p. 16.

26. "The Issue Globalists Don't Talk About," *International Management,* September 1987, p. 37.

One of the best examples of a successful standardized campaign was Philip Morris's Marlboro campaign in Europe. Marlboro's success as a leading brand began in the 1950s when the brand was repositioned to assure smokers that the flavor would be unchanged by the effect of the filter. The theme *"Come to where the flavor is. Come to Marlboro country"* became an immediate success in the United States and abroad. The brand led in West Germany with a 22 percent market share and was listed among the top three brands in most European markets.[27] In all overseas markets, the advertising theme makes use of the same type of ad used in the United States. The cowboy has become a symbol of freedom and evokes the same feelings among Americans, Brazilians, and Germans. (This phenomenon was discussed in Chapter 3 under the subject of reference groups.) Consequently, the cowboy is a relevant reference group for the German smoker, causing a positive identification. Marlboro's worldwide market share showed an increase every year since 1965 and reached sales of $9.4 billion in 1989. It was the world's most profitable consumer good, surpassing even Coca-Cola.[28]

Levi Strauss, the world's largest clothing manufacturer, created a very successful advertising campaign for its European operations. Focusing on its traditional denim jeans, the "Launderette" commercial showed a young man walking into a 1950s launderette, stripping to his boxer shorts, and washing his Levi jeans to the sound of Marvin Gaye's soul music "I Heard It Through the Grapevine."[29] The commercial was later used in many international markets. Local rules, however, required a number of adaptations. Levi could not show the original commercial in the United States because another company held the copyright to the music. For Brazil and Australia, Levi had to reshoot the commercials because local regulations required that commercials had to be made in those countries. In many Southeast Asian countries, local censors denied the company the right to run the commercial.

Warner Lambert Co. is developing a revitalized image for Chiclets gum. While advertisements in the past were created on a country-by-country basis with no central theme, research showed that Chiclets faced low visibility across many countries. The new positioning and campaign are targeted to the 18- to 24-year-old consumer. The commercial, shot in the sand dunes of northern Brazil, includes a desert shack occupied by a young man and a monkey. By rattling a Chiclets box they summon an international audience ranging from geishas to English school boys. The tag line in English is "Chiclets make cool things happen." Hoping to use the ad worldwide, Warner Lambert wanted to maximize the impact of its advertising expenditures.[30]

As these examples show us, specific factors will either allow or prevent standardization of some parts of an advertising campaign. The nature of these factors will be the topic of the following section.

27. "Cigarette Makers Now Look to Enhanced Big Grand Fire Power," *Financial Times,* April 26, 1990, p. 13.
28. "Defending the Rights of Marlboro Man," *Economist,* April 21, 1990, p. 84.
29. "Ads Astride the World," p. 16.
30. "Chiclets Tries New Language," *Advertising Age International,* April 19, 1993, p. I-1.

Requirements for Standardized Campaigns   For a company to launch a worldwide standardized campaign, some requirements first have to be met. These requirements center around the name, packaging, awareness, competitive situation, and consumer or customer attitudes.

The need for a standardized brand name or trademark is viewed by many companies as a prerequisite to a standardized campaign. Not only should the name be written in identical format, but it should also be pronounced identically. The major product 7UP, sold in about 80 markets worldwide, is consistently pronounced in the English language in all countries.[31]

Trademarks or corporate logos can also help in achieving greater standardization of corporate campaigns. Such well-known logos as Kodak's or General Electric's are used the world over.

Whirlpool, one of the world's largest manufacturers of domestic appliances, formed a joint venture in Europe with Philips in 1989. The two companies combined their European operations, with Whirlpool as majority partner. As a result, Whirlpool became the world's largest appliance maker, overtaking Electrolux of Sweden. All appliances were to be marketed under Philips Whirlpool. The joint venture resulted in a market share of 12 percent in Europe, compared to leader Electrolux's 22 percent. In the U.S. market, the positions were reversed, with Whirlpool's 30 percent and Electrolux's 15 percent market share.[32]

Since Whirlpool was largely unknown to European consumers, the company undertook a pan-European advertising campaign costing some $110 million over several years. The advertising was the result of some exhaustive testing of housewives in the United Kingdom, France, Spain, and Austria. Two test campaigns were not universally accepted, forcing Whirlpool to develop a new campaign that was based on features that had tested positive in both test campaigns.[33] The introductory TV spot featured a woman and her son moving through an ultramodern, computer-animated house from one electric appliance to another while a voice-over described the economic and ecological advantages of using Philips Whirlpool and its reliability. However, some parts of the commercials had to be reshot to account for different washing machine configurations in Europe: the French and Finnish versions show top-loading washers, the others feature front-loaders.[34]

The TV campaign was to use the same ads in eleven countries. The strategy was to combine Philips' reputation for reliability with the U.S. firm's image of innovation and eventually create a pan-European brand recognition that would completely phase out the Philips name by 1998. The phase-out is planned to take place country by country, depending on how fast Whirlpool can establish its own identity.[35]

31. ''Man in the Green Box Sells 7UP in World Markets,'' *Advertising Age,* May 19, 1975, p. 25.
32. ''Whirlpool Striving to Clean Up Europe,'' *Advertising Age,* March 5, 1990, p. 30.
33. ''Women of Europe Put Whirlpool in a Spin,'' *Financial Times,* March 1, 1990, p. 11a.
34. ''Whirlpool Striving,'' p. 30.
35. ''Whirlpool Seeks European Identity,'' *Financial Times,* January 13, 1990, p. 10.

To aid the prospective customer in identifying the advertised product with the actual one placed in retail stores, consumer products manufacturers in particular aim at packages that are of standardized appearance. Despite differences in sizes, these packages carry the same design in terms of color, layout, and name. Nonstandardized packages cannot be featured in a standardized campaign, of course. Naturally, this concern is of much greater interest to consumer products companies because the package has to double both as a protective and as a promotional device.

Because products may be at different stages of their product life cycles in different countries, a need for different types of advertising may emerge due to the various levels of customer awareness. Typically, a campaign during the earlier stages of the product life cycle concentrates on the product category since many prospective customers may not have heard about it. In later stages, with more intensive competition, the campaign tends to shift toward emphasizing the product's advantages over competitive products.

Consider the experience of Procter & Gamble when advertising first became available in former East Germany.[36] P&G developed a series of advertisements for TV that feature specific information on a product's function rather than the typical ads situated in lifestyle situations aired for West German consumers. The company found that consumer products such as fabric softeners, liquid detergents, and household cleaners were misused and the reusable containers intended to cut down on garbage were given to children as toys. The company expected that at some future time it would be able to air the same TV commercials throughout reunited Germany.

As companies enter new markets, they can expect to find different competitive situations that require an adjustment in the advertising campaign. Competing with a different group of companies and being placed in the position of an outsider often demand a change from the advertising policy used in the domestic market, where these firms tend to have a strong position. The French company, Source Perrier, entered the U.S. market with its Perrier mineral water by using a snob appeal. Emphasizing the product's noncaloric attributes, Perrier was positioned as an alternative to soft drinks or alcoholic beverages. With a premium price, Perrier was geared toward more-affluent adults.[37] In European markets, where Perrier was well entrenched and the drinking of mineral water accepted by a vast number of consumers, such an approach would not have yielded the same results.

Suntory, the leading Japanese whiskey distiller, dominates its domestic market with about a 60 percent market share. When entering the United States, however, the company also chose the snob appeal for people who looked for something special. Suntory's print advertising promoted its whiskey as ''slightly east of Scotch.'' This campaign was specifically created for the U.S. market and differed substantially from Suntory's Japanese advertising, which included a substantial amount of television commercials.[38]

36. ''Lifestyle Ads Irk East Europeans,'' *Advertising Age,* October 8, 1990, p. 56.
37. ''Perrier: The Astonishing Success of an Appeal to Affluent Adults,'' *Business Week,* January 22, 1979, p. 64.
38. ''The Liquor Industry's Aggressive New Ad Blitz,'' *Business Week,* March 20, 1978, p. 174.

A U.S. company that found itself in the role of an outsider in foreign markets was Anheuser-Busch. The largest U.S. beer brewer started to invade several foreign markets with tailor-made campaigns. In both Germany and France, the company promoted its beer as "the beer for the men of the West."[39] This campaign took into account the company's situation as a newcomer competing against highly reputed local brewers.

These three examples show companies with solid leadership positions at home entering foreign markets as outsiders. They were forced by this circumstance to develop advertising programs substantially different from those used in their home markets.

Land of the Soft Sell: Advertising in the Japanese Market

Japan is the world's second-largest advertising market, with a total of $28 million (in 1988) and growing at a faster rate than most other markets.[40] Advertising accounted for 1.2 percent of GNP in 1988, still behind the 2.5 percent for the United States.[41] The dominant style of advertising in Japan used a subtle approach of "soft sell" compared to the "hard sell" typical in the United States or the "wit" prevalent in the United Kingdom.[42]

Given different cultural backgrounds, it is quite normal to expect differences in advertising appeals due to varying consumer attitudes. Japan offers several examples that contrast with experiences in the United States or Europe. In Japan, consumers tend to be moved more by emotion than by logic, in contrast to North Americans or Europeans.[43] According to Gregory Clark, a European teaching at Sophia University in Tokyo, the Japanese are culturally oriented to consider the mood, style, and sincerity demonstrated by a deed more important than its content. Consequently, consumers are searching for ways to be emotionally convinced about a product. This leads to advertising that rarely mentions price, occasionally even omits the actual features or qualities of a product, and shies away from competitive advertising aimed at competing firms. This type of advertising is further supported by the Japanese language, which even has a verb *(kawasarern)* to describe the process of being convinced to buy a product contrary to one's own rational judgment.

Some differences are further elaborated by James Herendeen, an American executive working for one of the largest Japanese advertising agencies, Dai-Ichi Kikaku.[44] Japanese advertising has a strong nonverbal component; uses a contemporary Japanese language; frequently shows man-woman, mother-child, or even father-daughter relationships; demonstrates Japanese humor; and above all stresses long-term relationships. There is also

39. "Anheuser Tries Light Beer Again," *Business Week,* June 29, 1981, p. 136.

40. "Where Global Ambitions Come Unstuck," *Financial Times,* February 1, 1990, p. 9.

41. "Land of the Hardening Sell," *Economist,* September 10, 1988, p. 89.

42. "In the Land of the Soft Sell," *Financial Times,* February 9, 1990, p. 20.

43. "Emotion, Not Logic, Sways the Japanese Consumer," *Japan Economic Journal,* April 22, 1980, p. 24.

44. James Herendeen, "How to Japanize Your Creative," *International Advertiser,* September–October 1980, p. 22.

some evidence of the individual's place in Japanese society in the use of evocative pictures or events to indicate individual values. With respect to the emotional tendency, Herendeen suggests the use of nonverbal communication or things that lead to inference rather than direct understanding. Also important is the product origin and the need to present the product as being right for the Japanese. This requires a strong corporate identity program to establish a firm's credibility in the Japanese market.

Research conducted for the Nikkei Advertising Research Institute in Japan on advertising expressions used in Japan, South Korea, Taiwan, the United States, and France showed the high degree of nonverbal communication in Asia.[45] The study found that sentences of less than four phrases or words appeared in 50.1 percent of Japanese ads, 81.6 percent in Korea, 80.6 percent in Taiwan, but only 22.6 percent in the United States and 21.3 percent in France. The same study also compared the number of foreign words appearing in advertising headlines. Japan, with 39.2 percent, used the highest number of foreign words, followed by Taiwan with 32.1 percent, Korea with 15.7 percent, and France with 9.1 percent. The United States used foreign words in only 1.8 percent of the headlines investigated. This underlines the strong Japanese interest in foreign countries and words, particularly those of the English language. A later study confirmed the Japanese preference for less-wordy advertising copy and a greater reliance on mood or symbolism.[46]

The need for a strong corporate image was emphasized in an annual survey of leading Japanese and foreign firms.[47] Table 15.1 contains the ratings for both domestic and foreign-based food manufacturers active in the Japanese market. The Japanese firms with high ratings tended to be of long standing, technologically superior, diversified, and employing high-quality personnel. Japanese consumers tended to buy these companies' products even if prices were high. The products were also used as gifts. The need for a strong corporate image also exists in the Japanese industrial goods market.

Although one may conclude that U.S. products do not sell in Japan, the reality shows that this is not necessarily so. Japanese television commercials are full of U.S. themes, use many U.S. stars or heroes, and frequently have U.S. landscapes or backgrounds. By using U.S. stars in their commercials, Japanese companies give the impression that these products are very popular in the United States.

Given the Japanese interest in and positive attitudes toward many U.S. cultural themes, such strategies have worked out well for Japanese advertisers. This is why Nissan asked Paul Newman to drive its new car, Skyline, in its ads and why John Travolta was asked to appear in an ad sipping a new semialcoholic fruit juice.[48] When Mitsubishi Electric paid rock singer Madonna a reported $650,000 for the right to use fragments of a rock tour, the company's VCR sales doubled in three months, whereas competitors experienced

45. *Japan Economic Journal,* December 23, 1980, p. 33.

46. Jae W. Hong, Aydin Muderrisoglu, and George M. Zinkhan, "Cultural Differences and Advertising Expression: A Comparative Content Analysis of Japanese and U.S. Magazine Advertising," *Journal of Advertising,* 16, no. 1 (1987), pp. 55–62.

47. *Japan Economic Journal,* December 23, 1980, pp. 33, 34.

48. "U.S. Sets the Pace Despite Growing Pride in Things Japanese," *International Herald Tribune,* October 1, 1984, p. 12.

TABLE 15.1 ● Ranking of Food Manufacturers in Japan (Percentage of Respondents Rating Companies as Excellent)

Foreign-affiliated companies			*Japanese makers*		
1	Coca-Cola (Japan)	66.4%	1	Ajinomoto	83.7%
2	Ajinomoto General Foods	56.7	2	Snow Brand Milk Products	83.5
3	Lipton Japan	46.5	3	Suntory	82.2
4	Twinings	45.0	4	Kirin Brewery	81.6
5	Nestlé Japan	43.9	5	Morinaga Milk Ind.	80.7
6	PepsiCo (Japan)	30.7	6	Kikkoman Shoyu	77.3
7	McDonald's	29.9	7	Taiyo Fishery	71.0
8	Brookbond	27.5	8	Nippon Suisan	68.2
9	Kirin-Seagram	20.8	9	Lotte	62.8
10	Yamazaki Nabisco	20.8	10	Calpis	61.3

Source: Japan Economic Journal, December 23, 1980, p. 33. Reprinted by permission.

only a 15 percent increase.[49] Actress Faye Dunaway was paid some $900,000 by the Tokyo department store Parco for saying only, "This is an ad for Parco."[50] In contrast to U.S. testimonials, however, Japanese advertisers tend to use foreign stars as actors using the product but not openly endorsing it.

A more recent development is the use of Japanese in an international setting. This leads to the use of Japanese models or businesspeople in foreign settings, such as Matsushita's ad depicting a jazz-loving employee visiting the United States, where he is given a welcoming embrace by his friend who happens to be a black New Orleans saxophone player. Asahi, a successful Japanese brewery that launched the dry beer, used actual Japanese professionals working in the United States in a series of ads in Japan to show that "the brains created in Japan are becoming successful abroad."[51] It is part of a Japanese tendency to strive for product awareness only; advertisements are devoid of any mention of the product itself. As a result, comparative advertising rarely exists in Japan; also before-and-after claims are seldom used. According to some experts, Western advertising is designed to make the product look superior, whereas Japanese advertising is aimed at making it desirable.[52]

49. "Madonna in Japan," *Fortune,* September 15, 1986, p. 9.
50. Ibid.
51. "Tokyo TV Ads Portray Japanese as the Savvy International Type," *Wall Street Journal,* October 11, 1990, p. B6.
52. "Advertising: Upping a Youthful Image," *Financial Times,* October 22, 1986, p. VI.

Using a new approach, Dentsu developed an advertisement videogame in 1993 to help promote Ajinomoto mayonnaise. The game, played on a Nintendo Famizan machine, includes three adventures and a kitchen. After completing the adventures, the participants enter the kitchen, where they use utensils and food ingredients, including Ajinimoto products, to prepare foods. The videogame is meant to be used with children and mothers to develop a long-term preference for Ajinomoto's brand.[53]

Advertising in Japan has differed also from western practice in its management and structure. In Japan, the conflict of interest rules did not apply, and competing brands could be handled by the same agency. The market was dominated by Dentsu, by far Japan's largest agency and one of the world's largest advertising agencies. Dentsu is the Japanese media's largest single customer, accounting for some 20 percent of all newspaper ads and about 15 percent of all TV advertising. As such, Dentsu usually commands the best price and the best space in the press.[54] None of the other major advertising markets in the world is dominated by a single local agency.

The Impact of Recent Changes in Eastern Europe

With the political changes in eastern Europe, advertising suddenly became available to foreign companies and is developing as an acceptable economic activity. It has been hampered by the fact that commercial advertising as known in the open economies had been used largely for political purposes and to advertise excess goods. In Hungary, Procter & Gamble replaced its campaign for Blend-a-Med toothpaste because the claim ''Reduces cavities by 80 percent'' reminded consumers of the false statements used by the Communists.[55] When the markets in eastern Europe opened up, changes had to come both in the media policy of these countries and in the acceptability of advertising.

Residents of East Germany had been exposed to advertising through access to West German TV and some publications. However, because East German residents had little exposure to some of these new consumer goods, the approach to advertising there was usually different than that for the same company in West Germany.[56] Ford purchased one-minute TV commercials in each of the forty-one soccer world championship games aired in East Germany. Ford's approach for East Germany was less creative than its approach for West Germany, described as a ''down-to-earth good commercial.'' Many companies about to launch their products in East Germany had to postpone advertising efforts until distribution to local residents was assured.

In other eastern European nations, advertising is likewise in the early phases of development. The present infrastructure is radically different from what international firms are

53. David Kilburn, ''Dentsu Already Deep into Interactive,'' *Advertising Age,* November 1, 1993, p. 22.

54. ''In the Land,'' p. 20.

55. ''Road to E. Europe Paved with Marketing Mistakes,'' *Advertising Age International,* October 26, 1992, p. I-21.

56. ''E. Germany Gets New Ad Efforts,'' *Advertising Age,* July 2, 1990, p. 4.

used to. Few full-service advertising agencies exist. Many western agencies are now developing local offices, some as joint ventures with local managers.

In Hungary, about 150 advertising agencies are said to exist. About 100 of those have been formed since the early 1980s. Total advertising spending is estimated at no more than $140 million (1990). Of the top ten agencies, four are government owned, including the top two. The other six have foreign partners, including some leading international agencies such as McCann-Erickson since 1988. Some of these joint ventures are expected to be turned into wholly owned agencies in the near future. These agencies attract both Hungarian and international companies.[57] The liberalization of the Hungarian economy has also brought new media. Aside from the opening of local print, *Business Week* and *Playboy* were two among many international publications offering Hungarian-language editions and accepting print advertising.[58]

Nowhere have the changes been more pronounced than in the former Soviet Union. The Soviet government had decided only in February 1988 that marketing would become a priority under perestroika.[59] Total advertising spending in the Soviet Union by foreign companies was estimated at only $10 million annually, with most of it going toward trade fairs.[60] Outside posters and neon signs were among the first signs of advertising to appear, with Samsung and Goldstar, both of South Korea, among the first firms to pay the $200,000 in annual fees for two spots in Moscow or Leningrad.[61]

As eastern European markets make the transition from communism to capitalism, there are some significant opportunities to build brand awareness quickly. For example, only 5 percent of Russians could name Snickers as a candy bar in 1992. One year later, after a campaign featuring the Rolling Stones' ''(I Can't Get No) Satisfaction,'' 82 percent could name Snickers.[62] As Russia's population of 218 million citizens grows more prosperous, the opportunities for consumer products will grow.

Procter & Gamble is exporting several brands to Russia, among them Crest toothpaste and Camay soap. Colgate Palmolive, one of the world leaders in toothpaste, is importing Colgate toothpaste from an Indian company. Both companies can sell whatever they can ship.[63] Colgate had previously given away hundreds of thousands of toothpaste samples. When the company exhibited in a trade show in Moscow and gave away free samples, local residents stood in line for two hours. Many were reported to have returned to the end of the line for another sample. With strong interest among international firms to even-

57. ''Western Ad Agencies Push into Hungary,'' *Advertising Age,* June 11, 1990, p. 43.

58. ''Playboy Shifts Image in Hungary,'' *Advertising Age,* August 6, 1990, p. 24; ''*Business Week* to Break into Hungary,'' *Advertising Age,* March 12, 1990, p. 56.

59. ''UK Helps to Make Advertising and Promotion a Priority of Perestroika,'' *Financial Times,* December 8, 1988, p. 12.

60. ''Look but Don't Touch,'' *Economist,* June 16, 1990, p. 118.

61. ''UK Helps to Make.''

62. ''In Moscow, the Attack of the Killer Brands,'' *Business Week,* January 10, 1994, p. 40.

63. ''Colgate, P&G Pack for Road to Russia,'' *Advertising Age,* March 12, 1990, p. 56.

tually be present in the large Russian consumer market, several international advertising agencies have set up shop in Moscow, Young & Rubicam and Ogilvy & Mather among them.

Global Advertising

Global advertising received a considerable amount of attention in the 1980s and is now considered the most controversial topic in international advertising. The debate was triggered by Professor Theodore Levitt, who argues in an article and in his book, *The Marketing Imagination,* that markets are becoming increasingly alike worldwide and that the trend is toward a global approach to marketing.[64]

Interestingly, a study of 605 European consumers found that, while there was a strong preference for global products, consumers preferred advertising for local products. In many cases, the most memorable ads were of local brands, but the preferred product was a foreign brand! This indicates that more than advertising is needed to influence consumer behavior.[65]

Levitt's ideas were applied to the field of international advertising by Saatchi & Saatchi, a British advertising agency that rose to prominence on the basis of its global campaigns.[66] Saatchi & Saatchi claimed that worldwide brands would soon become the norm and that such an advertising challenge could only be handled by worldwide agencies. One such advertising campaign, for Procter & Gamble's Pampers, has been used successfully throughout the world.

Proponents of global advertising cite several trends as indicators of what the future of international advertising will be.[67] Consumer tastes, needs, and purchasing patterns are said to be converging. This can be supported by the converging trends in demographics across many countries. At the forefront of these trends has been the decline of the nuclear family, both in North America and in many countries around the globe. In most countries, more women are working. Similarly, divorce trends are increasingly pointing in the same direction in North America, Europe, and other developed countries. This has changed the role of women in society almost everywhere.

Standards of living have risen in many countries, and earlier differences among nations have been reduced. In addition to these demographic trends, common media such as films, television, and music are creating cultural convergence as well. These developments are said to reduce cultural barriers among countries; such barriers are expected to

64. Theodore Levitt, ''The Globalization of Markets,'' *Harvard Business Review,* May–June 1983, p. 92; *The Marketing Imagination* (New York: Free Press, 1983); *International Herald Tribune,* October 1, 1984, p. 7 (interview with Theodore Levitt).

65. Nancy Giges, ''Europeans Buy Outside Goods, but Like Local Ads,'' *Advertising Age International,* April 27, 1992, p. I-1.

66. ''Saatchi & Saatchi Will Keep Gobbling,'' *Fortune,* June 23, 1986, p. 36.

67. ''Advertising by Saatchi & Saatchi Compton,'' *New York Times,* January 22, 1984, p. 87.

be reduced even more through satellite television networks covering many countries with identical programs.

One of the stronger believers in global advertising, British Airways, broke new ground in its industry by airing the well-known "Manhattan" TV commercial in 1983. Designed by Saatchi & Saatchi, the spot showed the flight across the Atlantic and the landing on the island of Manhattan as an expression of British Airways flying as many passengers annually across the Atlantic as people lived in Manhattan. In 1989, the same advertising agency designed a new global campaign for British Airways, featuring some four thousand people greeting each other and interspersed with the creation of a smiling face when viewed from the air. The commercial was produced in the U.S. Midwest and directed by a well-known movie director. The company believes that the strong visual value allows it to use the production everywhere, resulting in a global campaign production cost of about half the traditional cost of creating advertising for each market.[68]

Researchers who studied 2,628 global advertisements found visual ads were more universally understood. Visuals have the obvious advantage of not being culturally specific. The researchers also found that most global ads are linked to the brand with the visual image helping to register the brand in the consumer's mind.[69]

For a global strategy to be successful, experience indicates that four requirements must be fulfilled. First, the product must be able to deliver the same benefit in each market. Second, the market or the product category development in each market must be at the same level in terms of product life cycle, penetration, and usage. Third, the competitive environment must be similar in each market. This refers to the type of competition and the nature of the competitive products encountered. And fourth, the heritage of the brand must not be restricted to particular countries, and the brand history must be similar in the various markets.[70]

Many marketing professionals are skeptical about the claims for global advertising.[71] However, many observers agree that global marketing may be an advantage for products aimed at the very affluent market in many countries, because these highly affluent and mobile consumers can be thought of as living in a global village.[72] Products included may range from diamonds to whiskey to very expensive watches. Because of the many local differences that become evident in making up a global advertising campaign, many advertising agency executives remain dubious about the prospect for large-scale global advertising. Instead, more-regionalized approaches, such as for Europe or for Asia, may be more appropriate at this time than going directly to a global approach.[73]

68. "BA's Warm Approach," *Financial Times,* December 28, 1989, p. 8.

69. M. Roland Jeannet, "Global Advertising," presentation made at 1988 Annual Conference of UK Advertising Agency Planners, London, 1988.

70. Jerome B. Kernan and Teresa J. Domzal, "International Advertising: To Globalize, Visualize," *Journal of International Consumer Marketing* 5, no. 4 (1993), pp. 51–71.

71. "Global Marketing Debated," *New York Times,* November 13, 1985, p. D21.

72. Rena Bartos, "And What About the Consumer Who Brushes His Teeth with Shampoo?" *International Herald Tribune,* October 1, 1984, p. 8.

73. "Prof. Real World's Lesson for Levitt," *Advertising Age,* January 6, 1986, p. 17.

A number of companies have begun the process of developing regional or global brands:

● Campbell Biscuits Europe has launched Biscuits Maison in France, Germany, Belgium, and the Netherlands.[74]

● Grand Metropolitan is promoting Burger King, Green Giant, and Häagen Dazs worldwide.[75]

● Fuji Photo Film and Nissan are both developing pan-European brands.[76]

● Johnson & Johnson has established a joint venture with Merck to launch Dolormin, an ibuprofen analgesic, as a Eurobrand.[77]

● Revlon has begun to develop a global name for all its products.[78]

● Helena Rubenstein, for its new line of suncare products, is using a single campaign in eighty-three countries.[79]

What may be more likely to happen is a modularized approach to international advertising. A company may select some features as standard for all its advertising while localizing some others. Pepsi-Cola chose this approach in its 1986 international campaign. The company wanted to use modern music in connection with its products while still using some local identification. As a result, with the assistance of Ogilvy & Mather, its advertising agency, Pepsi-Cola hired the U.S. singer Tina Turner, who teamed up in a big concert setting with local rock stars from six countries singing and performing the Pepsi-Cola theme song. In the commercials, the local rock stars are shown together with Tina Turner. Except for the footage of the local stars, all the commercials are identical. For other countries, local rock stars are spliced into the footage so that they also appear to be on stage with Tina Turner. By shooting the commercials all at once, the company saved in production costs. The overall concept of the campaign can be extended to some thirty countries without forcing local subsidiaries or bottlers to come up with their own campaigns.[80]

74. ''Unification Spurs Multinational Intros in Europe,'' *Advertising Age International,* January 18, 1993, p. I-3.

75. ''How Martin Sees Grand Met's Global Role,'' *Advertising Age International,* April 27, 1992, p. I-1.

76. ''Japan Rethinks Branding in Europe,'' *Advertising Age,* July 13, 1993, p. S-1.

77. ''J&J, Merck Ready First Euro Brand,'' *Advertising Age International,* October 26, 1992, p. I-1.

78. ''Revlon Eyes Global Image; Picks Y&R,'' *Advertising Age,* January 11, 1993, p. 1.

79. ''From Cookies to Appliances Pan-Euro. Efforts Build,'' *Advertising Age International,* June 22, 1992, p. I-1.

80. ''Advertising: Tina Turner Helping Pepsi's Global Effort,'' *New York Times,* March 10, 1986, p. D13.

Global companies are finding that advertising jingles that become hit singles in the United States often become popular in other countries, therefore providing support for the brand. For example, the Coke theme song "First Time" became popular in the United States and then Europe, helping to boost global sales.[81]

Media Selections

The international marketer is faced with a variety of media across the world. Difficulties arise because not all media are available in all countries; if they are available, their technical quality or capability to deliver to the required audience may be limited. Therefore, aside from the considerations that concern domestic operations, international media decisions are influenced by the availability or accessibility of various media for advertisers and the media habits of the target country.

Media Availability

Advertisers in North America have become accustomed to the availability of a full range of media for advertising purposes. Aside from the traditional print media, consisting of newspapers and magazines, the North American advertiser has access to radio and television as well as billboards and cinemas. In addition, direct mail is available to any prospective client group.

Commercial radio is not available in Norway, Denmark, Sweden, Finland, Switzerland, Saudi Arabia, or many of the former eastern bloc countries. In Norway, Denmark, Sweden, and Saudi Arabia, not even commercial television is available for advertisers.[82] Consequently, a company marketing its products in several countries may find itself unable to apply the same media mix in all markets. Even when some media are available, access may be partially restricted. The use of commercials interspersed throughout programs on radio or television is common in North America, Japan, and Latin America, among others, but less so in Europe. In Germany, advertisers have access to commercial television only during a few blocks of time, several minutes long at several time slots.[83] Because the commercials are not shown at frequent intervals as interruptions to TV programming, viewership of these preannounced commercial blocks tends to be very low. In addition, the time available for commercials is limited to forty minutes daily. For the most preferred block on German television, the evening program, less than half of the firms applying will ever be able to obtain media time. Therefore some firms have avoided television altogether because they were unable to obtain frequent showings, which are necessary for a successful

81. "It's Got a Good Beat, You Can Dance to It and It Sells Coke," *Wall Street Journal,* August 20, 1993, p. A7B.

82. International Advertising Research Associates, *Fifteenth Survey of Advertising Expenditures in 1983* (New York: INRA, 1985).

83. "Werbung: Bis Zum Spaten Abend," *Der Spiegel,* November 22, 1981, p. 81.

campaign. In some countries, the available time for commercials is allocated for various product groups, often regardless of the number of competitors or products on the market. For some competitive product categories, new products may only be launched by reallocating a company's television time among its existing products. This lack of flexibility inhibits new product introduction in some consumer product categories where television would be the most efficient advertising medium.

Existing government regulations have also had a substantial impact on how much television advertising is used. In Europe, television time is freely available in the United Kingdom, Greece, Ireland, Portugal, Spain, and Italy.[84] In Italy, the breakup of the state monopoly resulted in the creation of several hundred commercial television stations alone.[85] In those countries, television advertising equals 30 to 50 percent of the print advertising volume. In European countries with restricted or limited access, television advertising amounts to 5 to 20 percent of the total amount spent on print advertising. In Sweden, television advertising is not allowed, and all advertising is in print (see Table 15.2).

The European market has changed significantly with the advent of satellite and cable TV, which offers significant competition to the two or three state-controlled stations in each country. In 1980, there were approximately 40 channels throughout the European Union; now there are 150 channels. The television advertising market has grown from $3.0 billion, or 15 percent of total advertising, in 1980 to $25.0 billion, or 29 percent of total advertising, in 1993.[86]

The growth of Asian economies and the opening of the eastern bloc have rapidly increased the size of the global television market. The breakdown of the one billion televisions in use follows:[87]

Europe and former Soviet Union	350,000
Asia	320,000
North America and Caribbean	200,000
Latin America	80,000
Middle East	40,000
Africa	10,000

The availability of media may also be limited by law. Most countries do not allow advertising for cigarettes or alcoholic beverages on television or radio, though they are usually permitted in print media. When the leading Japanese whiskey distiller Suntory entered the U.S. market, the company had to do without television, its preferred medium.[88] In Japan, Suntory had been estimated to have spent about $50 million annually on television advertising because no restrictions existed with respect to alcoholic beverages there.

84. "European Ads' Potential 'Vast,' " *Financial Times,* March 24, 1983, p. 10.
85. "U.S. Style TV Turns on Europe," *Fortune,* April 13, 1987, p. 95.
86. "Wired Planet," *Economist,* February 12, 1994, p. 12, Special section, A Survey of Television.
87. "Television—What if They're Right?" *Economist,* February 12, 1994, p. 4, Special section, A Survey of Television.
88. "The Liquor Industry's Aggressive New Ad Blitz," *Business Week,* March 20, 1978, p. 174.

TABLE 15.2 ● Guide to Advertising in Twenty-Two Countries

	Australia	Austria	Belgium	Brazil
Total advertising expenditure 1979	1,482 million	7,900 million	9,500 million	50,700 million
Local currency	Dollar	Shilling	Franc	Cruzeiro
Total expressed as a % of gross national product	1.46%	0.88%	0.3%	0.95%
Breakdown of advertising expenditure by principal media (% of total)				
TV	30.3	16.5	12.8	42.0
National press	10.6		31.0	
Regional press	29.4	25.3	10.8	22.5
Magazines/periodicals	7.6		28.7	9.5
Trade and technical	2.6	In "other"		
Radio	8.8	6.5	1.2	16.0
Cinema	1.6	0.3	1.2	0.5
Outdoor	9.1	4.2	14.3	3.5
Other	NA	47.2	NA	6.0
Proportion of households with TV sets	96%	91%	93%	54%
Proportion of households with color TVs	75%	44%	50%	30%
Number of TV channels accepting advertising/sponsorship	50	2	None but RTL Luxembourg is received	89
Advertising time in 24-hour period (approximate minutes)	154	20	62 (RTL)	360
Restrictions on TV advertising	No cigarettes	No tobacco, hard liquor; regulated drugs and foods; restrictions on children's advertising	No tobacco, alcohol	No alcohol, cigarettes, cigars, until 9 P.M.
	−DM, PC, PC	+DM, −AC, PC	−DM, PC, +AC	+DM, AC, PC

Note: NA = not available. * = insignificant amount. 0 = medium not used. DM = direct mail. AC = agency commission. PC = production cost.

Source: From William J. Hawkes' presentation of A. C. Nielsen Company material at the International Marketing Workshop AMA/MSI, March 1983. Reprinted by permission of A. C. Nielsen Company.

Canada	Switzerland	Germany	Spain	Ireland	France
3.008 million	981 million	10,786 million	64,800 million	45.1 million	17,400 million
Dollar	Franc	D. Mark	Peseta	Punt	Franc
1.16%	0.6%	0.8%	0.5%	0.6%	0.83%
16.6	12.1	9.6	33.0	32.1	9.5
*	55.9	48.1 }	29.4	32.6 }	
28.6	NA }			7.9 }	17.5
17.9	32.0 }	18.4 }	16.9	1.5 }	
19.1	NA	* }		* }	21.1
11.4	0	3.3	12.3	9.9	6.5
0	NA	0.8	1.9	*	1.0
6.4	NA	3.6	6.5	6.0	9.3
*	NA	16.2	NA	*	35.2
97%	84%	85%	95%	85%	92%
81%	53%	62%	30%	32%	33%
95	3	2	2	2	2
216 per channel	60	40	85	85	48
No cigarettes, liquor; regional restrictions on beer and children's advertising	No alcohol, tobacco, drugs, politics, religion	No cigarettes, religion, charities, narcotics, prescription drugs, children's advertising, cures	No tobacco, hard drinks	No tobacco, contraceptives, religion, politics	Many categories are excluded: alcohol, margarine, slimming products, tobacco products, etc.
+DM, PC, −AC	−DM, AC, PC	+DM, −AC, PC	−DM, AC, PC	−DM, AC, PC	+DM, AC, −PC

TABLE 15.2 ● Guide to Advertising in Twenty-Two Countries (*Continued*)

	Great Britain	Greece	Italy	Japan	Mexico
Total advertising expenditure 1979	2,219 million	3,735.6 million	1,186 billion	2,113 billion	9,660 million
Local currency	Pound	Drachma	Lira	Yen	Peso
Total expressed as a % of gross national product	1.34%	0.32%	0.35%	0.95%	0.36%
Breakdown of advertising expenditure by principal media (% of total)					
TV	22.1	46.4	19	35.5	65.0
National press			24	31.0	8.0
Regional press	48.0	27.8			NA
Magazines/periodicals			53	5.3	4.0
Trade and technical	22.3	20.0	NA	In "other"	1.0
Radio	2.4	4.6	4	5.0	15.0
Cinema	0.8	NA	NA	In "other"	4.0
Outdoor	4.4	1.1	NA	In "other"	2.5
Other	NA	NA	NA	23.1	0.5
Proportion of households with TV sets	94%	95%	96%	98%	43.8%
Proportion of households with color TVs	65%	5%	27%	96%	None
Number of TV channels accepting advertising/sponsorship	1	2	2+ many private stations	93	15
Advertising time in 24-hour period (approximate minutes)	80	120	27, excluding private stations	230	12 hours/ station
Restrictions on TV advertising	No contraceptives, cigarettes, politics, gambling, religion, or charities	No cigarettes, prescription drugs	No jewels, furs, newspapers, magazines, cigarettes, gambling, clinics and hospitals	No overstatement, comparison with competitors, sensual messages on commercial films	No liquor before 10 P.M.
	−DM, +AC, PC	−DM, PC, +AC	−DM, PC, +AC	+DM, AC, PC	−DM, PC, +AC

Netherlands	New Zealand	Portugal	Argentina	Sweden	United States	South Africa
3,825 million	195.5 million	1,462.5 million	1,028 billion	2,004 million	49,690 million	290 million
Florin	Dollar	Escudo	Peso	Kronar	Dollar	Rand
1.29%	1.12%	0.2%	1.27%	0.46%	2.1%	1.8% (GDP)
5.0	25.4	55	24.6	0	20.5	19.3
46.9	0			36	4.2	35.3
	48.1	29	42.3	41	25.1	4.1
8.7	6.6			16	5.9	16.3
3.6	NA		15.7		3.4	6.5
0.7	8.2	16	9.0	0	6.6	12.0
0.3	1.2	NA	1.4	1	0	2.1
6.1	0.3	NA	6.1	5	1.1	4.4
28.7	10.2	NA	0.9	NA	33.2	NA
97%	95%	NA	86%	93%	98%	26.5%
65%	70%	NA	18%	71%	83%	18.4%
2	2	2	38	None	728	1
30	260	30	10 hours/channel	0	Voluntary code: hour/station	24
No tobacco, political, religion; special legislation for pharmaceuticals, sweets, alcohol	No cigarettes, alcohol, feminine hygiene products, contraceptives, politics	No tobacco, gambling; liquor only after 9 P.M.; restrictions on medicines	No use of foreign words or slang; no attitudes against morals; no misuse of country symbols	NA	No tobacco, contraceptives, fortune tellers	No Sunday advertising; no spirits, wine, beer, cigarettes after 9 P.M. except Saturday; no "sensitive" products
+DM, AC, −PC	+DM, AC, +PC	−DM, PC, +AC		−DM	+DM, AC, PC	−DM, AC, PC

These examples demonstrate that, on an international basis, companies have to remain flexible with respect to their media plans. A company cannot expect to be able to use its preferred medium to the fullest extent everywhere. Consequently, international advertising campaigns will have to be designed with delivery over several media in mind.

Credibility of Advertising

Countries view the value of advertising in very different ways. In the United States, one study found that about two-thirds of the population felt abused by advertising.[89] In the United Kingdom, approval amounted to about 77 percent. In eastern Europe, where TV commercials were used to sell products generally considered too shoddy to sell, consumers became skeptical of advertising in general. This skepticism was enhanced by the fact that the former communist regimes frequently used advertising for propaganda purposes, thus undermining its credibility.[90]

In other countries, particularly those of the developing world, advertising tends to be held in much higher regard. Advertised products have more prestige, and those advertised on television are viewed by consumers as the most prestigious.

Differences in the credibility of advertising in general, and some media in particular, will have to be taken into consideration by the international firm. Companies may want to place a greater reliance on advertising in countries where its credibility is very high. In other countries, the use of alternative forms of communication may be stressed.

Media Habits

As the experienced media buyer for any domestic market knows, the media habits of the target market are a major factor in deciding which media to use. The same applies on the international level. However, substantial differences in media habits exist due to a number of factors that are of little importance to the domestic or single-country operation. First of all, the penetration of various media differs substantially from one country to another. Second, advertisers encounter radically different literacy rates in many parts of the world. And finally, they may find different cultural habits or traits that favor one medium over another regardless of the penetration ratios or literacy rates.

Ownership or usage of television, radio, newspapers, and magazines varies substantially from one country to another. Whereas the developed industrial nations show high penetration ratios for all three major media carriers, other countries of the Third World have few radio and television receivers or low newspaper circulation (see Table 15.2). In general, the use or penetration of all of these media increases with the average income of a country. In most countries, the higher income classes avail themselves first of the electronic media and newspapers. International marketers have to be aware that some media,

89. "Are Ads Your Favorite Reading?" *Economist,* September 5, 1981, p. 31.
90. "Lifestyle Ads," p. 56.

though generally accessible for the advertiser, may be only of limited use since they reach only a small part of the country's target population.

The literacy of a country's population is an important factor influencing media decisions. Though this is less of a concern for companies in the industrial products market, it is a crucial factor in consumer goods advertising. In countries where large portions of the population are illiterate, the use of print media is of limited value. (Please see Table 3.2 for literacy rates of selected countries.) Both radio and television have been used by companies to circumvent the literacy problem. Other media that are occasionally used for this purpose are billboards and cinemas. The absence of a high level of literacy has forced consumer goods companies to translate their advertising campaigns into media and messages that communicate strictly by sound or demonstration. Television and radio have been used most successfully to overcome this problem, but they cannot be used in areas where the penetration of such receivers is limited. Frequently, this applies particularly to countries that have low electronic media penetration and low literacy rates.

In most developed countries, detailed statistics available to advertisers document the time people spend in contact with any given medium. A survey conducted by A. C. Nielsen in 1980 determined that the average family in Tokyo, Japan, used a television set for eight hours and twelve minutes a day.[91] The corresponding figure for the United States amounted to six hours and four minutes. The difference between the U.S. and Japanese attitudes becomes even more apparent in a poll conducted in both countries.[92] People were asked which of the following items they would keep if they had to make do with all but one: television, newspapers, telephone, automobile, and refrigerator. The answers were as follows:

	United States	*Japan*
Television	3%	31%
Newspapers	6	23
Telephone	9	16
Automobile	39	15
Refrigerator	42	13

Consequently, 31 percent of the polled Japanese would rather give up all other four items to keep their television, whereas only 3 percent of the Americans felt that way.

In both the United States and Europe, viewership of television appears on the decline. This has caused some companies to make adjustments in the media mix for those areas. In other countries, particularly those of the Third World, media habits are rapidly shifting toward electronic media as ownership of radio and television receivers is becoming more common. For a more detailed summary of media habits in various countries, see Table 15.3.

91. *International Herald Tribune,* July 26, 1982.
92. Ibid.

TABLE 15.3 ● Advertising Expenditure Survey

1989 total advertising expenditure (current prices in local currency)			PRINT	TV	RADIO	CINEMA	OUTDOOR/ TRANSIT
			Percentage distribution of measured media				
Austria	10,535	(m AS)	55.1	30.4	13.5	1.0	NA
Belgium	47,095	(m BF)	57.3	28.8	0.9	1.8	11.1
Denmark	7,569	(m DKr)	87.9	8.1	1.4	0.7	1.8
Finland	5,136	(m FIM)	80.6	13.0	3.8	0.1	2.5
France	55,311	(m FF)	50.3	28.0	7.7	0.9	13.1
Germany	22,616	(m DM)	80.6	11.2	4.1	1.0	3.1
Greece	57,001	(m Dra)	45.1	40.8	7.3	0	6.8
Ireland	173	(m punt)	52.6	29.9	10.4	0	7.2
Italy	6,276	(bn lire)	42.8	51.5	1.6	0	4.1
Japan	5,072	(bn yen)	43.1	37.2	5.3	0	14.5
Netherlands	7,932	(m FL)	83.8	11.6	2.2	0.3	2.1
Norway	4,745	(m NKr)	94.3	1.6	0.8	1.2	2.1
Portugal	45,044	(m Esc)	37.0	47.6	8.8	0	6.6
Spain	860,000	(m Ptas)	52.9	30.1	11.1	0.8	5.1
Sweden	12,907	(m SKr)	94.3	0	0	0.9	4.8
Switzerland	4,776	(m SF)	75.7	7.5	2.0	1.1	13.7
United Kingdom	8,313	(m £)	63.6	30.3	2.1	0.5	3.6
U.S.A.	123,930	(m $)	58.1	31.0	2.1	0.5	3.6

Source: From *World Advertising Expenditures 1989,* Twenty-Fourth Survey (Marmaroneck, NY: Stardon Inra Hooper, 1989), pp. 10, 11, 42, 43.

Satellite Television

Satellite television channels, which are not subject to government regulations, have revolutionized television in many parts of the world. The impact of satellite television channels is nowhere felt more directly than in Europe.

The leader in this field of privately owned channels is Sky Channel, owned by Rupert Murdoch, who has substantial media interests in many countries. Sky Channel had reached 4.7 million homes in thirteen countries by the end of 1985, and it transmitted a maximum of seventeen hours per day. Sky claimed that about 10 percent of all TV viewers served watched its channel. About one-third of all advertising revenue was generated from U.S. companies, another one-third from Japanese, and some 20 percent from Continental

Europe. Advertisers include such well-known companies as Canon, Digital, NEC, Kodak, Mattel, Nikon, Panasonic, Ford, Toyota, Xerox, Remington, Siemens, and Unilever.[93]

Murdock purchased the Star Satellite System in 1993 for $525 million. It serves 45 million people from Egypt to Mongolia.[94] The Star System relies heavily on advertising revenue, which could reach $72 million with full use (it operated at 10 percent of this in 1992). Star's advertisers include Nike and Coca-Cola.[95]

Originally only available as English-speaking television, satellite channels are now available in several European languages, such as German, French, and Swedish. Some 42.9 million viewers tuned into satellite TV in Europe in 1989.[96] This represented a 70 percent increase over 1988. The average weekly viewing almost doubled to seven hours. One of the largest winners was CNN, with an increase of almost 184 percent.

With the advent of local-language satellite TV, more attractive than the traditional national TV channels, many viewers left the English-speaking channels of Sky and Super Channel.[97] Furthermore, satellite TV has not attracted as much advertising expenditures as first anticipated, with major advertisers only scheduling about 2 percent of their budgets on satellite TV.[98]

The presently existing satellite networks have not yet attracted a large number of advertisers. Companies still prefer an entire national audience, such as all of Germany, to a small segment throughout western Europe. However, a deal arranged between Gillette and the Murdoch group of broadcasting channels gave an indication as to what companies may be able to do in the future. In October 1986, Gillette began to air through Sky Channel in Europe. The same advertisement had been carried earlier by Murdock's Fox Broadcasting System in the United States and Network Ten, the group's Australian system. This arrangement allowed Gillette to show the same commercial in all three continents.[99]

Different firms use satellite television for different purposes. Polaroid used it to advertise its sunglasses on Super Channel, an English-language channel, to reach mostly younger people in the Netherlands. Polaroid found that the domestic Dutch TV channel reached an older audience, which was less appropriate for its products. On the other hand, Nissan used Super Channel to promote its corporate image in Europe. Nissan executives believed that the English-language channel would get superior results for the unification of its image.[100]

93. "Advertising Potential Elevated by Satellite," *Financial Times,* November 14, 1985, p. 12.

94. "Wired Planet."

95. "A Minefield of Uncertainty," *Financial Times—Cable and Satellite Broadcasting,* October 6, 1992, p. V, Special section.

96. "Europe's Satellite TV Viewers Soar," *Advertising Age,* September 24, 1990, p. 39.

97. "Auf Wiedersehen, Roops," *Economist,* September 17, 1988, p. 80.

98. "Satellite Broadcasting: Healthy Long-Term Outlook," *Financial Times,* March 14, 1989, p. V.

99. "Advertising: Global Network Beams Nearer," *Financial Times,* October 22, 1986, p. IV.

100. "Super Channel: A Test for the Global Concept," *Financial Times,* February 17, 1987, p. 11.

For satellite-shown commercials to be effective, companies have to be able to profit from a global brand name and a uniform logo. Also, language remains a problem. English is the common language of the majority of satellite channels; however, there is a trend toward local-language satellite.

Most observers admit that the availability of satellite commercial networks has already had an impact on the national regulatory boards of countries that tended to restrict or limit commercial air time. It is now expected that, even in Scandinavia, commercial television will become the norm. In other parts of Europe, existing commercial television time is not expected to lose out to other channels. This may substantially enlarge the TV advertising market in Europe.

Scheduling International Advertising

The general rule in scheduling advertising suggests that the company more or less duplicates the sales curve or seasonality of its product. Furthermore, depending on the complexity of the buying decision or the deliberation time, the media expenditures tend to peak before the actual sales peak. This practice, though somewhat generalized here, applies as well to international markets as to domestic. Differences may exist, however, due to different sales peaks in the year, vacations or religious holidays, and differences in the deliberation time with regard to purchases.

Sales peaks are influenced both by climatic seasons and by customs and traditions. Winter months in North America and Europe are summer months in some countries of the southern hemisphere, namely Australia, New Zealand, South Africa, and Argentina. This substantially influences the purchase of many consumer goods, such as clothing, vacation services, and travel. Vacations are particularly important for some European countries. In Europe, school summer vacations tend to be shorter than in the United States, but employees typically are granted four to five weeks, which is more than those granted to the average U.S. employee. With vacations concentrated in a few weeks during the summer, this can have a major impact on the advertising scheduling. A company will not want to engage in a major media campaign when a substantial segment of the population is traveling away from home. In Sweden, many public places are closed in July, and Italy and France concentrate their holidays in August. In Germany, vacations are staggered by region over the period of July and August. Religious holidays also may affect the placement or timing of advertising. During the Islamic Ramadan, usually celebrated over a month during July, many Moslem countries do not allow the placement of any advertising.

For industrial products, the timing of advertising in support of sales efforts may be affected by the budgetary cycles prevailing in a given country. For countries with large state-controlled sectors, heavy emphasis needs to be placed on the period before a new national or sector plan is developed. Private sector companies tend to be more influenced by their own budgetary cycles, usually coinciding with their fiscal years. In Japan, many companies begin their fiscal year in June rather than on January 1. To the extent that capital budgets are completed before the new fiscal year commences, products that require budgetary approval will need advertising support in advance of the budget completion.

The time needed to think about a purchase has been cited as a primary factor in deciding on the appropriate time by which the advertising peak is to precede the sales peak. In its domestic market, a company may have become accustomed to a given purchase deliberation time by its customers. Since the deliberation may be determined by income levels or other environmental factors, other markets may show different patterns. The purchase or replacement of a small electrical household appliance may be a routine decision for a North American household, and the purchase may occur whenever the need arises. In a country with lower income levels, such a purchase may be planned several weeks or even months ahead. Consequently, a company engaged in international advertising needs to carefully evaluate the underlying assumptions of its domestic advertising policies and not automatically assume that they apply elsewhere.

Reach Versus Frequency

Invariably, an advertiser will be forced to make a tradeoff between the number of target customers to be reached and the number of messages placed through the media. This reach versus frequency tradeoff is created by advertising budget limitations, which exist even in the largest organizations. Typically, consumer interest in the product is used as a guide to determine the frequency needed. This interest in any given product category may vary from country to country. Furthermore, in countries with otherwise extensive advertising, the existing "noise" may require a step-up in frequency to ensure that the messages actually get through to the targets. Consequently, international advertisers should not assume that the reach versus frequency tradeoff will be the same in different countries.

Organizing the International Advertising Effort

A major concern for international marketing executives centers around the organization of their company's international advertising effort. Key concerns are the role of centralization at the head office versus the roles that subsidiaries and the advertising agency should play. Marketers are aware that a more harmonious approach to the international advertising effort may enhance both the quality and efficiency of the total effort. Thus, organizing the effort deserves as much time as individual advertising decisions about individual products or campaigns. Thus, in this section, we will look in greater detail at advertising agency selection and the managerial issues of running an international advertising effort in a multinational corporation.

Agency Selection

International companies face a number of options with respect to working with a given advertising agency. Many companies first develop an agency relationship domestically and have to decide at one point if they expect their domestic agency to handle their international advertising business as well. In some foreign markets, companies need to select foreign agencies to work with them—a decision that may be left to the local subsidiaries or may be made by the head office alone. Recently, some agencies have banded together to form international networks to attract more international business.

Working with Domestic Agencies

When a company starts to grow internationally, it is not unusual for the domestic advertising agency to handle the international business as well. However, this is only possible when the domestic agency has international experience and international capability. Many smaller domestic agencies do not have international experience. Thus, companies are forced to make other arrangements. Frequently, the international company starts to appoint individual agencies in each of the various foreign markets where it is operating. This may be done with the help of the local subsidiaries or through the company's head-office staff. Before long, the company will end up with a series of agency relationships that may make international or global coordination very difficult.

PPG Industries' Automotive Finishes Group had been using a domestic agency for ten years when the company anticipated a substantial growth in its international business. PPG was looking to acquire several companies in Europe in addition to the two plants already in place. The company, therefore, switched all of its business from the domestic agency to Campbell-Ewald, which was organized as a network with many affiliates overseas.[101] To better coordinate its U.S. and international advertising campaigns, Goodyear requested that its domestic agency, J. Walter Thompson, closely work with its international agency, McCann-Erickson, on a global campaign, even though the advertising would not be identical.[102] By having the two agencies work together, Goodyear was assured that the resulting campaign would be coordinated and that the company would speak with the same voice worldwide.

Working with Local Agencies

The local agency relationship offers some specific advantages. First of all, the local advertising agency is expected to fully understand the local environment and is in a position to create advertising targeted to the local market. However, many firms question the expertise and professionalism of local agencies, particularly in countries where advertising is not as developed as in the major markets of North America and Europe.

Jaguar had some interesting experiences in penetrating the Saudi Arabian market.[103] Jaguar had its own advertising in the Middle East handled through a British agency. The Saudi audience reacted negatively to the Lebanese Arabic used in the copy. They also noticed that the visuals had been shot in the United Arab Emirates, because the drivers in the pictures were wearing black bands with long black strings at the back that weighted

101. ''PPG Finishes Switches Shops Citing New International Needs,'' *Industrial Marketing,* August 1981, p. 25.
102. ''Goodyear Pulls Back from Print,'' *New York Times,* November 5, 1986, p. D19.
103. ''The Sleek Cat Springs into the Saudi Market,'' *Financial Times,* November 2, 1985, p. 14.

down the Arabian headdress. Though this type of headdress was typical for that part of the Arabian Gulf region, it was not typical for Saudi Arabia. When the Jaguar importer in Saudi Arabia complained about the advertising, Jaguar looked for a local agency run by U.S. and British expatriates. However, this attempt was also a failure, and the account was finally shifted to a local agency run largely by Saudi managers. This agency relied heavily on high-quality visuals from Jaguar in the United Kingdom but wrote all of its own copy.[104]

Working with International Affiliates in Local Markets

Increasingly, international companies have the option of working with local affiliates of large international agencies. Often these agencies were locally founded and at some time sold a minority stake to larger foreign agencies. More recently, international agencies have acquired majority stakes or started new branches from scratch. The capabilities of these agencies depend on the extent that they can be supported by the owner's network. However, this trend has brought new sophistication and expertise to countries where little existed.

Until recently, the advertising agency business in South Korea was dominated by in-house agencies of large Korean companies controlling some 60 percent of billings. Smaller, independent shops served the rest. With full foreign ownership to be allowed as of 1991, many international agencies decided to set up shop in Korea. International companies have been the major clients of these recently formed agencies.[105] Similar developments have been observed in eastern European countries that are turning toward economic liberalization.

Working with International Advertising Networks

Many companies with extensive international operations find it too difficult and cumbersome to deal simultaneously with a large number of agencies, both domestic and international. For that reason, multinational firms have tended to concentrate their accounts with some large advertising agencies that operate their own networks. Among the leaders are Saatchi & Saatchi, McCann-Erickson (Interpublic Group), Young & Rubicam, J. Walter Thompson and Ogilvy & Mather (WPF Group), and BBDO (Omnicon Group).[106]

As companies develop global business, they are likely to change agencies. For example, Reebok International moved all its $140 million advertising budget to Leo Burnett, dismissing Chiat/Day. While praising the creative talent of Chiat/Day, Dave Ropes, Reebok vice president of marketing services, said, "We're moving from an entrepreneurial stage to a world global brand. To do that we need different resources. We need the strength of a global agency."[107] Ford Motor Co. concentrated its advertising worldwide in three major agencies.[108] Gillette used to work with thirty agencies worldwide but reduced to just two.

104. Ibid.
105. "Agencies Vie for Slice of Korea," *Advertising Age,* September 10, 1990, p. 25.
106. *"Advertising Age's* Top 10 Agencies of 1989," *Advertising Age,* March 26, 1990, p. S-1.
107. "Reebok Gives Chiat/Day the Boot," *New York Times,* September 13, 1993, p. D1.
108. "Global Ad Buys in Ford's Future," *Advertising Age,* April 23, 1990, p. 4.

The first generation of international networks was created by U.S.-based advertising agencies in the 1950s and 1960s. The major driving forces were clients, who encouraged their U.S. agencies to move into local markets where the advertising agencies were weak. Leaders in this process were J. Walter Thompson, Ogilvy & Mather, BBDO, and Young & Rubicam. The second wave of international networks was dominated by British entrepreneurs Saatchi & Saatchi and WPP, who assembled a series of international agency networks under one corporate name. Saatchi & Saatchi has two major international networks, Saatchi & Saatchi Advertising and BSB Worldwide. Other networks are being built by some of the French agencies, and the Japanese agencies are now also building their own networks through acquisition.[109]

International advertising networks are sought after because of their ability to quickly spread around the globe with one single campaign. Usually, only one set of advertisements will be made and then circulated among the local agencies. Working within the same agency guarantees consistency and a certain willingness to accept direction from a central location. If a company tries to coordinate a global effort alone, without the help of an international network, the burden of coordination largely rests with the company itself. Not all firms are geared or equipped for such an effort. Therefore, the international network is a convenience to multinational firms. Apple Computer, after years of letting international divisions handle all their own advertising, decided to centralize management of worldwide communications in its Cupertino, California, headquarters. Using BBDO Worldwide as its advertising agent, Apple wants to have the same brand identity and same campaigns globally.[110] Table 15.4 provides a list of leading world advertising agencies.

Not all companies find a network a necessity. Some advertisers argue that a company may profit from a single strategy but that the execution of this strategy in the various markets should be left to local agencies that are willing to work in an ad hoc network geared only to the company's needs. Acorn, a British manufacturer of minicomputers, had its U.K. agency develop a campaign with independent agencies in Germany and in New York. Acorn had a clear strategy for attacking the educational segment in all markets. However, because of the differences in each market, the company did not opt for a standardized advertising campaign. In the United Kingdom, where the company faced a very high penetration of households with personal computers, Acorn capitalized on the fact that it was chosen by the BBC, the leading broadcasting network. Major targets were parents, but opinion leaders in schools were also addressed. In the United States, Acorn targeted mostly decision-makers in schools and did not advertise to individual households. In Germany, the emphasis was more on creating a strong corporate identity. As a result, the company had three different campaigns, but all three of them aimed at the educational market segment that remained the cornerstone of Acorn's international marketing strategy.[111]

109. "Why the Colossal Cost Is Worth It," *Financial Times,* January 18, 1990, p. 13.
110. "Apple Wants United Worldwide Image," *Advertising Age,* April 12, 1993, p. 2.
111. "A Dichotomy in Campaign Style," *Financial Times,* January 26, 1984, p. 12.

TABLE 15.4 ● World's Top Fifty Advertising Organizations in 1992 (in Millions of Dollars)

Rank	Advertising organization, headquarters	Worldwide gross income, 1992	Worldwide capitalized billings, 1992
1	*WWP Group*, London (Ogilvy & Mather; J. Walter Thompson; Scall, McCabe, Sloves)	$2,813.5	$18,954.9
2	*Interpublic Group of Cos.*, New York (Lintas, Lowe Group; McCann-Erickson)	1,989.2	13,342.8
3	*Omnicom Group*, New York (BBDO; DDB Needham)	1,806.7	13,225.9
4	*Saatchi & Saatchi Co.*, London (Saatchi & Saatchi; Backer Spielvogel Bates)	1,969.5	11,575.4
5	*Dentsu Inc.*, Tokyo	1,387.6	10,477.3
6	*Young & Rubicam*, New York	1,072.3	7,879.0
7	*Euro RSCG*, Neuilly, France	951.2	6,887.6
8	*Grey Advertising*, New York	735.4	4,915.9
9	*Foote Cone & Belding*, Chicago	682.7	5,197.8
10	*Hakuhodo*, Tokyo	661.1	5,077.9
11	*Leo Burnett Co.*, Chicago	643.8	4,304.3
12	*Publicis-FCB Communications*, Paris	590.1	3,821.6
13	*D'Arcy Masius Benton & Bowles*, New York	558.4	4,700.7
14	*BDDP Worldwide*, Paris	293.0	1,999.2
15	*Bozell, Jacobs, Kenyon, & Eckhardt*, New York	231.0	1,805.0
16	*Tokyu Agency*, Tokyo	179.4	1,593.7
17	*Daiko Advertising*, Osaka	175.9	1,330.9
18	*N W Ayer*, New York	175.0	1,581.5
19	*Asatsu*, Tokyo	165.9	1,245.9
20	*Dai-Ichi Kikaku*, Tokyo	151.4	1,102.7
21	*Ketchum Communications*, Pittsburgh	132.8	1,002.0
22	*Dentsu, Y&R Partnership*, New York/Tokyo	132.3	927.1
23	*Chiat/Day*, Venice, California	124.9	933.7
24	*Ross Roy Group*, Bloomfield Hills, Michigan	111.5	743.3
25	*I&S Corp.*, Tokyo	107.4	854.4
26	*Lopex*, London	106.5	710.6
27	*Cheil Communications*, Seoul	103.5	385.5
28	*Yomiko Advertising*, Tokyo	101.3	867.2
29	*Gold Greenlees Trott*, London	100.7	742.7
30	*Asahi Advertising*, Tokyo	93.9	597.9
31	*FCA Group*, Suresnes, France	86.4	679.3

TABLE 15.4 ● World's Top Fifty Advertising Organizations in 1992 (in Millions of Dollars) *(Continued)*

Rank	Advertising organization, headquarters	Worldwide gross income, 1992	Worldwide capitalized billings, 1992
32	*TMP Worldwide*, New York	80.1	533.8
33	*Man Nen Sha*, Osaka	79.4	509.6
34	*GGK International*, Zurich	74.8	509.0
35	*Armando Testa International*, Turin, Italy	73.9	567.4
36	*Oricom Ltd*, Tokyo	62.9	614.4
37	*Nikkeisha*, Tokyo	61.0	360.7
38	*Clemenger/BBDO*, Melbourne, Australia	60.2	358.7
39	*DIMAC Direct*, Bridgeton, Missouri	57.7	163.5
40	*Sogei*, Tokyo	54.8	342.6
41	*Admarketing*, Los Angeles	54.7	329.7
42	*Earl Palmer Brown Cos.*, Bethesda, Maryland	53.5	415.1
43	*Hal Riney & Partners*, San Francisco	52.5	350.0
44	*Hill, Holliday, Connors, Cosmopulos*, Boston	50.7	338.0
45	*Chuo Senko*, Tokyo	50.4	360.0
46	*W. B. Doner & Co.*, Southfield, Michigan	49.9	399.6
47	*Ally & Gargano*, New York	47.6	371.1
48	*Oricom Inc.*, Seoul	47.6	162.4
49	*Bronner Slosberg Humphrey*, Boston	45.1	301.0
50	*Jordan, McGrath, Case & Taylor*, New York	43.5	370.0

Source: "World's Top 50 Advertising Organizations," from *Advertising Age*, April 14, 1993, p. 12. Used with permission.

Coordinating International Advertising

The role the international marketing executive plays in a company's international advertising effort may differ from firm to firm and depend on several factors. Outside factors, such as the nature of the market or competition, and company internal factors, such as company culture or philosophy, may lead some firms to adopt a more centralized approach in international advertising. Other firms, for different reasons, may prefer to delegate more authority to local subsidiaries and local agencies. Key factors that may cause a firm to either centralize or decentralize decision making for international advertising will be reviewed in the sections that follow.

External Factors Affecting Advertising Coordination   One of the most important factors influencing how companies allocate decision-making for international advertising is market diversity. For products or services where customer needs and interests are homogeneous across many countries, greater opportunities for standardization exist. For companies with relatively standardized products, pressures also point in the direction of centralized decision-making. Consequently, companies that face markets with very different customer needs or market systems and structures will work more toward decentralizing their international advertising decision-making. Local knowledge would be more important to the success of these firms.

The nature of the competition can also affect the way an international firm plans for advertising decision-making. Firms that essentially face local competition or different sets of competitors from country to country will find it more logical to delegate international advertising to local subsidiaries. On the other hand, if a company is competing everywhere with a few sets of firms, which are essentially global firms using a similar type of advertising, the need to centralize will be apparent.

Internal Factors Affecting Advertising Coordination   A company's own internal structure and organization can also greatly influence its options of either centralizing or decentralizing international advertising decision-making. The opportunities for centralizing are few when a company follows an approach of customizing advertising for each local market. However, when a company follows a standardized advertising format, a more centralized approach will be possible and probably even desirable.

Skill levels and efficiency concerns can also determine the level of centralization. Decentralization requires that the advertising skills of local subsidiaries and local agencies be sufficient to perform successfully. On the other hand, international advertising may not be centralized successfully in companies where the head-office staff does not possess a good appreciation of the international dimension of the firm's business. Decentralization is often believed to result in inefficiencies or decreased quality because a firm's budget may be spread over too many individual agencies. Instead of having a large budget in one agency, the firm has created minibudgets that may not be sufficient to obtain the best creative talent to work on its products. Centralization will often give access to better talent, though knowledge of the local markets may be sacrificed.

The managerial style of the international company may affect the centralization decision in advertising as well. Some companies pride themselves on giving a considerable amount of freedom to local subsidiary managers. Under such circumstances, centralizing advertising decisions will only be counterproductive. It has been observed with many multinational firms that the general approach taken by the company's top management toward international markets relates closely to its desire to centralize or decentralize international advertising. However, since the company's internal and external factors are subject to change over time, it can be expected that the decision to centralize or decentralize will never be a permanent one.

This change in internal company policy is illustrated by Colgate-Palmolive, a firm with strong beliefs in global marketing strategies. The company developed a strong central department with a director for worldwide advertising. This function was created following a long period of creating local advertising campaigns. Five years later, a new management reaffirmed its preference for locally created advertising and abolished the central control function.[112]

Conclusions

Few areas of international marketing are subject to hotter debate than international advertising. The complexity of dealing simultaneously with a large number of different customers in many countries, all speaking their own languages and subject to their own cultural heritage, offers a real challenge to the international marketer. International executives must find the common ground within these diverse influences so that coherent campaigns can still be possible.

The debate in the field has recently shifted from one of standardization versus customization to one of global versus nonglobal advertising. Proponents of global advertising point to the convergence of customer needs and the emergence of the "world consumer," a person who is becoming ever more homogeneous whether he or she lives in Paris, London, New York, or Tokyo. However, many aspects of the advertising environment remain considerably diverse. Although English is rapidly becoming a global language, most messages still have to be translated into local languages. Diverse regulations in many countries on the execution, content, and format of advertisements still make it very difficult to offer standardized solutions to advertising problems. Also, media availability to advertisers is substantially different in many parts of the world, so many companies still have to adapt their media mix to the local situation. Thus, many executives believe that considerable local content is necessary; therefore, they will give the local country organizations substantial responsibility for input and decision-making.

Most marketers realize that total customization is not desirable, because it will require that each market create and implement its own advertising strategies. Top creative talent is scarce everywhere, and better creative solutions tend to be the costlier ones. As a result, companies appear to be moving toward modularization, in which some elements of the advertising message are common to all advertisements while other elements are tailored to local requirements. To make customization work, however, companies cannot simply design one set of advertisements and later expect to adapt the content. Successful modularization requires that companies, from the very outset, plan for such a process by including and considering the full range of possibilities and requirements to be satisfied. This offers a considerable challenge to international marketing executives and their advertising partners.

---

112. "Colgate Aftershock: Advertising Strategy Changes Looming," *Advertising Age,* September 24, 1990, p. 2.

Questions for Discussion

1. What major factors affect the extension of an international advertising campaign into several countries?

2. How do you explain that some companies appear to be successful with very similar campaigns worldwide whereas fail with the same strategy?

3. What advice will you give to a U.S. firm interested in advertising in Japan, and what will you suggest to a Japanese firm interested in advertising in the United States?

4. What future do you see for global advertising?

5. What will be the impact of increased commercial satellite television on international advertising, both in the United States and abroad?

6. How will the advertising industry need to react to the new trends in international marketing?

For Further Reading

Alden, Dana L., Wayne D. Hoeyer, and Chol Lee. "Identifying Global and Culture-Specific Dimensions of Humor in Advertising." *Journal of Marketing,* April 1993, pp. 64–75.

Aydin, Nizam, Vern Terpstra, and Attila Yaprak. "The American Challenge in International Advertising." *Journal of Advertising,* 13, no. 4 (1984), pp. 49–57.

Boddewyn, J. J. "The Global Spread of Advertising Regulation." *MSU Business Topics,* Spring 1981, pp. 5–13.

Colvin, Michael, Roger Heeler, and Jim Thorpe. "Developing International Advertising Strategy." *Journal of Marketing,* Fall 1980, pp. 73–79.

Donnelly, James H., Jr., and John K. Ryans, Jr. "Standardized Global Advertising, a Call As Yet Unanswered." *Journal of Marketing,* April 1969, pp. 57–60.

Dunn, S. Watson, and E. S. Lorimor. *International Advertising and Marketing.* Columbus, Ohio: Grid, 1979.

Kanso, Ali. "International Advertising Strategies: Global Commitment to Local Vision." *Journal of Advertising Research,* January–February 1992, pp. 10–14.

Killough, James. "Improved Payoffs from Transnational Advertising." *Harvard Business Review,* July–August 1978, pp. 102–110.

Milavsky, J. Ronald. "Recent Journal and Trade Publication Treatments of Globalization in Mass Media Marketing and Social Change." *International Journal of Advertising,* 12, no. 1 (1993), pp. 45–56.

Miller, Richard. "Mixing Your Global Media." *Target Marketing,* July 1992, pp. 15–16.

Neelankavil, J. P., and Albert B. Stridsberg. *Advertising Self-Regulation: A Global Perspective.* New York: Hastings House, 1980.

Peebles, Dean M., and John K. Ryans, Jr. "Advertising as a Positive Force." *Journal of Advertising,* Spring 1978, pp. 48–52.

Peebles, Dean M., John K. Ryans, Jr., and Ivan R. Vernon. "Coordinating International Advertising." *Journal of Marketing,* January 1978, pp. 28–34.

Roth, Martin S. "Depth Versus Breadth Strategies for Global Brand Image Management." *Journal of Advertising,* June 1992, pp. 25–36.

Sandler, Dennis M., and David Shani. "Brand Globally but Advertise Locally: An Empirical Investigation." *International Marketing Review,* 9, no. 4 (1992), pp. 18–31.

Shao, Alan T., and John S. Hill. "Executing Transitional Advertising Campaigns: Do U.S. Agencies Have the Overseas Talent?" *Journal of Advertising Research,* January–February 1992, pp. 49–58.

Winters, Lewis C. "International Psychographics." *Marketing Research: A Magazine of Management and Applications,* September 1992, pp. 48–49.

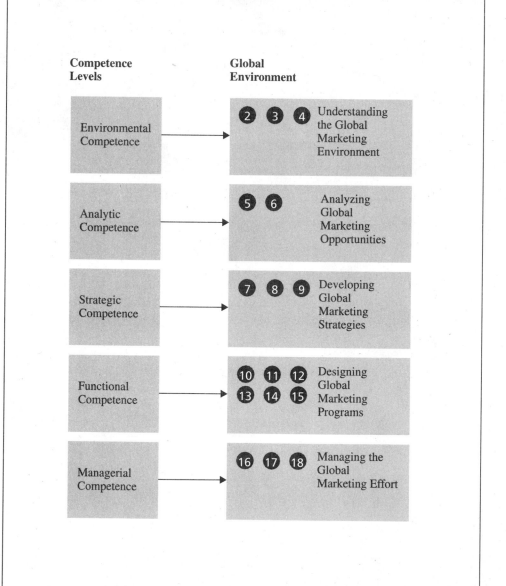

**Competence
Levels**

**Global
Environment**

Environmental
Competence

② ③ ④ Understanding
the Global
Marketing
Environment

Analytic
Competence

⑤ ⑥ Analyzing
Global
Marketing
Opportunities

Strategic
Competence

⑦ ⑧ ⑨ Developing
Global
Marketing
Strategies

Functional
Competence

⑩ ⑪ ⑫
⑬ ⑭ ⑮ Designing
Global
Marketing
Programs

Managerial
Competence

⑯ ⑰ ⑱ Managing the
Global
Marketing Effort

Part

5

Managing the Global Marketing Effort

Organizing International and Global Marketing

Planning and Controlling International and Global Marketing

The Export and Import Trade Process

TO BE SUCCESSFUL at international marketing, a company must do more than analyze markets and devise marketing programs. Increasingly, international companies run complex organizations with operating units in many different countries. The managerial challenges of running such diverse organizations are substantial and require skills that are different from those required by single-country organizations.

This final part of our text is devoted to issues involving the managerial competence of international and global marketing managers. Our goal is to show how managers can guide their operations more effectively in this very competitive global marketplace. In Chapter 16, we concentrate on organizational design issues for international firms and look at where the decision-making process should be concentrated. Chapter 17 focuses on how international firms should control their operations and marketing programs. The final chapter, Chapter 18, covers the various exporting and importing procedures faced by international marketing managers.

16

Organizing International and Global Marketing

● **AN IMPORTANT ASPECT** *of international marketing is the establishment of an appropriate organization. The organization must be able to formulate and implement strategies for each market. The objective is to develop a structure that will allow the firm to respond to distinct variations in each market while utilizing the company's appropriate experience from other markets and products. The key issue in establishing an international organization is deciding where to locate the international responsibility in the firm. The major dilemma facing international marketers involves the tradeoff between the need for an individual response to the local environment and the value of centralized knowledge and control. To be successful, companies need to find a proper balance between these two extremes.*

A number of organizational structures are suitable for different internal and external environmental factors. No one structure is best. In this chapter, we will examine the elements that affect the international marketing organization, the alternative organizational structures, common stages through which organizations evolve, the location of corporate global responsibility in an organization, and recent trends in international organization design.

Organizing: The Key to Strategy Implementation

The global marketplace offers numerous opportunities for astute marketers. To take advantage of these opportunities, they will develop strategies to fit the needs of diverse markets while capitalizing on economies of scale in centralized operations, centralized control, and experience in other markets. These strategies will be adapted to the internal and external environment so that they will prevail over the competition.[1] The final success of the strategy will be influenced by the selection of an appropriate organizational structure to implement that strategy.

The structure of an international organization should be congruent with the tasks to be performed, the need for product knowledge, and the need for market knowledge. It is difficult to select an organizational structure that can effectively and efficiently implement a marketing strategy while responding to the diverse needs of customers and the corporate staff. Chapter 17, ''Planning and Controlling International and Global Marketing,'' examines the simultaneous pressures for greater integration and greater diversity, which also create a significant tension in the development and control of an ideal organizational structure.

Elements Affecting the International Marketing Organization

The ideal structure of an organization should be a function of the products or services to be sold in the marketplace and the external and internal environments. Theoretically, the approach to developing such an organization is to analyze the specific tasks to be accomplished within an environment and then to design a structure that will complete these tasks most effectively. A number of other factors complicate the selection of an appropriate organization. In most cases, a company already has an existing organizational structure. As the internal and external environments change, companies will often change that structure. The search for an appropriate organizational structure must balance the forces for local responsiveness against the forces for global integration.[2]

It is important to understand the strengths and weaknesses of different organizational structures as well as the factors that encourage change in the structure. The diagram in Figure 16.1 reflects the elements that affect organizational design. In this section, we will discuss each of these elements individually.

1. Alfred D. Chandler, *Strategy and Structure* (Cambridge, Mass.: MIT Press, 1962).
2. Sumantra Ghoshal and Nitin Nohria, ''Horses for Courses: Organizational Forms for Multinational Corporations,'' *Sloan Management Review,* Winter 1993, p. 27.

FIGURE 16.1 ● Factors Affecting Organizational Design

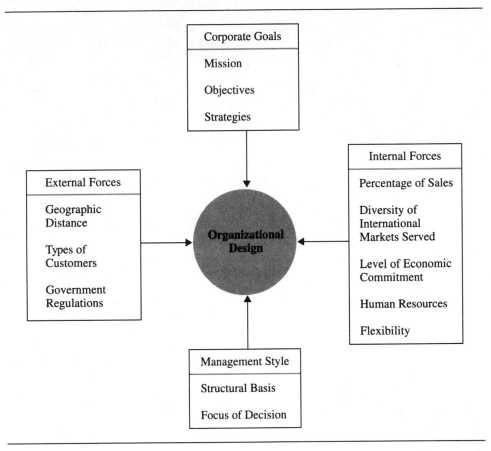

External Forces

The most important external factors are geographic distances, types of customers, and government regulations. In the international environment, each issue should be examined to determine its effect on the organization.

Geographic Distance   Technological innovations have somewhat eased the problem associated with physical distance. Companies, primarily in the United States and other developed countries, enjoy such conveniences as next-day mail, facsimile machines, teleconferencing, and rapid transportation. However, these benefits cannot be taken for granted. Distance becomes a distinct barrier when operations are established in less developed countries, where a simple phone call can take hours if not days to place. Even in developed countries, postal systems can be slow and telephone connections weak.

Geographic distance results in communication barriers, and one problem even high technology cannot solve is the time differentials. Managers in New York who reach an agreement over lunch will have a hard time finalizing the deal with their headquarters in London until the following day, as most executives in England will be on their way home for the evening. The five-hour difference results in lost communication time, which impedes rapid results in a divisional structure. If regular face-to-face meetings are required, physical distance affects the relationship between a subsidiary and its headquarters. For example, Matsushita Electric, known for its Panasonic brand of consumer electronics, keeps tight control over its European management, requiring senior executives to fly six thousand miles to the headquarters in Osaka as many as ten times per year.[3]

Types of Customers   A complete evaluation and understanding of the consumers within the marketplace enable companies to structure their organizations appropriately. The more homogeneous the consumers with respect to the product or service, the easier it will be for a firm to consolidate its efforts. As the main purpose of most companies is to serve the needs of the consumer, "decisions about organizing should start with a profound understanding of consumers." Who are the consumers? Where are they geographically located? What drives their purchasing decisions? Are there groups of consumers with similar needs in different countries? And finally, how can we create an organizational structure to get to these consumers and evoke the desired response?[4]

For example, ICI, the U.K.-based chemical company, reorganized its European operations from a set of product businesses that were marketed through national sales subsidiaries to a European organization. According to the company, the reason for the change was to "meet the needs of our customers. The single European market will affect the way in which our customers organize their own businesses. They will be looking for fewer suppliers and a more integrated relationship with companies supplying them."[5] Yoshihisa Tabuchi, president and chief executive officer (CEO) of Nomura Securities, the largest financial institution in the world, says the company's strategy depends on its clients. "Some businesses are inherently domestic, so why try to make them global? Retail brokerage is a good example. The style and structure we use to sell securities in Japan can't work in America and we would be foolish to try."[6] Here again we see that the structure must fit the customers.

3. "A Tortoise That Stays Within Its Shell," *Financial Times,* October 30, 1989, p. 13.

4. Sandra Vandermerwe, "Constructing Euro-Networks for Euro-Customers," paper presented to the European League for Economic Cooperation Symposium on Social Europe, May 1990, Utrecht, Holland, p. 1.

5. Clive Cookson, "ICI Proffers More Corporate Clout to Its Customers," *Financial Times,* September 7, 1990, p. 12.

6. Michael Schrage, "A Japanese Giant Rethinks Globalization: An Interview with Yoshihisa Tabuchi," *Harvard Business Review,* July–August 1989, p. 71.

Government Regulations   How various countries attract or repel foreign operations affects the structure of the organization. Laws involving imports, exports, taxes, hiring, and so on differ from country to country. Local taxes, statutory holidays, and political risk can deter a company from establishing a subsidiary or management center in a country. Many developing countries require a firm that establishes plants on their territory to hire, train, and develop local employees and to share ownership with the government or local citizens. These requirements for local investment and ownership may demand an organization with a local decision-making group.

Internal Forces

In addition to the external forces, internal factors will often impact the international organization. In this section, we examine these factors, including volume of international business, diversity of the markets being served, economic commitment to international business, available human resources, and flexibility within the company.

Percentage of International Sales   If only a small percentage of sales (1 percent to 10 percent) are international, a company will tend to have a simple organization with an export department. As the proportion of international sales increases relative to total sales, a company is more likely to change from an export department to an international division and then to to a worldwide organization.

Diversity of International Markets Served   As the number and diversity of international markets increase, the organization necessary to manage the marketing effort becomes more complex, and it requires a larger number of people to understand the markets and implement the strategies.

Level of Economic Commitment   A company unwilling or unable to allocate adequate financial resources to its international efforts will not be able to sustain a complex or costly international structure. The less-expensive organizational approaches to international marketing usually result in less control by the company on the local level. It is extremely important to build an organization that will provide the flexibility and resources to achieve the corporation's long-term goals for international markets.

Human Resources   Available and capable personnel are just as vital to a firm as financial resources. Some companies send top domestic executives to foreign operations and then find that these exported executives do not understand the nation's culture. The hiring of local executives is also difficult because competition for such people is extremely intense in many countries. Panasonic U.K. recruits graduates from British universities to develop local talent; the graduate trainees are sent to Japan for one year to absorb Japanese culture and discipline. The program is extremely popular. With a long-term approach to developing local talent, Panasonic prefers "to grow its own," whereas archrival Sony uses headhunters extensively to recruit local managers.[7] Because people are such an important resource in international organizations, many companies structure their organizations based on the availability of internationally trained executive talent. Also, more companies are developing cross-cultural training programs to help prepare executives for new environments.[8]

Flexibility   Although a rigid structure gives a firm more control over operations, it also restricts adaptability. When a company devises an organization structure, it must build in some flexibility, especially in the event of the need for future reorganization. A study of the implementation of a global strategy for seventeen products found that organizational flexibility was one of the key success factors. The structure needs to be flexible enough to respond to the needs of the consumers.[9] Companies that establish a perfect design for the present find themselves in trouble later on if the firm grows or declines.

Management Style

The management style of a company can be described in terms of its structure and its decision-making processes. These factors will influence the type of international organization the company will adopt.

Structural Basis   There are three basic options for the managerial structure of an organization: functional, market-based, or matrix. These options provide the foundation on which to design an organization. Figure 16.2 depicts the options a company has once it decides on the basic framework.

When American Standard restructured its company from a geographic organization to a product-based organization, it did so to encourage cross-fertilization of management skills and technology. Additionally, American Standard's corporate philosophy was to promote the best person. This policy meant that non-Americans not only ran most of the overseas divisions but also were moving into senior U.S. and global jobs. This philosophy enabled American Standard to shed its reputation as a U.S.-based company.[10]

The prospect of a unified Europe gave a number of firms the impetus to change their organizational structures. ICI, British Petroleum (BP), Unilever, Procter & Gamble, Electrolux, Philips, United Distillers, and many others reorganized to improve their abilities to respond to the needs of the European markets. For example, in 1987, United Distillers was a loose federation of twelve brand-owning fiefdoms that included Johnnie Walker, Dewar, and Haig. Each distilled its own whiskies and sold them around the world through third-

7. "A Tortoise That Stays," p. 13.

8. Mark Mendenhall and Gary Oddow, "Acculturation Profiles of Expatriate Managers: Implications for Cross-Cultural Training Programs," *Columbia Journal of World Business,* Winter 1986, p. 73.

9. Kamran Kashani, "Why Does Global Marketing Work—or Not Work?" *European Management Journal,* June 1990, p. 154.

10. Hugh D. Menzies, "Happy Days at American Standard," *Fortune,* September 22, 1980, p. 136.

FIGURE 16.2 ● Basis for Organizational Design

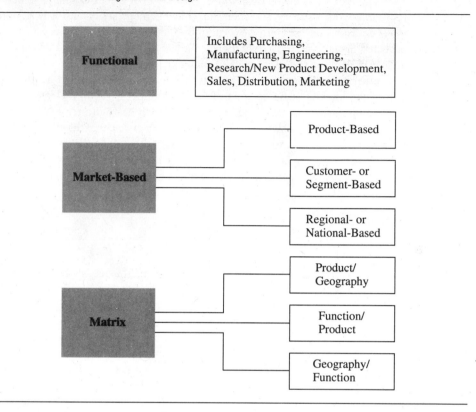

party distribution. There was a great deal of interbrand competition and cannibalization. The company decided to abolish the old product-based structure and introduce a simple regional structure that would place operational management in marketplaces: Europe, North America, Asia Pacific, and international (South America, the Middle East, and Africa). A central strategic unit was established to research and produce individual brand marketing plans and portfolio strategies and to handle new product development in a liaison with regional managers. The new organization focuses on the needs of each marketplace, without cannibalizing its own brands.[11]

Focus of Decision   Who makes what decisions guides the organizational design. If all decision-making responsibility is in the hands of headquarters, then the international operations should reflect this. There are many layers, or types, of decisions to be made from the purchasing of paper clips to the acquisition of a product line or a company.

11. Philip Rawstorne, ''Re-shaping United Distillers,'' *Financial Times,* June 13, 1990, p. 12.

The focus of decision is very much a function of the CEO's management style. Texaco reorganized its structure to reflect that management style: past CEO August Long had made decisions on even minor expenditures, and the company's success (or lack of success) reflected his authoritarian style. Later, Texaco was restructured to provide more authority and responsibility to lower levels of management.[12]

Over a ten-year period, Electrolux made over one hundred acquisitions to become one of the leading manufacturers of large appliances, vacuum cleaners, chain saws, and garden appliances. Because the company grew three-fold after 1981, there was pressure to develop a more formalized and centralized decision-making process. Sven Stork, one of the powerful product line managers, resisted this trend. "Either Electrolux places trust in its product line manager or introduces a corporate control system like ITT's under Harold Geneen with 1,000 staff. That would be poison for this company, it wouldn't work; and so we'd have to sell two-thirds of our product lines."[13]

Corporate Goals

Every company needs a mission. The mission is the business's framework: the values that drive the company and the belief the company has for itself. The glue that holds the company together, the mission answers four questions: (1) Why do we exist? (2) Where are we going? (3) What do we believe in? (4) What is our distinctive competence?[14]

After reviewing its mission, no company should begin establishing an international organization until it has reviewed and established its strategies and objectives. If the company anticipates future growth in international markets, then it must establish a structure that can evolve effectively and efficiently into a larger operation. Too often, shortsighted executives establish international operations that do not enable the managers to grow with the company when markets begin to expand. These managers are not equipped to take on any added responsibility. Additionally, headquarters fails to communicate short-term goals, long-range objectives, and sometimes even the total mission of the company. Inadequate communications result in an ambiguous corporate image and the inability to facilitate coordination of all marketing elements.

Recent authors go beyond the need for goals and objectives and call for "strategic intent." They argue that some companies that have risen to global leadership did so with a ten- to twenty-year quest for winning. Corporate leaders developed a strategic intent with slogans such as "Encircle Caterpillar" for Komatsu and "Beat Xerox" for Canon.

12. "Texaco Restoring Luster to the Star," *Business Week,* December 22, 1980, pp. 54–61.

13. Christopher Lorenz, "A Struggle Against Creeping Formality," *Financial Times,* June 26, 1989, p. 12.

14. Andrew Campbell, Marion Devine, and David Young, *A Sense of Mission* (London: Economist Books, 1990), pp. 19–41.

If the head of a company can develop this sense of winning throughout the company, it will stretch the organization to excel and achieve far greater goals.[15]

Types of International Organizations

The international marketplace offers many opportunities. To take advantage of these opportunities, a company must evaluate the options, develop a strategy, and establish an organization to implement the strategy. The organization should take into account all the factors affecting organizational design shown in Figure 16.1. In this section, we review the various types of international organizational structure.

Companies Without International Specialists

When many companies begin selling products to foreign markets, they are without a separate international organization or an international specialist. A domestically oriented company may begin to receive inquiries from foreign buyers who saw an advertisement in a trade magazine or attended a domestic trade show. The domestic staff will respond to the inquiry in the same fashion as it does other inquiries. Product brochures will be sent to the potential buyer for review. If sufficient interest exists on the part of both buyer and seller, then more communication (telex, airmail, faxes, telephone, personal visits) may transpire. With no specific individual designated to handle international business, it may be directed to a sales manager, an inside salesperson, a product manager, or an outside salesperson.

Companies without an international organization will obviously have limited costs. Of course, with no one responsible for international business, it will probably provide little or no sales and profit. Also, when the firm attempts to respond to the occasional inquiry, no one will understand the difficulties of translation into another language, the particular needs of the customer, the transfer of funds, fluctuating exchange rates, shipping, legal liabilities, or the other many differences between domestic and international business. As the number of international inquiries grows or management recognizes the potential in international markets, international specialists will be added to the domestic organization.

International Specialists and Export Departments

The complexities of selling a product to a variety of different countries encourages most domestically oriented firms to establish an international expertise. This can vary from having a part-time international specialist to a full staff of specialists organized into an

---

15. Gary Hamel and C. K. Prahalad, ''Strategic Intent,'' *Harvard Business Review,* May–June 1989, pp. 63–68.

export department or international department. Figure 16.3 illustrates an organization operating with an international specialist.

International specialists and export departments are primarily a sales function. They will respond to inquiries, exhibit at international trade shows, and handle export documentation, shipping, insurance, and financial matters. Also, the international specialist(s) will maintain contact with embassies, export financing agencies, and the Department of Commerce. All of these groups regularly publish requests for bid quotations from other countries. The international specialist or export department may use the services of an export agent, an export management company, or import intermediaries to assist in the process (see Chapter 12).

Hiring international specialists gives firms the ability to respond to, bid for, and process foreign business. The size of this type of organization will be directly related to the amount of international business handled. The costs should be minor when compared to the potential.

International specialist/export departments are often reactive rather than proactive in nature. These specialists do not usually evaluate the worldwide demand for a product or

FIGURE 16.3 ● Organization with an International Specialist

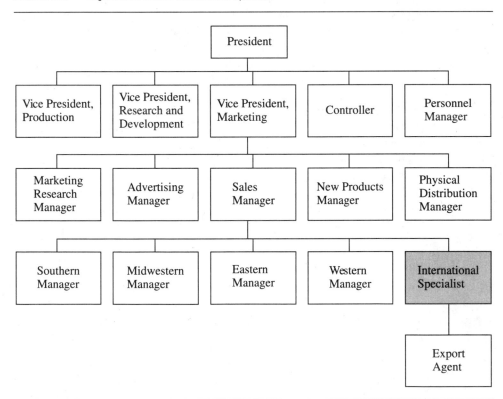

service, identify pockets of opportunities, develop a strategy to infiltrate these opportunities, or reap the rewards; they usually respond to inquiries. Also, because international sales are so small, the international specialist may have little opportunity to modify the current products or services to meet international market needs. In most cases, the products are sold as is, with no modification.

International Division

As sales to foreign markets become more important to the company and the complexity of coordinating the international effort extends beyond a specialist or a single department, a company may establish an international division. The international division normally will report to the president, thus having an equal status with other functions such as marketing, finance, and production. Figure 16.4 illustrates the organizational design of a firm using an international division.

The international division will be directly involved in the development and implementation of an international strategy. Heads of the international divisions will have mar-

FIGURE 16.4 ● Organization with an International Division

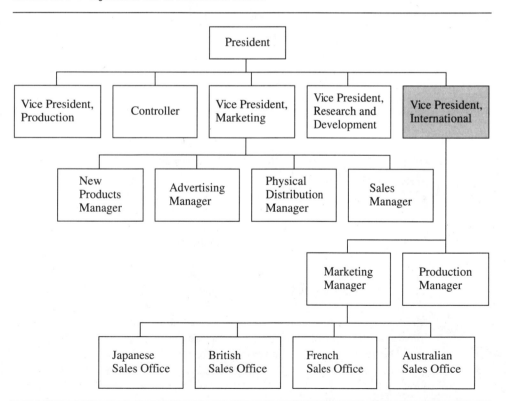

keting, sales, and possibly production managers reporting to him or them. These individuals focus their entire efforts on the international markets. It has been suggested that the international division is the best organizational alternative when international business represents 10 percent to 15 percent of the total business.[16]

An international division focuses on the international market at a high enough level in the organization to directly influence strategy. Also, the international division will begin to actively seek out market opportunities in foreign companies. The sales and marketing efforts in each country will be supported through a regional or local office. These offices will be able to understand the local environment, including legal requirements, customer needs, competition, and so on. This close contact with the marketplace improves the organization's ability to perform successfully.

Having an international division is obviously more expensive than having either no international focus or only a specialist. However, the increased cost will be offset by increased sales. An international division can be the transition stage between a domestically oriented and a globally oriented company. As a company begins to adopt a worldwide focus, the international organization will evolve into a broader entity.

Worldwide Organizations

As a firm recognizes the potential size of the global market, it begins to change from a domestic company doing some business overseas to a worldwide company doing business in a number of countries. A worldwide focus will normally result in a worldwide organizational design.

A company can choose to organize around four dimensions: geography, function, product, and business unit. The matrix organization, another possible type of worldwide organization, combines two or more of the four dimensions. We will discuss and illustrate each organizational alternative.

Geographic Organizational Structures   Geographic organizational designs focus on the need for an intimate knowledge of the company's customers and their environment. A geographic organization will allow a company the opportunity to understand local culture, economy, politics, law, and the competitive situation. There are two general types of geographic organizations, a regional management center and a country-based organization. In many cases, the regional management center and country-based organizations are combined.

Regional Management Centers   Regional management centers form a worldwide organization that focuses on one or more particular regions of the world, such as Europe, the Middle East, Latin America, North America, the Caribbean, or the Far East. Figure 16.5 illustrates the regional management structure of a worldwide geographic organization.

The reasons for using a regional geographic approach to organizational design are twofold. First, there is the pressure of size. Once a market reaches a certain size, the firm

16. "Learning the Rules for Global Selling," *Business Abroad,* November 1969, pp. 43–44.

FIGURE 16.5 ● Regional Management Centers

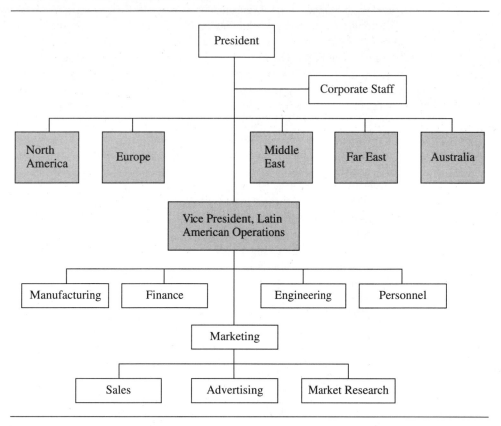

must have a staff focused on that region to maximize revenues from that area of the world and to protect the firm's assets. The second reason for a regional focus is the regional nature of markets. A group of countries located close together, and having similar social and cultural histories, climates, resources, and often languages, will have many similar needs for products. Often, these regional country groups have unified themselves for political and economic reasons; for example, the European Union (EU) is a regional group.

The regional approach to a worldwide organization has a number of benefits. It allows a company to locate marketing and manufacturing efforts to take advantage of regional agreements such as the EU or the North American Free Trade Agreement (NAFTA). Also, the regional approach puts the company in close contact with distributors, customers, and subsidiaries. Regional management will be able to respond to local conditions and react faster than a totally centralized organization, in which all decisions are made at the headquarters.

One of the disadvantages of a regional management center is cost. In general, overseas offices are expensive: international moving costs are high; executives living abroad usually receive additional compensation; and expenses for personnel, office space, communication, and travel are all higher. The increased costs of a regional office must be offset by increased organizational effectiveness, such as in generating sales and controlling costs.

Prior to the euphoria regarding 1992, many large international companies were organized on a national basis. The national organizations, including those in France, Germany, Italy, and the United Kingdom, often were coordinated through a regional management center, the European headquarters. The prospect of a single European market has caused companies to rethink their European organization, often reducing the role of the national organization in favor of a stronger Eurocentric management. A study of twenty multinational companies by A. T. Kearney found that a big benefit of a regional or pan-European structure is reduced finance function costs. The study showed that, by sharing accounting services such as accounts payables, billings, accounts receivables, and general ledger accounting, firms could save 35–45 percent of finance function costs.[17]

Restructuring of manufacturing and logistics in Europe is proceeding at a rapid pace as companies centralize production to lower costs and increase flexibility.[18] For example, Anglo Dutch Unilever, the world's second-largest manufacturer of consumer products (after Procter & Gamble) set up a new organization in 1990 called Lever Europe. This was a surprise move for Unilever, which has always been very decentralized, with each national organization having full autonomy to modify and market products as dictated by local conditions. Of course, the decentralization led to a hodgepodge of brands, resulting in the same liquid abrasive cleaner being called Cif, Jif, Vif, or Viss, depending on the country. Unilever is centralizing both marketing and manufacturing and reducing the autonomy and power of the country managers.[19] Unilever is attempting to balance the need for centralized requirements in research, finance, and packaging with the need to stay close to the markets.[20]

Country-Based Organizations The second type of geographic organization is the country-based organization, which utilizes a separate unit for each country. Figure 16.6 illustrates a simple country-based geographic organization.

A country-based organization resembles a regional management center, except that the focus is on a single country rather than a group of countries. For example, instead of having a regional management center in Brussels overseeing all European sales and operations, the company has an organizational unit in each country. The country-based organization can be extremely sensitive to local customs, laws, and needs, which may be different even though the countries participate in a regional organization such as the EU. With the unification of Europe came the acceptance of European-wide product standards,

17. "European Study Finds Companies Can Save 35–45% by Moving to Financial Shared Services," *A. T. Kearney news release,* December 16, 1993, p. 1.

18. George Taucher, "1992: The End to European National Organizations?" *International Business Communications,* 2, no. 3 (1990), pp. 4–7.

19. Ian Fraser, "Now Only the Name's Not the Same," *Eurobusiness,* April 1990, pp. 22–25.

20. Floris A. Maljers, "Inside Unilever: The Evolving Transnational Company," *Harvard Business Review,* September–October 1992, p. 48.

FIGURE 16.6 ● Country-Based Geographic Organization

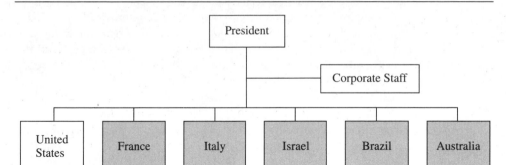

MK = Marketing
OP = Operations

the elimination of border restriction, and the moves to financial unity. These have caused many companies to look at Europe as a single market.

Country organizations are being eliminated or reduced in structure as pan-European organizations emerge.[21] Reckitt and Colman, the U.K.-based manufacturer of toiletries and household goods such as Brasso, has reorganized its corporate structure in response to 1992. Manufacturing operations have been consolidated so one or two factories will be making products for all of Europe, rather than having factories in each country making most products. Product marketing has also been reorganized into Eurobrand groups rather than by country.[22]

One of the difficulties of a country-based organization is that its cost is higher; therefore, the benefit of a local organization must offset its cost. The second difficulty involves the coordination with headquarters. If a company is involved in forty countries, it is difficult and cumbersome to have all forty country-based organizational units reporting to one or more people in the company's headquarters. The third problem of a country-based unit is that it may not take advantage of the regional groupings of countries discussed in Chapter 5. Regional trading agreements, such as the EU, make it valuable to coordinate activities in involved countries. Also, regional media, such as television and print media, often cut across country boundaries and require coordination.

21. Taucher, ''1992: The End?''
22. Christopher Parkes, ''Reckitt to Cut About 500 Jobs over Two Years,'' *Financial Times,* July 1, 1989, p. 22.

To deal with the shortcomings of a country-based organization, many firms combine the concepts of a regional management center and a country-based unit, as shown in Figure 16.7. Combining regional and country approaches minimizes many of the limitations of both designs, but it also adds an additional layer of management. Some executives think that the regional headquarters' additional layer reduces the country-level implementation of strategy rather than improves it. In order to receive benefits from a regional center in such a combined approach, there must be a value in a regional strategy. Each company must reach its own decision regarding the organization design, its cost, and its benefits.

Functional Organizational Structures   A second way of organizing a worldwide marketer is by function. In such an organization, the top executives in marketing, finance, production, accounting, and research and development all have worldwide responsibilities. For international companies, this type of organization is best for narrow or homogeneous product lines, with little variation between products or geographic markets. As shown in Figure 16.8, the functional organization is a simple structure. Each functional manager has worldwide responsibility for that function. Usually, the manager has people responsible for the function in regions or countries around the world.

FIGURE 16.7 ● Organization Using Both Country-Based Units and Regional Management Centers

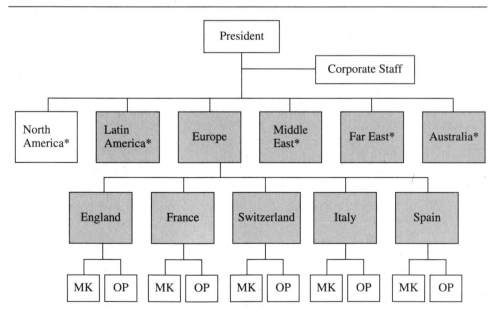

MK = Marketing
OP = Operations

*Under these regional offices would be country organizations similar to the European offices.

FIGURE 16.8 ● Functional Worldwide Organization

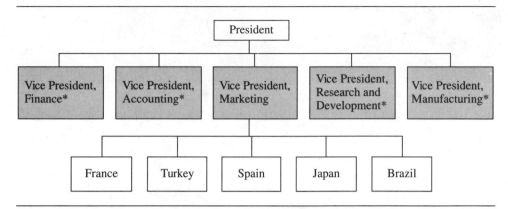

*Each functional vice president has managers of that function in the countries served reporting to him or her, as illustrated with the vice president, marketing.

Coca-Cola Company reorganized its marketing function worldwide from a country-focused organization to a worldwide functional organization. In the transition, market research and marketing operations that previously reported to the senior vice president of marketing U.S.A. were transferred to the newly formed global marketing division. With 90 percent of its earnings growth coming from overseas markets, Coca-Cola decided to shift the focus away from a U.S.-dominated structure to a global one.[23] Ford likewise went to a global functional organization, to eliminate the duplication of functions among regional organizations in the United States, Europe, Asia, and Latin America. Alexander Trotman, Ford's chairman, expected to save Ford two–three billion dollars per year by 2000, as well as to speed up development of new models.[24]

Product Organizational Structures   A third type of worldwide marketing organization is based on product line rather than on function or geographic area. The product group becomes responsible for the performance of the organizational unit, which incorporates marketing, sales, planning, and in some cases production. Other functions, such as legal, accounting, and finance, can be included in the product group or performed by the corporate staff.

Structuring by product line is common for companies with several unrelated product lines. The rationale for selecting a product versus a regional focus is that the differences between the marketing of the products is greater than the differences between the geographic markets. In the 1970s and 1980s, many global companies used a dual structure referred to as a matrix, which is discussed below. During the 1990s, a number of companies

23. Marcy Magiera, ''Coke's Zyman Fires Marketing Blitzkrieg,'' *Advertising Age,* August 30, 1993, p. 1.
24. ''A Global Tune-up for Ford,'' *Business Week,* May 2, 1994, p. 38.

FIGURE 16.9 ● Worldwide Product Organization

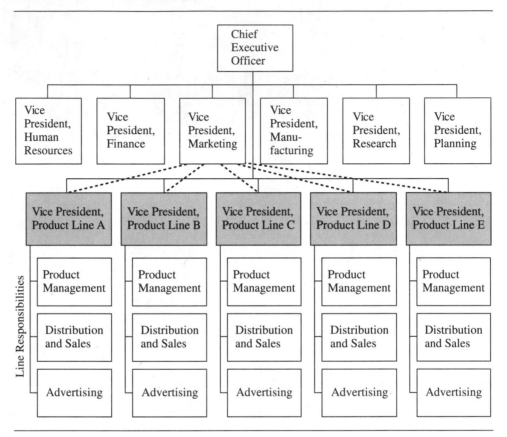

such as Philips and ICI have switched away from their geographic and product matrix to strong product divisions.[25] Typically, the end users for a product organization will vary by product line, so there is no advantage to having the marketing for the different product lines done by the same group. The product is the focus of the organizational structure shown in Figure 16.9.

A product organization concentrates management on the product line, which is an advantage when the product line constantly changes due to technology. The product focus also gives the organization excellent flexibility. Within a product group, management can control the product life cycle, adding and deleting products with a marginal effect on overall operations. Also, the firm can add new product groups as it adds new, unrelated products through acquisition.

Monsanto now has a global products organization. The transition was accompanied by a shift of the resins staff from St. Louis to Brussels. The previous organization "forced

25. Cookson, "ICI Proffers More," p. 12.

us to focus primarily on North America—at the expense of product and market opportunities elsewhere,'' according to Bill Slowikowski, head of Monsanto Resins.[26]

The product organization has its limitations.[27] Knowledge of specific areas may be limited, since each product group cannot afford a local organization. This lack of knowledge may cause the company to miss market opportunities. The managers of international product divisions can also be a problem. They can be ethnocentric and relatively disinterested in or uneasy with the international side of the business. Another limitation of a product organization is the lack of coordination in international markets. If each product group goes its own way, the company's international development may result in inefficiencies. For example, two product divisions separately may be purchasing advertising space in the same magazine, which will be more expensive than if the purchases are combined.

To offset the inefficiencies of a worldwide product organization, some companies provide for global coordination of activities such as advertising, customer service, and government relations. 3M shifted most strategic and operational responsibilities away from its national subsidiaries and into nineteen centralized product divisions, each with Europewide responsibility. The European business centers were quickly accepted because managers saw the need for pricing coordination, faster development and launch of new products, and better coordination of large customers in multiple countries.[28]

Matrix Organizational Structures   Some companies have become frustrated with the limitations of the one-dimensional geographic, product, and functional organization structures. In response to the limitation of single-dimension organizations, the matrix organization was developed. As shown in Figure 16.10, the matrix organization allows two dimensions of equal weight (here, geographic and product dimensions) in the organization structure and in decision-making responsibility. A matrix organization structure has a dual rather than a single chain of command, which means that many individuals will have two superiors. Firms tend to adopt matrix organizations when they need to be highly responsive to two dimensions (e.g., product and geography), when there are stringent constraints on financial or human resources, and when uncertainties generate very high information processing requirements.[29] P&G strengthened its global management matrix of product and geography for two reasons. First, the matrix organization can usually handle twice the volume of business with the same staff. Second, the matrix allows much quicker rollout of a product worldwide than was the case in the past with a country-based organization.[30]

26. Christopher Lorenz, ''When Head Office Goes Native,'' *Financial Times,* December 2, 1992, p. 11.

27. For a detailed discussion of a product organization, see William H. Davidson and Phillippe Haspeslagh, ''Shaping a Global Product Organization,'' *Harvard Business Review,* July–August 1982, pp. 125–132.

28. Christopher Lorenz, ''Facing Up to Responsibility,'' *Financial Times,* December 13, 1993, p. 10.

29. Paul R. Lawrence, Harvey F. Kolodny, and Stanley M. David, ''The Human Side of the Matrix,'' *Organization Dynamics,* Summer 1979, pp. 43–47.

30. Bill Sapority, ''Behind the Tumult at P&G,'' *Fortune,* March 7, 1994, p. 82.

FIGURE 16.10 ● Matrix Organization

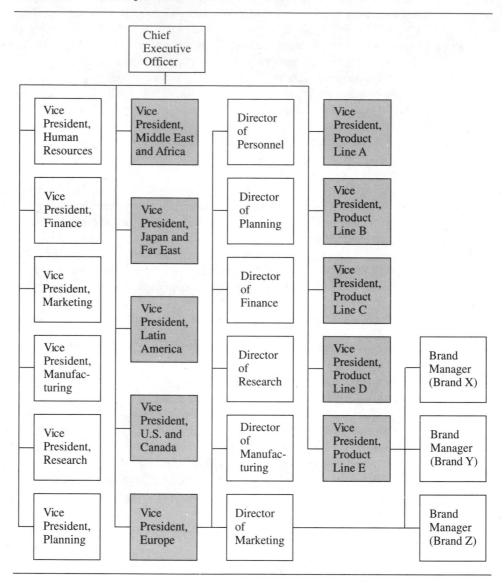

A matrix organization can include both product and geographic management components. Product management has worldwide responsibility for a specific product line, while geographic management is responsible for all product lines in a specific geographic area. These management structures overlap at the national product/market level.

The combination of different organizational objectives and dual reporting relationships fosters conflict and complexity. Power struggles are a common problem when a matrix organization is first established. The power struggle is the result of the dual reporting relationship. The power limits of the two relationships are tested as each side attempts to identify its place in the organization. Electrolux adopted a complex matrix organization with four dimensions:

Global product area managers: hot, cold, wet appliances

Regional marketing coordinators: Europe, the United States, and the rest of the world

Country level: product divisions

Country level: marketing/sales companies

The structure creates a number of tensions on the country, regional, and global level. Leif Johansson, product manager for white goods at Electrolux, said the structure is ''a quite impossible organization, but the only one that will work.'' Asked about eliminating or reducing the role of the country managers, as done by ICI, Unilever, and others, he said, ''That would be wrong, because they're damned good at their job—which includes defending their national interests, dealing with large retail customers and trade unions, as well as overseeing national salary structures. There is too much of a tendency to try to solve organizational problems by designing a structure that quiets conflicts rather than bringing them to the surface.''[31]

The key to successful matrix management is the degree to which managers in an organization can resolve conflict and achieve the successful implementation of plans and programs. The matrix organization requires a change in management behavior from traditional authority to an influence system based on technical competence, interpersonal sensitivity, and leadership.

A matrix or hybrid structure offers several advantages:

● It permits an organization to function better in an uncertain and changing environment.

● It increases potential for control and coordination.

● It gives more individuals the chance to develop from technical or functional specialists to generalists.

There has been a shift away from the geographic/divisional matrix toward global divisions. These global divisions have responsibility for a set of products worldwide. The shift has been part of the multinationals' quest for simple structures, faster decision-making, and greater global effectiveness.[32] Philips, Citibank, Ciba-Geigy, Texas Instruments, BP, and General Electric have all switched from matrix organizations to worldwide product divisions. The main problem with the matrix organization is that it assumes that product and geographic consideration are evenly balanced; in reality, few large, diversified companies

31. Christopher Lorenz, ''An Impossible Organization, but the Only One That Works,'' *Financial Times,* June 21, 1989, p. 14.

32. Christopher Lorenz, ''Re-appraising the Power Base of Regional Barons,'' *Financial Times,* March 26, 1990, p. 12.

have such a balance. A U.S.-based consumer goods firm with two major businesses, drugs and local-brand candy bars, found that the matrix organization did not work for these two products. Therefore, the company reorganized, putting its billion-dollar prescription drug division on a worldwide basis with close ties to headquarters and retaining the matrix organization for the over-the-counter drugs and the candy divisions.[33]

The matrix organization requires a substantial investment in dual budgeting, accounting, transfer pricing, and personnel evaluation systems. The additional complexity and cost of a matrix organization should be offset by the benefit of the dual focus, increased flexibility and sales, and economies of scale.

Strategic Business Units with Global Responsibilities   One of the most recent forms of organizational design is the *strategic business unit* (SBU). The SBU is an organizational group supporting products and technologies that serve an identified market and compete with identified competitors. The SBU may either be a separate organizational design, similar to a product organization, or it can be an organizational unit used only for the purpose of developing a business strategy for many products in a geographic area.

The increased penetration of global competition has forced many firms to set up SBUs to address the global markets and assess competition in developing a global business strategy. For example, both Coors (beer) and Norton Company (grinding wheels) have set up separate business units to explore the markets for ceramic products based on new high-performance ceramic technologies. These business units are particularly alert to the efforts of Japanese manufacturers such as Yokoyana, Sumatomo, and many others that are engaged in ceramics research, as well as of the Japanese Ministry of International Trade and Industry, which sponsors long-term ceramics research and development. Nestlé established seven strategic business units with worldwide strategic responsibilities for a set of businesses. With research, production, and marketing expertise, the SBUs have much more clout to direct decisions than in the previously powerful country headquarters. The new organization was also expected to reduce head office staff at Nestlé by 12 percent.[34]

The Life Cycle of International Organizations

Companies evolve as organizations over time. As their international involvement expands, the degree of organizational complexity increases and firms reorganize accordingly. As a firm moves from exporting a few goods to being a worldwide organization, it finds itself going through organizational changes with differing structures and focus. Organizations change to reflect the importance of different markets and the needs of the customer. As the amount of international business increases and the needs of the customers become more complex, the organization will change to reflect the market. Figure 16.11 depicts the

33. J. Quincy Hunsicker, "The Matrix in Retreat," *Financial Times,* October 25, 1982, p. 16.
34. Christopher Lorenz, "Lean Regime for a Fitter Future," *Financial Times,* May 6, 1992, p. 14.

FIGURE 16.11 ● Life Cycle of International Organizations

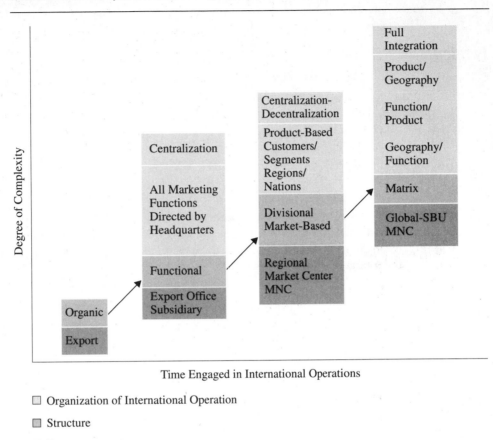

typical progression of the international organization's life cycle. Because this is a dynamic and integrative process, most companies do not follow this life cycle exactly, but the framework does provide a method by which to evaluate the degree of focus and responsibility.

Export

When the domestic market becomes saturated or a need is identified in foreign markets, companies begin exporting their product or services. The export department is still a function of and normally reports to the company and follows company procedures and strategies. Often, companies will first begin to receive inquiries from foreign companies about their products. Then an export person or department is established to process and respond to the foreign inquiries.

Foreign Sales Office

If the demand for the product increases and there appears to be a need to establish an office either to ease administrative procedures or to investigate new markets or refine old markets, then a company will normally establish an office in a foreign country. Usually, this office is under headquarters' control and acts according to home office directions.

Regional Market Center

Regional market centers act as filters between the headquarters and various country organizations. Regional market centers coordinate the marketing function of the branches so that they remain in line with corporate objectives. Regional market centers are normally organized along geographic lines; however, they may be organized along product groups or similar target markets.

Matrix Organizations

The matrix organization is the most complex and sophisticated structure. It requires a firm to be fully competent in the following areas:

1. Geographic knowledge
2. Product knowledge
3. Functional aspects, such as finance, production, and marketing
4. Customer/industry knowledge

Instead of focusing in one area—geographic or product organization—the matrix incorporates both, and each operates as a profit center. Matrix organizations allow low levels to have substantial authority; however, they require an open and flexible corporate culture/orientation for successful implementation.

Global Integration—Strategic Business Units

Fully advanced international companies with complete integration have begun to establish strategic business units. An SBU acts as a separate business and contains a group of products or technologies directed at a specific target market. SBUs are part of a formal structure but act primarily to determine strategies. As mentioned earlier in the chapter, a number of companies have moved from the geography/product division matrix to a global product division structure.

Trends in Global Organizations

Global companies are continually challenged by the need to adapt their organizations to the needs of the marketplace. They need to respond to three major challenges:

The need for efficiency

The need for responsiveness

The need for learning[35]

As companies compete on a worldwide basis, they need to develop global economies of scale. Instead of supporting manufacturing plants in each major market, products or components are standardized. Electrolux, Black & Decker, Unilever, and many other firms have rationalized their manufacturing to yield economies of scale. While the washing machine or power tool may vary from country to country, the motors can be standardized and manufactured in large volumes to reduce costs. The organizational structure needs to encourage this trend toward efficiency, which is why, as part of its complex matrix organization, Electrolux has three senior-level executives—"Mr. Hot" responsible for stoves and cookers, "Mr. Cold" for refrigerators and freezers, and "Mr. Wet" responsible for washers and dryers—who coordinate the manufacturing and marketing of their product lines across all markets.[36]

While some products such as soft drinks, watches, and perfume seem to be trending toward a single global brand, most markets vary by country. Even with the same global product, the market structure, competitors, regulations, and culture often will vary by country. Company organizations need to be able to balance their drive for global economies against the need to be responsive to local markets. Kao, the large Japanese detergent, soap, and personal care products manufacturer, developed technologically advanced factories with low costs. Unfortunately, Kao's attempts to enter the United States and Europe stalled. Kao failed because of its inability to understand the differences between markets and to adapt accordingly.[37] Failure to respond to local needs can undermine efforts toward global expansion.

The increased cost of R&D, shortened product life cycles, and consumer demand for the latest technology have increased the need for development and diffusion of worldwide learning. This learning is often related to R&D but can also include marketing or manufacturing learning. ITT's strategy of individually developing its telecommunication switch technology for each country without gaining any global expertise was one of the factors leading to that company's decline. On the other hand, P&G's seven years of research to develop a heavy-duty, liquid laundry detergent in Europe was quickly and successfully transferred to the United States in the form of Liquid Tide.

35. Christopher A. Bartlett and Sumantra Ghoshal, *Managing Across Borders* (London: Hutchinson Business Books, 1989), pp. 3–17.

36. Lorenz, "An Impossible Organization," p. 14.

37. Bartlett and Ghoshal, *Managing Across Borders,* pp. 3–17.

Christopher Bartlett and Sumantra Ghoshal interviewed 236 managers in diverse groups of nine companies—P&G, Kao, Unilever, ITT, Ericsson, NEC, GE, Philips, and Matsushita. Based on their research, they suggest that the challenges of global efficiency, local responsiveness, and global learning have become so strong that the global organization must respond to all these challenges simultaneously.[38]

Kenichi Ohmae argues against the trend toward global products. Being a global company begins with an attitude rather than a product. He suggests that the global company must position itself equidistant from the triad of major markets: Japan, the United States, and Europe. While tastes may vary, the broad movements among consumers are similar and offer opportunities. Ohmae believes the renaissance corporation should exploit whatever economies of scale, technology, or branding it has within the triad. In addition, the renaissance global corporation must be an ''insider'' in each of the triad markets. For example, Coca-Cola has 70 percent of the Japanese soft drink market. This is the result of heavy investment in Japan to understand the market and build the functional specialties needed. That is, Coca-Cola became an insider in Japan.[39]

Much of this chapter has focused on the company's formal structure, which establishes lines of authority and responsibility. In global organizations, the formal structure, while important, is only one part of the organizational challenge. The interpersonal relationships, decision-making process, and individual behavior of managers must also be responsive to the needs of the marketplace. Bartlett and Ghoshal argue that *people* are the key to managing complex strategies and organizations.

The task of molding an organization to respond to the needs of a global marketplace involves building a shared vision and developing human resources. A clear vision of the purpose of the company that is shared by everyone gives meaning and direction to each manager. For example, NEC, the Japanese electronics company, has a vision of computers and communications. The vision is simple and can be easily communicated across borders. Every manager can see the direction and relate individual behavior to the goal of building systems where computers and communication are interlinked to solve business problems.

Managers are a company's scarcest resource. The process of recruiting, selecting, training, and managing the human resources must help build a common vision and values. Matsushita (Panasonic) gives new white-collar workers six months of cultural and spiritual training. Philips has organization cohesion training, and Unilever's new hires go through indoctrination: such initial programs help to build vision and shared values. Managers also receive ongoing training. For example, Unilever brings four hundred to five hundred international managers from around the world to its international management training center. Unilever spends as much on training as it does on R&D, not only to upgrade skills but also to indoctrinate managers into the Unilever club and help build personal relationships and informal contacts that are more powerful than the formal systems or structures.[40]

38. Ibid., pp. 16–17.

39. Kenichi Ohmae, *The Borderless World* (London: Collins, 1990), pp. 26–30.

40. Christopher A. Bartlett and Sumantra Ghoshal, ''Matrix Management: Not a Structure, a Frame of Mind,'' *Harvard Business Review,* July–August 1990, pp. 138–145.

Conclusions

Organizing the marketing efforts of a company across a number of countries is a difficult process. As the scope of a company's international business changes, its organizational structure must be modified in accordance with the internal and external environments. As the number of countries in which a company is marketing increases, as product lines expand, and as objectives change, so will the organizations. In this chapter, we have reviewed the various organizations commonly used, showing the benefits of each. The dynamic nature of business requires a constant reevaluation of organizational structure with necessary modifications to meet the objectives of the firm.

Questions for Discussion

1. What aspects of the external environment cause structures of multicountry marketing organizations to be different from those of single-country marketing organizations?

2. What effect will the marketing strategy have on an international marketing organization? For example, if the key aspect of a computer manufacturer's strategy is to focus on three industries worldwide—banks, stockbrokers, and educational institutions—will the organization be different from that of another company that decides to focus on end users who require mainframe computers?

3. How does a single-country organization evolve into an international organization? What type of international organization is likely to develop first? Second? Why?

4. What actions will cause a company to develop an international marketing organization?

5. What are the pros and cons of a regional management center versus a product organization?

6. A country-based geographic structure responds well to the local culture and marketing. What will cause a company to switch from a country structure to a worldwide product organization?

7. Matrix organizations can be very costly and complex. What advantages do they offer to offset these problems?

8. In addition to the formal organization structure, how does the global company ensure that it is responding to the marketplace and achieving efficiency, local responsiveness, and global learning?

For Further Reading

Bartlett, Christopher A. "MNCs: Get Off the Reorganization Merry-Go-Round." *Harvard Business Review,* March–April 1983, pp. 138–146.

Bartlett, Christopher A., and Sumantra Ghoshal. *Managing Across Borders: The Transnational Solution.* Boston: Harvard Business School Press, 1989.

''Corporate Organization: Where in the World Is It Going?'' *Business International,* August 15, 1980, pp. 257–258.

David, Stanley M., and Paul R. Lawrence. ''Problems of Matrix Organization.'' *Harvard Business Review,* May–June 1978, pp. 134–136.

Davidson, William H., and Phillippe Haspeslagh. ''Shaping a Global Product Organization.'' *Harvard Business Review,* July–August 1982, pp. 125–132.

Doyle, Peter, John Saunders, and Veronica Wong. ''Competition in Global Markets: A Case Study of American and Japanese Competition in the British Market.'' *Journal of International Business Studies,* 3rd Quarter 1992, pp. 419–426.

Drake, Rodman, and Lee M. Caudill. ''Management of the Large Multinational: Trends and Future Changes.'' *Business Horizons,* May–June 1981, pp. 88–90.

Handy, Charles. *The Age of Unreason.* London: Hutchinson, 1989.

Handy, Charles. *Inside Organizations.* London: BBC Books, 1990.

Holmen, Milton G. ''Organizing and Staffing of Foreign Operations of Multinational Corporations.'' Paper presented at the Academy of International Business Meeting, New Orleans, October 25, 1980.

Howard, Robert. ''The Designer Organization: Italy's GFT Goes Global.'' *Harvard Business Review,* September–October 1991, pp. 28–44.

Laabs, Jennifer. ''Building a Global Management Team.'' *Personnel Journal,* 72, no. 8 (1993), p. 75.

Maruca, Regina Fazio. ''The Right Way to Go Global: An Interview with Whirlpool CEO David Whitwam.'' *Harvard Business Review,* March–April 1994, pp. 135–145.

Ohmae, Kenichi. *The Borderless World.* London: Collins, 1990.

Parker, Herbert S. ''Restructuring the Corporation.'' *Planning Review,* January–February 1987, pp. 46–48.

Picard, Jacques. ''Determinants of Centralization of Marketing Decision Making in Multinational Corporations.'' In *Marketing in the 80's.* Proceedings of the Educators' Conference. Chicago: American Marketing Association, 1980.

17

Planning and Controlling International and Global Marketing

● **THE PROCESSES OF** *planning and controlling are interrelated. Planning enables a company to understand the environment and develop a strategy. Controlling is the process of evaluating strategy implementation and managing the efforts of those people responsible for the strategy. Both planning and controlling are affected by to the specific organization structure (see Chapter 16), because the processes are completed within that structure. As the environment changes and new strategies are developed, the organization may change, which may affect the planning and controlling processes. For example, if a company changes from a functional organization, with all marketing decisions made at the headquarters in New York, to a geographic organization, with regional management centers in Paris, Tokyo, New York, and São Paulo, the planning and controlling processes will change. Figure 17.1 provides an overview of Chapter 17.*

The International Planning Process

Planning in the international environment is difficult because of the number of extraneous elements involved. Table 17.1 illustrates the differences between planning in a domestic setting and planning in an international one.

As shown in Table 17.1, numerous factors, such as language, political differences, currency fluctuations, and a lack of market data, increase the complexity of international

FIGURE 17.1 ● Planning and Controlling International Marketing

Planning Methods	Boston Consulting Group	General Electric/ McKinsey	Profit Impact of Marketing Strategy	Scenario Planning
Planning Process	Selecting Markets	Coordinating Planning Efforts	Decision-Making	Standardized Versus Decentralized
Control Process	Standards	Measurements and Evaluations	Correcting Deviations	

planning. These differences make developing and implementing international plans more difficult.

Strategic planning is a widely accepted practice of corporate business. The issue of globalization demands strategic research and thought in addressing increasingly complex and competitive world markets.[1] Often, global strategic planning takes place at the highest levels of a company. Relatively young, well-trained executives commonly provide the information and analysis for these high-level discussions and decisions. It is important to understand the process that the board or executive committee takes to make a strategic decision, as you may be the marketing manager implementing that decision.

As businesses move into international markets, the decision-makers are faced with increasingly complex alternatives.[2] Should we license in Brazil, export to South Africa, establish a joint venture in Kuwait, or set up a wholly owned subsidiary in Hong Kong?

1. See George Rabstejnek, ''Let's Get Back to the Basics of Global Strategy,'' *Journal of Business Strategy,* September–October 1989, p. 34.
2. Noel Capon, Chris Christodoulou, John U. Farley, James Hulbert, et al., ''Comparison of Corporate Planning Practice in American and Australian Manufacturing Companies,'' *Journal of International Business Studies,* Fall 1984, pp. 41–54.

TABLE 17.1 ● Domestic versus International Planning Factors

Domestic planning	International planning
1. Single language and nationality	1. Multilingual/multinational/multicultural factors
2. Relatively homogeneous market	2. Fragmented and diverse markets
3. Data available, usually accurate, and collection easy	3. Data collection a formidable task, requiring significantly higher budgets and personnel allocation
4. Political factors relatively unimportant	4. Political factors frequently vital
5. Relative freedom from government interference	5. Involvement in national economic plans; government influences affect business decisions
6. Individual corporation has little effect on environment	6. "Gravitational" distortion by large companies
7. Chauvinism helps	7. Chauvinism hinders
8. Relatively stable business environment	8. Multiple environments, many of which are highly unstable (but may be highly profitable)
9. Uniform financial climate	9. Variety of financial climates ranging from overconservative to wildly inflationary
10. Single currency	10. Currencies differing in stability and real value
11. Business "rules of the game" mature and understood	11. Rules diverse, changeable, and unclear
12. Management generally accustomed to sharing responsibilities and using financial controls	12. Management frequently autonomous and unfamiliar with budgets and controls

Source: William W. Cain, "International Planning: Mission Impossible?" *Columbia Journal of World Business,* July–August 1970, p. 58. Reprinted by permission.

Which project or combination of projects will meet our corporate objectives? The two dimensions that differentiate international from domestic strategic planning are the multiple countries that businesses market to and the modes of entry into those markets.

Planning Models

In this section, we review the various types of planning processes being used, their application to the international market, and the advantages and disadvantages of each procedure when used with the international markets. The most widely used approaches to planning are the following:

Boston Consulting Group (BCG) approach

General Electric/McKinsey (GE) approach

Profit impact of market strategy (PIMS)

Scenario planning[3]

Numerous articles and papers review and compare the various planning models as they apply to domestic markets. Using these domestic systems as a base, each approach will be examined as it is used for international markets.

At any point in time, a firm really consists of a number of businesses, such as divisions, products, or brands. When established, each of these businesses was expected to grow. The firm would encourage growth by expanding research and development, advertising, and promotional budgets for all but the declining products. In recent years, the cost and availability of capital have caused corporations to be much more selective in the financing of their businesses. The tendency has been for a firm to look at its individual businesses and decide which ones to build, maintain, phase down, or close down. Therefore, the job of planning has become one of evaluating current businesses and searching out new opportunities so that the mixture of businesses within the firm will provide the necessary growth and cash flow for growth. For international markets, the breakdown of a firm's activities into the different businesses, usually referred to as strategic business units (SBUs), is normally done on a product-by-country basis. Once the firm is broken down into SBUs, planning must classify them based on expected future potential. While the concept of an SBU is widely accepted, it does have limitations. For example, because vertically integrated businesses share facilities and their performances are interrelated, it may not be easy to neatly sort out business units.[4] One of the original classification schemes was developed by the Boston Consulting Group.

The Boston Consulting Group Approach The Boston Consulting Group (BCG) approach[5] classifies all current strategic business units into a business portfolio matrix, shown in Figure 17.2. This includes both current SBUs and potential or proposed opportunities. The proposed opportunities are normally an extension of the current business via expansion into a new country or new product. BCG's methodology classifies these businesses by market growth rate and market share. The market growth rate is the expected total market demand growth on an annualized basis. The market share is the company's relative share compared to the largest competitor. For example, a rate of 1.0 means the SBU has the same share as the next competitor, a 0.5 means it has one-half the share of the competitor ahead of it, and a 3.0 means it has a three times larger share than the next-largest competitor.

A firm's SBUs are evaluated and classified based on this approach. Market growth rate relates to the stage of the product life cycle, and relative market share is based on the

---

3. Richard G. Hamermesh, ''Making Planning Strategic,'' *Harvard Business Review,* July–August 1986, p. 115.

4. Rael T. Hussein, ''A Critical Review of Strategic Planning Models,'' *Quarterly Review of Marketing,* Spring–Summer 1987, p. 17.

5. Bruce D. Henderson, ''The Experience Curve Reviewed: IV. The Growth Share Matrix of the Product Portfolio,'' *Perspectives*, no. 135 (Boston: Boston Consulting Group, 1973).

FIGURE 17.2 ● Boston Consulting Group Matrix

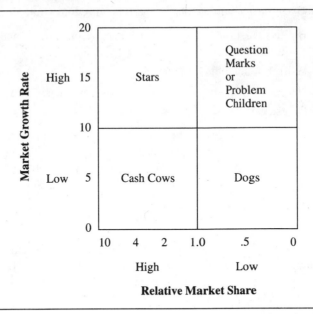

Source: PERSPECTIVES, No. 135, ''The Experience Curve–Reviewed, 14. The Growth Share Matrix or The Product Portfolio.'' Adapted by permission from THE BOSTON CONSULTING GROUP, Inc., 1973.

concept of market dominance. According to their positioning, products are classified as follows:

> *Dogs:* Low market share and low growth. Should break even. Not a source of cash.
>
> *Question marks or problem children:* Low market share and high market growth. These SBUs are cash users. Money must be spent to maintain market position. They could become either stars or dogs.
>
> *Stars:* High growth and high share. May break even or use cash to support high growth rate. Eventually, growth will slow down, and they will become cash cows.
>
> *Cash cows:* High market share and low market growth. As expected, these SBUs throw off cash to support other SBUs.[6]

To survive in the long term, a firm needs the proper balance of business in each area.

Over time, businesses will change their positions. Many SBUs start as problem children, then become stars, then cash cows, and finally dogs. The corporate planning function must work with the managers of each SBU to forecast the future mix of businesses in each

6. Bruce D. Henderson, *Henderson on Corporate Strategy* (Cambridge, Mass.: Abt Associates, 1979).

area. Then resources must be allocated, based on this forecast as well as on the corporate objectives. Firms will use one of the following four strategies:

Build: Invest for the future; forgo short-term earning while improving market position.

Hold: Maintain the current position.

Harvest: Generate short-term cash flow regardless of the long-term effect.

Divest: Sell or liquidate.

The most difficult part of using the BCG method is determining which level or unit of analysis to examine. For example, a firm may have only 5 percent of the world industrial pipe market, but it has 35 percent of the world industrial pipe market over fifteen inches in diameter and 58 percent of the Spanish industrial pipe market over twelve inches in diameter.

The method used most often when applying the BCG approach in international planning is to use one product compared by country, as shown in Figure 17.3. The suggested procedure is to develop the market portfolio material for the firm's own products and for those of major competitors. The analysis should be repeated in five years. This will assist management in deciding which countries to build, hold, harvest, or divest.

The BCG approach in international planning has the following major advantages:

- Requires a global view of the firm's business and its competition
- Provides a framework for analysis and comparison of business

FIGURE 17.3 ● Industrial Pipe: Market Portfolio

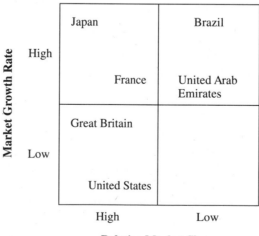

● Is a good basis for the formulation of marketing objectives for specific international markets

● Allows a convenient graphic form that is easily understood by executives

Although the BCG approach has had wide acceptance, it has also received criticism for oversimplifying the process.[7] The BCG approach assumes that high market share and high growth rate will result in success. However, research has raised some doubts about market growth and market share. There are a number of low market share businesses with high profitability. Often, problem children are the result of late entry to a market, which can change quickly with a leapfrog strategy using new technology. If a cash cow is continually milked and not given sufficient attention, it can dry up. General Electric has been criticized for feeding off its cash cows too much and not investing enough to upgrade and protect its consumer products.[8] Obviously, other internal and external factors also affect the success of a business. Even if you accept the basic premise of the BCG approach, there are still problems with defining the product, defining the market, measuring market growth, and measuring market dominance. These limitations apply to both international and domestic applications.

When companies use the BCG method for international markets with one product compared in several countries, the following four problems arise. First, the elements chosen for analysis are the countries. This may be wrong. Instead of looking at the countries by country market growth and market share for hair shampoo, maybe they should be analyzing the world portfolio for hair shampoo by product market—for example, the men's expensive shampoo market, children's shampoo market, or young women's shampoo market. The original BCG model ignores the interdependence of international markets. While the Paris operation may be a dog, using Paris as a production point for Greece, Italy, Spain, Portugal, and France may result in a cash cow or star.

Second, the BCG approach assumes a firm has extended experience with a product. Therefore, a high market share and more production experience will result in decreased costs. This concept becomes very gray when one starts to examine possible variations in input costs, such as capital, human resources, material, tariffs, inflation, exchange rates, and transportation for different countries.

Third, the BCG method assumes the motivations of international firms to be similar (e.g., profits, return on investment). This is not always true. Different countries emphasize different things. For some it is full employment and a favorable balance of payments. Others may desire low inflation. Also, a country's economic or social policies will affect the implementation of the BCG method.

Finally, the individual firm may have other objectives besides the generation of cash, such as gaining technical information, preventing competition, or establishing good relations with a local government. For example, Philips, the Dutch electronics giant, has argued

7. Peter W. Turnbull, ''A Review of Portfolio Planning Models for Industrial Marketing and Purchasing Management,'' *European Journal of Marketing*, 24, no. 3 (1990), p. 13.

8. John O'Shaughnessy, *Competitive Marketing: A Strategic Approach* (London: Allen & Unwin, 1984), pp. 24–25.

that it must keep its semiconductor business, which is a money-losing business. Philips executives maintain that without proprietary access to semiconductor know-how, the company's ability to compete with the Japanese in consumer electronics would be fatally undermined.[9]

The General Electric/McKinsey Approach[10]

General Electric and McKinsey management consultants worked together to develop the GE business screen, a multifactor assessment based on an analysis of factors relating to profitability. The approach is an extension of the BCG approach.

The GE screen uses the following factors to evaluate SBUs:

Industry attractiveness	Business strength
Market size	Relative market share
Market growth	Price competitiveness
Market diversity	Size, growth
Profit margins	Product quality
Competitive structure	Profitability
Technical role	Technological position
Cyclicality	Strengths and weaknesses
Environment	Knowledge of customers/market
Legal, human, social	Image, pollution, people

The GE approach rates each SBU, based on these factors for industry attractiveness and business strength.[11] Each factor is given a certain weight. A procedure of aggregating various executives' opinions on these weights results in high, medium, or low attractiveness and business strength ratings.[12] Each SBU is then located on GE's nine-cell business screen, shown in Figure 17.4.

As shown in the screen, the GE approach results in strategic decisions similar to those in the BCG approach. The three cells at the upper left show the SBUs in favorable industries with good business strengths. The firm should invest and grow with these cells. The three diagonal cells are in the middle. The firm needs to decide whether to maintain, improve, or harvest these SBUs. The three cells at the lower right are those SBUs with an overall low attractiveness; they are candidates for harvesting or divesting.

The principles of the GE approach have been modified and used in the international environment. As we mentioned in Chapter 6, Ford Motor Co.'s Tractor Division developed

9. Andrew Lorenz and Iain Jenkins, ''The Powerhorse That Blew a Fuse,'' *Sunday Times,* May 20, 1990, p. D9.

10. Information in this section is drawn from *Managing Strategies for the Future Through Current Crises* (Fairfield, Conn.: General Electric Company, 1975).

11. Francis J. Aguilar and Richard Hamermesh, ''General Electric: Strategic Position: 1981,'' Harvard Business School Case 9-381-174, p. 25.

12. Turnbull, ''A Review of Portfolio Planning Models,'' pp. 7–10.

FIGURE 17.4 ● GE's Business Screen for Evaluating SBUs

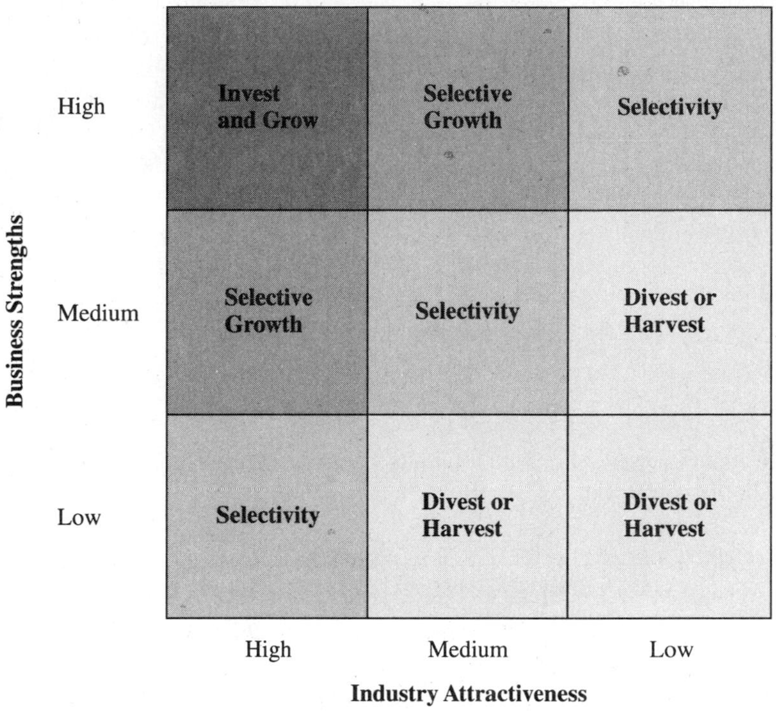

<table>
<tr><td rowspan="3" style="writing-mode: vertical-lr">Business Strengths</td><td>High</td><td>Invest and Grow</td><td>Selective Growth</td><td>Selectivity</td></tr>
<tr><td>Medium</td><td>Selective Growth</td><td>Selectivity</td><td>Divest or Harvest</td></tr>
<tr><td>Low</td><td>Selectivity</td><td>Divest or Harvest</td><td>Divest or Harvest</td></tr>
<tr><td></td><td></td><td>High</td><td>Medium</td><td>Low</td></tr>
<tr><td></td><td></td><td colspan="3">Industry Attractiveness</td></tr>
</table>

a strategic market portfolio evaluation system that focused on country attractiveness and competitive strengths.[13]

The GE approach has the same limitations as the BCG method. However, the GE method is more adaptable to international markets. Each firm can determine which factors are important to its success in an international market and can evaluate SBUs based on these factors. Unfortunately, little empirical work has been done on either approach in the international market. The GE approach is still two dimensional, using only the factors of country attractiveness and business strength. This ignores the form of entry. For example, the importance of political stability varies greatly, depending on whether a firm is exporting or involved in direct foreign investment.

In conclusion, the GE approach is useful for international companies. It provides more flexibility than the BCG approach, but its limitations should not be ignored.

13. Gilbert D. Harrell and Richard O'Kiefer, ''Multinational Strategic Market Portfolios,'' *MSU Business Topics,* Winter 1981, p. 12.

Profit Impact of Marketing Strategy (PIMS)[14]   The PIMS project was started in 1960 at General Electric. Over the years, the model was developed at the Harvard Business School, the Marketing Science Institute, and finally at the Strategic Planning Institute. The PIMS model database includes the history and performance of over 450 companies and three thousand businesses.[15] The model includes a computer-based regression model that utilizes the experience of the database to determine what explains (or drives) profitability.

Each business is described in terms of thirty-seven factors, such as growth rate, market share, product quality, and investment intensity. The PIMS model uses multivariate regression equations to establish relationships between these different factors and two separate measures of performance, specifically return on investment (ROI) and cash flow. PIMS research indicates that these performance measures are explained by general factors such as the following:

Market growth rate

Market share of business

Market share divided by share of three largest competitors

Degree of vertical integration

Working capital requirements per dollars of sales

Plant and equipment requirements per dollars of sales

Relative product quality

The PIMS model uses many more variables than either the BCG or GE approach. Using the thirty-seven factors, the model explains over 80 percent of the observed variation in profitability of the three thousand businesses in the database. Varta AG and Wiener-Verlag has $1 billion in sales through twenty profit centers in eight countries. Its business consists of paper manufacturing and printing. Through the BCG approach, it found that most of its businesses were classified as cash cows; therefore, they would be wise to take the cash and invest in high-growth businesses. Unfortunately, the group had very little surplus cash. So while the BCG technique was easy to apply and communicate, it gave little practical help. The company used the PIMS analysis to enhance its strategic planning. The twenty profit centers resulted in seventy SBUs, which were evaluated relative to the three thousand businesses in the database. The actual return on investment was calculated and compared to the return of companies with a comparable cost structure and competitive situation. The analysis showed a number of businesses that would achieve immediate profit improvement from operational changes such as reduced inventory. The analysis also showed which businesses were in a weak competitive position and the size of the invest-

14. Information in this section is drawn from Sidney Schoeffler, Robert D. Buzzell, and Donald F. Henry, ''Impact of Strategic Planning on Profit Performance,'' *Harvard Business Review,* March–April 1974, pp. 137–145.

15. Robert D. Buzzell and Bradley T. Gale, *The PIMS Principles: Linking Strategy to Performance* (New York: Free Press, 1987).

ment needed to improve the business. The Varta AG and Wiener-Verlag group of companies found PIMS far superior to the BCG model.[16]

There are three major criticisms of the PIMS model. First, since the model uses variables related to each other, multicollinearity results. Therefore, the impact of individual factors on performance cannot be clearly identified. Second, the PIMS results include only those companies still in the business. The higher profits may be the result of taking higher risks, but that does not take into account other companies that tried and failed.[17] Third, the technical procedure for eliminating extreme values of data input tends to bias the results and improve the model's appearance. Although all these criticisms are valid, the methodology of the PIMS approach is one of the best approaches available for domestic planning.

The outlook for an international PIMS model is optimistic, with over one thousand non-U.S. strategic business units. The PIMS model should analyze performance by the traditional criteria as well as by mode of entry. The form that a multinational business takes has a significant impact on costs, profitability, risks, and so on. Also, the PIMS model will probably be limited to product-by-country analysis. Although the data will be helpful, many products need to be analyzed on a product-by-market segment. Also, with the regional trade groups that have formed, such as ANCOM, ASEAN, EU, EFTA, and OPEC (see Table 5.6), many markets are becoming regionalized. This will also be an obstacle for the international PIMS model.

However, despite these limitations, the PIMS model may become one of the key international strategic planning models in the future. With the utilization of a multinational database, the PIMS model will be able to assist planners in deciding how to allocate resources to meet corporate objectives.

Scenario Planning[18]   The three strategic planning models discussed so far are referred to as portfolio models. These models do not take into consideration the impact of various external factors such as economic growth, energy costs, inflation, East/West relations, war, and economic fluctuations.

Scenario planning is a unique approach to strategic planning. With scenario planning, the multinational's business is broken down into business/country segments. A central or most probable scenario is developed regarding significant external variables such as energy costs, world politics, and inflation. Possible variants of this central scenario are also developed. Then the business/country segments are evaluated based on the central scenario and the variant scenarios. Ideally, investment decisions can be based on this analysis. A large, U.K.-based oil company was using scenario planning in the early 1970s. The company

16. George Kellinghusen and Klaus Wubbenhorts, "Strategic Control for Improved Performance," *Long Range Planning,* 23, no. 3 (1990), pp. 30–40.

17. George S. Day, *Analysis for Strategic Market Decisions* (New York: West, 1986), p. 153.

18. Information in this section is drawn from Harold F. Klein and Robert E. Linneman, "The Use of Scenarios in Corporate Planning—Eight Case Histories," *Long Range Planning,* October 1981, pp. 69–77.

had devised six possible scenarios, with a plan for each. When the Yom Kippur Arab-Israeli war took place in October 1973, followed by OPEC declaring an oil embargo, this company already had a plan they could implement immediately to deal with limited supply and a slowdown in the worldwide demand for oil.[19]

Scenario planning has limitations. First, the development of a central scenario and variants will be difficult. There will be many inputs to this scenario, with limited agreement. Second, analysis of the effect of each scenario will also be complex. For example, if a firm is selling pipe to the United Kingdom and the central scenario predicts oil prices will go up 10 percent per year, how will the firm evaluate the U.K. pipe market? Increased oil prices mean more tax revenues from North Sea oil, an increase in exports, a favorable impact on the balance of trade, the strengthening of the pound sterling, an increase in imports, and a decrease in the ability of the remaining U.K. industries to export.

Although scenario planning and contingency planning are useful techniques, they should be used to augment the portfolio methods—BCG, GE, and PIMS.

Global Business Planning—A Look to the Future

When the models for business planning (BCG, GE/McKinsey, and others) are applied to international business, they are criticized as being mere extensions of domestic models. The factors and criteria used in these approaches are too narrow and exclude factors that are international in nature. Researchers emphasize the need for adoption of a global portfolio perspective in order to determine the optional mix of countries, products, market segments, and modes of operation to achieve the desired long-term results.[20]

A global perspective on portfolio planning should allow a company to evaluate the extent of its involvement in international markets. Companies need to explore the opportunities for reallocating resources across countries, product line, and modes of operations. The benefits of participating in lead markets (see Chapter 11), understanding a major competitor's home market, and exploiting opportunities from specialized R&D talent must be assessed to identify the best allocation of resources to maximize the long-term profitability. When companies apply domestic approaches to the global environment, resources are often spread over wide geographic areas, with little attention given to the interdependencies of management decisions. An effective global portfolio strategy requires an integrated approach within the context of corporate objectives. Yoram Wind and Susan Douglas suggest that a global portfolio approach should:

1. Be built on conceptually attractive dimensions of risks and returns, as well as on any idiosyncratic criteria considered to be important to the company

2. Allow for differential weighting of the various dimensions

3. Allow for sequential analysis to reduce the cost and complexity of data collection

19. R. Jeffrey Ellis, *Managing Strategy in the Real World* (Lexington, Mass.: Lexington Books, 1988), pp. 107–119.
20. Turnbull, ''A Review of Portfolio Planning Models,'' pp. 14–15.

4. Integrate the available hard data with management's subjective judgments

5. Allow for a flexible structure capable of dealing with any unit of analysis or portfolio components

6. Be based on projected performance of the product/market/mode of entry and level and type of marketing activities under alternative scenarios

7. Offer guidelines for resource allocation among the portfolio components

8. Incorporate the scheduling of activities with the resource allocation procedure

9. Allow for easily implementable sensitivity to assess the impact of changes in assumptions and judgments or to stimulate likely outcomes of competitive activities and other environmental forces[21]

The International Marketing Planning Process

The complexity of international markets requires a structured approach to the planning process. Research into the practices of multinational companies has revealed a number of problems regarding the planning process. Among the problems identified were the following:

● Too much information of the wrong kind and a lack of useful information for planning

● A neglect of strategic or long-term planning

● Overemphasis on the plan as a control device instead of as a means to achieving the objectives

● A belief that forecasting and budgeting were market planning

● A separation of long-term and short-term plans, which precluded operational management from considering more desirable alternatives[22]

The heterogeneous nature of international markets and the difficulty of data collection require that the marketer take an organized approach to evaluating opportunities and preparing plans. Figure 17.5 illustrates an international marketing planning matrix.

The planning matrix is an organized approach to evaluating international opportunities. The matrix requires that the marketer evaluate the marketing planning variables at each level of decision-making. Levels of decision-making, which are located on the vertical axis, begin with the commitment decision. This first decision, whether or not to enter foreign markets, is based on the firm's objectives, its resources, and the opportunities available in international versus domestic markets. After making the commitment decision,

---

21. Yoram Wind and Susan Douglas, ''International Portfolio Analysis and Strategy: The Challenges of the 80s,'' *Journal of International Business Studies,* Fall 1981, p. 7. Reprinted by permission.

22. Tom Griffin, ''Marketing Planning: Observations on Current Practices and Recent Studies,'' *European Journal of Marketing,* 24, no. 12 (1989), pp. 21–22.

FIGURE 17.5 ● International Marketing Planning Matrix

International Decisions	Marketing Planning Variables					
	Situation Analysis	Problems-Opportunity Analysis	Objectives	Marketing Program	Marketing Budgets	Sales Vol. Cost/Profit Estimate
A. Commitment Decision						
B. Country Selection						
C. Mode of Entry						
D. Marketing Strategy						
E. Marketing Organization						

Source: Reprinted with permission from Helmut Becker and Hans B. Thorelli: *International Marketing Strategy,* Copyright © 1980, Pergamon Press PLC.

a company will select the country it wishes to enter. The country decision is based on evaluation of the environment, the demand, the corporate resources, and the financial projections. The mode of entering the selected country will be based on the firm's commitment decision, the country selection, and the cost/benefit evaluation of different modes of entry.

As discussed in Chapter 9, the mode of entry will also be affected by a variety of other factors, such as risk assessment and laws of foreign ownership. The marketing strategy will flow logically from the firm's objective in a market, which will include the marketing mix required to differentiate products in that environment. The market organization decision is related to the objective and strategy for each market. The organization structure will determine which people will be where, how decisions will be made, what information and services will go back and forth between the organizational unit and headquarters, and the budgeting control process. A recent study of seventy-nine businesses from twenty countries found that all companies prepared some type of marketing plan. In fact, when given the following standard model for a marketing plan, 65 percent said their process was very similar and 28 percent said it was somewhat similar.[23]

Model Marketing Plan

Situational analysis

 Environmental trends

 Market trends

 Strengths and weaknesses versus competition

Problems and opportunities based on situational analysis

Objectives of the plan

Strategies to achieve objectives

 Product, package, price, distribution, advertising, sales, target markets

Tactics to implement the strategies

 Sales forecast

 Estimate of income, expense, profit

 Method to evaluate overall effectiveness of plan

Selecting Markets

Only the largest international company with a product that appeals to all types of people in all environments can afford to be in all the countries of the world. Given the limited employee and financial resources of most companies, international activities must be narrowed to a selective set of countries. Given that most companies desire to be profitable in each market served and that profitability will be determined by the level of resources required to meet the competitive demands of the marketplace, it is important to maintain a critical mass of marketing resources. These resources include the cost of modifying the product to be competitive, the distribution coverage, and the advertising and direct sales coverage required to be competitive. This set of marketing resources must reach a critical mass in order to be effective and profitable. Figure 17.6 shows a grid for evaluating new foreign markets. The horizontal axis measures the market attractiveness of each country, and the vertical axis describes the company's position in each market with respect to the critical mass of marketing resources.

 Using the grid for selecting new markets will help a company focus its resources on the opportunities with the greatest profitability. It will also tend to concentrate market expansion in markets that are geographically close to current markets.

23. Ibid.

FIGURE 17.6 ● Grid for Evaluating Foreign Markets

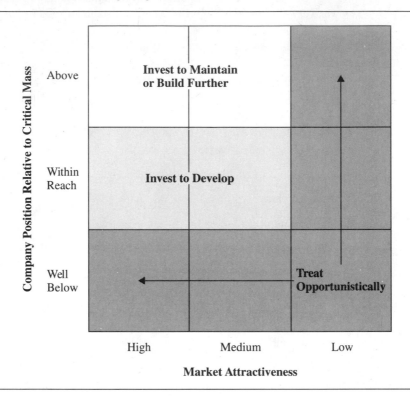

Source: Robert S. Attiyeh and David L. Wenner, "Critical Mass: Key to Export Profits." Reprinted from *Business Horizons,* December 1979. Copyright © 1979 by the Foundation for the School of Business at Indiana University. Used with permission.

Coordinating the Planning Process[24]

Coordinating the strategic planning process between the product marketing functions and the country managers is a challenging process. A natural tendency to emphasize the product element shortchanges the geographic element. To improve coordination of product management and country management while utilizing the expertise of each, General Electric has each *country* executive develop a comprehensive country opportunity plan that covers all products and strategies. The country executive's plan is compared to the plans of GE's individual strategic business units for that market. The combination of the two different

24. The information in this section is drawn from "Many Subs in One Country? Getting More Coordination Without Stifling Initiative," *Business International,* January 15, 1982, pp. 17–19.

organizations provides a rich pool of information on tactics and opportunities. The final plan integrates the product and country points of view, with conflicts identified and solutions proposed.

Hoechst, one of the largest global chemical companies, headquartered in Germany, uses a multilevel planning system to coordinate the different layers of management, as well as to get the full benefit of its knowledge and coordinate strategy from different parts of the company. The Hoechst planning system is illustrated in Figure 17.7. The top layer is strategic planning covering a ten-year horizon for products and regions. For example, what is Hoechst planning over the next ten years for agricultural operations and pharmaceuticals? In addition, what are the plans for Japan or France? Care is taken to ensure that the strategic goals match for products and regions. Strategic planning at Hoechst involves the following four steps:

1. Gathering internal data about markets, competitors, and capacities

2. Gathering and analyzing external data on world economics, industry dynamics, market trends, and key success factors

3. Developing strategic options and selecting a preferred solution

4. Developing an implementation plan with milestones identified and target dates set

The middle layer of Hoechst's system is operational planning. This process covers the next four years on a rolling forecast, which is revised each year. The first year is in detail, and the second to fourth years are in rougher outline. The bottom layer is a control system for following up and monitoring, on a quarterly basis, the progress of the operational plans. This allows deviations to be tracked and plans adjusted to deal with shocks, such as currency fluctuations. The planning system has proved successful, with Hoechst achieving a 1988 profit of 2.0 billion Deutsche marks, the largest in its 125-year history.[25]

Siemens, the world's fifth-largest electrical and electronics equipment maker, has a formalized communication phase between the product groups and the geographic structures; during this formal communication phase of the planning process, the product and country management meet to establish an understanding of each other's position. Eaton Corporation, organized around a worldwide product structure, found it necessary to inform managers of methods to respond to common environmental issues such as political conditions, taxes, inflation, and joint ownership. To share information and experience, regional coordinating committees that meet monthly were set up in Latin America and Europe. Danish firms were found to be behind other Europeans in adopting formalized planning systems, because they see planning as a matter of survival and prefer to minimize paper plans in favor of oral communication.[26]

25. Carol Kennedy, ''Hoechst: Re-positioning for a Global Market,'' *Long Range Planning,* 23, no. 3 (1990), pp. 16–22.
26. Robert Ackersley and William C. Harris, ''How Danish Companies Plan,'' *Long Range Planning,* 22, no. 6 (1989), p. 115.

FIGURE 17.7 ● Hoechst Planning System

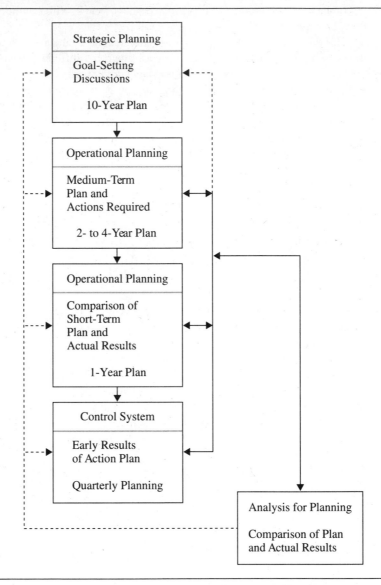

Source: Reprinted from LONG RANGE PLANNING, Vol. 23, No. 3, p. 18. Copyright 1990, with kind permission from Elsevier Science Ltd., The Boulevard, Langford Lane, Kidlington, OX5 1GB, UK.

TABLE 17.2 ● Degree of Local Management Autonomy According to Type of Marketing Decision

	Local marketing decision			
Degree of local management autonomy	*PRODUCT DESIGN*	*ADVERTISING APPROACH*	*RETAIL PRICE*	*DISTRIBUTION OUTLETS/1,000 POPULATION*
Primary authority rested with local management	30%	86%	74%	61%
Local management shared authority with other levels in organization	15	8	20	38
Decision primarily imposed upon local management	55 100%	6 100%	6 100%	1 100%
N (marketing programs observed)	N = 86	N = 84*	N = 84*	N = 86

*Classification information not available in two cases.

Source: R. J. Aylmer, "Who Makes Marketing Decisions in the Multinational Firm?" Reprinted from *Journal of Marketing,* October 1970, p. 26, published by the American Marketing Association.

Who Makes the Decisions?

Decision-making responsibility is dependent on several internal and external factors. What decisions are made within each line of command differs from firm to firm.

Table 17.2 summarizes a study of eighty-six separate marketing programs in nine U.S.-based international companies. The study determined the degree of local management autonomy with respect to various marketing decisions. The author of the report found that primary authority for the advertising, pricing, and distribution decisions were with local management. Only the product design decision was controlled primarily by headquarters and imposed on local management.

Culture can also influence the decision-making process. For example, at France's state-run Rhône Poulene, many managers expected to be told what to do by the hierarchy. After Rhône-Poulene acquired a number of overseas companies, it found the need to change its culture to speed up decision-making.[27]

Standardized Versus Decentralized Planning

When prospective markets can be grouped together as a result of homogeneous characteristics, then marketing decisions can often be standardized and applied to the markets.

27. "Rhône-Poulene—Building a Global Powerhouse," *Fortune,* July 26, 1993, pp. 96–97.

There are, however, certain marketing functions that cannot be completely standardized. A survey of one hundred senior executives in twenty-seven leading packaged-goods multinationals was conducted to determine the level of standardization for each of the elements in the marketing process. The results of this study are shown in Figure 17.8.

A study of seventeen attempts of standardization at U.S. and European multinationals found that one-half of the attempts failed. The researcher recommends: (1) more-uniform market research to determine the similarities and differences from country to country, (2)

FIGURE 17.8 ● Standardization of Marketing Decisions Among European Subsidiaries of Selected Multinational Enterprises

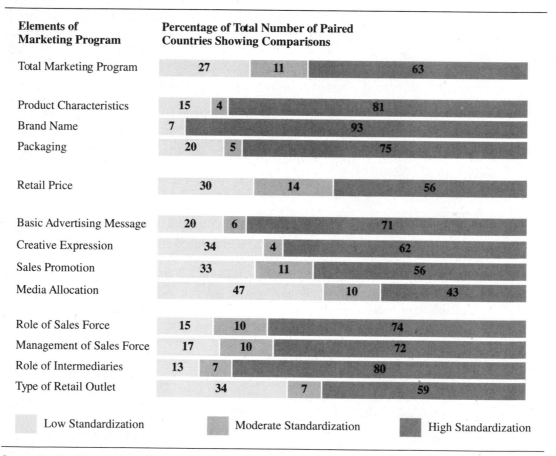

Elements of Marketing Program	Percentage of Total Number of Paired Countries Showing Comparisons (Low / Moderate / High)		
Total Marketing Program	27	11	63
Product Characteristics	15	4	81
Brand Name	7		93
Packaging	20	5	75
Retail Price	30	14	56
Basic Advertising Message	20	6	71
Creative Expression	34	4	62
Sales Promotion	33	11	56
Media Allocation	47	10	43
Role of Sales Force	15	10	74
Management of Sales Force	17	10	72
Role of Intermediaries	13	7	80
Type of Retail Outlet	34	7	59

Low Standardization   Moderate Standardization   High Standardization

use of local initiative and decision-making while implementing the strategy, (3) improved follow-up to identify and solve local implementation problems, (4) active participation from subsidiaries in the development of the strategy, and (5) increased flexibility to allow global standards to be modified or developed when dictated by local conditions.[28]

The single European market offers a new opportunity for companies to standardize. A survey of forty companies inside the European Union (EU) and forty companies outside the EU, from the European Free Trade Association (EFTA), North America, Australasia, and the Far East, revealed their views about the opportunities that a unified Europe presented. Both insiders and outsiders reported that a unified Europe would encourage them to centralize strategic market decision-making and advertising and promotion. Particularly the insiders thought that marketing operations should be decentralized to get close to the customer and delivery quality by the account management staff.[29] Others have argued that the global product and centralized approach will only apply to cosmopolitan products such as expensive watches and perfume, so marketers should continue to adapt products to meet local consumers' preferences.[30]

The annual operating plan is the most widely used process in most international firms.[31] Most firms combine their annual operating plan with a five-year plan. The planning process should be a major force for increasing the degree of integration and coordination between different entities of a global enterprise. According to James Hulbert and William Brandt, most of the problems with multinational planning lie with people, not with the planning systems.[32] According to John Lovering, finance director at Sears:

> Planning is very simple. It is deciding what to do, and making it happen. In my experience the second is much harder than the first. It is doomed to failure unless the necessary organizational steps are taken, and the use of strategic controls and reinforcing incentive and reward systems are central to this task. But as long as we remember that planning is a change agent, nothing more nothing less, we will not go far wrong. This means that the planning process must be consistent with the strategy and must help shape an appropriate culture and style. In these circumstances, the use of strategic planning processes can be genuinely helpful in ensuring a systematic approach to resource allocation and the maintenance of subsequent control.[33]

28. Kamran Kashani, ''Beware the Pitfalls of Global Marketing,'' *Harvard Business Review,* September–October 1989, pp. 91–98.

29. Sandra Vandermerwe, ''Strategies for a Pan European Market,'' *Long Range Planning,* 22, no. 3 (1989), pp. 50–51.

30. Jurgen Reichel, ''How Can Marketing Be Successfully Standardized for the European Market?'' *European Journal of Marketing,* 23, no. 7 (1989), pp. 60–67.

31. James M. Hulbert and William K. Brandt, *Managing the Multinational Subsidiary* (New York: Holt, Rinehart and Winston, 1980), pp. 35–64.

32. Ibid.

33. John Lovering, ''Brief Case: Developing a Strategic Planning and Control Process,'' *Long Range Planning,* 23, no. 2 (1990), pp. 112–114.

Controlling International Marketing Operations

Maintaining control of international operations is a growing concern in light of the increasing trend toward global companies. As a company becomes larger, it faces more critical decisions, and control over operations tends to dissipate. A company's planning process is usually based on a number of assumptions about country environments, competitors, pricing, government regulations, and so on. As a plan is implemented, the company must monitor its success, as well as the variables that were used to develop the plan. As the environment changes, so will the plan; therefore, a critical part of planning is control. Establishment of a system to control marketing activities in numerous markets is not an easy job. But if companies expect to achieve the goals they have set, then a control system must be established to regulate the activities for achieving the desired goals.

Variables That Affect Control

Several variables affect the degree and effectiveness of a control system for international operations. A number of these are described in the following sections.

Communication Systems   Effective communication systems facilitate control. Physical communication methods, such as the phone, mail, and personal visits, are greatly affected by both distance and location. The more sophisticated a country's telecommunications are, the easier the communication process is. Telecommunications technology greatly improved in the 1980s, with global optical fibers and satellite networks. Global voice mail, facsimile transmissions, and telephone communications have greatly enhanced communication and reporting.

Likewise, the closer the subdivision is to headquarters, the less chance there is to lose control. As physical distances separating headquarters and operating divisions increase, the time, expense, and potential for error increase. Physical distance also affects the speed with which changes can be implemented and problems can be detected.

Global information networks are becoming available that allow improved communication around the world. For example, Internet links millions of computer users, who have access to information, research, and services. These information superhighways are reducing many of the constraints of geography. Long term, these inexpensive global networks will allow for better control.[34]

Adequacy of Data   The accuracy and incompleteness of economic, industrial, and consumer data affect control. If the marketing plan and the goals for a particular country are based on inadequate data, then the ability to control and modify the marketing activities will be affected. For example, consider the goal of selling washing machines to Malaysia, maybe to achieve a 30 percent share of last year's market, which was estimated at 100,000 units. Therefore, the goal would be 30,000 units. But if the actual sales last year were only

34. Louise Kehoe, ''Casting the Net Worldwide,'' *Financial Times,* November 30, 1993, p. 11.

70,000 units because the government had exaggerated its report to indicate economic prosperity, then the goal of 30,000 units would be too high. It may also be difficult to get timely and accurate statistics, such as the level of inflation and disposable income, which will influence the marketing strategy.

Diversity of Environments   Currency values, legal structures, political systems, advertising options, number and type of public holidays, and cultural factors all influence the task of developing and controlling a marketing program. Due to this diversity of the local environments, there are continuous conflicts between the needs of the local situation and overall corporate goals. The issue of diversity must be reflected in the control system.

Management Philosophy   Management philosophy about whether the company should be centralized or decentralized will affect the development of a control system. A highly centralized management control system will require an effective communication system so that the headquarters staff has timely and accurate local input that may affect decision-making. The communication system must also allow decisions to be made quickly and transmitted to the local management for quick implementation. A decentralized management control system may not require the same type of communication system for day-to-day decision-making, but it will require a well-documented and -communicated set of objectives for each autonomous unit. These objectives will help guide local decision-making and control so that the corporate goals are achieved.

Size of International Operations   As the size of the international operation increases as a percentage of total sales, top management becomes more active in decision-making. One author found that as the size of a local affiliate grew, the frequency of decisions imposed by headquarters declined and the frequency of decisions shared with headquarters increased.[35]

Elements of a Control Strategy

Control is the cornerstone of management. Control provides the means to direct, regulate, and manage business operations. The implementation of a marketing program requires a significant amount of interaction among the individual areas of marketing (product development, advertising, sales), as well as the other functional areas (production, research and development, finance). The control system is used to measure these business activities, competitive reaction, and market reaction. Deviations from the planned activities and results are analyzed and reported so that corrective action can be taken.

   Many companies need to improve their control process. Without some type of control system, strategies that look good on paper never get implemented. Most strategies are long-term in nature and can often take a back seat to the short-term tactical decisions needed for quarterly results. One of the often overlooked strengths of Japanese companies

35. R. J. Aylmer, ''Who Makes the Decisions in the Multinational Firm?'' *Journal of Marketing*, October 1970, p. 26.

FIGURE 17.9 ● Strategic Control Processes of 18 Multinationals

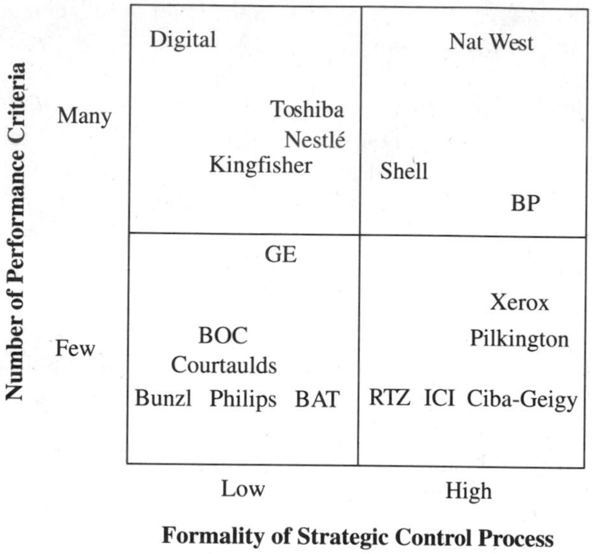

<table>
<tr><td rowspan="2" style="writing-mode: vertical-rl">Number of Performance Criteria</td><td>Many</td><td>Digital

　　　Toshiba
　　　Nestlé
　Kingfisher</td><td>Nat West

Shell
　　　　BP</td></tr>
<tr><td>Few</td><td>　　GE

　BOC
Courtaulds
Bunzl Philips BAT</td><td>　　　　Xerox
　　　Pilkington

RTZ ICI Ciba-Geigy</td></tr>
<tr><td></td><td></td><td>Low</td><td>High</td></tr>
</table>

Formality of Strategic Control Process

Source: Michael Goold, *Strategic Control* (London: Economist Books, 1990), p. 33. Reprinted by permission.

is their ability to develop and implement long-term strategies.[36] Through interviews with over fifty companies regarding their control systems, Michael Goold assessed control systems on two dimensions: number of performance criteria and formality of the strategic control process. Figure 17.9 summarizes the control systems of eighteen multinational companies. The research on these companies found that strategic control systems add value in the following ways:

● Forcing greater clarity and realism in planning
● Encouraging higher standards of performance
● Providing more motivation for business managers
● Permitting timely intervention by corporate management
● Ensuring that financial objectives do not overwhelm strategic objectives
● Defining responsibilities more clearly, making decentralization work better[37]

A control system has three basic elements: (1) the establishment of standards, (2) the measurement of performance against standards, and (3) the analysis and correction of any

36. Warren J. Keegan, ''Strategic Marketing Planning: The Japanese Approach,'' *International Marketing Review,* Autumn 1983, pp. 5–15.
37. Michael Goold, *Strategic Control* (London: Economist Books, 1990), p. 125.

deviations from the standards. Although control seemingly is a conceptually simple aspect of the management process, a wide variety of problems arise in international situations, resulting in inefficiencies and intracompany conflicts.

Companies have found many inefficiencies and redundancies in the way business is done. So, many are looking for ways to radically improve performance as well as reduce costs. ''Business process reengineering is the fundamental rethinking and radical design of business processes to achieve dramatic improvements in critical, contemporary measures of performance, such as costs, quality service and speed.''[38] Rank Xerox has developed a set of seven uniform basic processes to be used across all functional departments in Europe. The company expects to cut overheads by $200 million per year and improve productivity.[39]

Developing Standards Setting standards is an extremely important part of the control process because standards will direct the efforts of individual managers. To effectively influence the behavior of the managers who direct the international marketing programs, the standards must be clearly defined, accepted, and understood by these managers. Standard setting is driven by the corporate goals. Corporate goals are achieved through the effective and efficient implementation of a marketing strategy, on a local-country level. The standards should be related to the sources of long-term competitive advantage. In companies where the strategies are decentralized to a business, it is recommended that there be only four to six key objectives. Fewer objectives focus management's efforts without causing confusion about priorities.[40]

Control standards must be specifically tied to the strategy and based on the desired behavior of the local marketing people. The desired behavior should reflect the actions to be taken to implement the strategy, as well as performance standards that indicate the success of the strategy, such as increased market share or sales. Examples of *behavioral* standards include the type and amount of advertising, the distribution coverage, market research to be performed, and expected price levels. *Performance* standards can include trial rates by customers or sales by product line. In the 1990s, there has been a trend to broaden the measures of business performance beyond financial data. More and more companies are measuring quality, customer satisfaction, innovation, and market share.[41]

The standards should be set through a joint process with corporate headquarters personnel and the local marketing organization. Normally the standard setting will be done annually, when the operational business plan is established.

Management systems need to be somewhat consistent for comparability. For example, James River, the papermaking company, has a European joint venture with Oy Nokia of Finland and Cragnotti & Partners, an Italian merchant bank. The joint venture organization

38. Michael Hammer and James Champy, *Reengineering the Corporation* (New York: Harper Collins, 1993), p. 32.
39. Christopher Lorenz, ''Time to Get Serious,'' *Financial Times,* June 25, 1993, p. 9.
40. Goold, *Strategic Control,* p. 120.
41. Robert G. Eccles, ''The Performance Measurement Manifesto,'' *Harvard Business Review,* January–February 1991, p. 165.

acquired thirteen companies in ten countries. When comparing plant utilization, the company found some companies operated 330 days per year, allowing for holidays and maintenance, where other companies operated 350 days. To accurately measure results, the company found it needed to develop uniform standards and measurement systems.[42]

Measuring and Evaluating Performance   After standards are set, a process is required for monitoring performance. In order to monitor performance against standards, management must be able to observe current performance. Observation in the international environment is often impersonal through mail, cable, or telex, but it also can be personal through telephone, travel, or meetings. Much of the numerical information, such as sales and expenses, will be reported through the accounting system. Other items, such as the implementation of an advertising program, will be communicated through a report. The reporting system may be weekly, monthly, or quarterly. Motorola has found that a hybrid organization best suits the semiconductor business. Production and finance are directed from the center, and marketing and distribution are done locally, by geography. To measure this hybrid organization, the factories are evaluated on costs, quality, and timeliness of production, while the geographic territories are judged on sales, profit, and market share.[43]

Analyzing and Correcting Deviations from the Standards   The purpose of establishing standards and reporting performance is to ensure achievement of the corporate goals. To achieve these goals, management must evaluate performance versus standards and initiate actions where performance is below the standards set. Due to distance, communication, and cultural difference issues, the control process can be difficult in the international setting.

Control strategy can be related to the principle of the carrot and the stick, using both positive and negative incentives. On the positive side, outstanding performance may result in increased independence, more marketing dollars, and salary increases or bonuses for the managers. On the negative side, unsatisfactory performance can lead to the reduction of all the items associated with a satisfactory performance, as well as the threat of firing the managers responsible. The key to correcting deviations is to get the managers to understand and agree with the standards, then give them the ability to correct these deficiencies. This will often mean that the managers will be given some flexibility with resources. For example, if sales are down 10 percent, the ability to increase advertising or reduce prices may be necessary to offset the sales decline.

Making Strategic Control Work   Most companies do not have a formal strategic control system. Few define and monitor their strategic objectives as systematically as they monitor their budgets. While most managers can tell you within pennies how much the advertising expenditures are over or under the plan, few will be able to tell you the six milestones to

42. Janet Guyon, ''A Joint-Venture Papermaker Casts Net Across Europe,'' *Wall Street Journal,* December 7, 1992, p. B4.
43. ''Asia Beckons,'' *Economist,* May 30, 1992, p. 64.

TABLE 17.3 ● Making Formal Strategic Control Work

Issues	*Recommendations*
Selecting the right objectives	Based on analysis of competitive advantage
	Few in number
	Milestones that measure short-term progress
	Leading indicators of future performance
	Projects or action programs only if important for competitive advantage
Setting suitable targets	Precise and objectively measurable, if possible
	Proposed by business managers but stretched by the center
	Competitively benchmarked
	Consistent with budget targets: tradeoffs openly confronted and resolved
Creating pressure for strategic performance	Systematic progress monitoring and reviews
	Personal rewards indirectly tied to achievement of strategic targets
	Performance against strategic targets matters to top management and is the basis for corporate interventions
Strategic planning and strategic control	High-quality strategic planning needed as basis for strategic controls
	Strategic planning process used to review strategic progress
Formality without bureaucracy	Avoid large staff departments and lengthy reports
	Avoid specially gathered data
	Conduct reviews face to face
	Supplement formal reviews with informal contacts
	Be prepared to short-circuit formal process if necessary

Source: Michael Goold, *Strategic Control* (London: Economist Books, 1990), p. 199. Reprinted by permission.

implementing the 1993 strategy and the company's progress on each. To establish and get full value from a formal strategic control system, Michael Goold has made a number of recommendations, summarized in Table 17.3.

Conflict Between Headquarters and Subsidiaries

A universal problem facing international marketing executives is internal conflict between headquarters and subsidiaries. A study of 109 large U.S. and European multinationals and their worldwide subsidiaries found that this conflict was a bigger problem than competition,

TABLE 17.4 ● Key Problems Identified by Large U.S. and European Multinationals

Key problems identified by headquarters executives
- Lack of qualified personnel
- Lack of strategic thinking and long-range planning at subsidiary level
- Lack of marketing expertise at the subsidiary level
- Too little relevant communication between headquarters and subsidiaries
- Insufficient utilization of multinational marketing experience
- Restricted headquarters control of the subsidiaries

Key problems identified by subsidiary executives
- Excessive headquarters control procedures
- Excessive financial and marketing constraints
- Insufficient participation of subsidiaries in product decisions
- Insensitivity of headquarters to local market differences
- Shortage of useful information from headquarters
- Lack of multinational orientation at headquarters

Source: Adapted and reprinted by permission of the *Harvard Business Review.* ''Problems That Plague Multinational Marketers'' by Ulrich E. Wiechmann and Lewis G. Pringle (July–August 1979). Copyright © 1979 by the President and Fellows of Harvard College; all rights reserved.

political instability, or any of the other challenges of international marketing. Table 17.4 summarizes the results of the study.

Conflicts between two parts of a corporation are inevitable due to the natural differences in orientation and perception between the two groups. The subsidiary manager usually wants less control, more authority, and more local differentiation, whereas headquarters wants more detailed reporting and greater unification of geographically dispersed operations. This expected conflict is not bad. In fact, the conflict causes constant dialogue between different organizational levels during the planning and implementation of strategies. This dialogue will result in a balance between headquarters and subsidiary authority, global and local perspective, and standardization and differentiation of the international marketing mix.[44]

Some of the problems in planning and controlling international marketing operations can be reduced or eliminated. Common problems, such as deficiencies in the communications process, overemphasis on short-term issues, and failure to take full advantage of an organization's international experience, require open discussions between headquarters and subsidiary executives.

44. Ulrich E. Wiechmann and Lewis G. Pringle, ''Problems That Plague Multinational Marketers,'' *Harvard Business Review,* 57 (July–August 1979), p. 124.

Retaining Talented Global Managers

Many companies are shifting to a global marketing orientation. To successfully manage this shift to global marketing, companies must utilize and integrate well the talents of global managers. A recent survey of U.S. executives found that fewer than half of those sent abroad thought the posting helped their careers.[45] Companies that want to send good people overseas and keep them must change the status and handling of these posts. Five suggestions follow on how to motivate and retain talented global managers when making the shift to global marketing.

1. Encourage field managers to generate ideas and give them recognition for those ideas. R. J. Reynolds revitalized the Camel brand after a German subsidiary came up with a new positioning and copy strategy.

2. Include the country managers in the development of marketing strategies and programs. When Procter & Gamble introduced a sanitary napkin as a global product, local managers were encouraged to suggest changes in the global marketing program. Also, local managers were allowed to develop their own coupon and sales promotion programs.

3. Maintain a product portfolio of regional and global brands.

4. Allow country managers control of their marketing budgets, so they can respond to local consumer needs and competition.

5. Emphasize country managers' general management responsibilities that extend beyond the marketing function. Country managers who have risen through the marketing function often do not spend enough time on local manufacturing, industrial relations, and government affairs. Global marketing can free them to focus on and develop their skills in these other areas.[46]

Conclusions

The processes of planning marketing programs and controlling their implementation are the first and last steps in international marketing. Marketers must first evaluate the global environment and select opportunities, using one of the planning approaches. This process will lead to a strategy, which is implemented by the organization. Sometimes, the organization's structure will be changed in order to effectively implement the strategy. Finally, a system must be put in place to evaluate the implementation and measure progress toward the desired effect of the strategy.

45. Thomas A. Stewart, "How to Manage in the New Era," *Fortune,* January 15, 1990, p. 32.
46. John A. Quelch and Edward J. Hoff, "Customizing Global Marketing," *Harvard Business Review,* 64 (May–June 1986), p. 68.

The planning and controlling processes are critical parts of the marketing process that require communication and agreement from different parts of the organization. This is difficult. It is no surprise that the planning and controlling processes lead to conflict. However, they also promote understanding the world market, developing effective strategies, and successfully implementing the strategies with excellent results.

Questions for Discussion

1. You have recently been transferred from a domestic marketing division to the international marketing staff. Part of your new job is to review the planning process of each geographic marketing group—Europe, Asia, and South America. What differences can you expect from domestic planning?

2. What are the advantages and disadvantages of the Boston Consulting Group planning method when applied to international markets?

3. What are the advantages and disadvantages of the PIMS model over other planning methods that can be used for international planning?

4. What types of marketing decisions are usually left up to the local management? Why?

5. What is the purpose of a control system? How do you differentiate a good control system from a poor one?

6. Recent feedback for sales, profit, and market share indicates that your subsidiary in Japan has not implemented the strategy that was developed. How will you influence the management to focus more effort on successful strategy implementation?

7. Recently, you have lost four key international marketing people to other companies. You suspect that these losses indicate that the morale of your international executives is poor. What can be done to improve morale?

For Further Reading

Ansoff, H. Igor, and Edward J. McDonnell. *Implanting Strategic Management.* 2nd ed. Englewood Cliffs, N.J.: Prentice Hall, 1990.

Bartness, Andrew, and Keith Cerny. ''Building Competitive Advantage Through a Global Network of Capabilities.'' *California Management Review,* Winter 1993, pp. 78–103.

Becker, Helmut, and Hans B. Thorelli. ''Strategic Planning in International Marketing.'' In *International Marketing Strategy.* Eds. Hans Thorelli and Helmut Becker. New York: Pergamon, 1982, pp. 367–378.

Campbell, Andrew, Marion Devine, and David Young. *A Sense of Mission.* London: Economist Books, 1990.

Chakravarthy, Balaji S., and Howard V. Perlmutter. ''Strategic Planning for a Global Business.'' *Columbia Journal of World Business,* Summer 1985, pp. 3–10.

Day, George S. *Market Driven Strategy.* New York: Free Press, 1990.

Dymsza, William A. "Global Strategic Planning." *Journal of International Business Studies,* Summer 1985, pp. 169–183.

Gale, Bradley T., and Ben Branch. "Allocating Capital More Effectively." *Sloan Management Review,* Fall 1987, p. 21.

Goold, Michael, and Andrew Campbell. *Strategies and Styles: The Role of the Centre in Managing Diversified Corporations.* Oxford: Basil Blackwell, 1987.

Hamel, Gary, and C. K. Prahalad. "Managing Strategic Responsibility in the MNC." *Strategic Management Journal* 4 (1983), pp. 341–351.

Hamel, Gary, and C. K. Prahalad. "Strategic Intent." *Harvard Business Review,* May–June 1989, pp. 63–76.

Hulbert, James M., William K. Brandt, and Raimer Richers. "Marketing Planning in the Multinational Subsidiary: Practices and Problems." *Journal of Marketing,* Summer 1980, pp. 7–15.

Nowakoski, Christopher A. "International Performance Measurement." *Columbia Journal of World Business,* Summer 1982, pp. 53–57.

Pink, Alan I. H. "Strategic Leadership Through Corporate Planning at ICI." *Long Range Planning* 21, no. 1 (1988), pp. 18–25.

Porter, Michael E., ed. *Competition in Global Industries.* Boston: Harvard Business School Press, 1986.

Roth, Kendall, and Allen J. Morrison. "Implementing Global Strategy: Characteristics of Global Subsidiary Mandates." *Journal of International Business Studies,* Fourth Quarter 1992, pp. 715–735.

Wind, Yoram, and Susan Douglas. "International Portfolio Analysis and Strategy: The Challenge of the 80s." *Journal of International Business Studies,* Fall 1981, p. 7.

18

The Export and Import Trade Process

● **THROUGHOUT PREVIOUS CHAPTERS,** *we have maintained that exporting and importing are subsets of international marketing. We have also indicated that international and global marketing may take place without any physical movement of products across country borders, thereby taking an even broader view of international marketing. However, most companies will, as part of their international marketing activities, engage in some form of exporting or importing. This can take place in the form of shipments from the headquarters location to a foreign market or through cross-shipments among various subsidiaries. Invariably, such export or import shipments cause specific problems that we have not yet discussed and that can best be handled in a separate chapter such as this one.*

To deal with all the specific rules and regulations that can be found in today's complex international business environments is not possible—or necessary for our purposes. In this chapter, we will view the export and import mechanics from the point of view of a U.S.-based firm. However, many aspects of the export section, such as those related to pricing, are of universal application and would be of interest to all readers. The structure and components of the chapter are depicted in Figure 18.1.

FIGURE 18.1 ● Export and Import Trading Process

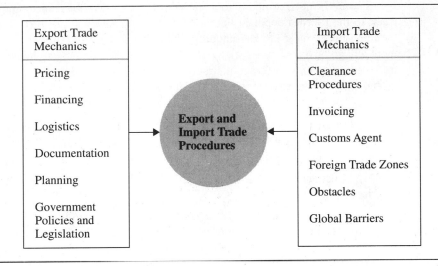

Export Trade Mechanics[1]

Any successful export activity of a firm should be based on a careful analysis of a company's export potential, as was discussed in Chapter 9. Techniques and approaches for such an analysis were covered in Chapters 5 and 6. Consequently, we start our discussion of export trade mechanics with the assumption that a potential market has been defined, measured, and located and that the company has made the decision to exploit the opportunity through exporting. Our focus is on the execution of a U.S. firm's export operation, paying special attention to pricing, financing, logistics, documentation, planning, and government policies that affect the individual firm.

Pricing

In Chapter 13, we described in detail the process by which companies determine prices for products to be shipped abroad. These methods of internal costing, profit analyses, and demand analyses can be applied to the export process. Peculiar to exporting, however, is the method of quoting prices. Foreign buyers need to know precisely where they will take over responsibility for the product—or what shipping costs the exporter is willing to assume. In the United States, it is customary to ship f.o.b. factory, freight collect, prepaid, charge, or COD. However, in export marketing, different terms are used worldwide.

1. This section has been adapted and based on *A Basic Guide to Exporting* (Washington, D.C.: U.S. Department of Commerce, International Trade Administration, 1994). Available from NTC Business Books, Lincolnwood, Illinois.

Figure 18.2 contains commonly used export quotations for a hypothetical shipment by a Peoria, Illinois, company to a client in Bogota, Colombia. The shipment is to go via truck to the railroad depot in Peoria and by rail to a New York pier. The products will then be shipped by sea to Barranquilla, Colombia. Following customs clearance, the shipment will go on by rail and truck to eventually reach the client's warehouse. In international trade, nearly twenty different alternatives exist for quoting the price of the merchandise, all indicating different responsibilities for the U.S. company or its Colombian client.

The most common terms used in quoting prices in international trade are these:

c.i.f.: Cost, insurance, freight, to a named port of import. Under this term, the seller quotes a price that includes the product, all transportation, and insurance to the point of unloading from the vessel or aircraft at the named destination.

c.f.: Cost and freight, similar to c.i.f. except that insurance of the shipment is not included.

f.a.s.: Free alongside ship, at a named port in the exporter's country. Under this term, the exporter quotes a price that includes the goods and any service and delivery charges to get the shipment alongside the vessel used for further transportation, but now at the buyer's expense.

f.o.b.: Free on board, includes the price of placing the shipment onto a specified vessel or aircraft, but further transportation will be the buyer's responsibility.

ex (named point of origin): Applies to a price for products at the point of origin and requires that the buyer assume all transportation charges.

The incorrect use of a delivery term can cause significant problems between the exporter and the buyer.[2]

When asked by a foreign buyer to quote a price, the exporter will have to quote a price that takes into consideration the methods of freight payment. In quoting a price, the company is advised to stipulate a price that easily allows the buyer to figure out total costs for the shipment. Usually, this means quoting a price c.i.f. foreign port. The foreign buyer can then estimate additional transportation charges for the final distance under known circumstances.

In the case of our example in Figure 18.2, the most meaningful quote for the Colombian buyer is c.i.f. Bogota. Quoting a price ex factory places the burden of estimating transportation entirely on the foreign buyer. But, as one may imagine, estimation of costs can be quite difficult to do from abroad. An exporter can do a great service to the buyer by quoting prices that reflect the final destination charges based on information from freight forwarders with experience in shipping to the foreign country. It also makes it easier for the buyer to compare prices from different companies if they are all quoted to one point, such as Bogota. Sometimes the buyer will request a specific type of price. For example,

2. *Incoterms* is a booklet of terms and their definitions. These are the internationally agreed-on terms used by international freight forwarders all over the world. *Incoterms* can be obtained from the International Chamber of Commerce, 801 Second Avenue, Suite 1204, New York, NY 10017.

FIGURE 18.2 ● Exporting Example

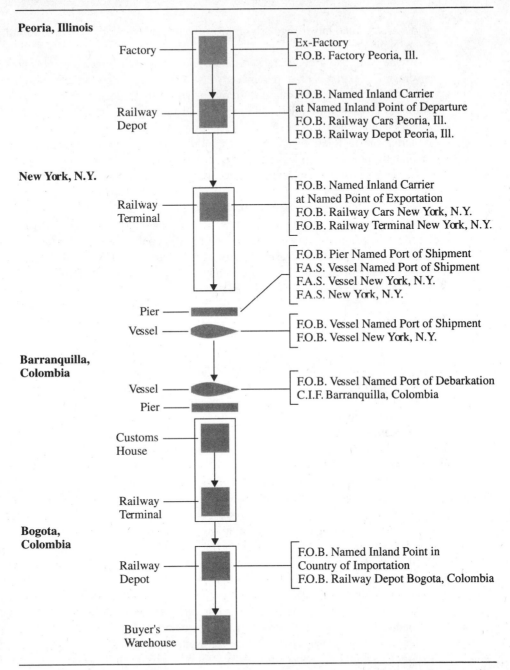

Peoria, Illinois

Factory ——— Ex-Factory
F.O.B. Factory Peoria, Ill.

Railway
Depot ——— F.O.B. Named Inland Carrier
at Named Inland Point of Departure
F.O.B. Railway Cars Peoria, Ill.
F.O.B. Railway Depot Peoria, Ill.

New York, N.Y.

Railway
Terminal ——— F.O.B. Named Inland Carrier
at Named Point of Exportation
F.O.B. Railway Cars New York, N.Y.
F.O.B. Railway Terminal New York, N.Y.

F.O.B. Pier Named Port of Shipment
F.A.S. Vessel Named Port of Shipment
F.A.S. Vessel New York, N.Y.
F.A.S. New York, N.Y.

Pier ———

Vessel ——— F.O.B. Vessel Named Port of Shipment
F.O.B. Vessel New York, N.Y.

**Barranquilla,
Colombia**

Vessel ——— F.O.B. Vessel Named Port of Debarkation
C.I.F. Barranquilla, Colombia

Pier ———

Customs
House

Railway
Terminal

**Bogota,
Colombia**

Railway
Depot ——— F.O.B. Named Inland Point in
Country of Importation
F.O.B. Railway Depot Bogota, Colombia

Buyer's
Warehouse

Source: Gerald R. Richter, "Basic Principles of Foreign Trade," in *International Trade Handbook,* ed. Leslie L. Lewis (Chicago: Dartnell Corporation, prepared in cooperation with the American Institute for Foreign Trade, 1965), p. 32. Used with permission.

if our Colombian buyer regularly imports from New York, he may request all prices be f.o.b. New York.

The computed freight, transportation, and insurance charges may also depend on the leverage the exporter or importer has with freight forwarders. In the example, the U.S. exporter may only have this one shipment going to Bogota, Colombia. Therefore, the shipping costs will be relatively high. Should the importer have several shipments that could be combined, average freight costs from New York to Colombia may be less. The exporter can facilitate the process by quoting several prices at various points along the shipment route and then leaving the choice to the buyer, who will select the best method.

Exporters should not underestimate the possibility of using the export pricing process as a selling tool, particularly when there are similar products available from other manufacturers. Also, different pricing strategies present obvious risks. For example, if you quote in a foreign currency rather than dollars, you assume the risk of exchange rate fluctuation. Even insurance costs can fluctuate: insurance rates doubled for goods being shipped to the Persian Gulf after Iraq's invasion of Kuwait on August 2, 1990.[3] Pricing for export involves many variables that require close examination. A miscalculation or misjudgment can often turn a profitable order to a losing order.

Financing

Chapter 13, on pricing, contained several sections on financing international marketing operations through, among others, export banks of various countries. Also discussed were noncash transactions such as barter and countertrade. These types of arrangements are not repeated in this chapter. This section focuses on various arrangements exporters can make to ensure payment for their merchandise and on credit methods that can be offered to foreign clients.

Although cash transactions can be desirable, this form of payment is rarely used. The shipment may be in transit for weeks or even months at a time, thus tying up the importer's capital. Also, the importer does not really know what was shipped until the products are in its possession. Consequently, most forms of payment are designed to protect both parties. When an exporter knows the foreign clients and fully trusts their financial integrity, shipments on *open account* may be arranged. Usually, the terms are arranged such that the foreign client can wait to make payment until the goods have arrived at their final destination. However, in this case, the exporter will have risked capital in the transaction.

Consignment sales is the method whereby credit is extended by the exporter. The exporter is not compensated until the products are physically sold by the importer. The consignment goods are often held in free trade zones (discussed later in the chapter) or in a bonded warehouse until sold by an agent or needed by the buyer. With appropriate payment, the consigned goods will be released to the buyer. This approach increases the exporter's capital costs because no funds are received until the goods are collected by the buyer.

3. ''Ship Insurance Rates Soar in Some Areas of Persian Gulf as Jan. 15 Deadline Nears,'' *Wall Street Journal,* January 10, 1991, p. A16.

To control both ownership and payment terms for international shipments, traders have developed the *draft,* or *bill of exchange.*[4] The draft is a formal order the exporter issues to the importer, specifying when the sum is to be paid to the third party, usually the exporter's bank. A triangular relationship is established with the issuer of the draft, the exporter, as drawer; the importer as drawee; and the payee as the recipient of the payment. Since the draft is a negotiable instrument, it can be sold, transferred, and discounted, and the exporter can use it to finance the shipment.

Exporters may use either a *sight draft* or a *time draft.* Sight drafts are used when the exporter desires to control the shipment beyond the point of original shipment, usually to ensure payment. In practice, the exporter endorses the bill of lading (B/L) and adds a sight draft on the correspondent bank of the exporter's bank. Along with the bill of lading and sight draft, other documents will be provided such as the packing list, invoice, consular invoices, and certificate of insurance. Once the documents have arrived, a transfer by way of endorsement to the importer will be made on payment in full at that bank. Consequently, the importer cannot take possession of the goods until payment has been made (on sight of documents). Yet, the importer is assured that the goods have actually been shipped as indicated by the accompanying documents.

Alternatively, transactions can be made in time drafts. This method specifies the period in which the payment is to be made. The payment period beginning on receiving the documents may be thirty, sixty, or ninety days or longer. Not only will drafts allow the exporter to control the shipment until proper payment occurs, but they also allow further financing by having the properly signed draft discounted with a bank before the agreed-upon payment term expires. In such a case, the banking system assumes the role of the creditor, thus reducing the capital risks of the exporter.

Also used quite frequently is a financial instrument called a *letter of credit.* With a letter of credit, the importer, or foreign buyer, finances the transaction, thus alleviating the credit burden on the exporter. With a letter of credit, the responsibility is in the hands of the importer. Once informed that the exporter will ship with a letter of credit (L/C), the importer will ask the bank to write an irrevocable L/C with a bank specified by the exporter on the latter's behalf. The importer will usually instruct the bank on the conditions of payment, typically against submission of all necessary documents, including a bill of lading. When the exporter has placed the shipment on the appropriate vessel, the company will go to the bank and turn over all documents associated with the transaction. When satisfied, the exporter's bank will pay out the funds and debit the importer's bank, which will in turn debit the importing company.

Overall, the irrevocable L/C has distinct advantages for the exporter because it represents a firm order that, once issued by the bank, cannot be canceled or revoked. For example, a company that sells machinery built to order can use the irrevocable L/C to guarantee that payment will be made. Time limits are placed on the L/C that protect the importer against an open-ended transaction. Should the exporter fail to ship and submit documents before the expiration date, the L/C would expire without any further respon-

4. Endel J. Kolde, *International Business Enterprise,* 2nd ed. (Englewood Cliffs, N.J.: Prentice Hall, 1973), pp. 289–290.

sibility on the part of the importer to finance the transaction. Any bank charges associated with the transaction are usually paid by the buyer. Letters of credit are normally prepared at commercial banks by a staff of back-office clerks. The paperwork required for each letter of credit, as well as the possibility of typing errors, can make the issuing of these instruments slow. Pressure from exports has motivated many banks to automate this process with computer technology to speed up the process so payments could be processed quickly.[5]

Letters of credit are a widely used instrument that has developed into several specialized forms over and above the standard irrevocable L/C described above. The following additional forms exist:

Revolving or periodic letters of credit allow for a repetition of the same transaction as soon as the previous amount has been paid by the bank that originated the L/C.

Cumulative letters of credit are opened to cover payments of partial shipments and/ or the use of the unused portion of the L/C for another transaction between the same parties.

Red clause letters of credit are used to permit partial cash payments to the beneficiary, or exporter, as an advance on the shipment without any documentation. Final payments are made only against full documentation, however.

Back-to-back letters of credit are issued based on an earlier L/C. This may be done if an exporter, in whose favor an L/C was opened by a foreign client, will use the original L/C as a basis or security to issue a second L/C in favor of a supplier for materials connected with that particular transaction.

Circular letters of credit are issued without designating any particular bank. The exporter may send documents to the issuing bank or present them to any bank that will send them on for collection.

Performance letters of credit are used to guarantee the completion of a contract undertaken abroad. They can be drawn upon if the exporter fails to meet performance requirements and are therefore also known under the term *performance bonds.*[6]

When a company exports to another country, such as a politically volatile area or with a new customer, guaranteeing payment of invoices is always a concern. A letter of credit is a relatively safe instrument to guarantee payment. In some cases, letters of credit may not be acceptable to the buyer, or they may not be practical. In the United States, exporters can turn to the Foreign Credit Insurance Association (FCIA) for assistance. The FCIA is an association of fifty marine and insurance casualty companies created in 1961 to insure U.S. exporters of goods and services against commercial and political risks. There are numerous risks with any foreign buyer. The firm can go out of business. The local

---

5. Jon Marks, ''Letters of Credit Are Beginning to Change, a Rich Link with the Past,'' *Financial Times,* June 1, 1989, Export Finance Section 7.

6. Kolde, *International Business Enterprise,* p. 294.

government can change standards. Natural disasters such as floods or earthquakes can eliminate the buyer's ability to pay. FCIA offers insurance to protect against a buyer's failure to pay. Most developed countries have some type of export insurance program similar to FCIA.

As we have seen, numerous options are available to arrange for payment in export transactions. The exporting company can, of course, select the particular type of transaction, always keeping in mind the needs and requirements of the buyer—who may, if offered better credit terms elsewhere, decide to place an order with a different company. The payment process is an important part of the transaction between the buyer and seller in an export situation; it can minimize the risks of exchange rate fluctuations and the process of dealing with a distant buyer or seller. Experienced exporters study government assistance and financing programs looking for creative ways to use these programs for the benefit of the buyer. For example, Biwater, a U.K. construction company, won a $550 million water supply contract in Malaysia through a combination of creative financing and support by the U.K. Aid and Trade Program.[7]

Logistics

The requirements of export logistics differ substantially from domestic operations, calling for special care on the part of the exporting firm. Practices must ensure that the shipment arrives in the best possible condition and at the lowest possible cost. To ensure that the products arrive in usable condition, export packages have to be prepared to avoid four typical problems: breakage, weight, moisture, and pilferage.

Export shipments often are subject to additional handling procedures, including the use of a sling for loading onto a vessel, nets to combine various items for loading, or conveyors, chutes, and other methods that put added stress and strain on the shipment and are frequently the cause of breakage. Once on board a vessel, the weight of other cargo placed on top of the shipment can also be hazardous. At the overseas destination, handling facilities are sometimes unsophisticated. Consequently, the cargo may be even dragged, pushed, or rolled during unloading, causing damage to the goods.

While packages are on a voyage, moisture is a constant problem due to condensation in the hold of a ship. This may even be so for vessels equipped with air conditioning and dehumidifiers. At the point of arrival, unloading may take place in the rain, and many foreign ports lack covered storage facilities. Furthermore, without adequate protection, theft and pilferage are common.

To avoid these problems, exporters are encouraged to add extra packaging to protect their cargo. However, overpacking should be avoided because both freight and customs are frequently assessed on the gross weight of the merchandise, resulting in unneeded charges for extra packaging. Airfreight usually requires less packaging than ocean freight, and container shipments can be used to provide added protection for the goods. Exporters are encouraged to check with carriers or marine insurance companies for advice on proper

7. Peter Montagnon, ''Export Credit: Unbundling—a Way Round Trade Barriers,'' *Financial Times,* November 7, 1990, p. 17.

packaging. For companies that are not equipped to do export packaging, professional companies provide this service for a moderate fee.

Equally important is the proper marking of the shipment. Although the destination should be marked clearly and in large stenciled letters of black waterproof ink, experienced exporters advise that, to avoid pilferage or theft, no additional facts be provided on the content of the packages. Where necessary, special handling instructions should be added in the language of the port of destination.

Arrangements for the actual shipping of a company's products can be made through the services of an international freight forwarder. In general, a freight forwarder licensed by the Federal Maritime Administration should be used because these agents are familiar with foreign import regulations, methods of shipping, and the requirements of U.S. export documentation. Not only will freight forwarders advise on freight costs and other related fees, but they can also make recommendations on packaging. Since the cost for their services is a legitimate export cost, exporters can add such costs to their prices charged to foreign customers. Aside from advising exporters, forwarders also make the necessary arrangements to clear shipments through customs, arrange for the actual shipping, and check for the necessary documents as described in the section below.

Documentation

To facilitate the transfer of goods out of the United States and through a foreign country's procedures, a series of export documents have to be prepared. Exporters prepare such documents with care, since export documents frequently have been used as a basis for obtaining trade credit from banks or collection from the buyer.

One requirement is a detailed export packing list, usually containing substantially more details about weight and volume than those used for domestic commerce. This packing list is used by shippers to reserve or book the necessary space on the vessel. Furthermore, port officials at the dock use this list to determine whether the correct cargo has been received. In addition, customs officials both in the United States and abroad use the packing list, and ultimately the buyer will want to check the goods against the list to verify that the entire shipment was received. To satisfy all these users, the packing list must contain not only a detailed description of the products for each packaging unit but also weights, volume, and dimensions in both metric and nonmetric terms.

Most countries have specific requirements for the marking and labeling of imports. Failure to comply can result in severe penalties. For example, Peru requires that all imports are labeled with the brand name, country of origin, and an expiration date on the product. Customs officials will refuse clearance of any imports not complying with the regulations. The importer must ship the goods out of Peru within sixty days, or they are seized and auctioned as abandoned goods. A basic guide published by the Department of Commerce for U.S. exporters will describe the required export documents and pertinent regulations for labeling, marking, and packing products for import. The pamphlet series entitled ''Preparing Shipment to (Country)'' helps avoid delays and penalties.[8]

8. ''Tools of the Export Trade,'' *Business America,* October 28, 1988, pp. 2–5.

The U.S. government requires that all export shipments be subject to a licensing procedure. Basically, there exist two types of export licenses. The *validated export license* must be secured for each individual order from the Office of Export Administration in Washington, D.C. Several types of products and commodities may fall into this category, such as chemicals, special types of plastic, advanced electronic and communications equipment, and scarce materials including petroleum. For defense products, licenses are issued by the Department of State. The requirement for a validated export license may apply for shipments of certain commodities to all countries or only to a limited number of countries. The entire mechanism was instituted to protect the United States' strategic position for reasons of foreign policy or national security or to regulate supply for select scarce products. Regulations are also subject to frequent changes depending on the political or economic climate prevailing at the time of decision.

All other products are subject to several types of *general licenses.* These are published general authorizations, each with a specific license symbol that is dependent on product category. Exporters must inquire at the Department of Commerce to obtain the correct general license symbol. Exporters usually check with the Department of Commerce before an order is accepted to determine the type of license required. Obtaining export licenses from the government has often been a slow process that can cause delays for the exporter. To reduce the paperwork and speed up the process, the Department of Commerce introduced two new systems. The Export License Application and Information Network (ELAIN) allows exporters to submit license applications electronically for all free world applications. When approved, the license is conveyed back to the exporter electronically. The System for Tracking Export License Applications (STELA) is a voice answering service that allows exporters to check the status of their license application. The new systems drastically cut processing time from an average of forty-six days in 1984 to fourteen days. For trusted trading nations, the processing time is often five days or less with the aid of the electronic systems.[9]

The exporter's *shipper's export declaration* has to be added to all shipments. It requires a declaration of the products in terms of the U.S. Customs Service definitions and classifications. In this form, the exporter must note the applicable license for the shipment. A sample of the shipper's export declaration is shown in Figure 18.3.

Most exporters also submit a series of documents to their customers to facilitate additional financing or handling at the point of destination. These documents may vary by country, method of payment, mode of transportation, and even by customer. The following documents may be required:

> *Commercial invoice.* In addition to the customary content, the invoice should indicate the origin of the products and export marks. Also needed is an antidiversion clause, such as "United States law prohibits disposition of these commodities to North Korea, Cambodia, or Cuba." When payment is against a letter of credit, the invoice should contain all necessary numbers and bank names.

9. "The Electronic Age of Export Licensing in ELAIN JOINS STELA to Cut Processing Time," *Business America,* February 29, 1988, pp. 7–11.

FIGURE 18.3 ● Shipper's Export Declaration

U.S. DEPARTMENT OF COMMERCE — BUREAU OF THE CENSUS · INTERNATIONAL TRADE ADMINISTRATION

FORM **7525-V** (1·1·88) **SHIPPER'S EXPORT DECLARATION** OMB No. 0607-0018

1a. EXPORTER *(Name and address including ZIP code)*		
	ZIP CODE	**2.** DATE OF EXPORTATION
b. EXPORTER'S EIN (IRS) NO.	**c.** PARTIES TO TRANSACTION ☐ Related ☐ Non-related	**3.** BILL OF LADING/AIR WAYBILL NO.

4a. ULTIMATE CONSIGNEE

b. INTERMEDIATE CONSIGNEE

5. FORWARDING AGENT

6. POINT (STATE) OF ORIGIN OR FTZ NO.	**7.** COUNTRY OF ULTIMATE DESTINATION

8. LOADING PIER *(Vessel only)*	**9.** MODE OF TRANSPORT *(Specify)*
10. EXPORTING CARRIER	**11.** PORT OF EXPORT
12. PORT OF UNLOADING *(Vessel and air only)*	**13.** CONTAINERIZED *(Vessel only)* ☐ Yes ☐ No

14. SCHEDULE B DESCRIPTION OF COMMODITIES

15. MARKS, NOS., AND KINDS OF PACKAGES   *(Use columns 17–19)*

D/F (16)	SCHEDULE B NUMBER (17)	CHECK DIGIT	QUANTITY – SCHEDULE B UNIT(S) (18)	SHIPPING WEIGHT *(Kilos)* (19)	VALUE (U.S. dollars, omit cents) *(Selling price or cost if not sold)* (20)

21. VALIDATED LICENSE NO./GENERAL LICENSE SYMBOL   **22.** ECCN *(When required)*

23. Duly authorized officer or employee | The exporter authorizes the forwarder named above to act as forwarding agent for export control and customs purposes.

24. I certify that all statements made and all information contained herein are true and correct and that I have read and understand the instructions for preparation of this document, set forth in the **"Correct Way to Fill Out the Shipper's Export Declaration."** I understand that civil and criminal penalties, including forfeiture and sale, may be imposed for making false or fraudulent statements herein, failing to provide the requested information or for violation of U.S. laws on exportation (13 U.S.C. Sec. 305; 22 U.S.C. Sec. 401; 18 U.S.C. Sec. 1001; 50 U.S.C. App. 2410).

Signature _____

Confidential - For use solely for official purposes authorized by the Secretary of Commerce (13 U.S.C. 301 (g)).

Title _____

Export shipments are subject to inspection by U.S. Customs Service and/or Office of Export Enforcement.

Date _____

25. AUTHENTICATION *(When required)*

This form may be printed by private parties provided it conforms to the official form. For sale by the Superintendent of Documents, Government Printing Office, Washington, D.C. 20402, and local Customs District Directors. The **"Correct Way to Fill Out the Shipper's Export Declaration"** is available from the Bureau of the Census, Washington, D.C. 20233.

Source: U.S. Department of Commerce.

Some countries even require special certification, at times in the language of that country, and a few countries may need signed invoices with notarization. The Commerce Department keeps a current list of all requirements by country.

Consular invoice. Some countries, particularly those of Latin America, require a special invoice in addition to the commercial invoice prepared in the language of the country and issued on official forms by the consulate. The forms are typically prepared by the forwarding agent.

Certificate of origin. Some countries may require a specific and separate statement that is normally countersigned by a recognized chamber of commerce. Based on this statement, import duties are assessed, if preferential rates are claimed, the inclusion of the certificate of origin is often necessary.

Inspection certificate. A foreign buyer may request that the products be inspected, typically by an independent inspection firm, with respect to quality, quantity, and conformity of goods as stated in the order and invoice.

Bill of lading. Bills of lading are issued in various forms, depending on the mode of transportation. The exporter endorses the B/L in favor of either the buyer or the bank financing the transaction. The B/L identifies the owner of the shipment and is needed to claim the products at the point of destination. The bill of lading provides *three* functions: (1) receipt for goods, (2) content for shipment, and (3) title to the goods, if consigned ''to the order of.''

Dock receipts or warehouse receipts. In cases in which the shipper or exporter is responsible for moving the goods not to the foreign destination but only to the U.S. port, a dock or warehouse receipt is usually required confirming that the shipment was actually received at the port for further shipment.

Certificate of manufacture. Such a certificate may be issued for cases in which the buyer intends to pay for the order before shipment. The certificate, combined with a commercial invoice, may be presented to a bank appointed by the buyer for early payment. More typical is to pay only against a B/L indicating that the merchandise has actually been shipped.

Insurance certificates. Particularly where the exporter is required to arrange for insurance, such certificates are usually necessary. They are negotiable instruments and must be endorsed accordingly.

Exporters pay careful attention to the specifications attached to letters of credit with respect to the required set of documents. The paying bank will only effect payment if all submitted documents fully conform to the specifications determined by the buyer. Mistakes can cause lengthy delays that can be costly to the exporter.

Planning Process

The plan for a firm's export operations is central to any successful exporting effort. The planning activities are designed as a guideline for the future instead of depending on chance to pursue export business. The export plan ensures that all activities are directed toward the achievement of preformulated objectives selected to ensure the long-term profitability of the firm. Planning allows a firm to develop its export business on its own terms instead of having it be dictated by foreign clients' demands.

Several aspects are part of a successful export plan. Initially, the company will have to select an appropriate time horizon for its planning process. Franklin Root suggests that the planning horizon be chosen so that the firm will be forced to raise fundamental and basic questions about the future direction and extent of the firm's export business.[10] Secondly, planning horizons should be long enough to project the effects of the firm's decisions. The normal plan is three to five years, though for some it may be as short as one year or as long as ten years.

The planning unit will target specific countries for each product. The combination of the various country or product plans is the corporate export plan. However, the effort will almost always start at the country or product level. Viewing export planning as a process, one can identify the three major steps shown in Figure 18.4: identifying and measuring market opportunities, developing an export strategy, and implementing the strategy.

The process of identifying and measuring market opportunities has been described in detail in Chapter 6. Essentially, to identify those that may be pursued, the plan has to start with a preliminary screening of the great many export markets that exist. The preliminary screening prevents any unnecessary effort being spent on markets that do not warrant any resources at this time. For the targeted markets, the market potentials will be estimated always keeping in mind that the potential may be measured at various levels (see Figure 6.3). As a next step, an estimate of the firm's sales potential for each market will determine the best possible outcome given the firm's competitive position. Where appropriate, market segments may be analyzed separately if the marketing strategy will require changes for each segment.

The development of the export strategy includes the setting of some objectives. Naturally, these objectives must be in line with the firm's capabilities and reflect the realities of the marketplace as derived from the analysis of the market opportunities. The specific objectives will differ by company. The objectives can include sales volume, market share, and profit expectations. The export plan should consider the potential market reaction to the firm's action and should recognize that competitors may adapt their marketing activities to planned changes.

Once export objectives have been clearly defined, the firm can go about planning the individual elements of the marketing mix. The product offering, including service, must be prepared, and allowances will have to be made for any required adjustments. Prices will be predetermined based on both the internal price structure and the demand situation. The export plan will include a detailed promotional plan outlining all the steps to be undertaken to promote the product in the target market. Finally, the plans for the distribution strategy will have to be included as well, containing both entry and local distribution approaches. The key to a successful plan is the relationship between the objectives and

10. Franklin R. Root, *Strategic Planning for Export Marketing* (Scranton, Penn.: International Textbook Company, 1966), pp. 4–7.

FIGURE 18.4 ● Export Planning Process

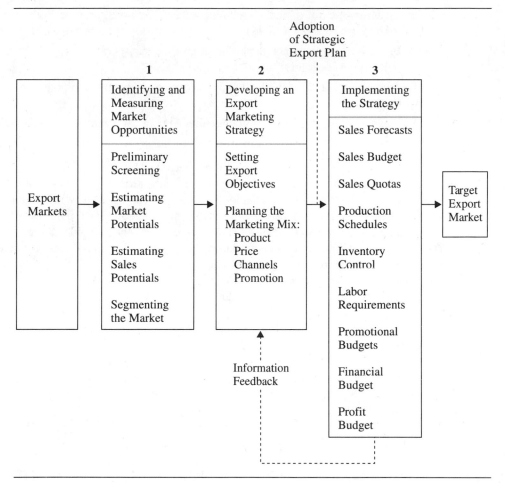

Source: Frankin R. Root, *Strategic Planning for Export Marketing* (Scranton, Penn.: International Textbook Company, 1966), p. 5.

the planned action. Management will have to ensure that the desired objectives can in fact be reached with the planned marketing mix.

Based on the detailed marketing mix plans, operational budgets are established. These budgets include:

1. Sales forecasts (in monetary and unit terms)

2. Sales budget (all planned sales-related expenditures)

3. Sales quotas (in monetary and unit terms)

4. Production schedules

5. Inventory control (including the requirements for inventories, in both domestic and foreign warehouse locations)

6. Employee requirements (the hiring of all necessary personnel to achieve the objectives set earlier)

7. Promotional budgets (with all expenses for advertising, exhibitions, and sales material)

8. Financial budget (for the capital requirements to carry out the planned effort)

9. Profit budget (as the final criterion and measuring device of the export operation)

Under ideal situations, operational budgets may be prepared for a number of alternative plans, with the final selection depending on the profitability of each of the scenarios. In a world where the present situation is constantly subject to new developments, a plan or the export effort over a period of three to five years may appear unnecessary or unwise. But even under rapidly changing situations, executives cannot avoid making some assumptions about the future. The export plan will bring discipline and cohesion to the process. Once the original assumptions have to be changed, modifications in the plan may have to be as made as well. However, as with any planning process, the export plan forces the company to think about its future in an organized fashion.

Government Export Policies and Legislation

There is no doubt that exports can greatly enhance the economy of any nation. The U.S. Congress found that exports were responsible for creating one out of every nine manufacturing jobs and generating one out of seven dollars of total U.S. goods produced.[11] Thus, governments frequently try to influence their country's export volume through legislation or direct government supports. To outline the export policies of all major countries is too difficult. Consequently, this section concentrates on the United States. Though the respective export policies of other countries may vary by specific objective or by approach, understanding the U.S. export policies will provide some conceptual background for the understanding of the policies of all countries and an appreciation for the important role governments can play.

Organization of U.S. Export Policies   The execution of the U.S. government's export policies lies with the Department of Commerce, whereas negotiations and policy advisement to the president are the responsibilities of the trade representative, a cabinet position. Also part of the U.S. export policymaking is the Export-Import Bank, an independent agency whose activities were described in Chapter 13.

The U.S. Department of Commerce coordinates the activities of 162 commercial attachés in sixty-five countries. Involved with U.S. embassies abroad, these attachés provide U.S. business with support at the local level. Also available are about 150 international

11. *Congressional Record,* 128, no. 134 (October 1, 1982).

trade specialists in thirty-two U.S. cities. An important aspect of the Commerce Department's activities is trade promotion programs that include permanent overseas trade fairs and seminars on exporting for U.S. businesspeople in the United States. With a budget of several million dollars, the department is now developing an automated information system that is expected to serve up to 50,000 subscribers in the United States.[12]

The Department of Commerce assists U.S. exporters with four export centers opened in January 1994 in Los Angeles, Miami, Chicago, and Baltimore. These centers provide one-stop shopping for businesses seeking markets abroad. In the past, companies interested in expanding abroad had nineteen agencies to deal with, all requiring separate paperwork. Now they deal with one contact for help.[13]

Most governments have some type of agency or program to support exporting initiatives. These programs are often targeted to the smaller company that does not have export experience. For example, Labelking, a small South London printer of adhesive labels for the food industry, relied on the advice of one of the thirty-one export development advisers hired and trained by the U.K. Department of Trade and Industry. The adviser helped Labelking assess the size of the European and U.S. market and enter the French and Iberian market.[14]

In addition to federal government programs, many states have established organizations and agencies to assist U.S. companies in their exporting efforts. In 1987, thirty-six states maintained offices abroad and programs at home to encourage export trade, particularly with smaller companies.[15] For example, C. M. Magnetics, a three-year-old company in Santa Fe Springs, California, received a $2.7 million order from China. This order was the direct result of efforts by the state of California's World Trade Commission. "Without their help," company president J. Carlos Macrel said of the agency, "we probably wouldn't be in business today."[16]

Though the resources committed on behalf of U.S. exports may appear substantial, the $30.5 million spent on the export development program for fiscal 1981 was substantially less than the corresponding budget of the Japan External Trade Organization (JETRO). JETRO is endowed with a budget of $48 million and is able to maintain a staff of about 600 in Japan and another 650 persons overseas.[17] This discrepancy in budget exists despite the fact that U.S. exports are almost twice the volume of Japan's exports. For many U.S. businesspeople, this difference in funding of export programs is symbolic of a lack of interest on the part of many government officials and legislators, who have accumulated a substantial amount of legislation that actually hinders U.S. exports. In the

12. "The New Export Policy Works like the Old—Badly," *Business Week,* July 21, 1980, p. 89.

13. "Greasing the Skids for Exports," *Business Week,* January 31, 1994, pp. 66–67.

14. Charles Batchelor, "A Napoleonic Drive, with a French Partner into Iberia," *Financial Times,* September 5, 1989, p. 12.

15. "Big Plans for Small Business: Firms Try to Boost Exports," *Insight,* July 13, 1987, p. 40.

16. "States Launch Efforts to Make Small Firms Better Exporters," *Wall Street Journal,* February 2, 1987, p. 25.

17. "New Export Policy," p. 90.

following section, we explore the various legislative and regulative disincentives that the United States and some other countries have accumulated.

Obstacles to U.S. Exports   The policies mentioned in this section are generally viewed as hindrances to commercial activity that ultimately affect U.S. exports. Consequently, U.S. exports are below potential. These policies typically have been enacted by Congress to achieve other political goals, such as environmental conservation.

The Foreign Corrupt Practices Act of 1977 was enacted as a result of published reports on corporate bribery of foreign nationals, initially triggered by the "United Brands affair" in Honduras. The company reportedly paid funds to that country's president to get favorable tax treatment on banana exports. Subsequent investigations by the Securities and Exchange Commission (SEC) and the U.S. government found scores of other U.S. companies guilty of the same practices. The resulting 1977 act places stringent restrictions on the type of payments that third-party agents can receive. Consequently, some U.S. companies have the expense accounts of their foreign representatives certified by U.S. consular officers. However, competitors from other major trading nations are not subject to such legislation, a fact that many U.S. businesspeople consider a disadvantage. A study of 207 U.S. exporters found that the most difficult aspect of international marketing in terms of ethical and moral problems is bribery. Thirty-four percent of the companies cited bribery as a problem, followed by 15 percent reporting government interference and 7 percent citing customs clearance.[18]

To build an export business, a company often will need to locate a staff of people in other countries. The cost of locating staff in other countries can be exorbitant. For example, a midlevel manager in the United States will earn $57,428 with salary and bonuses, while the same manager will be paid $103,550 in Switzerland or $95,834 in Germany.[19] These comparisons do not include the additional costs of housing, moving, and air travel back to the States that most companies provide for overseas employees.

The policy instituted under the Carter administration on nuclear power plant exports illustrates the effect of a political decision on foreign trade. The United States passed the Nuclear Non-Proliferation Act of 1978 requiring all governments that use enriched uranium from U.S. sources to obtain the U.S. government's permission in advance if the uranium is to be sent anywhere for reprocessing.[20] The retroactive law applied to most of the twenty-six loyal and trusted foreign customers, which would face a cutoff in supplies if this new feature was not approved by them.

The U.S. Nuclear Non-Proliferation Act was intended to enhance existing controls administered by the International Atomic Energy Agency (IAEA), based in Vienna, Austria. An international nonproliferation treaty, in effect since 1970, had been signed by over one hundred governments, including those who had purchased uranium under U.S. contracts. The act reflects the U.S. government's position that existing controls were not strict

18. Robert Armstrong, Bruce W. Stening, John K. Ryans, Larry Marks, and Michael Mayo, "International Marketing Ethics," *European Journal of Marketing,* 24, no. 10 (1990), p. 10.

19. "Hay European Salary Comparisons," *Eurobusiness,* December 1990, p. 70.

20. "How Carter's Nuclear Policy Backfired Abroad," *Fortune,* October 23, 1978, p. 124.

enough to prevent further proliferation of atomic weapons to nations that were on the verge of attaining such capabilities (Brazil, Argentina, Iran, Pakistan, and India among them).

Even before the enactment of the 1978 act, U.S. export sales of nuclear reactors had been declining since 1974 due to a tremendous overbooking of orders.[21] In 1971, U.S. manufacturers supplied all eight foreign orders for nuclear reactors but supplied only one of ten in 1976 and none of seven ordered in 1977. Foreign orders went to suppliers in Germany, France, and other countries that did not insist on rules such as those of the U.S. government. The loss of foreign orders for such nuclear reactors was further influenced by the U.S. government's decision to stop the development of the breeder reactor, which allowed for reprocessing of spent uranium and would have reduced the world's demand for raw uranium. However, other foreign governments, such as the French government, have continued to develop this new breeder technology and consequently have an advantage over U.S. companies such as Westinghouse and General Electric, which must compete with the older and simpler design. With each nuclear installation worth nearly one billion dollars, the effect on U.S. exports was substantial.

The U.S. government has also affected exports through politically motivated actions. Unilaterally, the United States employed trade embargoes against Cuba, Vietnam, and the Soviet Union. Most of these actions were imposed by the U.S. government alone and were not followed by other nations, thus giving the clear advantage to foreign countries. The cutoff of Soviet aid and the U.S. embargo devastated the Cuban economy. The lack of machinery imports has been especially damaging to the Cuban industrial base.[22] The 1994 lifting of the nineteen-year trade embargo on Vietnam opened this fast-growing market to U.S. companies. Within months of the embargo being lifted, Coke, Pepsi, IBM, Kodak, GE, Citibank, Boeing, and many others were doing business in Vietnam, hoping to get across to the seventy million consumers in one of the fastest-growing Asian countries.[23]

Sometimes, regulations that prevent exports are pushed by special-interest groups. Exports of U.S. lumber in the form of logs were severely hurt by a rule that prohibited exports of logs cut on U.S. government land in raw form. Congress prevented such sales to satisfy U.S. sawmill owners and their workers, who saw too many logs shipped to Japan, where they were cut to Japanese specifications that differed from those used in the United States. Since the majority of U.S. logs are cut on government land, each year several hundred million dollars worth of export sales were lost. The Japanese simply bought logs elsewhere rather than buying cut timber in the United States.[24]

The limitations of exports can also be at an international level. The Coordinating Committee on Multi-lateral Exports Control (COCOM), established in 1949, includes fifteen nations—Belgium, Canada, Denmark, France, Germany, Greece, Italy, Japan, Luxembourg, the Netherlands, Norway, Portugal, Turkey, the United Kingdom, and the United

21. "Why the Nuclear Power Race Worries the U.S.," *Business Week,* August 23, 1976, pp. 68–69.

22. "End of U.S. Embargo Would Revive Cuba," *Financial Times,* December 22, 1992, p. 4.

23. "Destination Vietnam, U.S. Companies Trail Rivals—but Not for Long," *Business Week,* February 14, 1994, pp. 26–27.

24. Lee Smith, "The Neglected Promise of Our Forests," *Fortune,* November 5, 1979, p. 112.

States. COCOM members agree on which products they will not sell to the Soviet Union and other Warsaw Pact countries such as Albania, North Korea, Vietnam, and China. Typical products include weapons, advanced computers, and atomic energy components. In 1985, COCOM limits cost U.S. industry $9.3 billion in lost sales, according to a National Science Foundation report. With the opening up of eastern Europe, COCOM is reducing its list of restricted products.[25]

Many business and political leaders have recognized the considerable negative effect of such rules for U.S. exports, and recent changes indicate a move toward fewer such restrictions. In 1994 the Clinton administration eliminated some of the final license controls on computers left over from the Cold War.[26]

Occasionally, U.S. companies have diverted export orders to foreign subsidiaries where such restrictions do not apply. In general, however, any company that depends on exports as a source of income is well advised to carefully monitor government legislations and acts, both domestically and abroad, since the potential effect can be either to create new opportunities or to prevent the exploitation of existing ones.

Import Trade Mechanics[27]

In many ways, the importer is concerned with the same trade mechanics as the exporter. Communications with foreign suppliers can be difficult due to distances involved, time changes, and cultural differences. Import trade makes use of the same price-quoting vocabulary as exporting does, and the payment mechanism is the same with respect to the use of letters of credit or open accounts. Finally, the logistic concerns of the importer are identical to those of the exporter, so that many of the points covered in the earlier portion of this chapter need not be repeated.

A substantial amount of effort is expended by importers to bring products through local customs. Not surprisingly, import requirements vary by nation and are numerous. In this section, we concentrate solely on the major import procedures as they apply to the United States. However, these procedures are indicative of the type of procedures employed in other countries. The Department of Commerce has a staff of specialists to help companies export. These specialists can explain the customs clearance procedures for most countries. Also, freight forwarders are very knowledgeable about customers' requirements and will assist in preparing the necessary documents.

25. "High-Tech Exports: Is the Dam Breaking?" *Business Week,* June 4, 1990, pp. 66–67.

26. "Greasing the Skids for Exports," p. 66.

27. The section on import trade mechanics was based on *Importing into the United States* (Washington, D.C.: Department of the Treasury, U.S. Custom Service, January 1989). Since these regulations are subject to frequent revisions, the interested reader is advised to obtain the latest information directly from the Customs Service.

Clearance Procedures

On reaching the United States, the recipient, or consignee, of the shipment will have to file an entry for the products or goods with U.S. Customs. The importer has the choice of filing for consumption or filing for storage. Under the second alternative, imported products may be stored for some time before they are officially entered for consumption in the United States, or they may be reexported.

Since the proper declaration of imported products requires some specific knowledge, many importers use the services of licensed customs brokers. A broker is empowered by the firm to act on its behalf at customs and file the necessary forms. To determine the customs status of a shipment, an examination is typically performed to check the following:

1. The value of the shipment to assess customs
2. The verification of required marking and labeling
3. Shipment of prohibited merchandise
4. Verification of invoicing and determination of either shortages or excess compared to the invoice

The importer will have to prepare all necessary forms to allow the U.S. Customs officials to make these determinations. Failure to meet these requirements may result in lengthy delays in clearing any shipment, unnecessary expenses on behalf of the importer, and higher fees charged by customs brokers.

Valuation of Shipments   U.S. Customs officers are required by law to find the value of the imported merchandise. Basically, customs value is determined by selecting the higher of either foreign value nor export value. *Foreign value* is based on the prices at which the imported merchandise is freely placed for sale in the country of origin in the usual wholesale quantities. The *export value* is the price at which the merchandise is freely offered for sale as an export to the United States in the major markets of the country of origin. When neither a foreign value nor export value can be found, the merchandise may be entered at the corresponding U.S. value at which such or similar merchandise is freely offered in the United States less the necessary allowance for bringing the products into the country. If a corresponding U.S. value does not exist, valuation can be based on the cost of production. In a few cases, valuation can be based on the U.S. selling price, which is based on the typical price for the same product offered in the United States.

Products that are subject to duty are assessed either *ad valorem* (a percentage of the established value), with a *specific duty* (a specific amount per unit of measurement), or with a *compound duty* (combination of ad valorem and specific duty). Though the U.S. Customs Office publishes a list of the various duties by type of product, an importer can find out by contacting the U.S. Customs Office with the following information:

● Complete description of the imported item
● Method of manufacture

- Specifications and analyses
- Quantities and costs of component materials
- Commercial designation of the product in the United States and identification of the primary use of the product

Given sufficient material as described above, the U.S. Customs Service can provide importers with a binding assessment on import duties that makes it possible to assess the entire landed cost for the importer for later use in pricing. No binding information is available via telephone or based on incomplete information.

Marking and Labeling   Unless otherwise stated, each product or article imported into the United States must be legibly marked in a conspicuous place, with the name of the country of origin stated in English so that the U.S. purchaser can easily determine the country of origin. In some cases, markings may be made on the containers rather than the articles themselves. Importers are advised to obtain the particular regulations or exemptions from the U.S. Customs Service. In case of a lack of proper markings, the U.S. Customs Service can assess a special marking duty unless the imported products are marked under customs supervision. In either case, the absence of the required markings can cause costly delays to the importer.

Prohibited or Restricted Merchandise   The importation of certain articles is either prohibited or restricted. It is impractical to list all the prohibited or restricted items. However, the major classes of items are shown in Table 18.1. Restricted items can be imported with proper clearance.

TABLE 18.1 ● Classes of Products That Are Prohibited or Restricted for Import into the United States

- *Alcoholic beverages:* Require a permit from Bureau of Alcohol, Tobacco and Firearms
- *Arms, ammunition, explosives:* Require a permit from Bureau of Alcohol, Tobacco and Firearms
- *Automobiles:* Must conform to federal motor vehicle safety standards
- *Coins, currencies, and stamps:* No replicas of U.S. or foreign items permitted
- *Eggs and egg products:* Subject to the Egg Products Inspection Act
- *Animals and plants:* Subject to regulations of the Animal or Plant Health Inspection Service
- *Electronic products:* Subject to the Radiation Control Act
- *Food, drugs, devices, cosmetics:* Subject to the federal Food, Drug and Cosmetics Act
- *Narcotic drugs:* Prohibited
- *Nuclear reactors and radioactive material:* Subject to the U.S. Atomic Energy Commission
- *Obscene, immoral, seditious matter:* Prohibited
- *Pesticides:* Subject to the federal Environmental Control Act
- *Wool, fur, textiles, and fabric products:* Subject to the Wool Products Labeling Act, the Textile Fiber Products Identification Act, the Flammable Fabrics Act, and the Fur Products Labeling Act

Invoicing Procedures For some special categories of merchandise, only a commercial invoice prepared in the same manner typical for commercial transactions is sufficient for U.S. Customs clearance. Quite frequently, either a special invoice or a commercial invoice is not available at the time of entry. In such instances, the importer can prepare a pro forma invoice by promising to deliver final invoices within six months of the date of entry. Also, a bond must usually be posted to cover the value of the estimated duties.

Inaccurate information can cause costly delays to both the importer and exporter. To provide for smooth clearance through customs, the U.S. importer should assume the responsibility of properly informing the foreign supplier. The Journal of Commerce, a private company, has a service called PIERS, which is a database of all imports and exports reported to the U.S. Customs in the forty-seven largest U.S. ports. The data are helpful for competitive and market research analysis.

Goods can be delayed at the port, waiting for the necessary paperwork before being shipped. There is a trend toward the use of electronic transmission of customers' documentation. TRADANET is a global service that allows companies to send the commercial invoice and customs clearance document to the importer while the goods are in transit. With these documents, the importer can clear the goods through customs.[28]

The Role of the Customs Agent

Since the handling of shipments through customs requires specialized knowledge, most companies employ outside specialized firms that are registered with U.S. Customs. Not only will these agents prepare the necessary invoices from information supplied by the importer, but they will also arrange for clearance through customs, inspection where necessary, payment of duties, and transport to the final destination. Frequently, such customs agents are also international freight forwarders, or freight forwarding firms with a specialized customs section. To allow the customs agent to act on behalf of the importer, a special power of attorney is granted that then identifies the customs agent as a legally empowered actor.

Free Trade Zones or Foreign Trade Zones[29]

Within the United States and elsewhere in the world, zones have been established where merchandise can be placed for unlimited time periods without the payment of duties. Duty will be assessed, however, as soon as the merchandise is transferred from the free trade zone.

---

28. Roy Price, ''Towards Paperless Exporting,'' *Industrial Marketing Digest,* 12, no. 3 (1987), pp. 63–66.

29. For a detailed discussion of the role of foreign trade zones in global marketing, see Patriya S. Tansuhaj and James W. Gentry, ''Firm Differences in Perceptions of the Facilitating Role of Foreign Trade Zones in Global Marketing and Logistics,'' *Journal of International Business Studies,* Spring 1987, pp. 29–33.

Such zones offer many advantages to both exporters or importers. For one, duty payable can tie up a substantial amount of working capital. The use of a free trade zone allows a firm to keep an inventory close by without prepaying duty. In addition, many importers may later want to reexport products to other countries and thus prefer to store the merchandise temporarily in a place where no duties have to be paid until the final destination is determined.

Free trade zones are also valuable as manufacturing sites. Any merchandise brought into such zones may be broken up, repackaged, assembled, sorted, graded, cleaned, or used in the manufacturing process with domestic material. The latter can be brought duty free into trade zones and reimported, again duty free, into the United States. Duty will have to be paid only on components or parts subject to duty rather than on the entire value.

Free trade zones exist in most countries and are typically attached to ports or airports. In some countries with low labor costs, free trade zones were established to allow for the further processing of semimanufactured goods originating from developed countries.[30] These goods are later reexported into the country of origin. Malaysia is one country that has allowed many foreign electronics companies to bring components for further assembly to Malaysian foreign trade zones. As a result, the foreign trade zones have ceased as a strictly distribution- or transportation-related phenomenon and are now incorporated by many international companies in their production or sourcing strategy.

Obstacles to Foreign Imports

Recently, there has been extensive political debate over protectionist measures for certain key U.S. industries. The trade law known as the "escape clause" authorizes the president to file a protecting grant for any industry that can prove that it is being hurt by imports.[31] The law dates back to the New Deal and President Franklin Roosevelt.

Nowhere have imports made a bigger impression than in the steel industry. In 1983, the United States imported roughly 20 percent of all its steel needs. U.S. companies claim that the steel is being "dumped" in our country at artificially low costs. Domestic companies blame foreign government subsidies for the low import cost. Hence, steelworkers and their companies are pushing government to protect U.S. markets against unreasonable foreign competition.

Consumers are the main beneficiaries of these imports. They are able to purchase quality at low cost. In addition, there are countless numbers of jobs involved with trade firms in imports. A recent estimate states that 194,000 jobs are related to auto imports alone.[32] Quotas have been the recent political answer to the conflict. However, a 15 percent

30. "Export for the Future—Sameen (Kenya) Duty Free Industrial Park," *Eurobusiness,* December 1990–January 1991, Special Section, Kenya.

31. Clyde H. Farnsworth, "Industry's New Assault on Imports," *New York Times,* January 27, 1984, p. D1.

32. "Imports, Often Blamed for Killing U.S. Jobs, Create New Ones Too," *Wall Street Journal,* February 29, 1984, p. 1.

import quota on steel is estimated to have the effect of raising consumer prices over 20 percent.[33] The conflict boils down to lower prices versus jobs.

Global Import Barriers

Goods do not flow freely from country to country. There are a host of impediments to the smooth flow of trade, such as import taxes, tariffs, quotas, and nontariff barriers (discussed in Chapters 2 and 4). The importing country can take a number of actions to slow down, block, or make importing unprofitable. For example, South Korea's trade deficit quadrupled to $1.0 billion in 1990. In response, it declared 94 percent of the U.S. exports to South Korea as luxury goods with tariffs and taxes. A large Westinghouse or Whirlpool refrigerator that sells for $1,700 in the United States costs $4,200 in Korea. If Korea did not relax some of these barriers, the United States would have responded by slapping retaliatory duties on Korea's Hyundai cars and Lucky-Goldstar VCRs.[34]

As the twelve countries of the European Union adopted over 280 directives to set business standards, U.S. businesses are finding many of the standards in favor European suppliers. For example, Hyster, the U.S. forklift truck manufacturer, found it needed to make twelve modifications to its forklift to comply with the new EU directive from Brussels.[35]

The manufacturers and farmers of the United States face a number of export barriers, which are being discussed through GATT negotiations, trade talks, and meetings of heads of state. The top ten barriers to trade are shown in Table 18.2.[36]

Japan has received a great deal of pressure to open its markets. And the United States is a leader in the fight to ease barriers that prevent goods from entering Japan, whose trade surplus averaged 30 billion dollars in the early 1980s.[37] Many foreign countries insist that trade is a two-way street; countries cannot expect to export unless they allow free and easy access to imports. Although the Japanese have been criticized for unfair trade practices, a recent survey indicated that 70 percent of Japanese consumers did not discriminate against imports.[38]

33. "Jobless Rate Off Despite Slowing of the Economy," *Wall Street Journal,* February 6, 1984, p. 5.

34. "Seoul's Crackdown on Imports May Be a Luxury It Can't Afford," *Business Week,* January 21, 1991, p. 46.

35. "AS EC Markets Unite, U.S. Exporters Face New Trade Barriers," *Wall Street Journal,* January 19, 1989, p. 1.

36. Rahul Jacob, "Export Barriers the U.S. Hates Most," *Fortune,* February 27, 1989, pp. 88–89.

37. "Japan—Headaches in the Labyrinth," *Financial Times,* September 19, 1983, Special Section, Japan, p. I.

38. "New Emphasis on Import Promotion," *Financial Times,* September 19, 1983, Special Section, Japan, p. VI.

TABLE 18.2 ● Export Barriers the United States Hates Most

Product	Countries	Barrier	Sales lost by U.S.*
Grain	European Union	Price supports, variable duties	$2.0 billion
Soybeans	European Union	Price supports	$1.4 billion
Rice	Japan	Ban	$300 million
Beef	European Union	Ban on growth hormones in livestock	$100 million
Commercial aircraft	Britain, France, Germany, Spain	Subsidies to Airbus Industrie	Over $850 million
Telecommunications equipment	European Union, South Korea	Standards stacked against imports	No estimate
Telecommunications satellites	Japan	Ban on import by government agencies	No estimate
Pharmaceuticals	Argentina, Brazil	No patent protection	Over $110 million
Videocassettes, films	Brazil	Requirements to subsidize and market local films	Over $40 million
Computer software	Thailand	Poor patent protection	No estimate

*Annual, estimated.

Source: Rahul Jacob, "Export Barriers the U.S. Hates Most," *Fortune*, February 27, 1989, p. 89. © 1989 The Time Inc. Magazine Company. All rights reserved.

Japan has greatly simplified import procedures under a four-point plan:

1. Establishment or changes of specifications or standards with the aim of conforming to foreign standards

2. The nature and aim of such establishment or changes to be made public in advance

3. The views of those affected both at home and abroad to be sought, with efforts made to reflect these views in improving procedures as soon as possible

4. Foreign inspection standards to be recognized as soon as possible and domestic inspection simplified

It is hoped these four points will help to increase harmony among trading nations.

Conclusions

This chapter has explained some of the procedural aspects of international marketing. Thorough knowledge of these trade mechanics is often a prerequisite for international marketers. All too frequently, an international strategy fails because some of these mechanics have been neglected.

However, this text cannot and does not specify all the regulations in force for any particular product category or country. We have provided a general background, listing the factors that may have to be investigated before a strategy can be implemented. The regulations described are also subject to change. Consequently, we suggest that close contact with specialists in this area be maintained so that executives responsible for international marketing activities can be kept abreast of new developments.

There is a trend around the world toward reducing barriers and opening markets. The rapid growth in global trade has made more countries interdependent. If Japan continues to protect its $6 billion rice market, the United States can limit the importation of Japanese cars. World leaders are working hard to open all markets, although it will take years to remove all the barriers. Close contact with your trade association will keep your firm up-to-date on the latest agreements between governments and the trade.

Questions for Discussion

1. Your company manufactures telephones at your plant in Scranton, Pennsylvania. South Korea wants a quote on 10,000 telephones. How should you quote so that it is convenient for the buyer?

2. Irrevocable letters of credit have become very popular. How do they protect the buyer and the seller?

3. When calculating the cost of a shipment of machinery for export, what additional costs will the exporter be faced with in addition to shipping and insurance?

4. Explain the possible uses of export documentation on a shipment of pipe from Los Angeles to Bolivia?

5. What are the critical elements of the export planning process? If you were asked to develop a plan for exporting gloves to South America, how would you do it?

6. What are the advantages and disadvantages of import limits in the United States? Use, for example, the import quotas on Japanese automobiles into the United States.

7. How can free trade zones be used by U.S. manufacturers?

For Further Reading

Attiyeh, Robert S., and David L. Wenner. "Critical Mass: Key to Exports." *Business Horizons,* December 1979, pp. 28–38.

Ayal, Igal. "Industry Export Performance: Assessment and Prediction." *Journal of Marketing,* Summer 1982, pp. 54–61.

Brasch, J. "Using Export Specialists to Develop Overseas Sales." *Harvard Business Review,* May–June 1981, pp. 6–8.

Carey, Ben. "Fine Tuning Harmonized System." *American Shipper,* September 1982, p. 100.

Dollar, David. "Import Quotas and the Product Cycle." *Quarterly Journal of Economics,* August 1987, pp. 615–632.

Filbert, William B. "The Licensing Process: Getting the Export License." *Export Today,* February 1984, pp. 60–63.

Fitzpatrick, Peter B., and Alan S. Zimmerman. *Essentials of Export Marketing.* New York: American Management Association, 1985.

"Export Activity in Developing Nations." *Journal of International Business Studies,* Spring–Summer 1978, pp. 95–102.

Hayes, John. "Who Sets the Standards?" *Forbes,* April 17, 1989, pp. 110–112.

McGuinness, Norman W., and Blair Little. "The Influence of Product Characteristics on the Export Performance of New Industrial Products." *Journal of Marketing,* Spring 1981, pp. 110–122.

Rabino, Samuel. "Tax Incentives to Export: Some Implications for Policy Makers." *Journal of International Business Studies,* 11, no. 1 (1980), pp. 74–85.

Root, Franklin R. *Entry Strategies for International Markets.* Lexington, Mass.: D. C. Heath, 1987.

Weiss, Kenneth D. *Building an Import-Export Business.* New York: John Wiley & Sons, 1987.

Yorio, V. *Adapting Products for Export.* New York: Conference Board, 1983.

Part

6

Cases

Case 1

Gillette International's TRAC II

In mid-1972, Gillette International's management was considering the introduction of its new shaving system, the TRAC II, in some of its foreign markets. The blade had been introduced only nine months earlier in the U.S. market with considerable success. However, existing blade production capacity was limited, and the company could not serve all markets at the same time. Consequently, management was carefully evaluating which markets should get top priority for the TRAC II and how to combine this market selection process with an appropriate pricing strategy. In addition, the company was keenly aware of its main competitors, Schick of the United States and Wilkinson of the United Kingdom. The introduction of Gillette's newest product, the Platinum Plus, had been successful in most foreign markets; however, a number of executives believed the Platinum Plus's performance was below potential and wanted to avoid some of these negative experiences with the TRAC II introduction.

COMPANY BACKGROUND

The Gillette Company was a Boston-based consumer goods manufacturer with annual sales in 1971 of $730

The case was prepared by Robert Howard under the direction of Jean-Pierre Jeannet, Visiting Professor at IMD and Professor of Marketing and International Business at Babson College. This case was prepared for class discussion rather than to illustrate either effective or ineffective handling of an administrative situation. This case was based on earlier work by Robert Roland, M.B.A. candidate at Babson College. Copyright © 1988 by IMD, Lausanne, Switzerland. The International Institute for Management Development (IMD), resulting from the merger between IMEDE, Lausanne, and IMI, Geneva, acquires and retains all rights. Not to be used or reproduced without written permission from IMD, Lausanne, Switzerland.

million. The company was best known for its shaving product line, which was marketed worldwide and where Gillette continued to be the major company both in the United States and abroad.

The company's main operating units were Gillette North America, Gillette International, and other companies under the Diversified Companies group (see Exhibit 1). Gillette North America included four product divisions: Safety Razor, Paper Mate, Toiletries, and Personal Care.

The Safety Razor Division was responsible for the Gillette shaving business within the United States. The Toiletries Division marketed such products as deodorants, antiperspirants, shaving creams, and hair grooming products for both men and women, including the leading brands Right Guard and Foamy.

The Personal Care Division marketed women's toiletry products such as hair sprays, cream rinses, home permanents, and hair conditioners, as well as a line of portable hair dryers (Max, Super Max, and Max Plus for Men). After only one year in national distribution, Gillette held second place in the competitive market for hand-held dryers.

Gillette's Paper Mate Division was responsible for marketing writing instruments in the United States and was the leader in porous point pens. The Paper Mate Division also sold ballpoint pens and refills, broadtip markers, and glue and had recently entered the lower price segment with a new line of ballpoint and porous point pens.

The Diversified Companies group included a range of recent acquisitions located both in the United States and abroad. Acquired in 1967, Braun AG of West Germany was a leading manufacturer of electric housewares. Its largest lines were electric razors, coffeemakers, digital clocks, and some photographic products. In electric shavers, Braun was the market leader in Germany and its products were distributed

EXHIBIT 1 ● Gillette Organization Chart

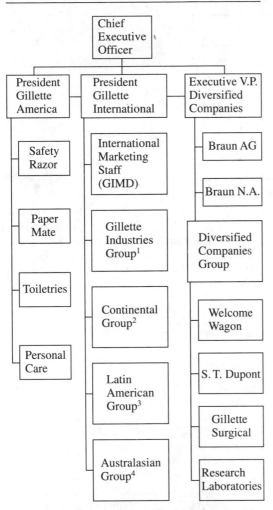

1. United Kingdom, S. Africa, and export departments to Ireland, Iceland, Greece, Eastern Europe, Near and Middle East, and African markets.
2. France, Germany, Italy, Spain, and affiliated sales companies in Scandinavia, Benelux, Alpine, and Portugal.
3. Argentina, Brazil, Colombia, Mexico, and Venezuela plus Latin American sales companies and export to Chile, Peru, Puerto Rico, Guatemala, Honduras, Costa Rica, Salvador, Nicaragua, Ecuador, Bolivia, Paraguay, Dominican Republic, Aruba, Curaçao, Guyana, Surinam, Barbados, and the Bahamas.
4. Australia, New Zealand, Japan, Hong Kong, and Southeast Asia.

Source: Company records.

in many European markets. Shavers were not sold in the United States due to a licensing agreement signed with an independent company in 1954 which was due to expire in 1975. Also part of this group was Welcome Wagon, a community service company acquired in 1971. Welcome Wagon was a service used by local businesses to acquaint new arrivals in the community with local companies and their services.

Safety Razor Division

The Safety Razor Division marketed Gillette's principal product line—shaving equipment and blades— in the U.S. market. Gillette was the world's leading blade manufacturer and the major factor in the U.S. market. The company marketed a full range of blades including double-edged stainless steel blades (Super Stainless Steel and Platinum Plus) as well as an older line of carbon steel blades (Super Blue, Blue, and Thin). Gillette sold its Techmatic Razor Blade and Lady Sure Touch on the band concept. In the United States, the Safety Razor Division also imported a line of disposable lighters under the name Cricket which was produced by Gillette's S. T. Dupont affiliate in France. Starting in the fall of 1971, the division began marketing the TRAC II, Gillette's latest shaving product based on a twin-blade shaving system. 1971 had brought record sales and profits for the division, and the outlook for 1972 indicated another top performance.

International Division

Gillette International was responsible for marketing the majority of Gillette's products abroad. The company sold its products in more than 170 countries and territories, with shaving products accounting for most of the volume. International sales had been steadily increasing as a percentage of corporate sales and accounted for more than 40 percent of Gillette's volume. Because of the higher profitability of international operations, Gillette International accounted for half of the company's profits, as seen in Exhibit 2.

The president of Gillette International was also the executive vice president for international operations at corporate headquarters in Boston. The president was supported by a staff of international marketing experts located at Gillette's International

EXHIBIT 2 ● The Gillette Company
Development of Sales and Profits, 1967–1971 (in Millions of Dollars)

Year	Total company		Blades and razors		Foreign operations	
	SALES	*NET PROFITS*	*SALES*	*NET PROFITS*	*SALES*	*NET PROFITS*
1967	$428	$57	$193	$38	$167	$20
1968	553	62	238	40	221	23
1969	610	65	250	44	256	29
1970	673	66	262	46	289	33
1971	730	62	270	41	327	33

Marketing Department (GIMD) in Boston. The staff was responsible for interacting with regional and country level managers on marketing, planning, and strategic issues and would set priorities for introduction when a supply of products was limited.

Reporting to Gillette International's president were four regional managers, each responsible for a group of markets. The Gillette Industries Group in London controlled Gillette operations in the United Kingdom and South Africa and export operations to Ireland, Iceland, Greece, Eastern Europe, the Middle East, and Africa. The group's only manufacturing facility was located in the United Kingdom.

Also located in London was the Continental Group, with responsibility for subsidiaries in France, Germany, Spain, and Italy. The Continental Group also controlled the marketing operations of affiliated sales companies in Scandinavia, the Benelux countries, Portugal, Switzerland, and Austria. This group's plant facilities were located in Germany, France, and Spain.

Gillette International's other two regional operations were based in Boston. The Latin America Group headed subsidiary operations in Argentina, Brazil, Colombia, Mexico, and Venezuela and was responsible for export and sales in Chile, Peru, Puerto Rico, and all of the countries in Central America and the Caribbean area. The group's manufacturing plants were located in Brazil, Argentina, Colombia, and Mexico.

Gillette International's fourth regional group was the Australasian Group with responsibility for Australia, New Zealand, Japan, Hong Kong, and Southeast Asia. Its major plant facility was located in Australia.

THE DEVELOPMENT OF SHAVING TECHNOLOGY

Carbon Steel Blades

King C. Gillette, the company founder, introduced the first safety razor in 1895. The company was granted an exclusive patent in 1904 on an improved version of its blade, which was followed by the development of the double-edged blade. In the 1930s, Gillette introduced carbon steel blades under the brand name Gillette Blue. These blades were thinner than earlier blades, had lacquer applied to the surface, and offered an improvement in shaving comfort and blade life.

The introduction of the Super Blue blade in 1960 represented a quantum step in technology. The Super Blue came with a silicon coated treatment which was baked on to give it extra hardness. This new process significantly improved the quality of shaving, although the shave quality tended to decline more rapidly than with previous blades after reaching a certain point. The blade was priced at 6.9 cents per unit and quickly became the standard in the industry. Customers once accustomed to the more comfortable shave of the Super Blue found it very difficult to return to the older carbon blades. For about eighteen months, Gillette was able to exploit this product advantage before competitors could introduce similar products.

Stainless Steel Blades

In August 1961, another quantum leap in shaving technology occurred when Wilkinson Sword, a U.K. company, introduced a Teflon coated stainless steel blade. The coating process was actually developed earlier by Gillette, and Wilkinson paid a royalty to Gillette for its use. Stainless steel was much harder than carbon steel and could absorb the high temperature generated in the Teflon coating process. However, because of this hardness, a stainless steel blade could not be sharpened as easily as a carbon blade. Stainless steel blades offered a high quality shave consistent over a relatively long time and were a considerable improvement for the user over carbon steel blades. Wilkinson introduced its new blade first in the United Kingdom and then launched it in the United States but did not have sufficient supply to satisfy the entire U.S. market. In response, both Gillette and Schick, the principal U.S. competitors, countered with crash development programs before Wilkinson could become fully established in major markets.

In 1963, Gillette introduced a Teflon coated stainless steel blade under the brand name Stainless (Silver Gillette in Europe). The major hurdle to overcome was the manufacturing process, as the new blades required specially designed equipment. The Stainless blades were improved by a factor of 2 to 3 in blade life over the carbon, double-edged blades. Gillette was able to maintain market leadership in the United States because Wilkinson moved too cautiously with its product rollout and did not have a fully developed marketing function.

In 1965, Gillette introduced its first modern shaving system consisting of the Techmatic razor band technology. Rather than using single blades one after another, the Techmatic came equipped with a cartridge that contained a band of blades. The user would never have to touch a single blade; thus the Techmatic offered added convenience although blade quality was equal to the stainless steel blades. Techmatic's introduction was well timed and had a lead of six months over all competitors, resulting in a 2 percent gain in market share. The Techmatic was Gillette's first entry into shaving systems other than the double-edged blade.

Platinum Treated Blades

In 1969, Gillette made another improvement in its blades by adding a platinum chromium alloy. This new blade, marketed in the United States under the brand name Platinum Plus, further increased blade life and shaving comfort but was not considered a technological breakthrough. The blade was also introduced in European markets under various names which included the word *platinum*.

In 1970 it was once more Wilkinson of the United Kingdom reaching the market with an innovation. Wilkinson launched its Wilkinson "Bonded" blade, consisting of a single blade enclosed in a plastic casing. The term *Bonded* meant that the blade remained permanently fixed in a cartridge. Although Gillette had been working on a twin blade cartridge, it was not ready for product launch at the time of the Wilkinson introduction. Fortunately for Gillette, Wilkinson did not have sufficient resources to make a major impact on the market.

In 1971, after combining Techmatic plastics knowledge with an innovative twin blade design, Gillette introduced the TRAC II. This was a major evolution from the single blade, double-edged razor and provided an entirely new concept in blade making. Although Wilkinson's Bonded razor gave the public its first experience with a cartridge product, the TRAC II represented the next step forward in cartridge design. Combined with Gillette's previous blade expertise, this shaving product was the most advanced in the industry in terms of quality and blade life (see Exhibit 3).

COMPETITION

Gillette Experience Prior to 1960

During the early development of the shaving industry, Gillette had almost no significant competition. The company got its first major break during World War I when U.S. soldiers were required to be clean shaven.

EXHIBIT 3 ● Blade Quality versus Blade Life

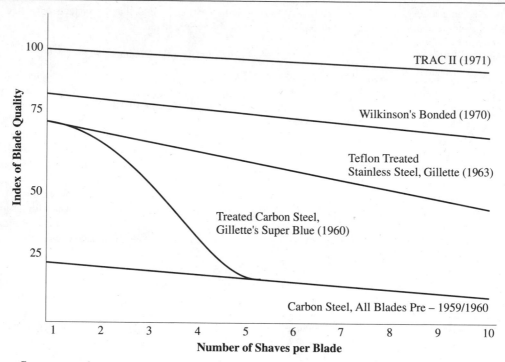

Source: Company records.

By the end of the war, Gillette had sold some 3.5 million razors and about 52 million blades to the military forces, giving Gillette a substantial advantage over other razor companies. Another big step occurred in 1939 when Gillette spent 50 percent of its entire advertising budget to sponsor the U.S. baseball World Series. By World War II, Gillette had the dominant share of the blade market. Market shares reached an all-time high in the early 1940s with 55–60 percent in the double-edged segment and about 40 percent of the entire market. The advent of television gave Gillette another boost.

Gillette did not face real double-edged blade competition in the United States or abroad until the early 1960s. Before that time, Wilkinson of the United Kingdom was not a major factor and Schick was only of minor concern in the United States. Gil-

lette was much more concerned with electric razors, particularly abroad, where the pricing of electric shavers tended to be lower than in the United States. With a smaller price gap between electric and wet shaving and with many customers preferring electric over wet shaving, Gillette was gaining market share in a stagnant or even declining segment.

Recent Developments: The Platinum Plus Experience

Gillette International's latest worldwide product introduction was the launch of Platinum Plus blades in early 1970. The Platinum Plus represented a product improvement and had been well received in the United States in the fall of 1969. In 1970, a number of key foreign markets were offered access to the Platinum Plus technology. However, because production machinery was only available in limited volume, Gillette had to introduce the product selectively. By 1972, all markets had been introduced to the Platinum Plus blade albeit with varied success.

From the outset, Gillette International gave its local managers considerable freedom in selecting the positioning strategy for the new blade. As a result, different countries chose different strategies. Some market introductions were unsuccessful by Gillette standards, and the company wanted to learn from these mistakes before introducing the TRAC II.

After reviewing the introduction of Platinum Plus in Europe, management came to a consensus on what had gone wrong. To gain further insight on the European scene, management looked closely at the U.K., German, and Brazilian experiences.

The U.K. subsidiary, faced with intensive competition in the U.K. market and a scarcity of retail shelf space, had decided to introduce Platinum Plus as its new top-of-the-line blade in place of Super Silver. Super Silver and Wilkinson's top blade had been similarly priced and selling at about the same volume. When Gillette withdrew Super Silver and introduced the higher priced Platinum Plus (with platinum coating), the company lost some of its share to Wilkinson because some users were unwilling to upgrade to the new product. As a result, Gillette lost overall market share and had not been able to regain it.

In West Germany, the Gillette subsidiary also faced intensive competition from Wilkinson. With a surplus of blade products in the retail trade, the German subsidiary opted to provide an improved product by adding a platinum coating to its top-of-the-line brand Super Silver and introduce the new product as Super Silver Platine. However, this variation brought only mixed success for Gillette.

By contrast, the Brazilian operation went ahead with the largely U.S. type strategy, by adding the new Platinum Plus to its existing product line, which included the Super Silver. This strategy proved successful. As a result of the Platinum Plus experience, management at Gillette International felt that local management should not decide on the introductory program. Rather than local companies proposing their own strategies, Gillette International's management preferred to give the local subsidiaries detailed instructions. If the decision did not suit the local market,

then local management could argue its case. At the start, however, there would be a more standardized marketing and positioning strategy largely based on the U.S. experience.

Schick in the United States and Abroad

Schick, a fully owned subsidiary of Warner Lambert, was Gillette's major competitor. Schick Safety Razor Co. manufactured injector and double-edged blades in the United States, Canada, Sweden, and the Netherlands as well as in Japan, where Schick was the dominant company in the wet shaving segment. Sales of Schick in 1972 were estimated at $47 million. In the United States and most other markets, Schick's market share was about one-third of Gillette's or less.

Schick's marketing strategy tended to emphasize print advertising or promotions such as free samples, in-store displays, or write-in offers. Schick was capable of introducing new blade types quickly and could be expected to react to Gillette within twelve to eighteen months after a new product introduction. But, like Gillette, Schick was constrained by the scarcity of machinery needed to introduce new products. In January 1972, Schick had entered Schick Super II, a product similar to TRAC II, into the shaving system market on the West Coast of the United States. By mid-1972, however, Schick Super II had still not reached full national distribution. Full-scale national television support had also not yet taken place. Most television exposure in the U.S. market was through partial sponsorship of the 1972 summer Olympics which were going on at the time.

Wilkinson on All Continents

Wilkinson, a British company, was not a serious competitor to Gillette until it introduced a treated stainless steel blade in 1961. Wilkinson had been marketing an untreated stainless blade since the mid-1950s with little success. Total sales for 1971 amounted to about £24 million ($60 million), of which the shaving portion accounted for about £18 million ($40 million). Wilkinson had experienced growth rates of 20 percent in recent years and had approximately 75 percent of its sales overseas.

Wilkinson operated its main manufacturing facilities in the United Kingdom, where it employed more than 1,300 people. The company's only other full manufacturing facility was in West Germany. Partial manufacturing and packaging were done in the United States, Australia, South Africa, and Spain.

When the treated, stainless steel blade was first introduced, Wilkinson did not have sufficient capacity to satisfy demand, and the result was only a 20 percent erosion of Gillette's U.K. market share. After its introduction in the United Kingdom, Wilkinson moved into the West German market in 1962 and, on a limited basis, into the United States at the end of 1962. In addition to capacity constraints, Wilkinson did not have a fully developed marketing operation outside its key markets and, thus, could never capitalize on the Teflon coated stainless steel blade. The only exception was the U.K. market, where Wilkinson's market share was larger than Gillette's.

Wilkinson's market share and market position differed considerably from market to market. As the major domestic producer, Wilkinson enjoyed a large share of the U.K. market. Its introduction of the "Bonded" razor ahead of Gillette had helped consolidate its market share further. It was estimated that Wilkinson's share was moving close to 50 percent for all blades sold in the United Kingdom. In Germany, Wilkinson continued to defend its share of about 30 percent. The same local subsidiary was also responsible for selling in Austria and Switzerland, where the company's market share had been increasing.

In Italy, Wilkinson had been able to increase its market share to about 20 percent as a result of introducing the Wilkinson Bonded system. Although Wilkinson maintained its own subsidiary in Italy, sales and distribution were handled by Colgate-Palmolive. In France, distribution and marketing were in the hands of Reckitt & Colman. In Spain, the company had started construction of full-scale manufacturing facilities which were expected to come on stream in 1974.

In other European countries, Wilkinson also relied on the distribution arrangements with established consumer products companies. In Denmark, Norway, Sweden, and Holland, Wilkinson products were marketed by Colgate-Palmolive. Wilkinson blades were marketed in Greece by Unilever, one of the world's largest consumer products companies, and in Ireland by Beecham, a U.K.-based personal products company. Distribution was also handled by Reckitt & Colman in South Africa, where Wilkinson's share had

increased beyond 10 percent with the introduction of the Bonded blade. Wilkinson blades were also distributed in many Middle Eastern countries out of a Beirut office.

In Asia, Wilkinson blades were marketed in Japan, Australia, and New Zealand. The Australian market position improved considerably with the introduction of the Bonded blade. In Japan, Wilkinson was marketed through Lion, a major Japanese personal products company.

In the United States, where Wilkinson's share was about 10 percent, marketing had been handled exclusively since 1970 by Colgate-Palmolive, the large, U.S.-based multinational consumer products company. In Canada, where Wilkinson had a market share of about 20 percent, its blades were distributed by John A. Houston Ltd. Throughout Latin America, Wilkinson used independent distributors to market in Brazil, Colombia, the Dominican Republic, Haiti, Paraguay, Uruguay, and Venezuela.

THE TRAC II OPPORTUNITY

Manufacturing Overview

The manufacturing process of the TRAC II system consisted of three distinct phases: the manufacturing of the blade, the manufacturing of cartridge parts, and the assembly of these blades and cartridge parts into the TRAC II system. Each one of these stages offered particular challenges to Gillette. The key problem, however, had turned from making the system work to adding sufficient capacity. Although it was difficult to forecast exactly how much blade capacity would be available for Gillette International, it was felt that each gain in annual volume of 150 million units would take twelve to eighteen months.

Blade Manufacture

The blade manufacturing process alone consisted of six stages. In the first stage a continuous strip of soft steel, purchased in coils the width of one blade, was mounted on a wheel for perforation. Perforations in the steel served as guides for additional blade cartridge components and also enabled soap and water to pass through. Oil used in cutting these perforations was removed before the steel passed into a hardening furnace with three temperature zones. The hardening gave the blades an extended life of eleven to fourteen shaves. After leaving the furnace, the steel was cooled in an annealing process before being rewound onto a wheel for sharpening.

In the sharpening process, the perforated and hardened steel strip was ground to remove rough steel from the blade's cutting edge, followed by rough sharpening and honing (refined sharpening process). Once the honing process had put a cutting edge on the blade, the steel strip was cut into individual blade lengths and the individual blades airblown onto blade holders. Blade holders transferred stacks of razor blades to blade magazines, which passed through a washing cycle before vacuum phase sputtering.

The contents of each magazine were automatically unloaded onto a sputtering knife. Twelve sputtering knives were positioned around a sputtering post of chromium and platinum with the cutting edge of the razor blades facing the sputtering post. Using a technique known as ion deposition, chromium and platinum were transferred from the sputtering post to the blades' cutting edge.

In the final step, the blade edges were coated with Teflon and passed through a sintering furnace which baked the Teflon onto the blade and enhanced the bonding of chromium and platinum to the razor's cutting surface.

Cartridge Assembly

Each TRAC II cartridge contained two individual razor blades, as well as several plastic and metal parts. Cartridge assembly began with black plastic guard caps that were fed from a bowl of caps into a chute, with each cap positioned so that its plastic alignment studs were face up.

The first razor blade in the cartridge assembly was set on a guard cap, with the plastic alignment studs passing through the blade perforations. A spacer was set on top of the first blade, followed by a second blade and, lastly, the top plastic guard cap. This was a very delicate operation since the relationship of the two blades to the cartridge was critical to providing shaving comfort. A slight pressure was applied to seal the assembled cartridge before it was moved to an automated inspection stage.

If the automated scanning device verified that all parts were included and properly aligned in the car-

tridge assembly, the cartridge was relayed to a dispenser tray. A plastic cartridge dispenser was positioned over the dispenser tray and five TRAC II cartridges pressed into place. Once assembled, these dispensers were transported to another area for final packaging. (For an overview of the manufacturing process, see Exhibit 4.)

Equipment as Bottleneck

Manufacturing equipment for the production of razor blades had specific requirements and was not purchased on the open market. Instead, Gillette produced its own equipment in company-owned tool shops in Boston, the United Kingdom, and France. For TRAC II production, new equipment was needed for blade perforation, hardening, and sharpening. New equipment was also needed for the production of plastic elements such as guard caps and dispensers as well as for assembly and loading operations. The longest lead times (twelve to eighteen months) were for the procurement of sharpening equipment. For plastic parts production, molds had to be produced which also required high precision tools.

For years, Gillette tool shops had been operating at full capacity. In recent years, Gillette had suffered from undercapacity in production, with output often a step or two behind actual demand for Gillette blades. As a result, Gillette's top management decided to add to existing capacity so that manufacturing capacity would always exceed demand by 10 percent. Consequently, just when the tool shops were busy providing this additional equipment, TRAC II increased the burden even more. It was estimated that Gillette was able to add about 150 million units of TRAC II (dispensers containing five cartridges) every twelve months, or about 12.5 million units per month. The Boston plant was using all its output to satisfy demand in the United States, and the North American division wanted still more products out of the newly planned capacity expansion. Given the nature of tool production, there was no short-term solution for expanding total output beyond the rate of 12.5 million units per month.[1]

1. The 150 million dispensers refer to annualized capacity increase; for example, after twelve months, the annualized output for the next twelve months would be increased by 150 million units (or 750 million blades).

EXHIBIT 4 ● Gillette TRAC II Manufacturing Overview

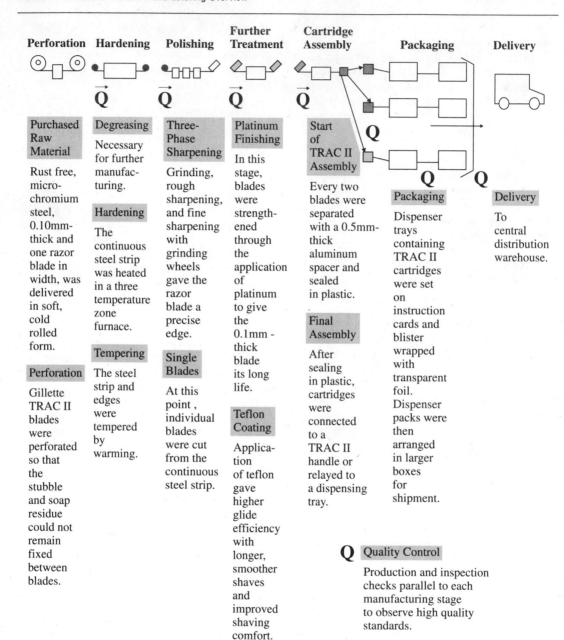

| Perforation | Hardening | Polishing | Further Treatment | Cartridge Assembly | Packaging | Delivery |

Purchased Raw Material

Rust free, micro-chromium steel, 0.10mm-thick and one razor blade in width, was delivered in soft, cold rolled form.

Perforation

Gillette TRAC II blades were perforated so that the stubble and soap residue could not remain fixed between blades.

Degreasing

Necessary for further manufac-turing.

Hardening

The continuous steel strip was heated in a three temperature zone furnace.

Tempering

The steel strip and edges were tempered by warming.

Three-Phase Sharpening

Grinding, rough sharpening, and fine sharpening with grinding wheels gave the razor blade a precise edge.

Single Blades

At this point, individual blades were cut from the continuous steel strip.

Platinum Finishing

In this stage, blades were strength-ened through the application of platinum to give the 0.1mm - thick blade its long life.

Teflon Coating

Applica-tion of teflon gave higher glide efficiency with longer, smoother shaves and improved shaving comfort.

Start of TRAC II Assembly

Every two blades were separated with a 0.5mm-thick aluminum spacer and sealed in plastic.

Final Assembly

After sealing in plastic, cartridges were connected to a TRAC II handle or relayed to a dispensing tray.

Packaging

Dispenser trays containing TRAC II cartridges were set on instruction cards and blister wrapped with transparent foil. Dispenser packs were then arranged in larger boxes for shipment.

Delivery

To central distribution warehouse.

Q Quality Control

Production and inspection checks parallel to each manufacturing stage to observe high quality standards.

PRICING ISSUES

Pricing was a main consideration in the launch of TRAC II abroad. Gillette International viewed pricing as the key to increasing market share and to maintaining or improving margins in each market. Pricing was dependent on a number of factors, any one of which could be used as a basis for selecting a final price policy. These factors were production costs, marketing costs, and competitor pricing.

Pricing Based on Production Costs

Production costs at Gillette were classified into two parts: manufacturing costs and initial investments costs. Manufacturing costs were defined as the sum of direct material, direct labor, and variable manufacturing overhead. The manufacturing costs of the new TRAC II were about twice the cost of the Platinum Plus blade, which averaged $.03 per unit. Initial investment costs for new processes at Gillette were normally 20 percent higher than prior blade processes. Added capital investment for the TRAC II, however, was substantially higher than for previous blade manufacturing processes because of the technology level and amounted to $10 million per 100 million units (dispensers at five blades each). As with the older line of blades, these investment costs would be reduced over time as volume increased and added equipment depreciated. A typical depreciation period was about six years. If the TRAC II were priced on the basis of total production costs, Gillette's typical ex-factory price for blades would give the company a gross margin of 70 percent. Out of this gross margin, the company would have to cover all direct marketing and general administrative expenses.

Pricing Based on Marketing Costs

Gillette's marketing costs tended to be higher for a new brand since the bulk of advertising expenditures would shift to the latest product. At the time of the TRAC II introduction, advertising expenditures for overseas markets were concentrated on Techmatic and Platinum Plus. If these expenditures were to be shifted to the TRAC II, management needed to decide on the changeover rate. Under ideal circumstances, these expenditures could be shifted at the same rate as customers upgraded brands. In the United States,

the Marketing Research Group had charted trade-up patterns since 1960. When the Super Blue was introduced, it cannibalized Blue Blade sales, enabling Super Blue to achieve predominant market share after only eighteen months. Similarly, when Platinum Plus was added to Gillette's product line, customers traded up from the stainless steel blade at roughly the same rate. This type of data was not available for countries other than the United States, but management felt it could use these data as an estimate for trends in the European marketplace.

Initial interest in and purchase of the TRAC II was particularly dependent on two things. One was the newness of the product. Management in Boston felt that once the TRAC II was launched, there would be a certain period of vulnerability because of its level of sophistication. Whether trading up from a previous Gillette product or switching brands, a consumer would have to spend an initial $1.50 for a TRAC II handle to accommodate TRAC II cartridges. Secondly, therefore, the potential for cartridge sales was dependent on the number of TRAC II handles. The only experience Gillette had had with such a sophisticated trade-up was the Techmatic. Excluding the Techmatic, all of Gillette's other successor blades were compatible with the same razor handle. Hence, the level of advertising had to be sufficient to generate early sales of the sophisticated TRAC II while at the same time balancing demand with a limited supply in each key market.

Pricing to Gain Market Share

The pricing policy chosen to cover production costs and advertising expenses would certainly influence market share. In the past, a new product would be priced at a certain premium over its predecessor. The size of this price premium would have varying effects on resulting market share. Given Gillette's pricing strategy with country by country differences, adding a 10–20 percent premium for a sophisticated new product such as TRAC II could result in success in some markets and low performance in others.

Past new product introductions served as an example. On average, Gillette's Super Blue sold at a 38 percent premium over Gillette's Blue. The first stainless steel blade, marketed as Super Silver in most European markets, was sold at about twice the retail price of the Super Blue.

The Gillette Techmatic was marketed at a substantial premium over the Platinum Plus. The amount of this price premium depended on the various competitive factors and differed from market to market. In 1971, the premium was about 50 percent over the Stainless Steel in both Germany and the United Kingdom. However, the price base was not identical, and actual retail prices for the two markets differed.

Given the key market data in Exhibits 5 and 6, Gillette management was concerned with creating a pricing policy that would lead to intracompany trade-up as well as intercompany brand switching.

Options for Gillette International

Having reviewed the manufacturing costs and anticipated demand patterns, Gillette management considered three pricing strategies: (1) in accordance with production cost differences, (2) at a constant premium over the now top Platinum Plus, or (3) at a uniform world price for all countries.

Pricing in relation to production costs would allow Gillette its existing margin structure and would take into consideration the new equipment investment. On the other hand, there were some markets

EXHIBIT 5 ● Size of Key Markets

Market	Estimated blade sales (1972) (in millions of blades)
United States	1,772
United Kingdom	361
West Germany	296
France	429
Italy	266
Spain	160
Canada	170
Argentina	250
Brazil	500
Mexico	310
Sweden	35
Holland	50
Japan	1,300

Source: Company records.

where margins were lower than desired, and a constant margin would not increase margins in these countries.

If management chose to price at a constant premium, there would be a real potential for price differences between markets. Such price differences between markets would not be easy to equilibrate once a product had been established at a certain price level. Furthermore, the differences could lead to product arbitrage (parallel imports).

The threat of parallel imports had always been a problem for Gillette and encouraged some managers to support the world pricing policy. Although this policy would alleviate parallel imports, it could put the TRAC II price out of reach in some markets, which would affect market share. And, although this policy would reduce product arbitrage, a uniform price would open up doors to competitors with various lower cost products and with identical products priced at a lower level.

Whichever policy was chosen, Gillette's management constantly had to keep the competition in mind. Gillette had to continue and increase its TRAC II supply with one-third of all new output going to the U.S. market. The decision to go international had been made, but only the remaining two-thirds of new output could be spread among those key markets.

Gillette had to move rapidly to reach its overseas markets before Schick introduced its Super II and before Wilkinson had a replacement for its own Bonded blade. The importance of getting to a market first was reinforced by the Marketing Research Group's findings on timing and market share. That meant, all things being equal regarding pricing, quality of product, and distribution, that the market share potentials to the second, third, and fourth entrants would be no more than 30 percent, 18 percent, and 12 percent, respectively, of the market leader.

Based on previous experience, the window of opportunity for the TRAC II would last twelve to eighteen months. Given that this time lead represented the number of months Schick and Wilkinson needed to invest several million dollars to achieve production capability, management had to make its decisions soon. Furthermore, the precise combination of pricing policy and selected target markets had to match and preserve Gillette's image as world leader in the shaving industry.

EXHIBIT 6 ● Key Market Shaving Data

	MALE POPULATION IN MILLIONS	PERCENTAGE OF WET SHAVERS	Share of market			Manufacturing		
			G	S	W	G	S	W
U.S.A.	67.6	73	58	23	10	X	X	
U.K.	19.7	72	40	3	42	X		X
W. Germany	21.7	40	59	6	31	X		X
France	17.4	50	65	23	5	X		
Italy	17.2	74	65	3	19			
Spain	11.7	48	70	17	4	X		X
Canada	7.4	58	55	23	19	X	X	
Argentina	8.1	75	95	1	0	X		
Brazil	21.5	97	85	3	4	X		
Mexico	10.0	95	80	5	0	X		
Sweden	3.1	39	54	45	1		X	
Holland	4.6	32	60	30	3		X	
Japan	40.0 (approx.)	n.a.	14	64	n.a.			

Source: Company records.

*Share of male wet shavers

Note: n.a. = not available
      G = Gillette
      S = Schick
      W = Wilkinson

Case 2

In August 1983, Malay Chadha and Suresh Metha,[1] General Manager and Marketing Manager of Wiltech shaving products, were reviewing the preceding year's sales. Wiltech had introduced a complete line of five products in July 1982 and had succeeded in associating the Wiltech name with the quality image and reputation of Wilkinson Sword. However, actual sales had been far below target figures, and the low sales volume contrasted poorly to industrywide sales of 1,850 million rupees versus Wiltech's 27 million rupees.[2] Therefore, Chadha and Metha had to consider what changes in Wiltech's marketing program could increase sales to the desired level. Such changes would require a complete review of Wiltech's pricing, advertising, and distribution strategies. Wiltech needed to improve the near-term situation, while also considering its long-term goal to become India's market leader in shaving products. In addition, an established multinational competitor was planning new plant construction.

Metha felt that prices could be maintained if

1. Disguised names.
2. Ten rupees (Rs.) = $1 in 1983.

This case was prepared by Robert Howard under the direction of Jean-Pierre Jeannet, Visiting Professor at IMD and Professor of Marketing and International Business at Babson College. This case was prepared for class discussion rather than to illustrate either effective or ineffective handling of an administrative situation. This case was based on earlier work by Sameer Kaji, M.B.A. candidate at Babson College. Copyright © 1988 by IMD, Lausanne, Switzerland. The International Institute for Management Development (IMD), resulting from the merger between IMEDE, Lausanne, and IMI, Geneva, acquires and retains all rights. Not to be used or reproduced without written permission from IMD, Lausanne, Switzerland.

Wiltech introduced one new blade and positioned its existing five brands more effectively. Chadha, on the other hand, believed that Wiltech had focused too much on India's wealthier segments and that prices should be adjusted. Chadha also saw that export opportunities existed and strongly favored trading with the Soviet Union. A detailed plan had to be ready in one week for presentation to the board. Despite this deadline, Chadha and Metha were unable after two days to agree on what Wiltech's problems were and how to correct them. High humidity and record temperatures did not help spirits as the two resumed their discussion.

WILTECH BACKGROUND

In 1979, Wilkinson Sword, the U.K. shaving systems company, entered into a licensing agreement to expand its international presence into India. Wiltech, for Wilkinson technology, was funded by Asian Cables Corporation Limited and the government-owned Karnataka State Industrial Investment Development Corporation. Equity participation was shared among Asian Cables (25 percent), the state government (26 percent), and the public (49 percent). The licensing agreement required Wilkinson to construct a manufacturing facility in Belagola, 100 miles from the central Wiltech office in Bangalore, Karnataka (see Exhibit 1). Wiltech's licensing terms included the following payments to Wilkinson:

1. £130,000[3] for design, drawings, and documentation

2. £260,000 for plant installation and commissioning

3. £0.66 = $1.

EXHIBIT 1 ● The Indian Subcontinent

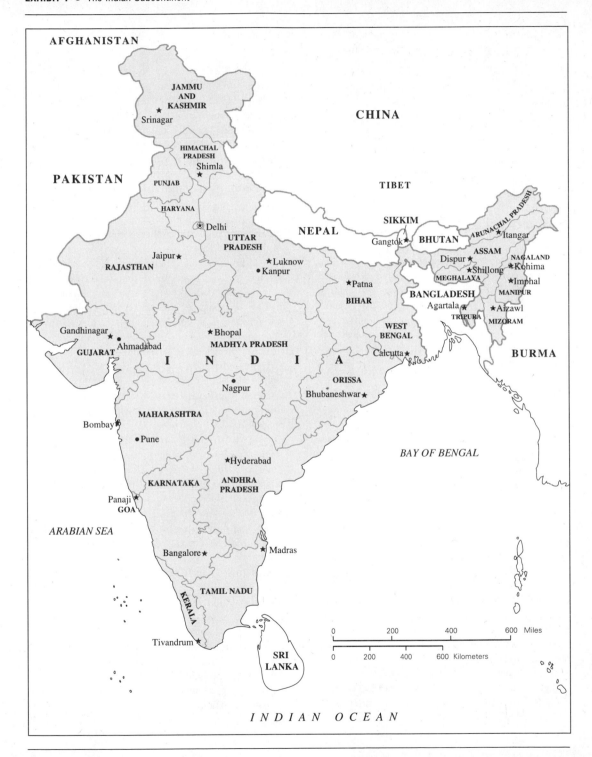

3. From the start of commercial production, a 2 percent royalty on all products sold, up to five years or £175,000, whichever came first

Wilkinson paid a tax of 20 percent to the Indian government on items 1 and 2 in three installments. A gratis time commitment of 7,840 worker hours by Wilkinson engineers was also included in this payment plan. Moreover, to ensure continued interest in the project, Wilkinson's chief executive and technical director were appointed to Wiltech's board of directors.

Wilkinson's Role in Shaving History

Wilkinson Sword was founded by Henry Nock in 1772 to manufacture personal and military defense weapons. Nock and his partner, James Wilkinson, emphasized close tolerances, quality control, and innovation in the design of their products. This attention to detail led to being appointed gun and sword makers for the British royalty—an honor which has continued to the present day. Henry Wilkinson, son of James, took full control of the business in 1825 and, in 1898, extended Wilkinson's image as a maker of quality steel cutting edges from swords to razor blades. Starting with the Pall Mall safety razor, Wilkinson maintained its position as a leader in shaving comfort and technology and pioneered several shaving breakthroughs.

One of Wilkinson's more recent innovations was the use of stainless steel. Double-edged carbon steel blades had been the industry norm until Wilkinson introduced its double-edged, stainless steel blades in 1956. Wilkinson developed their stainless steel blades further by coating them with Teflon and introduced these to the marketplace in 1961. A combination of product quality and a two-year lead time allowed Wilkinson to increase its U.K. market share from 7 percent to 45 percent, with similar gains in other countries. In 1970, Wilkinson championed another first in shaving technology when it launched its bonded shaving system. The bonded shaving system, which contained a single blade permanently fixed inside a cartridge, was available throughout the world by the end of 1974. And, in 1976, Wilkinson introduced its adjustable twin blade cartridge system, similar to the Gillette TRAC II.

THE INDIAN MARKET

India in Transition

After gaining political independence from Great Britain in 1947, India attempted a series of centrally planned economic programs. From 1950 onward, however, the rate of economic expansion continued to remain only 1.5 percent ahead of the rate of population growth. Attempts to speed up India's growth rate began in the 1970s, when forces emerged calling for reforms to move the country away from the planning process by freeing the private sector, reducing the dominance of the public sector, and liberalizing import policy insofar as it restricted the importation of new technologies.

Indira Gandhi accelerated these efforts to attract foreign investment and raise the standard of living. Attempts to attract foreign business did not, however, include relaxing the laws on foreign ownership. India's leaders were concerned about foreign exchange shortages and, as a result, preferred to encourage the production of import substitutes and licensing arrangements with foreign firms. Although Wilkinson Sword was the first to negotiate such a licensing arrangement in the shaving industry, it was inevitable that other multinational competitors would soon follow.

Such firms were attracted to the Indian shaving market for a number of reasons, one of which was its potential size. In 1981, India's population was estimated at 685 million and was expected to reach 844 million by 1990 and 994 million by 2000. This population was slow at urbanization by Western standards, and only 23 percent of the country resided in urban areas. Within this group of 156 million urban dwellers, 42 million (27 percent) lived in India's twelve metropolitan cities (see Exhibit 2). India's youth represented a disproportionate amount of the total population with 40 percent of the country under the age of fifteen and only 9 percent of the country fifty-five or older (see Exhibit 3).

Exacting descriptions of Indian society by income level were not available. Instead, the Center for Monitoring the Indian Economy classified Indian society into approximate income groups according to five-member families (see Exhibit 4). Beyond an urban versus rural reference, information in Exhibit 4

EXHIBIT 2 ● Distribution and Growth of India's Population[1]

	1981	*1971*	*1961*	*1951*	*1901*
Number of Towns	3,245	2,636	2,421	2,890	1,851
Urban Population (in millions)	156.2	109.1	78.9	62.4	25.9
Urban as a Percentage of Total Population	23.3	19.9	18.0	17.3	10.8
Percentage of Towns					
Class I (Includes metro. cities[2])	6.7	5.6	4.3	2.6	1.4
Class II	8.3	6.9	5.4	3.3	2.3
Class III	22.8	22.1	19.0	11.6	7.4
Class IV	32.3	33.1	30.8	21.8	21.4
Class V	22.9	25.7	31.5	40.0	40.9
Class VI	7.1	6.5	9.1	20.6	26.7
Total	100.0	100.0	100.0	100.0	100.0
Percentage of Urban Population in					
Class I	60.4	55.8	50.2	43.4	25.8
Class II	11.7	11.3	11.1	10.4	10.8
Class III	14.4	16.3	17.5	16.0	16.0
Class IV	9.5	11.3	13.0	14.0	20.9
Class V	3.6	4.7	7.3	13.1	20.2
Class VI	0.5	0.5	0.9	3.2	6.3
Total	100.0	100.0	100.0	100.0	100.0

1. The definition of *urban* adopted in the 1981 census, as in the previous two censuses, was as follows:
    (a) All statutory towns with a Municipal Corporation, Municipal Board, Cantonment Board, or Notified Town Area, etc.
    (b) All other places with (i) a minimum population of 5,000, (ii) at least 75% of male working population engaged in nonagricultural and allied activity, and (iii) a density of population of at least 400 per square kilometer (1,000 per sq. mile)
    An urban agglomeration is defined as one consisting of one or more towns, including in some cases villages or parts of a village which can be considered as urbanized and contiguous to the town or towns concerned.
    Urban agglomeration has been treated as a single unit. Class I towns (called cities) are those with a population of 100,000 and above; Class II: 50,000 to 99,999; Class III: 20,000 to 49,999; Class IV: 10,000 to 19,999; Class V: 5,000 to 9,999; and Class VI: less than 5,000.
    All figures for 1981 except the all-India urban ratio (23.3%) exclude Assam and Jammu and Kashmir.

2. Metropolitan cities have populations of 1 million or more and include Calcutta, Bombay, Delhi, Madras, Bangalore, Hyderabad, Ahmadabad, Kanpur, Pune, Nagpur, Lucknow, and Jaipur.

Source: Statistical Outline of India 1986–1987. Tata Services Limited, Department of Economics and Statistics, Bombay House, Bombay, pp. 32, 46. Reprinted by permission.

EXHIBIT 3 ● Age Distribution of India's Population

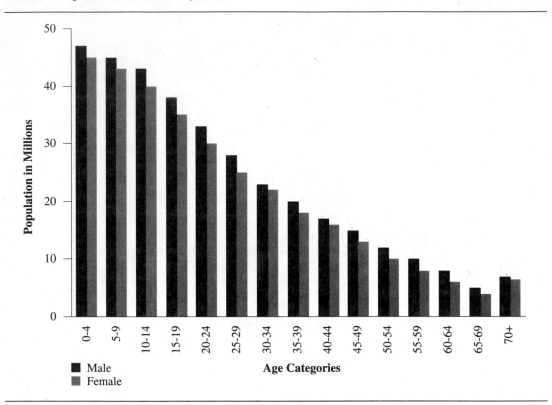

did not indicate how India's consumer wealth was distributed countrywide. These data were available on a per capita income basis for each of India's states (see Exhibit 5).

In addition to a tremendous diversity in population and income distribution, there were fifteen major languages, 1,650 dialects, and several religions spread throughout India's 25 states and union territories. This diversity made it difficult to come up with any one best description of an ''average'' consumer in the shaving market. There was sufficient evidence, however, that indicated the majority of Indian males shaved each day and that it was considered a prerequisite prior to beginning the day's activities. Those who did not shave were considered unclean and unable to participate in religious practices or other daily activities. The research also revealed that consumers were dissatisfied with India's current shaving products, yet were unaware of alternatives.

The government expansion of agricultural and social programs, as well as the more liberal industrial policies, created enthusiasm for investment as India entered the mid-1980s. Hence, with the indications that consumers were ready for alternative shaving products, Wiltech saw an excellent chance to secure a place in the Indian market.

The Indian Shaving Market

Worldwide, shaving markets were classified into wet and dry segments, the dry segment corresponded to electric and cordless razors, the wet segment to a variety of razors and blades. In India, the dry shaving market was insignificant, and most males used wet

EXHIBIT 4 ● Structure of Indian Society

Position	Group	Annual income per five-member family	Education	Standard of living
Top 1%—ruling elites living in larger cities	(a) Big owners of all types of business and property (land, factories, trading, transport, contracting, and brokering) (b) Leaders of central, state, and local governments, cooperatives, and ruling parties; most members of central and state legislatures (c) Top leaders of large national or metropolitan trade unions	> Rs. 500,000	Varies	Opulent; conspicuous consumers
Next 4%—supporting power elite living in cities	(a) Medium owners of business and property, and very rich farmers (b) Second-rank political leaders of ruling parties and first-rank leaders of opposition parties (c) Top bureaucrats and technocrats at all levels of government (d) Top executives in large public- and private-sector business units (e) More-affluent self-employed professionals (doctors, lawyers, etc.)	Rs. 100,000–500,000	Generally well educated (tertiary level)	Fairly affluent; good housing, furnishings, cars, TVs, telephones, sound systems, other durables
Next 5%—relatively prosperous by Indian standards; living in urban areas	(a) Small property owners and rich farmers (b) Petty bureaucrats, junior and medium business executives, and other supervisory cadre (c) Workers and employees organized in unions (d) Second-rank leaders of large trade unions; (e) Less-affluent self-employed (f) Others in ''middle class''	Rs. 15,000–100,000	Generally well educated	Generally good housing, moderately furnished, some durables

EXHIBIT 4 ● Structure of Indian Society (*Continued*)

Position	Group	Annual income per five-member family	Education	Standard of living
Next 10%— above average by Indian standards; living in urban areas	(a) Upper-middle farmers (b) Owners of very small business and property (c) Supervisory and lower staff in unorganized business (d) Others regarded as lower middle class	Rs. 10,000– 15,000	Poorly educated but literate	Barely tolerable housing and furnishing; some durables
Next 30%— barely above poverty line; living in towns and large villages	(a) Middle farmers (b) Lowest layers of employees in unorganized sector (c) Lowest layer of self-employed (d) Urban people in low-paid jobs	Rs. 6,000– 10,000	Half literate, other half illiterate	Level of poverty visible to visitors
Last 50%— below poverty line; living in villages	(a) Poor farmers (b) Irregularly employed, underemployed, and unemployed (c) Tribals/scheduled castes (d) Landless agricultural laborers	< Rs. 6,000	Illiterate	Abject poverty, bare subsistence

Note: Indications and figures are approximate and indicate only broad magnitudes. Incomes include fringe benefits, open and hidden perquisites, and black-market income. Farmers generally live in villages, but some have been grouped with the urban population for simplification of presentation.

Source: India: Limited Avenues to an Unlimited Market, Business International, 1985, pp. 14–15. Reprinted by permission.

shaving products. Razors and blades in India could be further classified by the type of steel used: carbon or stainless. Wiltech had two types of stainless steel products: (1) double-edged blades with a cutting edge on each side, and (2) twin blades, where two blades were carefully positioned above each other in a cartridge. The term *shaving system* referred to blades packaged and purchased in conjunction with a razor.

Segmentation

In the shaving industry, market size, sales volume, and market share were typically described in terms of blades sold. After 1961, stainless steel blades became the industry standard worldwide. In India, however, the market transition from carbon steel to stainless steel did not begin until the mid-1970s and by 1983 was still not complete.

In 1983, the value of the entire Indian razor blade market was Rs. 439 million, three-quarters from stainless steel and the balance from carbon steel blades. Of a total 1,434 million blades sold, stainless steel blades accounted for 67 percent and carbon steel 33 percent. These two blade segments were also classified demographically, urban versus rural (see Exhibit 6), with urban consumers classified further according to town class (see Exhibit 7).

EXHIBIT 5 ● 1983–1984 Per Capita Income by State (in Rupees)

State	Per capita income
Andhra Pradesh	1,955
Assam	1,762
Bihar	1,174
Gujarat	2,795
Haryana	3,147
Himachal Pradesh	2,230
Jammu & Kashmir	1,820
Karnataka	1,957
Kerala	1,761
Madhya Pradesh	1,636
Maharashtra	3,032
Manipur	1,673
Orissa	1,339*
Punjab	3,691
Rajasthan	1,881
Tamil Nadu	1,827
Tripura	1,206**
Uttar Pradesh	1,567
West Bengal	2,231
Delhi	3,928
Goa, Daman & Diu	3,479
Pondicherry	3,693

Note: Owing to differences in source material used, the figures for different states are not strictly comparable.
*1982–1983.
**1980–1981.
Source: Statistical Outline of India 1986–1987. Tata Services Limited, Department of Economics and Statistics, Bombay House, Bombay, p. 22. Reprinted by permission.

EXHIBIT 6 ● Urban versus Rural Blade Consumption in India (in Millions of Blades)

	Blade type		
Area	STAINLESS STEEL	CARBON STEEL	TOTAL
Urban	672.7	130.3	803
Rural	288.3	342.7	631
Total	961.0	473.0	1,434

EXHIBIT 7 ● Urban Blade Consumption by Town Class Distribution (in Millions of Blades)

	Blade type		
Town class	STAINLESS STEEL	CARBON STEEL	TOTAL
Metropolitan	193.3	23.4	216.7
Class I	229.8	35.2	265.0
Class II	90.2	16.9	107.1
Class III	82.3	24.8	107.1
Class IV	77.1	30.0	107.1
Total	672.7	130.3	803.0

Source: Company records.

COMPETITION IN THE INDIAN RAZOR BLADE MARKET

Malhotra Group

The Harbanslal Malhotra Group of companies was formed in the late 1940s after India achieved its independence. In 1954, the government of India banned imports of several consumer goods to preserve scarce foreign exchange reserves. Razor blades were thus prohibited from legally entering the country, which gave the Malhotra Group a near monopoly. In the next three decades, the Malhotra Group enjoyed substantial gains in market share and was virtually unchallenged until Wiltech entered the scene.

Malhotra's product lines consisted of four different double-edged blades and three shaving system products. Malhotra's biggest seller was the Topaz brand. Although the Topaz was made of local steel,

EXHIBIT 8 ● Pre-Wiltech Brand Positioning of Razor Blades in India

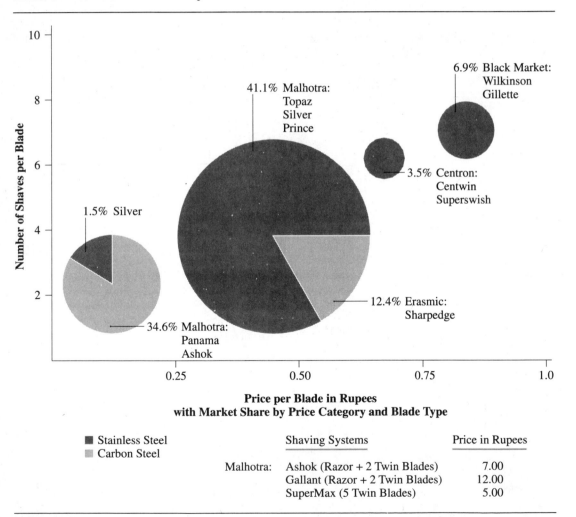

Price per Blade in Rupees
with Market Share by Price Category and Blade Type

■ Stainless Steel
▨ Carbon Steel

	Shaving Systems	Price in Rupees
Malhotra:	Ashok (Razor + 2 Twin Blades)	7.00
	Gallant (Razor + 2 Twin Blades)	12.00
	SuperMax (5 Twin Blades)	5.00

Source: Company records.

it was Malhotra's popular blade. Aimed at users in cities and smaller towns, Topaz was priced at 45 paise[4] per blade and sold in packs of five. Malhotra also had slightly less expensive blades, each of which sold in packs of five. Their respective names and prices were Silver Prince at 35 paise, Ashok at 30 paise, and Panama at 30 paise. Malhotra had a near perfect monopoly with its three shaving systems—Ashok, Gallant, and SuperMax, all priced in the Rs. 7–12 category.

Malhotra's product line was able to meet the diverse needs of the entire Indian shaving market, urban and rural as well as the carbon and stainless steel segments. This diverse market was reached by the Malhotra Group's 300 salesmen and 1,000 stockists (inventory-carrying distributors). Malhotra maintained strong market awareness with a unique promotion strategy, sponsoring a variety of sporting events and musical concerts aimed at Indians in the 25–40 age group. The combination of a broad product line, an aggressive pricing policy, a promotion level three to four times that of Wiltech, and a longtime presence in the Indian shaving market all contributed to Malhotra's 82 percent market share and its image as a leader in the Indian market.

Centron and Erasmic

Aside from Malhotra, the only other significant participants in India's razor market were Centron and Erasmic. Both firms made only blades and, hence, depended on Malhotra and black-market shaving systems for the sale of their blades. Centron was a small manufacturer that concentrated sales in India's eastern region. Centron offered two blades in the 60–65 paise category: the Superswish and the Centwin, both in packs of five. In the 1970s, Centron was acquired by Brooke Bond, a large multinational which marketed tea all over the country. Although Centron's operations concentrated on a limited region, Brooke Bond had an extensive, national distribution network which Wiltech management expected would be used countrywide to attack the razor market. Erasmic was another domestic manufacturer but marketed its blades primarily in northern India. Erasmic's blades were priced at 45 paise and in packs of five.

4. One rupee equals 100 paise.

Black-Market Blades

Blades sold on the black market were either Wilkinson or Gillette and typically cost 70 paise to 1 rupee each. Gillette International marketed the majority of Gillette's products abroad and was Wilkinson's most serious competitor in the worldwide shaving market. Gillette knew that Indian consumers were willing to buy its shaving products on the black market and would, therefore, welcome an opportunity to enter the Indian marketplace legally. India's improved political and economic climate motivated Gillette management to establish a joint venture with Poddar of Calcutta. Gillette planned to manufacture its products by 1986 and, despite being a few years behind Wiltech, would use its full resources to secure a share of India's market.

Each of these competitors sought to differentiate itself from the others to protect the respective markets. One result of this differentiation was a wide range in razor blade prices. (The range of prices and product segments are summarized in a brand positioning chart in Exhibit 8.)

MARKETING PRACTICES IN INDIA

India's Distribution Channels

After leaving a factory, blades in India were shipped to and temporarily stored at company-owned depots. Depots were usually located in one or more states in such a way as to minimize interstate sales. Intrastate sales were preferred because of differing tax rates among India's states.

India's vast size affected physical distribution. Unlike North America or Europe, India did not have retail distribution chains organized at the national level; instead, outlets would receive merchandise from the nearest depot. As it was difficult to handle many towns from a single point, each town would have a stockist (distributor) to supply the town's retailers. Stockists, of which there were an estimated 25,000 in India, received their shipments from a nearby depot after conversing with a salesman. Stockists' stores typically averaged only 500 square feet, but they played an important role in the distribution process. These distributors served as wholesalers in India, granting credit and stocking the consumer products their retail customers requested.

Retail outlets also played a major role in India's distribution system. Large retail outlets (such as grocery stores, general stores, and pharmacies) averaged 175 square feet and sold items consumed on a daily basis. Each large retail outlet usually had two to three salesmen in addition to the owner.

Small retail outlets were so limited in space that they had virtually no shelf space for razor blade display, nor could they carry any inventory. Because of these space limitations, a retailer never purchased case lots, only individual units usually less than 100 rupees in value. Small retail outlets were far more numerous than their larger competitors and could be found on almost every street corner even in residential areas. These small retail outlets also sold items consumed on a daily basis, but their limited space often required repeated same-day sales calls in areas with heavy sales, furthering the need for local stockists. Because of limited display space, the consumer could not usually see any blades and would simply ask for a package of blades, allowing the retailer to make the brand decision. To guarantee brand sales, it was customary in India to provide retailers with incentives such as cash or gifts (for example, imported Scotch) at festival times or as an end-of-year bonus. (For a distribution flowchart and 1983 data on blades sold through urban outlets, see Exhibits 9 and 10.)

Advertising in the Subcontinent

Media options for advertising in India consisted of television, radio, cinema, print, and outdoor. Traditionally, television advertising had not been used as heavily as in the West. However, this practice had begun to change over the last decade as incoming multinationals and other large companies responded to the rising number of television viewers. The advent of television advertising in India had, in fact, redefined the rules of consumer marketing. The success of products like Maggi, Vicco, Rasna, and Niki Tasha was attributed to television promotion. For most consumer products, television, cinema, and magazine advertising were preferred because they could project creative and colorful messages.

Statistics for television ownership were not available for smaller towns, but it was estimated that one television per thirty individuals was available in larger cities such as Bombay, Delhi, Calcutta, Bangalore, and Madras. Although the single, government-owned television channel would broadcast only in the late evening and at night, it reached 70 percent of India's population. Broadcasting began at 6 P.M. with the regional telecast via regional stations and was followed by a national broadcast from 8 to 11 P.M., which usually included advertiser sponsored programs.

Advertising was only permitted before and after the news or program. Advertisements during the local broadcast were normally in the local language, while those aired on the national broadcast would be in Hindi or English. The Sunday feature film at 6 P.M. and televised sporting events were the most popular advertising spots. For satisfactory exposure, most firms purchased thirty-second television spots at Rs. 7,000–10,000 which they would run for a three-month period.

Television advertisements could also be used in cinemas. Advertisements were aired before the film and during the ten-minute intermission. Cinema was India's most popular form of entertainment, with approximately 11,000 theatres and an industry producing around 800 films a year. The cost of cinema advertising varied from town to town and within towns from locality to locality. Countrywide, costs could be as low as Rs. 25 per week or as high as Rs. 1,000 per week, with Rs. 300 per week considered average in

EXHIBIT 9 ● Flowchart of Wiltech Distribution Channels

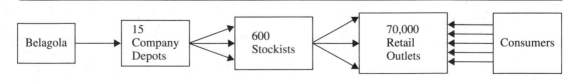

EXHIBIT 10 ● Volume of Razor Blades Sold Through Urban Outlets (in Millions of Blades)

	Blade type		
Outlet	STAINLESS STEEL	CARBON STEEL	TOTAL
Groceries	262.4	58.8	321.2
General Stores	228.7	36.3	265.0
Other	174.9	33.9	208.8
Drugstores	6.7	1.3	8.0
Total	672.7	130.3	803.0

Source: Company records.

urban markets. The shaving industry considered television and cinema to be the most effective media for advertising, because the entire shaving process could be visualized with audio reinforcement of the message.

Unlike television, access to radio was more evenly dispersed throughout the country, reaching 87 percent of the population. In 1983, there was one radio for every eight individuals in India. The one national and several regional radio stations were all government owned. Advertisements from the national station were given in Hindi, the national language, whereas the local stations advertised in the local language. On average, radio spots lasted thirty seconds and cost Rs. 1,000–1,500 per slot, depending on the time of day. Although radio reached a larger population than television, it was not widely used by the shaving industry as it lacked a visual message.

Print media in India, various newspapers, as well as twenty to twenty-five magazines, reached a total of 54 million people countrywide. These media were considered important in a campaign's introductory phase, but were not frequently continued, due to limited audio-visual capacity, after consumers had reached a certain level of awareness. A full-page advertisement in a daily with a circulation of 200,000 copies per day would cost Rs. 10,000–15,000 per day. Magazines were read frequently and had a circulation of 20,000–100,000 copies per month. The cost of a single full-page advertisement would vary between Rs. 25,000 and Rs. 50,000, depending on the magazine and the advertisement's placement.

Outdoor advertising in India included billboards and posters at bus stops, outside buses, on overhead footbridges, on the doors and sides of retail shops, and on the external walls of buildings and compounds. Like newspapers, outdoor advertising tended to be used for special promotion campaigns or during the introductory phase of a new product. The cost of an average outdoor advertising campaign was Rs. 30,000 per month.

WILTECH'S COMPETITIVE POSITION

The Wiltech Product Line

All Wiltech blades had the traditional Wilkinson ''gothic arch'' shape, which enhanced blade strength and extended blade life by about 40 percent over normal blades. After the rough gothic arch production step, Wiltech blades were sharpened, smoothed, and coated with Teflon. To ensure product continuity between the United Kingdom and India, Wiltech maintained strict quality control (QC) checks at each of its operations. Random samples from every lot were sent to Wilkinson in the United Kingdom for inspection. Each QC report through the middle of 1983 confirmed that Wiltech's products were meeting international standards. And, typical of many shaving products, Wiltech blades fit any brand of handle—both Indian and foreign.

Savage was Wiltech's premium blade with the same quality as imported Wilkinson blades due to a triple coating of chromium nitride, ceramic, and Teflon applied in the last stage of manufacturing. This coating gave each blade a 100 percent greater life than the regular Teflon-coated blades. Savage's packaging was also superior to Wiltech's other blades. Savage blades were wrapped in specially treated rustproof paper which had a dab of petroleum jelly on each corner to hold the blades firmly in place. Each pack contained five blades plus a top card that served both as a label and to give instructions on blade use. A purchase reminder card was placed between the fourth and fifth blades and each pack was wrapped in polystyrene and then cellophane before being shipped. A package of five Savage blades cost Rs. 4.90.

Wiltedge, with the same specifications as all Wilkinson blades, was marketed as Wiltech's most popular brand. Wiltedge had only Teflon coating, and its packaging was less elaborate than Savage's. Wiltedge blades had both an inner wrapper and an outer wrapper and were packed in a cardboard tuck. A package of five Wiltedge blades cost Rs. 3.

Wilzor was India's only scientifically designed two-piece razor and came with separable handle and shaving head. The shaving head contained double-edged blades adjusted to the optimum shaving angle. Alone, the Wilzor razor cost Rs. 13.10.

Wilman II represented Wilkinson's fixed twin blade shaving system. The Wilman was the only twin blade shaving product manufactured in India and had coatings of chromium, ceramic, and Teflon. Designed with a lightweight, heat resistant holder, and two blades adjusted at a precise angle, the Wilman II was the newest shaving concept. Wilman II was offered as a system or a gift pack, both with two twin cartridges, and sold for 13.60 rupees and 28.40 rupees, respectively. Wilman II refill packs of five twin blades were also available for Rs. 14.50.

Wiltessa was another first in the Indian shaving market, the only ladies' shaving system. The Wiltessa received the same process treatment as Wilman II and was specially designed for women's shaving needs. The Wiltessa was made of pink plastic and sold with two twin cartridges for Rs. 15.20.

Positioning the Wiltech Product Line

In 1982, Wiltech management felt that the superior quality of its products justified charging premium prices. As a result, Malay Chadha and Suresh Metha agreed to price Wiltech's line higher than the competition. Given India's market characteristics and the level of Wiltech's manufacturing technology, management decided to focus on stainless steel blades in the urban market. Within the urban market, management selected a target audience of males over sixteen years old earning more than Rs. 1,000 per month. To win this audience, Chadha and Metha selected Savage and Wiltedge, the two brands felt to offer the greatest potential. Savage was promoted as Wiltech's premium blade and aimed at those using black-market blades and dissatisfied users of India's own premium blades. Wiltedge promotion was aimed at consumers of India's popular blades, offering higher satisfaction

as well as a chance to upgrade to a higher quality product.

Wiltech's managers believed that a low awareness level of blade alternatives meant heavy promotion. Consequently, from May 1982 to March 1983, Wiltech spent Rs. 7,653,000 on advertising and promotion, scaling back in April 1983 when they felt initial brand awareness had been achieved. Press expenditures included six English magazines with nationwide coverage at a cost of Rs. 50,000 per magazine. Four regional magazines with local language were also used at a cost of Rs. 25,000 per magazine. The English magazines had circulations of up to 100,000 versus the regional magazines with a circulation of about 60,000 each.

The Wiltech Distribution Network

To minimize the risk of product introduction, Wiltech test marketed its line with apparent success in Bangalore, Bombay, and New Delhi. As these cities were considered representative of countrywide market behavior, Wiltech felt encouraged and decided to pursue

Advertising Expenditures (in Thousands of Rupees)

	May 1982– March 1983	Proposed April 1983– March 1984
Cinema Screening	773	1,546
TV Screening	238	987
Press	5,224	1,110
Others	416	285
Boarding	436	616
Film Production Costs	171	—
TV Production Costs	37	—
Radio Production Costs	—	155
POP Costs (leaflets, posters)	358	838
TOTAL	7,653	5,527

countrywide distribution. Wiltech's fifteen depots throughout India housed stock on a transitory basis; the eight primary depots received stock directly from the plant, whereas the seven secondary depots received their stock from the nearest regional office or from a primary depot.

In addition to Wiltech's central office in Bangalore, the company had regional offices in New Delhi, Bombay, and Calcutta. Each office had a regional manager with three area sales managers, six sales supervisors, and twenty-seven salesmen. Each Wiltech salesman was responsible for a particular territory and was paid a fixed salary of Rs. 800–1,200 per month. Additional incentives existed for meeting monthly target volume, market trends, competitive activities, and stock availability. For successfully meeting targets, they received a Rs. 350 monthly bonus and for meeting quarterly targets, Rs. 500.

Salesmen had to ensure that the orders of Wiltech's 600 stockists and all retailers were met and that posters portraying the company's products were distributed to retail outlets. In metropolitan areas, a salesman handled one stockist and 600–700 retail outlets. Stockists were visited daily and retailers twice a month. Salesmen covering smaller towns handled an average of ten to twelve stockists and 800–1,000 retail outlets. These stockists were visited once or twice a month. With stockists earning 7 percent and retailers 15 percent, Wiltech faithfully provided its distribution channels with standard operating margins. Classifying stockists and retailers as outlets, Wiltech's 81 salesmen reached 70,000 of India's 500,000 outlets by August 1983. Sales staff salaries, allowances, and touring expenses accounted for 50–60 percent of Wiltech's marketing expenditures, excluding advertising and promotion.

OPTIONS FOR WILTECH INDIA

Price Reduction with New Advertising

Wiltech had anticipated a volume of 3 to 4 million blades per month for Savage and 4 to 5 million for Wiltedge, but actual sales were only one million and 700,000 blades per month, respectively. Since each of Wiltech's brands was priced above the competition, Chadha felt that the pricing policy had caused the lower than expected sales volume. He therefore proposed reducing prices along with a new communication policy.

If the Savage and Wiltedge, priced at R. 1 and 60 paise per blade, respectively, were each lowered by 10 paise, they should be more competitive with black-market blades at R. 0.7–1 and the 45-paise Topaz blade from Malhotra. Furthermore, if Wiltech did choose the price reduction strategy, Chadha felt that the company should reposition Wiltedge as a mass blade, which would require a new communication strategy. Having established Wiltech as a blade manufacturer of international standards, Chadha believed that a new advertising campaign should concentrate on product awareness rather than product quality.

Entry into the Rural Sector

Metha, on the other hand, felt that Wiltech needed more sales in India's rural sector, with consumers far from cities and modern telecommunications. Metha was aware that this segment, comprising primarily farmers, provided half of India's market share and used mostly carbon steel blades in the 20–35 paise range. Unless Wiltech introduced a blade in the same price range, it could only sell brands priced about twice as high as rural customers were paying. To succeed with existing brands in this segment would require an educational campaign that demonstrated (1) that stainless steel blades were more comfortable than carbon steel, and (2) Wiltech's blades, which were twice as expensive, could give at least twice as many shaves as Malhotra's Ashok, Panama, or Silver Prince blades.

India as an Export Base

In addition to taking corrective action for Wiltech's domestic strategy, Chadha wanted to review the advantages of using India as an export base to the U.S.S.R. and the Middle East. India's diplomatic relations with these countries had led to several successful commercial opportunities over the years; in 1981/1982, access to the Soviet market accounted for 19.3 percent of all Indian exports. Consumer goods were particularly important, as the U.S.S.R. purchased 83 percent of India's cosmetics and detergent exports and 45 percent of India's coffee exports. Their bilateral trade agreement provided India with Soviet crude oil and capital equipment. The biggest advantage was that neither had to pay with scarce hard currency; trade was conducted in Indian rupees, with rupee surpluses or deficits carried into the following year.

As an incentive to preserve scarce foreign exchange earnings, the Indian government granted tax breaks to firms committing production to exports. In 1982/1983, Wiltech's exports were only 2–3 percent of total sales but yielded a tax break of Rs. 47,000. The size of this tax break would be substantially larger if export volume were increased. Chadha did not foresee a problem in capacity utilization if domestic demand continued to be lower than originally expected.

Wiltech could continue to use the market channels originally developed by Asian Cables Corporation, which had provided its 2–3 percent export base. However, if Chadha decided to boost exports, he would have to increase contacts with foreign trade organizations in the U.S.S.R. and attend exhibitions where contact with the right officials could be made.

Capacity Utilization

	Actual production (in millions of units)	Installed capacity (in millions of units)
Double-edged Blades	28.2	100.00
Shaving Systems and Twin Blade Units	5.4	20.00
Razor Handles	0.8	5.00
Two-Piece Systems	0.2	0.25

EXHIBIT 11 ● Financial Data for Wiltech India 1982

Sales (in Rupees)	27,200,000
Variable Costs	21,729,000
Fixed Costs (depreciation, financing, staff salaries, and marketing costs)	8,856,000
	30,585,000
Operating Result	(3,385,000)

The Soviet reputation on negotiating was the only drawback to this option that Chadha could see. The Soviets could offer margins of 5–6 percent but had been known to offer as little as 1–2 percent on certain products. On the other hand, Soviet central planners always placed bulk orders for an entire year. Success in the U.S.S.R. and the Middle East would certainly be noted at Wilkinson headquarters in England. Market achievements in these regions would fit in with Wilkinson's worldwide perspective and could lead to a substantial career move for Chadha.

After two days, Chadha and Metha had little time left to work out Wiltech's strategy for fiscal 1984 but were still unable to identify the key issues and how they should be handled. They had to consider Gillette's anticipated 1986 market entry and how to respond if Malhotra used its standard tactic of flooding the marketplace with shaving products via product line expansion. Another concern was Centron's acquisition by Brooke Bond, a large multinational, clearly indicating that yet another international competitor with vast resources was targeting the Indian shaving market. All these factors reinforced the need for Wiltech to make the right moves and to do so in a timely manner. (Refer to Exhibit 11.)

Case 3

P.T. Food Specialties—Indonesia (FSI)

On Tuesday morning, January 21, 1981, Ian Souter, marketing manager of FSI, was congratulating himself on having gotten an early start, as the Jakarta traffic seemed even worse than normal. He had allowed himself some extra time in order to prepare the agenda for a ten o'clock meeting with his staff. On the way to the office he asked the driver to turn on the radio in order to catch the beginning of the English language news. One block from the office he was reeling with shock as he learned that the Indonesian government was banning all TV advertising as of April 1, 1981. As the car pulled into his parking space, it occurred to him that his entire organization, his marketing strategies and campaigns, and his own job structure had become obsolete in one single day.

P.T. FOOD SPECIALTIES (FSI)

FSI was owned jointly by Nestlé S.A., a large multinational food products company, and a group of Indonesian investors. Nestlé S.A. had been founded in Vevey, Switzerland, in 1867 by Henri Nestlé as a small producer of milk products. In 1905, it merged with the Anglo-Swiss Condensed Milk Co. Between 1905 and 1980, this merged unit expanded rapidly, becoming Switzerland's largest multinational company and the largest company in the food industry in the world. In 1905, Nestlé already had eighty factories, 300 sales offices, and twelve subsidiaries worldwide. By 1980, the Nestlé group produced revenues of almost SFr. 24.5 billion through its sales offices and factories in more than 100 countries worldwide. Prior to 1972, Nestlé operated under the name Indonepro Distributors Inc. as the importer and distributor of Nestlé's products to Indonesia. In 1972, it began operating as a manufacturer and marketer of food products. It had discontinued its distribution operations after the introduction of an Indonesian law that restricted distribution activities to companies that were wholly owned by Indonesians. Since 1972, FSI had lost the right to sell its products directly to retailers or consumers.[1]

In 1981, FSI produced and marketed six products in Indonesia. The most important of these was MILKMAID SWEETENED CONDENSED MILK. Introduced in 1972 after a long history of importation, MILKMAID accounted for roughly 40 percent of FSI's annual turnover and was perhaps the least profitable of its six products. The Indonesian sweetened condensed milk market was both very large and competitive. It was dominated by three large organizations, Frisian Flag (with 50 percent of the market), Indo Milk, in conjunction with the Australian Dairy Board (with 34 percent of the market), and FSI (with 15 percent of the market). A 14 ounce can of MILKMAID had a selling price of approximately 400 rupiah in 1981.[2]

DANCOW powdered milk had also been introduced in 1972. It was sold in two forms, regular and instant. In 1981 DANCOW accounted for

This case was prepared by Barbara Priovolos under the supervision of Visiting Professor Jean-Pierre Jeannet as a basis for class discussion rather than to illustrate either effective or ineffective handling of an administrative situation. Copyright © 1982 by IMD, Lausanne, Switzerland. The International Institute for Management Development (IMD), resulting from the merger between IMEDE, Lausanne, and IMI, Geneva, acquires and retains all rights. Not to be used or reproduced without written permission from IMD, Lausanne, Switzerland.

1. In 1981, $1 = SFr. 2.
2. In 1981, 300 rupiah = SFr. 1; 625 rupiah = $1.

approximately 30 percent of FSI's total revenue. It was also one of FSI's most profitable products. The Indonesian powdered milk market was dominated by two large organizations. FSI had a 45 percent market share, and Frisian Flag had a 52 percent market share. The balance of the market was held by several imported brands. A 454 gram package (about one pound) of DANCOW regular carried a suggested retail price of 1,200 rupiah in 1981.

In 1978, FSI had introduced two infant cereals into Indonesia. Neither of these products was to be used as a breast milk substitute. CERELAC contained powdered milk, whereas NESTUM did not. These had become two of FSI's most profitable products and accounted for approximately 10 percent of FSI's annual revenue. The infant cereal market was fairly small, but FSI controlled almost 63 percent of it. The balance of the branded cereals was supplied largely by one local producer, P.T. Sari Husada, whose brand SNM had a 31 percent share of the market. All other brands, most of them imported, shared the remaining 6 percent of the market. Homemade cereals were very popular, and although few firm data were available on the subject, FSI executives believed that the vast majority of the children's cereal consumed in Indonesia was homemade. A 400 gram box of CERELAC and a 250 gram box of NESTUM had 1981 retail prices of 1,000 rupiah and 750 rupiah, respectively.

MILO, a chocolate-malted powder that was mixed with milk to produce a high energy drink, accounted for 8 percent of FSI's revenue. It was a moderately profitable product that had been introduced in 1974. The market for MILO was thought to be fairly small. It consisted primarily of children who used MILO as a ''growing up'' high nutrition drink and sports conscious adults who used it as a high energy drink. FSI had approximately 45 percent of this market segment. It shared the market with the Ovaltine brand, which had a 47 percent market share, and the Malcoa brand, which had an 8 percent market share. In 1981, the retail price for MILO was 100 rupiah for a 350 gram box.

PRODUCT DISTRIBUTION

Products found their way from the factory to the consumer's cupboard through a rather intricate series of distributors and wholesalers. SFI itself had only two customers. It sold all of its output to one of two main distributors, a Chinese-Indonesian company and a Pribumi, or native Indonesian, company. These two main distributors sold FSI's products to subdistributors or to agents for subdistributors. The approximately forty-five subdistributors then sold the products to wholesalers or directly to small shops. As a result FSI's products changed hands a minimum of four times, and often as many as six times, on their way from the factory to the consumer. See Exhibit 1 for a diagram of this distribution network.

FSI suggested price levels for both the retail and the wholesale outlets and paid for, although did not arrange, product transportation from the factory to the retailer. It also employed marketing personnel who served as advisers to the subdistributors and the retailers. Twenty area supervisors advised the subdistributors with regard to stock hygiene, merchandising, and promotional activities. They also trained subdistributor sales personnel to set up in-store displays, point-of-sale selling materials, and on-the-shelf product arrangement for maximum consumer impact. This type of support was considered by FSI executives as crucial. Many Indonesian retailers saw little difference between having a product in the store and making a product available, or even attractive, to the customer. Many retailers ordered products that were left in cartons behind desks, in storage rooms, or in similar areas well out of reach of the consumer. This marketing support was also consistent with the marketing advice of businessmen based in Indonesia who believed that personalized attention was an effective marketing tool in Indonesia.

In most cases, the subdistributors were grateful for the help provided by the area supervisors. Some conflicts of interest did occasionally occur. The subdistributors had a short-term view of business. They were generally most interested in products that were currently selling in large volumes. The area supervisor was interested in marketing every product and in building the market for new products, thus ensuring that the FSI brand was associated with goodwill and confidence in the mind of the extremely brand loyal Indonesian consumer. See Exhibit 2 for retail distribution data for FSI's products and its competitors' products.

EXHIBIT 1 ● Product Distribution

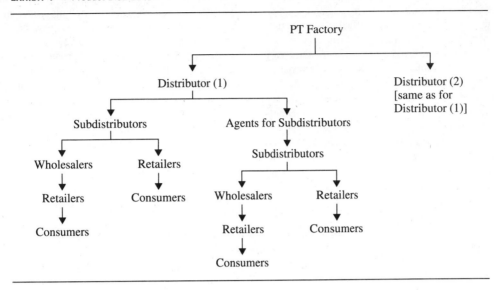

The FSI marketing office also included one national sales coordinator, to whom all of the area supervisors reported, and one product executive for each FSI product group. The product executives were responsible for developing and implementing supplemental promotional activities for their products, both trade oriented and consumer oriented, and for monitoring their products in the Indonesian market. See Exhibit 3 for the FSI Marketing Department organization chart.

THE INDONESIAN BUSINESS CLIMATE

In 1981, Indonesia was the fifth largest country in the world in terms of population, behind China, India, the U.S.S.R., and the U.S.A. Its 150 million people lived on approximately 6,000 of the roughly 13,000 islands that, straddling 5,000 kilometers (3,000 miles) of equator, made up Indonesia. It was a country of uncharted jungles and densely populated cities. Twenty percent of all Indonesians were city dwellers, and two-thirds of them lived on the islands of Java, Madura, and Bali. These islands contained only 7 percent of Indonesia's land mass and were among the most

densely populated areas on earth. Indonesia's capital city of Jakarta was home to seven million people. See Exhibit 4 for a map of Indonesia.

The Indonesian people were of more than 300 different ethnic groups, most of them of Malaysian origin. More than 90 percent of the population were followers of Islam, giving Indonesia the world's largest Moslem population. Although more than 300 languages and dialects were in regional use, the national language of Bahasa Indonesia was believed to be understood by all but the most remote village dwellers.

Indonesia had been under Dutch colonial rule for almost 300 years prior to its occupation by the Japanese between 1942 and 1945. In 1945, two days after the surrender of the Japanese, Indonesia made a unilateral declaration of independence. In 1949, the Netherlands unconditionally recognized the sovereignty of Indonesia. The political climate of Indonesia was stable. Its president, Suharto, had been in power since 1965. Although he was considered by many to be slow in initiating reforms that would stimulate economic growth, his leadership had been credited with reducing inflation from over 200 percent in the mid-1960s to under 10 percent in 1981, opening up

Indonesia to some private and foreign investment, reducing the rate of its population growth, and bringing the country to the brink of self-sufficiency in rice production, after having been the world's largest rice importer for many years. Indonesia was a country very rich in natural resources but with a very poor population. It was a country that was deeply preindustrial but one with a pocket of high technology industries.

Indonesia was a member of OPEC and the largest oil producer in Southeast Asia. It had proven reserves of 14 billion barrels and an estimated 50 billion barrels of reserves yet to be officially confirmed. Oil export earnings accounted for 75 percent of its foreign income in 1981. Oil was not the only important natural resource in Indonesia. Indonesia was the world's second largest producer of liquified natural gas and largest producer of tin. It also produced significant quantities of bauxite, nickel, coal, iron, manganese, gold, silver, copper, phosphates, and sulphur. Nevertheless, the Indonesian economy was primarily agricultural. Agriculture, forestry and fishing employed two-thirds of the Indonesian labor force and accounted for almost one-third of GNP. Small farms produced food for domestic consumption as well as

EXHIBIT 2 ● Retail Distribution—P.T.

MILKMAID	
	● Distribution largely urban
	● 80% supermarkets, 16% independent shops, 20% bazaar shops stock[1] product
	● Sweetened condensed milk as a product category sells[2]
	0.5% volume through supermarkets
	30% volume through independent shops
	70.5% volume through bazaar shops

DANCOW

● Distribution largely urban

	Standard	Instant	
Supermarkets	97%	90%	stock product
Independent shops	15%	10%	
Bazaar shops	30%	20%	

● Full cream powdered milk as a product category sells
   2% volume through supermarkets
   35% volume through independent shops
   63% volume through bazaar shops

CERELAC/NESTUM

● Exclusively urban distribution

	CERELAC	NESTUM	
Supermarkets	95%	94%	stock product
Independent shops	10%	10%	
Bazaar shops	20%	27%	

MILO

● Exclusively urban distribution with concentration in 5 or 6 main towns

● 98% of supermarkets, 12% of independent shops, 37% of bazaar shops stock product

● Tonic food beverages sell
   5% volume through supermarkets
   32% volume through independent shops
   64% volume through bazaar shops

1. Percentage of retail shops that sell that particular Nestlé brand.
2. Percentage of total volume of that product category industrywide selling through specific retail trade category.

EXHIBIT 2 ● Retail Distribution—Competitors (*Continued*)

Competition to MILKMAID

Frisian Flag

91% of all supermarkets
60% of independent shops ⎬ stock product
60% of bazaar shops

Indomilk

91% of all supermarkets
31% of independent shops ⎬ stock product
39% of bazaar shops

Respective market shares

Frisian Flag   50%
Indomilk   34%
MILKMAID   16%

Competition to DANCOW

Frisian Flag Standard

97% of all supermarkets
27% of independent shops ⎬ stock product
46% of bazaar shops

Frisian Flag Instant

98% of all supermarkets
14% of independent shops ⎬ stock products
22% of bazaar shops

Respective market shares

DANCOW Std.   27%
DANCOW Inst.   18.3%
Frisian Flag Std. 43.2%
Frisian Flag Inst. 8.6%

Competition to NESTUM/CERELAC

SNM

84% of all supermarkets
11% of independent shops ⎬ stock product
22% of bazaar shops

Nutricia

91% of all supermarkets
3.5% of independent shops ⎬ stock product
4.3% of bazaar shops

Respective market shares

NESTUM   22%
CERELAC   41%
SNM   31%
All Others   6%

Competition to MILO

Ovaltine

98% of all supermarkets
10.7% of independent shops ⎬ stock product
24.7% of bazaar shops

Malcoa

91% of all supermarkets
4% of independent shops ⎬ stock product
10% of bazaar shops

Respective market shares

MILO   45.0%
Ovaltine   47.0%
Malcoa   8.0%

EXHIBIT 3 ● P.T. Food Specialties Marketing Department

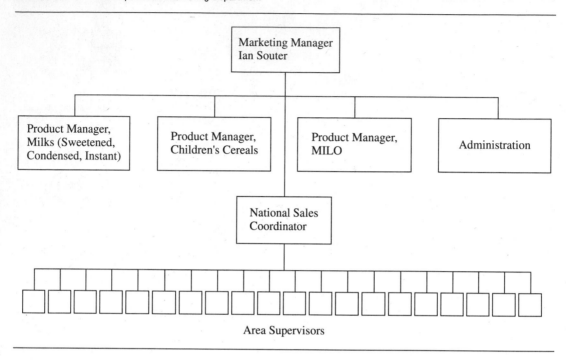

natural rubber, coffee, pepper, and tobacco for export. Large plantations, holdovers from its colonial days, produced Indonesia's most important agricultural exports: timber, rubber, coffee, tea, palm oil, and sugar.

The Indonesian manufacturing sector was very small, accounting for less than 5 percent of exports and only 7 percent of GNP. The trading sector of the economy, wholesale and retail, accounted for approximately 16 percent of the GNP and was dominated by Indonesia's Chinese minority. Until 1965, Indonesia's five million Chinese had had a virtual monopoly of business and manufacturing activities within the country, and their influence in 1981 was still considerable.

In 1981, Indonesia had at least $10 billion in hard currency reserves that did not benefit the economy due to an underdeveloped banking and financial services sector. Poverty was acute in Indonesia, and many of its income statistics were misleading. Although the per capita income was about $370 per year, the concentration of wealth was such that certain economists estimated that 40 percent of the population existed on less than $90 per year.

Income Distribution for Indonesia

Economic segment	Percentage of population	Monthly disposable income (in rupiahs)
A	3%–5%	100,000
B	13%–18%	75,000–100,000
C	25%–30%	50,000–75,000
D	29%–30%	30,000–50,000
E	34%	30,000

EXHIBIT 4 ● Map of Indonesia

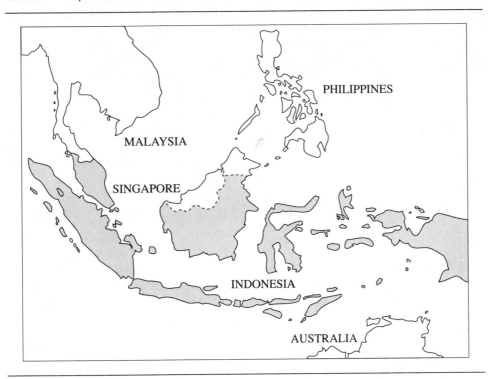

The Indonesian population could be classified into five separate economic classes in terms of disposable household income.[3]

FSI'S MARKETING MIX

As marketing manager, Ian Souter had generally emphasized developing customized campaigns for each of FSI's six products. The campaign budgets were divided between "above the line" mass media activities and "below the line" consumer promotion and trade promotion activities. In line with Nestlé and FSI company policy, which called for mass media pro-

3. Each household contained approximately seven people. This classification was based on the best estimates of foreign businessmen operating in Indonesia during 1981.

motion in order to build long term brand loyalty and confidence in their products, 60 percent to 90 percent of a campaign's budget was spent on mass media advertising. FSI executives felt that price promotions produced customers who only used the product while it was selling for the reduced price. These customers were likely to change brands again as soon as other manufacturers lowered their own prices. See Exhibit 5 for media spend data and Exhibit 6 for media cost data.

Souter felt that the 1980 MILKMAID campaign had been especially important. Souter had, in an effort to increase market share, attempted to reposition MILKMAID from a "growing up" children's drink to an "energy" drink for all ages. In 1980, FSI had for the first time created its own TV campaign for MILKMAID rather than using a campaign that had been developed by the Nestlé subsidiaries in Malaysia

EXHIBIT 5 ● Media Spending—per Product 1979 to 1981 (Planned)

Media product						*1979 (in millions of rupiah)*			
Media product	TV	Radio	Newspaper	Magazine	Cinema	Outdoor (form & amount)	Trade Promotion (form & amount)	Consumer promotion (form & amount)	Total
Sweetened Condensed Milk (MILKMAID)	40.55	7.73	—	7.66	0.01	—	0.60	—	56.55
DANCOW Instant	37.43	—	0.83	17.04	—	—	0.85	—	56.15
DANCOW Standard	22.46	—	8.69	—	11.90	—	0.52	—	43.57
NESTUM	29.82	—	—	—	—	—	—	3.87	33.69
CERELAC	42.97	—	—	—	—	—	—	3.59	46.56
MILO	33.07	—	—	—	—	2.00	0.07	0.45	35.59
TOTAL	206.30	7.73	9.52	24.70	11.91	2.00	2.04	7.91	272.11

EXHIBIT 5 ● Media Spending—per Product 1979 to 1981 (Planned) (*Continued*)

Media product						*1980 (in millions of rupiah)*			
Media product	TV	Radio	Newspaper	Magazine	Cinema	Outdoor (form & amount)	Trade promotion (form & amount)	Consumer promotion (form & amount)	Total
Sweetened Condensed Milk (MILKMAID)	65.14	12.91	—	12.23	0.03	—	0.50	0.07	90.88
DANCOW Instant	65.71	—	—	26.82	—	—	0.77	—	93.30
DANCOW Standard	36.97	—	13.19	—	11.40	—	0.65	—	62.21
NESTUM	72.90	—	—	—	—	—	0.11	2.40	75.41
CERELAC	51.73	—	—	—	—	—	0.11	2.24	54.08
MILO	90.82	—	6.29	21.21	—	0.24	2.79	2.04	123.39
TOTAL	383.27	12.91	19.48	60.26	11.43	0.24	4.93	6.75	499.27

EXHIBIT 5 ● Media Spending—per Product 1979 to 1981 (Planned) (*Continued*)

	1981, planned as of January 20, 1981 (in millions of rupiah)								
Media product	*TV*	*Radio*	*Newspaper*	*Magazine*	*Cinema*	*Outdoor (form & amount)*	*Trade promotion (form & amount)*	*Consumer promotion (form & amount)*	*Total*
Sweetened Condensed Milk (MILKMAID)	120.0	20.1	—	17.6	2.3	—	18.0	3.0	181.0
DANCOW Instant	124.0	—	—	66.0	—	—	13.0	30.0	233.0
DANCOW Standard	50.0	—	—	38.8	11.2	—	18.0	4.0	122.0
NESTUM	91.0	—	—	29.0	—	—	5.5	5.5	131.0
CERELAC	90.0	—	—	—	—	—	5.5	6.0	101.5
MILO	120.0	—	—	30.0	—	—	20.0	28.0	198.0
TOTAL	595.0	20.1	—	184.4	13.5	—	80.0	76.5	966.5

or the Philippines. This change in direction was seen by Souter as very important. Developing his own campaign had been both a lengthy and at times frustrating process. However, it had given him the ability to adapt his campaign to the Indonesian market by using Indonesian actors, actresses, and locations.

All of FSI's advertisements required approval by the Nestlé home office staff in Switzerland. In addition, working with the relatively inexperienced Indonesian film and creative personnel was frustrating even at the best of times. Thus the process of creating an Indonesian campaign required almost six months versus the two to three months that were required when already approved Malaysian or Philippine ads were adapted for use in Indonesia.

DANCOW powdered milk was promoted in two versions. The instant version received 90 percent of the promotional funds. DANCOW instant, or "the 4 second milk," had been the first locally produced instant milk in Indonesia. It had been a huge success. The instant form had, since its introduction, been ad-

vertised on TV and in women's magazines. Because the brand name was the same for both the instant and standard varieties it was believed that the standard form also benefited from the advertisements for the instant form. The ad budget for the standard form was used for newspaper and cinema slide advertisements.

FSI's two infant cereals were both mass marketed and promoted to the medical profession with the help of samples and literature. CERELAC, the milk based cereal, had been introduced using TV ads that had been developed in Malaysia. This reliance on Malaysian TV advertisements had continued, as had the product's success in the marketplace. NESTUM, a nonmilk cereal, had been introduced with magazine advertisements and had experienced very moderate initial sales. In mid-1979, a TV campaign for NESTUM was introduced, and sales increased dramatically. The TV campaign and the impressive sales results both continued throughout 1980.

MILO was advertised primarily on television with some backup advertisements in women's

EXHIBIT 6 ● January 20, 1981 Media Costs—Development and Production

In Thousands of Rupiah

Media	Cost to Develop One Spot	Cost to Broadcast One Spot	
		Prime Time or Urban	Not Prime Time or Regional
TV		476.7	75.7
Radio	287.0	2.0	0.05
Newspaper	102.0	217.3	52.1
Magazine	2,300.0	1,358.9	

Outdoor Media	Fixed Investment /Unit*
A-Boards: Inside Stadium Outside Stadium	20,000 15,000
Billboards: Strategic Location Ordinary Location	25,000 15,000
Footbridges	140,000

A-Boards: In stadium/outside.
Billboard: Strategic location/ordinary.

*All quotes include taxes and annual maintenance.

magazines and children's comic books. It was also the only FSI product advertised in outdoor media. At selected sports events, MILO had been advertised using A-boards (wooden signs placed back to back to form an A shape) around the entrance area to the event. Occasionally, these A-boards had also been used along parade routes.

TELEVISION ADVERTISING IN INDONESIA

Souter believed that:

There is no substitute for television. Without television my job, the job of marketing these products, would be nearly impossible, and the job of introducing a new product would be entirely impossible.

There is no other marketing tool in Indonesia that can ever come close to reaching exactly my market with exactly my message, the message that FSI products are consistently high quality products, products that one ought to use.

There were approximately two million television sets in Indonesia in 1981. They could tune into one government owned network, Televisi Republik, Indonesia (TVRI). Television advertisements were carried during two "blocks" per day, as well as before, during, and at the end of programs or sports events that the advertiser itself had sponsored. The early evening advertising block, from 17:30 to 18:00, was for regionally based commercials. The late evening block, from 21:00 to 21:30, was immediately before the late evening news break and carried national advertisements.

Some Western businessmen operating in Indonesia believed that television advertising in Indonesia, thanks to a happy and rare coincidence of business need and cultural forces working together, pleased just about everyone. Indonesia's television audience seemed to eagerly await the televised signals that one of the twice daily commercial breaks was about to begin. Cartoon type drawings of consumer product packages bearing generic names such as coffee, soap, or milk lined up on the screen, and a butterfly flew into view to alight briefly on several packages, as if to select them for its own use. Many marketing executives felt that the television appearance of a commercial product was as appealing to the Indonesian consumer as those packages were to that butterfly. To the Indonesian consumer, it was the sign that the product was of high quality, dependable, "real," and deserving of their confidence and trust.

Although firm statistics on television viewership did not exist, FSI executives believed that Indonesia's two million television sets were located almost entirely in urban areas. Beginning in the late 1970s, the Indonesian government supported a program to put a television set in every village for educational purposes. The number of sets involved in this program was never made clear. FSI executives also estimated that 11 percent of the televisions were in use during the early evening advertising break and that 24 percent were in use during the late evening advertising

break. They were not sure who was watching. They felt that during the early break it was primarily children and domestic household help. Souter continued:

I can control television advertising. I know, roughly, who sees it and when they see it, I know what they see, and I can judge how they interpret it because the visuals are so powerful. I can produce a TV campaign 1,000 times more efficiently than any other mass media campaign. Or, for that matter, any other marketing or promotion effort whatsoever. That is not to say that producing a TV campaign is easy. It's not! But other campaigns are much more difficult to create—and much, much, much more difficult to implement.

When a television campaign was employed for an FSI product, it was used to create the themes that were repeated and reflected by advertisements in other media. Souter believed that every product's ad campaign needed to be cohesive and self-reinforcing. To ensure this, he always developed TV campaigns first and then designed the radio, magazine, cinema, outdoor, and point of sale advertisements to reinforce and support the initially designed television message.

Not only FSI but all its competitors as well felt that television advertising was the most important factor in a product's marketing success. Competition for the forty to sixty second advertising "spots" was breathtaking. Advertising spots were distributed by the government bureaucracy specifically charged with this mission. Simply filing a request for a spot entailed making one's way around an obstacle course of problems that governmental bureaucrats throughout the world seemed so skilled in designing. At this point, simple arithmetic brought the real scope of this situation into focus. FSI's experience, which it believed to be similar to that of most other advertisers as well, was that roughly one in every ten requests was granted. On average, FSI was granted three national and five regional spots per month. In order to increase its television presence, FSI sponsored each year eight to ten nationally televised series, twelve to fifteen nationally televised sports events, and several regionally televised programs.

Television campaigns were also costly. One hundred million rupiahs per year per product were required for an effective television campaign. Each regional spot cost about 300,000 rupiahs to broadcast and each national spot cost about 750,000 rupiahs to broadcast. In addition, the production costs for one spot, in both a 60 second and a 40 second version, were about ten million rupiahs.

Two phrases highlighted both the advantages television advertising provided for a marketing manager operating in Indonesia in 1981 and the relative disadvantages of other media forms and promotional efforts: ''ability to control'' and ''not labor intensive.''

The production and broadcast of a television ad required the management and cooperation of a small team of professionals. Production required more people than might have been required in a country with a more experienced television establishment. However, one could identify fairly easily who was needed and what they needed to do. Similarly, to broadcast an advertisement was not a difficult task. Once permission had been granted, the result was available for all to see and to monitor. In addition to the ability to self-monitor a TV campaign, both TVRI and the advertising agencies provided certificates of broadcast for each broadcasted spot.

INDONESIA'S OTHER MASS MEDIA

Radio networks, in contrast with television, were operated only regionally. There were one government owned station that serviced major cities and many private stations that served both cities and rural areas. The radio networks were characterized by their variety in format, location, and language. A radio campaign with national coverage cost 40 to 50 million rupiahs and required the participation of 70 to 80 different radio stations. Local radio spots were arranged through local advertising agents. Neither the station nor the agents provided certificates to confirm that the ad had actually been broadcast. It was extremely difficult for FSI head office personnel to ensure or confirm that the radio ads that they had paid for had been aired.

Obtaining the translations for the regional stations posed another problem when using radio adver-

tisements. According to Souter, ''no two Indonesians will ever agree on an exact translation.'' The translation of only three advertisements into three dialects had recently required ''months and months'' to complete. The Indonesian radio ''population'' was believed to be many times that of its TV population, so that, theoretically at least, radio could have had as much, if not more, penetration value as TV.

Radio advertising could be booked throughout the day. The times most in demand, though, were early morning (workdays began around 7:00) and early evening before the TV was tuned in. During the Moslem fasting month in June or July, advertisements for food and drink could be carried only after sunset.

Advertising in cinemas was fairly common in Indonesia. Most cinema advertising was in the form of slides that were shown before the start of the film. FSI had advertised MILKMAID in cinemas in smaller towns but had not been very satisfied with the effectiveness of this medium. Indonesian cinemas were of two classes. Class A cinemas were in major cities and were very expensive to attend, especially when good or well-known films were being shown. Class B cinemas were in smaller towns. They were less expensive to attend and were often rather shabby in appearance. Operational problems plagued both classes of cinema. In FSI's experience, the slides, when they were shown at all, were often presented out of sequence or upside down.

FSI used some of Indonesia's magazines having national circulations for full page color advertisements that reflected its television advertisements. In magazine advertising, its strategy was to cluster together several ads in several magazines in order to create an impact. It would then use these advertisements in cycles. For two months the clustered ads would appear in several different magazines and then, for one month, no magazine advertisements would be employed. When magazine advertising was the only mass medium used for a product, as had been initially the case for NESTUM, a yearly ad budget of 56 million rupiahs was required to obtain what it felt was an effective penetration.

High caliber magazines were costly to the consumer. They had newsstand prices of between 800 and 1,000 rupiahs per issue and were generally issued bimonthly. This high cost led to very high readership figures per issue. Advertising agency personnel multiplied circulation estimates by eight to compute actual readership. For its market, FSI executives felt that a multiple of five was more realistic. It was, however, very difficult, if not impossible, to estimate readership at all due to the very poor circulation figures that were available. Audited circulation figures were virtually unavailable, and some FSI executives believed that the only way to really know who read which magazines was to survey the market by themselves.

Indonesia had six general interest magazines. Three of these were women's magazines which reported on fashion, decorating, and cooking. These had very impressive European formats. *Femina* and *Kartini* were aimed at the upper class housewife, and *Gadis* was designed for younger women. Research figures seemed to indicate that readership duplication was approximately 60 percent within this category. *Intisari,* a *Reader's Digest* style monthly; *Tempo,* a *Time* style magazine; and *Executif,* for high level business executives, had not been used often by FSI. However, these magazines were very popular among Indonesia's elite.

FSI used newspaper advertising primarily for special promotions and as a signal to the trade that FSI was very interested in supporting a given product. Souter felt that newspaper advertising was of strategic importance in dealing with the trade. Newspaper market penetration seemed to be fairly low. It was also a medium that was more effective in reaching a male audience than a female audience. Agency figures indicated that total readership was five times circulation figures. Although again circulation figures were considered to be very unreliable, FSI executives accepted a multiple of three in terms of their own market. New ads needed to be created for all newspaper campaigns because magazine artwork did not reproduce effectively in black and white. Souter estimated that 40 million rupiahs were required, over a three month period, for an effective newspaper campaign.

The range of newspapers was very wide. Probably the most important ones were the two Jakarta based nationals *Kompas* and *Sinar Harapan.* Their primary circulation was in Jakarta. In other important regional markets, they were very often second in circulation after the local newspaper. There were two rather low circulation English language newspapers,

the *Observer* and the *Indonesian Times;* these were not cited by FSI. In addition, a Chinese newspaper with a small but very influential readership was available. The advertising rates for the national and Chinese newspapers were much higher than those of the other newspapers.

Outdoor advertising was very popular in Indonesia, although FSI had rarely employed it. Billboards in shimmering or plain versions, footbridges, bus stop shelters, and A-boards were all used for advertising purposes. Souter believed that few of the outdoor advertising opportunities were appropriate for FSI because of the nature of their products. Outdoor locations soon became dirty, especially those in crowded cities. He did not feel that a dirty environment was appropriate for food products. Nevertheless, many of FSI's competitors did make use of outdoor advertisements. A second problem with outdoor advertisements was the negotiations involved in arranging them. Various "fees" and taxes were often imposed on the advertisers for which no receipt was ever given.

Outdoor advertisements were not inexpensive, and each form had its own particular drawbacks. Billboards needed to be leased for three to five years at a time, payable in advance. Bus stop shelters advertising different brands of the same products tended to line up one after the other. A similar problem arose with A-boards. These were often used temporarily at the entrance to sports events or along parade routes. They would often be massed so close together that the impact of each board was substantially reduced.

Pedestrian footbridges were an expensive, but popular, advertising medium. A company could build, for approximately 15 million rupiahs, a pedestrian footbridge over a crowded street. The company would become liable for all maintenance charges and the ever popular annually negotiated tax. In return, advertisements could be painted on the bridge for five years. At one time FSI executives had considered building such a bridge but had decided against it on the basis of cost and their reluctance to negotiate the "taxes."

TRADE BASED PROMOTION

Indonesia's wholesalers and retailers always welcomed trade based promotions that involved distributing premiums such as drinking glasses, which were a particular favorite, or product samples. These were promotions that they could easily participate in. To them, the immediate nature of the reward was a tremendous allure. They disliked coupon type promotions that required them to give up something first by accepting less money for a product or accepting only a coupon for a product in anticipation of later reimbursement by the company sponsoring the promotion. The concept of a monetary society was new to some retailers, who were far more comfortable being barter traders.

TUESDAY AFTERNOON

It was late in the afternoon of Tuesday, January 21, 1981, and Ian Souter had spent the day reviewing the marketing campaigns for each of the six products that FSI manufactured and marketed in Indonesia. He now had less than ten weeks to redesign and implement a ''non-television'' campaign for each of those products. The campaigns needed to be finalized by mid-March for their April introductions. He needed to meet those deadlines despite the delays and interruptions that he had come to expect during his three years in Indonesia. He felt that his list of campaign and promotion ideas would serve as the basis for a very intensive review meeting the next day with the staff of the Fortune Advertising Agency, which had served FSI for twenty-two years, and his own superiors.

Case 4

Nippon Vicks K.K.

In March of 1983, Masahiro Horita, product manager for Nippon Vicks' acne care business, was uncertain what to recommend to further grow the "Clearasil" business in Japan. Clearasil had been introduced nationally in 1979 and quickly reached a volume of 2.5 million packages. Nippon Vicks K.K. had been unable to expand volume beyond that point despite a general expansion of the market. Sales volume had recently dropped to a rate of 2 million packages per year. Horita felt under increasing pressure to remedy the situation, particularly given a period of intense competitive activity in early 1983.

During the last twelve months, Horita had held several discussions with head office executives on Clearasil strategy for Japan. He was expected to come up with a final proposal to be presented at the marketing strategy review meeting to be held at the end of this month. Despite extensive consultations, there still existed a substantial disagreement between Horita's views and those held by division head office personnel.

COMPANY BACKGROUND

Richardson-Vicks

Richardson-Vicks was a leading worldwide marketer of branded consumer products in the areas of health care, personal care, nutritional care, and home care. Corporate sales amounted to $1,115 million for the fiscal year ending June 30, 1982.

The Vicks name was recognized around the world for treatment of the common cold. In the United States, 25 percent of all consumer expenditures in this category went to purchase Vicks products. Abroad, Vicks cough drops were market leaders from Germany to Japan. "VapoRub," originally introduced in 1906, was marketed in more than 100 countries. Cold care provided for the original base of Richardson-Vicks, and in 1983 the company continued to add new products to that segment. The company had recently moved to expand its noncold health care products by adding an antacid, "Tempo," and acquiring "Percogesic" from Du Pont's Endo Laboratories as an entry into the analgesic market.

Richardson-Vicks had been in the personal care business since 1958 and expanded this segment through product development and acquisitions. "Oil of Olay" was the leading adult skin care product in the world with sales of more than $150 million. The company marketed several teenage skin care products. Clearasil was the leading acne product in the United States, Germany, and Japan. "Topex," another entry in the acne care category, was the leader in the benzoyl peroxide segment in many international markets. The company also sold several shampoo brands, toothpaste, and denture care products in many non-U.S. markets.

International Division

International operations accounted for slightly more than half of Richardson-Vicks' sales in 1982. With $303.8 million in sales for 1982, Vicks International Europe/Africa Division represented more than half of the company's foreign sales. Headquartered in Paris, the division's leading brands were "Kukident" denture care products, Vicks cough drops, Oil of Olay beauty fluid, and Clearasil acne care products.

The Vicks International Americas/Far East Division included Canada, Latin America, and the Far East. Sales for the Western Hemisphere (Americas) amounted to $136.9 million, and other areas (mostly Far East) totaled $137.9 million. Leading products of this division, headquartered in Westport, Connecticut, included "Choco Milk," a powdered chocolate nutritional supplement, Clearasil acne care products, "Larin" candy products, Oil of Olay beauty fluid, "Colac" laxative, Vicks cold products, and a line of insecticides.

Nippon Vicks K.K.

Nippon Vicks K.K. (NVKK) was a wholly owned subsidiary of Richardson-Vicks, Inc. The Japanese subsidiary was incorporated in 1964 and had experienced rapid growth. Sales grew from 1.8 billion yen in 1972/1973 to 11 billion yen in 1981/1982 and were expected to reach 13 billion yen in 1983/1984.[1] NVKK maintained its corporate offices in Osaka and operated a manufacturing plant near Nagoya, where about half of NVKK's staff was employed.

NVKK's leading product was Colac, accounting for about one-half of the company's sales. Colac was the leading laxative in Japan with a market share of about 40 percent. Other products marketed were Vicks cough drops, Vicks VapoRub, and two infant care products, "Milton" and "Milgard." With about 15 percent of NVKK's sales, Clearasil was an important contributor to the company's profitability. NVKK was one of the most successful foreign subsidiaries operating in Japan, and its brands enjoyed a leadership position in their market segments. NVKK had been particularly successful in introducing consumer products in Japan for which domestic products did not exist.

THE U.S. MARKET FOR SKIN CARE PRODUCTS

When the Clearasil business was acquired by Richardson-Vicks in 1960, total value amounted to U.S. $2.3 million. By 1980, Clearasil sales represented

1. 250 yen = $1 U.S.; 1 billion yen = $4 million U.S.

about U.S. $30 million and consisted of Clearasil Regular Tinted Cream, Clearasil Soap, Clearasil Stick, Clearasil Vanishing Formula, Clearasil Medicated Cleanser, Clearasil Antibacterial Acne Lotion, and most recently New Super Strength Clearasil Creams and Clearasil Antibacterial Soap.

The target audience for acne care products were almost all teenagers. The most typical skin problems faced by this group were pimples, oily skin, and blackheads. It was estimated that about 20 percent of the target audience represented new users each year. Although this was a teenage product, mothers were believed to make the selection in six out of ten occasions for boys and three out of ten for girls.

About 50 percent of the target population used treatment products, up from 35 percent in 1975. Of the 50 million teenagers, only 25 million were users of treatment products, 10 percent had clear skin, and 40 percent represented potential new users. Clearasil was the market leader with Clearasil creams accounting for about 25 percent of dollar value and 30 percent of unit value.

The treatment market in the U.S. had undergone substantial changes in the 1970s. Prior to 1975, sulfur and resorcinol, used in Clearasil, were the only approved treatment agents for creams. In 1975, the Federal Drug Administration cleared benzoyl peroxide in strength of up to 10 percent. This provided an opportunity for a new brand, Oxy 5, and later Oxy 10 (indicating the percentage of benzoyl peroxide), marketed by Norcliff-Thayer, a unit of Revlon. Oxy began to erode Clearasil's market share, a trend that was stopped only when Richardson-Vicks launched New Super Strength Clearasil Cream with 10 percent benzoyl peroxide in 1979. Clearasil's market share as a result rebounded, and the brand continued to dominate the acne treatment segment.

In the U.S., Clearasil was heavily supported by advertising. Budgeted expenditures in 1980 accounted for about U.S. $5 million, or 25 percent of all advertising expenditures for the category. Richardson-Vicks employed a strategy in the U.S. that was closer to a two-way action benefit.

THE SKIN CARE MARKET IN JAPAN

In Japan, skin care products were a part of the personal care industry. Since acne products were targeted

EXHIBIT 1 ● Japanese Skin Care Industry: Segmentation

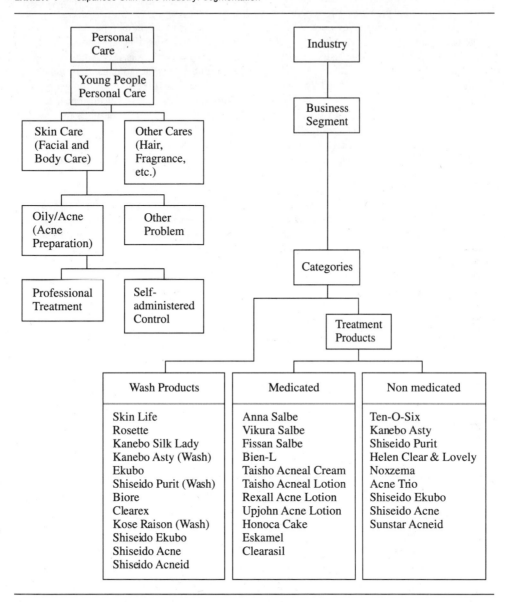

for people in their teens and early twenties, the acne products were part of the young people's personal care segment. Two principal categories were offered: skin care, including facial and body care, and ''other'' cares, consisting of hair care, fragrances, etc. See Exhibit 1.

The youth skin care market included 21.6 million consumers between the ages of 12 and 24, both male and female. Some 77 percent, or 16.6 million young people, suffered some type of skin problems. About 51 percent, or 11.0 million, suffered from acne, or pimples. There was no difference between male or female populations when it came to acne suffering. See Exhibit 2.

About the remaining 47 percent, or about 5.2 million of acne sufferers, were characterized as treaters. A very small percentage of these would search out professional help. Treaters were described as acne

sufferers using a specific acne product other than ordinary bar soap.

Some 53 percent of Japanese acne sufferers fell into the category of nontreaters. ''Pimples are the symbol of youth'' was a common saying in Japan, according to Horita. ''Japanese in general consider that the time will be coming for everyone to have pimples, and that they will disappear automatically. It was just a matter of time until they would disappear.'' Nontreaters used only ordinary bar soap to wash their face.

About 38 percent of treaters used ''wash products'' only, such as toiletry facial wash products, toiletry bar soaps, and cosmetic facial soaps. The wash-only group was 60 percent female. Wash products were marketed as preventatives.

About 44 percent of treaters used treatment products only. Of those, 70 percent were Clearasil users.

EXHIBIT 2 ● Japanese Skin Care Market: Young People

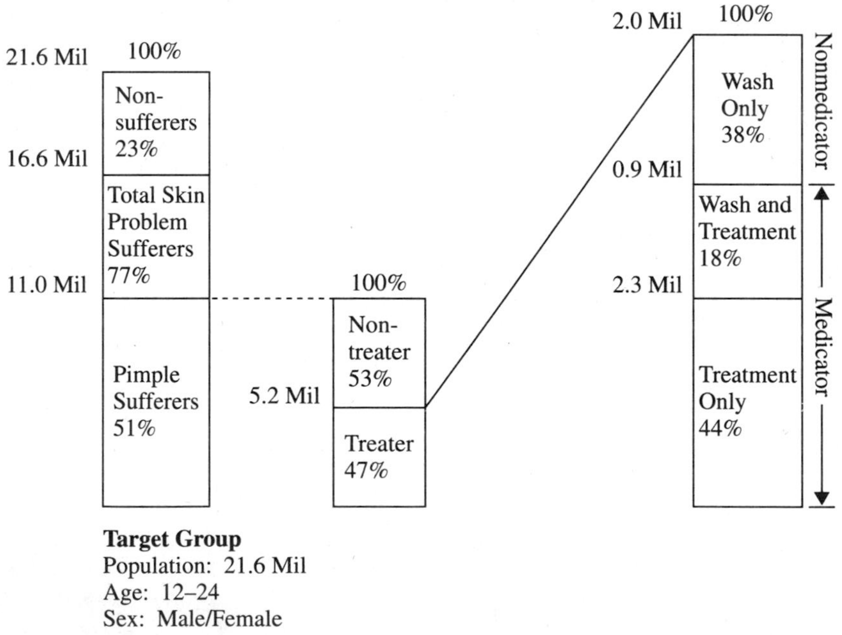

Target Group
Population: 21.6 Mil
Age: 12–24
Sex: Male/Female

Source: Post 24 A&U Tokyo (July 1981).

Users of treatment products were about equally divided between male and female users.

The third and smallest group of treaters, 18 percent of all treaters, were simultaneous users of treatment products and wash products.

Products for Acne Treatment

"Before Clearasil's relaunch in 1978, there was no product on the market advertised exclusively for acne treatment. NVKK and Clearasil created this market," explained Horita.

Treatment products were classified either as drug or quasi-drug. The difference between the two categories depended on the product's ingredients and its registration with the Japanese Drug Administration. Clearasil was drug registered.[2]

Competitors in this category included a number of domestic and foreign brands including Upjohn Acne Lotion, Rexall Acne Lotion, Taisho Acneal Cream, and Taisho Acneal Lotion. None of these products was actively supported by promotional campaigns, and all were priced between 700 yen and 1,200 yen per unit. Most of the manufacturers were pharmaceutical companies that tended to concentrate on ethical drugs that required promotion directed at the medical profession and distribution through drugstore outlets.

The quasi-drug acne treatment products consisted of a number of products positioned largely for acne prevention. These products were licensed under a different procedure and were prevented by law to be positioned for treatment. Major competitors were Kanebo Asty, Shiseido Purit, Helene Curtis, Clear and Lovely, Noxema, and Acne Trio. These included some of the largest Japanese cosmetic companies. Prices for these products ranged from 500 to 1,500 yen.

There was a difference between the two product categories with respect to product claims and distribution. Drug registered products could claim to treat and cure acne. Quasi-drug products at most could claim to prevent acne from occurring. If a company decided to license a product as a drug, that product's distribution was restricted to drugstores only. Quasi-

2. The term *drug-registered* is identical with medicated product, and *quasi-drug* with nonmedicated, as used elsewhere in this case.

drug products could be sold through a variety of outlets including drugstores, supermarkets, and department stores.

"Wash" Products

On a unit basis, "wash" products accounted for the largest share of the acne market in Japan. That share had been expanding and was estimated at more than 50 percent for the most recent two-month Nielsen period. There were seven subcategories in this wash market. See Exhibit 3.

Major competitors included Gyunyu Sekken with its Skin Life soap priced at 150 yen for a 46 gram bar, and Kao Sekken Biore cleansing foam (300 yen for a 60 gram tube). Kao was Japan's leading soap and detergent company.

The wash category had consistently gained in market share compared to the drug and quasi-drug categories. However, the leading brands—Ekubo and Biore—had not been exclusively positioned as acne products. These three leading wash brands were supported by mass media and marketed for general skin care. It was in the wash products category that competitive activity was particularly strong. This category had witnessed several new product entries in the past two months. See Exhibit 4.

MARKET CHANNELS

All of NVKK's products fell into the proprietary drug category. Consequently, distribution was standardized for all products. About 2,000 companies competed in the proprietary trade, but only about 175 employed 100 or more people. Proprietary drugs (OTC) accounted for 15 percent of all drug sales in Japan, compared to ethical drugs with 85 percent.

NVKK used the same channels as its Japanese competitors. Sales were made from the factory to a group of primary wholesalers. Some of these in turn sold to a number of subwholesalers. The subwholesalers distributed NVKK's products through a large number of retail outlets which included general drugstores and various types of chain drugstores. Because NVKK products could only be sold through drugstores, the company did not maintain contacts with discount stores, department stores, and convenience stores that did not have drug corners.

EXHIBIT 3 ● Japanese Wash Market

Segment	Target	Benefits
Cosmetic cleansers (lotion, cream, gel)	Female adults Makeup users	Removes makeup and dirt thoroughly Refreshing Dirt free
Cosmetic facial soap (Honey cake, moon drops)	All females Normal/dry skin, primarily	After washing, leaves skin smooth and moist Less irritation
Toiletry bar soap by cosmetic company	Females	Keeps skin smooth and moist Refreshing
Toiletry facial wash (Biore, Silk Lady)	All females Normal/dry skin primarily	After washing, leaves skin smooth and moist Less irritation Good for preventing pimples (secondary) Good for delicate skin
Specialized facial soap	Females with delicate skin	Good for face washing for very delicate/sensitive skin
Medicated soap	Younger males/females	Sterilizes skin Good for preventing pimples Treatment for skin disease
Medicated soap for sterilization	People with skin problems	Sterilizes skin

EXHIBIT 3 ● Japanese Wash Market (*Continued*)

Support	*Price/size/form*	*Distribution*	*Others*
Deep cleansing After feeling by product foam	Wide range of product forms	Cosmetic store	Use as part of daily makeup routine
			Personal use only
			Double usage with facial soap
Ingredients (honey, lemon, etc.)	Transparent bar soap	Cosmetic store (chain store)	Personal use
Appearance	Premium price		
Perfume	(1,000–1,500)		
Company image			
Product line by skin type	Medium price bar soap	All distribution channel	Personal–family
Special ingredient (MFP)	Mainly cream type	All distribution channel	Quasi drug
	Several sizes		Personal use– family use
Company image	Medium price (300–600)		
No perfume	Premium price (1,000–2,000)	Cosmetic/drug- store (specialized)	Only for sensitive skin
No coloring			
No irritants			
Weak acidity same as skin			
Ingredients			
Antibacterial ingredients	Low–medium	Drugstore– cosmetic	Specialized purpose only (pimple, allergy)
Drying effects			
Ingredients	Small size	Drugstore only	
	Medium–high		

EXHIBIT 4 ● Competitive Actions

Acne Preparations
Trend of Consumer Sales (Units)

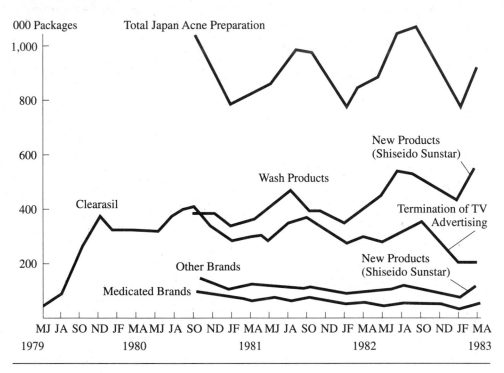

Wholesale Drug Distribution

NVKK used about 60 primary wholesalers which, together with their branches, maintained about 250 sales offices. Primary wholesalers were granted non-exclusive sales territories, which resulted in, at times, very keen competition among various branch offices. "For this kind of trade, 60 primary wholesalers is probably a moderate figure," explained Nagata, NVKK's national sales manager. A large Japanese competitor would maintain up to 200 primary wholesalers. NVKK's top 5 primary wholesalers accounted for about 57 percent of NVKK's total sales volume, the next 5 for 14 percent, while the smallest 25 were responsible for only 8 percent of NVKK sales. See Exhibit 5.

The role of the primary wholesaler was to dis-tribute the products both directly and through smaller subwholesalers. In the Japanese drug trade there existed about 2,700 wholesalers of all types. Of those, about 500 carried ethical products only, and 2,200 carried both ethical and proprietary drugs or only the latter category. Among the top 100 wholesalers, 25 specialized in ethical products only. The rest carried both proprietary and ethical lines. Some of these also carried toiletry products. "Of the about 1,000 wholesalers involved in proprietary drugs, we cover about 160," said Nagata, "and they maintain another 96 sales branches among themselves."

Of NVKK's primary wholesalers, only one concentrated in proprietary products accounting for 5 percent of NVKK's volume. Another eight primary wholesalers, accounting for 59 percent of sales,

EXHIBIT 5 ● Distribution Channels

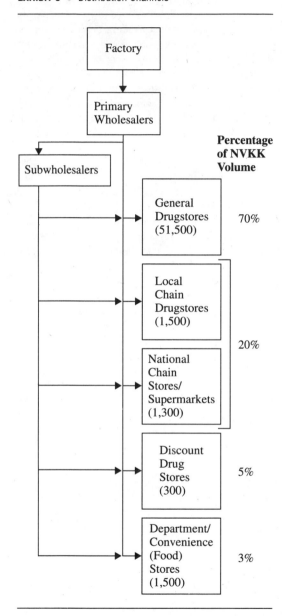

Percentage of NVKK Volume

Factory → Primary Wholesalers → Subwholesalers	
General Drugstores (51,500)	70%
Local Chain Drugstores (1,500) / National Chain Stores/ Supermarkets (1,300)	20%
Discount Drug Stores (300)	5%
Department/ Convenience (Food) Stores (1,500)	3%

carried both proprietary and toiletry products. The remainder of its volume was accounted for by primary wholesalers carrying both drug categories.

Retail Drug Distribution

"NVKK has achieved virtually 100 percent penetration of the drug-related retail trade" declared Nagata. General drugstores were the most important retail segment, accounting for 70 percent of NVKK's volume. There were about 51,500 such stores in Japan. Most of these stores were small and had less than six employees. Two-thirds of all stores had only one or two employees. They accounted for 40 percent market share. In Japan, only 1 percent of all drugstores had more than six employees. These larger stores accounted for only 7 percent of the general drugstore sales.

The second most important group was the national and local chain drugstores. This category included about 2,800 drugstores. They accounted for 20 percent of NVKK's volume. The local chains numbered about 1,500 stores. Another 1,300 outlets in this segment were accounted for by national chain stores, for example, Kokumin and Higuchi, or supermarkets with drug corners such as Daiei or Jusco. These chains maintained drug corners and employed a licensed pharmacist.

With about 300 outlets, local discount drugstores were small in numbers but accounted for 5 percent of NVKK's volume. These were individually managed stores operated on a discount basis. The department store and convenience store segment included about 1,500 outlets and accounted for only 3 percent of NVKK's volume. This last segment included 1,000 drugstore corners in department stores and about 500 in convenience food stores. Most convenience food stores did not have drug sections.

In 1980, the typical drugstore's retail sales consisted of the following product categories:

Drugs	51%
Cosmetics	12
Toiletries	9
Medical supplies	9
Other	19

Drug sales were further subdivided into the following categories:

Nutritional and tonic drugs	30.8%
Psychotropic drugs (includes cold remedies and sleeping pills)	19.0

Gastrointestinal drugs	16.2
External skin drugs	15.8
Respiratory tract drugs	4.3
Others	13.9

NVKK's Sales Organization

NVKK's sales force consisted of five branch managers and twenty-five salesmen. They focused their activities on NVKK's primary wholesalers, the sub-wholesalers, and NVKK's largest 1,500 retail customers. In urban areas, primary wholesalers were visited weekly, and twice per month in rural areas. Both sub-wholesalers and top retailers were visited once per month.

NVKK's sales force was responsible for distributing all of the company's eight products in national distribution, as well as any test markets the company might run. For its size, NVKK maintained a small sales force. In accordance with NVKK's reliance on a pull strategy that included heavy use of consumer advertising, NVKK's sales force was primarily used to maintain good relationships with wholesalers and to solve minor problems. Almost all orders were telephoned to NVKK by its wholesalers. In contrast, NVKK's Japanese competitors in the drug market tended to follow more of a "push" campaign, with a greater reliance on personal selling.

NVKK's price structure offered the average retailer a 30 percent gross margin. Subwholesalers bought at 64 percent of list, and the average primary wholesaler's purchase price was 60 percent of list. Although retailer margins for NVKK products were the same as for competitor products, NVKK wholesale margins were 3 to 4 percent below those of other major advertised brands. "NVKK follows much more of a pull strategy than other Japanese competitors in this field, who tend to emphasize more of a push strategy," commented Nagata.

RECENT COMPETITIVE DEVELOPMENTS

Starting in February 1983, competition in the acne preparation market had been very active. This activity was largely concentrated on the quasi-drug and wash segments of the acne market. In February, Shiseido added Acne Wash Foam as a line extension to its Ekubo wash product line. Also in February, Sunstar launched a set of wash products and a quasi-drug spot lotion under the brand name Acneid. In March, Shiseido introduced a series of six wash products, including both wash and quasi-drug lotions, under the Acne brand name. That same month Kanebo added a drug-registered acne cream, Mydate Acne Fresh, as an extension of its Mydate lotion and moisturizer wash products.

These new entries differed from existing cosmetic products insofar as they were exclusively positioned as acne products. Previously, products were either integrated into an existing line of cosmetics or represented a complete acne cosmetic line. These new wash products were registered as quasi-drug cosmetics with acne prevention as the key benefit. The new entries were distributed through a wide range of channels typical of cosmetic products.

The Ekubo line was produced and distributed by Shiseido, Japan's largest cosmetics company. The line included Ekubo Washing Foam, Milky Cream, Lemon Fresh, Milky Fresh, Milky Cream Soft, and Deodorant. The Ekubo Acne Foam came in two sizes of twenty grams and eighty grams, priced at 180 yen and 460 yen, respectively. The key benefit was "washing with it prevents acne." The line was supported by advertising in TV, magazines, outdoors, and informational leaflets and brochures.

Shiseido's later entry, Acne, was an entirely new line of six products consisting of:

Acne Soap	75 grams	600 yen
Acne Washing Foam	75 grams	1,000 yen
		(equals U.S. $4.00)
Acne Pack	75 grams	1,200 yen
Acne Lotion	75 grams	1,200 yen
Acne Skin Milk	75 grams	1,200 yen
Acne Spot Touch	10 ml	1,000 yen

These products appeared to be primarily targeted at consumers aged 15 to 17, both male and female, with the age group 18 to 24 as a secondary target. The introduction was supported with heavy TV, magazine, newspaper, and outdoor advertising.

Sunstar, Japan's leading marketer of toothpaste,

introduced Acneid, its first entry into the acne preparation market:

Acneid Washing Foam	60 grams	600 yen
Acneid Washing Foam S	60 grams	600 yen
Acneid Soap	60 grams	600 yen
Acneid Lotion	30 ml	700 yen

These products were fully supported with advertising in TV, magazine, outdoor, and point-of-purchase brochures.

Kanebo, Japan's second largest cosmetics company, introduced a medicated cream, Mydate Acne Fresh (30 grams at 600 yen), as a line extension for its Mydate series that included Clean Fresh cream, Milky Moist moisturizer, and Lotion Fresh.

CLEARASIL'S PERFORMANCE IN JAPAN

Skin-toned Clearasil had been marketed without advertising support in Japan from mid-1961 until early 1974. It had reached a unit volume of only 44,500 units at a consumer price of 300 yen. It was taken off the market together with other small-volume items in conjunction with a reorganization of NVKK's sales efforts.

Test Market Experience

NVKK decided to test market a reformulated version of Clearasil acne skin cream in 1978. The reformulated product was a "vanishing spot cream" that could be applied to acne on a person's face. Given its effective medicated ingredients, the product was designed to open the acne pimple head, to drain the pimple without the need for squeezing, and finally to dry the acne pimples. The reformulated Clearasil was virtually identical to the product sold in the United States at that time. It did not contain benzoyl peroxide as that was not an approved ingredient in Japan. It was packaged in an 18 gram tube wrapped in a carton.

NVKK tested Clearasil in two test markets between July 1978 and June 1979. The two markets, Hiroshima and Shizuoka, represented about 4.5 percent of the total Japanese market and were supported with spot television advertising. Clearasil was priced at 700 yen per package at the consumer level and was distributed through drugstores only. Given Clearasil's registration as an OTC proprietary product, NVKK was restricted to the drugstore channel. "We chose to register Clearasil as a proprietary (OTC) drug product because we believe it was a marketing advantage," explained Horita.

The test market results were very encouraging. Factory shipments amounted to about 122,000 packages over a twelve-month period. National rollout was commenced in July 1979 and was completed by October. It was supported by TV advertisement exclusively, and the consumer price was increased to 900 yen. Factory shipments for the first twelve months after national introduction amounted to 2,560,000 packages. The company had not expected to reach this sales level for at least another year. Factory shipments remained at about the same level for the 1980/1981 fiscal year but began to decrease to 2,308,000 packages in 1981/1982 and 2,031,000 packages for the 1982/1983 fiscal year. For a detailed history of Clearasil's performance over the period 1979–1983, see Exhibit 6.

Throughout this time, NVKK supported Clearasil heavily with advertising. Advertising expenditures averaged about 70 percent of sales for the first three years after the national launch.

Dane Battiato, NVKK's marketing director, commented: "In our business it is typical to spend lots of money on advertising. When we first launch a new brand in a market, we are prepared to investment-spend beyond the normal level of advertising for a certain period. At Richardson-Vicks, we use a hurdle rate of 18 percent ROI for investment projects. With Clearasil, we can only reach normal product contribution if we cut marketing expenditures back to about 40 percent of the current level while holding sales."

Strategic Decisions on Clearasil

Horita believed NVKK management had reached a point where some critical decisions had to be made with respect to Clearasil's direction in Japan. "It bothers me that we cannot expand volume beyond the earlier reached levels of 2.5 million packages while the rest of the market is expanding rapidly."

In reviewing Clearasil's progress to date, management concluded that neither pricing nor product

EXHIBIT 6 ● Clearasil Product Performance

	Time period	Sales units	Clearasil unit share %	Value (000 yen)	Clearasil sales share %
1979	S/O	261,400	9.9	190,097	14.3
	N/D	373,380	11.0	271,092	17.0
1980	J/F	334,060	9.8	242,297	14.4
	M/A	314,280	10.9	228,591	15.0
	M/J*	312,520	54.9	227,290	53.8
	J/A	385,340	45.3	298,146	45.9
	S/O	403,720	39.4	339,445	42.4
	N/D	325,870	36.2	227,498	40.6
1981	J/F	278,430	36.1	239,166	40.7
	M/A	295,680	36.1	251,942	39.9
	M/J	287,290	33.3	244,303	37.1
	J/A	358,610	36.2	306,242	41.1
	S/O	380,030	39.7	324,731	43.5
	N/D	320,350	37.0	273,877	41.9
1982	J/F	284,670	37.5	243,623	42.7
	M/A	305,290	36.0	260,285	40.2
	M/J	296,540	33.6	253,132	37.4
	J/A	333,300	31.8	283,883	35.8
	S/O	356,500	33.6	303,375	38.1
	N/D	300,210	32.2	252,702	36.7
1983	J/F	216,300	28.7	182,790	33.0
	M/A**	212,410	22.9	108,447	26.5

*New definition of segment by Nielsen Company.

**Estimated by NVKK executives for period March/April 1983.

formulation was at the root of the problem. Horita pointed to indications that Clearasil's advertising was not communicating as well as it should. In order to restore Clearasil's volume growth, the advertising strategy might have to be changed.

Another opportunity for Clearasil was to expand into the wash segment by launching a Clearasil soap. This would give NVKK a chance to participate in the fastest growing acne preparation segment, the wash products, with the possibility of launching additional line extensions at a later time.

CLEARASIL ADVERTISING IN JAPAN

Clearasil's advertising was centered around the theme used worldwide by Richardson-Vicks. The key component was the documentation of Clearasil's three-way action:

1. Clearasil opens the acne/pimple head.

2. Clearasil drains the inside of the acne pimple without squeezing.

3. Clearasil dries the acne pimple.

From the outset, Clearasil was positioned as a unique and highly effective medicated cream with a special three-way action unsurpassed in its ability to clear up acne and thereby improve the appearance and social confidence of acne sufferers.

For the test market and the first year of national launch, NVKK used two TV commercials produced locally, both in a 30-second and 15-second version around two themes, "High School" and "Date." The same themes were used until mid-1980 when a revised version, "Adolescence," was introduced. Starting January 1981, a new commercial titled "Testimonial" was used in 30-second and 15-second versions to be followed a year later by still another new campaign titled "Disarming." See Exhibit 7.

The "High School" and "Date" Campaigns

The "High School" and "Date" versions of Clearasil were the initial commercials aired during both the test market period and during the first twelve months of national distribution. The campaign was designed to position Clearasil as *the* specific acne treatment product in a market where specific acne treatment products had never been actively marketed. See Exhibit 8.

The copy objectives were to make the point that

EXHIBIT 7 ● Clearasil TV Campaign History

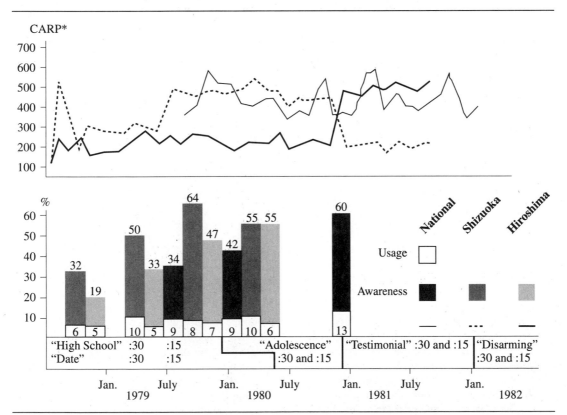

*CARP = Cumulative Audience Rating Point (people rating) shows gross coverage over the total people of each target area.

Clearasil was specifically formulated to deal with acne, was a serious medicated product for treatment of acne, and would contribute to the improvement of the complexion of users. The advertising had to communicate Clearasil's three-way action and that it was suitable for all ages of the primary target audience, and to imply that it provided some form of social reward.

Change to the "Adolescence" Campaign

By the end of 1979, Horita concluded that the "High School" and "Date" campaigns worked well as introductory campaigns to build brand awareness. In fact, the campaigns had surpassed all NVKK objectives. However, Horita believed that the two commercials did not wear very well over time. The commercials were too similar to each other because they both relied on the three-way-action demonstration. Furthermore, low interest scores were indications of problems with the commercials.

Drawing on unused footage from the "High School" commercials, a new commercial entitled "Adolescence" was produced. There was, of course, little difference in copy compared to the earlier version. The major differences were new visuals on other aspects of school life. See Exhibit 9.

The "Testimonial" Campaign

Successive research indicated that the previous campaigns successfully communicated with and generated trial among the sufferer/treater segment. The campaign failed to generate sufficient trial among the sufferer-nontreater segment because Clearasil was perceived as a very serious and specific product, possibly too medical, due to the overall serious tone of the commercials and the continuous use of the three-way-action demonstration.

The "Testimonial" campaign was produced to increase trial among the nontreater segment, which was identified as the key source for future volume growth for the brand. A documentary approach similar to Australian and Mexican testimonial commercials was used. These commercials featured testimonial comments in quick cut sequences depicting teenagers who suffered from acne and who shared their various ideas on remedies and their advice with the television audience in a frank and natural way.

The three-way-action of earlier commercials was made slightly shorter and lighter in tone but NVKK retained the basic copy points and animation flow. NVKK added a new end benefit "clear and smooth" and dropped the reference to "acne treatment cream." Both a spring and summer version of the "Testimonial" campaign were produced. The media mix strategy remained unchanged. See Exhibit 10.

Testing of the "Testimonial" commercials against the earlier campaigns showed little improvement in interest, involvement and effectiveness. In those categories, the "Testimonial" campaign was rated in the fourth, or lowest, quartile compared to average scores achieved by Japanese commercials.

The poor results of pre-/posttest among nontreaters despite high copy comprehension convinced NVKK executives that the "Testimonial" campaign could not live up to their expectations. An earlier study had shown that almost 70 percent of acne sufferers in the past year did not treat their acne other than washing with regular soap. It was increasingly clear that Clearasil could only grow as expected if an effective way to reach nontreaters could be found. Past campaigns were found amateurish (61%) and dull (45%). A low interest test score of 480 was observed with a sharp drop during the explanation of the three-way action. By comparison, for pharmaceutical products interest scores of 510 to 520 were considered average; 550 or more was viewed as very good. Many commercials on the air scored in the 525 to 530 range. See Exhibit 11.

The Change to the "Disarming" Campaign

To more effectively communicate with nontreaters, a new "Disarming" commercial was produced. A new format for expressing the three-way action was considered necessary. The previous approach created the impression that the product worked very quickly—that is, overnight—which was not the case. Furthermore, the three-way action was perceived as having been worn out. However, the three-way action was perceived to be the most impressive and important aspect of Clearasil. See Exhibit 12.

The new campaign also had to address the impression that Clearasil was for serious sufferers only and was not appropriate for light sufferers. The product was perceived as too strong for people with

EXHIBIT 8 ● Story Board for "Date" Campaign, 1978/1979, June 14, 1978

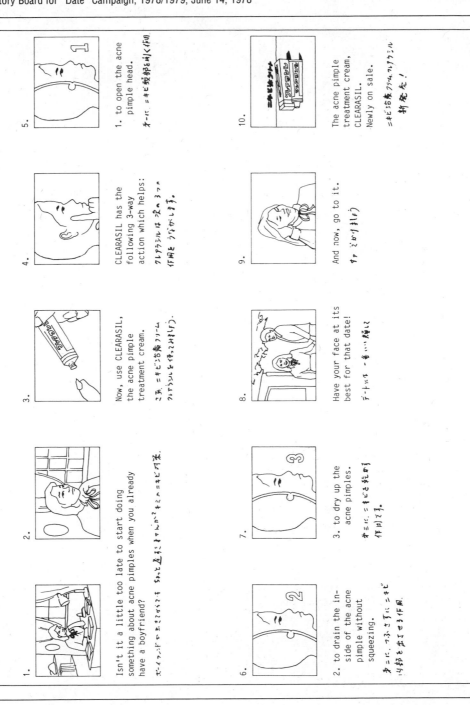

1.
Isn't it a little too late to start doing something about acne pimples when you already have a boyfriend?
オーイ、パーティーに出にくいですよ。こんと、思っと先にまたニキビのことを…ニキビニ…

2.
Now, use CLEARASIL, the acne pimple treatment cream.
さあ、ニキビにお薬クリームクレアシルを使って、2日間します。

3.
CLEARASIL has the following 3-way action which helps:
クレアシルは次の3つの作用とうごかします。

4.
1. to open the acne pimple head.
オーバーニキビの頭部をひらく作用

5.
[blank - numbered 1]

6.
2. to drain the inside of the acne pimple without squeezing.
オニに…プラスにニキビの内部を出にさせる作用

7.
3. to dry up the acne pimples.
オミニ…ニキビを乾燥作用とする。

8.
Have your face at its best for that date!
デートには一番いい顔に

9.
And now, go to it.
サアごおりましょう

10.
The acne pimple treatment cream, CLEARASIL. Newly on sale.
ニキビお薬クリーム、クレアシル 新発売！

EXHIBIT 8 ● Story Board for "Date" Campaign (*Continued*)

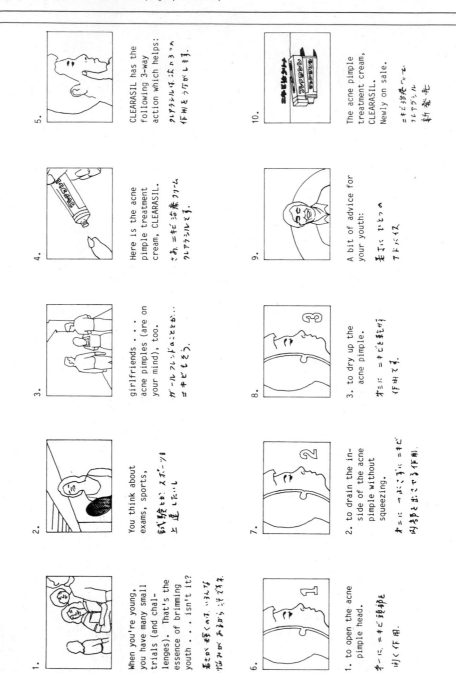

1. When you're young, you have many small trials (and challenges). That's the essence of brimming youth . . . isn't it?

髪とかお肌とか、いろんな
悩みが あるから、ごくろうさん。

2. You think about exams, sports,

試験とか、スポーツを
上達したい。

3. girlfriends . . . acne pimples (are on your mind), too.

ガール フレンド . . .
ニキビ も そう。

4. Here is the acne pimple treatment cream, CLEARASIL.

さあ、ニキビ 治療 クリーム
クレアラシル です。

5. CLEARASIL has the following 3-way action which helps:

クレアラシル は 次の 3 つ の
作用 を うながし ます。

6. 1. to open the acne pimple head.

オー ﾙ、ニキビ 頭部 を
ひらく 作用.

7. 2. to drain the inside of the acne pimple without squeezing.

オ二 に、ニキビ の
内部 と を だ して る 作用.

8. 3. to dry up the acne pimple.

オ三 に、ニキビ を 乾かす
作用 です.

9. A bit of advice for your youth:

若 さ に、ひとつ
アドバイス

10. The acne pimple treatment cream, CLEARASIL. Newly on sale.

ニキビ治療クリーム、
クレアラシル
新発売

EXHIBIT 9 ● Story Board for "Adolescence" Campaign, 1980, August 27, 1980

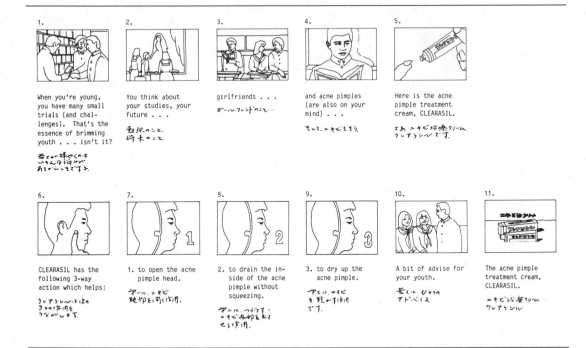

1.	2.	3.	4.	5.
When you're young, you have many small trials (and challenges). That's the essence of brimming youth . . . isn't it?	You think about your studies, your future . . .	girlfriends . . .	and acne pimples (are also on your mind) . . .	Here is the acne pimple treatment cream, CLEARASIL.
6.	7.	8.	9.	10.	11.
CLEARASIL has the following 3-way action which helps:	1. to open the acne pimple head.	2. to drain the inside of the acne pimple without squeezing.	3. to dry up the acne pimple.	A bit of advise for your youth.	The acne pimple treatment cream, CLEARASIL.

sensitive skin and was not "fashionable" because its image was inconsistent with that of a serious medicine. The previous execution of the "social reward" aspect was felt to be obvious, forced, and thus unpleasant to the viewer. While the concept of teenagers giving advice to other teenagers was acceptable, its execution was judged to be "preachy" in tone.

With respect to tone and image, the commercials were considered to be dark, gloomy, boring, repetitious, not lively, and lacking a modern contemporary "feeling." Contributing to this was the absence of music, the use of a male narrator, the execution of the three-way action with its worn-out image and the fixed pattern of setting up the acne problem, on to three-way action explanation, and then to end benefit. Furthermore, some of the characters in the commercials were not felt to be typical of contemporary teenagers.

A serious and direct approach to acne problems by highlighting disadvantages of acne sufferers was not responsive to nontreaters. Research showed that nontreaters were not seriously concerned about acne. "Do not worry about it" was the most often mentioned reason among nontreaters for not treating acne.

Dissatisfaction with Past Advertising Campaigns

During the first twelve months of the national campaign, Clearasil achieved an advertising intensity of about 14,700 GRPs in the two key regions of Japan, Kanto and Kansai, compared to a total of 18,888 GRPs and 19,947 GRPs, respectively, for all acne preparation products.[3] In March of 1980, Ekubo and

3. GRP = gross rating point. GRP equals the sum of all airings of the program or spot announcement during a given time period. For example, a once-a-week program constantly recording a 15 percent rating (or 15 percent of TV homes covered) results in 60 GRPs for a four-week period.

EXHIBIT 10 ● Story Board for "Testimonial" Campaign

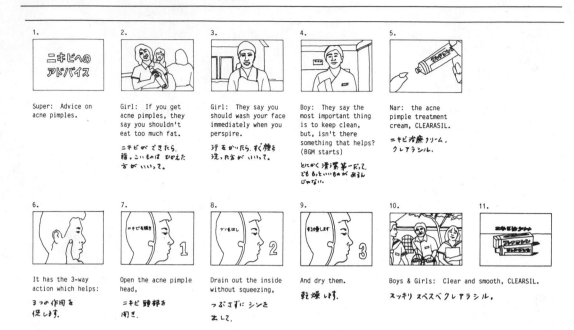

1.
Super: Advice on acne pimples.

2.
Girl: If you get acne pimples, they say you shouldn't eat too much fat.

ニキビが できたら、脂、こいものは ひかえた 方が いいって。

3.
Girl: They say you should wash your face immediately when you perspire.

汗を かいたら、すぐ 顔を 洗った方が いいって。

4.
Boy: They say the most important thing is to keep clean, but, isn't there something that helps? (BGM starts)

とにかく 清潔第一だって、でも もっと いいものが あるし じゃない。

5.
Nar: the acne pimple treatment cream, CLEARASIL.

ニキビ治療クリーム、クレアラシル。

6.
It has the 3-way action which helps:

3つの作用を 促します。

7.
Open the acne pimple head,

ニキビ 頭部を 開き、

8.
Drain out the inside without squeezing,

つぶさずに シンを 出して、

9.
And dry them.

乾燥します。

10.
Boys & Girls: Clear and smooth, CLEARSIL.

スッキリ スベスベ クレアラシル。

11.

Biore entered the market with budgets two to three times larger than Clearasil's for the March/June period of 1980. During the 1980/1981 period, Clearasil maintained its advertising at the same earlier level while Ekubo spent about 60% less and Biore maintained a level of slightly less than half of Clearasil's GRPs. During both years, Clearasil was the most advertised brand, with a 45.9 percent share of GRPs. For more details, see Exhibit 13.

Horita, who had been off the brand from the end of 1979 due to an eighteen months stay at the division's head office, became concerned about Clearasil's advertising in July of 1981. In his new position as creative development coordinator for all of NVKK's new products, he supervised some tests on Clearasil's advertising effectiveness on the "Adolescent" campaign. Interviewed teenagers connected the commercials with *dassai,* a slang word used for a crumpled looking middle manager, somebody who was neither chic nor sophisticated. "In terms of U.S. equivalent, this comes close to the 'Columbo' role

played by Peter Falk in the U.S. detective movie series," explained Brian Taylor, one of the U.S. expatriate managers at NVKK. What Horita was concerned about was that the teenagers believed only a dassai could create such a commercial. Even worse was the connection between dassai and *kusai,* the Japanese equivalent of "something disgusting."

Throughout this time period, NVKK had regularly measured consumer attitudes. Testing was done in the Tokyo area and in both of Clearasil's test markets. The results of the tests are shown in Exhibit 14.

"The data indicate a significant decrease in the satisfaction of Clearasil users," commented Mr. Horita, the brand manager. "At the same time, our brand awareness was ahead of objective. In our test markets, we expected a brand awareness of 50 to 60 percent after twelve months; instead, we achieved figures at 80 percent.

"Obviously, we are not getting our message

EXHIBIT 11 ● Clearasil TV Commercials' Test Ratings for "Testimonial" Campaign

	"High School"	*"Date"*	*"Testimonial"* summer version	
	30 SEC SCORE	*30 SEC SCORE*	*30 SEC SCORE*	*QUARTILE*
INTEREST				
Profile Curve Score	479	466	438	(4)
INVOLVEMENT				
Commercial Image Index	15%	12%	8%	(4)
COMMUNICATION				
A. Comprehension of Copy Point	48%	64%	42%	(2)
Comprehension of Sales Message	77	78	50	(1)
B. Recall of Brand Name	57	35	95	(1)
Recall of Copy Point	24	32	19	(2)
EFFECTIVENESS				
Pre-/Postscore	+8%	+4%	+3%	(4)
			+5	(4)
Persuasion Score	37	30	25	(4)

across as effectively as we wanted. Our interest scores for both commercials were below average compared to the typical Japanese commercial. Where we did very well was in the comprehension of copy points, sales message, and copy point recall. However, despite the excellent comprehension scores, the Clearasil commercials scored low on pre/post effectiveness and persuasion." See Exhibit 11.

Withdrawal of Advertising Support in November 1982

In the fall of 1982, it became clear that Vicks' latest campaign, "Disarming," was no more successful than previous ones. Interest curves in theater testing dropped even more. "As it did not make sense to support Clearasil with a campaign that did not meet our communications objective, we decided to withdraw all advertising support in November 1982. For the last five months, we have not put any advertising expenditures behind Clearasil," explained Horita.

The impact of the advertising withdrawal was felt almost immediately in figures on consumer offtake collected regularly for NVKK. Market share for Clearasil dropped to a low of 23 percent as compared to more than one-third in earlier periods. The biggest winners were the wash products. The share of wash products reached 57 percent for the most recent period. See Exhibit 15.

Advertising in Japan

A specialist in Japanese advertising gave the following explanation: "When a Western businessman

EXHIBIT 12 ● Story Board for "Disarming" Campaign, January 22, 1982

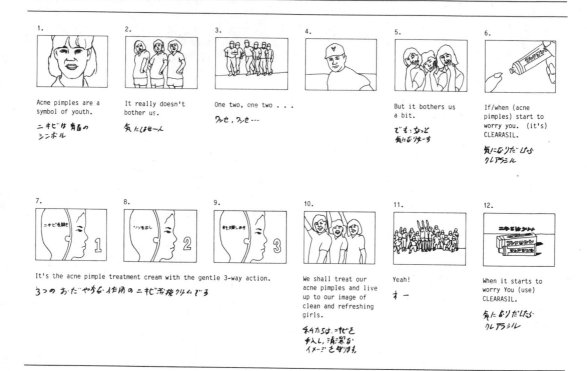

1. Acne pimples are a symbol of youth.
ニキビは 青春の シンボル

2. It really doesn't bother us.
気にしてませーん

3. One two, one two . . .
ワッセ, ワッセ・・・

5. But it bothers us a bit.
でも, ちょっと 気になります

6. If/when (acne pimples) start to worry you. (it's) CLEARASIL.
気になりだしたら クレアラシル

7./8./9. It's the acne pimple treatment cream with the gentle 3-way action.
3つの おだやかな 作用の ニキビ治療クリームである

10. We shall treat our acne pimples and live up to our image of clean and refreshing girls.
私たちは ニキビを 治入し, 清潔な イメージを 守ります。

11. Yeah!
オー

12. When it starts to worry You (use) CLEARASIL.
気になりだしたら クレアラシル

enters his hotel room in Japan and turns on the switch of his TV and watches the Japanese commercials, he invariably complains that they seem to be heavy on mood elements and often difficult to even understand what they were selling. On the other hand, Japanese businessmen complain on returning from the U.S. about the heavy verbiage in the U.S. commercials. How could the viewer, they would ask, stand being talked at so incessantly?"

When tested in Japan, U.S. and Japanese commercials ranked differently. Japanese commercials tended to score higher in "execution interest," whereas U.S. commercials scored higher on the "image index." The key difference was "copy recall," where Japanese commercials ranked overwhelmingly lower than U.S. commercials. There was little difference in brand recall, pre/post attitude shift, and product interest.

McCann-Erickson, NVKK's advertising agency in Japan, described the Japanese style of advertising as "understated" or "nonlinear." There was a saying that in Japan "you don't go into somebody's living room without first taking your shoes off." Consequently, Japanese advertising showed more "respect" for the consumer by being less direct.

Japanese consumers perceived little difference in the quality or technical superiority of various products. Often they were not knowledgeable about product details, such as ingredients in medicine. Because most products were in general believed to be equal, no comparative advertising was used in Japan. In the opinion of one of the executives, "you sell your product by becoming your consumer's friend."

For OTC products, word-of-mouth communications were very important and, together with store recommendations, outranked advertising as a source for

EXHIBIT 13 ● Acne Preparation Advertising Expenditures (in GRPs), 1979–1981

	TOTAL	1979						1980					
		JULY	AUG.	SEPT.	OCT.	NOV.	DEC.	JAN.	FEB.	MAR.	APR.	MAY	JUNE
Kanto													
Clearasil (7/79)	7,308	278	649	709	895	752	738	558	560	600	590	463	516
Ekubo (3/80)	4,847	—	—	—	—	—	—	—	—	1,805	1,185	1,271	588
Biore (3/80)	2,058	—	—	—	—	—	—	—	—	216	1,571	159	112
Skin Life	653	73	95	49	—	4	130	109	75	62	56	—	—
Noxzema	1,113	256	635	—	—	—	91	—	18	16	20	77	—
Asty	1,104	—	—	—	—	—	—	—	—	1,104	—	—	—
Clearex	60	—	—	—	—	—	—	—	—	—	—	—	60
Jelleje	—	—	—	—	—	—	—	—	—	—	—	—	—
Silk Lady	1,745	—	—	—	—	—	—	—	—	—	1,068	237	440
Total	18,888	607	1,379	758	895	756	959	667	653	3,801	4,490	2,207	1,716
Kansai													
Clearasil	7,447	262	682	671	848	626	626	611	474	574	941	560	572
Ekubo	4,741	—	—	—	—	—	—	—	—	1,605	1,195	1,354	587
Biore	2,164	—	—	—	—	—	—	—	—	68	1,781	183	129
Skin Life	612	59	97	28	—	7	132	110	54	68	57	—	—
Noxzema	973	181	601	—	—	—	67	—	18	15	23	68	—
Asty	1,072	—	—	—	—	—	—	—	—	1,072	—	—	—
Clearex	78	—	—	—	—	—	—	—	—	—	—	—	78
Jelleje	—	—	—	—	—	—	—	—	—	—	—	—	—
Silk Lady	2,860	—	—	—	—	—	—	—	—	—	1,819	526	515
Total	19,947	502	1,380	699	848	633	825	721	546	3,402	5,819	2,691	1,881

Source: MEH.

EXHIBIT 13 ● Acne Preparation Advertising Expenditures (in GRPs), 1979–1981 *(Continued)*

		1980						1981					
	TOTAL	JULY	AUG.	SEPT.	OCT.	NOV.	DEC.	JAN.	FEB.	MAR.	APR.	MAY	JUNE
Kanto													
Clearasil	7,089	513	812	456	468	442	812	848	509	625	569	478	557
Ekubo	4,197	1,574	916	443	255	284	212	105	80	93	80	94	61
Biore	3,138	674	170	83	208	614	109	260	46	71	558	165	180
Skin Life	736	35	15	27	16	7	100	166	95	137	116	22	—
Noxzema	1,865	121	260	212	156	170	128	3	—	125	126	415	149
Asty	—	—	—	—	—	—	—	—	—	—	—	—	—
Clearex	79	79	—	—	—	—	—	—	—	—	—	—	—
Acne Trio	515	—	—	—	—	—	—	—	—	—	—	—	515
Jelleje	—	—	—	—	—	—	—	—	—	—	—	—	—
Silk Lady	1,445	—	—	—	—	—	—	—	—	—	922	523	—
Total	19,064	2,996	2,173	1,221	1,103	1,517	1,361	1,382	730	1,051	2,371	1,697	1,462
Kansai													
Clearasil	7,492	553	857	536	452	477	825	941	518	725	605	509	494
Ekubo	4,561	1,690	1,000	479	320	305	264	125	83	76	75	85	59
Biore	3,427	752	234	83	249	666	116	278	77	101	517	216	138
Skin Life	934	33	19	29	16	6	120	216	141	180	151	23	—
Noxzema	1,876	275	266	236	—	190	100	5	—	125	124	400	155
Asty	—	—	—	—	—	—	—	—	—	—	—	—	—
Clearex	99	99	—	—	—	—	—	—	—	—	—	—	—
Acne Trio	—	—	—	—	—	—	—	—	—	—	—	—	—
Silk Lady	1,729	—	—	—	—	—	—	—	—	—	1,002	727	—
Total	20,118	3,402	2,376	1,363	1,037	1,644	1,425	1,565	819	1,207	2,474	1,960	846

Source: MEH.

EXHIBIT 14 ● Attribute Ratings on Clearasil (Among Clearasil Users)

	Tokyo			Shizuoka				Hiroshima			
	Post 6	Post 12	Post 24	Post 6	Post 12	Post 18	Post 24	Post 6	Post 12	Post 18	Post 24*
Base	153 %	75 %	85 %	142 %	155 %	150 %	98 %	111 %	148 %	155 %	115 %
Leaves skin feeling clean	23	23	13	20	13	14	15	17	28	25	25
Leaves skin smooth	22	15	15	12	12	6	10	10	21	18	16
Not greasy	37	36	23	28	23	26	17	32	42	37	35
Does not irritate skin	34	33	20	19	19	20	21	24	37	29	38
Fast working	44	33	19	22	24	41	34	27	30	37	37
Dries up oily skin	37	29	22	25	21	47	28	26	34	37	38
Helps open pimples	35	35	23	22	20	34	33	20	28	31	46
Can use with assurance	NA	36	26	NA	NA	NA	23	NA	NA	NA	44
Disappears into skin	25	19	14	17	12	13	11	18	27	32	25
Helps prevent pimples	30	28	19	21	13	18	14	31	36	39	38
Improves appearance of facial skin	NA	15	14	NA	NA	NA	11	NA	NA	NA	21
Helps clear up pimples	47	36	23	24	21	35	28	32	37	41	45
Helps drain pimples	43	32	21	24	19	37	33	26	39	36	43
Is a medicine	NA	24	20	NA	NA	NA	15	NA	NA	NA	25
Is a product that suits me	NA	24	21	NA	NA	NA	18	NA	NA	NA	24
Is a contemporary product	NA	21	19	NA	NA	NA	10	NA	NA	NA	27
Is a cosmetic	NA	6	2	NA	NA	NA	4	NA	NA	NA	6

*Indicates twenty-four months after launch in that area.

EXHIBIT 15 ● Clearasil Consumer Off-Take, Spring 1983

	80/81	*81/82*	*82/83*	*83 J/F*
Total Market	5,226	5,301	5,695	753
% Change Y/A		+1.4%	+7.4%	
Clearasil	1,973	1,943	1,642	216
% Change Y/A		−1.5%	−15.5%	
% Share	37.8%	36.7%	28.8%	28.7%
Medicated Brands	354*	338	280	36
% Change Y/A		−4.5%	−17.2%	
% Share	6.8%	6.4%	4.9%	4.9%
Other Brands	594*	567	661	84
% Change Y/A		−4.5%	+16.6%	
% Share	11.4%	10.7%	11.6%	11.2%
Wash Products	1,831*	2,445	3,104	415
% Change Y/A		+33.5%	+27.0%	
% Share	35.0%	46.1%	54.5%	55.2%

*These data 80 S/O–81 M/J.

Units in thousands.

Y/A = change year/after, or change from prior year.

product decisions. For both drug and cosmetics buyers, store recommendations were frequently solicited. Some 90 percent of buyers asked "always" or "sometimes" before purchasing.

THE OPPORTUNITY FOR LINE EXTENSION

As Horita was working on a solution for Clearasil's advertising problem, he also investigated opportunities to participate in the rapidly growing wash segment. "With most of the competitive activities right now taking place in the wash category, we should definitely consider entering with our own wash product," explained Horita. "Growth in the wash-only segment has outpaced growth in the treatment-only segment."

During the past few months, NVKK had a bar soap under test that could be marketed as Clearasil Soap. "We should see the Clearasil franchise as a business on its own with opportunities to expand into various categories, but all under the Clearasil franchise." The soap had been marketed by Richardson-Vicks in other countries under the Clearasil name and was thus available to NVKK. However, corporate policy did not allow a "prevents acne" claim, which the Japanese government allowed as a claim for medicated soaps.

Product concept tests had already been carried out. Results indicated that a price of about 450 yen per package would be appropriate. The soap would be classified as a drug-registered bar soap. Product usage tests indicated that treaters evaluated the product more positively than did the general population. In general, test scores on Clearasil Soap were equal to or better than those for Clearasil Cream a few years ago. However, since NVKK had no prior experience with a drug-registered soap in Japan, there was no control group to compare its soap against.

Distribution Requirements for Entering Wash Category

Several options existed for NVKK's entry into the wash segment. Horita had to consider not only whether NVKK should enter this segment but also how this might be done. In addition, any initiative needed to be coordinated with actions for Clearasil cream.

"Entry into the wash product segment has some important consequences for distribution," commented Mr. Nagata, the sales manager. In Japan, bar soaps were sold primarily through supermarkets and department stores. Only cosmetic soaps were sold in important volumes through drug and cosmetic stores. Bar soap for bath use was a very popular gift item among Japanese, with about 90 percent of the volume sold through department stores. Cosmetic soap was sold 75 percent through cosmetic stores or the cosmetic section in supermarkets, with drugstores accounting for 25 percent. "For us to be successful with a soap, we have to open more channels into the cosmetic stores, supermarkets, and department store segment. Right now, we don't have these channels.

"To appreciate the buying environment at the store level, you have to understand that soaps are treated as a toiletry product category. Although we may be selling to the same store, wholesaler and buyer choices are different from OTC products."

Japanese drugstores were notorious for their small size and crowded conditions. A typical drugstore was about 300 square feet in size. Arrangements included a U-shaped main counter and one or two middle aisles. Drug products, including Clearasil, were displayed behind the main counter and had to be specifically requested by the customer. Toiletries were typically displayed in one of the center aisles. In many instances, the wholesaler supplying toiletry products to a drugstore would differ from a wholesaler supplying drug products. In the case of chain drugstores, the buyer for toiletries was not identical to the buyer of drug products.

In cosmetic stores, a similar arrangement with a U-shaped main counter existed. Soaps would typically be displayed in one of the center aisles as a separate category, with another aisle reserved for other toiletry products. Frequently, the supplying wholesalers for those categories were not identical, making it difficult, for example, for a drug wholesaler supplying a cosmetics store to add a product category that had traditionally been supplied by another wholesaler. Supermarkets and department stores typically bought from wholesalers that combined cosmetic and toiletry lines.

"Right now, only 5 of our primary wholesalers and 60 subwholesalers carry both proprietary drugs and toiletries," remarked Nagata, the sales manager. "To develop the same network in toiletries takes time. Ideally, we need other toiletry products and/or an entire new line to accomplish this. To give us adequate coverage in toiletries we need 60 to 70 primary and another 80 to 100 subwholesalers."

Competition in the Toiletry Sector

Japanese competitors in the toiletry segment employed various distribution and sales strategies. Sunstar, Japan's largest marketer of toothpaste, made nonexclusive use of primary wholesalers, as did NVKK. Kao, the largest Japanese detergent and toiletry company, often referred to as the "Procter & Gamble of Japan," had its own sales company. This firm maintained numerous local joint ventures with wholesalers. For Tokyo, the company operated under Tokyo Kao Sales Co. and was owned 50 percent by Kao. These joint venture sales companies sold directly to retailers. Yet another approach was followed by Lion, a large toiletry company, whose major products were detergents, toiletry, and toothpaste. Lion also employed primary wholesalers but had its own sales groups inside each primary wholesaler that gave exclusive attention to its own products. Although Mr. Nagata was unsure, he believed that these sections were funded by Lion. Both Kanebo and Shiseido were classified as "affiliated chains." "Chain" products were marketed directly to retailers. The Kanebo chain included about 15,000 cosmetic stores. Kanebo's sales force numbered 250 salesmen. The Shiseido chain consisted of 28,000 stores. Shiseido employed about 1,800 salesmen and about 10,000 demonstrators-merchandisers.

SEARCHING FOR A NEW ADVERTISING APPROACH

"Our original approach to advertising Clearasil in Japan has been to follow quite closely the approaches used around the world for this brand. The three-way action is the basic product support that has become the cornerstone to Clearasil advertising worldwide. It worked everywhere, and it certainly also worked in the early campaign in Japan," explained Horita. "Typical advertising in Japan is much more subtle than advertising used in the United States. There is clearly a soft-sell approach, and frequently the product is mentioned only briefly at the end."

Robert Whelan, the product manager for Vicks cough drops in Japan, explained Richardson-Vicks' advertising approach as follows: "In the United States, we believe that the advertising message should explain the benefit of a product, supply some rationale or reason for saying it, and offer some opportunity to distinguish the product from the competition with some credibility about the claimed advantages. To give up any of these elements would be a major change from past practices."

Harold Todd, president of NVKK, commented, "The Clearasil situation is very complex. Here we are with a commercial that scores very high on recall but low on interest. Horita would like to eliminate the three-way action part that has been the key to the product's success worldwide. Maybe it is true. But originally, we were successful with just that approach. Maybe we are simply telling the story the wrong way? There are pros and cons on both sides. But certainly at this point I don't have enough confidence to simply take the three-way action out."

NVKK's Advertising Approach for Other Products

With the exception of Colac, a laxative sold only in Japan, NVKK followed an advertising policy that was similar to the one used by other Richardson-Vicks subsidiaries. The TV commercials, while produced in Japan, followed the usual approach of product benefit and support claim. In virtually all other product areas, NVKK was the market leader by a wide margin.

Colac, the laxative, was different since it was only marketed in Japan. Accounting for almost half of NVKK's sales, Colac was a success story. Colac's advertising focused entirely on brand personality with no defined, rational exposition of support. Imagery and mood were used extensively in the earlier part of all Colac commercials to symbolize some of the key benefits promised. Later in the commercials, what would appear to most observers to be just a conventional product introduction shot, is in fact the "clincher" in the eyes of the Japanese consumers.

Division Views

When the decision was made to relaunch Clearasil in Japan, the division argued strongly for the three-way action approach which had proved successful in Brazil and Australia. Already at that time, Horita had felt uncomfortable with that approach. Although NVKK's top executives shared Horita's concern, they went along with the division's arguments of "why don't you try it." As a result, the Japanese campaign was built on the extensive documentation supplied by the division, which included advertising strategy, logo, packaging, layouts, etc.

Following Horita's transfer to the divisional head office in Westport, Connecticut, NVKK followed the original strategy. Although Horita returned to Japan in mid-1981, he was not put back on Clearasil until spring of 1982. In the meantime, divisional management had changed, and Horita, convinced that the existing policies would lead nowhere, tried again to get the division to accept a change. Two major meetings were held in Japan. "So far, the division has not accepted our point of view yet," said Horita. "Perhaps they felt that I did not listen to anyone and that I was stubborn. After all, other countries work with the three-way action. Why should Japan be an exception?"

Horita's Views

Horita himself was uncertain as to what approach he should suggest. "We started out with a largely U.S. approach with emphasis on the three-way action argument. When our scores turned out low, we reduced the three-way action component by making it shorter or lighter, thus moving more into the direction of a Japanese approach. However, our scores got worse, not better. Now I am no longer convinced that moving to an even more typical Japanese style advertising would actually improve the situation. On the other hand, I have all along felt that the three-way action argument was kind of obvious to the Japanese consumer and it encouraged overexpectation of product performance. Its constant repetition just does not help.''

For the upcoming meeting on Clearasil marketing strategy in Japan, Horita wanted to take an integrated approach to his business in Japan. ''I don't see the Clearasil cream or the possibility of a Clearasil soap as two distinctly different issues. Instead, I would like to present an overall strategy for our Clearasil business in Japan and integrate both cream and soap under this umbrella.''

Case 5

Interactive Computer Systems Corp.[1]

In September 1980, Peter Mark, marketing manager of Interactive Computer Systems Corporation, was faced with a perplexing conflict between his company's USA sales group and the European subsidiaries. The USA sales group had begun to sell a display controller which had been developed in Europe. The product had been selling in Europe for several years, and sales were relatively strong. Now, however, several major European customers had begun to purchase the product through their USA offices and ship it back to Europe. The Europeans were complaining that the U.S. pricing was undercutting theirs and that they were losing sales volume which was rightfully theirs. Both the U.S. and European groups claimed that their pricing practices followed corporate guidelines and met the profit objectives set for them.

INTERACTIVE COMPUTER SYSTEMS CORP.

Interactive Computer Systems Corporation (ICS), headquartered in Stamford, Connecticut, was a large, multinational manufacturer of computer systems and equipment. The company made a range of computer

1. Names and data are disguised.

All prices and costs are stated in U.S. dollars.

This case was prepared by Visiting Professor Jean-Pierre Jeannet as a basis for class discussion rather than to illustrate either effective or ineffective handling of an administrative situation. Copyright © 1981 by IMD, Lausanne, Switzerland. The International Institute for Management Development (IMD), resulting from the merger between IMEDE, Lausanne, and IMI, Geneva, acquires and retains all rights. Not to be used or reproduced without written permission from IMD, Lausanne, Switzerland.

systems and was best known for its small, or "mini," computers. ICS was considered one of the industry leaders in that segment of the computer industry, which included such companies as Data General, Digital Equipment, Prime Computer, Masscomp, and Hewlett-Packard.

The company was primarily a U.S. based corporation, with the majority of its engineering and manufacturing facilities located in the eastern United States. In addition, ICS had manufacturing facilities in Canada, Singapore, West Germany, and Brazil and a joint venture in South Korea.

Sales were conducted throughout most of the non-Communist world by means of a number of sales subsidiaries with sales offices located in Canada, Mexico, Brazil, Argentina, Chile, Japan, Australia, and several European countries. Elsewhere, sales were conducted through a network of independent agents and distributors.

PRODUCT LINE

The ICS line of products was centered around a family of 16-bit minicomputer systems. *Mini-computer* was the popular term referring to small to medium sized computer systems, which were used in a wide variety of applications including industrial control, telecommunications systems, laboratory applications, and small business systems. "Sixteen-bit" refers to the size of the computer "word," or unit of data. These systems were different from the large computer systems of IBM, Univac, and Honeywell, which had word sizes of 32–36 bits.

In addition to the computer central processing units (CPUs) and memory units, ICS produced a line of peripheral devices required for making complete computer systems. These included devices such as magnetic tape units, disk storage units, line printers, card readers, video and hard-copy terminals, display units, and laboratory and industrial instrumentation interface units. These various peripherals were used as appropriate and combined with the final computer systems to meet the specific customer's requirements. ICS produced most of these products in-house, but some, such as line printers and card readers, were purchased to ICS specifications from companies specializing in those products, such as Data Products and Documentation.

ICS manufactured several central processing units, which were positioned in price and performance to form a product family. They all had similarity of design, accepted (executed) the same computer instructions, and ran on the same operating system (master control programs). The difference was in speed, complexity, and cost. The purchaser was able to select the model which economically met the performance requirements of the intended application.

This family of CPUs, together with the wide range of available peripheral devices, formed a family of computer systems offering a considerable range of price and performance but with compatible characteristics and programming.

COMMUNICATIONS INTERFACES

A communications interface was a peripheral device used for transmitting data to or from the computer system. This could either be:

- A terminal on which a user could enter data, for example on a typewriter-like keyboard, and have data displayed, typically on either a video screen or as hard copy on a typewriter-like printer.
- Other computers, either of the same type or from a different manufacturer.

MODEL 431
COMMUNICATIONS INTERFACE

The specific product in question was the model 431 communications interface, a four-line programmable multiplexer.

The 431 consisted of one electronic circuit module which plugged into the I/O (input/output) "bus" of the computer (a bus was an electrical cable or wiring on which data signals flowed in some organized manner). It provided the interface for four separate communications lines, which were connected by means of specially designed connectors on the module. Such multiline interfaces were typically called multiplexers after the manner in which they worked internally. They offered the advantages of more efficient space utilization and lower per-line costs compared with the normal alternative of a separate single-line interface per line. Depending on the computer vendor, multiplexers come in various sizes such as 2, 4, 6, 8, 16, 32, and 64 lines.

ICS already had 4-, 8-, and 16-line multiplexers in its line of high volume standard products. The specified advantage of the 431 was its programmable nature. It could be loaded with software to handle any of several different protocols directly in the interface, using its own microprocessor on the module. It also performed error checking and moved data directly to or from the main computer memory. Since these functions had previously all been performed by a program running in the computer, the 431 relieved the computer of this load and freed it up to do other work. The result was a net improvement in system speed and power.

The model 431 was designed in 1977 at ICS's small European engineering facility assigned to its

EXHIBIT 1 ● Model 431 Sales Volume (Units), Selected Countries

	1977	1978	1979	1980 (forecast)
Germany	30	100	110	100
U.K.	5	40	60	70
France	10	20	50	40
Canada	0	0	5	5
Switzerland	3	20	30	15
Australia	0	0	10	30
U.S.A.	0	2	80	200

German subsidiary, Interactive Computers GmbH, in Frankfurt and was manufactured there for shipment worldwide to those ICS subsidiaries who were selling the 431. Sales had initially started in Europe and then spread to other areas. Sales volumes are given in Exhibit 1.

INTERSUBSIDIARY TRANSACTIONS

With the exception of the Korean joint venture, all of ICS's subsidiaries were wholly owned, and products moved freely between them. ICS had set up its procedures and accounting systems in line with the fact that it was basically a U.S. based company manufacturing a uniform line of products for sales worldwide through various sales subsidiaries. For the major product lines, the only differences by countries were line voltages and some minor adaptations to comply with local government regulations.

Although the subsidiaries in the various countries were essentially sales subsidiaries functioning as sales offices to sell products in those countries, they were separately incorporated entities and wholly owned subsidiaries, operating under the laws of that particular country. Careful accounting of all transactions between the parent company and the subsidiaries had to be maintained for the purpose of import duties and local taxes.

When a customer ordered a computer system, the order was processed in the subsidiary and then transmitted back to the parent company (ICS) in the United States to have the system built. The order paperwork listed the specific hardware items (CPU, memory size, tape and disk units, etc.) wanted by the customer, and each system was built specifically to order. The component pieces were built by ICS in volume to meet the requirements of these specific customer systems orders. Like most companies, ICS expended a great amount of effort attempting to accurately forecast the mix of products it would need to meet customer orders.

When the customer's system, or any product, was shipped to the subsidiary, the subsidiary "bought" it from the parent at an intercompany discounted price, or "transfer price," of list minus 20 percent. The level of subsidiary transfer price discount was established with two factors in mind:

- It was the primary mechanism by which Interactive repatriated profits to the U.S. parent corporation.
- The 20 percent subsidiary margin was designed to give the subsidiaries positive cash flow to meet their local expenses such as salaries, facilities, benefits, travel, and supplies.

Import duties were paid on the discounted (list minus 20 percent) transfer price value according to the customs regulations of the importing country. Some typical import duties for computer equipment are shown in Exhibit 2.

Most countries were quite strict on import/export and customs duties and required consistency in all transactions. Therefore, all shipments were made at the same discounted transfer price, including shipments among subsidiaries and shipments back to the United States.

PRICING

ICS set prices worldwide based on U.S. price lists, which were referred to as "Master Price Lists," or MPLs. Prices in each country were based on the MPL

EXHIBIT 2 ● Import Duties for Computer Equipment for Selected Countries[1]

U.S.A	5.1%
Canada	8.8
Japan	9.8
Australia	2
EEC[2]	None between EEC countries; 6.7% from outside EEC countries

[1]These are typical amounts only. The topic of customs duties is quite complex. It varies with the type of goods, even within an industry (computer systems may be one rate, while computer terminals may be another, higher rate and parts a third rate), and by country of origin.

[2]European Economic Community (Common Market) consisting of the U.K., France, Germany, Italy, Belgium, Netherlands, Ireland, Denmark, and Luxembourg. *Note:* Duty calculated on a "CIF" basis—cost of the product plus insurance and freight.

plus an uplift factor to cover the increased cost of doing business in those countries. Some of these extra costs were:

- Freight and duty, in those countries where it was included in the price (in some countries, duties were paid for separately by the customer).

- Extended warranty: in some countries, the customary warranty periods were longer than in the United States, for example, one year versus ninety days.

- Cost of subsidiary operations and sales costs, to the extent that they exceed the normal selling costs in the United States.

- Cost of currency hedging: in order to be able to publish a price list in local currency, ICS bought U.S. dollars in the money futures market.

Uplift factors were periodically reviewed and adjusted if needed to reflect changes in the relative cost of doing business in each country. Typical uplift factors for some selected countries are shown in Exhibit 3.

Each subsidiary published its own price list in local currency. The list was generated quarterly by use of a computer program which took a tape of all the MPL entries and applied the uplift and a fixed currency exchange rate which had been set for the fiscal year. This price list was used by all salespeople

EXHIBIT 3 ● Typical Country Uplift Factors: Local Price = Master Price List + Uplift %

U.K.	8%
Germany	15
France	12
Switzerland	17
Sweden	15
Australia	12
Brazil	20
Canada	5

in the subsidiary as the official listing of products offered and their prices.

SPECIAL PRODUCTS

In addition to its standard line of products which were sold worldwide in volume, ICS had a number of lower volume, or specialized, products. The model 431 communications interface was considered one of these. Specialized products were typically not on the MPL, and prices were set locally by each subsidiary wherever they were sold. They were either quoted especially on request for quote basis or added to a special price list supplement produced by each country. This was a common procedure in the computer industry. IBM, for example, had several products "available on an RPQ (request product quotation) basis" only.

To support the sales of the specialized products, ICS had a separate team of specialists, with one or more specialists in each subsidiary. They were responsible for the pricing of their products and had a high degree of independence in setting prices in each subsidiary. The specialist or team in each subsidiary was responsible for all aspects of the sales of their assigned products and essentially ran a business within a business.

For the purposes of internal reporting to management, the specialists were measured on achieving a profit before tax, or PBT, of 15 percent, which was the ICS goal. The results were shown on a set of internal reports which were separate from the legal books of the subsidiary. The purpose of the internal reports was to give ICS management more information on the profitability of its various product lines. These reports took the form of a series of profit and loss statements of operation by line of product with overhead and indirect costs allocated on a percentage of revenue basis. For these internal P&L reports, the cost of goods was the actual cost of manufacture (internal cost) plus related direct costs instead of the discounted price paid by subsidiaries and shown on their official statements of operation.

431 SALES IN EUROPE

The model 431 communications interface was designed in 1977 by the European engineering group in

Frankfurt as a follow-up to some special engineering contracts for European customers. It was introduced in the European market in 1978, where it grew in popularity.

The 431 was produced in Frankfurt only on a low volume production line. The manufacturing and other direct costs amounted to U.S. $1,500 per unit. Because there were no tariffs within the EEC and shipping costs were covered by allocated fixed costs, there were no other direct costs. The allocated fixed costs in Europe were running at 47 percent of revenue. Thus, a contribution margin of 62 percent was required to achieve a 15 percent PBT. Based on these costs, a list price of U.S. $3,900 had been set within the EEC. The resulting P&L is shown in Exhibit 4.

Because of the popularity of this product, it had been listed on the special products price list in most European countries. Within the EEC, the price had been set at the same level, with any variation due only to local currency conversions. In European countries outside the EEC, the price was increased to cover import duties.

At the above price, the 431 had gained market acceptance and had grown in popularity, especially in Germany, the United Kingdom, and France. Its customers included several large European based multinational companies of major importance to ICS in Europe. These customers designed specific system configurations and added programming to perform specified applications and shipped the systems to other countries, either to their own subsidiaries for internal use (for example, a factory) or to customers abroad.

431 SALES IN U.S.A.

The 431 was brought to the attention of the U.S. sales group in two different ways. In sales contacts with U.S. operations of some European customers, ICS was told of the 431 and asked to submit price and availability schedules for local purchase in the U.S.A. U.S. customers expressed irritation at being told that the model was not available in the United States.

Secondly, the U.S. sales force also heard of the 431 from their European counterparts at sales meetings, where the Europeans explained how the 431 had been important in gaining large accounts.

As a result of this pressure from customers and the sales force, the U.S. special products specialists obtained several units for evaluation and in 1979 made the 431 available for sale in the United States.

Originally, the U.S. specialists set the price equal to the European price of $3,900. However, it became obvious that the U.S. market was more advanced and more competitive, with customers expecting more performance at that price. As a result the price had to be reexamined.

The 431 was obtained from Frankfurt at the internal cost of $1,500. Transportation costs were estimated at $200. In the USA accounting system, import duties and transportation were not charged directly and were absorbed by general overhead. This came about because ICS was primarily an exporter from the United States, with very little importing taking place. Consequently, it was felt that import costs were negligible. Thus, the only direct cost was the $1,500 internal cost. Overhead and allocated fixed expenses in the United States averaged 35 percent.

The result was, as shown in Exhibit 5, a revised price of $3,000 with a contribution margin of 50 percent and a PBT of 15 percent—the ICS goal. Following this analysis, the U.S. price was reduced to $3,000. The 431 was not listed on the main U.S.A. price list but was quoted only on an RPQ basis. Subsequently, this price was also listed on special products price list supplements which were prepared by the U.S. product specialists and handed out to the sales force in each district.

EXHIBIT 4 ● Model 431 European Profit Analysis (in U.S. dollars)

European List Price	U.S. $3,900
Manufacturing and Other Direct Costs	1,500
Contribution Margin	2,400
	62%
Allocated Fixed Costs (47%)	1,833
PBT	U.S. $ 567
	14.5%

EXHIBIT 5 ● Model 431 U.S.A. Profit Analysis

U.S.A. List Price	$3,000
Manufacturing Cost	1,500
Contribution Margin	1,500
	50%
Allocated Fixed Costs (35%)	1,050
PBT	$ 450
	15%

CURRENT SITUATION

The repricing of the 431 to $3,000 was instrumental in boosting U.S. sales. The sales volume continued to grow, and some large customers were captured. These customers included existing ICS customers who previously used other, lower-performance communications interfaces or had bought somewhat equivalent devices from other companies who made "plug compatible" products for use with ICS computers. Also, a good volume of sales was being obtained from the U.S. operations of European multinationals who were already familiar with the product. ICS's U.S. group, who had first viewed the European designed product with suspicion, was now more confident about it.

But the Europeans were not entirely happy with the situation. Recently, they had started complaining to ICS management that the U.S. pricing of the 431 was undercutting the European price. This was causing pressure on the European subsidiaries to reduce their price for the 431 below the $3,900 they needed to meet their profitability goals. Pressure was coming from customers who knew the U.S. price and from European salespeople who, as a result of travel to the United States or discussions with U.S. colleagues, knew the U.S. price and what the uplifted European price "was supposed to be."

The price difference had also been noticed by several of ICS's larger European multinational customers. They started buying the 431 through their U.S. offices and reexporting it, both back to Europe and to other countries.

So far, three customers had done this, two Ger-

man firms and one French customer. Several additional customers were showing definite signs of "shopping around."

This loss of customers to the United States was particularly painful to the Europeans. They had invested considerable amounts of effort into cultivating these customers.

In addition, the customers still expected to receive technical and presales support from their local ICS office (that is, European) as well as warranty and service support, regardless of where they placed the purchase order. Attempts to discuss this with the customers or persuade them to purchase in Europe had not been successful. Typical reactions had been "That's ICS's problem" (U.K. customer) and "But are you not one company?" (German customer).

In brief, the ICS European subsidiaries were complaining that they were "being denied the profitable results of their own work" by the unfair pricing practices of the U.S. parent company.

In the eyes of the U.S. team, however, they were pricing in accordance with corporate guidelines to achieve a 15 percent PBT. They also maintained that the market did not allow them to price the 431 any higher. Furthermore, they felt that they were simply exercising their right to set their own country prices to maximize profits within their specific country market.

The U.S. group was so pleased with the U.S. market acceptance of the 431 that they wanted to begin an aggressive promotion. As an important part of this, they were now planning to add the 431 on the official ICS U.S. price list. This was viewed as a key to higher sales since, especially in the United States, products tended to be sold from the regular price list, and the sales force tended to lose or ignore special price list supplements.

At this point, both the European and U.S. specialists were upset with each other. Both sides maintained that they were following the rules but that the actions of "the other side" were harming their success and profitability.

It had been a long day, and it was time to go home. As he turned his car out into the traffic on High Ridge Road, Mark was still feeling confused about the issues and wondering what should be done.

Case 6

American Hospital Supply—Japan Corporation

In the spring of 1975, executives of AHS-Japan, under the direction of F. Nakamoto, the company president, met to discuss the possible method of entering the Japanese dental equipment market. The company was a subsidiary of American Hospital Supply, Inc., and had introduced two of its parent company's product lines very successfully during the last five years. It was now up to the executive team to select a strategy and to submit the proposal to its parent company for endorsement. The selection process was made particularly difficult by the nature of the distribution system and the strength of AHS-Japan's potential competitors.

AHS-JAPAN CORPORATION

AHS-Japan Corporation was originally established in 1968 as a branch of the American Hospital Supply Corporation. Just recently, its status had been changed to a subsidiary following the liberalization of the Japanese investment regulations that earlier had not allowed a foreign company to own the majority of the share capital of a subsidiary in Japan. The original mission of the branches was to sell a product line similar to the parent company's with a possibility for

●

This case was prepared by Jean-Pierre Jeannet, Professor of Marketing and International Business at Babson College, while teaching as Visiting Lecturer at Keio University Graduate School of Business in Tokyo. This case was prepared for the sole purpose of class discussion rather than to illustrate either effective or ineffective handling of an administrative situation. Copyright © 1980, Jean-Pierre Jeannet.

local production later on. At the outset, the company carried only medical equipment, such as surgical equipment for operating rooms and intensive-care or critical-care units. In 1971, diagnostic reagents were introduced as the second major product line. The planned introduction of dental equipment would represent the third major product line for AHS-Japan, with further additions planned every one to two years. The company had been successful practically from its inception, growing from originally three employees in 1968 to about fifty at the present time. Sales had shown a growth pattern of 50 percent compounded annually.

AMERICAN HOSPITAL SUPPLY CORPORATION BACKGROUND

American Hospital Supply was formed in 1922 as the first distributor specializing solely in products for hospitals. The company had concentrated on this segment for many years before introducing other product lines such as dental equipment and materials or scientific instruments. Today, the original hospital supply business accounted for about 50 percent of total sales of U.S. $1,002 million in 1974. The other major segments were science (32 percent of sales), medical and dental specialties (11 percent), and pharmaceuticals (7 percent). (See Exhibit 1.) The company had integrated backward over the years, producing approximately 45 percent of its sales through its own manufacturing subsidiaries. The approximately 24,100 employees serviced more than 140 countries through about 50 production centers and 120 sales or distribution centers. The product line comprised about 100,000 items.

EXHIBIT 1 ● Group Net Sales and Net Earnings

	1975		1974		1973		1972		1971	
NET SALES (IN MILLIONS OF DOLLARS)										
Hospital	$ 323.2	29%	$268.7	27%	$213.7	26%	$181.7	26%	$168.7	28%
Science Specialties	355.9	31	312.6	32	300.2	36	242.9	35	197.7	33
Medical Specialties	72.4	6	67.5	7	52.7	6	44.1	6	39.1	6
Pharmaceutical	91.1	8	74.8	8	62.0	7	54.9	8	51.0	9
Capital Goods	60.0	5	55.9	6	49.4	6	43.8	6	42.4	7
Dental	46.9	4	41.7	4	34.3	4	30.9	4	25.2	4
Dietary	43.8	4	39.6	4	30.0	4	24.0	4	21.2	4
Services	92.1	8	79.3	8	57.9	7	46.0	7	34.9	6
International	81.8	7	71.2	7	53.7	6	38.1	6	28.4	5
Unallocated eliminations and adjustments	(23.8)	(2)	(25.4)	(3)	(16.5)	(2)	(12.7)	(2)	(12.4)	(2)
	$1143.4	100%	$985.9	100%	$837.4	100%	$693.7	100%	$596.2	100%
Total international sales	$ 202.9	18%	$168.8	17%	$125.2	15%	$ 97.4	14%	$ 81.0	14%

AHS INTERNATIONAL OPERATIONS

AHS organized its international operations as a separate corporate group directed by a president. For 1974, net sales amounted to $104.2 million, of which $33 million represented exports by U.S. subsidiaries to AHS companies and clients outside the U.S. and Canada. Net earnings amounted to $2.4 million on International Group companies and another $6.1 million on the export transactions. The International Group had the responsibility for coordination of all domestic export shipments as well as direct responsibility for foreign-based operations. It has always been the strategy of AHS to concentrate on major markets with a sufficiently high level of health care to justify local operations. As a result, the group operated its 23 operations concentrated on just 14 markets.

PRODUCT LINES IN JAPAN

AHS-Japan's first product introduction consisted of a portion of the parent company's medical equipment line. Due to the competitive nature of the Japanese market, special emphasis was put on sophisticated products, particularly those with a focus on cardiac disease applications. As a result, the product line consisted of heart valves, pacers, bypass or intra-aortic balloon pumps, and surgical instruments for open-heart surgery.

As a newcomer to the market, the company found the distribution problem particularly vexing. The market for medical instruments consisted of hospitals and clinical laboratories and some general practitioners. The larger hospitals and clinics sought their equipment directly from domestic manufacturers, importing companies, or foreign affiliated subsidiaries

EXHIBIT 1 ● Group Net Sales and Net Earnings (*Continued*)

	1975		1974		1973		1972		1971	
NET EARNINGS (IN MILLIONS OF DOLLARS)										
Hospital	$ 19.3	35%	$ 13.7	29%	$ 10.0	25%	$ 7.5	21%	$ 6.1	21%
Science Specialties	16.5	30	14.6	31	13.6	33	12.3	34	10.7	35
Medical Specialties	6.8	12	5.9	13	3.7	9	3.4	10	2.6	8
Pharmaceutical	6.3	12	5.0	11	4.9	12	5.1	14	5.4	18
Capital Goods	3.0	6	2.3	5	2.2	5	2.0	6	2.1	7
Dental	2.4	4	2.6	6	1.8	4	1.5	4	0.4	1
Dietary	2.3	4	1.5	3	0.8	2	0.5	1	0.1	—
Services	1.8	3	3.0	6	1.6	4	0.9	3	0.6	2
International	.2	—	2.4	5	3.1	8	1.9	5	2.3	8
Unallocated interest, eliminations, and adjustments	(3.4)	(6)	(4.4)	(9)	(0.7)	(2)	0.6	2	(0.1)	—
	$ 55.2	100%	$ 46.6	100%	$ 41.0	100%	$ 35.7	100%	$ 30.2	100%
Total international earnings	$ 10.5	19%	$ 10.9	23%	$ 7.9	19%	$ 4.9	14%	$ 3.2	10%

Sales and earnings for each market group include their respective export and Canadian operations. Appropriate eliminations have been made to reflect group results on a consolidated basis. Normal income tax provisions, less tax incentives and adjustments, are reflected within reported group earnings.

The International Group has responsibility for coordination of all domestic export shipments as well as direct responsibility for foreign-based operations. Total international net sales and net earnings shown as separate amounts include Canadian operations and United States exports, royalties from foreign sources, income from foreign investments, and foreign exchange gains and losses in addition to the International Group foreign-based operations.

Unallocated eliminations and adjustments reflect transactions between groups as well as corporate interest income and expense and other miscellaneous adjustments. Such unallocated interest expense after taxes amounted to $3.2 million in 1975 and $3.6 million in 1974. Other corporate office expenses have been allocated to group operations on the basis of sales and number of employees in each group.

in Japan. All three of the above sources for medical equipment, however, also sold through a group of 27 specialized wholesalers who partially sold directly to smaller hospitals and clinics or resold to about 150 regional dealers. As it turned out, the 27 specialized primary wholesalers had strong ties to already established importers or domestic manufacturers and were therefore not willing to adopt a product line that was competing with one of their established suppliers. Furthermore, AHS-Japan's cardiac equipment was of the highest sophistication, requiring the sales force to be fully trained in and knowledgeable about heart surgery, something that trade salesmen of both primary and regional wholesalers could not be expected to be. This situation led to AHS-Japan's decision to sell directly to end users (see Exhibit 2).

EXHIBIT 2 ● Distribution Channels for Medical Equipment and Devices

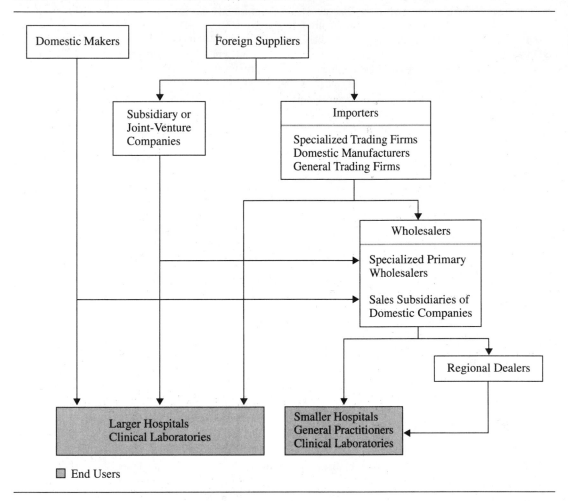

Following the introductory period, AHS-Japan continued to monitor the activities of medical equipment wholesalers in Japan. The company discovered that operating margins were relatively low, with net earnings averaging about 1 percent compared to 5.5 percent for AHS-US or 5 to 10 percent for typical U.S. dealers. While gross margins tended to be similar to those of the United States, Japanese intermediaries engaged in many additional activities and services of value to both suppliers and customers that were normally not performed by a wholesaler in the United States. Besides shipping goods to the customers, wholesalers gave general service, maintained excellent customer relations before and after the sale, collected valuable market information, sold repeat orders, and collected funds from their customers. Despite their gross margins,[1] these service functions

1. Gross margins for medical products varied substantially and depended on individual products. Items with low unit value and a large volume in repeat orders might carry margins as low as 15 percent. For equipment that required sophisticated service, long lead times, and relatively high unit value, the gross margins might be as high as 30 percent.

tended to reduce the net profit margin below a level typical for the United States. AHS-Japan also noted that wholesalers in Japan were able to carry out all of these functions at a lesser cost than a U.S. subsidiary due to their lower wages.

As a result, AHS-Japan decided later to include wholesalers in its distribution effort for medical equipment. The resulting savings in manpower, particularly since salesmen did not have to make monthly collection calls, added to AHS-Japan's sales productivity. Today, close to 80 percent of its sales were transacted through wholesalers or distributors. But the company believed these wholesalers to remain weak in promotion and technical after-sales service. Consequently, these two aspects continued to be supplied by AHS-Japan. As a result, AHS-Japan has been very successful competing with medical equipment in Japan.

Following the successful introduction of medical equipment, American Hospital Supply Corporation (AHSC) introduced clinical and diagnostic reagents. This product of the pharmaceutical industry was sold to the same targets as the medical equipment: hospitals, clinics, and general practitioners. Domestic producers only shipped about 30 percent of reagents directly, mostly to large hospitals or clinics; 70 percent was sold to 188 specialized primary wholesalers who partially sold directly to hospitals or supplied small regional wholesalers. These latter ones were not really necessary except that local governments preferred to deal with regional wholesalers. Foreign competitors could either sell through independent importers or distributors or could form a joint venture company in partnership with a Japanese company. Since clinical reagents had to be kept under refrigeration with special equipment, AHSC had to find a way to obtain cooperation of some of these primary wholesalers who supplied the largest market segment. Since it was very difficult to obtain their cooperation as a newcomer, AHS-Japan decided on a production joint venture with Green Cross Co., a highly respected drug manufacturer who also marketed whole blood. International Reagents Corporation, the JV manufacturing company, was then able to distribute its reagents through fifty of the primary wholesalers with the help of Green Cross Co. (See Exhibit 3 for marketing channels.) Again, the product introduction was successful.

OPPORTUNITIES IN THE DENTAL EQUIPMENT MARKET

The market for dental equipment and materials in Japan was one of the largest in the world. There were approximately 40,000 dentists in Japan, and about 2,000 entered the field each year. They spent approximately $500 million in 1975 for both equipment and materials. Materials included all items that were actually used up or consumed by the dentist in his practice, about $300 million annually. This amount was very high because it included precious metals, particularly gold, which accounted for 60 percent of the total used for fillings or tooth repair. Dental equipment, consisting of items such as chairs, lighting, handpieces, drills, etc., amounted to about $200 million annually. This latter segment of the market was of prime interest to AHS-Japan Corporation. Japan's 40,000 practicing dentists were trained in the country's twenty-seven dental colleges. Their income was relatively secure, because Japan's National Health Insurance Plan limited the amounts to be charged for a typical service. As a result, Japanese dentists had a tendency to see many more patients than their colleagues in Western countries—often forty to fifty per day. Since the equipment of a dental practice represented a very large outlay, Japanese dentists turned to the equipment manufacturers for help to finance their initial costs.

The market for dental equipment was essentially dominated by three firms: Yoshida, Morita, and Osada. Together they accounted for 80 percent of the market. Yoshida, with a market share of 30 percent, was selling equipment manufactured by itself. Morita, also with a market share of 30 percent, had a licensing arrangement with Ritter, a major dental company in the United States. In contrast to the United States, where a dentist might combine equipment from several manufacturers into a total package, the Japanese dentist only chose one manufacturer, who then provided the total service. To attract dental college graduates, the leading companies even assisted in planning, locating, and renting suitable buildings for dental practices and, in addition, provided the loans directly to the dentists to purchase or finance the practice. In the United States, the dentists typically received loans from a bank on their own, without involving the dental equipment manufacturer. Of course, the Japanese system provided for a very strong tie between the dentists and the major manufacturers. To assist in the servicing of its equipment, each manufacturer provided expert repair service through an extensive servicing network. It was believed that the "new" market to dental college graduates represented about 60 percent of the equipment market.

The remainder of the market consisted of replacement sales to established dentists and expansion of dental practices. This included most of the 40,000 practicing dentists. This segment of the market was dominated by twenty large wholesalers with strong contacts to the many retailers, or dealers, who were in almost daily contact with their dentists to supply

not only replacement equipment but primarily dental materials. The leading equipment manufacturers also used these intermediaries to sell in the replacement market.

Sharing the same distribution channel were the manufacturers of dental materials. This $300 million market consisted of 60 percent precious metals, primarily gold and silver. The market had been growing at a rate of 10 to 15 percent. The market for materials in Japan was dominated by a few large firms, with the top three alone accounting for 70 percent of the market. G.C. Dental Industries was the leader with 28 percent, followed by Sankin with 22 percent and Shofu with 20 percent of the market. These manufacturers made extensive use of the 800 to 900 large and

EXHIBIT 3 ● Distribution Channels for Clinical Diagnostic Reagents

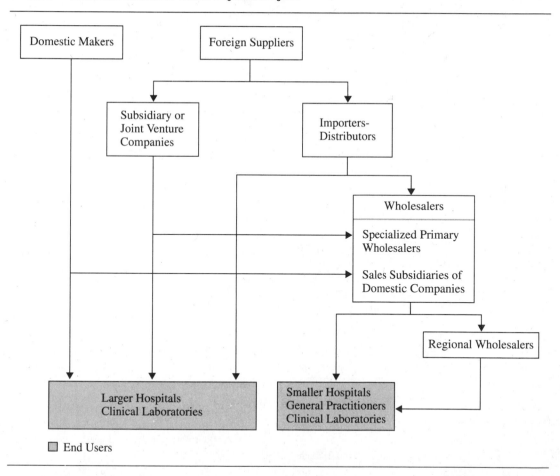

EXHIBIT 4 ● Distribution Channels for Dental Industry

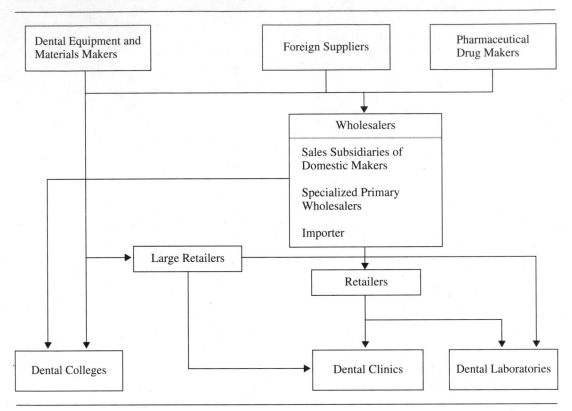

small retailers by selling to them either directly or through primary wholesalers (see Exhibit 4 for more details).

Sales to dentists took place almost on a daily basis. A retailer carrying one of the leading lines typically called the dentist in the morning and asked for the needs of the day. Orders were then accepted and shipped almost immediately. Contrary to equipment purchases, dentists sought materials from a number of manufacturers, "cherry picking" each line for its best products.

AHS-JAPAN'S LINE OF DENTAL EQUIPMENT

It was planned to introduce primarily handpieces, or "drills," and dental units (see Exhibits 5 and 6) made

by American Hospital Supply's midwest subsidiary.[2] The handpieces and dental units were generally regarded as the best in the industry, both in the United States and in Japan. While more expensive than competitive products by about 25 percent, they offered considerable benefits compared to other handpieces. Drill speeds were as high as 450,000 rpm, though some local competitors' products achieved even higher speeds. The speed could be gradually adjusted from zero to top speed with a foot pedal, whereas local competitors had no adjustable speed or foot

2. Midwest did not produce any other dental equipment such as chairs, lamps, etc.

EXHIBIT 5 ● Midwest Handpieces

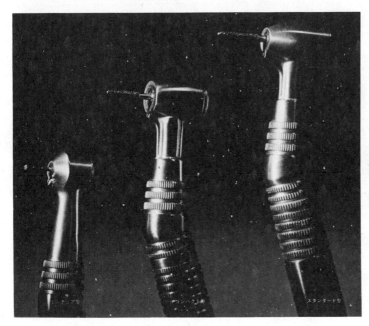

《エアータービン コントラアングル》
クワイエットエアー
スタンダード型
コンパクト型
ミニチュア型

回転ブレが無く、長寿命
磨耗の少ない特殊ボールベアリングと独特のメタルチャックシステムの採用により、バーのセンターリングは抜群。回転ブレが無いだけでなく、耐久性も連続回転試験で延べ800時間と、他社製品の2倍以上です。

強力で安定したトルク特性
高効率タービンと独自の軸受機構により、低速回転や加圧操作中においても安定した強いトルクを発揮します。

冷却効果の大きいスプレー
ヘッド先端のノズルからは冷却水が霧状になって噴出。形成歯牙を直接、効果的に冷やします。

ミッドウェスト社独自の4ホール方式
コントラ内には4本の（ドライブエアー用、エキゾーストエアー用、チップエアー用、水用）が独立して組込まれていますので――

① ●2ホール式よりさらに音が低くなります。
② ●スプレーの他にチップエアーだけ独立して使えます。
③ ●排気をユニットに回収するので清潔です。

①水 ②ドライブエアー ③エキゾーストエアー ④チップエアー

pedal. And finally, AHS units were generally considered to be superior to competitors' in styling.

Japanese dentists considered accuracy, quality, and high speed the primary criteria in selecting handpieces. In general, American equipment was highly regarded among Japanese dentists, many of whom knew Midwest equipment from their trips to conferences in the United States and Europe. In fact, some of them had purchased Midwest handpieces abroad or had written directly to the factory in the United States. In the past, Midwest had filled these orders despite the absence of a servicing network to assist the dentists.

The dental units were to sell at about 4.5 million yen,[3] compared to simpler ones available for as little as 2.5 million. Due to the expensive nature of AHS-Japan's equipment, the company considered the top 5 to 10 percent of practicing dentists as its main target market. Such dentists typically had been in business for several years and had achieved a relatively high income. When replacing equipment, they were more interested in status and willing to pay a premium price for what was considered the "Cadillac" of the industry. Of course, the products had to be adjusted to the Japanese environment. Because Japanese dentists

3. 250 yen = $1 U.S.

EXHIBIT 5 ● Midwest Handpieces (*Continued*)

〈エアータービン ハンドピース〉
ツルートルクショーティ Ⅰ型 Ⅱ型

低速使用時にも充分なトルク
エアータービンの高速回転を強力なトルクに変える画期的な
伝達装置。これが粘り強く安定した低速回転を実現しました。

優れた耐久性
回転部分の軸受けには特殊ボールベアリングを使用。長時間
にわたる苛酷な使用に耐えます。またエアーを動力源とします
から電気的トラブルなどに悩まされることなく、ほとんど故障
知らずです。

振動のないスムーズな回転
ボールベアリングの使用に加えて、ミッドウェスト独自のメタル
チャック方式の採用がバーの回転ブレを皆無にしました。ドリ
オット型のアタッチメント装置の場合もシッカリと安定します。

コントラ型の専用アタッチメントも用意
強力なトルクをそのままコントラアングルとしても使用できる専用
アタッチメントを用意しました。特にバランスを重視。交換操作は
ワンタッチです。

回転速度が自由にコントロールできる
ミッドウェストアメリカン社のユニットと組合せれば回転数を
フットペダルで自由にコントロール。どの回転領域でも有効な
力を発揮します。

チップエアー、スプレーが使用可能
必要に応じてスプレーホースを取付けることにより、チップエア
ー及びスプレーが使えます。

● Ⅰ型
変速リングを切換えることに
より、低速（200～6,000rpm）
から高速（6,000～25,000
rpm）まで自由に回転スピード
をコントロールできます。

● Ⅱ型
200～6,000rpmの低速領域
で高性能を発揮。回転スピー
ドのコントロールは自在です。

■専用アタッチメント（別売）

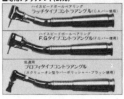
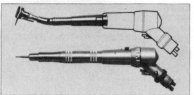

---

were smaller than their American colleagues, they preferred somewhat smaller chairs and lighter handpieces. Also, electricity in Japan was not everywhere the same: the western part used sixty cycles and eastern part fifty cycles. Some adjustment to the dental units was required, since in rural areas Japanese dentists worked on the traditional tatami (straw) mats and it was not possible to screw the equipment to the floor as was the case in urban areas or in the United States.

To facilitate such local adjustments, AHS-Japan planned to import the equipment initially from Midwest and later to move into local assembly, with local production as the ultimate goal. However, such adjustments to both dental units and equipment for an otherwise standardized product line would only be possible if AHS-Japan could guarantee sufficient sales volume to make the changes profitable.

SELECTION OF DISTRIBUTION CHANNEL

There were four basic options for AHS-Japan's entry into the dental equipment field. The company could (a) go directly to dentists with its own distribution setup or (b) use existing wholesalers and retailers to go to the market. The next two alternatives involved (c) some form of cooperation with one of the leading dental equipment manufacturers or (d) aligning themselves with a leading dental material supply manufacturer.

AHS-Japan had set several objectives for the introduction. The company wanted to become an important factor in the market, with a goal of a 10 percent market share for handpieces and 5 percent for dental units. Also, it was important to portray reliability, and if some form of arrangement were to be negotiated, it would have to be with a first-class company. And, finally, AHS-Japan wanted to open up

EXHIBIT 6 ● Midwest Dental Unit

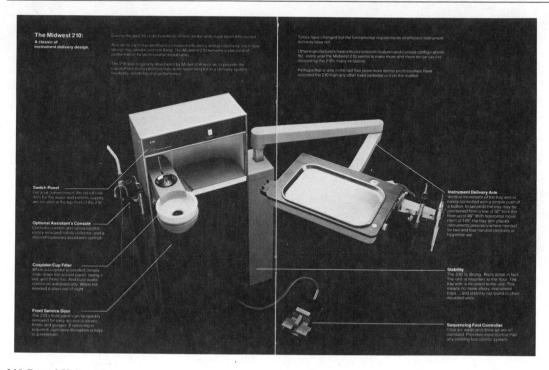

210 Dental Unit

Basic Unit (right- or left-   610090   Three Handpiece AUTOMATIC Activation and Syringe
handed versions)
                                                         Two Handpiece AUTOMATIC Activation and Syringe

                                                         Two Handpiece MANUAL Activation and Syringe

Basic Unit Includes: Midwest Tri-Clear® Syringe and Hose

                                                         Counter Balanced Tray Arm with:
                                                            a. Height adjustment button
                                                            b. Spray control knob
                                                            c. Water for handpiece cooling
                                                            d. Stainless steel tray
                                                            e. Warm water for three-way Tri-Clear Syringe
                                                            f. Air pressure gauge

                                                         Concealed Cuspidor with Automatic Flush and Gravity Drain

                                                         Concealed Cup Filler

                                                         Master Electric Switch

                                                         Flat Working Top

                                                         Variable Speed Foot Controller with Chip Air

                                                         Light Adapter Opening and Bracket
                                                         (Light Post Must Be Obtained from Light Manufacturer)

                                                         Duplex Electrical Outlet in Unit Base

EXHIBIT 6 ● Midwest Dental Unit (*Continued*)

---

210 Dental Unit (Continued)

Air Line Filter with Automatic Moisture Drain

Fused Electrical Service

Counterbalanced Accent Panel

Hydrocolloid and Drain Connection with Flow Adjustment

Dual Water Filtration System

Straight Handpiece Tubing with Midwest or Borden Back End

210 Dental Unit Accessories

Evacuation System	611467	Fittings for Central Suction Hi Volume Evacuation. Includes Solids Collector with Remote Switch for Central Pump and Saliva Ejector
	611472	Self-Contained Air Venturi Hi Volume Evacuation System with Fittings
Burner	303795	Bunsen Burner with Fittings
Syringe	611476	Tri-Clear® Syringe with Fittings (Auxiliary Syringe on Assistant's Console and Custom Installations)
Hoses	611328	Coiled Midwest 4-Hole Tubing (When Purchased with Unit) Also Available with Borden 2- and 3-Hole Tubing
	611329	Coiled Syringe Hose (When Purchased with Unit)
	731074	Fiber-optic Hose Installed 5′ Straight Hose with 10′ Fiber-optic Bundle
	731075	Coiled Fiber-optic Hose Installed

210 Dental Unit Accessories (Continued)

Oraluminator	731076	Oraluminator III Light Source with Remote Control Unit. Mounting Holes Predrilled in 210 Side Panel and Tray Bottom
HVE Hose	611481	Second HVE Hose (Central Vacuum Only)
Syringe	280022	Tri-Clear® Syringe
Installation Kit	610117	Kit for Field Installation of Assistant's Tri-Clear Syringe on 210 Unit (Does Not Include Syringe)
Tray Arm Lock	611494	U.S. Navy Tray Arm Locking Mechanism

---

channels for additional dental product introductions at a later time, both in the equipment and the materials segments of the market.

Alternative A: Going Direct

This would require AHS-J to sell directly to dentists, either to new graduates of dental colleges or estab-lished dentists, by use of a specially trained sales force. At this time, AHS-J did not have sufficient manpower to handle such a task, but additional personnel with sufficient qualifications could be hired and trained. AHS-J would also have to provide an extensive service network that could back up its selling effort. This was the option chosen for introduction of its medical equipment line.

Alternative B: Using Existing Intermediaries

AHS-J had the option of selling to its targets through the 29 primary wholesalers and 800 to 900 large and small retailers. Essentially, this was the channel used by the leading manufacturers for the replacement portion of their business. It would be necessary to gain the cooperation of a number of the primary wholesalers so that, in combination with their respective retail accounts, satisfactory coverage of the market could be established.

Using these intermediaries, however, would entail AHS-J assisting in the sales task by training the distributor sales personnel. Technical service, however, would have to be provided by AHS-J, since wholesalers and retailers were historically weak in that area. To some extent, this was the alternative selected for the medical equipment line following its successful initial introduction.

Alternative C: Cooperation with a Dental Equipment Manufacturer

The Japanese equipment manufacturers, which were now selling their own handpieces and dental units, were believed to be interested in using AHS-J's line as a new, top-of-the-line addition for dentists who were willing to pay for the added performance of Midwest equipment. Management believed that any one of the three leading manufacturers would be interested in carrying the line. Service could of course be handled by the Japanese manufacturer. However, management expected that whichever would be chosen as a distributor would require an exclusive arrangement for the Japanese market.

Alternative D: Cooperation with a Dental Materials Manufacturer

Over the past few years, manufacturers of dental materials had made attempts to invade the equipment market with their own products. Management therefore believed that any of the leading three materials manufacturers would be willing to carry the Midwest line as its entry into the dental equipment market. Sales would take place primarily through wholesalers and retailers which was the customary channel for the material segment of the dental market. Service would have to be provided in conjunction with AHS-J, since that was an important factor in the market.

THE REALITIES OF THE JAPANESE DISTRIBUTION SYSTEM

The choice of any of these basic alternatives greatly depended on AHS-J's objectives for its dental line in the Japanese market and on the "realities" of the Japanese distribution system, both in general and with respect to dental equipment and material.

One of the overriding factors in any Japanese distribution or business arrangement was the nature of the personal contact with one's business partners. In general, the Japanese did not like to conduct business with strangers, be that an unknown company or an unknown salesman. This often required that a businessman who wanted to see a particular person had to have an appropriate introduction. At best, this would be a good personal friend of the person to be visited, maybe even someone the latter was beholden to. Also, the higher the status of the person making an introduction, the better for later business. When no one could be found to give an introduction, sometimes a bank could serve as a reference. In any case, it was extremely difficult to see someone without an introduction, particularly when both the company and the person were unknown.

Another reality of business relationships was the loyalty displayed to existing contacts or associates. This was particularly strong in the channel structure. Over the years, manufacturers had become very close to their distributors and wholesalers, making it difficult for some to enact policies that would harm the other. Manufacturers would, whenever possible, tie wholesalers to their operations by granting liberal trade credit. Wholesalers in turn would do likewise with "their" retailers. As a result, a retailer would often be hesitant to carry a new, or even competitive, product from another wholesaler for fear of alienating his established supplier and hence endangering his source of financing. Such ties also existed between retailers and customers. In the extreme, a market could at times be virtually locked up through existing relationships making it extremely difficult for a newcomer to enter.

With respect to trends in the dental market, one important factor was the attempt by both the equipment manufacturers and material producers to invade each other's territory. Both groups maintained strong controls with "their" loyal group of wholesalers and retailers, ensuring the "Big Three" of each group coverage of the entire Japanese market.

It was these general factors, combined with AHS-J's intermediate and long-term objectives, that the company's management had to consider. Whatever the company decided, it would also have to gain the support of its parent organization.

Case 7

General Concepts

During spring of 1977, William P. Edwards, director of corporate marketing communications of General Concepts, was conducting a review of his company's approach to international advertising. During the last four years, the European subsidiaries had become more independent in their approach to advertising causing General Concepts to present a sometimes different image to its worldwide clientele. It was up to Edwards to choose from several possible alternatives a workable structure for General Concepts' international advertising, keeping in mind General Concepts' corporate goals and the realities of the marketplace.

COMPANY HISTORY

General Concepts was incorporated in 1966 as a manufacturer of small and medium sized general purpose digital computers. The company grew very quickly from sales of $2 million in 1969 to sales of over $180 million for fiscal year 1976 (see Exhibits 1 and 2 for financial summaries). At the same time, the company expanded its product line to include peripheral computer equipment, software and software services, and maintenance and training services for its clients.

●

This case was prepared by John Bleh, Research Assistant, under the direction of Jean-Pierre Jeannet, Professor of Marketing and International Business at Babson College, as a basis for class discussion rather than to illustrate either effective or ineffective handling of an administrative situation. Copyright © 1987 by Jean-Pierre Jeannet.

Traditionally, the electronic data processing industry had been characterized by a rapid technological process and price reductions. Some of the company's competitors, such as Digital Equipment Corporation, were long established companies, with substantially greater resources than General Concepts. There were, however, also a number of competitors smaller than General Concepts. Since small and medium scale general purpose digital computers were usually sold outright rather than leased, manufacturers were attracted by the relative ease of entry into this market segment compared to large computers, where leasing terms required substantial financial resources on the part of the seller. Despite this tough competitive climate, and without benefit of exact industry statistics, General Concepts' management felt the company was one of the major manufacturers of small and medium scale general purpose digital computers for industrial and scientific applications. By the end of fiscal year 1976, a total of 33,900 units had been shipped to customers, compared with 3,150 units just four years before.

PRODUCT LINES

The company's product line consists of three basic segments: central processors, software, and peripheral equipment.

Central processors were marketed under the trademarks of Orion, MicroOrion, and Satellite. From a design point of view, all Orion line computers used the same central processor and peripheral equipment, although performance and price of each model were different. All Orion computers were 16-bit binary computers using medium and large-scale integration, with four accumulators, two of which could be used as index registers. Parts, service, and additional

717

EXHIBIT 1 ● Financial Summary (in Thousands of Dollars, except per Share Data)

	1976	1975	1974	1973	1972	1971	1970	1969
Expenditures for property, plant, and equipment	15,277	7,344	6,458	6,674	3,897	770	456	102
Current assets	137,523	102,865	61,137	41,227	30,232	23,020	5,225	854
Current liabilities	50,337	25,721	26,595	14,152	7,600	2,677	1,175	523
Working capital	87,186	77,144	34,542	27,075	22,632	20,343	4,050	331
Stockholders' equity	114,787	92,224	48,809	37,245	27,080	21,446	4,377	429
Per share data:								
Outstanding shares (000)	9,839	8,787	8,386	8,421	7,980	6,976	5,946	4,841
Net income per share	$2.11	1.53	1.21	.81	.49	.22	.11	(.06)
Return on average assets	14.4%	13.6%	16.0%	15.4%				
Return on average equity	20.1%	19.1%	23.5%	20.8%				
Cumulative computers shipped	33,900	25,500	19,300	11,000	4,170	1,710	690	110
Employees at year-end	6,190	3,610	3,650	1,910	840	480	240	90

	1977 (estimate)	1976	1975	1974	1973	1972	1971	1970	1969
Net sales	$250,000	$180,000	$119,611	$92,952	$59,558	$30,324	$15,341	$7,035	$2,000
Costs and expenses		141,104	94,659	73,910	47,491				
Income from operations		38,896	24,952	19,042	12,067	3,897	1,561	433	(300)
Other income, principally interest		2,832	1,368	889	1,145			200	32
Interest expense		(406)	(365)	(437)	(141)				
Income before income taxes		41,322	25,955	19,494	13,071				
Provisions for income taxes		19,295	12,479	9,368	(6,220)				
Net income		$ 22,027	$ 13,476	$10,126	$ 6,851	$ 3,897	$ 1,561	$ 633	$ (268)

EXHIBIT 2 ● Consolidated Balance Sheet

	September 25, 1976
ASSETS	
Current assets:	
Cash	$ 597,000
Short-term investments, at cost and accrued interest, which approximates market	35,716,000
Accounts receivable, less allowance for doubtful accounts of $2,500,000 in 1977 and $2,200,000 in 1976	46,853,000
Inventories	54,009,000
Prepaid expenses	348,000
Total current assets	137,523,000
Property, plant, and equipment, at cost	39,676,000
Less accumulated depreciation	12,075,000
Total property, plant, and equipment, net	27,601,000
	$165,124,000
LIABILITIES AND STOCKHOLDERS' EQUITY	
Current liabilities:	
Notes payable, including accrued interest	$ 5,466,000
Accounts payable	19,576,000
Accrued payroll and commissions	2,685,000
Federal, state, and foreign income taxes	15,665,000
Deferred income taxes	4,515,000
Other accrued expenses	2,430,000
Total current liabilities	50,337,000
Stockholders' equity:	
Common stock, $.01 par value:	
Authorized—20,000,000 shares	
Issued—	
9,574,000 shares at September 24, 1977	
9,474,000 shares at September 25, 1976	95,000
Capital in excess of par value	58,245,000
Retained earnings	56,488,000
	114,828,000
Less: Treasury stock at cost (48,000 shares)	1,000
Note receivable from sale of stock	40,000
Deferred compensation	—
Total stockholders' equity	114,787,000
	$165,124,000

equipment for old and new models were continuously kept available. Orion computers were mostly sold to original equipment manufacturers (OEMs) to be added to machines or systems for controlling discrete assembly line operations, monitoring continuous production processes, testing, production planning, inventory management, and environmental surveillance. Furthermore, Orion computers had been successfully employed in scientific and engineering problem solving, medical and scientific laboratory analysis, and education. Orion models were marketed under model numbers Orion 120/121/122, Orion 80/82, Orion 84, ORION 2, ORION 83, ORION 3/300 and SC/400 (see Exhibit 3).

As a more powerful extension of the Orion models, the SATELLITE line was developed in 1975. The three models S/10, S/20, and C/30 were aimed at large and complex applications in both general scientific and business operations. For this latter segment, the C/30 was equipped with a commercial instruction set, report generating program, and a data file management system. Within the first twelve months of introduction, over 1,000 SATELLITE systems had been

installed at an average value of about $60,000 per system.

The MicroORION, introduced in 1976, was a family of microprocessors but also available as a fully equipped computer with software and peripheral equipment.

General Concepts also marketed peripheral equipment to satisfy the needs of clients who preferred to purchase systems as complete packages. Produced and sold were teletypewriters, paper tape readers and punches, cathode ray tube terminals, magnetic disc memories, magnetic tape equipment, line printers, plotters, card readers, communications controllers, multiplexors, and analog-to-digital as well as digital-to-analog converters.

In conjunction with its central processors, General Concepts developed and offered an extensive list of *software products* to be used with its ORION, SATELLITE, and MicroORION lines. Such software systems could be sought on a prepared basis or, if contracted by the customer, developed to fit special needs.

Not yet on sale but planned for introduction

EXHIBIT 3 ● Chart of Computer Families

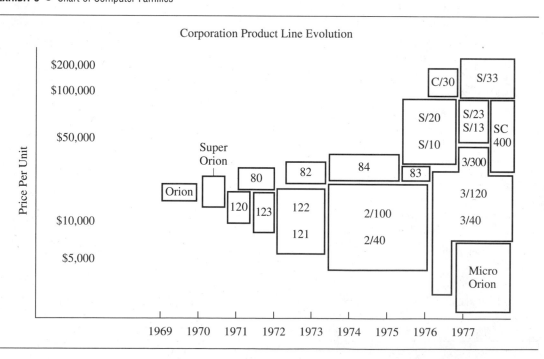

within the next few months was a new family of small business computers, the SC/400 family. The product family was designed for business information processing for small to medium sized companies with sales ranging from $500,000 to $20 million. Also, the SC/400 computers could be used by departments or regional offices at large corporations as part of a distributed processing network. Operated on a transaction-by-transaction basis rather than batch process and with as many as nine stations operating simultaneously and independently, the system offered advantages not presently available in other small business systems. The SC/400 family, made up of three models, was priced from $30,000 to $90,000 per system.

SALES AND DISTRIBUTION

While manufacturers of large computer systems, such as IBM, sold their products directly to end users, small computers were generally sold through intermediaries. General Concepts was typical of such small computer manufacturers, selling about 30 percent of its products directly to end users and 70 percent through four major types of intermediaries: original equipment manufacturers (OEMs), systems integrators, industrial distributors, and retail stores or dealers (see Exhibit 4).

Direct sales were made by more than 420 sales engineers and 220 systems engineers operating from various sales offices in the United States and abroad. With the increase in direct sales activities, General Concepts developed a more specialized sales force such as for micro products, technical systems, or commercial systems. In some cases, sales representatives were targeted at special industry segments such as medicine, banking, or government.

OEMs had long been the most important segment for small computer manufacturers. These companies combined computer hardware (central processors, terminals, storage equipment, etc.) with other equipment to produce products such as electronic cash registers, body scanning equipment, microfiche developers, or numerically controlled machine tools to be sold under the OEM's own name. The small computer was actually "buried" inside the OEM's product. In many instances, the end user of the product was not aware of the supplier of the computer portion contained in the end product.

Systems integrators (SIs) and small business systems suppliers formed the fastest growing segment in the distribution of small computers. Unlike OEMs, SIs bought their computers already assembled into a system from a single computer vendor, such as General Concepts. SIs added value to the product they resold in the form of application software designed to do a specific job: inventory control, order entry, accounting, and so on. Many SIs were originally service bureaus that had accepted data processing work for clients who had insufficient in-house information processing capacity or capabilities. Some SIs also offered installation assistance, diagnostic help, and field maintenance. Since the demand for application software and support had exceeded the capabilities of both the traditional and minicomputer vendors, this segment could be expected to continue its rapid development and growth.

Industrial distributors were an important distribution channel for all those computer products sold in large numbers approaching the sale of a commodity. Microprocessors (also called computer on a chip) or operator terminals were bought by users on that basis as components for their own products. The strength of the industrial distributor was to offer an immediate local supply of the components to the OEMs.

Retail distributors formed the latest distribution segment. The "computer store" displayed small computer systems or microprocessors of several manufacturers for purchase by individuals. Originally frequented by hobbyists, computer stores increasingly served small businesses by assisting them in selecting computers on the basis of ease of use, pricing, and overall capability.

Service and maintenance of General Concepts' products was supported by about 800 field engineers, both to fulfill product warranty service and to service installed machines on a service contract basis.

GC'S ADVERTISING STRATEGY

GC's communication strategy was dominated by the existence of three primary customer groups: OEMs, systems houses, and direct end users. GC's advertising was primarily directed at this latter group, the clients that bought GC equipment directly from the manufacturer and, to a smaller degree, from systems

EXHIBIT 4 ● Channels of Distribution

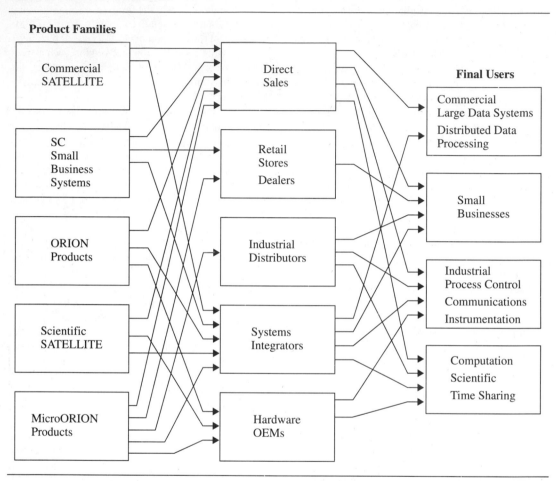

Product Families

Commercial SATELLITE	Direct Sales	**Final Users**
SC Small Business Systems	Retail Stores Dealers	Commercial Large Data Systems Distributed Data Processing
ORION Products	Industrial Distributors	Small Businesses
Scientific SATELLITE	Systems Integrators	Industrial Process Control Communications Instrumentation
MicroORION Products	Hardware OEMs	Computation Scientific Time Sharing

As can be seen in the graph above, while sale of computers directly to users by General Concepts has increased substantially, the systems integrators, distributors, and retail channels have become increasingly important. Many of the product and service departments described in this section should stimulate this rapid growth further in the year ahead.

houses. These customers again could be divided into two main user groups: clients for business data service processing and clients who used GC products primarily for science, industrial computing, and process control of manufacturing operations. GC had to communicate its products' features to these prospective clients.

GC believed that there was a difference in target group for computers for business use versus scientific or manufacturing control use. The main target group for computers with application for business data proc-

essing were corporate managers, particularly presidents, VPs of finance, and chief operating officers, in addition to data processing executives. The important aspect was to justify a choice of acquiring little-known GC computers instead of machines manufactured by larger mainframe companies such as IBM and Honeywell. GC's strategy was to reduce the risk as perceived by company executives for such a decision by using a message that was essentially nontechnical. This approach was selected since nontechnical executives, or generalists, had to make a technical, or data processing, decision with little knowledge of the hardware aspects of the computers to be chosen.

GC therefore occupied the position of a newcomer or outsider in the market for small computers. To compete against its better known competitors such as Digital Equipment Company or Hewlett-Packard, GC selected a communications strategy that depicted the company as unique, often bizarre, a company with a chip on its shoulder, using advertising copy that paid little attention to plain facts. Recognizing that technical or line managers paid greater attention to the products themselves whereas corporate officers were primarily risk averse, GC often chose testimonials of successful applications of its computers as a basis for its message development.

With respect to the scientific and industrial applications, corporate managers were involved to a lesser extent. Technical managers such as manufacturing managers, research directors, senior systems engineers, and scientists had a somewhat greater influence on the selection process. These technical managers were more likely to select a piece of equipment on its technical merit alone. As a result, technical or product oriented copy played a somewhat larger role for this market segment than for business data processing applications.

GC advertising in the United States was almost exclusively in print. Due to the fact that corporate management was the primary audience, about 75 percent of the advertising expenditures were concentrated on the *Wall Street Journal* and *Business Week.* Additional space was bought in other leading executive magazines such as *Forbes, Dun's,* and *Fortune.*

GENERAL CONCEPTS' INTERNATIONAL OPERATIONS

From its early existence, General Concepts had been selling abroad. Total international sales as a percentage of total corporate sales grew from 23 percent in 1971 to 41 percent in 1976. This rapid growth brought about the formation of many subsidiaries, particularly in Europe, and the establishment of production units in South Korea and Hong Kong. General Concepts' international sales developed as follows for 1971–1977:

	Sales in dollars	*Percentage of consolidated sales*
1971	$ 3.4M	23%
1972	7.8	26
1973	17.2	29
1974	25.1	27
1975	42.8	39
1976	72.3	41
1977 (est.)	80.0	—

General Concepts had seventeen wholly owned foreign sales subsidiaries and two production subsidiaries. Aside from European sales subsidiaries, General Concepts maintained subsidiaries in Canada, Australia, New Zealand, Brazil, Venezuela, and Israel. Japan was served through a licensing agreement with Nippon Computer Corp. since 1971. Whenever new products were introduced, they were made available to all the sales subsidiaries simultaneously, both in the United States and abroad.

GENERAL CONCEPTS' EUROPEAN OPERATIONS

General Concepts maintained eleven wholly owned sales subsidiaries in each of the following countries:

	Year formed
United Kingdom	1971
Germany	1971
Spain	1971
France	1972
Netherlands	1972
Austria	1972
Italy	1973
Sweden	1974
Switzerland	1974
Denmark	1975
Belgium	1975

European sales had shown the same rapid development as sales in the domestic market or other international sales, quickly growing from about $1 million, or 7 percent of corporate sales in 1971, to about $50 million, or about 30 percent of corporate sales in 1976. In general, European area sales represented 70 percent of General Concepts' international sales. The bulk of these European sales was accounted for by the subsidiaries in the United Kingdom, Germany, and Spain, in that order of importance.

As a result of General Concepts' rapid growth in Europe, several changes in its operational set-up had to be made. The most important move came in 1972 when General Concepts consolidated under the direction of Jack Bailey, since succeeded by Steve Blair, all its European subsidiaries into General Concepts Europe, Inc., with operations headquartered in Paris. Blair, vice president Europe for General Concepts, controlled the European subsidiaries through four area managers, each of whom had three to four subsidiaries assigned. A specialized group of staff personnel was maintained at the office of General Concepts Europe in Paris. (See Exhibit 5.)

The managers of the local subsidiaries maintained a considerable degree of autonomy over their operations inasmuch as each subsidiary was a separate profit center. In line with their P&L responsibility, subsidiary managers decided which products to carry in their product line and how to budget for their marketing expenditures, including advertising.

INTERNATIONAL ADVERTISING AT GENERAL CONCEPTS THROUGH 1976

In the early stages of market development, all advertising for Europe was done in the United States by Henderson, Sloan, Williams, Inc., New York, one of the leading advertising agencies in the United States. Henderson also made all media purchases in New York. With the formation of General Concepts Europe in 1972, the newly appointed vice president Europe had a communications manager reporting to himself, located in Paris. This communications manager also worked on PR assignments. Essentially, all creative work, however, was done by Henderson and then sent to Europe. No clear-cut advertising policy existed, and Europe's largest subsidiary, General Concepts Limited in the United Kingdom, had about

ten advertisements produced locally by a small, technically oriented advertising agency.

In 1973, Edwards was hired as director, corporate communications. During his first trip to Paris that same year, Edwards hired Alain Ray to fill the recently vacated position of communications manager. Ray had come to General Concepts from Hewlett-Packard's European headquarters in Geneva, Switzerland.

While in Paris, Edwards made a number of changes in the reporting structure as well. He decided to centralize all advertising for Europe under Ray. Each major subsidiary hired its own marketing communications expert, called MCE, responsible to Ray in Paris who in turn reported directly to Edwards at General Concepts' headquarters in Connecticut.

Creative work continued to be done by Henderson in New York for the U.S. market. This material was sent to Ray in Paris, who, together with his MCEs for the various countries, made suggestions as to how the advertising could be adapted to each individual market. All space purchased for print media continued to be handled in New York by Henderson, Sloan, Williams.

In 1973, Henderson introduced an independent agency "network" to better control the series of changes made in the various countries' advertising. These agencies, selected by Henderson in Germany, Spain, and the United Kingdom, allowed the adaptations to be made with the same degree of continuity or oneness throughout all markets but with changes for each local market as needed. This additional measure of decentralization was felt necessary to allow local changes while continuing to project the same image in all European countries. So by 1974, Ray had about seven MCEs reporting to himself but continued to report to Edwards.

In 1975, two important events substantially affected General Concepts' approach to international advertising. First, Edwards left the company (to return about two years later to assume the same position). In the same year still, Henderson, Sloan, Williams, General Concepts' advertising agency for several years, was fired, and the account was assigned to Nazzaro Associates, Inc., in Los Angeles, with E. Richard Steele as account executive. Since Nazzaro was not asked initially to handle European advertising, Ray at General Concepts Europe assumed greater control,

EXHIBIT 5 ● Organization Chart

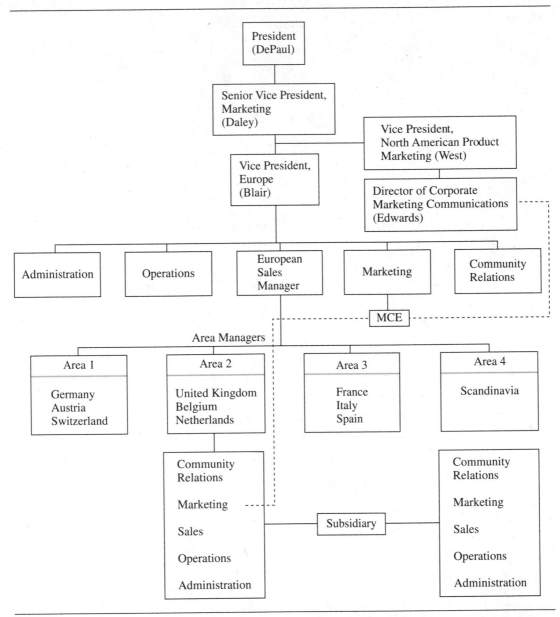

continuing to work with each local agency. Local subsidiaries were allowed to appoint and/or continue with their own local advertising agencies to either adapt U.S. creative work from Nazzaro or to create their own material. Only after the creation of the advertis-

ing did it have to be submitted to Ray in Paris. As a result, General Concepts' advertising began to assume a different look in each country, with Nazzaro in Los Angeles essentially used for General Concepts' North American business only. By 1976, General

Concepts Europe had, in the eyes of the U.S. parent company, become sufficiently mature to handle its advertising more independently. As a result, Ray reported now directly to the new VP in Europe, Larry J. Bailey. Any adaptations made in Europe were only checked by William P. Edwards, who had returned to General Concepts in 1977 with the title of corporate director of marketing communications.

PROBLEMS WITH GENERAL CONCEPTS' EUROPEAN ADVERTISING

Ever since its entry into the European market General Concepts had to face situations that at times differed significantly from its U.S. environment. General Concepts' approach of being unique, at times even bizarre, led to the creation of advertisements that in the eyes of General Concepts' European subsidiaries were ill suited for their markets and could not be adapted.

General Concepts had experienced three basic difficulties with the extension of all its ads to Europe. First, General Concepts in the United States used minority groups in its advertisements. European subsidiaries were opposed to using such pictures with minority members on the grounds that Europeans could not identify with black computer specialists since many companies had no blacks in such positions. Second, the direct naming of a competitor, a practice often used by General Concepts, was accepted only in the United Kingdom and against the law in most other countries. For all other European subsidiaries a different message had to be created. And finally the sweepstake campaigns so successful in the United States were outlawed in many European countries, Germany among them, and were eventually only instituted in the United Kingdom and Sweden.

The difficulty of General Concepts' advertising situation was best expressed by three very successful U.S. ads that all were either substantially changed or not run at all in Europe. General Concept used one ad with ''hillbillies,'' capitalizing on the wide knowledge and positive general attitude toward such persons in the United States. However, when General Concepts tried to run the same ad in Europe its subsidiaries objected since such hillbillies did not exist as a separate identifiable group in Europe nor was there an appropriate concept to express it, therefore

completely losing the desirable message of the ad.

A similar reaction was found toward General Concepts' ''Redneck'' ad depicting General Concepts' computers as breaking the speed barrier without paying the price: hence, identification with the ''redneck'' sheriff as a folk hero. But this image did not exist in Europe, and the ad would have lost its punch line. Furthermore, the Italian subsidiary objected since in Italy nobody wearing a uniform, either police, military, or otherwise, could be depicted in advertising. And one ad, showing a picture of a man hanging by his thumbs to visualize the result of ''One test of a computer company is the kind of support you get after the sale,'' was rejected by General Concepts' German subsidiary since the meaning of the ad conveyed a sense of terrorism in Germany. Another successful U.S. ad, with the slogan ''With some computer companies you can end up paying for more company than computer,'' showed a steak with a lot of fat indicating the overhead associated with General Concepts' bigger competitors. However, when the message was translated for German customers, the meaning communicated by the picture turned out to be just the opposite one because the steak with fat had a positive connotation to Germans. And finally, General Concepts had some problems with the ad ''When your business expands and your computer can't, where does that leave you?'' combined with the picture of a single hand holding a bag. In the United Kingdom, the same meaning was expressed by the phrase ''don't get left holding the baby,'' while in France the expression centered around ''being in a basket of crabs.''

In general, General Concepts' creative philosophy did not always translate very well since the U.S. idiom in terms of both copy and visual could not be extended abroad. These problems were most extreme with Germany, somewhat less with Italy and France, while both Scandinavia and particularly the United Kingdom offered greater opportunities for General Concepts' U.S. approach.

An additional problem was created by General Concepts' U.S. advertising emphasizing products only and therefore not developing any company image ads as requested by its subsidiaries. Since in many European countries General Concepts was not very well known, some subsidiaries, notably the Italian unit, were authorized to create special advertisements to improve their markets' awareness of General Concepts as a small computer manufacturer. In 1976, Nazzaro had recommended that each area develop testimonial ads for its area. That program was ongoing and apparently successful.

ALTERNATIVES TO GENERAL CONCEPTS' APPROACH TO ADVERTISING IN EUROPE

Upon his return to General Concepts, Edwards and Nazzaro felt that General Concepts' advertising in Europe had to be revised to follow general corporate philosophy and present a uniform image to all customers, both domestic and foreign. Over the last two years, General Concepts' advertising in the various European countries had become fragmented and did not offer the uniform image it once had.

General Concepts aimed at presenting a unified look to all its customers all over the world, and this goal was presently not achieved in Europe. This desire for a unified look had already resulted in a corporate identity program to cover the corporate mark, stationery, business cards, printed sales promotion material, personal identifications, product identification, and signage. The program was put forward in a manual with a cover letter written by DePaul, General Concepts' president (see Exhibit 6). The program did not pertain to the company's worldwide advertising effort. Furthermore, Edwards felt he lacked leverage with Ray reporting to Bailey to exercise any kind of control or influence over Europe's advertising. While the mechanics of the advertising side were well taken care of, General Concepts Europe depended largely on these small local agencies for creative input as well as for marketing expertise.

In Edwards' view, leverage, mechanics, creative input, and marketing expertise, combined with people relationships among different ad agencies and subsidiaries, substantially affected productivity and advertising quality. Since the subsidiaries had selected their own agencies, people relationships were likely to be good. However, Edwards believed that without additional control he could not significantly influence the European subsidiaries' advertising approach. In his words, "Control does not necessarily mean direct control. It means a method to project a better understanding of what General Concepts wants in all of its communication endeavors."

As he approached the decision, Edwards believed he had four basic alternatives to improve General Concepts' present setup in Europe: (a) assign authority to Nazzaro Associates for both domestic and European advertising; (b) have General Concepts create a "network" of different European advertising agencies selected by Edwards for better control and assigned to each subsidiary; (c) keep present European agencies but coordinate their efforts through General Concepts in Southern California; and finally (d) assign the creative strategy and execution of the international advertising program to a large New York agency with its own network of international affiliates in place.

At about the same time as Edwards was reviewing his alternatives in Europe, Nazzaro Associates also became dissatisfied with General Concepts' setup and proposed its own solution to the problem. Nazzaro wanted the responsibility to create advertising for General Concepts' domestic and international business, which meant that it was Nazzaro who supplied the creative work for all General Concepts ads. However, Nazzaro did not have any foreign affiliates to carry out this proposal on its own. To compensate for this lack of foreign contacts, Steele proposed that Nazzaro affiliate with Ed Hopkins Europe, a large and well-known international advertising agency headquartered in New York, who would supply the foreign expertise to Nazzaro. Ed Hopkins had its European headquarters in Paris and subsidiaries in European countries where General Concepts' own subsidiaries were located. Under Steele's plan, Nazzaro would supply drafts of all creative work to Ed Hopkins in Paris. Ed Hopkins' people would review the potential need for changes by contacting their own locally affiliated agencies, who would discuss each proposed advertisement with General Concepts' local MCEs. The reviewed proposals would then be returned to Nazzaro with any changes indicated. Proposed concept changes would also be added. The final result would be advertising concepts and copy that could be adopted by all subsidiaries with only local translation done under the supervision of the local Ed Hopkins affiliate. Advertising media space would be purchased by Ed Hopkins Europe under coordination with local subsidiaries.

Of course, as an alternative, General Concepts could create its own network of affiliated advertising

EXHIBIT 6 ●

A CORPORATE IDENTITY PROGRAM
FOR GENERAL CONCEPTS CORPORATION

General Concepts is one of the world's fastest growing organizations, in one of the fastest growing industries.

As we continue to expand worldwide, it is essential that the company maintain a clear and consistent visual identity with customers, employees, and other important audiences.

The enclosed is an interim guideline that covers the major aspects of General Concepts' corporate identity program.

The elements of the program reflect the "face" of the company—progressive, experimental, innovative, fast moving.

Through these elements, we hope to create a thread of graphic continuity woven into our worldwide corporate identity program in all areas whether it be brochure, sending a bill, plus all of the numerous other ways you influence and communicate with our public.

I urge everyone to use this manual as the standard for corporate identity.

Robert DePaul
President

---

agencies. Such a network would be coordinated through General Concepts Europe in Paris. General Concepts would select in each country an appropriate agency who would be assigned to work with its local subsidiary. Nazzaro creative work would be circulated to each advertising agency, which would discuss the proposal with its assigned General Concepts subsidiary and review the creative necessary changes. These comments would be sent to John Clarke (who reported to Ray) at General Concepts Europe who in turn would confer with Richard Steele at Nazzaro. Edwards believed it would not be easy to select good agencies in each country. At the present time, he had no particular agencies in mind. Besides, Nazzaro had worked with the present network and found it wholly lacking. In production requirements alone (film screens for publication, etc.) the problems were monumental when you added the language barrier and the constant need to convert to metric measures.

A third alternative for Edwards was to work with those agencies already selected by each subsidiary but to attempt to control their creative output. He felt that

if each agency were required to execute its creative work locally under the guidance of General Concepts' general advertising directives and if each agency were required to submit all creative to General Concepts Southern California office for approval, some measure of common approach to General Concepts' image in Europe could be achieved. In fact, it would be up to Edwards and his office to coordinate Nazzaro creative strategy with the proposals from Europe to provide for the common image desired by General Concepts.

A fourth alternative available to Edwards was the selection of a large New York based advertising agency with good connections in Europe through either affiliates or subsidiaries. This agency would be given authority to execute General Concepts' advertising strategy outside the United States, based upon Nazzaro's initial creative proposals. This move meant to revert to the pre-1974/75 policy. While no serious discussions had taken place, Edwards thought that Marsteller might be a possibility to take charge under this alternative.

POTENTIAL REACTION BY AFFECTED PARTIES

In Edwards' view, all four alternative proposals reflected a considerable improvement over status quo. The adaptation of any of the alternatives would present General Concepts with additional leverage over the execution of its advertising in Europe, improve the creative input, and add some additional marketing expertise for the subsidiaries. While all four alternatives increased General Concepts' control over its European advertising, the four proposals, of course, did so to varying degrees, with Nazzaro's alternative or the big New York agency approach to be favored over the other alternatives.

An important consideration was also the views and possible reaction among General Concepts' European subsidiaries. Edwards knew that personal chemistry played a very important role in advertising and that the imposition of any agency selection in General Concepts' local subsidiaries might create tensions along that way. If the four proposals were presented to the subsidiaries for a free vote, he was convinced that the subsidiaries would prefer to continue to work with their own agencies over any other choice.

Edwards knew that it was up to him to determine the direction of General Concepts' advertising approach in Europe. With present European measured media expenditures for 1977 at $500,000 and European budget expenditures for the next fiscal year of approximately $700,000, he was determined to reach a decision that could be acceptable to most of the parties concerned.

Case 8

Puritan-Bennett Corporation Boston Division

As he stepped into the elevator at the Skyline Hotel in London, John Sweeney, vice president and general manager of the Boston Division of Puritan-Bennett Corporation, reflected on his problems and frustrations with the British market. He had been with Ray Oglethorpe, vice president for sales and marketing, and Bob Taylor, vice president for international operations, since early morning. It was a typical day for London in late November of 1983. They had been trying to determine the best distribution for Puritan-Bennett medical products in Europe for next year. John Sweeney suspected that some parent company current channels did not meet division needs.

Earlier that day they had met with Adamson and Carr Ltd., Puritan-Bennett's British distributor, to discuss plans and forecasts for division and corporate product lines. The three vice presidents had then reviewed the situation in the United Kingdom and the rest of Europe.

PURITAN-BENNETT CORPORATION

Puritan-Bennett Corporation was founded in 1913 as the Puritan Company, a welding supply manufacturer

and distributor. The company emphasized the manufacture and supply of medical gas and equipment. It had pioneered development of oxygen as a medicinal agent. The company manufactured and sold three product lines: medical, aviation, and industrial, with medical products accounting for the largest percentage of sales (Exhibit 1).

In 1956, acquisition of the Bennett Company accelerated corporate growth in the United States and abroad. The company, now known as Puritan-Bennett, had sales offices worldwide for medical, aviation, and industrial product lines. Expansion continued in the late 1970s and early 1980s through acquisition and research and development. In 1978 the medical line was extended by purchase of the Foregger Company, a manufacturer of operating room equipment. The Boston Division was acquired in 1981 (Exhibit 2).

DEVELOPMENT OF THE BOSTON DIVISION

In 1978, John Sweeney acquired the assets of a bankrupt company and started LSE Corporation. The firm initially employed a total of four people, including Sweeney. LSE had a small manufacturing facility. Included in the purchase was a line of screening spirometers in the process of development. The company specialized in developing and selling a full line of spirometers, used in doctors' offices and industrial clinics as screening devices to diagnose lung dysfunction (Exhibit 3). Until this time, most spirometry had been done in hospitals. While the test took only a few minutes of a patient's time, evaluation of test results was time consuming (about thirty minutes) and cumbersome. When a physician suspected a patient might be suffering from chronic obstructive pulmo-

EXHIBIT 1 ● Five-Year Financial Summary, Corporate and Subsidiaries (All dollar amounts in thousands, except common share data)

	1983	*1982*	*1981*	*1980*	*1979*
Operating Results					
Net Sales					
Bennett Division	$ 48,525	$ 47,505	$ 53,382	$ 47,464	$ 40,817
Puritan Division	37,944	35,859	33,889	29,431	26,903
Boston Division	5,614	5,208	1,282	—	—
Total Medical	92,083	88,572	88,553	76,895	67,720
Aviation Division	12,772	14,161	18,437	17,863	14,764
Industrial Division	4,890	4,424	5,562	5,361	5,262
Total Net Sales	109,745	107,157	112,552	100,119	87,746
Gross Profit	45,551	40,757	47,748	38,910	34,289
Percentage of Sales	41.5%	38.0%	42.4%	38.9%	39.1%
Marketing, Research & Administrative Expense	41,348	40,877	37,401	30,517	26,425
Operating Profit (Loss)	4,203	(120)	10,347	8,393	7,864
Other Income (Expense)	(407)	(6,551)	540	20	(81)
Income (Loss) Before Income Taxes	3,796	(6,671)	10,887	8,413	7,783
Percentage of Sales	3.4%	—	9.7%	8.4%	8.9%
Provision for (Benefit from) Income Taxes	1,220	(4,412)	4,335	3,628	3,118
Effective Tax Rate	32.1%	66.1%	39.8%	43.1%	40.1%
Net Income (Loss)	2,576	(2,259)	6,552	4,785	4,665
Percentage of Sales	2.3%	—	5.8%	4.8%	5.3%
Financial Data					
Net Working Capital	$ 39,126	$ 36,037	$ 39,079	$ 37,789	$ 34,761
Current Ratio	2.5	3.3	3.9	4.6	4.3
Long-Term Debt	9,131	6,089	7,599	7,327	8,813
Debt/Equity Ratio	13.0%	9.4%	10.9%	11.5%	14.3%
Stockholders' Equity	60,922	58,622	61,932	56,464	52,805
Return on Average Stockholders' Equity	4.3%	—	11.1%	8.8%	9.1%
Common Share Data					
Earnings (Loss)	$ .87	$ (.78)	$ 2.27	$ 1.66	$ 1.62
Dividends Declared	.40	.40	.40	.40	.40
Net Book Value	20.62	20.28	21.45	19.62	18.37
Average Number of Shares Outstanding	2,947,652	2,889,444	2,883,588	2,876,471	2,873,084
Other Data					
Depreciation and Amortization	$ 4,677	$ 4,865	$ 4,672	$ 4,197	$ 4,305
Capital Expenditures	7,287	6,415	7,057	3,933	4,851
Plant and Equipment, Net	30,710	27,996	28,666	26,682	27,087
Total Assets	$ 99,894	$ 83,204	$ 86,241	$ 77,015	$ 74,479
Number of Employees	1,893	1,869	2,080	1,978	1,837

EXHIBIT 2 ● Corporate Organization Chart

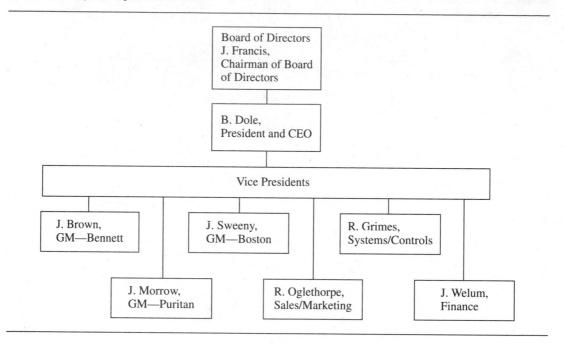

nary disease (COPD), he or she would recommend the patient be tested at a hospital.

A pioneer in the field, LSE offered within three years a broad range of microprocessing spirometers which allowed a doctor or nurse to evaluate test results in only five minutes. Improvements in technology led to a competitive price. In 1979 the top-of-the-line spirometer sold for $7,000 in the United States, and in 1981 for $4,500. John Sweeney's small company had grown to $3 million in sales and to an approximate 30 percent market share in the United States.

Puritan-Bennett acquired LSE Corporation in 1981 as part of an expansion program to increase the number of product lines and to upgrade the level of its microprocessing technology. An innovator in microprocessing spirometers, LSE met the parent company's need. Shortly after the merger, the renamed Boston Division joined another Puritan-Bennett acquisition, a firm manufacturing noninvasive blood pressure monitors. Noninvasive blood pressure mon-

itors measured blood pressure during surgery, during stress testing, and for chronically or critically ill patients (Exhibit 4). The newly organized Boston Division developed, coordinated, and manufactured spirometers and monitoring devices. Sales and responsibilities were divided between the division, which sold to individual physicians, and the company, which sold to hospitals and clinics. The Boston Division manufactured all spirometers in-house. Some monitoring devices were assembled from a combination of in-house product parts and purchased components. Others were imported through an arrangement with a Finnish company.

The Boston Division had recently moved to a larger manufacturing and sales facility in Wilmington, Massachusetts. The division employed seventy people to manufacture and sell spirometers and other division products. Three engineers researched and developed innovative pulmonary diagnostic and monitoring products.

EXHIBIT 3 ● PS600 Spirometer

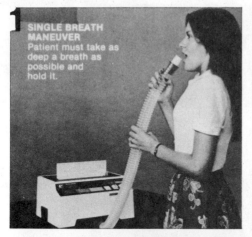

1 SINGLE BREATH MANEUVER Patient must take as deep a breath as possible and hold it.

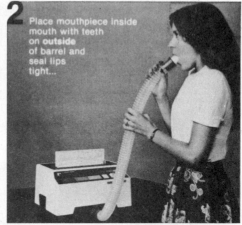

2 Place mouthpiece inside mouth with teeth on **outside** of barrel and seal lips tight...

3 Exhale the air as **force-fully** as possible from the beginning and keep exhaling until all the air is emp-tied out...

4 Remove mouthpiece and breathe normally.

MVV MANEUVER (Page 21 in Manual)

CAUTION: The MVV (Maximum Breathing Capacity) is a breathing stress test and should not be performed on patients with heart problems unless supervised by a physician.

1. Subject should take a deep breath before placing mouthpiece inside mouth with teeth on outside of barrel and lips sealed tight.
2. Instruct the subject to then breathe out and in as **rapidly** and **deeply** as possible.
3. Encourage the subject to continue to breathe in and out for a minimum of 10-12 seconds before telling them to stop.

FEF$_{25-75}$

This is the Forced Expiratory Flow during the middle 50% of the FVC curve.**

FEF$_{200-1200}$

This is the Forced Expiratory Flow between 0.2 liters and 1.2 liters.**

**If desired, this parameter may be calculated using the technique described on page 19 of the VS400 Operating Manual.

PURITAN-BENNETT CORPORATION

PURITAN-BENNETT CORPORATION OF MASSACHUSETTS
BOSTON DIVISION
265 BALLARDVALE STREET, WILMINGTON, MA 01887
(617) 657-8650 (800) 225-5344 TELEX 94-9467

EXHIBIT 4 ● D4000 Noninvasive Blood Pressure Monitor

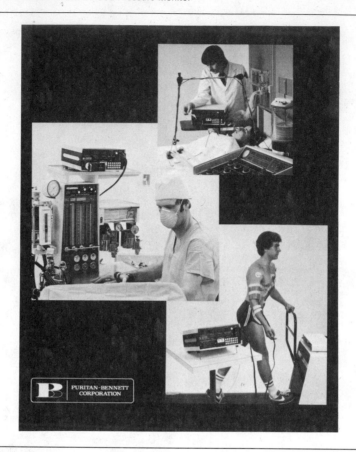

PURITAN-BENNETT CORPORATION

The Boston Division was most closely aligned with the Bennett Division, one of several Puritan-Bennett units. The Bennett Division sold life-supporting medical equipment, primarily ventilators, to hospitals. Ventilators assumed respiratory function, either short term for patients under anesthesia in the recovery room or in intensive care, or long term for terminally ill patients.

The Bennett Division had succeeded with its newest product, the 7200 Microprocessor Ventilator, which had sold well in the United States since introduction in 1983. Benefits of the new product included increased breathing ease for the patient, better oper-

ator control over ventilatory parameters, and lower operating costs. Products were competitively priced in the United States at $10,000 to $12,000 (Exhibit 5).

BACKGROUND ON SPIROMETRY

Spirometers were used to measure lung capacity and to diagnose lung dysfunctions. Lung dysfunctions could be categorized as restrictive, reducing volume (vital lung capacity), or obstructive, reducing flow through the airways, or a combination of both.

EXHIBIT 5 ● 7200 Microprocessor Ventilator

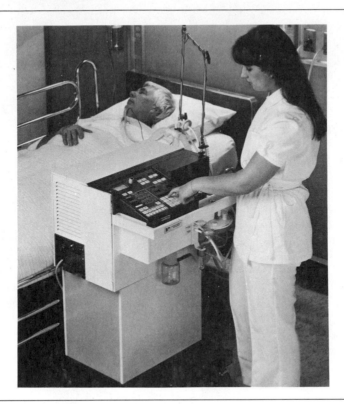

Spirometers were used in early diagnosis of chronic obstructive pulmonary disease (COPD), the sixth leading cause of death in the United States in 1980. Grouped under COPD were bronchitis, asthma, and emphysema. Leading causes of COPD were smoking, air pollution, occupational pollution, infection, heredity, aging, and allergies.

As depicted in Exhibit 6, air initially enters the body through the nose and mouth, then passes through the pharynx, larynx, trachea, bronchi, and bronchioles. At the chest cavity the trachea branches into two bronchi. Each bronchus subdivides, forming tiny tubes called bronchioles which open into small air sacks called alveoli. The alveoli form clusters around the bronchioles and unite into lobes. Each alveolus contains a meshlike network of capillaries, or

tiny blood cells. The lungs carry oxygen to the body by the air passage to the thin walls of the alveoli. Blood then absorbs the oxygen. The average office worker inhales 400 cubic feet of air each day, and the body absorbs an average of 20 cubic feet of oxygen.

Spirometer manufacturers had benefited in 1979 when U.S. health officials mandated spirometry for certain high risk groups. High risk groups included textile industry employees exposed to cotton dust, miners susceptible to black lung, and asbestos industry employees. A voluntary medical group had determined standards for spirometry, and government regulations later incorporated these standards. Some spirometer manufacturers were temporarily forced out of the market when their products failed to meet the new standards.

EXHIBIT 6 ● The Respiratory System

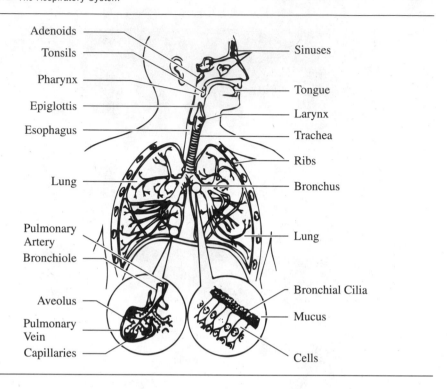

Adenoids
Tonsils
Pharynx
Epiglottis
Esophagus
Lung
Pulmonary
Artery
Bronchiole
Aveolus
Pulmonary
Vein
Capillaries

Sinuses
Tongue
Larynx
Trachea
Ribs
Bronchus
Lung
Bronchial Cilia
Mucus
Cells

BOSTON DIVISION SPIROMETRY PRODUCT LINE

Puritan-Bennett spirometers analyzed volume displacement and rate of airflow. The VS400 and the PS600 measured the volume of air inspired and expired and calculated flow. The DS705 and the ES800 measured the flow of air expired and calculated volume based on expiration speed and time (Exhibit 7). To perform the test, a patient inhaled deeply and exhaled forcefully into a tube connected to the spirometer. The test was repeated three times.

The VS400 and PS600 produced tracings of individual single breaths and maximum voluntary ventilation (MVV). While the VS400 still required hand calculations of pulmonary function parameters, the more advanced PS600 included a microprocessor to compute test results automatically. This innovation was considered key to the division's continued growth. The Boston Division was also working on an Apple software package allowing a physician to automate storage and retrieval of patient records on an Apple personal computer.

MONITORING PRODUCT LINE

Puritan-Bennett's Boston Division also manufactured monitors. Noninvasive blood pressure monitors were the only line of monitors produced in-house. Other monitors were imported from Europe for sale throughout the Western Hemisphere.

Blood pressure monitors measured the pressure blood exerted on arteries throughout the body. Blood pressure level depended on the rate of heart contraction, the amount of blood in the circulatory system, and the elasticity of arteries. Blood pressure was continuously monitored during surgery. Patients with

EXHIBIT 7 ● Spirometers

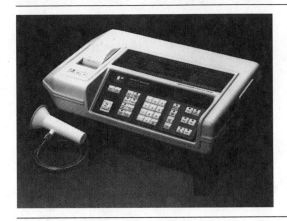 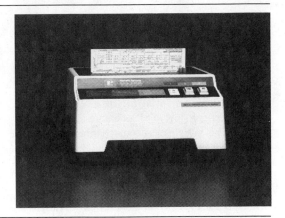

chronic diseases and those convalescing from acute diseases also required monitoring. Serious illness and surgery could alter blood pressure and thus needed to be controlled. A regular part of health checks, blood pressure screenings were particularly important for older people because blood pressure may rise with age.

Blood pressure was measured by pumping air into a bag or cuff fastened around the arm. Inflation continued until blood flow stopped. This measure, called systolic pressure, represented blood pressure when the heart contracted. Pressure when the heart relaxed between beats was called diastolic pressure.

The Puritan-Bennett D4000 and D4001 monitors could be used anywhere in a hospital and provided automatic inflation and deflation. The devices employed a patented infrasonde technique to monitor blood pressure continuously. Digital display of the blood pressure reading facilitated use by physicians or nurses. The product was designed for continuous monitoring rather than one-time screening.

THE U.S. MARKET FOR SPIROMETERS

The Boston Division, particularly strong in the U.S., enjoyed a 30 percent market share. Spirometer sales had reached $4 million in 1983 and were expected to account for 50 percent of Boston Division sales in 1984. There were 467,000 practicing physicians in the United States. Spirometers were used in doctors' offices, hospitals, and clinics. Boston Division strength

lay in the doctors' office segment, which included more than 100,000 physicians. The U.S. medical profession had begun to emphasize preventive health care, and John Sweeney believed that approximately 38 percent of practicing physicians could benefit from owning a spirometer. He estimated that only 30 percent of respiratory specialists or general practitioners currently employed spirometers in office. Spirometers were Puritan-Bennett's only medical product marketed to physicians' offices.

Physicians used spirometers primarily as a screening device. Lung screening was common in a variety of medical situations in the United States. Hospital admissions, preoperative checks, and annual checkups for senior citizens and smokers required lung screening as a part of regular test procedure. Many industries such as asbestos and mining regularly screened employees for lung dysfunction due to inhalation of dust or chemicals.

Most U.S. hospitals maintained respiratory therapy departments and pulmonary laboratories. Respiratory therapy departments treated lung problems early and monitored changes in patient progress during therapy. The spirometer was used for a five minute simple screening test of patients undergoing therapy before and after medication. The pulmonary laboratory evaluated chronically ill patients. Large pulmonary laboratory equipment cost from $50,000 to $75,000. Tests using such equipment were more extensive than those using spirometers and took longer to perform. The spirometer quickly screened large numbers of people, while the pulmonary laboratory equipment was used to evaluate treatment of patients identified as already having a lung dysfunction.

PURITAN-BENNETT CORPORATE MARKETING EFFORT IN THE UNITED STATES

Puritan-Bennett employed fifty-five salespersons to sell medical products to all operating divisions of a hospital. This sales force accounted for approximately $80 million in sales in 1983. Until 1983, Puritan-Bennett had sold through distributors in the U.S. market, with a trained sales force giving missionary support for all product lines. In early 1983, Puritan-Bennett began to sell equipment directly to hospitals. The decision to develop a direct sales force was based on two criteria. First, many distributors were not expanding sales volume according to company expectations. Second, the company expansion program was creating conflict. As Puritan-Bennett added new products to its line, it found that some dealers already carried similar competitive products. Furthermore, Puritan-Bennett's new technology for its 7200 microprocessing ventilator required extensive training for a highly technical sale. As the company continued to expand, these problems were expected to continue. Puritan-Bennett also used the cost savings on distribution margins to lower its prices. Selling costs now averaged 20 percent of sales.

BOSTON DIVISION U.S. MARKETING EFFORTS

Three segments composed division spirometry sales: hospitals accounting for 20 percent of total volume, industry with 20 percent, and physicians with 60 percent. Hospital sales were made by Puritan-Bennett's corporate sales force. The Boston Division had sole responsibility for marketing spirometers to private physicians and industrial users through 100 dealers. Most division volume came from the top 40 percent of these dealers. Dealers ranged from highly specialized ones to others carrying a broad line of medical equipment, accessories, and disposables. The best distributors were specialized either by area of medical expertise, such as cardiac or respiratory, or by end-user, such as hospitals or physicians' offices. Dealers were supported by a ten person missionary sales force

reporting to the division office in Wilmington. Three area managers representing east, central, and west regions reported to sales manager Bob Glinski. The missionary sales force was divided among the three regions. Bob Conley, one of the original employees at LSE, acted as marketing manager. Sales were strong in regions of the United States where environmental or industrial influences created respiratory problems.

John Sweeney liked the combination of dealers and support sales staff and felt they had been key to division success in the United States, particularly in the physician segment.

The physician's office spirometry market was still developing. The selling approach was less technical but required that the salesperson be able to stimulate primary demand by identifying potential users and key customers and by offering creative financial plans. Key customers were doctors or researchers who, through speeches and/or publications, were influential within their professions.

Monitor equipment sales were expected to grow to 50 percent of division sales. Noninvasive blood pressure monitors were to account for one-third of this volume. Noninvasive blood pressure monitors represented a rapidly growing market and required a highly technical sale. Unlike spirometers, monitors did not represent a new concept in medicine, but successful selling required a thorough technical understanding of the product. These products were sold directly to hospital users. John Sweeney estimated market share worldwide at 5 percent.

The United States represented about 50 percent of the world market for spirometers. Major industrial nations composed the remaining 50 percent. Sweeney estimated that 80 percent of the spirometry market outside of the United States consisted of sales to hospitals.

Puritan-Bennett and the Boston Division sold medical products through dealers at 25 percent off list price. Division gross margin was 55 percent, with selling costs averaging 20 percent of sales.

BOSTON DIVISION INTERNATIONAL MARKETING EFFORT

John Sweeney believed that to survive in today's medical equipment industry a company must have an international sales base. The bankrupt company Sweeney acquired in 1978 had sold nearly $1 million in spirometers in Europe in 1977. Reorganization of that company into LSE Corporation had left ill feelings with its German distributor, prompting Sweeney to seek a new distribution network. In 1979 he visited trade shows and signed on new distributors.

In spite of John Sweeney's efforts, initial attempts at European sales for LSE were not successful. Sweeney feared the small size of his organization was a major drawback in dealing with European distributors. LSE merged with Puritan-Bennett in 1981, partially in the hope that as part of a larger company the new division would gain greater leverage with distributors. Continual spirometer improvements had been made, and Sweeney was convinced that spirometers would sell in the European market if distributors paid more attention to his products. Special sourcing was required, however, to overcome limitations caused by the relative strength of the U.S. dollar versus other currencies.

Marketing spirometers in Europe required changing electrical wires and switches and programming for ''normal'' reference values by country. These changes had already been made for the United Kingdom, and the division was working on changes for other countries as well.

Because in Europe pulmonary laboratories existed for treatment of chronically ill patients, there were no respiratory therapy departments. Furthermore, little screening occurred for hospital admission and preparation for operations. Screening in physician offices was developing at a slower rate than in the United States. Sweeney believed this market had potential. Rising costs of hospital care worldwide evoked interest in products for use in doctor's offices or at home. European and Japanese participants at conventions of the American Lung Association, as well as other pulmonary specialists, voiced growing interest in nonhospital screening and treatment techniques.

PURITAN-BENNETT INTERNATIONAL SALES ORGANIZATION

Following the merger, the Boston Division depended upon Puritan-Bennett's international sales division for overseas sales.

The International Division channeled all sales through independent distributors. International sales reached $20 million in 1983. The vice president of international sales, Bob Taylor, was based at the head office in Kansas City. International operations were divided into three geographical areas. Les Fuller was area manager for Europe and the Middle East. The other divisions were Latin America, smallest of the three in terms of sales, and the Far East, largest in sales but employing fewer people than the European division.

There were three European area sales representatives. One representative, based in Germany, covered German speaking countries, including Germany, Austria, and Switzerland, as well as Eastern Europe. Another representative, based in France, covered France, Italy, Belgium, and Spain. A third representative, in the United Kingdom, covered the United Kingdom and Scandinavia. A fourth representative responded for the Middle East.

Puritan-Bennett had entered Europe before 1970 on an export basis. In the mid-1970s, the company had expanded its international commitment by forming a service organization in England. Puritan-Bennett's International Division had sold only ventilators, marketing directly to hospitals. Hospital doctors and nurses were the key decision makers in the purchase decision.

Puritan-Bennett U.K. Limited was the company's only wholly owned sales and distribution subsidiary. Based in Chichester, England, it imported and sold medical equipment to European distributors and performed technical service for distributors. Contact with end users was restricted to key customers or new product introductions. The U.K. operation employed ten people.

In Europe, Puritan-Bennett's larger distributors carried a full line of medical equipment and supplies. Smaller distributors concentrated on a specific medical expertise. It was very difficult to find distributors which fit the entire product line but were not already carrying a competitor's product.

Spirometers were sold to Puritan-Bennett U.K. at 25 percent off U.S. list price. Duty and freight added 11 percent to landed costs. Puritan-Bennett U.K. used a markup of 20 percent. Average transportation costs of 10 percent within the European marketplace were paid by the final distributor. The local distributor expected a 50 percent markup on landed costs.

Stiff price competition threatened any U.S. company operating in Europe. The strong U.S. dollar, as well as transportation and tariff costs, made price competition difficult. Puritan-Bennett relied on technical superiority of its products. Continued strength of the U.S. dollar intensified the price differential between U.S. and European or Japanese products.

EXPERIENCE IN THE UNITED KINGDOM

Puritan-Bennett's U.K. distributor for 10 years, Adamson and Carr was owned by a larger firm which manufactured cardiac care equipment. Adamson and Carr distributed products not only for its parent company but also for other medical equipment manufacturers. Following their visit earlier this day, Sweeney, Taylor, and Oglethorpe worried about low 1984 forecasts for ventilators, projected by A&C at five to eight units. When pressured, A&C revised to 10 to 20 units, still far below the estimate of 50 to 100 units predicted for Germany by Puritan-Bennett's German distributor. John Sweeney believed that sales in the United Kingdom should be similar to those in Germany. Touring the A&C plant, Sweeney noticed what appeared to be inventory buildup of A&C parent company products. Parent company cardiac care equipment had an average price of $3,000 to $12,000.

With A&C, Puritan-Bennett benefited from an installed sales base. Sales management, sales training, order processing, accounting, and inventory management adequately met the needs of both Puritan-Bennett and A&C's parent.

The distributor employed twelve salespeople who had established key contacts at hospitals with recovery rooms (RRs), intensive care units (ICUs), and critical care units (CCUs), all important in marketing the A&C cardiac care line. These contacts provided access to anesthesiology departments which were major users of monitoring and support equipment.

A&C had recently sold few noninvasive blood pressure monitors or spirometers and hesitated to expand that part of its product line. Prior to this time, A&C had carried Vitalograph spirometers. Vitalograph, a major European competitor of Puritan-Bennett, had now decided to sell direct in the United Kingdom.

Under socialized medicine, the government provided almost all health care. This meant that most testing and screening, including spirometry, was done in hospitals.

Previously the International Division had enjoyed good sales results with Bennett ventilators in the United Kingdom. Price increases and greater sophistication lowered late generation sales. The International Division had experienced similar distribution problems in other European countries. Ventilators sold well in the Middle East, Japan, and Germany. Sales in Spain were building, and sales in Italy held promise.

EXPERIENCE IN GERMANY

Strong ventilator sales in Germany had reached $3 million, 10 percent of U.S. sales. Puritan-Bennett Corporation used Carl A. Hoyer GmbH as its independent distributor. The International Division had enjoyed a good relationship with Hoyer for many years. Hoyer specialized in ventilation and respiratory products. Hoyer distributed for several companies, and Puritan-Bennett ventilator sales represented 50 percent of volume. Hoyer had a strong technical orientation and employed ten salespersons for Germany and Switzerland.

Hoyer was a good source of new product information for Puritan-Bennett. Because of their technical orientation, Hoyer salespeople helped Puritan-Bennett define new needs in the medical equipment market and identified new products in development by Puritan-Bennett competitors. Hoyer desired to expand its product line but only within the hospital segment. Already Hoyer carried a competitor's noninvasive blood pressure equipment. Germany had a large industrial base, making spirometry viable. Spirometry and blood pressure monitoring were both reimbursable through public and private health insurance programs.

The Puritan-Bennett U.K. subsidiary supported Hoyer activities. As in other European countries, this support included active missionary sales work. Puritan-Bennett participated in medical conventions, sponsored direct mailings, sought and referred dealer leads from other regions, and supported medical research using papers mentioning Puritan-Bennett products. Almost all missionary efforts in Europe centered on ventilators.

EXPERIENCE IN JAPAN

Amco Japan Ltd. was Puritan-Bennett's Japanese distributor. Amco Japan distributed throughout Japan, emphasizing high tech medical equipment. The medical equipment industry consisted of two segments: instruments and accessories or added features, and disposables. Disposables were those products which were consumed or would wear out and had to be thrown away. They included patient circuits, tubes, and mouthpieces. Amco Japan had emphasized technical equipment sales, featuring disposables and accessories as incremental business.

The Japanese distributor had no manufacturing facility. Amco Japan had begun with kidney dialysis equipment and broadened its product line to high tech medical equipment as the industry matured. Amco was second only to Hoyer in international sales volume for Puritan-Bennett. Twelve to fifteen salespeople, organized by specialty in terms of product function, called almost exclusively on hospitals. Amco Japan carried products from several different companies and desired to maintain a broad product line.

Most other Japanese distributors were large firms with internal specialization, either by end user or by area of medical specialty, such as respiratory or cardiac care.

Amco Japan was Boston Division's largest distributor of noninvasive blood pressure monitors. Introducing the Boston Division spirometer, Amco would face strong domestic competition. Heavy industry and heavy smoking habits created a viable market for spirometry, a reimbursable medical expense.

Bream headed sales for the Far East. The International Division maintained two offices to serve the Far East, one in Hong Kong and one on the U.S. West Coast. Puritan-Bennett had no representative based in Japan. Amco provided warehouses.

COMPETITION FOR VENTILATORS, SPIROMETERS, AND MONITORS

Puritan-Bennett was one of three leading competitors in the worldwide ventilation market. The others were

Siemens and Bourns. Based in Germany, Siemens sold direct throughout Europe and the United States. Bourns Ltd., a British company, sold its Bear ventilator direct in the United States and the United Kingdom. Bourns was less active on the continent than Puritan-Bennett or Siemens.

Siemens ventilators had microprocessors and cost $15,000. The Bourns Bear 20 ventilator at $10,000 had no microprocessor.

Noninvasive blood pressure monitoring was rapidly expanding and attracting new entrants. First in the market with its Dinamap monitor, Critikon became world leader and marketed direct in the United States and Europe, selling elsewhere via distributor. John Sweeney counted eight international competitors selling noninvasive blood pressure monitors. Most used a mix of direct sales and distributors. Many, like Datascope, were between one and two years old, rapidly gaining sales volume.

Competition in spirometry existed in countries where industry, pollution, and smoking prevailed and where government or private medical insurance reimbursed spirometry.

Puritan-Bennett dominated U.S. office spirometry with 30 percent market share but held only a negligible share of the non-U.S. market. Tariffs and duties impeded manufacturers in this price competitive market. These extra costs resulted in end user prices sometimes 50 percent above prices of European manufactured spirometers.

Vitalograph, Ltd., a British company and Puritan-Bennett's largest competitor, dominated the European spirometer market. Vitalograph sold direct in the United Kingdom but used distributors throughout the rest of Europe.

Before technological developments by LSE and later by the Boston Division, Vitalograph had sold the most widely used spirometer in the United States. Vitalograph European prices ranged from $1,150 for the basic model to $5,000 for the top-of-the-line model. Vitalograph offered no spirometer with microprocessing but had designed personal computer software to sell with the spirometer. A physician or nurse would connect the volume mechanism with a computer.

Puritan-Bennett's International Division and Vitalograph shared many European distributors, notably in Italy, Austria, and the Netherlands. Vitalograph was not represented in Japan, and its U.S. market share had declined. Vitalograph did all manufacturing in the United Kingdom. Its sales volume equaled that of the Boston Division.

Litton Industries operated two subsidiaries, Hellig A.G. in Germany and Mijnhardt A.G. in the Netherlands. Both produced spirometers under the name Vicatest. Vicatest, a small part of this very large company, was fighting to gain a stronger position in the spirometry market. Vicatest sold direct in the Netherlands and Germany but used distributors throughout the rest of Europe. Vicatest had entered neither Japanese nor U.S. markets. The product line included Vicatest 3 with microprocessing. Vicatest priced items 33–35 percent below those of the Boston Division.

The Chest Co., a Japanese firm new to the European market, sold spirometers priced below Puritan-Bennett's by 50 percent in Europe and 25 percent in the United States.

The Warren E. Collins Company of Braintree, Massachusetts, sold in both the United States and Europe but had not substantially dented the spirometry market in Europe. Jones Medical Instrument Company competed primarily in the United States but had begun to compete overseas. Other U.S. companies attempted to enter the international market as industrialized countries increased concern for preventive health care. A U.S. National Health Institute study showed strong correlation between lung capacity and heart disease. Early detection of reduced lung capacity might decrease patient risk if followed by early treatment or behavior change.

Spirometer manufacturers faced a new group of competitors. With technological breakthroughs leading to cost and time savings, manufacturers of large pulmonary laboratory systems showed interest in the screening market. System manufacturers included Warren E. Collins and the Gould Company in the United States and Jaeger A.G. in Germany.

CORPORATE STRATEGY

The late 1970s and early 1980s marked significant change for Puritan-Bennett. Through acquisitions and intensified R&D activities, the company adopted a more innovative position in the marketplace, incorporating electronics and microprocessing into its products. Puritan-Bennett also broadened its product line. This dual positioning strategy of broad and innovative product lines increasingly mandated international rather than domestic focus.

In the past decade, European and Japanese competitors had entered the U.S. market. Entry into foreign markets would allow Puritan-Bennett to know foreign competitors before they entered the United States. John Sweeney felt that presence in a foreign market could buy time for a U.S. firm. By competing well on foreign soil, Puritan-Bennett could instill reluctance by European or Japanese firms to enter the United States.

International presence supported the company desire to maintain a leading edge in technology. "This allows us a window on technology," said John Sweeney. "U.S. doctors do not have all the answers. We need worldwide contacts with doctors and researchers." An example of new techniques developed outside the United States, high frequency ventilation was most widely used in Germany, and therefore the German market provided the best place for feedback.

Different regulatory environments confirmed the importance of an international base. The U.S. Federal Drug Administration (FDA) could inhibit rapid introduction of new technologies. If Puritan-Bennett introduced a product in its foreign markets first, it would begin earlier payback of the initial investment. Puritan-Bennett discovered that, despite approvals required, the process was fast in the United Kingdom and in Germany. In France, the process known as "homologation" was cumbersome and difficult. The *Koseisho* procedure in Japan was well defined and predictable within a clear time frame.

With greater emphasis on innovation, Puritan-Bennett rapidly increased its R&D investment. Seeking a larger sales base would allow the company to spread initial investment cost over larger unit sales. This was true for all medical products, both hospital and physician office segments.

U.S. firms were at a cost disadvantage in many international markets because of labor, tariffs, transportation, and the strong U.S. dollar. Product quality and differentiation were therefore essential for success in Europe or Japan.

INTERNATIONAL PARTNERSHIP WITH A FINNISH FIRM

In 1981, Puritan-Bennett entered a partnership with the Datex Division of Instrumentarium, a Finnish company manufacturing hospital monitoring products. Instrumentarium had sought U.S. market entry as a first step to expansion throughout the Western Hemisphere.

The initial agreement focused on one product, a carbon dioxide monitor that measured the carbon dioxide [CO_2] level of patients in surgery or patients under ventilation in respiratory therapy. The monitor measured carbon dioxide levels breath to breath, providing continuous feedback on the oxygen-carbon dioxide exchange.

Because John Sweeney's division marketed all monitoring products, he was asked to oversee the partnership. Monitors were produced in Finland and sold by Puritan-Bennett in the United States through its distribution network. In 1983, when Puritan-Bennett began direct sales to hospitals, Finnish products were handled by the Kansas City based corporate sales group. The Boston Division continued to coordinate all activities with the Finnish company.

Since conclusion of the original agreement, the two companies had broadened their cooperation, expanding the product line to include an anesthesia brain monitor. This equipment monitored the brain waves of a patient under anesthesia and functioned with other Puritan-Bennett products. The two companies were in negotiation to add monitoring devices to both Instrumentarium and Puritan-Bennett product lines. Further agreement gave Puritan-Bennett responsibility for the entire Western Hemisphere by adding sales to Canada and Latin America.

Puritan-Bennett and Instrumentarium had entered joint product development projects. Instrumentarium was to develop specific products to fit the Puritan-Bennett line, either by complementing it or working in conjunction with an existing Puritan-Bennett product.

Elsewhere Instrumentarium sold monitors through dealers. In Germany and Switzerland it had used Carl A. Hoyer GmbH. The Finnish company used a different dealer in the United Kingdom and enjoyed strong sales there.

Both Puritan-Bennett and Instrumentarium were pleased with the relationship to date. They considered the possibility of a marketing joint venture in one or two key markets. The joint venture could market both the current line and any new products. Both companies felt that a joint venture could maximize their effectiveness. They were still in the early stages of target identification.

ALTERNATIVE DISTRIBUTION CHANNELS

As Taylor, Sweeney, and Oglethorpe reviewed distribution channels at their meeting in the Skyline lobby, they recognized several viable alternatives. Considering the United Kingdom as an example, they knew they could keep their current distributor, seek a new distributor, or use a direct sales force.

All three gentlemen agreed that ventilator sales projected by Grant at A&C were unacceptably low. The new generation 7200 model had sold well in the United States. Previous experience with A&C had been satisfactory, and Puritan-Bennett did not want to create tensions in its European distribution chain by dropping an established distributor after an extended relationship.

Puritan-Bennett could seek a new distributor. Bob Taylor was concerned about the time it would take to establish and to train a new distributor. He believed it might require two or three years to reach adequate volume.

A direct sales force was also possible. Puritan-Bennett currently sold $500,000 in disposables for ventilators already installed in the United Kingdom. Bob Taylor considered this to be ''captive'' business regardless of any change in channels. Disposables revenue would adequately cover the cost of adding salespeople to Puritan-Bennett U.K. Ltd. John Sweeney estimated that the cost of maintaining a sales force approached $70,000 per salesperson.

CONCLUSION

Growing product lines and innovations were important for the three vice presidents to consider when examining distribution channels. Training a new distributor and subsequent high volume could take two or three years, particularly for ventilators because this equipment required a highly technical approach. Medical equipment sales demanded commitment from a sales organization, and finding a strong distributor could be difficult. A direct sales force guaranteed early commitment but might not have immediate access to necessary channels. Hard feelings by distributors already providing good volume and service should not be risked.

John Sweeney considered how his division's products could and should fit with Bennett Division ventilators. One reason LSE had joined Puritan-Bennett was to improve international distribution by better access to European distributors. Another consideration was future broadening of the Boston Division product line. Expansion was expected to continue in all medical product lines. Sweeney wanted to determine which channels could best accommodate expansion.

Case 9

The SWATCH Project

"This watch is the product which will reintroduce Switzerland to the low and middle price market. It is the first step of our campaign to regain dominance of the world watch industry," said Dr. Ernst Thomke, president of ETA SA, a subsidiary of Asuag and Switzerland's largest watch company. Ernst Thomke had made this confident declaration about SWATCH to Franz Sprecher, project marketing consultant, in late spring 1981. Sprecher had accepted a consulting assignment to help ETA launch the watch, which was at that time still in the handmade prototype phase and as yet unnamed. This new watch would come in a variety of colored plastic cases and bracelets with an analog face. ETA had designed an entire production process exclusively for SWATCH. This new process was completely automated and built the quartz movement directly into the watch case. Sprecher's key concern was how to determine a viable proposal for moving this remarkable new product from the factory in Grenchen, Switzerland, into the hands of consumers all over the world.

COMPANY BACKGROUND: ETA, EBAUCHES, AND ASUAG

SWATCH was only one brand within a large consortium of holding companies and manufacturing units

●

This case was prepared by Susan W. Nye and Barbara Priovolos under the direction of Visiting Professor Jean-Pierre Jeannet as a basis for class discussion rather than to illustrate either effective or ineffective handling of an administrative situation. Copyright © 1985 by IMD, Lausanne, Switzerland. The International Institute for Management Development (IMD), resulting from the merger between IMEDE, Lausanne, and IMI, Geneva, acquires and retains all rights. Not to be used or reproduced without written permission from IMD, Lausanne, Switzerland.

controlled by Allgemeine Schweizer Uhrenindustrie (Asuag, or General Company of Swiss Watchmaking). SWATCH was to be produced by ETA, a movement manufacturer, which was part of Ebauches SA, the subsidiary company overseeing watch movement production within the Asuag organization.

Asuag was founded in 1931 when the Swiss government orchestrated the consolidation of a wide variety of small watchmakers. The major purpose of this consolidation was to begin rationalization of a highly fragmented, but vital, industry suffering the effects of one world war and a global depression. By 1981, Asuag had become the largest Swiss producer of watches and watch components. Asuag was the third largest watchmaker in the world, behind two Japanese firms, Seiko and Citizen. Asuag had a total of 14,499 employees, 83 percent of whom worked within Switzerland. Asuag accounted for about one-third of all Swiss watch exports, which were estimated at SFr. 3.1 billion in 1980.[1] Major activities were movement manufacture and watch assembly. Bracelets, cases, dials, and crystals were sourced from independent suppliers.

Ebauches SA, a wholly owned subsidiary of Asuag, controlled the various movement manufacturers. The Swiss government played an important role in encouraging and funding Ebauches' formation in 1932. An "Ebauche" was the base upon which the movement was built, and Ebauches companies produced almost all of the movements used in watches produced by Asuag group companies. Sixty-five percent of Ebauches production was used by Asuag group companies, and the rest was sold to other Swiss watch manufacturers. Ebauches SA recorded sales of SFr. 675.0 million in 1980, a 3.1 percent increase

---

1. U.S. $1 = SFr. 2.00; SFr. 1 = U.S. $0.50.

over the previous year. Ebauches companies employed a total of 6,860 people, 90 percent of them in Switzerland.

ETA SA, the manufacturer of SWATCH, produced a full range of watch movements and was known as the creator of the ultrathin movements used in expensive watches. The quality of ETA movements was so renowned that some watches were marked with ''ETA Swiss Quartz'' as well as the name brand. ETA movements were distributed on a virtual quota basis to a select group of watch manufacturers. The demand for its movements had always equaled or exceeded its production capacity. In 1980, ETA employed over 2,000 people and produced more than 14 million watch movements for revenues of approximately SFr. 362 million and profits of about SFr. 20 million.

Dr. Ernst Thomke had joined ETA as president in 1978. Early in his career, he had worked as an apprentice in production at ETA. He left the watch industry to pursue university degrees in chemistry and cancer research, earning both a Ph.D. and a medical degree. He then moved on to a career in research at British-owned Beecham Pharmaceutical. Thomke did not stay in the lab for long. He moved into the marketing department, where he boosted Beecham sales with ski trips and concerts for physicians and their families. His unorthodox selling techniques led to skyrocketing sales. He looked for a new challenge when faced with a transfer to another country. His colleagues at Asuag and throughout the watch industry described Thomke as a tough negotiator and as iron willed. After joining ETA he agreed to provide advertising and support allowances to movement customers. However, these agreements stated that ETA only provided aid if it had a role in product planning and strategy formulation.

THE GLOBAL WATCH INDUSTRY

To understand the global watch industry, three key variables were considered: watch technology, watch price, and the watch's country of origin.

Watch Movement Technology

Watch design underwent a revolutionary change in the early 1970s when traditional mechanical movement technology was replaced with electronics. A mechanical watch's energy source came from a tightened mainspring which was wound by the user. As the spring unwound, it drove a series of gears to which the watch hands were attached; the hands moved around the analog (or numerical) face of the watch to indicate the time. Highly skilled workers were required to produce and assemble the movements in accurate mechanical watches, and the Swiss were world renowned in this area.

The first electronic watch was built by a Swiss engineer, Max Hetzel, in 1954, but it was U.S. and Japanese companies that first commercialized electronic technology. Bulova, a U.S. company, was the first to bring an electronic watch to market in the early 1960s, based upon tuning-fork technology. A vibrating tuning fork stimulated the gears' movements and moved the hands on a traditional analog face. At the end of the decade, quartz crystal technology began to appear in the marketplace. An electric current was passed through a quartz crystal to stimulate high frequency vibration. This oscillation could be converted to precise time increments with a step motor. Quartz technology was used to drive the hands on traditional analog watches and led to an innovation: digital displays. Digital watches had no moving parts, and the conventional face and hands were replaced with digital readouts. Electronic watches revolutionized the industry because, for the first time, consumers could purchase an inexpensive watch with accuracy within one second per day or less.

Ebauches-owned companies had been involved in electronic watch technology since its pioneering stages. In 1962, Ebauches was among a number of Swiss component manufacturers and watch assembly firms which established the ''Centre Electronique Horlogère'' (CEH). The center's immediate goal was to develop a movement which could compete with Bulova's tuning-fork movement. CEH was never able to successfully produce a tuning-fork movement which did not violate Bulova's patents. In 1968, Ebauches entered into a licensing agreement with Bulova to manufacture and sell watches using Bulova's tuning-fork technology. In 1969, CEH introduced its first quartz crystal models, and Ebauches subsequently took over manufacture and marketing for the new movement, introducing its first quartz line in 1972.

Ebauches also worked with the U.S. electronic firm, Texas Instruments, and FASEC[2] in the early 1970s to pursue integrated circuit and display technology. By 1973, Ebauches was producing movements or watches for three generations of electronic technology: tuning-fork, quartz analog, and digital. Ebauches did not stay in the assembled watch market for long and returned to its first mission of producing and supplying watch movements to Asuag companies. Between 1974 and 1980 the Swiss watch industry as a whole spent SFr. 1 billion toward investment in new technology, and Asuag accounted for half the expenditure. Ebauches Electronique on Lake Neuchâtel was a major use of investment funds and was created to produce electronic components.

Price

Price was the traditional means of segmenting the watch market into three categories. "AA" and "A" watches were sold at prices above SFr. 1,200 and accounted for 42 percent of the total value of watches sold and 2 percent of total volume. "B" watches priced at SFr. 120–1,200 made up 25 percent of the market in value and 12 percent in units. "C" watches were priced under SFr. 120 and accounted for 33 percent of the market in value and 86 percent of total units.

PLAYERS IN THE GLOBAL WATCH INDUSTRY

Japan, Hong Kong, and Switzerland together accounted for almost 75 percent of total world watch production. In 1980, watch producers worldwide were faced with inventory buildups at factory warehouses and retail stores. A worldwide recession had slowed demand for watches, and overproduction compounded the problem. Projections for 1980 were not being met, and factory-based price-cutting, particularly by large producers, was becoming common as a substitute for production cuts.

2. FASEC was a laboratory for joint research in semiconductors, integrated circuits, and lasers. It was formed in 1966 by the Swiss Watch Federation (FHS), Brown Boveri, Landis & Gyr, and Philips of the Netherlands.

The Swiss Watch Industry

The Swiss watchmakers' position was viewed by many industry observers as being more precarious than others. Since 1970, when the Swiss accounted for 80 percent, their share of the world watch market in units had declined to 25 percent of the world's watch exports. The Swiss ranked third in unit production but remained first in the value of watches sold. Twenty-five percent of all Swiss watch factories were permanently shut down during the 1970s, and 30,000 workers lost their jobs.

Despite extensive factory and company shutdowns within the Swiss industry, in 1981 the Swiss still owned the rights to 10,000 registered brand names, although less than 3,000 were actively marketed. Most Swiss watches were priced in the mid- to expensive price ranges, above SFr. 100 ex-factory and SFr. 400 retail. In 1981, industry analysts were congratulating the Swiss for their adherence to the upper price segments, because the low-price segments were beginning to turn weak. Industry observers also noted that the Swiss seemed to be emerging from a decade of uncertainty and confusion and were focusing on higher quality segments of the watch market. Swiss component manufacturers had been supplying their inexpensive components to Far East assemblers, and analysts believed that this practice would continue.

Swiss watch manufacturers generally fell into one of three categories. First, there were the well-established, privately owned companies which produced expensive, handmade watches. These firms included Rolex, Patek-Philippe, Vacheron Constantin, Audemars-Piguet, and Piaget. For the most part, these firms were in good health financially. Stressing high quality as the key selling point, these manufacturers maintained tight control through vertical integration of the entire production and marketing processes from movement and component production through assembly and out into the market. The recession had cost them some customers, but these had been replaced by new Middle Eastern clients.

Second, there were a number of relatively small, privately owned companies that concentrated on watch components—bracelets, crystals, faces, hands, or movements. This group included an ETA competitor, Ronda SA. The financial health of these companies was mixed.

The third sector of the industry was the largest participants, Asuag and Société Suisse de l'Industrie Horlogère (SSIH). SSIH was an organization similar to but smaller than Asuag, producing 10 percent of all Swiss watch and movements output. Its most famous brand, Omega, had for years been synonymous with high quality. Omega had recently run into trouble and had been surpassed by the Asuag brand Rado as Switzerland's best-selling watch. In June 1981, SSIH announced a loss of SFr. 142 million for the fiscal year ending March 31, 1981. This loss gave SSIH a negative net worth of SFr. 27.4 million. A consortium of Swiss banks and the Zurich trading group Siber Hegner & Co., AG were brought together to save the company.

In the late 1970s, Asuag and SSIH began working in a cooperative effort to cut costs through the use of common components. However, this effort did not affect individual brand identities or brand names. Industry analysts did not rule out the eventual possibility of a full merger. Asuag was noted for its strength in production and quality but was reported to have a weakness in the marketing function. SSIH was noted for strong marketing skills but had recently been faced with a slippage in product quality. It was believed that both companies would stand to gain from closer ties in research and production.

The watch industry played a significant role in Switzerland's economy. The banks and the government took a serious interest in its operations and the performance of individual companies. Between 1934 and 1971 the Swiss government made it illegal to open, enlarge, transform, or transfer any watch manufacturing plant without government permission. This action was justified as a defensive move to combat potential unemployment due to foreign competition. It was also illegal to export watch components and watchmaking technology without a government issued permit. The government essentially froze the industry by dictating both prices and the supplier-manufacturer relationship. These constraints were gradually removed beginning in 1971 and by 1981 were no longer in effect.

The Japanese Watch Industry

Japan was the world's second largest watch producer in 1980 with approximately 67.5 million pieces, up

from 12.2 million pieces in 1970. The growth of the watch industry in Japan was attributed to the Japanese watchmakers' ability to commercialize the electronic watch. K. Hattori, which marketed the Seiko, Alba, and Pulsar brands, was Japan's largest watchmaker and responsible for approximately 42 million units. Selling under three different brand names allowed Hattori to compete across a broad price range. Seiko watches fell into the "B" category. Alba and Pulsar competed in the "C" range.

Casio entered the watch market in 1975, selling low cost digital watches. Philip Thwaites, the U.K. marketing manager, described Casio as follows: "Casio's strategy is simple, we aim to win market share by cutting prices to the bone." Casio's product line was exclusively digital. The company was noted for adding "gadgetry" to its watches, such as timers, stopwatches, and calculators. In Casio's view, the watch was no longer just a timepiece but a "wrist instrument."

In contrast to Switzerland, Japan's "big three" watch producers, the Hattori group, Casio, and Citizen, had a combined product line of fewer than twelve brands. All three firms were fully integrated, producing movements and most components and assembling and distributing worldwide through wholly owned distribution subsidiaries. These watchmakers made extensive use of automated equipment and assembly line production techniques.

The Watch Industry in Hong Kong

Hong Kong manufacturers had only entered the market in 1976, but by 1980 unit output had reached 126 million units. Ten major producers accounted for an estimated 70 percent of total volume. Watch design costs were minimized by copying Swiss and Japanese products. As many as 800 "loft workshops" were in operation in the late 1970s. These facilities could be started at low cost and ran with minimum overheads. The expanded capacity led to the rapid fall of Hong Kong watch prices: prices of simple watches in the SFr. 15-20 range in 1978 dropped to SFr. 10 the next year, with margins of less than SFr. 1. Hong Kong watches were sold under private label in minimum lot sizes of 1,000–2,000 units, with average ex-factory costs of SFr. 20 for mechanical watches and SFr. 50 for quartz analog and SFr. 10 for electronic digitals.

Most watchmaking activity in Hong Kong was concentrated on assembly. The colony had become Switzerland's client for watch components and movements. Swiss movement exports to Hong Kong had grown from 13.3 million pieces in 1977 to 38.5 million in 1980.

THE POPULARIUS PROJECT

The SWATCH project began under the code name ''Popularius.'' Thomke's goal was to discover what the market wanted and then to supply it. He told his engineers that he wanted a plastic, analog watch that could be produced at less than SFr. 10 and sold ex-factory at SFr. 15. He also wanted to use the technology which ETA had developed for its high priced, ultrathin ''Delirium'' movements to enter the low priced watch segment. Thomke was convinced that ETA's long term viability and profitability depended on increasing the company's volume and integrating downstream into fully assembled watch production and marketing. Thomke had seen the demand for ETA movements dwindle when exports of finished Swiss watches declined from 48 million pieces in 1970 to 28.5 million in 1980. The mass market ''C'' watch had all but disappeared from Swiss production, replaced by inexpensive Japanese and Hong Kong models. The Swiss manufacturers pushed their products up-market, and sales value of exports moved from SFr. 2,383.7 million in 1970 to SFr. 3,106.7 million in 1980.

With electronic technology, movements were no longer a major cost factor in the end price of a watch. The average price of an ETA movement was SFr. 18 and applied whether the watch sold ex-factory at SFr. 80 or SFr. 500. Thomke wanted to increase ETA volume output and knew that Asuag transfer pricing policies made this difficult. Asuag was a loose consortium of companies, each operating as an independent profit center. Transfer pricing reflected this fact. At each point of production and sales—movements, components, assembly and through the distribution channels—a profit was taken by the individual unit. Thomke believed that this system weakened the Swiss brands' competitive position for the volume business which his movement business needed to be profitable. Thomke believed that if he wanted to introduce a successful new product, he would need to sell it to 1

percent of the world's population, which amounted to about 10 percent of the ''C'' market segment. He knew that the Japanese companies were fully integrated and that the Hong Kong assemblers, which already operated with low overheads, were moving increasingly toward full integration.

Thomke knew he could turn over the Popularius project to another Asuag unit, but he did not have a great deal of confidence in the production and marketing capabilities of Asuag branded watch assemblers. ETA was the only company within the Asuag group which had extensive experience in automated manufacturing. If the Popularius was to succeed as the latest entry in the low price market, it would have to be produced in an automated environment. Furthermore, Thomke had watched many of the finished watch companies steadily lose market share to Japanese and Hong Kong competitors over the last decade, and he had little confidence in their marketing capabilities. ETA currently sold 65 percent of its output to Asuag companies, and Thomke wanted to reduce this dependence. He planned to use the Popularius as ETA's own entry into the finished watch market (Exhibit 1).

ETA engineers and technicians, responding to Thomke's specifications, developed the Popularius. To meet the low unit ex-factory price was no small accomplishment. A cost analysis at that time showed that the required components without assembly would have cost SFr. 20. Quartz technology provided accuracy within one second per day, and the watch was waterproof, shock resistant, and powered by a readily available and inexpensive three year battery. The watch weighed twenty grams and was eight mm thick with an analog face. The face and strap were made of durable mat finished plastic, and the strap was attached with a special hinge flush with the face. It was considered stylish and attractive. Further aesthetic enhancements could be made with the careful selection of color and face design. Ultrasonic welding produced a finished product which would not be reopened after it left the assembly line. In the event of failure, designers believed, the watch was essentially unrepairable and would be replaced rather than repaired. Batteries were replaceable by the owner and inserted in the back of the watch (Exhibit 2).

The product line was, at that time, limited to one size, a large ''man's'' watch, which could be

EXHIBIT 1 ● Comparison of Ebauches SA Sales to World Market

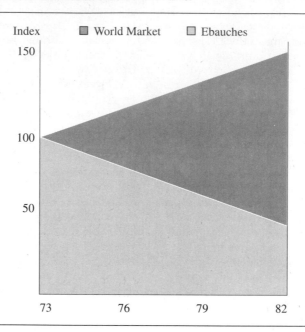

produced in a number of solid colors with several designs or patterns on the face. Although a 25 percent smaller version for women and children was being considered, no definite introduction plans had as yet been developed. Management believed that the young were a potentially strong secondary market for the new product. A number of ideas were in development for "novelty" watches with special functions, a button watch, and special colors and motifs. A day/date calendar with a quick reset feature was available. The production system was designed for strict quality control conditions to produce highly reliable watches. The movement was designed with a theoretical life of thirty years, and Popularius would be sold with a one year guarantee.

Manufacturing Systems for Popularius

The ability to produce and sell a watch with the Popularius features, for a low price, was largely dependent upon unique production technology developed at ETA. ETA's product development staff was respected throughout the watch industry for its technical abilities in mass production. Its production technology was considered by industry observers to be equal to that of the best Japanese companies. In the early stages of electronic movement production, even with high priced luxury movements, automated assembly was not only possible but a practical means of production. The production equipment planned for Popularius was entirely Swiss made and would in its final form consist of a fully automated production line that consumed raw materials at one end and delivered complete watches at the other.

ETA technology built the movement right into the base of the watch and required only 51 parts versus the 90 to 150 parts found in most electronic and mechanical watches. ETA had already used this technology to create the "Delirium," the world's thinnest movement, measuring .98 mm at its thickest point. These movements were used in high-precision luxury watches measuring 2.4 mm at their thickest point and selling at retail SFr. 40,000.

The Popularius production process and the

EXHIBIT 2 ● Photograph of the Product

SWATCH.
THE REVOLUTIONARY NEW TECHNOLOGY.

swatch ✚

SWATCH. THE NEW WAVE IN SWISS WATCHES.

equipment that made the technology possible were protected by seven patents. The ETA technical staff felt that it would be impossible for a competitor to duplicate Popularius, especially at low ex-factory price, because the watch was closely linked to its unique production process. ETA engineers had already invested nearly two years on this project, including the efforts of 200 employees and more than SFr. 10 million in research and development funds.

Production was still limited to hand production of prototype watches and watches for test marketing purposes. ETA expected the line to have semi- but not full automation with forecasted production levels of 600,000 men's watches and 150,000 smaller versions for women or children in the first year. Fully automated lines which would produce 2 million units per year were targeted for the second year. Production goals of 3 million units had been set for the third year. Production quotas for later years had not yet been finalized. Management expressed the desire to reach production and sales levels of 5 million units after three years (Exhibit 3).

Initially it was expected that full unit cost could go as high as SFr. 16. As volume increased the per unit cost would drop, and the full unit cost was expected to be less than SFr. 10 at production levels of 5 million watches per annum. The project was not considered technically feasible at annual production levels below 5 million, and higher volume was expected to drive the unit price just below SFr. 7. Asuag pricing and costing policy suggested that individual projects should reach contribution margins of 60 percent for marketing, sales and administrative expenses, fixed costs and profits. Each size model would require a separate production line. Within each line, economic order runs were 10,000 units for each color and 2,000 units for each face style. Maximum annual production per line was 2 million units, and the initial cost of installing a line was SFr. 5 million, including engineering costs of SFr. 2 million. Additional assembly lines could be installed at an estimated cost of SFr. 3 million. Production costs included depreciation of this equipment over four years. The equipment occupied space which was already available, and no additional real estate investments were expected.

ETA had applied for special financing packages with local authorities. No response had as yet been received. However, obtaining the necessary financing was not viewed as a problem.

Initial plans suggested a marketing budget of SFr. 5 per unit. The brand was expected to break even in the third year and begin earning profits for ETA in the fourth year. Per unit marketing costs were expected to decline as volume increased. Decisions as to how the budgeted marketing funds would be distributed had not been finalized. It was expected that they would be divided between ETA and its distributors, but on what basis and how the "campaigns" would be coordinated could not be decided until distribution agreements had been finalized. Thomke was a firm believer in joint ventures and wanted to develop 50/50 relationships with distributors.

Still to be decided were questions of packaging, advertising, production line composition, and distribution. Packaging alternatives centered around who should do it. ETA needed to decide if the product would leave the factory prepackaged and ready to

EXHIBIT 3 ● Projected Marketing Costs and Profits for SWATCH

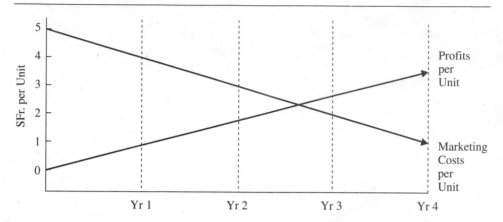

Per Unit:
Full Cost to Produce = SFr. 10 (with Long Range Target of Less than SFr. 7,
                              Including Depreciation for Production Machinery)
Ex-Factory Price = SFr. 15
Contribution Margin for Marketing Costs and Profit = SFr. 5

hang or display, or be shipped in bulk and packaged by the distributor or retailer, or even be sold "as is." Advertising budgets and campaigns had not been finalized. The size of the budgets and the question of whether or not advertising costs would be shared between ETA and the distributors were still open. The advertising agencies had not yet been chosen, and no media decisions had been finalized.

DISTRIBUTING POPULARIUS

Sprecher felt that distribution was the most important and problematic of the issues still outstanding. Discussions at ETA on developing an introduction strategy were confined to five industrial markets. Although it was not as yet definitive, the emerging consensus seemed to be that distribution would begin in Switzerland, the United States, the United Kingdom, France, and West Germany. Distribution in Japan, other industrialized countries, and certain developing countries was also being discussed for a later date.

Market and Country Selection

A major motivation in choosing the target entry markets would be the probability of gaining high volume sales. Thomke had in mind a goal of reaching an annual potential volume of 1 percent of the country's population in each targeted market. The United States would be an important market for Popularius success. It was the world's single largest watch market, and success with a product in the United States often signaled global success. Thomke planned to keep the watch priced below $30 in the United States. Germany and the United Kingdom were significantly large in terms of population but could be difficult markets to enter, because they were known to be particularly price sensitive. Germany was also noted as being particularly slow in accepting new innovations in consumer goods. Switzerland was chosen because it was the home market. ETA management assumed that their next move would be into Canada and the rest of Europe. If ETA decided to enter Japan and the LCDs, management would have some special considerations. Japan would be a particularly difficult market to crack, because almost all "B" and "C" class watches sold in Japan were produced domestically. Furthermore, Sprecher had heard that Seiko was considering plans for introducing a new quartz analog watch which would be priced under SFr. 50. The LCDs of Africa and Latin America provided ETA with opportunities for volume sales. Sprecher expected that consumers in these markets would use price as the only criteria for choosing a watch. Selling the Popularius to LCDs would put ETA in competition with the Hong Kong producers' inexpensive digital watches.

Selecting Distributing Organizations

Within each market there was a range of distribution alternatives. But a fundamental need was a central marketing, sales, and distribution unit within ETA with sole responsibility for "Popularius." However, at that time, there was no marketing or sales department within the ETA organization. ETA's products, watch movements, had always been distributed to a select and consistent group of users. Distribution at ETA had essentially been a question of arranging "best way" shipping, letters of credit, and insurance. The annual costs of establishing a central marketing division within ETA was estimated at SFr. 1–1.5 million. This figure would cover management and administrative salaries for a marketing manager, regional managers, product managers, service, sales planning, and advertising and promotion planning. Sprecher believed that eight to ten people would be required for adequate staffing of the department. Furthermore, he estimated that wholly owned subsidiaries in any of the major target markets could be staffed and run at a similar cost.

Contracting individual, independent marketing organizations in each country and then coordinating the marketing, sales, and distribution from the Grenchen office would, Sprecher believed, allow ETA to retain a much greater degree of control over the product. He felt that this type of organization would allow ETA to enter the market slowly and to learn about it gradually without having to relinquish control.

Following Thomke's suggestion, throughout the summer of 1981 Sprecher took a number of trips to

the United States to determine possible solutions to this and other marketing problems. Sprecher's agenda included visits to a number of distributors, advertising agencies, and retail stores. Sprecher completed his investigation with visits to some of the multinational advertising agencies' Zurich offices. Sprecher made his rounds with a maquette which he described as an "ugly, little black strap." The Popularius prototype still had a number of bugs to iron out, and Sprecher could only make promises of the variety of colors and patterns which were planned.

The United States would be essential to Popularius success because it was the world's largest watch market. Thomke and Sprecher also believed that the U.S. market would be more open to this new idea and felt they would gain the best advice from U.S. distributors and advertising agencies (Exhibit 4).

Retailer and Wholesaler Reactions

Sprecher began his first U.S. trip with a visit to Zales Corporation. The Zales organization included both a large jewelry and watch wholesale business and a chain of jewelry stores. Sprecher met with a high level marketing manager, who responded positively to the product but said that Zales could not seriously consider it at this early stage. He invited Sprecher to return when the project was further along. Zales management did advise Sprecher that if ETA decided to go ahead with the project and start production and sales, then "do it right." Doing it "right" meant heavy spending on advertising, point-of-purchase displays and merchandising, and aggressive pricing.

Sprecher also paid a visit to Gluck and Company. Gluck was a jewelry, watch, and accessory wholesaler operating in the low price end of the market. An aggressive trader, Gluck operated mainly on price, and much of its business involved single lots or short term arrangements to catalog and discount houses. Gluck executives told Sprecher that they did not believe in advertising but relied on low prices to push goods through the distribution chain and into the hands of the customer. If Gluck agreed to take on Popularius, it would have to be sold with a retail price of under SFr. 40. Sprecher attempted to discuss the possibility of a long term relationship between ETA and Gluck, but the wholesaler did not appear particularly interested.

EXHIBIT 4A ● Retail Watch Purchases in the United States: Summary of Market Research

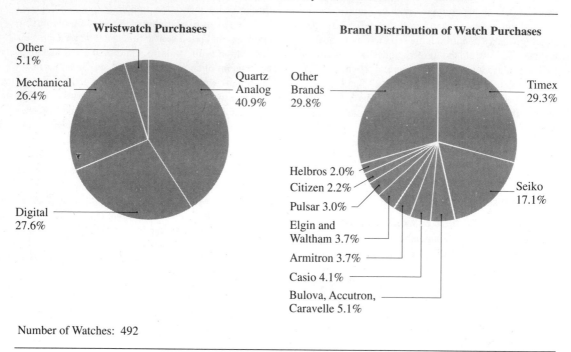

Wristwatch Purchases

Other 5.1%
Mechanical 26.4%
Quartz Analog 40.9%
Digital 27.6%

Brand Distribution of Watch Purchases

Other Brands 29.8%
Timex 29.3%
Seiko 17.1%
Helbros 2.0%
Citizen 2.2%
Pulsar 3.0%
Elgin and Waltham 3.7%
Armitron 3.7%
Casio 4.1%
Bulova, Accutron, Caravelle 5.1%

Number of Watches: 492

EXHIBIT 4B ● Retail Watch Purchases in the United States: Watch Purchases by Retail Price (Sample Size = 465)

	% Quartz analog	% Digital	% Mechanical
Number of watches	200	135	130
Price categories			
$1,000 or more	.5%	.7%	1.5%
$300 to $999	4.0	.7	1.5
$100 to $299	38.0	8.9	14.6
$50 to $99	33.5	31.9	35.4
$30 to $49	24.0	57.8	47.0

Note: 46.6 percent of all watches are purchased on sale or discount.

EXHIBIT 4C ● Retail Watch Purchases in the United States: Watch Purchases by Outlet Type (Sample Size = 485)

	% Watches (all)	% Analog quartz	% Digital
Number of items	485	198	134
Jewelry Store	27.6%	34.3%	12.0%
Department Store	26.2	26.3	27.6
Discount Store	16.7	14.7	23.1
Catalog Showroom	10.3	14.7	10.4
Mail Order	5.4		11.2
Wholesaler	2.1		1.5
Drugstore	5.1		6.0
Flea Market	0.4		
Other Outlets	6.2		7.5

EXHIBIT 4D ● Retail Watch Purchases in the United States: Distribution of Watch and Jewelry Purchase Prices by Age of Purchaser

	18–24 yrs.	25–34 yrs.	35–54 yrs.	55 and over
Number of customers	150	419	821	431
$25 to $49	39.4%	39.6%	35.7%	32.3%
$50 to $99				
$100 to $299	20.7	24.8	25.3	28.5
$300 to $999	27.3	25.3	26.7	27.6
$1,000 or more	11.3	8.8	9.0	10.4

Sprecher's reception at Bulova's New York offices was very different from Gluck. The first reaction of Andrew Tisch, president of the company, was that the Popularius should be packaged as a fashion watch. Tisch, was had substantial experience in consumer goods marketing and believed that Popularius should be heavily advertised and promoted, suggested a budget of SFr. 20 million. He was sufficiently impressed with the project and voiced some interest in establishing a separate company with ETA to market the watch.

Considering OEM Arrangements

Sprecher was concerned that he might be taking a "hit-or-miss" approach to his investigation and decided to pay a visit to Arthur Young and Company. Arthur Young was among the largest accounting firms in the world, one of the "Big Eight," and was noted for its industry analysis and consulting. Sprecher visited Arthur Young to see if its consultants might have some suggestions on potential partners for ETA. The accounting firm put together a proposal on how to attack the problem of finding a distribution partner. Sprecher was well aware that his investigation was still incomplete, and he returned to Switzerland with the Arthur Young proposal to work out a new agenda of visits.

Included in the Arthur Young proposal was the possibility of turning all marketing responsibilities of Popularius over to an independent company. Sprecher investigated this possibility and entered into negoti-ations with two well-known multinational consumer good companies: Timex and Duracell. Both of these companies had their own extensive and established distribution channels. ETA executives believed that an agreement with either of these two firms might provide Popularius with a virtual guarantee of high volume sales due to the extensive and intensive marketing resources at both.

The Duracell Proposal   Duracell produced and distributed high quality batteries worldwide and was interested in becoming the exclusive distributor of Popularius. Contact was initiated with the U.S. battery company's general manager in Zurich and followed up by a visit at Duracell's U.S. headquarters. The company had a distribution system in place which covered the entire globe. Duracell batteries were sold through drugstores, supermarkets, and hardware stores. Duracell made batteries for watches as well and therefore had some contacts in the retail watch trade. The company employed an experienced and well-trained sales force and had a wealth of marketing knowledge. Duracell had unused distribution capacity, and its management was looking for extensions to the product line and felt that an electronic watch could be complementary to and a logical extension of Duracell batteries.

Sprecher felt that an agreement with Duracell could be interesting but was concerned that ETA was being relegated to the role of product supplier, with little or no impact on marketing decisions. Duracell wanted to establish itself in an original equipment manufacture relationship with ETA. Duracell would buy the watch from ETA and then control the product's marketing strategy. ETA would be supplying the product, the product's name, and some marketing funds but would be left out of most mass marketing decisions. Furthermore, while Duracell continued to express interest, it was proceeding at what ETA executives considered to be a snail's pace. In late summer, Duracell management informed ETA that they were continuing their evaluation of Popularius as a product and that their investigation of its potential market was still incomplete.

The Timex Organization Timex was known for producing durable, inexpensive watches. The U.S.-based company had become famous in the late 1950s and 1960s for circumventing traditional watch outlets and jewelry stores and distributing through mass outlets such as drug, department, and hardware stores and even cigar stands. At its peak, Timex had sold watches through an estimated 2.5 million retail outlets. In 1982, Timex had an estimated 100,000 to 150,000 worldwide. Timex and ETA were considering the possibility of ETA production of a limited range of watches under the Timex name. The Timex Popularius would be produced in black with a different, but ETA approved, design. The hinge which attached the plastic strap to the watch case would be different, and "Swiss Made" would not be stamped on the face. Timex was willing to guarantee a minimum annual order of 600,000 units, at SFr. 10 ex-factory price.

Sprecher knew that ETA executives considered private label production as a viable option which could be implemented in either the introductory phase of distribution or later when the brand was well established. However, they felt that the Timex arrangement had some drawbacks. First, they perceived the Timex organization as somewhat stodgy and bureaucratic, and ETA executives were unsure as to how close a working relationship they could establish with Timex management. Second, Timex seemed to want Popularius for "nothing." Sprecher did not think that they could keep Popularius to a SFr. 50 retail price and gain a profit in the Timex agreement. Sprecher considered the Timex distribution system very costly. Sprecher estimated that Timex watches were distributed with a retail price of 4 to 4.5 times the ex-factory

watch price. ETA wanted to maintain a 3 to 3.5 ex-factory ratio. Sprecher believed that the Timex system was costly because it used a direct sales force as well as two middlemen (distributor and broker) to get watches into the retail store. Finally, ETA management was also concerned with Timex's most recent performance. The company had been steadily losing market share.

Positioning Options

Toward the end of his second trip to the States, Sprecher hit upon the "perfect" name for the new product—SWATCH. He had arranged to spend two weeks with the advertising agency Lintas SSC&B to work on developing a possible product and advertising strategy. This arrangement initiated a quasi-partnership between the two firms; Lintas invested its time and talent in the Popularius project and would receive payment later if they were to get the advertising account.

Lintas had been influenced by their work with another client, Monet, a producer of costume jewelry. Monet supported its products with heavy point-of-sale promotion activities. Lintas believed that this kind of promotion would be beneficial to Popularius.

Lintas saw a number of positioning options for the Popularius: a (new) Swiss watch, a second watch, an activity watch, a fashion watch, or a combination of images. The agency had suggested approaching the Popularius positioning with a combination of a fashion and sports image while emphasizing the watch's Swiss origin. The copy staff was excited about stressing the Swiss watch concept and the contraction S'watches was repeated throughout their notes. Sprecher looked at the abbreviation and was struck by the idea of taking it one step further to SWATCH, and the Popularius finally had a name.

Considering Direct Mail

Back in Switzerland, Sprecher continued interviewing advertising agencies. He visited the Zurich office of McCann-Erickson, a large multinational advertising agency, to discuss advertising strategy and to look into the mail-order market. McCann-Erickson made an investigation of the mail-order market for the SWATCH in West Germany. The purpose of this study was to demonstrate what a mail-order approach might accomplish for SWATCH.

McCann-Erickson's proposal suggested using mail order as an initial entry strategy for SWATCH. This arrangement would later be expanded into a mail-order business through specialized companies with a full range of watches and jewelry. Target group would be young men and women between 20 and 29 years, as well as people who "stay young." The target group would be motivated and interested in fashion, pop culture, and modern style.

To achieve sufficient penetration of the target market, which the agency estimated at 12.5 million, advertising support of about SFr. 1 million would have to be spent. Orders were estimated anywhere from 50,000 units to 190,000. This estimate included volume of 4,500 to 18,000 for a test market with total advertising costs of about SFr. 150,000. The effort would be organized in two waves, one in spring and a second in the fall.

Additional costs to be considered were mailing at SFr. 2.50 per unit as well as an unknown amount for coupon handling. Furthermore, experience indicated that about 10 percent of all orders would not be paid.

Considering an Exclusive Distributorship

Zales had suggested that Sprecher contact Ben Hammond, a former Seiko distributor for the southwestern region of the U.S. Sprecher was unable to make this contact, but Thomke followed up on this lead on a separate visit to the United States in late summer. Ben Hammond, president of Bhamco, was interested in the exclusive distribution rights for North America for SWATCH and a second Asuag brand, Certina. Bhamco was a gem stone firm, and Hammond had been in the jewelry and watch business in the southwest for several years. Up until the recent past, he had been the southwest distributor for Seiko. Hammond reported that he and Seiko had had a falling out when the Japanese manufacturer opened a parallel distribution system, selling its watches through new distributors to mass merchandise and discounters in direct competition to its traditional outlets and "exclusive" distributors. He proposed to start a new company, Swiss Watch Distribution Center (SWDC), and wanted an agreement for three years. Hammond

was very enthusiastic about the SWATCH and told Thomke that he could "sell it by the ton." Hammond projected first year sales of 500,000 units, growing to 1.2 million and 1.8–2 million in years two and three and then leveling off at 2.5 million.

Hammond felt that the watch should be positioned as a fashion item and sold through jewelry and fine department stores. He believed that a heavy advertising and point-of-sale budget would be important to gaining large volume sales and felt that SFr. 5 per watch was a reasonable figure. Furthermore, after his experience at Seiko, he promised a careful monitoring of consumer takeoff and a close relationship with retail buyers to avoid discounting and to give service support. Based in Texas, Hammond had substantial financial backing from a group of wealthy investors. He planned to begin initial efforts in the Southwest and then promised to spread rapidly to all major U.S. cities and Canada.

Next Week's Meeting

Thomke had just returned from the United States and briefed Sprecher on his meeting with Ben Hammond. Thomke was anxious to get moving on the project and planned to make a proposal to Pierre Renggli, the president of Asuag, in mid-September, less than three weeks away. At the end of the briefing, they had scheduled a strategy planning session for the next week. Sprecher now had less than one week to evaluate his information and to prepare his proposals for Thomke in preparation for their final presentation to Renggli. Sprecher knew that Thomke expected to receive approval for ETA production and marketing of SWATCH at that presentation. Sprecher knew that his proposals to Thomke needed to be operationally feasible, and with a target launch date of January 1, 1982, available implementation time was short. Sprecher knew that they could pursue negotiations with some of the companies which he had visited or "go it alone" with a direct sales force. Sprecher needed to balance the economic restraints which required minimum annual sales volume of 5 million with Thomke's desire to keep strategic control of the product within ETA. Sprecher needed to consider ETA's lack of marketing experience and what that would mean in the international marketplace.

Case 10

Tissot: Competing in the Global Watch Industry

One sunny afternoon in May 1985, Dr. Ernst Thomke drove his Porsche through the Jura mountains; he was on his way to Bienne for a Tissot strategy session. After more than a decade of declining sales, layoffs, and factory closings, the popular business press was proclaiming the return of the Swiss watch industry. Much of the credit for the resurrection had been given to Thomke, president of Ebauches SA, one of the SMH companies, and initiator of a new low priced Swiss fashion watch: the SWATCH. Thomke believed that the predictions of a revived Swiss watch industry were premature. He had accepted the considerable task of giving the Asuag brands, and particularly Tissot, a hard look to formulate new strategies to bring the Asuag group profitably in the second half of the 1980s and beyond. Specifically, his goal was to increase SMH total volume from 7 million to 50 million units. As his Porsche sped through the countryside he considered the past and future trends for the global watch industry, and he asked himself, ''How can Tissot grow and profit?''

In 1985, the future trends for the global watch industry were anything but clear. Over the past fifteen years, the industry had experienced radical changes.

●

This case was prepared by Susan W. Nye under the supervision of Visiting Professor Jean-Pierre Jeannet as a basis for class discussion rather than to illustrate either effective or ineffective handling of an administrative situation. Copyright © 1985 by IMD, Lausanne, Switzerland. The International Institute for Management Development (IMD), resulting from the merger between IMEDE, Lausanne, and IMI, Geneva, acquires and retains all rights. Not to be used or reproduced without written permission from IMD, Lausanne, Switzerland.

Innovation in products, production, and marketing were all key factors in the volatility which marked a period of rapid entry (often followed by rapid exit) of new competitors and the departure of some established producers.

In 1970 the global watch industry was dominated by Swiss watch manufacturers. By 1975 the competitive field had expanded, and key players came from Switzerland, Japan, and the United States. By the early 1980s the U.S. had all but disappeared as a contender, and Hong Kong was the world's largest exporter in units in the industry, with 326.4 million watches and movements in 1984. Japan ranked second in number and value of units produced. Between 1970 and 1984, the Swiss dropped to third place in unit volume as their assembled watch exports dwindled from 48 million to 17 million pieces. However, Switzerland continued to rank first in value of watch exports, SFr. 3.4 billion in 1984 (see Exhibit 1).

THE WATCH INDUSTRY IN SWITZERLAND

The Swiss watch industry was concentrated in the Jura along the western border of Switzerland. The Swiss had conquered the world market with mechanical watches and had developed a reputation for fine craftsmanship, elegance, and style. Swiss companies produced 80 percent of the watches selling for SFr. 1,200 or more and virtually all top priced watches. A large portion of these watches were still mechanical.

Until the early 1970s, Swiss watchmaking was intensely specialized and fragmented, with a rigid structure which had remained unchanged for centuries. Major changes began in the 1970s with several mergers involving sizable firms and important initiatives in both horizontal and vertical integration.

EXHIBIT 1A ● Total Production of Watches and Watch Movements Worldwide, 1960–1984 (in Millions of Pieces)[1]

1960	1970	1975	1980	1982	1983	1984
98.0	174.0	220.0	300.0	330.0	370.0	n.a.

[1]Without other timepieces as penwatches, and so on.
Source: Swiss Watch Federation. Used by permission.

EXHIBIT 1B ● Watch Production by Country, 1960–1983 (Percentage of Worldwide Unit Production)

	1960	1970	1975	1980	1982	1983
Switzerland	43.0%	42.0%	32.0%	18.4%	10.8%	9.3%
Japan	7.2	13.7	14.0	22.5	24.7	26.1
Hong Kong	—	—	—	18.5	30.0	35.0
U.S.A.	9.7	11.5	12.5	4.0	—	—
E. Ger.	20.5	14.5	16.7	15.7	14.8	13.2
France	5.6	6.3	7.6	3.3	2.9	2.2
W. Ger.	8.0	4.7	4.3	2.2	1.2	1.1

Source: Swiss Watch Federation. Used by permission.

EXHIBIT 1C ● Watch Exports—Watches and Movements, 1960–1984 (in Millions of Francs)

	1960	1970	1975	1980	1982	1984
Switz.*	1159.2	2383.7	2764.3	3106.7	3091.9	3397.3
Japan	16.4	399.3	835.1	1911.1	1908.5	2876.2
Hong Kong	—	63.1	246.1	1855.6	1779.0	2091.2
France	26.2	78.1	209.3	265.0	218.3	233.7
W. Germany	83.6	129.6	140.2	171.7	175.4	231.4

*Including nonassembled movements.
Source: Swiss Watch Federation. Used by permission.

EXHIBIT 1D ● Watch Exports—Watches and Movements, 1960–1984 (in Millions of Pieces)

	1960	*1970*	*1975*	*1980*	*1982*	*1984*
Switz.*	42.6	73.4	71.2	51.0	45.7	46.9
Japan	0.1	11.4	17.1	48.3	63.6	94.7
Hong Kong	—	5.7	16.1	126.1	213.7	326.4
France	1.3	4.4	9.5	9.8	8.4	6.2
W. Germany	3.8	4.1	9.5	4.5	4.7	5.5

*Including nonassembled movements.

Source: Swiss Watch Federation. Used by permission.

EXHIBIT 1E ● Exports as a Percentage of Total Pieces Produced, 1960–1984

	1960	*1970*	*1975*	*1980*	*1982*	*1984*
Switz. (E)	97%	97%	97%	97%	97%	97%
Japan	2	48	57	72	80	n.a.
Hong Kong	—	100	100	100	100	100
France	24	40	57	*	*	*
W. Germany	48	50	*	*	*	*

(E) = estimation.

n.a. = not available.

*Not available; because of reexports, exports are larger than production.

Source: Swiss Watch Federation. Used by permission.

EXHIBIT 1F ● Assembled Watches as a Percentage of Watches and Movements Exported (Value)

	1960	*1970*	*1975*	*1980*	*1982*	*1984*
Switz.	81.3%	86.1%	87.9%	85.9%	91.5%	92.9%
Japan	51.6	83.6	92.1	90.6	87.6	85.0
Hong Kong	97.1	100.0	96.6	95.4	96.9	96.7
France	87.7	93.8	93.8	88.7	91.5	94.4
W. Germany	91.1	88.7	90.6	89.0	92.0	94.8

Source: Swiss Watch Federation. Used by permission.

EXHIBIT 1G ● Assembled Watches as a Percentage of Watches and Movements Exported (Pieces)

	1960	*1970*	*1975*	*1980*	*1982*	*1984*
Switz.	73.7%	73.6%	71.7%	55.9%	59.3%	55.2%
Japan	29.0	64.8	78.1	75.5	67.5	60.6
Hong Kong	98.2	100.0	98.1	94.4	95.6	92.1
France	n.a.	89.5	90.4	81.6	79.0	94.4
W. Germany	89.3	88.9	85.5	69.0	74.4	72.6

n.a. = not available.

Source: Swiss Watch Federation. Used by permission.

The Swiss watch industry was essentially a group of industries. Traditionally, the Swiss had operated on a two tier system: component manufacturing and assembly. In 1934 the Swiss government had instituted laws that made it illegal to open, enlarge, transfer, or transform any watchmaking facilities without government permission. Exports of components and movements were also illegal without permission, as was the export of watchmaking machinery. These regulations were instituted to protect the Swiss watch industry against foreign competition. The government began deregulating the industry in 1971, and in 1985 these laws were no longer in effect.

Swiss watch firms generally fell into one of three categories. First, there had been a large number of "one-man-and-a-boy" and other small enterprises which produced components or movements or put purchased parts into cases. These firms marketed on the basis of long-established personal contacts. Included in this category were the piecework assemblers. A significant portion of inexpensive mechanical watches were assembled by Jura farmers during the winter as in-home piecework. Second were the well-established, privately owned watchmakers which produced expensive, handmade watches. And finally, there was the Asuag-SSIH organization, which was a group of companies representing approximately 35 percent of total Swiss exports of watches and movements.

Watches and movements declined from 11.9 percent to 7.2 percent of total Swiss exports from 1970 to 1980. At the start of the 1970s there were 1,618 watchmaking firms in the industry; this figure had fallen to 634 by 1984. Between 1970 and 1984 the full-time labor force producing watches shrank from 89,500 to 31,000. Layoffs due to the shrinking demand for mechanical watches were exacerbated by automation, rationalization, and concentration initiated throughout the Swiss watch industry.

SMH

Corporate Background

In an effort to resuscitate the industry, a consortium of seven Swiss banks orchestrated a merger between SSIH and Asuag in 1982. They provided the merger with a capital and cash infusion totaling more than SFr. 700 million. In return, the bank gained 97 percent ownership of the combine and planned to sell shares to the public when it returned to profitability, estimated at five to ten years. Turnaround began in 1984 with sales totaling SFr. 1,582.4 million and after-tax profits of SFr. 26.5 million. In February 1985, it was announced that control would be returned to private investors.

Asuag, short for Allgemeine Schweizer Uhrenindustrie, was the largest producer of watches and watch components in Switzerland, accounting for about one-third of total Swiss watch exports and 25 percent of production in Switzerland. Asuag had been founded in 1931 when the Swiss government orchestrated the consolidation of a wide variety of small watchmakers to strengthen the industry during the worldwide depression.

Movements were produced by the twelve subsidiaries of Ebauches SA, including ETA. ETA was the largest Swiss movement manufacturer. ETA produced a full range of movements but was best known as a producer of high quality, expensive ultrathin watch movements used for luxury watches. Ebauches companies sold 65 percent of their production volume to the Asuag-SSIH brands. Ebauches' sales had dropped from 51.1 million to 32.1 million pieces between 1973 and 1984. During this period the world market for movements had grown from 215 million to 350 million units. Ebauches' world market share dropped from 23.8 to 9.2 percent.

Asuag's brands of finished watches included Longines, Eterna, Certina, and Rado. Rado was the largest selling midpriced Swiss watch, with annual sales of about 1 million units. Fifty-five percent of Asuag's production was in finished watches. Asuag began losing money in 1977, reporting an accumulated net loss of SFr. 129 million in 1982.

Société Suisse de l'Industrie Horlogère (SSIH) had been the second largest watch company in Switzerland, responsible for 10 percent of total output. SSIH was made up of a diverse group of companies producing watches and movements in all price categories. SSIH group companies included Omega, Tissot, and Economic Time.

SSIH had encountered severe financial problems in the late 1970s. In 1977 the Zurich-based trading group Siber Hegner & Co. AG, a major international distributor of Swiss watches, including Omega and Tissot, provided SSIH with a capital infusion of SFr. 32.5 million. A rescue plan was devised which deemphasized the lower price end of the market. Siber Hegner management concentrated on electronic quartz models which sold at prices above SFr. 235. Tissot watch prices were pushed upward, and Tissot models were sold in the SFr. 235 to 1,500 range. Omega watches were priced above SFr. 600 at retail. Companies producing at the low price end of the market were sold off, and inexpensive watch production was reduced from 69.2 to 19.7 percent of total. At the same time, the product mix was shifted, and electronic watches increased from 8.9 percent of total in 1976 to 47.9 percent of total sales in 1980. Siber Heg-

ner provided a cash infusion for research and development and a worldwide advertising campaign. Acquisitions and joint ventures were arranged to improve integration, although management, production, marketing, and sales remained decentralized.

Initially, turnaround was successful, with profits in 1979 allowing for the first dividend payment since 1974. Profitability was short lived, and in June 1981, SSIH announced a loss of SFr. 142 million for the year ending March 31, 1981, giving the company a net loss of SFr. 27.4 million. A consortium of Swiss banks in an effort to bail out the company provided cash and credit valued at almost SFr. 230 million in return for 96.5 percent equity in the recapitalized company.

Tissot SA

Thomke described Tissot, and most Asuag-SSIH watches, as a "branded commodity." The individual companies produced their products under recognized brand names, but Thomke felt that the watches had been poorly developed in terms of brand image and personality. Thomke believed the weak image had led to the decline in Tissot sales (Exhibit 2). His goal was to create a workable brand strategy and identity for Tissot. In May 1985, Thomke believed that Tissot had gained the reputation of an "inexpensive" Omega.

The company produced about 400,000 watches in 1984, for watch sales of SFr. 42 million. The average retail price for a Tissot watch was about SFr. 375. Strongest sales volume was from watches in the SFr. 300–700 range. Retail prices ranged from SFr. 75 to 800 for stainless steel and gold plated watches. A second, smaller line of gold watches sold for between SFr. 1,000 and 5,000. Tissot watches were sold in Europe: Switzerland, West Germany, Italy, Scandinavia, and the United Kingdom. Tissot was also sold in Brazil, South Africa, Hong Kong, Singapore, and Japan. Tissot had been withdrawn from the U.S. market in the 1970s but Thomke wanted to reintroduce it to the United States as soon as possible.

Tissot production was limited to assembly. Employment at the factory had declined from a high of 1,200 to 200. All components and movements were purchased from Asuag-SSIH or independent companies. At the start of 1985, Tissot workers were assembling a product line of some 300 styles, each produced

EXHIBIT 2 ● Tissot World Sales, 1981–1984

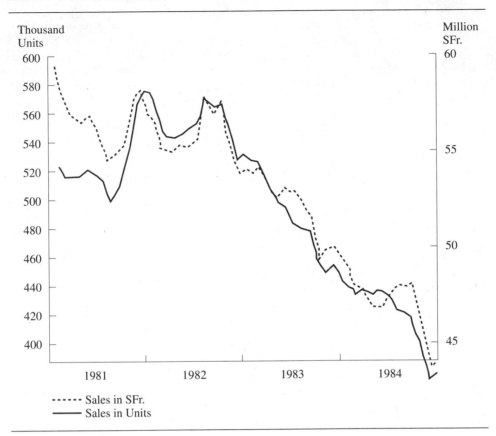

Thousand Units / Million SFr.

----- Sales in SFr.
——— Sales in Units

in a woman's and man's model and in a number of different metals and combinations. Thomke had already assigned ten engineers at Tissot to review the product line and production process.

Tissot shared Omega's distribution at both the wholesale and retail level. Almost all Omega wholesalers were independent distributors. A total of 12,000 retail stores, mostly jewelry stores and a few "high class" department stores carried Tissot watches. The majority of its watch sales came from the top 3,000 stores. Ex-factory prices ranged from SFr. 60 to 2,000. Both wholesalers and retailers provided advertising and promotion support, but all promotion activities had to be initiated by Tissot.

Thomke was aware that if he wanted to build up a strong image for Tissot, he would have to increase his marketing and promotion expenditure. Asuag-SSIH set targets for marketing and profit margins (MPM) for each brand. Thomke felt that a 50 percent margin would give a brand adequate funds for marketing and profit. Only his latest product, SWATCH, came close to that figure, followed by Rado with almost 30 percent. A target MPM of 15 percent had been set for Tissot for 1984, but Thomke had learned that the actual margin had been closer to 10 percent.

Thomke believed that the MPM had been squeezed by wholesalers because of the slow turnover for Tissot watches. Wholesalers demanded a margin of 28 to 45 percent for Tissot watches. Explaining the situation, Thomke said, "Tissot has never recovered the sales and market share it lost to Seiko and Citizen in the 1970s. Sales to retailers have slowed considerably, and consumer demand is down. To encourage wholesalers to keep Tissot in inventory, the company granted more liberal wholesaler margins, at the expense of marketing funds and profits."

Thomke felt that it was still possible to build up the brand and reestablish a strong wholesale network. However, he realized that this was an expensive proposition. He was prepared to invest 18 to 20 percent of sales in promotion, but to have any effect he needed a promotion budget of SFr. 12 million for Europe alone. Thomke estimated that the company could spend SFr. 6–8 million in Germany, Tissot's largest market in 1985. This figure would be divided with one half targeted for media advertising and the rest for point-of-sale promotion. If handled correctly, promotion activities would give Tissot the strong image which Thomke felt was essential to successful watch sales.

WATCHMAKING TECHNOLOGY

Designing a Watch Collection

Watches covered a broad spectrum in terms of style and price, ranging from sport watches, for informal or daytime wear, to luxury dress watches, which were pieces of jewelry. It could take three years to bring a watch from the drawing board to the market. A watch collection was made up of as many as thirty to forty lines. Each line had up to 1,000 models. A watch line was differentiated by case shape, design, and the movement. The differences between models were cosmetic variations in color and types of materials or due to slight variations in technology, such as day/date calendars or self-winding mechanisms.

Watch cases were made in precious metals, standard steel, brass, and plastic. The cases of many expensive luxury watches were decorated with semiprecious and precious stones, such as lapis lazuli, diamonds, and sapphires. Watch cases were made in two or three pieces. Two pieces, the back and front, were standard and held the watch together. For better watches a separate rim held the crystal in place. The rim provided designers with more flexibility when developing new models and gave the watches a finer finish.

Watch crystals were pieces of thin glass or plastic which protected the hands and dial and came in three types. The least expensive were plastic, followed by mineral glass and sapphire glass. Sapphire glass was very hard and could not be scratched or chipped.

Straps or bracelets held the watch on the wrist and came in a variety of materials. Straps came in leather, plastic, and cloth ribbons. Bracelets were made from precious metals, standard steel, brass, and plastic. Precious and semiprecious stones were often set into the bracelets of luxury watches. Up until the 1970s, most watches were sold with leather straps. In the past fifteen years, fashion had changed, and most watches were purchased with bracelets.

Timekeeping Technology

Every watch was composed of four basic elements: a time base, a source of energy, a transmission, and a display. The movement was the watch's time base. Movements came in two major categories: mechanical and electronic. Mechanical movements were driven by the release of energy from an unwinding spring. Electronic watches ran on an electric battery. Energy was transmitted through a series of gears, a motor, or integrated circuits to the hands of analog watches. These hands moved around the dial to display time. Integrated circuits were used to transmit time to digital watches, and time was displayed numerically in a frame on the watch case.

Mechanical Watch Movements

The movement was a complex set of 100 or more tiny parts. While all mechanical watch movements operated on the same principle, there was a great deal of variety in watch quality. Friction and wear had to be minimized to ensure long term accuracy of the tiny moving parts. To minimize friction, jewels were placed at all the movement's critical pivot and contact points. Fifteen was the standard number of jewels, but high-quality movements might contain as many as thirty. Contrary to popular belief, adding more jewels did not necessarily indicate increased quality, or cost to production. These internal jewels were synthetic and relatively inexpensive. It was the overall care and craftsmanship that went into the watches that created the expense and not the jewels themselves.

The precision and accuracy found in high quality jewel-lever watches required micromechanical engineering expertise. A variety of modifications could be made to a spring-powered watch which added to the complexity of the interior design but not the basic mechanism. Refinements, such as improved accuracy, miniaturization, water resistance, and self-wind technology, rather than radical new developments had occurred. Calendars and chronographs, as well as watches with start/stop mechanisms, were also possible.

Pin-lever watches, also called "roskopfs" after their inventor, had metal pins instead of jewels on the escapement mechanism gear teeth. Roskopf's original goal in inventing this watch had been to make the movement so simple that watches could be made affordable to everyone (Exhibit 3).

Electronic Movements

A Swiss engineer, Max Hetzel, invented the first electronic watch in 1954. This development was largely possible due to advances in miniature batteries and electric motors during World War II. Initially, electronics did not represent a big departure from mechanical technology nor offer substantially better accuracy. While the energy source was replaced with electronics, the transmission and regulating components remained unchanged.

The tuning-fork watch, developed in the 1960s, represented a significant change to the traditional principles of determining time. A small battery in the watch sent an electric current to the tuning fork and stimulated it to vibrate at 360 cycles per second. The vibrations were transmitted to a set of gears which drove the hands on the watch face. Tuning-fork watches, if properly adjusted, were accurate to within one minute per month.

The quartz crystal watch began appearing in the marketplace at the end of the 1960s. An electric current was passed through a quartz crystal to stimulate high frequency vibration which could be converted into precise time increments. Microcircuitry subdivided the crystal's frequency into an electric pulse which drove the watch. The pulse operated a tiny electric stepping motor or was transmitted through con-

EXHIBIT 3 ● Wristwatch Purchases in the United States

Wristwatch Purchases

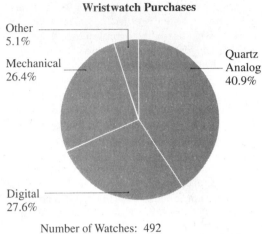

Number of Watches: 492
(Total Number of Surveyed Buyers: 492)

Source: National Jewelers/HTI.
    Consumer Survey 1983.

ductors and integrated circuits to drive the gears and watch hands.

In 1972, digital watches appeared for the first time. These watches had no moving parts, and the conventional face and hands were replaced with digital readouts. Early digital watches used light emitting diodes (LED) to show the time. With this technology, users pressed a button for time display. LED watches required a great deal of power, and batteries lasted no longer than one year. Liquid crystal diodes (LCD) came on the market in 1972; these watches displayed the time continually. These watches were considerably more conservative in energy usage, and batteries lasted from three to five years or longer.

Early electronic watches were not fully water- and shockproofed, and the batteries often malfunctioned in hot, humid climates. However, within a short period of time, technological advances led to electronic watches which were water proof to depths of thirty meters, shockproof, and able to withstand tropical climates.

Designing electronic watches for women had initially created problems as well as opportunities. To create models which fit a woman's smaller wrist required considerable miniaturization of the movement and battery. Creating smaller movements led to increased design flexibility. Improvements in miniaturization and advancement in large-scale integrated circuits (LSI) and battery technology allowed manufacturers to add special functions without excessive bulk. Watches began to take on the appearance of multifunction instruments. Runners, skin divers, sailors, and other sports enthusiasts bought watches which would provide them with waterproofing and sophisticated chronograph functions. Travelers were afforded the opportunity to buy watches with multiple time zone functions and alarms. Watches were also available with calculators and radios, and progress was being made toward a television watch (Exhibit 3).

Producing Watches

Movements, hands, cases, and bracelets were assembled to produce a complete watch. Mechanical watch quality was dependent on the care taken in assembly as well as the quality of the individual components. High quality mechanical movements were made by hand, and a combination of semi- and highly skilled craftsmen was needed. Mechanical watch assembly was done in batches. Highly skilled workers were essential at the final stages of production, for finishing and adjusting to produce high quality, finely finished, accurate movements and watches.

While the term *pin-lever* refers specifically to the replacement of jewels with metal pins, roskopfs were made from lower quality grade materials. Labor requirements for roskopfs were reduced with semi- or unskilled labor working in batch production.

Electronic movements for analog watches combined micromechanical and electronic engineering. The electronic regulating mechanism simplified the production process which could be run in an automated setting with semiskilled labor. Movements for digital watches were radically different from analog watches. These watches had no moving parts, and time was programmed onto a silicon chip. Unskilled labor could be used to assemble digital watches, which were assembled in batches and on automated assembly lines.

Both mechanical and electronic watch reliability was tied to the number of inspections the manufacturer made. For midpriced and expensive watches, 100 percent inspection occurred at several points during the process. Tests were made for water- and shockproofing as well as accuracy.

Costs of production were a function of a company's degree of integration and automation, material costs, and the local wage rates. Material costs were based on the quality of the watch produced. With roskopf watches, labor constituted a significant portion of variable costs, but as the watches moved up-market, the materials, fine stainless steel, sapphire crystals, and eventually precious metals and decorative jewels played the major role in the watch's ex-factory price. Watchmakers could improve their variable costs by assembling at volumes above 10,000 pieces. Assemblers producing 100,000–500,000 units per year could benefit from component supplier discounts which were as high as 20–25 percent. Beyond this point, cost improvements could only be realized with new production processes, automation, and robotics. Wages for the Swiss watch industry averaged SFr. 12 per hour. Most Swiss watchmakers sought a 30 percent gross margin. In Japan, average hourly wages for factory workers were SFr. 7.20. Japanese producers had an average gross margin of 40 percent. In Hong Kong, manufacturers kept their ex-factory prices low with inexpensive but highly productive piecework labor, averaging under SFr. 10 per day, fewer inspections, and cheaper materials. Gross margins of approximately 10–15 percent were typical for Hong Kong manufacturers (Exhibit 4).

SEGMENTING THE GLOBAL WATCH INDUSTRY

Price Segments

Price has been a traditional means of segmenting the watch market into three categories. The first group was low price, "C," watches and included all watches sold at retail for under SFr. 120. Roskopf watches and inexpensive digitals competed in this market. These watches accounted for 33 percent of total value of global watch sales and 86 percent of unit volume. The midprice, or "B" watches, ranged from SFr. 120–700 at retail. This sector represented 25 percent of sales in Swiss francs and 12 percent of

EXHIBIT 4A ● Breakdown of Production Costs

For a Swiss watch with an ex-factory price of SFr. 390, variable cost breakdown was estimated as follows:

case	70
bracelet	90
dial	50
crystal	18
movement	18 (50 for mechanical)
hands	5
Total materials costs	251
Assembly and quality control	25
Margin	114
Ex-factory	390
Wholesalers' margin	260
Retailers' margin	650
Consumer price	1,300

For Japanese watchmakers producing a watch with ex-factory of SFr. 250, breakdown of costs and margins was as follows:

Total variable costs	150
Margin	100
Ex-factory	250
Wholesalers' margin	60–90
Retailers' margin	310–340
Consumer price	630–700

For Hong Kong makers producing a watch with ex-factory cost of SFr. 80, breakdown of variable costs was as follows:

case and dial	15
bracelet	15
crystal	15
movement	18
hands	2
Total materials costs	65
Assembly and quality control	6
Manufacturer's margin 10%	8
Ex-factory	80
Wholesalers' margin	30
Retailers' margin	55–110
Consumer price	165–220

Source: Asuag-SSIH and interviews with industry experts.

total units for 1984. Electronic watches dominated both the "C" and the "B" price segments.

The third category was the top priced watches. The retail price of "A" watches ranged from SFr. 700 to 5,000. Manufacturers of luxury watches, "AA" class, sold to a small exclusive group willing to pay several thousand Swiss francs for a special, custom design jeweled watch. Precious stones and/or metal used in the watch face and bracelet accounted for the major portion of the "A" and "AA" watch prices. This was particularly true for electronic watches, where movements averaged SFr. 18. About 27 per-

EXHIBIT 4B ● Breakdown of Costs and Margins for Traditional "B" Watches (by Country of Origin)

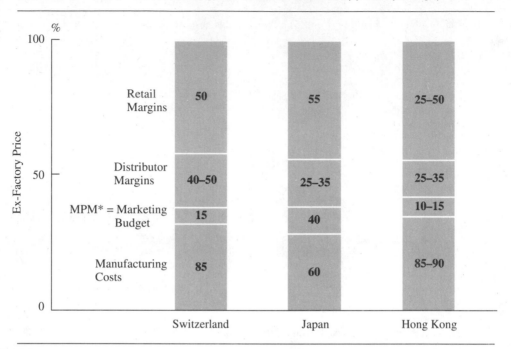

*Manufacturing and profit margins.

cent of the value of total watches and 2 percent of pieces sold worldwide were from the "A" tier. "AA" watches accounted for 16 percent of global watch sales in Swiss francs but less than .5 percent of total units. Mechanical watches still dominated the high priced segments (Exhibit 5).

Evaluating timekeeping technology was difficult for consumers. When shopping for watches, consumers chose a particular price level and expected a certain level of technical proficiency, style, and intangibles such as prestige. Quartz technology changed the price/accuracy ratio. Before the electronic watch, accuracy was bought with expensive, finely engineered jewel-lever watches. With the introduction of electronics, watches with accuracy of plus or minus fifteen seconds per month could be purchased for as little as $9.95.

Geographic Segments

Technologies and price have had an impact on the world markets for watches. Historically the major importer of finished watches, the United States was often the launching ground for new products, and success in this market indicated strong possibility of global success. The strong dollar and improving U.S. economy in 1984–1985 had a positive impact on the sales and profits of Swiss and Japanese watch companies. Europe and Japan were also strong markets for watches in all price categories. However, throughout the 1960s and 1970s, new opportunities for watch sales had opened up in the oil producing countries in the Middle East and in less developed countries (LDCs).

In the 1960s, watch producers began to move

EXHIBIT 5 ● Watch Purchases in the United States at Retail Prices

No. of items	% Watches (490)*	% Quartz analog (200)	% Digital (135)	% Mechanical (130)
$1,000 or more	.8	.5	.7	1.5
$300 to $999	2.4	4.0	.7	1.5
$100 to $299	23.5	38.0	8.9	14.6
$50 to $99	33.5	33.5	31.9	35.4
$25 to $49	39.8	24.0	57.8	47.0

*Total 490 responses for consumer survey.

Source: National Jeweler/HTI.
         Consumer Survey 1983.

EXHIBIT 6A ● Major Importers of Swiss Watches and Movements (in Millions of Pieces)

	1960	1970	1975	1980	1982	1984
Hong Kong	1.9	10.0	11.3	12.5	4.1	4.9
United States	12.4	19.2	.12.0	5.9	3.6	4.6
Germany	1.3	2.9	5.0	4.9	3.6	4.0
Italy	1.2	2.6	2.6	2.5	2.3	3.0
France	0.2	0.7	0.8	1.6	1.9	2.2
Japan	0.2	1.0	1.6	0.7	0.7	2.0
United Kingdom	1.7	6.1	6.3	3.2	1.9	1.9
Saudi Arabia	0.2	3.4	1.1	1.0	1.2	0.9
Arab Emirates			1.4	1.9	1.3	0.8
Spain	0.8	2.5	1.9	1.3	1.1	0.8
Total 10 largest markets	19.9	48.4	44.0	35.5	21.7	25.1
Total worldwide	41.0	71.4	65.8	51.0	31.3	32.2

Source: Swiss Watch Federation. Used by permission.

EXHIBIT 6B ● Major Importers of Swiss Watches and Movements (in Millions of Swiss Francs)

	1960	1970	1975	1980	1982	1984
United States	250.6	482.2	348.6	379.7	407.8	598.7
Hong Kong	76.6	242.6	257.6	401.6	344.1	351.5
Italy	70.1	153.9	194.0	256.4	287.7	300.3
Germany	48.2	135.3	195.6	241.7	212.4	246.6
Saudi Arabia*	12.2	92.0	84.0	201.9	271.9	233.1
France	10.6	38.6	75.6	123.3	152.0	169.8
Japan	14.1	88.0	172.5	109.0	120.3	167.1
Singapore	38.3	45.1	58.3	79.7	106.2	150.3
United Kingdom	43.1	131.3	176.6	125.3	127.2	139.9
Arab Emirates*	—	—	59.4	71.7	94.9	82.1
Total 10 largest markets	563.8	1,409.0	1,622.2	1,990.3	2,124.5	2,439.4
Total worldwide	1,146.3	2,362.2	2,720.3	2,917.5	3,011.0	3,298.8

*Saudi Arabia with Arab Emirates in 1960 and 1970.

Source: Swiss Watch Federation. Used by permission.

EXHIBIT 6C ● Major Importers of Japanese Watches and Movements (In Millions of Pieces)

	1980	1982	1983
Hong Kong	14.2	23.0	28.3
United States	7.5	10.3	11.8
Germany	3.4	2.7	3.1
Italy	0.8	0.8	1.1
France	1.1	1.9	2.6
Canada	0.8	0.7	1.0
United Kingdom	1.1	1.7	2.2
Saudi Arabia	2.1	2.8	3.9
Arab Emirates	0.6	1.3	1.4
Spain	0.5	2.0	2.1
Total 10 largest markets	32.1	47.2	57.5
Total worldwide	48.3	63.6	76.0

Source: Swiss Watch Federation. Used by permission.

EXHIBIT 6D ● Major Importers of Japanese Watches and Movements (in Millions of Swiss Francs)

	1980	1982	1983
United States	316.9	372.9	403.4
Hong Kong	383.7	471.0	580.8
Italy	40.9	33.3	47.6
Germany	142.4	94.4	88.0
Saudi Arabia	107.3	94.8	158.3
France	72.0	73.0	95.5
Canada	44.6	39.6	51.1
Singapore	18.3	29.9	23.0
United Kingdom	54.3	56.0	56.7
Arab Emirates	24.5	42.4	58.9
Total 10 largest markets	1,205.0	1,306.4	1,563.2
Total worldwide	1,918.5	1,925.4	2,224.7

Source: Swiss Watch Federation. Used by permission.

EXHIBIT 6E ● Major Importers of Watches and Movements from Hong Kong (in Millions of Pieces)

	1980	1982	1983
Canada	2.9	8.6	10.2
United States	32.6	81.7	119.2
Germany	11.5	15.6	20.5
Italy	4.6	5.2	8.0
France	6.6	4.8	4.2
Japan	5.9	8.2	12.4
United Kingdom	9.7	10.4	12.6
Saudi Arabia	2.4	6.4	7.1
Arab Emirates	1.4	3.9	6.2
Spain	4.2	9.5	14.8
Total 10 largest markets	81.8	154.3	215.2
Total worldwide	126.1	213.7	284.1

Source: Swiss Watch Federation. Used by permission.

EXHIBIT 6F ● Major Importers of Watches and Movements from Hong Kong (in Millions of Swiss Francs)

	1980	1982	1984
United States	469.4	591.3	671.7
Canada	56.7	63.3	57.8
Italy	62.7	34.9	40.8
Germany	194.9	129.4	145.9
Saudi Arabia	58.9	102.3	100.5
France	88.5	34.2	22.8
Japan	69.5	65.1	84.7
Singapore	43.8	46.8	34.2
United Kingdom	139.0	82.6	76.3
Arab Emirates	25.7	59.6	57.0
Total 10 largest markets	1,209.0	1,209.4	1,291.5
Total worldwide	1,859.7	1,779.6	1,915.3

Source: Swiss Watch Federation. Used by permission.

into the LDC market with inexpensive roskopf watches. This market was taken over by inexpensive digitals in the early 1970s. However, the initial success of the cheap digital in this market was short lived, and consumers returned to mechanical watches. The miniature batteries in the quartz watch were very expensive in these regions, sometimes more than the original cost of the watch. By 1984, this problem had been solved, and inexpensive electric watches again dominated the LDC market.

A new opportunity for watch manufacturers developed in industrialized countries, with children providing a new and growing market for inexpensive watches. Until the 1960s most received their first watch in their mid- to late teens, often as a gift. Roskopf watches opened up the market to children in the 7 to 10 year range. A major portion of these purchases were novelty watches, with cartoon and storybook characters, sold as gifts for children.

The market for expensive watches moved to the Middle East in the early 1970s. The rest of the world was caught in a recession, largely due to escalating oil and gas prices, and demand for high price luxury items fell off. Buyers in the oil producing countries had both the money and the interest to purchase luxury goods. The Swiss were particularly adept at meeting the changing fashions and tastes of this new luxury segment and provided expensive, luxury watches with lapis lazuli, coral, diamonds and turquoise (Exhibit 6).

TRENDS IN WATCHES DISTRIBUTION

Wholesale Distributors

Watch distributors played an essential role in linking the manufacturer to the retailer. Distributors generally sold one or perhaps two noncompeting brands.

Wholesalers expected exclusive distribution rights for the brand for a given region. Distributors maintained a sales force to sell to and service retailers. They purchased watches outright and maintained a local inventory.

Manufacturers expected their distributors to participate in promotion activities. Distributors attended trade fairs and contributed to advertising, mailing expenses, and point-of-purchase display materials.

The distributor was responsible to find and oversee adequate watch repair services. Watch repair was a key issue for watches in the "B," "A," and "AA" categories. This service need had led to a close working relationship between the producer, distributor, and retailer. The distributor found and licensed watch repair services and jewelers with watch repair capabilities. For especially difficult repairs, the distributor helped arrange for work to be sent back to the factory. With inexpensive, "throwaway" watches, repairs were less critical or nonexistent. Importers of "C" level watches had greater freedom in channel selection. Mass merchandisers, drugstores, and even supermarkets were used to distribute watches to end users. Some of these watches were sold with a guarantee, and rather than repair, a replacement was offered.

Most watch manufacturers had agreements with independent distributors. The Japanese and some of the private Swiss firms operated wholly or partially owned marketing and sales subsidiaries in their foreign markets. Twenty-five to 35 percent was the standard markup granted wholesalers and importers of Japanese and Hong Kong watches. This figure increased to 40 percent or more for importers of most Swiss watches.

Retailers

A wide variety of retailers sold watches to the end user, including jewelry and department stores, mass merchandisers, and mail order catalogs.

An estimated 40 percent of worldwide watch sales came from jewelry stores. Watch manufacturers benefited from the jeweler's selling expertise and personal interaction with consumers. Watches sold in exclusive jewelry and department stores benefited from the store's deluxe or fashion image. Fine gold, mechanical watches were a natural extension of the jew-

eler's product line, and most were capable of minor watch repairs and cleaning. When electronics were initially introduced, some jewelry stores resisted the new technology. Electronics were not within the jeweler's extensive training. Within a short period of time, however, customer demand and refinements to the technology moved quartz watches into jewelry stores worldwide.

Jewelry stores had been the traditional outlet for watch sales until the mid-1950s. The rapid growth in roskopf and later in inexpensive digital watch sales was accompanied by channel diversification, and watches moved into new outlets: drugstores, department stores, and supermarkets. Retail watch sales in the United States had been influenced by channel diversification, and in 1983 less than 30 percent of watches sold in the U.S. were purchased in jewelry stores (Exhibit 7).

Stock turn for a "B," "A," or "AA" watch could be as low as two times per year at retail, and phasing out older models and cleaning out the pipeline could take two to three years. "C" watches generally moved more quickly, with four to six stock turns per year.

Jewelry stores and department stores were accustomed to a 50–55 percent markup. Mass mer-

EXHIBIT 7A ● Watch Purchases by Outlet Type in the United States

Number of items	% Analog	% Digital	% Watches (485)
Jewelry store	34.3	12.0	27.6
Department store	26.3	27.6	26.2
Discount store	14.7	23.1	16.7
Catalog showroom	14.7	10.4	10.3
Mail order	14.7	11.2	5.4
Wholesaler	2.5	1.5	3.1
Drugstore	2.0	6.0	5.1
Flea market*			2.4
Other outlets	3.0	7.5	6.2

*Flea markets accounted for less than 1% of all categories.

EXHIBIT 7B ● Cost of Purchases in Main Outlets

Number of items	$1000+ (40)	$300–999 (173)	$100–299 (485)	$50–99 (466)	$25–49 (657)
Jewelry Store	70.0%	69.4%	49.1%	34.6%	27.2%
Department Store		6.9	16.7	22.5	27.9
Discount Store	2.5	1.7	5.8	9.7	10.5
Catalog Showroom	5.0	5.2	8.9	9.4	7.3
Other Outlets	22.5	16.8	19.5	23.8	27.1

EXHIBIT 7C ● Brand Distribution of Watch Purchases in the United States

Brand Distribution of Watch Purchases

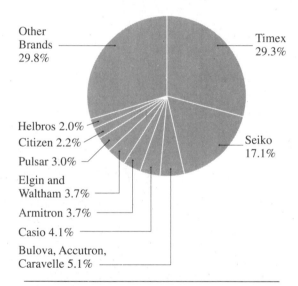

Source: National Jeweler/HTI.
   Consumer Survey 1983.

chandisers' margins varied and went as low as 25 percent.

COMPETITORS IN THE GLOBAL WATCH INDUSTRY

Timex

Timex, a U.S. company, began selling inexpensive mechanical watches in the late 1950s. Most Timex watches fell into the "C" range, with prices ranging from under SFr. 15 to just over SFr. 250.

The company developed into a manufacturer of mass-produced, hard alloy pin-lever watches. Manufacturing was mechanized, simplified, and standardized. When the company's pricing plan called for a 30 percent markup at the retail level, jewelry stores refused to carry the watches. Timex moved into mass outlets such as drug, department, and hardware stores, and even cigar stands. The number of outlets for Timex watches in 1985 was estimated between 100,000 and 150,000, down from a high of 2.5 million in the 1960s. By the late 1960s, 50 percent of all watches sold in the United States were Timex. In 1985, Timex had capacity to produce 15 million watches.

Timex had an advertising budget of approximately SFr. 20 million, most of which was spent on television sports events. Timex produced a large number of styles but did not promote any single model or style. The company was known for its "takes a licking and keeps on ticking" slogan promoting Timex durability.

Timex began limited production of digital watches in 1972. By the mid-1970s the company was feeling pressure from new entrants from Japan, and the U.S. sales support for mechanical watches was withdrawn, and Timex attempted to increase its digital capacity and to gain electronics capabilities rapidly. As a mechanical watch manufacturer, Timex had been fully integrated but used outside sources for electronic components. The company's initial entries to the digital market were poorly received, and sales declined to SFr. 1 billion in 1979. During the 1970s the company faced significant losses, which amounted to SFr. 260 million by the end of 1982. These losses were expected to escalate.

In the 1980s, Timex moved into consumer electronics, computers, and home health care products and refocused its watch business to try to halt its profit slide and plant closings. In 1981, Timex invested in a British home-computer company founded by inventor Clive Sinclair. The computer had little capacity but had the lowest price on the market. In 1982, fierce price competition in the home-computer market squeezed margins, and the price was cut in half to approximately SFr. 100. The company also lost sales to competitors such as Commodore, which offered more power for about SFr. 180. Timex management viewed the watch industry as splitting into two parts: jewelry and wrist instruments. Timex reported that its development plans would emphasize the wrist-instrument business with multifunction watches.

Texas Instruments, Inc.

In 1975 a number of U.S. electronics companies entered the industry with digital watches and circuits for electronic movements. Finding themselves with excess capacity, an estimated 100 chip producers entered the watch market. Most started as suppliers of movements and components and integrated forward into production and assembly of complete watches. In the early days of digital watch sales, demand far outstripped capacity. In spite of this fact, the electronics companies continually pushed price down in a market share war which eventually destroyed this attempted entry into the watch business.

Texas Instruments (TI) was the largest of the semiconductor and computer companies to enter the watch industry. Its consumer electronics division began in the early 1970s with hand-held calculators. The company then broadened this line with watches, home computers, and educational products.

Watch manufacturing at TI began in 1976, when its first LED, plastic-cased watch with a SFr. 40 price tag was introduced. One month later the price was cut in half. TI developed a digital watch that could be made from TI built parts on automated equipment. Prices were set to undercut the mechanical watch competition, with a goal to gain a large piece of both the U.S. and global market. Prices were set to reflect budgeted future volumes.

While TI had surprised the competition with reduced prices, it was caught off-guard with advances in digital display readouts. To provide a full line of products, the company imported seven out of thirteen of its basic lines from Hong Kong, including its multifunction watches. The corporation reported SFr. 6.4 billion in sales in 1979, SFr. 800 million of which came from consumer goods. The division showed a pretax profit of SFr. 4 million, down from pretax US$74 million in 1978. Profits continued to slide and TI moved out of the watch industry in 1982.

Casio Computer Company

In 1974, Casio, a Japanese computer company, entered the market and claimed 12 percent share of all Japanese watches sold within five years. Casio watches were sold in the "C" price range. Casio manufactured its watches in highly automated factories. Its product line was limited to digital watches, many of them multifunctional with stopwatches, timers, and calculators. Casio management has been quoted as saying: "People should own at least three watches." In 1985, Casio was selling an estimated 30 million watches per year. The Casio name was clearly linked worldwide with multifunction watches.

Casio's first entry into the digital market was priced at SFr. 180, and initial sales were weak. As the company's watch prices began to fall, sales doubled annually from 1974 to 1980.

Casio was among the first electronic watch producers to determine that the electronic watch's greatest appeal was technical rather than aesthetic. The company urged its department and mass merchandise store retailers to display its watches in the camera, calculator, or stereo department, rather than the jewelry department. Casio management felt that sales personnel at these counters understood electronic equipment better than jewelry salespeople and could therefore answer customer questions.

The Hong Kong Watchmakers

Hong Kong entered the watch market in a major way in 1976, specializing in inexpensive electronic and mechanical watches. Hong Kong watch manufacturers did not sell under their own company or brand name. Private label watches were produced and sold in minimum lots of 1,000–2,000 pieces per model.

Ten major producers accounted for an estimated 70 percent of total volume, but as many as 800 "loft workshops" were also operating. These production facilities could be started at low cost and run with minimum overheads. Hong Kong was the world's largest watch exporter and was responsible for 326.4 million units in 1984; total value was SFr. 2,091.2 million. Most watch production in Hong Kong was limited to assembly. Inexpensive components and movements were purchased in large lot sizes. Hong Kong manufacturers kept their design costs minimal or nonexistent by producing copies and near-copies of watches displayed at trade fairs and in jewelry stores. Average ex-factory prices were SFr. 25 for a mechanical, SFr. 60 for quartz analog, and SFr. 12 for electronic digitals. Hong Kong watch prices began to fall rapidly in the late 1970s. Simple watches selling for SFr. 18–20 in 1978 dropped to SFr. 12 in one year, and margins shrank to less than SFr. 1.

Counterfeiting was a fairly common practice among small Hong Kong manufacturers. A counterfeit copied the original watch design and was marked with the brand name. This practice was generally avoided by the large producers, who beginning in the early 1980s were seeking entry into the international watch establishment. Counterfeiting was a significant problem faced by European and Japanese producers. Unlike technological innovations, it was very difficult to establish patents or copyrights on designs. Firms could begin to protect their brand name by establishing a company or joint venture within Hong Kong.

SWATCH Watch SA

SWATCH was a plastic, quartz analog watch. SWATCH was sold at SFr. 15 ex-factory and SFr. 50 at retail in Switzerland. Prices outside of Switzerland were slightly higher, and the top price was $30 in the United States. The product was available in twelve styles, which changed twice per year, in a woman's and a man's model.

SWATCH WATCH was an Asuag-SSIH company under the direction of Ernst Thomke. It was founded in 1985 when it was split off from its original producer ETA. SWATCH WATCH remained within the Ebauches group of Asuag-SSIH. Within two years of its introduction in 1982, the brand had hit sales of 3.5 million units. Sales for 1985 were expected to reach 7.5 million units. In 1985, SWATCH management was concerned that the company's already constrained capacity could become an increasingly significant problem over the next few years. The product was produced on a fully automated and robotized assembly line, and the hands were the only component purchased from an outside source. The company had enjoyed rapid decline in production costs per watch. Thomke had met and surpassed his original target production cost of SFr. 10 per watch.

From introduction it had been positioned for active people, as a sport or fashion accessory and not as a time piece. The watch sold in jewelry and department stores. The company had spent heavily on promotion and advertising, budgeting approximately SFr. 5 per watch for marketing expense and profits.

SWATCH invested SFr. 20 million in marketing efforts and was expected to spend SFr. 30 million in 1985. SWATCH was sold in 19 industrial countries, approximately 50 percent of all SWATCHes in the United States. In the majority of markets, independent distributors were employed. However, SWATCH WATCH USA was a wholly owned subsidiary which controlled distribution in the United States. SWATCH WATCH USA played a significant role in the creation of marketing strategy and planning for the watch.

Seiko

Seiko, part of the K. Hattori Company, began marketing an electronic, quartz watch in 1969 and emerged as the market volume leader in the global watch industry within ten years. In 1984 the company reported annual sales of SFr. 3.8 billion for watches and clocks. Seiko brand watches fell within the "B" category. But the company competed in the "C" segment watches with the Alba and Larus labels, high "C" or low "B" segment with the Pulsar label, and "A" segment with the Jean Lassale brand. In 1984 the company sold 55 million watches, 22 million under the Seiko brand.

Seiko had been using assembly line production since the mid-1950s. Following the example of the Detroit automobile factories, its engineers designed assembly lines, and unskilled laborers were employed in most production. The firm was fully integrated, manufacturing key components, jewels, and even watchmaking machinery. Seiko was among the first to initiate large scale production and sales of electronic watches.

Seiko had been protected from foreign competitors in its domestic market. Only expensive watches, about 5 percent of total units and 20 percent of total value of Japanese purchases, were imported. Almost all of the low- to midprice watches purchased in Japan were produced by Seiko or one of its two domestic competitors, Citizen and Casio. Japanese companies produced some low priced movements for Hong Kong manufacturers. However, movements for "B" watch production were not exported to Hong Kong.

Seiko used the United States as a market for initial entry, where they gained a reputation which they then sold worldwide. The company offered fewer than 400 quartz and mechanical models in the United States, but over 2,300 worldwide. These models included analog, digital, and multifunction watches. Plans called for an expansion of the number of styles sold in the U.S. and a broadening of the price range at the upper and lower ends of the market.

Seiko owned sales subsidiaries in all of its major markets. Seiko watches were sold in jewelry and department stores. It had also established service centers in all of its major markets. This service allowed the customer to bring or mail a repair problem directly to the company, bypassing the jeweler. Seiko spent as much as SFr. 80–100 million annually in worldwide advertising, mostly television, to sell its quartz watches. Seiko had created a strong brand image based on its quartz technology and accuracy.

While Seiko was a formidable competitor of the Swiss watch industry, Japanese consumers were a major market for Swiss luxury watches. Throughout the 1970s and 1980s, Swiss luxury watches were considered a status symbol in Japan. In 1981, Seiko moved into the luxury market, at home and abroad, when it purchased a small Swiss watch producer Jean Lassale. The company's plan was to combine Swiss design and elegance with Japanese engineering and technical skill in electronics.

By 1970 both Seiko and its Japanese competitor Citizen had diversified into new businesses with internal development, mergers, and acquisitions. Included in the expanded product line were consumer electronic products such as computers, software, calculators, high-speed printers, miniature industrial robots, office equipment and machine tools, and even fashion department stores. As Seiko faced the 1990s, these product lines were expected to become an increasingly important part of the company's total sales and profits. In 1970, clocks and watches represented 99 percent of Seiko sales, but by 1983 that share had dropped to 40 percent. Top executives at Seiko expected this figure to continue to decline to 30 percent by 1990.

Longines SA

Longines was well known internationally but losing money when it was acquired by Asuag in 1974. Longines was developed into the group's premiere, or top-priced, brand and began contributing to profits in 1976.

After joining Asuag, Longines' prices began to climb as the company edged its way into the high-priced "A" watch segment. The first Swiss manufacturer to produce electronic watches in 1969, Longines' product mix was 50 percent electronic. In 1985, average ex-factory price for Longines watches was SFr. 450 to 500.

Longines produced at levels of about 500,000 watches per year. Investments were made in more efficient machines to reduce dependence on skilled labor, and the number of different types of movements and other precision parts was cut back. Longines continued to make about thirty lines, each with many variations.

Longines put all of its promotion money behind its leader model, the "Conquest." Management felt that the top priced "Conquest" best represented the overall style of the collection. "The Longines Style" campaign was supported with an advertising and promotion budget of 10 percent of total sales, and this sum was matched by Longines agents. Advertisements were placed in international and local media.

In 1984, Longines introduced a new watch line, the Conquest VHP. VHP stood for "very high precision," and the watch promised accuracy within one second per month. The gun metal–colored titanium and gold watch contained two quartz crystals. The first was the timekeeper, and the second compensated for vibrations and effects of the weather. The watch sold for SFr. 1,650 at retail, and initial response from the marketplace was very positive. Advertising for the new line stressed the watch's Swiss origin with the heading "Swiss Achievement."

Rolex

Rolex, with its prestigious "Oyster" line, was perhaps the best known of the Swiss luxury watch manufacturers. Rolex was a private company, owned by a foundation. The company was responsible for about 5.5 percent of Switzerland's watch exports by volume, with estimated annual export of 400,000 units, valued at SFr. 700–800 million. Rolex did not disclose its domestic sales.

Ninety percent of all Rolex watches were produced with mechanical movements housed in gold or platinum cases. The Oyster line was described as a premium sports watch. Retail Oyster watch prices ranged from SFr. 800 for stainless steel watches to SFr. 14,000 for solid gold watches. Production was semiautomated, and Geneva housewives made up a large part of the semiskilled labor. Skilled workers were required for hand assembly in the final stages of production. The company always allowed production to lag slightly behind demand.

Throughout the turbulent 1970s, the company had stayed consistently with the luxury sport watch market. Rolex limited advertising to the higher-priced Oyster line. Rolex also had a second line, Cellini, of high priced luxury dress watches. The company resisted entry into the electronic age; only 10 percent of the Rolex line was electronic. There was some speculation that in the next three to five years quartz watches would rise to 30 percent of total output. In 1983, quartz production was limited to watches under the Tudor brand, at the low end of Rolex's market, and were priced below SFr. 1,200. The Tudor watches were not advertised and did not bear the Rolex name.

In 1985, the Rolex catalog included three Oyster quartz models.

Rolex employed wholly owned marketing subsidiaries in nineteen countries. The Geneva headquarters worked through the subsidiaries to license jewelers to sell and service its watches. The subsidiaries provided sales and service support to local retailers and watch repairers. Maintaining adequate service coverage was important in an era of throwaway watches. For example, the New York subsidiary licensed seventy watch repairers to service Rolex watches. Distribution to retail outlets was based on a quota system. Subsidiaries were also used to maintain tight control over retail prices; Rolex did not permit any discounting. Promotion and advertising expenditures were estimated at 10 percent of sales. This expenditure was matched by the wholesalers and retailers.

Piaget SA

Piaget SA was founded by George Piaget in 1874, and in 1985 was still a family business directed by the founder's grandsons and great-grandsons. The company's workshops produced approximately 15,000 handmade watches each year at prices ranging from SFr. 4,000 to 400,000. The company carried a large collection of luxury watches for both men and women, producing approximately 1,200 models.

Only gold and/or platinum were used to encase the watch movements, and many of the watches were decorated with precious stones. Both mechanical and quartz models were included in the Piaget collection. Piaget was the only producer of luxury dress watches which was fully integrated. The company produced the world's thinnest mechanical watches: 1.2mm for a hand wind model, and 2mm for an automatic. Historically, the Piaget line was limited to dress watches, but the company entered the sports watch market in 1980.

Worldwide, Piaget watches were carried by 400 retailers. They tended to be the most prestigious stores in their areas and were located to be accessible to potential luxury watch buyers. Whenever possible, the watchmaker preferred retailers to carry only Piaget in their luxury dress watch line. Annual advertising expenditure for Piaget was estimated at SFr. 3 million, excluding the United States. About 55 percent of this expense was paid for by Piaget, and the rest was contribution from distributors and retailers.

Other Swiss manufacturers producing luxury dress watches included Audemars-Piguet, Patek-Philippe, and Vacheron & Constantin. All three were smaller than Piaget, producing less than 15,000 watches per year, and followed similar strategies.

Ebel

Ebel was founded in 1911 by Eugene Blum. The company described its transition in the 1970s as a renaissance.

In 1974 the third generation of Blums, Pierre-Alain, took over the company. When Pierre-Alain Blum became president, Ebel's fifty employees were making private label watches. With new management, Ebel began to take a closer look at the customers of its chief client Cartier. Within a short period of time, Ebel began branded watch production, and employment grew to 500 people. 1984 sales were estimated between SFr. 150 and 170 million.

The company's growth came about with the development of a unique one piece watch case and bracelet construction which became the base for the Ebel collection. Ebel's goal was to design and maintain a "classic," timeless collection, and the company did not plan to make major annual changes to its line. Ebel watches sold at retail SFr. 1,000 to 15,000. The company had five models and realized 90 percent of its sales from the top three. The company's goal was to create a strong brand image. Using its leader model, Ebel promoted its watch lines with the slogan "architects of time."

Ebel moved into electronic movements in 1978. With that change in technology the company enjoyed a boost in sales. In 1985, Ebel was assembling 300,000 units per year. The company maintained tight control over its suppliers. Ebel had production and development contracts with its movement suppliers and partial ownership of its case and bracelet manufacturer. The company still assembled private label watches for Cartier. In 1975, sales to Cartier had represented 90 percent of sales; 10 years later these sales represented less than 50 percent of total. It was estimated that Cartier sales provided about 25 percent of Ebel's profits in 1984.

Blum maintained close personal contact with the end customer, with frequent visits to jewelry stores. His goal was to keep a close eye on stock levels at jewelry stores and avoid a buildup of stocks in the distribution channels. He also wanted to ensure that the jewelry store's image was in line with the Ebel image.

In addition to its "architects of time" media advertising, Ebel also used sports sponsorship as a means of building an image with the public. Ebel became one of the first watch companies to actively use sporting events for its watches' promotion. Ebel sponsorships included a soccer team in Geneva and tennis and golf matches.

In the 1980s, Ebel was broadening its business activities. It expanded its product line by becoming the distributor for Schaeffer pens. Ebel also entered the clothing business with the American firm, Fenn, Wright and Manson. They opened a boutique in Geneva, and others were in the planning stages. Finally, Ebel was the agent for Olivetti computers for the French speaking part of Switzerland. The distribution company employed twelve people, including programmers.

Recent Entrants in the Watch Industry

A new group of "outsiders" and "newcomers" has entered the global watch industry. Many of these companies (or the current ownership) have been operating for ten years or less. With few exceptions, these "watchmakers" subcontracted all production and assembly, mostly in Switzerland. The watches were then positioned in the market as high fashion pieces.

Included in this group were Raymond Weil, founded in 1976. Within ten years the company reached annual sales levels of approximately 300,000 quartz watches, at prices ranging from SFr. 500 to 1,700. All work was subcontracted to companies and individual component manufacturers and assemblers in the Jura region of Switzerland. The company employed fifteen people for design, marketing, and sales and administration. One-third of all wholesale activities were captively held.

Weil's success in the watch industry was attributed to the company's sense of style and fashion. A new collection was introduced each year, with six woman's and six man's watches. Weil was constantly responding to changes in consumer tastes and the latest trend. His 1985 spring collection was named for a hit movie, *Amadeus,* a biography of the life of Mozart. Raymond Weil had a limited budget for its advertising and promotion expenditures, relying on a few well-placed messages and style to sell its products.

Cartier watches were classic in design and limited to fifteen different models. Cartier subcontracted its watches from Ebel. The Cartier watch lines did include models which sold for as much as SFr. 100,000. Most Cartier watches sold at prices ranging from SFr. 1,200 to 25,000. Most Cartier watches were quartz. Selling at a level of 450,000 units per year, the watch was an addition to the company's collection of accessories and jewelry. The watches were sold through the company's specialized retail stores, independent boutiques, and jewelry and fashionable department stores all over the world. Watch advertising and promotion expenses were minimized because the company's name was well recognized in the marketplace and the watch fell under the umbrella of the company's other accessories.

Gucci watches were sold by an independent entrepreneur who licensed the Gucci name. These "A" watches were sold at Gucci shops and by independent jewelers and high fashion department stores and boutiques. Annual volumes for Gucci watches were estimated at 400,000 units. The company did not advertise heavily and relied on the Gucci name for prestigious name brand identity.

SUMMARY

Thomke knew that a number of options were open to him to bring Tissot from its current status of a "branded commodity." He estimated that relaunch in Europe would be a minimum of SFr. 12 million. Costs for reintroducing Tissot to the United States would be even greater. To afford these marketing expenses, Tissot marketing and profit margins would have to improve, and sales volumes would have to grow. Thomke knew he could shift prices and was considering pushing Tissot prices downward to the bottom of the "B" group. A downward price shift would require a considerable increase in volume if the Tissot brand was to be profitable. The producer's margin decreased as watches moved down-market to the "B" and "C" segments. Thomke knew that producers of expensive watches which had a strong positive image with consumers could command high ex-factory prices. This provided the luxury watch firms considerable margins for marketing expenditures and profit.

Thomke believed that to operate profitably a watch had to capture at least 10 percent of its market segment. He wanted to produce a workable brand strategy which would allow Tissot to gain at least 10 percent of its segment. Thomke had several key factors to consider. The fast paced technological changes of the 1970s had slowed, and the traditional watch buying market was maturing. However, he saw that nontraditional approaches in the industry had allowed new entrants such as Raymond Weil and SWATCH to successfully gain footholds and profits in the global watch industry.

Case 11

The World Paint Industry, 1992

In early 1993, Herman Scopes, chief executive officer (CEO) of ICI Paints, was reviewing the company's 1992 results.

The past few years have brought tremendous changes to the industry; we have gone from expansion to recession in the most important markets, and mergers have brought about a reshuffling of the top ten paint makers. As we look to the 1990s, it has become clear that the rules by which paint companies prospered in the 1980s may no longer apply. To be a leader in the future, it will be necessary to understand changes in traditional practices such as level of integration, segment choice, country selection, resource allocation, technology choice, and key success factors. How will the paint industry look in five or even ten years, and what implications does this have for major players?

OVERVIEW

In 1991, the world paints and coatings industry was valued at $46 billion at suppliers' prices, corresponding to a volume of 13.5 billion liters. Generally speaking, the industry included a range of products such as

●

This note was prepared by Robert C. Howard under the direction of Jean-Pierre Jeannet, Professor of Marketing at IMD and Professor of Marketing and International Business at Babson College (U.S.A.). This note is a substantial revision of ''The World Paint Industry,'' GM 451, and is based on both publicly available material and industry sources. Copyright © 1993 by IMD, Lausanne, Switzerland. The International Institute for Management Development (IMD), resulting from the merger between IMEDE, Lausanne, and IMI, Geneva, acquires and retains all rights. Not to be used or reproduced without written permission from IMD, Lausanne, Switzerland.

pigmented coatings, or paints, as well as unpigmented coatings like stain and varnish, used to decorate and/or protect different surfaces (substrates). Worldwide, a close correlation existed between a country's per capita income level and coatings consumption, so forecast rates of gross domestic product (GDP) growth often served as a predictor for trends in the overall demand for coatings. In concert with the robust growth in GDP in the 1980s, industry sales grew rapidly in the five years to 1988. From 1989 on, however, coatings sales slowed significantly as a result of the downturn in the global economy.

Over the next few years, analysts believed, several factors would influence the competitive dynamics of the paint industry. Among them were the growing environmental movement, new growth opportunities in central and eastern Europe, and changes in retailing. Among these factors, some industry observers believed that the environmental movement was likely to play the most significant role in the 1990s, by changing the way paint companies manufactured and marketed their products. And because changes in manufacturing and marketing had important consequences for companies' cost structures, most analysts believed that the worldwide restructuring and rationalization processes that had dominated the industry during the previous decade would continue, albeit somewhat less intensively due to the recessionary climate.

USER SEGMENTS

In the industry, analysts and participants alike divided coatings sales into two main classes: decorative or architectural paints, used in decorating buildings and homes, and industrial coatings, which provided functional properties and added value to manufactured

EXHIBIT 1 ● World Paint Sales by Market Sector

1991
13,500 ML*

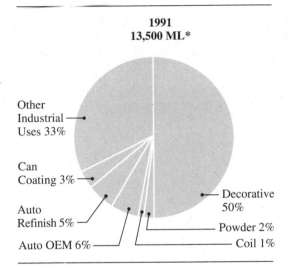

Other Industrial Uses 33%

Can Coating 3%

Auto Refinish 5%

Auto OEM 6%

Decorative 50%

Powder 2%

Coil 1%

Note: Excludes central and eastern Europe, the Middle East, and the African continent.

*ML = million liters.

EXHIBIT 2 ● World Paint Sales by Market Region

1991
13,500 ML

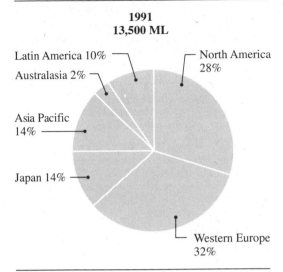

Latin America 10%

Australasia 2%

Asia Pacific 14%

Japan 14%

North America 28%

Western Europe 32%

Region definitions:
1. Western Europe = the United Kingdom, France, Germany (including former East Germany), Italy, Spain, Portugal, Belgium, the Netherlands, Denmark, Finland, Norway, Sweden, Austria, Ireland, Greece, and Turkey.
2. North America = the United States and Canada.
3. Asia Pacific = India, Pakistan, Sri Lanka, Thailand, Malaysia, Singapore, Indonesia, Taiwan, Hong Kong, China, and Korea.
4. Australasia = Australia and New Zealand.
5. Latin America = Brazil, Argentina, Mexico, Ecuador, Uruguay, Colombia, and Chile.
6. Excludes commonwealth of independent states, eastern Europe, the Middle East, and Africa.

*ML = million liters.

goods. Typically, decorative coatings were high volume, were low priced, and commanded low margins. Industrial coatings, on the other hand, were high priced and focused on niche markets. (Refer to Exhibit 1 and 2, respectively, for a breakdown of world paint sales by market sector and region.)

Decorative Paints

By far, decorative coatings was the largest single segment in the industry. Overall, the potential demand for decorative coatings in any country was influenced by climate, construction methods, and life style, together with the collective successes of the local paint industry in presenting its offering to private and professional consumers in a readily accessible and attractive form. From this base line, variations in demand were driven primarily by changes in real disposable income and in real interest rates, the latter already being an indicator of the level of construction activity and house moves.

In the decorative segment, paint sales were further classified according to two major user groups—professional and do-it-yourself (DIY)—each of which accounted for roughly half the sales in the segment. Typically, DIY users applied paint using a brush, while professional painters also used brushes but sometimes spray guns, as well. As the name implied, the professional market consisted of professional painters, further subdivided into restorers, new housing contractors, and commercial contractors. Sales to the professional market were either through small, independent stores or branches of manufacturers. The second segment consisted of individual DIY users, who bought paint through a variety of retail stores.

In 1991, the decorative segment accounted for 50 percent of the value of all paint sold in the world, or roughly 6.67 billion liters. Geographically, North America accounted for 30 percent of these sales; Western Europe, 32 percent; Japan, 9 percent; and the rest of the world, 29 percent. One industry observer pointed out that, despite the size of Japan's population and economy, decorative paints accounted for a surprisingly small share of the country's coatings sales. He attributed this to the fact that traditional domestic architecture in Japan, with its paper partitions, meant that millions of square feet of walls were not painted. In order of importance, major competitors in this segment were ICI of the United Kingdom, Sherwin-

Williams from the United States, Akzo from the Netherlands, Casco-Nobel from Sweden, and BASF from Germany (as shown in Exhibit 3).

Industrial Paints

In contrast to decorative coatings, demand for industrial coatings depended on a country's manufacturing profile, vehicles versus electronics or furniture versus textiles, for example. That is, industrial coatings tended to have more specialized uses than decorative coatings and included paint for cars, ships, planes, boats, white goods, cans, and thousands of other applications. In this segment, properties such as corrosion, abrasion resistance, and the ability to withstand high temperature or wet weather were important pur-

EXHIBIT 3 ● World Decorative Architectural Majors by Region

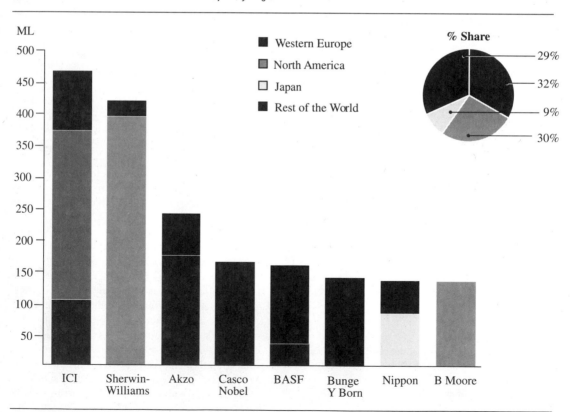

chase criteria. To monitor the market, participants further classified industrial coatings according to application: automotive OEMs (original equipment manufacturers), automotive refinish, can coatings, powder, coil, marine, and wood finishes. Each segment had its own particular customer group and usually required its own technology and application base.

Automotive OEM   The automotive OEM paint segment consisted of paint sales to automobile manufacturers—usually global companies—for use in their assembly plants. In this segment, users applied coatings by immersing an entire car body in a "paint bath" in which the paint carried an electric charge opposite from that of the car body, resulting in a corrosion resistant finish. Because of the service requirements associated with maintaining electrolytic paint baths, as well as the desire to provide a consistent color wherever cars were assembled, automotive OEM customers preferred paint suppliers that were both local and global in nature. That is, customers favored suppliers able to provide a consistent color around the world yet, at the same time, deliver local service. As a result, paint manufacturers tended to locate their factories close to automotive assembly plants and stationed their personnel permanently at automotive sites. When purchasing coatings, automotive OEM customers usually maintained a major supplier for each top coat and base coat and a second supplier for smaller-volume applications "to keep the big ones honest."

In 1991, the volume of paint sold to car manufacturers was roughly 791 million liters, or 6 percent of the industry volume, with sales distributed among North America, 22 percent; Western Europe, 27 percent; and Japan, 34 percent. In decreasing order of sales, leading competitors were PPG, Kansai, Nippon, BASF, Du Pont, Hoechst, ICI, and Akzo (as shown in Exhibit 4). Of these eight players, only PPG and BASF were considered to be global competitors; both Kansai and Nippon secured the majority of their sales in their home market.

Automobile Vehicle Refinishing   The refinish segment included paints and coatings for repairing automobiles. Although the color of a refinished automobile was expected to match its original color, refinish formulations—applied using spray guns—were quite different from the formulations used in the automotive OEM segment. Typically, refinish customers were small paint shops which needed quick and frequent deliveries, usually on a daily basis. Paint manufacturers normally supplied these customers with mixing schemes through local distributors, who combined basic colors and shades with solvents to obtain a correct color match. Because there were some 10,000 different shades and some sixty different colors to select from, a refinish company had to have access to the color and paint shops of car manufacturers. And, because automobile makers wanted to ensure that, if necessary, car owners could get their cars refinished wherever they were purchased, car manufacturers were interested in worldwide coverage. Not surprisingly, refinish paint manufacturers profited when they had access to all locations of a car maker, so that they could supply the widest possible color range in any geographic market. Although the volume of paint sold in this market was smaller than the automotive OEM segment, it was a larger segment by value due to its higher sales price and was, in fact, the most profitable segment in the industry.

Worldwide, the refinish segment accounted for 5 percent of industry sales, which were distributed among North America, 39 percent; Western Europe, 23 percent; and Japan, 13 percent (refer to Exhibit 5). In this segment, only ten paint manufacturers were considered significant players, and no new competitor had entered since the 1950s. In 1991, Du Pont was the world leader in the refinish segment, followed by BASF, PPG, and Sherwin-Williams.

Can Coatings   As the name implies, can coatings were applied inside tin and aluminum cans to make them corrosion resistant for use as food or beverage containers. In 1991, can coating sales were concentrated among four groups: Continental Can, Pechiney-Triangle (which included former American Can and National Can), Carnaud-MetalBox, and Crown Cork and Seal, as well as their licensees, all of which operated canning lines around the globe. Because these canning companies were expected to provide a consistent taste for globally marketed products such as Coca-Cola, they in turn expected their suppliers to provide local service at each of their canning sites. Even where can coatings were not identical, a considerable part of the coating technology could be used

EXHIBIT 4 ● World Auto OEM Majors by Region

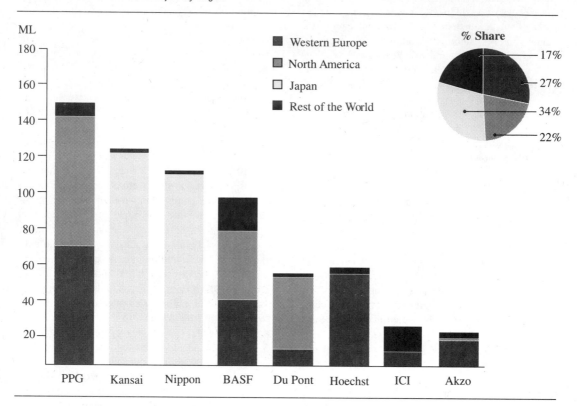

for customers with similar applications. A coating developed for sardines in Portugal, for example, might also be suitable for Norwegian sardine packers.

In 1991, the can coating segment accounted for only 3 percent of the world paint market, with sales distributed among North America, 41 percent; Europe, 27 percent; and Japan, 16 percent. Major competitors included BASF, Midland, and Valspar (as shown in Exhibit 6).

Powder Paints In contrast to other coatings, powder paints were 100 percent solids in the form of pigmented resin powders, usually electrostatically sprayed onto a grounded metal substrate and then cured by heat. Because powder paint could be applied in layers of fifty–sixty microns—five times as thick

as wet paint—it was far more durable and retained its color longer than wet paints. With an ability to resist abrasions for up to twenty years, powder paint was ideal for coating domestic appliances such as washing machines or refrigerators, as well as metal surfaces on the outside of buildings, which were subject to extreme weather conditions. Despite these advantages, powder paint had two limitations. First, because powder paint left thick layers, it could not be used in applications such as can coating, where thin layers of coating were a must. Second, because powder coatings had to be cured by heat, there was an upper limit to the size of an object which could be coated.

Other than the functional properties they imparted to a given substrate, powder paints had a major

EXHIBIT 5 ● World Refinish Majors by Region

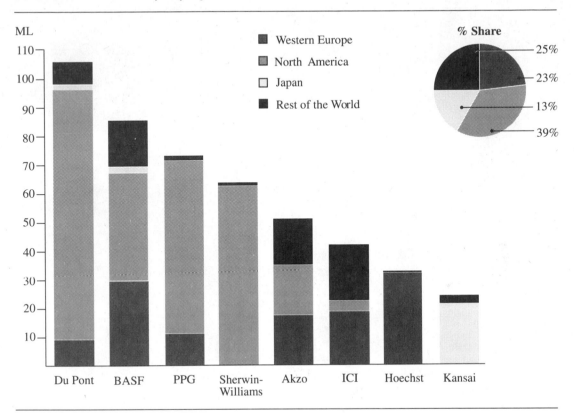

advantage over solvent-borne paints in that they released no toxic fumes into the atmosphere. As well as reducing emissions, powder coatings avoided the problem of waste disposal, as any stray powder was collected and reused. By contrast, wet paint always had a residual waste which had to be disposed of.

Worldwide, the market for powder coatings was growing 10–20 percent per year and was seen as a possible substitute for up to 50 percent of paint being applied to metal. In Europe, where the powder process was pioneered, the substitution already amounted to roughly 20 percent, compared to about 10 percent in the United States. Although major user groups included automotive component suppliers, the metal furniture industry, and domestic appliance manufac-

turers, most powder makers were also looking into applying colored coatings to inferior grades of plastic, thus enabling them to compete with the attractive high-quality plastics used for chairs and garden furniture. As one analyst pointed out, the trick was to develop a paint that could be cured at relatively low temperatures, so that it did not melt the plastic. Other potential new applications included car engine blocks, baskets inside automatic washing machines, and the steel reinforcement bars used in concrete. One analyst commented that manufacturers were also experimenting with high-gloss powder finishes that could eventually be used for car bodywork.

Worldwide, powder coatings accounted for only 2 percent of industry sales and were distributed

EXHIBIT 6 ● World Can Coatings Majors by Region

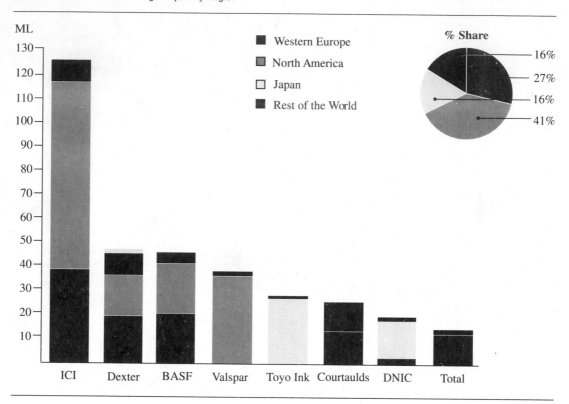

among Europe, 54 percent; North America, 21 percent; and Japan, 10 percent. In order of millions of kilograms sold, major competitors were Courtaulds, DSM, Becker, Ferro, ICI, Morton, Hoechst, and Evode (as shown in Exhibit 7).

Coil Coatings   The coil-coating segment derived its name from coiled steel or aluminum, which was given a decorative or industrial coating before the main manufacturing step or construction process. Typically, steel or aluminum coils were unrolled on automatic lines and the coating was applied by roller or spray. They were dried and hardened, and then the metal was coiled up again for shipment to manufacturers. Upon receipt, manufacturers could bend or

stamp the metal into a required shape—such as a refrigerator cabinet or building cladding—without damaging the painted surface. In Europe, coil-coating customers included major metal producers such as British Steel, Sollac of France, Phoenix (part of the Belgian Cockerill group), Hoescht of Germany, Svenska Stal of Sweden, and La Magona of Italy.

In 1991, roughly 60 percent of coil-coated steel and 50 percent of coil-coated aluminum in Europe went to the building sector. Other important outlets were the automotive industry, domestic appliances, and packages. Also in Europe, it was estimated that, although manufacturers produced roughly 2.2 million tons of painted steel per year in the form of car and commercial vehicle bodies, 95 percent of that steel

EXHIBIT 7 ● World Powder Majors by Region

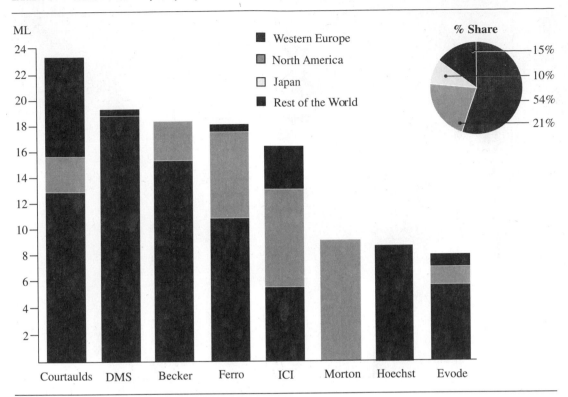

PAINT MANUFACTURING

Raw Materials

was painted after assembly. In other words, the industry used only 110,000 tons of prepainted coil, and coil coaters hoped that more European manufacturers would follow the example of Nissan's Sunderland, U.K., plant, which used precoated car body panels.

In terms of world paint sales, coil coatings represented less than 1 percent, or roughly 181 million liters, of industry sales. Geographically, these sales were concentrated in Europe, 34 percent; North America, 33 percent; and Japan, 22 percent (as shown in Exhibit 8). The suppliers of coating materials to the coil coaters included large paint companies such as Nippon, Kansai, Akzo, Valspar, ICI, Morton, Becker, and PPG, as well as specialized companies like Coats Coatings, part of Total, the French state-owned oil company which made materials for metal packaging.

In general, coatings consisted of three main ingredients: resins, solvents, and pigments, plus small amounts of additives (as shown in Exhibit 9). The resin, also called the binder, accounted for about 40 percent of raw material costs. It was the resin that acted as the film forming component in paint, produced a thick film or smooth surface once a paint had dried, and gave paint its durability. Solvents, accounting for some 10 percent of raw material costs, were commodity chemicals in liquid form and allowed a paint to remain fluid before application, yet evaporated during the drying process. As a rule, either water or petrochemical derivatives were used as solvents.

EXHIBIT 8 ● World Coil Majors by Region

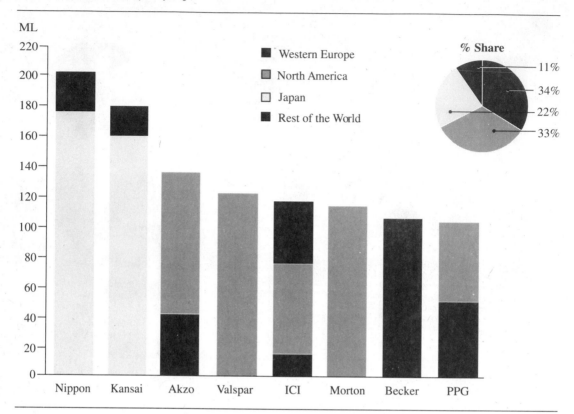

ML

Legend:
- Western Europe
- North America
- Japan
- Rest of the World

% Share: 11%, 34%, 22%, 33%

Companies (x-axis): Nippon, Kansai, Akzo, Valspar, ICI, Morton, Becker, PPG

Pigments, the ingredients that gave paint their colors, were either organic or inorganic in nature; of all pigments, titanium dioxide—that is, white pigment—was the most widely used. In the chemical trade, pigments were considered fine chemicals and usually accounted for 35–40 percent of raw material costs. Lastly, additives accounted for about 15 percent of raw material costs and included a wide range of items such as catalysts for drying, biocides, surfactants, antidegradants, and rheology (flow) modifiers.

Typically, paint ingredients were purchased in bulk, then mixed and packaged by a paint manufacturer before distribution. Combined, the cost of raw materials ranged between 30 and 55 percent of ex-factory costs, depending on application. As one observer pointed out, however, because many paint companies were in fact divisions of larger chemical companies, some players such as BASF or DSM were also active in the industry as raw material suppliers. Generally speaking, paint subsidiaries of chemical companies produced roughly two-thirds of their own resins in-house, although the number could vary considerably from one manufacturing site to the next. Stand-alone companies, on the other hand, tended to produce only 20–30 percent of their resins themselves.

Paint Technology and Research

Historically, paint companies concentrated their R&D on reformulating combinations of existing resins, solvents, pigments, and additives. However, the proportion and type of ingredient used in a paint formulation did have to be adjusted, as a function of the substrate to which it was applied—for example, to the climate

EXHIBIT 9 ● Surface Coating Raw Materials

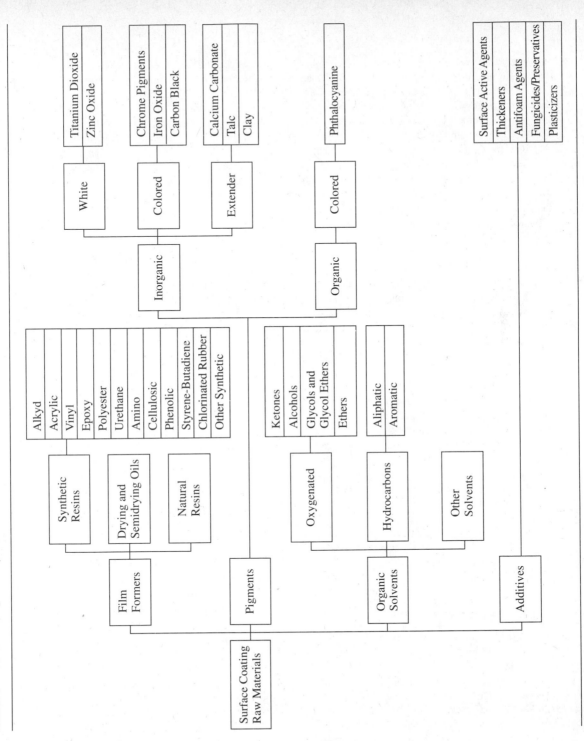

Source: Martin Staber; DSM Chemicals.

and other factors pertinent to the application. In 1991, there were not only coatings for special functional uses or environments such as heat and freeze resistance, there were also weldable and moldable paints and paints for squash courts and swimming pools, as well as coatings with biocidal, antireflective, fluorescent, intumescent, or even temperature-indicating properties. In short, because paint formulations had to decorate and protect an extensive variety of substrates—including metal alloys, concrete, and rigid and flexible plastics—they accounted for the increasingly technical nature of paint technology and the growing importance of R&D.

Since the resin had the largest influence on the properties of coatings, paint research was primarily concerned with developing new resins, possibly resulting in a technological and competitive advantage. While older resins tended to be soluble only in petrochemically derived solvents, newer resins were either water soluble or dry powders. In the industry, only those paint manufacturers that were part of major chemical firms engaged in serious resin research, while the remainder relied on merchant suppliers; in 1991, major paint companies spent roughly 4–5 percent of sales on R&D. At such firms—such as at Hoechst and Du Pont—research was carried out either centrally or in smaller dedicated groups that were part of the paint organizations (such as at BASF and ICI). Resin suppliers, on the other hand, because they were often removed from paint applications, tended to collaborate with their customers on research projects. While the development of a paint formulation from existing ingredients might take two to three man-months, the development of a new resin typically required twenty-five to thirty man-years at $100,000 each per year.

Paint Industry Economics

As noted, paint manufacturers showed varying degrees of integration, depending on the existence and size of a parent chemical company. Typically, smaller firms not affiliated with chemical conglomerates showed less integration and tended to buy their raw materials in the open market, often from the same chemical firms that operated paint companies. On the open market, resins were available from merchant suppliers such as Rohm & Haas, Union Carbide, Dow

Chemical, and Ciba-Geigy, as well as captive sources. At Rohm & Haas, it was believed that some 300–500 scientists worked on resin development. Among the top twelve paint companies, ICI both had in-house capability and operated a merchant house (ICI Resins) independently. In the five years preceding 1992, the level of investment required to manufacture a resin had increased from $500 to $1,000 per ton. The fact that resin manufacturing costs had doubled in only five years stemmed from the costly pollution abatement equipment manufacturers were required to install to neutralize hazardous byproducts created during manufacturing. At $1,000 per ton, a typical plant of 6,000 tons required an investment of $6 million, corresponding to $20 million and $100 million, respectively, in resin and paint sales. In terms of asset utilization, resin companies typically had 40 percent of their sales tied up in working capital and fixed assets. (Refer to Exhibit 10 for a summary of leading European resin producers and their market shares in different resin categories.)

Solvents and additives differed from resins in that they offered no strategic value in paint formulation and were widely available in the open market. At times, the availability of certain additives might be constrained, but for most items, several suppliers existed. Similarly, paint makers purchased pigments from a range of suppliers. Titanium dioxide, for example, was available from Du Pont, SCM, Finn Titan, Tioxide (ICI), and Ishihara. Although both Du Pont and ICI had in-house or related suppliers, they also sold their pigments on the open market. Color pigments were supplied by specialist suppliers, including Ciba-Geigy, Hoechst, ICI, and Bayer.

In summary, paint economics differed by application segment. While raw material costs tended to average 30–55 percent of ex-factory price, direct labor conversion costs averaged 5–10 percent, and indirect manufacturing costs, including depreciation for equipment, averaged 15 percent. Distribution, transportation, and logistics accounted for about 5 percent, R&D as much as 7 percent, marketing and selling ranged from 5 to 15 percent, and overhead about 10 percent, giving a pretax profit of 7–15 percent of sales. In general, successful paint companies experienced an asset turnover of 2.5–3.0, and assets tended to be equally split between fixed and working capital. With a 10 percent return on sales, it was not

EXHIBIT 10 ● Market Share of Leading European Resin Producers, 1992

	%		%
Alkyds		**Saturated polyester**	
DSM	25	Bayer	25
Cray Valley	20	Hoechst	17
Hoechst	15	BASF	12
Bayer	10	Others	46
Other	30	**Polyurethanes**	
Epoxies		Bayer	60
Ciba-Geigy	30	DSM	20
Dow	25	Rhône-Poulenc	5
Shell	25	Others	15
Others	20	**Phenolics**	
Acrylic emulsions		Hoechst	30
Rohm & Haas	20	BP Chemicals	22
Rohm	17	DSM	15
Vinamul	15	Others	33
Others	48	**Aminos**	
Vinyl emulsions		BASF	30
Hoechst	25	Dyno	28
Vinamul	15	BIP	17
Wacker	10	Hoechst	10
Others	50	Others	15
Unsaturated polyester		**Vinyl dispersions**	
BASF	18	BASF	25
DSM	15	Wacker	22
Hoechst	15	Hüls	15
Bayer	14	Hoechst	10
Others	38	Others	28

Source: IRL.

uncommon for a company to achieve a return on net assets (RONA) of 25–30 percent. (For an overview of paint manufacturing cost structure as a function of paint type, refer to Exhibit 11.)

TRENDS

For the remainder of the 1990s, industry analysts believed the level and nature of competition in the world paint industry would be characterized by a growing environmental movement, continued economic pressures, further globalization of the industry, the new markets in Eastern Europe, the strengthening of markets in the Asia Pacific region, and changes in retailing.

Environmental Movement

Over the next several years, health and environmental factors were liable to have the biggest impact on the paint industry. Because the manufacturing and industrial application of paint was a major source of air pollution through excessive emission of volatile organic compounds (VOCs), the United States and Europe had passed a variety of statutory instruments, codes, and safety regulations aimed at phasing out VOCs as well as inorganic pigments that contained heavy metals like lead and cadmium. In the latter case, regulators hoped that manufacturers would switch to less hazardous organic pigments. Because of the intensive research required to develop a new paint formulation, however, the new guidelines posed a formidable challenge to manufacturers.

Originally, aqueous paint formulations were introduced in the 1950s as an alternative to solvent-based formulations in the decorative segment and were promoted on the basis of their reduced odor and ease of cleanup. Though such water-borne coatings grew to account for 30 percent of all decorative coatings by the mid-1970s, the environmental movement acted as an additional sales impetus, and in 1992 roughly 70 percent of all decorative coatings were aqueous in nature. By the turn of the century, it was expected, 85 percent of all decorative coatings would be aqueous. Just as manufacturers replaced volatile organic compounds with water in decorative coatings in the 1980s and early 1990s, some companies began developing aqueous formulations for industrial appli-

cations. However, powder coatings did provide an alternative solution to the problem of eliminating VOCs. By the year 2010, one executive believed, aqueous formulations would represent approximately 20 percent of all industrial coatings, with powder equaling 30–35 percent and solvent-based systems accounting for the balance.

Aside from affecting what went into paints, the new guidelines also influenced how paints were made and how effluents were disposed of, as well as the application methods used by customers. In Europe, for example, the European Coil Coating Association (ECCA) was trying to convince more manufacturers to buy precoated coil, on the basis that it provided both a cost and quality advantage over competitors who painted products afterward. The economic argument in favor of paying a premium price for precoated steel instead of operating an in-house paint shop was likely to become stronger as environmental regulations became more stringent. However, car or appliance manufacturers could still respond by switching from traditional to powder paints rather than give up their own coating facilities. In other words, if coil coatings could be shown to be a more cost effective and environmentally friendly solution, companies which developed new resins for use in aqueous and powder paint formulations—containing organic instead of inorganic pigments—might not necessarily have an advantage.

Economic Pressures

From 1989 on, virtually every participant in the world paint industry had seen its sales slow down or decline as a result of the global recession. Though sales were forecast to grow at 2.5–3.0 percent once the economy entered a recovery, internal pressures were expected to remain. In particular, increasingly sophisticated coating formulations meant that R&D costs would account for a growing percentage of paint manufacturers' expenditures. When these costs were combined with the higher costs of organic versus inorganic pigments, as well as the technical service costs associated with some of the newer coatings, margins were expected to narrow. Though large paint manufacturers were better prepared to live with tight margins, as they knew that it would speed a further rationalization of the industry, smaller members did not have the

EXHIBIT 11 ● Paint Manufacturing Cost Structure

	Raw material	Direct labor conversion	Indirect manufacturing plus depreciation	R & D and technical service	Logistics and transport	Marketing and selling	Overhead	PBT	Average export price/liter
Decorative paint	40%	5%	12%	3%	4%	18%	8%	10%	$3.00
Can coating	50	5	13	6	3	8	7	8	2.00
Automotive refinish	30	9	14	8	5	12	9	13	6.50
Automotive OEM	50	7	13	10	3	6	8	3	4.50
Coil	55	8	12	8	4	5	6	2	6.00
Powder	55	10	10	7	5	5	6	2	4.50/kg

same resources or staying power. To contain costs, some of these smaller companies had begun joint purchasing of raw materials, a cooperative effort some believed might lead to further intercompany partnerships.

Globalization

Though European companies had set the pace in the restructuring of the world paint industry in the 1980s, analysts believed that global competition from United States and Japanese paint makers in the international arena would increase. As one example, in the four years preceding 1991, Sherwin-Williams had moved from fourth to second place, after ICI, pushing PPG and BASF from second and third to third and fourth place, respectively. One industry spokesman commented that the worldwide merger and acquisition activities were merely part of the globalization of the paint industry, which at the start of the 1990s was driven by three factors: first, the need to service customers with international manufacturing operations—those making cans or domestic appliances or assembling vehicles; second, the need to service customers dealing with the aftercare of internationally traded products such as vehicles and ships; last, the need to amortize the ever growing costs of research, product development, and marketing over a broad volume base.

Eastern Europe

During 1989, communist dictatorships across central and eastern Europe were replaced by a variety of governments which, in general, expressed their commitment to develop market economies. Analysts believed that these developments would influence the coatings business in two ways. First, the newly opened markets and their paint manufacturers were expected to be the targets of firms already established in the West, possibly altering global market shares. Second, once the legal issues surrounding privatization became clear, the surviving paint companies in central and eastern Europe were expected to restructure their own operations and market their coatings at home and abroad. (Because of the political changes, 1988 was the most recent year for which data were available on the markets in central and eastern Europe. In Poland, the former Czechoslovakia, and Hungary, estimated data were available on each of the user segments familiar to analysts and participants in the West. In the remaining markets in the region, however, paint sales were classified simply as decorative or industrial, as shown in Exhibit 12.)

EXHIBIT 12 ● Coatings Information for Central and Eastern Europe

| | | Segment volume as % of total | | | | | |
| | | | Industrial | | | | |
Country	1988 PAINT VOLUME (MILLIONS OF LITERS)	DECORATIVE	AUTO OEM	AUTO REF.	CAN	COIL	POWDER
Poland	300	35%	1%	3%	<1%	<1%	<1%
Czechoslovakia	128	40	2	4	<1	<1	<1
Hungary	116	25	1	1	1	1	1
Yugoslavia	135	29			71		
Bulgaria	33	21			79		
CIS	3,100	33			67		

Note: Other accounts for balance in first three markets.

Asia Pacific

With slow growth throughout the majority of western paint markets, coatings companies still had the prospect of faster growth in the Asia Pacific region, backed by the industrialization of those countries' economies. From low bases, countries such as Malaysia, Indonesia, and Vietnam were expected to show double digit annual growth through 2002 (as shown in Exhibit 13). As a result of this region's sales po-

tential, analysts expected a growing involvement by paint manufacturers in the form of direct investment or joint ventures.

Retailing

Traditionally, decorative paints had been sold in small shops or hardware stores, but recent developments in the DIY segment were substantially changing the retailing process. In recent years, in fact, the DIY

EXHIBIT 13 ● Projected Usage of Paints to 2002 for the Asia Pacific Region (in Thousands of Tons)

	1992	*1997*	*2002*
Far East			
China	940.0	1,200.0	1,565.0
Hong Kong	72.5	97.0	125.0
Japan	2,050.0	2,263.0	2,625.0
South Korea	422.0	760.0	1,220.0
Taiwan	335.0	565.0	912.0
All Far East	**3,819.5**	**4,885.0**	**6,447.0**
Southeast Asia			
Brunei	0.2	0.4	0.6
Cambodia	0.5	1.0	2.0
Indonesia	102.0	146.5	235.4
Malaysia	87.0	154.0	214.0
Philippines	232.0	290.0	415.0
Singapore	69.0	94.5	130.0
Thailand	66.5	82.6	120.0
Vietnam	9.0	15.0	26.0
All Southeast Asia	**566.2**	**784.0**	**1,143.0**
Oceania			
Australia	175.0	190.0	215.2
Fiji	2.2	2.6	3.0
New Zealand	30.0	33.1	37.5
Papua New Guinea	0.4	0.5	0.8
All Oceania	**207.6**	**226.2**	**256.2**
All Asia Pacific	**4,593.3**	**5,895.2**	**7,846.5**

Source: IRL.

segment had increased its share to slightly over half the decorative market, a trend that was expected to continue, at the expense of professional painters. In part, the increased share reflected a change in the way consumers viewed paint. Though once considered a lowly commodity, at the start of the 1990s, domestic paint was beginning to be seen as a household fashion accessory, adding value to the object it coated. In other words, the market for household paint, like that for beans, soap, and fish fingers, had become retail led and susceptible to all the pressures which afflicted grocery producers. While the supermarket's rise to eminence in food and packaged goods took thirty years, the storming of the trade by DIY superstores happened in only ten years.

Worldwide, these developments were most evident in Anglo-Saxon countries—the United Kingdom, the United States, and Australia, to a lesser degree in northern Europe, and considerably less in southern Europe. To clarify, in the late 1960s and early 1970s, specialist store chains like High Street in the United Kingdom and Sherwin-Williams in the United States replaced most small shops. Thereafter, variety department stores and supermarkets such as Woolworth, Sears, JCPenney, and Montgomery Ward in the United States and Tesco in the United Kingdom took the lead in retailing decorative paints. At one point, it was reported that Sears had reached a 30 percent U.S. market share through its own branding. In concert with the growing popularity of variety department stores and supermarkets, however, DIY superstores or sheds soon gained importance. In the United States, for example, the opening of stores like Home Depot cut Sears' market share in half. In the United Kingdom, the number of specialist stores declined from about 20,000 in 1979 to some 11,000 in 1988, and large DIY chains—such as B&Q, Texas, and Pay Less—accounted for 65 percent of all sector sales.

Throughout this retailing cycle, the marketing task of the paint manufacturer changed at each turn. In the first cycle, independent distributors and wholesalers gave way to manufacturer-owned stores and outlets. When the chains took over, increased buying power led to bargaining over shelf space. Thereafter, the supermarket or departmentalized variety stores bought private labels. Finally, the superstores narrowed the brand choice by typically carrying just one

advertised brand and their own private label. Inevitably, the reduced number of brands led to the disappearance of many retail paint suppliers.

COMPETITION

Despite the takeover activity of the 1980s, there were roughly 10,000 paint companies still active around the world in 1991. In general, these competitors could be grouped into two categories: large multinational companies and, primarily, domestic manufacturers. In the first category, the ten largest companies accounted for 35 percent of industry sales, employed hundreds if not thousands of people, and were sometimes part of larger chemical companies. Typically, these players made and marketed coatings products in all, or almost all, of the industry's market segments, having attained their size by acquiring smaller companies.

By the year 2000, one company spokesman predicted, the share of the paint business by the top ten coatings firms would exceed 50 percent, and this consolidation within the coatings industry would probably occur at a faster pace in western Europe than elsewhere. As evidence, he mentioned the emergence of Casco-Nobel from Sweden; in the four years 1986–1990, the company had more than quadrupled the size of its paint business in Europe by a series of acquisitions. Elsewhere in Europe, substantial positions had been established—particularly in decorative—by Total and Sigma, part of Petrofina, the state-owned oil company of Belgium. (Refer to Exhibit 14 for a summary of the top paint companies' sales by volume, Exhibit 15 for sales by region, and Exhibit 16 for sales by segment.)

At the other end of the spectrum, small companies had sales under $10 million and employed fewer than ten persons. Normally, these smaller manufacturers concentrated production on one or a few segments, usually in their home markets, and sometimes augmented their sales by OEM relationships with other specialist paint companies.

In Japan, paint companies operated under significantly different conditions than competitors in the West, due to the country's *keiretsu*, or "societies of business." There were two types of keiretsu: supply and bank centered. Generally speaking, supply keiretsu were groups of companies integrated along a

EXHIBIT 14 ● World League Table, 1991

Company	Country	Approximate volume (in millions of liters)
1. ICI	United Kingdom	805
2. Sherwin-Williams	United States	533
3. PPG	United States	515
4. BASF	W. Germany	500
5. Akzo	Netherlands	490
6. Nippon	Japan	350
7. Casco-Nobel	Sweden	350
8. Courtaulds	United Kingdom	300
9. Kansai	Japan	280
10. Du Pont	United States	265
11. Valspar	United States	200
12. Sigma	Belgium	180

supplier chain dominated by a major manufacturer. Bank keiretsu, on the other hand, were large industrial combines consisting of up to fifty companies, centered around a bank. In addition to interlocking directorships and cross-shareholdings, bank keiretsu provided a way to share risks and a mechanism for allocating investment to strategic industries. In 1992, the six major bank-centered keiretsu in Japan were Sumitomo, Mitsubishi, Mitsui, Dai Ichi Kangyo, Fuyo, and Sanwa.

In those keiretsu where both paint and automobile companies existed—such as Sanwa, Sumitomo, and Fuyo—paint companies derived much of their application know-how and revenue from sales to the automobile company within their respective ''business society.'' However, when they first began, Japanese paint companies had little, if any, paint technology and would acquire know-how through licensing. Because of having had licensing agreements, these same paint companies were prevented from expanding independently into North America and Europe, and they could access these regions only through business partnerships such as a joint venture

or strategic alliance with a local player. (Exhibit 17 gives an overview of company relationships in the world paint industry.) In the Asia Pacific region, though, Japanese companies were by far among the area's key players (as shown in Exhibit 18).

ICI

In 1991, Imperial Chemical Industries of the United Kingdom reported total sales of $22.1 billion. Of this amount, ICI Paints—the largest paint manufacturer in the world—accounted for 13 percent, or $2.9 billion, in sales and was one of the more profitable companies within the ICI Group. Around the world, ICI Paints was a formidable competitor in decorative paints, which accounted for 62 percent of its sales. In the United Kingdom alone, ICI's Dulux product line accounted for an estimated 37 percent of all decorative retail paint sales and included Dulux Vinyl Silk Emulsion, Dulux Matt Emulsion, Dulux Vinyl Soft Sheen, Dulux Satinwood, Dulux Gloss Finish, Dulux Non-Drip Gloss, Dulux Definitions, Dulux Undercoat,

EXHIBIT 15 ● World Paint Majors by Region

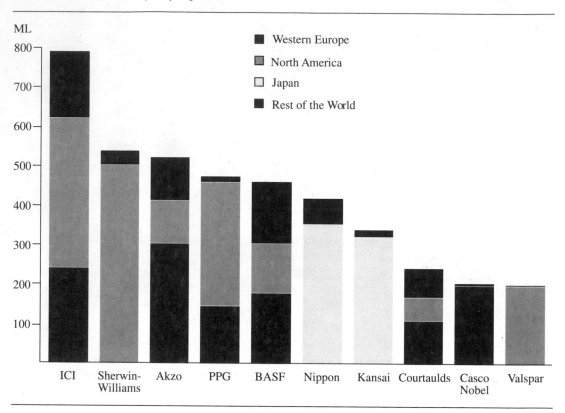

Dulux Options, and Dulux Weathershield. Dulux was also known for its Natural Hints product line, consisting of 9–10 shades of off-white colors. After decorative, can coating accounted for 16 percent; automotive refinish, 5 percent; automotive OEM, 3.4 percent; powder, 2 percent; coil coatings, 1.5 percent; and other, the balance of ICI Paints' sales. Geographically, 30 percent of ICI Paints' sales came from western Europe, 48 percent from North America, 10 percent from the Asia Pacific region, 10 percent from Australasia, and 1 percent from Latin America.

Despite ICI Paints' worldwide strength in the decorative segment, it was not the biggest in many regional markets. For example, Sherwin-Williams

was bigger in the United States, while Akzo and Casco-Nobel dominated in Europe. To bolster its presence in these markets, ICI Paints was not opposed to acquiring or merging parts of its business with other companies or forming joint ventures. In 1992, for example, ICI Paints expanded its European decorative business by acquiring a network of thirty trade branches in France from Master Peintures; the deal also included sales through a number of independent wholesalers. With annual sales approaching $35 million, the new network was expected to provide the base for further growth in the decorative segment. Also in Europe, together with Du Pont, ICI had formed a joint venture in automotive coatings called IDAC, aimed at securing 20 percent of the western

EXHIBIT 16 ● World Paint Majors by Application Segment

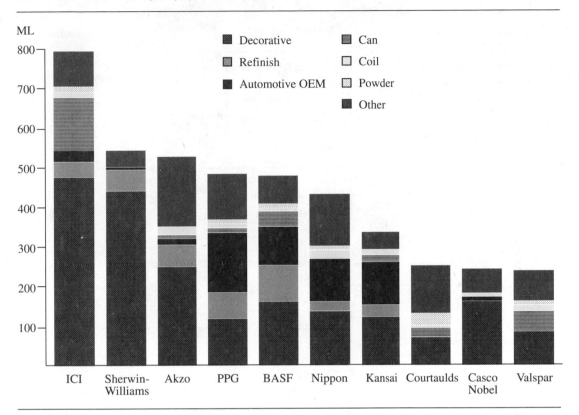

ML

Legend:
- Decorative
- Refinish
- Automotive OEM
- Can
- Coil
- Powder
- Other

Companies: ICI, Sherwin-Williams, Akzo, PPG, BASF, Nippon, Kansai, Courtaulds, Casco Nobel, Valspar

European market for vehicle refinishing. And in the same year, the ICI Paints World Packaging Group announced a partnership with Nippon Oil to make, distribute, and service ICI Paints' packaging coatings for food and beverage cans and closures in Japan. As well, ICI Paints bought the refinish business of Barnices Valentine, the leading producer of automotive refinishes in Spain, with one-third of the segment in that market. Herman Scopes, CEO of ICI Paints, commented, "We were strong elsewhere in this segment but before this, not in Spain."

Scopes attributed the subsidiary's success in a recessionary environment to three factors. First, from 1989 on, ICI Paints had trimmed its fixed costs; second, it had developed what Scopes called a "realis-tic" approach to pricing. By the latter, he meant that the company had succeeded in increasing prices in areas where ICI had a superior product or service base. The third factor benefiting the company's financial performance was, in mid-1990, a drop in raw material costs for pigments. He added that, in a recessionary climate, one of his biggest challenges was to continue to develop the paint business. To that end, he mentioned that Asia accounted for about 20 percent of ICI Paints' sales and had been growing at roughly 10 percent annually. To help meet demand, in 1992 the company began constructing a $15 million paint plant in China, just across the border from Hong Kong, and in the same year commissioned a can coatings plant in Taiwan.

EXHIBIT 17 ● International Cooperation on Paints and Coatings

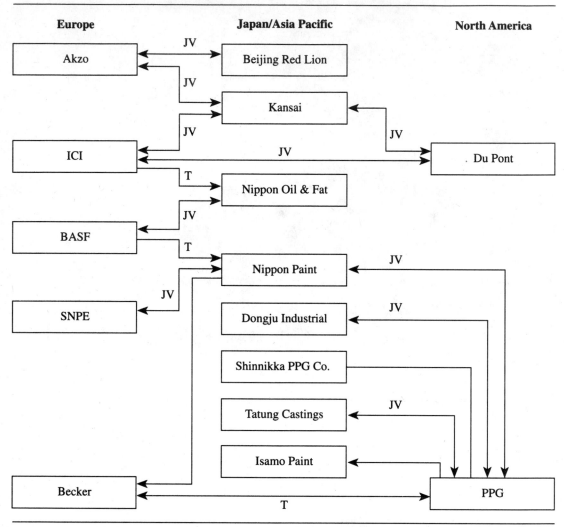

Notes: T = technical tie-up.
        JV = joint venture.
        OEM = original equipment manufacturing.
        Arrows indicate the flow of products and technologies.

EXHIBIT 18 ● Leading Paint Companies in the Asia Pacific Region*

Company	Home country	Market share %
Kansai Paint	Japan	7.46
Nippon Paint	Japan	6.87
Dainippon Toryo	Japan	2.84
ICI	UK	2.52
Courtaulds	UK	1.59
Chugoku	Japan	1.45
Shinto Paint	Japan	1.37
Wattyl	Australia	1.19
Jotun	Norway	0.59
Akzo	Netherlands	0.45
All others		73.67

*Excluding Japan.

Source: IRL.

Also in the Asia Pacific region—in Malaysia, Indonesia, and Thailand—the company had invested in new production units. In Malaysia, this would be ICI's second paint plant, with a planned completion date of late 1993 or early 1994. The $25 million plant would double capacity of decorative paints, while its existing plant would continue to produce automotive, refinish, and can coatings. In Indonesia, where ICI's plant reached maximum capacity, the company was planning to build a plant similar to the one in Malaysia. For Thailand, where ICI Paints was the market leader in can coatings, the company planned to triple production of decorative coatings, beginning in 1995. Expansion in each of these markets was part of ICI's plan to establish a stronghold in the Asia Pacific region in order to compete more strongly with Japanese products.

In addition to expanding existing operations, ICI was also merging and selling off parts of its business. In the United States, for example, in 1991, the company began merger discussions with Ferro, the powder coatings company. Though the deal was never concluded, the proposed merger of Ferro and ICI would have made that company the worldwide leader in powder coatings. Also, ICI sold the Canadian portion of its automotive OEM business to PPG in 1991. According to one spokesman, the sale coincided with the automotive industry's plan to reduce the number of suppliers as it globalized, to ensure consistent standards worldwide.

To stay competitive throughout the 1990s, ICI Paints had been investing up to 5 percent of sales in R&D and had focused its efforts on converting solvent-based products to water-based coatings. By the third quarter of 1991, according to Scopes, the company had already converted 75 percent of its coatings. More recently, ICI unveiled Aquabase, which it claimed was the first water-based metallic paint for automotive refinishing. The product was scheduled for a 1993 introduction in Europe, where the company estimated auto repairs accounted for 117,000 tons per year of VOC emissions. In the United Kingdom, Aquabase was expected to be priced 5–10 percent higher than conventional refinishing paints, and as much as 30 percent higher in Italy and Germany. Despite the premium price, ICI maintained that its customers would be able to avoid costly VOC emissions abatement equipment. ICI also planned to introduce the product in the U.S. automotive refinish market—the largest such market in the world—later in 1994. Additional goals included completing the integration of Glidden—the U.S. paint maker acquired in 1986—into ICI's global operations, reducing breakeven to 80 percent of 1991 levels and achieving a return on net assets of 35 percent by the end of 1993.

Sherwin-Williams

In 1991, Sherwin-Williams, with net sales of $2.54 million and net income of $128,223, was the second largest producer of paints and coatings in the industry. Geographically, the company and the bulk of its 16,700 employees were based in North America, which also accounted for 93 percent of the company's sales. At Sherwin-Williams, coating products fell into one of two business segments: the Paint Stores Segment or the Coatings Segment.

In the Paint Stores Segment—a network of roughly 2,000 company-operated paint and wall covering stores in the United States and Canada—paint, wall coverings, floor coverings, window treatments, spray equipment, and other associated paint products were marketed by store personnel and direct sales representatives to DIY customers, professional painters, painting contractors, industrial maintenance customers, home builders, property managers, and architects. With brands such as Dutch Boy, Martin-Senour, and Kem-Tone, Sherwin-Williams' paint stores underscored the firm's strength in decorative coatings, which accounted for 81 percent of its sales.

In contrast to the Paint Stores Segment, Sherwin-Williams' Coatings Segment consisted of five operating divisions: Consumer, Automotive, Specialty, Transportation Services, and the International Group. Typically, each division participated in the manufacture, distribution, and sale of coatings and related products. The Automotive Division, for example, sold directly to independent automotive body shops, dealerships, fleet owners, production shops, OEMs, and marine after-market accounts through a network of company-operated automotive branches, supported by a direct sales staff, and through jobbers and wholesale distributors. The automotive refinish segment accounted for 12 percent of Sherwin-Williams' sales and included brands such as Martin-Senour, Acme, and Rogers. Products for the Specialty Division, on

the other hand, were marketed through mass merchandisers, home centers, automotive chains, sanitary supply marketers, and maintenance distribution channels, and they included the Krylon and Illinois Bronze brands—aerosol paints acquired from Borden in 1990.

Outside North America, Sherwin-Williams products were manufactured and sold through subsidiaries and thirty-nine licensees in thirty countries; the majority of the licensees' sales were in South America. For the future, Sherwin-Williams intended to develop new business by establishing subsidiaries, joint ventures, and licensees in selected countries. Late in 1991, for example, Sherwin-Williams' Automotive Division signed an agreement with Herberts GmbH of Germany (the industrial coatings subsidiary of Hoechst) to utilize its technology with Sherwin-Williams' extensive marketing network to distribute Standox—a premium refinish product for top-of-the-line European automobiles—in the United States and Canada.

PPG

PPG Industries, Inc. had businesses in three main areas: Glass Coatings and Resins, Chemicals, and Medical & Diagnostics. In 1991, net sales for all groups amounted to $5.7 billion, of which $2.2 billion came from coatings and resins. One observer commented that the emergence of PPG's coatings and resins business as a world player in only eight years was considered one of the most impressive feats in the industry. In contrast to other coatings companies in the 1980s, which grew by acquiring companies which were unfamiliar, the licensees bought by PPG were companies it knew well, ones that were selling in the same segment abroad as PPG was in at home. That is, it stopped being a supplier to other paint companies and went directly to the customer. With no problems of corporate indigestion, analysts believed that PPG had up to a five-year lead on the competition in terms of fine-tuning its management structure.

In the industry, PPG was considered the toughest competitor in the automotive OEM market, which accounted for 32 percent of its sales. To a large extent, PPG's strength in this market stemmed from its process know-how in electrocoating car body technology, which, in turn, enabled car makers to provide their anticorrosion guarantees. PPG also offered its automotive customers a wide range of services and products—including prime coats, top coats, sealants, and adhesives. Then, too, PPG was known for working in partnership with its automotive customers to provide high-performance finishes with products that were environmentally sound and that reduced the cost of application. During 1991, for Buick's Le Sabre car model, for example, PPG provided its new HWB base coat, a waterborne product that improved environmental performance for customers while providing a high-quality appearance. In addition, PPG supplied a majority of the coatings, including waterborne base coats and electrodeposition primers, for the General Motors car model Saturn.

In addition to supplying directly to the automotive OEM market, PPG sold its automotive refinishes to the after-market, primarily through distributors, which accounted for 16 percent of its sales. In the decorative segment, which represented 23 percent of PPG's sales, the company competed with its Pittsburgh and Lucite paint brands, its Olympic brand of stains and paints, and its new Waterguard waterproofer sealants. Typically, PPG's decorative products were sold through independent distributors, paint dealers, mass merchandisers, and home centers. Remaining segments and their contribution to PPG sales were can, 3 percent; coil, 2 percent; powder, less than 1 percent; and other, the remainder. Geographically, 68 percent of the company's sales were in North America, 29 percent in western Europe, and the balance spread around the rest of the world.

At PPG, principal production facilities for coatings and resins were located in North America and western Europe; North American facilities consisted of fifteen plants in the United States, one in Canada, and one in Mexico. Additionally, Coatings and Resins operated twelve service centers in the United States, two in Canada, and one in Mexico, all of which provided just-in-time delivery and service to automotive assembly plants. Outside North America, PPG operated four plants in Italy, three plants in Spain, two plants in France, and one plant each in England and Germany. In Asia, PPG had a 50:50 joint venture with Dongju Industrial in South Korea and a 25 percent interest in Tatung Coatings in Taiwan. And, in Japan, PPG had a distribution agreement with Isamu Paint to distribute the company's automotive refinish prod-

ucts. As well, PPG had a 50:50 joint venture with the Nippon Steel Chemical Company, called Shinnikka PPG, to manufacture and market coatings for industrial applications in the Japanese market.

In the future, PPG intended to focus on global expansion and develop new technologies that met its customers' paint needs in terms of appearance, performance, and health and environmental safeguards. To this end, in 1991, PPG bought ICI Canada's automotive OEM business to further enhance its position in Canada, where it was already established as a supplier of cationic electrodeposition primers and high-solids top coats. Also in Canada, PPG installed an automotive service and warehouse facility to supply top coats to two Chrysler assembly plants.

Elsewhere, PPG formed a joint venture with Becker of Sweden to market and distribute automotive OEM coatings. Other recent highlights included the establishment of a major coating applications center in Italy to test finishes and application processes for automotive customers throughout Europe. Specific financial objectives for the future included an 18 percent return on equity, 4 percent real sales growth per year, and 3 percent annual improvement in output per employee.

BASF

In 1991, BASF was the world's largest chemical company and divided its business into six major activities: Oil and Gas, Products for Agriculture, Plastics and Fibers, Chemicals, Dyestuffs and Finishing Products, and Consumer Products. In 1991, sales and income from the BASF Group of companies were $28 billion and $1.3 billion, respectively.

Within the BASF Group of companies, the Dyestuffs and Finishing Products Division had primary responsibility for BASF paint products and, in 1991, recorded sales and income of $4.8 billion and $416 million, respectively. By segment, decorative accounted for 34 percent of BASF's paint sales and included the company's Glasurit and Herbol brands of house paints and coatings. In the automotive OEM segment, accounting for 21 percent of BASF's sales, the company was well known in Europe for its registered Cathodip cathodic electrodeposition process as well as its two-coat metallic finishes. In the refinish segment, which represented 18 percent of the company's sales, BASF sold a complete range of paints and priming materials, and it distributed this product line worldwide under the Glasurit and R-M brand names. Thereafter, can coatings accounted for 10 percent; powder and coil, less than 1 percent each; and other, the balance of BASF's coating sales. Geographically, BASF's sales were concentrated among western Europe, 39 percent, where it was represented by BASF Lacke & Farben AG; North America, 25 percent, where it was referred to as the Coating & Inks Division of BASF Corporation in North America; and Latin America, 36 percent, where the company operated under the name Glasurit do Brazil.

For the 1990s, observers believed that filling in the holes in its geographic coverage would continue to be important at BASF. To this end, BASF had acquired Pinturas Aurolin, a Mexican family business that supplied the automotive market and had approximately 40 percent of the local market. And in Europe, BASF announced plans to upgrade its paints and dyes factory in Spain, which specialized in paint for the automotive and metal industries. In France, in 1991, BASF Peintures & Encres had invested $53 million in equipment to produce water-based inks and paints, increasing capacity by some 30 percent. In the former East Germany, BASF had also announced plans to set up a $48 million water-based car paints plant and had signed a cooperation agreement with Lackfabrikzeitz to produce furniture paints and film coatings for BASF.

In Turkey, BASF had recently agreed to cooperate with Yasar Holding in the field of automotive OEM paints. In the Turkish market, Yasar Dyosad was a leader in automotive OEM paints and had an exclusive license to use all of BASF's know-how, including technology for Japanese car makers. Also in 1991, in Japan, BASF and Nippon Oil & Fats jointly formed BASF Nichiyu Coatings R&D to consolidate coatings technologies from Japan, Europe, and North America. Under the terms of the venture, BASF and Nippon Oil & Fats would cross-license automotive OEM coatings technologies, Nippin Oil & Fats would market technologies in Japan, and BASF would handle technologies outside Japan.

In Brazil in 1992, BASF's local subsidiary—Glasurit do Brazil—announced plans to build three new units in São Paulo: a $30 million resins plant, a $20 million dispersion paint unit, and a $20 million soluble paints unit. Modernization of an existing refinish plant was expected to absorb another $20 million.

To stay one step ahead of German environmental regulations, considered the toughest in the world, BASF in 1992 entered into an environmental partnership with Rethman Entsorgungswirtschaft and Rheinisch-Westfaelische TUV for waste disposal, use of unavoidable waste, and advice to customers on reducing and avoiding products which were not environmentally friendly; in the refinish segment, the concept had been taken up by 70 percent of BASF's clientele. Furthermore, over 70 percent of the R&D activities of the BASF group in the coatings sector was devoted to active environmental or compliance coatings. Other environmental firsts at BASF included the development of a high-solids (low solvent content) antirust coating for cars and pigments that contained no lead or cadmium.

Akzo

With headquarters in the Netherlands, the Akzo Group operated companies in more than fifty countries, organized in five divisions: Fibers, Salt and Basic Chemicals, Chemicals, Coatings, and Pharmaceuticals. In 1991, net sales for the group were $9 billion, 25 percent ($2.25 billion) of which came from Coatings (employing some 14,000 persons). Worldwide, Akzo's coatings sales were concentrated in Europe and North America, at 57 percent and 22 percent, respectively, of all sales.

The decorative segment was by far the single most important segment at Akzo, accounting for 48 percent of all the Coatings Division's sales. The ranking of the other segments was, in decreasing order, the refinish segment, 10 percent of sales; automotive OEM, 4 percent; coil, 3 percent; can, 1 percent; powder, less than 1 percent; and other, the remainder. In the automotive refinish segment, Akzo's position had increased in recent years, despite the decline in overall demand. Among the company's recent successes in this segment was the Autoclear MS program, a paint system that permitted customers to use clearcoats at various levels of automation. And, in 1991, customers also showed continued interest in Akzo's Mixit—a computer-controlled paint mixing system used to select from thousands of shades and colors to obtain a perfect match in automotive refinishing.

Other achievements included the introduction of heat release and toxicity compliant paint formulations for civilian aircraft interiors, and infrared reflecting, low visibility, and chemical agent resistant coatings for the defense industry. Additional developments included plans to build a distribution center and plant for water-based paints in Spain and, in France, an investment of $13.3 million for construction of a completely automated plant. At Akzo, management hoped that the new plant would allow it to increase its 12 percent share of the French paint market by over 3 percent by 1997.

To improve the geographic distribution of its coatings activities, Akzo in 1991 acquired the U.K. paints operation of Macpherson, which was expected to increase Akzo's U.K. market share from 8 percent to 20 percent and nearly double sales to $132 million. Macpherson manufactured professional decorative and DIY paints under its own name brand, as well as Valspar and various private labels. And, on a worldwide basis, Akzo swapped its engineering plastics business for the powder coatings portion of DSM. The management of Akzo believed that, in so doing, they would expand the company's powder coatings business in Europe and the United States.

In Asia, Akzo opened a $5 million coatings plant in Singapore to cater to the region's furniture, aerospace, and car industries. According to one spokesman, the Singapore facility complemented the company's existing operations in Thailand and Indonesia. In China, Akzo announced plans to form a joint venture with Beijing Red Lion Coatings to market Akzo's complete line of automotive finishes and related products in China. As well, it would contract out production to Beijing Red Lion Coatings.

In eastern Europe, Akzo formed a venture in 1990 with TVK, one of the leading Hungarian paint makers. Also, Akzo had initiated talks with Chemolak, Czechoslovakia's second biggest coatings producer, with a local market share of 30 percent.

Other projects included improving the company's cost structure, part of which included reducing the number of production sites. Aside from the Asian operations mentioned above, Akzo had manufacturing operations in Europe: in the Netherlands, Germany, Belgium, Austria, Denmark, Spain, France, the United Kingdom, and Greece. In North America, manufacturing sites existed in both the United States and Canada and, in Latin America, in Brazil, Mexico, and Argentina.

Nippon Paint

The Nippon Paint Co. Ltd was the second largest coatings manufacturer in Japan, where it was under the influence of the Sumitomo group. In its home market, domestic sales represented 83 percent of Nippon Paint's 1991 $1.2 billion in turnover; outside Japan, the company's sales were concentrated in countries in the Asia Pacific region. By segment, decorative represented 32 percent of Nippon's sales, followed by automotive OEM, 26 percent; refinish and coil, 5 percent each; can and powder, less than 1 percent each; with "other" accounting for the balance.

In and outside Japan, Nippon was renowned for its electrodeposition paint technology and its concentration on the automotive sector. To this end, Nippon Paint had operated fairly closely with PPG in the past but recently had started to act more independently. In the United States, for example, Nippon Paint entered into a joint venture, managed by a former PPG executive, to promote Nippon Paints' powder coatings in the United States. And in France, the company established a joint venture with SNPE Chemie de Paris to develop a new family of specialty products for use in the coatings and engineering plastics industries.

In Malaysia, where Nippon Paint had a 32 percent market share, the company announced plans in 1992 to expand its production facilities and to double capacity by the end of 1993. And, in China, Nippon Paint and Wuthelam Holding of Singapore planned to construct an $11 million paint factory in the Pudong economic zone. The new factory, one of five being planned by the two partners, was to be fully owned by Wuthelam and Nippon Paint and would be operated by Nipsea Holding, a 40/60 joint venture between Nippon Paint and Wuthelam. Elsewhere in Asia, in 1992, Nippon Paint started up a 500 ton per year powder coatings plant in Thailand to produce powders for its Thai customers—primarily serving as suppliers of car and household equipment components to Japanese companies.

Recently, Nissan, Nippon Oil & Fats, Kansai Paint, Nippon Paint, and BASF-Tanave jointly developed an automobile paint that reportedly withstood scratches and acid rain 60 percent better than existing automotive paints. And, in 1991, Nippon formed a pollution-free metal-coating system in which wash water was recycled. In the same year, the company formulated a self-polishing marine paint with a copper-based growth inhibitor for ship bottoms. The new paint contained cuprous oxide and a copper acrylate copolymer that underwent hydrolysis over a long period of time, thus renewing the growth inhibition effect and the self-polishing caused by water action against a ship's surface.

Other technological developments at Nippon Paint included a paint that could be broken down and recycled, a special coating for construction applications designed for fast drying and effective on iron constructions in cold weather. Still other innovations included Nippe Metalcoat, a thin coating for automobile body panels that greatly improved corrosion resistance. Initially developed in 1989 with the co-operation of Nippon Steel Corp and Sumitomo Metal Industries, Nippon Paint licensed the manufacturing technology for its Nippe Metalcoat to PPG, as well as to Becker of Sweden.

Courtaulds

Based in the United Kingdom, Courtaulds was an international specialty materials company employing some 23,000 people in thirty-nine countries. Courtaulds based its business strength on polymer technology, surface science, and cellulose chemistry and specialized in products for protection and/or decoration in a wide range of demanding environments. It organized its business into five areas: Coatings, Performance Materials, Packaging, Chemicals, and Fibers & Films. In 1991, Coatings accounted for 34 percent, or $1.1 billion, of Courtaulds' turnover, with an operating profit of $99 million and a 9 percent return on sales.

With operations in thirty-six countries and manufacturing facilities in twenty-five countries, Courtaulds was the world leader in marine and yacht paints. In addition to antifouling coatings for the ship-building, shipping, yacht, and leisure markets, Courtaulds was also a leader in heavy-duty coatings for onshore steel and concrete applications and for offshore rigs. More recently, Courtaulds had become a leader in powder coatings for industrial and architec-

tural applications and for consumer durable white goods markets. In this segment, its Interpon brand was a leading powder coating.

In the decorative segment, Courtaulds was a major producer in the United States and Australia under the Porter and Taubmans brands, respectively. Recently, Courtaulds had introduced a one-coat Ranch paint, complete with a six-year durability guarantee, reported to be as durable as three-coat paint systems. In can coatings, Courtaulds was a major producer in Europe, Brazil, and the Asia Pacific region. In coil, the company was also a major producer in Europe and the Asia Pacific region for coatings used to protect steel in architectural and appliance uses. Aside from its coatings products, Courtaulds also provided a rapid and flexible service to smaller industrial users through a network of local service centers, collectively referred to as Cromadex.

In summary, Courtaulds' sales were distributed by segment as follows: decorative, 23 percent; can, 11 percent; powder, 10 percent; coil, 3 percent; automotive OEM, 1 percent; with other accounting for 52 percent of sales, largely to customers in the shipping industry—in which Courtaulds had an estimated 30 percent market share. Geographically, Courtaulds' sales were concentrated in western Europe, 44 percent; North America, 25 percent; Australasia, 15 percent; South America, 10 percent; and the Asia Pacific region, 6 percent.

In 1991, Veneziani Zonca Vernici of Italy sold its ship paints division to Courtaulds, already the world's largest ship paint producer. In the same year, PPG sold its U.K. defense and coatings activities to Courtaulds, which through its other businesses was active in specialty materials, sealants, adhesives, coatings, and advanced products for the defense and aerospace industries. Similarly, in 1992, Courtaulds acquired ICI's aerospace and defense coatings business activities in Germany, France, and the United Kingdom.

Elsewhere in 1991, Courtaulds formed a joint venture in Taiwan to produce powder coatings. One spokesman commented that the joint venture would enable Courtaulds, which already had a South Korean subsidiary, to meet the boom in Southeast Asian markets for powder coatings. And in India, Courtaulds had a 40 percent stake in Shalimar Paint, which conducted R&D on coatings for wood finishing, waterborne paints, and a new generation of marine and chemical resistant coatings, as well as coil and powder coatings. In Australia, Raffles Paints was sold to Courtaulds in 1992.

Kansai Paint

In Japan, Kansai was the largest paint maker and specialized in industrial coatings for automobiles. In part, this stemmed from Kansai's belonging to the Sanwa Group, along with Daihatsu Motor. For fiscal year 1991, the company reported a turnover of $1.24 billion and a profit before tax of $68 million.

By segment, automotive OEM customers accounted for 37 percent of Kansai's sales; decorative, 33 percent; refinish, 7 percent; coil, 5 percent; can, 4 percent; powder, less than 1 percent; and other, roughly 13 percent, most of which was accounted for by coatings sales to the marine sector. Geographically, Japan represented 95 percent of Kansai's sales; outside the domestic market, the company had sales primarily in the Asia Pacific region. Recently, though, Kansai had formed a joint venture with Du Pont in the United States to supply local Japanese car manufacturers, or ''transplants,'' with the same paint it supplied those car makers in Japan.

At its Singapore facility, Kansai planned to double paint capacity for ships and containers in 1991 by building a $5.8 million plant, complete with a technical laboratory. In Singapore, industry analysts believed that Kansai had a 13 percent market share, 80 percent of which was accounted for by marine and container coatings. According to one company spokesman, over the next few years, Kansai aimed to increase exports from Singapore to China, Dubai, and Southeast Asia by 10 percent, from the current 50 percent share of total exports. In a separate plan, Kansai also announced it would double capacity at its Malaysian paint facility. In China, Kansai formed a joint venture—Tianjin Kansai Paint & Chemicals—in 1992 to produce container coatings and high performance rust protection coatings for iron and steel.

Outside Asia, Kansai tended to access markets via licensing or other agreements. In Hungary, for example, Kansai was involved in a joint venture with Akzo and IDAC to produce paint coatings for Suzuki, the Japanese car maker. Kansai supervised and improved coatings products, while IDAC transferred Kansai's coatings technology to Akzo.

Niche Players

Aside from the larger multinational companies, a number of smaller paint firms operated around the world. In the United Kingdom, for example, Sonneborn & Rieck targeted relatively small segments and tried to service them better than larger firms. In its traditional segment—painting wood—the company worked to high specifications such as those of the Ministry of Defence and kept out of the low margin, high volume consumer business. In coating metals, it concentrated on developing environmentally acceptable water-based liquid paints and powder coatings. Likewise, Grebe, a German company, specialized in heavy-duty paint for the roofs of railway rolling stock. In addition, Grebe had moved into other specialty areas such as high performance coatings for ovenware, coil coatings for the steel industry, and nonstick coatings for frying pans. By concentrating their business on specialization and service, niche players such as Sonneborn & Rieck and Grebe commanded product prices up to five times higher than a simple decorative or industrial paint, so there was less need for a large sales volume to support technical services and marketing.

Case 12

ICI Paints (A): Strategy for Globalization

"We at ICI Paints aspire to the number one position globally in the paint business. Our goal is to make ICI Paints the first choice among paint suppliers to whom a customer anywhere in the world would turn if he were seeking a long-term supply relationship," said Herman Scopes, PEO (Principal Executive Officer) of ICI Paints. "Now, we are already the world's leader if measured in market share, sales volume, or liters of paint produced. However, we have not yet been able to translate this position into superior financial performance. To get there, we will have to become much better at learning from each other and at transferring best practice from one operation to another."

INDUSTRY PROFILE

The world paint market was estimated at some £20[1] billion at ex-factory level and some 12 billion liters. Growth was expected to average 2–3 percent through the next decade.

1. In 1988, £1.00 = $1.50.

This case was prepared by Jean-Pierre Jeannet, Professor of Marketing and International Business at Babson College, and Adjunct Professor at IMD, as a basis for class discussion rather than to illustrate either effective or ineffective handling of a business situation. Copyright © 1990 by IMD, Lausanne, Switzerland. The International Institute for Management Development (IMD), resulting from the merger between IMEDE, Lausanne, and IMI, Geneva, acquires and retains all rights. Not to be used or reproduced without written permission from IMD, Lausanne, Switzerland.

North America accounted for 31 percent of the market by volume, followed by Europe (29 percent), Japan (13 percent), Asia Pacific (11 percent), and the rest of the world (16 percent). In the more mature paint markets of North America and Europe, annual growth was expected to be below GNP growth, whereas in the newly industrializing countries growth was expected to be in line with GNP growth. Long term, the three principal paint user areas of Europe, North America, and Asia Pacific were expected to become of equal size and account for 75 percent of the world market (refer to Exhibit 1).

Major application segments included decorative uses (50 percent), industrial uses (37 percent), coatings for cans (3 percent), automotive OEM (6 percent), car repair and refinishing (4 percent; see Exhibit 2).

There were approximately 10,000 paint manufacturers worldwide. Leading paint companies, aside from ICI, PPG, and BASF, were Sherwin-Williams (United States), Akzo (Netherlands), Nippon (Japan), International-Courtaulds (United Kingdom), Kansai (Japan), Du Pont (United States), and Valspar (United States). The top ten companies shared 30 percent of the world paint market in 1988. That share was expected to increase over the next decade.

COMPANY PROFILE

ICI Paints was the world's largest paint manufacturer, with a sales volume of £1.5 billion, or 8 percent of the world market, and an annual output of 800 million liters, or 7 percent of world volume. The company operated some sixty-four manufacturing plants in twenty-nine countries. Licensees operated in another

EXHIBIT 1 ● World Paint Industry Profile by Region (12,000 Million Liters Worth $35 Billion at Suppliers' Prices)

By Region

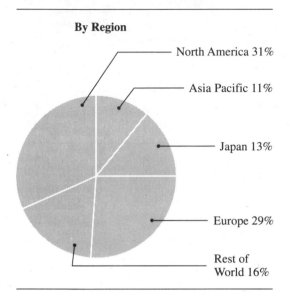

- North America 31%
- Asia Pacific 11%
- Japan 13%
- Europe 29%
- Rest of World 16%

EXHIBIT 2 ● World Paint Volume by Market Segment

Volume 12,000 ML*

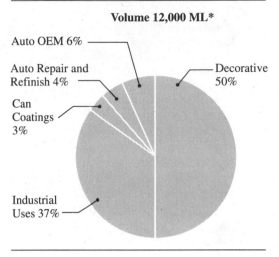

- Auto OEM 6%
- Auto Repair and Refinish 4%
- Can Coatings 3%
- Decorative 50%
- Industrial Uses 37%

*ML = million liters.

fourteen countries (refer to Exhibit 3). ICI was about 70 percent larger than its next biggest competitor, PPG Industries.

ICI Paints was part of the Consumer and Specialty Products sector of ICI. The division accounted for about 12 percent of total ICI turnover and 7 percent of its trading profit. Sales in 1988 (excluding sales by related companies) had reached £1.363 billion, with a trading profit of £98 million resulting in a return of 7.2 percent of sales. ICI Paints' profitability was on a par with BASF, its leading European competitor, and about twice that of its Japanese competitors. ICI Paints had been a consistent performer in an industry that had been characterized by considerable restructuring (refer to Exhibit 4).

ICI's market position varied considerably by market segment. The company was the world leader in the decorative and can coatings areas, a major player in automotive refinishes, one of the smaller automotive OEM players, and also held positions in powder, coil coatings, and other industrial coatings. ICI was absent from the marine paints sector (refer to Exhibit 5).

Decorative Paint Segment

About 57 percent of ICI Paints' business was accounted for by the decorative segment, which included paints and coatings used for the protection and decoration of industrial, commercial, and residential buildings. ICI was the world's largest producer of decorative paints, both for professional and do-it-yourself (DIY) users. The company marketed its Dulux brands in the United Kingdom, Australia, New Zealand, and a few other Asian markets; the Valentine brand in France; Ducolux in Germany; and Glidden Spred in the United States, which was acquired as part of the acquisition of Glidden in 1986. Glidden was the inventor of waterborne latex paints for popular emulsions. Although trading under different brands, ICI was the leader in most of these markets, particularly in the premium end of the market.

Most decorative paint was used where produced, with little cross-shipping, due to its low value. ICI tended to meet different local players country by country.

The wholesaling structure and retailing industry as well as the role of the DIY market varied consid-

EXHIBIT 3 ● ICI Paints Territorial Spread

ICI Paints Manufacturing Companies	ICI Minority Holdings	Companies Manufacturing Under License
Australia	Botswana	Colombia
Canada	Malawi	Cyprus
Eire	Indonesia	Japan
Fiji	Nigeria	Jordan
France	South Africa	Kenya
India	Zimbabwe	South Korea
Italy		Portugal
Madagascar		Saudi Arabia
Malaysia		Sudan
Mexico		Trinidad
New Zealand		Turkey
Pakistan		Venezuela
Papua New Guinea		Yemen
Singapore		
Spain		
Sri Lanka		
Taiwan		
Thailand		
United Kingdom		
Uruguay		
United States		
West Germany		

erably from one country to another. Furthermore, there was little economy of scale effect in this business. Some 500 paint companies competed in this segment in Italy alone. Paint formulations also had to be adjusted to local use conditions such as prevailing surfaces, building materials, and climate.

Despite these local differences, some commonalities existed. "Attitudes to what consumers want are far more common than different," commented John Thompson, ICI Paints' planning manager. "We have done market research in Turkey, Italy, and Columbus, Ohio, and the same overall pattern emerges: the

woman in a household determines when a surface is to be painted, and she determines the color. The husband selects the brand, usually on the basis of price and technique, although women are increasingly also making this decision. In terms of paint application, it is about evenly split between husbands and wives."

Can Coating Segment

Although the can coating segment, with worldwide sales of £800 million, accounted for only 3 percent of the world paint market, it accounted for 11 percent of

EXHIBIT 4 ● ICI Paints Financial Performance, 1985–1989

Sales (£m)

Operating profit

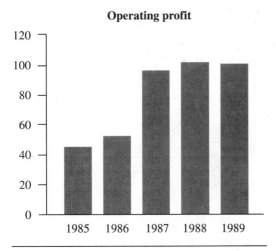

EXHIBIT 5 ● ICI Volume by Market Segment

Volume 800 ML

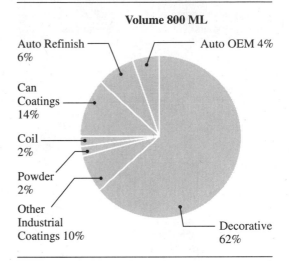

*ML = million liters.

inside of every can was a crucial part for a successful canning operation. Consequently, this part of the paint industry was viewed as a high technology application.

Customers were concentrated, with major use in the hands of four groups and their licensees: Continental Can, Pechiney-Triangle (included former American Can and National Can), Carnaud–MetalBox, and Crown Cork and Seal. These can manufacturers operated canning lines all over the world, and they expected the suppliers to follow them everywhere with a consistent product ensuring same tastes for globally marketed products such as Coca-Cola.

Coating products had to be developed for each application and depended on the particular food or beverage as well as on the type of metal or aluminum container used. Customers were increasingly looking for simplifications and tended to look for a narrower technology range.

In this business, it was important to be able to make the development effort go around. A new product for sardines might be developed in Portugal but might have applications for Norwegian packers as well. Success depended on avoiding duplication of

ICI business, or £165 million, representing about 28 percent market share and giving it world leadership. Some 46 percent of the market was in North America, followed by Europe (24 percent) and Asia Pacific (22 percent). Major competitors were BASF, Midland, and Valspar.

The coatings were used on the inside of tin or aluminum cans for food or beverage containers, making them corrosion resistant. This thin layer on the effort in applications development. Although coatings were usually not identical, a considerable part of the concept development could be widely applicable to other customers with the same applications.

ICI had acquired some eleven coatings companies over the years, including Holden (Birmingham) with operations in Europe, Marsden (United Kingdom), Wiederhold (Germany), Attivilac (Italy), and Glidden (United States). In Europe, ICI had strong operations in Rouen, France, where its Holden operation was located near the Carnaud company. The French operation had thus always been strong in food applications. Glidden, on the other hand, enjoyed a 80 percent market share in the United States for beverage cans.

ICI had targeted the can coating segment for major growth and planned to increase its market share to 40 percent of the world market, up from 28 percent currently. A new production facility was planned for Taiwan. As part of this expansion strategy, the company combined all of its various can coatings businesses under the same leadership in a single packaging group. Prior to that change, can coatings had been part of the larger group for general industry coatings.

Major changes were also contemplated for development. Work was conducted to transfer Glidden's aluminum can coatings technology to steel and tin plate. Also under review was a decision whether or not to site a new development center in Singapore or Malaysia to service the growing Asia Pacific markets. Other research initiatives were considered on basic background chemistry and how to develop this for the canning industry.

Automotive OEM Paint Segment

The automotive paint segment consisted of paint sales made to automobile manufacturers for use in their assembly plants. Worldwide, this segment represented 5 percent of the paint market. Major markets were North America (31 percent), Europe (32 percent), and Japan (26 percent). Leading competitors were PPG, BASF, Kansai, Nippon, Du Pont, Hoechst, and ICI, in order of importance.

ICI's market share was about 6 percent worldwide, ranking it number seven out of eight international players. Most of its sales were in Europe, followed by the Asia Pacific area (exclusive of Japan) and North America, with major local markets in Malaysia, Australia, and Canada. ICI was considered technically good but commercially weak in this segment. The company was a leader in the initial development of electrolytic paint and in the development of water-based top coat paints (Aquabase) for automotive users. The latest product was first introduced by GM in Canada and was now being introduced by Volvo in Sweden. Other European manufacturers were testing it, and ICI had granted a license to a Japanese company.

"This is an incestuous industry," remarked John Thompson, ICI Paints' planning manager. The customer base was largely globally operating companies and technologically very demanding. The technical service requirements of customers required paint suppliers to station technical service personnel permanently on location. As a result, the automotive companies preferred suppliers located at their doorsteps. This led to scattering factories close to assembly plants. In the United States, major paint companies would typically have several plants. Trends were away from multiple sourcing, which had kept local players alive, toward single sourcing and worldwide deals. Typically, a customer maintained a major supplier each for top coats and base coats, with a second supplier for smaller volume applications "to keep the big ones honest."

This segment was technically very demanding. PPG had reached segment leadership by developing electrolytic techniques key for the important base coating of car bodies. The initial development was actually made by ICI, but it was PPG which had made a commercial success out of the invention. At that time, PPG occasionally achieved single-source status through the installation of "hole-in-the-wall" plants, where the company was producing adjacent to the paint shops of the assembly plant.

Although the particular paint applications, such as color, were developed for each customer, a substantial part of the basic research had worldwide applications. Technical spinoffs were also possible for other paint segments, such as the refinish sector (with modifications in formulations due to the different paint applications methods), and for industrial components in areas such as the domestic appliance industry. This was one of the reasons why many players stayed in this segment despite low profitability or losses.

ICI had a very narrow geographic base in this segment and currently lacked platforms for major expansion. As a result, ICI engaged in a joint venture with Du Pont called IDAC, on a 50:50 basis, to supply the Western European automotive market. Du Pont had most of its automotive paint business in the United States and was therefore relatively weak in Europe. Du Pont's area of strength was in the top coat business, with GM and Ford as major customers in the United States. The IDAC goal was to reach a 20 percent market share in Europe during the early 1990s.

Automotive Refinish Paint Segment

The refinish segment included paints and coatings for repairing automobiles. The segment accounted for 4 percent of world sales and had the highest price per liter (£3.34). It was considered the most profitable paint segment. North America accounted for 36 percent of the world market, followed by Europe (30 percent) and Asia Pacific (25 percent).

Only ten paint manufacturers competed significantly in the refinish sector. Among those, only Sherwin-Williams of the United States and Rock of Japan did not also compete in the automotive OEM market. No new competitor had entered since the 1950s.

The world leader was BASF as a result of its recent acquisition of Inmont in the United States, followed by Du Pont and ICI. ICI was the largest refinish supplier outside the United States. Its Autocolor brand led in the United Kingdom and was well known in Europe. In France, the company was the leader with its Valentine brand. ICI had a color inventory of some 30,000 formulas to match the stock colors of virtually all vehicle manufacturers. ICI's matching capability was developed in the U.K. market, where a wide variety of car models was on the road following the decline of the local U.K. car industry.

Customers were largely small paint shops that needed quick and frequent deliveries, typically on a daily basis. Paint manufacturers supplied their customers with mixing schemes through local distributors who would combine the basic colors and shades with solvents to obtain the correct color match. There were some 10,000 different shades and some sixty different colors to select from. For ICI, this resulted in some 30,000 different formulas, partly as a result of different application techniques for the same shades and colors. A recent trend was in the direction of color mixing at the end-user location, using color systems supplied by the paint manufacturer. Recently, ICI had placed a computerized management system at the disposal of its customers.

To compete in this business, a company had to have access to the color and paint shops of the car manufacturers to obtain the needed information. Automobile manufacturers wanted to make sure that their customers could get their cars repaired wherever they were marketed. As an example, a company like Toyota was interested in worldwide coverage. Refinish paint manufacturers profited if they could have access to all car manufacturers, wherever they were located, so that they could supply the widest possible color range in any geographic market.

Powder Paint Segment

Powder paints was the fastest growing segment and represented an alternative technology for traditional wet paint rather than a particular application segment. Growing 10–20 percent annually, the segment had attracted many large companies as well as smaller suppliers. Leaders were International-Courtaulds (United Kingdom), Ferro (United States), ICI, and DSM (Netherlands).

Powder coatings were a precisely formulated mixture of pigment and resin which was sprayed using electrostatic spray guns. The sprayed item, a metal object, was then heated for about ten minutes to cure the surface. Coatings had been developed for heat resistance or chemical resistance. The major benefits for users were the reduced emissions such as solvents used with wet paints and the reduced need for waste disposal. Major user groups were the automotive component suppliers, the metal furniture industry, and domestic appliance manufacturers. Powder paint could conceivably substitute up to 50 percent of the paint being applied to metal. In Europe, where the produce was pioneered, the substitution already amounted to about 20 percent, compared to about 10 percent in the United States, an amount that was, however, growing rapidly.

While the technology itself had become basic, there was room to develop many applications. ICI had selected some specific applications for further development, such as domestic appliances and architectural components. ICI had concluded a joint venture with Nippon Oil & Fats of Japan in Malaysia. About half of ICI's powder volume was in the United States, about 40 percent in Europe, and the rest spread over many countries. In the United States, ICI was tied for first place with Morton but was only sixth in Europe.

General Industrial Paint Segment

Some £250 million of ICI Paints' business was part of the general industrial paint category, which included general industrial liquid paints, wood finishes, adhesives, ink, and others. Two-thirds of this segment was allied in some way to its four core business areas, such as adhesives in the United States or metal can printing. Another part consisted of stand-alone businesses, not necessarily connected to core sectors, such as inks for screen printing in Germany. In these segments, ICI did not compete consistently throughout the world and had only selected local pockets of excellence.

STRATEGY

ICI Paints aimed at world leadership and profitable growth. The company intended to concentrate on its key paint businesses on a global basis and wanted to exploit particular regional opportunities in the EC and Asia Pacific regions. ICI believed that a commitment to R&D and innovation was an essential part of industry leadership.

Organizationally, ICI aspired to become a marketing driven organization that was quality and customer focused, health and safety conscious, and environmentally responsible.

Organization

ICI management believed it was essential to have a global organization and management structure which would be both global and territory centered, support R&D centers of excellence in certain locations, and maximize resources and synergy between businesses, operations, and locations.

ICI Paints was organized along both geographic and business lines (refer to Exhibit 6). Reporting to the PEO were three regional heads (chief executives) for Europe, North America, and Asia Pacific. Each chief executive had P&L responsibility for the entire paint business in his area. The North American chief executive was also the head of Glidden, ICI Paints' major U.S. operating unit.

Reporting to each chief executive were several managers with country or territorial responsibility, called TGMs (territorial general managers) and BAGMs (short for business area general managers), for the four core sectors: decorative, can, automotive refinish and OEM, and powder. In some situations, BAGMs were identical with TGMs. In general, P&L results were a joint responsibility of BAGMs and TGMs.

At the territory or country level, BAGMs existed for the core business areas to the extent that each country had business in each of the four core sectors. Each territory also had other paint businesses. The percentage of sales in the latter category varied across territories, with higher percentages reported for some developing markets in Asia and lower percentages in the developed markets of Europe and North America.

Decision Making

Major decisions were always discussed and decided by the International Business Team (IBT) chaired by Herman Scopes, its PEO. Eight executives were members of the IBT, including the PEO and the three chief executives. The ICI Paints Group was led by Herman Scopes as its PEO and the seven members of the International Business Team (IBT). Part of the IBT were the three chief executives for North America, Europe, and Asia/Pacific/Australia regions, as well as four other executives with either functional or segment responsibility (refer to Exhibit 7). The IBT met six to eight times per year at various locations.

Executives were nominated to the IBT because of their ability to contribute broadly to the development of the ICI Paints Group rather than their specialties or specific skills. Once part of the IBT, members were assigned "portfolios" based on their own talents and experience, occasionally resulting in changes when the personnel constellation changed in the IBT.

EXHIBIT 6 ● Organization Chart

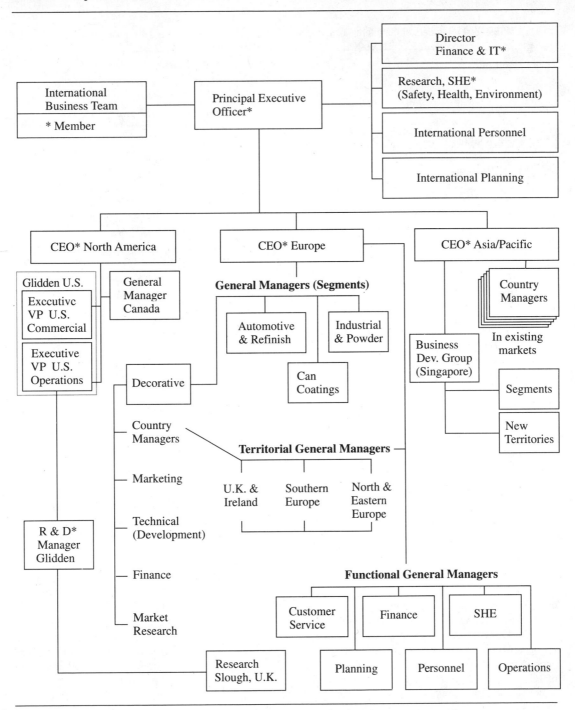

EXHIBIT 7 ● Members of the International Business Team (IBT)

Herman Scopes	PEO ICI Paints
John Dumble	Chief Executive North America President Glidden
Doug Curlewis	Chief Executive Europe International Leader Decorative Paint
Richard Stillwell	Chief Executive Asia Pacific/Australia
John Danzeisen	Finance Director International Leader Powder International Leader Finance Function International Leader IT Function
Alex Ramig	International Leader R&D
Brian Letchford	International Leader Automotive Refinish and OEM (designated International Leader Can)
Quintin Knight	International Leader Can Coatings (retiring in March 1990)

International Leaders not part of the IBT:

June Thomason	Operations Manager Glidden International Leader Operations
Ian Cope	International Leader Management Development

An important aspect of the way ICI Paints operated was its use of international leaders (ILs). IL positions existed for each of its four core business areas (decorative, can coatings, automotive, and powder) as well as for five functional areas: finance, information technology, operations, R&D, and management development. The ILs for three of these five areas were members of the IBT.

The ILs of the core sectors had the roles of facilitators or coordinators. These international leaders did not have P&L responsibility. However, they were responsible for the development of global strategies for each of their assigned core sectors. Powder was coordinated out of the United States, decorative out of Europe (by the chief executive Europe), and automotive and can coatings from Europe (head of that sector for Europe).

Strategies were developed at the business level by the international leaders and their teams and were then proposed to the International Business Team.

COORDINATING CORE BUSINESS SEGMENTS

The strategy making and coordination process differed considerably across the four core business areas.

The *decorative world strategy* consisted of three major elements. First, ICI Paints was to pursue quality leadership in all markets where the company was competing. It was understood that this meant setting the pace in the sector and pursuing a premium price. Second, there was to be a drive toward running a world brand, Dulux, the only world consumer paint brand in existence. This goal included having a consistent role for Dulux as the aspirational brand in all

ICI decorative paint markets. Third, ICI was to use the fact that it was the largest paint producer worldwide and should thus be able to maximize its resources in key functional areas.

Coordination was hampered by the fact that local operating companies considered their competitive situations to be unique. Glidden in the United States did not compete in the premium sector at all, and its market share was only about 10 percent, compared to 40 percent in the United Kingdom, or the three brand product line in Australia. To launch Dulux as a premium brand in the United States would entail a marketing investment of about $50 million over four–five years with a seven-year payback period for a required 5 percent market share. Glidden executives were not convinced that this strategy would be successful in the United States.

Due to the differences encountered, the IL for the sector had pursued a "consultative mode," meeting about twice annually with the key executives from the various operating companies. In addition, the IL had frequent individual meetings with operating executives and territorial managers.

In the *automotive sector*, the IL positions for the OEM and refinish segments were combined. For refinishes, where ICI had major positions in Europe and Australia only, the strategy was fairly heavily led from the center. Involved were key managers from Europe and Australia, with others "mostly along for the ride." A major point of discussion was ICI's future strategy in the United States, where it had no position at that time. Glidden executives were very interested in entering the refinish sector. However, a "greenfield approach" (i.e., starting up with no previous capability) was considered difficult, and yet no ready candidates for acquisition existed.

In the automotive OEM segment, the IL role consisted largely of outside contacts with Du Pont, ICI's partner for Europe, and frequent negotiations with Japanese companies on technology transfers that might result in obtaining business for ICI from Japanese transplant operations in Canada, Australia, Southeast Asia, India, and Pakistan, all countries where ICI was active in the OEM business.

Coordination in the *can coatings sector* was very close and involved a formal business area review team under the leadership of the IL for can coatings. The team consisted of the key players worldwide in ICI Paints, who met several times each year. A major challenge here was to devise a strategy in view of the increased concentration among customers. Despite ICI's leading market position, the company could not dictate prices. The resulting squeeze on margins had reduced profitability, and a new strategy would have to be devised to lead the company out of this "commodity hole."

For the *general industrial paint sector*, no IL had been appointed. These businesses were led in various ways. Businesses that were closely affiliated with one of the four core areas were attached to the IL teams of those areas. Others were left under the direction of the territorial management. Some businesses not directly tied to the paint business were kept as long as they were meeting required profitability targets.

Coordinating at the Functional Level

The ILs for the five key functions undertook their roles in different ways. For all functional ILs, however, the objectives were similar. ICI wanted to transfer skills, experience, and best practice around its group operating companies. It also wished to accelerate the innovation process (as distinctly different from the invention process). And finally, the desire, as elsewhere in the business, was to simplify and focus on operational aspects, not just to "spin wheels."

For the finance area, this largely involved the enforcement of corporate guidelines and practice around the Paint Group. For information technology (IT), the mission was still vague. One of the jobs was to encourage and promote the use of IT where appropriate, often convincing chief executives to make the necessary investments. The coordinating activities had led to a policy of using DEC equipment for technical applications and IBM for commercial and operational tasks.

In operations, efforts were undertaken to spread efficient production procedures across the group. Here, ICI relied on Glidden's skill as a low-cost producer.

In the R&D area, there had been a long-held conviction that technology was driven by the automotive and industrial market, such as coil coatings. ICI Paints was now moving the emphasis of its R&D brainpower to new fields such as decorative, can coatings, and powders, which was beginning to yield exciting results.

Coordinating the various functions was a challenging task since many of its operating companies had different corporate origins, were acquired from various sources, and represented different nationalities and cultures.

Current Organizational Issues for ICI Paints Worldwide

Over the past years, ICI's organization had undergone considerable changes. Aside from its territorial focus, it introduced the idea of ILs for segments and functions. However, the company encountered a major obstacle in the fact that much of its production assets were shared. It was believed that some fifty of its sixty-four plants were common sites for a number of paint products and segments. This meant that the business segments were largely responsible for business volume, but the BAGMs did not have full asset responsibility. At this time, not more than 75 percent of the company assets could be clearly attributed to individual business lines.

Aside from the organization issues and the challenges faced by each of the four core sectors, ICI Paints needed to leverage the benefit of its being the largest global player into a superior financial performance.

OPPORTUNITIES FOR ICI PAINTS

ICI Paints faced a number of opportunities in different geographic areas and various paint segments. These opportunities had to be seen in relationship to its own resources. "Although ICI is a very large corporation with considerable financial resources, it is not realistic to expect that we can do everything," said Thompson. "We still need to keep in mind that our profitability, while on a par with the best paint competitors, is below average for ICI as a whole." Some typical opportunities (not an exhaustive list, however) were:

ICI Paints' Opportunities in Japan

ICI Paints, despite its world leadership, did not have a direct presence in the Japanese market. For some time, the company had been considering an opportunity to go beyond licensing but was unsure about

the appropriate entry strategy. Considered were approaches ranging from exporting to joint ventures, making an acquisition, or even a greenfield start-up. Furthermore, which paint business to launch first in Japan was an unresolved question. Another question was how to relate any operation to the rest of ICI's business in Japan.

ICI Paints had virtually no direct sales in Japan. From time to time, decorative paint had been supplied by its Southeast Asian factories for sale as Japanese brands. Dulux Australia had supplied solid emulsion to be sold by Nippon Paints in the small Japanese DIY market.

The company's current presence in Japan consisted of two full-time ICI Japan employees—one long-serving and performing a liaison job with licensees plus color standards collection from Japanese automakers for ICI's refinish business, and the other recently appointed as a technical coordinator for submission of can coatings products for approval by the can manufacturers.

ICI had also concluded a series of licensing agreements, some granting technology to Japanese companies and others gaining access to Japanese technology. ICI granted automotive OEM licensees to Kansai, NOF, and Shinto, while obtaining licenses in the same area from Kansai and NOF. Furthermore, a powder coatings license was granted to Shinto while an industrial electrocoat license was obtained from the same company. A flexible packaging refinish license was granted to Rock, which in turn granted ICI a refinish license. A can coatings license, due to expire in 1991, was also granted to Dai Nippon Inks.

ICI Paints considered it inopportune to enter the general paints business. Instead, an entry through one of its key segments was viewed as more promising. Best opportunities appeared in can coatings and powder paints.

Powder paints were viewed as having a major opportunity in Japan due to the high concentration of metal based industries (automobile, appliances) dominated by firms such as Matsushita, Hitachi, and Mitsubishi.

The market for powder coatings was estimated at about 18,000 tons, or 8 percent of the world market. This was equal to the U.K. market but smaller than the market for powder coatings for Italy. The cost of building a factory was estimated at about $3 million with break-even volume of about 1,500 tons annually. Some $500,000–$750,000 of the original investment might be saved if the investment could be made together with ICI Films, another ICI international business, because the same buildings could be used. However, there were no production or marketing synergies between films and powder coatings.

In the can coatings sector, the opportunity was also tempting. Japan was a major market for metal cans, particularly in the beverage sector with three leading brewers, Kirin, Asahi, and Sapporo, as well as international soft drink firms such as Coca-Cola and Pepsi-Cola. The soft drink firms were global companies which were already indirect customers of ICI Paints elsewhere.

The Japanese can-making market was dominated by Toyo Seikan (the second largest can maker in the world), Mitsubishi, and Daiwa. They supplied coated cans directly to major users. Can users, such as beverage companies, often looked for suppliers who could serve them on a worldwide basis. Can coatings were typically formulated to the specific requirements of a customer.

The Japanese market for can coatings was estimated at some 70 million liters, or about 17.5 percent of the world market. A greenfield investment would cost about $15 million. The annual break-even point depended considerably on the particular product mix achieved. However, annual operating costs would be about $4 million, with another $1 million required for technical support. This would result in a break-even volume of about 5 million liters. On the other hand, licensing fees averaged about 3 percent of sales, with a minimum annual payment of $150,000.

ICI Paints needed a presence in Japan as part of its strategy to reach its goal of 40 percent market share worldwide in the can coatings sector. Major risks were a drain on critical resources such as human resources, capital funds, and the need for "patient money" to do well in Japan.

Present suppliers for can coatings included Dainippon, an old ICI Paints licensee of an earlier generation of coatings technology. Market leaders were Toyo Ink and Dainippon (DNIC), which accounted for about 50 percent and 40 percent of the Japanese market, respectively. In the present Japanese market, ICI Paints could compete with superior technology.

No other foreign company maintained a base in Japan for can coatings.

The major question remained on how to proceed. A joint venture with Toyo Sekan appeared possible. It was not clear, however, how to develop a local technology base, how to do the manufacturing and staffing. Another issue was how fast to proceed.

ICI Paints' Decorative Opportunities in the United States

ICI Paints had undertaken a recent attempt to investigate the possibilities of entering the premium paint segment in the United States. The difficulty of this strategy was underlined by the fact that such a premium segment was very small in the United States, amounting to about 12 percent of the market for DIY paint, compared to the United Kingdom, where it represented almost 40 percent of the decorative paint market. In the United States, regional companies such as Benjamin Moore and Pratt & Lambert were leaders in that segment.

Glidden, acquired in 1986, had pursued a low-price strategy that had resulted in enormous success. Sometimes described as "pile it high and price it low," Glidden was able to expand its business from just 4 percent market share to 17 percent currently in the DIY market, expanding its brand into national distribution and reaching the leading brand position in the U.S. market. By contrast, Sears (supplied by De Soto) had dropped from 30 percent to just 16 percent market share in the same fifteen-year time period. Furthermore, Glidden also achieved a 10 percent share in the contractor market aimed at painters and professionals.

At first, ICI Paints in the United Kingdom believed it might pave the way for a launch of a premium decorative brand in the United States by sending one of its own people to the U.S. operation. The assignment was to investigate if ICI's premium brand Dulux might be launched in the United States at some time in the future. Actually selected by Glidden, this British executive was soon isolated and "cocooned," which rendered his situation untenable, and no progress was achieved in resolving the issue whether a premium strategy might work in the United States. "It was like sending a 'Brit' to the 'Colonials,' " commented Herman Scopes, ICI Paints PEO. "This experience taught us that some other approach would have to be chosen.''

ICI Paints set up a study team consisting of both Glidden and ICI Paints executives. Scopes thought it might be helpful to "park" the idea of a position on global branding around Dulux and to look at the market more objectively. The output of the study was to be fed into a global review of ICI's decorative paint business. In the meantime, ICI's Canadian operation had agreed to launch a premium brand under the Dulux name.

Automotive Refinish Opportunity in the United States

The automotive refinish segment was a very stable market with only four major players: Du Pont, BASF/ Inmont, PPG, and Sherwin-Williams. These top four accounted for 90 percent of the market. This segment was highly profitable, with return on sales ranging from 18 to 24 percent and return on net assets (RONAs) of around 40 percent. The market consisted of some 60,000 body shops supplied through local jobbers via company-owned warehouses. Warehouse distributors played a decreasingly important role as they were usually not specialized enough.

The refinish segment in the United States was subject to a number of changes. One major factor was the increase in car imports into the United States, which tended to increase the range of products requiring refinishing. New top coat technologies adopted by car manufacturers required new refinishes and continued technological improvements on the part of the paint manufacturers. More sophisticated body shop equipment, such as controlled environments to counter solvent emission into the air, constantly forced adjustment in the refinish formulas. Furthermore, there was a trend toward supplying body shops with color mixing schemes rather than factory-packaged colors, shifting the mixing forward into the body shop as each job required it.

In the opinion of John Thompson, ICI Paints' planning manager, key to success in this segment was color performance, followed by technical service to body shops, then environmental friendliness, training opportunities for paint sprayers, and finally delivery service. Price was viewed as much less important than any of the above five criteria.

Several theoretical entry options existed. The first was through a major acquisition. "Who would sell such a beautiful business?" John Thompson asked. Acquisitions of a smaller player would not be big enough to make a difference. A greenfield entry was likely to be slow. Akzo, the large Dutch paint manufacturer, had been working at it for ten years and had still only achieved a 3 percent market share. There was an opportunity to enter regionally, with expansion to national distribution later on.

The financial resources required to develop this segment were considerable. Depending on the approach chosen, the pace of expansion, and the company's skill and success, a maximum negative accumulated cash flow of about \$30–\$50 million for a national introduction would have to be considered. Thompson considered the necessary volume for break-even to be 5 percent market share of a significant regional market and 4 percent market share nationally.

SELECTING A COURSE FOR THE FUTURE

ICI Paints management approached the future with some confidence. 1989 had been another good year for the paints business, with total sales of £1,628 million and a trading profit of £100 million. Volume in the major decorative DIY markets of the United States and the United Kingdom were affected by the depressed housing markets in both countries. Competitively, however, Glidden was able to assume clear brand leadership for decorative paints in the United States. Dulux Australia enjoyed record profits following the integration of an acquisition. Sales in Southeast Asia achieved strong growth with the successful introduction of new paint product lines and a joint venture in Hong Kong to develop business with China PRC.

In the can coatings segment, ICI was able to increase its world market share. Its position in Europe was strengthened through an acquisition in Spain (Quimilac SA). Powder paint continued to experience strong growth in Europe.

Case 13

ICI Paints (B) (Abridged): Considering a Global Product Organization

In the spring of 1993, Herman Scopes, chief executive officer (CEO) of ICI Paints, was having a discussion with the members of the company's International Business Team (IBT) about how the paint industry had changed over the past few years.

The passage of time has increasingly impressed upon us the rate at which markets are becoming international and global in nature. Over the past few years, ICI Paints has become an agglomeration of companies; global, but not necessarily globally managed. Moreover, as a result of past practices, we have an organizational structure that is, for the most part, based on geographic regions, not global product lines. As I look at the present business environment, however, I wonder whether that is the best arrangement and how the remainder of the IBT views the situation. Specifically, is our regional management structure, which has served us well in the past, appropriate for the rest of the decade?

In contrast to regional executives, who managed several of the company's products in one or more

●

This case was prepared by Robert C. Howard under the direction of Jean-Pierre Jeannet, Professor at IMD and Professor of Marketing and International Business at Babson College (U.S.A.), as a basis for class discussion rather than to illustrate either effective or ineffective handling of a business situation. Copyright © 1993 by IMD, Lausanne, Switzerland. The International Institute for Management Development (IMD), resulting from the merger between IMEDE, Lausanne, and IMI, Geneva, acquires and retains all rights. Not to be used or reproduced without written permission from IMD, Lausanne, Switzerland.

countries, some felt that ICI Paints should appoint worldwide business leaders with global product line responsibility. Doing so, however, raised all kinds of questions—such as the ability to maintain a local image in, say, North America and Asia with a product manager based in the United Kingdom. Adopting an organization based on global product lines also raised communication issues: would people feel able to relate to a product line organization that was worldwide in scope? Despite the potential problems, a global product organization offered distinct advantages in terms of allocating resources, deciding priorities, and making investment decisions. For Herman Scopes and his colleagues on the IBT, the question was whether the company should move from a regional to a global product organization and, if so, how.

IMPERIAL CHEMICAL INDUSTRIES PLC

The Imperial Chemical Industries (ICI) was formed in 1926 by the merger of Great Britain's four major chemical companies: Nobel Industries Limited, the United Alkali Company, the British Dyestuffs Corporation, and Brunner, Mond, and Company Limited. At that time, the newly formed ICI was divided into nine groups: alkalis, cellulose products, dyestuffs, explosives, fertilizers, general chemicals, rubberized fabrics, lime, and metals. Beginning in the 1930s, ICI's dyemakers used their knowledge of chemistry to diversify into plastics, specialty chemicals, and pharmaceuticals—higher margin products that later became ICI's core businesses. In 1991, those core businesses were structured along product and geographic lines into four principal areas: Bioscience Products, Specialty Chemicals and Materials, Industrial Chemicals, and Regional Businesses. In the same year, the ICI Group reported a turnover of $22.1 billion and profits of $1.8 billion and employed 128,600 persons around the world.

Sometime in the early 1990s, executives began considering breaking up ICI into smaller companies. In doing so, it was proposed, new companies would be better prepared to devote the amount of management attention and resources needed in an industry where the return on investment had gradually declined over the preceding twenty years. Had the reorganization occurred in 1992, ICI would have been split into two companies; one was to retain the company name with interests in industrial chemicals, paints, and explosives, while the other company—with the proposed name of Zeneca—was to include drugs, pesticides, seeds, and specialty chemicals. (Exhibit 1 gives financial data on how the two firms would have looked if they had been split in 1992.)

Organization of ICI Paints

In 1991, ICI Paints was the largest paint manufacturer in the world and accounted for $2.9 billion, or 13 percent, of all sales within the ICI Group of companies. In the same year, ICI Paints operated manufacturing plants in twenty-four countries, had licensees in an additional sixteen countries, all of which manufactured and marketed coatings in the company's main application segments: decorative, automotive OEM, automotive refinish, can, powder, and coil. (Refer to Exhibit 2 for a list of ICI Paints manufacturing companies, minority holdings, and licensees.)

Like other multinationals, ICI Paints traditionally structured its operations on the basis of individual markets. That is, executives had profit and loss responsibility for the full range of ICI products within a given market. Following the acquisitions of the 1980s, however, the management of ICI Paints felt that its customers could be better served by managers with a multicountry product line responsibility. To this end, ICI brought the management of Mexico, Canada, and the United States together under a regional CEO who reported to Herman Scopes in the United Kingdom. Similarly, regional constructs were devised for Europe and Asia. By 1990, the array of ICI Paints' subsidiaries and licensees was organized along geographic and business lines (as shown in Exhibit 3).

EXHIBIT 1 ● 1992 ICI-Zeneca Turnover and Operating Profit (Loss)

Turnover ($ million)		Operating profit (loss) ($ million)
	Zeneca	
228	Trading & Misc.	(18.2)
1,429	Specialties	39.5
1,961	Agrochemicals & Seeds	129.9
2,447	Pharmaceuticals	741.8
	New ICI	
2,827	Materials	(38)
5,396	Industrial Chemicals	(25.8)
2,052	Regional Businesses	12.2
836	Explosives	89.7
2,402	Paints	174.8

EXHIBIT 2 ● ICI Paints Territorial Spread

ICI Paints manufacturing companies	*ICI minority holdings*	*Companies manufacturing under license*
Australia	Botswana	Brazil
Canada	Malawi	Colombia
Ireland	South Africa	Cyprus
Fiji	Zimbabwe	Ecuador
France		Japan
India		Jordan
Indonesia		Kenya
Italy		Korea
Malaysia		Madagascar
Mexico		Portugal
New Zealand		Saudi Arabia
Pakistan		Sudan
Papua New Guinea		Trinidad
Singapore		Turkey
Spain		Venezuela
Taiwan		Yemen
Thailand		
United Kingdom		
United States		
West Germany		

Within his respective region, each regional CEO had profit and loss responsibility for the entire paint business. Also, within each region and reporting to the regional CEO, ICI Paints had country managers, territorial general managers (TGMs), and business area general managers (BAGMs). As the name implied, country and territorial managers supervised more than one of ICI Paints' product lines on a geographic basis, while business area general managers concentrated on the products of only one of ICI Paints' application segments. Because the latter were not required unless an individual segment reached a certain size, territorial general and business area general managers were sometimes one and the same person. In those areas where both existed, profit and loss results were a shared responsibility.

At ICI Paints, major decisions were always discussed and decided upon by an International Business Team (IBT), chaired by Herman Scopes. Additional members included the three regional CEOs, and four other executives with either functional or segment responsibility (as shown in Exhibit 4). Typically executives were nominated to the IBT because of their ability to contribute to the development of the ICI Paints Group rather than their specialties or specific skills. Once part of the IBT, members were assigned "portfolios" based on their own talents and experience. Occasionally, these responsibilities changed

EXHIBIT 3 ● Previous Organization Chart (1988–1990)

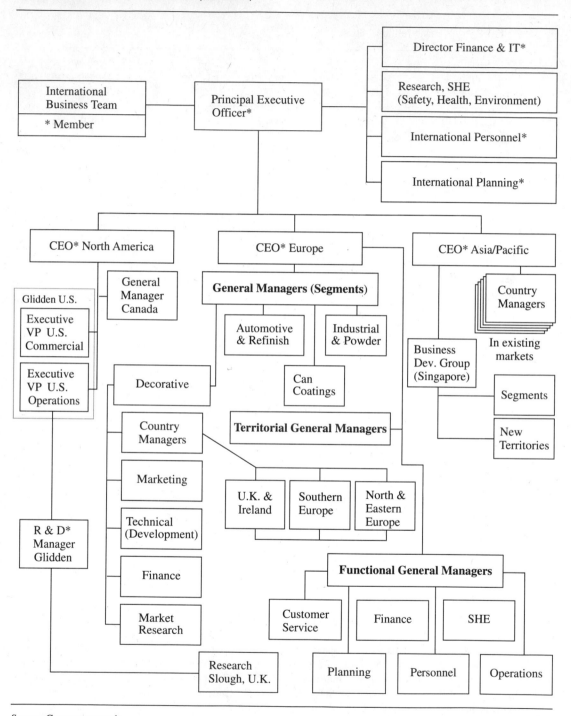

Source: Company records.

*International Business Team Member

EXHIBIT 4 ● Members of the International Business Team (IBT)

Herman Scopes	CEO Paints
John Danzeisen	Chief Executive North America
Peter Kirby	Chief Executive Asia Pacific
Denis Wright	Chief Executive Europe International Leader Decorative
Adrian Auer	Chief Financial Officer
Nigel Clark	International Leader Operations and Personnel
Brian Letchford	International Leader Automotive and Can Coatings
Alex Ramig	International Leader R&D
John Thompson	Chief Planner

when there was a change in the composition of the IBT.

Yet another important aspect of the way ICI Paints operated was its use of international leaders (ILs), persons drawn from each of the company's core business areas as well as three out of five of the following functional areas: finance, information technology, operations, research & development, and management development. Typically, international leaders drawn from the core businesses acted as facilitators or coordinators. And, though they did not have profit and loss responsibility, international leaders were responsible for developing global strategies in their respective application segment. Most recently, the company had appointed a worldwide safety, health, and environment (SHE) executive whose presence as an IL increased management's awareness of environmental issues.

Though the strategy making and coordination processes differed among ICI's application segments in general, strategies were developed at the business, or operational, level by the international leaders and their teams. In turn, these strategies were proposed to the International Business Team, which met six to eight times per year in various locations.

ICI PAINTS' COMPETITIVE POSITION

Worldwide, ICI Paints' competitive position varied as a function of region and application segment (as shown in Exhibit 5; for comparison with competition see Exhibit 6).

Decorative

By far, decorative paints was ICI's strongest product line, accounting for 62 percent of the company's 1991 sales. Despite ICI Paints' worldwide strength in the decorative segment, however, it was not the biggest in some regional markets, and market shares varied considerably by country. In western Europe, for example, ICI had only a 5 percent market share, behind Akzo with 8 percent and Casco-Nobel with 7 percent. In the United Kingdom, on the other hand, ICI's Dulux product line accounted for an estimated 37 percent of all retail paint sales and included Dulux Vinyl Silk Emulsion, Dulux Matt Emulsion, Dulux Vinyl Soft Sheen, Dulux Satinwood, Dulux Gloss Finish, Dulux Non-Drip Gloss, Dulux Definitions, Dulux Undercoat, Dulux Options, and Dulux Weathershed. Dulux was also known for its Natural Hints product line, consisting of nine–ten shades of off-white colors.

In North America, ICI Paints, through Glidden (its U.S. subsidiary), had an estimated 13 percent share of market, second only to Sherwin-Williams with 20 percent and well ahead of Benjamin Moore with 7 percent. And though ICI Paints had no decorative paint sales in Japan, it had a 5 percent market share in the rest of the Asia Pacific region, second only to Nippon Paint with 6 percent.

Industrial

Automotive Refinish   After the decorative segment, the automotive refinish segment was ICI Paints' largest segment, representing roughly 13 percent of company turnover. Similar to the decorative segment, sales of paint in the automotive refinish segment varied by region. In western Europe, for example, ICI Paints had an estimated 11 percent market share, behind Hoechst with 19 percent; BASF, 18 percent; and even Akzo at 11 percent. In North America, ICI had only a 1 percent share of the refinish market, well behind Du Pont with 31 percent; PPG and Sherwin-Williams with 22 percent each; BASF, 13 percent;

EXHIBIT 5 ● Breakdown of ICI Paints Sales by Region and Application Segment

Segment	% Market share by region			Application segment's share (%) of total ICI Paint revenues
	EUROPE	N. AMERICA	ASIA PACIFIC	
Decorative	5	13	5	
Auto OEM	4	0	15	3.4
Auto Ref.	11	1	14	13
Can	32	44	19	9
Coil	2	10	6	1.6
Powder	4	14	2	2

EXHIBIT 6 ● ICI's Principal Paint Competitors

	Coating as % of group sales	1990 m. litres	Sales $ million	RONA ave 1987–90	Key market sectors	Significant direct competition with ICI
International						
PPG	38%	515	1,963	26%	Motors, Refinish Dec.—U.S.A.	Refinish Decorative—U.S.A.
BASF	7%	485	c. 1,945	<15%	Motors, Refinish, Can	Refinish, Can
AKZO	23%	485	2,160	15%	Dec.—Europe Refinish, Motors	Decorative—Europe Refinish
Courtaulds	31%	300	1,767	25%	Marine, Can, Powders, Dec.	Can, Powders Decorative—Australia
Regional—Americas						
Sherwin-Williams	100%	535	2,338	26%	Dec., Refinish	Decorative
Du Pont	3%	265	c. 1,160	?	Motors, Refinish	
Valspar	100%	230	539	24%	Dec., Can, Wood, Coil	Can
Regional—Europe						
Casco Nobel	37%	250	892	20%	Dec., Coil, Wood Gen. Industrial	Decorative—U.K.
Hoechst	4%	220	1,160	c. 10%	Motors, Refinish	Refinish
Regional—Asia						
Nippon	100%	350	1,374	20%	Motors, Refinish Marine, Dec., Coil	Decorative Refinish, Motors
Kansai	100%	275	1,080	19%	Motors, Refinish, Dec. Marine, Can, Coil	Refinish, Motors
ICI	**13%**	**805**	**2,927**	**17%**	**Dec., Refinish, Can Powders**	

and Akzo, a 6 percent market share. Despite having no sales in this segment in Japan, ICI was in first place in the Asia Pacific region with a 14 percent market share, ahead of Korea Chemical with 13 percent; Kansai, 6 percent; and Kunsul and Nippon, each with 5 percent of the market.

Automotive OEM   With only 3.4 percent of ICI Paints' total sales, the automotive OEM coatings segment was among the smaller of the company's product lines. In western Europe, ICI had only a 4 percent share of this market segment, well behind PPG with 31 percent; Hoechst, 25 percent; BASF, 18 percent; and Akzo, 8 percent. In 1991, ICI sold the Canadian portion of its automotive OEM business to PPG. Thereafter, in North America and Japan, ICI was not present in the automotive OEM segment. In the rest of the Asia Pacific region, though, the company had a 15 percent market share in this segment, second to Korea Chemical with 23 percent but well ahead of Dong Ju with 9 percent, Goodlas Nerolac with 7 percent, and Daihan and Shen Yan with 5 percent each.

Can   Worldwide, can coatings accounted for roughly 9 percent of ICI Paints' sales. Geographically, ICI was a distant leader in western Europe, with a 32 percent market share, well ahead of BASF with 16 percent, Dexter with 15 percent, and Courtaulds with 11 percent. ICI was also a formidable competitor in can coatings in North America, with 44 percent of the market, more than twice the share of its closest rival, Valspar, with 20 percent and considerably ahead of BASF and Dexter with 12 percent and 10 percent of the market segment, respectively. Despite a strong presence in western Europe and North America in can coatings, ICI had no sales in this segment in Japan. It was, however, by far the leader in the rest of the Asia Pacific region, with 19 percent of that market. In terms of market shares, its closest rivals in that part of the world were Courtaulds and Kunsul, each with a 9 percent share of market.

Coil   In 1991, sale of coil coatings by ICI accounted for a mere 1.6 percent of all sales; in western Europe, several competitors led in this segment. In decreasing order of market share, these competitors were Becker, 18 percent; Sigma, 13 percent; Casco-Nobel, 12 percent; PPG, 9 percent; Akzo and Courtaulds, 7 percent

each; Kemira, 3 percent; and BASF, Dexter, Grebe, Hoechst, Salchi, and ICI, 2 percent each. In the North American coil coating segment, ICI was tied for fourth place with Lilly at a 10 percent market share; Valspar was the leader with 21 percent, followed by Morton, 19 percent, and Akzo, 16 percent. As with its other coatings, ICI had no sales in Japan but did have 6 percent of the Asia Pacific market for coil coatings, behind Nippon, 22 percent; Kansai, 17 percent; Korea Chemical, 13 percent; and Daihan, 10 percent.

Powder   Powder coatings represented approximately 2 percent of ICI Paints' 1991 sales and, in western Europe, accounted for 4 percent of all sales in that segment. Powder competitors with greater market shares were DSM, 13 percent; Becker, 11 percent; Courtaulds, 9 percent; and Hoechst, 6 percent. In North America, ICI's powder paints had a 14 percent market share, second only to Morton with 17 percent, yet still ahead of Ferro with 13 percent; Valspar, 12 percent; and Fuller O'Brien, 9 percent. In the Asia Pacific region, ICI's powder coatings had only a 2 percent share of market; there, leading competitors and their market shares were Daihan and Korea Chemical, 15 percent each; Jotun, 9 percent; Chokwang, 4 percent; and Kunsul, 3 percent. To bolster its presence in the powder segment, in 1991, ICI began merger discussions with Ferro. Though the deal was never concluded, a merger of Ferro and ICI would have made that company the worldwide leader in powder coatings.

DESIGNING AN ORGANIZATION FOR THE 1990s

At ICI Paints, management sought to have an organization in the 1990s that was both global and territory oriented, that supported R&D centers of excellence in certain locations, and that maximized resources among the company's different operations and locations. At the same time, the company intended to concentrate on its key application segments on a global basis and wanted to exploit opportunities in the European Community and Asia Pacific regions.

ICI Paints' organization had already evolved over time, and by 1992 several changes had been made (refer to Exhibit 7). In both the North American and European regions, territorial general managers had been eliminated, moving the entire organization

EXHIBIT 7 ● Present Organization Chart (1992)

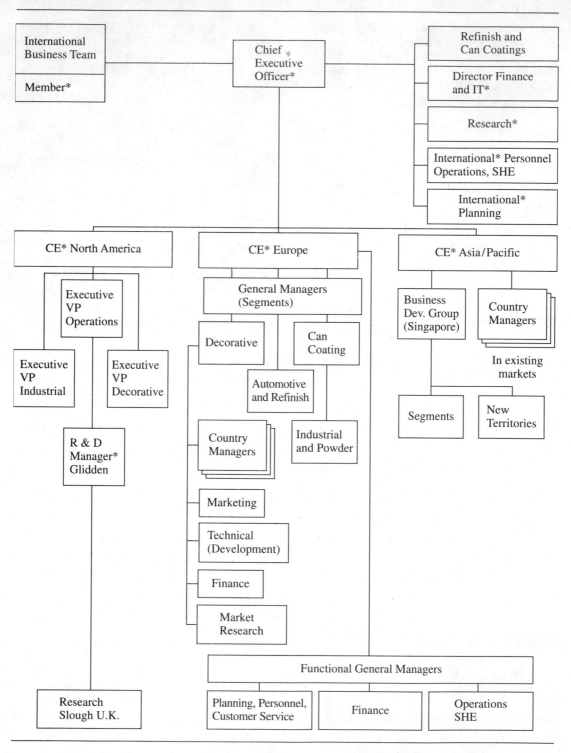

away from a territorial approach to more brand-oriented structure.

Upon review, some of ICI Paints' executives felt that, in order to succeed in the future, the company needed to focus more directly on and better coordinate the activities of its main application segments. To this end, executives cited four advantages in moving toward a global product organization. First, it was believed that a global product organization would enhance ICI's ability to serve a customer base that was itself becoming increasingly global. For customers with global operations—such as can coating companies and automobile makers—a single product and service package that was applicable worldwide was bound to be appealing.

Second, executives cited the substantial cost benefits of standardizing ICI's products. To emphasize this point, it was mentioned that reducing the number of the company's refinish top coats from twenty-four to ten would save upwards of $17 million on a product line with an annual turnover of approximately $300 million.

Third, executives believed that a global product organization would have additional benefits in terms of resource allocation. As an example, one manager mentioned that, with increasingly expensive pollution abatement equipment, it did not make sense to have as many manufacturing plants. Rather, he stressed, the company should consider consolidating the number of plants and upgrading the remainder to world-class manufacturing standards. In fact, it was believed that some thirty of the company's sixty-four plants were common sites for a number of paint products.

Last, the executive mentioned that, in a truly global product organization, there would be a much greater chance to transfer experience from one market to another. For example, he described how an application developed for a can coating customer in North America, while not identical, had a number of parallels to the needs faced by can coating customers in Europe.

In contrast to these advantages, another group of executives pointed out that, although some of ICI Paints' customer needs had become global, there were still substantial differences among individual markets. In the U.S. decorative segment, for example, Glidden had a 13 percent market share, was priced below other brands, and was distributed to DIY cus-tomers through mass merchandising outlets such as Wal-Mart. Because Glidden did not compete in the premium sector, it was seldom purchased by small-scale professional users like interior decorators. In contrast to Glidden in the United States, ICI's premium brand—Dulux—had a 37 percent market share in the United Kingdom. As a result, in 1993, ICI launched the Glidden brand in the United Kingdom, aiming it toward commercial contractors—a segment in which Dulux had been weak. John Thompson commented further:

To establish Dulux as a global brand, the U.S. market might be the next logical step. However, we estimated that a countrywide launch would cost ICI Paints $50 million over four to five years. An important issue would be not only determining the timing of such a large-scale project but also resolving the positioning of Glidden versus Dulux.

In conjunction with trying to establish a global brand, the group went on to say that reducing the number of paint formulations and standards might well yield savings, but at the risk of jeopardizing ICI's sensitivity to local market conditions. "How would you feel," he asked, "if you worked at Anheuser-Busch and your 'local' can coating salesman was in fact based in the U.K.?" Then, too, the executives pointed out that in theory it was easy to reduce the number of manufacturing plants. In practice, however, local management and governments would hardly be receptive to the unemployment created due to such restructuring. As well, the executives mentioned that, because many of ICI Paints' production assets were shared, business area general managers were largely responsible for business volume in an application segment, yet did not have full asset responsibility. In fact, no more than 75 percent of the company's assets could be clearly attributed to individual product lines.

SUMMARY

Before meeting with the IBT again, Scopes reviewed in his mind how his industry had changed and, in particular, what those changes implied for the organizational structure of ICI Paints. He recalled the words of one industry analyst who said that the worldwide merger and acquisition activities of the 1980s were merely part of the ongoing globalization of the paint industry. At the start of the 1990s, the analyst believed, the globalization process was driven by three factors: first, the need to service customers with international manufacturing operations such as can makers, vehicle assembly, and domestic appliances; second, the need to service customers dealing with the aftercare of internationally traded products such as vehicles and ships; last, the need to amortize the ever growing costs of research, product development, and marketing over a broad volume base. With these thoughts in mind, Scopes turned to the IBT to renew the discussion on developing a new organizational structure at ICI Paints and the role of the territorial general managers, the business area general managers, and particularly the international leaders in the 1990s.

Case 14

The Worldwide Robotics Industry, 1987

INTRODUCTION

In the fall of 1987, Stelio Demark, president of ASEA Robotics AB[1] (hereafter referred to as ASEA), was looking back on a period of rapid growth for his company. ASEA had become the leading robot supplier in Europe and was second in the United States, making it one of the world's foremost robot companies. With about 2,000 robots to be shipped, turnover was expected to reach Skr. 1,300 million for the fiscal year ending December 31, 1987. Despite the company's success, Stelio was concerned about the direction of the business.

We are witnessing an explosion of orders in complete systems at the local subsidiary level. I believe that we have to completely rethink the way we run our business, because despite rapid growth our profitability has not been satisfactory. Currently, nobody earns a respectable *ROI in this industry, and the real question is how to organize a company to achieve that in robotics in the 1990s.*

INDUSTRY OVERVIEW

In 1961, Unimation installed the first industrial robot at a General Motors factory in New Jersey. The following two decades were a time of slow growth in the robotics industry, and by 1980 only 23,000 robots had been installed worldwide. However, beginning in the early 1980s, sales increased sharply, and by 1986 the worldwide base of installed robots had reached 130,000. In the same year, total expenditures in the robotics industry reached $1.5 billion, with four-fifths of this value accounted for by unit hardware, or naked robots, and the balance by systems. By 1992 the worldwide robotics market was expected to have a value of $2.5 billion, with industry shipments approaching 47,000 units.

THE ROBOT AS A TOOL

Robots were a logical development in the process of industrial automation, which began in the nineteenth century. Yet, unlike "fixed sequence" manipulators designed for a single task, robots could be programmed to perform a range of jobs on different workpieces. Typically, robots consisted of a mechanical unit with a jointed arm and a computer system that served as the controller for specific applications. In addition, robots could be equipped with adaptive controls to detect and correct workpiece imperfections. (Refer to Exhibit 1 for a picture of a robot.)

One way to evaluate robots was to correlate per unit production costs with batch size or order volume (as seen in Exhibit 2). Where the batch size was small, manual labor was usually the most economical

---

1. ASEA AB, the parent company of ASEA Robotics AB, merged with Brown Boveri & Cie AG of Switzerland on January 4, 1988. Since the merger, the company has operated under the official name of ABB Robotics, ABB-R for short.

EXHIBIT 1 ● Example of a Naked Robot

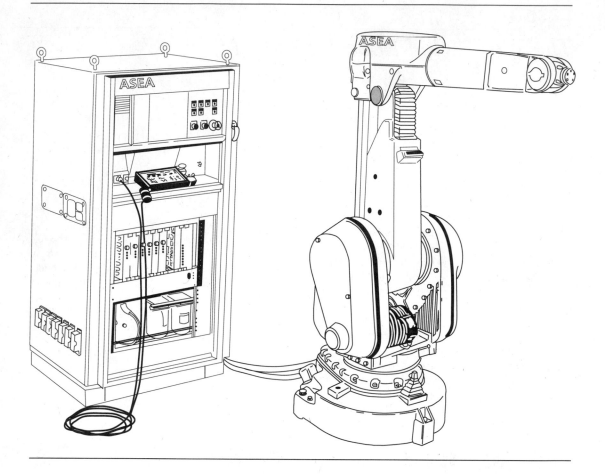

production method. On the other hand, for mass production of uniform components, special-purpose machines were justified. For products in between, a robotics system was often the most cost effective solution. In addition to lowering production costs, robots often provided a safer working environment by minimizing employee exposure to hazards such as paint fumes or welding gases.

Robot Flexibility

Flexibility was the cornerstone of robot technology. Aside from their ability to move and assemble components in a variety of shapes, sizes, and materials, robots could also perform process operations such as painting, polishing, and gluing.

Robots had yet another advantage over conventional production machines in that they did not need to be replaced or retooled when product design changes were implemented. Alternatively, it was possible to increase the utilization of such standard and often costly production machines by combining them with robots. In this context, robots served as one of the main tools in the larger manufacturing automation industry forecast to reach $100 billion in sales by 1990.

EXHIBIT 1 ● *(Continued)*

Technical Data

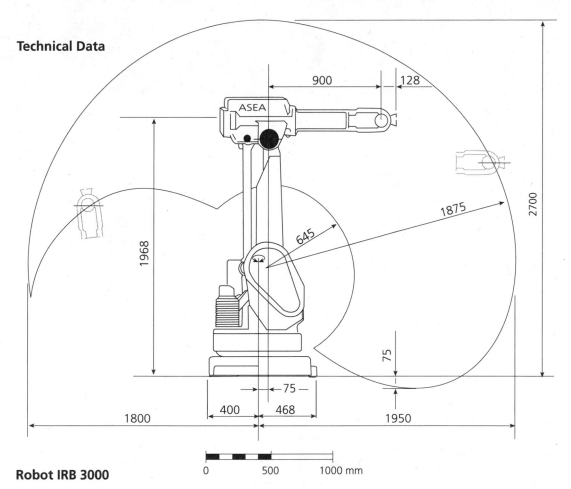

Robot IRB 3000

Axis	Type of motion	Work area	Max. speed
1	Rotation	= 180°	106°/s
2	Arm motion	+90° to -110°	100°/s
3	Arm motion	= 60°	87°/s
4	Rotary motion	= 200°	223°/s
5	Bending motion	= 120°	224°/s
6	Rotary motion	= 250°	213°/s

Number of servo-driven axes
In the robot   6
External   6

Handling capacity   30 kg

Repeatability   =0.15 mm
                           (ISO/TC 184/SC)

Power consumption
In service   2kW
At stand–by   0.3 kW

Environmental requirements
Degree of protection (robot
and control cabinet)   IP54
Ambient temperature   +5°C – + 45°C
Relative humidity   max. 90%

EXHIBIT 1 ● *(Continued)*

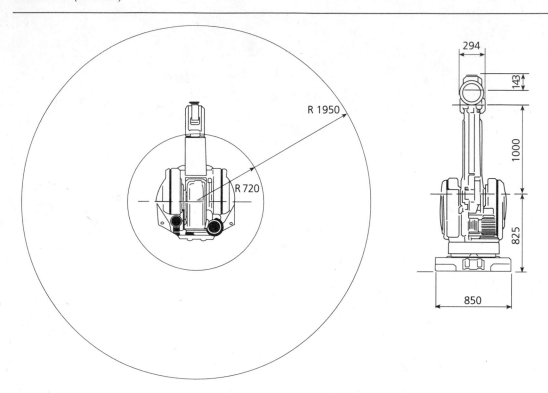

CONTROL SYSTEM S3

Programming capacity

Number of main programs	1
Number of subprograms	max. 9999
Program memory	32 kword (64 kbyte)
Number of positions	max. 2500
Battery backup time	min. 1000 hours
TCP positions	1 fixed, 19 definable
TCL	1 fixed, 19 definable

Inputs/outputs

Digital	64 in, 64 out
Analog	4 in, 4 out

Man-machine communication

Programming method	interactive dialogue in conjunction with joystick control of the robot
Number of menus	6 (standard)
System messages	plain text
Languages	English + choice of 3 x 3

FEATURES

Integrated electrical and air supply
Standardized peripheral equipment
Overload protection
Soft servo
Automatic restart function
Tool coordinates
Palletizing function
Gripper alignment function
Adaptive control of TCP
Program listing
Display screen
Computer link
Off-line programming
Image processing system

EXHIBIT 2 ● Range of Effectiveness for Industrial Robots

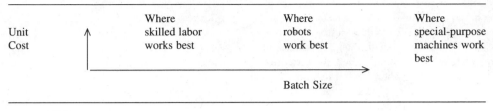

Source: ASEA.

Robot Complexity

Robots could be pneumatically, hydraulically, or electrically powered. The advantage of electrically controlled robots was their accuracy, reliability, and low energy requirements. The servo systems of electrically controlled robots allowed movements to be repeated with high accuracy. This made them ideal for complex applications which demanded a high degree of precision. Electrically powered robots were the quietest and had far fewer maintenance requirements than pneumatic or hydraulic robots. Although the latter were often cheaper than electrically powered robots, lower initial costs could be offset by more expensive tooling, higher operating and maintenance costs, and longer downtimes. Electric robots were the newest and, by 1987, the predominant robot type in use, although hydraulic robots could be used for special applications or very high weight applications.

Robot Selection Criteria

A major consideration in robot selection was the work to be done. For example, simple robots were acceptable when production involved large batches with little retooling. Sophisticated robots, on the other hand, were more appropriate for tasks requiring complex movements such as arc welding, cleaning of castings, deburring, and grinding/polishing.

Robots were differentiated from one another on the basis of working range, weight handling capacity, number of axes, speed, and accuracy. Range was the distance a robot could reach and defined a robot's working space. In general, robots used in the automotive industry had the longest reach, often determined by the length of a car. Weight capacity was

another criterion for selecting robots. In general, robots were sold for lightweight (up to 30 kg), medium weight (up to 90 kg), and heavyweight (more than 90 kg) applications.

The more sophisticated a robot, the higher the number of axes, or degrees of freedom. Specifically, degrees of freedom included base rotation, radial arm movement, vertical arm movement, pitching wrist movement, rolling wrist movement, and wrist yaw. Robots with five axes could handle most tasks and represented approximately 80 percent of the installed base of robots.

Robot speed, measured in either millimeters/second or degrees/second, described the maximum operating speed at which a robot could function with a defined payload.

Accuracy or repeatability referred to a robot's ability to return to a given point in space. Repeatability, measured in terms of millimeters (e.g., $+/-0.10$ mm), was one of the most important criteria to consider in purchasing a robot, as it affected the quality of final products.

MANUFACTURING ROBOTS

Industrial robots were specialized products and did not lend themselves to the mass production techniques of other industries. Typical manufacturing volumes per model range were in the low thousands per year. The research and development costs required to bring out one new model (controller and machine) were estimated to be $15 million and were usually recovered over five years. On average, a robotics company had an R&D team of thirty people per model, but smaller teams were possible as the number of models from one manufacturer increased. One industry analyst commented that although fixed costs had been 50 percent of sales, the percentage had increased in recent years due to the industry's maturing nature and increasing specialization. Consequently, research and development costs, once 10 percent of sales, had increased over the years to 15 percent, with no certainty of leveling off in the near future. Remaining cost components (such as selling) accounted for 15 percent, training 5 percent, finance 5 percent, and overhead 10 percent.

One factor that contributed to a robot's cost was its degree of sophistication. Robot sophistication and cost underwent a number of changes in the early 1980s as electrical components and microprocessors dropped in price. Generally, the larger a robot's microprocessor, the more quickly it operated, the more efficiently it performed, and the broader the range of functions it covered.

Segmenting the Robotics Industry

The worldwide robotics industry could be segmented geographically, by industry sector, or by application. Geographically, robots were concentrated in economically advanced countries, where manufacturing and hence automation first appeared. (Exhibit 3 summarizes the 1986 and 1992 forecasted revenue by geographic region.)

Segmentation by Industry Sector

The volume of robots used in the automobile industry allowed the market to be divided into automotive and nonautomotive segments. In 1987, one automotive segment, including assembly and component manufacturing, accounted for 49 percent of robot industry sales and was expected to account for 44 percent of sales by 1992.

The major nonautomotive categories included electronics, white goods, and "other." Examples of applications in the electronics industry included assembly automation, materials handling/machine tending, gluing and sealing, and surface treatment (coating). In addition to the applications found in the automotive and electronics industries, "other" included plastic molding, heat treatment, brick manu-

EXHIBIT 3 ● Geographic Distribution of Robotics Industry Revenue

Region	Estimated % 1987	Forecasted % 1992
Asia	42	36
North America	33	35
Europe	22	25
Rest of World	3	4
Total	100	100

Asia = Hong Kong, Japan, Korea, People's Republic of China, Singapore, and Taiwan.
North America = Canada and the United States.
Source: Dataquest.

facturing, glass manufacturing, inspection/testing, and education/research. In 1987, the electronics and "other" categories accounted for 21 percent and 30 percent of industry sales and, by 1992, were expected to grow to 24 percent and 32 percent, respectively.

Segmentation by Application

Application segments included spot welding, arc welding, gluing and sealing, materials handling/machine tending, final assembly automation, process (deburring, grinding, and polishing), and painting. Spot welding, which joined metals using electrical resistance heat and an applied pressure, was one of the first applications to be automated using robots. Up to 80 percent of this segment's sales were to automobile manufacturers, where car panels were tacked together with a line of spot welds. The spot welding segment was characterized by large projects and long negotiation periods. In 1987 spotwelding represented 18 percent of all robot applications with 3,691 units shipped worldwide at a value of $264 million. Although sales were forecast to increase to $289 million in 1988, spot welding was expected to decline as a percentage of all applications to 15 percent by 1992. In 1987, spot welding revenues and shipments were as follows:

Region	Automotive ($000)	Units	Nonautomotive ($000)	Units
Asia	76,000	1,312	25,000	452
North America	68,000	783	20,000	234
Europe	53,000	613	13,000	164
Rest of World	7,000	103	2,000	31

Source: Dataquest.

In contrast to spot welding, arc welding was used to form continuous seams when an electric arc bridged an electrode and a workpiece. Where welding was normally carried out under unpleasant conditions and experienced welders were difficult to find, robots were a proven success in both the spot and arc welding segments.

At $304 million, arc welding represented 20 percent of all applications in 1987 with worldwide shipments of 3,936 units. For 1988, sales were forecast at $339 million, and this segment was expected to grow to 23 percent of all applications by 1992. Revenues in 1987 for the arc welding application segment were as follows:

Region	Automotive ($000)	Units	Nonautomotive ($000)	Units
Asia	72,000	1,360	28,000	497
North America	36,000	500	32,000	296
Europe	50,000	609	74,000	534
Rest of World	6,000	90	6,000	51

Source: Dataquest.

Gluing and sealing was an application segment often grouped in "other." With sales of $152 million, "other" represented 10 percent of applications in 1987 and included processes such as deburring, grinding/polishing, and cutting. This segment was expected to grow to $171 million in 1988 and maintain a 10 percent share of market into 1992. In 1987, revenues in this category were distributed as follows:

Region	Automotive ($000)	Units	Electronic ($000)	Units	Other ($000)	Units
Asia	37,000	764	16,000	427	18,000	370
North America	26,000	253	8,000	63	18,000	167
Europe	14,000	173	3,000	33	8,000	81
Rest of World	2,000	32	1,000	11	1,000	16

Source: Dataquest.

Materials handling was often heavy, repetitive, and boring for human operators and included tasks such as palletizing, stacking, and packing. Where hazardous and/or delicate materials were involved, robotization allowed continuous and easy-to-run operations. Machine tending, or loading/unloading of machines, reduced dead time in a job characterized by a shortage of skilled labor with high wage rates.

In 1987, the materials handling and machine tending segments had a combined 23 percent share of all applications and $345 million in sales with 6,933 robots shipped worldwide. This segment was expected to have sales of $385 million in 1988 and to maintain its 23 percent share through 1992. In 1987, revenues for the materials handling/machine tending segment as a function of industry were:

Region	Automotive ($000)	Units	Electronic ($000)	Units	Other ($000)	Units
Asia	39,000	816	71,000	3,069	36,000	501
North America	37,000	476	24,000	450	40,000	424
Europe	45,000	555	11,000	152	30,000	329
Rest of World	6,000	75	2,000	42	4,000	46

Source: Dataquest.

Spray painting/coating was also an unpleasant task for human operators because of paint fumes and the associated health risks. Moreover, the inconsistent quality and low productivity of manual painters in this segment was readily improved with robots that reduced labor and raw material costs. Painting represented 9 percent of all applications in 1987 with estimated revenues of $135 million and industry shipments of 1,047 robots. Sales in 1988 were expected to increase only slightly to $139 million and, by 1992, this segment was expected to represent only 7 percent of all applications. Revenues for the painting segment of the robotics industry in 1987 were:

Region	Automotive ($000)	Units	Electronic ($000)	Units	Other ($000)	Units
Asia	12,000	194	1,000	14	3,000	63
North America	58,000	285	3,000	21	22,000	174
Europe	24,000	177	1,000	14	7,000	75
Rest of World	3,000	24	—	—	1,000	8

Source: Dataquest.

Assembly automation was one of the largest segments in robotics and covered virtually all branches of industry and all robot sizes. However, the complexity of this segment varied, and a number of robotics suppliers inexperienced at offering "systems" solutions reported to have lost money. This segment represented 20 percent of the worldwide robotics market in 1987 and had sales of $289 million corresponding to 6,904 robots. In 1988, sales were expected to reach $333 million and by 1992 were forecast to represent 22 percent of all applications. The spread of revenues in assembly by industry and region in 1987 was:

Region	Automotive ($000)	Units	Electronic ($000)	Units	Other ($000)	Units
Asia	15,000	293	104,000	3,962	26,000	345
North America	25,000	394	57,000	1,017	19,000	301
Europe	11,000	149	15,000	223	10,000	120
Rest of World	2,000	23	3,000	55	2,000	22

Source: Dataquest.

(Refer to Exhibit 4 for a comparative positioning of
U.S., European, and Japanese robot companies.)

EXHIBIT 4 ● Comparative Positioning of U.S., European, and Japanese Robot Companies

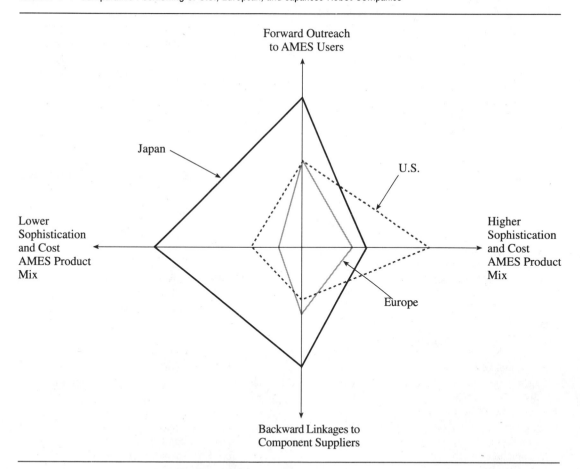

Note: AMES = Automatic Manufacturing Equipment and Systems.

MAJOR PLAYERS IN THE WORLD ROBOTICS INDUSTRY

Robot manufacturers had to combine all the technologies on which robots depended, including mechanics, electronics software engineering, computers, and communications. In addition to this diverse technology base, robotics firms had to be familiar with their customers' manufacturing processes. This range of technologies and process know-how explained why firms in the industry had such varied origins. Most of the early players in robotics came from other industries where automation brought immediate productivity gains. As such, shipbuilders and automobile manufacturers leveraged their welding expertise into spot and arc welding robots, and industrial electric companies used their electrical knowledge to transform robots from pneumatic or hydraulic driven tools to electrically powered machines. Once these initial entrants saturated the robotics segments in which they had their expertise, they began linking up with other firms to broaden their overall product offering. As robotics developed into an industry with its own identity, a number of start-up companies entered the business. By the end of 1987, there were an estimated 300 companies worldwide that manufactured and/or marketed robots. (Refer to Exhibit 5 for company sales and market share data.)

From the middle 1980s onward, the robotics industry showed an increasing trend toward internationalization as seen by the number of sales and technology agreements between suppliers in the world's three main robot markets. (For an overview of international industrial cooperation in the robotics industry as of 1985, refer to Exhibit 6.)

One important development in the robotics industry was the entry of companies such as IBM and Digital Equipment Corporation. As early as 1980, Kenneth G. Bosomworth, president of International Resource Development Inc., commented that it was only a matter of time before such companies started selling robots. ''The mechanics involved have been largely perfected, minimizing the value of machine tool expertise. Now it's becoming increasingly important for a robot company to have electronics and software capabilities.'' The entry of these large computer companies set the robot industry in perspective as part of the larger factory automation industry, with its 1990 estimated value of $100 billion.

North American–based Players

North America was the second largest geographic market for robots and in 1986 had an installed base of 25,000. Unimation installed the world's first industrial robot in 1961 and had achieved a market share of 40 percent in 1983, with sales of about $71 million. Shortly after Unimation's acquisition by Westinghouse, the market shifted to electrically powered robots and away from Unimation's hydraulically powered ones. Although Unimation responded to the switch in technology, it was felt that the company had lost major market share to GMF, the joint venture formed by General Motors and Fanuc of Japan in 1982.

Westinghouse Electric established itself as a player in the robotics industry when it purchased Unimation in 1983. To speed its entry into the robotics and factory automation markets at home and abroad, Westinghouse established licensing agreements with Olivetti in Italy and with Komatsu and Mitsubishi in Japan. In 1986, Westinghouse Electric had robotics sales of $52 million and an estimated market share of 12.4 percent in the worldwide machining/other segment, and systems revenue accounted for 54 percent of sales (Dataquest). Westinghouse Electric manufactured the Puma robot family. In 1983 the company was working on vision, force sensing, and conveyor tracking.

Based on a report that the robotics market would decline by 20–30 percent from 1986 to 1987, Westinghouse chose to change its strategy. Westinghouse turned away from making stand-alone robots on a large scale to supplying integrated automation solutions. Furthermore, Westinghouse closed Unimation and formed an Automation Division, which combined marketing, sales engineering, and other robotics and automated products–related operations. In 1987, Westinghouse also began a factory automation joint venture with Matsushita Electric Industrial. By the end of 1987, Westinghouse robotics had gone through tough times, and its continuation was open to question.

General Motors Fanuc Robotics Corp. (GMF) was based in Michigan and was formed in 1982 as a joint venture between General Motors and Fanuc in Japan. From GM's perspective, the deal was aimed at automating GM plants with low-cost hardware from Fanuc. Fanuc, on the other hand, gained access to

EXHIBIT 5 ● Company Sales by Application Segment and Application Market Share by Revenue

Sales by segment ($ million)		Market share by revenue	Units
U.S.-based Vendors			
General Motors–Fanuc			
Assembly	$14	4.7%	154
Materials Handling/Machine Loading	21	5.7	272
Painting	80.1	44.0	162
Spot Welding	40	10.3	527
Arc Welding	8	2.7	140
Machining/Other	23.1	14.0	241
DeVilbiss			
Painting	17.9	9.8	183
Arc Welding	2.1	0.7	21
Machining/Other	1.1	0.6	5
Cincinatti Milacron			
Assembly	2.4	0.8	18
Materials Handling/Maching Loading	8.2	2.2	81
Spot Welding	65.8	17.0	510
Arc Welding	1.4	0.5	9
Machining/Other	1.9	1.2	14
General Electric			
Assembly	0.5	0.2	6
Materials Handling/Machine Loading	3.2	0.9	32
Spot Welding	0.6	0.2	6
Arc Welding	4.4	1.5	44
Machining/Other	1.5	0.9	15
Prab			
Materials Handling/Machine Loading	14.5	4.0	111
Spot Welding	1.0	0.2	7
Machining/Other	3.9	2.3	30
Japanese-based Vendors			
Fanuc			
Assembly	9.0	3.0	262
Materials Handling/Machine Loading	18.0	4.9	512

EXHIBIT 5 ● *(Continued)*

Sales by segment ($ million)		Market share by revenue	Units
Painting	3.0	1.6	63
Spot Welding	18.0	4.6	360
Arc Welding	3.0	1.0	63
Machining/Other	9.0	5.4	226
Yaskawa			
Assembly	5.6	1.9	111
Materials Handling/Machine Loading	6.1	1.7	122
Spot Welding	13.3	3.4	266
Arc Welding	67.2	22.6	?
Machining/Other	18.9	11.4	377
Kawasaki			
Assembly	4.6	1.5	85
Materials Handling/Machine Loading	3.0	0.8	57
Painting	3.8	2.1	31
Spot Welding	57.8	14.9	737
Arc Welding	1.5	0.5	26
Machining/Other	5.3	3.2	39
Nachi-Fujikoshi			
Assembly	6.4	2.1	115
Materials Handling/Machine Loading	4.5	1.2	81
Painting	1.9	1.1	17
Spot Welding	43.5	11.2	783
Arc Welding	6.4	2.2	115
Machining/Other	1.3	0.8	23
European-based Vendors			
ASEA			
Assembly	15.2	5.1	167
Materials Handling/Machine Loading	70.3	19.2	774
Spot Welding	26.6	6.9	293
Arc Welding	68.4	23.0	753
Machining/Other	9.5	5.7	105

EXHIBIT 5 ● *(Continued)*

Sales by segment ($ million)		Market share by revenue	Units
KUKA			
Assembly	0.5	0.2	6
Materials Handling/Machine Loading	15	4.1	174
Spot Welding	30	7.7	348
Arc Welding	1.5	0.5	17
Machining/Other	3.0	1.8	35

GM's Flexible Automation Systems (FAS) unit—a group of sixty people with several years of experience in robot systems development. In 1986, GMF had sales of $186 million versus $16 million in its founding year. Its customer base had increased from 20 customers in 1982 to 650 in 1986, and as number one in the United States, it had a 30 percent share of that market versus 8 percent in 1982. Eric Mittelstadt, president of GMF, attributed its success to strong customer commitment with support that ranged from applications engineering to parts and service. On a worldwide basis, GMF had 11 percent of the 1986 robotics market, with systems sales estimated at 25 percent of total revenue (Dataquest).

When the automotive market for robotics collapsed in 1986/87, GMF targeted nonautomotive segments. Hence, GMF signed a contract with DeVilbiss to market electric painting robots. The deal combined the strengths of GMF, the largest overall robot vendor in the United States, with the world's biggest installer of painting robots. Both companies were allowed to market and service each other's products as well as their own line of painting robots.

In 1987, GMF consolidated its six locations from Troy, Michigan, to a new building at Auburn Hills, Michigan, and established centralized engineering, demonstration, training, and other services. Also in 1987, GMF secured major European sales with large orders to Peugeot in France and SAAB in Sweden, ASEA's home country. Across Europe, GMF was expected to pursue an aggressive strategy.

In the future, GMF planned to diversify and sell robots to several different industries, including electronics, aerospace, and food processing. To this end, GMF was customizing its standard line of robots to meet the needs of nonautomotive customers. It developed new robots for these markets, some of which could be used in "clean room" manufacturing applications. By diversifying along these lines, GMF planned to maintain a 50/50 split in sales between automotive and nonautomotive customers.

Cincinnati Milacron was a world leader in machine tools, systems, and precision measuring equipment and, until 1985, was the leading U.S. robot manufacturer. Despite its leading role, Cincinnati Milacron had made a profit in only one of the eleven preceding years. In December 1985, this company announced a write-off of $52 million in its robotic and machine tool operations and was still working off a substantial backlog of previous orders. In 1986, 26 percent of Cincinnati Milacron's $80 million revenue came from systems, and the company had 4.7 percent of the worldwide robotics market (Dataquest).

General Electric entered the robotics business in the middle 1970s after automating many of its own plants. From 1980 onward, GE entered into a number of licensing agreements, joint ventures, and acquisitions to become a one-stop robotics supplier of factory automation systems. Among these moves were licensing agreements with Italy's OEA SpA, Japan's Hitachi, and West Germany's Volkswagen. To try and secure the European market, GE established an

EXHIBIT 6 ● International Industrial Cooperation on Robots

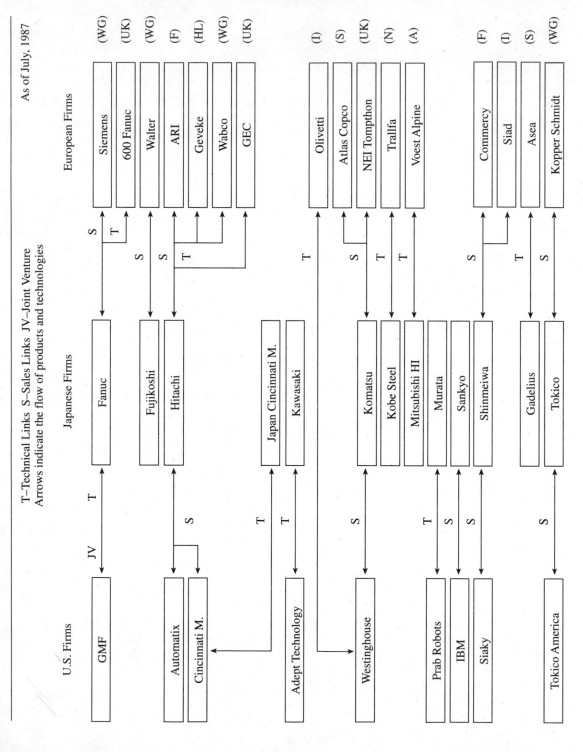

T–Technical Links S–Sales Links JV–Joint Venture
Arrows indicate the flow of products and technologies

As of July, 1987

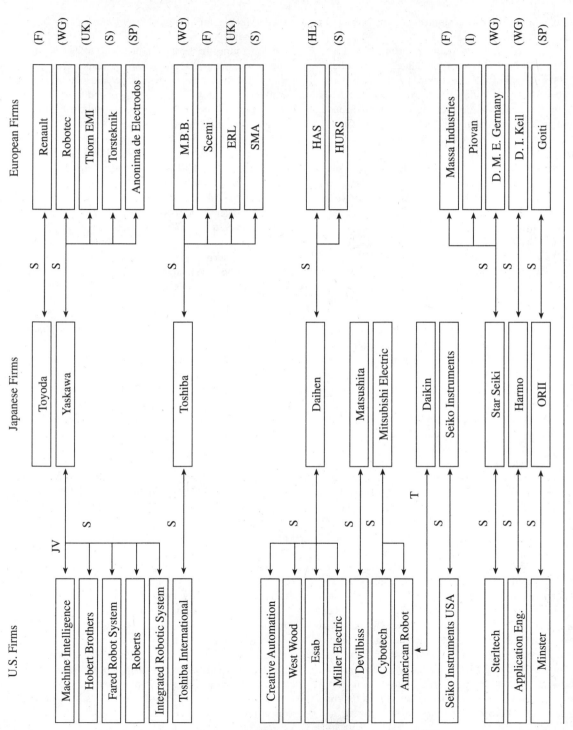

European Firms

Japanese Firms

U.S. Firms

Source: Japanese Industrial Robot Association.

automation systems customer training center in Frankfurt in 1985.

Despite GE's 1982 announcement to be a lead supplier in the "factory of the future," it lost at least $200 million in 1985 and decided to enter a joint venture with Fanuc. Initiated in January 1987, the $200 million robotics joint venture built on Fanuc's strengths in manufacturing machine tool controls and GE's expertise in robotics technology. In addition to research, the joint venture covered manufacturing and marketing. By the end of 1987, GE-Fanuc had sales of approximately $250 million, but GE planned to stop manufacturing robots. Instead, Fanuc would manufacture all robots in Japan, and GE's extensive distribution channels would be used to market Fanuc products with GE software in the United States.

Prab was based in Kalamazoo, Michigan, and specialized in robots for heavy weights and the materials handling/machine tending segments. In 1987, Prab received nonexclusive rights to market ASEA robots. ASEA also designated Prab as a systems integrator on materials handling and transfer applications. Under the terms of the agreement, ASEA manufactured original equipment robots, and Prab integrated heavy materials systems and parts transfer applications.

An agreement was designed to increase the sales and market penetration of both companies. The sales and service agreement provided for the sale of ASEA robots, controllers, software, and peripheral equipment by Prab's nationwide sales force for integration into Prab automation systems. Prab's initial emphasis for ASEA products was in nonautomotive markets with the intention to expand into other areas. The ASEA-Prab agreement resulted in termination of a previous Prab-GDA (West Germany) agreement. The withdrawal of Prab from robotics production was seen by many in the industry as a move into marketing and systems work. Prab sold its robots in Australia and New Zealand through distributors and in South America through an agent. In Japan, Prab had granted an exclusive license to Murata Machines Ltd. to manufacture and sell robots in Japan and other Far East countries. Prab also had a licensing agreement with Can-Eng Manufacturing, Ltd., to manufacture and sell robots in Canada. Fabrique Nationale in Belgium was Prab's European licensee, manufacturing and selling robots throughout western Europe, Africa, and Scandinavia.

In contrast to the five and six axes robots of the above manufacturers, Adept built a name for itself using SCARA (selective compliance assembly robot arm) robots with only 3 axes. Adept had used these robots to penetrate the light assembly and small parts materials handling markets. In 1986, Adept had sales of $25 million with $16.3 million in assembly and $8.7 million in materials handling. These sales corresponded to 281 and 151 robots and secured 5.4 percent and 2.4 percent, respectively, of the worldwide segments for Adept.

IBM entered the robotics market in 1982 with a system linked to its personal computer. IBM concentrated on the small parts assembly market with SCARA robots imported from Sankyo Seiki in Japan. SCARA robots were invented in Japan and moved only on a horizontal plane. This was suitable for flexible assembly operations where the robot could be changed from one product to another with a mere change in program, eliminating the need for additional robots. In 1986, IBM sold 240 robots valued at $8 million and had an estimated 2.7 percent of the worldwide assembly market.

Intelledex was almost unheard of in Europe, but in the United States it competed with Adept, Seiko, and IBM. Intelledex concentrated on light assembly in the automotive and electronics industries.

Japan-based Players

Japan was the largest user of robots and had an installed base of 93,000 systems at the end of 1986, by JIRA definitions. By ECE definition, the figure was closer to 50,000. Japan was also at the forefront of robotics hardware and was expected to remain so over the next several years. One example of a hardware advantage was in controls, where the Japanese tailored control modules to fit particular robotics applications. This was in contrast to western firms which tailored robot platforms instead of controls. Another Japanese competitive advantage was a design facility that allowed them to implement changes and offer more products. As a result, Japanese companies had bigger product ranges than western competitors. With a range of products in each application, the Japanese could have a more specific robot, usually at a lower price.

Despite their capabilities in microelectronics and hardware, the Japanese were not as sophisticated in software development as many firms in the United States—a disadvantage when attempting total systems integration. And, unlike western firms where robotics operations were treated as independent profit centers, financing in many Japanese firms came from a parent industrial group. This reflected the Japanese view that robots served a public relations role for the entire industrial group.

Fanuc stood for Fuji Automatic Numerical Control and was formed by Fujitsu in 1955 to enter the factory automation business. Fanuc was the world leader in numerical controls (NCs) for machine tools, lathes, and milling machines. It was NCs that played a major role in transforming the capabilities of a simple machine into a robot with a range of functions. Fanuc gained access to GM's robot technology with a joint venture in 1982 and sold the robots in Japan at low prices. The joint venture also gave Fanuc an opportunity to better integrate GM's robots with systems in the emerging factory of the future, positioning Fanuc in the systems integration market.

In its 1987 joint venture with General Electric, Fanuc gained access to the large U.S. market, specializing in programmable controllers. One of the more valuable gains was GE's automated production systems: IBM or Digital computers modified to GE specifications. In 1987, Fanuc decided to increase production specialization by producing all hardware in Japan and all software in the United States. Software was produced at Fanuc's two 50/50 joint venture companies: GMF Robotics Corporation in Michigan and GE Fanuc Automation Corporation. Both joint ventures imported Fanuc hardware from Japan, added their own software, and sold the finished products as U.S. products. Fanuc licensed to GM in the United States, the 600 Group in Britain, and Siemens in Germany.

Yaskawa Electric Manufacturing was established in 1915 and had an excellent reputation for manufacturing motors. One of the parent company's subsidiaries, Yaskawa Electric Data Inc., specialized in floppy disk drive (FDD) development and combined this expertise with its knowledge of servomotor technology. This combination gave Yaskawa an advantage in the development of motors for industrial robots. Yaskawa enjoyed a strong home market for

arc welding robots and was continuing to broaden its activities into materials handling and process applications. In 1986, Yaskawa had sales of $111 million, with 20 percent of its revenues attributed to systems. Yaskawa's world market share was 6.5 percent, and the company was expected to expand into other applications, broadening its product offering with new robots at a low cost.

Yaskawa claimed to be the first Japanese robot manufacturer to set up an overseas sales network. Yaskawa's distributors included Hobart Brothers, Inc., in the United States and GKN Lincoln in Great Britain. Yaskawa had cooperative ventures with Torsteknik Company of Sweden, Messer Gresheim of West Germany, and Alcas of Italy. Messer Gresheim's welding equipment, power supplies, and welding pacs strengthened Yaskawa's position in European welding segments. Yaskawa also had technological agreements with Feado Robot Systems in Japan, Barrons Engineering in South Africa, and A.N.I. Perkins in Australia. Yaskawa sales agreements were with Robotec of West Germany, Thorn EMI in Britain, Torsteknik in Sweden, and Anonima de Electrodos in Spain.

Kawasaki Heavy Industries began operations in 1896 as a shipbuilder and was the company with the longest history in that industry. Kawasaki Heavy Industries was the nucleus of the Kawasaki group, had a broad range of experience in heavy machinery and engineering, and was one of the first to market spot welding robots. One part of the Kawasaki group specialized in robots and got its start in North America as a licensee to Unimation. More recently, Kawasaki had established a technical link with Adept. In 1986, Kawasaki Heavy Industries had 4.5 percent of the world robotics market, an estimated 14.9 percent of the world spot welding segment, and 34 percent of its $76 million sales was represented by systems revenue (Dataquest). In 1987, Kawasaki established itself further in the U.S. robotics market with its own organization and a new spot welding robot.

Matsushita Electric in 1986 had sales of $100 million and a worldwide market share of 5.9 percent (Dataquest). Dataquest estimated that Matsushita Electric held a 13.7 percent share of the materials handling/machine tending segment and was number one in assembly with a 16.7 percent share. Matsushita's stake in assembly was underscored by the fact that, in 1983, 75 percent of its robot sales were accounted for by robots designed to insert electronic components [*Nihon Keizai Shimbun* (Tokyo), 21, no. 1058, International Weekly Edition, 1–3].

Other important Japanese players were *Nachi-Fujikoshi, Toshiba,* and *Hitachi.* Nachi-Fujikoshi was one of Japan's leading bearing manufacturers and ranked first in cutting tools. Nachi-Fujikoshi claimed to be the first to produce heavy-duty robots in Japan and in the past had supplied both spot welding and arc welding robots to GE. In 1986, Nachi-Fujikoshi held 3.8 percent of the world robotics market. Toshiba was a world leader in machine tool manufacturing and had agreements to sell robots through Messerschmidt-Boelkow-Bolm in Germany, Switzerland, and Austria; through Scemi in France; and through SMA in Sweden. In 1986, Toshiba had sales of $73 million and about 4.3 percent of the world robotics market. It was also estimated that Toshiba had market shares of 9.0 percent in the materials handling/machine tending segment, 9.8 percent in assembly, and 0.9 percent in spot welding. Toshiba revenues for these segments were $33 million, $29.3 million, and $3.7 million, respectively. Hitachi had a technical link and licensing agreement with General Electric in the United States and also licensed to GEC and Lansing Bagnall in the United Kingdom. In 1986, Hitachi had total sales of $36 million and an estimated market share of 8.5 percent in arc welding that accounted for $25.2 million of its revenues.

European-based Players

Western Europe was the third largest market for robots, with the installed base concentrated in three countries. In 1986 the three countries with the most robots were West Germany with 12,400, France with 7,500, and the United Kingdom with approximately 3,800 (United Nations Economic and Social Council ENG.AUT/AC.1/R.31/Add.4 and references therein).

ASEA Robotics was number one in the European market with a market share of approximately 25 percent (Dataquest). ASEA was late in entering the spot welding market segment and did not have a product in this segment until 1983 versus some competitors who had twenty years of spot welding experience. The United States was ASEA's single biggest market where it had 200 employees in ASEA Robotics, Inc.

By the end of 1987, this area of the company's sales had grown 10 percent to $45 million, despite the downward trend in the industry. With a market share of approximately 12 percent, ASEA was in second place in the United States behind GMF and expected a market expansion during 1988.

ASEA's start in the robotics industry grew out of a desire to improve its own business. This began in the mid- to late 1970s and followed on the purchase of NC machines and an ASEA climate that favored investment in production engineering. This climate found ASEA executives asking if they could make their own robots. ASEA consequently made and installed its very first robots in its own factories, where they were used for handling and tending. Shortly thereafter, ASEA began to sell these robots and approached ESAB to integrate robots with ESAB equipment for welding applications. ESAB marketed welding process equipment to a variety of industries around the world. The arc welding expertise offered by ESAB expanded ASEA's robot offering into a new application segment. Traditionally, ASEA's expertise had been in electronic control technology, not welding. ESAB provided ASEA with welding components to be attached to a robot arm and, in a sense, allowed ASEA to offer robotized arc welding at an early stage.

ASEA's electric drive technology and ESAB's arc welding expertise were later combined when SAAB figured ASEA into its welding automation plans. SAAB, the Swedish automobile and aerospace firm, gave ASEA the opportunity to develop a spot welding robot for the automotive industry via on-site testing and refinement. ESAB/ASEA knowledge in welding automation and SAAB's willingness to be a "futuristic" customer helped to establish ASEA in the robotics industry. That these three firms were all within one geographic area, spoke one language, and had the same culture further contributed to ASEA's success.

ASEA Robotics had made a number of alliances and several acquisitions over the years. Among these were Trallfa Robot of Norway, partially acquired (51 percent) in 1985. Trallfa was a leading manufacturer of robots for the painting and surface finishing sector, and its acquisition strengthened ASEA's export operations. Trallfa products consequently filled a void in the ASEA line, previously concentrated on arc welding and other metalworking applications. The acquisition also saved ASEA from having to modify electric robots for painting and its associated spark hazards.

In 1986, ASEA acquired VS Technology group (Luton, England), a robotics system integrator. VS Technology was known for design and manufacture of automated welding and assembly lines for European automotive and domestic appliance industries. VS Technology had a history of being a line builder serving the automotive industry. VST's recent moves into machine vision and related areas were directed toward producing smaller parts for the electronics industry. The move gave ASEA the ability to compete more fully on complete and advanced systems.

In 1986, ASEA Inc. underwent an internal reorganization that created two business divisions. The automotive division focused specifically on that industry, while the industrial automation division focused on a variety of other customers. Each division had total business responsibility for its activities. The restructuring was part of a larger effort to consolidate operations within ASEA, thereby reducing costs and lowering manpower requirements. By the end of 1986, ASEA's product offering was substantially greater than only a few years prior, and the company achieved a worldwide presence with 11.2 percent of the robotics market. In 1986, 30 percent of ASEA's $190 million in revenue was accounted for by systems (Dataquest).

In 1987, ASEA relocated robot production from the United States to Sweden. The move was part of an effort to consolidate robot manufacturing to one plant from six worldwide. The plant manufactured ASEA's entire line of industrial robots and also produced semis for ASEA robotics plants in the United States, Japan, France, and Spain. Also in 1987, ASEA sold its line of pneumatic materials-handling robots to MHU Robotics.

In Japan, ASEA was represented by ASEA Robotics/Gadelius (GAR) with a market share of 2–3 percent. ASEA products had an initial reputation of being overpriced in Japan, despite their high quality and precision (*Business Week,* June 27, 1983). ASEA moved to counter this in 1983 by manufacturing in Kobe—a move that reportedly lowered costs by 12–13 percent (*Business Week,* June 27, 1983). In both the United States and Japan, ASEA expanded by setting up large, well-equipped robotics centers that of-

fered customers service and support facilities along with systems engineering and hardware (*Business Week,* June 27, 1983).

Cloos was a family-owned company based in Germany which had developed its reputation as a leader in the arc welding segments and for delivering turnkey welding systems. Cloos changed its role as a robot manufacturer specialized in arc welding after it bought von Jungheinrich in 1986. The acquisition of von Jungheinrich, which developed and manufactured robot controls, complemented Cloos's previous strengths. In addition to growth by acquisition, Cloos built up its software and engineering departments and was able to target other applications. For the late 80s and 90s, Cloos planned to expand its application base to those areas which built upon its traditional arc welding expertise. Other applications where welding know-how could be leveraged included flame and plasma cutting as well as laser welding and cutting. Cloos also stated its desire to enter water-jet cutting, gluing, and sealing and possibly the materials handling segments (*Roboter,* February 1988).

With 1986 sales revenues of $70 million, Cloos had a 23.5 percent market share of the worldwide arc welding segment (Dataquest). In the United States, Cloos was represented by Cloos International Inc., established in 1985. In Europe, Cloos worked closely through agents and was represented in Great Britain, Austria, and the U.S.S.R. Markets in South America, Africa, and the Far East were cultivated through individual projects. Cloos's vision of the future for the robotics industry was that only a few key players would survive. Management believed that customers would ask robot suppliers to take on more responsibility as applications became more specific and as customers moved to integrate those applications into single "systems" solutions. For the future, the Cloos team planned to adjust to customer needs as far as its products and market conditions warranted.

Also based in Germany was *KUKA*—an acronym for *Keller und Knappich, Augsburg*—founded in 1898 as an acetylene works. KUKA had a successful history as a welding equipment supplier with oxy-acetylene welding devices as early as 1905, the first electric spot welding gun in Germany in 1936 and supplied the first welding transfer line to Volkswagen in 1956. KUKA's entry into robotics began in 1971 when it supplied the first welding transfer line equipped with U.S.-made robots to Daimler-Benz. From 1980 onward the company's role in robotics grew substantially. In 1981, KUKA was the first to market freely programmable continuous path control systems with sensors for multiaxis robots. In 1982 the firm acquired Expert Automation Inc. in the United States and a controlling interest in LSW Maschinenfabrik GmbH in Bremen, Germany. These acquisitions complemented KUKA's strengths and helped it to offer fully automated assembly cells with robots and vision systems. In addition to Germany, where KUKA had an estimated one-half of its sales, the company had subsidiaries in the United Kingdom, Belgium, France, Spain, Denmark, and India. KUKA also had a licensing agreement with the U.S.S.R., cooperation agreements with DEA in Italy on assembly robots and Schindler-Digitron in Switzerland on automated guided vehicles. KUKA was organized into four main groups: robots, transfer lines, assembly systems, and special welding systems, of which the first two represented nearly 90 percent of the total business. The company's background in welding was represented by its strength in the spot welding segment, where its application know-how and system capacity were a bonus. These gave KUKA a competitive advantage as a supplier of spot welding robots and as an automotive line builder and supplier. Unlike other robot companies, KUKA used its robots as a tool for selling systems. To a certain extent, KUKA was a systems house making its own mechanical robot arms. By the end of 1986, KUKA had sales of $50 million and was expecting to increase its presence in gluing and sealing as well as the materials handling segments.

Two other European competitors were *Reis Robot* and *Comau.* Reis Robot had its primary market in Germany, where it concentrated on nonautomotive customers. Reis manufactured robots for general transfer work, robots for handling tools and workpieces in machining cells, and used low prices as a central part of an aggressive strategy. Comau, which specialized in automotive and NC machine tools, started in robotics by working with Fiat. Comau determined design capabilities and limitations of robots and production lines and, in 1985, was bought by Fiat. In the same year, Comau and Digital announced the formation of a joint venture called Sesam, aimed at the European and world market in computer inte-

grated manufacturing. Sesam combined Comau's strengths in flexible manufacturing systems with Digital's knowledge of computers and concentrated on systems engineering—procuring and setting up equipment for flexible automation systems.

SELECTING A ROBOT SUPPLIER

Variables in Robotics Demand

Factors influencing the purchase of robots at a national level included general economic conditions, financial structures, and government policies such as subsidies. At the level of the firm, demand pull for robotics was determined by the role of manufacturing strategy in company planning policies and an attitude conducive to trying new technology. The purchase of robotics and manufacturing automation in general was favored by firms which sought reduced costs via increases in volume production and by firms which sought flexibility in response to market conditions. From a buyer's perspective, this meant being able to make 200X, 500Y and 300Z, as opposed to only 1000A.

Installing a Robot System

Robotic systems required considerable investment, not only in capital but also in engineering time, installation, and start-up. In a well-planned installation, a robot system usually paid for itself in two–four years. A major consideration in robot selection was the actual work to be done. Simple robots were acceptable when production involved large batches with little retooling, such as materials handling/machine tending. Sophisticated robots were more appropriate for such tasks as cleaning castings, deburring, grinding/polishing, arc welding, and gluing/sealing, because they involved complex patterns of movement.

Robots were sold "naked" (nonengineered, but with a controller) or in conjunction with "systems" that contained related peripheries, computers, engineering solutions, and software. Naked robots varied in price from $50,000 for simpler models to over $100,000 for the more sophisticated machines. The latter were more easily and economically adapted to different machining requirements, tools, and fixtures.

Systems were often assembled using components from a variety of manufacturers and could have as many as forty robots. An example of such a system was car body assembly, where an entire production line was automated. Unlike the relatively easy to design hardware, systems varied in complexity and necessitated a great deal of industrial engineering expertise. To achieve a satisfactory result, one or more engineers had to design a system based on a customer's particular needs, conduct a feasibility study with robots and select those robots best suited to the task. When operating across borders, this often required cooperative efforts with foreign manufacturers. This latter point was particularly true for the Japanese, where robot companies did not have a systems house capability. Instead a customer acted on his own behalf by integrating a system himself or by contacting an independent systems house. The Japanese also had to rely on local systems integrators in Europe, but in the United States they tended to bring in their own people.

The Marketing Process

From the customer's viewpoint, a robot could be purchased directly from a manufacturer or a systems integrator. ASEA distribution was characteristic of the larger robotics companies, referring to its sales outlets as Robot Centers. In addition to hardware sales, Robot Centers provided the engineering expertise to set up a complete system, including service and training. All robotics companies sold directly to customers. Where robotics companies differed, however, was in the nature of that sale. Aside from selling its own hardware, the larger robotics companies sold their engineering, or "systems," expertise. When that expertise was purchased separately, customers could specify the brand of hardware.

An alternative to buying robots directly from a manufacturer was for customers to go to independent systems integrators. These independents were also known as systems houses; they tended to be local and, in robotics, played the same role as a third-party programmer in the computer industry. Whether owned by a larger robot company or by an independent, integrators sold custom-designed manufacturing solutions. Smaller companies tended to rely more on engineered solutions than larger companies. Systems integrators might select robots and related equipment from several suppliers, competing with robot com-

panies in that they might select a limited number of a robot company's accessory or auxiliary product offerings. Among the independent systems integrators were Thyssen in Europe, Ingersoll Rand in the United States, and Budd & Co. in Canada. (Refer to Exhibit 7 for a summary of the robot distribution process.)

The extent of value added for a naked robot, its package, and the entire system depended on a specific application. An arc welding system served as an example. The naked robot, consisting of the platform and controls, would be sold for about $70,000. The required package to make it an arc welding robot consisted of a power pack ($15,000), an electrode feeder ($15,000), a torch cleaner ($1,000), and arc welding software and controls ($9,000), for a total of about $40,000. This package was added to the costs of the

EXHIBIT 7 ● Distribution Process for Robots (Example ASEA Robotics, Trends 1983–1988)

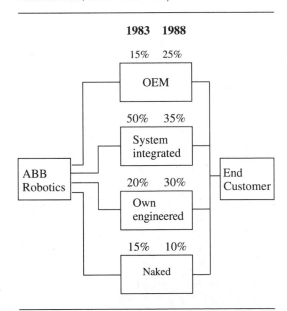

Notes: OEM: mainly ESAB
Syst. Integr: chosen mainly by customer
Own Engineered: value added deliveries
Naked: mainly integrated by customer

OEM, such as ESAB of Sweden, when that company purchased naked robots from a robot supplier such as ASEA, resulting in a packaged robot price of $110,000. When integrated into a complete manufacturing system, the systems integrator would combine the robot package with the necessary transfer equipment that moved pieces to and from the welding station and performed installation. As part of a complete line, the single robot would cost $300,000, or about four times its naked value. Of the systems integrator's $190,000 added value, about 25 percent accounted for his gross margin, the rest was spent on hardware. Typically, the integrator's margin was 10 percent for handling and 25 percent for know-how expressed in engineering man-hours sold for studies, plans, and so on (refer to Exhibit 8).

The price of a robot varied as a function of application (see Exhibit 9). Because assembly robots had fewer variations and therefore less flexibility than other robots, they were the most expensive to install when one added system costs to the cost of the naked robot. Of the estimated $1,485 million in robotics sales for 1987, $365 million was accounted for by installation or systems work (Dataquest).

Training

Training was important for those in robotics because of the need to apply the technology at the shop floor level. Further objectives of training were to avoid the misuse of robot technology and to minimize faults unnecessarily blamed on the robot. A few robotics companies such as ASEA had been so successful at training that it became a business in its own right, in addition to robot sales. ASEA offered general robotics courses, and it was not uncommon for these courses to be attended by people who purchased competitors' robots.

Changing Buyer Behavior

Sales in the initial stage of the robotics trade were characterized by naked robots and a few peripheries. Some viewed robots as a sophisticated but nonetheless "commodity" hardware and pressed for fixed pricing. This pressure, in addition to the robotics industry's own changing cost structure, squeezed the profit margins of many robot manufacturers. The changing cost structure in the industry did not facilitate pricing policy. Nick Rizvi, Corporate Staff Spe-

---

EXHIBIT 8 ● Value Added for Arc Welding Robot System

Value Added for Arcwelding Robot System

Robot Supplier		OEM Supplier		Systems Integrator	
Naked robot	M a r g i n	Peripheral equipment for arcwelding	M a r g i n	Transfer and line equipment	Systems integrator margin
$70,000		$110,000		$300,000	

Elements: Platform   Power Pac
          Control   Electrode Feeder
          Control   Arc Welding Controls
          Accessories Torch Cleaner

EXHIBIT 9 ● Distribution of Robot Costs

Application	Basic robot cost	Accessories	Installation
Welding	55%	30%	15%
Handling	67	22	11
Machining	45	35	20
Machine Tending	55	20	25
Painting	70	24	6
Assembly	40	35	25

Source: Le Nouvel Automatisme, June 1982.

cial Projects at ASEA Robotics, expressed his views on manufacturing in the robotics industry and its effect on pricing.

In the earlier days of the robot industry, manufacturers and western manufacturers in particular concentrated their manufacturing on a few robots with the same basic control. The end result was a somewhat limited range of robots, one of which could be selected and, if necessary, adjusted to fit an application. The Japanese, on the other hand, had a different philosophy in that they chose to manufacture robots with a variety of controls. This coincided with a Japanese design facility that allows them to implement changes and offer more products. Furthermore, that design facility allows them to do in four–five months what takes us about twelve months. Consequently, they have a broader product range for a given application that can be marketed as "more specific" for a customer's needs. And, when you add in the Japanese development and finance costs versus those of Western firms, those "more specific" robots can be sold for 10–15 percent less than their competitors' robots.

The Japanese "design facility" was seen by some in the industry as a major advantage. Given the pressures to manufacture in volume to meet high investment costs, robot makers tried to secure their share of industry shipments, using one of two general strategies. The larger competitors sought to be "one-stop" robotics suppliers and covered virtually all application segments. Consequently, larger firms such as ASEA and GMF had wider product offerings, with up to twelve robot models. Smaller firms, however, stressed their expertise in one or two application segments and offered two or three models. Each model was characterized by a combination of axes, weight handling capacity, speed, and accuracy. Some firms, such as Adept and Prab, had proven their success using these variables rather than applications to segment the market.

Nick Rizvi shared his thoughts on the dynamics of the robot industry.

The rules of the robotics game appear to have changed; it is no longer clear what the future rules will be. Where we were once safe selling naked robots, we now need to take bigger risks and sell complete systems. To meet that growing systems demand, we must find sufficient human resources with diverse engineering backgrounds. The financial risks associated with bidding in the systems area are not small either. Yet if we abandon systems work, we will lose our credibility as a robot manufacturer. What do we need to do differently in the future to succeed as well as we have in the past?

Case 15

ASEA Robotics AB (A)

INTRODUCTION

In October of 1987, Stelio Demark, president of ASEA Robotics AB,[1] looked with satisfaction on a market report just passed to him by Nick Rizvi, head of corporate projects, indicating that in 1986 ASEA Robotics AB had just edged GMF from its leadership position and had become the world's largest robot supplier, with sales of $190 million and a market share of 11.2 percent (refer to Exhibit 1). Reflecting on the challenges still ahead, Stelio Demark commented:

Just like everybody else in this industry,[2] we are still not making a satisfactory return in this business. Our company faces considerable challenges in the next few years. We need to make a number of key decisions as to which market segment and which geographic areas we should emphasize and how we should streamline our business with respect to its product offering, marketing, manufacturing and R&D. The next five years will be crucial with respect to turning this into a profitable business for our company.

CORPORATE BACKGROUND

The ASEA group, trading under the legal name of ASEA AB (AB stands for Inc. in Swedish), was one of the world's ten leading electrical equipment companies. Founded in Sweden in 1883, ASEA group sales were $8,950 million in 1987, with a net income of $641 million. Sales in 1987 were some 12 percent above 1986 levels. The company employed over 70,000 persons, approximately half of which worked outside Sweden. With its head office located in Vasteras, sixty miles outside Stockholm, ASEA was one of Sweden's largest publicly quoted companies. Shares were traded on the Stockholm, Copenhagen, Helsinki, and London stock exchanges, the OTC in Germany, and NASDAQ in the United States. (For a five year summary of the ASEA Group's financial position, refer to Exhibit 2.)

The ASEA Group was a major producer in the areas of energy, transportation, and industrial equipment. Its major European competitors in those fields were Siemens of Germany, Brown Boveri & Cie of Switzerland, and General Electric in the United Kingdom. Hitachi, Toshiba, and Mitsubishi were ASEA's major Japanese competitors; General Electric and Westinghouse were the major energy competitors in the United States.

When Percy Barnevik became chief executive officer (CEO) in the early 1980s, ASEA was

1. ASEA AB, the parent company of ASEA Robotics AB, merged with Brown Boveri & Cie AG of Switzerland on January 4, 1988. Since the merger, the company operated under the official name of ABB Robotics AB, ABB-R for short.

2. For background on the robotics industry, see Case 14, "The Worldwide Robotics Industry, 1987."

This case was prepared by Professor Jean-Pierre Jeannet, Visiting Professor at IMD and Professor of Marketing and International Business at Babson College, Wellesley, Mass., with the assistance of Research Associate Robert C. Howard. This case was prepared for class discussion only and not to illustrate either effective or ineffective handling of a business situation. Copyright © 1989 by IMD, Lausanne, Switzerland. The International Institute for Management Development (IMD), resulting from the merger between IMEDE, Lausanne, and IMI, Geneva, acquires and retains all rights. Not to be used or reproduced without written permission from IMD, Lausanne, Switzerland.

EXHIBIT 1 ● Worldwide Robotics Industry Market Share, 1986

Company	Total revenue (millions of U.S. dollars)	Market share by revenue
ABB	$ 190.0	11.2%
GMF	186.2	11.0
Yaskawa	111.0	6.5
Matsushita	100.0	5.9
Cincinnati	79.7	4.7
Kawasaki	76.0	4.5
Toshiba	73.3	4.3
Cloos	70.0	4.1
Nachi	64.0	3.8
Fanuc	60.0	3.5
Unimation	51.8	3.0
KUKA	50.0	2.9
Hitachi	36.0	2.1
Others	550.7	32.5
Total	$1,698.7	100.0%

significantly restructured along nine different industry groups, the largest accounting for some 20 percent of sales. In the beginning of 1986, ASEA began to incorporate many of its divisions as separate companies, a process that was expected to continue. The following business segments were part of the ASEA Group:

The *Power Plants* segments consisted of ASEA-Atom, ASEA Generation, ASEA Stal and its subsidiaries, and other foreign subsidiaries. The Power Plants segment manufactured plants for the generation of hydro, nuclear, and other thermal power, as well as heat production plants. A number of growth niches existed in this business as a result of new technology and market demands for energy conservation, efficiency, and a cleaner environment. In 1987 this segment accounted for 5.3 percent of group sales, with nuclear power plants representing 24 percent of the segment's volume.

Power Transmission included ASEA Relays, ASEA Transmission, ASEA Transformers, ASEA Switchgear, and related foreign subsidiaries. This business segment accounted for 13.4 percent of group volume and constituted one of ASEA's most technology intensive areas. ASEA was a world leader in high voltage transmission and reactive power compensation—a method used to lower losses in large power networks. The power transmission industry was characterized by worldwide overcapacity and low growth.

Power Distribution as a business segment included ASEA Distribution, ASEA Kabel and its subsidiaries, Elektrokoppar, and related foreign subsidiaries. The business segment marketed low and medium switchgear and apparatus, cables and capacitors, and manufactured wire, strip, and conductors from aluminum and copper. Power Distribution was concentrated on domestic markets and often required local production or adaptation of products to meet local needs. This segment was heavily oriented toward Sweden and represented approximately 9.5 percent of group volume.

EXHIBIT 2 ● ASEA Group Financial Summary (SKr., in thousands)

	1983	1984	1985	1986	1987
Order bookings	27,255	35,635	39,358	47,438	56,165
Invoices sales	30,589	36,600	41,652	46,601	52,271
Earnings after financial income and expense	1,970	2,337	2,413	2,425	2,725
Adjusted stockholders' equity	6,593	7,419	8,635	10,532	11,570
Total capital	32,175	37,087	41,618	47,154	59,040
Capital expenditures for property, plant & equipment	1,077	1,063	1,427	2,069	2,097
Capital expenditures for acquisitions	358	260	1,009	2,137	2,111
Average number of employees	56,660	58,434	60,979	63,124	72,868
Operating earnings/invoiced sales (%)	7.9	7.6	6.4	6.1	6.7
Return on capital employed (%)	16.5	17.8	16.8	18.2	16.2
Return on equity (%)	18.3	18.8	16.7	15.0	15.0
Debt-equity ratio	1.07	0.98	1.18	1.01	1.36
Interest coverage ratio	2.80	2.92	2.85	2.40	2.74
Net income per share (50% tax*)	16.00	18.90	19.60	19.60	22.10
Net income per share, fully diluted (50% tax*)	—	—	18.70	19.30	21.60
Net income per share according to equity accounting method (paid tax*)	28.70	32.60	35.60	35.30	29.60
Net income per share according to equity accounting method, fully diluted (paid tax*)	—	—	34.00	34.70	29.00
Dividend per share*	4.00	4.70	6.00	7.00	8.00**

*Adjusted for stock dividends.

**1987: proposed.

Note: Translation rates on December 31, 1987: $1.00 = SKr. 5.84; £1.00 = SKr. 10.84.

Transportation Equipment consisted of ASEA Traction and its subsidiaries, ASEA Truck, Haegglund & Soener, and related foreign subsidiaries. This business segment comprised mass transit systems, electric locomotives, all-terrain carriers, marine deck cranes, hydraulic equipment, and forklift trucks. In railway vehicles, ASEA had a strong position because it was one of the few manufacturers that offered a full range of products from locomotives and railroad cars to electrification systems, all from the same vendor. In 1987, the Transportation Equipment segment's volume was 7.0 percent of group sales.

The *Industrial Equipment* business segment included ASEA Automation, ASEA Drives, ASEA-Hafo, ASEA Metallurgy, Stal Refrigeration, ASEA Robotics, and related foreign subsidiaries. This segment consisted of equipment for improving productivity in the metallurgical and process industries, industrial robots, electronic components, and refrigeration plants. Parts of this sector were undergoing a shakeout, and margins had consequently been under pressure since the early 1980s. In 1987, this segment accounted for some 11.7 percent of group volume.

The *Financial Services* business segment was formed at the end of 1985 and accounted for some 7.7 percent of group volume. Its purpose was to increase ASEA's return on its liquid assets and provide sales support for ASEA's industrial businesses. Leasing, financing, foreign exchange management, trading, and countertrade were increasingly part of ASEA's industrial sales, and a presence in these businesses made ASEA's other business segments more competitive.

The *Flaekt Group* represented ASEA's largest business segment, with 22.6 percent of group volume. Flaekt AB, where ASEA had a 51 percent interest, focused on environmental control, both indoors and outdoors. Flaekt's base was air and energy technology with flue gas treatment representing an important part of the segment's business. The group's sales depended to a large extent on industrialized countries, where sales derived from general investment levels and legislation requirements of public authorities.

Standard Finished Goods was made up of ASEA Cylinda, ASEA Motors, ASEA Selfa and its subsidiaries, ASEA Skandia, and related foreign subsidiaries. This segment included an electrical wholesale business, electric motors, low voltage apparatus, and household appliances and in 1987 represented 10.0 percent of group volume. *Other Operations* included semifinished goods, power utility operations, telecommunications, service, and installation. Most of the companies in this segment were service companies and required a local presence in each country. Low capital expenditures and high margins gave this group a steady cash flow. In 1987, Other Operations accounted for 12.8 percent of ASEA's group volume.

DEVELOPMENT OF ASEA ROBOTICS

ASEA Robotics, first established in 1974, had achieved a consolidated sales volume of $250 million in 1987. The company employed some 1,500 persons worldwide, had R&D expenditures of 10 percent of sales, and was the clear market leader in Europe and a strong number two in the United States. ASEA Robotics also maintained sales representations in twenty countries.

ASEA got its start in the robotics business by combining its internal experience in robotics applications with that in electronics to build the world's first all electric robot. ASEA produced approximately 6,000 units of the first robot models, the IRB 6 and IRB 60 (short for industrial robot), most of which are still in operation after 70,000 hours of use. The IRB 6 was launched in 1974, the same year that the ASEA Electronics Division designated Robotics as its own profit center in Vasteras, Sweden. Vasteras was ASEA's corporate hometown, where Robotics was given considerable freedom in development. ASEA's start in the robotics industry grew out of the desire to improve its own manufacturing efficiency. This began in the mid- to late 1960s and followed on the purchase of NC machines and an ASEA climate that favored investment in production engineering. This climate found ASEA executives asking if they could make their own robots. ASEA consequently made and installed its first robots in its own factories, where they were used for handling and tending. Shortly thereafter, ASEA began to sell these robots and approached ESAB to develop a robot for welding applications. ESAB marketed welding process equipment to a variety of industries around the world and was a clear number one worldwide for arc welding applications. ESAB corporate sales amounted to about SKr. 12 billion ($2 billion). The arc welding expertise offered by ESAB expanded ASEA's robot offering into a new application segment. Traditionally, ASEA's expertise had been in electronic control technology—not welding. ESAB provided ASEA with welding components to be attached to a robot arm and, in a sense, allowed ASEA to make a robot capable of being integrated with ESAB equipment.

The division grew slowly at first and reached a volume of only 250 robots by 1980. After 1980, new management gave the business added attention and incorporated ASEA Robotics as a separate company in 1985. Thereafter, ASEA Robotics entered a period of rapid growth. From 1980 to 1987, annual output increased from 250 to 2,000 robots; the company expanded aggressively into the United States and Japan and set up production units in France and Spain. ASEA's expertise in robotics continued to grow in this time frame, and by the end of 1987 the company had products for arc and spot welding, painting/surface finishing, materials handling/machine tending, gluing, assembly, process, and a range of other applications and an installed base of nearly 10,000 robots (refer to Exhibit 3).

ASEA was late in entering the spot welding market segment and did not have a product in this segment until 1983, whereas some competitors had twenty years of spot welding experience. In the United States, ASEA's single biggest market, the company had 200 employees and was in second place, behind GMF. (Refer to Exhibit 4.)

ASEA Robotics had established a number of alliances and made several acquisitions over the years. Among these was Trallfa Robot of Norway, partially acquired (51 percent) in 1985. Trallfa was a leading manufacturer of robots for the painting and surface finishing sector, and its acquisition strengthened ASEA's export operations. Trallfa products consequently filled a void in the ASEA line, previously concentrated on arc welding and other metalworking applications. The acquisition also saved ASEA from having to modify electric robots for painting and its associated spark hazards.

In Japan, ASEA was represented by ASEA Robotics/Gadelius (GAR). ASEA products had an initial

EXHIBIT 3 ● ASEA Accumulated Application Experience, 1987

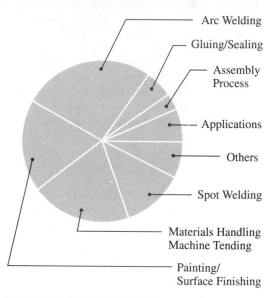

Total: approximately 10,000 robots

- Arc Welding
- Gluing/Sealing
- Assembly Process
- Applications
- Others
- Spot Welding
- Materials Handling Machine Tending
- Painting/ Surface Finishing

Total: approximately 10,000 robots

reputation of being overpriced in Japan, despite their high quality and precision (*Business Week,* June 27, 1983). ASEA moved to counter this in 1983 by manufacturing in Kobe—a move that reportedly lowered costs by 12–13 percent (*Business Week,* June 27, 1983). In both the United States and Japan, ASEA expanded by setting up large, well-equipped robotics centers, offering customers service and support facilities along with systems engineering and hardware (*Business Week,* June 27, 1983).

THE ASEA ROBOTICS PRODUCT LINE

The ASEA product line grew systematically from its original product, the IRB 6, to a full line of seven robot models, the Trallfa paint robot, and a range of accessories to equip robots for their various

EXHIBIT 4 ● Robotics Market Shares, 1987

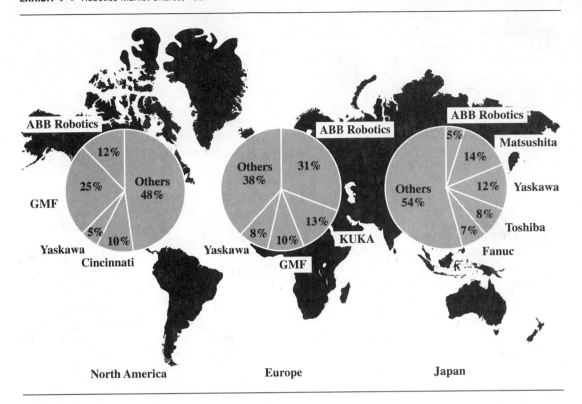

North America   Europe   Japan

EXHIBIT 5 ● Milestones in the Development of ASEA Robotics

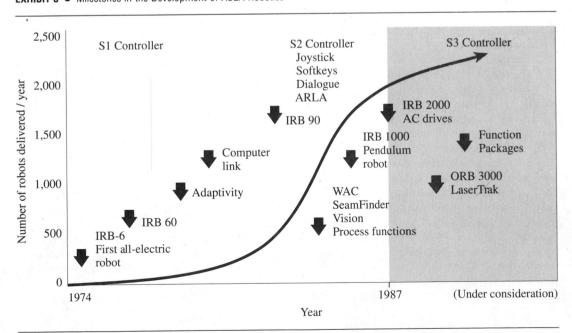

applications. (Refer to Exhibit 5 for a summary of ASEA's major milestones.)

The *IRB 6/2* was ASEA's first industrial robot (IRB) and, at its introduction in 1974, the first electrically powered robot. It handled loads up to six kilograms, and had an accuracy of $+/-0.1$ millimeter. The IRB 6/2 had five axes of rotation and was designed for applications that required great precision and uniform production. As such the IRB 6/2 was well suited for arc welding, gluing, polishing, deburring, inspection, and assembly.

The *IRB 60/2* was ASEA's heavy duty industrial robot designed to handle payloads of up to sixty kilograms with an accuracy of $+/-0.4$ millimeters. As with all ASEA robots, the IRB 60/2 had an alphanumeric display with a choice of languages, dust-proof touch sensitive buttons, and a logic control. The five-axis IRB 60 was ideal for materials handling, machine tending, and hazardous tasks such as cleaning of castings.

The *IRB 90S/2* was a flexible automated spot welding system suited for severe working environments. The IRB 90S/2 was sold either as a complete six-axis spot welding system or in a variety of configurations from a naked robot on up. The IRB 90S/2 had a unique water, air, and current (WAC) supply inside the robot arm so that cables would not hinder its working space. The IRB 1000 was a pendular type robot for small parts assembly. This model was a fast and accurate tool for the assembly segment of the robotics market.

The *IRB 2000* was a six-axis robot with a payload capacity of ten kilograms. This was supplemented by the *IRB 3000*, also a six-axis industrial robot, with a handling capacity of thirty kilograms and a reach of up to two meters. The IRB 2000 and 3000 were ASEA's family of multiapplication robots, ideally suited for materials handling and machine tending. Their extended reach also made them ideal for arc and stud welding, adhesive dispensing, deburring, water-jet cutting, and laser cutting tasks.

The *IRB 9000* was a six-axis industrial robot dedicated to spot welding with a payload capacity of up to 140 kilograms. Each naked robot included an integrated control unit and was usually sold with a number of accessories. The control unit acted as the digital communications link to the equipment that a robot served. The control unit was compact and easy to use, and its quality reflected ASEA's range of know-how in the diverse robotics industry.

The ASEA Group also sold *cell controllers* that could be used to control an entire manufacturing cell. In addition to robotics systems and cell controllers, ASEA offered a full range of grippers, laser-based seam finders and seam trackers, image processing systems, and other accessories which, when combined in a function package, formed ASEA's ''solutions'' business approach.

The recent addition of the IRB 2000 and the IRB 3000 had substantially improved ASEA's competitiveness for applications against competition that had already offered a third integrated mechanical wrist movement. Commented Nick Rizvi, head of corporate projects at ASEA Robotics AB,

When you do not have a robot ideally suited to a specific client application, you often end up designing something from scratch. This is usually more expensive than offering a standard robot solution. Some of our competitors had models of the IRB 2000 and 3000 type that were so specific they drove down the price level for our systems solutions. Consequently, we were competing for systems or turnkey solutions against specifically designed robots, which had a negative impact on our profitability.

Although it was difficult to classify a line of robots on a single dimension, one common approach was to look at weight handling capacity. Typical weight categories were:

0–6 kg	IRB 6, IRB 1000
6–10	IRB 2000
15–25	IRB 3000
30–60	IRB 60
80–100	IRB 90
100+	IRB 9000

For some applications, such as spot welding, heavy weight capacity plus reach (i.e., big robot arms) were important. ASEA's line was concentrated initially in the lower categories; it was not until 1983 that the IRB 90 came into the market. The recent entry of the IRB 9000 extended ASEA's product range into the heavy handling category.

An essential part of all ASEA robots were the electronic controllers. As Rizvi commented, "In fact, for us a naked robot always means the robot platform *and* the controller cabinet." ASEA used the same controllers for all its robots. The present S3 generation had been in use since the mid-1980s, and work on a third generation controller (S4) was under way.

ASEA's strategy of having the same controller set it apart from its Japanese competitors. "The Japanese offer a modular set of controllers which they can adapt to individual requirements," Rizvi commented. "It puzzles us how they can do this." The advantage of scaling the controller down or up as needed also resulted in cost efficiency.

Japanese competitors of ASEA appeared to have a larger product line, with a more limited range in weight handling capacity for each model. "As soon as you move away from your 'best' range for a robot, the customer usually overbuys and, as a result, has higher acquisition costs. With a product line of, say, ten rather than five robots, you can beat your competitor for the 'in-between' applications. What we have also noticed is that our Japanese competitors can get a new model out in just four–five months, whereas we need six–eight months for major product changes."

ASEA ROBOTICS MARKET POSITION

By the end of 1987, ASEA Robotics had an installed base of about 10,000 robots, approximately 65 percent in Europe, 15 percent in North America, and 10 percent in Japan and Australia. Corresponding market shares were Europe, 31 percent; North America, 12 percent; and Asia, 5 percent. Growth had been impressive, surpassing 2,000 units in 1986 and $200 million worldwide in consolidated sales in 1987.

ASEA's Position by Application Areas

Of ASEA's 10,000 installed robots, about 8,000 were for automotive applications. Leading applications were arc welding, painting and surface finishing, materials handling and machine tending, and spot weld-

ing. Less frequent were applications for gluing and sealing, assembly, and process applications. (Refer to Exhibit 6.)

ASEA's Competitive Position in Europe

ASEA's market position differed considerably by region. Europe was the company's strongest market, where it was by far the market leader with 31 percent, followed by KUKA (West Germany) with 13 percent, GMF with 10 percent, and Yaskawa of Japan with 8 percent. Some ten companies shared the remainder of the market. ASEA's market share varied from country to country, however. For example, ASEA dominated in Sweden with about 60 percent and was also the market leader in Spain, the United Kingdom, and Germany. ASEA held second place in both France and

EXHIBIT 6 ● ASEA Robotics Installed Base in Automotive Segment

Total: approximately 8,000 robots

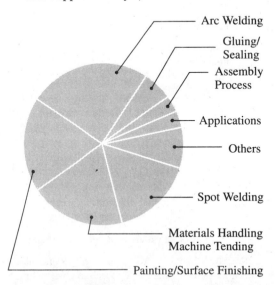

Total: approximately 8,000 robots

Italy, behind ACMA, a French company, and Comau, an Italian supplier, respectively.

In general, there was a consensus within ASEA

Robotics that the company's strength could be rated by application, based on available products, application know-how, and installed base.

	First	*Second*	*Third*
Arc Welding	ASEA	Yaskawa	KUKA
Spot Welding	KUKA	ASEA	Comau
Gluing/Sealing	GMF	KUKA	ASEA
Handling	ASEA	Cincinnati	Unimation
Machine Tending	Cincinnati	ASEA	Unim./Yaskawa
Assembly	ASEA	Unimation	Yaskawa
Process	ASEA	Cincinnati	Unimation
Painting	ASEA	GMF/Behr	Graco

Likewise, a consensus existed with respect to customer perceptions and ASEA's position against six key competitors in Europe.

ASEA led in most categories. In price levels and

price flexibility, only KUKA was rated below ASEA. Trends indicated that ASEA, KUKA, GMF, and Yaskawa were gaining volume, whereas Cincinnati and Unimation were declining.

	First	*Second*	*Third*
Market Image	ASEA	KUKA	Yaskawa
Product Technology	ASEA	KUKA	Yaskawa
Application Know-how	ASEA	KUKA	Comau
Financial Position	ASEA/GMF	Comau	KUKA
Operational Resources	ASEA	Yaskawa	Comau
Price Levels	Yaskawa	Unimation	Cincinnati/Comau
Price Flexibility	Yaskawa	Cincinnati/Comau	Unimation
Nonauto Penetration	Yaskawa	ASEA	Unimation
Automotive Penetration	KUKA	ASEA/Com./Cin.	—
Local Presence	ASEA	Unimation	KUKA
Market Share	ASEA	KUKA	GMF

ASEA's Competitive Position in the U.S. Market

In the United States, ASEA enjoyed second place, with a 12 percent share as opposed to GMF with 25 percent, Cincinnati with 10 percent, Yaskawa with 5 percent, followed by Unimation and KUKA. All other

manufacturers accounted for 48 percent of the market but had shares of 2 percent or less. GMF's share consisted of shipments mainly to GM's own plants.

As with Europe, there was a general belief at ASEA that the company's strength could be rated by application area as follows:

	First	Second	Third
Arc Welding	Yaskawa	ASEA	KUKA
Spot Welding	KUKA	Cincinnati	GMF
Gluing/Sealing	GMF	Cincinnati	KUKA (ASEA 4th)
Handling	ASEA	Cincinnati	GMF
Tending	ASEA	Cincinnati	GMF
Assembly	GMF	ASEA	KUKA
Process	ASEA	GMF	Cincinnati
Painting	GM	ASEA	

And, in comparison to the competition, ASEA employees believed the company's position could be approximated as follows:

	First	Second	Third
Market Image	GMF/KUKA	—	ASEA
Product Technology	KUKA	ASEA	Yaskawa
Application Know-how	KUKA	ASEA	Yaskawa
Financial Position	ASEA/GMF	—	KUKA
Operational Resources	GMF	ASEA	Cincinnati
Price Levels	Yaskawa/GMF	—	Unimation
Price Flexibility	Yaskawa/GMF	—	Unimation
Nonauto Penetration	Unimation	Yaskawa	GMF
Automotive Penetration	GMF/ASEA	—	Cincinnati/KUKA
Local Presence	GMF	Yaskawa	ASEA
Market Share	GMF	ASEA	Cincinnati

As far as competitive trends were concerned, GMF, ASEA, Yaskawa, and KUKA were all viewed as gaining strength, whereas Cincinnati and Unimation were seen as losing ground.

The United States was ASEA's single biggest market, with a growth rate of 10 percent in 1987 and an approximate volume of $45 million despite negative growth trends in the market. Employment had increased to 200 by 1987.

ASEA's Position in the Japanese Market

ASEA's position in the Japanese market, the world's largest robotics market, was number five, behind four Japanese companies. Matsushita was the leader with 14 percent, followed by Yaskawa (12 percent), Toshiba (8 percent), Fanuc (7 percent), and ASEA (5 percent). Other manufacturers accounted for 54 percent of the Japanese market. In Japan, ASEA was

represented by Gadelius, another company owned by
ASEA Corporation. ASEA products were initially
considered overpriced in Japan despite their high
quality and reputation. Local manufacturing in 1983
allowed the company to lower costs by about 10–15
percent.

THE ORGANIZATION OF THE ASEA ROBOTICS GROUP

Within ASEA Corporation, the robotics group was
organized as a business area. Sales and P&L results
were consolidated for the entire group, headed by
Bjorn Weichbrodt. Sales of the business group
amounted to about $250 million for 1987. Weichbrodt
also acted as president of ASEA Robotics Inc.
(U.S.A.). He was assisted by Stelio Demark, who was
responsible for European robot companies and was
president of ASEA Robotics AB in Sweden.

The business area management was assisted by
an Advisory International Strategy Group consisting
of the business area manager (Weichbrodt), head of
ASEA Robotics AB in Sweden (Demark), the heads
of local robotics sales organizations (Germany, Italy,
Japan, U.S.A.), and the business development manager. A small staff group comprising business development, controlling, and productivity also reported to
the business area manager. ASEA Robotics AB
(ROB) in Vasteras, Sweden, was the largest single
unit in the robotics business group. It comprised the
manufacturing organization, engineering, and research. ROB also had sales responsibility for the
Swedish market.

ASEA maintained sales units in eleven European
countries, the United States, Canada, Australia, and
Japan. Some sales companies (UDBs) were separately
incorporated (dedicated sales companies) (United
States, Germany, United Kingdom) but for the most
part were divisions within country sales organizations
maintained by ASEA for the entire corporate product
line. In all countries, however, ASEA Robotics had
separately identifiable units with a dedicated staff. Reporting was in the form of a matrix, with both the
business area management and local country management jointly responsible for the business result. This
meant that in France, for example, the UDB manager
reported to the country manager as well as the robot-

ics business area manager for financial results. Although the robotics area management had a considerable amount of control over local divisions, it did
not have sole decision-making authority in such issues as personnel.

Marketing Organization at ASEA Robotics

Marketing was essentially in the hands of ASEA's
robot centers located in the key areas. There were
twenty-six robot centers in existence, fourteen of
those in Europe, five in the Americas, and six in the
Pacific Rim countries (refer to Exhibit 7). Three countries, the United States (3), Sweden (2), and Japan (3)
had more than one robot center.

The role of the robot center was to project ASEA
Robotics' customer and sales service closer to its customer base. They provided full coverage for sales,
engineering, training, and service. Engineering services ranged from feasibility studies to systems
configuration to on-site installation. Robot center engineers had to have good knowledge of many manufacturing processes, production engineering, tooling,
and related disciplines. A typical robot center had a
staff of fifteen to forty. Combined employment of all
of ASEA's robot centers was about 700, including
those with complete systems capacity.

The robot centers were a solution to the lack of
distribution channels when ASEA started in this field.
The company had no contact to the key customer automotive segment. The robot centers were often located in buildings separate from the country sales organization for the corporation. In the United Kingdom
the robot center was in Birmingham near the center
of the U.K. car industry.

"Other robot manufacturers have solved this differently," Nick Rizvi said. "The Japanese had a customer in Japan that was sophisticated enough to buy
only naked robots and to perform the integration and
engineering in-house. In Europe, very few companies
could do this. When the Japanese sell in Europe, they
use systems houses that provide the package service
to their clients locally. We at ASEA are unique
in having created our own direct sales channel in all
key markets."

The activities at ASEA robot centers covered basic areas. Each center was expected to perform sales,
engineering, training, and service to clients in its area.

EXHIBIT 7 ● ASEA Robotics Robot Center Locations

Region		Robot center location
Europe	Austria	Brunn am Gebirge
	Belgium	Zaventem
	Denmark	Odense
	Finland	Espoo
	France	Persan
	Germany	Friedberg
	Holland	Apeldoorn
	Italy	Milan
	Norway	Bryne
	Spain	Sabadell
	Sweden	Gothenburg, Vasteras
	Switzerland	Zurich
	United Kingdom	Luton
The Americas	Brazil	São Paulo
	Canada	Toronto, Ontario
	United States	New Berlin & Milwaukee, Wisconsin; Troy & Detroit, Michigan; Irving, Texas; White Plains, New York
Japan and Australia	Australia	Melbourne
	Japan	Kobe, Tokyo, Nagoya & Hiroshima
	New Zealand	Auckland
	Singapore	

Systems Engineering at ASEA Robotics

The ASEA robot centers purchased naked robots from ROB in Sweden (platform and control). Based on their own customer contacts, they would equip the robots for the required application by using already existing accessories. If available, accessories were also sourced from ROB in Sweden. The robot centers were in a position to deliver a fully engineered package for a client if needed.

"One of our principal problems," Demark commented, "is the growing tendency to get involved in such engineering efforts at the robot center level. About 50 man-years, or about one-third of our total engineering effort, is now devoted to customizing robots to client needs. This represents 90 percent of our systems development effort."

Local tailoring could involve making robots available on a trial basis to clients. "We found that a number of robots were floating around in various places, which represented a capital tie-up of about $2.5 million."

Sales to OEMs

About 25 percent of ASEA's annual unit volume went to the OEMs, such as ESAB who equipped the naked robots with its own application packages. For this segment, no engineering was necessary.

Robot Economics

Although end-user prices varied by application, a typical end-user price for an ASEA robot fully equipped and installed amounted to about $150,000. The robot center would source it to about $75,000 from ROB in Sweden. The rest was value added by the robot center, consisting of about $30,000 for cell engineering and $50,000 for value added.

Training Activities at Robot Center

Training of customer employees was viewed as an important activity. ASEA offered one-week courses to customers for operators, programmers, and maintenance engineers at its robot centers. However, instead of selling training as a package only (representing about 1 percent of product price), ASEA began to sell training as a separate product. By 1987, training revenue represented some 10 percent of corporate revenue, or $25 million. This service was viewed as important because personnel tended to change and customers always had new employees who needed to be trained. In 1987 alone, about 4,000 people attended ASEA's courses.

ASEA offered regularly scheduled courses on topics such as operations, basic and advanced programming, safety, mechanical service, electronic service, and preventive maintenance. On special request, courses could be held at a client's site, and seminars on robotics in general could also be offered.

Service

The manpower needs for ASEA's robot service were relatively low. However, spare parts usage was high and had reached 25 percent of total robotics revenue ($62.5 million). ASEA was in a position to fly in parts and personnel anytime on short notice.

"Imagine that a car manufacturer's line is down because a single robot malfunctions. Given that a typical production cycle is three cars per minute, a one-minute shutdown will cost a lost value of three cars, or easily $30,000," Demark explained. As a result, most robot users needed to stock ample spare parts nearby and used to train their own maintenance staff.

Manufacturing Operations

ASEA's manufacturing strategy evolved considerably over time. In its initial phase, all manufacturing of robot platforms and controls took place in Vasteras in Sweden. In the early 1980s, ASEA realized that local acceptance in some markets would be helped if local manufacturing were established. This led to assembly operations in France, Japan, and the United States. However, this was found to be uneconomical, and in a third phase, manufacturing was again centralized in Vasteras, where a completely new plant was built.

The robot manufacturing center was a 15,000 square meter (165,000 square feet) area facility with an annual capacity of 3,000 naked robots. It manufactured both platforms and control systems. Delivery was four–six weeks from the order date. The manufacturing control system allowed a simultaneous release policy, which meant that an order was released for manufacturing only when "all the screws were in."

As a result of the newly adopted manufacturing system, local stocks of naked robots were felt unnecessary. Across the entire business area, inventory and work in process were to be kept at less than 20 percent of sales.

ASEA emphasized efficiency and had achieved a significant drop in its unit costs in 1987. Labor costs were expected to be reduced further in 1988 and onward. ASEA management expected to be able to offset any inflationary pressures with increased efficiency.

The manufacturing performed at ASEA Robotics in Vasteras largely consisted of assembling robots and systems testing before shipping. This was reflected in a very high content of purchased material, which amounted to more than half of total product costs. Concentrating on assembly alone allowed ASEA to invest its funds into R&D, marketing, and product line expansion without other fixed investments into manufacturing.

Research and Development Activities at ASEA Robotics[3]

For the entire robotics business area, the R&D effort was carried out by about 200 engineers. The total expenditures were estimated at $25 million, or about 15 percent of the volume in naked robots ($75,000 units, 2,000 units). About 150 man-years of engineering were performed at ROB in Vasteras, the remaining at the various robot centers.

Research at Vasteras (ROB) consisted of 120 man-years in development of new models (IRBs), work on controls, improving the mechanical parts of the existing line, and work on necessary computers and servo drives. Most of these resources went into the development of the IRB 2000, the IRB 3000, and the S3. Whenever a new model was introduced, the maintenance R&D requirements increased correspondingly, having reached about 40 percent of development man-years in 1987.

About eighty man-years were invested into application development, which included the adaptation of a naked robot to a specific task. More than half, or about fifty man-years, were spent in ASEA's various robot centers in response to special client requests. The bulk of this was carried out, however, in the larger sales companies (Germany, United States, Japan, France, United Kingdom, and Sweden).

Demark considered ASEA's present investment of about 120 man-years in development as a basic requirement to maintain ASEA's technological standing as a leading robot manufacturer.

"A new robot generation/model requires an investment of about SKr. 100 million. If I want to keep R&D at maximum 10 percent of naked robot sales, I need a volume of at least 2,000 units over the life of the model to cover my initial R&D investment. With an expected life of ten years, the minimum annual volume is about 200 robots per year."

"Most of our competitors do not have the volume we have. I just cannot see how they can make it given the heavy R&D costs," Demark said. Among the leading Europeans, KUKA (600–700 units annually), Comau (200–300 units), and Acma (300 units) were below ASEA's level. Although he was not

3. The data in this section have been disguised.

sure, Demark suspected that his Japanese competitors (Yaskawa, etc.) were able to treat R&D as a corporate expense and did not allocate it directly to the product line. "To them, robotics is a way to show that they were modern and at the edge of new technologies."

Pricing Robots at ASEA

"In general, we are 10–15 percent above the Japanese price level with our robots," Rizvi explained, "Although not all robots delivered the same performance, the Japanese can always beat you on a price/performance basis, as they do now in the United States."

Rizvi indicated that some buyers were learning to differentiate between initial acquisition costs and the costs of running and maintaining a robot. In the long term, ASEA robots had demonstrated a higher up-time stability which, if applied over the total economic life of a robot, would lead to a long-term running cost advantage for ASEA. Despite consistent cost reductions by ASEA, the 10–15 percent price difference vis-à-vis its Japanese competitors had not disappeared.

Currency fluctuations played a role as well. For ASEA, costs were based on the Swedish krona. However, other major competitors had difficulties as well. KUKA of Germany was in the same situation, and the Japanese had seen the yen appreciate substantially during the preceding two years. If there were any winners, it was the U.S.-based manufacturers. However, some of those were battered due to a considerable slowdown in new factory orders for the U.S. automobile industry.

ASEA Robotics' Competitive Situation

Management at ASEA Robotics considered several areas of strength when competing in the marketplace. First of all, ASEA had an orientation toward selling solutions rather than only products. Its broad range of products and accessories gave ASEA the capability to compete for a multitude of applications. Over time, the company had gained diverse application know-how. The company profited from the existence of its robot center concepts, and it also had moderate systems resources to provide the delivery of complete systems fully equipped with robots, accessories, and the necessary software. ASEA had shown an aggressive approach to R&D, had extensive training and service capabilities, and was recognized worldwide for quality and reliability.

At a recent meeting in Sweden, robot center managers developed a ranking system, with different categories and numbers, thought to approximate the importance of key success factors and possible sources of competitive advantage. A score of 0 was an indication of very poor performance in relation to the market and competitors; a score of 5 indicated very good or near perfect performance.

Ranking	Possible key success factors	Ranking	Possible sources of competitive advantage
1	Product costs	1	Exchangeability
1	Distribution costs	1	Exhange of people
2	Efficiency in business	1	Be prepared to take control of EDP opportunities
2	Competitors' knowledge	2	Information exchange
		2	Ease of communications
2	Anticipate market needs	2	Market flexibility
3	Volume	2	Multinational customer handling
3	Profitability	2	Application documentation
3	Professionalism	3	Quick throughput time
3	Market knowledge	3	Selective marketing nucleus
4	Product quality	3	Diversified production program
4	Global market	3	Correct organization size
4	Financial strength	3	Control features
3/4	Good management	3	Solutions
		3	Flexible organization
		4	Worldwide organization
		5	Broad range of products

Case 16

ASEA Robotics AB (B)

INTRODUCTION

"Looking at the next phase of our development, we have to rethink the way we do business in a number of areas," said Stelio Demark, president of ASEA Robotics AB[1] in Vasteras, Sweden. "Our plans for 1988 and 1989 need to reflect first of all a need to improve profitability towards the eventual goal of 20 percent on invested capital. This means we have to balance the needs for profitability and growth better. Furthermore, we have been pulled into several systems contracts that give me concern about how we tackle this business. At the same time, we have to think how we want to deal with our competitive situation in spot welding and assembly application, where we have traditionally been weak."

LONG-TERM PROFITABILITY OF ASEA ROBOTICS

"Our corporation expects us eventually to earn 20 percent on capital employed in our operation," De-

1. See Case 14, "The Worldwide Robotics Industry, 1987," and Case 15, "ASEA Robotics AB (A)," for further background.

●

This case was prepared by Jean-Pierre Jeannet, Visiting Professor at IMD and Professor of Marketing and International Business at Babson College, Wellesley, Mass., with the assistance of Robert Howard, research associate at IMD. This case was prepared for class discussion only and not to illustrate either effective or ineffective handling of an administrative situation. Copyright © 1989 by IMD, Lausanne, Switzerland. The International Institute for Management Development (IMD), resulting from the merger between IMEDE, Lausanne, and IMI, Geneva, acquires and retains all rights. Not to be used or reproduced without written

mark explained. "With $250 million in sales, employed net assets (total assets minus debt) are about $100 million. A return of 20 percent, or $20 million, amounts to a return of 8 percent on sales. Right now, most of our competitors are losing money on their robot operations."

Growth at ASEA over the past five years had been considerable. The company had moved from about 1,000 units in 1982 to 2,000 units in 1987, requiring a heavy investment in R&D and the expansion of the robot center concept. It was clear to Demark that targeted profitability could not be reached immediately and that progress had to come over time.

OPPORTUNITIES IN ASSEMBLY SEGMENT

Assembly applications, representing a worldwide volume of about 7,000 robots, or about 27 percent of all installations, was equal in size to materials handling/machine tending. It was made up of robots with a small to a very large handling capacity and a wide range of user industries.

To date, ASEA had about 200 installed robots for assembly applications with automotive customers. Annual sales for the entire applications amounted to about 100 units of varying sizes, about 75 percent of it in Europe. Due to the extensive customization, assembly robots sales tended to involve a large amount of systems design work. These were often complex technical installations which had to be priced before the work was completed. Cost overruns had occurred, partly because solutions tended to be novel.

The segment itself offered vast potential, and a considerable amount of attention was being spent on it. Experts believed that assembly was going to be the next major investment area for flexible automation. The largest market was the consumer electronics industry, a user segment that was not very familiar to ASEA's robot centers, which were mostly centered on automotive users and applications.

Demark felt that a comprehensive effort aimed at the entire assembly segment would require a large-scale product development effort. Among other things, ASEA would have to develop a SCARA (selective compliance assembly robot arm) robot, get into clean room classifications, communications facilities, and so on. Furthermore, ASEA would have to undertake a considerable marketing effort because its contacts with the electronics industry were almost nonexistent. "The electronics industry business culture differs widely from what we are used to with our traditional customers such as the automotive industry."

A second approach consisted of concentrating more narrowly on assembly of products already known to ASEA and on industry segments where contacts existed. This would result in equipping naked robots with the necessary accessories for some clearly identified tasks but staying away from full-scale design of entire systems or assembly lines. Since the end user would still require robots to be integrated into a system, ASEA would have to work closely with partners. That is, OEMs could buy naked robots from ASEA, adding value by equipping them with needed accessories. Or systems houses could perform the integrating function for customers by buying robots with accessories from various suppliers.

To develop a suitable package of accessories for the various assembly tasks required additional R&D efforts. Each package was estimated to require five–ten man-years of engineering. ASEA's existing range of robots was considered sufficient for assembly tasks with the exception of microassembly (very small parts). Leaving the assembly segment all together was a third option, but this would again endanger ASEA's idea of full partnership with the important automotive industry.

EXPANDING INTO SYSTEMS BUSINESS

In the fall of 1986, when orders for robot systems began to expand, Demark became concerned. "We were taking in a lot of systems business in many of our robot centers, exposing ourselves to considerable

risks. We needed to become clear on how we wanted to run this to avoid the losses which have occasionally occurred."

ASEA divided the robot business into three elements. The first element consisted of the robot platform, the control cabinet, and the accessories, which together were called a "naked" robot. A second element consisted of tools, fixtures, magazines to stock parts, and similar items and was referred to as a package. The third element included transfer devices, inspection devices, and all the necessary controls to integrate the robot package into a production process (refer to Exhibit 1).

The extent of value added for a naked robot, its package, and the entire system depended on a specific application. An arc welding system served as an example (refer to Exhibit 2). The naked robot, consisting of the platform and controls, would be sold for about $70,000. The required package to make it an arc welding robot consisted of a power pack ($16,000), an electrode feeder ($16,000), a torch cleaner ($1,000), and arc welding software and controls ($9,000), for a total of about $42,000. This package was increased by ESAB when that company purchased naked robots from ASEA, resulting in a packaged robot price of $110,000. When integrated into a complete manufacturing system, the systems integrator would combine the robot package with the necessary transfer equipment that moved pieces to and from the welding station and performed installation. As part of a complete line, the single robot would cost $300,000, or about four times its naked value. Of the systems integrator's $190,000 added value, about 25 percent accounted for the gross margin; the rest was spent on hardware. Typically, the integrator's margin was 10 percent for handling and 15 percent for know-how expressed in engineering man-hours sold for studies, plans, and so on.

"The basic attraction of going into the systems business is the high gross margins due to high value added," explained Nick Rizvi, manager for corporate projects at ASEA Robotics AB in Vasteras. "At the naked robot level, we get a gross margin of about 15 percent. The systems integrator assumes the role of the general contractor and typically has to deliver the entire robot system according to a prearranged package price." Contracting gross margins were high, but

EXHIBIT 1 ● Robot Systems

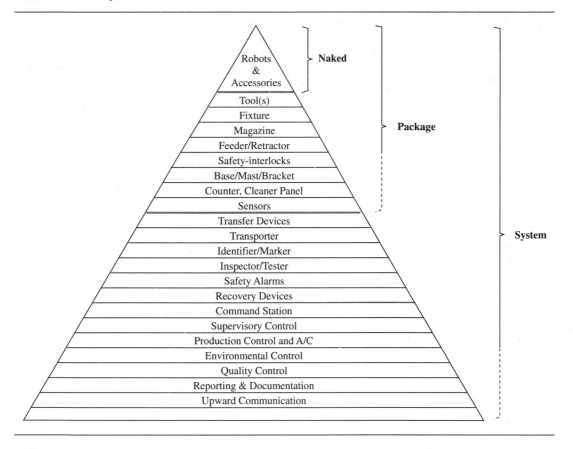

the contractor had to pay for all engineering, planning, and installation expenses, which on average led to net profit margins of only 2 percent. If there were cost overruns or unexpected events, the extra expenses could easily wipe out the entire profit on a project or even result in a loss.

There were also market factors that pushed companies like ASEA into the systems business. Automotive customers who used to buy naked robots and do their own engineering were increasingly expecting this service from suppliers. Of the major robot companies in Europe, only KUKA and Comau had systems experience, because these firms were essentially line builders who integrated backward into robot pro-

duction. But an entire line of twenty-five to eighty robots could exceed the price of $10 million, making it risky business for independent systems houses whose financial base was very narrow. As a result, large companies like KUKA and Comau gained a competitive advantage, but they would spec their own robots into a line.

More recently, automotive clients had realized that a fixed cost contract could risk financial ruin for its suppliers. They took steps toward a process called "simultaneous engineering." The entire project was divided into several steps, and release of funds was for one step at a time. "They recognized that they should not kill suppliers," Rizvi explained. "Now

EXHIBIT 2 ● Arc Welding Function Package

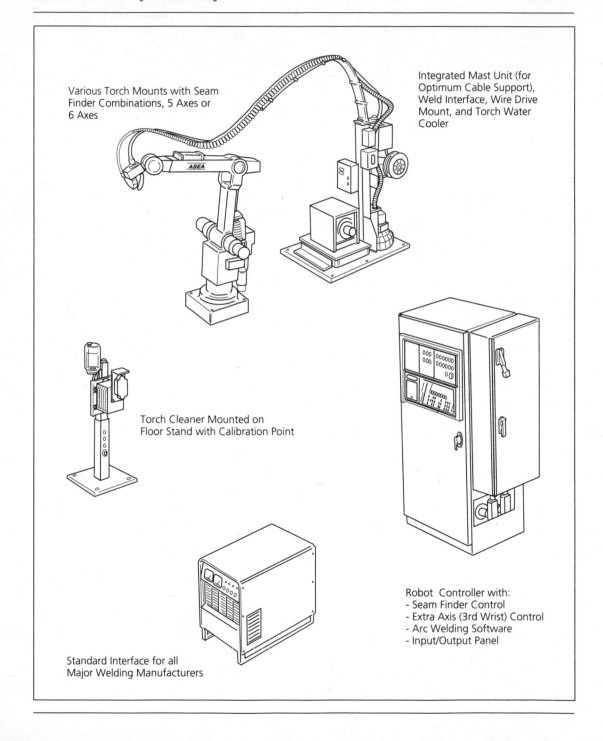

Various Torch Mounts with Seam Finder Combinations, 5 Axes or 6 Axes

Integrated Mast Unit (for Optimum Cable Support), Weld Interface, Wire Drive Mount, and Torch Water Cooler

Torch Cleaner Mounted on Floor Stand with Calibration Point

Robot Controller with:
- Seam Finder Control
- Extra Axis (3rd Wrist) Control
- Arc Welding Software
- Input/Output Panel

Standard Interface for all Major Welding Manufacturers

they tell suppliers to go ahead with this concept but to report regularly on progress.''

The systems business in Europe was dominated by a large number of medium-sized firms. Rizvi believed there were only about a dozen firms in Europe with more than 100 employees. By contrast, KUKA employed 400 and Comau 1,500 in their systems business. However, there were as many reasons for entering as for staying away from the systems business, according to Rizvi. ''For a typical system of about DM 30 million ($20 million), the robot content can be expected at about 10 percent, or $2 million, which is the equivalent of about twenty-five naked robots. The average net profitability of a systems integrator is 2 percent, or $400,000.'' The low percentage of robots as part of a total system spoke against becoming a systems supplier, whereas the additional feedback gained from client contacts would speak for it. One manager recalled a recent situation where a German company was rumored to have lost as much as DM 100 million on one contract alone due to unanticipated cost overruns.

At the time, ASEA had a number of systems orders. However, Demark considered only ASEA Robotics AB in Sweden and the U.S. company, ASEA Robotics in New Berlin and Milwaukee, to have real systems strengths. ASEA acquired one systems house in the United Kingdom in 1986, operating in 1988 under the name of ASEA Robotics Ltd. in Luton. All other robot centers were not considered experienced enough to enter the systems business.

Demark believed that ASEA had a number of different alternatives. Based on past experience, he realized that a successful systems business required close monitoring and concentrating on repeat orders to avoid cost overruns on installations not well known. It was still an open question if the present organization should be improved to add systems competence to robot centers or if systems orders should be restricted to those parts of ASEA where competence already existed. An alternative route was to build a separate organization for the systems business by building or acquiring independent systems houses.

EMPHASIS ON ROBOT PACKAGES

The bridge between the naked robot and the integrated system was the robot package that equipped a naked robot to perform a given task such as arc welding, gluing, or deburring. Where ASEA sold through OEMs, the function capability was added by the OEM. However, many times ASEA equipped naked robots for a given task, and in some instances this was done repeatedly. ''The experience has been that our robot centers end up providing the application package. But frequently, it is done on a one-time basis without regard to what other robot centers may have done when confronted with a similar situation elsewhere,'' Demark said.

Up to now, ASEA had concentrated its development resources almost exclusively on basic robot development. A push into application packages would represent a redirection. At the robot center levels, however, where approximately fifty man-years of development took place, this effort was almost exclusively aimed at developing customized solutions for specific applications. However, Demark felt it had occurred in a decentralized way.

''When our robot centers sell a naked robot to an OEM or an end user, they often have to explain how the robot might be used to perform a given function. In the process, we give our customers a considerable amount of applications knowledge free of charge because it is so difficult to sell engineering advice as a hardware supplier. However, if we already had tailor-made solutions for given applications, we could sell the robot as a package and get paid for it.

''The value added of an applications package varied from application to application. A typical range was from 30 to 75 percent on top of the base robot. ASEA executives believed that the profitability on the packaging elements was about the same as for the naked robot, an approximate 10–15 percent contribution after hardware and engineering.

A preliminary review resulted in a list of some 200 potential function applications. ASEA called these function packages an applications oriented standard robot system which was predesigned and tested. It was adapted to a complete solution, including a well-defined basic set of products to fulfill a specified production task on the shop floor with a minimum of systems engineering.

Initially, function packages were based on successful deliveries in installations rather than new applications. They consisted of basic products (robots, controls, accessories) with selected subsupplier products combined with complete sales and engineering documentation. Furthermore, it was anticipated that marketing and sales tools were included so that all robot centers could use the package, and that support tools for applications engineers and systems integrators would be included. Demark also felt that these function packages could generate feedback for product development, which might result in a platform for a more complete application oriented product line.

"What bothers me now," Demark said, "is the fact that we tailor these function packages to our customer needs on a robot center basis. If the Spanish subsidiary finishes and engineers a press tending application for a customer, no system exists to ensure that if the Dutch subsidiary meets the same problem next month, they will have access to the Spanish solution. In fact, some fifty man-years of engineering time at our subsidiaries and robot centers is largely devoted to this type of customization, which prevents us from drawing standardized solutions from our experience."

There were a number of key questions still unsolved regarding more function packages. Demark realized that the key lay in complete and thorough documentation for each package, which could be put at the disposal of all robot centers. Although required engineering man-years for each package was expected to vary, Demark considered an average of five–ten man-years per package realistic.

Implementation of this program depended on a number of variables. Demark needed to consider how important function packages were for ASEA. If he wanted to proceed with this program, how quickly it could be implemented needed to be decided now. Which engineering resources would be made available? Demark had only indirect control over the engineering resources at those robot centers which were part of ASEA Corp. sales organizations abroad. How much of those fifty man-years of engineering capacity could be mobilized for the development of function packs?

Nick Rizvi of Corporate Projects at ASEA Robotics thought about the way the industry had changed during the mid 1980s. Robotics companies were being divided into two camps: the smaller companies that concentrated on selling only robots to specialized customer segments, and the larger companies that offered complete system solutions. Amidst these changes, Japanese manufacturers were raising the quality of off-the-shelf products and avoiding the systems market. Where the Japanese could not win on robot sophistication, they were expected to compete on price. This placed additional pressure on non-Japanese firms to compete in the less profitable systems side of the robotics business. Nick Rizvi commented on the trend, "Companies have come and gone in this industry. Obviously the ticket is expensive. What do we do now that we're here and want to stay? How do we focus our efforts to be more profitable? We are profitable in naked robots, but we are being dragged into the systems business to maintain our credibility as a robot manufacturer. How do we protect the profitable side of our business, given our lack of experience in bidding and project management in the systems area?"

CONCLUSION

Demark and other senior executives at ASEA Robotics looked at their plans for the next few years. To move toward the expected profitability of about 20 percent on invested capital would require an additional contribution of $20 million. At the same time, pressures were on ASEA's limited R&D budget and the need to balance short-term with longer-term needs.

Name and Company Index

Subject Index